ذلك الكتاب لا ريب فيه

PART 1
Alif-Lam-Mim

Isaac, Jacob and the Tribes were Jews or Christians? Say: do you know better than Allah? Ah! Who is more unjust than those who conceal the testimony they have from Allah? But Allah is not unmindful of what you do!

141. That was a people that have passed away. They shall reap the fruit of what they did, and you of what you do! Of their merits there is no question in your case:

وَاِسْحٰقَ وَيَعْقُوبَ وَالْاَسْبَاطِ

كَانُوْا هُوْدًا اَوْ نَصٰرٰى ۗ قُلْ ءَاَنْتُمْ

اَعْلَمُ اَمِ اللّٰهُ ۗ وَمَنْ اَظْلَمُ مِمَّنْ

كَتَمَ شَهَادَةً عِنْدَهٗ مِنَ اللّٰهِ ۗ

وَمَا اللّٰهُ بِغَافِلٍ عَمَّا تَعْمَلُوْنَ ۝

تِلْكَ اُمَّةٌ قَدْ خَلَتْ ۚ لَهَا مَا

كَسَبَتْ وَلَكُمْ مَّا كَسَبْتُمْ ۚ وَلَا

تُسْئَلُوْنَ عَمَّا كَانُوْا يَعْمَلُوْنَ ۝

but if they turn back, it is they who are in schism; but Allah will suffice you as against them, and He is the All-Hearing, the All-Knowing.

138. (Our religion) takes its hue from Allah: and who can give better hue than Allah? And it is He Whom we worship.

139. Say: will you dispute with us about Allah, seeing that He is our Lord and your Lord; that we are responsible for our doings and you for yours; and that we are sincere (in our faith) in Him?

140. Or do you say that Abraham, Isma'il

وَاِنْ تَوَلَّوْا فَاِنَّمَا هُمْ فِىْ شِقَاقٍ ۚ

فَسَيَكْفِيْكَهُمُ اللّٰهُ ۚ وَهُوَ السَّمِيْعُ

الْعَلِيْمُ ۞ صِبْغَةَ اللّٰهِ ۚ وَمَنْ

اَحْسَنُ مِنَ اللّٰهِ صِبْغَةً ۫ وَّنَحْنُ

لَهٗ عٰبِدُوْنَ ۞ قُلْ اَتُحَآجُّوْنَنَا

فِى اللّٰهِ وَهُوَ رَبُّنَا وَرَبُّكُمْ ۚ

وَلَنَآ اَعْمَالُنَا وَلَكُمْ اَعْمَالُكُمْ ۚ

وَنَحْنُ لَهٗ مُخْلِصُوْنَ ۞ اَمْ

تَقُوْلُوْنَ اِنَّ اِبْرٰهٖمَ وَاِسْمٰعِيْلَ

the True, and he joined not gods with Allah."

136. Say: "We believe in Allah, and the revelation given to us, and to Abraham, Isma'il, Isaac, Jacob, and the Tribes, and that given to Moses and Jesus, and that given to (all) prophets from their Lord: we make no difference between one and another of them: and we bow to Allah (in Islam)."

137. So if they believe as you believe, they are indeed on the right path;

حَنِيفًا ۚ وَمَا كَانَ مِنَ الْمُشْرِكِينَ ۝

قُولُوا آمَنَّا بِاللّٰهِ وَمَا أُنْزِلَ

إِلَيْنَا وَمَا أُنْزِلَ إِلَى إِبْرَاهِمَ

وَإِسْمَعِيلَ وَإِسْحَقَ وَيَعْقُوبَ

وَالْأَسْبَاطِ وَمَا أُوتِيَ مُوسٰى

وَعِيسٰى وَمَا أُوتِيَ النَّبِيُّونَ مِنْ

رَّبِّهِمْ ۚ لَا نُفَرِّقُ بَيْنَ أَحَدٍ مِّنْهُمْ

وَنَحْنُ لَهُ مُسْلِمُونَ ۝ فَإِنْ آمَنُوا

بِمِثْلِ مَا آمَنْتُمْ بِهِ فَقَدِ اهْتَدَوْا

to his sons: "What will you worship after me?" They said: "We shall worship your Allah and the Allah of your fathers, of Abraham, Isma'il and Isaac, - the one (True) Allah: to Him we bow (in Islam)."

134. That was a people that has passed away. They shall reap the fruit of what they did, and you of what you do! Of their merits there is no question in your case!

135. They say: "Become Jews or Christians if any would be guided (to salvation)." Say you: "No! (I would rather) the Religion of Abraham

لِبَنِيْهِ مَا تَعْبُدُوْنَ مِنْ بَعْدِىْ

قَالُوْا نَعْبُدُ اِلٰهَكَ وَاِلٰهَ اٰبَآئِكَ

اِبْرٰهٖمَ وَاِسْمٰعِيْلَ وَاِسْحٰقَ اِلٰهًا

وَّاحِدًا ۚ وَّنَحْنُ لَهٗ مُسْلِمُوْنَ ۝

تِلْكَ اُمَّةٌ قَدْ خَلَتْ ۚ لَهَا مَا

كَسَبَتْ وَلَكُمْ مَّا كَسَبْتُمْ ۚ وَلَا

تُسْـَٔلُوْنَ عَمَّا كَانُوْا يَعْمَلُوْنَ ۝

وَقَالُوْا كُوْنُوْا هُوْدًا اَوْ نَصٰرٰى

تَهْتَدُوْا ۗ قُلْ بَلْ مِلَّةَ اِبْرٰهٖمَ

Him We chose and rendered pure in this world: and he will be in the Hereafter in the ranks of the Righteous.

131. Behold! His Lord said to him: "Bow (your will to Me):" He said: "I bow (my will) to the Lord and Cherisher of the Universe."

132. And this was the legacy that Abraham left to his sons, and so did Jacob; "Oh my sons! Allah has chosen the Faith for you; then die not except in the Faith of Islam."

133. Were you witnesses when death appeared before Jacob? Behold, he said

وَلَقَدِ اصْطَفَيْنٰهُ فِى الدُّنْيَا وَاِنَّهُ فِى الْاٰخِرَةِ لَمِنَ الصّٰلِحِيْنَ ۞

اِذْ قَالَ لَهُ رَبُّهٗۤ اَسْلِمْ قَالَ اَسْلَمْتُ لِرَبِّ الْعٰلَمِيْنَ ۞

وَوَصّٰى بِهَاۤ اِبْرٰهٖمُ بَنِيْهِ وَيَعْقُوْبُ ۗ يٰبَنِىَّ اِنَّ اللّٰهَ اصْطَفٰى لَكُمُ الدِّيْنَ فَلَا تَمُوْتُنَّ اِلَّا وَاَنْتُمْ مُّسْلِمُوْنَ ۞

اَمْ كُنْتُمْ شُهَدَآءَ اِذْ حَضَرَ يَعْقُوْبَ الْمَوْتُ ۙ اِذْ قَالَ

our progeny a people Muslim, bowing to you (will); and show us our place for the celebration of (due) rites; and turn unto us (in Mercy); for you are the Oft-returning, Most Merciful.

129. "Our Lord! Send among them an Apostle of their own, who shall rehearse Your Signs to them and instruct them in scripture and wisdom, and sanctify them: for you are the Exalted in Might, the Wise."

130. And who turns away from the religion of Abraham but such as debase their souls with folly?

ذُرِّيَّتِنَآ أُمَّةً مُّسْلِمَةً لَّكَ

وَأَرِنَا مَنَاسِكَنَا وَتُبْ عَلَيْنَا

إِنَّكَ أَنتَ التَّوَّابُ الرَّحِيمُ ۝

رَبَّنَا وَابْعَثْ فِيهِمْ رَسُولًا

مِّنْهُمْ يَتْلُوا عَلَيْهِمْ ءَايَتِكَ

وَيُعَلِّمُهُمُ الْكِتَبَ وَالْحِكْمَةَ

وَيُزَكِّيهِمْ إِنَّكَ أَنتَ الْعَزِيزُ

الْحَكِيمُ ۝ وَمَن يَرْغَبُ عَن مِّلَّةِ

إِبْرَٰهِمَ إِلَّا مَن سَفِهَ نَفْسَهُ

and feed its people with fruits,- such of them as believe in Allah and the Last Day." He said: "(Yes), and such as reject Faith,- for a while will I grant them their pleasure, but will soon drive them to the torment of Fire, - an evil destination (indeed)!"

127. And remember Abraham and Isma'il raised the foundations of the House (With this prayer): "Our Lord! Accept (this service) from us: for You are the All-Hearing, the All-Knowing.

128. "Our Lord! Make of us Muslims, bowing to You (Will), and of

وَّارْزُقْ اَهْلَهُ مِنَ الثَّمَرٰتِ مَنْ

اٰمَنَ مِنْهُمْ بِاللّٰهِ وَالْيَوْمِ الْاٰخِرِ ؕ

قَالَ وَمَنْ كَفَرَ فَاُمَتِّعُهُ قَلِيْلًا

ثُمَّ اَضْطَرُّهُ اِلٰى عَذَابِ النَّارِ ؕ

وَبِئْسَ الْمَصِيْرُ ۞ وَاِذْ يَرْفَعُ

اِبْرٰهٖمُ الْقَوَاعِدَ مِنَ الْبَيْتِ

وَاِسْمٰعِيْلُؕ رَبَّنَا تَقَبَّلْ مِنَّاؕ اِنَّكَ

اَنْتَ السَّمِيْعُ الْعَلِيْمُ ۞ رَبَّنَا

وَاجْعَلْنَا مُسْلِمَيْنِ لَكَ وَمِنْ

will make you an Imam to the Nations." He pleaded: "And also (Imams) from my offspring!" He answered: "But My Promise is not within the reach of evil-doers."

125. And remember We made the House a place of assembly for men and a place of safety; and take you the station of Abraham as a place of prayer; and We covenanted with Abraham and Isma'il, that they should sanctify My House for those who compass it round, or use it as a retreat, or bow, or prostrate themselves (therein in prayer).

126. And remember Abraham said: "My Lord, make this a City of Peace,

جَاعِلُكَ لِلنَّاسِ اِمَامًا ۚ قَالَ

وَمِنْ ذُرِّيَّتِيْ ۚ قَالَ لَا يَنَالُ عَهْدِي

الظّٰلِمِيْنَ ۞ وَاِذْ جَعَلْنَا الْبَيْتَ

مَثَابَةً لِّلنَّاسِ وَاَمْنًا ۚ وَاتَّخِذُوْا

مِنْ مَّقَامِ اِبْرٰهٖمَ مُصَلًّى ۚ وَعَهِدْنَآ

اِلٰى اِبْرٰهٖمَ وَاِسْمٰعِيْلَ اَنْ طَهِّرَا

بَيْتِيَ لِلطَّآئِفِيْنَ وَالْعٰكِفِيْنَ

وَالرُّكَّعِ السُّجُوْدِ ۞ وَاِذْ قَالَ اِبْرٰهٖمُ

رَبِّ اجْعَلْ هٰذَا بَلَدًا اٰمِنًا

therein, - the loss is their own.

122. O Children of Israel! Call to mind the special favour which I bestowed upon you, and that I preferred you to all others (for My Message).

123. Then guard yourselves against a Day when one soul shall not avail another, nor shall compensation be accepted from her nor shall intercession profit her nor shall anyone be helped (from outside).

124. And remember that Abraham was tried by his Lord with certain commands, which he fulfilled: He said: "I

بِهٖ فَاُولٰٓئِكَ هُمُ الْخٰسِرُوْنَ ۝

يٰبَنِيْٓ اِسْرَآءِيْلَ اذْكُرُوْا نِعْمَتِيَ

الَّتِيْٓ اَنْعَمْتُ عَلَيْكُمْ وَاَنِّيْ

فَضَّلْتُكُمْ عَلَى الْعٰلَمِيْنَ ۝ وَاتَّقُوْا

يَوْمًا لَّا تَجْزِيْ نَفْسٌ عَنْ نَّفْسٍ

شَيْئًا وَّلَا يُقْبَلُ مِنْهَا عَدْلٌ

وَّلَا تَنْفَعُهَا شَفَاعَةٌ وَّلَا هُمْ

يُنْصَرُوْنَ ۝ وَاِذِ ابْتَلٰٓى اِبْرٰهٖمَ

رَبُّهٗ بِكَلِمٰتٍ فَاَتَمَّهُنَّ ۛ قَالَ اِنِّيْ

of the Blazing Fire.

120. Never will the Jews or the Christians be satisfied with you unless you follow their form of religion. Say: "The Guidance of Allah, - that is the (only) Guidance." Were you to follow their desires after the knowledge which has reached you, then would you find neither Protector nor Helper against Allah.

121. Those to whom We have sent the Book study it as it should be studied: they are the ones that believe therein: those who reject faith

الْجَحِيْمِ ۞ وَلَنْ تَرْضٰى عَنْكَ

الْيَهُوْدُ وَلَا النَّصٰرٰى حَتّٰى تَتَّبِعَ

مِلَّتَهُمْ ۗ قُلْ اِنَّ هُدَى اللّٰهِ

هُوَ الْهُدٰى ۗ وَلَئِنِ اتَّبَعْتَ

اَهْوَآءَهُمْ بَعْدَ الَّذِيْ جَآءَكَ

مِنَ الْعِلْمِ ۙ مَا لَكَ مِنَ اللّٰهِ مِنْ

وَّلِيٍّ وَّلَا نَصِيْرٍ ۞ اَلَّذِيْنَ اٰتَيْنٰهُمُ

الْكِتٰبَ يَتْلُوْنَهٗ حَقَّ تِلَاوَتِهٖ ۙ

اُولٰٓئِكَ يُؤْمِنُوْنَ بِهٖ ۗ وَمَنْ يَّكْفُرْ

and the earth: when He decrees a matter, He says to it: "Be," and it is.

118. Those without knowledge said: "Why does not Allah speak to us? Or why does a Sign not come to us?" So said the people before them words of similar import. Their hearts are alike. We have indeed made clear the Signs for any people who hold firmly to Faith (in their hearts).

119. Surely We have sent you in truth as a bearer of glad tidings and a warner: but of you no question shall be asked of the Companions

وَالْاَرْضِ ؕ وَاِذَا قَضٰۤى اَمْرًا

فَاِنَّمَا يَقُوْلُ لَهٗ كُنْ فَيَكُوْنُ ۞

وَقَالَ الَّذِيْنَ لَا يَعْلَمُوْنَ لَوْلَا

يُكَلِّمُنَا اللّٰهُ اَوْ تَاْتِيْنَاۤ اٰيَةٌ ؕ

كَذٰلِكَ قَالَ الَّذِيْنَ مِنْ قَبْلِهِمْ

مِّثْلَ قَوْلِهِمْ ؕ تَشَابَهَتْ قُلُوْبُهُمْ ؕ

قَدْ بَيَّنَّا الْاٰيٰتِ لِقَوْمٍ يُّوْقِنُوْنَ ۞

اِنَّاۤ اَرْسَلْنٰكَ بِالْحَقِّ بَشِيْرًا

وَّنَذِيْرًا ۙ وَّلَا تُسْـَٔلُ عَنْ اَصْحٰبِ

fitting that such should themselves enter them except in fear.
For them there is nothing but
disgrace in this world, and in the
world to come, an exceeding
torment.

115. To Allah belong the East and
the West: whithersoever you
turn, there is the Presence of
Allah. For Allah is All-Pervading,
All-Knowing.

116. They say: "Allah has begotten a son": Glory be to Him. - No,
to Him belongs all that is in the
heavens and on earth: everything
renders worship to Him.

117. To Him is due the primal
origin of the heavens

كَانَ لَهُمْ أَنْ يَّدْخُلُوهَآ إِلَّا
خَآئِفِيْنَ ۚ لَهُمْ فِي الدُّنْيَا
خِزْيٌ وَّلَهُمْ فِي الْاٰخِرَةِ عَذَابٌ
عَظِيْمٌ ۞ وَلِلّٰهِ الْمَشْرِقُ وَالْمَغْرِبُ
فَأَيْنَمَا تُوَلُّوْا فَثَمَّ وَجْهُ اللّٰهِ
إِنَّ اللّٰهَ وَاسِعٌ عَلِيْمٌ ۞ وَقَالُوا
اتَّخَذَ اللّٰهُ وَلَدًا ۙ سُبْحٰنَهٗ ۚ بَلْ
لَّهٗ مَا فِي السَّمٰوٰتِ وَالْاَرْضِ ۚ
كُلٌّ لَّهٗ قٰنِتُوْنَ ۞ بَدِيْعُ السَّمٰوٰتِ

(to stand) upon"; and the Christians say: "The Jews have nothing (to stand) upon." Yet they (Profess to) study the (same) Book. Like unto their word is what those say who know not; but Allah will judge between them in their dispute on the Day of Judgment.

114. And who is more unjust than he who forbids that in places for the worship of Allah, Allah's name should be celebrated?- Whose zeal is (in fact) to ruin them? It was not

عَلٰى شَىْءٍ ۚ وَّقَالَتِ النَّصٰرٰى

لَيْسَتِ الْيَهُوْدُ عَلٰى شَىْءٍ ۙ وَّهُمْ

يَتْلُوْنَ الْكِتٰبَ ۗ كَذٰلِكَ قَالَ

الَّذِيْنَ لَا يَعْلَمُوْنَ مِثْلَ قَوْلِهِمْ ۚ

فَاللّٰهُ يَحْكُمُ بَيْنَهُمْ يَوْمَ الْقِيٰمَةِ

فِيْمَا كَانُوْا فِيْهِ يَخْتَلِفُوْنَ ۝

وَمَنْ أَظْلَمُ مِمَّنْ مَّنَعَ مَسٰجِدَ

اللّٰهِ أَنْ يُّذْكَرَ فِيْهَا اسْمُهٗ

وَسَعٰى فِيْ خَرَابِهَا ۚ أُولٰٓئِكَ مَا

Allah sees well all that you do.

111. And they say: "None shall enter Paradise unless he be a Jew or a Christian." Those are their (vain) desires. Say: "Produce your proof if you are truthful."

112. No, - whoever submits his whole self to Allah and is a doer of good, - He will get his reward with his Lord; on such shall be no fear, nor shall they grieve.

113. The Jews say: "The Christians have nothing

اللهُ بِمَا تَعۡمَلُوۡنَ بَصِيۡرٌ ۞

وَقَالُوۡا لَنۡ يَّدۡخُلَ الۡجَنَّةَ اِلَّا

مَنۡ كَانَ هُوۡدًا اَوۡ نَصٰرٰى ؕ تِلۡكَ

اَمَانِيُّهُمۡ ؕ قُلۡ هَاتُوۡا بُرۡهَانَكُمۡ

اِنۡ كُنۡتُمۡ صٰدِقِيۡنَ ۞   بَلٰى ۫

مَنۡ اَسۡلَمَ وَجۡهَهٗ لِلّٰهِ وَهُوَ

مُحۡسِنٌ فَلَهٗۤ اَجۡرُهٗ عِنۡدَ رَبِّهٖ ۪ وَلَا

خَوۡفٌ عَلَيۡهِمۡ وَلَا هُمۡ يَحۡزَنُوۡنَ ۞

وَقَالَتِ الۡيَهُوۡدُ لَيۡسَتِ النَّصٰرٰى

they could turn you (people) back to infidelity after you have believed, from selfish envy, after the Truth has become Manifest to them: but forgive and overlook, till Allah accomplish His purpose; for Allah has power over all things.

110. And be steadfast in prayer and regular in charity: and whatever good you send forth for your souls before you, you shall find it with Allah: for

يَرُدُّوْنَكُمْ مِّنْ بَعْدِ اِيْمَانِكُمْ

كُفَّارًا ۚ حَسَدًا مِّنْ عِنْدِ

اَنْفُسِهِمْ مِّنْ بَعْدِ مَا تَبَيَّنَ

لَهُمُ الْحَقُّ ۚ فَاعْفُوْا وَاصْفَحُوْا

حَتّٰى يَأْتِىَ اللّٰهُ بِاَمْرِهٖ ۚ اِنَّ

اللّٰهَ عَلٰى كُلِّ شَىْءٍ قَدِيْرٌ ۝

وَاَقِيْمُوا الصَّلٰوةَ وَاٰتُوا الزَّكٰوةَ ۚ

وَمَا تُقَدِّمُوْا لِاَنْفُسِكُمْ مِّنْ

خَيْرٍ تَجِدُوْهُ عِنْدَ اللّٰهِ ۗ اِنَّ

has power over all things?

107. Do you not know that to Allah belongs the dominion of the heavens and the earth? And besides Him you have neither patron nor helper.

108. Would you question your Apostle as Moses was questioned of old? But whoever changes from Faith to Unbelief, has strayed without doubt from the even way.

109. Quite a number of the People of the Book wish

عَلٰى كُلِّ شَىْءٍ قَدِيْرٌ ۞ اَلَمْ تَعْلَمْ

اَنَّ اللّٰهَ لَهٗ مُلْكُ السَّمٰوٰتِ

وَالْاَرْضِ ۖ وَمَا لَكُمْ مِّنْ دُوْنِ

اللّٰهِ مِنْ وَّلِيٍّ وَّلَا نَصِيْرٍ ۞

اَمْ تُرِيْدُوْنَ اَنْ تَسْـَٔلُوْا رَسُوْلَكُمْ

كَمَا سُئِلَ مُوْسٰى مِنْ قَبْلُ ۗ

وَمَنْ يَّتَبَدَّلِ الْكُفْرَ بِالْاِيْمَانِ

فَقَدْ ضَلَّ سَوَآءَ السَّبِيْلِ ۞ وَدَّ

كَثِيْرٌ مِّنْ اَهْلِ الْكِتٰبِ لَوْ

to those without Faith is a grie-vous Punishment.

105. It is never the wish of those without Faith among the People of the Book, nor of the Pagans, that anything good should come down to you from your Lord. But Allah will choose for His special Mercy whom He will - for Allah is Lord of grace abounding .

106. None of Our revelations do We abrogate or cause to be forgotten, but We substitute something better or similar: do you not know that Allah

وَلِلْكٰفِرِيْنَ عَذَابٌ اَلِيْمٌ ۝ مَا

يَوَدُّ الَّذِيْنَ كَفَرُوْا مِنْ اَهْلِ

الْكِتٰبِ وَلَا الْمُشْرِكِيْنَ اَنْ

يُّنَزَّلَ عَلَيْكُمْ مِّنْ خَيْرٍ مِّنْ

رَّبِّكُمْ ۭ وَاللّٰهُ يَخْتَصُّ بِرَحْمَتِهٖ

مَنْ يَّشَاءُ ۭ وَاللّٰهُ ذُو الْفَضْلِ

الْعَظِيْمِ ۝ مَا نَنْسَخْ مِنْ اٰيَةٍ

اَوْ نُنْسِهَا نَاْتِ بِخَيْرٍ مِّنْهَاۤ

اَوْ مِثْلِهَا ۭ اَلَمْ تَعْلَمْ اَنَّ اللّٰهَ

And they learned what harmed them, not what profited them. And they knew that the buyers of (magic) would have no share in the happiness of the Hereafter. And vile was the price for which they did sell their souls, if they but knew!

103. If they had kept their Faith and guarded themselves from evil, far better had been the reward from their Lord, if they but knew!

104. O you men of Faith! Say not (to the Apostle) words of ambiguous import, but words of respect; and listen (to him):

وَيَتَعَلَّمُونَ مَا يَضُرُّهُمْ وَلَا
يَنْفَعُهُمْ ۚ وَلَقَدْ عَلِمُوا لَمَنِ اشْتَرَاهُ
مَا لَهُ فِي الْآخِرَةِ مِنْ خَلَاقٍ ۚ
وَلَبِئْسَ مَا شَرَوْا بِهِ أَنْفُسَهُمْ ۚ
لَوْ كَانُوا يَعْلَمُونَ ۝ وَلَوْ أَنَّهُمْ
آمَنُوا وَاتَّقَوْا لَمَثُوبَةٌ مِّنْ عِنْدِ
اللّٰهِ خَيْرٌ ۚ لَوْ كَانُوا يَعْلَمُونَ ۝
يَا أَيُّهَا الَّذِينَ آمَنُوا لَا تَقُولُوا
رَاعِنَا وَقُولُوا انْظُرْنَا وَاسْمَعُوا

the blasphemers were, not
Solomon, but the evil ones,
teaching men magic, and such
things as came down at Babylon
to the Angels Harut and Marut.
But neither of these taught
anyone (such things) without
saying: "We are only for trial; so
do not blaspheme." They learned
from them the means to sow
discord between man and wife.
But they could not thus harm
anyone except by Allah's permission.

وَمَا كَفَرَ سُلَيْمَٰنُ وَلَٰكِنَّ الشَّيَٰطِينَ

كَفَرُوا يُعَلِّمُونَ النَّاسَ السِّحْرَ

وَمَآ أُنْزِلَ عَلَى الْمَلَكَيْنِ بِبَابِلَ

هَارُوتَ وَمَارُوتَ ۚ وَمَا يُعَلِّمَٰنِ

مِنْ أَحَدٍ حَتَّىٰ يَقُولَآ إِنَّمَا نَحْنُ

فِتْنَةٌ فَلَا تَكْفُرْ ۖ فَيَتَعَلَّمُونَ

مِنْهُمَا مَا يُفَرِّقُونَ بِهِ بَيْنَ

الْمَرْءِ وَزَوْجِهِ ۚ وَمَا هُم بِضَآرِّينَ

بِهِ مِنْ أَحَدٍ إِلَّا بِإِذْنِ اللَّهِ

but those who are perverse.

100. Is it not (the case) that every time they make Covenant, some party among them throw it aside? - No, most of them are faithless.

101. And when there came to them an Apostle from Allah, confirming what was with them, a party of the people of the Book threw away the Book of Allah behind their backs, as if (it had been something) they did not know!

102. They followed what the evil ones gave out (falsely) against the power of Solomon:

إِلَّا الْفَاسِقُونَ ۝ أَوَ كُلَّمَا عَاهَدُوا

عَهْدًا نَّبَذَهُ فَرِيقٌ مِّنْهُمْ

بَلْ أَكْثَرُهُمْ لَا يُؤْمِنُونَ ۝

وَلَمَّا جَآءَهُمْ رَسُولٌ مِّنْ عِندِ

اللهِ مُصَدِّقٌ لِّمَا مَعَهُمْ نَبَذَ

فَرِيقٌ مِّنَ الَّذِينَ أُوتُوا الْكِتَابَ

كِتَابَ اللهِ وَرَآءَ ظُهُورِهِمْ كَأَنَّهُمْ

لَا يَعْلَمُونَ ۝ وَاتَّبَعُوا مَا تَتْلُوا

الشَّيَاطِينُ عَلَى مُلْكِ سُلَيْمَانَ

they do.

97. Say: whoever is an enemy to Gabriel - for he has brought down the (revelation) to your heart by Allah's will, a confirmation of what went before, and guidance and glad tidings for those who believe,

98. Whoever is an enemy to Allah and His Angels and Apostles, to Gabriel and Michael,- certainly Allah is an enemy to those who reject Faith.

99. We have sent down to you Manifest Signs (Ayat); and none reject them

يَعْمَلُونَ ۞ قُلْ مَنْ كَانَ عَدُوًّا

لِّجِبْرِيلَ فَإِنَّهُ نَزَّلَهُ عَلَى

قَلْبِكَ بِإِذْنِ اللهِ مُصَدِّقًا

لِّمَا بَيْنَ يَدَيْهِ وَهُدًى

وَبُشْرَى لِلْمُؤْمِنِينَ ۞ مَنْ كَانَ

عَدُوًّا لِّلّٰهِ وَمَلَائِكَتِهِ وَرُسُلِهِ

وَجِبْرِيلَ وَمِيكَالَ فَإِنَّ اللهَ

عَدُوٌّ لِّلْكَافِرِينَ ۞ وَلَقَدْ أَنْزَلْنَا

إِلَيْكَ آيَاتٍ بَيِّنَاتٍ وَمَا يَكْفُرُ بِهَا

anyone else, then seek you for death, if you are sincere."

95. But they will never seek for death, on account of the (sins) which their hands have sent on before them. And Allah is Well-Acquainted with the wrong-doers.

96. You will indeed find them, of all people, most greedy of life,- even more than the idolators: each one of them wishes he could be given a life of a thousand years: but the grant of such life will not save him from (due) punishment. For Allah sees well all that

النَّاسِ فَتَمَنَّوُا الْمَوْتَ إِنْ كُنْتُمْ

صٰدِقِيْنَ ۝ وَلَنْ يَّتَمَنَّوْهُ أَبَدًاۢ

بِمَا قَدَّمَتْ أَيْدِيْهِمْ ۗ وَاللّٰهُ

عَلِيْمٌۢ بِالظّٰلِمِيْنَ ۝ وَلَتَجِدَنَّهُمْ

أَحْرَصَ النَّاسِ عَلٰى حَيٰوةٍ ۚ

وَمِنَ الَّذِيْنَ أَشْرَكُوْا ۛ يَوَدُّ

أَحَدُهُمْ لَوْ يُعَمَّرُ أَلْفَ سَنَةٍ ۚ

وَمَا هُوَ بِمُزَحْزِحِهٖ مِنَ الْعَذَابِ

أَنْ يُّعَمَّرَ ۗ وَاللّٰهُ بَصِيْرٌۢ بِمَا

and you did behave wrongfully.

93. And remember We took your covenant and We raised above you (the towering height) of Mount (Sinai): (Saying): "Hold firmly to what We have given you, and pay heed (to the Law)": they said: "We hear, and we disobey": and they had to drink into their hearts (of the taint) of the calf because of their Faithlessness. Say: "Vile indeed are the behests of your Faith if you have any faith!"

94. Say: "If the last Home, with Allah, be for you specially, and not for

وَاَنْتُمْ ظٰلِمُوْنَ ۞ وَاِذْ اَخَذْنَا

مِيْثَاقَكُمْ وَرَفَعْنَا فَوْقَكُمُ

الطُّوْرَ ؕ خُذُوْا مَآ اٰتَيْنٰكُمْ بِقُوَّةٍ

وَّاسْمَعُوْا ؕ قَالُوْا سَمِعْنَا وَعَصَيْنَا

وَاُشْرِبُوْا فِيْ قُلُوْبِهِمُ الْعِجْلَ

بِكُفْرِهِمْ ؕ قُلْ بِئْسَمَا يَاْمُرُكُمْ بِهٖٓ

اِيْمَانُكُمْ اِنْ كُنْتُمْ مُّؤْمِنِيْنَ ۞

قُلْ اِنْ كَانَتْ لَكُمُ الدَّارُ الْاٰخِرَةُ

عِنْدَ اللّٰهِ خَالِصَةً مِّنْ دُوْنِ

the punishment of those who reject Faith.

91. When it is said to them, "Believe in what Allah has sent down," they say, "We believe in what was sent down to us": yet they reject all besides, even if it be Truth confirming what is with them. Say: "Why then have you slain the prophets of Allah in times gone by, if you did indeed believe?"

92. There came to you Moses with clear (Signs); yet you worshipped the calf (even) after that,

عَذَابٌ مُّهِينٌ ۞ وَاِذَا قِيْلَ

لَهُمْ اٰمِنُوْا بِمَآ اَنْزَلَ اللّٰهُ

قَالُوْا نُؤْمِنُ بِمَآ اُنْزِلَ عَلَيْنَا

وَيَكْفُرُوْنَ بِمَا وَرَآءَهٗ وَهُوَ

الْحَقُّ مُصَدِّقًا لِّمَا مَعَهُمْ ۗ قُلْ

فَلِمَ تَقْتُلُوْنَ اَنْۢبِيَآءَ اللّٰهِ مِنْ

قَبْلُ اِنْ كُنْتُمْ مُّؤْمِنِيْنَ ۞

وَلَقَدْ جَآءَكُمْ مُّوْسٰى بِالْبَيِّنٰتِ

ثُمَّ اتَّخَذْتُمُ الْعِجْلَ مِنْ بَعْدِهٖ

from of old they had prayed for victory against those without Faith, - when there comes to them that which they (should) have recognised, they refuse to believe in it but the curse of Allah is on those without Faith.

90. Miserable is the price for which they have sold their souls, in that they deny (the revelation) which Allah has sent down, in insolent envy that Allah of His Grace should send it to any of His servants He pleases: thus they have drawn on themselves Wrath upon Wrath. And humiliating is

مِنْ قَبْلُ يَسْتَفْتِحُونَ عَلَى

الَّذِيْنَ كَفَرُوْا ۖ فَلَمَّا جَآءَهُمْ

مَّا عَرَفُوْا كَفَرُوْا بِهٖ فَلَعْنَةُ

اللّٰهِ عَلَى الْكٰفِرِيْنَ ۝ بِئْسَمَا

اشْتَرَوْا بِهٖۤ اَنْفُسَهُمْ اَنْ يَّكْفُرُوْا

بِمَاۤ اَنْزَلَ اللّٰهُ بَغْيًا اَنْ

يُّنَزِّلَ اللّٰهُ مِنْ فَضْلِهٖ عَلَى

مَنْ يَّشَآءُ مِنْ عِبَادِهٖ فَبَآءُوْ

بِغَضَبٍ عَلٰى غَضَبٍ ۚ وَلِلْكٰفِرِيْنَ

Mary clear (Signs) and strengthened him with the holy spirit. Is it that whenever there comes to you an Apostle with what you yourselves desire not, you are puffed up with pride? - some you called impostors, and others you slay!

88. They say, "Our hearts are the wrappings (which preserve Allah's Word: we need no more)." No, Allah's curse is on them for their blasphemy: little is it they believe.

89. And when there comes to them a Book from Allah, confirming what is with them,- although

مَرْيَمَ الْبَيِّنَتِ وَاَيَّدْنَهُ بِرُوْحِ
الْقُدُسِ ۚ اَفَكُلَّمَا جَآءَكُمْ رَسُوْلٌۢ
بِمَا لَا تَهْوٰۤى اَنْفُسُكُمُ اسْتَكْبَرْتُمْ ۚ
فَفَرِيْقًا كَذَّبْتُمْ وَ فَرِيْقًا
تَقْتُلُوْنَ ۞ وَ قَالُوْا قُلُوْبُنَا غُلْفٌ ۚ
بَلْ لَّعَنَهُمُ اللّٰهُ بِكُفْرِهِمْ
فَقَلِيْلًا مَّا يُؤْمِنُوْنَ ۞ وَ لَمَّا
جَآءَهُمْ كِتٰبٌ مِّنْ عِنْدِ اللّٰهِ
مُصَدِّقٌ لِّمَا مَعَهُمْ ۙ وَ كَانُوْا

but disgrace in this life? - and on the Day of Judgment they shall be consigned to the most grievous Chastisement, for Allah is not unmindful of what you do.

86. These are the people who buy the life of this world at the price of the Hereafter: their Chastisement shall not be lightened nor shall they be helped.

87. We gave Moses the Book and followed him up with a succession of Apostles; We gave Jesus the son of

اِلَّا خِزْىٌ فِى الْحَيٰوةِ الدُّنْيَا ۖ

وَيَوْمَ الْقِيٰمَةِ يُرَدُّوْنَ اِلٰٓى اَشَدِّ

الْعَذَابِ ۗ وَمَا اللّٰهُ بِغَافِلٍ عَمَّا

تَعْمَلُوْنَ ۞ اُولٰٓئِكَ الَّذِيْنَ اشْتَرَوُا

الْحَيٰوةَ الدُّنْيَا بِالْاٰخِرَةِ ۖ فَلَا

يُخَفَّفُ عَنْهُمُ الْعَذَابُ وَلَا هُمْ

يُنْصَرُوْنَ ۞ وَلَقَدْ اٰتَيْنَا مُوْسَى

الْكِتٰبَ وَقَفَّيْنَا مِنْ بَعْدِهٖ

بِالرُّسُلِ ۖ وَاٰتَيْنَا عِيْسَى ابْنَ

can bear witness.

85. After this it is you, the same people, who slay among yourselves, and banish a party of you from their homes; assist (their enemies) against them, in guilt and rancour; and if they come to you as captives, you ransom them, though it was not lawful for you to banish them. Then is it only a part of the Book that you believe in, and do you reject the rest? But what is the reward for those among you who behave like this

تَشْهَدُوْنَ ۞ ثُمَّ اَنْتُمْ هٰٓؤُلَآءِ

تَقْتُلُوْنَ اَنْفُسَكُمْ وَتُخْرِجُوْنَ

فَرِيْقًا مِّنْكُمْ مِّنْ دِيَارِهِمْ

تَظٰهَرُوْنَ عَلَيْهِمْ بِالْاِثْمِ

وَالْعُدْوَانِ ۗ وَاِنْ يَّاْتُوْكُمْ اُسٰرٰى

تُفٰدُوْهُمْ وَهُوَ مُحَرَّمٌ عَلَيْكُمْ

اِخْرَاجُهُمْ ۗ اَفَتُؤْمِنُوْنَ بِبَعْضِ

الْكِتٰبِ وَتَكْفُرُوْنَ بِبَعْضٍ ۚ فَمَا

جَزَآءُ مَنْ يَّفْعَلُ ذٰلِكَ مِنْكُمْ

worship none but Allah; treat
with kindness your parents and
kindred, and or-phans and those
in need; speak fair to the people;
be steadfast in prayer; and
practise regular charity. Then did
you turn back, except a few
among you, and you backslide
(even now).

84. And remember We took
your covenant (to this effect):
shed no blood amongst you, nor
turn out your own people from
your homes: and this you
solemnly ratified, and to this you

لَا تَعْبُدُونَ إِلَّا اللّٰهَ وَبِالْوَالِدَيْنِ
اِحْسَانًا وَّذِى الْقُرْبٰى وَالْيَتٰمٰى
وَالْمَسٰكِيْنِ وَقُوْلُوْا لِلنَّاسِ حُسْنًا
وَّاَقِيْمُوا الصَّلٰوةَ وَاٰتُوا الزَّكٰوةَ ؕ
ثُمَّ تَوَلَّيْتُمْ إِلَّا قَلِيْلًا مِّنْكُمْ
وَاَنْتُمْ مُّعْرِضُوْنَ ۞ وَاِذْ اَخَذْنَا
مِيْثَاقَكُمْ لَا تَسْفِكُوْنَ دِمَآءَكُمْ
وَلَا تُخْرِجُوْنَ اَنْفُسَكُمْ مِّنْ
دِيَارِكُمْ ثُمَّ اَقْرَرْتُمْ وَاَنْتُمْ

a promise from Allah, for He never breaks His promise? Or is it that you say of Allah what you do not know?"

81. No, those who seek gain in evil, and are girt round by their sins, - they are companions of the Fire: therein shall they abide (for ever).

82. But those who have faith and work righteousness, they are companions of the Garden: therein shall they abide (for-ever).

83. And remember We took a covenant from the Children of Israel (to this effect):

عِنْدَ اللهِ عَهْدًا فَلَنْ يُّخْلِفَ

اللهُ عَهْدَهٗٓ اَمْ تَقُوْلُوْنَ عَلَى

اللهِ مَا لَا تَعْلَمُوْنَ ۞ بَلٰى مَنْ

كَسَبَ سَيِّئَةً وَّاَحَاطَتْ بِهٖ

خَطِيْٓئَتُهٗ فَاُولٰٓئِكَ اَصْحٰبُ النَّارِ ۚ

هُمْ فِيْهَا خٰلِدُوْنَ ۞ وَالَّذِيْنَ

اٰمَنُوْا وَعَمِلُوا الصّٰلِحٰتِ اُولٰٓئِكَ

اَصْحٰبُ الْجَنَّةِ ۚ هُمْ فِيْهَا خٰلِدُوْنَ ۞

وَاِذْ اَخَذْنَا مِيْثَاقَ بَنِيْٓ اِسْرَآءِيْلَ

the Book, but (see therein their own) desires, and they do nothing but conjecture.

79.   Then woe to those who write the Book with their own hands, and then say: "This is from Allah," to traffic with it for miserable price! - woe to them for what their hands do write, and for the gain they make thereby.

80.   And they say: "The Fire shall not touch us but for a few numbered days:" Say: "Have you taken

الْكِتٰبَ اِلَّاۤ اَمَانِيَّ وَاِنْ هُمْ

اِلَّا يَظُنُّوْنَ ۞ فَوَيْلٌ لِّلَّذِيْنَ

يَكْتُبُوْنَ الْكِتٰبَ بِاَيْدِيْهِمْ ثُمَّ

يَقُوْلُوْنَ هٰذَا مِنْ عِنْدِ اللّٰهِ

لِيَشْتَرُوْا بِهٖ ثَمَنًا قَلِيْلًا ۚ

فَوَيْلٌ لَّهُمْ مِّمَّا كَتَبَتْ اَيْدِيْهِمْ

وَوَيْلٌ لَّهُمْ مِّمَّا يَكْسِبُوْنَ ۞

وَقَالُوْا لَنْ تَمَسَّنَا النَّارُ اِلَّاۤ

اَيَّامًا مَّعْدُوْدَةً ۚ قُلْ اَتَّخَذْتُمْ

knowingly after they understood it.

76.   Behold! when they meet the
men of Faith, they say: "We
believe": but when they meet
each other in private, they say:
"Shall you tell them what Allah
has revealed to you, that they
may engage you in argument
about it before your Lord?"- Do
you not understand (their aim)?

77.   Do they not know that Allah
knows what they conceal and
what they reveal?

78.   And there are among them
illiterates, who know not

بَعْدِ مَا عَقَلُوهُ وَهُمْ يَعْلَمُوْنَ ۞

وَاِذَا لَقُوا الَّذِيْنَ اٰمَنُوْا قَالُوْٓا

اٰمَنَّا ۚ وَاِذَا خَلَا بَعْضُهُمْ اِلٰى

بَعْضٍ قَالُوْٓا اَتُحَدِّثُوْنَهُمْ بِمَا

فَتَحَ اللّٰهُ عَلَيْكُمْ لِيُحَآجُّوْكُمْ

بِهٖ عِنْدَ رَبِّكُمْ ؕ اَفَلَا تَعْقِلُوْنَ ۞

اَوَلَا يَعْلَمُوْنَ اَنَّ اللّٰهَ يَعْلَمُ

مَا يُسِرُّوْنَ وَمَا يُعْلِنُوْنَ ۞

وَمِنْهُمْ اُمِّيُّوْنَ لَا يَعْلَمُوْنَ

like a rock and even worse in hardness. For among rocks there are some from which rivers gush forth; others there are which when split asunder send forth water; and others which sink for fear of Allah. And Allah is not unmindful of what you do.

75. Can you (O you men of Faith) entertain the hope that they will believe in you?- Seeing that a party of them heard the Word of Allah, and perverted it

كَالْحِجَارَةِ أَوْ أَشَدُّ قَسْوَةً ۚ وَإِنَّ

مِنَ الْحِجَارَةِ لَمَا يَتَفَجَّرُ مِنْهُ

الْأَنْهَارُ ۚ وَإِنَّ مِنْهَا لَمَا يَشَّقَّقُ

فَيَخْرُجُ مِنْهُ الْمَاءُ ۚ وَإِنَّ مِنْهَا

لَمَا يَهْبِطُ مِنْ خَشْيَةِ اللّٰهِ ۗ وَمَا

اللّٰهُ بِغَافِلٍ عَمَّا تَعْمَلُونَ ۝

أَفَتَطْمَعُونَ أَنْ يُؤْمِنُوا لَكُمْ وَقَدْ

كَانَ فَرِيقٌ مِنْهُمْ يَسْمَعُونَ

كَلَامَ اللّٰهِ ثُمَّ يُحَرِّفُونَهُ مِنْ

sound and without blemish". They said: "Now you has brought the truth." Then they offered her in sacrifice, but not with good-will.

72. And remember you slew a man and fell into a dispute among yourselves as to the crime: but Allah was to bring forth what you did hide.

73. So We said: "Strike the (body) with a piece of the (heifer)." Thus Allah brings the dead to life and shows you His Signs: perchance you may understand.

74. Thenceforth were your hearts hardened: they became

مُسَلَّمَةٌ لَّا شِيَةَ فِيهَا ۚ قَالُوا

الْـٰٔنَ جِئْتَ بِالْحَقِّ ۚ فَذَبَحُوهَا

وَمَا كَادُوا يَفْعَلُونَ ۞ وَإِذْ

قَتَلْتُمْ نَفْسًا فَادَّارَٰٔتُمْ فِيهَا ۖ

وَاللَّهُ مُخْرِجٌ مَّا كُنتُمْ تَكْتُمُونَ ۞

فَقُلْنَا اضْرِبُوهُ بِبَعْضِهَا ۚ كَذَٰلِكَ

يُحْىِ اللَّهُ الْمَوْتَىٰ وَيُرِيكُمْ ءَايَٰتِهِ

لَعَلَّكُمْ تَعْقِلُونَ ۞ ثُمَّ قَسَتْ

قُلُوبُكُم مِّنۢ بَعْدِ ذَٰلِكَ فَهِىَ

you Lord to make plain to us her colour." He said: "He says: a fawn-coloured heifer, pure and rich in tone, the admiration of beholders!"

70. They said: "Beseech on our behalf you Lord to make plain to us what she is: to us are all heifers alike: we wish indeed for guidance, if Allah wills."

71. He said: "He says: a heifer not trained to till the soil or water the fields;

رَبَّكَ يُبَيِّن لَّنَا مَا لَوْنُهَا ۚ

قَالَ اِنَّهٗ يَقُوْلُ اِنَّهَا بَقَرَةٌ

صَفْرَآءُ فَاقِعٌ لَّوْنُهَا تَسُرُّ

النّٰظِرِيْنَ ۞ قَالُوا ادْعُ لَنَا

رَبَّكَ يُبَيِّن لَّنَا مَا هِيَ ۙ اِنَّ

الْبَقَرَ تَشٰبَهَ عَلَيْنَا ۚ وَاِنَّا اِنْ

شَآءَ اللّٰهُ لَمُهْتَدُوْنَ ۞ قَالَ

اِنَّهٗ يَقُوْلُ اِنَّهَا بَقَرَةٌ لَّا ذَلُوْلٌ

تُثِيْرُ الْاَرْضَ وَلَا تَسْقِى الْحَرْثَ ۚ

to his people: "Allah commands that you sacrifice a heifer". They said: "Makes you a laughing-stock of us?" He said: "Allah save me from being an ignorant (fool)!"

68. They said: "Beseech on our behalf you Lord to make plain to us what (heifer) it is!" He said; "He says: the heifer should be neither too old nor too young, but of middling age. Now do what you are commanded!"

69. They said: "Beseech on our behalf

لِقَوْمِهٖ اِنَّ اللّٰهَ يَأْمُرُكُمْ اَنْ

تَذْبَحُوا بَقَرَةً قَالُوْٓا اَتَتَّخِذُنَا

هُزُوًا قَالَ اَعُوْذُ بِاللّٰهِ اَنْ

اَكُوْنَ مِنَ الْجٰهِلِيْنَ ۞ قَالُوا

ادْعُ لَنَا رَبَّكَ يُبَيِّنْ لَّنَا مَا

هِيَ ۗ قَالَ اِنَّهٗ يَقُوْلُ اِنَّهَا

بَقَرَةٌ لَّا فَارِضٌ وَّلَا بِكْرٌ ۗ

عَوَانٌۢ بَيْنَ ذٰلِكَ ۗ فَافْعَلُوْا

مَا تُؤْمَرُوْنَ ۞ قَالُوا ادْعُ لَنَا

you may fear Allah."

64. But you turned back there-after: had it not been for the Grace and Mercy of Allah to you, you had surely been among the lost.

65. And well you knew those amongst you who transgressed in the matter of the Sabbath: We said to them: "Be you apes, des-pised and rejected."

66. So We made it an example to their own time and to their posterity, and a lesson to those who fear Allah.

67. And remember Moses said

تَتَّقُوۡنَ ۞ ثُمَّ تَوَلَّيۡتُمۡ مِّنۡ

بَعۡدِ ذٰلِكَ ۚ فَلَوۡلَا فَضۡلُ اللّٰهِ

عَلَيۡكُمۡ وَرَحۡمَتُهُ لَكُنۡتُمۡ مِّنَ

الۡخٰسِرِيۡنَ ۞ وَلَقَدۡ عَلِمۡتُمُ الَّذِيۡنَ

اعۡتَدَوۡا مِنۡكُمۡ فِى السَّبۡتِ فَقُلۡنَا

لَهُمۡ كُوۡنُوۡا قِرَدَةً خٰسِئِيۡنَ ۞

فَجَعَلۡنٰهَا نَكَالًا لِّمَا بَيۡنَ

يَدَيۡهَا وَمَا خَلۡفَهَا وَمَوۡعِظَةً

لِّلۡمُتَّقِيۡنَ ۞ وَاِذۡ قَالَ مُوۡسٰى

and went on transgressing.

62. Those who believe (in the Qur'an), and those who follow the Jewish (scriptures), and the Christians and the Sabians,- and who believe in Allah and the Last Day, and work righteousness, shall have their reward with their Lord; on them shall be no fear, nor shall they grieve.

63. And remember We took your covenant and We raised above you (the towering height) of Mount (Sinai): (Saying): "Hold firmly to what We have given you and bring (ever) to remembrance what is therein: perchance

وَّكَانُوْا يَعْتَدُوْنَ ۞ اِنَّ الَّذِيْنَ اٰمَنُوْا وَالَّذِيْنَ هَادُوْا وَالنَّصٰرٰى وَالصّٰبِئِيْنَ مَنْ اٰمَنَ بِاللّٰهِ وَالْيَوْمِ الْاٰخِرِ وَعَمِلَ صَالِحًا فَلَهُمْ اَجْرُهُمْ عِنْدَ رَبِّهِمْ وَلَا خَوْفٌ عَلَيْهِمْ وَلَا هُمْ يَحْزَنُوْنَ ۞ وَاِذْ اَخَذْنَا مِيْثَاقَكُمْ وَرَفَعْنَا فَوْقَكُمُ الطُّوْرَ خُذُوْا مَآ اٰتَيْنٰكُمْ بِقُوَّةٍ وَّاذْكُرُوْا مَا فِيْهِ لَعَلَّكُمْ

its pot-herbs, and cucumbers, its garlic, lentils, and onions." He said: "Will you exchange the better for the worse? Go you down to any town, and you shall find what you want!" They were covered with humiliation and misery; they drew on themselves the wrath of Allah. This because they went on rejecting the Signs of Allah and slaying His Messengers without just cause. This because they rebelled

بَقْلِهَا وَقِثَّآئِهَا وَفُوْمِهَا وَعَدَسِهَا

وَبَصَلِهَا ۚ قَالَ اَتَسْتَبْدِلُوْنَ الَّذِیْ

هُوَ اَدْنٰی بِالَّذِیْ هُوَ خَیْرٌ ۚ

اِهْبِطُوْا مِصْرًا فَاِنَّ لَكُمْ مَّا

سَاَلْتُمْ ۗ وَضُرِبَتْ عَلَیْهِمُ الذِّلَّةُ

وَالْمَسْكَنَةُ ۖ وَبَآءُوْ بِغَضَبٍ مِّنَ

اللّٰهِ ۗ ذٰلِكَ بِاَنَّهُمْ كَانُوْا یَكْفُرُوْنَ

بِاٰیٰتِ اللّٰهِ وَیَقْتُلُوْنَ النَّبِیّٖنَ

بِغَیْرِ الْحَقِّ ۗ ذٰلِكَ بِمَا عَصَوْا

for his people; We said: "Strike the rock with your staff." Then gushed forth therefrom twelve springs. Each group knew its own place for water. So eat and drink of the sustenance provided by Allah, and do no evil nor mischief on the (face of the) earth.

61. And remember you said: "O Moses! We cannot endure one kind of food (always); so beseech your Lord for us to produce for us of what the earth grows,-

لِقَوۡمِهٖ فَقُلۡنَا اضۡرِبۡ بِّعَصَاكَ

الۡحَجَرَ ۚ فَانۡفَجَرَتۡ مِنۡهُ اثۡنَتَا

عَشۡرَةَ عَيۡنًا ؕ قَدۡ عَلِمَ كُلُّ

اُنَاسٍ مَّشۡرَبَهُمۡ ؕ كُلُوۡا وَاشۡرَبُوۡا

مِنۡ رِّزۡقِ اللّٰهِ وَلَا تَعۡثَوۡا فِی

الۡاَرۡضِ مُفۡسِدِیۡنَ ۝ وَاِذۡ قُلۡتُمۡ

یٰمُوۡسٰی لَنۡ نَّصۡبِرَ عَلٰی طَعَامٍ

وَّاحِدٍ فَادۡعُ لَنَا رَبَّكَ یُخۡرِجۡ

لَنَا مِمَّا تُنۡۢبِتُ الۡاَرۡضُ مِنۡ

58. And remember We said: "Enter this town, and eat of the plenty therein as you wish; but enter the gate with humility, in posture and in words, and We shall forgive you your faults and increase (the portion of) those who do good."

59. But the transgressors changed the word from that which had been given them; so We sent on the transgressors a plague from heaven, for that they infringed (Our command) repeatedly.

60. And remember Moses prayed for water

وَاِذْ قُلْنَا ادْخُلُوْا هٰذِهِ الْقَرْيَةَ

فَكُلُوْا مِنْهَا حَيْثُ شِئْتُمْ رَغَدًا

وَّادْخُلُوا الْبَابَ سُجَّدًا وَّقُوْلُوْا

حِطَّةٌ نَّغْفِرْ لَكُمْ خَطٰيٰكُمْ ۗ وَسَنَزِيْدُ

الْمُحْسِنِيْنَ ۞ فَبَدَّلَ الَّذِيْنَ

ظَلَمُوْا قَوْلًا غَيْرَ الَّذِيْ قِيْلَ

لَهُمْ فَاَنْزَلْنَا عَلَى الَّذِيْنَ ظَلَمُوْا

رِجْزًا مِّنَ السَّمَآءِ بِمَا كَانُوْا

يَفْسُقُوْنَ ۞ وَاِذِ اسْتَسْقٰى مُوْسٰى

"O Moses! We shall never believe in you until we see Allah manifestly," but you were dazed with thunder and lighting even as you looked on.

56. Then We raised you up after your death: you had the chance to be grateful.

57. And We gave you the shade of clouds and sent down to you manna and quails, saying: "Eat of the good things We have provided for you:" (But they rebelled); to us they did not harm, but they harmed their own souls.

يٰمُوْسٰى لَنْ نُّؤْمِنَ لَكَ حَتّٰى
نَرَى اللّٰهَ جَهْرَةً فَاَخَذَتْكُمُ
الصّٰعِقَةُ وَ اَنْتُمْ تَنْظُرُوْنَ ۝
ثُمَّ بَعَثْنٰكُمْ مِّنْۢ بَعْدِ مَوْتِكُمْ
لَعَلَّكُمْ تَشْكُرُوْنَ ۝ وَ ظَلَّلْنَا
عَلَيْكُمُ الْغَمَامَ وَ اَنْزَلْنَا عَلَيْكُمُ
الْمَنَّ وَ السَّلْوٰى كُلُوْا مِنْ
طَيِّبٰتِ مَا رَزَقْنٰكُمْ وَمَا ظَلَمُوْنَا
وَلٰكِنْ كَانُوْۤا اَنْفُسَهُمْ يَظْلِمُوْنَ ۝

there was a chance for you to be grateful.

53. And remember We gave Moses the Scripture and the Criterion (Between right and wrong): there was a chance for you to be guided aright.

54. And remember Moses said to his people: "O my people! You have indeed wronged yourselves by your worship of the calf: so turn (in repentance) to your Maker, and slay yourselves (the wrong-doers); that will be better for you in the sight of your Maker." Then He turned towards you (in forgiveness): for He is Oft-returning, Most Merciful.

55. And remember you said:

بَعْدِ ذٰلِكَ لَعَلَّكُمْ تَشْكُرُوْنَ ۞ وَاِذْ

اٰتَيْنَا مُوْسَى الْكِتٰبَ وَالْفُرْقَانَ

لَعَلَّكُمْ تَهْتَدُوْنَ ۞ وَاِذْ قَالَ

مُوْسٰى لِقَوْمِهٖ يٰقَوْمِ اِنَّكُمْ

ظَلَمْتُمْ اَنْفُسَكُمْ بِاتِّخَاذِكُمُ

الْعِجْلَ فَتُوْبُوْٓا اِلٰى بَارِئِكُمْ

فَاقْتُلُوْٓا اَنْفُسَكُمْ ۚ ذٰلِكُمْ خَيْرٌ لَّكُمْ

عِنْدَ بَارِئِكُمْ ۚ فَتَابَ عَلَيْكُمْ ۚ اِنَّهٗ

هُوَ التَّوَّابُ الرَّحِيْمُ ۞ وَاِذْ قُلْتُمْ

and punishments, slaughtered your sons and let your women-folk live; therein was a tremendous trial from your Lord.

50. And remember We divided the sea for you and saved you and drowned Pharaoh's people within your very sight.

51. And remember We appointed forty nights for Moses, and in his absence you took the calf (for worship), and you did grievous wrong.

52. Even then We did forgive you;

الْعَذَابَ يُذَبِّحُونَ أَبْنَاءَكُمْ

وَيَسْتَحْيُونَ نِسَاءَكُمْ ۚ وَفِى ذَٰلِكُمْ

بَلَاءٌ مِّن رَّبِّكُمْ عَظِيمٌ ۝ وَإِذْ

فَرَقْنَا بِكُمُ الْبَحْرَ فَأَنْجَيْنَاكُمْ

وَأَغْرَقْنَا آلَ فِرْعَوْنَ وَأَنْتُمْ

تَنْظُرُونَ ۝ وَإِذْ وَاعَدْنَا مُوسَىٰ

أَرْبَعِينَ لَيْلَةً ثُمَّ اتَّخَذْتُمُ

الْعِجْلَ مِن بَعْدِهِ وَأَنْتُمْ

ظَالِمُونَ ۝ ثُمَّ عَفَوْنَا عَنكُم مِّن

to meet their Lord, and that they are to return to Him.

47. O, Children of Israel! Call to mind the (special) favour which I bestowed upon you, and that I preferred you to all others (for My Message).

48. Then guard yourselves against a day when one soul shall not avail another nor shall intercession be accepted for her, nor shall compensation be taken from her, nor shall anyone be helped (from outside).

49. And remember, We delivered you from the people of Pharaoh: they set you hard tasks

مُلْقُوْنَ رَبِّهِمْ وَاَنَّهُمْ اِلَيْهِ

رٰجِعُوْنَ ۞ يٰبَنِيْۤ اِسْرَآءِيْلَ اذْكُرُوْا

نِعْمَتِيَ الَّتِيْۤ اَنْعَمْتُ عَلَيْكُمْ وَاَنِّيْ

فَضَّلْتُكُمْ عَلَى الْعٰلَمِيْنَ ۞ وَاتَّقُوْا

يَوْمًا لَّا تَجْزِيْ نَفْسٌ عَنْ

نَّفْسٍ شَيْئًا وَّلَا يُقْبَلُ مِنْهَا

شَفَاعَةٌ وَّلَا يُؤْخَذُ مِنْهَا عَدْلٌ

وَّلَا هُمْ يُنْصَرُوْنَ ۞ وَاِذْ نَجَّيْنٰكُمْ

مِّنْ اٰلِ فِرْعَوْنَ يَسُوْمُوْنَكُمْ سُوْۤءَ

42. And cover not Truth with falsehood, nor conceal the Truth when you know (what it is).

43. And be steadfast in prayer; practise regular charity; and bow down your heads with those who bow down (in worship).

44. Do you enjoin right conduct on the people, and forget (to practise it) yourselves, and yet you study the Scripture? Will you not understand?

45. No, seek (Allah's) help with patient perseverance and prayer: it is indeed hard, except to those who bring a lowly spirit,-

46. Who bear in mind the certainty that they are

وَلَا تَلْبِسُوا الْحَقَّ بِالْبَاطِلِ

وَتَكْتُمُوا الْحَقَّ وَأَنْتُمْ تَعْلَمُونَ ۞

وَأَقِيمُوا الصَّلٰوةَ وَاٰتُوا الزَّكٰوةَ

وَارْكَعُوا مَعَ الرَّاكِعِينَ ۞ أَتَأْمُرُونَ

النَّاسَ بِالْبِرِّ وَتَنْسَوْنَ أَنْفُسَكُمْ

وَأَنْتُمْ تَتْلُونَ الْكِتٰبَ ۚ أَفَلَا

تَعْقِلُونَ ۞ وَاسْتَعِينُوا بِالصَّبْرِ

وَالصَّلٰوةِ ۚ وَإِنَّهَا لَكَبِيرَةٌ إِلَّا عَلَى

الْخٰشِعِينَ ۞ الَّذِينَ يَظُنُّونَ أَنَّهُمْ

reject Faith and belie Our Signs, they shall be companions of the Fire; they shall abide therein."

40. O Children of Israel! Call to mind the (special) favour which I bestowed upon you, and fulfil your covenant with Me as I fulfil My Covenant with you, and fear none but Me.

41. And believe in what I reveal, confirming the revelation which is with you, and be not the first to reject Faith therein, nor sell My Signs for a small price; and fear Me, and Me alone.

كَفَرُوا وَكَذَّبُوا بِاٰيٰتِنَا اُولٰٓئِكَ

اَصْحٰبُ النَّارِ هُمْ فِيْهَا خٰلِدُوْنَ ۞

يٰبَنِيْٓ اِسْرَآءِيْلَ اذْكُرُوْا نِعْمَتِيَ

الَّتِيْٓ اَنْعَمْتُ عَلَيْكُمْ وَاَوْفُوْا

بِعَهْدِيْٓ اُوْفِ بِعَهْدِكُمْ وَاِيَّايَ

فَارْهَبُوْنِ ۞ وَاٰمِنُوْا بِمَآ اَنْزَلْتُ

مُصَدِّقًا لِّمَا مَعَكُمْ وَلَا تَكُوْنُوْٓا

اَوَّلَ كَافِرٍۭ بِهٖ وَلَا تَشْتَرُوْا بِاٰيٰتِيْ

ثَمَنًا قَلِيْلًا وَاِيَّايَ فَاتَّقُوْنِ ۞

We said: "Get you down, all (you people), with enmity between yourselves. On earth will be your dwelling-place and your means of livelihood for a time."

37. Then learnt Adam from his Lord words (of repentance), and his Lord turned toward him; for He is Oft-returning, Most Merciful.

38. We said: "Get you down all from here; and if, as is sure, there comes to you Guidance from Me, whosoever follows My guidance, on them shall be no fear, nor shall they grieve.

39. "But those who

وَقُلْنَا اهْبِطُوا بَعْضُكُمْ لِبَعْضٍ

عَدُوٌّ ۖ وَلَكُمْ فِى الْأَرْضِ مُسْتَقَرٌّ

وَّمَتَاعٌ اِلَى حِينٍ ۞ فَتَلَقَّى اٰدَمُ

مِنْ رَّبِّهٖ كَلِمَاتٍ فَتَابَ عَلَيْهِ ۚ

اِنَّهٗ هُوَ التَّوَّابُ الرَّحِيمُ ۞ قُلْنَا

اهْبِطُوا مِنْهَا جَمِيعًا ۚ فَاِمَّا

يَأْتِيَنَّكُمْ مِّنِّى هُدًى فَمَنْ

تَبِعَ هُدَاىَ فَلَا خَوْفٌ عَلَيْهِمْ

وَلَا هُمْ يَحْزَنُونَ ۞ وَالَّذِينَ

to the Angels: "Bow down to Adam" and they bowed down: not so Iblis: he refused and was haughty: he was of those who reject Faith.

35. We said: "O Adam! Dwell you and your wife in the Garden; and eat of the bountiful things therein as (where and when) you will; but approach not this you, or you run into harm and trans-gression."

36. Then did Satan make them slip from the (Garden), and get them out of the state (of felicity) in which they had been.

لِلْمَلٰٓئِكَةِ اسْجُدُوْا لِاٰدَمَ

فَسَجَدُوْٓا اِلَّآ اِبْلِيْسَ ؕ اَبٰى

وَاسْتَكْبَرَ ۖ وَكَانَ مِنَ الْكٰفِرِيْنَ ۞

وَقُلْنَا يٰٓاٰدَمُ اسْكُنْ اَنْتَ

وَزَوْجُكَ الْجَنَّةَ وَكُلَا مِنْهَا

رَغَدًا حَيْثُ شِئْتُمَا ۖ وَلَا تَقْرَبَا

هٰذِهِ الشَّجَرَةَ فَتَكُوْنَا مِنَ

الظّٰلِمِيْنَ ۞ فَاَزَلَّهُمَا الشَّيْطٰنُ

عَنْهَا فَاَخْرَجَهُمَا مِمَّا كَانَا فِيْهِ

if you are right."

32. They said: "Glory to You, of knowledge we have none, save what You has taught us: in truth it is You Who are perfect in knowledge and wisdom."

33. He said: "O Adam! Tell them their natures." When he had told them, Allah said: "Did I not tell you that I know the secrets of heaven and earth, and I know what you reveal and what you conceal?"

34. And behold, We said

إِن كُنتُمْ صَٰدِقِينَ ۝ قَالُوا

سُبْحَٰنَكَ لَا عِلْمَ لَنَآ إِلَّا مَا

عَلَّمْتَنَآ إِنَّكَ أَنتَ الْعَلِيمُ

الْحَكِيمُ ۝ قَالَ يَٰٓـَٔادَمُ أَنۢبِئْهُم

بِأَسْمَآئِهِمْ فَلَمَّآ أَنۢبَأَهُم

بِأَسْمَآئِهِمْ قَالَ أَلَمْ أَقُل

لَّكُمْ إِنِّىٓ أَعْلَمُ غَيْبَ السَّمَٰوَٰتِ

وَالْأَرْضِ وَأَعْلَمُ مَا تُبْدُونَ

وَمَا كُنتُمْ تَكْتُمُونَ ۝ وَإِذْ قُلْنَا

to the angels: "I will create a vicegerent on earth." They said: "Will you place therein one who will make mischief therein and shed blood?- while we do celebrate Your praises and glorify Your holy (name)?" He said: "I know what you know not."

31. And He taught Adam the nature of all things; then He placed them before the Angels, and said: "Tell me the nature of these

رَبُّكَ لِلْمَلَٰٓئِكَةِ اِنِّىْ جَاعِلٌ

فِى الْاَرْضِ خَلِيْفَةً ۖ قَالُوْٓا

اَتَجْعَلُ فِيْهَا مَنْ يُّفْسِدُ

فِيْهَا وَيَسْفِكُ الدِّمَآءَ ۚ وَنَحْنُ

نُسَبِّحُ بِحَمْدِكَ وَنُقَدِّسُ لَكَ ۗ

قَالَ اِنِّىْٓ اَعْلَمُ مَا لَا تَعْلَمُوْنَ ۝

وَعَلَّمَ اٰدَمَ الْاَسْمَآءَ كُلَّهَا

ثُمَّ عَرَضَهُمْ عَلَى الْمَلَٰٓئِكَةِ ۙ

فَقَالَ اَنْۢبِـُٔوْنِىْ بِاَسْمَآءِ هٰٓؤُلَآءِ

and do mischief on earth: cause losses (only) to themselves.

28. How can you reject the faith in Allah? - seeing that you were without life, and He gave you life; then will He cause you to die, and will again bring you to life; and again to Him will you return.

29. It is He Who has created for you all things that are on earth; moreover His design comprehended the heavens, for He gave order and perfection to the seven firmaments; and of all things He has perfect knowledge.

30. Behold, your Lord said

وَيُفْسِدُونَ فِى الْأَرْضِ أُولَٰٓئِكَ

هُمُ الْخَٰسِرُونَ ۝ كَيْفَ تَكْفُرُونَ

بِاللَّهِ وَكُنْتُمْ أَمْوَٰتًا فَأَحْيَاكُمْ

ثُمَّ يُمِيتُكُمْ ثُمَّ يُحْيِيكُمْ ثُمَّ

إِلَيْهِ تُرْجَعُونَ ۝ هُوَ الَّذِى

خَلَقَ لَكُمْ مَّا فِى الْأَرْضِ

جَمِيعًا ثُمَّ اسْتَوَىٰٓ إِلَى السَّمَآءِ

فَسَوَّىٰهُنَّ سَبْعَ سَمَٰوَٰتٍ وَهُوَ

بِكُلِّ شَىْءٍ عَلِيمٌ ۝ وَإِذْ قَالَ

Those who believe know that it is truth from their Lord; but those who reject Faith say: "What means Allah by this similitude?" By it He causes many to stray, and many He leads into the right path; but He causes not to stray, except those who forsake (the path),-

27. Those who break Allah's Covenant after it is ratified, and who sunder what Allah has ordered to be joined,

فَاَمَّا الَّذِيْنَ اٰمَنُوْا فَيَعْلَمُوْنَ

اَنَّهُ الْحَقُّ مِنْ رَّبِّهِمْ ۚ وَاَمَّا

الَّذِيْنَ كَفَرُوْا فَيَقُوْلُوْنَ مَاذَآ

اَرَادَ اللّٰهُ بِهٰذَا مَثَلًا ۘ يُضِلُّ

بِهٖ كَثِيْرًا ۙ وَّيَهْدِيْ بِهٖ كَثِيْرًا ۚ

وَمَا يُضِلُّ بِهٖۤ اِلَّا الْفٰسِقِيْنَ ۙ ۞

الَّذِيْنَ يَنْقُضُوْنَ عَهْدَ اللّٰهِ

مِنْۢ بَعْدِ مِيْثَاقِهٖ ۖ وَيَقْطَعُوْنَ

مَآ اَمَرَ اللّٰهُ بِهٖۤ اَنْ يُّوْصَلَ

righteousness, that their portion is Gardens beneath which rivers flow. Every time they are fed with fruits therefrom, they say: "Why, this is what we were fed with before," for they are given things in similitude; and they have therein companions pure (and holy); and they abide therein (for ever).

26. Allah disdains not to use the similitude of things, lowest as well as highest.

الصّٰلِحٰتِ اَنَّ لَهُمْ جَنّٰتٍ

تَجْرِىْ مِنْ تَحْتِهَا الْاَنْهٰرُ

كُلَّمَا رُزِقُوْا مِنْهَا مِنْ ثَمَرَةٍ

رِّزْقًا ۙ قَالُوْا هٰذَا الَّذِىْ

رُزِقْنَا مِنْ قَبْلُ وَاُتُوْا بِهٖ

مُتَشَابِهًا ۙ وَلَهُمْ فِيْهَآ اَزْوَاجٌ

مُّطَهَّرَةٌ ۙ وَّهُمْ فِيْهَا خٰلِدُوْنَ ۝

اِنَّ اللّٰهَ لَا يَسْتَحْىٖٓ اَنْ يَّضْرِبَ

مَثَلًا مَّا بَعُوْضَةً فَمَا فَوْقَهَا ۚ

rivals unto Allah when you know (the truth).

23.   And if you are in doubt as to what We have revealed from time to time to Our servant, then produce a Sura like thereof; and call your witnesses or helpers (if there are any) besides Allah, if your (doubts) are true.

24.   But if you cannot- and of a surety you cannot- then fear the Fire whose fuel is men and stones,- which is prepared for those who reject Faith.

25.   But give glad tidings to those who believe and work

لِلّٰهِ اَنْدَادًا وَّاَنْتُمْ تَعْلَمُوْنَ ۞

وَاِنْ كُنْتُمْ فِيْ رَيْبٍ مِّمَّا نَزَّلْنَا

عَلٰى عَبْدِنَا فَاْتُوْا بِسُوْرَةٍ مِّنْ

مِّثْلِهٖ ۖ وَادْعُوْا شُهَدَآءَكُمْ مِّنْ

دُوْنِ اللّٰهِ اِنْ كُنْتُمْ صٰدِقِيْنَ ۞

فَاِنْ لَّمْ تَفْعَلُوْا وَلَنْ تَفْعَلُوْا

فَاتَّقُوا النَّارَ الَّتِيْ وَقُوْدُهَا النَّاسُ

وَالْحِجَارَةُ ۖ اُعِدَّتْ لِلْكٰفِرِيْنَ ۞

وَبَشِّرِ الَّذِيْنَ اٰمَنُوْا وَعَمِلُوا

their faculty of hearing and seeing; for Allah has power over all things.

21. O you people! Adore your Guardian-Lord, who created you and those who came before you, that you may have the chance to learn righteousness;

22. Who has made the earth your couch, and the heavens your canopy; and sent down rain from the heavens; and brought forth therewith Fruits for your sustenance; then set not up

بِسَمْعِهِمْ وَأَبْصَارِهِمْ ۚ اِنَّ

اللّٰهَ عَلَىٰ كُلِّ شَيْءٍ قَدِيرٌ ۞

يَٰٓأَيُّهَا النَّاسُ اعْبُدُوا رَبَّكُمُ

الَّذِى خَلَقَكُمْ وَالَّذِينَ مِن

قَبْلِكُمْ لَعَلَّكُمْ تَتَّقُونَ ۞ الَّذِى

جَعَلَ لَكُمُ الْأَرْضَ فِرَاشًا

وَّالسَّمَآءَ بِنَآءً ۖ وَّأَنْزَلَ مِنَ

السَّمَآءِ مَآءً فَأَخْرَجَ بِهِ مِنَ

الثَّمَرَٰتِ رِزْقًا لَّكُمْ ۖ فَلَا تَجْعَلُوا

they will not return (to the path).

19. Or (another similitude) is that of a rain-laden cloud from the sky: in it are zones of darkness, and thunder and lightning: they press their fingers in their ears to keep out the stunning thunder-clap, as if they are in terror of death. But Allah is ever round the rejecters of Faith!

20. The lightning all but snatches away their sight; every time the light (helps) them, they walk therein, and when the darkness grows on them, they stand still. And if Allah willed, He could take away

فَهُمْ لَا يَرْجِعُونَ ۝ أَوْ كَصَيِّبٍ

مِّنَ السَّمَاءِ فِيهِ ظُلُمَاتٌ وَّرَعْدٌ

وَّبَرْقٌ يَجْعَلُونَ أَصَابِعَهُمْ

فِيٓ اٰذَانِهِمْ مِّنَ الصَّوَاعِقِ

حَذَرَ الْمَوْتِ وَاللّٰهُ مُحِيطٌ

بِالْكٰفِرِينَ ۝ يَكَادُ الْبَرْقُ يَخْطَفُ

أَبْصَارَهُمْ كُلَّمَآ أَضَآءَ لَهُمْ

مَّشَوْا فِيهِ وَإِذَآ أَظْلَمَ عَلَيْهِمْ

قَامُوْا وَلَوْ شَآءَ اللّٰهُ لَذَهَبَ

on them, and give them rope in their wrong-doing; so they will wander like blind ones (here and there).

16. These are they who have bartered Guidance for error: but their traffic is profitless, and they have lost true direction.

17. Their similitude is that of a man who kindled a fire; when it lighted all around him, Allah took away their light and left them in utter darkness. So they could not see.

18. Deaf, dumb, and blind,

بِهِمۡ وَيَمُدُّهُمۡ فِى طُغۡيَانِهِمۡ

يَعۡمَهُونَ ۞ أُولَٰٓئِكَ ٱلَّذِينَ

ٱشۡتَرَوُاْ ٱلضَّلَٰلَةَ بِٱلۡهُدَىٰ فَمَا

رَبِحَت تِّجَٰرَتُهُمۡ وَمَا كَانُواْ

مُهۡتَدِينَ ۞ مَثَلُهُمۡ كَمَثَلِ

ٱلَّذِى ٱسۡتَوۡقَدَ نَارًا فَلَمَّآ

أَضَآءَتۡ مَا حَوۡلَهُۥ ذَهَبَ ٱللَّهُ

بِنُورِهِمۡ وَتَرَكَهُمۡ فِى ظُلُمَٰتٍ

لَّا يُبۡصِرُونَ ۞ صُمُّۢ بُكۡمٌ عُمۡىٌ

but they realise (it) not.

13. When it is said to them: "Believe as the others believe:" They say: "Shall we believe as the fools believe?" No, of a surety they are the fools, but they do not know.

14. When they meet those who believe, they say: "We believe;" but when they are alone with their evil ones, they say: "We are really with you: we (were) only jesting."

15. Allah will throw back their mockery

وَلٰكِنْ لَّا يَشْعُرُوْنَ ۞ وَاِذَا

قِيْلَ لَهُمْ اٰمِنُوْا كَمَآ اٰمَنَ

النَّاسُ قَالُوْٓا اَنُؤْمِنُ كَمَآ

اٰمَنَ السُّفَهَآءُ ۚ اَلَآ اِنَّهُمْ هُمُ

السُّفَهَآءُ وَلٰكِنْ لَّا يَعْلَمُوْنَ ۞

وَاِذَا لَقُوا الَّذِيْنَ اٰمَنُوْا قَالُوْٓا

اٰمَنَّا ۚ وَاِذَا خَلَوْا اِلٰى شَيٰطِيْنِهِمْ ۙ

قَالُوْٓا اِنَّا مَعَكُمْ ۙ اِنَّمَا نَحْنُ

مُسْتَهْزِءُوْنَ ۞ اَللّٰهُ يَسْتَهْزِئُ

they do not (really) believe.

9. They think they would deceive Allah and those who believe, but they only deceive themselves, and realise (it) not!

10. In their hearts is a disease; and Allah has increased their disease: And grievous is the Chastaisement they (incur), because they are false (to themselves).

11. When it is said to them: "Make not mischief on the earth," they say: "Why, we only want to make peace!"

12. Of a surety, they are the ones who make mischief,

هُمْ بِمُؤْمِنِيْنَ ۞ يُخٰدِعُوْنَ اللّٰهَ

وَالَّذِيْنَ اٰمَنُوْا ۚ وَمَا يَخْدَعُوْنَ

اِلَّاۤ اَنْفُسَهُمْ وَمَا يَشْعُرُوْنَ ۞ فِيْ

قُلُوْبِهِمْ مَّرَضٌ ۙ فَزَادَهُمُ اللّٰهُ

مَرَضًا ۚ وَلَهُمْ عَذَابٌ اَلِيْمٌۢ ۙ بِمَا

كَانُوْا يَكْذِبُوْنَ ۞ وَاِذَا قِيْلَ

لَهُمْ لَا تُفْسِدُوْا فِى الْاَرْضِ ۙ

قَالُوْۤا اِنَّمَا نَحْنُ مُصْلِحُوْنَ ۞

اَلَاۤ اِنَّهُمْ هُمُ الْمُفْسِدُوْنَ

5.　　They are on (true) guidance, from their Lord, and it is these who will prosper.

6.　　As to those who reject Faith, it is the same to them whether you warn them or do not warn them; they will not believe.

7.　　Allah has set a seal on their hearts and on their hearing, and on their eyes is a veil; great is the Chastisement they (incur).

8.　　Of the people there are some who say: "We believe in Allah and the Last Day;" but

اُولَٰٓئِكَ عَلَىٰ هُدًى مِّن رَّبِّهِمْ

وَاُولَٰٓئِكَ هُمُ الْمُفْلِحُونَ ۞ اِنَّ

الَّذِينَ كَفَرُوا سَوَآءٌ عَلَيْهِمْ

ءَاَنذَرْتَهُمْ اَمْ لَمْ تُنذِرْهُمْ

لَا يُؤْمِنُونَ ۞ خَتَمَ اللهُ عَلَىٰ

قُلُوبِهِمْ وَعَلَىٰ سَمْعِهِمْ ۚ وَعَلَىٰٓ

اَبْصَارِهِمْ غِشَاوَةٌ ۖ وَلَهُمْ عَذَابٌ

عَظِيمٌ ۞ وَمِنَ النَّاسِ مَن يَقُولُ

اٰمَنَّا بِاللهِ وَبِالْيَوْمِ الْاٰخِرِ وَمَا

Al-Baqarah (The Heifer)

Bismillahir-Rahmanir-Rahim

1. Alif-Lam-Mim.
2. This is the Book; in it is guidance sure, without doubt, to those who fear Allah;
3. Who believe in the Unseen, are steadfast in prayer, and spend out of what We have provided for them;
4. And who believe in the Revelation sent to you, and sent before your time, and (in their hearts) have the assurance of the Hereafter.

سُورَةُ الْبَقَرَةِ

بِسْمِ اللهِ الرَّحْمٰنِ الرَّحِيمِ

الٓمّٓ ۚ ذٰلِكَ الْكِتٰبُ لَا رَيْبَ ۛ فِيهِ ۛ

هُدًى لِّلْمُتَّقِينَ ۙ الَّذِينَ يُؤْمِنُونَ

بِالْغَيْبِ وَيُقِيمُونَ الصَّلٰوةَ وَمِمَّا

رَزَقْنٰهُمْ يُنْفِقُونَ ۙ وَالَّذِينَ يُؤْمِنُونَ

بِمَا أُنْزِلَ إِلَيْكَ وَمَا أُنْزِلَ مِنْ

قَبْلِكَ ۚ وَبِالْآخِرَةِ هُمْ يُوقِنُونَ ۗ

Al-Fatiha (The Opening)

Bismillahir-Rahmanir-Rahim

(In the Name of Allah, Most Gracious, Most Merciful)

1. Praise be to Allah, the Cherisher and Sustainer of the Worlds;

2. Most Gracious, Most Merciful;

3. Master of the Day of Judgment.

4. You do we worship, and Your aid do we seek.

5. Show us the straight way.

6. The way of those on whom You have bestowed Your Grace, those whose (portion) is not wrath, and who do not go astray.

أَنَّهُمْ مُّلَقُوا اللهِ ۚ كَمْ مِّنْ

فِئَةٍ قَلِيلَةٍ غَلَبَتْ فِئَةً

كَثِيرَةً بِإِذْنِ اللهِ ۗ وَاللهُ

مَعَ الصَّبِرِينَ ۩ وَلَمَّا بَرَزُوْا

لِجَالُوتَ وَجُنُودِهِ قَالُوْا

رَبَّنَا أَفْرِغْ عَلَيْنَا صَبْرًا

وَّثَبِّتْ أَقْدَامَنَا وَانْصُرْنَا عَلَى

الْقَوْمِ الْكٰفِرِينَ ۩ فَهَزَمُوْهُمْ

بِإِذْنِ اللهِ ۙ وَقَتَلَ دَاوُدُ

"Allah will test you at the stream: if any drinks of its water, he goes not with my army: only those who taste not of it go with me: a mere sip out of the hand is excused." But they all drank of it, except a few. When they crossed the river, - he and the faithful ones with him, - they said: "This day we cannot cope with Goliath and his forces." But those who were convinced

إِنَّ اللَّهَ مُبْتَلِيكُمْ بِنَهَرٍ ۚ فَمَنْ

شَرِبَ مِنْهُ فَلَيْسَ مِنِّيْ وَمَنْ

لَّمْ يَطْعَمْهُ فَإِنَّهُ مِنِّيْ

إِلَّا مَنِ اغْتَرَفَ غُرْفَةً بِيَدِهٖ ۚ

فَشَرِبُوْا مِنْهُ إِلَّا قَلِيْلًا

مِّنْهُمْ ۚ فَلَمَّا جَاوَزَهٗ هُوَ

وَالَّذِيْنَ اٰمَنُوْا مَعَهٗ ۙ قَالُوْا

لَا طَاقَةَ لَنَا الْيَوْمَ بِجَالُوْتَ

وَجُنُوْدِهٖ ۚ قَالَ الَّذِيْنَ يَظُنُّوْنَ

Allah grants His authority to whom He pleaseth. Allah cares for all, and He knows all things."

248. And (further) their Prophet said to them: "A Sign of his authority is that there shall come to you the Ark of the Covenant, with (an assurance) therein of security from your Lord, and the relics left by the family of Moses and the family of Aaron, carried by Angels. In this is a symbol for you if you indeed have faith."

249. When Talut set forth with the armies, he said:

وَاللّٰهُ يُؤْتِيْ مُلْكَهٗ مَنْ يَّشَآءُ ؕ

وَاللّٰهُ وَاسِعٌ عَلِيْمٌ ۟ وَقَالَ ﴿٢٤٧﴾

لَهُمْ نَبِيُّهُمْ اِنَّ اٰيَةَ مُلْكِهٖٓ اَنْ

يَّاْتِيَكُمُ التَّابُوْتُ فِيْهِ سَكِيْنَةٌ

مِّنْ رَّبِّكُمْ وَبَقِيَّةٌ مِّمَّا تَرَكَ

اٰلُ مُوْسٰى وَاٰلُ هٰرُوْنَ تَحْمِلُهُ

الْمَلٰٓئِكَةُ ؕ اِنَّ فِيْ ذٰلِكَ لَاٰيَةً

لَّكُمْ اِنْ كُنْتُمْ مُّؤْمِنِيْنَ ۟ۚ ﴿٢٤٨﴾ فَلَمَّا

فَصَلَ طَالُوْتُ بِالْجُنُوْدِ ۙ قَالَ

to fight, they turned back, except a small band among them. But Allah has full knowledge of those who do wrong.

247. Their Prophet said to them: "Allah has appointed Talut as king over you." They said: "How can he exercise authority over us when we are better fitted than he to exercise authority, and he is not even gifted, with wealth in abundance?" He said: "Allah has chosen him above you, and has gifted him abundantly with knowledge and bodily prowess:

عَلَيْهِمُ الْقِتَالُ تَوَلَّوْا اِلَّا قَلِيْلًا

مِّنْهُمْ ۗ وَاللّٰهُ عَلِيْمٌۢ بِالظّٰلِمِيْنَ ۩

وَقَالَ لَهُمْ نَبِيُّهُمْ اِنَّ اللّٰهَ قَدْ

بَعَثَ لَكُمْ طَالُوْتَ مَلِكًا ۗ قَالُوْٓا

اَنّٰى يَكُوْنُ لَهُ الْمُلْكُ عَلَيْنَا

وَنَحْنُ اَحَقُّ بِالْمُلْكِ مِنْهُ وَلَمْ

يُؤْتَ سَعَةً مِّنَ الْمَالِ ۗ قَالَ اِنَّ

اللّٰهَ اصْطَفٰىهُ عَلَيْكُمْ وَزَادَهٗ

بَسْطَةً فِى الْعِلْمِ وَالْجِسْمِ ۗ

and to Him shall be your return.

246. Have you not turned your vision to the Chiefs of the Children of Israel after (the time of) Moses? They said to a prophet (that was) among them: "Appoint for us a king, that we may fight in the cause of Allah." He said: "Is it not possible, if you were commanded to fight, that you will not fight?" They said: "How could we refuse to fight in the cause of Allah, seeing that we were turned out of our homes and our families?" But when they were commanded

وَاِلَيۡهِ تُرۡجَعُوۡنَ ۞ اَلَمۡ تَرَ اِلَى

الۡمَلَاِ مِنۡ بَنِىۡۤ اِسۡرَآءِيۡلَ مِنۡۢ

بَعۡدِ مُوۡسَى ۘ اِذۡ قَالُوۡا لِنَبِىٍّ لَّهُمُ

ابۡعَثۡ لَنَا مَلِكًا نُّقَاتِلۡ فِىۡ سَبِيۡلِ

اللّٰهِ ۚ قَالَ هَلۡ عَسَيۡتُمۡ اِنۡ كُتِبَ

عَلَيۡكُمُ الۡقِتَالُ اَلَّا تُقَاتِلُوۡا ؕ

قَالُوۡا وَمَا لَنَاۤ اَلَّا نُقَاتِلَ فِىۡ

سَبِيۡلِ اللّٰهِ وَقَدۡ اُخۡرِجۡنَا مِنۡ

دِيَارِنَا وَاَبۡنَآئِنَا ؕ فَلَمَّا كُتِبَ

were thousands (in number), for fear of death? Allah said to them: "Die"! Then He restored them to life. For Allah is full of bounty to mankind, but Most of them are ungrateful.

244. Then fight in the cause of Allah, and know that Allah hears and knows all things.

245. Who is he that will loan to Allah a beautiful loan, which Allah will double unto his credit and multiply many times? It is Allah that giveth (you) Want or Plenty,

اُلُوْفٌ حَذَرَ الْمَوْتِ فَقَالَ لَهُمُ

اللهُ مُوْتُوْا ثُمَّ اَحْيَاهُمْ اِنَّ

اللهَ لَذُوْ فَضْلٍ عَلَى النَّاسِ

وَلٰكِنَّ اَكْثَرَ النَّاسِ لَا يَشْكُرُوْنَ ۝

وَقَاتِلُوْا فِيْ سَبِيْلِ اللهِ وَاعْلَمُوْٓا

اَنَّ اللهَ سَمِيْعٌ عَلِيْمٌ ۝ مَنْ

ذَا الَّذِيْ يُقْرِضُ اللهَ قَرْضًا

حَسَنًا فَيُضٰعِفَهٗ لَهٗٓ اَضْعَافًا

كَثِيْرَةً ؕ وَاللهُ يَقْبِضُ وَيَبْصُۜطُ ۗ

a year's maintenance and residence; but if they leave (the
residence), there is no blame on
you for what they do with
themselves, provided it is
reasonable. And Allah is Exalted
in Power, Wise.

241. For divorced women Maintenance (should be provided) on
a reasonable (scale). This is a duty
on the righteous.

242. Thus does Allah make clear
His Signs to you: in order that you
may understand.

243. Did you not turn by vision
to those who abandoned their
homes, though they

مَتَاعًا اِلَى الْحَوْلِ غَيْرَ اِخْرَاجٍ

فَاِنْ خَرَجْنَ فَلَا جُنَاحَ عَلَيْكُمْ

فِيْ مَا فَعَلْنَ فِيْٓ اَنْفُسِهِنَّ مِنْ

مَّعْرُوْفٍ ۗ وَاللّٰهُ عَزِيْزٌ حَكِيْمٌ ۞

وَلِلْمُطَلَّقٰتِ مَتَاعٌۢ بِالْمَعْرُوْفِ ۗ

حَقًّا عَلَى الْمُتَّقِيْنَ ۞ كَذٰلِكَ

يُبَيِّنُ اللّٰهُ لَكُمْ اٰيٰتِهٖ لَعَلَّكُمْ

تَعْقِلُوْنَ ۞ اَلَمْ تَرَ اِلَى الَّذِيْنَ

خَرَجُوْا مِنْ دِيَارِهِمْ وَهُمْ

forget liberality between your-selves. For Allah sees well all that you do.

238. Guard strictly your (habit of) prayers, especially the Middle Prayer; and stand before Allah in a devout (frame of mind).

239. If you fear (an enemy), pray on foot, or riding, (as may be most convenient), but when you are in security, celebrate Allah's praises in the manner He has taught you, which you knew not (before).

240. Those of you who die and leave widows should bequeath for their widows

تَنْسَوُا الْفَضْلَ بَيْنَكُمْ ؕ اِنَّ اللّٰهَ

بِمَا تَعْمَلُوْنَ بَصِيْرٌ ۞ حٰفِظُوْا

عَلَى الصَّلَوٰتِ وَالصَّلٰوةِ الْوُسْطٰى

وَقُوْمُوْا لِلّٰهِ قٰنِتِيْنَ ۞ فَاِنْ

خِفْتُمْ فَرِجَالًا اَوْ رُكْبَانًا ۚ فَاِذَاۤ

اَمِنْتُمْ فَاذْكُرُوا اللّٰهَ كَمَا

عَلَّمَكُمْ مَّا لَمْ تَكُوْنُوْا تَعْلَمُوْنَ ۞

وَالَّذِيْنَ يُتَوَفَّوْنَ مِنْكُمْ وَيَذَرُوْنَ

اَزْوَاجًا ۖ وَصِيَّةً لِّاَزْوَاجِهِمْ

dower; but bestow on them (a suitable gift), the wealthy according to his means, and the poor according to his means; - a gift of a reasonable amount is due from those who wish to do the right thing.

237. And if you divorce them before consummation, but after the fixation of a dower for them, then the half of the dower (is due to them), unless they remit it or (the man's half) is remitted by him in whose hands is the marriage tie; and the remission (of the man's half) is the nearest to righteousness. And do not

فَرِيضَةً ۚ وَمَتِّعُوهُنَّ عَلَى الْمُوسِعِ قَدَرُهُ وَعَلَى الْمُقْتِرِ قَدَرُهُ ۚ مَتَاعًا بِالْمَعْرُوفِ ۖ حَقًّا عَلَى الْمُحْسِنِينَ ۞ وَإِن طَلَّقْتُمُوهُنَّ مِن قَبْلِ أَن تَمَسُّوهُنَّ وَقَدْ فَرَضْتُمْ لَهُنَّ فَرِيضَةً فَنِصْفُ مَا فَرَضْتُمْ إِلَّا أَن يَعْفُونَ أَوْ يَعْفُوَ الَّذِي بِيَدِهِ عُقْدَةُ النِّكَاحِ ۚ وَأَن تَعْفُوا أَقْرَبُ لِلتَّقْوَىٰ ۚ وَلَا

make a secret contract with them except in terms honourable, nor resolve on the tie of marriage till the term prescribed is fulfilled. And know that Allah knows what is in your hearts, and take heed of Him; and know that Allah is Oft-forgiving, Most Forbearing.

236. There is no blame on you if you divorce women before consummation or the fixation of their

تُوَاعِدُوْهُنَّ سِرًّا اِلَّا اَنْ

تَقُوْلُوْا قَوْلًا مَّعْرُوْفًا ۬ وَلَا

تَعْزِمُوْا عُقْدَةَ النِّكَاحِ حَتّٰى

يَبْلُغَ الْكِتٰبُ اَجَلَهٗ ۪ وَاعْلَمُوْۤا

اَنَّ اللّٰهَ يَعْلَمُ مَا فِيْۤ اَنْفُسِكُمْ

فَاحْذَرُوْهُ ۚ وَاعْلَمُوْۤا اَنَّ اللّٰهَ

غَفُوْرٌ حَلِيْمٌ ۞ لَا جُنَاحَ عَلَيْكُمْ

اِنْ طَلَّقْتُمُ النِّسَآءَ مَا لَمْ

تَمَسُّوْهُنَّ اَوْ تَفْرِضُوْا لَهُنَّ

months and ten days: when they have fulfilled their term, there is no blame on you if they dispose of themselves in a just and reasonable manner. And Allah is well acquainted with what you do.

235. There is no blame on you if you make an offer of betrothal or hold it in your hearts. Allah knows that you cherish them in your hearts: but do not

اَشْهُرٍ وَّعَشْرًا فَاِذَا بَلَغْنَ

اَجَلَهُنَّ فَلَا جُنَاحَ عَلَيْكُمْ

فِيْمَا فَعَلْنَ فِيْۤ اَنْفُسِهِنَّ

بِالْمَعْرُوْفِ وَاللّٰهُ بِمَا تَعْمَلُوْنَ

خَبِيْرٌ ۝ وَلَا جُنَاحَ عَلَيْكُمْ

فِيْمَا عَرَّضْتُمْ بِهٖ مِنْ

خِطْبَةِ النِّسَاۤءِ اَوْ اَكْنَنْتُمْ

فِيْۤ اَنْفُسِكُمْ عَلِمَ اللّٰهُ اَنَّكُمْ

سَتَذْكُرُوْنَهُنَّ وَلٰكِنْ لَّا

and after due consultation, there is no blame on them. If you decide on a foster-mother for your offspring, there is no blame on you, provided you pay (the mother) what you offered, on equitable terms. But fear Allah and know that Allah sees well what you do.

234. If any of you die and leave widows behind, they shall wait concerning themselves four

مِنْهُمَا وَتَشَاوُرٍ فَلَا جُنَاحَ

عَلَيْهِمَا ۗ وَإِنْ أَرَدْتُّمْ أَنْ

تَسْتَرْضِعُوٓا أَوْلَادَكُمْ فَلَا

جُنَاحَ عَلَيْكُمْ إِذَا سَلَّمْتُمْ مَّا

اٰتَيْتُمْ بِالْمَعْرُوْفِ ۗ وَاتَّقُوا اللّٰهَ

وَاعْلَمُوٓا أَنَّ اللّٰهَ بِمَا تَعْمَلُوْنَ

بَصِيْرٌ ۞ وَالَّذِيْنَ يُتَوَفَّوْنَ

مِنْكُمْ وَيَذَرُوْنَ أَزْوَاجًا

يَّتَرَبَّصْنَ بِأَنْفُسِهِنَّ أَرْبَعَةَ

233. The mothers shall give suck to their offspring for two whole years, if the father desires to complete the term. But he shall bear the cost of their food and clothing on equitable terms. No soul shall have a burden laid on it greater than it can bear. No mother shall be treated unfairly on account of her child. Nor father on account of his child, an heir shall be chargeable in the same way. If they both decide on weaning, by mutual consent,

وَالْوَالِدَاتُ يُرْضِعْنَ اَوْلَادَهُنَّ

حَوْلَيْنِ كَامِلَيْنِ لِمَنْ اَرَادَ

اَنْ يُّتِمَّ الرَّضَاعَةَ ۚ وَعَلَى

الْمَوْلُوْدِ لَهٗ رِزْقُهُنَّ وَكِسْوَتُهُنَّ

بِالْمَعْرُوْفِ ۚ لَا تُكَلَّفُ نَفْسٌ

اِلَّا وُسْعَهَا ۚ لَا تُضَآرَّ وَالِدَةٌ

بِوَلَدِهَا وَلَا مَوْلُوْدٌ لَّهٗ بِوَلَدِهٖ

وَعَلَى الْوَارِثِ مِثْلُ ذٰلِكَ ۚ

فَاِنْ اَرَادَا فِصَالًا عَنْ تَرَاضٍ

And fear Allah, and know that Allah is well acquainted with all things.

232. When you divorce women, and they fulfil the term of their ('Iddat), do not prevent them from marrying their (former) husbands, if they mutually agree on equitable terms. This instruction is for all among you, who believe in Allah and the Last Day. That is (the course making for) most virtue and purity among you. And Allah knows, and you know not.

وَاتَّقُوا اللّٰهَ وَاعْلَمُوْۤا اَنَّ اللّٰهَ

بِكُلِّ شَىْءٍ عَلِيْمٌ ۞ وَاِذَا طَلَّقْتُمُ

النِّسَآءَ فَبَلَغْنَ اَجَلَهُنَّ فَلَا

تَعْضُلُوْهُنَّ اَنْ يَّنْكِحْنَ اَزْوَاجَهُنَّ

اِذَا تَرَاضَوْا بَيْنَهُمْ بِالْمَعْرُوْفِ ؕ

ذٰلِكَ يُوْعَظُ بِهٖ مَنْ كَانَ

مِنْكُمْ يُؤْمِنُ بِاللّٰهِ وَالْيَوْمِ الْاٰخِرِ ؕ

ذٰلِكُمْ اَزْكٰى لَكُمْ وَاَطْهَرُ ؕ وَاللّٰهُ

يَعْلَمُ وَاَنْتُمْ لَا تَعْلَمُوْنَ ۞

women, and they fulfil the term of their ('Iddat), either take them back on equitable terms or set them free on equitable terms; but do not take them back to injure them, (or) to take undue advantage; if any one does that; he wrongs his own soul. Do not treat Allah's Signs as a jest, but solemnly rehearse Allah's favours on you, and the fact that He sent down to you the Book and Wisdom, for your instruction.

النِّسَآءَ فَبَلَغْنَ أَجَلَهُنَّ

فَأَمْسِكُوْهُنَّ بِمَعْرُوْفٍ أَوْ

سَرِّحُوْهُنَّ بِمَعْرُوْفٍ ۖ وَلَا

تُمْسِكُوْهُنَّ ضِرَارًا لِّتَعْتَدُوْا ۚ

وَمَنْ يَّفْعَلْ ذٰلِكَ فَقَدْ ظَلَمَ

نَفْسَهٗ ۚ وَلَا تَتَّخِذُوْا اٰيٰتِ اللّٰهِ

هُزُوًا ۖ وَّاذْكُرُوْا نِعْمَتَ اللّٰهِ

عَلَيْكُمْ وَمَآ أَنْزَلَ عَلَيْكُمْ مِّنَ

الْكِتٰبِ وَالْحِكْمَةِ يَعِظُكُمْ بِهٖ ۚ

ordained by Allah; so do not transgress them if any do transgress the limits ordained by Allah, such persons wrong (themselves as well as others).

230. So if a husband divorces his wife (irrevocably), he cannot, after that, re-marry her until after she has married another husband and he has divorced her. In that case there is no blame on either of them if they re-unite, provided they feel that they can keep the limits ordained by Allah. Such are the limits ordained by Allah, which He makes plain to those who understand.

231. When you divorce

اللهِ فَلَا تَعْتَدُوْهَا ۚ وَمَنْ

يَّتَعَدَّ حُدُوْدَ اللهِ فَأُولٰٓئِكَ هُمُ

الظّٰلِمُوْنَ ۞ فَاِنْ طَلَّقَهَا فَلَا

تَحِلُّ لَهٗ مِنْۢ بَعْدُ حَتّٰى تَنْكِحَ

زَوْجًا غَيْرَهٗ ؕ فَاِنْ طَلَّقَهَا فَلَا

جُنَاحَ عَلَيْهِمَاۤ اَنْ يَّتَرَاجَعَاۤ اِنْ

ظَنَّاۤ اَنْ يُّقِيْمَا حُدُوْدَ اللهِ ؕ

وَتِلْكَ حُدُوْدُ اللهِ يُبَيِّنُهَا

لِقَوْمٍ يَّعْلَمُوْنَ ۞ وَاِذَا طَلَّقْتُمُ

but men have a degree (of advantage) over them. And Allah is Exalted in Power, Wise.

229. A divorce is only permissible twice: after that, the parties should either hold together on equitable terms, or separate with kindness. It is not lawful for you, (men), to take back any of your gifts (from your wives), except when both parties fear that they would be unable to keep the limits ordained by Allah. If you (judges) do indeed fear that they would be unable to keep the limits ordained by Allah, there is no blame on either of them if she give something for her freedom. These are the limits

وَلِلرِّجَالِ عَلَيْهِنَّ دَرَجَةٌ ۖ وَاللّٰهُ

عَزِيزٌ حَكِيمٌ ۞ الطَّلَاقُ مَرَّتَٰنِ ۖ

فَإِمْسَاكٌ بِمَعْرُوفٍ أَوْ تَسْرِيحٌ

بِإِحْسَانٍ ۗ وَلَا يَحِلُّ لَكُمْ أَن

تَأْخُذُوا مِمَّآ ءَاتَيْتُمُوهُنَّ شَيْئًا

إِلَّآ أَن يَخَافَآ أَلَّا يُقِيمَا حُدُودَ

اللّٰهِ ۖ فَإِنْ خِفْتُمْ أَلَّا يُقِيمَا

حُدُودَ اللّٰهِ فَلَا جُنَاحَ عَلَيْهِمَا

فِيمَا افْتَدَتْ بِهِ ۗ تِلْكَ حُدُودُ

Allah hears and knows all things.

228. Divorced women shall wait concerning themselves for three monthly periods. Nor is it lawful for them to hide what Allah has created in their wombs, if they have faith in Allah and the Last Day. And their husbands have the better right to take them back in that period, if they wish for reconciliation. And women shall have rights similar to the rights against them, according to what is equitable;

اللهُ سَمِيعٌ عَلِيمٌ ۝ وَالْمُطَلَّقٰتُ

يَتَرَبَّصْنَ بِأَنْفُسِهِنَّ ثَلٰثَةَ

قُرُوْٓءٍ ۗ وَلَا يَحِلُّ لَهُنَّ اَنْ

يَّكْتُمْنَ مَا خَلَقَ اللهُ فِيْٓ

اَرْحَامِهِنَّ اِنْ كُنَّ يُؤْمِنَّ

بِاللهِ وَالْيَوْمِ الْاٰخِرِ ۗ وَبُعُوْلَتُهُنَّ

اَحَقُّ بِرَدِّهِنَّ فِيْ ذٰلِكَ اِنْ

اَرَادُوْٓا اِصْلَاحًا ۗ وَلَهُنَّ مِثْلُ

الَّذِيْ عَلَيْهِنَّ بِالْمَعْرُوْفِ

or making peace between persons; for Allah is One Who hears
and knows all things.

225. Allah will not call you to
account for thoughtlessness in
your oaths, but for the intention
in your hearts; and He is Oft-
forgiving, Most Forbearing.

226. For those who take an oath
for abstention from their wives, a
waiting for four months is
ordained; if then they return,
Allah is Oft-forgiving, Most
Merciful.

227. But if their intention is firm
for divorce,

وَتُصْلِحُوْا بَيْنَ النَّاسِ ۚ وَاللّٰهُ

سَمِيْعٌ عَلِيْمٌ ۞ لَا يُؤَاخِذُكُمُ

اللّٰهُ بِاللَّغْوِ فِيْۤ اَيْمَانِكُمْ وَلٰكِنْ

يُّؤَاخِذُكُمْ بِمَا كَسَبَتْ قُلُوْبُكُمْ ۗ

وَاللّٰهُ غَفُوْرٌ حَلِيْمٌ ۞ لِلَّذِيْنَ

يُؤْلُوْنَ مِنْ نِّسَآئِهِمْ تَرَبُّصُ

اَرْبَعَةِ اَشْهُرٍ ۚ فَاِنْ فَآءُوْ

فَاِنَّ اللّٰهَ غَفُوْرٌ رَّحِيْمٌ ۞

وَاِنْ عَزَمُوا الطَّلَاقَ فَاِنَّ

you may approach them in any manner , time, or place ordained for you by Allah. For Allah loves those who turn to Him constantly and He loves those who keep themselves pure and clean.

223. Your wives are as a tilth unto you; so approach your tilth when or how you will; but do some good act for your souls beforehand; and fear Allah. And know that you are to meet Him (in the Hereafter), and give (these) good tidings to those who believe.

224. And make not Allah's (name) an excuse in your oaths against doing good, or acting rightly,

حَتّٰى يُؤْمِنُوا ۚ وَلَعَبْدٌ مُؤْمِنٌ خَيْرٌ

مِّنْ مُّشْرِكٍ وَّلَوْ اَعْجَبَكُمْ ۗ اُولٰٓئِكَ

يَدْعُوْنَ اِلَى النَّارِ ۖ وَاللّٰهُ يَدْعُوۡۤا

اِلَى الْجَنَّةِ وَالْمَغْفِرَةِ بِاِذْنِهٖ ۚ

وَيُبَيِّنُ اٰيٰتِهٖ لِلنَّاسِ لَعَلَّهُمْ

يَتَذَكَّرُوْنَ ۞ وَيَسْئَلُوْنَكَ عَنِ

الْمَحِيْضِ ۖ قُلْ هُوَ اَذًى ۙ فَاعْتَزِلُوا

النِّسَآءَ فِى الْمَحِيْضِ ۙ وَلَا تَقْرَبُوْهُنَّ

حَتّٰى يَطْهُرْنَ ۚ فَاِذَا تَطَهَّرْنَ

220. (Their bearings) on this life and the Hereafter. They ask you concerning orphans. Say: "The best thing to do is what is for their good; if you mix their affairs with yours, they are your brethren; but Allah knows the man who means mischief from the man who means good. And if Allah had wished, He could have put you into difficulties: He is indeed Exalted in Power, Wise."

221. Do not marry unbelieving women (idolators), until they believe: a slave woman who believes is better than an unbelieving woman, even though she allures you. Nor marry (your girls) to unbelievers until they believe: a man slave who believes is better than an unbeliever, even though he allures you. Unbelievers do (but) beckon you to the Fire. But Allah beckons by His Grace to the Garden (of Bliss) and forgiveness, and makes His Signs clear to mankind so that they may celebrate His praise.

222. They ask you concerning women's courses. Say: they are a hurt and a pollution: so keep away from women in their courses, and do not approach them until they are clean. But when they have purified themselves,

فَأْتُوْهُنَّ مِنْ حَيْثُ أَمَرَكُمُ

اللّٰهُ ۚ إِنَّ اللّٰهَ يُحِبُّ التَّوَّابِيْنَ

وَيُحِبُّ الْمُتَطَهِّرِيْنَ ۝ نِسَاؤُكُمْ

حَرْثٌ لَّكُمْ ۖ فَأْتُوْا حَرْثَكُمْ

أَنّٰى شِئْتُمْ ۖ وَقَدِّمُوْا لِأَنْفُسِكُمْ ۚ

وَاتَّقُوا اللّٰهَ وَاعْلَمُوْا أَنَّكُمْ

مُّلٰقُوْهُ ۗ وَبَشِّرِ الْمُؤْمِنِيْنَ ۝

وَلَا تَجْعَلُوا اللّٰهَ عُرْضَةً

لِّأَيْمَانِكُمْ أَنْ تَبَرُّوْا وَتَتَّقُوْا

فِى الدُّنْيَا وَالْاٰخِرَةِ ۗ وَيَسْئَلُوْنَكَ

عَنِ الْيَتٰمٰى ۗ قُلْ اِصْلَاحٌ لَّهُمْ

خَيْرٌ ۗ وَاِنْ تُخَالِطُوْهُمْ فَاِخْوَانُكُمْ ۗ

وَاللّٰهُ يَعْلَمُ الْمُفْسِدَ مِنَ الْمُصْلِحِ ۗ

وَلَوْ شَآءَ اللّٰهُ لَاَعْنَتَكُمْ ۗ اِنَّ

اللّٰهَ عَزِيْزٌ حَكِيْمٌ ۝ وَلَا تَنْكِحُوا

الْمُشْرِكٰتِ حَتّٰى يُؤْمِنَّ ۗ وَلَاَمَةٌ

مُّؤْمِنَةٌ خَيْرٌ مِّنْ مُّشْرِكَةٍ وَّلَوْ

اَعْجَبَتْكُمْ ۗ وَلَا تُنْكِحُوا الْمُشْرِكِيْنَ

and those who suffered exile and fought (and strove and struggled) in the path of Allah, - they have the hope of the Mercy of Allah: and Allah is Oft-forgiving, Most Merciful.

219. They ask you concerning wine and gambling. Say: "In them is great sin, and some profit, for men; but the sin is greater than the profit." They ask you how much they are to spend; Say: "What is beyond your needs." Thus dose Allah make clear to you His Signs: in order that you may consider -

وَالَّذِيْنَ هَاجَرُوْا وَجَهَدُوْا فِيْ

سَبِيْلِ اللّٰهِ ۙ أُولٰٓئِكَ يَرْجُوْنَ

رَحْمَتَ اللّٰهِ ۗ وَاللّٰهُ غَفُوْرٌ رَّحِيْمٌ ۞

يَسْـَٔلُوْنَكَ عَنِ الْخَمْرِ وَالْمَيْسِرِ ۗ

قُلْ فِيْهِمَآ إِثْمٌ كَبِيْرٌ وَّمَنَافِعُ

لِلنَّاسِ ۖ وَإِثْمُهُمَآ أَكْبَرُ مِنْ نَّفْعِهِمَا ۗ

وَيَسْـَٔلُوْنَكَ مَاذَا يُنْفِقُوْنَ ۚ

قُلِ الْعَفْوَ ۗ كَذٰلِكَ يُبَيِّنُ اللّٰهُ

لَكُمُ الْاٰيٰتِ لَعَلَّكُمْ تَتَفَكَّرُوْنَ ۞

Tumult and oppression are worse than slaughter. Nor will they cease fighting you until they turn you back from your faith if they can. And if any of you turn back from their faith and die in unbelief, their works will bear no fruit in this life and in the Hereafter; they will be companions of the Fire and will abide therein.

218. Those who believed

عِنْدَ اللّٰهِ ۚ وَالْفِتْنَةُ أَكْبَرُ مِنَ

الْقَتْلِ ۗ وَلَا يَزَالُوْنَ يُقَاتِلُوْنَكُمْ

حَتّٰى يَرُدُّوْكُمْ عَنْ دِيْنِكُمْ

إِنِ اسْتَطَاعُوْا ۚ وَمَنْ يَّرْتَدِدْ

مِنْكُمْ عَنْ دِيْنِهٖ فَيَمُتْ وَهُوَ

كَافِرٌ فَأُولٰٓئِكَ حَبِطَتْ أَعْمَالُهُمْ

فِى الدُّنْيَا وَالْاٰخِرَةِ ۚ وَأُولٰٓئِكَ

أَصْحٰبُ النَّارِ ۖ هُمْ فِيْهَا

خٰلِدُوْنَ ۝ إِنَّ الَّذِيْنَ اٰمَنُوْا

it. But it is possible that you dislike a thing which is good for you, and that you love a thing which is bad for you. But Allah knows, and you know not.

217. They ask you concerning fighting in the Prohibited Month. Say: "Fighting therein is a grave (offence); but graver still in the sight of Allah to prevent access to the path of Allah, to deny Him, to prevent access to the Sacred Mosque, and drive out its members."

لَّكُمْ ۚ وَعَسٰۤى اَنْ تَكْرَهُوْا شَيْئًا

وَّهُوَ خَيْرٌ لَّكُمْ ۚ وَعَسٰۤى اَنْ

تُحِبُّوْا شَيْئًا وَّهُوَ شَرٌّ لَّكُمْ ؕ وَاللّٰهُ

يَعْلَمُ وَاَنْتُمْ لَا تَعْلَمُوْنَ ۩

يَسْـَٔلُوْنَكَ عَنِ الشَّهْرِ الْحَرَامِ

قِتَالٍ فِيْهِ ؕ قُلْ قِتَالٌ فِيْهِ

كَبِيْرٌ ؕ وَصَدٌّ عَنْ سَبِيْلِ اللّٰهِ

وَكُفْرٌۢ بِهٖ وَالْمَسْجِدِ الْحَرَامِ

وَاِخْرَاجُ اَهْلِهٖ مِنْهُ اَكْبَرُ

and were so shaken in spirit that even the Apostle and those of faith who were with him cried: "When (will come) the help of Allah?" Ah! Verily, the help of Allah is (always) near!

215. They ask you what they should spend (in charity). Say: Whatever you spend that is good, is for parents and kindred and orphans and those in want and for wayfarers. And whatever you do that is good, - Allah knows it well.

216. Fighting is prescribed for you, and you dislike

وَزُلْزِلُوْا حَتّٰى يَقُوْلَ الرَّسُوْلُ

وَالَّذِيْنَ اٰمَنُوْا مَعَهٗ مَتٰى نَصْرُ

اللّٰهِ ۗ اَلَاۤ اِنَّ نَصْرَ اللّٰهِ قَرِيْبٌ ۞

يَسْـَٔلُوْنَكَ مَاذَا يُنْفِقُوْنَ ۗ قُلْ

مَاۤ اَنْفَقْتُمْ مِّنْ خَيْرٍ فَلِلْوَالِدَيْنِ

وَالْاَقْرَبِيْنَ وَالْيَتٰمٰى وَالْمَسٰكِيْنِ

وَابْنِ السَّبِيْلِ ؕ وَمَا تَفْعَلُوْا مِنْ

خَيْرٍ فَاِنَّ اللّٰهَ بِهٖ عَلِيْمٌ ۞

كُتِبَ عَلَيْكُمُ الْقِتَالُ وَهُوَ كُرْهٌ لَّ

but the People of the Book, after the clear Signs came to them, did not differ among themselves, except through selfish contumacy. Allah by His Grace guided the believers to the Truth, concerning that wherein they differed. For Allah guided whom He will to a path that is straight.

214. Or do you think that you shall enter the Garden (of Bliss) without such (trials) as came to those who passed away before you? They encountered suffering and adversity,

فِيْهِ ۚ وَمَا اخْتَلَفَ فِيْهِ اِلَّا الَّذِيْنَ

اُوْتُوْهُ مِنْۢ بَعْدِ مَا جَآءَتْهُمُ

الْبَيِّنٰتُ بَغْيًۢا بَيْنَهُمْ ۚ فَهَدَى اللّٰهُ

الَّذِيْنَ اٰمَنُوْا لِمَا اخْتَلَفُوْا فِيْهِ مِنَ

الْحَقِّ بِاِذْنِهٖ ۗ وَاللّٰهُ يَهْدِيْ مَنْ

يَّشَآءُ اِلٰى صِرَاطٍ مُّسْتَقِيْمٍ ۝ اَمْ

حَسِبْتُمْ اَنْ تَدْخُلُوا الْجَنَّةَ وَلَمَّا

يَاْتِكُمْ مَّثَلُ الَّذِيْنَ خَلَوْا مِنْ

قَبْلِكُمْ ۗ مَسَّتْهُمُ الْبَاْسَآءُ وَالضَّرَّآءُ

Allah is strict in punishment.

212. The life of this world is alluring to those who reject Faith, and they scoff at those who believe. But the righteous will be above them on the Day of Resurrection; for Allah bestows His abundance without measure on whom He will.

213. Mankind was one single nation, and Allah sent Messengers with glad tidings and warnings; and with them He sent the Book in truth, to judge between people in matters wherein they differed;

اللهُ شَدِيْدُ الْعِقَابِ ۞ زُيِّنَ لِلَّذِيْنَ

كَفَرُوا الْحَيٰوةُ الدُّنْيَا وَيَسْخَرُوْنَ

مِنَ الَّذِيْنَ اٰمَنُوْا ۘ وَالَّذِيْنَ اتَّقَوْا

فَوْقَهُمْ يَوْمَ الْقِيٰمَةِ ۗ وَاللهُ يَرْزُقُ

مَنْ يَّشَاۤءُ بِغَيْرِ حِسَابٍ ۞ كَانَ

النَّاسُ أُمَّةً وَّاحِدَةً ۗ فَبَعَثَ اللهُ

النَّبِيّٖنَ مُبَشِّرِيْنَ وَمُنْذِرِيْنَ ۖ

وَاَنْزَلَ مَعَهُمُ الْكِتٰبَ بِالْحَقِّ

لِيَحْكُمَ بَيْنَ النَّاسِ فِيْمَا اخْتَلَفُوْا

you backslide after the clear (Signs) have come to you, then know that Allah is Exalted in Power, Wise.

210. Will they wait until Allah comes to them in canopies of clouds, with Angels (in His train) and the question is (thus) settled? But to Allah do all questions go back (for decision).

211. Ask the Children of Israel how many clear (Signs) We have sent them. But if any one, after Allah's favour has come to him, substitutes (something else),

زَلَلۡتُمۡ مِّنۡۢ بَعۡدِ مَا جَآءَتۡكُمُ

الۡبَيِّنٰتُ فَاعۡلَمُوۡۤا اَنَّ اللّٰهَ عَزِيۡزٌ

حَكِيۡمٌ ۞ هَلۡ يَنۡظُرُوۡنَ اِلَّاۤ اَنۡ

يَّاۡتِيَهُمُ اللّٰهُ فِيۡ ظُلَلٍ مِّنَ

الۡغَمَامِ وَالۡمَلٰٓئِكَةُ وَقُضِىَ الۡاَمۡرُ ؕ

وَاِلَى اللّٰهِ تُرۡجَعُ الۡاُمُوۡرُ ۞ سَلۡ

بَنِىۡۤ اِسۡرَآءِيۡلَ كَمۡ اٰتَيۡنٰهُمۡ مِّنۡ

اٰيَةٍ بَيِّنَةٍ ؕ وَمَنۡ يُّبَدِّلۡ نِعۡمَةَ

اللّٰهِ مِنۡۢ بَعۡدِ مَا جَآءَتۡهُ فَاِنَّ

mischief.

206. When it is said to him, "Fear Allah", he is led by arrogance to (more) crime. Enough for him is Hell; - an evil bed indeed (to lie on)!

207. And there is the type of man who gives his life to earn the pleasure of Allah: and Allah is full of kindness to (His) devotees.

208. O you who believe! Enter into Islam whole-heartedly; and follow not the footsteps of the Satan; for he is to you an avowed enemy.

209. If

الْفَسَادَ ۞ وَإِذَا قِيْلَ لَهُ اتَّقِ

اللهَ اَخَذَتْهُ الْعِزَّةُ بِالْاِثْمِ

فَحَسْبُهُ جَهَنَّمُ وَلَبِئْسَ الْمِهَادُ ۞

وَمِنَ النَّاسِ مَنْ يَّشْرِيْ نَفْسَهُ

ابْتِغَآءَ مَرْضَاتِ اللهِ وَاللهُ

رَءُوْفٌ بِالْعِبَادِ ۞ يٰٓاَيُّهَا الَّذِيْنَ

اٰمَنُوا ادْخُلُوْا فِى السِّلْمِ كَآفَّةً

وَلَا تَتَّبِعُوْا خُطُوٰتِ الشَّيْطٰنِ

اِنَّهُ لَكُمْ عَدُوٌّ مُّبِيْنٌ ۞ فَاِنْ

on him, and if any one stays on, there is no blame on him, if his aim is to do right. Then fear Allah, and know that you will surely be gathered unto Him.

204. There is the type of man whose speech about this world's life may dazzle you, and he calls Allah to witness about what is in his heart; yet he is the most contentious of enemies.

205. When he turns his back, His aim everywhere is to spread mischief through the earth and destroy crops and cattle. But Allah loves not

عَلَيْهِ ۚ وَمَنْ تَأَخَّرَ فَلَا اِثْمَ عَلَيْهِ

لِمَنِ اتَّقٰى ۚ وَاتَّقُوا اللّٰهَ وَاعْلَمُوْۤا

اَنَّكُمْ اِلَيْهِ تُحْشَرُوْنَ ۞ وَمِنَ

النَّاسِ مَنْ يُّعْجِبُكَ قَوْلُهٗ فِي

الْحَيٰوةِ الدُّنْيَا وَيُشْهِدُ اللّٰهَ

عَلٰى مَا فِيْ قَلْبِهٖ ۙ وَهُوَ اَلَدُّ

الْخِصَامِ ۞ وَاِذَا تَوَلّٰى سَعٰى فِي

الْاَرْضِ لِيُفْسِدَ فِيْهَا وَيُهْلِكَ

الْحَرْثَ وَالنَّسْلَ ۚ وَاللّٰهُ لَا يُحِبُّ

men who say: "Our Lord! Give us (Your bounties) in this world!" But they will have no portion in the Hereafter.

201. And there are men who say: "Our Lord! Give us good in this world and good in the Hereafter, and save us from the torment of the Fire!"

202. To these will be allotted what they have earned; and Allah is quick in account.

203. Celebrate the praises of Allah during the Appointed Days. But if any one hastens to leave in two days, there is no blame

النَّاسِ مَنْ يَّقُوْلُ رَبَّنَآ اٰتِنَا

فِى الدُّنْيَا وَمَا لَهٗ فِى الْاٰخِرَةِ

مِنْ خَلَاقٍ ۝ وَمِنْهُمْ مَّنْ يَّقُوْلُ

رَبَّنَآ اٰتِنَا فِى الدُّنْيَا حَسَنَةً

وَّفِى الْاٰخِرَةِ حَسَنَةً وَّقِنَا عَذَابَ

النَّارِ ۝ اُولٰٓئِكَ لَهُمْ نَصِيْبٌ مِّمَّا

كَسَبُوْا ۚ وَاللّٰهُ سَرِيْعُ الْحِسَابِ

۝ وَاذْكُرُوا اللّٰهَ فِىْ اَيَّامٍ مَّعْدُوْدٰتٍ

فَمَنْ تَعَجَّلَ فِىْ يَوْمَيْنِ فَلَآ اِثْمَ

Then when you pour down from (Mount) Arafat, celebrate the praises of Allah at the Sacred Monument, and celebrate His praises as He has directed you, even though, before this, you went astray.

199. Then pass on at a quick pace from the place whence it is usual for the multitude so to do, and ask for Allah's forgiveness. For Allah is Oft-forgiving, Most Merciful.

200. So when you have accomplished your holy rites, celebrate the praises of Allah, as you used to celebrate the praises of your fathers, - even, with far more heart and soul. There are

فَاِذَاۤ اَفَضْتُمْ مِّنْ عَرَفٰتٍ فَاذْكُرُوا

اللّٰهَ عِنْدَ الْمَشْعَرِ الْحَرَامِ ۖ

وَاذْكُرُوْهُ كَمَا هَدٰىكُمْ ۚ وَاِنْ

كُنْتُمْ مِّنْ قَبْلِهٖ لَمِنَ الضَّآلِّيْنَ ۝

ثُمَّ اَفِيْضُوْا مِنْ حَيْثُ اَفَاضَ

النَّاسُ وَاسْتَغْفِرُوا اللّٰهَ ۚ اِنَّ

اللّٰهَ غَفُوْرٌ رَّحِيْمٌ ۝ فَاِذَا قَضَيْتُمْ

مَّنَاسِكَكُمْ فَاذْكُرُوا اللّٰهَ كَذِكْرِكُمْ

اٰبَآءَكُمْ اَوْ اَشَدَّ ذِكْرًا ۗ فَمِنَ

and know that Allah is strict in punishment.

197. For Hajj are the months well known. If any one undertakes that duty therein, let there be no obscenity, nor wickedness, nor wrangling in the Hajj. And whatever good you do, (be sure) Allah knows it. And take a provision (with you) for the journey, but the best of pro-visions is right conduct. So fear Me, o you that are wise.

198. It is no crime in you if you seek of the bounty of your Lord (during pilgrimage).

وَاعْلَمُوْٓا اَنَّ اللّٰهَ شَدِيْدُ الْعِقَابِ ۞ اَلْحَجُّ اَشْهُرٌ مَّعْلُوْمٰتٌ ۚ فَمَنْ فَرَضَ فِيْهِنَّ الْحَجَّ فَلَا رَفَثَ وَلَا فُسُوْقَ ۙ وَلَا جِدَالَ فِى الْحَجِّ ۗ وَمَا تَفْعَلُوْا مِنْ خَيْرٍ يَّعْلَمْهُ اللّٰهُ ۗ وَتَزَوَّدُوْا فَاِنَّ خَيْرَ الزَّادِ التَّقْوٰى ۚ وَاتَّقُوْنِ يٰٓاُولِى الْاَلْبَابِ ۞ لَيْسَ عَلَيْكُمْ جُنَاحٌ اَنْ تَبْتَغُوْا فَضْلًا مِّنْ رَّبِّكُمْ ۚ

(necessitating shaving), (he should) in compensation either fast, or feed the poor, or offer sacrifice; and when you are in peaceful conditions (again), if any one wishes to continue the 'umra or the Hajj, he must make an offering, such as he can afford, but if he cannot afford it, he should fast three days during the Hajj and seven days on his return, making ten days in all. This is for those whose household is not in (the precincts of) the Sacred Mosque. And fear Allah,

فَفِدْيَةٌ مِّنْ صِيَامٍ اَوْ صَدَقَةٍ
اَوْ نُسُكٍ ۚ فَاِذَآ اَمِنْتُمْ ۫ فَمَنْ
تَمَتَّعَ بِالْعُمْرَةِ اِلَى الْحَجِّ فَمَا
اسْتَيْسَرَ مِنَ الْهَدْيِ ۚ فَمَنْ لَّمْ
يَجِدْ فَصِيَامُ ثَلٰثَةِ اَيَّامٍ فِي
الْحَجِّ وَسَبْعَةٍ اِذَا رَجَعْتُمْ ۭ
تِلْكَ عَشَرَةٌ كَامِلَةٌ ۭ ذٰلِكَ
لِمَنْ لَّمْ يَكُنْ اَهْلُهٗ حَاضِرِي
الْمَسْجِدِ الْحَرَامِ ۭ وَاتَّقُوا اللّٰهَ

and know that Allah is with those who restrain themselves.

195. And spend of your substance in the cause of Allah, and make not your own hands contribute to (your) destruction; but do good; for Allah loves those who do good.

196. And complete the Hajj or 'umra in the service of Allah. But if you are prevented (from completing it), send an offering for sacrifice, such as you may find, and do not shave your heads until the offering reaches the place of sacrifice. And if any of you is ill, or has an ailment in his scalp,

وَٱعْلَمُوْٓا اَنَّ اللّٰهَ مَعَ الْمُتَّقِيْنَ ۝

وَاَنْفِقُوْا فِيْ سَبِيْلِ اللّٰهِ وَلَا

تُلْقُوْا بِاَيْدِيْكُمْ اِلَى التَّهْلُكَةِ ۚ

وَاَحْسِنُوْٓا اِنَّ اللّٰهَ يُحِبُّ الْمُحْسِنِيْنَ ۝

وَاَتِمُّوا الْحَجَّ وَالْعُمْرَةَ لِلّٰهِ ۚ فَاِنْ

اُحْصِرْتُمْ فَمَا اسْتَيْسَرَ مِنَ الْهَدْيِ ۚ

وَلَا تَحْلِقُوْا رُءُوْسَكُمْ حَتّٰى يَبْلُغَ

الْهَدْيُ مَحِلَّهٗ ۚ فَمَنْ كَانَ مِنْكُمْ

مَّرِيْضًا اَوْ بِهٖٓ اَذًى مِّنْ رَّاْسِهٖ

مغ

Such is the reward of those who suppress Faith.

192. But if they cease, Allah is Oft-forgiving, Most Merciful.

193. And fight them on until there is no more tumult or oppression, and there prevail justice and faith in Allah; but if they cease, let there be no hostility except to those who practise oppression.

194. The prohibited month for the prohibited month, - and so for all things prohibited, - there is the law of equality. If then any one transgresses the prohibition against you, transgress you likewise against him. But fear Allah,

كَذَٰلِكَ جَزَآءُ الْكَٰفِرِينَ ۞ فَإِنِ

انتَهَوْا فَإِنَّ اللهَ غَفُورٌ رَّحِيمٌ ۞

وَقَٰتِلُوهُمْ حَتَّىٰ لَا تَكُونَ فِتْنَةٌ

وَيَكُونَ الدِّينُ لِلَّهِ ۖ فَإِنِ انتَهَوْا

فَلَا عُدْوَانَ إِلَّا عَلَى الظَّٰلِمِينَ ۞

الشَّهْرُ الْحَرَامُ بِالشَّهْرِ الْحَرَامِ

وَالْحُرُمَٰتُ قِصَاصٌ ۚ فَمَنِ اعْتَدَىٰ

عَلَيْكُمْ فَاعْتَدُوا عَلَيْهِ بِمِثْلِ

مَا اعْتَدَىٰ عَلَيْكُمْ ۚ وَاتَّقُوا اللهَ

so that you may achieve success.

190. Fight in the cause of Allah those who fight you, but do not transgress limits; for Allah loveth not transgressors.

191. And slay them wherever you catch them, and turn them out from where they have turned you out; for tumult and oppression are worse than slaughter; but fight them not at the Sacred Mosque, unless they (first) fight you there; but if they fight you, slay them.

لَعَلَّكُمْ تُفْلِحُوْنَ ۞ وَقَاتِلُوْا فِيْ

سَبِيْلِ اللّٰهِ الَّذِيْنَ يُقَاتِلُوْنَكُمْ

وَلَا تَعْتَدُوْا ۗ اِنَّ اللّٰهَ لَا يُحِبُّ

الْمُعْتَدِيْنَ ۞ وَاقْتُلُوْهُمْ حَيْثُ

ثَقِفْتُمُوْهُمْ وَاَخْرِجُوْهُمْ مِّنْ

حَيْثُ اَخْرَجُوْكُمْ وَالْفِتْنَةُ اَشَدُّ

مِنَ الْقَتْلِ ۚ وَلَا تُقٰتِلُوْهُمْ عِنْدَ

الْمَسْجِدِ الْحَرَامِ حَتّٰى يُقٰتِلُوْكُمْ

فِيْهِ ۚ فَاِنْ قٰتَلُوْكُمْ فَاقْتُلُوْهُمْ

among yourselves for vanities, nor use it as bait for the judges, with intent that you may eat up wrongfully and knowingly a little of (other) people's property.

189. They ask you concerning the New Moons. Say: they are but signs to mark fixed periods of time in (the affairs of) men, and for Pilgrimage. It is no virtue if you enter your houses from the back: it is virtue if you fear Allah. Enter houses through the proper doors: and fear Allah

بَيْنَكُمْ بِالْبَاطِلِ وَتُدْلُوا بِهَآ

اِلَى الْحُكَّامِ لِتَأْكُلُوا فَرِيقًا

مِّنْ اَمْوَالِ النَّاسِ بِالْاِثْمِ

وَاَنْتُمْ تَعْلَمُوْنَ ۞ يَسْئَلُوْنَكَ

عَنِ الْاَهِلَّةِ ۚ قُلْ هِيَ مَوَاقِيْتُ

لِلنَّاسِ وَالْحَجِّ ۚ وَلَيْسَ الْبِرُّ

بِاَنْ تَأْتُوا الْبُيُوْتَ مِنْ ظُهُوْرِهَا

وَلَكِنَّ الْبِرَّ مَنِ اتَّقَىٰ ۚ وَأْتُوا

الْبُيُوْتَ مِنْ اَبْوَابِهَا ۚ وَاتَّقُوا اللّٰهَ

Allah has ordained for you, and eat and drink, until the white thread of dawn appear to you distinct from its black thread; then complete your fast till the night appears; but do not associate with your wives while you are in retreat in the mosques. Those are Limits (set by) Allah: do not go near to those. Thus does Allah make clear His Signs to men: that they may learn self-restraint.

188. And do not eat up your property

اللَّهُ لَكُمْ وَ كُلُوا وَاشْرَبُوا حَتّٰى

يَتَبَيَّنَ لَكُمُ الْخَيْطُ الْأَبْيَضُ

مِنَ الْخَيْطِ الْأَسْوَدِ مِنَ الْفَجْرِ

ثُمَّ أَتِمُّوا الصِّيَامَ إِلَى الَّيْلِ

وَ لَا تُبَاشِرُوهُنَّ وَ أَنْتُمْ عٰكِفُوْنَ

فِي الْمَسٰجِدِ تِلْكَ حُدُوْدُ اللَّهِ

فَلَا تَقْرَبُوْهَا كَذٰلِكَ يُبَيِّنُ

اللَّهُ اٰيٰتِهٖ لِلنَّاسِ لَعَلَّهُمْ

يَتَّقُوْنَ ۝ وَ لَا تَأْكُلُوا أَمْوَالَكُمْ

I listen to the prayer of every suppliant when he calls on Me: let them also, with a will, listen to My call, and believe in Me: that they may walk in the right way.

187. Permitted to you, on the night of the fasts, is the approach to your wives. They are your garments and you are their garments. Allah knows what you used to do secretly among yourselves; but He turned to you and forgave you; so now associate with them, and seek what

اُجِيْبُ دَعْوَةَ الدَّاعِ اِذَا دَعَانِ

فَلْيَسْتَجِيْبُوْا لِيْ وَلْيُؤْمِنُوْا بِيْ

لَعَلَّهُمْ يَرْشُدُوْنَ ۩ اُحِلَّ لَكُمْ

لَيْلَةَ الصِّيَامِ الرَّفَثُ اِلٰى

نِسَآئِكُمْ ۗ هُنَّ لِبَاسٌ لَّكُمْ وَاَنْتُمْ

لِبَاسٌ لَّهُنَّ ۗ عَلِمَ اللهُ اَنَّكُمْ

كُنْتُمْ تَخْتَانُوْنَ اَنْفُسَكُمْ

فَتَابَ عَلَيْكُمْ وَعَفَا عَنْكُمْ ۚ فَالْـٰٔنَ

بَاشِرُوْهُنَّ وَابْتَغُوْا مَا كَتَبَ

for guidance and judgment (between right and wrong). So every one of you who is present (at his home) during that month should spend it in fasting, but if any one is ill, or on a journey, the prescribed period (should be made up) by days later. Allah intends every facility for you; He does not want to put you to difficulties. (He wants you) to complete the prescribed period, and to glorify Him in that He has guided you; and perchance you shall be grateful.

186. When My servants ask you concerning Me, I am indeed close (to them):

انتصار

مِنَ الْهُدٰى وَالْفُرْقَانِ ۚ فَمَنْ

شَهِدَ مِنْكُمُ الشَّهْرَ فَلْيَصُمْهُ ۚ

وَمَنْ كَانَ مَرِيْضًا اَوْ عَلٰى سَفَرٍ

فَعِدَّةٌ مِّنْ اَيَّامٍ اُخَرَ ۗ يُرِيْدُ

اللّٰهُ بِكُمُ الْيُسْرَ وَلَا يُرِيْدُ

بِكُمُ الْعُسْرَ وَلِتُكْمِلُوا الْعِدَّةَ

وَلِتُكَبِّرُوا اللّٰهَ عَلٰى مَا هَدٰىكُمْ

وَلَعَلَّكُمْ تَشْكُرُوْنَ ۝ وَاِذَا سَاَلَكَ

عِبَادِيْ عَنِّيْ فَاِنِّيْ قَرِيْبٌ ۗ

184. (Fasting is) for a fixed number of days; but if any of you is ill, or on a journey, the prescribed number (should be made up) from days later. For those who can do it (with hardship), is a ransom, the feeding of one that is indigent. But he that will give more, of his own free will, - it is better for him. And it is better for you that you fast, if you only knew.

185. Ramadhan is the (month) in which was sent down the Qur'an, as a guide to mankind, also clear (Signs)

أَيَّامًا مَّعْدُودَاتٍ فَمَنْ كَانَ

مِنْكُمْ مَّرِيضًا أَوْ عَلَى سَفَرٍ

فَعِدَّةٌ مِّنْ أَيَّامٍ أُخَرَ وَعَلَى

الَّذِينَ يُطِيقُونَهُ فِدْيَةٌ

طَعَامُ مِسْكِينٍ فَمَنْ تَطَوَّعَ

خَيْرًا فَهُوَ خَيْرٌ لَّهُ وَأَنْ تَصُومُوا

خَيْرٌ لَّكُمْ إِنْ كُنْتُمْ تَعْلَمُونَ ۝

شَهْرُ رَمَضَانَ الَّذِي أُنْزِلَ فِيهِ

الْقُرْآنُ هُدًى لِّلنَّاسِ وَبَيِّنَتٍ

Allah-fearing.

181. If anyone changes the bequest after hearing it, the guilt shall be on those who make the change. For Allah hears and knows (all things).

182. But if anyone fears partiality or wrong-doing on the part of the testator, and makes peace between (the parties concerned), there is no wrong in him: for Allah is Oft-forgiving, Most Merciful.

183. O you who believe! Fasting is prescribed to you as it was prescribed to those before you, that you may (learn) self-restraint,-

الْمُتَّقِيْنَ ۝ فَمَنْ بَدَّلَهٗ بَعْدَ مَا

سَمِعَهٗ فَإِنَّمَآ اِثْمُهٗ عَلَى الَّذِيْنَ

يُبَدِّلُوْنَهٗ ۚ اِنَّ اللّٰهَ سَمِيْعٌ عَلِيْمٌ ۝

فَمَنْ خَافَ مِنْ مُّوْصٍ جَنَفًا اَوْ

اِثْمًا فَاَصْلَحَ بَيْنَهُمْ فَلَآ اِثْمَ

عَلَيْهِ ۚ اِنَّ اللّٰهَ غَفُوْرٌ رَّحِيْمٌ ۝

يٰٓاَيُّهَا الَّذِيْنَ اٰمَنُوْا كُتِبَ عَلَيْكُمُ

الصِّيَامُ كَمَا كُتِبَ عَلَى الَّذِيْنَ

مِنْ قَبْلِكُمْ لَعَلَّكُمْ تَتَّقُوْنَ ۝

then grant any reasonable demand, and compensate him with handsome gratitude, this is a concession and a Mercy from your Lord. After this whoever exceeds the limits shall be in grave Chastisement.

179. In the Law of Equality there is (saving of) Life to you, o you men of understanding; that you may restrain yourselves.

180. It is prescribed, when death approaches any of you, if he leave any goods that he make a bequest to parents and next of kin, according to reasonable usage; this is due from

فَاتِّبَاعٌ بِالْمَعْرُوفِ وَأَدَآءٌ إِلَيْهِ

بِإِحْسَانٍ ذَٰلِكَ تَخْفِيفٌ مِّن

رَّبِّكُمْ وَرَحْمَةٌ فَمَنِ اعْتَدَىٰ

بَعْدَ ذَٰلِكَ فَلَهُ عَذَابٌ أَلِيمٌ ۝

وَلَكُمْ فِي الْقِصَاصِ حَيَوٰةٌ يَٰٓأُولِي

الْأَلْبَابِ لَعَلَّكُمْ تَتَّقُونَ ۝ كُتِبَ

عَلَيْكُمْ إِذَا حَضَرَ أَحَدَكُمُ الْمَوْتُ

إِن تَرَكَ خَيْرًا ۙ الْوَصِيَّةُ لِلْوَالِدَيْنِ

وَالْأَقْرَبِينَ بِالْمَعْرُوفِ حَقًّا عَلَى

charity; to fulfil the contracts which you have made; and to be firm and patient, in pain (or suffering) and a diversity, and throughout all periods of panic. Such are the people of truth, the Allah-fearing.

178. O you who believe! The law of equality is prescribed to you in cases of murder: the free for the free, the slave for the slave, the woman for the woman. But if any remission is made by the brother of the slain,

الزَّكٰوةَ وَالْمُوفُونَ بِعَهْدِهِمْ إِذَا

عَاهَدُوْا وَالصّٰبِرِيْنَ فِى الْبَأْسَآءِ

وَالضَّرَّآءِ وَحِيْنَ الْبَأْسِ أُولٰٓئِكَ

الَّذِيْنَ صَدَقُوْا وَأُولٰٓئِكَ هُمُ

الْمُتَّقُوْنَ ۝ يٰٓأَيُّهَا الَّذِيْنَ اٰمَنُوْا

كُتِبَ عَلَيْكُمُ الْقِصَاصُ فِى

الْقَتْلٰى اَلْحُرُّ بِالْحُرِّ وَالْعَبْدُ

بِالْعَبْدِ وَالْأُنْثٰى بِالْأُنْثٰى

فَمَنْ عُفِيَ لَهُ مِنْ أَخِيْهِ شَىْءٌ

seek causes of dispute in the Book are in a schism Far (from the purpose).

177. It is not righteousness that you turn your faces toward East or West; but it is righteousness - to believe in Allah and the Last Day, and the Angels, and the Book, and the Messengers; to spend of your substance, out of love for Him, for your kin, for orphans, for the needy, for the wayfarer, for those who ask, and for the ransom of slaves; to be steadfast in prayer, and practice regular

اخْتَلَفُوْا فِى الْكِتٰبِ لَفِىْ شِقَاقٍ

بَعِيْدٍ ۞ لَيْسَ الْبِرَّ اَنْ تُوَلُّوْا

وُجُوْهَكُمْ قِبَلَ الْمَشْرِقِ وَالْمَغْرِبِ

وَلٰكِنَّ الْبِرَّ مَنْ اٰمَنَ بِاللّٰهِ

وَالْيَوْمِ الْاٰخِرِ وَالْمَلٰٓئِكَةِ وَالْكِتٰبِ

وَالنَّبِيّٖنَ ۚ وَاٰتَى الْمَالَ عَلٰى حُبِّهٖ

ذَوِى الْقُرْبٰى وَالْيَتٰمٰى وَالْمَسٰكِيْنَ

وَابْنَ السَّبِيْلِ ۙ وَالسَّآئِلِيْنَ وَفِى

الرِّقَابِ ۚ وَاَقَامَ الصَّلٰوةَ وَاٰتَى

in the Book, and purchase for them a miserable profit, - they swallow into themselves nothing but Fire; Allah will not address them on the Day of Resurrection. Nor purify them: grievous will be their Chastisement.

175. They are the ones who buy Error in place of Guidance and Torment in place of Forgiveness. Ah! What boldness (they show) for the Fire!

176. (Their doom is) because Allah sent down the Book in truth but those who

مِنَ الۡكِتٰبِ وَيَشۡتَرُوۡنَ بِهٖ ثَمَنًا

قَلِيۡلًا ۙ اُولٰٓئِكَ مَا يَاۡكُلُوۡنَ فِيۡ

بُطُوۡنِهِمۡ اِلَّا النَّارَ وَلَا يُكَلِّمُهُمُ

اللّٰهُ يَوۡمَ الۡقِيٰمَةِ وَلَا يُزَكِّيۡهِمۡ ۖ

وَلَهُمۡ عَذَابٌ اَلِيۡمٌ ۞ اُولٰٓئِكَ

الَّذِيۡنَ اشۡتَرَوُا الضَّلٰلَةَ بِالۡهُدٰى

وَالۡعَذَابَ بِالۡمَغۡفِرَةِ ۚ فَمَآ اَصۡبَرَهُمۡ

عَلَى النَّارِ ۞ ذٰلِكَ بِاَنَّ اللّٰهَ نَزَّلَ

الۡكِتٰبَ بِالۡحَقِّ ۗ وَاِنَّ الَّذِيۡنَ

void of wisdom.

172. O you who believe! Eat of the good things that We have provided for you and be grateful to Allah, if it is Him you worship.

173. He has only forbidden you dead meat, and blood, and the flesh of swine, and that on which any other name has been invoked besides that of Allah. But if one is forced by necessity, without wilful disobedience, nor transgressing due limits, - then is he guiltless. For Allah is Oft-forgiving, Most Merciful.

174. Those who conceal Allah's revelations

يَعْقِلُونَ ۞ يَا أَيُّهَا الَّذِينَ اٰمَنُوا

كُلُوا مِنْ طَيِّبَاتِ مَا رَزَقْنَاكُمْ

وَاشْكُرُوا لِلّٰهِ إِنْ كُنْتُمْ إِيَّاهُ

تَعْبُدُونَ ۞ إِنَّمَا حَرَّمَ عَلَيْكُمُ

الْمَيْتَةَ وَالدَّمَ وَلَحْمَ الْخِنْزِيرِ

وَمَا أُهِلَّ بِهِ لِغَيْرِ اللّٰهِ فَمَنِ

اضْطُرَّ غَيْرَ بَاغٍ وَّلَا عَادٍ فَلَا إِثْمَ

عَلَيْهِ إِنَّ اللّٰهَ غَفُورٌ رَّحِيمٌ ۞

إِنَّ الَّذِينَ يَكْتُمُونَ مَا أَنْزَلَ اللّٰهُ

what is evil and shameful, and that you should say of Allah that of which you have no knowledge.

170. When it is said to them: "Follow what Allah has revealed:" They say: "No! we shall follow the ways of our fathers." What! even though their fathers were void of wisdom and guidance?

171. The parable of those who reject Faith is as if one were to shout like a goat-herd, to things that listen to nothing but calls and cries: deaf, dumb, and blind, they are

بِالسُّوْٓءِ وَالْفَحْشَآءِ وَاَنْ تَقُوْلُوْا

عَلَى اللّٰهِ مَا لَا تَعْلَمُوْنَ ۞ وَاِذَا

قِيْلَ لَهُمُ اتَّبِعُوْا مَآ اَنْزَلَ اللّٰهُ

قَالُوْا بَلْ نَتَّبِعُ مَآ اَلْفَيْنَا عَلَيْهِ

اٰبَآءَنَا ؕ اَوَلَوْ كَانَ اٰبَآؤُهُمْ لَا

يَعْقِلُوْنَ شَيْئًا وَّلَا يَهْتَدُوْنَ ۞

وَمَثَلُ الَّذِيْنَ كَفَرُوْا كَمَثَلِ الَّذِيْ

يَنْعِقُ بِمَا لَا يَسْمَعُ اِلَّا دُعَآءً

وَّنِدَآءً ؕ صُمٌّۢ بُكْمٌ عُمْيٌ فَهُمْ لَا

follow (them) : they would see the Chastisement, and all relations between them would be cut off.

167. And those who followed would say: "If only We had one more chance, we would clear ourselves of them, as they have cleared themselves of us." Thus will Allah show them (the fruits of) their deeds as (nothing but) regrets. Nor will there be a way for them out of the Fire.

168. O you people! Eat of what is on earth, lawful and good; and do not follow the footsteps of the Satan, for he is to you an avowed enemy.

169. For he commands you

ٱتَّبَعُوا۟ وَرَأَوُا۟ ٱلْعَذَابَ وَتَقَطَّعَتْ

بِهِمُ ٱلْأَسْبَابُ ۝ وَقَالَ ٱلَّذِينَ

ٱتَّبَعُوا۟ لَوْ أَنَّ لَنَا كَرَّةً فَنَتَبَرَّأَ مِنْهُمْ

كَمَا تَبَرَّءُوا۟ مِنَّا ۗ كَذَٰلِكَ يُرِيهِمُ

ٱللَّهُ أَعْمَالَهُمْ حَسَرَٰتٍ عَلَيْهِمْ ۖ وَمَا

هُم بِخَٰرِجِينَ مِنَ ٱلنَّارِ ۝ يَٰٓأَيُّهَا

ٱلنَّاسُ كُلُوا۟ مِمَّا فِى ٱلْأَرْضِ حَلَٰلًا

طَيِّبًا وَلَا تَتَّبِعُوا۟ خُطُوَٰتِ ٱلشَّيْطَٰنِ ۚ

إِنَّهُ لَكُمْ عَدُوٌّ مُّبِينٌ ۝ إِنَّمَا يَأْمُرُكُم

which trail like their slaves between the sky and the earth;- (here) indeed are Signs for a people that are wise.

165. Yet there are men who take (for worship) others besides Allah, as equal (with Allah): they love them as they should love Allah. But those of Faith are over-flowing in their love for Allah. If only the unrighteous could see, behold, they would see the Chastisement; that to Allah belongs all power, and Allah will strongly enforce the Chastisement.

166. Then would those who are followed clear themselves of those who

الْمُسَخَّرِ بَيْنَ السَّمَآءِ وَالْاَرْضِ

لَاٰيٰتٍ لِّقَوْمٍ يَّعْقِلُوْنَ ۞ وَمِنَ

النَّاسِ مَنْ يَّتَّخِذُ مِنْ دُوْنِ اللّٰهِ

اَنْدَادًا يُّحِبُّوْنَهُمْ كَحُبِّ اللّٰهِ ۚ

وَالَّذِيْنَ اٰمَنُوْۤا اَشَدُّ حُبًّا لِّلّٰهِ ۗ

وَلَوْ يَرَى الَّذِيْنَ ظَلَمُوْۤا اِذْ يَرَوْنَ

الْعَذَابَ ۙ اَنَّ الْقُوَّةَ لِلّٰهِ جَمِيْعًا ۙ

وَّاَنَّ اللّٰهَ شَدِيْدُ الْعَذَابِ ۞ اِذْ

تَبَرَّاَ الَّذِيْنَ اتُّبِعُوْا مِنَ الَّذِيْنَ

163. And your God is One God (Allah) There is no god but He, Most Gracious, Most Merciful.

164. Behold! In the creation of the heavens and the earth; in the alternation of the night and the day; in the sailing of the ships through the ocean for the profit of mankind; in the rain which Allah sends down from the skies, and the life which He gives therewith to an earth that is dead; in the beasts of all kinds that He scatters through the earth; in the change of the winds, and the clouds

وَاِلٰهُكُمْ اِلٰهٌ وَّاحِدٌ ۚ لَآ اِلٰهَ اِلَّا هُوَ

الرَّحْمٰنُ الرَّحِيْمُ ۞ اِنَّ فِىْ خَلْقِ

السَّمٰوٰتِ وَالْاَرْضِ وَاخْتِلَافِ الَّيْلِ

وَالنَّهَارِ وَالْفُلْكِ الَّتِىْ تَجْرِىْ

فِى الْبَحْرِ بِمَا يَنْفَعُ النَّاسَ

وَمَآ اَنْزَلَ اللّٰهُ مِنَ السَّمَآءِ مِنْ

مَّآءٍ فَاَحْيَا بِهِ الْاَرْضَ بَعْدَ

مَوْتِهَا وَبَثَّ فِيْهَا مِنْ كُلِّ دَآبَّةٍ

وَّتَصْرِيْفِ الرِّيٰحِ وَالسَّحَابِ

the Book, - on them shall be Allah's curse, and the curse of those entitled to curse, -

160. Except those who repent and make amends and openly declare (the Truth): to them I turn; for I am Oft-returning, Most Merciful.

161. Those who reject Faith, and die rejecting, - on them is Allah's curse, and the curse of angels, and of all mankind;

162. They will abide therein: their Chastisement will not be lightened, nor will respite be their (lot).

الْكِتٰبُ أُولٰٓئِكَ يَلْعَنُهُمُ اللهُ

وَيَلْعَنُهُمُ اللّٰعِنُوْنَ ۞ إِلَّا الَّذِيْنَ

تَابُوْا وَأَصْلَحُوْا وَبَيَّنُوْا فَأُولٰٓئِكَ

أَتُوْبُ عَلَيْهِمْ ۚ وَأَنَا التَّوَّابُ

الرَّحِيْمُ ۞ إِنَّ الَّذِيْنَ كَفَرُوْا

وَمَاتُوْا وَهُمْ كُفَّارٌ أُولٰٓئِكَ عَلَيْهِمْ

لَعْنَةُ اللهِ وَالْمَلٰٓئِكَةِ وَالنَّاسِ

أَجْمَعِيْنَ ۞ خٰلِدِيْنَ فِيْهَا ۚ لَا يُخَفَّفُ

عَنْهُمُ الْعَذَابُ وَلَا هُمْ يُنْظَرُوْنَ ۞

on whom (descend) blessings from Allah, and Mercy, and they are the ones that receive guidance.

158. Behold! Safa and Marwa are among the Symbols of Allah. So if those who visit the House in the Season or at other times, should compass them round, it is no sin in them. And if any one obeys his own impulse to good,- be sure that Allah is He Who recognises and knows.

159. Those who conceal the clear (Signs) We have sent down, and the Guidance, after We have made it clear for the people in

عَلَيْهِمْ صَلَوٰتٌ مِّنْ رَّبِّهِمْ وَرَحْمَةٌ ۖ

وَأُولَٰٓئِكَ هُمُ الْمُهْتَدُونَ ۞ إِنَّ

الصَّفَا وَالْمَرْوَةَ مِنْ شَعَآئِرِ اللَّهِ ۖ

فَمَنْ حَجَّ الْبَيْتَ أَوِ اعْتَمَرَ فَلَا

جُنَاحَ عَلَيْهِ أَنْ يَّطَّوَّفَ بِهِمَا ۚ

وَمَنْ تَطَوَّعَ خَيْرًا فَإِنَّ اللَّهَ شَاكِرٌ

عَلِيمٌ ۞ إِنَّ الَّذِينَ يَكْتُمُونَ

مَآ أَنْزَلْنَا مِنَ الْبَيِّنَٰتِ وَالْهُدَىٰ

مِنْۢ بَعْدِ مَا بَيَّنَّٰهُ لِلنَّاسِ فِى

for Allah is with those who patiently persevere.

154. And say not of those who are slain in the way of Allah: "They are dead." No, they are living, though you perceive (it) not.

155. Be sure we shall test you with something of fear and hunger, some loss in goods or lives or the fruits (of your toil), but give glad tidings to those who patiently persevere,

156. Who say, when afflicted with calamity: "To Allah We belong, and to Him is our return":-

157. They are those

إِنَّ اللّٰهَ مَعَ الصّٰبِرِيْنَ ۞ وَلَا

تَقُوْلُوْا لِمَنْ يُّقْتَلُ فِيْ سَبِيْلِ

اللّٰهِ اَمْوَاتٌ ؕ بَلْ اَحْيَاءٌ وَّلٰكِنْ

لَّا تَشْعُرُوْنَ ۞ وَلَنَبْلُوَنَّكُمْ بِشَيْءٍ

مِّنَ الْخَوْفِ وَالْجُوْعِ وَنَقْصٍ

مِّنَ الْاَمْوَالِ وَالْاَنْفُسِ وَالثَّمَرٰتِ ؕ

وَبَشِّرِ الصّٰبِرِيْنَ ۞ الَّذِيْنَ اِذَآ

اَصَابَتْهُمْ مُّصِيْبَةٌ ۙ قَالُوْٓا اِنَّا

لِلّٰهِ وَاِنَّآ اِلَيْهِ رٰجِعُوْنَ ۞ اُولٰٓئِكَ

so fear them not, but fear Me; and that I may complete My favours on you, and you may (consent to) be guided;

151. A similar (favour have you already received) in that We have sent among you an Apostle of your own, rehearsing to you Our Signs, and sanctifying you, and instructing you in Scripture and Wisdom, and in new knowledge.

152. Then you remember Me; I will remember you. Be grateful to Me, and reject not Faith.

153. O you who believe! Seek help with patient perseverance and prayer;

فَلَا تَخْشَوْهُمْ وَاخْشَوْنِى وَلِأُتِمَّ

نِعْمَتِى عَلَيْكُمْ وَلَعَلَّكُمْ تَهْتَدُوْنَ ۝

كَمَا أَرْسَلْنَا فِيْكُمْ رَسُوْلًا مِّنْكُمْ

يَتْلُوْا عَلَيْكُمْ اٰيٰتِنَا وَيُزَكِّيْكُمْ

وَيُعَلِّمُكُمُ الْكِتٰبَ وَالْحِكْمَةَ

وَيُعَلِّمُكُمْ مَّا لَمْ تَكُوْنُوْا تَعْلَمُوْنَ ۝

فَاذْكُرُوْنِىْ أَذْكُرْكُمْ وَاشْكُرُوْا لِىْ

وَلَا تَكْفُرُوْنِ ۝ يٰٓأَيُّهَا الَّذِيْنَ

اٰمَنُوا اسْتَعِيْنُوْا بِالصَّبْرِ وَالصَّلٰوةِ

149. From wheresoever you start forth, turn your face in the direction of the Sacred Mosque; that is indeed the truth from your Lord. And Allah is not unmindful of what you do.

150. So from wheresoever you start forth, turn your face in the direction of the Sacred Mosque; and wheresoever you are, turn your face to it: that there be no ground of dispute against you among the people, except those of them that are bent on wickedness;

وَمِنْ حَيْثُ خَرَجْتَ فَوَلِّ وَجْهَكَ

شَطْرَ الْمَسْجِدِ الْحَرَامِ ۖ وَإِنَّهُ

لَلْحَقُّ مِنْ رَّبِّكَ ۗ وَمَا اللَّهُ بِغَافِلٍ

عَمَّا تَعْمَلُونَ ۞ وَمِنْ حَيْثُ

خَرَجْتَ فَوَلِّ وَجْهَكَ شَطْرَ

الْمَسْجِدِ الْحَرَامِ ۚ وَحَيْثُ مَا

كُنْتُمْ فَوَلُّوا وُجُوهَكُمْ شَطْرَهُ

لِئَلَّا يَكُونَ لِلنَّاسِ عَلَيْكُمْ

حُجَّةٌ إِلَّا الَّذِينَ ظَلَمُوا مِنْهُمْ

be in the wrong.

146. The people of the Book know this as they know their own sons; but some of them conceal the truth which they themselves know.

147. The Truth is from your Lord; so be not at all in doubt.

148. To each is a goal to which Allah turns him; then strive together (as in a race) towards all that is good. Wheresoever you are, Allah will bring you together. For Allah has power over all things.

الظّٰلِمِيْنَ ۩ اَلَّذِيْنَ اٰتَيْنٰهُمُ الْكِتٰبَ

يَعْرِفُوْنَهٗ كَمَا يَعْرِفُوْنَ اَبْنَآءَهُمْ ۖ

وَاِنَّ فَرِيْقًا مِّنْهُمْ لَيَكْتُمُوْنَ

الْحَقَّ وَهُمْ يَعْلَمُوْنَ ۩ اَلْحَقُّ

مِنْ رَّبِّكَ فَلَا تَكُوْنَنَّ مِنَ

الْمُمْتَرِيْنَ ۩ وَلِكُلٍّ وِّجْهَةٌ هُوَ

مُوَلِّيْهَا فَاسْتَبِقُوا الْخَيْرٰتِ ؕ اَيْنَ

مَا تَكُوْنُوْا يَأْتِ بِكُمُ اللّٰهُ جَمِيْعًا ؕ

اِنَّ اللّٰهَ عَلٰى كُلِّ شَيْءٍ قَدِيْرٌ ۩

in that direction. The people of the Book know well that that is the truth from their Lord. Nor is Allah unmindful of what they do.

145. Even if you were to bring to the people of the Book all the Signs (together), they would not follow your Qibla; nor are you going to follow their Qibla; nor indeed will they follow each other's Qibla. If you after the knowledge has reached you, were to follow their (vain) desires, - then would you indeed (clearly)

شَطْرَهٗ ۗ وَ اِنَّ الَّذِيْنَ اُوْتُوا الْكِتٰبَ

لَيَعْلَمُوْنَ اَنَّهُ الْحَقُّ مِنْ رَّبِّهِمْ ؕ

وَ مَا اللّٰهُ بِغَافِلٍ عَمَّا يَعْمَلُوْنَ ۝

وَ لَئِنْ اَتَيْتَ الَّذِيْنَ اُوْتُوا الْكِتٰبَ

بِكُلِّ اٰيَةٍ مَّا تَبِعُوْا قِبْلَتَكَ ۚ وَ مَا

اَنْتَ بِتَابِعٍ قِبْلَتَهُمْ ۚ وَ مَا بَعْضُهُمْ

بِتَابِعٍ قِبْلَةَ بَعْضٍ ؕ وَ لَئِنِ اتَّبَعْتَ

اَهْوَآءَهُمْ مِّنْ بَعْدِ مَا جَآءَكَ

مِنَ الْعِلْمِ ۙ اِنَّكَ اِذًا لَّمِنَ

who followed the Apostle from those who would turn on their heels (from the Faith). Indeed it was (a change) momentous, except to those guided by Allah. And never would Allah make your faith of no effect. For Allah is to all people most surely full of kindness, Most Merciful.

144. We see the turning of your face (for guidance) to the heavens: now shall We turn you to a Qibla that shall please you. Turn then your face in the direction of the Sacred Mosque: Wherever you are, turn your faces

يَتَّبِعُ الرَّسُوْلَ مِمَّنْ يَّنْقَلِبُ عَلٰى

عَقِبَيْهِ ۚ وَاِنْ كَانَتْ لَكَبِيْرَةً اِلَّا

عَلَى الَّذِيْنَ هَدَى اللّٰهُ ۗ وَمَا كَانَ

اللّٰهُ لِيُضِيْعَ اِيْمَانَكُمْ ۚ اِنَّ اللّٰهَ

بِالنَّاسِ لَرَءُوْفٌ رَّحِيْمٌ ۞ قَدْ

نَرٰى تَقَلُّبَ وَجْهِكَ فِى السَّمَآءِ ۚ

فَلَنُوَلِّيَنَّكَ قِبْلَةً تَرْضٰىهَا ۚ فَوَلِّ

وَجْهَكَ شَطْرَ الْمَسْجِدِ الْحَرَامِ ۗ

وَحَيْثُ مَا كُنْتُمْ فَوَلُّوْا وُجُوْهَكُمْ

142. The fools among the people will say: "What has turned them from the Qibla to which they were used?" Say: To Allah belong both East and West: He guides whom He will to a Way that is straight.

143. Thus, have We made of you an Ummat justly balanced, that you might be witnesses over the nations, and the Apostle a witness over yourselves; and We appointed the Qibla to which you were used, only to test those

سَيَقُوْلُ السُّفَهَآءُ مِنَ النَّاسِ

مَا وَلّٰىهُمْ عَنْ قِبْلَتِهِمُ الَّتِيْ كَانُوْا

عَلَيْهَا ۚ قُلْ لِّلّٰهِ الْمَشْرِقُ وَالْمَغْرِبُ ۚ

يَهْدِيْ مَنْ يَّشَآءُ اِلٰى صِرَاطٍ

مُّسْتَقِيْمٍ ۞ وَكَذٰلِكَ جَعَلْنٰكُمْ

اُمَّةً وَّسَطًا لِّتَكُوْنُوْا شُهَدَآءَ

عَلَى النَّاسِ وَيَكُوْنَ الرَّسُوْلُ

عَلَيْكُمْ شَهِيْدًا ۗ وَمَا جَعَلْنَا الْقِبْلَةَ

الَّتِيْ كُنْتَ عَلَيْهَآ اِلَّا لِنَعْلَمَ مَنْ

پاره

سَيَقُوْلُ

(۲)

PART 3
Tilkar-Rusul

Most Merciful.

90. But those who reject Faith after they accepted it, and then go on adding to their defiance of Faith, - never will their repentance be accepted; for they are those who have (of set purpose) gone astray.

91. As to those who reject Faith, and die rejecting, - never would be accepted from any such as much gold as the earth contains, though they should offer it for ransom. For such is (in store) a Chastisement grievous, and they will find no helpers.

رَّحِيْمٌ ۞ اِنَّ الَّذِيْنَ كَفَرُوْا بَعْدَ

اِيْمَانِهِمْ ثُمَّ ازْدَادُوْا كُفْرًا لَّنْ

تُقْبَلَ تَوْبَتُهُمْ ۚ وَاُولٰٓئِكَ هُمُ

الضَّآلُّوْنَ ۞ اِنَّ الَّذِيْنَ كَفَرُوْا

وَمَاتُوْا وَهُمْ كُفَّارٌ فَلَنْ

يُّقْبَلَ مِنْ اَحَدِهِمْ مِّلْءُ

الْاَرْضِ ذَهَبًا وَّلَوِ افْتَدٰى بِهٖ ؕ

اُولٰٓئِكَ لَهُمْ عَذَابٌ اَلِيْمٌ

وَّمَا لَهُمْ مِّنْ نّٰصِرِيْنَ ۞

that the Apostle was true and that Clear Signs had come unto them? But Allah guides not a people unjust.

87.   Of such the reward is that on them (rests) the curse of Allah, and His Angels, and of all mankind; -

88.   In that will they dwell; nor will their Chastisement be lightened, nor respite be (their lot); -

89.   Except for those that repent (even) after that, and make amends; for verily Allah is Oft-Forgiving,

اَنَّ الرَّسُوْلَ حَقٌّ وَّجَآءَهُمُ

الْبَيِّنٰتُ ۚ وَاللّٰهُ لَا يَهْدِى الْقَوْمَ

الظّٰلِمِيْنَ ۞ اُولٰٓئِكَ جَزَآؤُهُمْ اَنَّ

عَلَيْهِمْ لَعْنَةَ اللّٰهِ وَالْمَلٰٓئِكَةِ

وَالنَّاسِ اَجْمَعِيْنَ ۞ خٰلِدِيْنَ

فِيْهَا ۚ لَا يُخَفَّفُ عَنْهُمُ الْعَذَابُ

وَلَا هُمْ يُنْظَرُوْنَ ۞ اِلَّا

الَّذِيْنَ تَابُوْا مِنْۢ بَعْدِ ذٰلِكَ

وَاَصْلَحُوْا ۟ فَاِنَّ اللّٰهَ غَفُوْرٌ

Jacob, and the Tribes, and in (the Books) given to Moses, Jesus, and the Prophets, from their Lord: we make no distinction between one and another among them, and to Allah do we bow our will (in Islam)."

85.   If anyone desires a religion other than Islam (submission to Allah), never will it be accepted of him; and in the Hereafter he will be in the ranks of those who have lost (all spiritual good).

86.   How shall Allah guide those who reject Faith after they accepted it and bore witness

وَيَعْقُوبَ وَالْأَسْبَاطِ وَمَا أُوتِيَ

مُوسَى وَعِيسَى وَالنَّبِيُّونَ مِنْ

رَّبِّهِمْ لَا نُفَرِّقُ بَيْنَ أَحَدٍ

مِّنْهُمْ وَنَحْنُ لَهُ مُسْلِمُونَ ۞

وَمَنْ يَبْتَغِ غَيْرَ الْإِسْلَامِ

دِينًا فَلَنْ يُقْبَلَ مِنْهُ وَهُوَ

فِي الْآخِرَةِ مِنَ الْخَاسِرِينَ ۞

كَيْفَ يَهْدِى اللَّهُ قَوْمًا

كَفَرُوا بَعْدَ إِيمَانِهِمْ وَشَهِدُوا

and I am with you among the witnesses."

82. If any turn back after this, they are perverted transgressors.

83. Do they seek for other than the Religion of Allah? - while all creatures in the heavens and on the earth have, willingly or unwillingly, bowed to His Will (accepted Islam), and to Him shall they all be brought back.

84. Say: "We believe in Allah, and in what has been revealed to us and what was revealed to Abraham, Isma'il, Isaac,

وَاَنَا مَعَكُمْ مِّنَ الشّٰهِدِيْنَ ۞

فَمَنْ تَوَلّٰى بَعْدَ ذٰلِكَ فَاُولٰٓئِكَ

هُمُ الْفٰسِقُوْنَ ۞ اَفَغَيْرَ دِيْنِ

اللّٰهِ يَبْغُوْنَ وَلَهٗٓ اَسْلَمَ مَنْ

فِى السَّمٰوٰتِ وَالْاَرْضِ طَوْعًا

وَّكَرْهًا وَّاِلَيْهِ يُرْجَعُوْنَ ۞

قُلْ اٰمَنَّا بِاللّٰهِ وَمَآ اُنْزِلَ

عَلَيْنَا وَمَآ اُنْزِلَ عَلٰٓى

اِبْرٰهِيْمَ وَاِسْمٰعِيْلَ وَاِسْحٰقَ

for Lords and Patrons. What! would he bid you to unbelief after you have bowed your will (to Allah in Islam)?

81. Behold! Allah took the covenant of the Prophets, saying: "I give you a Book and Wisdom; then comes to you an Apostle, confirming what is with you; do you believe in him and render him help." Allah said: "Do you agree, and take this My Covenant as binding on you?" They said: "We agree." He said: "Then bear witness,

أَرْبَابًا أَيَأْمُرُكُم بِالْكُفْرِ بَعْدَ

إِذْ أَنتُم مُّسْلِمُونَ ۞ وَإِذْ

أَخَذَ اللّٰهُ مِيثَاقَ النَّبِيِّۦنَ

لَمَآ ءَاتَيْتُكُم مِّن كِتَٰبٍ

وَّحِكْمَةٍ ثُمَّ جَآءَكُمْ رَسُولٌ

مُّصَدِّقٌ لِّمَا مَعَكُمْ لَتُؤْمِنُنَّ

بِهِۦ وَلَتَنصُرُنَّهُۥ قَالَ ءَأَقْرَرْتُمْ

وَأَخَذْتُمْ عَلَىٰ ذَٰلِكُمْ إِصْرِى

قَالُوٓا أَقْرَرْنَا قَالَ فَاشْهَدُوا

Allah, and (well) they know it!

79. It is not (possible) that a man, to whom is given the Book, and Wisdom, and the Prophetic Office, should say to people: "Be you my worshippers rather than Allah's": on the contrary (he would say) "Be you worshippers of Him Who is truly the Cherisher of all: for you had been taught by the Book, and as you read it still."

80. Nor would he instruct you to take Angels and Prophets

اللهِ الْكَذِبَ وَهُمْ يَعْلَمُوْنَ ۞

مَا كَانَ لِبَشَرٍ اَنْ يُّؤْتِيَهُ

اللهُ الْكِتٰبَ وَالْحُكْمَ وَالنُّبُوَّةَ

ثُمَّ يَقُوْلَ لِلنَّاسِ كُوْنُوْا

عِبَادًا لِّيْ مِنْ دُوْنِ اللهِ وَلٰكِنْ

كُوْنُوْا رَبَّانِيّٖنَ بِمَا كُنْتُمْ

تُعَلِّمُوْنَ الْكِتٰبَ وَبِمَا كُنْتُمْ

تَدْرُسُوْنَ ۞ وَلَا يَاْمُرَكُمْ اَنْ

تَتَّخِذُوا الْمَلٰٓئِكَةَ وَالنَّبِيّٖنَ

the Hereafter: nor will Allah (deign to) speak to them or look at them on the Day of Judgment, nor will He cleanse them (of sin): they shall have a grievous Chastisement.

78. There is among them a section who distort the Book with their tongues: (as they read) you would think it is a part of the Book, but it is no part of the Book; and they say, "That is from Allah," but it is not from Allah: it is they who tell a lie against

الْاٰخِرَةِ وَلَا يُكَلِّمُهُمُ اللّٰهُ وَلَا

يَنْظُرُ اِلَيْهِمْ يَوْمَ الْقِيٰمَةِ

وَلَا يُزَكِّيْهِمْ ۖ وَلَهُمْ عَذَابٌ

اَلِيْمٌ ۞ وَاِنَّ مِنْهُمْ لَفَرِيْقًا

يَلْوٗنَ اَلْسِنَتَهُمْ بِالْكِتٰبِ

لِتَحْسَبُوْهُ مِنَ الْكِتٰبِ وَمَا

هُوَ مِنَ الْكِتٰبِ ۚ وَيَقُوْلُوْنَ

هُوَ مِنْ عِنْدِ اللّٰهِ وَمَا هُوَ

مِنْ عِنْدِ اللّٰهِ ۚ وَيَقُوْلُوْنَ عَلَى

stood demanding, because, they
say, "there is no call on us (to keep
faith) with these ignorant
(Pagans)." But they tell a lie
against Allah, and (well) they
know it.

76. No, those that keep their
plighted faith and act aright,
surely Allah loves those who act
aright.

77. As for those who sell the
faith they owe to Allah and their
own plighted word for a small
price, they shall have no portion
in

عَلَيْهِ قَآئِمًا ۗ ذٰلِكَ بِاَنَّهُمْ

قَالُوْا لَيْسَ عَلَيْنَا فِى الْاُمِّيّٖنَ

سَبِيْلٌ ۚ وَيَقُوْلُوْنَ عَلَى اللّٰهِ

الْكَذِبَ وَهُمْ يَعْلَمُوْنَ ۞ بَلٰى

مَنْ اَوْفٰى بِعَهْدِهٖ وَاتَّقٰى

فَاِنَّ اللّٰهَ يُحِبُّ الْمُتَّقِيْنَ ۞

اِنَّ الَّذِيْنَ يَشْتَرُوْنَ بِعَهْدِ

اللّٰهِ وَاَيْمَانِهِمْ ثَمَنًا قَلِيْلًا

اُولٰٓئِكَ لَا خَلَاقَ لَهُمْ فِى

that those (receiving such revelation) should engage you in
argument before your Lord?"
Say: "All bounties are in the hand
of Allah: He grants them to
whom He pleases: and Allah
cares for all, and He knows all
things."

74.   For His Mercy He specially
chooses whom He pleases; for
Allah is the Lord of bounties
unbounded.

75.   Among the People of the
Book are some who, if entrusted
with a hoard of gold, will
(readily) pay it back; others, who,
if entrusted with a single silver
coin, will not repay it unless you
constantly

يُحَآجُّوْكُمْ عِنْدَ رَبِّكُمْ ۚ قُلْ

اِنَّ الْفَضْلَ بِيَدِ اللّٰهِ يُؤْتِيْهِ

مَنْ يَّشَآءُ ۚ وَاللّٰهُ وَاسِعٌ عَلِيْمٌ ۟

يَّخْتَصُّ بِرَحْمَتِهٖ مَنْ يَّشَآءُ ۚ

وَاللّٰهُ ذُو الْفَضْلِ الْعَظِيْمِ ۟

وَمِنْ اَهْلِ الْكِتٰبِ مَنْ اِنْ

تَأْمَنْهُ بِقِنْطَارٍ يُّؤَدِّهٖۤ اِلَيْكَ ۚ

وَمِنْهُمْ مَّنْ اِنْ تَأْمَنْهُ بِدِيْنَارٍ

لَّا يُؤَدِّهٖۤ اِلَيْكَ اِلَّا مَا دُمْتَ

do you clothe Truth with false-hood, and conceal the Truth, while you have knowledge?

72.   A section of the People of the Book say: "Believe in the morning what is revealed to the believers, but reject it at the end of the day; perchance they may (themselves) turn back;

73.   "And believe no one unless he follows your religion." Say: "True guidance is the Guidance of Allah: (fear you) lest a revelation be sent to someone (else) like that which was sent unto you? Or

تَلْبِسُوْنَ الْحَقَّ بِالْبَاطِلِ وَتَكْتُمُوْنَ

الْحَقَّ وَاَنْتُمْ تَعْلَمُوْنَ ۞ وَ قَالَتْ

طَّآئِفَةٌ مِّنْ اَهْلِ الْكِتٰبِ اٰمِنُوْا

بِالَّذِيْٓ اُنْزِلَ عَلَى الَّذِيْنَ اٰمَنُوْا

وَجْهَ النَّهَارِ وَاكْفُرُوْٓا اٰخِرَهٗ

لَعَلَّهُمْ يَرْجِعُوْنَ ۞ وَلَا تُؤْمِنُوْٓا

اِلَّا لِمَنْ تَبِعَ دِيْنَكُمْ قُلْ اِنَّ

الْهُدٰى هُدَى اللّٰهِ اَنْ يُّؤْتٰٓى

اَحَدٌ مِّثْلَ مَآ اُوْتِيْتُمْ اَوْ

gods with Allah.

68. Without doubt, among men, the nearest of kin to Abraham, are those who follow him, as are also this Apostle and those who believe: and Allah is the Protector of those who have Faith.

69. It is the wish of a section of the People of the Book to lead you astray. But they shall lead astray (not you), but themselves, and they do not perceive!

70. You People of the Book! Why reject you the Signs of Allah, of which you are (yourselves) witnesses?

71. You People of the Book! Why

الْمُشْرِكِينَ ۞ اِنَّ اَوْلَى النَّاسِ

بِاِبْرٰهِيْمَ لَلَّذِيْنَ اتَّبَعُوْهُ وَهٰذَا

النَّبِيُّ وَالَّذِيْنَ اٰمَنُوْا ۚ وَاللّٰهُ وَلِيُّ

الْمُؤْمِنِيْنَ ۞ وَدَّتْ طَّآئِفَةٌ مِّنْ

اَهْلِ الْكِتٰبِ لَوْ يُضِلُّوْنَكُمْ ۚ

وَمَا يُضِلُّوْنَ اِلَّاۤ اَنْفُسَهُمْ وَمَا

يَشْعُرُوْنَ ۞ يٰۤاَهْلَ الْكِتٰبِ لِمَ

تَكْفُرُوْنَ بِاٰيٰتِ اللّٰهِ وَاَنْتُمْ

تَشْهَدُوْنَ ۞ يٰۤاَهْلَ الْكِتٰبِ لِمَ

Abraham, when the Torah and the Gospel were not revealed till after him? Have you no understanding?

66. Ah! You are those who fell to disputing (even) in matters of which you had some knowledge! But why dispute you in matters of which you have no knowledge? It is Allah Who knows, and you who know not!

67. Abraham was not a Jew nor yet a Christian; but he was true in Faith, and bowed his will to Allah's (which is Islam), and he joined not

اِبْرٰهِیْمَ ؕ وَمَاۤ اُنْزِلَتِ التَّوْرٰىةُ

وَالْاِنْجِیْلُ اِلَّا مِنْۢ بَعْدِهٖ ؕ اَفَلَا

تَعْقِلُوْنَ ۟ۨ هٰاۤ اَنْتُمْ هٰۤؤُلَآءِ

حَاجَجْتُمْ فِیْمَا لَکُمْ بِهٖ عِلْمٌ

فَلِمَ تُحَآجُّوْنَ فِیْمَا لَیْسَ لَکُمْ

بِهٖ عِلْمٌ ؕ وَاللّٰهُ یَعْلَمُ وَاَنْتُمْ

لَا تَعْلَمُوْنَ ۟ مَا کَانَ اِبْرٰهِیْمُ

یَهُوْدِیًّا وَّلَا نَصْرَانِیًّا وَّلٰکِنْ کَانَ

حَنِیْفًا مُّسْلِمًا ؕ وَمَا کَانَ مِنَ

the Wise.

63. But if they turn back, Allah has full knowledge of those who do mischief.

64. Say: "O People of the Book! come to common terms as between us and you: that we worship none but Allah; that we associate no partners with Him; that we erect not, from among ourselves, lords and patrons other than Allah." If then they turn back, you say: "Bear witness that we (at least) are Muslims (bowing to Allah's Will)."

65. You People of the Book! Why dispute you about

الْحَكِيمُ ۞ فَإِنْ تَوَلَّوْا فَإِنَّ اللّٰهَ

عَلِيمٌ بِالْمُفْسِدِينَ ۞ قُلْ يَا أَهْلَ

الْكِتَابِ تَعَالَوْا إِلٰى كَلِمَةٍ سَوَآءٍ

بَيْنَنَا وَبَيْنَكُمْ أَلَّا نَعْبُدَ إِلَّا

اللّٰهَ وَلَا نُشْرِكَ بِهٖ شَيْئًا وَلَا

يَتَّخِذَ بَعْضُنَا بَعْضًا أَرْبَابًا

مِّنْ دُونِ اللّٰهِ فَإِنْ تَوَلَّوْا

فَقُولُوا اشْهَدُوا بِأَنَّا مُسْلِمُونَ ۞

يَا أَهْلَ الْكِتَابِ لِمَ تُحَآجُّونَ فِيْ

Allah alone; so be not of those who doubt.

61. If any one disputes in this matter with you, now after (full) knowledge has come to you, say: "Come! let us gather together,- our sons and your sons, our women and your women, our- selves and yourselves: then let us earnestly pray, and invoke the curse of Allah on those who lie!"

62. This is the true account: there is no god except Allah; and Allah - He is indeed the Exalted in Power,

رَّبِّكَ فَلَا تَكُنْ مِّنَ الْمُمْتَرِيْنَ ۟

فَمَنْ حَاجَّكَ فِيْهِ مِنْ بَعْدِ مَا

جَآءَكَ مِنَ الْعِلْمِ فَقُلْ تَعَالَوْا

نَدْعُ اَبْنَآءَنَا وَاَبْنَآءَكُمْ وَنِسَآءَنَا

وَنِسَآءَكُمْ وَاَنْفُسَنَا وَاَنْفُسَكُمْ ۖ

ثُمَّ نَبْتَهِلْ فَنَجْعَلْ لَّعْنَتَ اللّٰهِ

عَلَى الْكٰذِبِيْنَ ۟ اِنَّ هٰذَا لَهُوَ

الْقَصَصُ الْحَقُّ ۚ وَمَا مِنْ اِلٰهٍ

اِلَّا اللّٰهُ ۚ وَاِنَّ اللّٰهَ لَهُوَ الْعَزِيْزُ

with terrible agony in this world and in the Hereafter, nor will they have anyone to help."

57. "As to those who believe and work righteousness, Allah will pay them (in full) their reward; but Allah loves not those who do wrong."

58. "This is what We rehearse unto you of the Signs and the Message of Wisdom."

59. The similitude of Jesus before Allah is as that of Adam; He created him from dust, then said to him: "Be," and he was.

60. The Truth (comes) from

عَذَابًا شَدِيدًا فِى الدُّنْيَا

وَالْاٰخِرَةِ وَمَا لَهُمْ مِنْ نّٰصِرِيْنَ

۞ وَاَمَّا الَّذِيْنَ اٰمَنُوْا وَعَمِلُوا الصّٰلِحٰتِ

فَيُوَفِّيْهِمْ اُجُوْرَهُمْ ۭ وَاللّٰهُ لَا يُحِبُّ

الظّٰلِمِيْنَ ۞ ذٰلِكَ نَتْلُوْهُ عَلَيْكَ

مِنَ الْاٰيٰتِ وَالذِّكْرِ الْحَكِيْمِ ۞

اِنَّ مَثَلَ عِيْسٰى عِنْدَ اللّٰهِ كَمَثَلِ

اٰدَمَ ۭ خَلَقَهٗ مِنْ تُرَابٍ ثُمَّ قَالَ

لَهٗ كُنْ فَيَكُوْنُ ۞ اَلْحَقُّ مِنْ

54. And (the unbelievers) plotted and planned, and Allah too planned, and the best of planners is Allah.

55. Behold! Allah said: "O Jesus! I will take you and raise you to Myself and clear you (of the falsehoods) of those who blaspheme; I will make those who follow you superior to those who reject Faith, to the Day of Resurrection: then shall you all return unto me, and I will judge between you of the matters wherein you dispute."

56. "As to those who reject Faith, I will punish them

وَمَكَرُوا وَمَكَرَ اللهُ ۚ وَاللهُ خَيْرُ الْمَاكِرِينَ ۞ اِذْ قَالَ اللهُ يٰعِيْسٰى اِنِّىْ مُتَوَفِّيْكَ وَرَافِعُكَ اِلَىَّ وَمُطَهِّرُكَ مِنَ الَّذِيْنَ كَفَرُوْا وَجَاعِلُ الَّذِيْنَ اتَّبَعُوْكَ فَوْقَ الَّذِيْنَ كَفَرُوْا اِلٰى يَوْمِ الْقِيٰمَةِ ۚ ثُمَّ اِلَىَّ مَرْجِعُكُمْ فَاَحْكُمُ بَيْنَكُمْ فِيْمَا كُنْتُمْ فِيْهِ تَخْتَلِفُوْنَ ۞ فَاَمَّا الَّذِيْنَ كَفَرُوْا فَاُعَذِّبُهُمْ

So fear Allah, and obey me."

51.   "It is Allah Who is my Lord and your Lord; then worship Him. This is a Way that is straight."

52.   When Jesus found unbelief on their part, he said: "Who will be my helpers to (the work of) Allah?" Said the Disciples: "We are Allah's helpers: we believe in Allah, and you bear witness that we are Muslims."

53.   "Our Lord! We believe in what You have revealed, and we follow the Apostle; then write us down among those who bear witness."

فَاتَّقُوا اللّٰهَ وَ اَطِيْعُوْنِ ۞ اِنَّ

اللّٰهَ رَبِّيْ وَ رَبُّكُمْ فَاعْبُدُوْهُ ؕ

هٰذَا صِرَاطٌ مُّسْتَقِيْمٌ ۞ فَلَمَّاۤ

اَحَسَّ عِيْسٰى مِنْهُمُ الْكُفْرَ قَالَ

مَنْ اَنْصَارِيْۤ اِلَى اللّٰهِ ؕ قَالَ

الْحَوَارِيُّوْنَ نَحْنُ اَنْصَارُ اللّٰهِ ۚ اٰمَنَّا

بِاللّٰهِ ۚ وَ اشْهَدْ بِاَنَّا مُسْلِمُوْنَ ۞

رَبَّنَاۤ اٰمَنَّا بِمَاۤ اَنْزَلْتَ وَ اتَّبَعْنَا

الرَّسُوْلَ فَاكْتُبْنَا مَعَ الشّٰهِدِيْنَ ۞

by Allah's leave: and I heal those born blind, and the lepers, and I quicken the dead, by Allah's leave; and I declare to you what you eat, and what you store in your houses. Surely therein is a Sign for you if you did believe;"

50. "(I have come to you), to attest the Torah which was before me. And to make lawful to you part of what was (before) forbidden to you; I have come to you with a Sign from your Lord.

بِاِذۡنِ اللّٰهِ ۚ وَاُبۡرِئُ الۡاَكۡمَهَ

وَالۡاَبۡرَصَ وَاُحۡىِ الۡمَوۡتٰى بِاِذۡنِ

اللّٰهِ ۚ وَاُنَبِّئُكُمۡ بِمَا تَاۡكُلُوۡنَ وَمَا

تَدَّخِرُوۡنَ ۙ فِىۡ بُيُوۡتِكُمۡ ؕ اِنَّ فِىۡ

ذٰلِكَ لَاٰيَةً لَّكُمۡ اِنۡ كُنۡتُمۡ

مُّؤۡمِنِيۡنَ ۞ وَمُصَدِّقًا لِّمَا بَيۡنَ

يَدَىَّ مِنَ التَّوۡرٰىةِ وَلِاُحِلَّ لَكُمۡ

بَعۡضَ الَّذِىۡ حُرِّمَ عَلَيۡكُمۡ

وَجِئۡتُكُمۡ بِاٰيَةٍ مِّنۡ رَّبِّكُمۡ ۟ قف

when no man has touched me?"
He said: "Even so: Allah creates
what He wills: when He has
decreed a Plan, He but says to it,
"Be," and it is!"

48. "And Allah will teach him
the Book and Wisdom, the Torah
and the Gospel,"

49. "And (appoint him) an
Apostle to the Children of Israel,
(with this message): "'I have
come to you, with a Sign from
your Lord, in that I make for you
out of clay, as it were, the figure of
a bird, and breathe into it, and it
becomes a bird

وَلَمْ يَمْسَسْنِي بَشَرٌ ۖ قَالَ كَذٰلِكِ

اللّٰهُ يَخْلُقُ مَا يَشَاءُ ۚ اِذَا قَضٰۤى

اَمْرًا فَاِنَّمَا يَقُوْلُ لَهٗ كُنْ

فَيَكُوْنُ ۩ وَيُعَلِّمُهُ الْكِتٰبَ وَالْحِكْمَةَ

وَالتَّوْرٰةَ وَالْاِنْجِيْلَ ۩ وَرَسُوْلًا

اِلٰى بَنِىْۤ اِسْرَآءِيْلَ ۙ اَنِّىْ قَدْ

جِئْتُكُمْ بِاٰيَةٍ مِّنْ رَّبِّكُمْ ۙ اَنِّىْۤ

اَخْلُقُ لَكُمْ مِّنَ الطِّيْنِ كَهَيْئَةِ

الطَّيْرِ فَاَنْفُخُ فِيْهِ فَيَكُوْنُ طَيْرًا

as to which of them should be charged with the care of Mary: nor were you with them when they disputed (the point).

45. Behold! The Angels said: "O Mary! Allah gives you glad tidings of a Word from Him: his name will be Christ Jesus, the son of Mary, held in honour in this world and the Hereafter and of (the company of) those nearest to Allah;"

46. "He shall speak to the people in infancy and in maturity. And he shall be (of the company) of the righteous."

47. She said: "O my Lord! How shall I have a son

اَيُّهُمْ يَكْفُلُ مَرْيَمَ وَمَا كُنْتَ

لَدَيْهِمْ اِذْ يَخْتَصِمُوْنَ ۞ اِذْ قَالَتِ

الْمَلٰٓئِكَةُ يٰمَرْيَمُ اِنَّ اللّٰهَ

يُبَشِّرُكِ بِكَلِمَةٍ مِّنْهُ ٝ اسْمُهُ

الْمَسِيْحُ عِيْسَى ابْنُ مَرْيَمَ

وَجِيْهًا فِى الدُّنْيَا وَالْاٰخِرَةِ وَمِنَ

الْمُقَرَّبِيْنَ ۞ وَيُكَلِّمُ النَّاسَ فِى

الْمَهْدِ وَكَهْلًا وَّمِنَ الصّٰلِحِيْنَ ۞

قَالَتْ رَبِّ اَنّٰى يَكُوْنُ لِى وَلَدٌ

days but with signals. Then celebrate the praises of your Lord again and again, and glorify Him in the evening and in the morning."

42.   Behold! The Angels said: "O Mary! Allah has chosen you and purified you - chosen you above the women of all nations.

43.   "O Mary! Worship your Lord devoutly: prostrate yourself and bow down (in prayer) with those who bow down."

44.   This is part of the tidings of the things unseen, which We reveal unto you (O Apostle!) by inspiration: you were not with them when they cast lots with arrows,

أَيَّامٍ اِلَّا رَمْزًا ۗ وَاذْكُرْ رَّبَّكَ

كَثِيرًا وَّسَبِّحْ بِالْعَشِىِّ وَالْاِبْكَارِ ۞

وَاِذْ قَالَتِ الْمَلٰٓئِكَةُ يٰمَرْيَمُ اِنَّ

اللّٰهَ اصْطَفٰكِ وَطَهَّرَكِ وَاصْطَفٰكِ

عَلٰى نِسَآءِ الْعٰلَمِيْنَ ۞ يٰمَرْيَمُ

اقْنُتِيْ لِرَبِّكِ وَاسْجُدِيْ وَارْكَعِيْ

مَعَ الرّٰكِعِيْنَ ۞ ذٰلِكَ مِنْ اَنْۢبَآءِ

الْغَيْبِ نُوْحِيْهِ اِلَيْكَ ۗ وَمَا كُنْتَ

لَدَيْهِمْ اِذْ يُلْقُوْنَ اَقْلَامَهُمْ

"Allah does give you glad tidings of Yahya, confirming the truth of a Word from Allah, and (be besides) noble, chaste, and a Prophet, - of the (goodly) company of the righteous."

40. He said: "O my Lord! How shall I have a son, seeing I am very old, and my wife is barren?" "Thus," was the answer, "does Allah accomplish what He wills."

41. He said: "O my Lord! Give me a Sign!" "Your Sign," was the answer, "shall be that you shall speak to no man for three

اَنَّ اللّٰهَ يُبَشِّرُكَ بِيَحْيٰى

مُصَدِّقًۢا بِكَلِمَةٍ مِّنَ اللّٰهِ

وَسَيِّدًا وَّحَصُوْرًا وَّنَبِيًّا مِّنَ

الصّٰلِحِيْنَ ۞ قَالَ رَبِّ اَنّٰى

يَكُوْنُ لِيْ غُلٰمٌ وَّقَدْ بَلَغَنِيَ

الْكِبَرُ وَامْرَاَتِيْ عَاقِرٌ ۚ قَالَ

كَذٰلِكَ اللّٰهُ يَفْعَلُ مَا يَشَآءُ ۞

قَالَ رَبِّ اجْعَلْ لِّيْۤ اٰيَةً ۗ قَالَ

اٰيَتُكَ اَلَّا تُكَلِّمَ النَّاسَ ثَلٰثَةَ

(her) chamber to see her, he found her supplied with sustenance. He said: "O Mary! Wherefrom (comes) this to you?" She said: "From Allah: for Allah porovides sustenance to whom He pleases without measure."

38. There did Zakariya pray to his Lord, saying: "O my Lord! Grant for me from You a progeny that is pure: for You are He who hears prayer!"

39. While he was standing in prayer in the chamber, the Angels called to him:

الْمِحْرَابَ وَجَدَ عِنْدَهَا رِزْقًا

قَالَ يَمَرْيَمُ اَنّٰى لَكِ هٰذَا ۖ

قَالَتْ هُوَ مِنْ عِنْدِ اللّٰهِ ۖ اِنَّ

اللّٰهَ يَرْزُقُ مَنْ يَّشَآءُ بِغَيْرِ

حِسَابٍ ۞ هُنَالِكَ دَعَا زَكَرِيَّا

رَبَّهٗ ۚ قَالَ رَبِّ هَبْ لِيْ مِنْ

لَّدُنْكَ ذُرِّيَّةً طَيِّبَةً ۚ اِنَّكَ

سَمِيْعُ الدُّعَآءِ ۞ فَنَادَتْهُ الْمَلٰٓئِكَةُ

وَهُوَ قَآئِمٌ يُّصَلِّيْ فِى الْمِحْرَابِ ۙ

hear and know all things."

36. When she delivered (the baby girl) she said: "O my Lord! Behold! I am delivered of a female child!"- and Allah knew best what she brought forth - "And no wise is the male like the female. I have named her Mary, and I commend her and her offspring to Your protection from Satan, the Rejected."

37. Right graciously did her Lord accept her: He made her grow in purity and beauty: to the care of Zakariya was she assigned. Every time that he entered

السَّمِيعُ الْعَلِيمُ ۞ فَلَمَّا وَضَعَتْهَا

قَالَتْ رَبِّ إِنِّي وَضَعْتُهَا أُنثَىٰ

وَاللَّهُ أَعْلَمُ بِمَا وَضَعَتْ وَلَيْسَ

الذَّكَرُ كَالْأُنثَىٰ وَإِنِّي سَمَّيْتُهَا

مَرْيَمَ وَإِنِّي أُعِيذُهَا بِكَ

وَذُرِّيَّتَهَا مِنَ الشَّيْطَانِ الرَّجِيمِ ۞

فَتَقَبَّلَهَا رَبُّهَا بِقَبُولٍ حَسَنٍ

وَأَنبَتَهَا نَبَاتًا حَسَنًا وَّكَفَّلَهَا

زَكَرِيَّا طُ كُلَّمَا دَخَلَ عَلَيْهَا زَكَرِيَّا

32. Say: "Obey Allah and His Apostle": but if they turn back, Allah loves not those who reject Faith.

33. Allah did choose Adam and Noah, the family of Abraham, and the family of 'Imran above all people, -

34. Offspring, one of the other: and Allah hears and knows all things.

35. Behold! A woman of 'Imran said: "O my Lord! I do dedicate unto You what is in my womb for Your special service: so accept this of me: for You

قُلْ اَطِيعُوا اللّٰهَ وَالرَّسُوْلَ ۚ فَاِنْ

تَوَلَّوْا فَاِنَّ اللّٰهَ لَا يُحِبُّ الْكٰفِرِيْنَ ۞

اِنَّ اللّٰهَ اصْطَفٰٓى اٰدَمَ وَنُوْحًا

وَّاٰلَ اِبْرٰهِيْمَ وَاٰلَ عِمْرٰنَ عَلَى

الْعٰلَمِيْنَ ۙ ۞ ذُرِّيَّةً ۢ بَعْضُهَا مِنْ

بَعْضٍ ؕ وَاللّٰهُ سَمِيْعٌ عَلِيْمٌ ۞

اِذْ قَالَتِ امْرَاَتُ عِمْرٰنَ رَبِّ

اِنِّيْ نَذَرْتُ لَكَ مَا فِيْ بَطْنِيْ

مُحَرَّرًا فَتَقَبَّلْ مِنِّيْ ؕ اِنَّكَ اَنْتَ

has power over all things.

30. "On the Day when every soul will be confronted with all the good it has done, and all the evil it has done, it will wish there were a great distance between it and its evil. But Allah cautions you (to remember) Himself. And Allah is full of kindness to those that serve Him."

31. Say: "If you do love Allah, follow me: Allah will love you and forgive you your sins: for Allah is Oft-forgiving, Most Merciful."

عَلٰى كُلِّ شَىْءٍ قَدِيْرٌ ۞ يَوْمَ

تَجِدُ كُلُّ نَفْسٍ مَّا عَمِلَتْ

مِنْ خَيْرٍ مُّحْضَرًا ۚ وَّمَا عَمِلَتْ

مِنْ سُوْٓءٍ ۚ تَوَدُّ لَوْ اَنَّ بَيْنَهَا وَبَيْنَهٗٓ

اَمَدًۢا بَعِيْدًا ۗ وَيُحَذِّرُكُمُ اللّٰهُ

نَفْسَهٗ ۗ وَاللّٰهُ رَءُوْفٌۢ بِالْعِبَادِ ۞

قُلْ اِنْ كُنْتُمْ تُحِبُّوْنَ اللّٰهَ

فَاتَّبِعُوْنِيْ يُحْبِبْكُمُ اللّٰهُ وَيَغْفِرْ

لَكُمْ ذُنُوْبَكُمْ ۗ وَاللّٰهُ غَفُوْرٌ رَّحِيْمٌ ۞

28.   Let not the believers take for friends or helpers unbelievers rather than believers: if any do that, in nothing will there be help from Allah: except that it be to guard yourselves from them. But Allah cautions you (to remember) Himself; for the final goal is to Allah.

29.   Say: "Whether you hide what is in your hearts or reveal it, Allah knows it all: He knows what is in the heavens, and what is on earth. And Allah

لَا يَتَّخِذِ الْمُؤْمِنُوْنَ الْكٰفِرِيْنَ اَوْلِيَاءَ

مِنْ دُوْنِ الْمُؤْمِنِيْنَ ۚ وَمَنْ يَّفْعَلْ

ذٰلِكَ فَلَيْسَ مِنَ اللّٰهِ فِيْ شَىْءٍ

اِلَّاۤ اَنْ تَتَّقُوْا مِنْهُمْ تُقٰةً ۗ

وَيُحَذِّرُكُمُ اللّٰهُ نَفْسَهٗ ۗ وَاِلَى

اللّٰهِ الْمَصِيْرُ ۝ قُلْ اِنْ تُخْفُوْا

مَا فِيْ صُدُوْرِكُمْ اَوْ تُبْدُوْهُ

يَعْلَمْهُ اللّٰهُ ۗ وَيَعْلَمُ مَا فِي

السَّمٰوٰتِ وَمَا فِي الْاَرْضِ ۗ وَاللّٰهُ

of Power (and Rule), You give power to whom You please, and You strip off power from whom You please: You endow with honour whom You please, and You bring low whom You please: in Your hand is all good. Verily, over all things You have power.

27. "You cause the night to gain on the day, and You cause the day to gain on the night; You bring the living out of the dead, and You bring the dead out of the living; and You give sustenance to whom You please, without measure."

الْمُلْكَ تُؤْتِى الْمُلْكَ مَنْ تَشَآءُ

وَتَنْزِعُ الْمُلْكَ مِمَّنْ تَشَآءُ وَتُعِزُّ

مَنْ تَشَآءُ وَتُذِلُّ مَنْ تَشَآءُ

بِيَدِكَ الْخَيْرُ ۖ إِنَّكَ عَلَى كُلِّ شَىْءٍ

قَدِيرٌ ۝ تُوْلِجُ الَّيْلَ فِى النَّهَارِ

وَتُوْلِجُ النَّهَارَ فِى الَّيْلِ ۖ وَتُخْرِجُ

الْحَىَّ مِنَ الْمَيِّتِ وَتُخْرِجُ

الْمَيِّتَ مِنَ الْحَىِّ ۖ وَتَرْزُقُ

مَنْ تَشَآءُ بِغَيْرِ حِسَابٍ ۝

of Allah, to settle their dispute, but a party of them turn back and decline (the arbitration).

24. This because they say: "The Fire shall not touch us but for a few numbered days": their forgeries deceive them as to their own religion.

25. But how (will they fare) when We gather them together against a Day about which there is no doubt, and each soul will be paid out just what it has earned, without (favour or) injustice?

26. Say: "O Allah! Lord

اللهِ لِيَحْكُمَ بَيْنَهُمْ ثُمَّ يَتَوَلّٰى

فَرِيْقٌ مِّنْهُمْ وَهُمْ مُّعْرِضُوْنَ ۞

ذٰلِكَ بِاَنَّهُمْ قَالُوْا لَنْ تَمَسَّنَا

النَّارُ اِلَّاۤ اَيَّامًا مَّعْدُوْدٰتٍ ۪

وَّغَرَّهُمْ فِيْ دِيْنِهِمْ مَّا كَانُوْا

يَفْتَرُوْنَ ۞ فَكَيْفَ اِذَا جَمَعْنٰهُمْ

لِيَوْمٍ لَّا رَيْبَ فِيْهِ ۪ وَوُفِّيَتْ

كُلُّ نَفْسٍ مَّا كَسَبَتْ وَهُمْ لَا

يُظْلَمُوْنَ ۞ قُلِ اللّٰهُمَّ مٰلِكَ

21.   As to those who deny the Signs of Allah and in defiance of right, slay the prophets, and slay those who teach just dealing with mankind, announce to them a grievous Chastisement.

22.   They are those whose works will bear no fruit in this world and in the Hereafter, nor will they have anyone to help.

23.   Has you not turned your vision to those who have been given a portion of the Book? They are invited to the Book

اِنَّ الَّذِيْنَ يَكْفُرُوْنَ بِاٰيٰتِ اللّٰهِ

وَيَقْتُلُوْنَ النَّبِيّٖنَ بِغَيْرِ حَقٍّ

وَّيَقْتُلُوْنَ الَّذِيْنَ يَأْمُرُوْنَ بِالْقِسْطِ

مِنَ النَّاسِ فَبَشِّرْهُمْ بِعَذَابٍ

اَلِيْمٍ ۞ اُولٰٓئِكَ الَّذِيْنَ حَبِطَتْ

اَعْمَالُهُمْ فِى الدُّنْيَا وَالْاٰخِرَةِ

وَمَا لَهُمْ مِّنْ نّٰصِرِيْنَ ۞ اَلَمْ

تَرَ اِلَى الَّذِيْنَ اُوْتُوْا نَصِيْبًا

مِّنَ الْكِتٰبِ يُدْعَوْنَ اِلٰى كِتٰبِ

through envy of each other, after knowledge had come to them. But if any deny the Signs of Allah, Allah is swift in calling to account.

20.   So if they dispute with you, say: "I have submitted my whole self to Allah and so have those who follow me." And say to the People of the Book and to those who are unlearned: "Do you (also) submit yourselves?" If they do, they are in right guidance, but if they turn back, your duty is to convey the Message; and in Allah's sight are (all) His servants.

مِنْ بَعْدِ مَا جَآءَهُمُ الْعِلْمُ

بَغْيًا بَيْنَهُمْ ۚ وَمَنْ يَّكْفُرْ بِاٰيٰتِ

اللّٰهِ فَإِنَّ اللّٰهَ سَرِيعُ الْحِسَابِ ۞

فَإِنْ حَآجُّوكَ فَقُلْ أَسْلَمْتُ

وَجْهِيَ لِلّٰهِ وَمَنِ اتَّبَعَنِ ۗ وَقُلْ

لِّلَّذِينَ أُوتُوا الْكِتٰبَ وَالْأُمِّيِّنَ

ءَأَسْلَمْتُمْ ۚ فَإِنْ أَسْلَمُوْا فَقَدِ

اهْتَدَوْا ۚ وَإِنْ تَوَلَّوْا فَإِنَّمَا عَلَيْكَ

الْبَلٰغُ ۗ وَاللّٰهُ بَصِيْرٌ بِالْعِبَادِ ۞

Part – 3   32   Ale-Imran–3

forgive us, then, our sins, and save us from the agony of the Fire;"-

17. Those who show patience, firmness and self-control; who are true (in word and deed); who worship devoutly; who spend (in the way of Allah); and who pray for forgiveness in the early hours of the morning.

18. There is no Allah but He: that is the witness of Allah, His Angels, and those endued with knowledge, standing firm on justice. There is no Allah but He, the Exalted in Power, the Wise.

19. The Religion before Allah is Islam (submission to His Will): nor did the People of the Book dissent therefrom except

فَاغْفِرْ لَنَا ذُنُوبَنَا وَقِنَا عَذَابَ

النَّارِ ۞ اَلصّٰبِرِيْنَ وَالصّٰدِقِيْنَ

وَالْقٰنِتِيْنَ وَالْمُنْفِقِيْنَ وَالْمُسْتَغْفِرِيْنَ

بِالْاَسْحَارِ ۞ شَهِدَ اللّٰهُ اَنَّهٗ لَاۤ

اِلٰهَ اِلَّا هُوَ وَالْمَلٰٓئِكَةُ وَاُولُوا

الْعِلْمِ قَآئِمًۢا بِالْقِسْطِ ط لَاۤ اِلٰهَ

اِلَّا هُوَ الْعَزِيْزُ الْحَكِيْمُ ط اِنَّ

الدِّيْنَ عِنْدَ اللّٰهِ الْاِسْلَامُ وَمَا

اخْتَلَفَ الَّذِيْنَ اُوْتُوا الْكِتٰبَ اِلَّا

and (wealth of) cattle and well-tilled land. Such are the possessions of this world's life; but in nearness to Allah is the best of the goals (to return to).

15. Say: Shall I give you glad tidings of things for better than those? For the righteous are Gardens in nearness to their Lord, with rivers flowing beneath; therein is their eternal home; with companions pure (and holy); and the good pleasure of Allah. For in Allah's sight are (all) His servants, -

16. (Namely), those who say: "Our Lord! we have indeed believed:

وَالْاَنْعَامِ وَالْحَرْثِ ذٰلِكَ مَتَاعُ

الْحَيٰوةِ الدُّنْيَا ۚ وَاللهُ عِنْدَهٗ

حُسْنُ الْمَاٰبِ ۞ قُلْ اَؤُنَبِّئُكُمْ

بِخَيْرٍ مِّنْ ذٰلِكُمْ ۚ لِلَّذِيْنَ اتَّقَوْا

عِنْدَ رَبِّهِمْ جَنّٰتٌ تَجْرِیْ مِنْ

تَحْتِهَا الْاَنْهٰرُ خٰلِدِيْنَ فِيْهَا

وَاَزْوَاجٌ مُّطَهَّرَةٌ وَّرِضْوَانٌ مِّنَ

اللهِ ؕ وَاللهُ بَصِيْرٌۢ بِالْعِبَادِ ۞

الَّذِيْنَ يَقُوْلُوْنَ رَبَّنَاۤ اِنَّنَاۤ اٰمَنَّا

in the two armies that met (in combat): one was fighting in the cause of Allah, the other resisting Allah; these saw with their own eyes twice their number. But Allah does support with His aid whom He pleases. In this is a warning for such as have eyes to see."

14.   Fair in the eyes of men is the love of things they covet: women and sons; heaped-up hoards of gold and silver; horses branded (for breed and excellence);

فِي فِئَتَيْنِ الْتَقَتَا ۚ فِئَةٌ تُقَاتِلُ

فِي سَبِيلِ اللَّهِ وَأُخْرَىٰ كَافِرَةٌ

يَرَوْنَهُمْ مِّثْلَيْهِمْ رَأْيَ الْعَيْنِ ۚ

وَاللَّهُ يُؤَيِّدُ بِنَصْرِهِ مَن يَشَاءُ ۚ

إِنَّ فِي ذَٰلِكَ لَعِبْرَةً لِّأُولِي

الْأَبْصَارِ ۝ زُيِّنَ لِلنَّاسِ حُبُّ

الشَّهَوَاتِ مِنَ النِّسَاءِ وَالْبَنِينَ

وَالْقَنَاطِيرِ الْمُقَنْطَرَةِ مِنَ الذَّهَبِ

وَالْفِضَّةِ وَالْخَيْلِ الْمُسَوَّمَةِ

reject Faith, - neither their possessions nor their (numerous) progeny will avail them anything against Allah: they are themselves but fuel for the Fire.

11.   (Their plight will be) no better than that of the people of Pharaoh, and their predecessors: they denied our Signs, and Allah called them to account for their sins. For Allah is strict in punishment.

12.   Say to those who reject Faith: "Soon will you be vanquished and gathered together to Hell, - an evil bed indeed (to lie on)!

13.   "There has already been for you a Sign

كَفَرُوْا لَنْ تُغْنِىَ عَنْهُمْ اَمْوَالُهُمْ

وَلَا اَوْلَادُهُمْ مِّنَ اللّٰهِ شَيْئًا ۤ

وَاُولٰٓئِكَ هُمْ وَقُوْدُ النَّارِ ۞ كَدَاْبِ

اٰلِ فِرْعَوْنَ ۙ وَالَّذِيْنَ مِنْ قَبْلِهِمْ ۚ

كَذَّبُوْا بِاٰيٰتِنَا ۚ فَاَخَذَهُمُ اللّٰهُ

بِذُنُوْبِهِمْ ۗ وَاللّٰهُ شَدِيْدُ الْعِقَابِ ۞

قُلْ لِّلَّذِيْنَ كَفَرُوْا سَتُغْلَبُوْنَ

وَتُحْشَرُوْنَ اِلٰى جَهَنَّمَ ۚ وَبِئْسَ

الْمِهَادُ ۞ قَدْ كَانَ لَكُمْ اٰيَةٌ

And those who are firmly grounded in knowledge say: "We believe in the Book; the whole of it is from our Lord:" and none will grasp the Message except men of understanding.

8.   "Our Lord!" (they say), "Let not our hearts deviate now after you have guided us, but grant us mercy from Your Own Presence; for You are the Grantor of bounties without measure.

9.   "Our Lord! You are He that will gather mankind together against a Day about which there is no doubt; for Allah never fails in His promise."

10.   Those who

وَالرَّاسِخُونَ فِي الْعِلْمِ يَقُوْلُوْنَ

اٰمَنَّا بِهٖ ۙ كُلٌّ مِّنْ عِنْدِ رَبِّنَا ۚ

وَمَا يَذَّكَّرُ اِلَّا اُولُوا الْاَلْبَابِ ۞

رَبَّنَا لَا تُزِغْ قُلُوْبَنَا بَعْدَ اِذْ

هَدَيْتَنَا وَهَبْ لَنَا مِنْ لَّدُنْكَ

رَحْمَةً ۚ اِنَّكَ اَنْتَ الْوَهَّابُ ۞

رَبَّنَا اِنَّكَ جَامِعُ النَّاسِ

لِيَوْمٍ لَّا رَيْبَ فِيْهِ ۚ اِنَّ اللّٰهَ لَا

يُخْلِفُ الْمِيْعَادَ ۞ اِنَّ الَّذِيْنَ

in the wombs as He pleases. There is no Allah but He, the Exalted in Might, the Wise.

7.   He it is Who has sent down to you the Book: in it are verses basic or fundamental (of established meaning); they are the foundation of the Book: others are allegorical. But those in whose hearts is perversity follow the part thereof that is allegorical, seeking discord, and searching for its hidden meanings, but no one knows its hidden meanings except Allah.

فِى الْاَرْحَامِ كَيْفَ يَشَآءُ ۚ لَاۤ اِلٰهَ

اِلَّا هُوَ الْعَزِيْزُ الْحَكِيْمُ ۞ هُوَ

الَّذِىْۤ اَنْزَلَ عَلَيْكَ الْكِتٰبَ

مِنْهُ اٰيٰتٌ مُّحْكَمٰتٌ هُنَّ اُمُّ

الْكِتٰبِ وَاُخَرُ مُتَشٰبِهٰتٌ ؕ فَاَمَّا

الَّذِيْنَ فِىْ قُلُوْبِهِمْ زَيْغٌ

فَيَتَّبِعُوْنَ مَا تَشَابَهَ مِنْهُ

ابْتِغَآءَ الْفِتْنَةِ وَابْتِغَآءَ تَاْوِيْلِهٖ ۚ

وَمَا يَعْلَمُ تَاْوِيْلَهٗۤ اِلَّا اللّٰهُ

(step by step), in truth, the Book, confirming what went before it; and He sent down the Law (of Moses) and the Gospel (of Jesus) before this,

4. As a guide to mankind, and He sent down the criterion (of judgment between right and wrong). Then those who reject Faith in the Signs of Allah will suffer the severest Chastisement, and Allah is Exalted in Might, Lord of Retribution.

5. From Allah, verily nothing is hidden on earth or in the heavens.

6. He it is Who shapes you

الْكِتَبَ بِالْحَقِّ مُصَدِّقًا لِّمَا

بَيْنَ يَدَيْهِ وَأَنْزَلَ التَّوْرٰةَ

وَالْاِنْجِيْلَ ۙ مِنْ قَبْلُ هُدًى

لِّلنَّاسِ وَأَنْزَلَ الْفُرْقَانَ ۗ اِنَّ

الَّذِيْنَ كَفَرُوْا بِاٰيٰتِ اللّٰهِ لَهُمْ

عَذَابٌ شَدِيْدٌ ۗ وَاللّٰهُ عَزِيْزٌ

ذُو انْتِقَامٍ ۗ اِنَّ اللّٰهَ لَا يَخْفٰى

عَلَيْهِ شَيْءٌ فِي الْاَرْضِ وَلَا

فِي السَّمَآءِ ۗ هُوَ الَّذِيْ يُصَوِّرُكُمْ

a burden like that which you did lay on those before us; our Lord! Lay not on us a burden greater than we have strength to bear. Blot out our sins, and grant us forgiveness. Have mercy on us. You are our Protector; help us against those who stand against Faith."

Ale-Imran (The Family of Imran)

Bismillahir-Rahmanir-Rahim

1.   Alif-Lam-Mim.

2.   Allah! There is no Allah but He, - the Living, the Self-Subsisting, Eternal.   3.   It is He Who sent down to you

اِصْرًا كَمَا حَمَلْتَهُ عَلَى الَّذِينَ

مِنْ قَبْلِنَا رَبَّنَا وَلَا تُحَمِّلْنَا

مَا لَا طَاقَةَ لَنَا بِهِ وَاعْفُ

عَنَّا وَاغْفِرْ لَنَا وَارْحَمْنَا أَنْتَ

مَوْلَىٰنَا فَانْصُرْنَا عَلَى الْقَوْمِ

الْكَافِرِينَ ۝

بِسْمِ اللّٰهِ الرَّحْمٰنِ الرَّحِيمِ

الٓمٓ ۝ اللّٰهُ لَا إِلَٰهَ إِلَّا هُوَ

الْحَيُّ الْقَيُّومُ ۝ نَزَّلَ عَلَيْكَ

as do the men of faith. Each one (of them) believes in Allah, His Angels, His Books, and His Apostles. "We make no distinction (they say) between one and another of His Apostles." And they say: "We hear, and we obey: (we seek) your forgiveness, our Lord, and to You is the end of all journeys."

286. On no soul does Allah place a burden greater than it can bear. It gets every good that it earns, and it suffers every ill that it earns. (Pray:) "Our Lord! Condemn us not if we forget or fall into error; our Lord! Lay not on us

وَالْمُؤْمِنُوْنَ ۚ كُلٌّ اٰمَنَ بِاللّٰهِ

وَمَلٰٓئِكَتِهٖ وَكُتُبِهٖ وَرُسُلِهٖ ۚ لَا

نُفَرِّقُ بَيْنَ اَحَدٍ مِّنْ رُّسُلِهٖ ۚ

وَقَالُوْا سَمِعْنَا وَاَطَعْنَا غُفْرَانَكَ

رَبَّنَا وَاِلَيْكَ الْمَصِيْرُ ۞ لَا

يُكَلِّفُ اللّٰهُ نَفْسًا اِلَّا وُسْعَهَا ۚ

لَهَا مَا كَسَبَتْ وَعَلَيْهَا مَا اكْتَسَبَتْ ۚ

رَبَّنَا لَا تُؤَاخِذْنَآ اِنْ نَّسِيْنَآ اَوْ

اَخْطَأْنَا ۚ رَبَّنَا وَلَا تَحْمِلْ عَلَيْنَا

evidence; for whoever conceals it, - his heart is tainted with sin. And Allah Knows all that you do.

284. To Allah belongs all that is in the heavens and on earth. Whether you show what is in your minds or conceal it, Allah calls you to account for it. He forgives whom He pleases, and punishes whom He pleases. For Allah has power over all things.

285. The Apostle believes in what has been revealed to him from his Lord,

الشَّهَادَةَ ۖ وَمَنْ يَكْتُمْهَا فَإِنَّهٗٓ

اٰثِمٌ قَلْبُهٗ ۗ وَاللّٰهُ بِمَا تَعْمَلُوْنَ

عَلِيْمٌ ۞ لِلّٰهِ مَا فِى السَّمٰوٰتِ

وَمَا فِى الْاَرْضِ ۗ وَاِنْ تُبْدُوْا مَا

فِىْٓ اَنْفُسِكُمْ اَوْ تُخْفُوْهُ يُحَاسِبْكُمْ

بِهِ اللّٰهُ ۗ فَيَغْفِرُ لِمَنْ يَّشَآءُ

وَيُعَذِّبُ مَنْ يَّشَآءُ ۗ وَاللّٰهُ عَلٰى

كُلِّ شَىْءٍ قَدِيْرٌ ۞ اٰمَنَ الرَّسُوْلُ

بِمَآ اُنْزِلَ اِلَيْهِ مِنْ رَّبِّهٖ

scribe nor witness suffer harm. If you do (such harm), it would be wickedness in you. So fear Allah; for it is Allah that teaches you. And Allah is Well Acquainted with all things.

283. If you are on a journey, and cannot find a scribe, a pledge with possession (may serve the purpose). And if one of you deposits a thing on trust with another, let the trustee (faithfully) discharge his trust, and let him fear his Lord. Conceal not

يُضَآرَّ كَاتِبٌ وَّلَا شَهِيدٌ ۗ

وَإِن تَفْعَلُوا فَإِنَّهُ فُسُوقٌ بِكُمْ ۗ

وَاتَّقُوا اللَّهَ ۖ وَيُعَلِّمُكُمُ اللَّهُ ۗ

وَاللَّهُ بِكُلِّ شَىْءٍ عَلِيمٌ ۝

وَإِن كُنتُمْ عَلَىٰ سَفَرٍ وَّلَمْ

تَجِدُوا كَاتِبًا فَرِهَٰنٌ مَّقْبُوضَةٌ ۖ

فَإِنْ أَمِنَ بَعْضُكُم بَعْضًا

فَلْيُؤَدِّ الَّذِى اؤْتُمِنَ أَمَانَتَهُ

وَلْيَتَّقِ اللَّهَ رَبَّهُ ۗ وَلَا تَكْتُمُوا

witnesses should not refuse when they are called on (for evidence). Disdain not to reduce to writing (your contract) for a future period, whether it be small or big: it is juster in the sight of Allah, more suitable as evidence, and more convenient to prevent doubts among your-selves but if it be a transaction which you carry out on the spot among yourselves, there is no blame on you if you reduce it not to writing. But take witness when-ever you make a commercial contract; and let neither

يَأْبَ الشُّهَدَآءُ إِذَا مَا دُعُوا

وَلَا تَسْـَٔمُوا أَن تَكْتُبُوهُ صَغِيرًا

أَوْ كَبِيرًا إِلَىٰ أَجَلِهِ ۚ ذَٰلِكُمْ

أَقْسَطُ عِندَ اللَّهِ وَأَقْوَمُ

لِلشَّهَادَةِ وَأَدْنَىٰ أَلَّا تَرْتَابُوا

إِلَّا أَن تَكُونَ تِجَارَةً حَاضِرَةً

تُدِيرُونَهَا بَيْنَكُمْ فَلَيْسَ

عَلَيْكُمْ جُنَاحٌ أَلَّا تَكْتُبُوهَا

وَأَشْهِدُوا إِذَا تَبَايَعْتُمْ وَلَا

anything of what he owes. If the party liable is mentally deficient, or weak, or unable himself to dictate, let his guardian dictate faithfully, and get two witnesses, out of your own men, and if there are not two men, then a man and two women, such as you choose, for witnesses, so that if one of them errs, the other can remind her. The

شَيْئًا ۚ فَاِنْ كَانَ الَّذِىْ عَلَيْهِ

الْحَقُّ سَفِيْهًا اَوْ ضَعِيْفًا اَوْ لَا

يَسْتَطِيْعُ اَنْ يُّمِلَّ هُوَ فَلْيُمْلِلْ

وَلِيُّهٗ بِالْعَدْلِ ۚ وَاسْتَشْهِدُوْا

شَهِيْدَيْنِ مِنْ رِّجَالِكُمْ ۚ فَاِنْ

لَّمْ يَكُوْنَا رَجُلَيْنِ فَرَجُلٌ

وَّامْرَاَتٰنِ مِمَّنْ تَرْضَوْنَ مِنَ

الشُّهَدَآءِ اَنْ تَضِلَّ اِحْدٰىهُمَا

فَتُذَكِّرَ اِحْدٰىهُمَا الْاُخْرٰى ۚ وَلَا

to Allah. Then shall every soul be paid what it earned, and none shall be dealt with unjustly.

282. O you who believe! When you deal with each other, in transactions involving future obligations in a fixed period of time, reduce them to writing. Let a scribe write down faithfully as between the parties: let not the scribe refuse to write: as Allah has taught him, so let him write. Let him who incurs the liability dictate, but let him fear his Lord Allah, and not diminish

اِلَى اللّٰهِ ۛ ثُمَّ تُوَفّٰى كُلُّ نَفْسٍ

مَّا كَسَبَتْ وَهُمْ لَا يُظْلَمُوْنَ ۝

يٰٓاَيُّهَا الَّذِيْنَ اٰمَنُوْٓا اِذَا تَدَايَنْتُمْ

بِدَيْنٍ اِلٰٓى اَجَلٍ مُّسَمًّى فَاكْتُبُوْهُ ۭ

وَلْيَكْتُبْ بَّيْنَكُمْ كَاتِبٌۢ بِالْعَدْلِ ۠

وَلَا يَاْبَ كَاتِبٌ اَنْ يَّكْتُبَ كَمَا

عَلَّمَهُ اللّٰهُ فَلْيَكْتُبْ ۚ وَلْيُمْلِلِ

الَّذِيْ عَلَيْهِ الْحَقُّ وَلْيَتَّقِ

اللّٰهَ رَبَّهٗ وَلَا يَبْخَسْ مِنْهُ

for usury, if you are indeed believers.

279. If you do it not, take notice of war from Allah and His Apostle: but if you turn back, you shall have your capital sums: deal not unjustly, and you shall not be dealt with unjustly.

280. If the debtor is in a difficulty, grant him time till it is easy for him to repay. But if you remit it by way of charity, that is best for you if you only knew.

281. And fear the Day when you shall be brought back

الرِّبٰوٓا اِنْ كُنْتُمْ مُّؤْمِنِيْنَ ۝

فَاِنْ لَّمْ تَفْعَلُوْا فَاْذَنُوْا بِحَرْبٍ

مِّنَ اللّٰهِ وَرَسُوْلِهٖ ۚ وَاِنْ تُبْتُمْ

فَلَكُمْ رُءُوْسُ اَمْوَالِكُمْ ۚ لَا

تَظْلِمُوْنَ وَلَا تُظْلَمُوْنَ ۝ وَاِنْ

كَانَ ذُوْ عُسْرَةٍ فَنَظِرَةٌ اِلٰى

مَيْسَرَةٍ ۚ وَاَنْ تَصَدَّقُوْا خَيْرٌ

لَّكُمْ اِنْ كُنْتُمْ تَعْلَمُوْنَ ۝

وَاتَّقُوْا يَوْمًا تُرْجَعُوْنَ فِيْهِ

they will abide therein (for ever).

276. Allah will deprive usury of all blessing, but will give increase for deeds of charity: for He loves not creatures ungrateful and wicked.

277. Those who believe, and do deeds of righteousness, and establish regular prayers and regular charity, will have their reward with their Lord: on them shall be no fear, nor shall they grieve.

278. O you who believe! Fear Allah, and give up what remains of your demand

هُمْ فِيهَا خَلِدُونَ ۞ يَمْحَقُ

اللهُ الرِّبوا وَيُرْبِى الصَّدَقَٰتِ

وَاللهُ لَا يُحِبُّ كُلَّ كَفَّارٍ أَثِيمٍ ۞

إِنَّ الَّذِينَ اٰمَنُوا وَعَمِلُوا

الصَّلِحَٰتِ وَأَقَامُوا الصَّلوٰةَ وَاٰتَوُا

الزَّكوٰةَ لَهُمْ أَجْرُهُمْ عِنْدَ رَبِّهِمْ

وَلَا خَوْفٌ عَلَيْهِمْ وَلَا هُمْ

يَحْزَنُونَ ۞ يَٰأَيُّهَا الَّذِينَ اٰمَنُوا

اتَّقُوا اللهَ وَذَرُوا مَا بَقِيَ مِنَ

nor shall they grieve.

275. Those who devour interest will not stand except as stand one whom the Satan one by his touch has driven to madness. That is because they say: "Trade is like interest," but Allah has permitted trade and forbidden interest. Those who after receiving direction from their Lord, desist, shall be pardoned for the past; their case is for Allah has (to judge); but those who repeat (the offence) are Companions of the Fire:

وَلَا هُمْ يَحْزَنُوْنَ ۞ الَّذِيْنَ يَأْكُلُوْنَ

الرِّبٰوا لَا يَقُوْمُوْنَ اِلَّا كَمَا يَقُوْمُ

الَّذِيْ يَتَخَبَّطُهُ الشَّيْطٰنُ مِنَ

الْمَسِّ ذٰلِكَ بِاَنَّهُمْ قَالُوْۤا اِنَّمَا

الْبَيْعُ مِثْلُ الرِّبٰوا وَاَحَلَّ اللّٰهُ

الْبَيْعَ وَحَرَّمَ الرِّبٰوا فَمَنْ جَآءَهٗ

مَوْعِظَةٌ مِّنْ رَّبِّهٖ فَانْتَهٰى فَلَهٗ

مَا سَلَفَ وَاَمْرُهٗۤ اِلَى اللّٰهِ وَمَنْ

عَادَ فَاُولٰٓئِكَ اَصْحٰبُ النَّارِ

Allah's cause are restricted (from travel), and cannot move about in the land, seeking (for trade or work): the ignorant man thinks, because of their modesty, that they are free from want. You shall know them by their (unfailing) mark: they beg not importunately from all the sundry. And whatever of good you give, be assured Allah knows it well.

274. Those who (in charity) spend of their goods by night and by day, in secret and in public, have their reward with their Lord: on them shall be no fear,

سَبِيلِ اللّٰهِ لَا يَسْتَطِيعُوْنَ ضَرْبًا

فِي الْأَرْضِ يَحْسَبُهُمُ الْجَاهِلُ

أَغْنِيَآءَ مِنَ التَّعَفُّفِ تَعْرِفُهُمْ

بِسِيْمَاهُمْ لَا يَسْئَلُوْنَ النَّاسَ

إِلْحَافًا وَمَا تُنْفِقُوْا مِنْ خَيْرٍ

فَإِنَّ اللّٰهَ بِهِ عَلِيْمٌ ۝ الَّذِيْنَ

يُنْفِقُوْنَ أَمْوَالَهُمْ بِالَّيْلِ وَالنَّهَارِ

سِرًّا وَّعَلَانِيَةً فَلَهُمْ أَجْرُهُمْ

عِنْدَ رَبِّهِمْ وَلَاخَوْفٌ عَلَيْهِمْ

that is best for you: it will remove from you some of your (stains of) evil. And Allah is Well Acquainted with what you do.

272. It is not required of you (O Apostle), to set them on the right path, but Allah sets on the right path whom He pleases. Whatever of good you give benefits your own souls, and you shall only do so seeking the "Face" of Allah. Whatever good you give, shall be rendered back to you, and you shall not be dealt with unjustly.

273. (Charity is) for those in need, who, in

فَهُوَ خَيْرٌ لَّكُمْ ۚ وَيُكَفِّرُ عَنْكُمْ مِّنْ

سَيِّاٰتِكُمْ ۚ وَاللّٰهُ بِمَا تَعْمَلُوْنَ

خَبِيْرٌ ۞ لَيْسَ عَلَيْكَ هُدٰىهُمْ

وَلٰكِنَّ اللّٰهَ يَهْدِىْ مَنْ يَّشَآءُ ۗ

وَمَا تُنْفِقُوْا مِنْ خَيْرٍ فَلِاَنْفُسِكُمْ ۚ

وَمَا تُنْفِقُوْنَ اِلَّا ابْتِغَآءَ وَجْهِ

اللّٰهِ ۚ وَمَا تُنْفِقُوْا مِنْ خَيْرٍ يُّوَفَّ

اِلَيْكُمْ وَاَنْتُمْ لَا تُظْلَمُوْنَ ۞

لِلْفُقَرَآءِ الَّذِيْنَ اُحْصِرُوْا فِىْ

and bounties. And Allah cares for all and He knows all things.

269. He grants wisdom to whom He pleases; and he to whom wisdom is granted receives indeed a benefit overflowing; but none will grasp the Message but men of understanding.

270. And whatever you spend in charity or devotion, be sure Allah knows it all. But the wrong-doers have no helpers.

271. If you disclose (acts of) charity, even so it is well, but if you conceal them, and make them reach those (really) in need,

مِنْهُ وَفَضْلًا ۗ وَٱللّٰهُ وَاسِعٌ عَلِيمٌ ۞

يُؤْتِى ٱلْحِكْمَةَ مَن يَشَآءُ ۚ وَمَن

يُؤْتَ ٱلْحِكْمَةَ فَقَدْ أُوتِىَ خَيْرًا

كَثِيرًا ۗ وَمَا يَذَّكَّرُ إِلَّآ أُولُوا

ٱلْأَلْبَابِ ۞ وَمَآ أَنفَقْتُم مِّن نَّفَقَةٍ

أَوْ نَذَرْتُم مِّن نَّذْرٍ فَإِنَّ ٱللّٰهَ

يَعْلَمُهُ ۗ وَمَا لِلظّٰلِمِينَ مِنْ أَنصَارٍ ۞

إِن تُبْدُوا ٱلصَّدَقٰتِ فَنِعِمَّا هِىَ ۖ

وَإِن تُخْفُوهَا وَتُؤْتُوهَا ٱلْفُقَرَآءَ

to you (His) Signs; that you may consider.

267. O you who believe! Give of the good things which you have (honourably) earned, and of the fruits of the earth which We have produced for you, and do not ever aim at getting anything which is bad, in order that out of it you may give away something, when you yourselves would not receive it except with closed eyes. And know that Allah is Free of all wants, and Worthy of all praise.

268. Satan threatens you with poverty and bids you to conduct unseemly. Allah promises you His forgiveness

لَكُمُ الْاٰيٰتِ لَعَلَّكُمْ تَتَفَكَّرُوْنَ ۞

يٰٓاَيُّهَا الَّذِيْنَ اٰمَنُوْٓا اَنْفِقُوْا مِنْ

طَيِّبٰتِ مَا كَسَبْتُمْ وَمِمَّاۤ اَخْرَجْنَا

لَكُمْ مِّنَ الْاَرْضِ ۪ وَلَا تَيَمَّمُوا

الْخَبِيْثَ مِنْهُ تُنْفِقُوْنَ وَلَسْتُمْ

بِاٰخِذِيْهِ اِلَّاۤ اَنْ تُغْمِضُوْا فِيْهِ ؕ

وَاعْلَمُوْٓا اَنَّ اللّٰهَ غَنِيٌّ حَمِيْدٌ ۞

اَلشَّيْطٰنُ يَعِدُكُمُ الْفَقْرَ وَيَاْمُرُكُمْ

بِالْفَحْشَآءِ ۚ وَاللّٰهُ يَعِدُكُمْ مَّغْفِرَةً

it yield a double increase of harvest, and if it receives not heavy
rain, light moisture suffices it.
Allah sees well whatever you do.

266. Does any of you wish that he
should have a garden with date-
palms and vines and streams
flowing underneath, and all
kinds of fruit, while he is stricken
with old age, and his children are
not strong (enough to look after
themselves) - that it should be
caught in a whirlwind, with fire
therein, and be burnt up? Thus
does Allah make clear

أُكُلَهَا ضِعْفَيْنِ ۚ فَإِنْ لَّمْ يُصِبْهَا

وَابِلٌ فَطَلٌّ ۗ وَاللهُ بِمَا تَعْمَلُوْنَ

بَصِيْرٌ ۝ أَيَوَدُّ أَحَدُكُمْ أَنْ تَكُوْنَ

لَهُ جَنَّةٌ مِّنْ نَّخِيْلٍ وَّأَعْنَابٍ

تَجْرِيْ مِنْ تَحْتِهَا الْأَنْهٰرُ ۙ لَهُ

فِيْهَا مِنْ كُلِّ الثَّمَرٰتِ ۙ وَأَصَابَهُ

الْكِبَرُ وَلَهُ ذُرِّيَّةٌ ضُعَفَآءُ ۖ

فَأَصَابَهَآ إِعْصَارٌ فِيْهِ نَارٌ

فَاحْتَرَقَتْ ۗ كَذٰلِكَ يُبَيِّنُ اللهُ

but believe neither in Allah nor in the Last Day. They are in parable like a hard, barren rock, onwhich is a little soil: on it falls heavy rain, which leaves it (just) a bare stone. They will be able to do nothing with what they have earned. And Allah guides not those who reject faith.

265. And the likeness of those who spend their substance, seeking to please Allah and to strengthen their souls, is as a garden, high and fertile: heavy rain falls on it but makes

وَلَا يُؤْمِنُ بِاللهِ وَالْيَوْمِ الْاٰخِرِ

فَمَثَلُهُ كَمَثَلِ صَفْوَانٍ عَلَيْهِ

تُرَابٌ فَاَصَابَهُ وَابِلٌ فَتَرَكَهُ

صَلْدًا ۗ لَا يَقْدِرُوْنَ عَلٰى شَيْءٍ

مِّمَّا كَسَبُوْا ۗ وَاللهُ لَا يَهْدِى

الْقَوْمَ الْكٰفِرِيْنَ ۞ وَمَثَلُ الَّذِيْنَ

يُنْفِقُوْنَ اَمْوَالَهُمُ ابْتِغَاءَ مَرْضَاتِ

اللهِ وَتَثْبِيْتًا مِّنْ اَنْفُسِهِمْ كَمَثَلِ

جَنَّةٍ بِرَبْوَةٍ اَصَابَهَا وَابِلٌ فَاٰتَتْ

in the cause of Allah, and follow not up their gifts with reminders of their generosity or with injury, - for them their reward is with their Lord: on them shall be no fear, nor shall they grieve.

263. Kind words and the covering of faults are better than charity followed by injury. Allah is free of all wants, and He is Most Forbearing.

264. O you who believe! Waste not your charity by reminders of your generosity or by injury, - like those who spend their substance to be seen of men,

فِىْ سَبِيْلِ اللّٰهِ ثُمَّ لَا يُتْبِعُوْنَ

مَاۤ اَنْفَقُوْا مَنًّا وَّلَاۤ اَذًى لَّهُمْ

اَجْرُهُمْ عِنْدَ رَبِّهِمْ وَلَا خَوْفٌ

عَلَيْهِمْ وَلَا هُمْ يَحْزَنُوْنَ ۞ قَوْلٌ

مَّعْرُوْفٌ وَّمَغْفِرَةٌ خَيْرٌ مِّنْ

صَدَقَةٍ يَّتْبَعُهَاۤ اَذًى وَاللّٰهُ غَنِىٌّ

حَلِيْمٌ ۞ يٰۤاَيُّهَا الَّذِيْنَ اٰمَنُوْا لَا

تُبْطِلُوْا صَدَقٰتِكُمْ بِالْمَنِّ وَالْاَذٰى

كَالَّذِىْ يُنْفِقُ مَالَهٗ رِئَآءَ النَّاسِ

to you; put a portion of them on every hill and call to them: they will come to you (flying) with speed. Then know that Allah is Exalted in Power, Wise."

261. The parable of those who spend their substance in the way of Allah is that of a grain of corn: it groweth seven ears, and each ear has a hundred grains. Allah giveth manifold increase to whom He pleases: and Allah careth for all and He knows all things.

262. Those who spend their substance

اِلَيْكَ ثُمَّ اجْعَلْ عَلٰى كُلِّ جَبَلٍ

مِّنْهُنَّ جُزْءًا ثُمَّ ادْعُهُنَّ يَأْتِيْنَكَ

سَعْيًا ۚ وَاعْلَمْ اَنَّ اللّٰهَ عَزِيْزٌ

حَكِيْمٌ ۞ مَثَلُ الَّذِيْنَ يُنْفِقُوْنَ

اَمْوَالَهُمْ فِيْ سَبِيْلِ اللّٰهِ كَمَثَلِ

حَبَّةٍ اَنْۢبَتَتْ سَبْعَ سَنَابِلَ فِيْ

كُلِّ سُنْۢبُلَةٍ مِّائَةُ حَبَّةٍ ۗ وَاللّٰهُ

يُضٰعِفُ لِمَنْ يَّشَاءُ ۗ وَاللّٰهُ وَاسِعٌ

عَلِيْمٌ ۞ الَّذِيْنَ يُنْفِقُوْنَ اَمْوَالَهُمْ

a Sign for the people, look further at the bones, how We bring them together and clothe them with flesh." When this was shown clearly to him, he said: "I know that Allah has power over all things."

260. Behold! Abraham said: "My Lord! Show me how you gives life to the dead." He said: "Do you not then believe?" He said: "Yes! but to satisfy my own understanding." He said: "Take four birds; tame them to turn

ايَةً لِّلنَّاسِ وَانْظُرْ اِلَى الْعِظَامِ

كَيْفَ نُنْشِزُهَا ثُمَّ نَكْسُوهَا

لَحْمًا ۚ فَلَمَّا تَبَيَّنَ لَهُ ۙ قَالَ

اَعْلَمُ اَنَّ اللّٰهَ عَلٰى كُلِّ شَىْءٍ

قَدِيرٌ ۝ وَاِذْ قَالَ اِبْرٰهٖمُ رَبِّ

اَرِنِىْ كَيْفَ تُحْىِ الْمَوْتٰى ۚ قَالَ

اَوَلَمْ تُؤْمِنْ ۚ قَالَ بَلٰى وَلٰكِنْ

لِّيَطْمَئِنَّ قَلْبِىْ ۚ قَالَ فَخُذْ

اَرْبَعَةً مِّنَ الطَّيْرِ فَصُرْهُنَّ

passed by a hamlet, all in ruins to its roofs. He said: "Oh! How shall Allah bring it (ever) to life, after (this) its death?" But Allah caused him to die for a hundred years, then raised him up (again). He said: "How long did you tarry (thus)?" He said: (Perhaps) a day or part of a day." He said: "No you hast tarried thus a hundred years; but look at your food and your drink; they show no signs of age; and look at your donkey: and that We may make of you

مَرَّ عَلٰى قَرْيَةٍ وَّهِىَ خَاوِيَةٌ

عَلٰى عُرُوْشِهَا ۚ قَالَ اَنّٰى يُحْىٖ

هٰذِهِ اللّٰهُ بَعْدَ مَوْتِهَا ۚ فَاَمَاتَهُ

اللّٰهُ مِائَةَ عَامٍ ثُمَّ بَعَثَهٗ ۗ

قَالَ كَمْ لَبِثْتَ ۗ قَالَ لَبِثْتُ

يَوْمًا اَوْ بَعْضَ يَوْمٍ ۗ قَالَ بَلْ

لَّبِثْتَ مِائَةَ عَامٍ فَانْظُرْ اِلٰى

طَعَامِكَ وَشَرَابِكَ لَمْ يَتَسَنَّهْ ۚ

وَانْظُرْ اِلٰى حِمَارِكَ وَلِنَجْعَلَكَ

to one who disputed with Abraham about his Lord, because Allah had granted him power? Abraham said: "My Lord is He Who gives life and death." He said: "I give life and death". Said Abraham: "But it is Allah that causes the sun to rise from the East: do you then cause him to rise from the West." Thus was he confounded who (in arrogance) rejected Faith. Nor does Allah give guidance to a people unjust.

259. Or (take) the similitude of one who

اِلَى الَّذِى حَاجَّ اِبْرٰهٖمَ فِى

رَبِّهٖ اَنْ اٰتٰىهُ اللّٰهُ الْمُلْكَ

اِذْ قَالَ اِبْرٰهٖمُ رَبِّىَ الَّذِى

يُحْىٖ وَيُمِيْتُ قَالَ اَنَا اُحْىٖ

وَاُمِيْتُ قَالَ اِبْرٰهٖمُ فَاِنَّ اللّٰهَ

يَاْتِى بِالشَّمْسِ مِنَ الْمَشْرِقِ

فَاْتِ بِهَا مِنَ الْمَغْرِبِ فَبُهِتَ

الَّذِى كَفَرَ وَاللّٰهُ لَا يَهْدِى

الْقَوْمَ الظّٰلِمِيْنَ ۝ اَوْ كَالَّذِى

whoever rejects evil and believes in Allah has grasped the most trustworthy hand-hold, that never breaks. And Allah hears and knows all things.

257. Allah is the Protector of those who have faith: from the depths of darkness He will lead them forth into light. Of those who reject Faith the patrons are the evil ones: from light they will lead them forth into the depths of darkness. They will be Companions of the Fire, to dwell therein (for ever).

258. Have you not turned your vision

فَمَنْ يَكْفُرْ بِالطَّاغُوتِ وَيُؤْمِنْ

بِاللهِ فَقَدِ اسْتَمْسَكَ بِالْعُرْوَةِ

الْوُثْقَىٰ لَا انْفِصَامَ لَهَا ۗ وَاللهُ

سَمِيعٌ عَلِيمٌ ۞ اللهُ وَلِيُّ الَّذِينَ

اٰمَنُوْا يُخْرِجُهُمْ مِّنَ الظُّلُمٰتِ اِلَى

النُّوْرِ ۗ وَالَّذِيْنَ كَفَرُوْا اَوْلِيٰٓـؤُهُمُ

الطَّاغُوتُ يُخْرِجُوْنَهُمْ مِّنَ النُّوْرِ

اِلَى الظُّلُمٰتِ ۗ اُولٰٓئِكَ اَصْحٰبُ النَّارِ

هُمْ فِيْهَا خٰلِدُوْنَ ۞ اَلَمْ تَرَ

the heavens and on earth. Who is
there can intercede in His
presence except as He permits?
He knows what (appears to His
creatures as) before or after or
behind them. Nor shall they
compass of His knowledge
except as He wills. His Throne
does extend over the heavens and
the earth, and He feels no fatigue
in guarding and preserving
them: for He is the Most High, the
Supreme (in glory).

256. Let there be no compulsion
in religion: Truth stands out clear
from Error:

السَّمٰوٰتِ وَمَا فِى الْأَرْضِ مَنْ

ذَا الَّذِى يَشْفَعُ عِنْدَهُ اِلَّا

بِاِذْنِهِ يَعْلَمُ مَا بَيْنَ اَيْدِيْهِمْ

وَمَا خَلْفَهُمْ وَلَا يُحِيْطُوْنَ بِشَىْءٍ

مِّنْ عِلْمِهِ اِلَّا بِمَا شَآءَ وَسِعَ

كُرْسِيُّهُ السَّمٰوٰتِ وَالْاَرْضَ وَلَا

يَـُٔوْدُهُ حِفْظُهُمَا وَهُوَ الْعَلِىُّ

الْعَظِيْمُ ۝ لَا اِكْرَاهَ فِى الدِّيْنِ

قَدْ تَّبَيَّنَ الرُّشْدُ مِنَ الْغَىِّ

If Allah had so willed, they would not have fought each other; but Allah fulfills His plan.

254. O you who believe! Spend out of (the bounties) We have provided for you, before the Day comes when no bargaining (will avail), nor friendship nor inter-cession. Those who reject Faith they are the wrong-doers.

255. Allah! There is no god but He, - the Living, the Self-sub-sisting, Eternal. No slumber can seize Him nor sleep. His are all things in

وَلَوْ شَآءَ اللهُ مَا اقْتَتَلُوا وَلٰكِنَّ

اللهَ يَفْعَلُ مَا يُرِيدُ ۝ يٰٓأَيُّهَا

الَّذِيْنَ اٰمَنُوْا أَنْفِقُوْا مِمَّا

رَزَقْنٰكُمْ مِّنْ قَبْلِ أَنْ يَّأْتِيَ

يَوْمٌ لَّا بَيْعٌ فِيْهِ وَلَا خُلَّةٌ

وَّلَا شَفَاعَةٌ وَالْكٰفِرُوْنَ هُمُ

الظّٰلِمُوْنَ ۝ اللهُ لَآ اِلٰهَ اِلَّا

هُوَ الْحَيُّ الْقَيُّوْمُ ۚ لَا تَأْخُذُهٗ

سِنَةٌ وَّلَا نَوْمٌ ۗ لَهٗ مَا فِي

253. Those Apostles We endowed with gifts, some above others: to one of them Allah spoke; others He raised to degrees (of honour); to Jesus the son of Mary We gave clear (Signs), and strengthened him with the holy spirit. If Allah had so willed, succeeding generations would not have fought among each other, after clear (Signs) had come to them, but they (chose) to wrangle, some believing and others rejecting.

تِلْكَ الرُّسُلُ فَضَّلْنَا بَعْضَهُمْ

عَلَى بَعْضٍ مِنْهُمْ مَنْ كَلَّمَ اللهُ

وَرَفَعَ بَعْضَهُمْ دَرَجَاتٍ وَاٰتَيْنَا

عِيْسَى ابْنَ مَرْيَمَ الْبَيِّنَاتِ

وَاَيَّدْنَاهُ بِرُوْحِ الْقُدُسِ وَلَوْ

شَاءَ اللهُ مَا اقْتَتَلَ الَّذِيْنَ

مِنْ بَعْدِهِمْ مِّنْ بَعْدِ مَا جَاءَتْهُمُ

الْبَيِّنَاتُ وَلٰكِنِ اخْتَلَفُوْا فَمِنْهُمْ

مَّنْ اٰمَنَ وَمِنْهُمْ مَّنْ كَفَرَ

مطابع الفتح الإسلامية

پاره

تِلْكَ الرُّسُلُ

(۳)

ذَٰلِكَ ٱلْكِتَٰبُ لَا رَيْبَ فِيهِ

PART 4
Lan Tanalu

foster-sisters; your wives'
mothers; your step-daughters
under your guardianship, born of
your wives to whom you have
gone in, - no prohibition if you
have not gone in; - (those who
have been) wives of your sons
proceeding from your loins; and
two sisters in wedlock at one and
the same time, except for what is
past; for Allah is Oft-Forgiving,
Most Merciful;

وَأَخَوَاتُكُم مِّنَ الرَّضَاعَةِ وَأُمَّهٰتُ
نِسَآئِكُمْ وَرَبَآئِبُكُمُ الّٰتِى فِى
حُجُورِكُم مِّن نِّسَآئِكُمُ الّٰتِى
دَخَلْتُم بِهِنَّ فَإِن لَّمْ تَكُونُوا
دَخَلْتُم بِهِنَّ فَلَا جُنَاحَ عَلَيْكُمْ
وَحَلَآئِلُ أَبْنَآئِكُمُ الَّذِينَ مِنْ
أَصْلَابِكُمْ وَأَن تَجْمَعُوا بَيْنَ
الْأُخْتَيْنِ إِلَّا مَا قَدْ سَلَفَ
إِنَّ اللهَ كَانَ غَفُورًا رَّحِيمًا ۞

when you have gone in to each other, and they have taken from you a solemn covenant?

22. And marry not women whom your fathers married,- except what is past: it was shameful and odious, - an abominable custom indeed.

23. Prohibited to you (for marriage) are: - your mothers, daughters, sisters; father's sisters, mother's sisters; brother's daughters, sister's daughters; foster-mothers (who gave you suck),

وَقَدْ اَفْضٰى بَعْضُكُمْ اِلٰى بَعْضٍ

وَّ اَخَذْنَ مِنْكُمْ مِّيْثَاقًا غَلِيْظًا ۩

وَلَا تَنْكِحُوْا مَا نَكَحَ اٰبَآؤُكُمْ

مِّنَ النِّسَآءِ اِلَّا مَا قَدْ سَلَفَ

اِنَّهٗ كَانَ فَاحِشَةً وَّمَقْتًا

وَسَآءَ سَبِيْلًا ۩ حُرِّمَتْ عَلَيْكُمْ

اُمَّهٰتُكُمْ وَبَنٰتُكُمْ وَاَخَوٰتُكُمْ وَعَمّٰتُكُمْ

وَخٰلٰتُكُمْ وَبَنٰتُ الْاَخِ وَبَنٰتُ

الْاُخْتِ وَاُمَّهٰتُكُمُ الّٰتِيْٓ اَرْضَعْنَكُمْ

of open lewdness; on the contrary live with them on a footing of kindness and equity. If you take a dislike to them it may be that you dislike a thing, and Allah brings about through it a great deal of good.

20.   But if you decide to take one wife in place of another, even if you had given the latter a whole treasure for dower, take not the least bit of it back: will you take it by slander and a manifest wrong?

21.   And how could you take it

بِفَاحِشَةٍ مُّبَيِّنَةٍ وَعَاشِرُوهُنَّ

بِالْمَعْرُوفِ فَإِنْ كَرِهْتُمُوهُنَّ

فَعَسَى أَنْ تَكْرَهُوا شَيْئًا وَّيَجْعَلَ

اللهُ فِيهِ خَيْرًا كَثِيرًا ۝ وَإِنْ

أَرَدْتُّمُ اسْتِبْدَالَ زَوْجٍ مَّكَانَ

زَوْجٍ وَّآتَيْتُمْ إِحْدَاهُنَّ قِنْطَارًا

فَلَا تَأْخُذُوا مِنْهُ شَيْئًا

أَتَأْخُذُونَهُ بُهْتَانًا وَّإِثْمًا

مُّبِينًا ۝ وَكَيْفَ تَأْخُذُونَهُ

of those who continue to do evil, until death faces one of them, and he says, "Now have I repented indeed;" nor of those who die rejecting Faith: for them have We prepared a Punishment most grievous.

19. O you who believe! You are forbidden to inherit women against their will. Nor should you treat them with harshness, that you may take away part of the dower you have given them,- except where they have been guilty

لِلَّذِينَ يَعْمَلُونَ السَّيِّئَاتِ حَتَّى

إِذَا حَضَرَ أَحَدَهُمُ الْمَوْتُ قَالَ

إِنِّي تُبْتُ الْآنَ وَلَا الَّذِينَ

يَمُوتُونَ وَهُمْ كُفَّارٌ أُولَٰئِكَ

أَعْتَدْنَا لَهُمْ عَذَابًا أَلِيمًا ۝

يَا أَيُّهَا الَّذِينَ آمَنُوا لَا يَحِلُّ

لَكُمْ أَن تَرِثُوا النِّسَاءَ كَرْهًا

وَلَا تَعْضُلُوهُنَّ لِتَذْهَبُوا بِبَعْضِ

مَا آتَيْتُمُوهُنَّ إِلَّا أَن يَأْتِينَ

Allah ordain for them some (other) way.

16. If two men among you are guilty of lewdness, punish them both. If they repent and amend, leave them alone; for Allah is Oft-Returning, Most Merciful.

17. Allah accepts the repentance of those who do evil in ignorance and repent soon afterwards; to them will Allah turn in mercy: for Allah is full of knowledge and wisdom.

18. Of no effect is the repentance

اللّٰهُ لَهُنَّ سَبِيلًا ۞ وَالَّذٰنِ

يَاۡتِيٰنِهَا مِنۡكُمۡ فَاٰذُوۡهُمَا ۚ فَاِنۡ

تَابَا وَاَصۡلَحَا فَاَعۡرِضُوۡا عَنۡهُمَا ؕ

اِنَّ اللّٰهَ كَانَ تَوَّابًا رَّحِيۡمًا ۞

اِنَّمَا التَّوۡبَةُ عَلَى اللّٰهِ لِلَّذِيۡنَ

يَعۡمَلُوۡنَ السُّوۡٓءَ بِجَهَالَةٍ ثُمَّ

يَتُوۡبُوۡنَ مِنۡ قَرِيۡبٍ فَاُولٰٓئِكَ

يَتُوۡبُ اللّٰهُ عَلَيۡهِمۡ ؕ وَكَانَ اللّٰهُ

عَلِيۡمًا حَكِيۡمًا ۞ وَلَيۡسَتِ التَّوۡبَةُ

therein (for ever) and that will be the supreme achievement.

14. But those who disobey Allah and His Apostle and transgress His limits will be admitted to a Fire, to abide therein: and they shall have a humiliating punishment.

15. If any of your women are guilty of lewdness, take the evidence of four (reliable) witnesses from amongst you against them; and if they testify, confine them to houses until death do claim them, or

فِيهَا ۚ وَذٰلِكَ الْفَوْزُ الْعَظِيمُ ﴿١٣﴾

وَمَنْ يَّعْصِ اللّٰهَ وَرَسُوْلَهٗ

وَيَتَعَدَّ حُدُوْدَهٗ يُدْخِلْهُ نَارًا

خَالِدًا فِيْهَا ۖ وَلَهٗ عَذَابٌ

مُّهِيْنٌ ﴿١٤﴾ وَالّٰتِيْ يَأْتِيْنَ الْفَاحِشَةَ

مِنْ نِّسَآئِكُمْ فَاسْتَشْهِدُوْا

عَلَيْهِنَّ اَرْبَعَةً مِّنْكُمْ ۚ فَاِنْ

شَهِدُوْا فَاَمْسِكُوْهُنَّ فِى الْبُيُوْتِ

حَتّٰى يَتَوَفّٰهُنَّ الْمَوْتُ اَوْ يَجْعَلَ

one of the two gets a sixth; but if more than two, they share in a third; after payment of legacies and debts; so that no loss is caused (to any one). Thus is it ordained by Allah; and Allah is All-Knowing, Most Forbearing.

13. Those are limits set by Allah: those who obey Allah and His Apostle will be admitted to Gardens with rivers flowing beneath, to abide

وَاحِدٍ مِّنْهُمَا السُّدُسُ فَإِنْ

كَانُوْٓا اَكْثَرَ مِنْ ذٰلِكَ فَهُمْ

شُرَكَآءُ فِى الثُّلُثِ مِنْۢ بَعْدِ

وَصِيَّةٍ يُّوْصٰى بِهَآ اَوْ دَيْنٍ

غَيْرَ مُضَآرٍّ ۚ وَصِيَّةً مِّنَ اللّٰهِ ۗ

وَاللّٰهُ عَلِيْمٌ حَلِيْمٌ ۞ تِلْكَ

حُدُوْدُ اللّٰهِ ۚ وَمَنْ يُّطِعِ اللّٰهَ

وَرَسُوْلَهٗ يُدْخِلْهُ جَنّٰتٍ تَجْرِىْ

مِنْ تَحْتِهَا الْاَنْهٰرُ خٰلِدِيْنَ

after payment of legacies and debts. In what you leave, their share is a fourth, if you leave no child; but if you leave a child, they get an eighth; after payment of legacies and debts. If the man or woman whose inheritance is in question, has left neither ascendants nor descendants, but has left a brother or a sister, each

مِمَّا تَرَكْنَ مِنْ بَعْدِ وَصِيَّةٍ

يُوصِيْنَ بِهَآ أَوْ دَيْنٍ وَلَهُنَّ

الرُّبُعُ مِمَّا تَرَكْتُمْ إِنْ لَّمْ

يَكُنْ لَّكُمْ وَلَدٌ فَإِنْ كَانَ

لَكُمْ وَلَدٌ فَلَهُنَّ الثُّمُنُ مِمَّا

تَرَكْتُمْ مِنْ بَعْدِ وَصِيَّةٍ

تُوصُوْنَ بِهَآ أَوْ دَيْنٍ وَإِنْ

كَانَ رَجُلٌ يُّوْرَثُ كَلٰلَةً أَوِ

امْرَأَةٌ وَّلَهُ أَخٌ أَوْ أُخْتٌ فَلِكُلِّ

brothers (or sisters) the mother has a sixth. (The distribution in all cases is) after the payment of legacies and debts. You know not whether your parents or your children are nearest to you in benefit. These are settled portions ordained by Allah; and Allah is All-Knowing, All-Wise.

12. In what your wives leave, your share is a half, if they leave no child; but if they leave a child, you get a fourth;

إِخْوَةٌ فَلِأُمِّهِ السُّدُسُ مِنْ

بَعْدِ وَصِيَّةٍ يُّوصٰى بِهَآ أَوْ دَيْنٍ

اٰبَآؤُكُمْ وَأَبْنَآؤُكُمْ لَا تَدْرُوْنَ

أَيُّهُمْ أَقْرَبُ لَكُمْ نَفْعًا

فَرِيْضَةً مِّنَ اللّٰهِ إِنَّ اللّٰهَ

كَانَ عَلِيْمًا حَكِيْمًا ۝ وَلَكُمْ

نِصْفُ مَا تَرَكَ أَزْوَاجُكُمْ إِنْ

لَّمْ يَكُنْ لَّهُنَّ وَلَدٌ فَإِنْ

كَانَ لَهُنَّ وَلَدٌ فَلَكُمُ الرُّبُعُ

a blazing Fire!

11. Allah (thus) directs you as regards your children's (inheritance): to the male, a portion equal to that of two females: if only daughters, two or more, their share is two-thirds of the inheritance; if only one, her share is a half. For parents, a sixth share of the inheritance to each, if the deceased left children; if no children, and the parents are the (only) heirs, the mother has a third; if the deceased left

سَعِيرًا ۞ يُوصِيكُمُ اللهُ فِىٓ أَوْلَادِكُمْ

لِلذَّكَرِ مِثْلُ حَظِّ الْأُنثَيَيْنِ فَإِن

كُنَّ نِسَآءً فَوْقَ اثْنَتَيْنِ فَلَهُنَّ

ثُلُثَا مَا تَرَكَ وَإِن كَانَتْ وَاحِدَةً

فَلَهَا النِّصْفُ وَلِأَبَوَيْهِ لِكُلِّ

وَاحِدٍ مِّنْهُمَا السُّدُسُ مِمَّا

تَرَكَ إِن كَانَ لَهُ وَلَدٌ فَإِن لَّمْ

يَكُن لَّهُ وَلَدٌ وَوَرِثَهُ أَبَوَاهُ

فَلِأُمِّهِ الثُّلُثُ فَإِن كَانَ لَهُ

8. But if at the time of division other relatives, or orphans, or poor, are present, feed them out of the (property), and speak to them words of kindness and justice.

9. Let those (disposing of an estate) have the same fear in their minds as they would have for their own if they had left a helpless family behind: let them fear Allah, and speak words of appropriate (comfort).

10. Those who unjustly eat up the property of orphans, eat up a Fire into their own bodies: they will soon be enduring

وَإِذَا حَضَرَ الْقِسْمَةَ أُولُوا الْقُرْبٰى

وَالْيَتٰمٰى وَالْمَسٰكِيْنُ فَارْزُقُوْهُمْ

مِّنْهُ وَقُوْلُوْا لَهُمْ قَوْلًا مَّعْرُوْفًا ۞

وَلْيَخْشَ الَّذِيْنَ لَوْ تَرَكُوْا مِنْ

خَلْفِهِمْ ذُرِّيَّةً ضِعٰفًا خَافُوْا

عَلَيْهِمْ فَلْيَتَّقُوا اللّٰهَ وَلْيَقُوْلُوْا قَوْلًا

سَدِيْدًا ۞ إِنَّ الَّذِيْنَ يَأْكُلُوْنَ

أَمْوَالَ الْيَتٰمٰى ظُلْمًا إِنَّمَا يَأْكُلُوْنَ

فِيْ بُطُوْنِهِمْ نَارًا ۖ وَسَيَصْلَوْنَ

their growing up. If the guardian is well-off, let him claim no remuneration, but if he is poor, let him have for himself what is just and reasonable. When you release their property to them, take witnesses in their presence: but all-sufficient is Allah in taking account.

7.   From what is left by parents and those nearest related there is a share for men and a share for women, whether the property be small or large, - a determinate share.

اَنْ يَّكْبُرُوْا ۚ وَمَنْ كَانَ غَنِيًّا

فَلْيَسْتَعْفِفْ ۚ وَمَنْ كَانَ فَقِيْرًا

فَلْيَأْكُلْ بِالْمَعْرُوْفِ ۚ فَاِذَا دَفَعْتُمْ

اِلَيْهِمْ اَمْوَالَهُمْ فَاَشْهِدُوْا عَلَيْهِمْ ۚ

وَكَفٰى بِاللّٰهِ حَسِيْبًا ۞ لِلرِّجَالِ

نَصِيْبٌ مِّمَّا تَرَكَ الْوَالِدٰنِ

وَالْاَقْرَبُوْنَ ۖ وَلِلنِّسَآءِ نَصِيْبٌ مِّمَّا

تَرَكَ الْوَالِدٰنِ وَالْاَقْرَبُوْنَ مِمَّا

قَلَّ مِنْهُ اَوْ كَثُرَ ۚ نَصِيْبًا مَّفْرُوْضًا ۞

any part of it to you, take it and enjoy it with right good cheer.

5.   To those weak of under-standing make not over your property, which Allah has made a means of support for you, but feed and clothe them therewith, and speak to them words of kindness and justice.

6.   Make trial of orphans until they reach the age of marriage; if then you find sound judgment in them, release their property to them; but consume it not waste-fully, nor in haste against

لَكُمْ عَنْ شَىْءٍ مِّنْهُ نَفْسًا فَكُلُوهُ

هَنِيْئًا مَّرِيْئًا ۞ وَلَا تُؤْتُوا السُّفَهَآءَ

أَمْوَالَكُمُ الَّتِيْ جَعَلَ اللّٰهُ لَكُمْ

قِيٰمًا وَّارْزُقُوْهُمْ فِيْهَا وَاكْسُوْهُمْ

وَقُوْلُوْا لَهُمْ قَوْلًا مَّعْرُوْفًا ۞

وَابْتَلُوا الْيَتٰمٰى حَتّٰى إِذَا بَلَغُوا

النِّكَاحَ فَإِنْ اٰنَسْتُمْ مِّنْهُمْ

رُشْدًا فَادْفَعُوا إِلَيْهِمْ أَمْوَالَهُمْ

وَلَا تَأْكُلُوْهَا إِسْرَافًا وَّبِدَارًا

and devour not their substance (by mixing it up) with your own. For this is indeed a great sin.

3.   If you fear that you shall not be able to deal justly with the orphans, marry women of your choice, two, or three, or four; but if you fear that you shall not be able to deal justly (with them), then only one, or (a captive) that your right hands possess, that will be more suitable, to prevent you from doing injustice.

4.   And give the women (on marriage) their dower as a free gift; but if they, of their own good pleasure, remit

وَلَا تَأْكُلُوٓا أَمْوَالَهُمْ إِلَىٰٓ أَمْوَالِكُمْ

إِنَّهُۥ كَانَ حُوبًا كَبِيرًا ۞ وَإِنْ

خِفْتُمْ أَلَّا تُقْسِطُوا فِى الْيَتَٰمَىٰ

فَانْكِحُوا مَا طَابَ لَكُمْ مِّنَ

النِّسَآءِ مَثْنَىٰ وَثُلَٰثَ وَرُبَٰعَ

فَإِنْ خِفْتُمْ أَلَّا تَعْدِلُوا فَوَاحِدَةً

أَوْ مَا مَلَكَتْ أَيْمَانُكُمْ ذَٰلِكَ أَدْنَىٰٓ

أَلَّا تَعُولُوا ۞ وَءَاتُوا النِّسَآءَ

صَدُقَٰتِهِنَّ نِحْلَةً فَإِنْ طِبْنَ

An-Nisaa (The Women)

Bismillahir-Rahmanir-Rahim

1. O mankind! Fear your Guardian-Lord, who created you from a single person, created, of like nature, his mate, and from them twain scattered (like seeds) countless men and women;- reverence Allah, through Whom you demand your mutual (rights), and (reverence) the wombs (that bore you): for Allah ever watches over you.

2. To orphans restore their property (when they reach their age), nor substitute (your) worthless things for (their) good ones;

بِسۡمِ اللّٰهِ الرَّحۡمٰنِ الرَّحِيۡمِ

يٰۤاَيُّهَا النَّاسُ اتَّقُوۡا رَبَّكُمُ

الَّذِىۡ خَلَقَكُمۡ مِّنۡ نَّفۡسٍ

وَّاحِدَةٍ وَّخَلَقَ مِنۡهَا زَوۡجَهَا

وَبَثَّ مِنۡهُمَا رِجَالًا كَثِيۡرًا وَّنِسَآءً ۚ

وَاتَّقُوا اللّٰهَ الَّذِىۡ تَسَآءَلُوۡنَ بِهٖ

وَالۡاَرۡحَامَ ؕ اِنَّ اللّٰهَ كَانَ عَلَيۡكُمۡ

رَقِيۡبًا ۞ وَاٰتُوا الۡيَتٰمٰۤى اَمۡوَالَهُمۡ

وَلَا تَتَبَدَّلُوا الۡخَبِيۡثَ بِالطَّيِّبِ ۖ

among the People of the Book, those who believe in Allah, in the revelation to you, and in the revelation to them, bowing in humility to Allah: they will not sell the Signs of Allah for a miserable gain! for them is a reward with their Lord, and Allah is swift in account.

200. O you who believe! Persevere in patience and constancy; vie in such perseverance; strengthen each other; and fear Allah; that you may prosper.

مِنْ اَهْلِ الْكِتٰبِ لَمَنْ يُّؤْمِنُ

بِاللّٰهِ وَمَآ اُنْزِلَ اِلَيْكُمْ وَمَآ

اُنْزِلَ اِلَيْهِمْ خٰشِعِيْنَ لِلّٰهِ ۙ لَا

يَشْتَرُوْنَ بِاٰيٰتِ اللّٰهِ ثَمَنًا

قَلِيْلًا ۗ اُولٰٓئِكَ لَهُمْ اَجْرُهُمْ

عِنْدَ رَبِّهِمْ ۗ اِنَّ اللّٰهَ سَرِيْعُ

الْحِسَابِ ۝١٩٩ يٰٓاَيُّهَا الَّذِيْنَ اٰمَنُوا

اصْبِرُوْا وَصَابِرُوْا وَرَابِطُوْا ۟

وَاتَّقُوا اللّٰهَ لَعَلَّكُمْ تُفْلِحُوْنَ ۝٢٠٠

from the Presence of Allah, and from His Presence is the best of rewards."

196. Let not the strutting about of the unbelievers through the land deceive you:

197. Little is it for enjoyment: their ultimate abode is Hell: what an evil bed (to lie on)!

198. On the other hand, for those who fear their Lord, are Gardens, with rivers flowing beneath; therein are they to dwell (for ever), - a gift from the Presence of Allah; and that which is in the Presence of Allah is the best (bliss) for the righteous.

199. And there are, certainly,

مِّنْ عِنْدِ اللهِ ۗ وَاللهُ عِنْدَهُ

حُسْنُ الثَّوَابِ ۝ لَا يَغُرَّنَّكَ تَقَلُّبُ

الَّذِيْنَ كَفَرُوْا فِى الْبِلَادِ ۝

مَتَاعٌ قَلِيْلٌ ثُمَّ مَأْوٰىهُمْ جَهَنَّمُ ۗ

وَبِئْسَ الْمِهَادُ ۝ لٰكِنِ الَّذِيْنَ

اتَّقَوْا رَبَّهُمْ لَهُمْ جَنّٰتٌ تَجْرِيْ

مِنْ تَحْتِهَا الْأَنْهٰرُ خٰلِدِيْنَ

فِيْهَا نُزُلًا مِّنْ عِنْدِ اللهِ ۗ وَمَا

عِنْدَ اللهِ خَيْرٌ لِّلْأَبْرَارِ ۝ وَإِنَّ

of Judgment: for You never break Your promise."

195. And their Lord has accepted of them, and answered them: "Never will I suffer to be lost the work of any of you, be he male or female: you are members, one of another: those who have left their homes, or been driven out therefrom, or suffered harm in My Cause, or fought or been slain, - verily, I will blot out from them their iniquities, and admit them into Gardens with rivers flowing beneath; - A reward

القِيٰمَةِ ۖ اِنَّكَ لَا تُخْلِفُ الْمِيْعَادَ ۞

فَاسْتَجَابَ لَهُمْ رَبُّهُمْ اَنِّیْ لَاۤ

اُضِیْعُ عَمَلَ عَامِلٍ مِّنْکُمْ مِّنْ

ذَکَرٍ اَوْ اُنْثٰی ۚ بَعْضُکُمْ مِّنْ بَعْضٍ ۚ

فَالَّذِیْنَ هَاجَرُوْا وَ اُخْرِجُوْا مِنْ

دِیَارِهِمْ وَ اُوْذُوْا فِیْ سَبِیْلِیْ

وَ قٰتَلُوْا وَ قُتِلُوْا لَاُکَفِّرَنَّ عَنْهُمْ

سَیِّاٰتِهِمْ وَ لَاُدْخِلَنَّهُمْ جَنّٰتٍ

تَجْرِیْ مِنْ تَحْتِهَا الْاَنْهٰرُ ۚ ثَوَابًا

of the Fire."

192. "Our Lord! Any whom You admit to the Fire, truly You covered (them) with shame, and never will wrong-doers find any helpers!"

193. "Our Lord! We have heard the call of one calling (us) to Faith, 'Believe you in the Lord,' and we have believed. Our Lord! Forgive us our sins, blot out from us our iniquities, and take to yourself our souls in the company of the righteous."

194. "Our Lord! Grant us what You promised unto us through Your Apostles, and save us from shame on the Day

النَّارَ ۞ رَبَّنَآ اِنَّكَ مَنْ تُدْخِلِ

النَّارَ فَقَدْ اَخْزَيْتَهٗ ۗ وَمَا

لِلظّٰلِمِيْنَ مِنْ اَنْصَارٍ ۞ رَبَّنَآ

اِنَّنَا سَمِعْنَا مُنَادِيًا يُّنَادِيْ

لِلْاِيْمَانِ اَنْ اٰمِنُوْا بِرَبِّكُمْ

فَاٰمَنَّا ۖ رَبَّنَا فَاغْفِرْ لَنَا ذُنُوْبَنَا

وَ كَفِّرْ عَنَّا سَيِّاٰتِنَا وَتَوَفَّنَا مَعَ

الْاَبْرَارِ ۞ رَبَّنَا وَاٰتِنَا مَا وَعَدْتَّنَا

عَلٰى رُسُلِكَ وَلَا تُخْزِنَا يَوْمَ

of the heavens and the earth; and Allah has power over all things.

190. Behold! In the creation of the heavens and the earth, and the alternation of night and day,- there are indeed Signs for men of understanding, -

191. Men who celebrate the praises of Allah, standing, sitting, and lying down on their sides, and contemplate the (wonders of) creation in the heavens and the earth, (with the thought): "Our Lord! Not for nothing have you created (all) this! Glory to You! Give us salvation from the Chastisement

السَّمٰوٰتِ وَالْأَرْضِ ۗ وَاللّٰهُ عَلٰى

كُلِّ شَىْءٍ قَدِيْرٌ ۞ اِنَّ فِىْ خَلْقِ

السَّمٰوٰتِ وَالْأَرْضِ وَاخْتِلَافِ

الَّيْلِ وَالنَّهَارِ لَاٰيٰتٍ لِّأُولِى

الْأَلْبَابِ ۞ الَّذِيْنَ يَذْكُرُوْنَ

اللّٰهَ قِيٰمًا وَّقُعُوْدًا وَّعَلٰى جُنُوْبِهِمْ

وَيَتَفَكَّرُوْنَ فِىْ خَلْقِ السَّمٰوٰتِ

وَالْأَرْضِ ۚ رَبَّنَا مَا خَلَقْتَ هٰذَا

بَاطِلًا ۚ سُبْحٰنَكَ فَقِنَا عَذَابَ

of the Book, to make it known and clear to mankind, and not to hide it; but they threw it away behind their backs, and purchased with it some miserable gain! and vile was the bargain they made!

188. Think not that those who exult in what they have brought about, and love to be praised for what they have not done, - think not that they can escape the Chastisement. For them is a Chastisement grievous indeed.

189. To Allah belongeth the dominion

الْكِتٰبَ لَتُبَيِّنُنَّهٗ لِلنَّاسِ وَلَا

تَكْتُمُوْنَهٗ ۖ فَنَبَذُوْهُ وَرَآءَ ظُهُوْرِهِمْ

وَاشْتَرَوْا بِهٖ ثَمَنًا قَلِيْلًا ۖ

فَبِئْسَ مَا يَشْتَرُوْنَ ۝ لَا

تَحْسَبَنَّ الَّذِيْنَ يَفْرَحُوْنَ بِمَآ

اَتَوْا وَّيُحِبُّوْنَ اَنْ يُّحْمَدُوْا

بِمَا لَمْ يَفْعَلُوْا فَلَا تَحْسَبَنَّهُمْ

بِمَفَازَةٍ مِّنَ الْعَذَابِ ۚ وَلَهُمْ

عَذَابٌ اَلِيْمٌ ۝ وَلِلّٰهِ مُلْكُ

the fire and admitted to the Garden will have attained the object (of Life): for the life of this world is but goods and chattels of deception.

186. You shall certainly be tried and tested in your possessions and in your personal selves; and you shall certainly hear much that will grieve you, from those who received the Book before you and from those who worship many gods. But if you persevere patiently, and guard against evil, - then that will be a deter-mining factor in all affairs.

187. And remember Allah took a covenant from the People

النَّارِ وَأُدْخِلَ الْجَنَّةَ فَقَدْ فَازَ

وَمَا الْحَيْوةُ الدُّنْيَا اِلَّا مَتَاعُ

الْغُرُوْرِ ۞ لَتُبْلَوُنَّ فِيْ اَمْوَالِكُمْ

وَاَنْفُسِكُمْ وَلَتَسْمَعُنَّ مِنَ الَّذِيْنَ

اُوْتُوا الْكِتَبَ مِنْ قَبْلِكُمْ وَمِنَ

الَّذِيْنَ اَشْرَكُوْا اَذًى كَثِيْرًا

وَاِنْ تَصْبِرُوْا وَتَتَّقُوْا فَاِنَّ

ذٰلِكَ مِنْ عَزْمِ الْاُمُوْرِ ۞ وَاِذْ

اَخَذَ اللهُ مِيْثَاقَ الَّذِيْنَ اُوْتُوا

Say: "There came to you Apostles before me, with Clear Signs and even with what you ask for: why then did you slay them, if you speak the truth?"

184. Then if they reject you, so were rejected Apostles before you, who came with Clear Signs, Books of dark prophecies, and the Book of Enlightenment.

185. Every soul shall have a taste of death: and only on the Day of Judgment shall you be paid your full recompense. Only he who is saved far from

قُلْ قَدْ جَآءَكُمْ رُسُلٌ مِّنْ

قَبْلِىْ بِالْبَيِّنٰتِ وَبِالَّذِىْ قُلْتُمْ

فَلِمَ قَتَلْتُمُوْهُمْ اِنْ كُنْتُمْ

صٰدِقِيْنَ ۞ فَاِنْ كَذَّبُوْكَ فَقَدْ

كُذِّبَ رُسُلٌ مِّنْ قَبْلِكَ

جَآءُوْ بِالْبَيِّنٰتِ وَالزُّبُرِ وَالْكِتٰبِ

الْمُنِيْرِ ۞ كُلُّ نَفْسٍ ذَآئِقَةُ

الْمَوْتِ ۗ وَاِنَّمَا تُوَفَّوْنَ اُجُوْرَكُمْ

يَوْمَ الْقِيٰمَةِ ۗ فَمَنْ زُحْزِحَ عَنِ

Allah is indigent and we are rich!"- We shall certainly record their word and (their act) of slaying the Prophets in defiance of right, and We shall say: "Taste the Chastisement of the Scorching Fire!"

182. "This is because of the (unrighteous deeds) which your hands sent on before you: for Allah never harms those who serve Him."

183. They (also) said: "Allah took our promise not to believe in an Apostle unless he showed us a sacrifice consumed by fire (from heaven)."

قف لازم

اللّٰهَ فَقِيْرٌ وَّ نَحْنُ اَغْنِيَآءُ

سَنَكْتُبُ مَا قَالُوْا وَ قَتْلَهُمُ

الْاَنْبِيَآءَ بِغَيْرِ حَقٍّ وَّ نَقُوْلُ

ذُوْقُوْا عَذَابَ الْحَرِيْقِ ۝ ذٰلِكَ

بِمَا قَدَّمَتْ اَيْدِيْكُمْ وَ اَنَّ

اللّٰهَ لَيْسَ بِظَلَّامٍ لِّلْعَبِيْدِ ۝

اَلَّذِيْنَ قَالُوْآ اِنَّ اللّٰهَ عَهِدَ

اِلَيْنَآ اَلَّا نُؤْمِنَ لِرَسُوْلٍ حَتّٰى

يَاْتِيَنَا بِقُرْبَانٍ تَاْكُلُهُ النَّارُ

and do right, you have a reward without measure.

180. And let not those who covetously withhold of the gifts which Allah has given them of His Grace, think that it is good for them: no, it will be the worse for them: soon shall the things which they covetously withheld be tied to their necks like a twisted collar, on the Day of Judgment. To Allah belongs the heritage of the heavens and the earth; and Allah is Well-Acquainted with all that you do.

181. Allah has heard the taunt of those who say: "Truly,

وَتَتَّقُوْا فَلَكُمْ اَجْرٌ عَظِيْمٌ ۝

وَلَا يَحْسَبَنَّ الَّذِيْنَ يَبْخَلُوْنَ

بِمَاۤ اٰتٰهُمُ اللّٰهُ مِنْ فَضْلِهٖ

هُوَ خَيْرًا لَّهُمْ ؕ بَلْ هُوَ شَرٌّ

لَّهُمْ ؕ سَيُطَوَّقُوْنَ مَا بَخِلُوْا بِهٖ

يَوْمَ الْقِيٰمَةِ ؕ وَلِلّٰهِ مِيْرَاثُ

السَّمٰوٰتِ وَالْاَرْضِ ؕ وَاللّٰهُ بِمَا

تَعْمَلُوْنَ خَبِيْرٌ ۟ ۝ لَقَدْ سَمِعَ

اللّٰهُ قَوْلَ الَّذِيْنَ قَالُوْۤا اِنَّ

is good for themselves: We grant them respite that they may grow in their iniquity: but they will have a shameful punishment.

179. Allah will not leave the believers in the state in which you are now, until He separates what is evil from what is good. Nor will He disclose to you the secrets of the Unseen. But He chooses of His Apostles (for the purpose) whom He pleases. So believe in Allah. And His Apostles: and if you believe

خَيْرٌ لِّاَنْفُسِهِمْ ۚ اِنَّمَا نُمْلِىْ لَهُمْ

لِيَزْدَادُوْۤا اِثْمًا ۚ وَلَهُمْ عَذَابٌ

مُّهِيْنٌ ۞ مَا كَانَ اللّٰهُ لِيَذَرَ

الْمُؤْمِنِيْنَ عَلٰى مَاۤ اَنْتُمْ عَلَيْهِ

حَتّٰى يَمِيْزَ الْخَبِيْثَ مِنَ الطَّيِّبِ ۗ

وَمَا كَانَ اللّٰهُ لِيُطْلِعَكُمْ عَلَى

الْغَيْبِ وَلٰكِنَّ اللّٰهَ يَجْتَبِىْ مِنْ

رُّسُلِهٖ مَنْ يَّشَآءُ ۖ فَاٰمِنُوْا

بِاللّٰهِ وَرُسُلِهٖ ۚ وَاِنْ تُؤْمِنُوْا

those grieve you who rush headlong into Unbelief: not the least harm will they do to Allah: Allah's plan is that He will give them no portion in the Hereafter, but a severe punishment.

177. Those who purchase Unbelief at the price of Faith, - not the least harm will they do to Allah, but they will have a grievous punishment.

178. Let not the unbelievers think that Our respite to them

يَحْزُنْكَ الَّذِينَ يُسَارِعُونَ فِي

الْكُفْرِ اِنَّهُمْ لَنْ يَّضُرُّوا اللهَ

شَيْئًا يُرِيدُ اللهُ اَلَّا يَجْعَلَ

لَهُمْ حَظًّا فِي الْاٰخِرَةِ وَلَهُمْ

عَذَابٌ عَظِيمٌ ۞ اِنَّ الَّذِينَ

اشْتَرَوُا الْكُفْرَ بِالْاِيْمَانِ لَنْ

يَّضُرُّوا اللهَ شَيْئًا وَلَهُمْ

عَذَابٌ اَلِيمٌ ۞ وَلَا يَحْسَبَنَّ

الَّذِينَ كَفَرُوا اَنَّمَا نُمْلِي لَهُمْ

army is gathering against you": and frightened them: but it (only) increased their Faith: they said: "For us Allah does suffice, and He is the best Disposer of affairs."

174. And they returned with Grace and Bounty from Allah: no harm ever touched them: for they followed the good pleasure of Allah: and Allah is the Lord of bounties unbounded.

175. It is only the Satan that suggests to you the fear of his votaries: be you not afraid of them, but fear Me, if you have Faith.

176. Let not

النَّاسَ قَدْ جَمَعُوْا لَكُمْ فَاخْشَوْهُمْ

فَزَادَهُمْ اِيْمَانًا ۖ وَّقَالُوْا حَسْبُنَا

اللّٰهُ وَنِعْمَ الْوَكِيْلُ ۙ فَانْقَلَبُوْا

بِنِعْمَةٍ مِّنَ اللّٰهِ وَفَضْلٍ لَّمْ

يَمْسَسْهُمْ سُوْٓءٌ ۙ وَّاتَّبَعُوْا رِضْوَانَ

اللّٰهِ ۗ وَاللّٰهُ ذُوْ فَضْلٍ عَظِيْمٍ ۙ

اِنَّمَا ذٰلِكُمُ الشَّيْطٰنُ يُخَوِّفُ

اَوْلِيَآءَهٗ ۖ فَلَا تَخَافُوْهُمْ وَخَافُوْنِ

اِنْ كُنْتُمْ مُّؤْمِنِيْنَ ۙ وَلَا

them (in their bliss), the (martyrs) glory in the fact that on them is no fear, nor have they (cause to) grieve.

171. They glory in the Grace and the bounty from Allah, and in the fact that Allah lets not the reward of the faithful to be lost (in the least).

172. Of those who answered the call of Allah and the Apostle, even after being wounded, those who do right and refrain from wrong, have a great reward;-

173. Men said to them: "A great

بِهِمْ مِّنْ خَلْفِهِمْ اَلَّا خَوْفٌ

عَلَيْهِمْ وَلَا هُمْ يَحْزَنُوْنَ ۞

يَسْتَبْشِرُوْنَ بِنِعْمَةٍ مِّنَ اللّٰهِ

وَفَضْلٍ ۙ وَّاَنَّ اللّٰهَ لَا يُضِيْعُ

اَجْرَ الْمُؤْمِنِيْنَ ۞ اَلَّذِيْنَ اسْتَجَابُوْا

لِلّٰهِ وَالرَّسُوْلِ مِنْ بَعْدِ مَاۤ

اَصَابَهُمُ الْقَرْحُ ۛ لِلَّذِيْنَ اَحْسَنُوْا

مِنْهُمْ وَاتَّقَوْا اَجْرٌ عَظِيْمٌ ۞

اَلَّذِيْنَ قَالَ لَهُمُ النَّاسُ اِنَّ

they conceal.

168. (They are) the ones that say, (of their brethren slain), while they themselves sit (at ease): "If only they had listened to us they would not have been slain." Say: "Avert death from your own selves, if you speak the truth."

169. Think not of those who are slain in Allah's way as dead. No, they live, finding their sustenance in the Presence of their Lord;

170. They rejoice in the Bounty provided by Allah: and with regard to those left behind, who have not yet joined

يَكْتُمُونَ ۩ ٱلَّذِينَ قَالُوا لِإِخْوَانِهِمْ

وَقَعَدُوا لَوْ أَطَاعُونَا مَا قُتِلُوا

قُلْ فَادْرَءُوا عَنْ أَنفُسِكُمُ

ٱلْمَوْتَ إِن كُنتُمْ صَٰدِقِينَ ۩

وَلَا تَحْسَبَنَّ ٱلَّذِينَ قُتِلُوا فِي

سَبِيلِ ٱللَّهِ أَمْوَٰتًا ۚ بَلْ أَحْيَآءٌ

عِندَ رَبِّهِمْ يُرْزَقُونَ ۩ فَرِحِينَ

بِمَآ ءَاتَىٰهُمُ ٱللَّهُ مِن فَضْلِهِۦ

وَيَسْتَبْشِرُونَ بِٱلَّذِينَ لَمْ يَلْحَقُوا

166. What you suffered on the day the two armies met, was with the leave of Allah, in order that He might test the believers,-

167. And the hypocrites also. These were told: "Come, fight in the way of Allah, or (at least) drive (the foe from your city)." They said: "Had we known there would be a fight, we should certainly have followed you." They were that day nearer to Unbelief than to Faith, saying with their lips what was not in their hearts but Allah has full knowledge of all

وَمَآ اَصَابَكُمْ يَوْمَ الْتَقَى الْجَمْعٰنِ

فَبِاِذْنِ اللّٰهِ وَلِيَعْلَمَ الْمُؤْمِنِيْنَ ۞

وَلِيَعْلَمَ الَّذِيْنَ نَافَقُوْا ۚ وَقِيْلَ

لَهُمْ تَعَالَوْا قَاتِلُوْا فِيْ سَبِيْلِ

اللّٰهِ اَوِ ادْفَعُوْا ۗ قَالُوْا لَوْ نَعْلَمُ

قِتَالًا لَّا تَّبَعْنٰكُمْ ۗ هُمْ لِلْكُفْرِ

يَوْمَئِذٍ اَقْرَبُ مِنْهُمْ لِلْاِيْمَانِ ۚ

يَقُوْلُوْنَ بِاَفْوَاهِهِمْ مَّا لَيْسَ

فِيْ قُلُوْبِهِمْ ۗ وَاللّٰهُ اَعْلَمُ بِمَا

the believers when He sent among them an Apostle from among themselves, rehearsing unto them the Signs of Allah, sanctifying them, and instructing them in Scripture and Wisdom, while, before that, they had been in manifest error.

165. What! When a single disaster smites you, although you smote (your enemies) with one twice as great, do you say?- "Wherefrom is this?" Say (to them): "It is from yourselves: for Allah has power over all things."

الْمُؤْمِنِينَ اِذْ بَعَثَ فِيهِمْ رَسُوْلًا

مِّنْ اَنْفُسِهِمْ يَتْلُوْا عَلَيْهِمْ

اٰيٰتِهٖ وَيُزَكِّيْهِمْ وَيُعَلِّمُهُمُ

الْكِتٰبَ وَالْحِكْمَةَ ۚ وَاِنْ كَانُوْا

مِنْ قَبْلُ لَفِيْ ضَلٰلٍ مُّبِيْنٍ ۝

اَوَلَمَّا اَصَابَتْكُمْ مُّصِيْبَةٌ قَدْ

اَصَبْتُمْ مِّثْلَيْهَا ۙ قُلْتُمْ اَنّٰى هٰذَا ۗ

قُلْ هُوَ مِنْ عِنْدِ اَنْفُسِكُمْ ۗ اِنَّ

اللَّهَ عَلٰى كُلِّ شَيْءٍ قَدِيْرٌ ۝

(ever) be false to his trust. If any person is so false, he shall, on the Day of Judgment, restore what he misappropriated; then shall every soul receive its due, - whatever it earned, - and none shall be dealt with unjustly.

162. Is the man who follows the good pleasure of Allah like the man who draws on himself the wrath of Allah, and whose abode is in Hell? - a woeful refuge!

163. They are in varying grades in the sight of Allah, and Allah sees well all that they do.

164. Allah did confer a great favour on

اَنْ يَّغُلَّ ۚ وَمَنْ يَّغْلُلْ يَأْتِ

بِمَا غَلَّ يَوْمَ الْقِيٰمَةِ ۚ ثُمَّ

تُوَفّٰى كُلُّ نَفْسٍ مَّا كَسَبَتْ

وَهُمْ لَا يُظْلَمُوْنَ ۝ اَفَمَنِ

اتَّبَعَ رِضْوَانَ اللّٰهِ كَمَنْ بَآءَ

بِسَخَطٍ مِّنَ اللّٰهِ وَمَأْوٰىهُ جَهَنَّمُ ۚ

وَبِئْسَ الْمَصِيْرُ ۝ هُمْ دَرَجٰتٌ

عِنْدَ اللّٰهِ ۗ وَاللّٰهُ بَصِيْرٌۢ بِمَا

يَعْمَلُوْنَ ۝ لَقَدْ مَنَّ اللّٰهُ عَلَى

from about you: so pass over (their faults), and ask for (Allah's) forgiveness for them; and consult them in affairs (of moment). Then, when you have taken a decision, put your trust in Allah. For Allah loves those who put their trust (in Him).

160. If Allah helps you, none can overcome you: if He forsakes you, who is there, after that, that can help you? In Allah, then, let believers put their trust.

161. No prophet could

مِنْ حَوْلِكَ ۖ فَاعْفُ عَنْهُمْ

وَاسْتَغْفِرْ لَهُمْ وَشَاوِرْهُمْ فِى

الْأَمْرِ ۖ فَإِذَا عَزَمْتَ فَتَوَكَّلْ

عَلَى اللهِ ۚ إِنَّ اللهَ يُحِبُّ

الْمُتَوَكِّلِينَ ۞ إِنْ يَّنْصُرْكُمُ اللهُ

فَلَا غَالِبَ لَكُمْ ۖ وَإِنْ يَّخْذُلْكُمْ

فَمَنْ ذَا الَّذِى يَنْصُرُكُمْ مِّنْ

بَعْدِهِ ۚ وَعَلَى اللهِ فَلْيَتَوَكَّلِ

الْمُؤْمِنُونَ ۞ وَمَا كَانَ لِنَبِىٍّ

It is Allah that gives Life and Death, and Allah sees well all that you do.

157. And if you are slain, or die, in the way of Allah, forgiveness and mercy from Allah are far better than all they could amass.

158. And if you die, or are slain, lo! it is unto Allah that you are brought together.

159. It is part of the Mercy of Allah that you deal gently with them. Were you to be severe or harsh-hearted, they would have broken away

وَاللّٰهُ يُحْىٖ وَيُمِيْتُ ۗ وَاللّٰهُ بِمَا

تَعْمَلُوْنَ بَصِيْرٌ ۞ وَلَىِٕنْ قُتِلْتُمْ

فِيْ سَبِيْلِ اللّٰهِ اَوْ مُتُّمْ

لَمَغْفِرَةٌ مِّنَ اللّٰهِ وَرَحْمَةٌ

خَيْرٌ مِّمَّا يَجْمَعُوْنَ ۞ وَلَىِٕنْ

مُّتُّمْ اَوْ قُتِلْتُمْ لَاِلَى اللّٰهِ

تُحْشَرُوْنَ ۞ فَبِمَا رَحْمَةٍ مِّنَ

اللّٰهِ لِنْتَ لَهُمْ ۚ وَلَوْ كُنْتَ

فَظًّا غَلِيْظَ الْقَلْبِ لَانْفَضُّوْا

- it was Satan who caused them to fail, because of some (evil) they had done. But Allah has blotted out (their fault): for Allah is Oft-Forgiving, Most Forbearing.

156. O you who believe! Be not like the unbelievers, who say of their brethren, when they are travelling through the Earth or engaged in fighting: "If they had stayed with us, they would not have died, or been slain." This that Allah may make it a cause of sighs and regrets in their hearts.

اِنَّمَا اسْتَزَلَّهُمُ الشَّيْطٰنُ بِبَعْضِ

مَا كَسَبُوْا ۚ وَلَقَدْ عَفَا اللّٰهُ

عَنْهُمْ ۗ اِنَّ اللّٰهَ غَفُوْرٌ حَلِيْمٌ ۝

يٰٓاَيُّهَا الَّذِيْنَ اٰمَنُوْا لَا تَكُوْنُوْا

كَالَّذِيْنَ كَفَرُوْا وَقَالُوْا لِاِخْوَانِهِمْ

اِذَا ضَرَبُوْا فِى الْاَرْضِ اَوْ

كَانُوْا غُزًّى لَّوْ كَانُوْا عِنْدَنَا

مَا مَاتُوْا وَمَا قُتِلُوْا ۚ لِيَجْعَلَ

اللّٰهُ ذٰلِكَ حَسْرَةً فِى قُلُوْبِهِمْ ۗ

They say (to themselves): "If we had had anything to do with this affair, we should not have been in the slaughter here." Say: "Even if you had remained in your homes, those for whom death was decreed would certainly have gone forth to the place of their death"; but (all this was) that Allah might test what is in your breasts and purge what is in your hearts. For Allah knows well the secrets of your hearts.

155. Those of you who turned back on the day the two hosts met

يَقُوْلُوْنَ لَوْ كَانَ لَنَا مِنَ الْأَمْرِ

شَيْءٌ مَّا قُتِلْنَا هٰهُنَا ۗ قُلْ لَّوْ

كُنْتُمْ فِيْ بُيُوْتِكُمْ لَبَرَزَ الَّذِيْنَ

كُتِبَ عَلَيْهِمُ الْقَتْلُ إِلٰى

مَضَاجِعِهِمْ ۚ وَلِيَبْتَلِيَ اللهُ

مَا فِيْ صُدُوْرِكُمْ وَلِيُمَحِّصَ

مَا فِيْ قُلُوْبِكُمْ ۗ وَاللهُ عَلِيْمٌۢ

بِذَاتِ الصُّدُوْرِ ۝ إِنَّ الَّذِيْنَ

تَوَلَّوْا مِنْكُمْ يَوْمَ الْتَقَى الْجَمْعٰنِ

of all that you do.

154. After (the excitement) of the distress, He sent down calm on a band of you overcome with slumber, while another band was stirred to anxiety by their own feelings, moved by wrong suspicions of Allah - suspicions due to ignorance. They said: "What affair is this of our?" Say you: "Indeed, this affair is wholly Allah's." They hide in their minds what they dare not reveal to you.

بِمَا تَعْمَلُوْنَ ۩ ثُمَّ اَنْزَلَ

عَلَيْكُمْ مِّنْ بَعْدِ الْغَمِّ اَمَنَةً

نُّعَاسًا يَّغْشٰى طَآئِفَةً مِّنْكُمْ ۙ

وَطَآئِفَةٌ قَدْ اَهَمَّتْهُمْ اَنْفُسُهُمْ

يَظُنُّوْنَ بِاللّٰهِ غَيْرَ الْحَقِّ ظَنَّ

الْجَاهِلِيَّةِ ۚ يَقُوْلُوْنَ هَلْ لَّنَا

مِنَ الْاَمْرِ مِنْ شَىْءٍ ۗ قُلْ اِنَّ

الْاَمْرَ كُلَّهٗ لِلّٰهِ ۗ يُخْفُوْنَ فِىْٓ

اَنْفُسِهِمْ مَّا لَا يُبْدُوْنَ لَكَ

hanker after this world and some that desire the Hereafter. Then did He divert you from your foes in order to test you. But He forgave you: for Allah is full of grace to those who believe.

153. Behold! You were climbing up the high ground, without even casting a side glance at any one, and the Apostle in your rear was calling you back. There did Allah give you one distress after another by way of requital, to teach you not to grieve for (the booty) that had escaped you and for (the ill) that had befallen you. For Allah is Well Aware

يُّرِيدُ الدُّنْيَا وَمِنْكُمْ مَّنْ يُّرِيدُ

الْاٰخِرَةَ ۚ ثُمَّ صَرَفَكُمْ عَنْهُمْ

لِيَبْتَلِيَكُمْ ۚ وَلَقَدْ عَفَا عَنْكُمْ ۗ وَاللّٰهُ

ذُوْ فَضْلٍ عَلَى الْمُؤْمِنِيْنَ ۝

اِذْ تُصْعِدُوْنَ وَلَا تَلْوٗنَ عَلٰۤى

اَحَدٍ وَّالرَّسُوْلُ يَدْعُوْكُمْ فِيْۤ

اُخْرٰىكُمْ فَاَثَابَكُمْ غَمًّا بِغَمٍّ

لِّكَيْلَا تَحْزَنُوْا عَلٰى مَا فَاتَكُمْ

وَلَا مَاۤ اَصَابَكُمْ ۗ وَاللّٰهُ خَبِيْرٌ

of the unbelievers, for that they joined companions with Allah, for which He had sent no authority: their abode will be the Fire: and evil is the home of the wrong-doers!

152. Allah did indeed fulfil His promise to you when you with His permission were about to annihilate your enemy,- until you flinched and fell to disputing about the order, and disobeyed it after He brought you in sight (of the booty) which you covet. Among you are some that

اَلَّذِیْنَ کَفَرُوا الرُّعْبَ بِمَاۤ

اَشْرَکُوْا بِاللّٰهِ مَا لَمْ یُنَزِّلْ

بِهٖ سُلْطٰنًا ؕ وَ مَاْوٰىهُمُ النَّارُ ؕ

وَ بِئْسَ مَثْوَی الظّٰلِمِیْنَ ۝

وَ لَقَدْ صَدَقَکُمُ اللّٰهُ وَعْدَهٗۤ

اِذْ تَحُسُّوْنَهُمْ بِاِذْنِهٖ ۚ حَتّٰۤی

اِذَا فَشِلْتُمْ وَ تَنَازَعْتُمْ فِی

الْاَمْرِ وَ عَصَیْتُمْ مِّنْۢ بَعْدِ مَاۤ

اَرٰىکُمْ مَّا تُحِبُّوْنَ ؕ مِنْکُمْ مَّنْ

and help us against those that resist Faith."

148. And Allah gave them a reward in this world, and the excellent reward of the Hereafter. For Allah Loves those who do good.

149. O you who believe! If you obey the unbelievers, they will drive you back on your heels, and you will turn back (from Faith) to your own loss.

150. No, Allah is your Protector, and He is the best of helpers.

151. Soon shall We cast terror into the hearts

وَانْصُرْنَا عَلَى الْقَوْمِ الْكٰفِرِيْنَ ۝

فَاٰتٰهُمُ اللّٰهُ ثَوَابَ الدُّنْيَا

وَحُسْنَ ثَوَابِ الْاٰخِرَةِ ؕ وَاللّٰهُ

يُحِبُّ الْمُحْسِنِيْنَ ۝ يٰۤاَيُّهَا

الَّذِيْنَ اٰمَنُوۤا اِنْ تُطِيْعُوا

الَّذِيْنَ كَفَرُوْا يَرُدُّوْكُمْ عَلٰۤى

اَعْقَابِكُمْ فَتَنْقَلِبُوْا خٰسِرِيْنَ ۝

بَلِ اللّٰهُ مَوْلٰىكُمْ ۚ وَهُوَ خَيْرُ

النّٰصِرِيْنَ ۝ سَنُلْقِيْ فِيْ قُلُوْبِ

And swiftly shall We reward those that (serve Us with) gratitude.

146. How many of the Prophets fought (in Allah's way), and with them (fought) large bands of godly men? But they never lost heart if they met with disaster in Allah's way, nor did they weaken (in will) nor give in. And Allah loves those who are firm and steadfast.

147. All that they said was: "Our Lord! Forgive us our sins and anything we may have done that transgressed our duty: establish our feet firmly,

مِنْهَا ۗ وَسَنَجْزِى الشّٰكِرِيْنَ ۝

وَكَاَيِّنْ مِّنْ نَّبِىٍّ قٰتَلَ مَعَهٗ

رِبِّيُّوْنَ كَثِيْرٌ ۚ فَمَا وَهَنُوْا

لِمَاۤ اَصَابَهُمْ فِىْ سَبِيْلِ اللّٰهِ

وَمَا ضَعُفُوْا وَمَا اسْتَكَانُوْا ۗ

وَاللّٰهُ يُحِبُّ الصّٰبِرِيْنَ ۝ وَمَا

كَانَ قَوْلَهُمْ اِلَّاۤ اَنْ قَالُوْا

رَبَّنَا اغْفِرْ لَنَا ذُنُوْبَنَا وَاِسْرَافَنَا

فِىْۤ اَمْرِنَا وَثَبِّتْ اَقْدَامَنَا

the Apostles that passed away
before him. If he died or were
slain, will you then turn back on
your heels? If any did turn back
on his heels, not the least harm
will he do to Allah; but Allah (on
the other hand) will swiftly
reward those who (serve Him)
with gratitude.

145. Nor can a soul die except by
Allah's leave, the term being
fixed as by writing. If any do
desire a reward in this life, We
shall give it to him; and if any do
desire a reward in the Hereafter,
We shall give it to him.

خَلَتْ مِنْ قَبْلِهِ الرُّسُلُ أَفَإِنْ

مَاتَ أَوْ قُتِلَ انْقَلَبْتُمْ عَلَى

أَعْقَابِكُمْ وَمَنْ يَنْقَلِبْ عَلَى

عَقِبَيْهِ فَلَنْ يَضُرَّ اللهَ شَيْئًا

وَسَيَجْزِى اللهُ الشَّاكِرِينَ ۝ وَمَا

كَانَ لِنَفْسٍ أَنْ تَمُوتَ إِلَّا

بِإِذْنِ اللهِ كِتَابًا مُؤَجَّلًا وَمَنْ

يُّرِدْ ثَوَابَ الدُّنْيَا نُؤْتِهِ مِنْهَا

وَمَنْ يُّرِدْ ثَوَابَ الْآخِرَةِ نُؤْتِهِ

loves not those that do wrong.

141. Allah's object also is to purge those that are true in Faith and to deprive of blessing Those that resist Faith.

142. Did you think that you would enter Heaven without Allah testing those of you who fought hard (in His Cause) and remained steadfast?

143. You did indeed wish for death before you met him: now you have seen him with your own eyes, (and you flinch!)

144. Muhammad is no more than an Apostle: many were

لَا يُحِبُّ الظّٰلِمِيْنَ ۞ وَلِيُمَحِّصَ

اللّٰهُ الَّذِيْنَ اٰمَنُوْا وَيَمْحَقَ

الْكٰفِرِيْنَ ۞ اَمْ حَسِبْتُمْ اَنْ

تَدْخُلُوا الْجَنَّةَ وَلَمَّا يَعْلَمِ اللّٰهُ

الَّذِيْنَ جٰهَدُوْا مِنْكُمْ وَيَعْلَمَ

الصّٰبِرِيْنَ ۞ وَلَقَدْ كُنْتُمْ تَمَنَّوْنَ

الْمَوْتَ مِنْ قَبْلِ اَنْ تَلْقَوْهُ

فَقَدْ رَاَيْتُمُوْهُ وَاَنْتُمْ تَنْظُرُوْنَ ۞

وَمَا مُحَمَّدٌ اِلَّا رَسُوْلٌ ۚ قَدْ

138. Here is a plain statement to men, a guidance and instruction to those who fear Allah.

139. So lose not heart, nor fall into despair: for you must gain mastery if you are true in Faith.

140. If a wound has touched you, be sure a similar wound has touched the others. Such days (of varying fortunes) We give to men and men by turns: that Allah may know those that believe, and that He may take to Himself from your ranks Martyr-witnesses (to Truth). And Allah

هٰذَا بَيَانٌ لِّلنَّاسِ وَهُدًى

وَّمَوْعِظَةٌ لِّلْمُتَّقِيْنَ ۞ وَلَا تَهِنُوْا

وَلَا تَحْزَنُوْا وَأَنْتُمُ الْأَعْلَوْنَ

اِنْ كُنْتُمْ مُّؤْمِنِيْنَ ۞ اِنْ

يَّمْسَسْكُمْ قَرْحٌ فَقَدْ مَسَّ

الْقَوْمَ قَرْحٌ مِّثْلُهُ ۚ وَتِلْكَ

الْأَيَّامُ نُدَاوِلُهَا بَيْنَ النَّاسِ ۚ

وَلِيَعْلَمَ اللّٰهُ الَّذِيْنَ اٰمَنُوْا

وَيَتَّخِذَ مِنْكُمْ شُهَدَآءَ ۗ وَاللّٰهُ

sins except Allah? - and are never obstinate in persisting knowingly in (the wrong) they have done.

136. For such the reward is forgiveness from their Lord, and Gardens with rivers flowing underneath, - an eternal dwelling: how excellent a recompense for those who work (and strive)!

137. Many were the Ways of Life that have passed away before you: travel through the earth, and see what was the end of those who rejected Truth.

الذُّنُوبَ اِلَّا اللهُ ۙ وَلَمْ يُصِرُّوْا

عَلٰى مَا فَعَلُوْا وَهُمْ يَعْلَمُوْنَ ۝

اُولٰٓئِكَ جَزَآؤُهُمْ مَّغْفِرَةٌ مِّنْ

رَّبِّهِمْ وَجَنّٰتٌ تَجْرِيْ مِنْ

تَحْتِهَا الْاَنْهٰرُ خٰلِدِيْنَ فِيْهَا ؕ

وَنِعْمَ اَجْرُ الْعٰمِلِيْنَ ۝ قَدْ

خَلَتْ مِنْ قَبْلِكُمْ سُنَنٌ ۙ

فَسِيْرُوْا فِي الْاَرْضِ فَانْظُرُوْا

كَيْفَ كَانَ عَاقِبَةُ الْمُكَذِّبِيْنَ ۝

from your Lord, and for a Garden whose width is that (of the whole) of the heavens and of the earth, prepared for the righteous, -

134. Those who spend (freely), whether in prosperity, or in adversity; who restrain anger, and pardon (all) men; - for Allah loves those who do good; -

135. And those who, having done something to be ashamed of, or wronged their own souls, earnestly bring Allah to mind, and ask for forgiveness for their sins, - and who can forgive

مِنْ رَّبِّكُمْ وَجَنَّةٍ عَرْضُهَا

السَّمٰوٰتُ وَالْأَرْضُ أُعِدَّتْ

لِلْمُتَّقِيْنَ ۙ الَّذِيْنَ يُنْفِقُوْنَ

فِى السَّرَّآءِ وَالضَّرَّآءِ وَالْكٰظِمِيْنَ

الْغَيْظَ وَالْعَافِيْنَ عَنِ النَّاسِ ؕ

وَاللّٰهُ يُحِبُّ الْمُحْسِنِيْنَ ۚ

وَالَّذِيْنَ إِذَا فَعَلُوْا فَاحِشَةً

أَوْ ظَلَمُوْا أَنْفُسَهُمْ ذَكَرُوا اللّٰهَ

فَاسْتَغْفَرُوْا لِذُنُوْبِهِمْ ۛ وَمَنْ يَّغْفِرُ

and on earth. He forgiveth whom He pleases and punishes whom He pleases; but Allah is Oft-Forgiving, Most Merciful.

130. O you who believe! Devour not interest, doubled and multiplied; but fear Allah; that you may (really) prosper.

131. Fear the Fire, which is prepaired for those who reject Faith:

132. And obey Allah and the Apostle; that you may obtain mercy.

133. Be quick in the race for seeking forgiveness

وَمَا فِى الْأَرْضِ ۖ يَغْفِرُ لِمَنْ

يَّشَاءُ وَيُعَذِّبُ مَنْ يَّشَاءُ ۚ

وَاللّٰهُ غَفُوْرٌ رَّحِيْمٌ ۞ يٰٓأَيُّهَا

الَّذِيْنَ اٰمَنُوْا لَا تَأْكُلُوا الرِّبٰٓوا

أَضْعَافًا مُّضٰعَفَةً ۖ وَاتَّقُوا اللّٰهَ

لَعَلَّكُمْ تُفْلِحُوْنَ ۞ وَاتَّقُوا النَّارَ

الَّتِيْٓ أُعِدَّتْ لِلْكٰفِرِيْنَ ۞

وَأَطِيْعُوا اللّٰهَ وَالرَّسُوْلَ لَعَلَّكُمْ

تُرْحَمُوْنَ ۞ وَسَارِعُوْٓا إِلٰى مَغْفِرَةٍ

126. Allah made it but a message of hope for you, and an assurance to your hearts: (in any case) there is no help except from Allah, The Exalted, the Wise:

127. That He might cut off a fringe of the unbelievers or expose them to infamy, and they should then be turned back, frustrated of their purpose.

128. Not for you, (but for Allah), is the decision: whether He turn in mercy to them, or punish them; for they are indeed wrong-doers.

129. To Allah belongeth all that is in the heavens

وَمَا جَعَلَهُ اللهُ اِلَّا بُشْرٰى

لَكُمْ وَلِتَطْمَئِنَّ قُلُوبُكُمْ بِهٖ ۗ

وَمَا النَّصْرُ اِلَّا مِنْ عِنْدِ اللهِ

الْعَزِيزِ الْحَكِيمِ ۞ لِيَقْطَعَ طَرَفًا

مِّنَ الَّذِينَ كَفَرُوٓا اَوْ يَكْبِتَهُمْ

فَيَنْقَلِبُوْا خَآئِبِيْنَ ۞ لَيْسَ

لَكَ مِنَ الْاَمْرِ شَيْءٌ اَوْ يَتُوْبَ

عَلَيْهِمْ اَوْ يُعَذِّبَهُمْ فَاِنَّهُمْ

ظٰلِمُوْنَ ۞ وَلِلّٰهِ مَا فِى السَّمٰوٰتِ

helped you at Badr, when you were a insignificant little force; then fear Allah; thus may you show your gratitude.

124. Remember you said to the faithful: "Is it not enough for you that Allah should help you with three thousand Angels (specially) sent down?

125. "Yes, - if you remain firm, and act aright, even if the enemy should rush here on you in hot haste, your Lord would help you with five thousand Angels making a terrific onslaught."

نَصَرَكُمُ اللّٰهُ بِبَدۡرٍ وَّاَنۡتُمۡ

اَذِلَّةٌ ۖ فَاتَّقُوا اللّٰهَ لَعَلَّكُمۡ

تَشۡكُرُوۡنَ ۝ اِذۡ تَقُوۡلُ لِلۡمُؤۡمِنِيۡنَ

اَلَنۡ يَّكۡفِيَكُمۡ اَنۡ يُّمِدَّكُمۡ رَبُّكُمۡ

بِثَلٰثَةِ اٰلٰفٍ مِّنَ الۡمَلٰٓئِكَةِ

مُنۡزَلِيۡنَ ۝ بَلٰى ۚ اِنۡ تَصۡبِرُوۡا

وَتَتَّقُوۡا وَيَاۡتُوۡكُمۡ مِّنۡ فَوۡرِهِمۡ

هٰذَا يُمۡدِدۡكُمۡ رَبُّكُمۡ بِخَمۡسَةِ

اٰلٰفٍ مِّنَ الۡمَلٰٓئِكَةِ مُسَوِّمِيۡنَ ۝

but if some misfortune overtakes you, they rejoice at it. But if you are cons-tant and do right, not the least harm will their cunning do to you; for Allah encompasses about all that they do.

121. Remember that morning you did leave the household (early) to post the faithful at their stations for battle: and Allah hears and knows all things:

122. Remember two of your parties meditated cowardice; but Allah was their Protector, and in Allah should the faithful (ever) put their trust.

123. Allah had

وَاِنْ تُصِبْكُمْ سَيِّئَةٌ يَّفْرَحُوْا بِهَا ۚ

وَاِنْ تَصْبِرُوْا وَتَتَّقُوْا لَا يَضُرُّكُمْ

كَيْدُهُمْ شَيْئًا ۗ اِنَّ اللّٰهَ بِمَا

يَعْمَلُوْنَ مُحِيْطٌ ۞ وَاِذْ غَدَوْتَ

مِنْ اَهْلِكَ تُبَوِّئُ الْمُؤْمِنِيْنَ

مَقَاعِدَ لِلْقِتَالِ ۗ وَاللّٰهُ سَمِيْعٌ

عَلِيْمٌ ۞ اِذْ هَمَّتْ طَّآئِفَتٰنِ مِنْكُمْ

اَنْ تَفْشَلَا ۙ وَاللّٰهُ وَلِيُّهُمَا ۗ وَعَلَى

اللّٰهِ فَلْيَتَوَكَّلِ الْمُؤْمِنُوْنَ ۞ وَلَقَدْ

what their hearts conceal is far worse. We have made plain to you the Signs, if you have wisdom.

119. Ah! You are those who love them, but they love you not,- though you believe in the whole of the Book. When they meet you, they say, "We believe": but when they are alone, they bite off the very tips of their fingers at you in their rage. Say: "Perish in your rage; Allah knows well all the secrets of the heart."

120. If anything that is good befalls you, it grieves them;

وَمَا تُخْفِى صُدُورُهُمْ أَكْبَرُ قَدْ

بَيَّنَّا لَكُمُ الْآيَاتِ إِنْ كُنْتُمْ

تَعْقِلُونَ ۝ هَاأَنْتُمْ أُولَاءِ تُحِبُّونَهُمْ

وَلَا يُحِبُّونَكُمْ وَتُؤْمِنُونَ بِالْكِتَابِ

كُلِّهِ وَإِذَا لَقُوكُمْ قَالُوا آمَنَّا

وَإِذَا خَلَوْا عَضُّوا عَلَيْكُمُ الْأَنَامِلَ

مِنَ الْغَيْظِ قُلْ مُوتُوا بِغَيْظِكُمْ

إِنَّ اللَّهَ عَلِيمٌ بِذَاتِ الصُّدُورِ ۝

إِنْ تَمْسَسْكُمْ حَسَنَةٌ تَسُؤْهُمْ

(for ever).

117. What they spend in the life of this (material) world may be likened to a wind which brings a nipping frost: it strikes and destroys the harvest of men who have wronged their own souls: it is not Allah that has wronged them, but they wrong themselves.

118. O you who believe! Take not into your intimacy those outside your ranks: they will not fail to corrupt you. They only desire your ruin: rank hatred has already appeared from their mouths:

خَلِدُونَ ۞ مَثَلُ مَا يُنْفِقُونَ

فِى هٰذِهِ الْحَيٰوةِ الدُّنْيَا كَمَثَلِ

رِيحٍ فِيهَا صِرٌّ أَصَابَتْ حَرْثَ

قَوْمٍ ظَلَمُوٓا أَنْفُسَهُمْ فَأَهْلَكَتْهُ

وَمَا ظَلَمَهُمُ اللَّهُ وَلٰكِنْ أَنْفُسَهُمْ

يَظْلِمُونَ ۞ يٰٓأَيُّهَا الَّذِينَ اٰمَنُوا

لَا تَتَّخِذُوا بِطَانَةً مِّنْ دُونِكُمْ

لَا يَأْلُونَكُمْ خَبَالًا وَدُّوا مَا عَنِتُّمْ

قَدْ بَدَتِ الْبَغْضَاءُ مِنْ أَفْوَاهِهِمْ

and the Last Day; they enjoin what is right, and forbid what is wrong; and they hasten (in emulation) in (all) good works: they are in the ranks of the righteous.

115. Of the good that they do, nothing will be rejected of them; for Allah knows well those that do right.

116. Those who reject Faith, - neither their possessions nor their (numerous) progeny will avail them anything against Allah: they will be Companions of the Fire, - dwelling therein

وَالْيَوْمِ الْاٰخِرِ وَيَاْمُرُوْنَ
بِالْمَعْرُوْفِ وَيَنْهَوْنَ عَنِ الْمُنْكَرِ
وَيُسَارِعُوْنَ فِى الْخَيْرٰتِ ۚ وَاُولٰٓئِكَ
مِنَ الصّٰلِحِيْنَ ۝ وَمَا يَفْعَلُوْا مِنْ
خَيْرٍ فَلَنْ يُّكْفَرُوْهُ ؕ وَاللّٰهُ
عَلِيْمٌۢ بِالْمُتَّقِيْنَ ۝ اِنَّ الَّذِيْنَ
كَفَرُوْا لَنْ تُغْنِىَ عَنْهُمْ اَمْوَالُهُمْ
وَلَاۤ اَوْلَادُهُمْ مِّنَ اللّٰهِ شَيْئًا ؕ
وَاُولٰٓئِكَ اَصْحٰبُ النَّارِ ۚ هُمْ فِيْهَا

Part-4 9 Ale-Imran- 3

men; they draw on themselves wrath from Allah, and pitched over them is (the tent of) destitution. This because they rejected the Signs of Allah, and slew the prophets in defiance of right; this because they rebelled and transgressed beyond bounds.

113. Not all of them are alike: of the People of the Book are a portion that stand (for the right): they rehearse the Signs of Allah all night long, and they prostrate themselves in adora-tion.

114. They believe in Allah

النَّاسِ وَبَآءُوۡ بِغَضَبٍ مِّنَ

اللّٰهِ وَضُرِبَتۡ عَلَيۡهِمُ الۡمَسۡكَنَةُ ؕ

ذٰلِكَ بِاَنَّهُمۡ كَانُوۡا يَكۡفُرُوۡنَ

بِاٰيٰتِ اللّٰهِ وَيَقۡتُلُوۡنَ الۡاَنۡۢبِيَآءَ

بِغَيۡرِ حَقٍّ ؕ ذٰلِكَ بِمَا عَصَوۡا

وَّكَانُوۡا يَعۡتَدُوۡنَ ۝ لَيۡسُوۡا سَوَآءً ؕ

مِنۡ اَهۡلِ الۡكِتٰبِ اُمَّةٌ قَآئِمَةٌ

يَّتۡلُوۡنَ اٰيٰتِ اللّٰهِ اٰنَآءَ الَّيۡلِ

وَهُمۡ يَسۡجُدُوۡنَ ۝ يُؤۡمِنُوۡنَ بِاللّٰهِ

enjoining what is right, forbidding what is wrong, and believing
in Allah. If only the People of the
Book had faith, it were best for
them: among them are some who
have faith, but most of them are
perverted transgressors.

111. They will do you no harm,
barring a trifling annoyance; if
they come out to fight you, they
will show you their backs, and no
help shall they get.

112. Shame is pitched over them
(like a tent) wherever they are
found, except when under a
covenant (of protection) from
Allah and from

تَأْمُرُوْنَ بِالْمَعْرُوْفِ وَتَنْهَوْنَ

عَنِ الْمُنْكَرِ وَتُؤْمِنُوْنَ بِاللّٰهِ ۗ وَلَوْ

اٰمَنَ اَهْلُ الْكِتٰبِ لَكَانَ خَيْرًا

لَّهُمْ ۗ مِنْهُمُ الْمُؤْمِنُوْنَ وَاَكْثَرُهُمُ

الْفٰسِقُوْنَ ۞ لَنْ يَّضُرُّوْكُمْ اِلَّا اَذًى ۗ

وَاِنْ يُّقَاتِلُوْكُمْ يُوَلُّوْكُمُ الْاَدْبَارَ ۫

ثُمَّ لَا يُنْصَرُوْنَ ۞ ضُرِبَتْ

عَلَيْهِمُ الذِّلَّةُ اَيْنَ مَا ثُقِفُوْۤا

اِلَّا بِحَبْلٍ مِّنَ اللّٰهِ وَحَبْلٍ مِّنَ

the Chastisement for rejecting Faith."

107. But those whose faces will be (lit with) white, - they will be in (the light of) Allah's mercy: therein to dwell (for ever).

108. These are the Signs of Allah: We rehearse them to you in Truth: and Allah means no injustice to any of His creatures.

109. To Allah belongs all that is in the heavens and on earth: to Him do all questions go back (for decision).

110. You are the best of Peoples, evolved for mankind,

الْعَذَابُ بِمَا كُنْتُمْ تَكْفُرُوْنَ ۞

وَاَمَّا الَّذِيْنَ ابْيَضَّتْ وُجُوْهُهُمْ

فَفِيْ رَحْمَةِ اللّٰهِ ۖ هُمْ فِيْهَا

خٰلِدُوْنَ ۞ تِلْكَ اٰيٰتُ اللّٰهِ

نَتْلُوْهَا عَلَيْكَ بِالْحَقِّ ۗ وَمَا اللّٰهُ

يُرِيْدُ ظُلْمًا لِّلْعٰلَمِيْنَ ۞ وَلِلّٰهِ

مَا فِي السَّمٰوٰتِ وَمَا فِي الْاَرْضِ ۗ

وَاِلَى اللّٰهِ تُرْجَعُ الْاُمُوْرُ ۞ كُنْتُمْ

خَيْرَ اُمَّةٍ اُخْرِجَتْ لِلنَّاسِ

that is good, enjoining what is right, and forbidding what is wrong: they are the ones to attain felicity.

105. Be not like those who are divided amongst themselves and fall into disputations after receiving Clear Signs: for them is a dreadful Chastisement, -

106. On the Day when some faces will be (lit up with) white, and some faces will be (in the gloom of) black: to those whose faces will be black, (will be said): "Did you reject Faith after accepting it? Taste then

الْخَيْرِ وَيَأْمُرُونَ بِالْمَعْرُوفِ

وَيَنْهَوْنَ عَنِ الْمُنْكَرِ وَأُولٰٓئِكَ

هُمُ الْمُفْلِحُوْنَ ۞ وَلَا تَكُوْنُوْا

كَالَّذِيْنَ تَفَرَّقُوْا وَاخْتَلَفُوْا مِنْ

بَعْدِ مَا جَاءَهُمُ الْبَيِّنٰتُ ۖ وَأُولٰٓئِكَ

لَهُمْ عَذَابٌ عَظِيْمٌ ۞ يَوْمَ تَبْيَضُّ

وُجُوهٌ وَّتَسْوَدُّ وُجُوهٌ ۚ فَأَمَّا

الَّذِيْنَ اسْوَدَّتْ وُجُوهُهُمْ

أَكَفَرْتُمْ بَعْدَ إِيْمَانِكُمْ فَذُوْقُوا

a state of Islam.

103. And hold fast, all together, by the rope which Allah (stretches out for you), and be not divided among yourselves; and remember with gratitude Allah's favour on you; for you were enemies and He joined your hearts in love, so that by His Grace, you became brethren; and you were on the brink of the pit of Fire, and He saved you from it. Thus does Allah make His Signs clear to you: that you may be guided.

104. Let there arise out of you a band of people inviting to all

مُسْلِمُوْنَ ۝ وَاعْتَصِمُوْا بِحَبْلِ

اللّٰهِ جَمِيْعًا وَّلَا تَفَرَّقُوْا ۪ وَاذْكُرُوْا

نِعْمَتَ اللّٰهِ عَلَيْكُمْ اِذْ كُنْتُمْ

اَعْدَآءً فَاَلَّفَ بَيْنَ قُلُوْبِكُمْ

فَاَصْبَحْتُمْ بِنِعْمَتِهٖٓ اِخْوَانًا ۚ وَكُنْتُمْ

عَلٰى شَفَا حُفْرَةٍ مِّنَ النَّارِ

فَاَنْقَذَكُمْ مِّنْهَا ۗ كَذٰلِكَ يُبَيِّنُ اللّٰهُ

لَكُمْ اٰيٰتِهٖ لَعَلَّكُمْ تَهْتَدُوْنَ ۝

وَلْتَكُنْ مِّنْكُمْ اُمَّةٌ يَّدْعُوْنَ اِلَى

100. O you who believe! If you listen to a faction among the People of the Book, they would (indeed) render you apostates after you have believed!

101. And how would you deny Faith while unto you are rehearsed the Signs of Allah, and among you lives the Apostle? Whoever holds firmly to Allah will be shown a way that is straight.

102. O you who believe! Fear Allah as He should be feared, and die not except in

يَا أَيُّهَا الَّذِينَ آمَنُوا إِن تُطِيعُوا

فَرِيقًا مِّنَ الَّذِينَ أُوتُوا الْكِتَبَ

يَرُدُّوكُم بَعْدَ إِيمَانِكُمْ كَفِرِينَ ۞

وَكَيْفَ تَكْفُرُونَ وَأَنتُمْ تُتْلَى

عَلَيْكُمْ آيَتُ اللَّهِ وَفِيكُمْ رَسُولُهُ

وَمَن يَّعْتَصِم بِاللَّهِ فَقَدْ هُدِىَ

إِلَى صِرَاطٍ مُّسْتَقِيمٍ ۞ يَا أَيُّهَا

الَّذِينَ آمَنُوا اتَّقُوا اللَّهَ حَقَّ

تُقَاتِهِ وَلَا تَمُوتُنَّ إِلَّا وَأَنتُم

those who can afford the journey; but if any deny Faith, Allah stands not in need of any of His creatures.

98. Say: "O People of the Book! Why reject you the Signs of Allah, when Allah is Himself witness to all you do?"

99. Say: "O you People of the Book! Why obstruct you those who believe, from the path of Allah, seeking to make it crooked, while you were your-selves witnesses (to Allah's Covenant)? But Allah is not unmindful of all that you do."

حِجُّ الْبَيْتِ مَنِ اسْتَطَاعَ إِلَيْهِ
سَبِيلًا ۚ وَمَنْ كَفَرَ فَإِنَّ اللهَ
غَنِيٌّ عَنِ الْعَلَمِينَ ۝ قُلْ يٰٓأَهْلَ
الْكِتٰبِ لِمَ تَكْفُرُوْنَ بِاٰيٰتِ اللهِ
وَاللهُ شَهِيْدٌ عَلٰى مَا تَعْمَلُوْنَ
۝ قُلْ يٰٓأَهْلَ الْكِتٰبِ لِمَ تَصُدُّوْنَ
عَنْ سَبِيْلِ اللهِ مَنْ اٰمَنَ
تَبْغُوْنَهَا عِوَجًا وَّأَنْتُمْ شُهَدَآءُ ۚ
وَمَا اللهُ بِغَافِلٍ عَمَّا تَعْمَلُوْنَ ۝

a lie and attribute it to Allah, they are indeed unjust wrong-doers.

95. Say: "Allah speaks the Truth: follow the religion of Abraham, the staunch in faith; he was not of the Pagans."

96. The first House (of worship) appointed for men was that at Bakka (Makkah); full of blessing and of guidance for all kinds of beings.

97. In it are Signs Manifest; (for example), the Station of Abraham; whoever enters it attains security; pilgrimage thereto is a duty men owe to Allah, -

اللهِ الْكَذِبَ مِنْۢ بَعْدِ ذٰلِكَ

فَاُولٰٓئِكَ هُمُ الظّٰلِمُوْنَ ۞ قُلْ

صَدَقَ اللهُ فَاتَّبِعُوْا مِلَّةَ اِبْرٰهِيْمَ

حَنِيْفًا ؕ وَمَا كَانَ مِنَ الْمُشْرِكِيْنَ ۞

اِنَّ اَوَّلَ بَيْتٍ وُّضِعَ لِلنَّاسِ

لَلَّذِيْ بِبَكَّةَ مُبٰرَكًا وَّهُدًى

لِّلْعٰلَمِيْنَ ۞ فِيْهِ اٰيٰتٌۢ بَيِّنٰتٌ

مَّقَامُ اِبْرٰهِيْمَ ۚ وَمَنْ دَخَلَهٗ

كَانَ اٰمِنًا ؕ وَلِلّٰهِ عَلَى النَّاسِ

92. By no means shall you attain righteousness unless you give (freely) of that which you love; and whatever you give, of a truth Allah knows it well.

93. All food was lawful to the Children of Israel, except what Israel made unlawful for himself, before the Law (of Moses) was revealed. Say: "Bring you the Law and study it, if you be men of truth."

94. If any, after this, invent

لَنْ تَنَالُوا الْبِرَّ حَتّٰى تُنْفِقُوا

مِمَّا تُحِبُّونَ ۚ وَمَا تُنْفِقُوا مِنْ

شَيْءٍ فَاِنَّ اللهَ بِهٖ عَلِيْمٌ ۞

كُلُّ الطَّعَامِ كَانَ حِلًّا لِّبَنِيْٓ

اِسْرَآءِيْلَ اِلَّا مَا حَرَّمَ اِسْرَآءِيْلُ

عَلٰى نَفْسِهٖ مِنْ قَبْلِ اَنْ

تُنَزَّلَ التَّوْرٰىةُ ۚ قُلْ فَاْتُوا

بِالتَّوْرٰىةِ فَاتْلُوْهَآ اِنْ كُنْتُمْ

صٰدِقِيْنَ ۞ فَمَنِ افْتَرٰى عَلَى

ذَ ٰلِكَ الْكِتَابُ لَا رَيْبَ فِيهِ

پارہ

لَن تَنَالُوا

(۴)

بِسْمِ اللَّهِ الرَّحْمَٰنِ الرَّحِيمِ

PART 5
Wal-Muhsanaat

hypocrites will be in the lowest depths of the Fire: no helper will you find for them; -

146. Except for those who repent, mend (their lives), hold fast to Allah, and purify their religion as in Allah's sight: if so they will be (numbered) with the believers. And soon will Allah grant to the believers a reward of immense value.

147. What can Allah gain by your punishment, if you are grateful and you believe? No, it is Allah that recogniseth (all good), and knows all things.

الْمُنَفِقِينَ فِي الدَّرْكِ الْأَسْفَلِ مِنَ

النَّارِ وَلَنْ تَجِدَ لَهُمْ نَصِيرًا ۝

إِلَّا الَّذِينَ تَابُوا وَأَصْلَحُوا

وَاعْتَصَمُوا بِاللَّهِ وَأَخْلَصُوا دِينَهُمْ

لِلَّهِ فَأُولَٰئِكَ مَعَ الْمُؤْمِنِينَ

وَسَوْفَ يُؤْتِ اللَّهُ الْمُؤْمِنِينَ

أَجْرًا عَظِيمًا ۝ مَا يَفْعَلُ اللَّهُ

بِعَذَابِكُمْ إِنْ شَكَرْتُمْ وَآمَنْتُمْ

وَكَانَ اللَّهُ شَاكِرًا عَلِيمًا ۝

prayer, they stand without earnestness, to be seen of men, but little do they hold Allah in remembrance;

143. (They are) distracted in mind even in the midst of it, - being (sincerely) for neither one group nor for another. Whom Allah leaves straying, - never will you find for him the way.

144. O you who believe! Take not for friends unbelievers rather than believers: do you wish to offer Allah an open proof against yourselves?

145. The

الصَّلٰوةِ قَامُوْا كُسَالٰى ۙ يُرَآءُوْنَ

النَّاسَ وَلَا يَذْكُرُوْنَ اللّٰهَ اِلَّا

قَلِيْلًا ۖ ۞ مُّذَبْذَبِيْنَ بَيْنَ ذٰلِكَ ۖ

لَاۤ اِلٰى هٰؤُلَاۤءِ وَلَاۤ اِلٰى هٰؤُلَاۤءِ ۗ

وَمَنْ يُّضْلِلِ اللّٰهُ فَلَنْ تَجِدَ لَهٗ

سَبِيْلًا ۞ يٰۤاَيُّهَا الَّذِيْنَ اٰمَنُوْا لَا

تَتَّخِذُوا الْكٰفِرِيْنَ اَوْلِيَاۤءَ مِنْ دُوْنِ

الْمُؤْمِنِيْنَ ۚ اَتُرِيْدُوْنَ اَنْ تَجْعَلُوْا

لِلّٰهِ عَلَيْكُمْ سُلْطٰنًا مُّبِيْنًا ۞ اِنَّ

you do gain a victory from Allah, they say: "Were we not with you?"- but if the unbelievers gain a success, they say (to them): "Did we not gain an advantage over you, and did we not guard you from the believers?" But Allah will judge between you on the Day of Judgment. And never will Allah grant to the unbelievers a way (to triumph) over the believers.

142. The hypocrites - they think they are over-reaching Allah, but He will over-reach them: when they stand up to

كَانَ لَكُمْ فَتْحٌ مِّنَ اللهِ قَالُوٓا

اَلَمْ نَكُنْ مَّعَكُمْ ۖ وَاِنْ كَانَ

لِلْكٰفِرِيْنَ نَصِيْبٌ ۙ قَالُوٓا اَلَمْ

نَسْتَحْوِذْ عَلَيْكُمْ وَنَمْنَعْكُمْ مِّنَ

الْمُؤْمِنِيْنَ ۚ فَاللهُ يَحْكُمُ بَيْنَكُمْ

يَوْمَ الْقِيٰمَةِ ۗ وَلَنْ يَّجْعَلَ اللهُ

لِلْكٰفِرِيْنَ عَلَى الْمُؤْمِنِيْنَ سَبِيْلًا ۟ ﴿١٤١﴾

اِنَّ الْمُنٰفِقِيْنَ يُخٰدِعُوْنَ اللهَ

وَهُوَ خَادِعُهُمْ ۚ وَاِذَا قَامُوٓا اِلَى

among them? No, - all honour is with Allah.

140. Already has He sent you Word in the Book, that when you hear the signs of Allah held in defiance and ridicule, you are not to sit with them unless they turn to a different theme: if you did, you would be like them. For Allah will collect the hypocrites and those who defy Faith - all in Hell: -

141. (These are) the ones who wait and watch about you: if

عِنْدَهُمُ الْعِزَّةَ فَإِنَّ الْعِزَّةَ لِلّٰهِ

جَمِيْعًا ۗ وَقَدْ نَزَّلَ عَلَيْكُمْ فِى

الْكِتٰبِ اَنْ اِذَا سَمِعْتُمْ اٰيٰتِ

اللّٰهِ يُكْفَرُ بِهَا وَيُسْتَهْزَاُ بِهَا فَلَا

تَقْعُدُوْا مَعَهُمْ حَتّٰى يَخُوْضُوْا فِىْ

حَدِيْثٍ غَيْرِهٖ ۖ اِنَّكُمْ اِذًا مِّثْلُهُمْ ۗ

اِنَّ اللّٰهَ جَامِعُ الْمُنٰفِقِيْنَ

وَالْكٰفِرِيْنَ فِىْ جَهَنَّمَ جَمِيْعَا ۙ

الَّذِيْنَ يَتَرَبَّصُوْنَ بِكُمْ ۖ فَاِنْ

His Books, His Apostles, and the Day of Judgment, has gone far, far astray.

137. Those who believe, then reject Faith, then believe (again) and (again) reject Faith, and go on increasing in unbelief, - Allah will not forgive them nor guide them on the way.

138. To the hypocrites give the glad tidings that there is for them (but) a grievous Chastisement;

139. Yes, to those who take for friends unbelievers rather than believers: is it honour they seek

وَكُتُبِهٖ وَرُسُلِهٖ وَالْيَوْمِ الْاٰخِرِ

فَقَدْ ضَلَّ ضَلٰلًا بَعِيْدًا ۞ اِنَّ

الَّذِيْنَ اٰمَنُوْا ثُمَّ كَفَرُوْا ثُمَّ

اٰمَنُوْا ثُمَّ كَفَرُوْا ثُمَّ ازْدَادُوْا

كُفْرًا لَّمْ يَكُنِ اللّٰهُ لِيَغْفِرَ لَهُمْ

وَلَا لِيَهْدِيَهُمْ سَبِيْلًا ۞ بَشِّرِ

الْمُنٰفِقِيْنَ بِاَنَّ لَهُمْ عَذَابًا اَلِيْمًا ۞

الَّذِيْنَ يَتَّخِذُوْنَ الْكٰفِرِيْنَ اَوْلِيَآءَ

مِنْ دُوْنِ الْمُؤْمِنِيْنَ ۚ اَيَبْتَغُوْنَ

or your kin, and whether it be (against) rich or poor: for Allah can best protect both. Follow not the lusts (of your hearts), lest you swerve, and if you distort (justice) or decline to do justice, verily Allah is Well-Acquainted with all that you do.

136. O you who believe! Believe in Allah and His Apostle, and the scripture which He has sent to His Apostle and the scripture which He sent to those before (him). Any who denies Allah, His Angels,

وَالْاَقْرَبِيْنَ ۚ اِنْ يَّكُنْ غَنِيًّا اَوْ

فَقِيْرًا فَاللّٰهُ اَوْلٰى بِهِمَا ۚ فَلَا

تَتَّبِعُوا الْهَوٰٓى اَنْ تَعْدِلُوْا ۚ وَاِنْ

تَلْوٗٓا اَوْ تُعْرِضُوْا فَاِنَّ اللّٰهَ كَانَ

بِمَا تَعْمَلُوْنَ خَبِيْرًا ۝ يٰٓاَيُّهَا

الَّذِيْنَ اٰمَنُوْٓا اٰمِنُوْا بِاللّٰهِ وَرَسُوْلِهٖ

وَالْكِتٰبِ الَّذِيْ نَزَّلَ عَلٰى رَسُوْلِهٖ

وَالْكِتٰبِ الَّذِيْٓ اَنْزَلَ مِنْ قَبْلُ ۚ

وَمَنْ يَّكْفُرْ بِاللّٰهِ وَمَلٰٓئِكَتِهٖ

Allah to carry through all affairs.

133. If it were His will, He could destroy you, O mankind, and create another race; for He has power this to do.

134. If any one desires a reward in this life, in Allah's (gift) is the reward (both) of this life and of the hereafter: for Allah is He that hears and sees (all things).

135. O you who believe! stand out firmly for justice, as witnesses to Allah, even as against your-selves, or your parents,

بِاللّٰهِ وَكِيلًا ۞ اِنْ يَّشَاْ يُذْهِبْكُمْ

اَيُّهَا النَّاسُ وَيَاْتِ بِاٰخَرِيْنَ ؕ

وَكَانَ اللّٰهُ عَلٰى ذٰلِكَ قَدِيْرًا ۞

مَنْ كَانَ يُرِيْدُ ثَوَابَ الدُّنْيَا

فَعِنْدَ اللّٰهِ ثَوَابُ الدُّنْيَا وَالْاٰخِرَةِ ؕ

وَكَانَ اللّٰهُ سَمِيْعًۢا بَصِيْرًا ۞

يٰٓاَيُّهَا الَّذِيْنَ اٰمَنُوْا كُوْنُوْا

قَوّٰمِيْنَ بِالْقِسْطِ شُهَدَآءَ لِلّٰهِ

وَلَوْ عَلٰٓى اَنْفُسِكُمْ اَوِ الْوَالِدَيْنِ

from His all-reaching bounty: for Allah is He that cares for all and is Wise.

131. To Allah belong all things in the heavens and on earth. Verily We have directed the People of the Book before you, and you (O Muslims) to fear Allah. But if you deny Him, lo! unto Allah belong all things in the heavens and on earth, and Allah is free of all wants, worthy of all praise.

132. Yes, unto Allah belong all things in the heavens and on earth, and enough is

مِّنْ سَعَتِهٖ ۚ وَكَانَ اللّٰهُ وَاسِعًا

حَكِيْمًا ۞ وَلِلّٰهِ مَا فِى السَّمٰوٰتِ

وَمَا فِى الْاَرْضِ ۗ وَلَقَدْ وَصَّيْنَا

الَّذِيْنَ اُوْتُوا الْكِتٰبَ مِنْ قَبْلِكُمْ

وَاِيَّاكُمْ اَنِ اتَّقُوا اللّٰهَ ۚ وَاِنْ

تَكْفُرُوْا فَاِنَّ لِلّٰهِ مَا فِى السَّمٰوٰتِ

وَمَا فِى الْاَرْضِ ۗ وَكَانَ اللّٰهُ

غَنِيًّا حَمِيْدًا ۞ وَلِلّٰهِ مَا فِى

السَّمٰوٰتِ وَمَا فِى الْاَرْضِ ۗ وَكَفٰى

even though men's souls are swayed by greed. But if you do good and practise self-restraint, Allah is Well-Acquainted with all that you do.

129. You are never able to be fair and just as between women, even if it is your ardent desire: but turn not away (from one) altogether, so as to leave her (as it were) hanging (in the air). If you come to a friendly understanding, and practise self-restraint, Allah is Oft-Forgiving, Most Merciful.

130. But if they disagree (and must part), Allah will provide abundance for all

وَاُحْضِرَتِ الْاَنْفُسُ الشُّحَّ ۚ وَاِنْ
تُحْسِنُوْا وَتَتَّقُوْا فَاِنَّ اللّٰهَ
كَانَ بِمَا تَعْمَلُوْنَ خَبِيْرًا ۝
وَلَنْ تَسْتَطِيْعُوْۤا اَنْ تَعْدِلُوْا
بَيْنَ النِّسَآءِ وَلَوْ حَرَصْتُمْ فَلَا
تَمِيْلُوْا كُلَّ الْمَيْلِ فَتَذَرُوْهَا
كَالْمُعَلَّقَةِ ۚ وَاِنْ تُصْلِحُوْا وَتَتَّقُوْا
فَاِنَّ اللّٰهَ كَانَ غَفُوْرًا رَّحِيْمًا ۝
وَاِنْ يَّتَفَرَّقَا يُغْنِ اللّٰهُ كُلًّا

the portions prescribed, and yet whom you desire to marry, as also concerning the children who are weak and oppressed: that you stand firm for justice to orphans. There is not a good deed which you do, but Allah is Well-Acquainted therewith.

128. If a wife fears cruelty or desertion on her husband's part, there is no blame on them if they arrange an amicable settlement between themselves; and such settlement is best;

مَا كُتِبَ لَهُنَّ وَتَرْغَبُوْنَ اَنْ

تَنْكِحُوْهُنَّ وَالْمُسْتَضْعَفِيْنَ

مِنَ الْوِلْدَانِ وَاَنْ تَقُوْمُوْا

لِلْيَتٰمٰى بِالْقِسْطِ ۚ وَمَا تَفْعَلُوْا

مِنْ خَيْرٍ فَاِنَّ اللّٰهَ كَانَ بِهٖ

عَلِيْمًا ۝ وَاِنِ امْرَاَةٌ خَافَتْ

مِنْۢ بَعْلِهَا نُشُوْزًا اَوْ اِعْرَاضًا

فَلَا جُنَاحَ عَلَيْهِمَآ اَنْ يُّصْلِحَا

بَيْنَهُمَا صُلْحًا ؕ وَالصُّلْحُ خَيْرٌ

his whole self to Allah, does good, and follows the way of Abraham the true in Faith? For Allah did take Abraham for a friend.

126. But to Allah belong all things in the heavens and on earth: and He it is that encompasses all things.

127. They ask your instruction concerning the women. Say: Allah does instruct you about them: and (remember) what has been rehearsed unto you in the Book, concerning the orphans of women to whom you give not

وَجْهَهُ لِلّٰهِ وَهُوَ مُحْسِنٌ

وَّاتَّبَعَ مِلَّةَ اِبْرٰهِيْمَ حَنِيْفًا ۗ

وَاتَّخَذَ اللّٰهُ اِبْرٰهِيْمَ خَلِيْلًا ۝

وَلِلّٰهِ مَا فِى السَّمٰوٰتِ وَمَا فِى

الْاَرْضِ ۗ وَكَانَ اللّٰهُ بِكُلِّ شَىْءٍ

مُّحِيْطًا ۝ وَيَسْتَفْتُوْنَكَ فِى النِّسَآءِ ۗ

قُلِ اللّٰهُ يُفْتِيْكُمْ فِيْهِنَّ ۙ وَمَا

يُتْلٰى عَلَيْكُمْ فِى الْكِتٰبِ فِىْ

يَتٰمَى النِّسَآءِ الّٰتِىْ لَا تُؤْتُوْنَهُنَّ

123. Not your desires, nor those of the People of the Book (can prevail): whoever works evil, will be requited accordingly. Nor will he find, besides Allah, any protector or helper.

124. If any do deeds of righteousness, - be they male or female - and have faith, they will enter Heaven, and not the least injustice will be done to them.

125. Who can be better in religion than one who submits

قِيلًا ۞ لَيْسَ بِأَمَانِيِّكُمْ وَلَا

أَمَانِيِّ أَهْلِ الْكِتَٰبِ مَنْ

يَّعْمَلْ سُوٓءًا يُّجْزَ بِهِۦ وَلَا

يَجِدْ لَهُۥ مِنْ دُونِ اللَّهِ وَلِيًّا

وَّلَا نَصِيرًا ۞ وَمَنْ يَّعْمَلْ مِنَ

الصَّٰلِحَٰتِ مِنْ ذَكَرٍ أَوْ أُنثَىٰ

وَهُوَ مُؤْمِنٌ فَأُو۟لَٰٓئِكَ يَدْخُلُونَ

الْجَنَّةَ وَلَا يُظْلَمُونَ نَقِيرًا ۞

وَمَنْ أَحْسَنُ دِينًا مِّمَّنْ أَسْلَمَ

suffered a loss that is manifest.

120. Satan makes them promises, and creates in them false desires; but Satan's promises are nothing but deception.

121. They (his dupes) will have their dwelling in Hell, and from it they will find no way of escape.

122. But those who believe and do deeds of righteousness, - We shall soon admit them to Gardens, with rivers flowing beneath, - to dwell therein for ever. Allah's promise is the truth, and whose word can be truer than Allah's?

خَسِرَ خُسْرَانًا مُّبِينًا ۙ يَعِدُهُمْ

وَيُمَنِّيهِمْ ۖ وَمَا يَعِدُهُمُ الشَّيْطٰنُ

إِلَّا غُرُورًا ۞ أُولٰٓئِكَ مَأْوٰىهُمْ

جَهَنَّمُ ۚ وَلَا يَجِدُونَ عَنْهَا

مَحِيصًا ۞ وَالَّذِينَ اٰمَنُوا وَعَمِلُوا

الصّٰلِحٰتِ سَنُدْخِلُهُمْ جَنّٰتٍ

تَجْرِي مِنْ تَحْتِهَا الْأَنْهٰرُ

خٰلِدِينَ فِيهَا أَبَدًا ۚ وَعْدَ اللّٰهِ

حَقًّا ۚ وَمَنْ أَصْدَقُ مِنَ اللّٰهِ

leaving Him, call but upon female deities: they call but upon Satan the persistent rebel!

118. Allah did curse him, but he said: "I will take of Your servants a portion marked off;

119. "I will mislead them, and I will create in them false desires; I will order them to slit the ears of cattle, and to deface the (fair) nature created by Allah." Whoever, forsaking Allah, takes Satan for a friend, has of a surety

يَّدْعُوْنَ مِنْ دُوْنِهٖٓ اِلَّآ اِنَاثًا ۚ

وَاِنْ يَّدْعُوْنَ اِلَّا شَيْطٰنًا

مَّرِيْدًا ۙ ۞ لَّعَنَهُ اللّٰهُ ۘ وَقَالَ

لَاَتَّخِذَنَّ مِنْ عِبَادِكَ نَصِيْبًا

مَّفْرُوْضًا ۙ ۞ وَّلَاُضِلَّنَّهُمْ وَلَاُمَنِّيَنَّهُمْ

وَلَاٰمُرَنَّهُمْ فَلَيُبَتِّكُنَّ اٰذَانَ

الْاَنْعَامِ وَلَاٰمُرَنَّهُمْ فَلَيُغَيِّرُنَّ

خَلْقَ اللّٰهِ ۚ وَمَنْ يَّتَّخِذِ الشَّيْطٰنَ

وَلِيًّا مِّنْ دُوْنِ اللّٰهِ فَقَدْ

a reward of the highest (value).

115. If anyone contends with the Apostle even after guidance has been plainly conveyed to him, and follows a path other than that becoming to men of Faith, We shall leave him in the path he has chosen, and land him in Hell,- what an evil refuge!

116. Allah forgives not (the sin of) joining other gods with Him; but He forgives whom He pleases other sins than this: one who joins other gods with Allah has strayed far, far away (from the right).

117. (The Pagans),

أَجْرًا عَظِيمًا ۝ وَمَنْ يُّشَاقِقِ

الرَّسُولَ مِنْ بَعْدِ مَا تَبَيَّنَ

لَهُ الْهُدَى وَيَتَّبِعْ غَيْرَ سَبِيلِ

الْمُؤْمِنِينَ نُوَلِّهِ مَا تَوَلَّى وَنُصْلِهِ

جَهَنَّمَ ۚ وَسَآءَتْ مَصِيرًا ۝ إِنَّ

اللَّهَ لَا يَغْفِرُ أَنْ يُّشْرَكَ بِهِ

وَيَغْفِرُ مَا دُونَ ذٰلِكَ لِمَنْ

يَّشَآءُ ۚ وَمَنْ يُّشْرِكْ بِاللَّهِ فَقَدْ

ضَلَّ ضَلٰلًا بَعِيدًا ۝ إِنْ

their own souls astray, and to you they can do no harm in the least. For Allah has sent down to you the Book and wisdom and taught you what you knew not (before): and great is the Grace of Allah unto you.

114. In most of their secret talks there is no good: but if one exhorts to a deed of charity or justice or conciliation between men, (secrecy is permissible): to him who does this, seeking the good pleasure of Allah, We shall soon give

إِلَّآ أَنفُسَهُمْ وَمَا يَضُرُّونَكَ مِن

شَىْءٍ وَأَنزَلَ اللَّهُ عَلَيْكَ الْكِتَٰبَ

وَالْحِكْمَةَ وَعَلَّمَكَ مَا لَمْ تَكُنْ

تَعْلَمُ وَكَانَ فَضْلُ اللَّهِ عَلَيْكَ

عَظِيمًا ۞ لَّا خَيْرَ فِى كَثِيرٍ مِّن

نَّجْوَىٰهُمْ إِلَّا مَنْ أَمَرَ بِصَدَقَةٍ

أَوْ مَعْرُوفٍ أَوْ إِصْلَٰحٍ بَيْنَ

النَّاسِ وَمَن يَفْعَلْ ذَٰلِكَ ابْتِغَآءَ

مَرْضَاتِ اللَّهِ فَسَوْفَ نُؤْتِيهِ

Allah Oft-Forgiving, Most Merciful.

111. And if any one earns sin, he earns it against his own soul: for Allah is full of knowledge and wisdom.

112. But if any one earns a fault or a sin and throws it on to one that is innocent, he carries (on himself) (both) a falsehood and a flagrant sin.

113. But for the Grace of Allah to you and his Mercy, a party of them would certainly have plotted to lead you astray. But (in fact) they will only lead

الله غَفُورًا رَّحِيمًا ۞ وَمَن

يَّكْسِبْ اِثْمًا فَاِنَّمَا يَكْسِبُهُ

عَلٰى نَفْسِهِ ۖ وَكَانَ اللهُ عَلِيْمًا

حَكِيْمًا ۞ وَمَنْ يَّكْسِبْ خَطِيْئَةً

اَوْ اِثْمًا ثُمَّ يَرْمِ بِهٖ بَرِيْئًا

فَقَدِ احْتَمَلَ بُهْتَانًا وَّاِثْمًا

مُّبِيْنًا ۞ وَلَوْلَا فَضْلُ اللهِ

عَلَيْكَ وَرَحْمَتُهٗ لَهَمَّتْ طَّآئِفَةٌ

مِّنْهُمْ اَنْ يُّضِلُّوْكَ ۖ وَمَا يُضِلُّوْنَ

seeing that He is in their midst when they plot by night, in words that He cannot approve: and Allah does compass round all that they do.

109. Ah! These are the sort of men on whose behalf you may contend in this world; but who will contend with Allah on their behalf on the Day of Judgment, or who will carry their affairs through?

110. If any one does evil or wrongs his own soul but afterwards seeks Allah's forgiveness, he will find

وَهُوَ مَعَهُمْ إِذْ يُبَيِّتُوْنَ مَا

لَا يَرْضٰى مِنَ الْقَوْلِ ؕ وَكَانَ

اللّٰهُ بِمَا يَعْمَلُوْنَ مُحِيْطًا ۝

هٰٓاَنْتُمْ هٰٓؤُلَآءِ جٰدَلْتُمْ عَنْهُمْ

فِى الْحَيٰوةِ الدُّنْيَا ۫ فَمَنْ يُّجَادِلُ

اللّٰهَ عَنْهُمْ يَوْمَ الْقِيٰمَةِ اَمْ

مَّنْ يَّكُوْنُ عَلَيْهِمْ وَكِيْلًا ۝

وَمَنْ يَّعْمَلْ سُوْٓءًا اَوْ يَظْلِمْ

نَفْسَهٗ ثُمَّ يَسْتَغْفِرِ اللّٰهَ يَجِدِ

the Book in truth, that you might judge between men, as guided by Allah: so be not (used) as an advocate by those who betray their trust;

106. But seek the forgiveness of Allah; for Allah is Oft-Forgiving, Most Merciful.

107. Contend not on behalf of such as betray their own souls; for Allah loves not one given to perfidy and crime:

108. They may hide (their crimes) from men, but they cannot hide (them) from Allah,

الْكِتَبَ بِالْحَقِّ لِتَحْكُمَ بَيْنَ

النَّاسِ بِمَآ أَرَاكَ اللهُ ۖ وَلَا

تَكُنْ لِلْخَآئِنِينَ خَصِيمًا ۖ

وَّاسْتَغْفِرِ اللهَ ۖ إِنَّ اللهَ كَانَ

غَفُورًا رَّحِيمًا ۖ وَلَا تُجَادِلْ

عَنِ الَّذِينَ يَخْتَانُونَ أَنْفُسَهُمْ ۚ

إِنَّ اللهَ لَا يُحِبُّ مَنْ كَانَ

خَوَّانًا أَثِيمًا ۖ يَّسْتَخْفُونَ مِنَ

النَّاسِ وَلَا يَسْتَخْفُونَ مِنَ اللهِ

or lying down on your sides; but when you are free from danger, set up regular prayers: For such prayers are enjoined on believers at stated times.

104. And slacken not in following up the enemy: if you are suffering hardships, they are suffering similar hardships; but you have hope from Allah, while they have none. And Allah is full of knowledge and wisdom.

105. We have sent down to you

وَّعَلٰى جُنُوبِكُمْ ۚ فَاِذَا اطْمَاْنَنْتُمْ
فَاَقِيْمُوا الصَّلٰوةَ ۚ اِنَّ الصَّلٰوةَ
كَانَتْ عَلَى الْمُؤْمِنِيْنَ كِتٰبًا
مَّوْقُوْتًا ۞ وَلَا تَهِنُوْا فِى ابْتِغَآءِ
الْقَوْمِ ۗ اِنْ تَكُوْنُوْا تَاْلَمُوْنَ
فَاِنَّهُمْ يَاْلَمُوْنَ كَمَا تَاْلَمُوْنَ
وَتَرْجُوْنَ مِنَ اللّٰهِ مَا لَا
يَرْجُوْنَ ۗ وَكَانَ اللّٰهُ عَلِيْمًا
حَكِيْمًا ۞ اِنَّاۤ اَنْزَلْنَاۤ اِلَيْكَ

if you were negligent of your arms and your baggage, to assault you in a single rush. But there is no blame on you if you put away your arms because of the inconvenience of rain or because you are ill; but take (every) precaution for yourselves. For the unbelievers Allah has prepared a humiliating Punishment.

103. When you pass (Congregational) prayers, celebrate Allah's praises, standing, sitting down,

كَفَرُوْا لَوْ تَغْفُلُوْنَ عَنْ أَسْلِحَتِكُمْ

وَ أَمْتِعَتِكُمْ فَيَمِيْلُوْنَ عَلَيْكُمْ

مَّيْلَةً وَّاحِدَةً ۚ وَلَا جُنَاحَ عَلَيْكُمْ

إِنْ كَانَ بِكُمْ أَذًى مِّنْ مَّطَرٍ

أَوْ كُنْتُمْ مَّرْضٰى أَنْ تَضَعُوْۤا

أَسْلِحَتَكُمْ ۚ وَخُذُوْا حِذْرَكُمْ

إِنَّ اللّٰهَ أَعَدَّ لِلْكٰفِرِيْنَ عَذَابًا

مُّهِيْنًا ۞ فَإِذَا قَضَيْتُمُ الصَّلٰوةَ

فَاذْكُرُوا اللّٰهَ قِيٰمًا وَّقُعُوْدًا

for the unbelievers are unto you open enemies.

102. When you (O Apostle) are with them, and stand to lead them in prayer, let one party of them stand up (in prayer) with you, taking their arms with them: when they finish their prostrations, let them take their position in the rear. And let the other party come up which has not yet prayed - and let them pray with you, taking all precautions, and bearing arms: the unbelievers wish,

كَفَرُوا ۚ اِنَّ الْكٰفِرِيْنَ كَانُوْا

لَكُمْ عَدُوًّا مُّبِيْنًا ۞ وَاِذَا كُنْتَ

فِيْهِمْ فَاَقَمْتَ لَهُمُ الصَّلٰوةَ

فَلْتَقُمْ طَآئِفَةٌ مِّنْهُمْ مَّعَكَ

وَلْيَاْخُذُوْٓا اَسْلِحَتَهُمْ ۖ فَاِذَا

سَجَدُوْا فَلْيَكُوْنُوْا مِنْ وَّرَآئِكُمْ ۖ

وَلْتَاْتِ طَآئِفَةٌ اُخْرٰى لَمْ يُصَلُّوْا

فَلْيُصَلُّوْا مَعَكَ وَلْيَاْخُذُوْا

حِذْرَهُمْ وَاَسْلِحَتَهُمْ ۗ وَدَّ الَّذِيْنَ

in the earth many a refuge, wide and spacious: should he die as a refugee from home for Allah and His Apostle, His reward becomes due and sure with Allah: and Allah is Oft-Forgiving, Most Merciful.

101. When you travel through the earth, there is no blame on you if you shorten your prayers, for fear the unbelievers may attack you:

فِى الْاَرْضِ مُرْغَمًا كَثِيْرًا

وَّسَعَةً ۚ وَمَنْ يَّخْرُجْ مِنْ بَيْتِهٖ

مُهَاجِرًا اِلَى اللّٰهِ وَرَسُوْلِهٖ

ثُمَّ يُدْرِكْهُ الْمَوْتُ فَقَدْ وَقَعَ

اَجْرُهٗ عَلَى اللّٰهِ ۚ وَكَانَ اللّٰهُ

غَفُوْرًا رَّحِيْمًا ۞ وَاِذَا ضَرَبْتُمْ

فِى الْاَرْضِ فَلَيْسَ عَلَيْكُمْ

جُنَاحٌ اَنْ تَقْصُرُوْا مِنَ الصَّلٰوةِ ۖ

اِنْ خِفْتُمْ اَنْ يَّفْتِنَكُمُ الَّذِيْنَ

"Was not the earth of Allah spacious enough for you to move yourselves away (from evil)?" Such men will find their abode in Hell, - what an evil refuge! -

98. Except those who are (really) weak and oppressed - men, women, and children - who have no means in their power, nor (a guide-post) to direct their way.

99. For these, there is hope that Allah will forgive: for Allah does blot out (sins) and forgive again and again.

100. He who forsakes his home in the cause of Allah, finds

اَلَمْ تَكُنْ اَرْضُ اللهِ وَاسِعَةً
فَتُهَاجِرُوْا فِيْهَا ۚ فَأُولٰٓئِكَ مَأْوٰىهُمْ
جَهَنَّمُ ۚ وَسَآءَتْ مَصِيْرًا ۞ اِلَّا
الْمُسْتَضْعَفِيْنَ مِنَ الرِّجَالِ وَالنِّسَآءِ
وَالْوِلْدَانِ لَا يَسْتَطِيْعُوْنَ حِيْلَةً
وَّلَا يَهْتَدُوْنَ سَبِيْلًا ۞ فَأُولٰٓئِكَ
عَسَى اللهُ اَنْ يَّعْفُوَ عَنْهُمْ ۚ
وَكَانَ اللهُ عَفُوًّا غَفُوْرًا ۞ وَمَنْ
يُّهَاجِرْ فِيْ سَبِيْلِ اللهِ يَجِدْ

and persons than to those who sit (at home). Unto all (in Faith) has Allah promised good: but those who strive and fight has He distinguished above those who sit (at home) by a special reward,-

96.   Ranks specially bestowed by Him, and Forgiveness and Mercy. For Allah is Oft-Forgiving, Most Merciful.

97.   When angels take the souls of those who die in sin against their souls, they say: "In what (plight) were you?" They reply: "Weak and oppressed were we in the earth." They say:

وَاَنْفُسِهِمْ عَلَى الْقٰعِدِيْنَ دَرَجَةً ۖ

وَّكُلًّا وَّعَدَ اللّٰهُ الْحُسْنٰى ۖ وَفَضَّلَ

اللّٰهُ الْمُجٰهِدِيْنَ عَلَى الْقٰعِدِيْنَ

اَجْرًا عَظِيْمًا ۙ ٩٥ دَرَجٰتٍ مِّنْهُ

وَمَغْفِرَةً وَّرَحْمَةً ۖ وَكَانَ اللّٰهُ

غَفُوْرًا رَّحِيْمًا ٩٦ اِنَّ الَّذِيْنَ

تَوَفّٰهُمُ الْمَلٰٓئِكَةُ ظَالِمِيْ اَنْفُسِهِمْ

قَالُوْا فِيْمَ كُنْتُمْ ۖ قَالُوْا كُنَّا

مُسْتَضْعَفِيْنَ فِى الْاَرْضِ ۖ قَالُوْا

of a believer!" coveting the perishable goods of this life: with Allah are profits and spoils abundant. Even thus were you yourselves before, till Allah conferred on you His favours: therefore carefully investigate. For Allah is well aware of all that you do.

95. Not equal are those believers who sit (at home) and receive no hurt, and those who strive and fight in the cause of Allah with their goods and their persons. Allah has granted a grade higher to those who strive

مُؤْمِنًا تَبْتَغُوْنَ عَرَضَ الْحَيٰوةِ

الدُّنْيَا فَعِنْدَ اللهِ مَغَانِمُ كَثِيْرَةٌ

كَذٰلِكَ كُنْتُمْ مِّنْ قَبْلُ فَمَنَّ

اللهُ عَلَيْكُمْ فَتَبَيَّنُوْا ؕ اِنَّ اللهَ

كَانَ بِمَا تَعْمَلُوْنَ خَبِيْرًا ۞ لَا

يَسْتَوِى الْقٰعِدُوْنَ مِنَ الْمُؤْمِنِيْنَ

غَيْرُ أُولِى الضَّرَرِ وَالْمُجٰهِدُوْنَ فِى

سَبِيْلِ اللهِ بِاَمْوَالِهِمْ وَاَنْفُسِهِمْ ؕ

فَضَّلَ اللهُ الْمُجٰهِدِيْنَ بِاَمْوَالِهِمْ

for two months running: by way of repentance to Allah: for Allah has all knowledge and all wisdom.

93. If a man kills a believer intentionally, his recompense is Hell, to abide therein (for ever): and the wrath and the curse of Allah are upon him, and a dreadful Chastisement is prepared for him.

94. O you who believe! When you go abroad in the cause of Allah, investigate carefully, and say not to any one who offers you a salutation: "You are none

شَهْرَيْنِ مُتَتَابِعَيْنِ تَوْبَةً مِّنَ

اللّٰهِ ۗ وَكَانَ اللّٰهُ عَلِيْمًا حَكِيْمًا ۝

وَمَنْ يَّقْتُلْ مُؤْمِنًا مُّتَعَمِّدًا

فَجَزَآؤُهٗ جَهَنَّمُ خَالِدًا فِيْهَا

وَغَضِبَ اللّٰهُ عَلَيْهِ وَلَعَنَهٗ

وَأَعَدَّ لَهٗ عَذَابًا عَظِيْمًا ۝ يٰٓأَيُّهَا

الَّذِيْنَ اٰمَنُوْٓا اِذَا ضَرَبْتُمْ فِيْ

سَبِيْلِ اللّٰهِ فَتَبَيَّنُوْا وَلَا تَقُوْلُوْا

لِمَنْ أَلْقٰٓى اِلَيْكُمُ السَّلٰمَ لَسْتَ

kills a believer, it is ordained that he should free a believing slave, and pay compensation to the deceased's family, unless they remit it freely. If the deceased belonged to a people at war with you, and he was a believer, the freeing of a believing slave (is enough). If he belonged to a people with whom you have a treaty of Mutual alliance, compensation should be paid to his family, and a believing slave be freed. For those who find this beyond their means, (is prescribed) a fast

قَتَلَ مُؤْمِنًا خَطَأً فَتَحْرِيرُ

رَقَبَةٍ مُؤْمِنَةٍ وَّدِيَةٌ مُّسَلَّمَةٌ

اِلٰٓى اَهْلِهٖٓ اِلَّآ اَنْ يَّصَّدَّقُوْا

فَاِنْ كَانَ مِنْ قَوْمٍ عَدُوٍّ لَّكُمْ

وَهُوَ مُؤْمِنٌ فَتَحْرِيرُ رَقَبَةٍ

مُّؤْمِنَةٍ وَاِنْ كَانَ مِنْ قَوْمٍ

بَيْنَكُمْ وَبَيْنَهُمْ مِّيْثَاقٌ فَدِيَةٌ

مُّسَلَّمَةٌ اِلٰٓى اَهْلِهٖ وَتَحْرِيرُ رَقَبَةٍ

مُّؤْمِنَةٍ فَمَنْ لَّمْ يَجِدْ فَصِيَامُ

that wish to gain your confidence as well as that of their people: every time they are sent back to temptation, they succumb thereto: if they withdraw not from you nor give you (guarantees) of peace besides restraining their hands, seize them and slay them wherever you get them: in their case We have provided you with a clear argument against them.

92. Never should a believer kill a believer; but (if it so happens) by mistake, (compensation is due): if one (so)

أَخَرِينَ يُرِيدُونَ أَن يَأْمَنُوكُمْ

وَيَأْمَنُوا قَوْمَهُمْ كُلَّمَا رُدُّوٓا إِلَى

الْفِتْنَةِ أُرْكِسُوا فِيهَا فَإِن لَّمْ

يَعْتَزِلُوكُمْ وَيُلْقُوٓا إِلَيْكُمُ السَّلَمَ

وَيَكُفُّوٓا أَيْدِيَهُمْ فَخُذُوهُمْ

وَاقْتُلُوهُمْ حَيْثُ ثَقِفْتُمُوهُمْ

وَأُولَٰٓئِكُمْ جَعَلْنَا لَكُمْ عَلَيْهِمْ

سُلْطَٰنًا مُّبِينًا ۞ وَمَا كَانَ لِمُؤْمِنٍ

أَن يَقْتُلَ مُؤْمِنًا إِلَّا خَطَـًٔا وَمَن

take no friends or helpers from their ranks; -

90. Except those who join a group between whom and you there is a treaty (of peace), or those who approach you with hearts restraining them from fighting you as well as fighting their own people. If Allah had pleased, He could have given them power over you, and they would have fought you: therefore if they withdraw from you but fight you not, and (instead) send you (guarantees of) peace, then Allah has opened no way for you (to war against them).

91. Others you will find

تَتَّخِذُوا مِنْهُمْ وَلِيًّا وَّلَا نَصِيْرًا ۞

إِلَّا الَّذِيْنَ يَصِلُوْنَ اِلٰى قَوْمٍۭ بَيْنَكُمْ

وَ بَيْنَهُمْ مِّيْثَاقٌ اَوْ جَآءُوْكُمْ

حَصِرَتْ صُدُوْرُهُمْ اَنْ يُّقَاتِلُوْكُمْ

اَوْ يُقَاتِلُوْا قَوْمَهُمْ ۗ وَلَوْ شَآءَ اللّٰهُ

لَسَلَّطَهُمْ عَلَيْكُمْ فَلَقَاتَلُوْكُمْ ۚ فَاِنِ

اعْتَزَلُوْكُمْ فَلَمْ يُقَاتِلُوْكُمْ وَ اَلْقَوْا

اِلَيْكُمُ السَّلَمَ ۙ فَمَا جَعَلَ اللّٰهُ

لَكُمْ عَلَيْهِمْ سَبِيْلًا ۞ سَتَجِدُوْنَ

divided into two parties about the hypocrites? Allah has upset them for their (evil) deeds. Would you guide those whom Allah has thrown out of the Way? For those whom Allah has thrown out of the Way, never shall you find the Way.

89. They but wish that you should reject Faith, as they do, and thus be on the same footing (as they): but take not friends from their ranks until they flee in the way of Allah (from what is forbidden). But if they turn renegades, seize them and slay them wherever you find them; and (in any case)

الْمُنٰفِقِيْنَ فِئَتَيْنِ وَاللّٰهُ اَرْكَسَهُمْ

بِمَا كَسَبُوْا ۚ اَتُرِيْدُوْنَ اَنْ تَهْدُوْا

مَنْ اَضَلَّ اللّٰهُ ۚ وَمَنْ يُّضْلِلِ

اللّٰهُ فَلَنْ تَجِدَ لَهٗ سَبِيْلًا ۞

وَدُّوْا لَوْ تَكْفُرُوْنَ كَمَا كَفَرُوْا

فَتَكُوْنُوْنَ سَوَآءً فَلَا تَتَّخِذُوْا

مِنْهُمْ اَوْلِيَآءَ حَتّٰى يُهَاجِرُوْا فِيْ

سَبِيْلِ اللّٰهِ ۚ فَاِنْ تَوَلَّوْا فَخُذُوْهُمْ

وَاقْتُلُوْهُمْ حَيْثُ وَجَدْتُّمُوْهُمْ ۖ وَلَا

an evil cause, shares in its burden: and Allah has power over all things.

86. When a (courteous) greeting is offered you, meet it with a greeting still more courteous, or (at least) of equal courtesy. Allah takes careful account of all things.

87. Allah! There is no god but He: of a surety He will gather you together against the Day of Judgment, about which there is no doubt. And whose word can be truer than Allah's?

88. Why should you be

شَفَاعَةً سَيِّئَةً يَّكُنْ لَّهُ كِفْلٌ

مِّنْهَا ۚ وَكَانَ اللّٰهُ عَلٰى كُلِّ شَىْءٍ

مُّقِيتًا ۞ وَاِذَا حُيِّيْتُمْ بِتَحِيَّةٍ

فَحَيُّوْا بِاَحْسَنَ مِنْهَآ اَوْ رُدُّوْهَا ۗ

اِنَّ اللّٰهَ كَانَ عَلٰى كُلِّ شَىْءٍ

حَسِيْبًا ۞ اَللّٰهُ لَاۤ اِلٰهَ اِلَّا هُوَ ۚ

لَيَجْمَعَنَّكُمْ اِلٰى يَوْمِ الْقِيٰمَةِ لَا

رَيْبَ فِيْهِ ۗ وَمَنْ اَصْدَقُ مِنَ

اللّٰهِ حَدِيْثًا ۞ فَمَا لَكُمْ فِى

from them (direct). Were it not for the Grace and Mercy of Allah unto you, all but a few of you would have fallen into the clutches of Satan.

84. Then fight in Allah's cause - you are held responsible only for yourself - and motivate the believers. It may be that Allah will restrain the fury of the unbelievers; for Allah is the strongest in might and in punishment.

85. Whoever recommends and helps a good cause becomes a partner therein: and whoever recommends and helps

مِنْهُمْ وَلَوْلَا فَضْلُ اللّٰهِ عَلَيْكُمْ

وَرَحْمَتُهُ لَاتَّبَعْتُمُ الشَّيْطٰنَ إِلَّا

قَلِيلًا ۞ فَقَاتِلْ فِيْ سَبِيْلِ اللّٰهِ

لَا تُكَلَّفُ إِلَّا نَفْسَكَ وَحَرِّضِ

الْمُؤْمِنِيْنَ ۚ عَسَى اللّٰهُ أَنْ يَّكُفَّ

بَأْسَ الَّذِيْنَ كَفَرُوْا ۚ وَاللّٰهُ أَشَدُّ

بَأْسًا وَّأَشَدُّ تَنْكِيْلًا ۞ مَنْ

يَّشْفَعْ شَفَاعَةً حَسَنَةً يَّكُنْ

لَّهُ نَصِيْبٌ مِّنْهَا ۚ وَمَنْ يَّشْفَعْ

so keep clear of them, and put your trust in Allah, and enough is Allah as a disposer of affairs.

82. Do they not consider the Qur'an (with care)? Had it been from other than Allah, they would surely have found therein much discrepancy.

83. When there comes to them some matter touching (public) safety or fear, they divulge it. If they had only referred it to the Apostle, or to those charged with authority among them, the proper investigators would have tested it

فَاَعْرِضْ عَنْهُمْ وَتَوَكَّلْ عَلَى

اللّٰهِ ۚ وَكَفٰى بِاللّٰهِ وَكِيْلًا ۞ اَفَلَا

يَتَدَبَّرُوْنَ الْقُرْاٰنَ ۚ وَلَوْ كَانَ

مِنْ عِنْدِ غَيْرِ اللّٰهِ لَوَجَدُوْا

فِيْهِ اخْتِلَافًا كَثِيْرًا ۞ وَاِذَا

جَآءَهُمْ اَمْرٌ مِّنَ الْاَمْنِ اَوِ

الْخَوْفِ اَذَاعُوْا بِهٖ ۚ وَلَوْ رَدُّوْهُ

اِلَى الرَّسُوْلِ وَاِلٰۤى اُولِى الْاَمْرِ

مِنْهُمْ لَعَلِمَهُ الَّذِيْنَ يَسْتَنْۢبِطُوْنَهٗ

but whatever evil happens to you, is from your (own) soul. And We have sent you as an Apostle to (instruct) mankind. And enough is Allah for a Witness.

80. He who obeys the Apostle, obeys Allah: but if any turn away, We have not sent you to watch over their (evil deeds).

81. They have "Obedience" on their lips; but when they leave you, a section of them meditate all night on things very different from what you tell them. But Allah records their nightly (plots):

وَمَآ اَصَابَكَ مِنْ سَيِّئَةٍ فَمِنْ

نَّفْسِكَ وَاَرْسَلْنٰكَ لِلنَّاسِ رَسُوْلًا

وَكَفٰى بِاللّٰهِ شَهِيْدًا ۞ مَنْ يُّطِعِ

الرَّسُوْلَ فَقَدْ اَطَاعَ اللّٰهَ وَمَنْ

تَوَلّٰى فَمَآ اَرْسَلْنٰكَ عَلَيْهِمْ

حَفِيْظًا ۞ وَيَقُوْلُوْنَ طَاعَةٌ فَاِذَا

بَرَزُوْا مِنْ عِنْدِكَ بَيَّتَ

طَآئِفَةٌ مِّنْهُمْ غَيْرَ الَّذِيْ

تَقُوْلُ وَاللّٰهُ يَكْتُبُ مَا يُبَيِّتُوْنَ

78. "Wherever you are, death will find you out, even if you are in towers built up strong and high!" If some good befalls them, they say, "This is from Allah"; but if evil, they say, "This is from you (O Prophet)". Say: "All things are from Allah." But what has come to these people, that they fail to understand a single fact?

79. Whatever good, (O man!) happens to you, is from Allah;

اَيْنَ مَا تَكُوْنُوْا يُدْرِكْكُّمُ الْمَوْتُ

وَلَوْ كُنْتُمْ فِيْ بُرُوْجٍ مُّشَيَّدَةٍ ۗ

وَاِنْ تُصِبْهُمْ حَسَنَةٌ يَّقُوْلُوْا

هٰذِهٖ مِنْ عِنْدِ اللّٰهِ ۚ وَاِنْ

تُصِبْهُمْ سَيِّئَةٌ يَّقُوْلُوْا هٰذِهٖ

مِنْ عِنْدِكَ ۗ قُلْ كُلٌّ مِّنْ عِنْدِ

اللّٰهِ ۗ فَمَالِ هٰٓؤُلَآءِ الْقَوْمِ لَا

يَكَادُوْنَ يَفْقَهُوْنَ حَدِيْثًا ۝ مَآ

اَصَابَكَ مِنْ حَسَنَةٍ فَمِنَ اللّٰهِ ۚ

prayers and spend in regular charity? When (at length) the order for fighting was issued to them, behold! a section of them feared men as - or even more than - they should have feared Allah: they said: "Our Lord! Why have you ordered us to fight? Would You not grant us respite to our (natural) term, near (enough)?" Say: "Short is the enjoyment of this world: the Hereafter is the best for those who do right: never will you be dealt with unjustly in the very least!

الصَّلٰوةَ وَ اٰتُوا الزَّكٰوةَ ۚ فَلَمَّا

كُتِبَ عَلَيْهِمُ الْقِتَالُ اِذَا

فَرِيْقٌ مِّنْهُمْ يَخْشَوْنَ النَّاسَ

كَخَشْيَةِ اللّٰهِ اَوْ اَشَدَّ خَشْيَةً ۚ

وَ قَالُوْا رَبَّنَا لِمَ كَتَبْتَ عَلَيْنَا

الْقِتَالَ ۚ لَوْلَا اَخَّرْتَنَا اِلٰى اَجَلٍ

قَرِيْبٍ ۚ قُلْ مَتَاعُ الدُّنْيَا

قَلِيْلٌ ۚ وَ الْاٰخِرَةُ خَيْرٌ لِّمَنِ

اتَّقٰى ۚ وَ لَا تُظْلَمُوْنَ فَتِيْلًا ۝

town, whose people are oppressors; and raise for us from you one who will protect; and raise for us from You one who will help!"

76. Those who believe fight in the cause of Allah, and those who reject Faith fight in the cause of Evil: so fight you against the friends of Satan: feeble indeed is the cunning of Satan.

77. Have you not turned your vision to those who were told to hold back their hands (from fight) but establish regular

الْقَرْيَةِ الظَّالِمِ أَهْلُهَا وَاجْعَلْ لَنَا

مِنْ لَدُنْكَ وَلِيًّا وَاجْعَلْ لَنَا

مِنْ لَدُنْكَ نَصِيرًا ۞ اَلَّذِيْنَ

اٰمَنُوْا يُقَاتِلُوْنَ فِيْ سَبِيْلِ اللّٰهِ

وَالَّذِيْنَ كَفَرُوْا يُقَاتِلُوْنَ فِيْ

سَبِيْلِ الطَّاغُوْتِ فَقَاتِلُوْا اَوْلِيَآءَ

الشَّيْطٰنِ اِنَّ كَيْدَ الشَّيْطٰنِ كَانَ

ضَعِيْفًا ۞ اَلَمْ تَرَ اِلَى الَّذِيْنَ

قِيْلَ لَهُمْ كُفُّوْٓا اَيْدِيَكُمْ وَاَقِيْمُوا

74. Let those fight in the cause of Allah Who sell the life of this world for the Hereafter. To him who fights in the cause of Allah,- whether he is slain or gets victory - soon shall We give him a reward of great (value).

75. And why should you not fight in the cause of Allah and of those who, being weak, are ill-treated (and oppressed)?- Men, women, and children, whose cry is: "Our Lord! Rescue us from this

فَلْيُقَاتِلْ فِىْ سَبِيْلِ اللّٰهِ

الَّذِيْنَ يَشْرُوْنَ الْحَيٰوةَ الدُّنْيَا

بِالْاٰخِرَةِ ۚ وَمَنْ يُّقَاتِلْ فِىْ سَبِيْلِ

اللّٰهِ فَيُقْتَلْ اَوْ يَغْلِبْ فَسَوْفَ

نُؤْتِيْهِ اَجْرًا عَظِيْمًا ۞ وَمَا لَكُمْ

لَا تُقَاتِلُوْنَ فِىْ سَبِيْلِ اللّٰهِ

وَالْمُسْتَضْعَفِيْنَ مِنَ الرِّجَالِ

وَالنِّسَآءِ وَالْوِلْدَانِ الَّذِيْنَ

يَقُوْلُوْنَ رَبَّنَآ اَخْرِجْنَا مِنْ هٰذِهِ

Take your precautions, and either go forth in parties or go forth all together.

72. There are certainly among you men who would tarry behind: if a misfortune befalls you, they say: "Allah did favour us in that we were not present among them."

73. But if good fortune comes to you from Allah, they would be sure to say - as if there had never been ties of affection between you and them - "Oh! I wish I had been with them; a fine thing should I then have made of it!"

خُذُوا حِذْرَكُمْ فَانْفِرُوا ثُبَاتٍ

أَوِ انْفِرُوا جَمِيعًا ۞ وَإِنَّ مِنْكُمْ

لَمَنْ لَيُبَطِّئَنَّ فَإِنْ أَصَابَتْكُمْ

مُّصِيبَةٌ قَالَ قَدْ أَنْعَمَ اللهُ

عَلَيَّ إِذْ لَمْ أَكُنْ مَّعَهُمْ شَهِيدًا ۞

وَلَئِنْ أَصَابَكُمْ فَضْلٌ مِّنَ اللهِ

لَيَقُولَنَّ كَأَنْ لَّمْ تَكُنْ بَيْنَكُمْ

وَبَيْنَهُ مَوَدَّةٌ يَّلَيْتَنِي كُنْتُ

مَعَهُمْ فَأَفُوزَ فَوْزًا عَظِيمًا ۞

67. And We would then have given them from Our Presence a great reward;

68. And We would have shown them the Straight Way.

69. All who obey Allah and the Apostle are in the company of those on whom is the Grace of Allah, - of the Prophets (who teach), the sincere (lovers of Truth), the witnesses (who testify), and the righteous (who do good): ah! what a beautiful fellowship!

70. Such is the Bounty from Allah: and sufficient is it that Allah knows all.

71. O you who believe!

وَّاِذًا لَّاٰتَيْنٰهُمْ مِّنْ لَّدُنَّاۤ اَجْرًا

عَظِيْمًا ۞ وَّلَهَدَيْنٰهُمْ صِرَاطًا

مُّسْتَقِيْمًا ۞ وَمَنْ يُّطِعِ اللّٰهَ

وَالرَّسُوْلَ فَاُولٰٓئِكَ مَعَ الَّذِيْنَ

اَنْعَمَ اللّٰهُ عَلَيْهِمْ مِّنَ النَّبِيّٖنَ

وَالصِّدِّيْقِيْنَ وَالشُّهَدَآءِ وَالصّٰلِحِيْنَ ۚ

وَحَسُنَ اُولٰٓئِكَ رَفِيْقًا ۞ ذٰلِكَ

الْفَضْلُ مِنَ اللّٰهِ ۚ وَكَفٰى بِاللّٰهِ

عَلِيْمًا ۞ يٰۤاَيُّهَا الَّذِيْنَ اٰمَنُوا

Most Merciful.

65. But no, by your Lord, they can have no (real) Faith, until they make you judge in all disputes between them, and find in their souls no resistance against your decisions, but accept them with the fullest conviction.

66. If We had ordered them to sacrifice their lives or to leave their homes, very few of them would have done it: but if they had done what they were (actually) told, it would have been best for them, and would have gone farthest to strengthen their (faith);

رَّحِيمًا ۞ فَلَا وَرَبِّكَ لَا يُؤْمِنُونَ

حَتَّىٰ يُحَكِّمُوكَ فِيمَا شَجَرَ بَيْنَهُمْ

ثُمَّ لَا يَجِدُوا فِي أَنْفُسِهِمْ حَرَجًا

مِّمَّا قَضَيْتَ وَيُسَلِّمُوا تَسْلِيمًا ۞

وَلَوْ أَنَّا كَتَبْنَا عَلَيْهِمْ أَنِ اقْتُلُوا

أَنْفُسَكُمْ أَوِ اخْرُجُوا مِن دِيَارِكُم

مَّا فَعَلُوهُ إِلَّا قَلِيلٌ مِّنْهُمْ وَلَوْ

أَنَّهُمْ فَعَلُوا مَا يُوعَظُونَ بِهِ

لَكَانَ خَيْرًا لَّهُمْ وَأَشَدَّ تَثْبِيتًا ۞

"We meant no more than good-will and conciliation!"

63. Those men, - Allah knows what is in their hearts; so keep clear of them, but admonish them, and speak to them a word to reach their very souls.

64. We sent not an Apostle, but to be obeyed, in accordance with the Will of Allah. If they had only, when they were unjust to themselves, come to you and asked Allah's forgiveness, and the Apostle had asked forgiveness for them, they would have found Allah indeed Oft-Returning,

اَرَّدْنَاۤ اِلَّاۤ اِحْسَانًا وَّتَوْفِيْقًا ۞ اُولٰٓئِكَ الَّذِيْنَ يَعْلَمُ اللّٰهُ مَا فِيْ قُلُوْبِهِمْ فَاَعْرِضْ عَنْهُمْ وَعِظْهُمْ وَقُلْ لَّهُمْ فِيْۤ اَنْفُسِهِمْ قَوْلًاۢ بَلِيْغًا ۞ وَمَاۤ اَرْسَلْنَا مِنْ رَّسُوْلٍ اِلَّا لِيُطَاعَ بِاِذْنِ اللّٰهِ وَلَوْ اَنَّهُمْ اِذْ ظَّلَمُوْۤا اَنْفُسَهُمْ جَآءُوْكَ فَاسْتَغْفَرُوا اللّٰهَ وَاسْتَغْفَرَ لَهُمُ الرَّسُوْلُ لَوَجَدُوا اللّٰهَ تَوَّابًا

is to resort together for judgment (in their disputes) to the Satan, though they were ordered to reject him. But Satan's wish is to lead them astray far away (from the right).

61. When it is said to them: "Come to what Allah has revealed, and to the Apostle": you see the Hypocrites avert their faces from you in disgust.

62. How then, when they are seized by misfortune, because of the deeds which their hands have sent forth? Then they come to you, swearing by Allah:

أَنْ يَّتَحَاكَمُوْٓا إِلَى الطَّاغُوْتِ وَقَدْ

أُمِرُوْٓا أَنْ يَّكْفُرُوْا بِهِ ۗ وَيُرِيْدُ

الشَّيْطَنُ أَنْ يُّضِلَّهُمْ ضَلَلًۢا

بَعِيْدًا ۞ وَإِذَا قِيْلَ لَهُمْ تَعَالَوْا

إِلَى مَآ أَنْزَلَ اللّٰهُ وَإِلَى الرَّسُوْلِ

رَأَيْتَ الْمُنٰفِقِيْنَ يَصُدُّوْنَ عَنْكَ

صُدُوْدًا ۞ فَكَيْفَ إِذَآ أَصَابَتْهُمْ

مُّصِيْبَةٌۢ بِمَا قَدَّمَتْ أَيْدِيْهِمْ

ثُمَّ جَآءُوْكَ يَحْلِفُوْنَ بِاللّٰهِ ۗ إِنْ

believe! Obey Allah, and obey the Apostle, and those charged with authority among you. If you differ in anything among yourselves, refer it to Allah and His Apostle, if you do believe in Allah and the Last Day: that is best, and most suitable for final determination.

60. Have you not turned your vision to those who declare that they believe in the revelations that have come to you and to those before you? Their (real) wish

اٰمَنُوْٓا اَطِيْعُوا اللّٰهَ وَ اَطِيْعُوا

الرَّسُوْلَ وَ اُولِى الْاَمْرِ مِنْكُمْ

فَاِنْ تَنَازَعْتُمْ فِیْ شَیْءٍ فَرُدُّوْهُ

اِلَى اللّٰهِ وَ الرَّسُوْلِ اِنْ كُنْتُمْ

تُؤْمِنُوْنَ بِاللّٰهِ وَ الْيَوْمِ الْاٰخِرِ

ذٰلِكَ خَيْرٌ وَّ اَحْسَنُ تَاْوِيْلًا ۵۹

اَلَمْ تَرَ اِلَى الَّذِيْنَ يَزْعُمُوْنَ

اَنَّهُمْ اٰمَنُوْا بِمَآ اُنْزِلَ اِلَيْكَ

وَمَآ اُنْزِلَ مِنْ قَبْلِكَ يُرِيْدُوْنَ

Gardens, with rivers flowing beneath, - their eternal home: Therein shall they have companions pure and holy: We shall admit them to shades, cool and ever deepening.

58.   Allah does command you to render back your trusts to those to whom they are due; and when you judge between man and man, that you judge with justice: verily how excellent is the teaching which He gives you! for Allah is He Who hears and sees all things.

59.   O you who

جَنّٰتٍ تَجْرِيْ مِنْ تَحْتِهَا الْاَنْهٰرُ

خٰلِدِيْنَ فِيْهَاۤ اَبَدًا ۖ لَهُمْ فِيْهَاۤ

اَزْوَاجٌ مُّطَهَّرَةٌ ۖ وَّنُدْخِلُهُمْ ظِلًّا

ظَلِيْلًا ۝ اِنَّ اللّٰهَ يَاْمُرُكُمْ اَنْ

تُؤَدُّوا الْاَمٰنٰتِ اِلٰۤى اَهْلِهَا ۙ

وَاِذَا حَكَمْتُمْ بَيْنَ النَّاسِ اَنْ

تَحْكُمُوْا بِالْعَدْلِ ۚ اِنَّ اللّٰهَ

نِعِمَّا يَعِظُكُمْ بِهٖ ۗ اِنَّ اللّٰهَ كَانَ

سَمِيْعًا بَصِيْرًا ۝ يٰۤاَيُّهَا الَّذِيْنَ

and conferred upon them a great kingdom.

55. Some of them believed, and some of them averted their faces from him: and enough is Hell for a burning fire.

56. Those who reject Our Signs, We shall soon cast into the Fire: as often as their skins are roasted through, We shall change them for fresh skins, that they may taste the Chastisement: for Allah is Exalted in Power, Wise.

57. But those who believe and do deeds of righteousness, We shall soon admit to

وَاٰتَيْنٰهُمْ مُّلْكًا عَظِيْمًا ۞ فَمِنْهُمْ

مَّنْ اٰمَنَ بِهٖ وَمِنْهُمْ مَّنْ صَدَّ

عَنْهُ ۗ وَكَفٰى بِجَهَنَّمَ سَعِيْرًا ۞

اِنَّ الَّذِيْنَ كَفَرُوْا بِاٰيٰتِنَا سَوْفَ

نُصْلِيْهِمْ نَارًا ۗ كُلَّمَا نَضِجَتْ

جُلُوْدُهُمْ بَدَّلْنٰهُمْ جُلُوْدًا غَيْرَهَا

لِيَذُوْقُوا الْعَذَابَ ۗ اِنَّ اللّٰهَ

كَانَ عَزِيْزًا حَكِيْمًا ۞ وَالَّذِيْنَ

اٰمَنُوْا وَعَمِلُوا الصّٰلِحٰتِ سَنُدْخِلُهُمْ

to the unbelievers that they are better guided in the (right) way than the believers!

52. They are (men) whom Allah has cursed: and those whom Allah has cursed, you will find, have no one to help.

53. Have they a share in dominion or power? Behold, they give not a farthing to their fellow-men?

54. Or do they envy mankind for what Allah has given them of His Bounty? But We had already given the people of Abraham the Book and wisdom,

لِلَّذِينَ كَفَرُوا هَٰٓؤُلَآءِ أَهْدَىٰ مِنَ

الَّذِينَ ءَامَنُوا سَبِيلًا ۝ أُوْلَٰٓئِكَ

الَّذِينَ لَعَنَهُمُ اللَّهُ وَمَن يَلْعَنِ

اللَّهُ فَلَن تَجِدَ لَهُۥ نَصِيرًا ۝

أَمْ لَهُمْ نَصِيبٌ مِّنَ الْمُلْكِ

فَإِذًا لَّا يُؤْتُونَ النَّاسَ نَقِيرًا ۝

أَمْ يَحْسُدُونَ النَّاسَ عَلَىٰ مَآ

ءَاتَىٰهُمُ اللَّهُ مِن فَضْلِهِۦ فَقَدْ

ءَاتَيْنَآ ءَالَ إِبْرَٰهِيمَ الْكِتَٰبَ وَالْحِكْمَةَ

set up partners with Allah is to devise a sin most heinous indeed.

49. Have you not turned your vision to those who claim sanctity for themselves? No but Allah does sanctify whom He please. But never will they fail to receive justice in the least little thing.

50. See! how they invent a lie against Allah! but that by itself is a manifest sin!

51. Have you not turned your vision to those who were given a portion of the Book? They believe in sorcery and evil, and say

يُّشْرِكْ بِاللهِ فَقَدِ افْتَرٰۤى اِثْمًا

عَظِيْمًا ۞ اَلَمْ تَرَ اِلَى الَّذِيْنَ

يُزَكُّوْنَ اَنْفُسَهُمْ ۗ بَلِ اللهُ يُزَكِّىْ

مَنْ يَّشَآءُ وَلَا يُظْلَمُوْنَ فَتِيْلًا ۞

اُنْظُرْ كَيْفَ يَفْتَرُوْنَ عَلَى اللهِ

الْكَذِبَ ۗ وَكَفٰى بِهٖۤ اِثْمًا مُّبِيْنًا ۞

اَلَمْ تَرَ اِلَى الَّذِيْنَ اُوْتُوْا

نَصِيْبًا مِّنَ الْكِتٰبِ يُؤْمِنُوْنَ

بِالْجِبْتِ وَالطَّاغُوْتِ وَيَقُوْلُوْنَ

but few of them will believe.

47. O you People of the Book! Believe in what We have (now) revealed, confirming what was (already) with you, before We change the face and fame of some (of you) beyond all recognition, and turn them hindwards, or curse them as We cursed the Sabbath-breakers, for the decision of Allah must be carried out.

48. Allah forgives not that partners should be set up with Him; but He forgives anything else, to whom He pleases; to

يُؤْمِنُوْنَ اِلَّا قَلِيْلًا ۞ يَا يُّهَا

الَّذِيْنَ اُوْتُوا الْكِتٰبَ اٰمِنُوْا

بِمَا نَزَّلْنَا مُصَدِّقًا لِّمَا مَعَكُمْ

مِّنْ قَبْلِ اَنْ نَّطْمِسَ وُجُوْهًا

فَنَرُدَّهَا عَلٰٓى اَدْبَارِهَآ اَوْ نَلْعَنَهُمْ

كَمَا لَعَنَّآ اَصْحٰبَ السَّبْتِ ۚ وَكَانَ

اَمْرُ اللّٰهِ مَفْعُوْلًا ۞ اِنَّ اللّٰهَ لَا

يَغْفِرُ اَنْ يُّشْرَكَ بِهٖ وَيَغْفِرُ

مَا دُوْنَ ذٰلِكَ لِمَنْ يَّشَآءُ ۚ وَمَنْ

for a Protector, and Allah is enough for a Helper.

46. Of the Jews there are those who displace words from their (right) places, and say: "We hear and we disobey"; and "Hear what is not heard"; and "Ra'ina"; with a twist of their tongues and a slander to Faith. If only they had said: "We hear and we obey"; and "Do hear"; and "Do look at us"; it would have been better for them, and more proper; but Allah has cursed them for their Unbelief; and

وَلِيًّا ۚ وَّكَفٰى بِاللّٰهِ نَصِيْرًا ۞

مِنَ الَّذِيْنَ هَادُوْا يُحَرِّفُوْنَ

الْكَلِمَ عَنْ مَّوَاضِعِهٖ وَيَقُوْلُوْنَ

سَمِعْنَا وَعَصَيْنَا وَاسْمَعْ غَيْرَ

مُسْمَعٍ وَّرَاعِنَا لَيًّا بِاَلْسِنَتِهِمْ

وَطَعْنًا فِى الدِّيْنِ ۚ وَلَوْ اَنَّهُمْ

قَالُوْا سَمِعْنَا وَاَطَعْنَا وَاسْمَعْ

وَانْظُرْنَا لَكَانَ خَيْرًا لَّهُمْ وَاَقْوَمَ

وَلٰكِنْ لَّعَنَهُمُ اللّٰهُ بِكُفْرِهِمْ فَلَا

from offices of nature, or you have been in contact with women, and you find no water, then take for yourselves clean sand or earth, and rub therewith your faces and hands. For Allah does blot out sins and forgive again and again.

44. Have you not turned your vision to those who were given a portion of the Book? They traffic in error, and wish that you should lose the right path.

45. But Allah has full knowledge of your enemies: Allah is enough

مِّنكُم مِّنَ الْغَائِطِ أَوْ لٰمَسْتُمُ

النِّسَاءَ فَلَمْ تَجِدُوا مَاءً فَتَيَمَّمُوا

صَعِيدًا طَيِّبًا فَامْسَحُوا بِوُجُوهِكُمْ

وَأَيْدِيكُمْ ۗ إِنَّ اللّٰهَ كَانَ عَفُوًّا

غَفُورًا ۞ أَلَمْ تَرَ إِلَى الَّذِينَ

أُوتُوا نَصِيبًا مِّنَ الْكِتٰبِ

يَشْتَرُونَ الضَّلٰلَةَ وَيُرِيدُونَ

أَن تَضِلُّوا السَّبِيلَ ۞ وَاللّٰهُ

أَعْلَمُ بِأَعْدَائِكُمْ ۚ وَكَفَىٰ بِاللّٰهِ

you as a witness against these People!

42. On that day those who reject Faith and disobey the Apostle will wish that the earth were made one with them: but never will they hide a single fact from Allah!

43. O you who believe! Approach not prayers with a mind befogged, until you can understand all that you say, - nor in a state of ceremonial impurity (except when travelling on the road), until after washing your whole body. If you are ill, or on a journey, or one of you comes

بِكَ عَلَىٰ هَٰؤُلَاءِ شَهِيدًا ۩

يُّؤْمِنٍ يَّوَدُّ الَّذِينَ كَفَرُوا وَعَصَوُا

الرَّسُولَ لَوْ تُسَوَّىٰ بِهِمُ الْأَرْضُ

وَلَا يَكْتُمُونَ اللهَ حَدِيثًا ۩ يَٰأَيُّهَا

الَّذِينَ اٰمَنُوا لَا تَقْرَبُوا الصَّلٰوةَ

وَأَنْتُمْ سُكَارَىٰ حَتّٰى تَعْلَمُوا مَا

تَقُولُونَ وَلَا جُنُبًا اِلَّا عَابِرِي

سَبِيلٍ حَتّٰى تَغْتَسِلُوا ۚ وَاِنْ كُنْتُمْ

مَّرْضَىٰ اَوْ عَلَىٰ سَفَرٍ اَوْ جَاءَ اَحَدٌ

the Satan for their intimate, what a dreadful intimate he is!

39. And what burden were it on them if they had faith in Allah and in the Last Day, and they spent out of what Allah has given them for sustenance? For Allah has full knowledge of them.

40. Allah is never unjust in the least degree: If there is any good (done), He doubles it, and gives from His Own Presence a great reward.

41. How then if We brought from each People a witness, and We brought

الشَّيْطَانُ لَهُ قَرِينًا فَسَآءَ قَرِينًا ۩

وَمَاذَا عَلَيْهِمْ لَوْ اٰمَنُوْا بِاللّٰهِ

وَالْيَوْمِ الْاٰخِرِ وَاَنْفَقُوْا مِمَّا

رَزَقَهُمُ اللّٰهُ ۚ وَكَانَ اللّٰهُ بِهِمْ

عَلِيْمًا ۩ اِنَّ اللّٰهَ لَا يَظْلِمُ

مِثْقَالَ ذَرَّةٍ ۚ وَاِنْ تَكُ حَسَنَةً

يُّضٰعِفْهَا وَيُؤْتِ مِنْ لَّدُنْهُ

اَجْرًا عَظِيْمًا ۩ فَكَيْفَ اِذَا جِئْنَا

مِنْ كُلِّ اُمَّةٍ بِشَهِيْدٍ وَّجِئْنَا

the wayfarer (you meet), and what your right hands possess: for Allah loves not the arrogant, the vainglorious.

37.   (Nor) those who are niggardly or enjoin niggardliness on others, or hide the bounties which Allah has bestowed on them; for We have prepared, for those who resist Faith, a punishment that steeps them in contempt;-

38.   Nor those who spend of their substance, to be seen of men, but have no faith in Allah and the Last Day: if any take

وَابْنِ السَّبِيْلِ وَمَا مَلَكَتْ اَيْمَانُكُمْ

اِنَّ اللّٰهَ لَا يُحِبُّ مَنْ كَانَ

مُخْتَالًا فَخُوْرَا ۙ ۝ الَّذِيْنَ يَبْخَلُوْنَ

وَيَأْمُرُوْنَ النَّاسَ بِالْبُخْلِ

وَيَكْتُمُوْنَ مَآ اٰتٰهُمُ اللّٰهُ مِنْ

فَضْلِهٖ ۗ وَاَعْتَدْنَا لِلْكٰفِرِيْنَ عَذَابًا

مُّهِيْنًا ۙ ۝ وَالَّذِيْنَ يُنْفِقُوْنَ اَمْوَالَهُمْ

رِئَآءَ النَّاسِ وَلَا يُؤْمِنُوْنَ بِاللّٰهِ

وَلَا بِالْيَوْمِ الْاٰخِرِ ۗ وَمَنْ يَّكُنِ

a breach between them twain, appoint (two) arbiters, one from his family, and the other from hers; if they wish for peace, Allah will cause their reconciliation: for Allah has full knowledge, and is acquainted with all things.

36.   Serve Allah, and join not any partners with Him; and do good - to parents, kinsfolk, orphans, those in need, neighbours who are near, neighbours who are strangers, the companion by your side,

شِقَاقَ بَيْنِهِمَا فَابْعَثُوْا حَكَمًا

مِّنْ اَهْلِهٖ وَحَكَمًا مِّنْ اَهْلِهَا

اِنْ يُّرِيْدَآ اِصْلَاحًا يُّوَفِّقِ اللّٰهُ

بَيْنَهُمَا ؕ اِنَّ اللّٰهَ كَانَ عَلِيْمًا

خَبِيْرًا ۞ وَ اعْبُدُوا اللّٰهَ وَلَا

تُشْرِكُوْا بِهٖ شَيْئًا وَّبِالْوَالِدَيْنِ

اِحْسَانًا وَّبِذِى الْقُرْبٰى وَالْيَتٰمٰى

وَالْمَسٰكِيْنِ وَالْجَارِ ذِى الْقُرْبٰى

وَالْجَارِ الْجُنُبِ وَالصَّاحِبِ بِالْجَنْبِ

because Allah has given the one more (strength) than the other, and because they support them from their means. Therefore the righteous women are devoutly obedient, and guard in (the husband's) absence what Allah would have them guard. As to those women on whose part you fear disloyalty and ill-conduct, admonish them (first), (next), refuse to share their beds, (and last) beat them (lightly); but if they return to obedience, seek not against them means (of annoyance): for Allah is Most High, Great (above you all).

35. If you fear

بِمَا فَضَّلَ اللّٰهُ بَعْضَهُمْ عَلٰى

بَعْضٍ وَّبِمَآ اَنْفَقُوْا مِنْ اَمْوَالِهِمْ ۗ

فَالصّٰلِحٰتُ قٰنِتٰتٌ حٰفِظٰتٌ

لِّلْغَيْبِ بِمَا حَفِظَ اللّٰهُ ۗ وَالّٰتِيْ

تَخَافُوْنَ نُشُوْزَهُنَّ فَعِظُوْهُنَّ

وَاهْجُرُوْهُنَّ فِى الْمَضَاجِعِ

وَاضْرِبُوْهُنَّ ۚ فَاِنْ اَطَعْنَكُمْ فَلَا

تَبْغُوْا عَلَيْهِنَّ سَبِيْلًا ۗ اِنَّ اللّٰهَ

كَانَ عَلِيًّا كَبِيْرًا ۞ وَاِنْ خِفْتُمْ

is allotted what they earn, and to women what they earn: but ask Allah of His bounty. For Allah has full knowledge of all things.

33. To (benefit) every one, We have appointed shares and heirs to property left by parents and relatives. To those, also, to whom your right hand was pledged, give their due portion. For truly Allah is Witness to all things.

34. Men are the protectors and maintainers of women,

نَصِيبٌ مِّمَّا اكْتَسَبُوا ۖ وَلِلنِّسَآءِ

نَصِيبٌ مِّمَّا اكْتَسَبْنَ ۚ وَسْئَلُوا

اللّٰهَ مِنْ فَضْلِهٖ ۗ إِنَّ اللّٰهَ كَانَ

بِكُلِّ شَيْءٍ عَلِيْمًا ۞ وَلِكُلٍّ جَعَلْنَا

مَوَالِيَ مِمَّا تَرَكَ الْوَالِدَانِ

وَالْأَقْرَبُوْنَ ۚ وَالَّذِيْنَ عَقَدَتْ

أَيْمَانُكُمْ فَاٰتُوْهُمْ نَصِيْبَهُمْ ۚ إِنَّ

اللّٰهَ كَانَ عَلٰى كُلِّ شَيْءٍ شَهِيْدًا ۞

الرِّجَالُ قَوَّامُوْنَ عَلَى النِّسَآءِ

Allah has been to you Most Merciful!

30. If any do that in rancour and injustice, - soon shall We cast them into the Fire: and easy it is for Allah.

31. If you (but) eschew the most heinous of the things which you are forbidden to do, We shall expel out of you all the evil in you, and admit you to a gate of great honour.

32. And in no wise covet those things in which Allah has bestowed His gifts more freely on some of you than on others: to men

اللّٰهُ كَانَ بِكُمْ رَحِيمًا ۝ وَمَنْ

يَّفْعَلْ ذٰلِكَ عُدْوَانًا وَّظُلْمًا

فَسَوْفَ نُصْلِيهِ نَارًا ۚ وَكَانَ

ذٰلِكَ عَلَى اللّٰهِ يَسِيرًا ۝ إِنْ

تَجْتَنِبُوْا كَبَآئِرَ مَا تُنْهَوْنَ

عَنْهُ نُكَفِّرْ عَنْكُمْ سَيِّاٰتِكُمْ

وَنُدْخِلْكُمْ مُّدْخَلًا كَرِيمًا ۝

وَلَا تَتَمَنَّوْا مَا فَضَّلَ اللّٰهُ بِهٖ

بَعْضَكُمْ عَلٰى بَعْضٍ ۚ لِلرِّجَالِ

All-Wise.

27. Allah does wish to turn to you, but the wish of those who follow their lusts is that you should turn away (from Him),- far, far away.

28. Allah does wish to lighten your (difficulties): for man was created weak (in flesh).

29. O you who believe! Eat not up your property among your- selves in vanities: but let there be among you traffic and trade by mutual good-will: nor kill (or destroy) yourselves: for verily

حَكِيْمًا ۞ وَاللهُ يُرِيْدُ اَنْ يَّتُوْبَ

عَلَيْكُمْ وَيُرِيْدُ الَّذِيْنَ يَتَّبِعُوْنَ

الشَّهَوٰتِ اَنْ تَمِيْلُوْا مَيْلًا

عَظِيْمًا ۞ يُرِيْدُ اللهُ اَنْ يُّخَفِّفَ

عَنْكُمْ وَخُلِقَ الْاِنْسَانُ ضَعِيْفًا ۞

يٰٓاَيُّهَا الَّذِيْنَ اٰمَنُوْا لَا تَاْكُلُوْۤا

اَمْوَالَكُمْ بَيْنَكُمْ بِالْبَاطِلِ اِلَّاۤ

اَنْ تَكُوْنَ تِجَارَةً عَنْ تَرَاضٍ

مِّنْكُمْ وَلَا تَقْتُلُوْۤا اَنْفُسَكُمْ اِنَّ

taking paramours: when they are taken in wedlock, if they fall into shame, their punishment is half that for free women. This (permission) is for those among you who fear sin; but it is better for you that you practise self-restraint. And Allah is Oft-Forgiving, Most Merciful.

26. Allah does wish to make clear to you and to show you the ordinances of those before you; and (He does wish to) turn to you (in Mercy): and Allah is All-Knowing,

مُتَّخِذٰتِ اَخْدَانٍ ۚ فَاِذَآ اُحْصِنَّ

فَاِنْ اَتَيْنَ بِفَاحِشَةٍ فَعَلَيْهِنَّ

نِصْفُ مَا عَلَى الْمُحْصَنٰتِ مِنَ

الْعَذَابِ ۚ ذٰلِكَ لِمَنْ خَشِىَ

الْعَنَتَ مِنْكُمْ ۚ وَاَنْ تَصْبِرُوْا خَيْرٌ

لَّكُمْ ۚ وَاللّٰهُ غَفُوْرٌ رَّحِيْمٌ ۞ يُرِيْدُ

اللّٰهُ لِيُبَيِّنَ لَكُمْ وَيَهْدِيَكُمْ

سُنَنَ الَّذِيْنَ مِنْ قَبْلِكُمْ

وَيَتُوْبَ عَلَيْكُمْ ۚ وَاللّٰهُ عَلِيْمٌ

is All-Knowing, All-Wise.

25. If any of you have not the means wherewith to wed free believing women, they may wed believing girls from among those whom your right hands possess: and Allah has full knowledge about your faith. You are one from another: wed them with the leave of their owners, and give them their dowers, according to what is reasonable: they should be chaste, not lustful, nor

كَانَ عَلِيْمًا حَكِيْمًا ۞ وَمَنْ

لَّمْ يَسْتَطِعْ مِنْكُمْ طَوْلًا اَنْ

يَّنْكِحَ الْمُحْصَنٰتِ الْمُؤْمِنٰتِ

فَمِنْ مَّا مَلَكَتْ اَيْمَانُكُمْ مِّنْ

فَتَيٰتِكُمُ الْمُؤْمِنٰتِ ۚ وَاللّٰهُ اَعْلَمُ

بِاِيْمَانِكُمْ ۚ بَعْضُكُمْ مِّنْ بَعْضٍ ۚ

فَانْكِحُوْهُنَّ بِاِذْنِ اَهْلِهِنَّ

وَاٰتُوْهُنَّ اُجُوْرَهُنَّ بِالْمَعْرُوْفِ

مُحْصَنٰتٍ غَيْرَ مُسٰفِحٰتٍ وَّلَا

24. Also (prohibited are) women already married, except those whom your right hands possess: thus has Allah ordained (prohibitions) against you: except for these, all others are lawful, provided you seek (them in marriage) with gifts from your property, - desiring chastity, not lust. Seeing that you derive benefit from them, give them their dowers (at least) as prescribed; but if, after a dower is prescribed, you agree mutually (to vary it), there is no blame on you, and Allah

وَالْمُحْصَنٰتُ مِنَ النِّسَآءِ اِلَّا

مَا مَلَكَتْ اَيْمَانُكُمْ ۚ كِتٰبَ اللّٰهِ

عَلَيْكُمْ ۚ وَاُحِلَّ لَكُمْ مَّا وَرَآءَ

ذٰلِكُمْ اَنْ تَبْتَغُوْا بِاَمْوَالِكُمْ

مُّحْصِنِيْنَ غَيْرَ مُسٰفِحِيْنَ ۚ فَمَا

اسْتَمْتَعْتُمْ بِهٖ مِنْهُنَّ فَاٰتُوْهُنَّ

اُجُوْرَهُنَّ فَرِيْضَةً ۚ وَلَا جُنَاحَ

عَلَيْكُمْ فِيْمَا تَرَاضَيْتُمْ بِهٖ

مِنْۢ بَعْدِ الْفَرِيْضَةِ ۚ اِنَّ اللّٰهَ

تلك الكتب الاربعة

پاره

وَالْمُحْصَنٰتُ

(۵)

بِسْمِ اللَّهِ الرَّحْمَنِ الرَّحِيمِ

PART 6
La Yuhibbullaah

and in what has been revealed to him, never would they have taken them for friends and protectors, but most of them are rebellious wrong-doers.

82. Strongest among men in enmity to the believers will you find the Jews and Pagans; and nearest among them in love to the believers will you those who say, "We are Christians": because among these are men devoted to learning and men who have renounced the world, and they are not arrogant.

وَمَا أُنْزِلَ إِلَيْهِ مَا اتَّخَذُوهُمْ

أَوْلِيَاءَ وَلَٰكِنَّ كَثِيرًا مِّنْهُمْ

فَٰسِقُونَ ۞ لَتَجِدَنَّ أَشَدَّ النَّاسِ

عَدَاوَةً لِّلَّذِينَ آمَنُوا الْيَهُودَ

وَالَّذِينَ أَشْرَكُوا وَلَتَجِدَنَّ

أَقْرَبَهُم مَّوَدَّةً لِّلَّذِينَ آمَنُوا

الَّذِينَ قَالُوا إِنَّا نَصَارَىٰ

ذَٰلِكَ بِأَنَّ مِنْهُمْ قِسِّيسِينَ

وَرُهْبَانًا وَّأَنَّهُمْ لَا يَسْتَكْبِرُونَ ۞

and of Jesus the son of Mary: because they disobeyed and persisted in excesses.

79. Nor did they (usually) forbid one another the iniquities which they committed: evil indeed were the deeds which they did.

80. You see many of them turning in friendship to the unbelievers. Evil indeed are (the works) which their souls have sent forward before them (with the result), that Allah's wrath is on them, and in torment will they abide.

81. If only they had believed in Allah, in the Apostle,

وَعِيسَى ابْنِ مَرْيَمَ ذٰلِكَ بِمَا

عَصَوْا وَّ كَانُوْا يَعْتَدُوْنَ ۞ كَانُوْا

لَا يَتَنَاهَوْنَ عَنْ مُّنْكَرٍ فَعَلُوْهُ

لَبِئْسَ مَا كَانُوْا يَفْعَلُوْنَ ۞ تَرٰى

كَثِيْرًا مِّنْهُمْ يَتَوَلَّوْنَ الَّذِيْنَ

كَفَرُوْا لَبِئْسَ مَا قَدَّمَتْ لَهُمْ

أَنْفُسُهُمْ أَنْ سَخِطَ اللّٰهُ عَلَيْهِمْ

وَ فِى الْعَذَابِ هُمْ خٰلِدُوْنَ ۞

وَلَوْ كَانُوْا يُؤْمِنُوْنَ بِاللّٰهِ وَ النَّبِيِّ

something which has no power either to harm or benefit you? But Allah, - He it is that hears and knows all things."

77. Say: "O People of the Book! Exceed not in your religion the bounds (of what is proper), trespassing beyond the truth, nor follow the vain desires of people who went wrong in times gone by, - who misled many, and strayed (themselves) from the even way.

78. Curses were pronounced on those among the Children of Israel who rejected Faith, by the tongue of David

مَا لَا يَمْلِكُ لَكُمْ ضَرًّا وَّلَا

نَفْعًا ۚ وَاللّٰهُ هُوَ السَّمِيعُ

الْعَلِيمُ ۞ قُلْ يَآ أَهْلَ الْكِتٰبِ

لَا تَغْلُوا فِي دِينِكُمْ غَيْرَ الْحَقِّ

وَلَا تَتَّبِعُوٓا أَهْوَآءَ قَوْمٍ قَدْ

ضَلُّوا مِنْ قَبْلُ وَأَضَلُّوا كَثِيرًا

وَّضَلُّوا عَنْ سَوَآءِ السَّبِيلِ ۞

لُعِنَ الَّذِينَ كَفَرُوا مِنْ بَنِيٓ

إِسْرَآءِيلَ عَلَىٰ لِسَانِ دَاوٗدَ

the blasphemers among them.

74.   Why turn they not to Allah, and seek His forgiveness? For Allah is Oft-Forgiving, Most Merciful.

75.   Christ the son of Mary was no more than an Apostle; many were the Apostles that passed away before him. His mother was a woman of truth. They had both to eat their (daily) food. See how Allah does make His Signs clear to them; yet see in what ways they are deluded away from the truth!

76.   Say: "Will you worship, besides Allah,

كَفَرُوْا مِنْهُمْ عَذَابٌ اَلِيْمٌ ۞ اَفَلَا

يَتُوْبُوْنَ اِلَى اللهِ وَيَسْتَغْفِرُوْنَهٗ ۚ

وَاللهُ غَفُوْرٌ رَّحِيْمٌ ۞ مَا الْمَسِيْحُ

ابْنُ مَرْيَمَ اِلَّا رَسُوْلٌ ۚ قَدْ

خَلَتْ مِنْ قَبْلِهِ الرُّسُلُ ۚ

وَاُمُّهٗ صِدِّيْقَةٌ ۚ كَانَا يَأْكُلَانِ

الطَّعَامَ ۗ اُنْظُرْ كَيْفَ نُبَيِّنُ لَهُمُ

الْاٰيٰتِ ثُمَّ انْظُرْ اَنّٰى يُؤْفَكُوْنَ ۞

قُلْ اَتَعْبُدُوْنَ مِنْ دُوْنِ اللهِ

"O Children of Israel! Worship Allah, my Lord and your Lord." Whoever joins other Allah's with Allah, - Allah will forbid him the Garden, and the Fire will be his abode. There will for the wrong-doers be no one to help.

73. They do blaspheme who say: Allah is one of three in a Trinity: for there is no god except One God (Allah). If they desist not from their word (of blasphemy), verily a grievous Chastisement will befall

يٰبَنِىٓ اِسْرَآءِيلَ اعْبُدُوا اللّٰهَ

رَبِّى وَ رَبَّكُمْ ۖ اِنَّهٗ مَنْ يُّشْرِكْ

بِاللّٰهِ فَقَدْ حَرَّمَ اللّٰهُ عَلَيْهِ

الْجَنَّةَ وَ مَأْوٰىهُ النَّارُ ۖ وَ مَا

لِلظّٰلِمِينَ مِنْ اَنْصَارٍ ۞ لَقَدْ

كَفَرَ الَّذِينَ قَالُوٓا اِنَّ اللّٰهَ

ثَالِثُ ثَلٰثَةٍ ۘ وَ مَا مِنْ اِلٰهٍ

اِلَّآ اِلٰهٌ وَّاحِدٌ ۚ وَاِنْ لَّمْ يَنْتَهُوْا

عَمَّا يَقُوْلُوْنَ لَيَمَسَّنَّ الَّذِينَ

there came to them an Apostle with what they themselves desired not - some (of these) they called impostors, and some they (go so far as to) slay.

71. They thought there would be no trial (or punishment); so they became blind and deaf; yet Allah (in mercy) turned to them; yet again many of them became blind and deaf. But Allah sees well all that they do.

72. They do blaspheme who say: "Allah is Christ the son of Mary." But said Christ:

جَآءَهُمْ رَسُوْلٌ بِمَا لَا تَهْوٰٓى

اَنْفُسُهُمْ فَرِيْقًا كَذَّبُوْا وَ فَرِيْقًا

يَّقْتُلُوْنَ ۙ وَ حَسِبُوْۤا اَلَّا تَكُوْنَ

فِتْنَةٌ فَعَمُوْا وَصَمُّوْا ثُمَّ تَابَ

اللّٰهُ عَلَيْهِمْ ثُمَّ عَمُوْا وَصَمُّوْا

كَثِيْرٌ مِّنْهُمْ ۭ وَاللّٰهُ بَصِيْرٌۢ

بِمَا يَعْمَلُوْنَ ۙ لَقَدْ كَفَرَ الَّذِيْنَ

قَالُوْۤا اِنَّ اللّٰهَ هُوَ الْمَسِيْحُ

ابْنُ مَرْيَمَ ۭ وَقَالَ الْمَسِيْحُ

their obstinate rebellion and blasphemy. But sorrow you not over (these) people without Faith.

69. Those who believe (in the Qur'an), those who follow the Jewish (scriptures), and the Sabians and the Christians, - any who believe in Allah and the Last Day, and work righteousness, - on them shall be no fear, nor shall they grieve.

70. We took the covenant of the Children of Israel and sent them Apostles, every time,

أُنْزِلَ إِلَيْكَ مِنْ رَّبِّكَ طُغْيَانًا

وَّكُفْرًا فَلَا تَأْسَ عَلَى الْقَوْمِ

الْكٰفِرِيْنَ ۞ اِنَّ الَّذِيْنَ اٰمَنُوْا

وَالَّذِيْنَ هَادُوْا وَالصّٰبِئُوْنَ

وَالنَّصٰرٰى مَنْ اٰمَنَ بِاللهِ وَالْيَوْمِ

الْاٰخِرِ وَعَمِلَ صَالِحًا فَلَا خَوْفٌ

عَلَيْهِمْ وَلَا هُمْ يَحْزَنُوْنَ ۞ لَقَدْ

اَخَذْنَا مِيْثَاقَ بَنِيْۤ اِسْرَآئِيْلَ

وَاَرْسَلْنَاۤ اِلَيْهِمْ رُسُلًا ؕ كُلَّمَا

Apostle! Proclaim the (message) which has been sent to you from your Lord. If you did not, you would not have fulfilled and proclaimed His mission. And Allah will defend you from men (who mean mischief). For Allah guides not those who reject Faith.

68. Say: "O People of the Book! You have no ground to stand upon unless you stand fast by the Law, the Gospel, and all the revelation that has come to you from your Lord." It is the revelation that comes to you from your Lord, that increases in most of them

يَٰٓأَيُّهَا الرَّسُولُ بَلِّغْ مَآ أُنزِلَ إِلَيْكَ

مِن رَّبِّكَ ۖ وَإِن لَّمْ تَفْعَلْ فَمَا

بَلَّغْتَ رِسَالَتَهُۥ ۚ وَٱللّٰهُ يَعْصِمُكَ

مِنَ ٱلنَّاسِ ۗ إِنَّ ٱللّٰهَ لَا يَهْدِى

ٱلْقَوْمَ ٱلْكَٰفِرِينَ ۝ قُلْ يَٰٓأَهْلَ

ٱلْكِتَٰبِ لَسْتُمْ عَلَىٰ شَىْءٍ حَتَّىٰ

تُقِيمُوا۟ ٱلتَّوْرَىٰةَ وَٱلْإِنجِيلَ

وَمَآ أُنزِلَ إِلَيْكُم مِّن رَّبِّكُمْ ۚ

وَلَيَزِيدَنَّ كَثِيرًا مِّنْهُم مَّآ

loves not those who do mischief.

65. If only the People of the Book had believed and been righteous, We should indeed have blotted out their iniquities and admitted them to Gardens of Bliss.

66. If only they had stood fast by the Law, the Gospel, and all the revelation that was sent to them from their Lord, they would have enjoyed happiness from every side. There is from among them a party on the right course: but many of them follow a course that is evil.

67. O

يُحِبُّ الْمُفْسِدِينَ ۝ وَلَوْ أَنَّ

أَهْلَ الْكِتَٰبِ اٰمَنُوْا وَاتَّقَوْا لَكَفَّرْنَا

عَنْهُمْ سَيِّاٰتِهِمْ وَلَاَدْخَلْنٰهُمْ

جَنّٰتِ النَّعِيْمِ ۝ وَلَوْ أَنَّهُمْ أَقَامُوا

التَّوْرٰىةَ وَالْاِنْجِيْلَ وَمَا أُنْزِلَ

اِلَيْهِمْ مِّنْ رَّبِّهِمْ لَاَكَلُوْا مِنْ

فَوْقِهِمْ وَمِنْ تَحْتِ أَرْجُلِهِمْ

مِنْهُمْ أُمَّةٌ مُّقْتَصِدَةٌ ط وَكَثِيْرٌ

مِّنْهُمْ سَآءَ مَا يَعْمَلُوْنَ ۝ يٰأَيُّهَا

And be they accursed for the (blasphemy) they utter. No, both His hands are widely outstretched: He gives and spends (of His Bounty) as He pleases. But the revelation that comes to you from Allah increases in most of them their obstinate rebellion and blasphemy. Amongst them We have placed enmity and hatred till the Day of Judgment. Every time they kindle the fire of war, Allah does extinguish it; but they (ever) strive to do mischief on earth. And Allah

أَيْدِيهِمْ وَلُعِنُوْا بِمَا قَالُوْا ۘ

بَلْ يَدَاهُ مَبْسُوْطَتٰنِ ۙ يُنْفِقُ

كَيْفَ يَشَآءُ ؕ وَلَيَزِيْدَنَّ كَثِيْرًا

مِّنْهُمْ مَّاۤ اُنْزِلَ اِلَيْكَ مِنْ رَّبِّكَ

طُغْيَانًا وَّكُفْرًا ؕ وَاَلْقَيْنَا بَيْنَهُمُ

الْعَدَاوَةَ وَالْبَغْضَآءَ اِلٰى يَوْمِ

الْقِيٰمَةِ ؕ كُلَّمَاۤ اَوْقَدُوْا نَارًا

لِّلْحَرْبِ اَطْفَاَهَا اللّٰهُ ۙ وَيَسْعَوْنَ

فِى الْاَرْضِ فَسَادًا ؕ وَاللّٰهُ لَا

with the same but Allah knows fully all that they hide.

62. Many of them you see, racing each other in sin and rancour, and their eating of things forbidden. Evil indeed are the things that they do.

63. Why do not the Rabbis and the Doctors of Law forbid them from their (habit of) uttering sinful words and eating things forbidden? Evil indeed are their works.

64. The Jews say: "Allah's hand is tied up." Be their hands tied up

بِهٖ ۚ وَاللهُ اَعْلَمُ بِمَا كَانُوْا

يَكْتُمُوْنَ ۞ وَتَرٰى كَثِيْرًا مِّنْهُمْ

يُسَارِعُوْنَ فِي الْاِثْمِ وَالْعُدْوَانِ

وَاَكْلِهِمُ السُّحْتَ ۚ لَبِئْسَ مَا

كَانُوْا يَعْمَلُوْنَ ۞ لَوْلَا يَنْهٰىهُمُ

الرَّبّٰنِيُّوْنَ وَالْاَحْبَارُ عَنْ قَوْلِهِمُ

الْاِثْمَ وَاَكْلِهِمُ السُّحْتَ ۚ لَبِئْسَ

مَا كَانُوْا يَصْنَعُوْنَ ۞ وَقَالَتِ

الْيَهُوْدُ يَدُ اللهِ مَغْلُوْلَةٌ ۚ غُلَّتْ

before (us), and (perhaps) that most of you are rebellious and disobedient?"

60.   Say: "Shall I point out to you something much worse than this, (as judged) by the treatment it received from Allah? Those who incurred the Curse of Allah and His Wrath, those of whom some He transformed into apes and swine, those who worshipped evil; - these are (many times) worse in rank, and far more astray from the even path!"

61.   When they come to you, they say: "We believe": but in fact they enter with a mind against Faith, and they go out

قَبْلُ وَاَنَّ اَكْثَرَكُمْ فٰسِقُوْنَ ۞

قُلْ هَلْ اُنَبِّئُكُمْ بِشَرٍّ مِّنْ

ذٰلِكَ مَثُوْبَةً عِنْدَ اللّٰهِ مَنْ

لَّعَنَهُ اللّٰهُ وَغَضِبَ عَلَيْهِ

وَجَعَلَ مِنْهُمُ الْقِرَدَةَ وَالْخَنَازِيْرَ

وَعَبَدَ الطَّاغُوْتَ ط اُولٰٓئِكَ شَرٌّ

مَّكَانًا وَّاَضَلُّ عَنْ سَوَآءِ السَّبِيْلِ ۞

وَاِذَا جَآءُوْكُمْ قَالُوْٓا اٰمَنَّا وَقَدْ

دَّخَلُوْا بِالْكُفْرِ وَهُمْ قَدْ خَرَجُوْا

your religion for a mockery or sport,- whether among those who received the Scripture before you, or among those who reject Faith; but fear you Allah, if you have Faith (indeed).

58. When you proclaim your call to prayer they take it (but) as mockery and sport; that is because they are a people without understanding.

59. Say: "O People of the Book! Do you disapprove of us for no other reason than that we believe in Allah, and the revelation that has come to us and that which came

دِيْنَكُمْ هُزُوًا وَّلَعِبًا مِّنَ الَّذِيْنَ

اُوْتُوا الْكِتٰبَ مِنْ قَبْلِكُمْ وَالْكُفَّارَ

اَوْلِيَآءَ ۚ وَاتَّقُوا اللّٰهَ اِنْ كُنْتُمْ

مُّؤْمِنِيْنَ ۞ وَاِذَا نَادَيْتُمْ اِلَى

الصَّلٰوةِ اتَّخَذُوْهَا هُزُوًا وَّلَعِبًا ۚ

ذٰلِكَ بِاَنَّهُمْ قَوْمٌ لَّا يَعْقِلُوْنَ ۞

قُلْ يٰاَهْلَ الْكِتٰبِ هَلْ تَنْقِمُوْنَ

مِنَّا اِلَّا اَنْ اٰمَنَّا بِاللّٰهِ وَمَا

اُنْزِلَ اِلَيْنَا وَمَا اُنْزِلَ مِنْ

the Grace of Allah, which He will bestow on whom He pleases. And Allah encompasses all, and He knows all things.

55. Your (real) friends are (no less than) Allah, His Apostle, and the (fellowship of) believers,- those who establish regular prayers and regular charity, and they bow down humbly (in worship).

56. As to those who turn (for friendship) to Allah, His Apostle, and the (fellowship of) believers,- it is the fellowship of Allah that must certainly triumph.

57. O you who believe! Take not for friends and protectors those who take

فَضْلُ اللّٰهِ يُؤْتِيهِ مَنْ يَّشَآءُ

وَاللّٰهُ وَاسِعٌ عَلِيْمٌ ۞ اِنَّمَا

وَلِيُّكُمُ اللّٰهُ وَرَسُوْلُهٗ وَالَّذِيْنَ

اٰمَنُوا الَّذِيْنَ يُقِيْمُوْنَ الصَّلٰوةَ

وَيُؤْتُوْنَ الزَّكٰوةَ وَهُمْ رٰكِعُوْنَ ۞

وَمَنْ يَّتَوَلَّ اللّٰهَ وَرَسُوْلَهٗ

وَالَّذِيْنَ اٰمَنُوا فَاِنَّ حِزْبَ اللّٰهِ

هُمُ الْغٰلِبُوْنَ ۞ يٰٓاَيُّهَا الَّذِيْنَ

اٰمَنُوْا لَا تَتَّخِذُوا الَّذِيْنَ اتَّخَذُوا

swore their strongest oaths by Allah, that they were with you?" All that they do will be in vain, and they will fall into (nothing but) ruin.

54. O you who believe! If any from among you turn back from his Faith, soon will Allah produce a people whom He will love as they will love Him, - lowly with the believers, mighty against the rejecters, fighting in the Way of Allah, and never afraid of the reproaches of such as find fault. That is

اَقْسَمُوا بِاللهِ جَهْدَ اَيْمَانِهِمْ

اِنَّهُمْ لَمَعَكُمْ ۚ حَبِطَتْ اَعْمَالُهُمْ

فَاَصْبَحُوا خٰسِرِيْنَ ۞ يٰۤاَيُّهَا الَّذِيْنَ

اٰمَنُوْا مَنْ يَّرْتَدَّ مِنْكُمْ عَنْ

دِيْنِهٖ فَسَوْفَ يَاْتِى اللهُ بِقَوْمٍ

يُّحِبُّهُمْ وَيُحِبُّوْنَهٗۤ ۙ اَذِلَّةٍ عَلَى

الْمُؤْمِنِيْنَ اَعِزَّةٍ عَلَى الْكٰفِرِيْنَ

يُجَاهِدُوْنَ فِيْ سَبِيْلِ اللهِ

وَلَا يَخَافُوْنَ لَوْمَةَ لَآئِمٍ ۚ ذٰلِكَ

(for friendship) is of them. Verily Allah guideth not a people unjust .

52. Those in whose hearts is a disease - you see how eagerly they run about amongst them, saying: "We do fear lest a change of fortune bring us disaster." Ah! Perhaps Allah will give (you) victory, or a decision according to His Will. Then will they repent of the thoughts which they secretly harboured in their hearts.

53. And those who believe will say: "Are these the men who

فَإِنَّهُ مِنْهُمْ ۗ إِنَّ اللَّهَ لَا يَهْدِى

الْقَوْمَ الظَّالِمِينَ ۞ فَتَرَى الَّذِينَ

فِى قُلُوبِهِمْ مَّرَضٌ يُّسَارِعُونَ

فِيهِمْ يَقُولُونَ نَخْشَى أَنْ تُصِيبَنَا

دَآئِرَةٌ ۚ فَعَسَى اللَّهُ أَنْ يَّأْتِىَ

بِالْفَتْحِ أَوْ أَمْرٍ مِّنْ عِنْدِهِ

فَيُصْبِحُوا عَلَى مَآ أَسَرُّوا فِى

أَنْفُسِهِمْ نَادِمِينَ ۞ وَيَقُولُ

الَّذِينَ آمَنُوا أَهٰؤُلَآءِ الَّذِينَ

to you. And if they turn away, be assured that for some of their crime it is Allah's purpose to punish them. And truly most men are rebellious.

50. Do they then seek after a judgment of (the days of) ignorance? But who, for a people whose faith is assured, can give better judgment than Allah?

51. O you who believe! Take not the Jews and the Christians for your friends and protectors: they are but friends and protectors to each other. And he amongst you that turns to them

اللهُ اِلَيْكَ ۚ فَاِنْ تَوَلَّوْا فَاعْلَمْ

اَنَّمَا يُرِيْدُ اللهُ اَنْ يُّصِيْبَهُمْ

بِبَعْضِ ذُنُوْبِهِمْ ۗ وَاِنَّ كَثِيْرًا

مِّنَ النَّاسِ لَفٰسِقُوْنَ ۞ اَفَحُكْمَ

الْجَاهِلِيَّةِ يَبْغُوْنَ ۗ وَمَنْ اَحْسَنُ

مِنَ اللهِ حُكْمًا لِّقَوْمٍ يُّوْقِنُوْنَ ۞

يٰۤاَيُّهَا الَّذِيْنَ اٰمَنُوْا لَا تَتَّخِذُوا

الْيَهُوْدَ وَالنَّصٰرٰۤى اَوْلِيَآءَ ۘ بَعْضُهُمْ

اَوْلِيَآءُ بَعْضٍ ۚ وَمَنْ يَّتَوَلَّهُمْ مِّنْكُمْ

and an open way. If Allah had so willed, He would have made you a single people, but (His Plan is) to test you in what He have given you: so strive as in a race in all virtues. The goal of you all is to Allah; it is He that will show you the truth of the matters in which you dispute;

49. And this (He commands): Judge you between them by what Allah has revealed, and follow not their vain desires, but beware of them lest they beguile you from any of that (teaching) which Allah has sent down

وَّمِنْهَاجًا ۚ وَلَوْ شَآءَ اللهُ لَجَعَلَكُمْ

اُمَّةً وَّاحِدَةً وَّلٰكِنْ لِّيَبْلُوَكُمْ

فِيْ مَاۤ اٰتٰىكُمْ فَاسْتَبِقُوا الْخَيْرٰتِ ۗ

اِلَى اللهِ مَرْجِعُكُمْ جَمِيْعًا

فَيُنَبِّئُكُمْ بِمَا كُنْتُمْ فِيْهِ

تَخْتَلِفُوْنَ ۞ وَاَنِ احْكُمْ بَيْنَهُمْ

بِمَاۤ اَنْزَلَ اللهُ وَلَا تَتَّبِعْ

اَهْوَآءَهُمْ وَاحْذَرْهُمْ اَنْ

يَّفْتِنُوْكَ عَنْ بَعْضِ مَاۤ اَنْزَلَ

by what Allah has revealed therein. If any do fail to judge by (the light of) what Allah has revealed, they are (no better than) those who rebel.

48. To you We sent the Scripture in truth, confirming the scripture that came before it, and guarding it in safety: so judge between them by what Allah has revealed, and follow not their vain desires, diverging from the Truth that has come to you. To each among you have We prescribed a law

بِمَآ اَنْزَلَ اللهُ فِيْهِ ۗ وَمَنْ لَّمْ

يَحْكُمْ بِمَآ اَنْزَلَ اللهُ فَاُولٰٓئِكَ

هُمُ الْفٰسِقُوْنَ ۞ وَاَنْزَلْنَآ اِلَيْكَ

الْكِتٰبَ بِالْحَقِّ مُصَدِّقًا لِّمَا

بَيْنَ يَدَيْهِ مِنَ الْكِتٰبِ

وَمُهَيْمِنًا عَلَيْهِ فَاحْكُمْ بَيْنَهُمْ

بِمَآ اَنْزَلَ اللهُ وَلَا تَتَّبِعْ

اَهْوَآءَهُمْ عَمَّا جَآءَكَ مِنَ

الْحَقِّ ۚ لِكُلٍّ جَعَلْنَا مِنْكُمْ شِرْعَةً

And if any fail to judge by (the light of) what Allah has revealed, they are (no better than) wrong-doers.

46. And in their footsteps We sent Jesus the son of Mary, confirming the Law that had come before him: We sent him the Gospel: therein was guidance and light, and confirmation of the Law that had come before him: a guidance and an admonition to those who fear Allah.

47. Let the People of the Gospel judge

وَمَنْ لَّمْ يَحْكُمْ بِمَآ اَنْزَلَ
اللّٰهُ فَاُولٰٓئِكَ هُمُ الظّٰلِمُوْنَ ۞
وَقَفَّيْنَا عَلٰٓى اٰثَارِهِمْ بِعِيْسَى
ابْنِ مَرْيَمَ مُصَدِّقًا لِّمَا بَيْنَ
يَدَيْهِ مِنَ التَّوْرٰىةِ ۫ وَاٰتَيْنٰهُ
الْاِنْجِيْلَ فِيْهِ هُدًى وَّنُوْرٌ
وَّمُصَدِّقًا لِّمَا بَيْنَ يَدَيْهِ مِنَ
التَّوْرٰىةِ وَهُدًى وَّمَوْعِظَةً
لِّلْمُتَّقِيْنَ ۞ وَلْيَحْكُمْ اَهْلُ الْاِنْجِيْلِ

therefore fear not men, but fear
Me, and sell not My Signs for a
miserable price. If any do fail to
judge by (the light of) what Allah
has revealed, they are (no better
than) unbelievers.

45. We ordained therein for
them: "Life for life, eye for eye,
nose for nose, ear for ear, tooth for
tooth, and wounds equal for
equal." But if any one remits the
retaliation by way of charity, it is
an act of atonement for himself.

فَلَا تَخْشَوُا النَّاسَ وَاخْشَوْنِ

وَلَا تَشْتَرُوا بِاٰيٰتِى ثَمَنًا قَلِيلًا

وَمَنْ لَّمْ يَحْكُمْ بِمَآ اَنْزَلَ

اللّٰهُ فَاُولٰٓئِكَ هُمُ الْكٰفِرُوْنَ ۝

وَكَتَبْنَا عَلَيْهِمْ فِيْهَآ اَنَّ النَّفْسَ

بِالنَّفْسِ وَالْعَيْنَ بِالْعَيْنِ وَالْاَنْفَ

بِالْاَنْفِ وَالْاُذُنَ بِالْاُذُنِ وَالسِّنَّ

بِالسِّنِّ وَالْجُرُوْحَ قِصَاصٌ فَمَنْ

تَصَدَّقَ بِهٖ فَهُوَ كَفَّارَةٌ لَّهٗ

43. But why do they come to you for decision, when they have (their own) Law before them?-therein is the (plain) command of Allah; yet even after that, they would turn away. For they are not (really) people of Faith.

44. It was We Who revealed the Law (to Moses): therein was guidance and light. By its standard have been judged the Jews, by the Prophets who bowed (as in Islam) to Allah's Will, by the Rabbis and the Doctors of Law: for to them was entrusted the protection of Allah's Book, and they were witnesses there to:

وَكَيْفَ يُحَكِّمُوْنَكَ وَعِنْدَهُمُ

التَّوْرٰىةُ فِيْهَا حُكْمُ اللّٰهِ ثُمَّ

يَتَوَلَّوْنَ مِنْۢ بَعْدِ ذٰلِكَ ۚ وَمَاۤ

أُولٰٓئِكَ بِالْمُؤْمِنِيْنَ ۞ اِنَّاۤ أَنْزَلْنَا

التَّوْرٰىةَ فِيْهَا هُدًى وَّنُوْرٌ ۚ يَحْكُمُ

بِهَا النَّبِيُّوْنَ الَّذِيْنَ أَسْلَمُوْا

لِلَّذِيْنَ هَادُوْا وَالرَّبَّانِيُّوْنَ

وَالْأَحْبَارُ بِمَا اسْتُحْفِظُوْا مِنْ

كِتٰبِ اللّٰهِ وَكَانُوْا عَلَيْهِ شُهَدَآءَ ۚ

it is not Allah's Will to purify their hearts. For them there is disgrace in this world, and in the Hereafter a heavy Punishment.

42. (They are fond of) listening to falsehood, of devouring anything forbidden. If they do come to you, either judge between them, or decline to interfere. If you decline, they cannot hurt you in the least. If you judge, judge in equity between them. For Allah loves those who judge in equity.

الَّذِينَ لَمْ يُرِدِ اللهُ اَنْ يُّطَهِّرَ

قُلُوبَهُمْ ۚ لَهُمْ فِي الدُّنْيَا خِزْيٌ ۖ

وَّلَهُمْ فِي الْاٰخِرَةِ عَذَابٌ عَظِيمٌ ۙ ۞

سَمّٰعُونَ لِلْكَذِبِ اَكّٰلُونَ لِلسُّحْتِ ۚ

فَاِنْ جَآءُوكَ فَاحْكُمْ بَيْنَهُمْ

اَوْ اَعْرِضْ عَنْهُمْ ۚ وَاِنْ تُعْرِضْ

عَنْهُمْ فَلَنْ يَّضُرُّوكَ شَيْئًا ۖ وَاِنْ

حَكَمْتَ فَاحْكُمْ بَيْنَهُمْ بِالْقِسْطِ ۚ

اِنَّ اللهَ يُحِبُّ الْمُقْسِطِينَ ۞

"We believe" with their lips but whose hearts have no faith; or it be among the Jews, - men who will listen to any lie, - will listen even to others who have never so much as come to you. They change the words from their (right) times and places: they say, "If you are given this, take it, but if not, beware!" If any one's trial is intended by Allah you have no authority in the least for him against Allah. For such -

اٰمَنَّا بِاَفْوَاهِهِمْ وَلَمْ تُؤْمِنْ

قُلُوبُهُمْ ۚ وَمِنَ الَّذِيْنَ هَادُوْا ۛ

سَمّٰعُوْنَ لِلْكَذِبِ سَمّٰعُوْنَ لِقَوْمٍ

اٰخَرِيْنَ ۙ لَمْ يَاْتُوْكَ ۚ يُحَرِّفُوْنَ

الْكَلِمَ مِنْ بَعْدِ مَوَاضِعِهٖ ۚ يَقُوْلُوْنَ

اِنْ اُوْتِيْتُمْ هٰذَا فَخُذُوْهُ

وَاِنْ لَّمْ تُؤْتَوْهُ فَاحْذَرُوْا ۚ وَمَنْ

يُّرِدِ اللّٰهُ فِتْنَتَهٗ فَلَنْ تَمْلِكَ

لَهٗ مِنَ اللّٰهِ شَيْئًا ۚ اُولٰٓئِكَ

after his crime, and amends his conduct, Allah turns to him in forgiveness; for Allah is Oft-Forgiving, Most Merciful.

40. Do you not know that to Allah (alone) belongs the dominion of the heavens and the earth? He punishes whom He pleases, and He forgives whom He pleases: and Allah has power over all things.

41. O Apostle! Let not those grieve you, who race each other into unbelief: (whether it be) among those who say

بَعْدِ ظُلْمِهِ وَ أَصْلَحَ فَإِنَّ اللهَ

يَتُوبُ عَلَيْهِ ۚ إِنَّ اللهَ غَفُورٌ

رَّحِيمٌ ۞ أَلَمْ تَعْلَمْ أَنَّ اللهَ

لَهُ مُلْكُ السَّمٰوٰتِ وَالْأَرْضِ

يُعَذِّبُ مَنْ يَّشَآءُ وَيَغْفِرُ

لِمَنْ يَّشَآءُ ۚ وَاللهُ عَلٰى كُلِّ

شَىْءٍ قَدِيرٌ ۞ يٰٓأَيُّهَا الرَّسُولُ

لَا يَحْزُنْكَ الَّذِينَ يُسَارِعُونَ

فِى الْكُفْرِ مِنَ الَّذِينَ قَالُوٓا

to give as ransom for the Chastisement of the Day of Judgment, it would never be accepted of them, theirs would be a grievous Chastisement.

37. Their wish will be to get out of the Fire, but never will they get out therefrom: their Chastisement will be one that endures.

38. As to the thief, Male or female, cut off his or her hands: a punishment by way of example, from Allah, for their crime: and Allah is Exalted in Power.

39. But if the thief repents

لِيَفْتَدُوا بِهٖ مِنْ عَذَابِ يَوْمِ

الْقِيٰمَةِ مَا تُقُبِّلَ مِنْهُمْ ۚ وَلَهُمْ

عَذَابٌ اَلِيْمٌ ۞ يُرِيْدُوْنَ اَنْ

يَّخْرُجُوْا مِنَ النَّارِ وَمَا هُمْ

بِخٰرِجِيْنَ مِنْهَا ۖ وَلَهُمْ عَذَابٌ

مُّقِيْمٌ ۞ وَالسَّارِقُ وَالسَّارِقَةُ

فَاقْطَعُوْٓا اَيْدِيَهُمَا جَزَآءًۢ بِمَا

كَسَبَا نَكَالًا مِّنَ اللّٰهِ ؕ وَاللّٰهُ

عَزِيْزٌ حَكِيْمٌ ۞ فَمَنْ تَابَ مِنْۢ

a heavy Punishment is theirs in the Hereafter;

34. Except for those who repent before they fall into your power: in that case, know that Allah is Oft-Forgiving, Most Merciful.

35. O you who believe! Do your duty to Allah, seek the means of approach unto Him, and strive with might and main in His cause: that you may prosper.

36. As to those who reject Faith, - if they had everything on earth, and twice repeated,

الْاٰخِرَةِ عَذَابٌ عَظِيْمٌ ۞ اِلَّا

الَّذِيْنَ تَابُوْا مِنْ قَبْلِ اَنْ

تَقْدِرُوْا عَلَيْهِمْ ۚ فَاعْلَمُوْٓا اَنَّ اللّٰهَ

غَفُوْرٌ رَّحِيْمٌ ۞ يٰٓاَيُّهَا الَّذِيْنَ

اٰمَنُوا اتَّقُوا اللّٰهَ وَابْتَغُوْٓا اِلَيْهِ

الْوَسِيْلَةَ وَجَاهِدُوْا فِيْ سَبِيْلِهٖ

لَعَلَّكُمْ تُفْلِحُوْنَ ۞ اِنَّ الَّذِيْنَ

كَفَرُوْا لَوْ اَنَّ لَهُمْ مَّا فِي

الْاَرْضِ جَمِيْعًا وَّمِثْلَهٗ مَعَهٗ

Our Apostles with Clear Signs, yet, even after that, many of them continued to commit excesses in the land.

33. The punishment of those who wage war against Allah and His Apostle, and strive with might and main for mischief through the land is: execution, or crucifixion, or the cutting off of hands and feet from opposite sides, or exile from the land: that is their disgrace in this world, and

رُسُلُنَا بِالْبَيِّنَـٰتِ ثُمَّ اِنَّ

كَثِيرًا مِّنْهُمْ بَعْدَ ذَٰلِكَ فِي

الْاَرْضِ لَمُسْرِفُونَ ۞ اِنَّمَا جَزَٰٓؤُا

الَّذِينَ يُحَارِبُونَ اللّٰهَ وَرَسُولَهُ

وَيَسْعَوْنَ فِي الْاَرْضِ فَسَادًا

اَنْ يُّقَتَّلُوْٓا اَوْ يُصَلَّبُوْٓا اَوْ تُقَطَّعَ

اَيْدِيْهِمْ وَاَرْجُلُهُمْ مِّنْ خِلَافٍ

اَوْ يُنْفَوْا مِنَ الْاَرْضِ ذَٰلِكَ لَهُمْ

خِزْىٌ فِي الدُّنْيَا وَلَهُمْ فِي

"Was I not even able to be as this raven, and to hide the shame of my brother?" Then he became full of regrets –

32. On that account: We ordained for the Children of Israel that if any one slew a person – unless it be for murder or for spreading mischief in the land – it would be as if he slew the whole people: and if any one saved a life, it would be as if he saved the life of the whole people. Then although there came to them

اَعَجَزْتُ اَنْ اَكُوْنَ مِثْلَ هٰذَا

الْغُرَابِ فَاُوَارِيَ سَوْءَةَ اَخِيْ

فَاَصْبَحَ مِنَ النّٰدِمِيْنَ ۩ مِنْ

اَجْلِ ذٰلِكَ ۚ كَتَبْنَا عَلٰى بَنِيْ

اِسْرَآءِيْلَ اَنَّهٗ مَنْ قَتَلَ نَفْسًا

بِغَيْرِ نَفْسٍ اَوْ فَسَادٍ فِى الْاَرْضِ

فَكَاَنَّمَا قَتَلَ النَّاسَ جَمِيْعًا ۚ

وَمَنْ اَحْيَاهَا فَكَاَنَّمَا اَحْيَا

النَّاسَ جَمِيْعًا ۗ وَلَقَدْ جَآءَتْهُمْ

for I do fear Allah, the Cherisher of the worlds."

29. "For me, I intend to let you draw on yourself my sin as well as your, for you will be among the Companions of the Fire, and that is the reward of those who do wrong."

30. The (selfish) soul of the other led him to the murder of his brother: he murdered him, and became (himself) one of the lost ones.

31. Then Allah sent a raven, who scratched the ground, to show him how to hide the shame of his brother. "Woe is me!" said he;

اِنِّىۤ اَخَافُ اللّٰهَ رَبَّ الْعٰلَمِيْنَ ۞

اِنِّىۤ اُرِيْدُ اَنْ تَبُوۡٓاَ بِاِثْمِىۡ

وَاِثْمِكَ فَتَكُوۡنَ مِنْ اَصْحٰبِ

النَّارِ ۚ وَذٰلِكَ جَزٰٓؤُا الظّٰلِمِيْنَ ۞

فَطَوَّعَتْ لَهٗ نَفْسُهٗ قَتْلَ اَخِيْهِ

فَقَتَلَهٗ فَاَصْبَحَ مِنَ الْخٰسِرِيْنَ ۞

فَبَعَثَ اللّٰهُ غُرَابًا يَّبْحَثُ فِى

الْاَرْضِ لِيُرِيَهٗ كَيْفَ يُوَارِىۡ

سَوْءَةَ اَخِيْهِ ۚ قَالَ يٰوَيْلَتٰىۤ

the land: but sorrow you not over these rebellious people."

27. Recite to them the truth of the story of the two sons of Adam. Behold! They each presented a sacrifice (to Allah): it was accepted from one, but not from the other. Said the latter: "Be sure I will slay you." "Surely," said the former, "Allah does accept of the sacrifice of those who are righteous."

28. "If you do stretch your hand against me, to slay me, it is not for me to stretch my hand against you to slay you:

الْاَرْضِ ۚ فَلَا تَاْسَ عَلَى الْقَوْمِ
الْفٰسِقِيْنَ ۞ وَاتْلُ عَلَيْهِمْ نَبَاَ
ابْنَىْ اٰدَمَ بِالْحَقِّ ۘ اِذْ قَرَّبَا
قُرْبَانًا فَتُقُبِّلَ مِنْ اَحَدِهِمَا
وَلَمْ يُتَقَبَّلْ مِنَ الْاٰخَرِ ۘ قَالَ
لَاَقْتُلَنَّكَ ۘ قَالَ اِنَّمَا يَتَقَبَّلُ اللّٰهُ
مِنَ الْمُتَّقِيْنَ ۞ لَئِنْ بَسَطْتَّ
اِلَىَّ يَدَكَ لِتَقْتُلَنِىْ مَا اَنَا
بِبَاسِطٍ يَّدِىَ اِلَيْكَ لِاَقْتُلَكَ

if you have faith."

24. They said: "O Moses! While they remain there, never shall we be able to enter, to the end of time. Go you, and your Lord, and fight you two, while we sit here (and watch)."

25. He said: "O my Lord! I have power only over myself and my brother: so separate us from this rebellious people!"

26. Allah said: "Therefore will the land be out of their reach for forty years: in distraction will they wander through

اِنْ كُنْتُمْ مُّؤْمِنِيْنَ ۞ قَالُوْا

يٰمُوْسٰى اِنَّا لَنْ نَّدْخُلَهَا اَبَدًا

مَّا دَامُوْا فِيْهَا فَاذْهَبْ اَنْتَ

وَرَبُّكَ فَقَاتِلَا اِنَّا هٰهُنَا

قٰعِدُوْنَ ۞ قَالَ رَبِّ اِنِّيْ لَآ

اَمْلِكُ اِلَّا نَفْسِيْ وَاَخِيْ فَافْرُقْ

بَيْنَنَا وَبَيْنَ الْقَوْمِ الْفٰسِقِيْنَ ۞

قَالَ فَاِنَّهَا مُحَرَّمَةٌ عَلَيْهِمْ

اَرْبَعِيْنَ سَنَةً ۚ يَتِيْهُوْنَ فِى

back ignominiously, for then will you be overthrown, to your own ruin."

22. They said: "O Moses! In this land are a people of exceeding strength: never shall we enter it until they leave it: if (once) they leave, then shall we enter."

23. (But) among (their) Allah-fearing men were two on whom Allah had bestowed His Grace: they said: "Assault them at the (proper) gate: when once you are in, victory will be yours; but on Allah put your trust

أَدْبَارِكُمْ فَتَنْقَلِبُوْا خٰسِرِيْنَ ۩

قَالُوْا يٰمُوْسٰى اِنَّ فِيْهَا قَوْمًا

جَبَّارِيْنَ ۚ وَاِنَّا لَنْ نَّدْخُلَهَا حَتّٰى

يَخْرُجُوْا مِنْهَا ۚ فَاِنْ يَّخْرُجُوْا مِنْهَا

فَاِنَّا دٰخِلُوْنَ ۩ قَالَ رَجُلٰنِ

مِنَ الَّذِيْنَ يَخَافُوْنَ اَنْعَمَ

اللّٰهُ عَلَيْهِمَا ادْخُلُوْا عَلَيْهِمُ

الْبَابَ ۚ فَاِذَا دَخَلْتُمُوْهُ فَاِنَّكُمْ

غٰلِبُوْنَ ۚ ۬ وَعَلَى اللّٰهِ فَتَوَكَّلُوْۤا

but now has come unto you a bringer of glad tidings and a warner (from evil). And Allah has power over all things.

20. Remember Moses said to his People: "O my People! Call in remembrance the favour of Allah unto you, when He produced Prophets among you, made you kings, and gave you what He had not given to any other among the people.

21. "O my People! Enter the holy land which Allah has assigned unto you, and turn not

فَقَدْ جَآءَكُمْ بَشِيرٌ وَّنَذِيرٌ

وَاللّٰهُ عَلٰى كُلِّ شَىْءٍ قَدِيرٌ ۱۹

وَاِذْ قَالَ مُوسٰى لِقَوْمِهٖ يٰقَوْمِ

اذْكُرُوْا نِعْمَةَ اللّٰهِ عَلَيْكُمْ

اِذْ جَعَلَ فِيْكُمْ اَنْبِيَآءَ وَجَعَلَكُمْ

مُّلُوْكًا ۖ وَّاٰتٰىكُمْ مَّا لَمْ يُؤْتِ

اَحَدًا مِّنَ الْعٰلَمِيْنَ ۲۰ يٰقَوْمِ

ادْخُلُوا الْاَرْضَ الْمُقَدَّسَةَ الَّتِيْ

كَتَبَ اللّٰهُ لَكُمْ وَلَا تَرْتَدُّوْا عَلٰى

and his beloved." Say: "Why then does He punish you for your sins? No, you are but men, - of the men he has created: He forgives whom He pleases, and He punishes whom He pleases: and to Allah belongs the dominion of the heavens and the earth, and all that is between: and unto Him is the final goal (of all)."

19. O People of the Book! Now has come unto you, making (things) clear unto you, Our Apostle, after the break in (the series of) Our Apostles, lest you should say: "There came unto us no bringer of glad tidings and no warner (from evil)":

وَاحْجَآؤُهُمْ قُلْ فَلِمَ يُعَذِّبُكُمْ

بِذُنُوبِكُمْ ۖ بَلْ اَنْتُمْ بَشَرٌ مِّمَّنْ

خَلَقَ ۖ يَغْفِرُ لِمَنْ يَّشَآءُ وَيُعَذِّبُ

مَنْ يَّشَآءُ ۖ وَلِلّٰهِ مُلْكُ السَّمٰوٰتِ

وَالْاَرْضِ وَمَا بَيْنَهُمَا ۖ وَاِلَيْهِ

الْمَصِيرُ ۞ يٰاَهْلَ الْكِتٰبِ قَدْ

جَآءَكُمْ رَسُولُنَا يُبَيِّنُ لَكُمْ عَلٰى

فَتْرَةٍ مِّنَ الرُّسُلِ اَنْ تَقُوْلُوْا

مَا جَآءَنَا مِنْ بَشِيْرٍ وَّلَا نَذِيْرٍ

is Christ the son of Mary. Say: "Who then has the least power against Allah, if His Will were to destroy Christ the son of Mary, his mother, and all - every one that is on the earth? For to Allah belonges the dominion of the heavens and the earth, and all that is between. He creates what He pleases. For Allah has power over all things."

18. (Both) the Jews and the Christians say: "We are sons of Allah,

هُوَ الْمَسِيحُ ابْنُ مَرْيَمَ ۚ قُلْ

فَمَنْ يَّمْلِكُ مِنَ اللّٰهِ شَيْئًا

اِنْ اَرَادَ اَنْ يُّهْلِكَ الْمَسِيحَ

ابْنَ مَرْيَمَ وَ اُمَّهٗ وَ مَنْ فِي

الْاَرْضِ جَمِيعًا ۗ وَ لِلّٰهِ مُلْكُ

السَّمٰوٰتِ وَالْاَرْضِ وَمَا بَيْنَهُمَا ۚ

يَخْلُقُ مَا يَشَآءُ ۗ وَاللّٰهُ عَلٰى كُلِّ

شَيْءٍ قَدِيرٌ ۞ وَ قَالَتِ الْيَهُوْدُ

وَ النَّصٰرٰى نَحْنُ اَبْنٰٓؤُا اللّٰهِ

revealing to you much that you used to hide in the Book, and passing over much (that is now unnecessary). There has come to you from Allah a (new) light and a perspicuous Book,

16.   Wherewith Allah guides all who seek His good pleasure to ways of peace and safety, and leads them out of darkness, by His Will, unto the light, - guides them to a path that is straight.

17.   In blasphemy indeed are those that say that Allah

يُبَيِّنُ لَكُمْ كَثِيرًا مِّمَّا كُنْتُمْ

تُخْفُوْنَ مِنَ الْكِتٰبِ وَيَعْفُوْا

عَنْ كَثِيْرٍ ۚ قَدْ جَآءَكُمْ مِّنَ اللّٰهِ

نُوْرٌ وَّكِتٰبٌ مُّبِيْنٌ ۙ يَّهْدِيْ بِهِ

اللّٰهُ مَنِ اتَّبَعَ رِضْوَانَهٗ سُبُلَ

السَّلٰمِ وَيُخْرِجُهُمْ مِّنَ الظُّلُمٰتِ

اِلَى النُّوْرِ بِاِذْنِهٖ وَيَهْدِيْهِمْ

اِلٰى صِرَاطٍ مُّسْتَقِيْمٍ ۞ لَقَدْ

كَفَرَ الَّذِيْنَ قَالُوٓا اِنَّ اللّٰهَ

but forgive them, and overlook (their misdeeds): for Allah loves those who are kind.

14. From those, too, who call themselves Christians, We did take a covenant, but they forgot a good part of the message that was sent them: so We estranged them, with enmity and hatred between the one and the other, to the Day of Judgment. And soon will Allah show them what it is they have done.

15. O Pople of the Book! There has come to you Our Apostle,

مِنْهُمْ فَاعْفُ عَنْهُمْ وَاصْفَحْ

إِنَّ اللّٰهَ يُحِبُّ الْمُحْسِنِينَ ۞

وَمِنَ الَّذِينَ قَالُوا إِنَّا نَصَارَى

أَخَذْنَا مِيثَاقَهُمْ فَنَسُوا حَظًّا

مِّمَّا ذُكِّرُوا بِهِ فَأَغْرَيْنَا بَيْنَهُمُ

الْعَدَاوَةَ وَالْبَغْضَاءَ إِلَى يَوْمِ

الْقِيَامَةِ ۚ وَسَوْفَ يُنَبِّئُهُمُ اللّٰهُ

بِمَا كَانُوا يَصْنَعُونَ ۞ يَا أَهْلَ

الْكِتَابِ قَدْ جَاءَكُمْ رَسُولُنَا

your evils, and admit you to
Gardens with rivers flowing
beneath; but if any of you, after
this, resisteth Faith, he has truly
wandered from the path or
rectitude."

13. But because of their breach
of their covenant, We cursed
them, and made their hearts
grow hard; they change the
words from their (right) places
and forget a good part of the
message that was sent them, nor
will you cease to find them -
barring a few - ever bent on (new)
deceits:

سَيِّئَاتِكُمْ وَلَأُدْخِلَنَّكُمْ جَنَّتٍ

تَجْرِى مِنْ تَحْتِهَا الْأَنْهَرُ ۚ

فَمَنْ كَفَرَ بَعْدَ ذٰلِكَ مِنْكُمْ

فَقَدْ ضَلَّ سَوَآءَ السَّبِيْلِ ۝

فَبِمَا نَقْضِهِمْ مِّيْثَاقَهُمْ لَعَنّٰهُمْ

وَجَعَلْنَا قُلُوْبَهُمْ قٰسِيَةً ۚ يُحَرِّفُوْنَ

الْكَلِمَ عَنْ مَّوَاضِعِهٖ ۙ وَنَسُوْا حَظًّا

مِّمَّا ذُكِّرُوْا بِهٖ ۚ وَلَا تَزَالُ تَطَّلِعُ

عَلٰى خَآئِنَةٍ مِّنْهُمْ اِلَّا قَلِيْلًا

their hands from you: so fear Allah. And on Allah let believers put (all) their trust.

12.　Allah did (aforetime) take a covenant from the Children of Israel, and We appointed twelve captains among them. And Allah said: "I am with you: if you (but) establish regular prayers, practise regular charity, believe in my Apostles, honour and assist them, and loan to Allah a beautiful loan, verily I will wipe out from you

اَيْدِيَهُمْ عَنْكُمْ وَاتَّقُوا اللهَ ۚ وَعَلَى

اللهِ فَلْيَتَوَكَّلِ الْمُؤْمِنُوْنَ ۞

وَلَقَدْ اَخَذَ اللهُ مِيْثَاقَ بَنِيْ

اِسْرَآءِيْلَ ۚ وَبَعَثْنَا مِنْهُمُ اثْنَيْ

عَشَرَ نَقِيْبًا ۗ وَقَالَ اللهُ اِنِّيْ

مَعَكُمْ ۗ لَئِنْ اَقَمْتُمُ الصَّلٰوةَ

وَاٰتَيْتُمُ الزَّكٰوةَ وَاٰمَنْتُمْ بِرُسُلِيْ

وَعَزَّرْتُمُوْهُمْ وَاَقْرَضْتُمُ اللهَ

قَرْضًا حَسَنًا لَّاُكَفِّرَنَّ عَنْكُمْ

to piety: and fear Allah. For Allah is Well-Acquainted with all that you do.

9.   To those who believe and do deeds of righteousness has Allah promised forgiveness and a great reward.

10.   Those who reject Faith and deny Our Signs will be Companions of Hell-fire.

11.   O you who believe! Call in remembrance the favour of Allah unto you when certain men formed the design to stretch out their hands against you, but (Allah) held back

لِلتَّقْوٰى وَاتَّقُوا اللّٰهَ اِنَّ اللّٰهَ

خَبِيرٌۢ بِمَا تَعْمَلُوْنَ ۝ وَعَدَ اللّٰهُ

الَّذِيْنَ اٰمَنُوْا وَعَمِلُوا الصّٰلِحٰتِ

لَهُمْ مَّغْفِرَةٌ وَّاَجْرٌ عَظِيْمٌ ۝

وَالَّذِيْنَ كَفَرُوْا وَكَذَّبُوْا بِاٰيٰتِنَآ

اُولٰٓئِكَ اَصْحٰبُ الْجَحِيْمِ ۝ يٰٓاَيُّهَا

الَّذِيْنَ اٰمَنُوا اذْكُرُوْا نِعْمَتَ

اللّٰهِ عَلَيْكُمْ اِذْ هَمَّ قَوْمٌ اَنْ

يَّبْسُطُوْا اِلَيْكُمْ اَيْدِيَهُمْ فَكَفَّ

that you may be grateful.

7. And call in remembrance the favour of Allah unto you, and His Covenant, which He ratified with you, when you said: "We hear and we obey": and fear Allah, for Allah knows well the secrets of your hearts.

8. O you who believe! Stand out firmly for Allah, as witnesses to fair dealing, and let not the hatred of others to you make you swerve to wrong and depart from justice. Be just: that is next

لَعَلَّكُمْ تَشْكُرُوْنَ ۞ وَاذْكُرُوْا نِعْمَةَ

اللهِ عَلَيْكُمْ وَمِيْثَاقَهُ الَّذِىْ

وَاثَقَكُمْ بِهٖ ۚ اِذْ قُلْتُمْ سَمِعْنَا

وَاَطَعْنَا ۖ وَاتَّقُوا اللهَ ۗ اِنَّ اللهَ

عَلِيْمٌۢ بِذَاتِ الصُّدُوْرِ ۞ يٰٓاَيُّهَا

الَّذِيْنَ اٰمَنُوْا كُوْنُوْا قَوّٰمِيْنَ

لِلّٰهِ شُهَدَآءَ بِالْقِسْطِ ۖ وَلَا

يَجْرِمَنَّكُمْ شَنَاٰنُ قَوْمٍ عَلٰٓى

اَلَّا تَعْدِلُوْا ۚ اِعْدِلُوْا ۗ هُوَ اَقْرَبُ

If you are in a state of ceremonial impurity, bathe your whole body. But if you are ill, or on a journey, or one of you comes from offices of nature, or you have been in contact with women, and you find no water, then take for yourselves clean sand or earth, and rub therewith your faces and hands, Allah does not wish to place you in a difficulty, but to make you clean, and to complete his favour to you,

وَإِنْ كُنْتُمْ جُنُبًا فَاطَّهَّرُوْا ۚ وَإِنْ

كُنْتُمْ مَّرْضٰى أَوْ عَلٰى سَفَرٍ أَوْ

جَآءَ أَحَدٌ مِّنْكُمْ مِّنَ الْغَآئِطِ

أَوْ لٰمَسْتُمُ النِّسَآءَ فَلَمْ تَجِدُوْا

مَآءً فَتَيَمَّمُوْا صَعِيْدًا طَيِّبًا

فَامْسَحُوْا بِوُجُوْهِكُمْ وَأَيْدِيْكُمْ

مِّنْهُ ۚ مَا يُرِيْدُ اللّٰهُ لِيَجْعَلَ

عَلَيْكُمْ مِّنْ حَرَجٍ وَّلٰكِنْ يُّرِيْدُ

لِيُطَهِّرَكُمْ وَلِيُتِمَّ نِعْمَتَهٗ عَلَيْكُمْ

before your time, - when you give them their due dowers, and desire chastity, not lewdness, nor secret intrigues if any one rejects Faith, fruitless is his work, and in the Hereafter he will be in the ranks of those who have lost (all spiritual good).

6.   O you who believe! When you prepare for prayer, wash your faces, and your hands (and arms) to the elbows; rub your heads (with water); and (wash) your feet to the ankles.

قَبْلِكُمْ اِذَآ اٰتَيْتُمُوْهُنَّ اُجُوْرَهُنَّ

مُحْصِنِيْنَ غَيْرَ مُسٰفِحِيْنَ وَلَا

مُتَّخِذِىْٓ اَخْدَانٍ ۗ وَمَنْ يَّكْفُرْ

بِالْاِيْمَانِ فَقَدْ حَبِطَ عَمَلُهٗ ۖ وَهُوَ

فِى الْاٰخِرَةِ مِنَ الْخٰسِرِيْنَ ۞

يٰٓاَيُّهَا الَّذِيْنَ اٰمَنُوْٓا اِذَا قُمْتُمْ

اِلَى الصَّلٰوةِ فَاغْسِلُوْا وُجُوْهَكُمْ

وَاَيْدِيَكُمْ اِلَى الْمَرَافِقِ وَامْسَحُوْا

بِرُءُوْسِكُمْ وَاَرْجُلَكُمْ اِلَى الْكَعْبَيْنِ ۗ

eat what they catch for you, but pronounce the Name of Allah over it: and fear Allah; for Allah is swift in taking account.

5. This day are (all) things good and pure made lawful for you. The food of the People of the Book is lawful for you and yours is lawful unto them. (Lawful unto you in marriage) are (not only) chaste women who are believers, but chaste women among the People of the Book, revealed

فَكُلُوا مِمَّا أَمْسَكْنَ عَلَيْكُمْ

وَاذْكُرُوا اسْمَ اللهِ عَلَيْهِ ۚ

وَاتَّقُوا اللهَ ۚ إِنَّ اللهَ سَرِيعُ

الْحِسَابِ ۞ الْيَوْمَ أُحِلَّ لَكُمُ

الطَّيِّبَاتُ ۗ وَطَعَامُ الَّذِينَ أُوتُوا

الْكِتَابَ حِلٌّ لَّكُمْ ۖ وَطَعَامُكُمْ

حِلٌّ لَّهُمْ ۖ وَالْمُحْصَنَاتُ مِنَ

الْمُؤْمِنَاتِ وَالْمُحْصَنَاتُ مِنَ

الَّذِينَ أُوتُوا الْكِتَابَ مِن

but fear Me. This day have I perfected your religion for you, completed My Favour upon you, and have chosen for you Islam as your religion. But if any is forced by hunger, with no inclination to transgression, Allah is indeed Oft-Forgiving, Most Merciful.

4.   They ask you what is lawful to them (as food). Say: Lawful unto you are (all) things good and pure: and what you have taught your trained hunting animals (to catch) in the manner directed to you by Allah:

وَاخْشَوْنِ الْيَوْمَ اَكْمَلْتُ لَكُمْ

دِيْنَكُمْ وَاَتْمَمْتُ عَلَيْكُمْ نِعْمَتِيْ

وَرَضِيْتُ لَكُمُ الْاِسْلَامَ دِيْنًا ۚ

فَمَنِ اضْطُرَّ فِيْ مَخْمَصَةٍ غَيْرَ

مُتَجَانِفٍ لِّاِثْمٍ ۙ فَاِنَّ اللهَ غَفُوْرٌ

رَّحِيْمٌ ۞ يَسْئَلُوْنَكَ مَاذَآ اُحِلَّ

لَهُمْ ۗ قُلْ اُحِلَّ لَكُمُ الطَّيِّبٰتُ ۙ وَمَا

عَلَّمْتُمْ مِّنَ الْجَوَارِحِ مُكَلِّبِيْنَ

تُعَلِّمُوْنَهُنَّ مِمَّا عَلَّمَكُمُ اللهُ

to you (for food) are: dead meat, blood, the flesh of swine, and that on which has been invoked the name of other than Allah; that which has been killed by strangling, or by a violent blow, or by a headlong fall, or by being gored to death; that which has been (partly) eaten by a wild animal; unless you are able to slaughter it (in due form); that which is sacrificed on stone (altars); (forbidden) also is the division (of meat) by raffling with arrows: that is impiety. This day have those who reject Faith given up all hopes of your religion: yet fear them not

عَلَيْكُمُ الْمَيْتَةُ وَالدَّمُ وَلَحْمُ

الْخِنْزِيرِ وَمَآ أُهِلَّ لِغَيْرِ اللّٰهِ

بِهِۦ وَالْمُنْخَنِقَةُ وَالْمَوْقُوذَةُ

وَالْمُتَرَدِّيَةُ وَالنَّطِيحَةُ وَمَآ

أَكَلَ السَّبُعُ إِلَّا مَا ذَكَّيْتُمْ

وَمَا ذُبِحَ عَلَى النُّصُبِ وَأَن

تَسْتَقْسِمُوا بِالْأَزْلَامِ ذَٰلِكُمْ فِسْقٌ

الْيَوْمَ يَئِسَ الَّذِينَ كَفَرُوا

مِن دِينِكُمْ فَلَا تَخْشَوْهُمْ

to the Sacred House, seeking of the bounty and good pleasure of their Lord. But when you are clear of the sacred precincts and of pilgrim garb, you may hunt and let not the hatred of some people in (once) shutting you out of the Sacred Mosque lead you to transgression (and hostility on your part). Help you one another in righteousness and piety, but help you not one another in sin and rancour: fear Allah: for Allah is strict in punishment.

3. Forbidden

الْبَيْتَ الْحَرَامَ يَبْتَغُوْنَ فَضْلًا

مِّنْ رَّبِّهِمْ وَرِضْوَانًا ۚ وَإِذَا

حَلَلْتُمْ فَاصْطَادُوْا ۚ وَلَا يَجْرِمَنَّكُمْ

شَنَاٰنُ قَوْمٍ اَنْ صَدُّوْكُمْ عَنِ

الْمَسْجِدِ الْحَرَامِ اَنْ تَعْتَدُوْا ۘ

وَتَعَاوَنُوْا عَلَى الْبِرِّ وَالتَّقْوٰى ۖ

وَلَا تَعَاوَنُوْا عَلَى الْاِثْمِ

وَالْعُدْوَانِ ۖ وَاتَّقُوا اللّٰهَ ۖ اِنَّ

اللّٰهَ شَدِيْدُ الْعِقَابِ ۞ حُرِّمَتْ

Al-Ma'ida (The Table Spread)

Bismillahir-Rahmanir-Rahim

1. O you who believe! Fulfil (all) obligations. Lawful unto you (for food) are all four-footed animals, with the exceptions named: but animals of the chase are forbidden while you are in the sacred precincts or in pilgrim garb: for Allah does command according to His Will and Plan.

2. O you who believe! Violate not the sanctity of the Symbols of Allah, nor of the sacred month, nor of the animals brought for sacrifice, nor the garlands that mark out such animals, nor the people resorting

بِسْمِ اللهِ الرَّحْمٰنِ الرَّحِيْمِ

يٰۤاَيُّهَا الَّذِيْنَ اٰمَنُوْۤا اَوْفُوْا بِالْعُقُوْدِ ؕ اُحِلَّتْ لَكُمْ بَهِيْمَةُ الْاَنْعَامِ اِلَّا مَا يُتْلٰى عَلَيْكُمْ غَيْرَ مُحِلِّى الصَّيْدِ وَاَنْتُمْ حُرُمٌ ؕ اِنَّ اللهَ يَحْكُمُ مَا يُرِيْدُ ۞ يٰۤاَيُّهَا الَّذِيْنَ اٰمَنُوْا لَا تُحِلُّوْا شَعَآئِرَ اللهِ وَلَا الشَّهْرَ الْحَرَامَ وَلَا الْهَدْىَ وَلَا الْقَلَآئِدَ وَلَاۤ اٰمِّيْنَ

about those who leave no descendants or ascendants as heirs. If it is a man that dies, leaving a sister but no child, she shall have half the inheritance: if (such a deceased was) a woman, who left no child, her brother takes her inheritance: if there are two sisters, they shall have two-thirds of the inheritance (between them): if there are brothers and sisters, (they share), the male having twice the share of the female. Thus does Allah make clear to you (His Law), lest you err. And Allah has. knowledge of all things.

فِي الْكَلٰلَةِ ۚ اِنِ امْرُؤٌا هَلَكَ

لَيْسَ لَهٗ وَلَدٌ وَّلَهٗٓ اُخْتٌ فَلَهَا

نِصْفُ مَا تَرَكَ ۚ وَهُوَ يَرِثُهَآ اِنْ

لَّمْ يَكُنْ لَّهَا وَلَدٌ ۚ فَاِنْ كَانَتَا

اثْنَتَيْنِ فَلَهُمَا الثُّلُثٰنِ مِمَّا

تَرَكَ ۚ وَاِنْ كَانُوْٓا اِخْوَةً رِّجَالًا

وَّنِسَآءً فَلِلذَّكَرِ مِثْلُ حَظِّ

الْاُنْثَيَيْنِ ۗ يُبَيِّنُ اللّٰهُ لَكُمْ اَنْ

تَضِلُّوْا ۗ وَاللّٰهُ بِكُلِّ شَيْءٍ عَلِيْمٌ ۩

with a grievous Chastisement; nor will they find, besides Allah, any to protect or help them.

174. O mankind! Verily there has come to you a convincing proof from your Lord: for We have sent unto you a light (that is) manifest.

175. Then those who believe in Allah, and hold fast to Him,- soon will He admit them to Mercy and Grace from Himself, and guide them to Himself by a straight way.

176. They ask you for a legal decision. Say: Allah directs (thus)

عَذَابًا أَلِيمًا ۙ وَّلَا يَجِدُوْنَ لَهُمْ

مِّنْ دُوْنِ اللّٰهِ وَلِيًّا وَّلَا نَصِيْرًا ۞

يٰٓاَيُّهَا النَّاسُ قَدْ جَآءَكُمْ بُرْهَانٌ

مِّنْ رَّبِّكُمْ وَاَنْزَلْنَآ اِلَيْكُمْ نُوْرًا

مُّبِيْنًا ۞ فَاَمَّا الَّذِيْنَ اٰمَنُوْا

بِاللّٰهِ وَاعْتَصَمُوْا بِهٖ فَسَيُدْخِلُهُمْ

فِيْ رَحْمَةٍ مِّنْهُ وَفَضْلٍ ۙ

وَّيَهْدِيْهِمْ اِلَيْهِ صِرَاطًا مُّسْتَقِيْمًا ۞

يَسْتَفْتُوْنَكَ ۗ قُلِ اللّٰهُ يُفْتِيْكُمْ

Allah as a Disposer of affairs.

172. Christ disdains nor to serve and worship Allah, nor do the Angels, those nearest (to Allah): those who disdain His worship and are arrogant, - He will gather them all together unto Himself to (answer).

173. But those who believe and do deeds of righteousness, He will give their (due) rewards,- and more, out of His Bounty: but those who are disdainful and arrogant, He will punish

بِاللهِ وَكِيلًا ۩ لَنْ يَسْتَنْكِفَ

الْمَسِيحُ أَنْ يَّكُوْنَ عَبْدًا لِّلهِ

وَلَا الْمَلٰئِكَةُ الْمُقَرَّبُوْنَ ۚ وَمَنْ

يَّسْتَنْكِفْ عَنْ عِبَادَتِهٖ وَيَسْتَكْبِرْ

فَسَيَحْشُرُهُمْ اِلَيْهِ جَمِيْعًا ۞ فَاَمَّا

الَّذِيْنَ اٰمَنُوْا وَعَمِلُوا الصّٰلِحٰتِ

فَيُوَفِّيْهِمْ اُجُوْرَهُمْ وَيَزِيْدُهُمْ

مِّنْ فَضْلِهٖ ۚ وَاَمَّا الَّذِيْنَ

اسْتَنْكَفُوْا وَاسْتَكْبَرُوْا فَيُعَذِّبُهُمْ

in your religion: nor say of Allah anything but the truth. Christ Jesus the son of Mary was (no more than) an Apostle of Allah, and His Word, which He bestowed on Mary, and a Spirit proceeding from Him: so believe in Allah and His Apostles. Say not "Trinity" : desist: it will be better for you: for Allah is One God (Allah): glory be to Him: (far Exalted is He) above having a son. To Him belong all things in the heavens and on earth. And enough is

فِى دِينِكُمْ وَلَا تَقُوْلُوْا عَلَى اللهِ

اِلَّا الْحَقَّ اِنَّمَا الْمَسِيْحُ عِيْسَى

ابْنُ مَرْيَمَ رَسُوْلُ اللهِ وَكَلِمَتُهُ

اَلْقٰهَآ اِلٰى مَرْيَمَ وَرُوْحٌ مِّنْهُ

فَاٰمِنُوْا بِاللهِ وَرُسُلِهِ وَلَا

تَقُوْلُوْا ثَلٰثَةٌ اِنْتَهُوْا خَيْرًا لَّكُمْ

اِنَّمَا اللهُ اِلٰهٌ وَّاحِدٌ سُبْحٰنَهُ

اَنْ يَّكُوْنَ لَهُ وَلَدٌ لَهُ مَا فِى

السَّمٰوٰتِ وَمَا فِى الْاَرْضِ وَكَفٰى

Allah will not forgive them nor guide them to any way -

169. Except the way of Hell, to dwell therein for ever. And this to Allah is easy.

170. O mankind! The Apostle has come to you in truth from Allah: believe in him: it is best for you. But if you reject Faith, to Allah belong all things in the heavens and on earth: and Allah is All-Knowing, All-Wise.

171. O People of the Book! Commit no excesses

يَكُنِ اللّٰهُ لِيَغْفِرَ لَهُمْ وَلَا لِيَهْدِيَهُمْ

طَرِيقًا ۞ اِلَّا طَرِيقَ جَهَنَّمَ

خٰلِدِينَ فِيهَآ اَبَدًا ۚ وَكَانَ ذٰلِكَ

عَلَى اللّٰهِ يَسِيرًا ۞ يٰٓاَيُّهَا النَّاسُ

قَدْ جَآءَكُمُ الرَّسُولُ بِالْحَقِّ مِنْ

رَّبِّكُمْ فَاٰمِنُوا خَيْرًا لَّكُمْ ۚ وَاِنْ

تَكْفُرُوا فَاِنَّ لِلّٰهِ مَا فِي السَّمٰوٰتِ

وَالْاَرْضِ ۚ وَكَانَ اللّٰهُ عَلِيمًا

حَكِيمًا ۞ يٰٓاَهْلَ الْكِتٰبِ لَا تَغْلُوا

that mankind, after (the coming) of the Apostles, should have no plea against Allah: for Allah is Exalted in Power, Wise.

166. But Allah hears witness that what He has sent unto you He has sent from His (own) knowledge, and the Angels bear witness: but enough is Allah for a Witness.

167. Those who reject Faith and keep off (men) from the Way of Allah, have verily strayed far, far away from the Path.

168. Those who reject Faith and do wrong, -

لِلنَّاسِ عَلَى اللهِ حُجَّةٌ بَعْدَ الرُّسُلِ ۖ وَكَانَ اللهُ عَزِيزًا حَكِيمًا ۝ لٰكِنِ اللهُ يَشْهَدُ بِمَا أَنْزَلَ إِلَيْكَ أَنْزَلَهُ بِعِلْمِهِ ۖ وَالْمَلَائِكَةُ يَشْهَدُونَ ۚ وَكَفٰى بِاللهِ شَهِيدًا ۝ إِنَّ الَّذِينَ كَفَرُوا وَصَدُّوا عَنْ سَبِيلِ اللهِ قَدْ ضَلُّوا ضَلَالًا بَعِيدًا ۝ إِنَّ الَّذِينَ كَفَرُوا وَظَلَمُوا لَمْ

after him: We sent inspiration to
Abraham, Isma'il, Isaac, Jacob
and the Tribes, to Jesus, Job,
Jonah, Aaron, and Solomon, and
to David We gave the Psalms.

164. Of some Apostles We have
already told you the story; of
others We have not; - and to
Moses Allah spoke direct; -

165. Apostles who gave good
news as well as warning,

بَعْدِهٖ ۚ وَاَوْحَيْنَاۤ اِلٰۤى اِبْرٰهِيْمَ

وَاِسْمٰعِيْلَ وَاِسْحٰقَ وَيَعْقُوْبَ

وَالْاَسْبَاطِ وَعِيْسٰى وَاَيُّوْبَ

وَيُوْنُسَ وَهٰرُوْنَ وَسُلَيْمٰنَ ۚ

وَاٰتَيْنَا دَاوٗدَ زَبُوْرًا ۙ ١٦٣ وَرُسُلًا

قَدْ قَصَصْنٰهُمْ عَلَيْكَ مِنْ قَبْلُ

وَرُسُلًا لَّمْ نَقْصُصْهُمْ عَلَيْكَ ۚ

وَكَلَّمَ اللّٰهُ مُوْسٰى تَكْلِيْمًا ۚ ١٦٤ رُسُلًا

مُّبَشِّرِيْنَ وَمُنْذِرِيْنَ لِئَلَّا يَكُوْنَ

a grievous Punishment.

162. But those among them who are well-grounded in knowledge, and the believers, believe in what has been revealed to you and what was revealed before you: and (especially) those who establish regular prayer and practise regular charity and believe in Allah and in the Last Day: to them shall We soon give a great reward.

163. We have sent you inspiration, as We sent it to Noah and the Messengers

مِنْهُمْ عَذَابًا اَلِيْمًا ۞ لٰكِنِ

الرّٰسِخُوْنَ فِى الْعِلْمِ مِنْهُمْ

وَالْمُؤْمِنُوْنَ يُؤْمِنُوْنَ بِمَآ اُنْزِلَ

اِلَيْكَ وَمَآ اُنْزِلَ مِنْ قَبْلِكَ

وَالْمُقِيْمِيْنَ الصَّلٰوةَ وَالْمُؤْتُوْنَ

الزَّكٰوةَ وَالْمُؤْمِنُوْنَ بِاللّٰهِ وَالْيَوْمِ

الْاٰخِرِ ۗ اُولٰٓئِكَ سَنُؤْتِيْهِمْ اَجْرًا

عَظِيْمًا ۞ اِنَّآ اَوْحَيْنَآ اِلَيْكَ كَمَآ

اَوْحَيْنَآ اِلٰى نُوْحٍ وَّالنَّبِيّٖنَ مِنْ

159. And there is none of the People of the Book but must believe in him before his death; and on the Day of Judgment he will be a witness against them; -

160. For the iniquity of the Jews We made unlawful for them certain (foods) good and wholesome which had been lawful for them;- in that they hindered many from Allah's Way; -

161. That they took interest, though they were forbidden; and that they devoured men's substance wrongfully; - We have prepared for those among them who reject faith

وَإِنْ مِّنْ أَهْلِ الْكِتٰبِ إِلَّا

لَيُؤْمِنَنَّ بِهِ قَبْلَ مَوْتِهِ وَيَوْمَ

الْقِيٰمَةِ يَكُوْنُ عَلَيْهِمْ شَهِيْدًا ۞

فَبِظُلْمٍ مِّنَ الَّذِيْنَ هَادُوْا

حَرَّمْنَا عَلَيْهِمْ طَيِّبٰتٍ أُحِلَّتْ

لَهُمْ وَبِصَدِّهِمْ عَنْ سَبِيْلِ اللهِ

كَثِيْرًا ۞ وَّأَخْذِهِمُ الرِّبٰوا وَقَدْ

نُهُوْا عَنْهُ وَأَكْلِهِمْ أَمْوَالَ النَّاسِ

بِالْبَاطِلِ وَأَعْتَدْنَا لِلْكٰفِرِيْنَ

a grave false charge;

157. That they said (in boast), "We killed Christ Jesus the son of Mary, the Apostle of Allah"; - but they killed him not, nor crucified him, but so it was made to appear to them, and those who differ therein are full of doubts, with no (certain) knowledge, but only conjecture to follow, for of a surety they killed him not: -

158. No, Allah raised him up unto Himself; and Allah is Exalted in Power, Wise; -

بُهْتَانًا عَظِيمًا ۞ وَّقَوْلِهِمْ إِنَّا

قَتَلْنَا الْمَسِيحَ عِيسَى ابْنَ

مَرْيَمَ رَسُوْلَ اللّٰهِ ۚ وَمَا قَتَلُوْهُ

وَمَا صَلَبُوْهُ وَلٰكِنْ شُبِّهَ لَهُمْ

وَإِنَّ الَّذِيْنَ اخْتَلَفُوْا فِيْهِ

لَفِيْ شَكٍّ مِّنْهُ ۚ مَا لَهُمْ بِهٖ

مِنْ عِلْمٍ إِلَّا اتِّبَاعَ الظَّنِّ ۚ وَمَا

قَتَلُوْهُ يَقِيْنًا ۞ بَلْ رَّفَعَهُ اللّٰهُ

إِلَيْهِ ۚ وَكَانَ اللّٰهُ عَزِيْزًا حَكِيْمًا ۞

the gate with humility"; and (once again) We commanded them: "Transgress not in the matter of the Sabbath." And We took from them a solemn covenant.

155. (They have incurred divine displeasure): in that they broke their covenant; that they rejected the Signs of Allah; that they slew the Messengers in defiance of right; that they said, "Our hearts are the wrappings (which preserve Allah's Word; we need no more)"; - No, Allah has set the seal on their hearts for their blasphemy, and little is it they believe; -

156. That they rejected Faith; that they uttered against Mary

الْبَابَ سُجَّدًا وَّقُلْنَا لَهُمْ لَا

تَعْدُوْا فِي السَّبْتِ وَاَخَذْنَا

مِنْهُمْ مِّيْثَاقًا غَلِيْظًا ۞ فَبِمَا

نَقْضِهِمْ مِّيْثَاقَهُمْ وَكُفْرِهِمْ

بِاٰيٰتِ اللّٰهِ وَقَتْلِهِمُ الْاَنْبِيَآءَ

بِغَيْرِ حَقٍّ وَّقَوْلِهِمْ قُلُوْبُنَا

غُلْفٌ ۜ بَلْ طَبَعَ اللّٰهُ عَلَيْهَا

بِكُفْرِهِمْ فَلَا يُؤْمِنُوْنَ اِلَّا قَلِيْلًا ۞

وَّبِكُفْرِهِمْ وَقَوْلِهِمْ عَلٰى مَرْيَمَ

to them from heaven: indeed they asked Moses for an even greater (miracle), for they said: "Show us Allah in public," but they were dazed for their presumption, with thunder and lightning. Yet they wor-shipped the calf even after clear signs had come to them; even so We forgave them; and gave Moses manifest proofs of authority.

154. And for their covenant We raised over them (the towering height) of Mount (Sinai); and (on another occasion) We said: "Enter

عَلَيْهِمْ كِتٰبًا مِّنَ السَّمَآءِ فَقَدْ

سَاَلُوْا مُوْسٰٓى اَكْبَرَ مِنْ ذٰلِكَ

فَقَالُوْۤا اَرِنَا اللّٰهَ جَهْرَةً

فَاَخَذَتْهُمُ الصّٰعِقَةُ بِظُلْمِهِمْ

ثُمَّ اتَّخَذُوا الْعِجْلَ مِنْۢ بَعْدِ

مَا جَآءَتْهُمُ الْبَيِّنٰتُ فَعَفَوْنَا

عَنْ ذٰلِكَ ۚ وَ اٰتَيْنَا مُوْسٰى سُلْطٰنًا

مُّبِيْنًا ۞ وَ رَفَعْنَا فَوْقَهُمُ الطُّوْرَ

بِمِيْثَاقِهِمْ وَ قُلْنَا لَهُمُ ادْخُلُوا

others": and (those who) wish to take a course midway, -

151. They are in truth (equally) unbelievers; and We have prepared for unbelievers a humiliating Punishment.

152. To those who believe in Allah and His Apostles and make no distinction between any of the Apostles, We shall soon give their (due) rewards: for Allah is Oft-Forgiving, Most Merciful.

153. The People of the Book ask you to cause a book to descend

بِبَعْضٍ وَيُرِيدُونَ اَنْ يَّتَّخِذُوْا

بَيْنَ ذٰلِكَ سَبِيْلًا ۙ اُولٰٓئِكَ

هُمُ الْكٰفِرُوْنَ حَقًّا ۚ وَاَعْتَدْنَا

لِلْكٰفِرِيْنَ عَذَابًا مُّهِيْنًا

وَالَّذِيْنَ اٰمَنُوْا بِاللّٰهِ وَرُسُلِهٖ

وَلَمْ يُفَرِّقُوْا بَيْنَ اَحَدٍ مِّنْهُمْ

اُولٰٓئِكَ سَوْفَ يُؤْتِيْهِمْ اُجُوْرَهُمْ

وَكَانَ اللّٰهُ غَفُوْرًا رَّحِيْمًا

يَسْئَلُكَ اَهْلُ الْكِتٰبِ اَنْ تُنَزِّلَ

148. Allah loves not that evil should be noised abroad in public speech, except where injustice has been done; for Allah is He Who hears and knows all things.

149. Whether you publicise a good deed or conceal it or cover evil with pardon, verily Allah does blot out (sins) and has power (in the judgment of values).

150. Those who deny Allah and His Apostles, and (those who) wish to separate Allah from His Apostles, saying: "We believe in some but reject

لَا يُحِبُّ اللّٰهُ الْجَهْرَ بِالسُّوْءِ

مِنَ الْقَوْلِ اِلَّا مَنْ ظُلِمَ ؕ

وَكَانَ اللّٰهُ سَمِيْعًا عَلِيْمًا ۝ اِنْ

تُبْدُوْا خَيْرًا اَوْ تُخْفُوْهُ اَوْ تَعْفُوْا

عَنْ سُوْءٍ فَاِنَّ اللّٰهَ كَانَ عَفُوًّا

قَدِيْرًا ۝ اِنَّ الَّذِيْنَ يَكْفُرُوْنَ

بِاللّٰهِ وَرُسُلِهٖ وَيُرِيْدُوْنَ اَنْ

يُّفَرِّقُوْا بَيْنَ اللّٰهِ وَرُسُلِهٖ

وَيَقُوْلُوْنَ نُؤْمِنُ بِبَعْضٍ وَّنَكْفُرُ

پاره

لَا يُحِبُّ اللهُ

(٦)

PART 7
Wa Idha Sami'u

to each people its own doings. In the end will they return to their Lord, and We shall then tell them the truth of all that they did.

109. They swear their strongest oaths by Allah, that if a (special) Sign came to them, by it they would believe. Say: "Certainly (all) Signs are in the power of Allah: but what he wishes you (Muslims) realise that (even) if (special) Signs came, they will not believe?"

110. We (too) shall turn to (confusion) their hearts and their eyes, even as they refused to believe in this in the first instance: We shall leave them in their trespasses, to wander in distraction.

لِكُلِّ أُمَّةٍ عَمَلُهُمْ ثُمَّ إِلَى رَبِّهِمْ
مَّرْجِعُهُمْ فَيُنَبِّئُهُمْ بِمَا كَانُوا
يَعْمَلُونَ ۞ وَأَقْسَمُوا بِاللَّهِ جَهْدَ
أَيْمَانِهِمْ لَئِنْ جَآءَتْهُمْ ءَايَةٌ لَّيُؤْمِنُنَّ
بِهَا ۚ قُلْ إِنَّمَا ٱلْءَايَاتُ عِندَ اللَّهِ ۖ
وَمَا يُشْعِرُكُمْ أَنَّهَا إِذَا جَآءَتْ لَا
يُؤْمِنُونَ ۞ وَنُقَلِّبُ أَفْئِدَتَهُمْ وَأَبْصَارَهُمْ
كَمَا لَمْ يُؤْمِنُوا بِهِ أَوَّلَ مَرَّةٍ
وَنَذَرُهُمْ فِي طُغْيَانِهِمْ يَعْمَهُونَ ۞

do we explain the Signs by various (symbols): that they may say, "you have taught (us) diligently," and that We may make the matter clear to those who know.

106. Follow what you are taught by inspiration from your Lord: there is no Allah but He: and turn aside from those who join gods with Allah.

107. If it had been Allah's plan, they would not have taken false gods: but We made you not one to watch over their doings, nor are you set over them to dispose of their affairs.

108. Revile not those whom they call upon besides Allah, lest they out of spite revile Allah in their ignorance. Thus have We made alluring

نُصَرِّفُ الْاٰيٰتِ وَلِيَقُوْلُوْا دَرَسْتَ

وَلِنُبَيِّنَهٗ لِقَوْمٍ يَّعْلَمُوْنَ ۞ اِتَّبِعْ

مَاۤ اُوْحِيَ اِلَيْكَ مِنْ رَّبِّكَ ۚ لَاۤ اِلٰهَ

اِلَّا هُوَ ۚ وَاَعْرِضْ عَنِ الْمُشْرِكِيْنَ ۞

وَلَوْ شَاۤءَ اللّٰهُ مَاۤ اَشْرَكُوْا ۗ وَمَا

جَعَلْنٰكَ عَلَيْهِمْ حَفِيْظًا ۚ وَمَاۤ اَنْتَ

عَلَيْهِمْ بِوَكِيْلٍ ۞ وَلَا تَسُبُّوا الَّذِيْنَ

يَدْعُوْنَ مِنْ دُوْنِ اللّٰهِ فَيَسُبُّوا

اللّٰهَ عَدْوًۢا بِغَيْرِ عِلْمٍ ۗ كَذٰلِكَ زَيَّنَّا

has full knowledge of all things.

102. That is Allah, your Lord! there is no Allah but He, the Creator of all things: then worship Him: and He has power to dispose of all affairs.

103. No vision can grasp Him, but His grasp is over all vision: He is above all comprehension, yet is acquainted with all things.

104. "Now have come to you, from your Lord, proofs (to open your eyes): if any will see, it will be for (the good of) his own soul; if any will be blind, it will be to his own (harm): I am not (here) to watch over your doings."

105. Thus

بِكُلِّ شَىْءٍ عَلِيمٌ ۞ ذٰلِكُمُ اللهُ

رَبُّكُمْ لَا إِلٰهَ إِلَّا هُوَ خَالِقُ

كُلِّ شَىْءٍ فَاعْبُدُوهُ وَهُوَ عَلٰى

كُلِّ شَىْءٍ وَّكِيلٌ ۞ لَا تُدْرِكُهُ

الْأَبْصَارُ وَهُوَ يُدْرِكُ الْأَبْصَارَ

وَهُوَ اللَّطِيفُ الْخَبِيرُ ۞ قَدْ جَاءَكُمْ

بَصَائِرُ مِنْ رَّبِّكُمْ فَمَنْ أَبْصَرَ

فَلِنَفْسِهِ وَمَنْ عَمِيَ فَعَلَيْهَا وَمَا

أَنَا عَلَيْكُمْ بِحَفِيظٍ ۞ وَكَذٰلِكَ

each similar (in kind) yet different (in variety): when they begin to bear fruit, feast your eyes with the fruit and the ripeness thereof. Behold! In these things there are Signs for people who believe.

100. Yet they make the Jinns equals with Allah, though Allah did create the Jinns; and they falsely, having no knowledge, attribute to Him sons and daughters. Praise and glory be to Him! (for He is) above what they attribute to Him!

101. To Him is due the primal origin of the heavens and the earth: how can He have a son when He has no consort? He created all things, and He

مُشْتَبِهًا وَّغَيْرَ مُتَشَابِهٍ ۚ اُنْظُرُوا

اِلٰى ثَمَرِهٖ اِذَاۤ اَثْمَرَ وَيَنْعِهٖ ۚ اِنَّ

فِيْ ذٰلِكُمْ لَاٰيٰتٍ لِّقَوْمٍ يُّؤْمِنُوْنَ ۩

وَجَعَلُوْا لِلّٰهِ شُرَكَآءَ الْجِنَّ وَخَلَقَهُمْ

وَخَرَقُوْا لَهٗ بَنِيْنَ وَبَنٰتٍۭ بِغَيْرِ

عِلْمٍ ۚ سُبْحٰنَهٗ وَتَعٰلٰى عَمَّا يَصِفُوْنَ ۩

بَدِيْعُ السَّمٰوٰتِ وَالْاَرْضِ ۚ اَنّٰى

يَكُوْنُ لَهٗ وَلَدٌ وَّلَمْ تَكُنْ لَّهٗ

صَاحِبَةٌ ۚ وَخَلَقَ كُلَّ شَيْءٍ ۚ وَهُوَ

from a single person: here is a place of sojourn and a place of departure: We detail Our Signs for people who understand.

99. It is He Who sends down rain from the skies: with it We produce vegetation of all kinds: from some We produce green (crops), out of which We produce grain, heaped up (at harvest); out of the date-palm and its sheaths (or spathes) (come) clusters of dates hanging low and near: and (then there are) gardens of grapes, and olives, and pome-granates,

مِّن نَّفْسٍ وَّاحِدَةٍ فَمُسْتَقَرٌّ

وَّمُسْتَوْدَعٌ ۗ قَدْ فَصَّلْنَا الْاٰيٰتِ

لِقَوْمٍ يَّفْقَهُوْنَ ۞ وَهُوَ الَّذِيْۤ

اَنْزَلَ مِنَ السَّمَآءِ مَآءً ۚ فَاَخْرَجْنَا

بِهٖ نَبَاتَ كُلِّ شَيْءٍ فَاَخْرَجْنَا

مِنْهُ خَضِرًا نُّخْرِجُ مِنْهُ حَبًّا

مُّتَرَاكِبًا ۚ وَمِنَ النَّخْلِ مِنْ طَلْعِهَا

قِنْوَانٌ دَانِيَةٌ وَّجَنّٰتٍ مِّنْ

اَعْنَابٍ وَّالزَّيْتُوْنَ وَالرُّمَّانَ

He causes the living to issue from the dead, and He is the one to cause the dead to issue from the living. That is Allah: then how are you deluded away from the truth? **96.** He it is that cleaves the daybreak (from the dark): He makes the night for rest and tranquillity, and the sun and moon for the reckoning (of time): such is the judgment and ordering of (Him), the Exalted in Power, the Omniscient.

97. It is He Who makes the stars (as beacons) for you, that you may guide yourselves, with their help, through the dark spaces of land and sea: We detail Our Signs for people who know.

98. It is He Who has produced you

يُخْرِجُ الْحَىَّ مِنَ الْمَيِّتِ وَ مُخْرِجُ

الْمَيِّتِ مِنَ الْحَىِّ ذٰلِكُمُ اللهُ

فَاَنّٰى تُؤْفَكُوْنَ ۝ فَالِقُ الْاِصْبَاحِ

وَ جَعَلَ الَّيْلَ سَكَنًا وَّ الشَّمْسَ

وَ الْقَمَرَ حُسْبَانًا ذٰلِكَ تَقْدِيْرُ الْعَزِيْزِ

الْعَلِيْمِ ۝ وَ هُوَ الَّذِيْ جَعَلَ لَكُمُ

النُّجُوْمَ لِتَهْتَدُوْا بِهَا فِيْ ظُلُمٰتِ

الْبَرِّ وَ الْبَحْرِ قَدْ فَصَّلْنَا الْاٰيٰتِ

لِقَوْمٍ يَّعْلَمُوْنَ ۝ وَ هُوَ الَّذِيْ اَنْشَاَكُمْ

tell lies against Allah, and scorn-
fully to reject of His Signs!"

94.   "And behold! You come to
Us bare and alone as We created
you for the first time: you have left
behind you all (the favours) which
We bestowed on you: We see not
with you your intercessors whom
you thought to be partners in your
affairs: so now all relations
between you have been cut off, and
your (pet) fancies have left you in
the lurch!"

95.   It is Allah Who causes the
seed-grain and the date-stone to
split and sprout.

تَقُوْلُوْنَ عَلَى اللّٰهِ غَيْرَ الْحَقِّ

وَكُنْتُمْ عَنْ اٰيٰتِهٖ تَسْتَكْبِرُوْنَ ۞

وَلَقَدْ جِئْتُمُوْنَا فُرَادٰى كَمَا خَلَقْنٰكُمْ

اَوَّلَ مَرَّةٍ وَّ تَرَكْتُمْ مَّا خَوَّلْنٰكُمْ

وَرَآءَ ظُهُوْرِكُمْ ۚ وَمَا نَرٰى مَعَكُمْ

شُفَعَآءَكُمُ الَّذِيْنَ زَعَمْتُمْ اَنَّهُمْ

فِيْكُمْ شُرَكٰٓؤُاۡ ۚ لَقَدْ تَّقَطَّعَ بَيْنَكُمْ

وَضَلَّ عَنْكُمْ مَّا كُنْتُمْ تَزْعُمُوْنَ ۞

اِنَّ اللّٰهَ فَالِقُ الْحَبِّ وَالنَّوٰى

in this (Book), and they are constant in guarding their prayers.

93. Who can be more wicked than one who invents a lie against Allah, or says, "I have received inspiration," when he has received none, or (again) who says, "I can reveal the like of what Allah has revealed"? If you could but see how the wicked (do fare) in the flood of confusion at death! - the Angels stretch forth their hands, (saying),"Yield up your souls: this day shall you receive your reward, - a chastisement of shame, for that you used to

به وَهُمْ عَلَى صَلَاتِهِمْ يُحَافِظُونَ ۞

وَمَنْ أَظْلَمُ مِمَّنِ افْتَرَى عَلَى

اللهِ كَذِبًا أَوْ قَالَ أُوحِيَ إِلَيَّ

وَلَمْ يُوحَ إِلَيْهِ شَيْءٌ وَّمَنْ

قَالَ سَأُنْزِلُ مِثْلَ مَا أَنْزَلَ

اللهُ وَلَوْ تَرَى إِذِ الظَّالِمُونَ فِي

غَمَرَاتِ الْمَوْتِ وَالْمَلَائِكَةُ بَاسِطُوا

أَيْدِيهِمْ أَخْرِجُوا أَنْفُسَكُمُ الْيَوْمَ

تُجْزَوْنَ عَذَابَ الْهُونِ بِمَا كُنْتُمْ

which Moses brought? - a light and guidance to man: but you make it into (separate) sheets for show, while you conceal much (of its contents): therein were you taught that which you knew not - neither you nor your fathers." Say: "Allah (sent it down)": then leave them to plunge in vain discourse and trifling.

92.   And this is a Book which We have sent down, bringing blessings, and confirming (the revelations) which came before it: that you may warn the Mother of Cities and all around her. Those who believe in the Hereafter believe

الَّذِى جَآءَ بِهِ مُوسَى نُوْرًا وَّهُدًى

لِّلنَّاسِ تَجْعَلُوْنَهُ قَرَاطِيْسَ

تُبْدُوْنَهَا وَتُخْفُوْنَ كَثِيْرًا وَعُلِّمْتُمْ

مَّا لَمْ تَعْلَمُوْٓا اَنْتُمْ وَلَآ اٰبَآؤُكُمْ

قُلِ اللهُ ثُمَّ ذَرْهُمْ فِىْ خَوْضِهِمْ

يَلْعَبُوْنَ ۞ وَهٰذَا كِتٰبٌ اَنْزَلْنٰهُ

مُبٰرَكٌ مُّصَدِّقُ الَّذِىْ بَيْنَ يَدَيْهِ

وَلِتُنْذِرَ اُمَّ الْقُرٰى وَمَنْ حَوْلَهَا

وَالَّذِيْنَ يُؤْمِنُوْنَ بِالْاٰخِرَةِ يُؤْمِنُوْنَ

the Book, and authority, and prophethood: if these (their descendants) reject them, behold! We shall entrust their charge to a new people who reject them not.

90. Those were the (prophets) who received Allah's guidance: follow the guidance they received; say: "No reward for this do I ask of you: this is no less than a message for the nations."

91. No just estimate of Allah do they make when they say: "Nothing does Allah send down to man (by way of revelation)." Say: "Who then sent down the Book

الْكِتَبَ وَالْحُكْمَ وَالنُّبُوَّةَ ۚ فَإِنْ

يَّكْفُرْ بِهَا هٰٓؤُلَآءِ فَقَدْ وَكَّلْنَا بِهَا

قَوْمًا لَّيْسُوا بِهَا بِكٰفِرِينَ ۝ أُولٰٓئِكَ

الَّذِينَ هَدَى اللّٰهُ ۚ فَبِهُدٰىهُمُ

اقْتَدِهْ ۗ قُلْ لَّآ أَسْئَلُكُمْ عَلَيْهِ أَجْرًا ۗ

إِنْ هُوَ إِلَّا ذِكْرٰى لِلْعٰلَمِينَ ۝ وَمَا

قَدَرُوا اللّٰهَ حَقَّ قَدْرِهٖٓ إِذْ قَالُوا

مَآ أَنْزَلَ اللّٰهُ عَلٰى بَشَرٍ مِّنْ

شَىْءٍ ۗ قُلْ مَنْ أَنْزَلَ الْكِتٰبَ

and John, and Jesus and Elias: all in the ranks of the righteous:

86.　And Isma'il and Elisha, and Jonas, and Lot: and to all We gave favour above the nations:

87.　(To them) and to their fathers, and progeny and brethren: We chose them, and We guided them to a straight way.

88.　This is the guidance of Allah: He gives that guidance to whom He pleases, of His worshippers. If they were to join other gods with Him, all that they did would be vain for them.

89.　These were the men to whom We gave

وَيَحْيٰى وَعِيْسٰى وَاِلْيَاسَ ۖ كُلٌّ

مِّنَ الصّٰلِحِيْنَ ۙ ۝ وَاِسْمٰعِيْلَ وَالْيَسَعَ

وَيُوْنُسَ وَلُوْطًا ۚ وَكُلًّا فَضَّلْنَا عَلَى

الْعٰلَمِيْنَ ۙ ۝ وَمِنْ اٰبَآئِهِمْ وَذُرِّيّٰتِهِمْ

وَاِخْوَانِهِمْ ۚ وَاجْتَبَيْنٰهُمْ وَهَدَيْنٰهُمْ اِلٰى

صِرَاطٍ مُّسْتَقِيْمٍ ۝ ذٰلِكَ هُدَى اللّٰهِ

يَهْدِيْ بِهٖ مَنْ يَّشَآءُ مِنْ عِبَادِهٖ ۚ

وَلَوْ اَشْرَكُوْا لَحَبِطَ عَنْهُمْ مَّا كَانُوْا

يَعْمَلُوْنَ ۝ اُولٰٓئِكَ الَّذِيْنَ اٰتَيْنٰهُمُ

with wrong - that are (truly) in security, for they are on (right) guidance."

83. That was the reasoning about Us, which We gave to Abraham (to use) against his people: We raise whom We will, degree after degree: for your Lord is full of wisdom and knowledge.

84. We gave him Isaac and Jacob: all (three) guided: and before him, We guided Noah, and among his progeny, David, Solomon, Job, Joseph, Moses, and Aaron: thus do We reward those who do good:

85. And Zakariya

بِظُلْمٍ أُولَٰئِكَ لَهُمُ الْأَمْنُ وَهُم

مُّهْتَدُونَ ۝ وَتِلْكَ حُجَّتُنَا آتَيْنَاهَا

إِبْرَاهِيمَ عَلَىٰ قَوْمِهِ نَرْفَعُ دَرَجَاتٍ

مَّن نَّشَاءُ إِنَّ رَبَّكَ حَكِيمٌ عَلِيمٌ ۝

وَوَهَبْنَا لَهُ إِسْحَاقَ وَيَعْقُوبَ

كُلًّا هَدَيْنَا وَنُوحًا هَدَيْنَا مِن

قَبْلُ وَمِن ذُرِّيَّتِهِ دَاوُدَ وَسُلَيْمَانَ

وَأَيُّوبَ وَيُوسُفَ وَمُوسَىٰ وَهَارُونَ

وَكَذَٰلِكَ نَجْزِي الْمُحْسِنِينَ ۝ وَزَكَرِيَّا

Allah, when He (Himself) has guided me? I fear not (the beings) you associate with Allah: unless my Lord wills, (nothing can happen). My Lord comprehends in His knowledge all things. Will you not (yourselves) be admonished?

81. "How should I fear (the beings) you associate with Allah, when you fear not to give partners to Allah without any warrant having been given to you? Which of (us) two parties has more right to security? (Tell me) if you know.

82. "It is those who believe and confuse not their beliefs

اللهِ وَقَدْ هَدٰنِ ۚ وَلَاۤ اَخَافُ مَا

تُشْرِكُوْنَ بِهٖۤ اِلَّاۤ اَنْ يَّشَآءَ رَبِّىْ

شَيْـًٔا ۗ وَسِعَ رَبِّىْ كُلَّ شَىْءٍ عِلْمًا ۗ

اَفَلَا تَتَذَكَّرُوْنَ ۞ وَكَيْفَ اَخَافُ

مَاۤ اَشْرَكْتُمْ وَلَا تَخَافُوْنَ اَنَّكُمْ

اَشْرَكْتُمْ بِاللهِ مَا لَمْ يُنَزِّلْ بِهٖ

عَلَيْكُمْ سُلْطٰنًا ۚ فَاَىُّ الْفَرِيْقَيْنِ

اَحَقُّ بِالْاَمْنِ ۚ اِنْ كُنْتُمْ تَعْلَمُوْنَ ۞

اَلَّذِيْنَ اٰمَنُوْا وَلَمْ يَلْبِسُوْۤا اِيْمَانَهُمْ

he said: "This is my Lord." But when the moon set, he said: "Unless my Lord guide me, I shall surely be among those who go astray."

78.　　When he saw the sun rising in splendour, he said: "This is my Lord; this is the greatest (of all)." But when the sun set, he said: "O my people! I am indeed free from your (guilt) of giving partners to Allah."

79.　　"For me, I have set my face, firmly and truly, towards Him Who created the heavens and the earth, and never shall I give partners to Allah."

80.　　His people disputed with him. He said: "(Come) you to dispute with me, about

قَالَ هٰذَا رَبِّيْ ۚ فَلَمَّا اَفَلَ قَالَ

لَىِٕنْ لَّمْ يَهْدِنِيْ رَبِّيْ لَاَكُوْنَنَّ مِنَ

الْقَوْمِ الضَّاۗلِّيْنَ ۞ فَلَمَّا رَاَ الشَّمْسَ

بَازِغَةً قَالَ هٰذَا رَبِّيْ هٰذَاۤ اَكْبَرُ ۚ

فَلَمَّاۤ اَفَلَتْ قَالَ يٰقَوْمِ اِنِّيْ بَرِيْۤءٌ

مِّمَّا تُشْرِكُوْنَ ۞ اِنِّيْ وَجَّهْتُ وَجْهِيَ

لِلَّذِيْ فَطَرَ السَّمٰوٰتِ وَالْاَرْضَ

حَنِيْفًا وَّمَاۤ اَنَا مِنَ الْمُشْرِكِيْنَ ۞

وَحَاۤجَّهٗ قَوْمُهٗ ۚ قَالَ اَتُحَاۤجُّوْۤنِّيْ فِى

as well as that which is open. For He is the Wise, Well Acquainted (with all things).

74. Abraham said to his father Azar: "Do you take idols for gods? For I see you and your people in manifest error."

75. So also did We show Abraham the power and the laws of the heavens and the earth, that he might (with understanding) have certitude.

76. When the night covered him over, he saw a star: he said: "This is my Lord." But when it set, he said: "I love not those that set."

77. When he saw the moon rising in splendour,

وَالشَّهَادَةِ ۚ وَهُوَ الْحَكِيمُ الْخَبِيرُ ۩ وَإِذْ

قَالَ إِبْرٰهِيمُ لِأَبِيهِ اٰزَرَ أَتَتَّخِذُ

أَصْنَامًا اٰلِهَةً ۚ إِنِّي أَرٰىكَ وَقَوْمَكَ

فِي ضَلٰلٍ مُّبِينٍ ۩ وَكَذٰلِكَ نُرِيٓ

إِبْرٰهِيمَ مَلَكُوتَ السَّمٰوٰتِ وَالْأَرْضِ

وَلِيَكُونَ مِنَ الْمُوقِنِينَ ۩ فَلَمَّا جَنَّ

عَلَيْهِ الَّيْلُ رَاٰ كَوْكَبًا ۖ قَالَ هٰذَا

رَبِّي ۖ فَلَمَّآ أَفَلَ قَالَ لَآ أُحِبُّ

الْاٰفِلِينَ ۩ فَلَمَّا رَاٰ الْقَمَرَ بَازِغًا

friends calling, 'come to us', (vainly) guiding him to the path." Say: "Allah's gui-dance is the (only) guidance, and we have been directed to submit ourselves to the Lord of the worlds;-

72. "To establish regular pra-yers and to fear Allah: for it is to Him that we shall be gathered together."

73. It is He Who created the heavens and the earth in true (proportions): the day He says, "Be," it is. His word is the truth. His will be the dominion the day the trumpet will be blown. He knows the Unseen

أَصْحَبٌ يَّدْعُوْنَهُ إِلَى الْهُدَى ائْتِنَا

قُلْ إِنَّ هُدَى اللهِ هُوَ الْهُدَى

وَأُمِرْنَا لِنُسْلِمَ لِرَبِّ الْعٰلَمِيْنَ ۞

وَأَنْ أَقِيْمُوا الصَّلٰوةَ وَاتَّقُوْهُ وَهُوَ

الَّذِيْ إِلَيْهِ تُحْشَرُوْنَ ۞ وَهُوَ

الَّذِيْ خَلَقَ السَّمٰوٰتِ وَالْأَرْضَ

بِالْحَقِّ وَيَوْمَ يَقُوْلُ كُنْ فَيَكُوْنُ

قَوْلُهُ الْحَقُّ وَلَهُ الْمُلْكُ يَوْمَ

يُنْفَخُ فِى الصُّوْرِ عٰلِمُ الْغَيْبِ

protector or intercessor except Allah: if it offered every ransom, (or reparation), none will be accepted: such is (the end of) those who deliver themselves to ruin by their own acts: they will have for drink (only) boiling water, and for punishment, one most grievous: for they persisted in rejecting Allah.

71. Say: "Shall we indeed call on others besides Allah, - things that can do us neither good nor harm, - and turn on our heels after receiving guidance from Allah? - like one whom the evil ones have made into a fool, wandering bewildered through the earth, his

دُوْنِ اللهِ وَلِيٌّ وَّلَا شَفِيْعٌ وَاِنْ

تَعْدِلْ كُلَّ عَدْلٍ لَّا يُؤْخَذْ مِنْهَا

اُولٰٓئِكَ الَّذِيْنَ اُبْسِلُوْا بِمَا كَسَبُوْا

لَهُمْ شَرَابٌ مِّنْ حَمِيْمٍ وَّعَذَابٌ اَلِيْمٌ

بِمَا كَانُوْا يَكْفُرُوْنَ ۞ قُلْ اَنَدْعُوْا

مِنْ دُوْنِ اللهِ مَا لَا يَنْفَعُنَا وَلَا

يَضُرُّنَا وَنُرَدُّ عَلٰٓى اَعْقَابِنَا بَعْدَ

اِذْ هَدَانَا اللهُ كَالَّذِى اسْتَهْوَتْهُ

الشَّيٰطِيْنُ فِى الْاَرْضِ حَيْرَانَ لَهٗ

from them unless they turn to a different theme. If Satan ever makes you forget, then after recollection, sit not you in the company of those who do wrong.

69. On their account no responsibility falls on the righteous, but (their duty) is to remind them, that they may (learn to) fear Allah.

70. Leave alone those who take their religion to be mere play and amusement, and are deceived by the life of this world. But proclaim (to them) this (truth): that every soul delivers itself to ruin by its own acts: it will find for itself no

عَنْهُمْ حَتّٰى يَخُوْضُوْا فِيْ حَدِيْثٍ

غَيْرِهٖ ۚ وَاِمَّا يُنْسِيَنَّكَ الشَّيْطٰنُ

فَلَا تَقْعُدْ بَعْدَ الذِّكْرٰى مَعَ الْقَوْمِ

الظّٰلِمِيْنَ ۝ وَمَا عَلَى الَّذِيْنَ يَتَّقُوْنَ

مِنْ حِسَابِهِمْ مِّنْ شَيْءٍ وَّلٰكِنْ

ذِكْرٰى لَعَلَّهُمْ يَتَّقُوْنَ ۝ وَذَرِ الَّذِيْنَ

اتَّخَذُوْا دِيْنَهُمْ لَعِبًا وَّلَهْوًا وَّغَرَّتْهُمُ

الْحَيٰوةُ الدُّنْيَا وَذَكِّرْ بِهٖۤ اَنْ تُبْسَلَ

نَفْسٌ بِمَا كَسَبَتْ ۚ لَيْسَ لَهَا مِنْ

send calamities on you, from above and below, or to cover you with confusion in party strife, giving you a taste of mutual vengeance - each from the other." See how We explain the Signs by various (symbols); that they may understand.

66. But your people reject this, though it is the truth. Say: "Not mine is the responsibility for arranging your affairs;

67. For every message is a limit of time, and soon shall you know it."

68. When you see men engaged in vain discourse about Our Signs, turn away

يَّبْعَثَ عَلَيْكُمْ عَذَابًا مِّنْ فَوْقِكُمْ

اَوْ مِنْ تَحْتِ اَرْجُلِكُمْ اَوْ يَلْبِسَكُمْ

شِيَعًا وَّيُذِيْقَ بَعْضَكُمْ بَأْسَ

بَعْضٍ ۗ اُنْظُرْ كَيْفَ نُصَرِّفُ الْاٰيٰتِ

لَعَلَّهُمْ يَفْقَهُوْنَ ۞ وَكَذَّبَ بِهٖ

قَوْمُكَ وَهُوَ الْحَقُّ ۗ قُلْ لَّسْتُ

عَلَيْكُمْ بِوَكِيْلٍ ۞ لِّكُلِّ نَبَاٍ مُّسْتَقَرٌّ

وَّسَوْفَ تَعْلَمُوْنَ ۞ وَاِذَا رَاَيْتَ

الَّذِيْنَ يَخُوْضُوْنَ فِيْ اٰيٰتِنَا فَاَعْرِضْ

and they never fail in their duty.

62. Then are men returned unto Allah, their Protector, the (only) Reality: is not His the command? and He is the swiftest in taking account.

63. Say: "Who is it that deliveres you from the dark recesses of land and sea, when you call upon Him in humility and silent terror: 'If He only delivers us from these (dangers), (we vow) we shall truly show our gratitude'.?"

64. Say: "It is Allah that delivers you from these and all (other) distresses: and yet you worship false gods!"

65. Say: "He has power to

وَهُمْ لَا يُفَرِّطُونَ ۞ ثُمَّ رُدُّوا إِلَى

اللَّهِ مَوْلَاهُمُ الْحَقِّ اَلَا لَهُ الْحُكْمُ

وَهُوَ اَسْرَعُ الْحَاسِبِينَ ۞ قُلْ

مَنْ يُّنَجِّيكُمْ مِنْ ظُلُمَاتِ الْبَرِّ

وَالْبَحْرِ تَدْعُوْنَهُ تَضَرُّعًا وَّخُفْيَةً

لَئِنْ اَنْجَانَا مِنْ هٰذِهٖ لَنَكُوْنَنَّ

مِنَ الشَّاكِرِينَ ۞ قُلِ اللَّهُ يُنَجِّيكُمْ

مِّنْهَا وَمِنْ كُلِّ كَرْبٍ ثُمَّ اَنْتُمْ

تُشْرِكُوْنَ ۞ قُلْ هُوَ الْقَادِرُ عَلَى اَنْ

anything fresh or dry (green or withered), but is (inscribed) in a record clear (to those who can read).

60. It is He Who does take your souls by night, and has knowledge of all that you have done by day: by day does He raise you up again; that a term appointed be fulfilled; in the end unto Him will be your return; then will He show you the truth of all that you did.

61. He is the Irresistible, (watching) from above over His worshippers, and He sets guardians over you. At length, when death approaches one of you, Our Angels take his soul,

رَطْبٍ وَّلَا يَابِسٍ اِلَّا فِىْ كِتٰبٍ

مُّبِيْنٍ ۞ وَهُوَ الَّذِىْ يَتَوَفّٰىكُمْ

بِالَّيْلِ وَيَعْلَمُ مَا جَرَحْتُمْ بِالنَّهَارِ

ثُمَّ يَبْعَثُكُمْ فِيْهِ لِيُقْضٰٓى اَجَلٌ

مُّسَمًّى ثُمَّ اِلَيْهِ مَرْجِعُكُمْ ثُمَّ

يُنَبِّئُكُمْ بِمَا كُنْتُمْ تَعْمَلُوْنَ ۞

وَهُوَ الْقَاهِرُ فَوْقَ عِبَادِهٖ وَيُرْسِلُ

عَلَيْكُمْ حَفَظَةً ۗ حَتّٰٓى اِذَا جَآءَ

اَحَدَكُمُ الْمَوْتُ تَوَفَّتْهُ رُسُلُنَا

What you wish to see hastened, is not in my power. The command rests with none but Allah: He declares the truth, and He is the best of judges."

58. Say: "If what you would see hastened were in my power, the matter would be settled at once between you and me. But Allah knows best those who do wrong."

59. With Him are the keys of the Unseen, the treasures that none knows but He. He knows whatever there is on the earth and in the sea. Not a leaf does fall but with His knowledge: there is not a grain in the darkness (or depths) of the earth, nor

مَا تَسْتَعْجِلُوْنَ بِهٖ ۗ اِنِ الْحُكْمُ

اِلَّا لِلّٰهِ ۚ يَقُصُّ الْحَقَّ وَهُوَ خَيْرُ

الْفَاصِلِيْنَ ۞ قُلْ لَّوْ اَنَّ عِنْدِيْ مَا

تَسْتَعْجِلُوْنَ بِهٖ لَقُضِيَ الْاَمْرُ بَيْنِيْ

وَبَيْنَكُمْ ۗ وَاللّٰهُ اَعْلَمُ بِالظّٰلِمِيْنَ ۞

وَعِنْدَهٗ مَفَاتِحُ الْغَيْبِ لَا يَعْلَمُهَا

اِلَّا هُوَ ۗ وَيَعْلَمُ مَا فِى الْبَرِّ وَالْبَحْرِ ۗ

وَمَا تَسْقُطُ مِنْ وَّرَقَةٍ اِلَّا يَعْلَمُهَا

وَلَا حَبَّةٍ فِيْ ظُلُمٰتِ الْاَرْضِ وَلَا

and thereafter repented, and mended (his conduct), lo! He is Oft-Forgiving, Most Merciful.

55. Thus do We explain the Signs in detail: so that the way of the sinners may be shown up.

56. Say: "I am forbidden to worship those - others than Allah - whom you call upon." Say: "I will not follow your vain desires: if I did, I would stray from the path, and be not of the company of those who receive guidance."

57. Say: "For me, I (work) on a clear Sign from my Lord, but you reject Him.

ثُمَّ تَابَ مِنْ بَعْدِهِ وَأَصْلَحَ

فَإِنَّهُ غَفُورٌ رَّحِيمٌ ۞ وَكَذَٰلِكَ

نُفَصِّلُ الْآيَاتِ وَلِتَسْتَبِينَ سَبِيلُ

الْمُجْرِمِينَ ۞ قُلْ إِنِّي نُهِيتُ أَنْ

أَعْبُدَ الَّذِينَ تَدْعُونَ مِنْ دُونِ

اللَّهِ قُلْ لَّا أَتَّبِعُ أَهْوَاءَكُمْ

قَدْ ضَلَلْتُ إِذًا وَّمَا أَنَا مِنَ

الْمُهْتَدِينَ ۞ قُلْ إِنِّي عَلَىٰ بَيِّنَةٍ

مِّن رَّبِّي وَكَذَّبْتُمْ بِهِ مَا عِنْدِي

are they accountable for you, that you should turn them away, and thus be (one) of the unjust.

53. Thus did We try some of them by comparison with others, that they should say: "Is it these then that Allah has favoured from amongst us?" Does not Allah know best those who are grateful?

54. When those come to you who believe in Our Signs, say: "Peace be on you: your Lord has inscribed for Himself (the rule of) Mercy: verily, if any of you did evil in ignorance,

حِسَابِكَ عَلَيْهِمْ مِّنْ شَيْءٍ فَتَطْرُدَهُمْ

فَتَكُوْنَ مِنَ الظّٰلِمِيْنَ ۞ وَكَذٰلِكَ

فَتَنَّا بَعْضَهُمْ بِبَعْضٍ لِّيَقُوْلُوْا

اَهٰٓؤُلَآءِ مَنَّ اللّٰهُ عَلَيْهِمْ مِّنْ بَيْنِنَا ۗ

اَلَيْسَ اللّٰهُ بِاَعْلَمَ بِالشّٰكِرِيْنَ ۞

وَاِذَا جَآءَكَ الَّذِيْنَ يُؤْمِنُوْنَ

بِاٰيٰتِنَا فَقُلْ سَلٰمٌ عَلَيْكُمْ كَتَبَ

رَبُّكُمْ عَلٰى نَفْسِهِ الرَّحْمَةَ ۙ اَنَّهٗ

مَنْ عَمِلَ مِنْكُمْ سُوْٓءًا بِجَهَالَةٍ

revealed to me." Say: "Can the blind be held equal to the seeing?" Will you then consider not?

51. Give this warning to those in whose (hearts) is the fear that they will be brought (to judgment) before their Lord: except for Him they will have no protector nor intercessor: that they may guard (against evil).

52. Send not away those who call on their Lord morning and evening, seeking His Face. In nothing are you accountable for them, and in nothing

يُوْحٰٓى اِلَيَّ قُلْ هَلْ يَسْتَوِى

الْاَعْمٰى وَالْبَصِيْرُ اَفَلَا تَتَفَكَّرُوْنَ ۞

وَاَنْذِرْ بِهِ الَّذِيْنَ يَخَافُوْنَ اَنْ

يُّحْشَرُوْٓا اِلٰى رَبِّهِمْ لَيْسَ لَهُمْ

مِّنْ دُوْنِهٖ وَلِيٌّ وَّلَا شَفِيْعٌ لَّعَلَّهُمْ

يَتَّقُوْنَ ۞ وَلَا تَطْرُدِ الَّذِيْنَ

يَدْعُوْنَ رَبَّهُمْ بِالْغَدٰوةِ وَالْعَشِيِّ

يُرِيْدُوْنَ وَجْهَهٗ مَا عَلَيْكَ مِنْ

حِسَابِهِمْ مِّنْ شَىْءٍ وَّمَا مِنْ

except those who do wrong?

48. We send the Apostles only to give good news and to warn: so those who believe and mend (their lives), - upon them shall be no fear, nor shall they grieve.

49. But those who reject Our Signs, - them shall punishment touch, for that they ceased not from transgressing.

50. Say: "I tell you not that with me are the Treasures of Allah, nor do I know what is hidden, nor do I tell you I am an Angel. I but follow what is

إِلَّا الْقَوْمُ الظَّالِمُونَ ۝ وَمَا نُرْسِلُ

الْمُرْسَلِينَ إِلَّا مُبَشِّرِينَ وَمُنذِرِينَ

فَمَنْ آمَنَ وَأَصْلَحَ فَلَا خَوْفٌ

عَلَيْهِمْ وَلَا هُمْ يَحْزَنُونَ ۝

وَالَّذِينَ كَذَّبُوا بِآيَاتِنَا يَمَسُّهُمُ

الْعَذَابُ بِمَا كَانُوا يَفْسُقُونَ ۝

قُل لَّا أَقُولُ لَكُمْ عِندِي خَزَآئِنُ

اللَّهِ وَلَا أَعْلَمُ الْغَيْبَ وَلَا أَقُولُ

لَكُمْ إِنِّي مَلَكٌ إِنْ أَتَّبِعُ إِلَّا مَا

plunged in despair!

45. Of the wrong-doers the last remnant was cut off. Praise be to Allah, the Cherisher of the Worlds.

46. Say: "Think you, if Allah took away your hearing and your sight, and sealed up your hearts, who - a god other than Allah - could restore them to you?" See how We explain the Signs by various (symbols); yet they turn aside.

47. Say: "Think you, if the Punishment of Allah comes to you, whether suddenly or openly, will any be destroyed

مُّبْلِسُوْنَ ۝ فَقُطِعَ دَابِرُ الْقَوْمِ

الَّذِيْنَ ظَلَمُوْا ۚ وَالْحَمْدُ لِلّٰهِ رَبِّ

الْعٰلَمِيْنَ ۝ قُلْ اَرَءَيْتُمْ اِنْ اَخَذَ

اللّٰهُ سَمْعَكُمْ وَاَبْصَارَكُمْ وَخَتَمَ

عَلٰى قُلُوْبِكُمْ مَّنْ اِلٰهٌ غَيْرُ اللّٰهِ

يَاْتِيْكُمْ بِهٖ ۗ اُنْظُرْ كَيْفَ نُصَرِّفُ

الْاٰيٰتِ ثُمَّ هُمْ يَصْدِفُوْنَ ۝

قُلْ اَرَءَيْتَكُمْ اِنْ اَتٰىكُمْ عَذَابُ

اللّٰهِ بَغْتَةً اَوْ جَهْرَةً هَلْ يُهْلَكُ

many nations, and We afflicted the nations with suffering and adversity, that they might learn humility.

43. When the suffering reached them from Us, why then did they not learn humility? On the contrary their hearts became hardened, and Satan made their (sinful) acts seem alluring to them.

44. But when they forgot the warning they had received, We opened to them the gates of all (good) things, until, in the midst of their enjoyment of Our gifts, on a sudden, We called them to account, when lo! they were

أُمَمٍ مِّنْ قَبْلِكَ فَأَخَذْنَٰهُمْ

بِالْبَأْسَاءِ وَالضَّرَّاءِ لَعَلَّهُمْ

يَتَضَرَّعُونَ ۞ فَلَوْلَا إِذْ جَاءَهُم

بَأْسُنَا تَضَرَّعُوا وَلَٰكِن قَسَتْ

قُلُوبُهُمْ وَزَيَّنَ لَهُمُ الشَّيْطَٰنُ مَا

كَانُوا يَعْمَلُونَ ۞ فَلَمَّا نَسُوا مَا

ذُكِّرُوا بِهِ فَتَحْنَا عَلَيْهِمْ أَبْوَابَ

كُلِّ شَيْءٍ حَتَّىٰ إِذَا فَرِحُوا بِمَا

أُوتُوا أَخَذْنَٰهُم بَغْتَةً فَإِذَا هُم

Our Signs are deaf and dumb, - in the midst of darkness profound: whom Allah wills, He leaves to wander: whom He wills, He places on the way that is straight.

40. Say: "Think you to yourselves, if there come upon you the Wrath of Allah, or the Hour (that you dread), would you then call upon other than Allah? - (reply) if you are truthful!

41. "No,- On Him would you call, and if it be His will, He would remove (the distress) which occasioned your call upon Him, and you would forget (the false gods) which you join with Him!"

42. Before you We sent (Apostles) to

بِاٰيٰتِنَا صُمٌّ وَّبُكْمٌ فِي الظُّلُمٰتِ

مَنْ يَّشَاِ اللّٰهُ يُضْلِلْهُ وَمَنْ يَّشَاْ

يَجْعَلْهُ عَلٰى صِرَاطٍ مُّسْتَقِيْمٍ ۞

قُلْ اَرَءَيْتَكُمْ اِنْ اَتٰىكُمْ عَذَابُ

اللّٰهِ اَوْ اَتَتْكُمُ السَّاعَةُ اَغَيْرَ اللّٰهِ

تَدْعُوْنَ اِنْ كُنْتُمْ صٰدِقِيْنَ ۞

بَلْ اِيَّاهُ تَدْعُوْنَ فَيَكْشِفُ مَا

تَدْعُوْنَ اِلَيْهِ اِنْ شَاْءَ وَتَنْسَوْنَ

مَا تُشْرِكُوْنَ ۞ وَلَقَدْ اَرْسَلْنَا اِلٰى

then will they be turned unto Him.

37. They say: "Why is not a Sign sent down to him from his Lord?" Say: "Allah has certainly power to send down a Sign: but most of them understand not."

38. There is not an animal (that lives) on the earth, nor a being that flies on its wings, but (forms part of) communities like you. Nothing have we omitted from the Book, and they (all) shall be gathered to their Lord in the end.

39. Those who reject

اللهُ ثُمَّ اِلَيْهِ يُرْجَعُوْنَ ۩ وَقَالُوْا

لَوْلَا نُزِّلَ عَلَيْهِ اٰيَةٌ مِّنْ رَّبِّهٖ

قُلْ اِنَّ اللهَ قَادِرٌ عَلٰى اَنْ

يُّنَزِّلَ اٰيَةً وَّلٰكِنَّ اَكْثَرَهُمْ لَا

يَعْلَمُوْنَ ۩ وَمَا مِنْ دَآبَّةٍ فِى

الْاَرْضِ وَلَا طٰٓئِرٍ يَّطِيْرُ بِجَنَاحَيْهِ

اِلَّا اُمَمٌ اَمْثَالُكُمْ مَا فَرَّطْنَا فِى

الْكِتٰبِ مِنْ شَىْءٍ ثُمَّ اِلٰى رَبِّهِمْ

يُحْشَرُوْنَ ۩ وَالَّذِيْنَ كَذَّبُوْا

there is none that can alter the words (and decrees) of Allah. Already you have received some account of those Apostles.

35. If their spurning is hard on your mind, yet if you were able to seek a tunnel in the ground or a ladder to the skies and bring them a Sign, - (what good?). If it were Allah's will, He could gather them together unto true guidance: so be not you among those who are swayed by ignorance (and impatience)!

36. Those who listen (in truth), be sure, will accept: as to the dead, Allah will raise them up;

وَلَا مُبَدِّلَ لِكَلِمَٰتِ اللهِ ۚ وَلَقَدْ

جَآءَكَ مِنْ نَّبَإِى الْمُرْسَلِينَ ۝

وَإِنْ كَانَ كَبُرَ عَلَيْكَ اِعْرَاضُهُمْ

فَإِنِ اسْتَطَعْتَ اَنْ تَبْتَغِىَ نَفَقًا

فِى الْاَرْضِ اَوْ سُلَّمًا فِى السَّمَآءِ

فَتَأْتِيَهُمْ بِاٰيَةٍ ۚ وَلَوْ شَآءَ اللهُ

لَجَمَعَهُمْ عَلَى الْهُدٰى فَلَا تَكُونَنَّ

مِنَ الْجَٰهِلِينَ ۝ اِنَّمَا يَسْتَجِيبُ

الَّذِينَ يَسْمَعُونَ ۘ وَالْمَوْتٰى يَبْعَثُهُمُ

32. What is the life of this world but play and amusement? But best is the home in the hereafter, for those who are righteous. Will you not then understand?

33. We know indeed the grief which their words do cause you: it is not you they reject: it is the Signs of Allah, which the wicked contemn.

34. Rejected were the Apostles before you: with patience and constancy they bore their rejection and their wrongs, until Our aid did reach them:

وَمَا الْحَيٰوةُ الدُّنْيَا اِلَّا لَعِبٌ

وَّلَهْوٌ ؕ وَلَلدَّارُ الْاٰخِرَةُ خَيْرٌ لِّلَّذِيْنَ

يَتَّقُوْنَ ؕ اَفَلَا تَعْقِلُوْنَ ۞ قَدْ

نَعْلَمُ اِنَّهٗ لَيَحْزُنُكَ الَّذِىْ

يَقُوْلُوْنَ فَاِنَّهُمْ لَا يُكَذِّبُوْنَكَ

وَلٰكِنَّ الظّٰلِمِيْنَ بِاٰيٰتِ اللّٰهِ

يَجْحَدُوْنَ ۞ وَلَقَدْ كُذِّبَتْ رُسُلٌ

مِّنْ قَبْلِكَ فَصَبَرُوْا عَلٰى مَا

كُذِّبُوْا وَاُوْذُوْا حَتّٰى اَتٰىهُمْ نَصْرُنَا ؕ

when they are confronted with their Lord! He will say: "Is not this the truth?" They will say: "Yes, by our Lord!" He will say: "Taste you then the Chastisement, because you rejected Faith."

31. Lost indeed are they who treat it as a falsehood that they must meet Allah, - until on a sudden the hour is on them, and they say: "Ah! Woe unto us that we took no thought of it"; for they bear their burdens on their backs, and evil indeed are the burdens that they bear?

اِذْ وُقِفُوا عَلَى رَبِّهِمْ ۚ قَالَ

اَلَيْسَ هَٰذَا بِالْحَقِّ ۚ قَالُوا بَلَىٰ

وَرَبِّنَا ۚ قَالَ فَذُوقُوا الْعَذَابَ

بِمَا كُنْتُمْ تَكْفُرُونَ ۝ قَدْ خَسِرَ

اَلَّذِينَ كَذَّبُوا بِلِقَاءِ اللّٰهِ ۖ حَتَّىٰ

اِذَا جَاءَتْهُمُ السَّاعَةُ بَغْتَةً

قَالُوا يَٰحَسْرَتَنَا عَلَىٰ مَا فَرَّطْنَا

فِيهَا ۙ وَهُمْ يَحْمِلُونَ أَوْزَارَهُمْ

عَلَىٰ ظُهُورِهِمْ ۚ أَلَا سَاءَ مَا يَزِرُونَ ۝

they perceive it not.

27. If you could but see when they are confronted with the Fire! they will say: "Would that we were but sent back! then would we not reject the Signs of our Lord, but would be amongst those who believe!"

28. Yes, in their own (eyes) will become manifest what before they concealed. But if they were returned, they would certainly relapse to the things they were forbidden, for they are indeed liars.

29. And they (sometimes) say: "There is nothing except our life on this earth, and never shall we be raised up again."

30. If you could but see

يَشْعُرُوْنَ ۞ وَلَوْ تَرٰٓى اِذْ وُقِفُوْا

عَلَى النَّارِ فَقَالُوْا يٰلَيْتَنَا نُرَدُّ

وَلَا نُكَذِّبَ بِاٰيٰتِ رَبِّنَا وَنَكُوْنَ

مِنَ الْمُؤْمِنِيْنَ ۞ بَلْ بَدَا لَهُمْ

مَّا كَانُوْا يُخْفُوْنَ مِنْ قَبْلُ ۚ

وَلَوْ رُدُّوْا لَعَادُوْا لِمَا نُهُوْا

عَنْهُ وَاِنَّهُمْ لَكٰذِبُوْنَ ۞ وَقَالُوْٓا

اِنْ هِيَ اِلَّا حَيَاتُنَا الدُّنْيَا وَمَا

نَحْنُ بِمَبْعُوْثِيْنَ ۞ وَلَوْ تَرٰٓى

25. Of them there are some who (pretend to) listen to you; but We have thrown veils on their hearts, So they understand it not, and deafness in their ears; if they saw every one of the Signs, not they will believe in them; in so much that when they come to you, they (but) dispute with you; the unbelievers say: "These are nothing but tales of the ancients."

26. Others they keep away from it, and themselves they keep away; but they only destroy their own souls, and

وَمِنْهُمْ مَّنْ يَّسْتَمِعُ اِلَيْكَ

وَجَعَلْنَا عَلٰى قُلُوْبِهِمْ اَكِنَّةً

اَنْ يَّفْقَهُوْهُ وَفِيْٓ اٰذَانِهِمْ وَقْرًا ۭ

وَاِنْ يَّرَوْا كُلَّ اٰيَةٍ لَّا يُؤْمِنُوْا

بِهَا ۭ حَتّٰٓى اِذَا جَآءُوْكَ يُجَادِلُوْنَكَ

يَقُوْلُ الَّذِيْنَ كَفَرُوْٓا اِنْ هٰذَآ

اِلَّآ اَسَاطِيْرُ الْاَوَّلِيْنَ ۝ وَهُمْ

يَنْهَوْنَ عَنْهُ وَيَنْـَٔوْنَ عَنْهُ ۚ

وَاِنْ يُّهْلِكُوْنَ اِلَّآ اَنْفُسَهُمْ وَمَا

invents a lie against Allah or rejects His Signs? But verily the wrong-doers never shall prosper.

22. One day shall We gather them all together: We shall say to those who ascribed partners (to Us): "Where are the partners whom you (invented and) talked about?"

23. There will then be (left) no subterfuge for them but to say: "By Allah, our Lord, we were not those who joined gods with Allah."

24. Behold! how they lie against their own souls! But the (lie) which they invented will leave them in the lurch.

افْتَرٰى عَلَى اللهِ كَذِبًا اَوْ كَذَّبَ

بِاٰيٰتِهٖ ۗ اِنَّهٗ لَا يُفْلِحُ الظّٰلِمُوْنَ ۞

وَيَوْمَ نَحْشُرُهُمْ جَمِيْعًا ثُمَّ نَقُوْلُ

لِلَّذِيْنَ اَشْرَكُوْا اَيْنَ شُرَكَآؤُكُمُ

الَّذِيْنَ كُنْتُمْ تَزْعُمُوْنَ ۞ ثُمَّ

لَمْ تَكُنْ فِتْنَتُهُمْ اِلَّا اَنْ قَالُوْا

وَاللهِ رَبِّنَا مَا كُنَّا مُشْرِكِيْنَ ۞

اُنْظُرْ كَيْفَ كَذَبُوْا عَلٰى اَنْفُسِهِمْ

وَضَلَّ عَنْهُمْ مَّا كَانُوْا يَفْتَرُوْنَ ۞

this Qur'an has been revealed to me by inspiration, that I may warn you and all whom it reaches. Can you possibly bear witness that besides Allah there is another God?" Say: "No! I cannot bear witness!" Say: "But in truth He is the one Allah, and I truly am innocent of (your blasphemy of) joining others with Him."

20.   Those to whom We have given the Book know this as they know their own sons. Those who have lost their own souls refuse therefore to believe.

21.   Who does more wrong than he who

وَأُوحِيَ إِلَيَّ هَذَا الْقُرْآنُ

لِأُنْذِرَكُمْ بِهِ وَمَنْ بَلَغَ أَئِنَّكُمْ

لَتَشْهَدُونَ أَنَّ مَعَ اللَّهِ آلِهَةً

أُخْرَى قُلْ لَا أَشْهَدُ قُلْ إِنَّمَا

هُوَ إِلَهٌ وَاحِدٌ وَإِنَّنِي بَرِيءٌ مِمَّا

تُشْرِكُونَ ۝ الَّذِينَ آتَيْنَاهُمُ الْكِتَابَ

يَعْرِفُونَهُ كَمَا يَعْرِفُونَ أَبْنَاءَهُمُ

الَّذِينَ خَسِرُوا أَنْفُسَهُمْ فَهُمْ لَا

يُؤْمِنُونَ ۝ وَمَنْ أَظْلَمُ مِمَّنْ

16. "On that day, if the Chastisement is averted from any, it is due to Allah's Mercy; and that would be (Salvation), the obvious fulfilment of all desire.

17. "If Allah touch you with affliction, none can remove it but He; if He touch you with happiness, He has power over all things.

18. "He is the Irresistible, (watching) from above over His worshippers; and He is the Wise, Acquainted with all things."

19. Say: "What thing is most weighty in evidence?" Say: "Allah is Witness between me and you;

يُّصْرَفُ عَنْهُ يَوْمَئِذٍ فَقَدْ رَحِمَهُ

وَذٰلِكَ الْفَوْزُ الْمُبِيْنُ ۞ وَإِنْ

يَّمْسَسْكَ اللّٰهُ بِضُرٍّ فَلَا كَاشِفَ

لَهُ إِلَّا هُوَ ۖ وَإِنْ يَّمْسَسْكَ بِخَيْرٍ

فَهُوَ عَلٰى كُلِّ شَيْءٍ قَدِيْرٌ ۞

وَهُوَ الْقَاهِرُ فَوْقَ عِبَادِهِ ۖ

وَهُوَ الْحَكِيْمُ الْخَبِيْرُ ۞ قُلْ

اَيُّ شَيْءٍ اَكْبَرُ شَهَادَةً ۖ قُلِ

اللّٰهُ ۖ شَهِيْدٌۢ بَيْنِيْ وَبَيْنَكُمْ ۖ

13. To him belongs all that dwells (or lurketh) in the night and the day. For he is the one who hears and knows all things."

14. Say: "Shall I take for my protector any other than Allah, the Maker of the heavens and the earth? And He it is that feeds but is not fed." Say: "No! but I am commanded to be the first of those who bow to Allah (in Islam), and be not of the company of those who join gods with Allah."

15. Say: "I would, if I disobeyed my Lord, indeed have fear of the Chastisement of a Mighty Day.

وَلَهُ مَا سَكَنَ فِى الَّيْلِ وَالنَّهَارِ ۗ

وَهُوَ السَّمِيْعُ الْعَلِيْمُ ۞ قُلْ

اَغَيْرَ اللّٰهِ اَتَّخِذُ وَلِيًّا فَاطِرِ

السَّمٰوٰتِ وَالْاَرْضِ وَهُوَ يُطْعِمُ

وَلَا يُطْعَمُ ۗ قُلْ اِنِّيْٓ اُمِرْتُ

اَنْ اَكُوْنَ اَوَّلَ مَنْ اَسْلَمَ

وَلَا تَكُوْنَنَّ مِنَ الْمُشْرِكِيْنَ ۞

قُلْ اِنِّيْٓ اَخَافُ اِنْ عَصَيْتُ

رَبِّيْ عَذَابَ يَوْمٍ عَظِيْمٍ ۞ مَنْ

their scoffers were hemmed in by the thing that they mocked.

11. Say: "Travel through the earth and see what was the end of those who rejected Truth."

12. Say: "To whom belongs all that is in the heavens and on earth?" Say: "To Allah. He has inscribed for Himself (the rule of) Mercy. That He will gather you together for the Day of Judgment, there is no doubt whatever. It is they who have lost their own souls, that will not believe.

بِالَّذِينَ سَخِرُوا مِنْهُمْ مَّا كَانُوا

بِهِ يَسْتَهْزِءُوْنَ ۞ قُلْ سِيرُوْا

فِى الْأَرْضِ ثُمَّ انْظُرُوْا كَيْفَ

كَانَ عَاقِبَةُ الْمُكَذِّبِينَ ۞ قُلْ

لِّمَنْ مَّا فِى السَّمٰوٰتِ وَالْأَرْضِ

قُلْ لِّلّٰهِ ۚ كَتَبَ عَلٰى نَفْسِهِ

الرَّحْمَةَ ۚ لَيَجْمَعَنَّكُمْ اِلٰى يَوْمِ

الْقِيٰمَةِ لَا رَيْبَ فِيْهِ ۚ اَلَّذِينَ

خَسِرُوا اَنْفُسَهُمْ فَهُمْ لَا يُؤْمِنُوْنَ ۞

parchment, so that they could touch it with their hands, the unbelievers would have been sure to say: "This is nothing but obvious magic!"

8. They say: "Why is not an Angel sent down to him?" If we did send down an Angel, the matter would be settled at once, and no respite would be granted them.

9. If We had made it an Angel, We should have sent him as a man, and We should certainly have caused them confusion in a matter which they have already covered with confusion.

10. Mocked were (many) Apostles before you; but

قِرْطَاسٍ فَلَمَسُوهُ بِأَيْدِيهِمْ

لَقَالَ الَّذِينَ كَفَرُوْا إِنْ هٰذَآ

إِلَّا سِحْرٌ مُّبِيْنٌ ۞ وَ قَالُوْا

لَوْ لَآ أُنْزِلَ عَلَيْهِ مَلَكٌ ۗ وَلَوْ

أَنْزَلْنَا مَلَكًا لَّقُضِيَ الْأَمْرُ ثُمَّ

لَا يُنْظَرُوْنَ ۞ وَلَوْ جَعَلْنٰهُ مَلَكًا

لَّجَعَلْنٰهُ رَجُلًا وَّ لَلَبَسْنَا عَلَيْهِمْ

مَّا يَلْبِسُوْنَ ۞ وَلَقَدِ اسْتُهْزِئَ

بِرُسُلٍ مِّنْ قَبْلِكَ فَحَاقَ

mock at.

6. See they not how many of those before them We did destroy? - generations We had established on the earth, in strength such as We have not given to you - for whom We poured out rain from the skies in abundance, and gave (fertile) streams flowing beneath their (feet): yet for their sins We destroyed them, and raised in their wake fresh generations (to succeed them).

7. If We had sent down to you a written (message) on

يَسْتَهْزِءُوْنَ ۞ اَلَمْ يَرَوْا كَمْ

اَهْلَكْنَا مِنْ قَبْلِهِمْ مِّنْ

قَرْنٍ مَّكَّنّٰهُمْ فِى الْاَرْضِ

مَا لَمْ نُمَكِّنْ لَّكُمْ وَ اَرْسَلْنَا

السَّمَآءَ عَلَيْهِمْ مِّدْرَارًا ۙ وَّجَعَلْنَا

الْاَنْهٰرَ تَجْرِىْ مِنْ تَحْتِهِمْ

فَاَهْلَكْنٰهُمْ بِذُنُوْبِهِمْ وَاَنْشَاْنَا

مِنْۢ بَعْدِهِمْ قَرْنًا اٰخَرِيْنَ ۞

وَلَوْ نَزَّلْنَا عَلَيْكَ كِتٰبًا فِىْ

and then decreed a stated term (for you). And there is in His presence another determined term; yet you doubt within yourselves!

3. And He is Allah in the heavens and on earth. He knows what you hide, and what you reveal, and He knows the (recompense) which you earn (by your deeds).

4. But never did a single one of the Signs of their Lord reach them, but they turned away therefrom.

5. And now they reject the truth when it reaches them: but soon shall they learn the reality of what they used to

ثُمَّ قَضَى اَجَلًا وَاَجَلٌ مُّسَمًّى

عِنْدَهُ ثُمَّ اَنْتُمْ تَمْتَرُوْنَ ۝ وَهُوَ

اللّٰهُ فِى السَّمٰوٰتِ وَفِى الْاَرْضِ

يَعْلَمُ سِرَّكُمْ وَجَهْرَكُمْ وَيَعْلَمُ

مَا تَكْسِبُوْنَ ۝ وَمَا تَأْتِيْهِمْ مِّنْ

اٰيَةٍ مِّنْ اٰيٰتِ رَبِّهِمْ اِلَّا كَانُوْا

عَنْهَا مُعْرِضِيْنَ ۝ فَقَدْ كَذَّبُوْا

بِالْحَقِّ لَمَّا جَآءَهُمْ فَسَوْفَ

يَأْتِيْهِمْ اَنْبٰٓؤُا مَا كَانُوْا بِهٖ

that is the great salvation, (the fulfilment of all desires).

120. To Allah does belong the dominion of the heavens and the earth, and all that is therein, and it is He Who has power over all things.

Al-An'am (The Cattle)
Bismillahir -Rahmanir-Rahim

1. Praise to be Allah, Who created the heavens and the earth, and made the darkness and the light. Yet those who reject Faith hold (others) as equal with their Guardian-Lord.

2. He it is who created you from clay,

ذٰلِكَ الْفَوْزُ الْعَظِيْمُ ۞ لِلّٰهِ مُلْكُ

السَّمٰوٰتِ وَالْاَرْضِ وَمَا فِيْهِنَّ

وَهُوَ عَلٰى كُلِّ شَىْءٍ قَدِيْرٌ ۞

بِسْمِ اللّٰهِ الرَّحْمٰنِ الرَّحِيْمِ

اَلْحَمْدُ لِلّٰهِ الَّذِىْ خَلَقَ

السَّمٰوٰتِ وَالْاَرْضَ وَجَعَلَ

الظُّلُمٰتِ وَالنُّوْرَ ۣثُمَّ الَّذِيْنَ

كَفَرُوْا بِرَبِّهِمْ يَعْدِلُوْنَ ۞ هُوَ

الَّذِىْ خَلَقَكُمْ مِّنْ طِيْنٍ

amongst them; when You did take me up, You were the Watcher over them, and You are a Witness to all things.

118. "If You do punish them, they are Your servants: if You does forgive them, You are the Exalted in Power, the Wise."

119. Allah will say: "This is a day on which the truthful will profit from their truth: theirs are Gardens, with rivers flowing beneath, - their eternal home: Allah well-pleased with them, and they with Allah:

فِيهِمْ فَلَمَّا تَوَفَّيْتَنِي كُنْتَ أَنْتَ

الرَّقِيبَ عَلَيْهِمْ وَأَنْتَ عَلَى كُلِّ

شَيْءٍ شَهِيدٌ ۝ إِنْ تُعَذِّبْهُمْ

فَإِنَّهُمْ عِبَادُكَ وَإِنْ تَغْفِرْ لَهُمْ

فَإِنَّكَ أَنْتَ الْعَزِيزُ الْحَكِيمُ ۝ قَالَ

اللَّهُ هَذَا يَوْمُ يَنْفَعُ الصَّادِقِينَ

صِدْقُهُمْ لَهُمْ جَنَّاتٌ تَجْرِي مِنْ

تَحْتِهَا الْأَنْهَارُ خَالِدِينَ فِيهَا أَبَدًا

رَضِيَ اللَّهُ عَنْهُمْ وَرَضُوا عَنْهُ

as gods in derogation of Allah'?"
He will say: "Glory to You! Never
could I say what I had no right (to
say). Had I said such a thing, You
would indeed have known it.
You knowest what is in my heart,
though I know not what is in
Thine. For you know in full all
that is hidden.

117. "Never said I to them
anything except what You
commanded me to say, to wit,
'Worship Allah, my Lord and
your Lord'; and I was a witness
over them while I dwelt

اِلٰهَيْنِ مِنْ دُوْنِ اللهِ ۖ قَالَ

سُبْحٰنَكَ مَا يَكُوْنُ لِيْ اَنْ اَقُوْلَ

مَا لَيْسَ لِيْ ۛ بِحَقٍّ ۚ اِنْ كُنْتُ

قُلْتُهُ فَقَدْ عَلِمْتَهٗ ۚ تَعْلَمُ مَا فِيْ

نَفْسِيْ وَلَاۤ اَعْلَمُ مَا فِيْ نَفْسِكَ ۚ

اِنَّكَ اَنْتَ عَلَّامُ الْغُيُوْبِ ﴿١١٦﴾ مَا

قُلْتُ لَهُمْ اِلَّا مَاۤ اَمَرْتَنِيْ بِهٖۤ

اَنِ اعْبُدُوا اللهَ رَبِّيْ وَرَبَّكُمْ ۚ

وَكُنْتُ عَلَيْهِمْ شَهِيْدًا مَّا دُمْتُ

from heaven a table set (with viands), that there may be for us - for the first and the last of us - a solemn festival and a Sign from You; and provide for our sustenance, for You are the best Sustainer (of our needs)."

115. Allah said: "I will send it down unto you: but if any of you after that resists faith, I will punish him with a Chastisement such as I have not inflicted on any one among all the peoples."

116. And behold! Allah will say: "O Jesus the son of Mary! Did you say unto men, worship me and my mother

مَآئِدَةً مِّنَ السَّمَآءِ تَكُونُ لَنَا

عِيْدًا لِّاَوَّلِنَا وَاٰخِرِنَا وَاٰيَةً

مِّنْكَ وَارْزُقْنَا وَاَنْتَ خَيْرُ

الرّٰزِقِيْنَ ۩ قَالَ اللّٰهُ اِنِّيْ مُنَزِّلُهَا

عَلَيْكُمْ فَمَنْ يَّكْفُرْ بَعْدُ مِنْكُمْ

فَاِنِّيْٓ اُعَذِّبُهٗ عَذَابًا لَّآ اُعَذِّبُهٗٓ

اَحَدًا مِّنَ الْعٰلَمِيْنَ ۩ وَاِذْ قَالَ

اللّٰهُ يٰعِيْسَى ابْنَ مَرْيَمَ ءَاَنْتَ

قُلْتَ لِلنَّاسِ اتَّخِذُوْنِيْ وَاُمِّيَ

the Disciples, said: "O Jesus the son of Mary! Can your Lord send down to us a table set (with viands) from heaven?" Said Jesus: "Fear Allah, if you have faith."

113. They said: "We only wish to eat thereof and satisfy our hearts, and to know that you have indeed told us the truth; and that we ourselves may be witnesses to the miracle."

114. Said Jesus the son of Mary: "O Allah our Lord! Send us

الْحَوَارِيُّوْنَ يٰعِيْسَى ابْنَ مَرْيَمَ

هَلْ يَسْتَطِيْعُ رَبُّكَ اَنْ يُّنَزِّلَ

عَلَيْنَا مَآئِدَةً مِّنَ السَّمَآءِ ۚ قَالَ

اتَّقُوا اللّٰهَ اِنْ كُنْتُمْ مُّؤْمِنِيْنَ ۝

قَالُوْا نُرِيْدُ اَنْ نَّأْكُلَ مِنْهَا

وَتَطْمَئِنَّ قُلُوْبُنَا وَنَعْلَمَ اَنْ

قَدْ صَدَقْتَنَا وَنَكُوْنَ عَلَيْهَا مِنَ

الشّٰهِدِيْنَ ۝ قَالَ عِيْسَى ابْنُ

مَرْيَمَ اللّٰهُمَّ رَبَّنَا اَنْزِلْ عَلَيْنَا

and it becomes a bird by My leave, and you healed those born blind, and the lepers, by My leave. And behold ! You brought forth the dead by My leave. And behold! I did restrain the Children of Israel from (violence to) you when you showed them the clear Signs, and the unbelievers among them said: 'This is nothing but evident magic.'

111. "And behold! I inspired the Disciples to have faith in Me and Mine Apostle: they said, 'We have faith, and you bear witness that we bow to Allah as Muslims'".

112. Behold!

فَتَكُوْنُ طَيْرًا بِاِذْنِيْ وَتُبْرِئُ

الْاَكْمَهَ وَالْاَبْرَصَ بِاِذْنِيْ وَاِذْ

تُخْرِجُ الْمَوْتٰى بِاِذْنِيْ وَاِذْ كَفَفْتُ

بَنِيْ اِسْرَآءِيْلَ عَنْكَ اِذْ جِئْتَهُمْ

بِالْبَيِّنٰتِ فَقَالَ الَّذِيْنَ كَفَرُوْا

مِنْهُمْ اِنْ هٰذَآ اِلَّا سِحْرٌ مُّبِيْنٌ ۝

وَاِذْ اَوْحَيْتُ اِلَى الْحَوَارِيِّنَ اَنْ

اٰمِنُوْا بِيْ وَبِرَسُوْلِيْ قَالُوْٓا اٰمَنَّا

وَاشْهَدْ بِاَنَّنَا مُسْلِمُوْنَ ۝ اِذْ قَالَ

"What was the response you received (from men to your teaching)?" They will say: "We have no knowledge: it is You Who knows in full all that is hidden."

110. Then will Allah say: "O Jesus the son of Mary! Recount My favour to you and to your mother. Behold! I strengthened you with the holy Spirit, so that you did speak to the people in childhood and in maturity. Behold! I taught you the Book and Wisdom, the Law and the Gospel and behold! you make out of clay, as it were, the figure of a bird, by My leave, and you breathed into it

مَاذَآ اُجِبْتُمْ ۚ قَالُوْا لَا عِلْمَ لَنَا ۖ

اِنَّكَ اَنْتَ عَلَّامُ الْغُيُوْبِ ۞ اِذْ

قَالَ اللّٰهُ يٰعِيْسَى ابْنَ مَرْيَمَ اذْكُرْ

نِعْمَتِيْ عَلَيْكَ وَعَلٰى وَالِدَتِكَ ۘ

اِذْ اَيَّدْتُّكَ بِرُوْحِ الْقُدُسِ ۟ تُكَلِّمُ

النَّاسَ فِى الْمَهْدِ وَكَهْلًا ۚ وَاِذْ

عَلَّمْتُكَ الْكِتٰبَ وَالْحِكْمَةَ وَالتَّوْرٰةَ

وَالْاِنْجِيْلَ ۚ وَاِذْ تَخْلُقُ مِنَ الطِّيْنِ

كَهَيْـَٔةِ الطَّيْرِ بِاِذْنِيْ فَتَنْفُخُ فِيْهَا

among those who claim a lawful right: let them swear by Allah: "We affirm that our witness is truer than that of those two, and that we have not trespassed (beyond the truth): if we did, behold! the wrong be upon us!"

108. That is most suitable: that they may give the evidence in its true nature and shape, or else they would fear that other oaths would be taken after their oaths. But fear Allah, and listen (to His counsel): for Allah guides not a rebellious people:

109. One day will Allah gather the Apostles together, and ask:

الَّذِيْنَ اسْتَحَقَّ عَلَيْهِمُ الْأَوْلَيٰنِ

فَيُقْسِمٰنِ بِاللّٰهِ لَشَهَادَتُنَاۤ اَحَقُّ

مِنْ شَهَادَتِهِمَا وَمَا اعْتَدَيْنَاۤ اِنَّاۤ

اِذًا لَّمِنَ الظّٰلِمِيْنَ ۞ ذٰلِكَ اَدْنٰۤى

اَنْ يَّأْتُوْا بِالشَّهَادَةِ عَلٰى وَجْهِهَاۤ

اَوْ يَخَافُوْۤا اَنْ تُرَدَّ اَيْمَانٌۢ بَعْدَ

اَيْمَانِهِمْ ؕ وَاتَّقُوا اللّٰهَ وَاسْمَعُوْا ؕ

وَاللّٰهُ لَا يَهْدِى الْقَوْمَ الْفٰسِقِيْنَ ۞

يَوْمَ يَجْمَعُ اللّٰهُ الرُّسُلَ فَيَقُوْلُ

outside if you are journeying through the earth, and the chance of death befalls you (thus). If you doubt (their truth), detain them both after prayer, and let them both swear by Allah: "We wish not in this for any worldly gain, even though the (beneficiary) be our near relation: we shall hide not the evidence before Allah: if we do, then behold! the sin be upon us!"

107. But if it gets known that these two were guilty of the sin (of perjury), let two others stand forth in their places, - nearest in kin from

غَيْرِكُمْ اِنْ اَنْتُمْ ضَرَبْتُمْ فِى

الْاَرْضِ فَاَصَابَتْكُمْ مُّصِيْبَةُ الْمَوْتِ

تَحْبِسُوْنَهُمَا مِنْۢ بَعْدِ الصَّلٰوةِ

فَيُقْسِمٰنِ بِاللّٰهِ اِنِ ارْتَبْتُمْ لَا

نَشْتَرِيْ بِهٖ ثَمَنًا وَّلَوْ كَانَ ذَا

قُرْبٰى ۙ وَلَا نَكْتُمُ شَهَادَةَ ۙ اللّٰهِ

اِنَّاۤ اِذًا لَّمِنَ الْاٰثِمِيْنَ ۞ فَاِنْ

عُثِرَ عَلٰۤى اَنَّهُمَا اسْتَحَقَّاۤ اِثْمًا

فَاٰخَرٰنِ يَقُوْمٰنِ مَقَامَهُمَا مِنَ

void of knowledge and guidance?

105. O you who believe! Guard your own souls: if you follow (right) guidance, no hurt can come to you from those who stray. The goal of you all is to Allah: it is He that will show you the truth of all that you do.

106. O you who believe! When death approaches any of you, (take) witnesses among yourselves when making bequests,- two just men of your own (brotherhood) or others from

يَعْلَمُوْنَ شَيْئًا وَّلَا يَهْتَدُوْنَ ۞

يَاۤيُّهَا الَّذِيْنَ اٰمَنُوْا عَلَيْكُمْ

اَنْفُسَكُمْ ۚ لَا يَضُرُّكُمْ مَّنْ ضَلَّ

اِذَا اهْتَدَيْتُمْ ؕ اِلَى اللّٰهِ مَرْجِعُكُمْ

جَمِيْعًا فَيُنَبِّئُكُمْ بِمَا كُنْتُمْ

تَعْمَلُوْنَ ۞ يَاۤيُّهَا الَّذِيْنَ اٰمَنُوْا

شَهَادَةُ بَيْنِكُمْ اِذَا حَضَرَ اَحَدَكُمُ

الْمَوْتُ حِيْنَ الْوَصِيَّةِ اثْنٰنِ

ذَوَا عَدْلٍ مِّنْكُمْ اَوْ اٰخَرٰنِ مِنْ

and on that account lost their faith.

103. It was not Allah Who instituted (superstitions like those of) a slit-ear she-camel, or a she-camel let loose for free pasture, or idol sacrifices for twin-births in animals, or stallion-camels freed from work: it is blasphemers who invent a lie against Allah; but most of them lack wisdom.

104. When it is said to them: "Come to what Allah has revealed; come to the Apostle": they say: "Enough for us are the ways we found our fathers following." What! even though their fathers were

ثُمَّ أَصْبَحُوا بِهَا كَفِرِينَ ۞ مَا

جَعَلَ اللّٰهُ مِنْ بَحِيرَةٍ وَّلَا

سَآئِبَةٍ وَّلَا وَصِيلَةٍ وَّلَاحَامٍ

وَّلٰكِنَّ الَّذِينَ كَفَرُوا يَفْتَرُونَ

عَلَى اللّٰهِ الْكَذِبَ وَأَكْثَرُهُمْ لَا

يَعْقِلُونَ ۞ وَإِذَا قِيلَ لَهُمْ تَعَالَوْا

إِلٰى مَا أَنْزَلَ اللّٰهُ وَإِلَى الرَّسُولِ

قَالُوا حَسْبُنَا مَا وَجَدْنَا عَلَيْهِ

اٰبَآءَنَا ۗ أَوَلَوْ كَانَ اٰبَآؤُهُمْ لَا

"Not equal are things that are bad and things that are good, even though the abundance of the bad may dazzle you; so fear Allah, O you that understand; that (so) you may prosper."

101. O you who believe! Ask not questions about things which, if made plain to you, may cause you trouble. But if you ask about things when the Qur'an is being revealed, they will be made plain to you, Allah will forgive those: for Allah is Oft-Forgiving, Most Forbearing.

102. Some people before you did ask such questions,

لَا يَسْتَوِى الْخَبِيثُ وَالطَّيِّبُ وَلَوْ
أَعْجَبَكَ كَثْرَةُ الْخَبِيثِ فَاتَّقُوا
اللّٰهَ يَا أُولِى الْأَلْبَابِ لَعَلَّكُمْ
تُفْلِحُونَ ۞ يَا أَيُّهَا الَّذِينَ اٰمَنُوا
لَا تَسْئَلُوا عَنْ أَشْيَاءَ إِنْ تُبْدَ لَكُمْ
تَسُؤْكُمْ ۚ وَإِنْ تَسْئَلُوا عَنْهَا حِينَ
يُنَزَّلُ الْقُرْاٰنُ تُبْدَ لَكُمْ ۚ عَفَا
اللّٰهُ عَنْهَا ۗ وَاللّٰهُ غَفُورٌ حَلِيمٌ ۞
قَدْ سَأَلَهَا قَوْمٌ مِّنْ قَبْلِكُمْ

the Sacred House, an asylum of security for men, as also the Sacred months, the animals for offerings, and the garlands that mark them: that you may know that Allah has knowledge of what is in the heavens and on earth and that Allah is Well Acquainted with all things.

98. Know you that Allah is strict in punishment and that Allah is Oft-Forgiving, Most Merciful.

99. The Apostle's duty is but to proclaim (the message). But Allah knows all that you reveal and all that you conceal.

100. Say:

الْبَيْتَ الْحَرَامَ قِيَامًا لِّلنَّاسِ

وَالشَّهْرَ الْحَرَامَ وَالْهَدْىَ وَالْقَلَائِدَ

ذٰلِكَ لِتَعْلَمُوا أَنَّ اللّٰهَ يَعْلَمُ مَا

فِي السَّمٰوٰتِ وَمَا فِي الْأَرْضِ وَأَنَّ

اللّٰهَ بِكُلِّ شَيْءٍ عَلِيمٌ ۞ اِعْلَمُوا

أَنَّ اللّٰهَ شَدِيدُ الْعِقَابِ وَأَنَّ

اللّٰهَ غَفُورٌ رَّحِيمٌ ۞ مَا عَلَى

الرَّسُولِ إِلَّا الْبَلَاغُ وَاللّٰهُ يَعْلَمُ

مَا تُبْدُونَ وَمَا تَكْتُمُونَ ۞ قُلْ

or by way of atonement, the feeding of the indigent; or its equivalent in fasts: that he may taste of the chastisement of his deed. Allah forgives what is past: for repetition Allah will exact from him the chastisement. For Allah is Exalted, and Lord of Retribution.

96. Lawful to you is the pursuit of water-game and its use for food, - for the benefit of yourselves and those who travel; but forbidden is the pursuit of land-game; - as long as you are in the sacred precincts or in pilgrim garb. And fear Allah, to Whom you shall be gathered back.

97. Allah made the Ka'ba,

اَوْ كَفَّارَةٌ طَعَامُ مَسَاكِينَ اَوْ عَدْلُ

ذٰلِكَ صِيَامًا لِّيَذُوقَ وَبَالَ اَمْرِهٖ

عَفَا اللّٰهُ عَمَّا سَلَفَ وَمَنْ عَادَ

فَيَنْتَقِمُ اللّٰهُ مِنْهُ وَاللّٰهُ عَزِيزٌ

ذُو انْتِقَامٍ ۞ اُحِلَّ لَكُمْ صَيْدُ الْبَحْرِ

وَطَعَامُهٗ مَتَاعًا لَّكُمْ وَلِلسَّيَّارَةِ

وَحُرِّمَ عَلَيْكُمْ صَيْدُ الْبَرِّ مَا دُمْتُمْ

حُرُمًا وَاتَّقُوا اللّٰهَ الَّذِيْ اِلَيْهِ

تُحْشَرُونَ ۞ جَعَلَ اللّٰهُ الْكَعْبَةَ

in a little matter of game well within reach of your hands and your lances, that He may test who fears Him unseen: any who transgress thereafter, will have a grievous Chastisement.

95. O you who believe! Kill not game while in the sacred precincts or in pilgrim garb. If any of you does so intentionally, the compensation is an offering, brought to the Ka'ba, of a domestic animal equivalent to the one he killed, as adjudged by two just men among you;

بِشَىْءٍ مِّنَ الصَّيْدِ تَنَالُهُ

اَيْدِيكُمْ وَرِمَاحُكُمْ لِيَعْلَمَ اللّٰهُ

مَنْ يَّخَافُهُ بِالْغَيْبِ فَمَنِ اعْتَدٰى

بَعْدَ ذٰلِكَ فَلَهُ عَذَابٌ اَلِيْمٌ ۞

يٰٓاَيُّهَا الَّذِيْنَ اٰمَنُوْا لَا تَقْتُلُوا

الصَّيْدَ وَاَنْتُمْ حُرُمٌ وَمَنْ قَتَلَهُ

مِنْكُمْ مُّتَعَمِّدًا فَجَزَآءٌ مِّثْلُ مَا

قَتَلَ مِنَ النَّعَمِ يَحْكُمُ بِهِ ذَوَا

عَدْلٍ مِّنْكُمْ هَدْيًا بَالِغَ الْكَعْبَةِ

and obey the Apostle, and beware (of evil): if you do turn back, know you that it is Our Apostle's duty to proclaim (the message) in the clearest manner.

93. On those who believe and do deeds of righteousness there is no blame for what they ate (in the past), when they guard themselves from evil, and believe, and do deeds of righteousness, - (or) again, guard themselves from evil and believe, - (or) again, guard themselves from evil and do good. For Allah loves those who do good.

94. O you who believe! Allah does but make a trial of you

وَ أَطِيعُوا الرَّسُولَ وَ احْذَرُوا فَإِنْ

تَوَلَّيْتُمْ فَاعْلَمُوا أَنَّمَا عَلَى رَسُولِنَا

الْبَلَاغُ الْمُبِيْنُ ۝ لَيْسَ عَلَى

الَّذِيْنَ اٰمَنُوا وَ عَمِلُوا الصَّلِحٰتِ

جُنَاحٌ فِيْمَا طَعِمُوا إِذَا مَا اتَّقَوْا

وَّ اٰمَنُوا وَ عَمِلُوا الصَّلِحٰتِ ثُمَّ

اتَّقَوْا وَّ اٰمَنُوا ثُمَّ اتَّقَوْا وَّ أَحْسَنُوا

وَ اللّٰهُ يُحِبُّ الْمُحْسِنِيْنَ ۝ يٰٓأَيُّهَا

الَّذِيْنَ اٰمَنُوا لَيَبْلُوَنَّكُمُ اللّٰهُ

His Signs, that you may be grateful.

90. O you who believe! Intoxicants and gambling, (dedi-cation of) stones, and (divination by) arrows, are an abomination,- of Satan's handwork: eschew such (abomination), that you may prosper.

91. Satan's plan is (but) to excite enmity and hatred between you, with intoxicants and gambling, and hinder you from the remembrance of Allah, and from prayer: will you not then abstain?

92. Obey Allah,

اٰيٰتِهٖ لَعَلَّكُمْ تَشْكُرُوْنَ ۝ يٰٓاَيُّهَا

الَّذِيْنَ اٰمَنُوْٓا اِنَّمَا الْخَمْرُ وَالْمَيْسِرُ

وَالْاَنْصَابُ وَالْاَزْلَامُ رِجْسٌ مِّنْ

عَمَلِ الشَّيْطٰنِ فَاجْتَنِبُوْهُ لَعَلَّكُمْ

تُفْلِحُوْنَ ۝ اِنَّمَا يُرِيْدُ الشَّيْطٰنُ

اَنْ يُّوْقِعَ بَيْنَكُمُ الْعَدَاوَةَ وَالْبَغْضَآءَ

فِى الْخَمْرِ وَالْمَيْسِرِ وَيَصُدَّكُمْ عَنْ

ذِكْرِ اللّٰهِ وَعَنِ الصَّلٰوةِ ۚ فَهَلْ

اَنْتُمْ مُّنْتَهُوْنَ ۝ وَاَطِيْعُوا اللّٰهَ

89. Allah will not call you to account for what is futile in your oaths, but He will call you to account for your deliberate oaths: for expiation, feed ten indigent persons, on a scale of the average for the food of your families; or clothe them; or give a slave his freedom. If that is beyond your means, fast for three days. That is the expiation for the oaths you have sworn. But keep to your oaths. Thus does Allah make clear to you

لَا يُؤَاخِذُكُمُ اللّٰهُ بِاللَّغْوِ فِىۤ

اَيْمَانِكُمْ وَلٰكِنْ يُّؤَاخِذُكُمْ بِمَا

عَقَّدْتُّمُ الْاَيْمَانَ ۚ فَكَفَّارَتُهٗۤ اِطْعَامُ

عَشَرَةِ مَسٰكِيْنَ مِنْ اَوْسَطِ مَا

تُطْعِمُوْنَ اَهْلِيْكُمْ اَوْ كِسْوَتُهُمْ اَوْ

تَحْرِيْرُ رَقَبَةٍ ؕ فَمَنْ لَّمْ يَجِدْ

فَصِيَامُ ثَلٰثَةِ اَيَّامٍ ؕ ذٰلِكَ كَفَّارَةُ

اَيْمَانِكُمْ اِذَا حَلَفْتُمْ ؕ وَاحْفَظُوْۤا

اَيْمَانَكُمْ ؕ كَذٰلِكَ يُبَيِّنُ اللّٰهُ لَكُمْ

underneath,- their eternal home. Such is the recompense of those who do good.

86. But those who reject Faith and belie our Signs,- they shall be Companions of Hell-fire.

87. O you who believe! Make not unlawful the good things which Allah has made lawful for you, but commit no excess: for Allah loves not those given to excess.

88. Eat of the things which Allah has provided for you, lawful and good; but fear Allah, in Whom you believe.

تَحْتِهَا الْأَنْهَٰرُ خَٰلِدِينَ فِيهَا ۚ وَذَٰلِكَ

جَزَآءُ الْمُحْسِنِينَ ۞ وَالَّذِينَ كَفَرُوا

وَكَذَّبُوا بِـَٔايَٰتِنَآ أُو۟لَٰٓئِكَ أَصْحَٰبُ

الْجَحِيمِ ۞ يَٰٓأَيُّهَا الَّذِينَ ءَامَنُوا

لَا تُحَرِّمُوا طَيِّبَٰتِ مَآ أَحَلَّ اللَّهُ

لَكُمْ وَلَا تَعْتَدُوٓا ۚ إِنَّ اللَّهَ لَا

يُحِبُّ الْمُعْتَدِينَ ۞ وَكُلُوا مِمَّا

رَزَقَكُمُ اللَّهُ حَلَٰلًا طَيِّبًا ۚ وَاتَّقُوا

اللَّهَ الَّذِىٓ أَنتُم بِهِۦ مُؤْمِنُونَ ۞

83. And when they listen to the revelation received by the Apostle, you will see their eyes overflowing with tears, for they recognise the truth: they pray: "Our Lord! we believe; write us down among the witnesses.

84. "What cause can we have not to believe in Allah and the truth which has come to us, seeing that we long for our Lord to admit us to the company of the righteous?"

85. And for this their prayer has Allah rewarded them with Gardens, with rivers flowing

وَإِذَا سَمِعُوا مَا أُنْزِلَ إِلَى

الرَّسُولِ تَرَى أَعْيُنَهُمْ تَفِيضُ

مِنَ الدَّمْعِ مِمَّا عَرَفُوا مِنَ

الْحَقِّ يَقُولُونَ رَبَّنَا آمَنَّا فَاكْتُبْنَا

مَعَ الشَّاهِدِينَ ۞ وَمَا لَنَا لَا

نُؤْمِنُ بِاللَّهِ وَمَا جَاءَنَا مِنَ

الْحَقِّ وَنَطْمَعُ أَنْ يُدْخِلَنَا رَبُّنَا

مَعَ الْقَوْمِ الصَّالِحِينَ ۞ فَأَثَابَهُمُ

اللَّهُ بِمَا قَالُوا جَنَّاتٍ تَجْرِي مِنْ

ناشران الکتب الاسلامیة

پارہ

وَاِذَاسَمِعُوا

(٧)

بنك الكتب الإسلامية

PART 8
Walaw Annana

Hindering from the path of Allah those who believe in Him, and seeking in it something crooked; but remember how you were small in numbers, and He gave you increase. And hold in your mind's eye what was the end of those who did mischief."

87. "And if there is a party among you who believes in the message with which I have been sent, and a party which does not believe, hold yourselves in patience until Allah does decide between us: for He is the best to decide."

وَتَصُدُّوْنَ عَنْ سَبِيْلِ اللهِ

مَنْ اٰمَنَ بِهٖ وَتَبْغُوْنَهَا عِوَجًا

وَاذْكُرُوْا اِذْ كُنْتُمْ قَلِيْلًا

فَكَثَّرَكُمْ وَانْظُرُوْا كَيْفَ كَانَ

عَاقِبَةُ الْمُفْسِدِيْنَ ۞ وَاِنْ كَانَ

طَآئِفَةٌ مِّنْكُمْ اٰمَنُوْا بِالَّذِيْٓ

اُرْسِلْتُ بِهٖ وَطَآئِفَةٌ لَّمْ

يُؤْمِنُوْا فَاصْبِرُوْا حَتّٰى يَحْكُمَ اللهُ

بَيْنَنَا وَهُوَ خَيْرُ الْحٰكِمِيْنَ ۞

We sent Shu'aib, one of their own brethren: he said: "O my people! Worship Allah; You have no other Allah but Him. Now has come unto you a clear (Sign) from your Lord! so give just measure and weight, nor withhold from the people the things that are their due; and do no mischief on the earth after it has been set in order: that will be best for you, if you have Faith.

86. "And squat not on every road, breathing threats,

أَخَاهُمْ شُعَيْبًا ۗ قَالَ يَقَوْمِ

اعْبُدُوا اللَّهَ مَا لَكُم مِّنْ إِلَٰهٍ

غَيْرُهُ ۖ قَدْ جَاءَتْكُم بَيِّنَةٌ مِّن

رَّبِّكُمْ ۖ فَأَوْفُوا الْكَيْلَ وَالْمِيزَانَ

وَلَا تَبْخَسُوا النَّاسَ أَشْيَاءَهُمْ

وَلَا تُفْسِدُوا فِي الْأَرْضِ بَعْدَ

إِصْلَاحِهَا ۚ ذَٰلِكُمْ خَيْرٌ لَّكُمْ

إِن كُنتُم مُّؤْمِنِينَ ۝ وَلَا

تَقْعُدُوا بِكُلِّ صِرَاطٍ تُوعِدُونَ

in preference to women : you are indeed a people transgressing beyond bounds."

82. And his people gave no answer but this: they said, "Drive them out of your city: these are indeed men who want to be clean and pure!"

83. But We saved him and his family, except his wife: she was of those who tarried behind.

84. And We rained down on them a shower (of brimstone): then see what was the end of those who indulged in sin and crime!

85. To the Madyan people

شَهْوَةً مِّنْ دُوْنِ النِّسَآءِ ۚ بَلْ

أَنْتُمْ قَوْمٌ مُّسْرِفُوْنَ ۞ وَمَا كَانَ

جَوَابَ قَوْمِهٖٓ إِلَّآ أَنْ قَالُوْٓا

أَخْرِجُوْهُمْ مِّنْ قَرْيَتِكُمْ ۚ إِنَّهُمْ

أُنَاسٌ يَّتَطَهَّرُوْنَ ۞ فَأَنْجَيْنٰهُ

وَأَهْلَهٗٓ إِلَّا امْرَأَتَهٗ ۖ كَانَتْ

مِنَ الْغٰبِرِيْنَ ۞ وَأَمْطَرْنَا عَلَيْهِمْ

مَّطَرًا ۚ فَانْظُرْ كَيْفَ كَانَ عَاقِبَةُ

الْمُجْرِمِيْنَ ۞ وَإِلٰى مَدْيَنَ

an Apostle (of Allah)!"

78. So the earthquake took them unawares, and they lay prostrate in their homes in the morning!

79. So Salih left them, saying: "O my people! I did indeed convey to you the message for which I was sent by my Lord: I gave you good counsel, but you love not good counsellors!"

80. We also (sent) Lut: he said to his people: "Do you commit lewdness such as no people in creation (ever) committed before you?

81. "For you practise your lusts on men

الْمُرْسَلِينَ ۞ فَاَخَذَتْهُمُ الرَّجْفَةُ

فَاَصْبَحُوا فِي دَارِهِمْ جَاثِمِينَ ۞

فَتَوَلَّى عَنْهُمْ وَقَالَ يَا قَوْمِ

لَقَدْ اَبْلَغْتُكُمْ رِسَالَةَ رَبِّي

وَنَصَحْتُ لَكُمْ وَلَكِنْ لَّا تُحِبُّونَ

النَّاصِحِينَ ۞ وَلُوطًا اِذْ قَالَ

لِقَوْمِهِ اَتَاْتُونَ الْفَاحِشَةَ مَا

سَبَقَكُمْ بِهَا مِنْ اَحَدٍ مِّنَ

الْعَالَمِينَ ۞ اِنَّكُمْ لَتَاْتُونَ الرِّجَالَ

of the arrogant party among his people said to those who were reckoned powerless - those among them who believed: "Know you indeed that Salih is an Apostle from his Lord?" They said: "We do indeed believe in the revelation which has been sent through him."

76. The Arrogant party said: "For our part, we reject what you believe in."

77. Then they ham-strung the she-camel, and insolently defied the order of their Lord, saying: "O Salih! Bring about your threats, if you are

الَّذِينَ اسْتَكْبَرُوا مِن قَوْمِهِ

لِلَّذِينَ اسْتُضْعِفُوا لِمَنْ اٰمَنَ

مِنْهُمْ اَتَعْلَمُونَ اَنَّ صٰلِحًا مُّرْسَلٌ

مِّن رَّبِّهِ ۚ قَالُوٓا اِنَّا بِمَآ اُرْسِلَ

بِهٖ مُؤْمِنُونَ ۞ قَالَ الَّذِينَ

اسْتَكْبَرُوٓا اِنَّا بِالَّذِىٓ اٰمَنتُم بِهٖ

كٰفِرُونَ ۞ فَعَقَرُوا النَّاقَةَ وَعَتَوْا

عَنْ اَمْرِ رَبِّهِمْ وَقَالُوا يٰصٰلِحُ

ائْتِنَا بِمَا تَعِدُنَآ اِنْ كُنتَ مِنَ

your Lord! This she-camel of Allah is a Sign for you: so leave her to graze in Allah's earth, and let her come to no harm, or you shall be seized with a grievous punishment."

74. "And remember how He made you inheritors after the 'Ad people and gave you habitations in the land: you build for yourselves palaces and castles in (open) plains, and carve out homes in the mountains; so bring to remembrance the benefits (you have received) from Allah, and refrain from evil and mischief on the earth."

75. The leaders

رَّبِّكُمْ هٰذِهٖ نَاقَةُ اللّٰهِ لَكُمْ اٰيَةً

فَذَرُوْهَا تَاْكُلْ فِيْٓ اَرْضِ اللّٰهِ

وَلَا تَمَسُّوْهَا بِسُوْٓءٍ فَيَاْخُذَكُمْ

عَذَابٌ اَلِيْمٌ ۞ وَاذْكُرُوْٓا اِذْ جَعَلَكُمْ

خُلَفَآءَ مِنْۢ بَعْدِ عَادٍ وَّبَوَّاَكُمْ فِى

الْاَرْضِ تَتَّخِذُوْنَ مِنْ سُهُوْلِهَا

قُصُوْرًا وَّتَنْحِتُوْنَ الْجِبَالَ بُيُوْتًا

فَاذْكُرُوْٓا اٰلَآءَ اللّٰهِ وَلَا تَعْثَوْا فِى

الْاَرْضِ مُفْسِدِيْنَ ۞ قَالَ الْمَلَاُ

which you have devised - you and your fathers, - without authority from Allah? Then wait: I am amongst you, also waiting."

72. We saved him and those who adhered to him. By Our Mercy, and We cut off the roots of those who rejected Our Signs and did not believe.

73. To the Thamud people (We sent) Salih, one of their own brethren: he said: "O my people! Worship Allah: You have no other Allah but Him. Now has come unto you a clear (Sign) from

سَمَّيْتُمُوْهَاۤ اَنْتُمْ وَ اٰبَآؤُكُمْ مَّا نَزَّلَ

اللّٰهُ بِهَا مِنْ سُلْطٰنٍ ؕ فَانْتَظِرُوْۤا

اِنِّيْ مَعَكُمْ مِّنَ الْمُنْتَظِرِيْنَ ۝

فَاَنْجَيْنٰهُ وَ الَّذِيْنَ مَعَهٗ بِرَحْمَةٍ

مِّنَّا وَ قَطَعْنَا دَابِرَ الَّذِيْنَ كَذَّبُوْا

بِاٰيٰتِنَا وَ مَا كَانُوْا مُؤْمِنِيْنَ ۝ وَاِلٰى

ثَمُوْدَ اَخَاهُمْ صٰلِحًا ؔؕ قَالَ يٰقَوْمِ

اعْبُدُوا اللّٰهَ مَا لَكُمْ مِّنْ اِلٰهٍ

غَيْرُهٗ ؕ قَدْ جَآءَتْكُمْ بَيِّنَةٌ مِّنْ

that He made you inheritors after the people of Noah, and gave you a stature tall among the nations. Call in remembrance the benefits (you have received) from Allah: that so you may prosper."

70.   They said: "Do you come to us saying, that we may worship Allah alone, and give up the cult of our fathers? Bring us what you threaten us with, if so be that you tell the truth!"

71.   He said: "Punishment and wrath have already come upon you from your Lord: dispute you with me over names

اِذْ جَعَلَكُمْ خُلَفَآءَ مِنْۢ بَعْدِ

قَوْمِ نُوْحٍ وَّزَادَكُمْ فِى الْخَلْقِ

بَصْۜطَةً ۚ فَاذْكُرُوْۤا اٰلَآءَ اللّٰهِ لَعَلَّكُمْ

تُفْلِحُوْنَ ۞ قَالُوْۤا اَجِئْتَنَا لِنَعْبُدَ

اللّٰهَ وَحْدَهٗ وَنَذَرَ مَا كَانَ

يَعْبُدُ اٰبَآؤُنَا ۚ فَاْتِنَا بِمَا تَعِدُنَآ

اِنْ كُنْتَ مِنَ الصّٰدِقِيْنَ ۞ قَالَ

قَدْ وَقَعَ عَلَيْكُمْ مِّنْ رَّبِّكُمْ رِجْسٌ

وَّغَضَبٌ ۖ اَتُجَادِلُوْنَنِيْ فِيْۤ اَسْمَآءٍ

66. The leaders of the unbelievers among his people said: "Ah! We see you are an imbecile!" and "We think you are a liar!"

67. He said: "O my people! I am no imbecile, but (I am) an Apostle from the Lord and Cherisher of the Worlds!"

68. "I but fulfil towards you the duties of my Lord's mission: I am to you a sincere and trustworthy adviser."

69. "Do you wonder that there has come to you a message from your Lord through a man of your own people, to warn you? Call in remembrance

الْمَلَأُ الَّذِينَ كَفَرُوا مِنْ قَوْمِهِ

إِنَّا لَنَرَاكَ فِي سَفَاهَةٍ وَّإِنَّا

لَنَظُنُّكَ مِنَ الْكٰذِبِينَ ۞ قَالَ

يٰقَوْمِ لَيْسَ بِيْ سَفَاهَةٌ وَّلٰكِنِّيْ

۞ رَسُوْلٌ مِّنْ رَّبِّ الْعٰلَمِيْنَ

أُبَلِّغُكُمْ رِسٰلٰتِ رَبِّيْ وَأَنَا لَكُمْ

نَاصِحٌ أَمِيْنٌ ۞ أَوَعَجِبْتُمْ أَنْ

جَاءَكُمْ ذِكْرٌ مِّنْ رَّبِّكُمْ عَلٰى

رَجُلٍ مِّنْكُمْ لِيُنْذِرَكُمْ وَاذْكُرُوْا

your Lord, through a man of your own people, to warn you, - so that you may fear Allah and receive His Mercy?"

64. But they rejected him, and We delivered him, and those with him, in the Ark: but We overwhelmed in the flood those who rejected Our Signs. They were indeed a blind people!

65. To the 'Ad people, (We sent) Hud, one of their (own) brethren: he said: "O my people! Worship Allah! You have no other Allah but Him. Will you not fear (Allah)?"

كَمْ بِكُمْ عَلَىٰ رَجُلٍ مِّنْكُمْ

لِيُنْذِرَكُمْ وَلِتَتَّقُوْا وَلَعَلَّكُمْ

تُرْحَمُوْنَ ۞ فَكَذَّبُوْهُ فَأَنْجَيْنٰهُ

وَالَّذِيْنَ مَعَهٗ فِى الْفُلْكِ

وَاَغْرَقْنَا الَّذِيْنَ كَذَّبُوْا بِاٰيٰتِنَا ۚ

اِنَّهُمْ كَانُوْا قَوْمًا عَمِيْنَ

۞ وَاِلٰى عَادٍ اَخَاهُمْ هُوْدًا ۚ قَالَ

يٰقَوْمِ اعْبُدُوا اللّٰهَ مَا لَكُمْ مِّنْ

اِلٰهٍ غَيْرُهٗ ؕ اَفَلَا تَتَّقُوْنَ ۞ قَالَ

but Him. I fear for you the punishment of a dreadful day!"

60. The leaders of his people said: "Ah! We see you evidently wandering (in mind)."

61. He said: "O my people! No wandering is there in my (mind): on the contrary I am an Apostle from the Lord and Cherisher of the Worlds!"

62. "I but fulfil towards you the duties of my Lord's mission: sincere is my advice to you, and I know from Allah something that you know not."

63. "Do you wonder that there has come to you a message from

غَيْرُهُ ۚ إِنِّىٓ أَخَافُ عَلَيْكُمْ

عَذَابَ يَوْمٍ عَظِيمٍ ۞ قَالَ الْمَلَأُ

مِنْ قَوْمِهِ إِنَّا لَنَرَىٰكَ فِى

ضَلَٰلٍ مُّبِينٍ ۞ قَالَ يَٰقَوْمِ

لَيْسَ بِى ضَلَٰلَةٌ وَّلَٰكِنِّى رَسُولٌ

مِّنْ رَّبِّ الْعَٰلَمِينَ ۞ أُبَلِّغُكُمْ

رِسَٰلَٰتِ رَبِّى وَأَنصَحُ لَكُمْ وَأَعْلَمُ

مِنَ اللَّهِ مَا لَا تَعْلَمُونَ ۞ أَوَ

عَجِبْتُمْ أَن جَآءَكُمْ ذِكْرٌ مِّن

thereon, and produce every kind of harvest therewith: thus shall We raise up the dead: perchance you may remember.

58. From the land that is clean and good, by the will of its Cherisher, springs up produce, (rich) after its kind: but from the land that is bad, springs up nothing but that which is niggardly: thus do we explain the Signs by various (symbols) to those who are grateful.

59. We sent Noah to his people. He said: "O my people! Worship Allah! You have no other Allah

بِهِ الْمَآءَ فَاَخْرَجْنَا بِهٖ مِنْ كُلِّ
الثَّمَرٰتِ ۚ كَذٰلِكَ نُخْرِجُ الْمَوْتٰى
لَعَلَّكُمْ تَذَكَّرُوْنَ ۞ وَالْبَلَدُ الطَّيِّبُ
يَخْرُجُ نَبَاتُهٗ بِاِذْنِ رَبِّهٖ ۚ
وَالَّذِىْ خَبُثَ لَا يَخْرُجُ اِلَّا
نَكِدًا ۚ كَذٰلِكَ نُصَرِّفُ الْاٰيٰتِ
لِقَوْمٍ يَّشْكُرُوْنَ ۞ لَقَدْ اَرْسَلْنَا
نُوْحًا اِلٰى قَوْمِهٖ فَقَالَ يٰقَوْمِ
اعْبُدُوا اللّٰهَ مَا لَكُمْ مِّنْ اِلٰهٍ

55. Call on your Lord with humility and in private: for Allah loves not those who trespass beyond bounds.

56. Do no mischief on the earth, after it has been set in order, but call on Him with fear and longing (in your hearts): for the Mercy of Allah is (always) near to those who do good.

57. It is He Who sends the winds like heralds of glad tidings, going before His Mercy: when they have carried the heavy-laden clouds, We drive them to a land that is dead, make rain to descend

ادْعُوا رَبَّكُمْ تَضَرُّعًا وَخُفْيَةً

إِنَّهُ لَا يُحِبُّ الْمُعْتَدِينَ ۝

وَلَا تُفْسِدُوا فِي الْأَرْضِ بَعْدَ

إِصْلَاحِهَا وَادْعُوهُ خَوْفًا وَّطَمَعًا

إِنَّ رَحْمَتَ اللّٰهِ قَرِيبٌ مِّنَ

الْمُحْسِنِينَ ۝ وَهُوَ الَّذِي يُرْسِلُ

الرِّيحَ بُشْرًا بَيْنَ يَدَيْ رَحْمَتِهِ

حَتّٰى إِذَا أَقَلَّتْ سَحَابًا ثِقَالًا

سُقْنٰهُ لِبَلَدٍ مَّيِّتٍ فَأَنْزَلْنَا

our behaviour in the past." In fact they will have lost their souls, and the things they invented will leave them in the lurch.

54. Your Guardian-Lord is Allah, Who created the heavens and the earth in six days, and is firmly established on the Throne (of Authority): He draws the night as a veil over the day, each seeking the other in rapid succession: He created the sun, the moon, and the stars, (all) governed by laws under His command. Is it not His to create and to govern? Blessed be Allah, the Cherisher and Sustainer of the Worlds.

كُنَّا نَعْمَلُ ۗ قَدْ خَسِرُوۤا اَنْفُسَهُمْ

وَضَلَّ عَنْهُمْ مَّا كَانُوْا يَفْتَرُوْنَ ۞

اِنَّ رَبَّكُمُ اللّٰهُ الَّذِيْ خَلَقَ

السَّمٰوٰتِ وَالْاَرْضَ فِيْ سِتَّةِ اَيَّامٍ

ثُمَّ اسْتَوٰى عَلَى الْعَرْشِ ۖ يُغْشِى

الَّيْلَ النَّهَارَ يَطْلُبُهٗ حَثِيْثًا ۙ

وَّ الشَّمْسَ وَالْقَمَرَ وَالنُّجُوْمَ

مُسَخَّرٰتٍ بِاَمْرِهٖ ۗ اَلَا لَهُ الْخَلْقُ

وَالْاَمْرُ ۗ تَبٰرَكَ اللّٰهُ رَبُّ الْعٰلَمِيْنَ ۞

and as they were wont to reject Our Signs.

52. For We had certainly sent unto them a Book, based on knowledge, which We explained in detail, - a guide and a mercy to all who believe.

53. Do they just wait for the final fulfilment of the event? On the day the event is finally fulfilled, those who disregarded it before will say: "The Apostles of our Lord did indeed bring true (tidings). Have we no inter-cessors now to intercede on our behalf? Or could we be sent back? Then should we behave diffe-rently from

وَمَا كَانُوۡا بِاٰيٰتِنَا يَجۡحَدُوۡنَ ۵۱

وَلَقَدۡ جِئۡنٰهُمۡ بِكِتٰبٍ فَصَّلۡنٰهُ

عَلٰى عِلۡمٍ هُدًى وَّ رَحۡمَةً لِّقَوۡمٍ

يُّؤۡمِنُوۡنَ ۵۲ هَلۡ يَنۡظُرُوۡنَ اِلَّا

تَاۡوِيۡلَهٗ يَوۡمَ يَاۡتِيۡ تَاۡوِيۡلُهٗ

يَقُوۡلُ الَّذِيۡنَ نَسُوۡهُ مِنۡ قَبۡلُ

قَدۡ جَآءَتۡ رُسُلُ رَبِّنَا بِالۡحَقِّ

فَهَلۡ لَّنَا مِنۡ شُفَعَآءَ فَيَشۡفَعُوۡا

لَنَآ اَوۡ نُرَدُّ فَنَعۡمَلَ غَيۡرَ الَّذِيۡ

the Garden: no fear shall be on you, nor shall you grieve."

50.　The Companions of the Fire will call to the Companions of the Garden: "Pour down to us water or anything that Allah does provide for your sustenance." They will say: "Both these things has Allah forbidden to those who rejected Him."

51.　"Such as took their religion to be mere amusement and play, and were deceived by the life of the world." That day shall We forget them as they forgot the meeting of this day of theirs,

الْجَنَّةِ لَا خَوْفٌ عَلَيْكُمْ وَلَا أَنْتُمْ

تَحْزَنُونَ ۩ وَنَادَىٰ أَصْحَابُ النَّارِ

أَصْحَابَ الْجَنَّةِ أَنْ أَفِيضُوا

عَلَيْنَا مِنَ الْمَاءِ أَوْ مِمَّا

رَزَقَكُمُ اللَّهُ ۚ قَالُوا إِنَّ اللَّهَ

حَرَّمَهُمَا عَلَى الْكَافِرِينَ ۩ الَّذِينَ

اتَّخَذُوا دِينَهُمْ لَهْوًا وَلَعِبًا

وَغَرَّتْهُمُ الْحَيَوٰةُ الدُّنْيَا ۚ فَالْيَوْمَ

نَنْسَاهُمْ كَمَا نَسُوا لِقَاءَ يَوْمِهِمْ هٰذَا

but they will have an assurance (thereof).

47. When their eyes shall be turned towards the Companions of the Fire, they will say: "Our Lord! Send us not to the company of the wrong-doers."

48. The Men on the Heights will call to certain men whom they will know from their marks, saying: "Of what profit to you were your hoards and your arrogant ways?"

49. "Behold! Are these not the men whom you swore that Allah with His Mercy would never bless? Enter you

وَهُمْ يَطْمَعُونَ ۝ وَإِذَا صُرِفَتْ

أَبْصَارُهُمْ تِلْقَاءَ أَصْحَابِ النَّارِ

قَالُوا رَبَّنَا لَا تَجْعَلْنَا مَعَ الْقَوْمِ

الظَّالِمِينَ ۝ وَنَادَى أَصْحَابُ

الْأَعْرَافِ رِجَالًا يَعْرِفُونَهُمْ

بِسِيمَاهُمْ قَالُوا مَا أَغْنَى عَنْكُمْ

جَمْعُكُمْ وَمَا كُنْتُمْ تَسْتَكْبِرُونَ ۝

أَهَؤُلَاءِ الَّذِينَ أَقْسَمْتُمْ لَا

يَنَالُهُمُ اللَّهُ بِرَحْمَةٍ ادْخُلُوا

true?" They shall say, "Yes"; but a crier shall proclaim between them: "The curse of Allah is on the wrong-doers;" -

45. "Those who would hinder (men) from the path of Allah and would seek in it something crooked: they were those who denied the Hereafter."

46. Between them shall be a veil, and on the Heights will be men who would know every one by his marks: they will call out to the Companions of the Garden, "Peace on you": they will not have entered,

حَقًّا ۚ قَالُوۡا نَعَمۡ ۚ فَاَذَّنَ مُؤَذِّنٌۢ

بَيۡنَهُمۡ اَنۡ لَّعۡنَةُ اللّٰهِ عَلَى

الظّٰلِمِيۡنَ ۙ الَّذِيۡنَ يَصُدُّوۡنَ

عَنۡ سَبِيۡلِ اللّٰهِ وَيَبۡغُوۡنَهَا

عِوَجًا ۚ وَهُمۡ بِالۡاٰخِرَةِ كٰفِرُوۡنَ ۞

وَبَيۡنَهُمَا حِجَابٌ ۚ وَعَلَى الۡاَعۡرَافِ

رِجَالٌ يَّعۡرِفُوۡنَ كُلًّاۢ بِسِيۡمٰهُمۡ

وَنَادَوۡا اَصۡحٰبَ الۡجَنَّةِ اَنۡ

سَلٰمٌ عَلَيۡكُمۡ ۖ لَمۡ يَدۡخُلُوۡهَا

and they shall say: "Praise be to Allah, Who has guided us to this (felicity): never could we have found guidance, had it not been for the guidance of Allah: indeed it was the truth, that the Apostles of our Lord brought unto us." And they shall hear the cry: "Behold! The garden before you! You have been made its inheritors, for your deeds (of righteousness)."

44. The Companions of the Garden will call out to the Companions of the Fire: "We have indeed found the promises of our Lord to us true: have you also found your Lord's promises

وَقَالُوا الۡحَمۡدُ لِلّٰهِ الَّذِىۡ هَدٰىنَا
لِهٰذَا ۖ وَمَا كُنَّا لِنَهۡتَدِىَ لَوۡلَاۤ
اَنۡ هَدٰىنَا اللّٰهُ ۚ لَقَدۡ جَآءَتۡ
رُسُلُ رَبِّنَا بِالۡحَقِّ ۚ وَنُوۡدُوۡاۤ اَنۡ
تِلۡكُمُ الۡجَنَّةُ اُوۡرِثۡتُمُوۡهَا بِمَا
كُنۡتُمۡ تَعۡمَلُوۡنَ ۞ وَنَادٰىۤ اَصۡحٰبُ
الۡجَنَّةِ اَصۡحٰبَ النَّارِ اَنۡ قَدۡ
وَجَدۡنَا مَا وَعَدَنَا رَبُّنَا حَقًّا
فَهَلۡ وَجَدۡتُّمۡ مَّا وَعَدَ رَبُّكُمۡ

such is Our reward for those in sin.

41. For them there is Hell, as a couch (below) and folds of covering above: such is Our requital of those who do wrong.

42. But those who believe and work righteousness, - no burden do We place on any soul, but that which it can bear, - they will be Companions of the Garden, therein to dwell (for ever).

43. And We shall remove from their hearts any lurking sense of injury; - beneath them will be rivers flowing; -

وَكَذَٰلِكَ نَجْزِى الْمُجْرِمِينَ ۝

لَهُم مِّن جَهَنَّمَ مِهَادٌ وَّمِن

فَوْقِهِمْ غَوَاشٍ ۗ وَكَذَٰلِكَ نَجْزِى

الظَّٰلِمِينَ ۝ وَالَّذِينَ ءَامَنُوا

وَعَمِلُوا الصَّٰلِحَٰتِ لَا نُكَلِّفُ نَفْسًا

إِلَّا وُسْعَهَآ أُوْلَٰٓئِكَ أَصْحَٰبُ

الْجَنَّةِ هُمْ فِيهَا خَٰلِدُونَ ۝

وَنَزَعْنَا مَا فِى صُدُورِهِم مِّنْ

غِلٍّ تَجْرِى مِن تَحْتِهِمُ الْأَنْهَٰرُ

"Doubled for all" : but this you do not understand.

39. Then the first will say to the last: "See then! No advantage have you over us; so taste you of the Chastisement for all that you did."

40. To those who reject Our Signs and treat them with arrogance, no opening will there be of the gates of heaven, nor will they enter the Garden, until the camel can pass through the eye of the needle:

لِكُلٍّ ضِعْفٌ وَّلٰكِنْ لَّا تَعْلَمُوْنَ ۞

وَقَالَتْ اُوْلٰىهُمْ لِاُخْرٰىهُمْ فَمَا

كَانَ لَكُمْ عَلَيْنَا مِنْ فَضْلٍ

فَذُوْقُوا الْعَذَابَ بِمَا كُنْتُمْ

تَكْسِبُوْنَ ۞ اِنَّ الَّذِيْنَ كَذَّبُوْا

بِاٰيٰتِنَا وَاسْتَكْبَرُوْا عَنْهَا لَا

تُفَتَّحُ لَهُمْ اَبْوَابُ السَّمَاءِ وَلَا

يَدْخُلُوْنَ الْجَنَّةَ حَتّٰى يَلِجَ

الْجَمَلُ فِيْ سَمِّ الْخِيَاطِ

against themselves, that they had rejected Allah.

38. He will say: "Enter you in the company of the peoples who passed away before you - men and Jinns, - into the Fire." Every time a new people enters, it curses its sister-people (that went before), until they follow each other, all into the Fire. Says the last about the first: "Our Lord! It is these that misled us: so give them a double Chastisement in the Fire." He will say:

عَلَى أَنْفُسِهِمْ أَنَّهُمْ كَانُوا

كَٰفِرِينَ ۩ قَالَ ادْخُلُوا فِي أُمَمٍ

قَدْ خَلَتْ مِنْ قَبْلِكُمْ مِّنَ

الْجِنِّ وَالْإِنْسِ فِي النَّارِ ۚ

كُلَّمَا دَخَلَتْ أُمَّةٌ لَّعَنَتْ

أُخْتَهَا ۖ حَتَّى إِذَا ادَّارَكُوا فِيهَا

جَمِيعًا ۙ قَالَتْ أُخْرَاهُمْ لِأُولَاهُمْ

رَبَّنَا هَٰؤُلَاءِ أَضَلُّونَا فَآتِهِمْ

عَذَابًا ضِعْفًا مِّنَ النَّارِ ۚ قَالَ

and treat them with arrogance, - they are Companions of the Fire, to dwell therein (for ever).

37. Who is more unjust than one who invents a lie against Allah or rejects His Signs? For such, their portion appointed must reach them from the Book (of decrees): until, when Our Messengers (of death) arrive and take their souls, they say: "Where are the things that you used to invoke besides Allah?" They will reply, "They have left us in the lurch," and they will bear witness

وَاسۡتَكۡبَرُوۡا عَنۡهَآ اُولٰٓئِكَ اَصۡحٰبُ

النَّارِ ۖ هُمۡ فِيۡهَا خٰلِدُوۡنَ ۞

فَمَنۡ اَظۡلَمُ مِمَّنِ افۡتَرٰى عَلَى

اللّٰهِ كَذِبًا اَوۡ كَذَّبَ بِاٰيٰتِهٖ ۚ

اُولٰٓئِكَ يَنَالُهُمۡ نَصِيۡبُهُمۡ مِّنَ

الۡكِتٰبِ ۚ حَتّٰى اِذَا جَآءَتۡهُمۡ

رُسُلُنَا يَتَوَفَّوۡنَهُمۡ ۙ قَالُوۡۤا اَيۡنَ

مَا كُنۡتُمۡ تَدۡعُوۡنَ مِنۡ دُوۡنِ

اللّٰهِ ؕ قَالُوۡا ضَلُّوۡا عَنَّا وَشَهِدُوۡا

about Allah of which you have no knowledge.

34. To every people is a term appointed: when their term is reached, not an hour can they cause delay, nor (an hour) can they advance (it in anticipation).

35. O you Children of Adam! Whenever there come to you Apostles from amongst you, rehearsing My Signs unto you, - those who are righteous and mend (their lives), - on them shall be no fear nor shall they grieve.

36. But those who reject Our Signs

عَلَى اللّٰهِ مَا لَا تَعْلَمُوْنَ ۝

وَلِكُلِّ اُمَّةٍ اَجَلٌ ۚ فَاِذَا جَآءَ

اَجَلُهُمْ لَا يَسْتَأْخِرُوْنَ سَاعَةً

وَّلَا يَسْتَقْدِمُوْنَ ۝ يٰبَنِيْٓ اٰدَمَ

اِمَّا يَأْتِيَنَّكُمْ رُسُلٌ مِّنْكُمْ

يَقُصُّوْنَ عَلَيْكُمْ اٰيٰتِيْ ۙ فَمَنِ

اتَّقٰى وَاَصْلَحَ فَلَا خَوْفٌ

عَلَيْهِمْ وَلَا هُمْ يَحْزَنُوْنَ ۝

وَالَّذِيْنَ كَذَّبُوْا بِاٰيٰتِنَا

Say: They are, in the life of this world, for those who believe, (and) purely for them on the Day of Judgment. Thus do We explain the Signs in detail for those who understand.

33.   Say: The things that my Lord has indeed forbidden are: shameful deeds, whether open or secret; sins and trespasses against truth or reason; assigning of partners to Allah, for which He has given no authority; and saying things

قُلْ هِيَ لِلَّذِينَ اٰمَنُوْا فِي

الْحَيٰوةِ الدُّنْيَا خَالِصَةً يَّوْمَ

الْقِيٰمَةِ ۘ كَذٰلِكَ نُفَصِّلُ الْاٰيٰتِ

لِقَوْمٍ يَّعْلَمُوْنَ ۞ قُلْ اِنَّمَا

حَرَّمَ رَبِّيَ الْفَوَاحِشَ مَا ظَهَرَ

مِنْهَا وَمَا بَطَنَ وَالْاِثْمَ

وَالْبَغْيَ بِغَيْرِ الْحَقِّ وَاَنْ

تُشْرِكُوْا بِاللّٰهِ مَا لَمْ يُنَزِّلْ

بِهٖ سُلْطٰنًا وَّاَنْ تَقُوْلُوْا

the loss of their way; in that they took the Satan, in preference to Allah, for their friends and protectors, and think that they receive guidance.

31. O Children of Adam! Wear your beautiful apparel at every time and place of prayer: eat and drink: but waste not by excess, for Allah loves not the wasters.

32. Say: Who has forbidden the beautiful (gifts) of Allah, which He has produced for His servants, and the things, clean and pure, which (He has provided) for sustenance?

الضَّلَلَةُ ۚ إِنَّهُمُ اتَّخَذُوا

الشَّيَطِينَ أَوْلِيَآءَ مِن دُونِ اللَّهِ

وَيَحْسَبُونَ أَنَّهُم مُّهْتَدُونَ ۝

يَبَنِىٓ ءَادَمَ خُذُوا زِينَتَكُمْ عِندَ

كُلِّ مَسْجِدٍ وَّكُلُوا وَاشْرَبُوا

وَلَا تُسْرِفُوٓا ۚ إِنَّهُۥ لَا يُحِبُّ

الْمُسْرِفِينَ ۝ قُلْ مَنْ حَرَّمَ

زِينَةَ اللَّهِ الَّتِىٓ أَخْرَجَ

لِعِبَادِهِۦ وَالطَّيِّبَتِ مِنَ الرِّزْقِ

our fathers doing so"; and "Allah commanded us thus": Say: "No, Allah never commands what is shameful: do you say of Allah what you know not?"

29. Say: "My Lord has commanded justice; and that you set your whole selves (to Him) at every time and place of prayer, and call upon Him, making your devotion sincere as in His sight: such as He created you in the beginning, so shall you return."

30. Some He has guided: others have (by their choice) deserved

عَلَيْهَاۤ اٰبَآءَنَا وَاللّٰهُ اَمَرَنَا

بِهَا ؕ قُلْ اِنَّ اللّٰهَ لَا يَاْمُرُ

بِالْفَحْشَآءِ ؕ اَتَقُوْلُوْنَ عَلَى اللّٰهِ

مَا لَا تَعْلَمُوْنَ ۝ قُلْ اَمَرَ

رَبِّيْ بِالْقِسْطِ ۟ وَاَقِيْمُوْا وُجُوْهَكُمْ

عِنْدَ كُلِّ مَسْجِدٍ وَّادْعُوْهُ

مُخْلِصِيْنَ لَهُ الدِّيْنَ ؕ كَمَا

بَدَاَكُمْ تَعُوْدُوْنَ ۝ فَرِيْقًا

هَدٰى وَفَرِيْقًا حَقَّ عَلَيْهِمُ

the Signs of Allah, that they may receive admonition!

27. O you Children of Adam! Let not Satan seduce you, in the same manner as he got your parents out of the Garden, stripping them of their raiment, to expose their shame: for he and his tribe watch you from a position where you cannot see them: We made the Satan friends (only) to those without faith.

28. When they do anything that is shameful, they say: "We found

اٰيٰتِ اللّٰهِ لَعَلَّهُمْ يَذَّكَّرُوْنَ ۞

يٰبَنِيْٓ اٰدَمَ لَا يَفْتِنَنَّكُمُ الشَّيْطٰنُ

كَمَآ اَخْرَجَ اَبَوَيْكُمْ مِّنَ الْجَنَّةِ

يَنْزِعُ عَنْهُمَا لِبَاسَهُمَا لِيُرِيَهُمَا

سَوْاٰتِهِمَا ؕ اِنَّهٗ يَرٰىكُمْ هُوَ

وَقَبِيْلُهٗ مِنْ حَيْثُ لَا تَرَوْنَهُمْ ؕ

اِنَّا جَعَلْنَا الشَّيٰطِيْنَ اَوْلِيَآءَ

لِلَّذِيْنَ لَا يُؤْمِنُوْنَ ۞ وَاِذَا

فَعَلُوْا فَاحِشَةً قَالُوْا وَجَدْنَا

and bestow not upon us Your Mercy, we shall certainly be lost."

24. (Allah) said: "Get you down, with enmity between yourselves. On earth will be your dwelling-place and your means of live-lihood, - for a time."

25. He said: "Therein shall you live, and therein shall you die; but from it shall you be taken out (at last)."

26. O you Children of Adam! We have bestowed raiment upon you to cover your shame, as well as to be an adornment to you. But the raiment of righteousness, - that is the best. Such are among

وَتَرْحَمْنَا لَنَكُوْنَنَّ مِنَ الْخَسِرِيْنَ ۩

قَالَ اهْبِطُوْا بَعْضُكُمْ لِبَعْضٍ

عَدُوٌّ ۚ وَلَكُمْ فِي الْأَرْضِ مُسْتَقَرٌّ

وَّمَتَاعٌ اِلٰى حِيْنٍ ۩ قَالَ

فِيْهَا تَحْيَوْنَ وَفِيْهَا تَمُوْتُوْنَ

وَمِنْهَا تُخْرَجُوْنَ ۩ يٰبَنِيْٓ اٰدَمَ

قَدْ اَنْزَلْنَا عَلَيْكُمْ لِبَاسًا

يُّوَارِيْ سَوْاٰتِكُمْ وَرِيْشًا ۗ وَلِبَاسُ

التَّقْوٰى ۙ ذٰلِكَ خَيْرٌ ۚ ذٰلِكَ مِنْ

21. And he swore to them both, that he was their sincere adviser.

22. So by deceit he brought about their fall: when they tasted of the tree, their shame became manifest to them, and they began to sew together the leaves of the garden over their bodies. And their Lord called unto them: "Did I not forbid you that tree, and tell you that Satan was an avowed enemy unto you?"

23. They said: "Our Lord! We have wronged our own souls: If You forgive us not

وَقَاسَمَهُمَآ اِنِّى لَكُمَا لَمِنَ
النَّصِحِيْنَ ۙ فَدَلَّهُمَا بِغُرُوْرٍ ۚ
فَلَمَّا ذَاقَا الشَّجَرَةَ بَدَتْ لَهُمَا
سَوْاٰتُهُمَا وَطَفِقَا يَخْصِفٰنِ عَلَيْهِمَا
مِنْ وَّرَقِ الْجَنَّةِ ۚ وَنَادٰىهُمَا
رَبُّهُمَآ اَلَمْ اَنْهَكُمَا عَنْ تِلْكُمَا
الشَّجَرَةِ وَاَقُلْ لَّكُمَآ اِنَّ الشَّيْطٰنَ
لَكُمَا عَدُوٌّ مُّبِيْنٌ ۟ قَالَا رَبَّنَا
ظَلَمْنَآ اَنْفُسَنَا ۖ وَاِنْ لَّمْ تَغْفِرْ لَنَا

with you all.

19. "O Adam! Dwell you and your wife in the Garden, and enjoy (its good things) as you wish: but approach not this tree, or you run into harm and transgression."

20. Then began Satan to whisper suggestions to them, in order to reveal to them their shame that was hidden from them (before): he said: "Your Lord only forbade you this tree, lest you should become Angels or such beings as live for ever."

مِنْكُمْ أَجْمَعِينَ ۝ وَيٰٓاٰدَمُ اسْكُنْ

أَنْتَ وَزَوْجُكَ الْجَنَّةَ فَكُلَا مِنْ

حَيْثُ شِئْتُمَا وَلَا تَقْرَبَا هٰذِهِ

الشَّجَرَةَ فَتَكُونَا مِنَ الظّٰلِمِينَ ۝

فَوَسْوَسَ لَهُمَا الشَّيْطٰنُ لِيُبْدِيَ

لَهُمَا مَا وُرِيَ عَنْهُمَا مِنْ سَوْاٰتِهِمَا

وَقَالَ مَا نَهٰكُمَا رَبُّكُمَا عَنْ

هٰذِهِ الشَّجَرَةِ إِلَّا أَنْ تَكُونَا

مَلَكَيْنِ أَوْ تَكُونَا مِنَ الْخٰلِدِينَ ۝

15. (Allah) said: "Be you among those who have respite."

16. He said: "Because You have thrown me out of the way, I will lie in wait for them on Your straight way:"

17. "Then will I assault them from before them and behind them, from their right and their left: nor will You find, in most of them, gratitude (for Your mercies)."

18. (Allah) said: "Get out from here, disgraced and expelled. If any of them follow you, - Hell will I fill

قَالَ إِنَّكَ مِنَ الْمُنْظَرِينَ ۝

قَالَ فَبِمَا أَغْوَيْتَنِي لَأَقْعُدَنَّ

لَهُمْ صِرَاطَكَ الْمُسْتَقِيمَ ۝ ثُمَّ

لَآتِيَنَّهُمْ مِّنْ بَيْنِ أَيْدِيهِمْ

وَمِنْ خَلْفِهِمْ وَعَنْ أَيْمَانِهِمْ

وَعَنْ شَمَآئِلِهِمْ ۖ وَلَا تَجِدُ

أَكْثَرَهُمْ شَاكِرِينَ ۝ قَالَ اخْرُجْ

مِنْهَا مَذْءُومًا مَّدْحُورًا ۖ لَّمَنْ

تَبِعَكَ مِنْهُمْ لَأَمْلَأَنَّ جَهَنَّمَ

bow down to Adam, and they bowed down; not so Iblis; he refused to be of those who bow down.

12. (Allah) said: "What prevented you from bowing down when I commanded you?" He said: "I am better than he: You did create me from fire, and him from clay."

13. (Allah) said: "Get you down from here: it is not for you to be arrogant here: get out, for you are of the meanest (of creatures)."

14. He said: "Give me respite till the Day they are raised up."

اسْجُدُوا لِاٰدَمَ فَسَجَدُوْا اِلَّا

اِبْلِيْسَ لَمْ يَكُنْ مِّنَ السّٰجِدِيْنَ ۞

قَالَ مَا مَنَعَكَ اَلَّا تَسْجُدَ اِذْ

اَمَرْتُكَ ۗ قَالَ اَنَا خَيْرٌ مِّنْهُ ۚ

خَلَقْتَنِيْ مِنْ نَّارٍ وَّخَلَقْتَهٗ

مِنْ طِيْنٍ ۞ قَالَ فَاهْبِطْ مِنْهَا

فَمَا يَكُوْنُ لَكَ اَنْ تَتَكَبَّرَ فِيْهَا

فَاخْرُجْ اِنَّكَ مِنَ الصّٰغِرِيْنَ ۞

قَالَ اَنْظِرْنِيْ اِلٰى يَوْمِ يُبْعَثُوْنَ ۞

8. The balance that day will be true (to a nicety): those whose scale (of good) will be heavy, will prosper:

9. Those whose scale will be light, will find their souls in perdition for that they wrongfully treated Our Signs.

10. It is We Who have placed you with authority on earth, and provided you therein with means for the fulfilment of your life: small are the thanks that you give!

11. It is We Who created you and gave you shape; then We said the Angels

وَالۡوَزۡنُ يَوۡمَئِذِ الۡحَقُّ فَمَنۡ ثَقُلَتۡ

مَوَازِينُهُ فَاُولٰٓئِكَ هُمُ الۡمُفۡلِحُوۡنَ ۝

وَمَنۡ خَفَّتۡ مَوَازِينُهُ فَاُولٰٓئِكَ

الَّذِيۡنَ خَسِرُوۡۤا اَنۡفُسَهُمۡ بِمَا

كَانُوۡا بِاٰيٰتِنَا يَظۡلِمُوۡنَ ۝ وَلَقَدۡ

مَكَّنّٰكُمۡ فِى الۡاَرۡضِ وَجَعَلۡنَا

لَكُمۡ فِيۡهَا مَعَايِشَ ؕ قَلِيۡلًا مَّا

تَشۡكُرُوۡنَ ۝ وَلَقَدۡ خَلَقۡنٰكُمۡ ثُمَّ

صَوَّرۡنٰكُمۡ ثُمَّ قُلۡنَا لِلۡمَلٰٓئِكَةِ

your Lord, and follow not, as friends or protectors, other than Him. Little it is you remember of admonition.

4. How many towns have We destroyed (for their sins)? Our punishment took them on a sudden by night or while they slept for their afternoon rest.

5. When (thus) Our punishment took them, no cry did they utter but this: "Indeed we did wrong."

6. Then shall we question those to whom Our message was sent and those by whom We sent it.

7. And verily, We shall recount their whole story with knowledge, for We were never absent (at any time or place).

رَّبِّكُمۡ وَلَا تَتَّبِعُوۡا مِنۡ دُوۡنِهٖۤ أَوۡلِيَآءَ ؕ

قَلِيۡلًا مَّا تَذَكَّرُوۡنَ ۞ وَكَمۡ مِّنۡ

قَرۡيَةٍ أَهۡلَكۡنٰهَا فَجَآءَهَا بَاۡسُنَا

بَيَاتًا أَوۡ هُمۡ قَآئِلُوۡنَ ۞ فَمَا كَانَ

دَعۡوٰىهُمۡ اِذۡ جَآءَهُمۡ بَاۡسُنَاۤ اِلَّاۤ

اَنۡ قَالُوۡۤا اِنَّا كُنَّا ظٰلِمِيۡنَ ۞

فَلَنَسۡـَٔلَنَّ الَّذِيۡنَ اُرۡسِلَ اِلَيۡهِمۡ

وَلَنَسۡـَٔلَنَّ الۡمُرۡسَلِيۡنَ ۞ فَلَنَقُصَّنَّ

عَلَيۡهِمۡ بِعِلۡمٍ وَّمَا كُنَّا غَآئِبِيۡنَ ۞

(His) agents, inheritors of the earth: He has raised you in ranks, some above others: that He may try you in the gifts He has given you: for your Lord is quick in punishment: yet He is indeed Oft-Forgiving, Most Merciful.

Al-A'raf (The Heights)
Bismillahir-Rahmanir-Rahim

1.   Alif. Lam. Mim. Sad.

2.   A Book revealed unto you, - so let your heart be oppressed no more by any difficulty on that account, - that with it you mightest warn (the erring) and teach the believers.

3.   Follow (O men!) the revelation given unto you from

خَلَٰٓئِفَ الْأَرْضِ وَرَفَعَ بَعْضَكُمْ

فَوْقَ بَعْضٍ دَرَجَٰتٍ لِّيَبْلُوَكُمْ

فِي مَآ ءَاتَىٰكُمْ ۗ إِنَّ رَبَّكَ سَرِيعُ

الْعِقَابِ ۖ وَإِنَّهُ لَغَفُورٌ رَّحِيمٌ ۝

بِسْمِ اللَّهِ الرَّحْمَٰنِ الرَّحِيمِ

الٓمٓصٓ ۝ كِتَٰبٌ أُنزِلَ إِلَيْكَ

فَلَا يَكُن فِي صَدْرِكَ حَرَجٌ مِّنْهُ

لِتُنذِرَ بِهِۦ وَذِكْرَىٰ لِلْمُؤْمِنِينَ ۝

اتَّبِعُوا مَآ أُنزِلَ إِلَيْكُم مِّن

and my death, are (all) for Allah, the Cherisher of the Worlds:

163. No partner has He: this am I commanded, and I am the first of those who bow to His Will.

164. Say: "Shall I seek for (my) Cherisher other than Allah, when He is the Cherisher of all things (that exist)? Every soul draws the meed of its acts on none but itself: no bearer of burdens can bear of burdens can bear the burden of another. Your goal in the end is towards Allah: He will tell you the truth of the things wherein you disputed."

165. It is He Who has made you

وَمَمَاتِي لِلّٰهِ رَبِّ الْعٰلَمِينَ ۝

لَا شَرِيكَ لَهُ ۚ وَبِذٰلِكَ أُمِرْتُ

وَأَنَا أَوَّلُ الْمُسْلِمِينَ ۝ قُلْ أَغَيْرَ

اللّٰهِ أَبْغِي رَبًّا وَهُوَ رَبُّ كُلِّ

شَيْءٍ ۚ وَلَا تَكْسِبُ كُلُّ نَفْسٍ إِلَّا

عَلَيْهَا ۚ وَلَا تَزِرُ وَازِرَةٌ وِزْرَ

أُخْرَىٰ ۚ ثُمَّ إِلَىٰ رَبِّكُمْ مَّرْجِعُكُمْ

فَيُنَبِّئُكُمْ بِمَا كُنْتُمْ فِيهِ

تَخْتَلِفُونَ ۝ وَهُوَ الَّذِي جَعَلَكُمْ

Allah: He will in the end tell them the truth of all that they did.

160. He that does good shall have ten times as much to his credit: he that does evil shall only be recompensed according to his evil: no wrong shall be done unto (any of) them.

161. Say: "Verily, my Lord has guided me to a way that is straight, - a religion of right, - the path (trod) by Abraham the true in Faith, and he (certainly) joined not gods with Allah."

162. Say: "Truly, my prayer and my service of sacrifice, my life

اللّٰهُ ثُمَّ يُنَبِّئُهُمْ بِمَا كَانُوْا

يَفْعَلُوْنَ ۞ مَنْ جَآءَ بِالْحَسَنَةِ فَلَهٗ

عَشْرُ أَمْثَالِهَا ۚ وَمَنْ جَآءَ بِالسَّيِّئَةِ

فَلَا يُجْزٰى إِلَّا مِثْلَهَا وَهُمْ

لَا يُظْلَمُوْنَ ۞ قُلْ إِنَّنِيْ هَدٰىنِيْ

رَبِّيْ إِلٰى صِرَاطٍ مُّسْتَقِيْمٍ ۚ

دِيْنًا قِيَمًا مِّلَّةَ إِبْرٰهِيْمَ حَنِيْفًا ۚ

وَمَا كَانَ مِنَ الْمُشْرِكِيْنَ ۞ قُلْ

إِنَّ صَلَاتِيْ وَنُسُكِيْ وَمَحْيَايَ

your Lord (Himself), or certain of the Signs of your Lord! The day that certain of the Signs of your Lord do come, no good will it do to a soul to believe in them then if it believed not before nor earned righteousness through its faith. Say: "Wait you: we too are waiting."

159. As for those who divide their religion and break up into sects, you have no part in them in the least: their affair is with

يَأْتِيَ رَبُّكَ أَوْ يَأْتِيَ بَعْضُ

ءَايَتِ رَبِّكَ يَوْمَ يَأْتِي بَعْضُ

ءَايَتِ رَبِّكَ لَا يَنفَعُ نَفْسًا

إِيمَانُهَا لَمْ تَكُنْ ءَامَنَتْ مِن

قَبْلُ أَوْ كَسَبَتْ فِي إِيمَانِهَا خَيْرًا

قُلِ انتَظِرُوٓا إِنَّا مُنتَظِرُونَ ۝

إِنَّ الَّذِينَ فَرَّقُوا دِينَهُمْ

وَكَانُوا شِيَعًا لَّسْتَ مِنْهُمْ

فِي شَيْءٍ إِنَّمَآ أَمْرُهُمْ إِلَى

157. Or lest you should say: "If the Book had only been sent down to us, we should have followed its guidance better than they." Now then has come unto you a clear (Sign) from your Lord, - and a guide and a mercy: then who could do more wrong than one who rejects Allah's Signs, and turns away therefrom? In good time shall We requite those who turn away from Our Signs, with a dreadful Chastisement, for their turning away.

158. Are they waiting to see if the Angels come to them, or

اَوْ تَقُوْلُوْا لَوْ اَنَّا اُنْزِلَ عَلَيْنَا

الْكِتٰبُ لَكُنَّا اَهْدٰى مِنْهُمْ

فَقَدْ جَاءَكُمْ بَيِّنَةٌ مِّنْ رَّبِّكُمْ

وَهُدًى وَّرَحْمَةٌ فَمَنْ اَظْلَمُ

مِمَّنْ كَذَّبَ بِاٰيٰتِ اللّٰهِ وَصَدَفَ

عَنْهَا سَنَجْزِى الَّذِيْنَ يَصْدِفُوْنَ

عَنْ اٰيٰتِنَا سُوْءَ الْعَذَابِ بِمَا

كَانُوْا يَصْدِفُوْنَ ۞ هَلْ يَنْظُرُوْنَ

اِلَّا اَنْ تَاْتِيَهُمُ الْمَلٰٓئِكَةُ اَوْ

154. Moreover, We gave Moses the Book, completing (Our favour) to those who would do right, and explaining all things in detail, - and a guide and a mercy, that they might believe in the meeting with their Lord.

155. And this is a Book which We have revealed as a blessing: so follow it and be righteous, that you may receive mercy:

156. Lest you should say: "The Book was sent down to two Peoples before us, and for our part, we remained unacquainted with all that they learned by assiduous study:"

ثُمَّ اٰتَيْنَا مُوْسَى الْكِتٰبَ تَمَامًا

عَلَى الَّذِيْٓ اَحْسَنَ وَتَفْصِيْلًا

لِّكُلِّ شَيْءٍ وَّهُدًى وَّرَحْمَةً

لَّعَلَّهُمْ بِلِقَآءِ رَبِّهِمْ يُؤْمِنُوْنَ ۝

وَهٰذَا كِتٰبٌ اَنْزَلْنٰهُ مُبٰرَكٌ

فَاتَّبِعُوْهُ وَاتَّقُوْا لَعَلَّكُمْ تُرْحَمُوْنَ ۝

اَنْ تَقُوْلُوْٓا اِنَّمَآ اُنْزِلَ الْكِتٰبُ

عَلٰى طَآئِفَتَيْنِ مِنْ قَبْلِنَا

وَاِنْ كُنَّا عَنْ دِرَاسَتِهِمْ لَغٰفِلِيْنَ ۝

the age of full strength; give measure and weight with (full) justice; - no burden do We place on any soul, but that which it can bear; - whenever you speak, speak justly, even if a near relative is concerned; and fulfil the Covenant of Allah: thus does He command you, that you may remember.

153. Verily, this is My way, leading straight: follow it: follow not (other) paths: they will scatter you about from His (great) path: thus does He command you, that you may be righteous.

أَشُدَّهُ ۚ وَأَوْفُوا الْكَيْلَ وَالْمِيزَانَ

بِالْقِسْطِ ۚ لَا نُكَلِّفُ نَفْسًا إِلَّا

وُسْعَهَا ۖ وَإِذَا قُلْتُمْ فَاعْدِلُوا

وَلَوْ كَانَ ذَا قُرْبَىٰ ۚ وَبِعَهْدِ اللَّهِ

أَوْفُوا ۚ ذَٰلِكُمْ وَصَّاكُم بِهِ لَعَلَّكُمْ

تَذَكَّرُونَ ۝ وَأَنَّ هَٰذَا صِرَاطِي

مُسْتَقِيمًا فَاتَّبِعُوهُ ۖ وَلَا تَتَّبِعُوا

السُّبُلَ فَتَفَرَّقَ بِكُمْ عَن سَبِيلِهِ ۚ

ذَٰلِكُمْ وَصَّاكُم بِهِ لَعَلَّكُمْ تَتَّقُونَ ۝

be good to your parents; kill not your children on a plea of want; - We provide sustenance for you and for them; - come not nigh to shameful deeds, whether open or secret; take not life, which Allah has made sacred, except by way of justice and law: thus does He command you, that you may learn wisdom.

152. And come not nigh to the orphan's property, except to improve it, until he attain

وَبِالْوَالِدَيْنِ اِحْسَانًا ۚ وَلَا تَقْتُلُوْا

اَوْلَادَكُمْ مِّنْ اِمْلَاقٍ ۚ نَحْنُ

نَرْزُقُكُمْ وَاِيَّاهُمْ ۚ وَلَا تَقْرَبُوا

الْفَوَاحِشَ مَا ظَهَرَ مِنْهَا وَمَا

بَطَنَ ۚ وَلَا تَقْتُلُوا النَّفْسَ الَّتِيْ

حَرَّمَ اللّٰهُ اِلَّا بِالْحَقِّ ۚ ذٰلِكُمْ

وَصّٰىكُمْ بِهٖ لَعَلَّكُمْ تَعْقِلُوْنَ ۝

وَلَا تَقْرَبُوْا مَالَ الْيَتِيْمِ اِلَّا

بِالَّتِيْ هِيَ اَحْسَنُ حَتّٰى يَبْلُغَ

if it had been His Will, He could indeed have guided you all."

150. Say: "Bring forward your witnesses to prove that Allah did forbid so and so." If they bring such witnesses, be not you amongst them: nor follow you the vain desires of such as treat Our Signs as falsehoods, and such as believe not in the Hereafter: for they hold others as equal with their Guardian-Lord.

151. Say: "Come, I will rehearse what Allah has (really) prohibited you from": join not anything as equal with Him;

فَلَوۡ شَآءَ لَهَدٰىكُمۡ أَجۡمَعِيۡنَ ۝

قُلۡ هَلُمَّ شُهَدَآءَكُمُ الَّذِيۡنَ

يَشۡهَدُوۡنَ أَنَّ اللّٰهَ حَرَّمَ هٰذَا ۚ

فَإِنۡ شَهِدُوۡا فَلَا تَشۡهَدۡ مَعَهُمۡ ۚ

وَلَا تَتَّبِعۡ أَهۡوَآءَ الَّذِيۡنَ كَذَّبُوۡا

بِـَٔايٰتِنَا وَالَّذِيۡنَ لَا يُؤۡمِنُوۡنَ

بِالۡاٰخِرَةِ وَهُمۡ بِرَبِّهِمۡ يَعۡدِلُوۡنَ ۝

قُلۡ تَعَالَوۡا أَتۡلُ مَا حَرَّمَ رَبُّكُمۡ

عَلَيۡكُمۡ أَلَّا تُشۡرِكُوۡا بِهٖ شَيۡئًا

from people in guilt never will His wrath be turned back.

148. Those who give partners (to Allah) will say: "If Allah had wished, we should not have given partners to Him, nor would our fathers; nor should we have had any taboos." So did their ancestors argue falsely, until they tasted of Our wrath. Say: "Have you any (certain) knowledge? If so, produce it before us. You follow nothing but conjecture: you do nothing but lie."

149. Say: "With Allah is the argument that reaches home:

بَأْسُهُ عَنِ الْقَوْمِ الْمُجْرِمِينَ ۞

سَيَقُولُ الَّذِينَ أَشْرَكُوا لَوْ شَاءَ

اللهُ مَا أَشْرَكْنَا وَلَا آبَاؤُنَا وَلَا

حَرَّمْنَا مِنْ شَيْءٍ كَذَلِكَ كَذَّبَ

الَّذِينَ مِنْ قَبْلِهِمْ حَتَّى ذَاقُوا

بَأْسَنَا قُلْ هَلْ عِنْدَكُمْ مِنْ

عِلْمٍ فَتُخْرِجُوهُ لَنَا إِنْ تَتَّبِعُونَ إِلَّا

الظَّنَّ وَإِنْ أَنْتُمْ إِلَّا تَخْرُصُونَ ۞

قُلْ فَلِلَّهِ الْحُجَّةُ الْبَالِغَةُ

is forced by necessity, without wilful disobedience, nor transgressing due limits, - your Lord is Oft-Forgiving, Most Merciful.

146. For those who followed the Jewish Law, We forbade every (animal) with undivided hoof, and We forbade them that fat of the ox and the sheep, except what adheres to their backs or their entrails, or is mixed up with a bone: this in recompense for their wilful disobedience: for We are True (in Our ordinances).

147. If they accuse you of falsehood, say: "Your Lord is full of mercy all- embracing; but

اضْطُرَّ غَيْرَ بَاغٍ وَّلَا عَادٍ فَإِنَّ

رَبَّكَ غَفُورٌ رَّحِيمٌ ۞ وَعَلَى الَّذِينَ

هَادُوا حَرَّمْنَا كُلَّ ذِى ظُفُرٍ

وَمِنَ الْبَقَرِ وَالْغَنَمِ حَرَّمْنَا عَلَيْهِمْ

شُحُومَهُمَا إِلَّا مَا حَمَلَتْ ظُهُورُهُمَا

أَوِ الْحَوَايَا أَوْ مَا اخْتَلَطَ بِعَظْمٍ

ذَٰلِكَ جَزَيْنَاهُم بِبَغْيِهِمْ وَإِنَّا

لَصَادِقُونَ ۞ فَإِن كَذَّبُوكَ فَقُل

رَّبُّكُمْ ذُو رَحْمَةٍ وَاسِعَةٍ وَلَا يُرَدُّ

Allah ordered you such a thing? But who does more wrong than one who invents a lie against Allah, to lead astray men without knowledge? For Allah guides not people who do wrong.

145. Say: "I find not in the message received by me by inspiration any (meat) forbidden to be eaten by one who wishes to eat it, unless it be dead meat, or blood poured forth, or the flesh of swine, - for it is an abomination - or, what is impious, (meat) on which a name has been invoked, other than Allah's". But (even so), if a person

وَصَّىٰكُمُ اللّٰهُ بِهٰذَا فَمَنْ اَظْلَمُ

مِمَّنِ افْتَرَىٰ عَلَى اللّٰهِ كَذِبًا

لِّيُضِلَّ النَّاسَ بِغَيْرِ عِلْمٍ اِنَّ

اللّٰهَ لَا يَهْدِى الْقَوْمَ الظّٰلِمِيْنَ ۞

قُلْ لَّا اَجِدُ فِيْ مَا اُوْحِيَ اِلَيَّ

مُحَرَّمًا عَلَىٰ طَاعِمٍ يَّطْعَمُهُ اِلَّا

اَنْ يَّكُوْنَ مَيْتَةً اَوْ دَمًا مَّسْفُوْحًا

اَوْ لَحْمَ خِنْزِيْرٍ فَاِنَّهُ رِجْسٌ اَوْ

فِسْقًا اُهِلَّ لِغَيْرِ اللّٰهِ بِهٖ فَمَنِ

of sheep a pair, and of goats a pair; say, has He forbidden the two males, or the two females, or (the young) which the wombs of the two females enclose? Tell me with knowledge if you are truthful:

144. Of camels a pair, and oxen a pair; say, has He forbidden the two males, or the two females, or (the young) which the wombs of the two females enclose? - were you present when

مِنَ الضَّأْنِ اثْنَيْنِ وَمِنَ الْمَعْزِ

اثْنَيْنِ ۗ قُلْ ءَآلذَّكَرَيْنِ حَرَّمَ اَمِ

الْاُنْثَيَيْنِ اَمَّا اشْتَمَلَتْ عَلَيْهِ

اَرْحَامُ الْاُنْثَيَيْنِ ۗ نَبِّئُوْنِيْ بِعِلْمٍ اِنْ

كُنْتُمْ صٰدِقِيْنَ ۞ وَمِنَ الْاِبِلِ

اثْنَيْنِ وَمِنَ الْبَقَرِ اثْنَيْنِ ۗ قُلْ

ءَآلذَّكَرَيْنِ حَرَّمَ اَمِ الْاُنْثَيَيْنِ

اَمَّا اشْتَمَلَتْ عَلَيْهِ اَرْحَامُ

الْاُنْثَيَيْنِ ۗ اَمْ كُنْتُمْ شُهَدَآءَ اِذْ

and dates, and tilth with produce of all kinds, and olives and pomegranates, similar (in kind) and different (in variety): eat of their fruit in their season, but render the dues that are proper on the day that the harvest is gathered. But waste not by excess: for Allah loves not the wasters.

142. Of the cattle are some for burden and some for meat: eat what Allah has provided for you, and follow not the footsteps of Satan: for he is to you and avowed enemy.

143. (Take) eight (head of cattle) in (four) pairs:

وَّ النَّخْلَ وَ الزَّرْعَ مُخْتَلِفًا اُكُلُهٗ

وَ الزَّيْتُوْنَ وَ الرُّمَّانَ مُتَشَابِهًا

وَّ غَيْرَ مُتَشَابِهٍ ؕ كُلُوْا مِنْ ثَمَرِهٖۤ اِذَاۤ

اَثْمَرَ وَ اٰتُوْا حَقَّهٗ يَوْمَ حَصَادِهٖ ۫ۖ

وَ لَا تُسْرِفُوْا ؕ اِنَّهٗ لَا يُحِبُّ

الْمُسْرِفِيْنَ ۙ ۝ وَ مِنَ الْاَنْعَامِ حَمُوْلَةً

وَّ فَرْشًا ؕ كُلُوْا مِمَّا رَزَقَكُمُ اللّٰهُ

وَ لَا تَتَّبِعُوْا خُطُوٰتِ الشَّيْطٰنِ ؕ اِنَّهٗ

لَكُمْ عَدُوٌّ مُّبِيْنٌ ۙ ۝ ثَمٰنِيَةَ اَزْوَاجٍ ۚ

(for food) for our men, and forbidden to our women; but if it is still-born, then all have share therein. For their (false) attribution (of superstitions to Allah), He will soon punish them: for He is full of wisdom and knowledge.

140. Lost are those who slay their children, from folly, without knowledge, and forbid food which Allah has provided for them, inventing (lies) against Allah. They have indeed gone astray and heeded no guidance.

141. It is He Who produces gardens, with trellises and without,

لِّذُكُورِنَا وَمُحَرَّمٌ عَلَىٰ أَزْوَاجِنَا ۚ

وَإِن يَكُن مَّيْتَةً فَهُمْ فِيهِ

شُرَكَآءُ ۚ سَيَجْزِيهِمْ وَصْفَهُمْ ۚ إِنَّهُ

حَكِيمٌ عَلِيمٌ ۝ قَدْ خَسِرَ الَّذِينَ

قَتَلُوٓا أَوْلَٰدَهُمْ سَفَهًۢا بِغَيْرِ عِلْمٍ

وَحَرَّمُوا مَا رَزَقَهُمُ اللَّهُ افْتِرَآءً

عَلَى اللَّهِ ۚ قَدْ ضَلُّوا وَمَا كَانُوا

مُهْتَدِينَ ۝ وَهُوَ الَّذِىٓ أَنشَأَ

جَنَّٰتٍ مَّعْرُوشَٰتٍ وَغَيْرَ مَعْرُوشَٰتٍ

in their religion. If Allah had willed, they would not have done so: but leave alone them and their inventions.

138. And they say that such and such cattle and crops are taboo, and none should eat of them except those whom - so they say - We wish; further, there are cattle forbidden to yoke or burden, and cattle on which, (at slaughter), the name of Allah is not pronounced; - inventions against Allah's name: soon will He requite them for their inventions.

139. They say: "What is in the wombs of such and such cattle is specially reserved

دِينِهِمْ وَلَوْ شَاءَ اللّٰهُ مَا فَعَلُوهُ

فَذَرْهُمْ وَمَا يَفْتَرُونَ ۞ وَقَالُوا

هٰذِهِ أَنْعَامٌ وَّحَرْثٌ حِجْرٌ ۚ لَّا

يَطْعَمُهَا إِلَّا مَنْ نَّشَاءُ بِزَعْمِهِمْ

وَأَنْعَامٌ حُرِّمَتْ ظُهُورُهَا وَأَنْعَامٌ

لَّا يَذْكُرُونَ اسْمَ اللّٰهِ عَلَيْهَا

افْتِرَاءً عَلَيْهِ ۚ سَيَجْزِيْهِمْ بِمَا

كَانُوا يَفْتَرُونَ ۞ وَقَالُوا مَا فِيْ

بُطُونِ هٰذِهِ الْأَنْعَامِ خَالِصَةٌ

produced in abundance in tilth and in cattle, they assigned Him a share: they say, according to their fancies: "This is for Allah, and this" - for our "partners"! but the share of their" partners "reaches not Allah, while the share of Allah reaches their "partners" ! evil (and unjust) is their assignment!

137. Even so, in the eyes of most of the pagans, their "partners" made alluring the slaughter of their children, in order to lead them to their own destruction, and cause confusion

ذَرَأَ مِنَ الْحَرْثِ وَالْأَنْعَامِ نَصِيبًا

فَقَالُوا هَذَا لِلَّهِ بِزَعْمِهِمْ وَهَذَا

لِشُرَكَائِنَا ۖ فَمَا كَانَ لِشُرَكَائِهِمْ

فَلَا يَصِلُ إِلَى اللَّهِ ۖ وَمَا كَانَ

لِلَّهِ فَهُوَ يَصِلُ إِلَى شُرَكَائِهِمْ ۗ

سَاءَ مَا يَحْكُمُونَ ۝ وَكَذَلِكَ

زَيَّنَ لِكَثِيرٍ مِّنَ الْمُشْرِكِينَ

قَتْلَ أَوْلَادِهِمْ شُرَكَاؤُهُمْ

لِيُرْدُوهُمْ وَلِيَلْبِسُوا عَلَيْهِمْ

full of Mercy: if it were His will, He could destroy you, and in your place appoint whom He will as your successors, even as He raised you up from the posterity of other people.

134. All that has been promised unto you will come to pass: nor can you frustrate it (in the least bit).

135. Say: "O my people! Do whatever you can: I will do (my part): soon will you know who it is whose end will be (best) in the Hereafter: certain it is that the wrong-doers will not prosper."

136. Out of what Allah has

ذُو الرَّحْمَةِ ۚ اِنْ يَّشَأْ يُذْهِبْكُمْ

وَيَسْتَخْلِفْ مِنْۢ بَعْدِكُمْ مَّا يَشَآءُ

كَمَآ اَنْشَاَكُمْ مِّنْ ذُرِّيَّةِ قَوْمٍ

اٰخَرِيْنَ ۞ اِنَّ مَا تُوْعَدُوْنَ لَاٰتٍ ۙ

وَّمَآ اَنْتُمْ بِمُعْجِزِيْنَ ۞ قُلْ يٰقَوْمِ

اعْمَلُوْا عَلٰى مَكَانَتِكُمْ اِنِّيْ عَامِلٌ ۚ

فَسَوْفَ تَعْلَمُوْنَ ۙ مَنْ تَكُوْنُ لَهٗ

عَاقِبَةُ الدَّارِ ۗ اِنَّهٗ لَا يُفْلِحُ

الظّٰلِمُوْنَ ۞ وَجَعَلُوْا لِلّٰهِ مِمَّا

unto you My Signs, and warning you of the meeting of this Day of yours?" They will say: "We bear witness against ourselves." It was the life of this world that deceived them. So against themselves will they bear witness that they rejected Faith.

131. (The Apostles were sent) thus, for your Lord would not destroy for their wrong-doing men's habitations while their occupants were unwarned.

132. To all are degrees (or ranks) according to their deeds: for your Lord is not unmindful of anything that they do.

133. Your Lord is Self-sufficient,

عَلَيْكُمْ اٰيٰتِيْ وَيُنْذِرُوْنَكُمْ لِقَآءَ

يَوْمِكُمْ هٰذَا ۚ قَالُوْا شَهِدْنَا عَلٰى

اَنْفُسِنَا وَغَرَّتْهُمُ الْحَيٰوةُ الدُّنْيَا

وَشَهِدُوْا عَلٰى اَنْفُسِهِمْ اَنَّهُمْ

كَانُوْا كٰفِرِيْنَ ۝ ذٰلِكَ اَنْ لَّمْ

يَكُنْ رَّبُّكَ مُهْلِكَ الْقُرٰى بِظُلْمٍ

وَّاَهْلُهَا غٰفِلُوْنَ ۝ وَلِكُلٍّ دَرَجٰتٌ

مِّمَّا عَمِلُوْا ۗ وَمَا رَبُّكَ بِغَافِلٍ

عَمَّا يَعْمَلُوْنَ ۝ وَرَبُّكَ الْغَنِيُّ

"Our Lord! We made profit from each other: but (alas!) we reached our term - which You did appoint for us." He will say: "The Fire be your dwelling-place: you will dwell therein for ever, except as Allah wills." For your Lord is full of wisdom and knowledge.

129. Thus do we make the wrong-doers turn to each other, because of what they earn.

130. "O you assembly of Jinns and men! came there not unto you Apostles from amongst you, setting forth

الْاِنْسِ رَبَّنَا اسْتَمْتَعَ بَعْضُنَا

بِبَعْضٍ وَّبَلَغْنَآ اَجَلَنَا الَّذِیۤ

اَجَّلْتَ لَنَا ؕ قَالَ النَّارُ مَثْوٰىكُمْ

خٰلِدِیْنَ فِیْهَاۤ اِلَّا مَا شَآءَ اللّٰهُ ؕ

اِنَّ رَبَّكَ حَكِیْمٌ عَلِیْمٌ ۝

وَكَذٰلِكَ نُوَلِّیْ بَعْضَ الظّٰلِمِیْنَ

بَعْضًۢا بِمَا كَانُوْا یَكْسِبُوْنَ ۝

یٰمَعْشَرَ الْجِنِّ وَالْاِنْسِ اَلَمْ

یَاْتِكُمْ رُسُلٌ مِّنْكُمْ یَقُصُّوْنَ

thus does Allah (heap) the Chastisement on those who refuse to believe.

126. This is the way of your Lord, leading straight: We have detailed the Signs for those who receive admonition.

127. For them will be a Home of Peace in the presence of their Lord: He will be their Friend, because they practised (righteousness).

128. One day will He gather them all together, (and say): "O you assembly of Jinns! Much (toll) did you take of men." Their friends amongst men will say:

كَذٰلِكَ يَجْعَلُ اللهُ الرِّجْسَ

عَلَى الَّذِيْنَ لَا يُؤْمِنُوْنَ ۞ وَهٰذَا

صِرَاطُ رَبِّكَ مُسْتَقِيْمًا ۚ قَدْ

فَصَّلْنَا الْاٰيٰتِ لِقَوْمٍ يَّذَّكَّرُوْنَ ۞

لَهُمْ دَارُ السَّلٰمِ عِنْدَ رَبِّهِمْ وَهُوَ

وَلِيُّهُمْ بِمَا كَانُوْا يَعْمَلُوْنَ ۞

وَيَوْمَ يَحْشُرُهُمْ جَمِيْعًا ۚ يٰمَعْشَرَ

الْجِنِّ قَدِ اسْتَكْثَرْتُمْ مِّنَ

الْاِنْسِ ۚ وَقَالَ اَوْلِيٰٓؤُهُمْ مِّنَ

by Allah's Apostles." Allah knows best where (and how) to carry out His mission. Soon will the wicked be over-taken by humiliation before Allah, and a severe Punishment, for all their plots.

125. Those whom Allah (in His plan) wills to guide, - He opens their breast to Islam; those whom He wills to leave straying, - He makes their breast close and constricted, as if they had to climb up to the skies:

رُسُلُ اللهِ ۖ اللهُ أَعْلَمُ حَيْثُ
يَجْعَلُ رِسَالَتَهُ ۗ سَيُصِيبُ الَّذِينَ
أَجْرَمُوا صَغَارٌ عِنْدَ اللهِ
وَعَذَابٌ شَدِيدٌ بِمَا كَانُوا
يَمْكُرُونَ ۞ فَمَنْ يُرِدِ اللهُ
أَنْ يَهْدِيَهُ يَشْرَحْ صَدْرَهُ
لِلْإِسْلَامِ ۖ وَمَنْ يُرِدْ أَنْ يُضِلَّهُ
يَجْعَلْ صَدْرَهُ ضَيِّقًا حَرَجًا
كَأَنَّمَا يَصَّعَّدُ فِي السَّمَاءِ ۚ

amongst men, be like him who is in the depths of darkness, from which he can never come out? Thus to those without faith their own deeds seem pleasing.

123. Thus have We placed leaders in every town, its wicked men, to plot (and burrow) therein: but they only plot against their own souls, and they perceive it not.

124. When there comes to them a Sign (from Allah), they say: "We shall not believe until we receive one (exactly) like those received

فِي النَّاسِ كَمَنْ مَّثَلُهُ فِي

الظُّلُمَاتِ لَيْسَ بِخَارِجٍ مِّنْهَا

كَذَلِكَ زُيِّنَ لِلْكَافِرِينَ مَا كَانُوا

يَعْمَلُونَ ۞ وَكَذَلِكَ جَعَلْنَا فِي

كُلِّ قَرْيَةٍ أَكَابِرَ مُجْرِمِيهَا

لِيَمْكُرُوا فِيهَا ۚ وَمَا يَمْكُرُونَ

إِلَّا بِأَنْفُسِهِمْ وَمَا يَشْعُرُونَ ۞

وَإِذَا جَاءَتْهُمْ آيَةٌ قَالُوا لَنْ

نُّؤْمِنَ حَتَّى نُؤْتَى مِثْلَ مَا أُوتِيَ

those who earn sin will get due recompense for their "earnings."

121. Eat not of (meats) on which Allah's name has not been pronounced: that would be impiety. But the evil ones ever inspire their friends to contend with you if you were to obey them, you would indeed be Pagans.

122. Can he who was dead, to whom We gave life, and a light whereby he can walk

اِنَّ الَّذِيْنَ يَكْسِبُوْنَ الْاِثْمَ

سَيُجْزَوْنَ بِمَا كَانُوْا يَقْتَرِفُوْنَ ۝

وَلَا تَأْكُلُوْا مِمَّا لَمْ يُذْكَرِ اسْمُ

اللّٰهِ عَلَيْهِ وَاِنَّهٗ لَفِسْقٌ ؕ

وَاِنَّ الشَّيٰطِيْنَ لَيُوْحُوْنَ اِلٰى

اَوْلِيٰٓئِهِمْ لِيُجَادِلُوْكُمْ ۚ وَاِنْ

اَطَعْتُمُوْهُمْ اِنَّكُمْ لَمُشْرِكُوْنَ ۝

اَوَمَنْ كَانَ مَيْتًا فَاَحْيَيْنٰهُ

وَجَعَلْنَا لَهٗ نُوْرًا يَّمْشِيْ بِهٖ

118. So eat of (meats) on which Allah's name has been pronounced, if you have faith in His Signs.

119. Why should you not eat of (meats) on which Allah's name has been pronounced, when He has explained to you in detail what is forbidden to you - except under compulsion of necessity? But many do mislead (men) by their appetites unchecked by knowledge. Your Lord knows best those who transgress.

120. Eschew all sin, open or secret:

فَكُلُوا مِمَّا ذُكِرَ اسْمُ اللّٰهِ عَلَيْهِ

اِنْ كُنْتُمْ بِاٰيٰتِهٖ مُؤْمِنِيْنَ ۝

وَمَا لَكُمْ اَلَّا تَأْكُلُوا مِمَّا ذُكِرَ

اسْمُ اللّٰهِ عَلَيْهِ وَقَدْ فَصَّلَ

لَكُمْ مَّا حَرَّمَ عَلَيْكُمْ اِلَّا مَا

اضْطُرِرْتُمْ اِلَيْهِ وَاِنَّ كَثِيْرًا

لَّيُضِلُّوْنَ بِاَهْوَآئِهِمْ بِغَيْرِ عِلْمٍ

اِنَّ رَبَّكَ هُوَ اَعْلَمُ بِالْمُعْتَدِيْنَ ۝

وَذَرُوْا ظَاهِرَ الْاِثْمِ وَبَاطِنَهٗ

be then of those who doubt.

115. The word of your Lord does find its fulfilment in truth and in justice: none can change His Words: for He is the One Who hears and knows all.

116. Were you to follow the common run of those on earth, they will lead you away from the way of Allah. They follow nothing but conjecture: they do nothing but lie.

117. Your Lord knows best who strays from His way: He knows best who they are that receive His guidance.

تَكُوۡنَنَّ مِنَ الۡمُمۡتَرِيۡنَ ۝ وَتَمَّتۡ

كَلِمَتُ رَبِّكَ صِدۡقًا وَّ عَدۡلًا ؕ

لَا مُبَدِّلَ لِكَلِمٰتِهٖ ۚ وَهُوَ السَّمِيۡعُ

الۡعَلِيۡمُ ۝ وَاِنۡ تُطِعۡ اَكۡثَرَ مَنۡ

فِى الۡاَرۡضِ يُضِلُّوۡكَ عَنۡ سَبِيۡلِ

اللّٰهِ ؕ اِنۡ يَّتَّبِعُوۡنَ اِلَّا الظَّنَّ

وَاِنۡ هُمۡ اِلَّا يَخۡرُصُوۡنَ ۝ اِنَّ

رَبَّكَ هُوَ اَعۡلَمُ مَنۡ يَّضِلُّ عَنۡ

سَبِيۡلِهٖ ۚ وَهُوَ اَعۡلَمُ بِالۡمُهۡتَدِيۡنَ ۝

If your Lord had so planned, they would not have done it: so leave them and their inventions alone.

113. To such (deceit) let the hearts of those incline, who have no faith in the Hereafter: let them delight in it, and let them earn from it what they may.

114. Say: "Shall I seek for judge other than Allah? - when He it is Who has sent unto you the Book, explained in detail." They know full well, to whom We have given the Book, that it has been sent down from your Lord in truth. Never

وَلَوْ شَآءَ رَبُّكَ مَا فَعَلُوهُ

فَذَرْهُمْ وَمَا يَفْتَرُونَ ۝ وَلِتَصْغَىٰٓ

إِلَيْهِ أَفْـِٔدَةُ الَّذِينَ لَا يُؤْمِنُونَ

بِالْآخِرَةِ وَلِيَرْضَوْهُ وَلِيَقْتَرِفُوا

مَا هُمْ مُقْتَرِفُونَ ۝ أَفَغَيْرَ اللَّهِ

أَبْتَغِي حَكَمًا وَّهُوَ الَّذِيٓ أَنْزَلَ

إِلَيْكُمُ الْكِتَابَ مُفَصَّلًا وَالَّذِينَ

اٰتَيْنَاهُمُ الْكِتَابَ يَعْلَمُونَ أَنَّهُ

مُنَزَّلٌ مِّنْ رَّبِّكَ بِالْحَقِّ فَلَا

111. Even if We did send unto them Angels, and the dead did speak unto them, and We gathered together all things before their very eyes, they are not the ones to believe, unless it is in Allah's plan. But most of them ignore (the truth).

112. Likewise, did We make for every Messenger an enemy, Satan among men and Jinns, inspiring each other with flowery discourses by way of deception.

وَلَوْ أَنَّنَا نَزَّلْنَا إِلَيْهِمُ

الْمَلَٰٓئِكَةَ وَكَلَّمَهُمُ الْمَوْتَىٰ

وَحَشَرْنَا عَلَيْهِمْ كُلَّ شَىْءٍ

قُبُلًا مَّا كَانُوا لِيُؤْمِنُوٓا إِلَّآ

أَن يَشَآءَ اللَّهُ وَلَٰكِنَّ أَكْثَرَهُمْ

يَجْهَلُونَ ۝ وَكَذَٰلِكَ جَعَلْنَا

لِكُلِّ نَبِىٍّ عَدُوًّا شَيَٰطِينَ

الْإِنسِ وَالْجِنِّ يُوحِى بَعْضُهُمْ

إِلَىٰ بَعْضٍ زُخْرُفَ الْقَوْلِ غُرُورًا

پاره

وَلَوْ اَنَّنَا

(۸)

بسم الله الرحمن الرحيم

PART 9
Qaalal-Mala-u

38. Say to the unbelievers, if (now) they desist (from Unbelief), their past would be forgiven them; but if they persist, the punishment of those before them is already (a matter of warning for them).

39. And fight them on until there is no more tumult or oppression, and religion becomes Allah's in its entirety, but if they cease, surely Allah does see all that they do.

40. If they refuse, be sure that Allah is your Protector - the best to protect and the best to help.

قُلْ لِّلَّذِيْنَ كَفَرُوْٓا اِنْ يَّنْتَهُوْا

يُغْفَرْ لَهُمْ مَّا قَدْ سَلَفَ ۚ وَاِنْ

يَّعُوْدُوْا فَقَدْ مَضَتْ سُنَّتُ

الْاَوَّلِيْنَ ۝ وَقَاتِلُوْهُمْ حَتّٰى لَا

تَكُوْنَ فِتْنَةٌ وَّيَكُوْنَ الدِّيْنُ

كُلُّهٗ لِلّٰهِ ۚ فَاِنِ انْتَهَوْا فَاِنَّ اللّٰهَ

بِمَا يَعْمَلُوْنَ بَصِيْرٌ ۝ وَاِنْ تَوَلَّوْا

فَاعْلَمُوْٓا اَنَّ اللّٰهَ مَوْلٰىكُمْ ۚ

نِعْمَ الْمَوْلٰى وَنِعْمَ النَّصِيْرُ ۝

spend their wealth to hinder (man) from the path of Allah, and so will they continue to spend; but in the end they will have (only) regrets and sighs; at length they will be overcome: and the unbelievers will be gathered together to Hell;

37. In order that Allah may separate the impure from the pure, put the impure, one on another, heap them together, and cast them into Hell. They will be the ones to have lost.

يُنْفِقُوْنَ أَمْوَالَهُمْ لِيَصُدُّوْا عَنْ

سَبِيْلِ اللّٰهِ ۖ فَسَيُنْفِقُوْنَهَا ثُمَّ

تَكُوْنُ عَلَيْهِمْ حَسْرَةً ثُمَّ

يُغْلَبُوْنَ ۗ وَالَّذِيْنَ كَفَرُوْا اِلٰى

جَهَنَّمَ يُحْشَرُوْنَ ۙ لِيَمِيْزَ اللّٰهُ

الْخَبِيْثَ مِنَ الطَّيِّبِ وَيَجْعَلَ

الْخَبِيْثَ بَعْضَهٗ عَلٰى بَعْضٍ

فَيَرْكُمَهٗ جَمِيْعًا فَيَجْعَلَهٗ فِيْ

جَهَنَّمَ ۗ أُولٰٓئِكَ هُمُ الْخٰسِرُوْنَ ۙ

going to send it whilst they could ask for pardon.

34. But what plea have they that Allah should not punish them, when they keep out (men) from the Sacred Mosque - and they are not its guardians? No men can be its guardians except the righteous; but most of them do not understand.

35. Their prayer at the House (of Allah) is nothing but whistling and clapping of hands: (its only answer can be), "Taste you the Chastisement because you blasphemed."

36. The unbelievers

مُعَذِّبَهُمْ وَهُمْ يَسْتَغْفِرُوْنَ ۞

وَمَا لَهُمْ اَلَّا يُعَذِّبَهُمُ اللهُ وَهُمْ

يَصُدُّوْنَ عَنِ الْمَسْجِدِ الْحَرَامِ

وَمَا كَانُوْا اَوْلِيَآءَهٗ اِنْ اَوْلِيَآؤُهٗ

اِلَّا الْمُتَّقُوْنَ وَلٰكِنَّ اَكْثَرَهُمْ لَا

يَعْلَمُوْنَ ۞ وَمَا كَانَ صَلَاتُهُمْ

عِنْدَ الْبَيْتِ اِلَّا مُكَآءً وَّتَصْدِيَةً

فَذُوْقُوا الْعَذَابَ بِمَا كُنْتُمْ

تَكْفُرُوْنَ ۞ اِنَّ الَّذِيْنَ كَفَرُوْا

Our Signs are rehearsed to them, they say: "We have heard this (before): if we wished, we could say (words) like these: these are nothing but tales of the ancients."

32. Remember how they said: "O Allah if this is indeed the Truth from You, rain down on us a shower of stones form the sky, or send us a grievous Chastisement."

33. But Allah was not going to send them a Chastisement whilst you were amongst them; nor was He

تُتْلَى عَلَيْهِمْ ايٰتُنَا قَالُوا قَدْ

سَمِعْنَا لَوْ نَشَاءُ لَقُلْنَا مِثْلَ

هٰذَا اِنْ هٰذَا اِلَّا اَسَاطِيرُ

الْاَوَّلِيْنَ ۞ وَ اِذْ قَالُوا اللّٰهُمَّ

اِنْ كَانَ هٰذَا هُوَ الْحَقَّ مِنْ

عِنْدِكَ فَاَمْطِرْ عَلَيْنَا حِجَارَةً

مِّنَ السَّمَاءِ اَوِ ائْتِنَا بِعَذَابٍ

اَلِيْمٍ ۞ وَ مَا كَانَ اللّٰهُ لِيُعَذِّبَهُمْ

وَ اَنْتَ فِيْهِمْ وَ مَا كَانَ اللّٰهُ

but a trial; and that it is Allah with Whom lies your highest reward.

29. O you who believe! If you fear Allah, He will grant you a criterion (to judge between right and wrong), remove from you (all) evil (that may afflict) you, and forgive you: for Allah is the Lord of grace unbounded.

30. Remember how the unbelievers plotted against you, to keep you in bonds, or slay you, or get you out (of your home). They plot and plan, and Allah too plans; but the best of planners is Allah.

31. When

فِتْنَةٌ ۚ وَاَنَّ اللّٰهَ عِنْدَهٗ اَجْرٌ

عَظِيْمٌ ۩ يٰٓاَيُّهَا الَّذِيْنَ اٰمَنُوْۤا

اِنْ تَتَّقُوا اللّٰهَ يَجْعَلْ لَّكُمْ

فُرْقَانًا وَّيُكَفِّرْ عَنْكُمْ سَيِّاٰتِكُمْ

وَيَغْفِرْ لَكُمْ ۗ وَاللّٰهُ ذُو الْفَضْلِ

الْعَظِيْمِ ۩ وَاِذْ يَمْكُرُ بِكَ الَّذِيْنَ

كَفَرُوْا لِيُثْبِتُوْكَ اَوْ يَقْتُلُوْكَ اَوْ

يُخْرِجُوْكَ ۗ وَيَمْكُرُوْنَ وَيَمْكُرُ اللّٰهُ ۗ

وَاللّٰهُ خَيْرُ الْمٰكِرِيْنَ ۩ وَاِذَا

strict in punishment.

26.   Call to mind when you were a small (band), deemed weak through the land, and afraid that men might despoil and kidnap you; but He provided a safe asylum for you, strengthened you with His aid, and gave you good things for sustenance: that you might be grateful.

27.   O you that believe! Betray not the trust of Allah and the Apostle, nor misappropriate knowingly things entrusted to you.

28. And know you that your possessions and your progeny are

شَدِيدُ الْعِقَابِ ۞ وَاذْكُرُوْا اِذْ

اَنْتُمْ قَلِيْلٌ مُّسْتَضْعَفُوْنَ فِي

الْاَرْضِ تَخَافُوْنَ اَنْ يَّتَخَطَّفَكُمُ

النَّاسُ فَاٰوٰىكُمْ وَاَيَّدَكُمْ بِنَصْرِهٖ

وَرَزَقَكُمْ مِّنَ الطَّيِّبٰتِ لَعَلَّكُمْ

تَشْكُرُوْنَ ۞ يٰٓاَيُّهَا الَّذِيْنَ اٰمَنُوْا

لَا تَخُوْنُوا اللّٰهَ وَالرَّسُوْلَ وَتَخُوْنُوْٓا

اَمٰنٰتِكُمْ وَاَنْتُمْ تَعْلَمُوْنَ ۞

وَاعْلَمُوْٓا اَنَّمَآ اَمْوَالُكُمْ وَاَوْلَادُكُمْ

in them any good. He would indeed have made them listen: (as it is), if He had made them listen, they would but have turned back and declined (Faith).

24. O you who believe! Give your response to Allah and His Apostle, when He calls you to that which will give you life; and know that Allah comes in between a man and his heart, and that it is He to Whom you shall (all) be gathered.

25. And fear tumult or oppression, which affects not in particular (only) those of you who do wrong: and know that Allah is

فِيهِمْ خَيْرًا لَّأَسْمَعَهُمْ ۖ وَلَوْ

أَسْمَعَهُمْ لَتَوَلَّوا وَّهُم مُّعْرِضُونَ

۞ يَٰٓأَيُّهَا الَّذِينَ ءَامَنُوا اسْتَجِيبُوا

لِلَّهِ وَلِلرَّسُولِ إِذَا دَعَاكُمْ لِمَا

يُحْيِيكُمْ ۖ وَاعْلَمُوٓا أَنَّ اللَّهَ

يَحُولُ بَيْنَ الْمَرْءِ وَقَلْبِهِ

وَأَنَّهُۥٓ إِلَيْهِ تُحْشَرُونَ ۞ وَاتَّقُوا

فِتْنَةً لَّا تُصِيبَنَّ الَّذِينَ ظَلَمُوا

مِنكُمْ خَاصَّةً ۖ وَاعْلَمُوٓا أَنَّ اللَّهَ

your forces be to you even if they were multiplied: for verily Allah is with those who believe!

20. O you who believe! Obey Allah and His Apostle, and turn not away from him when you hear (him speak).

21. Nor be like those who say, "We hear," but listen not:

22. For the worst of beasts in the sight of Allah are the deaf and the dumb, - those who understand not.

23. If Allah had found

عَنْكُمْ فِئَتُكُمْ شَيْئًا وَّلَوْ كَثُرَتْ

وَاَنَّ اللّٰهَ مَعَ الْمُؤْمِنِيْنَ ۞

يٰاَيُّهَا الَّذِيْنَ اٰمَنُوْا اَطِيْعُوا

اللّٰهَ وَرَسُوْلَهٗ وَلَا تَوَلَّوْا عَنْهُ

وَاَنْتُمْ تَسْمَعُوْنَ ۞ وَلَا تَكُوْنُوْا

كَالَّذِيْنَ قَالُوْا سَمِعْنَا وَهُمْ

لَا يَسْمَعُوْنَ ۞ اِنَّ شَرَّ الدَّوَآبِّ

عِنْدَ اللّٰهِ الصُّمُّ الْبُكْمُ الَّذِيْنَ

لَا يَعْقِلُوْنَ ۞ وَلَوْ عَلِمَ اللّٰهُ

refuge (indeed)!

17. It is not you who slew them; it was Allah: when you threw (a handful of dust), it was not your act, but Allah's: in order that He might test the believers by a gracious trial from Himself: for Allah is He Who heareth and knoweth (all things).

18. That, and also because Allah is He Who makes feeble the plans and stratagems of the unbelievers.

19. (O unbelievers!) If you prayed for victory and judgment, now has the judgment come to you: if you desist (from wrong), it will be best for you: if you return (to the attack), so shall We. Not the least good will

الْمَصِيرُ ۞ فَلَمْ تَقْتُلُوهُمْ وَلٰكِنَّ

اللهَ قَتَلَهُمْ ۖ وَمَا رَمَيْتَ إِذْ

رَمَيْتَ وَلٰكِنَّ اللهَ رَمٰى ۚ وَلِيُبْلِيَ

الْمُؤْمِنِينَ مِنْهُ بَلَاءً حَسَنًا ۚ إِنَّ

اللهَ سَمِيعٌ عَلِيمٌ ۞ ذٰلِكُمْ وَأَنَّ

اللهَ مُوهِنُ كَيْدِ الْكٰفِرِينَ

۞ إِنْ تَسْتَفْتِحُوا فَقَدْ جَاءَكُمُ

الْفَتْحُ ۚ وَإِنْ تَنْتَهُوا فَهُوَ خَيْرٌ لَّكُمْ ۖ

وَإِنْ تَعُودُوا نَعُدْ وَلَنْ تُغْنِيَ

Allah is strict in punishment.

14. Thus (will it be said): "Taste then of the (punishment): for those who resist Allah, is the Chastisement of the Fire."

15. O you who believe! When you meet the unbelievers in hostile array, never turn your backs to them.

16. If any do turn his back to them on such a day - unless it be in a stratagem of war, or to retreat to a troop (of his own) - he draws on himself the wrath of Allah, and his abode is Hell, - an evil

اللهَ شَدِيْدُ الْعِقَابِ ۞ ذٰلِكُمْ

فَذُوْقُوْهُ وَ اَنَّ لِلْكٰفِرِيْنَ عَذَابَ

النَّارِ ۞ يٰٓاَيُّهَا الَّذِيْنَ اٰمَنُوْٓا

اِذَا لَقِيْتُمُ الَّذِيْنَ كَفَرُوْا

زَحْفًا فَلَا تُوَلُّوْهُمُ الْاَدْبَارَ ۞

وَمَنْ يُّوَلِّهِمْ يَوْمَىِٕذٍ دُبُرَهٗٓ اِلَّا

مُتَحَرِّفًا لِّقِتَالٍ اَوْ مُتَحَيِّزًا اِلٰى

فِئَةٍ فَقَدْ بَآءَ بِغَضَبٍ مِّنَ

اللهِ وَمَاْوٰىهُ جَهَنَّمُ ط وَبِئْسَ

your hearts, and to plant your feet firmly therewith.

12. Remember your Lord inspired the Angels (with the message): "I am with you: give firmness to the believers: I will instil terror into the hearts of the unbelievers: smite you above their necks and smite all their finger-tips off them."

13. This because they contended against Allah and His Apostle: if any contend against Allah and His Apostle,

عَلَىٰ قُلُوبِكُمْ وَيُثَبِّتَ بِهِ

الْأَقْدَامَ ۝ اِذْ يُوحِىٰ رَبُّكَ اِلَى

الْمَلَٰئِكَةِ اَنِّىٰ مَعَكُمْ فَثَبِّتُوا

الَّذِيْنَ اٰمَنُوْا ۚ سَاُلْقِىٰ فِىْ قُلُوبِ

الَّذِيْنَ كَفَرُوا الرُّعْبَ فَاضْرِبُوْا

فَوْقَ الْاَعْنَاقِ وَاضْرِبُوْا مِنْهُمْ

كُلَّ بَنَانٍ ۝ ذٰلِكَ بِاَنَّهُمْ

شَآقُّوا اللّٰهَ وَرَسُوْلَهٗ ۚ وَمَنْ

يُّشَاقِقِ اللّٰهَ وَرَسُوْلَهٗ فَاِنَّ

with a thousand of the Angels, ranks on ranks."

10. Allah made it but a message of hope, and an assurance to your hearts: (in any case) there is no help except from Allah: and Allah is Exalted in Power, Wise.

11. Remember He covered you with a sort of drowsiness, to give you calm as from Himself, and He caused rain to descend on you from heaven, to clean you therewith, to remove from you the stain of Satan, to strengthen

بِأَلْفٍ مِّنَ الْمَلَٰٓئِكَةِ مُرْدِفِينَ ۞

وَمَا جَعَلَهُ اللّٰهُ إِلَّا بُشْرَىٰ

وَلِتَطْمَئِنَّ بِهِ قُلُوبُكُمْ ۚ وَمَا

النَّصْرُ إِلَّا مِنْ عِنْدِ اللّٰهِ ۗ

إِنَّ اللّٰهَ عَزِيزٌ حَكِيمٌ ۞ إِذْ

يُغَشِّيكُمُ النُّعَاسَ أَمَنَةً مِّنْهُ

وَيُنَزِّلُ عَلَيْكُم مِّنَ السَّمَآءِ

مَآءً لِّيُطَهِّرَكُم بِهِ وَيُذْهِبَ

عَنكُمْ رِجْزَ الشَّيْطَانِ وَلِيَرْبِطَ

to death and they (actually) saw it.

7. Behold! Allah promised you one of the two (enemy) parties, that it should be yours: you wished that the one unarmed should be yours, but Allah willed to justify the Truth according to His words and to cut off the roots of the unbelievers;-

8. That He might justify Truth and prove Falsehood false, distasteful though it be to those in guilt.

9. Remember you implored the assistance of your Lord, and He answered you: "I will assist you

اِلَى الْمَوْتِ وَهُمْ يَنْظُرُوْنَ ۞ وَاِذْ

يَعِدُكُمُ اللّٰهُ اِحْدَى الطَّآئِفَتَيْنِ

اَنَّهَا لَكُمْ وَتَوَدُّوْنَ اَنَّ غَيْرَ

ذَاتِ الشَّوْكَةِ تَكُوْنُ لَكُمْ وَيُرِيْدُ

اللّٰهُ اَنْ يُّحِقَّ الْحَقَّ بِكَلِمٰتِهٖ

وَيَقْطَعَ دَابِرَ الْكٰفِرِيْنَ ۞ لِيُحِقَّ

الْحَقَّ وَيُبْطِلَ الْبَاطِلَ وَلَوْ كَرِهَ

الْمُجْرِمُوْنَ ۞ اِذْ تَسْتَغِيْثُوْنَ رَبَّكُمْ

فَاسْتَجَابَ لَكُمْ اَنِّيْ مُمِدُّكُمْ

put (all) their trust in their Lord;

3.   Who establish regular prayers and spend (freely) out of the gifts We have given them for sustenance:

4.   Such in truth are the believers: they have grades of dignity with their Lord, and forgiveness, and generous sustenance:

5.   Just as your Lord ordered you out of your house in truth, even though a party among the believers disliked it,

6.   Disputing with you concerning the truth after it was made manifest, as if they were being driven

بِهِمْ يَتَوَكَّلُوْنَ ۞ الَّذِيْنَ يُقِيْمُوْنَ

الصَّلٰوةَ وَمِمَّا رَزَقْنٰهُمْ يُنْفِقُوْنَ ۞

اُولٰٓئِكَ هُمُ الْمُؤْمِنُوْنَ حَقًّا ۚ لَهُمْ

دَرَجٰتٌ عِنْدَ رَبِّهِمْ وَمَغْفِرَةٌ

وَّرِزْقٌ كَرِيْمٌ ۞ كَمَآ اَخْرَجَكَ

رَبُّكَ مِنْۢ بَيْتِكَ بِالْحَقِّ ۖ

وَاِنَّ فَرِيْقًا مِّنَ الْمُؤْمِنِيْنَ

لَكٰرِهُوْنَ ۞ يُجَادِلُوْنَكَ فِي الْحَقِّ

بَعْدَ مَا تَبَيَّنَ كَاَنَّمَا يُسَاقُوْنَ

Al-Anfal (The Spoils of War)

Bismillahir-Rahmanir-Rahim

1. They ask you concerning (things taken as) spoils of war. Say: "(Such) spoils are at the disposal of Allah and the Apostle: so fear Allah, and keep straight the relations between yourselves: obey Allah and His Apostle, if you do believe."

2. For, believers are those who, when Allah is mentioned, feel a tremor in their hearts, and when they hear His Signs rehearsed, find their faith strengthened, and

بِسْمِ اللهِ الرَّحْمٰنِ الرَّحِيْمِ

يَسْـَٔلُوْنَكَ عَنِ الْاَنْفَالِ ۚ قُلِ

الْاَنْفَالُ لِلّٰهِ وَالرَّسُوْلِ ۚ فَاتَّقُوا

اللهَ وَاَصْلِحُوْا ذَاتَ بَيْنِكُمْ ۖ

وَاَطِيْعُوا اللهَ وَرَسُوْلَهٗٓ اِنْ

كُنْتُمْ مُّؤْمِنِيْنَ ۞ اِنَّمَا الْمُؤْمِنُوْنَ

الَّذِيْنَ اِذَا ذُكِرَ اللهُ وَجِلَتْ

قُلُوْبُهُمْ وَاِذَا تُلِيَتْ عَلَيْهِمْ

اٰيٰتُهٗ زَادَتْهُمْ اِيْمَانًا وَّعَلٰى

for any who have faith."

204. When the Qur'an is read, listen to it with attention, and hold your peace: that you may receive Mercy.

205. And do you (O reader!) bring your Lord to remembrance in your (very) soul, with humility and in reverence, without loudness in words, in the mornings and evenings; and be not you of those who are unheedful.

206. Those who are near to your Lord, disdain not to do Him worship: they celebrate His praises, and bow down before Him.

لِقَوْمٍ يُّؤْمِنُوْنَ ۝ وَاِذَا قُرِئَ
الْقُرْاٰنُ فَاسْتَمِعُوْا لَهُ وَاَنْصِتُوْا
لَعَلَّكُمْ تُرْحَمُوْنَ ۝ وَاذْكُرْ رَّبَّكَ
فِيْ نَفْسِكَ تَضَرُّعًا وَّخِيْفَةً
وَّدُوْنَ الْجَهْرِ مِنَ الْقَوْلِ
بِالْغُدُوِّ وَالْاٰصَالِ وَلَا تَكُنْ
مِّنَ الْغٰفِلِيْنَ ۝ اِنَّ الَّذِيْنَ عِنْدَ
رَبِّكَ لَا يَسْتَكْبِرُوْنَ عَنْ عِبَادَتِهٖ
وَيُسَبِّحُوْنَهٗ وَلَهٗ يَسْجُدُوْنَ ۝

201. Those who fear Allah, when a thought of evil from Satan assaults them, bring Allah to remembrance, and they see (aright)!

202. But their brethren (the evil ones) plunge them deeper into error, and never relax (their efforts).

203. If you bring them not a revelation, they say: "Why have you not got it together?" Say: "I but follow what is revealed to me from my Lord: this is (nothing but) lights from your Lord, and Guidance, and Mercy,

إِنَّ الَّذِينَ اتَّقَوْا إِذَا مَسَّهُمْ

طَائِفٌ مِّنَ الشَّيْطَانِ تَذَكَّرُوا

فَإِذَا هُم مُّبْصِرُونَ ۝ وَإِخْوَانُهُمْ

يَمُدُّونَهُمْ فِي الْغَيِّ ثُمَّ لَا

يُقْصِرُونَ ۝ وَإِذَا لَمْ تَأْتِهِم

بِآيَةٍ قَالُوا لَوْلَا اجْتَبَيْتَهَا ۚ

قُلْ إِنَّمَا أَتَّبِعُ مَا يُوحَى

إِلَيَّ مِن رَّبِّي ۚ هَٰذَا بَصَائِرُ

مِن رَّبِّكُمْ وَهُدًى وَّرَحْمَةٌ

besides Him, are unable to help you, and indeed to help themselves."

198. If you call them to guidance, they hear not. You will see them looking at you, but they see not.

199. Hold to forgiveness; command what is right; but turn away from the ignorant.

200. If a suggestion from Satan assails your (mind), seek refuge with Allah; for He hears and knows (all things).

مِنْ دُوْنِهِ لَا يَسْتَطِيْعُوْنَ نَصْرَكُمْ

وَلَآ اَنْفُسَهُمْ يَنْصُرُوْنَ ۩ وَاِنْ

تَدْعُوْهُمْ اِلَى الْهُدٰى لَا يَسْمَعُوْا

وَتَرٰىهُمْ يَنْظُرُوْنَ اِلَيْكَ وَهُمْ

لَا يُبْصِرُوْنَ ۩ خُذِ الْعَفْوَ

وَأْمُرْ بِالْعُرْفِ وَاَعْرِضْ عَنِ

الْجٰهِلِيْنَ ۩ وَاِمَّا يَنْزَغَنَّكَ

مِنَ الشَّيْطٰنِ نَزْغٌ فَاسْتَعِذْ

بِاللّٰهِ اِنَّهٗ سَمِيْعٌ عَلِيْمٌ ۩

if you are (indeed) truthful!

195. Have they feet to walk with? Or hands to lay hold with? Or eyes to see with? Or ears to hear with? Say: "Call your 'Allah-partners', scheme (your worst) against me, and give me no respite!

196. "For my Protector is Allah, Who revealed the Book (from time to time), and He will choose and befriend the righteous.

197. "But those you call upon

اِنْ كُنْتُمْ صٰدِقِيْنَ ۞ اَلَهُمْ

اَرْجُلٌ يَّمْشُوْنَ بِهَا ۗ اَمْ لَهُمْ

اَيْدٍ يَّبْطِشُوْنَ بِهَا ۗ اَمْ لَهُمْ

اَعْيُنٌ يُّبْصِرُوْنَ بِهَا ۗ اَمْ لَهُمْ

اٰذَانٌ يَّسْمَعُوْنَ بِهَا ۗ قُلِ ادْعُوْا

شُرَكَآءَكُمْ ثُمَّ كِيْدُوْنِ فَلَا

تُنْظِرُوْنِ ۞ اِنَّ وَلِيِّ اللّٰهُ الَّذِيْ

نَزَّلَ الْكِتٰبَ ۖ وَهُوَ يَتَوَلَّى

الصّٰلِحِيْنَ ۞ وَالَّذِيْنَ تَدْعُوْنَ

above the partners they ascribe to Him.

191. Do they indeed ascribe to Him as partners things that can create nothing, but are themselves created?

192. No aid can they give them, nor can they aid themselves!

193. If you call them to guidance, they will not obey: for you it is the same whether you call them or you hold your peace!

194. Verily those whom you call upon besides Allah are servants like unto you: call upon them, and let them listen to your prayer,

عَمَّا يُشْرِكُوْنَ ۞ اَيُشْرِكُوْنَ مَا لَا

يَخْلُقُ شَيْئًا وَّهُمْ يُخْلَقُوْنَ ۞

وَلَا يَسْتَطِيْعُوْنَ لَهُمْ نَصْرًا وَّلَآ

اَنْفُسَهُمْ يَنْصُرُوْنَ ۞ وَاِنْ تَدْعُوْهُمْ

اِلَى الْهُدٰى لَا يَتَّبِعُوْكُمْ سَوَآءٌ

عَلَيْكُمْ اَدَعَوْتُمُوْهُمْ اَمْ اَنْتُمْ

صَامِتُوْنَ ۞ اِنَّ الَّذِيْنَ تَدْعُوْنَ

مِنْ دُوْنِ اللّٰهِ عِبَادٌ اَمْثَالُكُمْ

فَادْعُوْهُمْ فَلْيَسْتَجِيْبُوْا لَكُمْ

who have faith."

189. It is He Who created you from a single person, and made his mate of like nature, in order that he might dwell with her (in love). When they are united, she bears a light burden and carries it about (unnoticed). When she grows heavy, they both pray to Allah their Lord, (saying): "If you give us a goodly child, we vow we shall (ever) be grateful."

190. But when He gives them a goodly child, they ascribe to others a share in the gift they have received: but Allah is exalted high

يُؤْمِنُوْنَ ۞ هُوَ الَّذِىْ خَلَقَكُمْ

مِنْ نَّفْسٍ وَّاحِدَةٍ وَّجَعَلَ

مِنْهَا زَوْجَهَا لِيَسْكُنَ اِلَيْهَا ۚ

فَلَمَّا تَغَشّٰهَا حَمَلَتْ حَمْلًا

خَفِيْفًا فَمَرَّتْ بِهٖ ۚ فَلَمَّاۤ اَثْقَلَتْ

دَّعَوَا اللّٰهَ رَبَّهُمَا لَىِٕنْ اٰتَيْتَنَا

صَالِحًا لَّنَكُوْنَنَّ مِنَ الشّٰكِرِيْنَ ۞

فَلَمَّاۤ اٰتٰىهُمَا صَالِحًا جَعَلَا لَهٗ

شُرَكَآءَ فِيْمَاۤ اٰتٰىهُمَا ۚ فَتَعٰلَى اللّٰهُ

the heavens and the earth. Only, all of a sudden will it come to you." They ask you as if you were eager in search thereof: say: "The knowledge thereof is with Allah (alone), but most men know not."

188. Say: "I have no power over any good or harm to myself except as Allah wills. If I had knowledge of the Unseen, I should have multiplied all good, and no evil should have touched me: I am but a warner, and a bringer of glad tidings to those

السَّمٰوٰتِ وَالْأَرْضِ ۚ لَا تَأْتِيكُمْ اِلَّا

بَغْتَةً ۗ يَسْـَٔلُوْنَكَ كَاَنَّكَ حَفِيٌّ

عَنْهَا ۗ قُلْ اِنَّمَا عِلْمُهَا عِنْدَ

اللّٰهِ وَلٰكِنَّ اَكْثَرَ النَّاسِ لَا

يَعْلَمُوْنَ ۝ قُلْ لَّآ اَمْلِكُ لِنَفْسِيْ

نَفْعًا وَّلَا ضَرًّا اِلَّا مَا شَآءَ اللّٰهُ ۗ وَلَوْ

كُنْتُ اَعْلَمُ الْغَيْبَ لَاسْتَكْثَرْتُ

مِنَ الْخَيْرِ ۛ وَمَا مَسَّنِيَ السُّوْٓءُ ۚ

اِنْ اَنَا اِلَّا نَذِيْرٌ وَّبَشِيْرٌ لِّقَوْمٍ

and all that Allah has created? (Do they not see) that it may well be that their terms is drawing to an end? In what message after this will they then believe?

186. To such as Allah rejects from His guidance, there can be no guide: He will leave them in their trespasses, wandering in distraction.

187. They ask you about the (final) Hour - when will be its appointed time? Say: "The knowledge thereof is with my Lord (alone): none but He can reveal as to when it will occur. Heavy were its burden through

وَمَا خَلَقَ اللّٰهُ مِنْ شَيْءٍ ۚ وَأَنْ

عَسَىٰ أَنْ يَّكُوْنَ قَدِ اقْتَرَبَ

أَجَلُهُمْ ۖ فَبِأَيِّ حَدِيْثٍۭ بَعْدَهٗ

يُؤْمِنُوْنَ ۞ مَنْ يُّضْلِلِ اللّٰهُ

فَلَا هَادِيَ لَهٗ ۚ وَيَذَرُهُمْ فِيْ

طُغْيَانِهِمْ يَعْمَهُوْنَ ۞ يَسْـَٔلُوْنَكَ

عَنِ السَّاعَةِ أَيَّانَ مُرْسَٰهَا ۖ

قُلْ إِنَّمَا عِلْمُهَا عِنْدَ رَبِّيْ ۖ لَا

يُجَلِّيْهَا لِوَقْتِهَآ إِلَّا هُوَ ۚ ثَقُلَتْ فِى

181. Of those We have created are people who direct (others) with truth. And dispense justice therewith.

182. Those who reject Our Signs, We will lead them step by step to rain while they know not;

183. Respite will I grant unto them: for My scheme is strong (and unfailing).

184. Do they not reflect? Their companion is not seized with madness: he is but a perspicuous warner.

185. Do they see nothing in the kingdome of the heavens and the earth

مَا كَانُوا يَعْمَلُونَ ۞ وَمِمَّنْ

خَلَقْنَا أُمَّةٌ يَّهْدُونَ بِالْحَقِّ

وَبِهِ يَعْدِلُونَ ۞ وَالَّذِينَ كَذَّبُوا

بِاٰيَاتِنَا سَنَسْتَدْرِجُهُمْ مِّنْ حَيْثُ

لَا يَعْلَمُونَ ۞ وَأُمْلِي لَهُمْ ۗ اِنَّ

كَيْدِي مَتِينٌ ۞ اَوَلَمْ يَتَفَكَّرُوا

مَا بِصَاحِبِهِمْ مِّنْ جِنَّةٍ ۗ اِنْ هُوَ

اِلَّا نَذِيرٌ مُّبِينٌ ۞ اَوَلَمْ يَنْظُرُوا

فِي مَلَكُوتِ السَّمٰوٰتِ وَالْاَرْضِ

179. Many are the Jinns and men we have made for Hell: they have hearts wherewith they understand not, eyes wherewith they see not, and ears wherewith they hear not. They are like cattle, - no more misguided: for they are heedless (of warning).

180. The most beautiful names belong to Allah: so call on him by them; but shun such men as use profanity in his names: for what they do, they will soon be requited.

وَلَقَدْ ذَرَأْنَا لِجَهَنَّمَ كَثِيْرًا

مِّنَ الْجِنِّ وَالْإِنْسِ ۖ لَهُمْ قُلُوْبٌ

لَّا يَفْقَهُوْنَ بِهَا ۖ وَلَهُمْ اَعْيُنٌ

لَّا يُبْصِرُوْنَ بِهَا ۖ وَلَهُمْ اٰذَانٌ

لَّا يَسْمَعُوْنَ بِهَا ۚ أُولٰٓئِكَ كَالْأَنْعَامِ

بَلْ هُمْ اَضَلُّ ۚ أُولٰٓئِكَ هُمُ

الْغٰفِلُوْنَ ۞ وَلِلّٰهِ الْأَسْمَاءُ الْحُسْنٰى

فَادْعُوْهُ بِهَا ۖ وَذَرُوا الَّذِيْنَ

يُلْحِدُوْنَ فِيْ اَسْمَائِهٖ ۚ سَيُجْزَوْنَ

if you attack him, he lolls out his tongue, or if you leave him alone, he (still) lolls out his tongue. That is the similitude of those who reject Our Signs; so relate the story; perchance they may reflect.

177. Evil as an example are people who reject Our Signs and wrong their own souls.

178. Whom Allah does guide, - he is on the right path: whom He rejects from His guidance, - such are the persons who perish.

إِنْ تَحْمِلْ عَلَيْهِ يَلْهَثْ اَوْ تَتْرُكْهُ يَلْهَثْ ۚ ذٰلِكَ مَثَلُ الْقَوْمِ الَّذِيْنَ كَذَّبُوْا بِاٰيٰتِنَا ۚ فَاقْصُصِ الْقَصَصَ لَعَلَّهُمْ يَتَفَكَّرُوْنَ ۞ سَآءَ مَثَلَا ۨالْقَوْمُ الَّذِيْنَ كَذَّبُوْا بِاٰيٰتِنَا وَاَنْفُسَهُمْ كَانُوْا يَظْلِمُوْنَ ۞ مَنْ يَّهْدِ اللّٰهُ فَهُوَ الْمُهْتَدِيْ ۚ وَمَنْ يُّضْلِلْ فَاُولٰٓئِكَ هُمُ الْخٰسِرُوْنَ ۞

after them: will You then destroy us because of the deeds of men who followed falsehood?"

174. Thus do We explain the Signs in detail; and perchance they may turn (unto Us).

175. Relate to them the story of the man to whom We sent Our Signs, but he passed them by: so Satan followed him up, and he went astray.

176. If it had been Our Will, We should have elevated him with Our Signs; but he inclined to the earth, and followed his own vain desires. His similitude is that of a dog:

بَعْدِهِمْ أَفَتُهْلِكُنَا بِمَا فَعَلَ

الْمُبْطِلُوْنَ ۝ وَكَذٰلِكَ نُفَصِّلُ

الْاٰيٰتِ وَلَعَلَّهُمْ يَرْجِعُوْنَ ۝ وَاتْلُ

عَلَيْهِمْ نَبَأَ الَّذِيْ اٰتَيْنٰهُ

اٰيٰتِنَا فَانْسَلَخَ مِنْهَا فَاَتْبَعَهُ

الشَّيْطٰنُ فَكَانَ مِنَ الْغٰوِيْنَ ۝

وَلَوْ شِئْنَا لَرَفَعْنٰهُ بِهَا وَلٰكِنَّهٗ

اَخْلَدَ اِلَى الْاَرْضِ وَاتَّبَعَ

هَوٰىهُ فَمَثَلُهٗ كَمَثَلِ الْكَلْبِ

and bring (ever) to remembrance what is therein; perchance you may fear Allah."

172. When your Lord drew forth from the Children of Adam - from their loins - their descendants, and made them testify concerning themselves, (saying): "Am I not your Lord (who cherishes and sustains you)?"- they said: "Yes! We do testify!" (This), lest you should say on the Day of Judgment: "Of this we were never mindful":

173. Or lest you should say: "Our fathers before us may have taken false gods, but we are (their) descendants

بِقُوَّةٍ وَّ اذْكُرُوْا مَا فِيْهِ لَعَلَّكُمْ

تَتَّقُوْنَ ۞ وَ اِذْ اَخَذَ رَبُّكَ مِنْ

بَنِيْۤ اٰدَمَ مِنْ ظُهُوْرِهِمْ ذُرِّيَّتَهُمْ

وَ اَشْهَدَهُمْ عَلٰۤى اَنْفُسِهِمْ ۚ اَلَسْتُ

بِرَبِّكُمْ ۗ قَالُوْا بَلٰى ۛ شَهِدْنَا ۛ

اَنْ تَقُوْلُوْا يَوْمَ الْقِيٰمَةِ اِنَّا

كُنَّا عَنْ هٰذَا غٰفِلِيْنَ ۙ ۞

اَوْ تَقُوْلُوْۤا اِنَّمَاۤ اَشْرَكَ اٰبَآؤُنَا

مِنْ قَبْلُ وَ كُنَّا ذُرِّيَّةً مِّنْۢ

that they would not ascribe to Allah anything but the truth? And they study what is in the Book. But best for the righteous is the home in the Here-after. Will you not understand?

170. As to those who hold fast by the Book and establish regular prayer, - never shall We suffer the reward of the righteous to perish.

171. When We raised the Mount over them, as if it had been a canopy, and they thought it was going to fall on them (We said): "Hold firmly to what We have given you,

مِيثَاقُ الْكِتَبِ أَنْ لَّا يَقُوْلُوْا

عَلَى اللهِ إِلَّا الْحَقَّ وَدَرَسُوْا

مَا فِيْهِ ۗ وَالدَّارُ الْأَخِرَةُ خَيْرٌ

لِّلَّذِيْنَ يَتَّقُوْنَ ۗ أَفَلَا تَعْقِلُوْنَ ۝

وَالَّذِيْنَ يُمَسِّكُوْنَ بِالْكِتٰبِ

وَأَقَامُوا الصَّلٰوةَ ۗ إِنَّا لَا نُضِيْعُ

أَجْرَ الْمُصْلِحِيْنَ ۝ وَإِذْ نَتَقْنَا

الْجَبَلَ فَوْقَهُمْ كَأَنَّهُ ظُلَّةٌ وَّظَنُّوْا

أَنَّهُ وَاقِعٌ بِهِمْ ۚ خُذُوْا مَا اٰتَيْنٰكُمْ

168. We broke them up into sections on this earth. There are among them some that are the righteous, and some that are the opposite. We have tried them with both prosperity and adversity: in order that they might turn (to Us).

169. After them succeeded an (evil) generation: they inherited the Book, but they chose (for themselves) the vanities of this world, saying (for excuse): "(Everything) will be forgiven us." (Even so), if similar vanities came their way, they would (again) seize them. Was not the covenant of the Book taken from them,

وَقَطَّعْنَاهُمْ فِى الْأَرْضِ أُمَمًا

مِّنْهُمُ الصّٰلِحُوْنَ وَمِنْهُمْ دُوْنَ

ذٰلِكَ وَبَلَوْنَاهُمْ بِالْحَسَنٰتِ

وَالسَّيِّاٰتِ لَعَلَّهُمْ يَرْجِعُوْنَ ۝

فَخَلَفَ مِنْ بَعْدِهِمْ خَلْفٌ

وَرِثُوا الْكِتٰبَ يَأْخُذُوْنَ عَرَضَ

هٰذَا الْأَدْنٰى وَيَقُوْلُوْنَ سَيُغْفَرُ لَنَا

وَإِنْ يَّأْتِهِمْ عَرَضٌ مِّثْلُهٗ

يَأْخُذُوْهُ أَلَمْ يُؤْخَذْ عَلَيْهِمْ

Evil; but We visited the wrong-doers with a grievous punishment because they were given to transgression.

166. When in their insolence they transgressed (all) prohibitions, We said to them: "Be you apes, despised and rejected."

167. Behold! Your Lord did declare that He would send against them, to the Day of Judgment, those who would afflict them with grievous Chastisement. Your Lord is quick in retribution, but He is also Oft-Forgiving, Most Merciful.

السُّوٓءِ وَاَخَذۡنَا الَّذِيۡنَ ظَلَمُوۡا

بِعَذَابٍۭ بَئِيۡسٍۭ بِمَا كَانُوۡا

يَفۡسُقُوۡنَ ۝ فَلَمَّا عَتَوۡا عَنۡ

مَّا نُهُوۡا عَنۡهُ قُلۡنَا لَهُمۡ كُوۡنُوۡا

قِرَدَةً خٰسِئِيۡنَ ۝ وَاِذۡ تَاَذَّنَ

رَبُّكَ لَيَبۡعَثَنَّ عَلَيۡهِمۡ اِلٰى

يَوۡمِ الۡقِيٰمَةِ مَنۡ يَّسُوۡمُهُمۡ سُوٓءَ

الۡعَذَابِ ۗ اِنَّ رَبَّكَ لَسَرِيۡعُ

الۡعِقَابِ ۖ وَاِنَّهٗ لَغَفُوۡرٌ رَّحِيۡمٌ ۝

but on the day they had no Sabbath, they came not: thus did We make a trial of them, for they were given to transgression.

164. When some of them said: "Why do you preach to a people whom Allah will destroy or visit with a terrible punishment?"- said the preachers: "To discharge our duty to your Lord, and perchance they may fear Him."

165. When they disregarded the warnings that had been given them, We rescued those who forbade

وَيَوْمَ لَا يَسْبِتُوْنَ لَا تَأْتِيْهِمْ

كَذَٰلِكَ نَبْلُوْهُمْ بِمَا كَانُوْا

يَفْسُقُوْنَ ۝ وَاِذْ قَالَتْ أُمَّةٌ

مِّنْهُمْ لِمَ تَعِظُوْنَ قَوْمًا اللَّهُ

مُهْلِكُهُمْ أَوْ مُعَذِّبُهُمْ عَذَابًا

شَدِيْدًا ۚ قَالُوْا مَعْذِرَةً اِلَى

رَبِّكُمْ وَلَعَلَّهُمْ يَتَّقُوْنَ ۝

فَلَمَّا نَسُوْا مَا ذُكِّرُوْا بِهٖٓ

أَنْجَيْنَا الَّذِيْنَ يَنْهَوْنَ عَنِ

your faults; We shall increase (the portion of) those who do good."

162. But the transgressors among them changed the word from that which had been given them so We sent on them a plague from heaven. For that they repeatedly transgressed.

163. Ask them concerning the town standing close by the sea. Behold! They transgressed in the matter of the Sabbath. For on the day of their Sabbath their fish did come to them, openly holding up their heads,

خَطِيئَتِكُمْ ۚ سَنَزِيدُ الْمُحْسِنِينَ ﴿١٩١﴾

فَبَدَّلَ الَّذِينَ ظَلَمُوا مِنْهُمْ

قَوْلًا غَيْرَ الَّذِي قِيلَ لَهُمْ

فَأَرْسَلْنَا عَلَيْهِمْ رِجْزًا مِّنَ

السَّمَاءِ بِمَا كَانُوا يَظْلِمُونَ ﴿١٩٢﴾

وَسْئَلْهُمْ عَنِ الْقَرْيَةِ الَّتِي

كَانَتْ حَاضِرَةَ الْبَحْرِ إِذْ

يَعْدُونَ فِي السَّبْتِ إِذْ تَأْتِيهِمْ

حِيتَانُهُمْ يَوْمَ سَبْتِهِمْ شُرَّعًا

its own place for water. We gave them the shade of clouds, and sent down to them manna and quails, (saying): "Eat of the good things We have provided for you": (but they rebelled); to Us they did no harm, but they harmed their own souls.

161. And remember it was said to them: "Dwell in this town and eat therein as you wish, but say the word of humility and enter the gate in a posture of humility: We shall forgive you

أُنَاسٍ مَّشْرَبَهُمْ ۖ وَظَلَّلْنَا عَلَيْهِمُ

الْغَمَامَ وَأَنْزَلْنَا عَلَيْهِمُ الْمَنَّ

وَالسَّلْوَىٰ ۖ كُلُوا مِنْ طَيِّبَٰتِ

مَا رَزَقْنَٰكُمْ ۚ وَمَا ظَلَمُونَا وَلَٰكِنْ

كَانُوا أَنْفُسَهُمْ يَظْلِمُونَ ۝ وَإِذْ

قِيلَ لَهُمُ اسْكُنُوا هَٰذِهِ

الْقَرْيَةَ وَكُلُوا مِنْهَا حَيْثُ

شِئْتُمْ وَقُولُوا حِطَّةٌ وَادْخُلُوا

الْبَابَ سُجَّدًا نَغْفِرْ لَكُمْ

who believes in Allah and His Words: follow him that (so) you may be guided."

159. Of the People of Moses there is a section who guide and do justice in the light of truth.

160. We divided them into twelve tribes or nations. We directed Moses by inspiration, when his (thirsty) people asked him for water: "Strike the rock with your staff": out of it there gushed forth twelve springs: each group knew

الْأُمِّيِّ الَّذِي يُؤْمِنُ بِاللّٰهِ وَكَلِمٰتِهِ

وَاتَّبِعُوهُ لَعَلَّكُمْ تَهْتَدُونَ ۞ وَمِنْ

قَوْمِ مُوْسٰٓى أُمَّةٌ يَّهْدُوْنَ بِالْحَقِّ

وَبِهِ يَعْدِلُوْنَ ۞ وَقَطَّعْنٰهُمُ

اثْنَتَيْ عَشْرَةَ أَسْبَاطًا أُمَمًا ۚ

وَأَوْحَيْنَآ إِلٰى مُوْسٰٓى إِذِ اسْتَسْقٰهُ

قَوْمُهٗٓ أَنِ اضْرِبْ بِّعَصَاكَ

الْحَجَرَ ۚ فَانْبَجَسَتْ مِنْهُ اثْنَتَا

عَشْرَةَ عَيْنًا ۗ قَدْ عَلِمَ كُلُّ

upon them. So it is those who believe in him, honour him, help him, and follow the light which is sent down with him, - it is they who will prosper."

158. Say: "O men! I am sent unto you all, as the Apostle of Allah, to Whom belongs the dominion of the heavens and the earth: there is no Allah but He: it is He that gives both life and death. So believe in Allah and His Apostle, the unlettered Prophet,

عَلَيْهِمْ ۚ فَالَّذِيْنَ اٰمَنُوْا بِهٖ

وَعَزَّرُوْهُ وَنَصَرُوْهُ وَاتَّبَعُوا

النُّوْرَ الَّذِيْۤ اُنْزِلَ مَعَهٗۤ ۙ

اُولٰٓئِكَ هُمُ الْمُفْلِحُوْنَ ۩ قُلْ

يٰۤاَيُّهَا النَّاسُ اِنِّيْ رَسُوْلُ

اللّٰهِ اِلَيْكُمْ جَمِيْعًا الَّذِيْ لَهٗ

مُلْكُ السَّمٰوٰتِ وَالْاَرْضِ ۚ لَاۤ

اِلٰهَ اِلَّا هُوَ يُحْيٖ وَيُمِيْتُ ۪

فَاٰمِنُوْا بِاللّٰهِ وَرَسُوْلِهِ النَّبِيِّ

do right, and pay Zakat, and those who believe in Our Signs;" -

157. "Those who follow the Apostle, the unlettered Prophet, whom they find mentioned in their own (scriptures), - in the Law (Tourat) and the Gospel; - for he commands them what is just and forbids them what is evil; he allows them as lawful what is good (and pure) and prohibits them from what is bad (and impure); he releases them from their heavy burdens and from the yokes that are

يَتَّقُونَ وَيُؤْتُونَ الزَّكٰوةَ وَالَّذِينَ

هُمْ بِاٰيٰتِنَا يُؤْمِنُونَ ۞ اَلَّذِينَ

يَتَّبِعُونَ الرَّسُولَ النَّبِيَّ الْأُمِّيَّ

الَّذِي يَجِدُونَهُ مَكْتُوبًا عِنْدَهُمْ

فِي التَّوْرَاةِ وَالْإِنْجِيلِ يَأْمُرُهُمْ

بِالْمَعْرُوفِ وَيَنْهٰهُمْ عَنِ الْمُنْكَرِ

وَيُحِلُّ لَهُمُ الطَّيِّبٰتِ وَيُحَرِّمُ

عَلَيْهِمُ الْخَبٰٓئِثَ وَيَضَعُ عَنْهُمْ

إِصْرَهُمْ وَالْأَغْلٰلَ الَّتِي كَانَتْ

among us? This is no more than trial from you: by it You cause whom You will to stray, and You lead whom You will into the right path. You are our Protector: so forgive us and give us Your mercy; for You are the best of those who forgive."

156. "And ordain for us that which is good, in this life and in the Hereafter: for we have turned unto You." He said: "With My punishment I visit whom I will; but My Mercy extends to all things. That (mercy) I shall ordain for those who

مِنَّا ۚ إِنْ هِيَ إِلَّا فِتْنَتُكَ ۚ تُضِلُّ

بِهَا مَنْ تَشَاءُ وَتَهْدِى مَنْ

تَشَاءُ ۖ أَنْتَ وَلِيُّنَا فَاغْفِرْ لَنَا

وَارْحَمْنَا ۖ وَأَنْتَ خَيْرُ الْغَافِرِينَ ۝

وَاكْتُبْ لَنَا فِي هَٰذِهِ الدُّنْيَا

حَسَنَةً وَّفِي الْآخِرَةِ إِنَّا هُدْنَا

إِلَيْكَ ۚ قَالَ عَذَابِي أُصِيبُ

بِهِ مَنْ أَشَاءُ ۖ وَرَحْمَتِي وَسِعَتْ

كُلَّ شَيْءٍ ۚ فَسَأَكْتُبُهَا لِلَّذِينَ

Most Merciful.

154. When the anger of Moses was appeased, he took up the Tablets: in the writing thereon was Guidance and Mercy for such as fear their Lord.

155. And Moses chose seventy of his people for Our place of meeting: when they were seized with violent quaking, he prayed: "O my Lord! If it had been Your Will You could have destroyed, long before, both them and me: would You destroy us for the deeds of the foolish ones

سَاحِيمٌ ۞ ۞ وَلَمَّا سَكَتَ عَنْ

مُّوسَى الْغَضَبُ أَخَذَ الْأَلْوَاحَ

وَفِى نُسْخَتِهَا هُدًى وَّرَحْمَةٌ

لِّلَّذِينَ هُمْ لِرَبِّهِمْ يَرْهَبُونَ ۞

وَاخْتَارَ مُوسَى قَوْمَهُ سَبْعِينَ

رَجُلًا لِّمِيقَاتِنَا ۚ فَلَمَّا أَخَذَتْهُمُ

الرَّجْفَةُ قَالَ رَبِّ لَوْ شِئْتَ

أَهْلَكْتَهُم مِّن قَبْلُ وَإِيَّايَ ۖ

أَتُهْلِكُنَا بِمَا فَعَلَ السُّفَهَاءُ

Forgive me and my brother! Admit us to Your mercy! For You are the Most Merciful of those who show mercy!"

152. Those who took the calf (for worship) will indeed be overwhelmed with wrath from their Lord, and with shame in this life: thus do We recompense those who invent (falsehoods).

153. But those who do wrong but repent thereafter and (truly) believe, - verily your Lord is thereafter Oft-Forgiving,

اغْفِرْ لِي وَلِأَخِي وَأَدْخِلْنَا فِي رَحْمَتِكَ وَأَنتَ أَرْحَمُ الرَّاحِمِينَ ۝

إِنَّ الَّذِينَ اتَّخَذُوا الْعِجْلَ سَيَنَالُهُمْ غَضَبٌ مِّن رَّبِّهِمْ وَذِلَّةٌ فِي الْحَيَوٰةِ الدُّنْيَا وَكَذٰلِكَ نَجْزِي الْمُفْتَرِينَ ۝

وَالَّذِينَ عَمِلُوا السَّيِّئَاتِ ثُمَّ تَابُوا مِن بَعْدِهَا وَآمَنُوا إِنَّ رَبَّكَ مِن بَعْدِهَا لَغَفُورٌ

Moses came back to his people, angry and grieved, he said: "Evil it is that you have done in my place in my absence: did you make haste to bring on the judgment of your Lord?" He put down the Tablets, seized his brother by (the hair of) his head, and dragged him to him. Aaron said: "Son of my mother! The people did indeed not listen to me, and went near to slaying me! Make not the enemies rejoice over my misfortune, nor count you me amongst the people of sin."

151. Moses prayed: "O my Lord!

رَجَعَ مُوْسٰى اِلٰى قَوْمِهٖ غَضْبَانَ

اَسِفًا ۚ قَالَ بِئْسَمَا خَلَفْتُمُوْنِىْ

مِنْ بَعْدِىْ ۚ اَعَجِلْتُمْ اَمْرَ

رَبِّكُمْ ۚ وَاَلْقَى الْاَلْوَاحَ وَاَخَذَ

بِرَأْسِ اَخِيْهِ يَجُرُّهٗۤ اِلَيْهِ ؕ قَالَ

ابْنَ اُمَّ اِنَّ الْقَوْمَ اسْتَضْعَفُوْنِىْ

وَكَادُوْا يَقْتُلُوْنَنِىْ ۖ فَلَا تُشْمِتْ

بِىَ الْاَعْدَآءَ وَلَا تَجْعَلْنِىْ مَعَ

الْقَوْمِ الظّٰلِمِيْنَ ۞ قَالَ رَبِّ

148. The people of Moses made, in his absence, out of their ornaments, the image of calf, (for worship) having lowing sound. Did they not see that it could neither speak to them, nor show them the way? They took it for worship and they did wrong.

149. When they repented, and saw that they had erred, they said: "If our Lord have not mercy upon us and forgive us, we shall indeed be of those who perish."

150. When

وَ اتَّخَذَ قَوْمُ مُوسَى مِنْ

بَعْدِهِ مِنْ حُلِيِّهِمْ عِجْلًا

جَسَدًا لَّهُ خُوَارٌ أَلَمْ يَرَوْا

أَنَّهُ لَا يُكَلِّمُهُمْ وَلَا يَهْدِيهِمْ

سَبِيلًا اتَّخَذُوهُ وَكَانُوا ظَالِمِينَ ۝

وَلَمَّا سُقِطَ فِىٓ أَيْدِيهِمْ وَرَأَوْا

أَنَّهُمْ قَدْ ضَلُّوا قَالُوا لَئِنْ

لَّمْ يَرْحَمْنَا رَبُّنَا وَيَغْفِرْ لَنَا

لَنَكُونَنَّ مِنَ الْخَاسِرِينَ ۝ وَلَمَّا

even if they see all the Signs, they will not believe in them; and if they see the way of right conduct, they will not adopt it as the way; but if they see the way of error, that is the way they will adopt. For they have rejected Our Signs, and failed to take warning from them.

147. Those who reject Our Signs and the meeting in the Hereafter, - vain are their deeds: can they expect to be rewarded except as they have wrought?

الْحَقَّ ۚ وَإِنْ يَّرَوْا كُلَّ اٰيَةٍ لَّا

يُؤْمِنُوْا بِهَا ۚ وَإِنْ يَّرَوْا سَبِيْلَ

الرُّشْدِ لَا يَتَّخِذُوْهُ سَبِيْلًا ۚ وَإِنْ

يَّرَوْا سَبِيْلَ الْغَيِّ يَتَّخِذُوْهُ

سَبِيْلًا ۚ ذٰلِكَ بِأَنَّهُمْ كَذَّبُوْا

بِاٰيٰتِنَا وَكَانُوْا عَنْهَا غٰفِلِيْنَ ۞

وَالَّذِيْنَ كَذَّبُوْا بِاٰيٰتِنَا وَلِقَآءِ

الْاٰخِرَةِ حَبِطَتْ أَعْمَالُهُمْ ۚ هَلْ

يُجْزَوْنَ إِلَّا مَا كَانُوْا يَعْمَلُوْنَ ۞

(other) men, by the mission I (have given you) and the words I (have spoken to you): take then the (revelation) which I give you, and be of those who give thanks."

145. And We ordained laws for him in the tablets in all matters, both commanding and explaining all things, (and said): "Take and hold these with firmness, and enjoin your people to hold fast by the best in the precepts: soon shall I show you the homes of the wicked, - (how they lie desolate)."

146. Those who behave arrogantly on the earth in defiance of right - them will I turn away from My Signs:

النَّاسِ بِرِسٰلٰتِيْ وَبِكَلَامِيْ ۖ فَخُذْ

مَآ اٰتَيْتُكَ وَكُنْ مِّنَ الشّٰكِرِيْنَ ۝

وَكَتَبْنَا لَهٗ فِي الْاَلْوَاحِ مِنْ

كُلِّ شَيْءٍ مَّوْعِظَةً وَّتَفْصِيْلًا

لِّكُلِّ شَيْءٍ ۚ فَخُذْهَا بِقُوَّةٍ

وَّأْمُرْ قَوْمَكَ يَأْخُذُوْا بِأَحْسَنِهَا ۚ

سَأُوْرِيْكُمْ دَارَ الْفٰسِقِيْنَ ۝

سَأَصْرِفُ عَنْ اٰيٰتِيَ الَّذِيْنَ

يَتَكَبَّرُوْنَ فِي الْاَرْضِ بِغَيْرِ

He said: "O my Lord! Show (Yourself) to me, that I may look upon You." Allah said: "By no means can you see Me (direct); but look upon the mount; if it abide in its place, then shall you see Me." When his Lord manifested His glory on the Mount, He made it as dust. And Moses fell down in a swoon. When he recovered his senses he said: "Glory be to You! to You I turn in repentance, and I am the first to believe."

144. (Allah) said: "O Moses! I have chosen you above

قَالَ رَبِّ أَرِنِيْ أَنْظُرْ اِلَيْكَ

قَالَ لَنْ تَرَانِيْ وَلٰكِنِ انْظُرْ

اِلَى الْجَبَلِ فَاِنِ اسْتَقَرَّ مَكَانَهٗ

فَسَوْفَ تَرَانِيْ ۚ فَلَمَّا تَجَلّٰى

رَبُّهٗ لِلْجَبَلِ جَعَلَهٗ دَكًّا وَّخَرَّ

مُوْسٰى صَعِقًا ۚ فَلَمَّا اَفَاقَ

قَالَ سُبْحٰنَكَ تُبْتُ اِلَيْكَ

وَاَنَا اَوَّلُ الْمُؤْمِنِيْنَ ۝ قَالَ

يٰمُوْسٰى اِنِّيْ اصْطَفَيْتُكَ عَلٰى

your male children and saved alive your females: in that was a momentous trial from your Lord.

142. We appointed for Moses thirty nights, and completed (the period) with ten (more): thus was completed the term (of communion) with his Lord, forty nights. And Moses had charged his brother Aaron (before he went up): "Act for me amongst my people: do right, and follow not the way of those who do mischief."

143. When Moses came to the place appointed by Us, and his Lord addressed him,

أَبْنَآءَكُمْ وَيَسْتَحْيُونَ نِسَآءَكُمْ

وَفِي ذَٰلِكُمْ بَلَآءٌ مِّنْ رَّبِّكُمْ

عَظِيمٌ ۩ وَوَاعَدْنَا مُوسَىٰ ثَلَٰثِينَ

لَيْلَةً وَأَتْمَمْنَٰهَا بِعَشْرٍ فَتَمَّ

مِيقَاتُ رَبِّهِ أَرْبَعِينَ لَيْلَةً

وَقَالَ مُوسَىٰ لِأَخِيهِ هَٰرُونَ

اخْلُفْنِي فِي قَوْمِي وَأَصْلِحْ وَلَا

تَتَّبِعْ سَبِيلَ الْمُفْسِدِينَ ۩ وَلَمَّا

جَآءَ مُوسَىٰ لِمِيقَاتِنَا وَكَلَّمَهُ رَبُّهُ

They said: "O Moses! Fashion for us a god like unto the gods they have." He said: "Surely you are a people without knowledge.

139. "As to these folk, - the cult they are in is (but) a fragment of a ruin, and vain is the (worship) which they practise."

140. He said: "Shall I seek for you a Allah other than the (true) Allah, when it is Allah who has endowed you with gifts above the nations?"

141. And remember We rescued you from Pharaoh's people, who afflicted you with the worst of penalties, who slew

قَالُوْا يٰمُوْسَى اجْعَلْ لَّنَآ اِلٰهًا

كَمَا لَهُمْ اٰلِهَةٌ ۚ قَالَ اِنَّكُمْ

قَوْمٌ تَجْهَلُوْنَ ۞ اِنَّ هٰٓؤُلَاۤءِ

مُتَبَّرٌ مَّا هُمْ فِيْهِ وَ بٰطِلٌ

مَّا كَانُوْا يَعْمَلُوْنَ ۞ قَالَ

اَغَيْرَ اللّٰهِ اَبْغِيْكُمْ اِلٰهًا وَّهُوَ

فَضَّلَكُمْ عَلَى الْعٰلَمِيْنَ ۞ وَاِذْ

اَنْجَيْنٰكُمْ مِّنْ اٰلِ فِرْعَوْنَ

يَسُوْمُوْنَكُمْ سُوْۤءَ الْعَذَابِ ۚ يُقَتِّلُوْنَ

a people, considered weak (and of no account), inheritors of lands in both east and west, - lands whereon We sent down Our blessings. The fair promise of your Lord was fulfilled for the Children of Israel, because they had patience and constancy, and We levelled to the ground the great works and fine buildings which Pharaoh and his people erected (with such pride).

138. We took the Children of Israel (with safety) across the sea. They came upon a people devoted entirely to some idols they had.

الْقَوْمَ الَّذِيْنَ كَانُوْا يُسْتَضْعَفُوْنَ
مَشَارِقَ الْأَرْضِ وَمَغَارِبَهَا الَّتِيْ
بَارَكْنَا فِيْهَا ۖ وَتَمَّتْ كَلِمَتُ رَبِّكَ
الْحُسْنَىٰ عَلَىٰ بَنِيْ إِسْرَآءِيْلَ ۙ
بِمَا صَبَرُوْا ۖ وَدَمَّرْنَا مَا كَانَ
يَصْنَعُ فِرْعَوْنُ وَقَوْمُهُ وَمَا
كَانُوْا يَعْرِشُوْنَ ۩ وَجَاوَزْنَا بِبَنِيْ
إِسْرَآءِيْلَ الْبَحْرَ فَأَتَوْا عَلَىٰ
قَوْمٍ يَّعْكُفُوْنَ عَلَىٰ أَصْنَامٍ لَّهُمْ ۚ

"O Moses! On our behalf call on your Lord in virtue of his promise to you: if you will remove the Chastisement from us, we shall truly believe in you, and we shall send away the Children of Israel with you."

135. But every time We removed the plague from them according to a fixed term which they had to fulfil, - behold! they broke their word!

136. So We exacted retribution from them: We drowned them in the sea, because they rejected Our Signs and failed to take warning from them.

137. And We made

يٰمُوْسَى ادْعُ لَنَا رَبَّكَ بِمَا عَهِدَ

عِنْدَكَ ۚ لَئِنْ كَشَفْتَ عَنَّا

الرِّجْزَ لَنُؤْمِنَنَّ لَكَ وَلَنُرْسِلَنَّ

مَعَكَ بَنِىْ اِسْرَآءِيْلَ ۞ فَلَمَّا

كَشَفْنَا عَنْهُمُ الرِّجْزَ اِلٰٓى اَجَلٍ

هُمْ بَالِغُوْهُ اِذَا هُمْ يَنْكُثُوْنَ ۞

فَانْتَقَمْنَا مِنْهُمْ فَاَغْرَقْنٰهُمْ فِى

الْيَمِّ بِاَنَّهُمْ كَذَّبُوْا بِاٰيٰتِنَا

وَكَانُوْا عَنْهَا غٰفِلِيْنَ ۞ وَاَوْرَثْنَا

Behold! In truth the omens of evil are theirs in Allah's sight, but most of them do not understand!

132. They said (to Moses): "Whatever be the Signs you bring, to work therewith your sorcery on us, we shall never believe in you."

133. So We sent (plagues) on them: wholesale death, locusts, lice, frogs, and blood: Signs openly self-explained: but they were steeped in arrogance, - a people given to sin.

134. Every time the Chastisement fell on them, they said:

اَلَآ اِنَّمَا طَآئِرُهُمْ عِنْدَ اللّٰهِ
وَلٰكِنَّ اَكْثَرَهُمْ لَا يَعْلَمُوْنَ ۝
وَقَالُوْا مَهْمَا تَأْتِنَا بِهٖ مِنْ اٰيَةٍ
لِّتَسْحَرَنَا بِهَا ۙ فَمَا نَحْنُ لَكَ
بِمُؤْمِنِيْنَ ۝ فَاَرْسَلْنَا عَلَيْهِمُ
الطُّوْفَانَ وَالْجَرَادَ وَالْقُمَّلَ
وَالضَّفَادِعَ وَالدَّمَ اٰيٰتٍ مُّفَصَّلٰتٍ ۙ
فَاسْتَكْبَرُوْا وَكَانُوْا قَوْمًا مُّجْرِمِيْنَ ۝
وَلَمَّا وَقَعَ عَلَيْهِمُ الرِّجْزُ قَالُوْا

and after you came to us." He said: "It may be that your Lord will destroy your enemy and make you inheritors in the earth; that so He may try you by your deeds."

130. We punished the people of Pharaoh with years (of droughts) and shortness of crops; that they might receive admonition.

131. But when good (times) came, they said, "This is due to us;" When gripped by calamity, they ascribed it to evil omens connected with Moses and those with him!

وَمِنْ بَعْدِ مَا جِئْتَنَا ۚ قَالَ عَسَىٰ

رَبُّكُمْ أَنْ يُّهْلِكَ عَدُوَّكُمْ

وَيَسْتَخْلِفَكُمْ فِى الْأَرْضِ فَيَنْظُرَ

كَيْفَ تَعْمَلُوْنَ ۩ وَلَقَدْ أَخَذْنَآ

اٰلَ فِرْعَوْنَ بِالسِّنِيْنَ وَنَقْصٍ

مِّنَ الثَّمَرَاتِ لَعَلَّهُمْ يَذَّكَّرُوْنَ ۩

فَإِذَا جَآءَتْهُمُ الْحَسَنَةُ قَالُوْا

لَنَا هٰذِهِ ۚ وَإِنْ تُصِبْهُمْ سَيِّئَةٌ

يَّطَّيَّرُوْا بِمُوْسَىٰ وَمَنْ مَّعَهٗ ۗ

Will you leave Moses and his people, to spread mischief in the land, and to abandon you and your gods?" He said: "Their male children will we slay; (only) their females will we save alive; and we have over them (power) irresistible."

128. Said Moses to his people: "Pray for help from Allah, and (wait) in patience and constancy: for the earth is Allah's, to give as a heritage to such of His servants as He pleases; and the end is (best) for the righteous.

129. They said: "We have had (nothing but) trouble, both before

أَتَذَرُ مُوسَى وَقَوْمَهُ لِيُفْسِدُوا

فِي الْأَرْضِ وَيَذَرَكَ وَآلِهَتَكَ ۚ

قَالَ سَنُقَتِّلُ أَبْنَاءَهُمْ وَنَسْتَحْيِ

نِسَاءَهُمْ وَإِنَّا فَوْقَهُمْ قَاهِرُونَ ﴿١٢٧﴾

قَالَ مُوسَى لِقَوْمِهِ اسْتَعِينُوا

بِاللَّهِ وَاصْبِرُوا ۖ إِنَّ الْأَرْضَ لِلَّهِ

يُورِثُهَا مَنْ يَشَاءُ مِنْ عِبَادِهِ ۖ

وَالْعَاقِبَةُ لِلْمُتَّقِينَ ﴿١٢٨﴾ قَالُوا

أُوذِينَا مِنْ قَبْلِ أَنْ تَأْتِينَا

the city to drive out its people: but soon shall you know (the consequences).

124. "Be sure I will cut off your hands and your feet on apposite sides, and I will cause you all to die on the cross."

125. They said: "For us, we are but sent back unto our Lord:

126. "But you do wreak your vengeance on us simply because we believed in the Signs of our Lord when they reached us! our Lord! pour out on us patience and constancy, and take our souls unto You as Muslims (who bow to Your Will)!

127. Said the chiefs of Pharaoh's people:"

الْمَدِينَةِ لِتُخْرِجُوا مِنْهَا أَهْلَهَا

فَسَوْفَ تَعْلَمُونَ ۞ لَأُقَطِّعَنَّ

أَيْدِيَكُمْ وَأَرْجُلَكُمْ مِنْ خِلَافٍ

ثُمَّ لَأُصَلِّبَنَّكُمْ أَجْمَعِينَ ۞ قَالُوٓا

إِنَّآ إِلَىٰ رَبِّنَا مُنقَلِبُونَ ۞ وَمَا

تَنقِمُ مِنَّآ إِلَّآ أَنْ ءَامَنَّا بِـَٔايَٰتِ

رَبِّنَا لَمَّا جَآءَتْنَا رَبَّنَآ أَفْرِغْ

عَلَيْنَا صَبْرًا وَتَوَفَّنَا مُسْلِمِينَ ۞

وَقَالَ الْمَلَأُ مِنْ قَوْمِ فِرْعَوْنَ

into Moses's mind by inspiration: "Throw (now) your staff": and behold! it swallows up straight away all the falsehoods which they fake!

118. Thus truth was confirmed, and all that they did was made of no effect.

119. So they (great ones) were vanquished there and then, and were made to look small.

120. But the sorcerers fell down prostrate in adoration.

121. Saying: "We believe in the Lord of the Worlds, -

122. "The Lord of Moses and Aaron."

123. Said Pharaoh: "Believe you in Him before I give you permission? Surely this is a trick which you have planned in

اِلٰى مُوْسٰٓى اَنْ اَلْقِ عَصَاكَ فَاِذَا

هِىَ تَلْقَفُ مَا يَأْفِكُوْنَ ۚ ۞ فَوَقَعَ

الْحَقُّ وَبَطَلَ مَا كَانُوْا يَعْمَلُوْنَ ۚ ۞

فَغُلِبُوْا هُنَالِكَ وَانْقَلَبُوْا صٰغِرِيْنَ ۚ ۞

وَاُلْقِىَ السَّحَرَةُ سٰجِدِيْنَ ۚ ۞ قَالُوْٓا

اٰمَنَّا بِرَبِّ الْعٰلَمِيْنَ ۙ ۞ رَبِّ

مُوْسٰى وَهٰرُوْنَ ۞ قَالَ فِرْعَوْنُ

اٰمَنْتُمْ بِهٖ قَبْلَ اَنْ اٰذَنَ لَكُمْ ۚ

اِنَّ هٰذَا لَمَكْرٌ مَّكَرْتُمُوْهُ فِى

112. And bring up to you all (our) sorcerers well-versed."

113. So there came the sorcerers to Pharaoh: they said, "Of course we shall have a (suitable) reward if we win!"

114. He said: "Yes, (and more),- for you shall in that case be (raised to posts) nearest (to my person)."

115. They said: "O Moses! Will you throw (first), or shall we have the (first) throw?"

116. Said Moses: "Throw you (first)." So when they threw, they bewitched the eyes of the people, and struck terror into them: for they showed a great (feat of) magic.

117. We put it

يَأْتُوكَ بِكُلِّ سَاحِرٍ عَلِيمٍ ۝

وَجَآءَ السَّحَرَةُ فِرْعَوْنَ قَالُوٓا

إِنَّ لَنَا لَأَجْرًا إِن كُنَّا نَحْنُ

الْغَالِبِينَ ۝ قَالَ نَعَمْ وَإِنَّكُمْ

لَمِنَ الْمُقَرَّبِينَ ۝ قَالُوا يَمُوسَىٰٓ إِمَّآ

أَن تُلْقِيَ وَإِمَّآ أَن نَّكُونَ نَحْنُ

الْمُلْقِينَ ۝ قَالَ أَلْقُوا ۖ فَلَمَّآ أَلْقَوْا

سَحَرُوٓا أَعْيُنَ النَّاسِ وَاسْتَرْهَبُوهُمْ

وَجَآءُو بِسِحْرٍ عَظِيمٍ ۝ وَأَوْحَيْنَآ

come with a Sign, show it forth, - if you tellest the truth."

107. Then (Moses) threw his staff, and behold! it was a serpent, plain (for all to see)!

108. And he drew out his hand, and behold! it was white to all beholders!

109. Said the chiefs of the people of Pharaoh: "This is indeed a sorcerer well-versed."

110. "His plan is to get you out of your land: then what is it you counsel?"

111. They said: "Keep him and his brother in suspense (for a while); and send to the cities men to collect -

جِئْتُ بِآيَةٍ فَأْتِ بِهَا إِنْ كُنْتَ

مِنَ الصَّادِقِينَ ۝ فَأَلْقَى عَصَاهُ

فَإِذَا هِيَ ثُعْبَانٌ مُبِينٌ ۝ وَنَزَعَ

يَدَهُ فَإِذَا هِيَ بَيْضَاءُ لِلنَّاظِرِينَ ۝

قَالَ الْمَلَأُ مِنْ قَوْمِ فِرْعَوْنَ

إِنَّ هَذَا لَسَاحِرٌ عَلِيمٌ ۝ يُرِيدُ

أَنْ يُخْرِجَكُمْ مِنْ أَرْضِكُمْ فَمَاذَا

تَأْمُرُونَ ۝ قَالُوا أَرْجِهْ وَأَخَاهُ

وَأَرْسِلْ فِي الْمَدَائِنِ حَاشِرِينَ ۝

with Our Signs to Pharaoh and his chiefs, but they wrongfully rejected them: so see what was the end of those who made mischief.

104. Moses said: "O Pharaoh! I am an Apostle from the Lord of the Worlds,-

105. One for whom it is right to say nothing but truth about Allah. Now have I come unto you (people), from your Lord, with a clear (Sign): so let the Children of Israel depart along with me."

106. (Pharaoh) said: "If indeed you have

بِـَٔايَٰتِنَآ إِلَىٰ فِرْعَوْنَ وَ مَلَإِيْهِ

فَظَلَمُوْا بِهَا ۚ فَانْظُرْ كَيْفَ كَانَ

عَاقِبَةُ الْمُفْسِدِيْنَ ۞ وَ قَالَ

مُوْسَىٰ يٰفِرْعَوْنُ إِنِّيْ رَسُوْلٌ

مِّنْ رَّبِّ الْعٰلَمِيْنَ ۞ حَقِيْقٌ

عَلَىٰ أَنْ لَّآ أَقُوْلَ عَلَى اللّٰهِ

إِلَّا الْحَقَّ ۚ قَدْ جِئْتُكُمْ بِبَيِّنَةٍ

مِّنْ رَّبِّكُمْ فَأَرْسِلْ مَعِيَ بَنِيْ

إِسْرَآءِيْلَ ۞ قَالَ إِنْ كُنْتَ

could not hear?

101. Such were the towns whose story We (thus) relate unto you: there came indeed to them their Apostles with clear (Signs): but they would not believe what they had rejected before. Thus does Allah seal up the hearts of those who reject Faith.

102. Most of them We found not men (true) to their covenant: but most of them We found rebellious and disobedient.

103. Then after them We sent Moses

يَسْمَعُوْنَ ۞ تِلْكَ الْقُرٰى نَقُصُّ

عَلَيْكَ مِنْ اَنْبَآئِهَا ۚ وَلَقَدْ

جَآءَتْهُمْ رُسُلُهُمْ بِالْبَيِّنٰتِ ۚ فَمَا

كَانُوْا لِيُؤْمِنُوْا بِمَا كَذَّبُوْا مِنْ

قَبْلُ ۚ كَذٰلِكَ يَطْبَعُ اللّٰهُ عَلٰى

قُلُوْبِ الْكٰفِرِيْنَ ۞ وَمَا وَجَدْنَا

لِاَكْثَرِهِمْ مِّنْ عَهْدٍ ۚ وَاِنْ

وَّجَدْنَاۤ اَكْثَرَهُمْ لَفٰسِقِيْنَ ۞

ثُمَّ بَعَثْنَا مِنْ بَعْدِهِمْ مُّوْسٰى

by night while they were asleep?

98. Or else did they feel secure against its coming in broad daylight while they played about (care-free)?

99. Did they then feel secure against the Plan of Allah? - but no one can feel secure from the Plan of Allah, except those (doomed) to ruin!

100. To those who inherit the earth in succession to its (previous) possessors, is it not a guiding, (lesson) that, if We so willed, We could punish them (too) for their sins, and seal up their hearts so that they

بَيَاتًا وَّهُمْ نَآئِمُوْنَ ۞ اَوَ

اَمِنَ اَهْلُ الْقُرٰٓى اَنْ يَّأْتِيَهُمْ

بَأْسُنَا ضُحًى وَّهُمْ يَلْعَبُوْنَ ۞

اَفَاَمِنُوْا مَكْرَ اللّٰهِ ۚ فَلَا يَأْمَنُ

مَكْرَ اللّٰهِ اِلَّا الْقَوْمُ الْخٰسِرُوْنَ ۞

اَوَلَمْ يَهْدِ لِلَّذِيْنَ يَرِثُوْنَ

الْاَرْضَ مِنْ بَعْدِ اَهْلِهَآ اَنْ

لَّوْ نَشَآءُ اَصَبْنٰهُمْ بِذُنُوْبِهِمْ ۚ

وَنَطْبَعُ عَلٰى قُلُوْبِهِمْ فَهُمْ لَا

We changed their suffering into prosperity, until they grew and multiplied, and began to say: "Our fathers (too) were touched by suffering and affluence" ... Behold! We called them to account of a sudden, while they realised not (their peril).

96. If the people of the towns had but believed and feared Allah, We should indeed have opened out to them (all kinds of) blessings from heaven and earth; but they rejected (the truth), and We brought them to book for their misdeeds.

97. Did the people of the towns feel secure against the coming of Our wrath

بَدَّلْنَا مَكَانَ السَّيِّئَةِ الْحَسَنَةَ

حَتّٰى عَفَوْا وَّقَالُوْا قَدْ مَسَّ

اٰبَآءَنَا الضَّرَّآءُ وَالسَّرَّآءُ فَاَخَذْنٰهُمْ

بَغْتَةً وَّهُمْ لَا يَشْعُرُوْنَ ۞ وَلَوْ

اَنَّ اَهْلَ الْقُرٰى اٰمَنُوْا وَاتَّقَوْا

لَفَتَحْنَا عَلَيْهِمْ بَرَكٰتٍ مِّنَ السَّمَآءِ

وَالْاَرْضِ وَلٰكِنْ كَذَّبُوْا فَاَخَذْنٰهُمْ

بِمَا كَانُوْا يَكْسِبُوْنَ ۞ اَفَاَمِنَ

اَهْلُ الْقُرٰى اَنْ يَّأْتِيَهُمْ بَأْسُنَا

Shu'aib became as if they had never been in the homes where they had flourished: the men who rejected Shu'aib - it was they who were ruined!

93. So Shu'aib left them, saying: "O my people! I did indeed convey to you the messages for which I was sent by my Lord: I gave you good counsel, but how shall I lament over a people who refuse to believe!"

94. Whenever We sent a Prophet to a town, We took up its people in suffering and adversity, in order that they might learn humility.

95. Then

شُعَيْبًا كَانُوا لَمْ يَغْنَوْا فِيهَا

الَّذِيْنَ كَذَّبُوا شُعَيْبًا كَانُوا

هُمُ الْخَسِرِيْنَ ۞ فَتَوَلَّى عَنْهُمْ

وَقَالَ يَقَوْمِ لَقَدْ اَبْلَغْتُكُمْ

رِسَلَتِ رَبِّيْ وَنَصَحْتُ لَكُمْ

فَكَيْفَ اَسَى عَلَى قَوْمٍ كَفِرِيْنَ ۞

وَمَآ اَرْسَلْنَا فِيْ قَرْيَةٍ مِّنْ

نَبِيٍّ اِلَّا اَخَذْنَا اَهْلَهَا بِالْبَاْسَاءِ

وَالضَّرَّآءِ لَعَلَّهُمْ يَضَّرَّعُوْنَ ۞ ثُمَّ

Our Lord. Our Lord can reach out to the utmost recesses of things by His knowledge. In the Allah is our trust. Our Lord! Decide You between us and our people in truth, for You are the best to decide."

90. The leaders, the unbelievers among his people, said: "If you follow Shu'aib, be sure then you are ruined!"

91. But the earthquake took them unawares, and they lay prostrate in their homes before the morning!

92. The men who reject

رَبَّنَا وَسِعَ رَبَّنَا كُلَّ شَىْءٍ

عِلْمًا عَلَى اللهِ تَوَكَّلْنَا رَبَّنَا

افْتَحْ بَيْنَنَا وَبَيْنَ قَوْمِنَا

بِالْحَقِّ وَأَنْتَ خَيْرُ الْفَاتِحِينَ ۝

وَقَالَ الْمَلَأُ الَّذِينَ كَفَرُوا

مِنْ قَوْمِهِ لَئِنِ اتَّبَعْتُمْ

شُعَيْبًا إِنَّكُمْ إِذًا لَّخَاسِرُونَ ۝

فَأَخَذَتْهُمُ الرَّجْفَةُ فَأَصْبَحُوا فِي

دَارِهِمْ جَاثِمِينَ ۝ الَّذِينَ كَذَّبُوا

88. The leaders, the arrogant party among his people, said: "O Shu'aib! We shall certainly drive you out of our city - (you) and those who believe with you; or else you (thou and they) shall have to return to our ways and religion." He said: "What! even though we do detest (them)?"

89. "We should indeed invent a lie against Allah, if we returned to your ways after Allah has rescued us therefrom; nor could we by any manner of means return thereto unless it be as in the will and plan of Allah,

قَالَ الْمَلَأُ الَّذِيْنَ اسْتَكْبَرُوْا

مِنْ قَوْمِهٖ لَنُخْرِجَنَّكَ يٰشُعَيْبُ

وَالَّذِيْنَ اٰمَنُوْا مَعَكَ مِنْ قَرْيَتِنَاۤ

اَوْ لَتَعُوْدُنَّ فِيْ مِلَّتِنَا ۚ قَالَ

اَوَلَوْ كُنَّا كٰرِهِيْنَ ۗ ﴿٨٨﴾ قَدِ افْتَرَيْنَا

عَلَى اللّٰهِ كَذِبًا اِنْ عُدْنَا فِيْ

مِلَّتِكُمْ بَعْدَ اِذْ نَجّٰنَا اللّٰهُ

مِنْهَا ۗ وَمَا يَكُوْنُ لَنَاۤ اَنْ

نَّعُوْدَ فِيْهَاۤ اِلَّاۤ اَنْ يَّشَاۤءَ اللّٰهُ

پاره

قَالَ الْمَلَاُ

(٩)

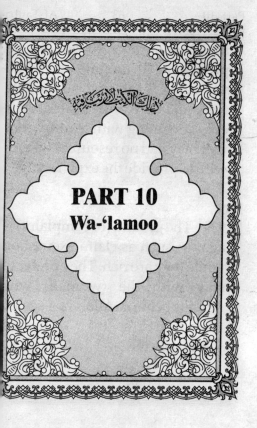

PART 10
Wa-'lamoo

those who came to you to be provided with mounts, and when you said, "I can find no mounts for you," they turned back, their eyes streaming with tears of grief that they had no resources wherewith to provide the expenses.

93. The ground (of complaint) is against such as claim exemption while they are rich. They prefer to stay with the (women) who remain behind: Allah has sealed their hearts; so they know not (what they miss).

الَّذِيْنَ اِذَا مَاۤ اَتَوْكَ لِتَحْمِلَهُمْ

قُلْتَ لَاۤ اَجِدُ مَاۤ اَحْمِلُكُمْ

عَلَيْهِ تَوَلَّوْا وَّاَعْيُنُهُمْ تَفِيْضُ

مِنَ الدَّمْعِ حَزَنًا اَلَّا يَجِدُوْا

مَا يُنْفِقُوْنَ ۞ اِنَّمَا السَّبِيْلُ

عَلَى الَّذِيْنَ يَسْتَاْذِنُوْنَكَ وَهُمْ

اَغْنِيَاۤءُ ۚ رَضُوْا بِاَنْ يَّكُوْنُوْا

مَعَ الْخَوَالِفِ وَطَبَعَ اللّٰهُ عَلٰى

قُلُوْبِهِمْ فَهُمْ لَا يَعْلَمُوْنَ ۞

and those who were false to Allah and His Apostle (merely) sat inactive. Soon will a grievous Chastisement seize the unbelievers among them.

91. There is no blame on those who are infirm, or ill, or who find no resources to spend (on the cause), if they are sincere (in duty) to Allah and His Apostle: no ground (of complaint) can there be against such as do right: and Allah is Oft-Forgiving, Most Merciful.

92. Nor (is there blame) on

وَقَعَدَ الَّذِيْنَ كَذَبُوا اللّٰهَ

وَرَسُوْلَهٗ ۚ سَيُصِيْبُ الَّذِيْنَ

كَفَرُوْا مِنْهُمْ عَذَابٌ اَلِيْمٌ ۞

لَيْسَ عَلَى الضُّعَفَآءِ وَلَا عَلَى

الْمَرْضٰى وَلَا عَلَى الَّذِيْنَ لَا

يَجِدُوْنَ مَا يُنْفِقُوْنَ حَرَجٌ

اِذَا نَصَحُوْا لِلّٰهِ وَرَسُوْلِهٖ ۚ مَا

عَلَى الْمُحْسِنِيْنَ مِنْ سَبِيْلٍ ۚ

وَاللّٰهُ غَفُوْرٌ رَّحِيْمٌ ۞ وَّلَا عَلَى

understand not.

88. But the Apostle, and those who believe with him, strive and fight with their wealth and their persons: for them are (all) good things: and it is they who will prosper.

89. Allah has prepared for them Gardens under which rivers flow, to dwell therein: that is the supreme felicity.

90. And there were, among the desert Arabs (also), men who made excuses and came to claim exemption;

يَّفْقَهُوْنَ ۞ لٰكِنِ الرَّسُوْلُ

وَالَّذِيْنَ اٰمَنُوْا مَعَهٗ جَاهَدُوْا

بِاَمْوَالِهِمْ وَاَنْفُسِهِمْ ۚ وَاُولٰٓئِكَ

لَهُمُ الْخَيْرٰتُ ۚ وَاُولٰٓئِكَ هُمُ

الْمُفْلِحُوْنَ ۞ اَعَدَّ اللّٰهُ لَهُمْ

جَنّٰتٍ تَجْرِىْ مِنْ تَحْتِهَا

الْاَنْهٰرُ خٰلِدِيْنَ فِيْهَا ۚ ذٰلِكَ

الْفَوْزُ الْعَظِيْمُ ۞ وَجَآءَ الْمُعَذِّرُوْنَ

مِنَ الْاَعْرَابِ لِيُؤْذَنَ لَهُمْ

Allah's plan is to punish them with these things in this world, and that their souls may perish in their (very) denial of Allah.

86. When a *Sura* comes down, enjoining them to believe in Allah and to strive and fight along with His Apostle, those with wealth and influence among them ask you for exemption, and say: "Leave us (behind): we would be with those who sit (at home)."

87. They prefer to be with (the women), who remain behind (at home): their hearts are sealed and so they

إِنَّمَا يُرِيْدُ اللهُ أَنْ يُّعَذِّبَهُمْ

بِهَا فِى الدُّنْيَا وَتَزْهَقَ أَنْفُسُهُمْ

وَهُمْ كٰفِرُوْنَ ۞ وَإِذَآ أُنْزِلَتْ

سُوْرَةٌ أَنْ اٰمِنُوْا بِاللهِ وَجَاهِدُوْا

مَعَ رَسُوْلِهِ اسْتَاْذَنَكَ أُولُوا

الطَّوْلِ مِنْهُمْ وَقَالُوْا ذَرْنَا

نَكُنْ مَّعَ الْقٰعِدِيْنَ ۞ رَضُوْا

بِأَنْ يَّكُوْنُوْا مَعَ الْخَوَالِفِ

وَطُبِعَ عَلٰى قُلُوْبِهِمْ فَهُمْ لَا

"Never shall you come out with me, nor fight an enemy with me: for you preferred to sit inactive on the first occasion: then sit you (now) with those who stayed behind."

84. Nor do you ever pray for any of them that dies, nor stand at his grave; for they rejected Allah and His Apostle, and died in a state of perverse rebellion.

85. Nor let their wealth nor their children dazzle you:

لَّنْ تَخْرُجُوْا مَعِيَ أَبَدًا وَّلَنْ
تُقَاتِلُوْا مَعِيَ عَدُوًّا ۭ إِنَّكُمْ
رَضِيتُمْ بِالْقُعُوْدِ أَوَّلَ مَرَّةٍ
فَاقْعُدُوْا مَعَ الْخٰلِفِيْنَ ۞ وَلَا
تُصَلِّ عَلٰۤى أَحَدٍ مِّنْهُمْ مَّاتَ
أَبَدًا وَّلَا تَقُمْ عَلٰى قَبْرِهٖ ۭ
إِنَّهُمْ كَفَرُوْا بِاللّٰهِ وَرَسُوْلِهٖ
وَمَاتُوْا وَهُمْ فٰسِقُوْنَ ۞ وَلَا
تُعْجِبْكَ أَمْوَالُهُمْ وَأَوْلَادُهُمْ

strive and fight, with their goods and their persons, in the cause of Allah: they said, "Go not forth in the heat." Say, "The Fire of Hell is fiercer in heat." If only they could understand!

82. Let them laugh a little: much will they weep: a recompense for the (evil) that they do.

83. If, then, Allah bring you back to any of them, and they ask your permission to come out (with you), say:

يُّجَاهِدُوْا بِاَمْوَالِهِمْ وَاَنْفُسِهِمْ

فِيْ سَبِيْلِ اللّٰهِ ۚ وَقَالُوْا لَا

تَنْفِرُوْا فِي الْحَرِّ ۗ قُلْ نَارُ

جَهَنَّمَ اَشَدُّ حَرًّا ۗ لَوْ كَانُوْا

يَفْقَهُوْنَ ۞ فَلْيَضْحَكُوْا قَلِيْلًا

وَّلْيَبْكُوْا كَثِيْرًا ۚ جَزَاءًۢ بِمَا

كَانُوْا يَكْسِبُوْنَ ۞ فَاِنْ رَّجَعَكَ

اللّٰهُ اِلٰى طَآئِفَةٍ مِّنْهُمْ

فَاسْتَاْذَنُوْكَ لِلْخُرُوْجِ فَقُلْ

on them: and they shall have a grievous Chastisement.

80. Whether you ask for their forgiveness, or not, (their sin is unforgivable): if you ask seventy times for their forgiveness, Allah will not forgive them: because they have rejected Allah and His Apostle: and Allah guides not those who are perversely rebellious.

81. Those who were left behind (in the Tabuk expedition) rejoiced in their inaction behind the back of the Apostle of Allah: they hated to

مِنْهُمْ وَلَهُمْ عَذَابٌ أَلِيمٌ ۞

اِسْتَغْفِرْ لَهُمْ أَوْ لَا تَسْتَغْفِرْ لَهُمْ

اِنْ تَسْتَغْفِرْ لَهُمْ سَبْعِينَ

مَرَّةً فَلَنْ يَّغْفِرَ اللهُ لَهُمْ

ذٰلِكَ بِأَنَّهُمْ كَفَرُوا بِاللهِ

وَرَسُولِهِ وَاللهُ لَا يَهْدِى

الْقَوْمَ الْفٰسِقِينَ ۞ فَرِحَ

الْمُخَلَّفُونَ بِمَقْعَدِهِمْ خِلٰفَ

رَسُولِ اللهِ وَكَرِهُوا أَنْ

whereon they shall meet Him: because they broke their covenant with Allah, and because they lied (again and again).

78. Know they not that Allah does know their secret (thoughts) and their secret counsels, and that Allah knows well all things Unseen?

79. Those who slander such of the believers as give themselves freely to (deeds of) charity, as well as such as can find nothing to give except the fruits of their labour, - and throw ridicule on them, - Allah will throw back their ridicule

يَلْقَوْنَهُ ۖ بِمَآ أَخْلَفُوا اللَّهَ مَا

وَعَدُوهُ وَبِمَا كَانُوا يَكْذِبُونَ ۞

أَلَمْ يَعْلَمُوٓا أَنَّ اللَّهَ يَعْلَمُ

سِرَّهُمْ وَنَجْوَىٰهُمْ وَأَنَّ

اللَّهَ عَلَّامُ الْغُيُوبِ ۞ الَّذِينَ

يَلْمِزُونَ الْمُطَّوِّعِينَ مِنَ

الْمُؤْمِنِينَ فِي الصَّدَقَتِ وَالَّذِينَ

لَا يَجِدُونَ إِلَّا جُهْدَهُمْ

فَيَسْخَرُونَ مِنْهُمْ ۖ سَخِرَ اللَّهُ

with a grievous Chastisement in this life and in the Hereafter: they shall have none on earth to protect or help them.

75.   Amongst them are men who made a covenant with Allah, that if He bestowed on them of His Bounty, they would give (largely) in charity, and be truly amongst those who are righteous.

76.   But when He did bestow of His Bounty, they became covetous, and turned back (from their covenant), averse (from its fulfilment).

77.   So He has put as a consequence hypocrisy into their hearts, (to last) till the Day,

اللهُ عَذَابًا اَلِيمًا فِي الدُّنْيَا

وَالْاٰخِرَةِ ۚ وَمَا لَهُمْ فِي الْاَرْضِ

مِنْ وَّلِيٍّ وَّلَا نَصِيرٍ ۞ وَمِنْهُمْ

مَّنْ عَاهَدَ اللهَ لَئِنْ اٰتٰنَا

مِنْ فَضْلِهِ لَنَصَّدَّقَنَّ وَلَنَكُوْنَنَّ

مِنَ الصّٰلِحِيْنَ ۞ فَلَمَّآ اٰتٰهُمْ

مِّنْ فَضْلِهِ بَخِلُوْا بِهِ وَتَوَلَّوْا

وَّهُمْ مُّعْرِضُوْنَ ۞ فَاَعْقَبَهُمْ

نِفَاقًا فِيْ قُلُوْبِهِمْ اِلٰى يَوْمِ

the unbelievers and the Hypocrites, and be firm against them.
Their abode is Hell, - an evil
refuge indeed.

74. They swear by Allah that
they said nothing (evil), but
indeed they uttered blasphemy,
and they did it after accepting
Islam; and they meditated a plot
which they were unable to carry
out: this revenge of theirs was
(their) only return for the bounty
with which Allah and His
Apostle had enriched them! If
they repent, it will be best for
them; but if they turn back (to
their evil ways), Allah will
punish them

الْكُفَّارَ وَالْمُنٰفِقِیْنَ وَاغْلُظْ عَلَیْهِمْ ۚ

وَمَأْوٰىهُمْ جَهَنَّمُ ؕ وَبِئْسَ الْمَصِیْرُ ۝

یَحْلِفُوْنَ بِاللّٰهِ مَا قَالُوْا ؕ وَلَقَدْ

قَالُوْا كَلِمَةَ الْكُفْرِ وَكَفَرُوْا

بَعْدَ اِسْلَامِهِمْ وَهَمُّوْا بِمَا لَمْ

یَنَالُوْا ۚ وَمَا نَقَمُوْۤا اِلَّاۤ اَنْ

اَغْنٰىهُمُ اللّٰهُ وَرَسُوْلُهٗ مِنْ

فَضْلِهٖ ؕ فَاِنْ یَّتُوْبُوْا یَكُ خَیْرًا

لَّهُمْ ۚ وَاِنْ یَّتَوَلَّوْا یُعَذِّبْهُمُ

Charity, and obey Allah and His Apostle. On them will Allah pour His mercy: for Allah is Exalted in power, Wise.

72. Allah has promised to believers, men and women, Gardens under which rivers flow, to dwell therein, and beautiful mansions in Gardens of everlasting bliss. But the greatest bliss is the good pleasure of Allah: that is the supreme felicity.

73. O Prophet! Strive hard against

الزَّكٰوةَ وَيُطِيعُوْنَ اللّٰهَ وَرَسُوْلَهٗ ۚ

اُولٰٓئِكَ سَيَرْحَمُهُمُ اللّٰهُ ؕ اِنَّ

اللّٰهَ عَزِيْزٌ حَكِيْمٌ ۝ وَعَدَ اللّٰهُ

الْمُؤْمِنِيْنَ وَالْمُؤْمِنٰتِ جَنّٰتٍ

تَجْرِيْ مِنْ تَحْتِهَا الْاَنْهٰرُ

خٰلِدِيْنَ فِيْهَا وَمَسٰكِنَ طَيِّبَةً

فِيْ جَنّٰتِ عَدْنٍ ؕ وَرِضْوَانٌ مِّنَ

اللّٰهِ اَكْبَرُ ؕ ذٰلِكَ هُوَ الْفَوْزُ

الْعَظِيْمُ ۝ يٰٓاَيُّهَا النَّبِيُّ جَاهِدِ

the People of Noah, and 'Ad, and Thamud; the People of Abraham, the men of Midian, and the cities overthrown. To them came their Apostles with clear Signs. It is not Allah Who wrongs them, but they wrong their own souls.

71. The believers, men and women, are protectors one of another: they enjoin what is just, and forbid what is evil: they observe regular Prayers, practise regular

قَوْمِ نُوْحٍ وَّعَادٍ وَّثَمُوْدَهُ

وَقَوْمِ اِبْرٰهِيْمَ وَاَصْحٰبِ مَدْيَنَ

وَالْمُؤْتَفِكٰتِ ۚ اَتَتْهُمْ رُسُلُهُمْ

بِالْبَيِّنٰتِ ۚ فَمَا كَانَ اللّٰهُ

لِيَظْلِمَهُمْ وَلٰكِنْ كَانُوْا اَنْفُسَهُمْ

يَظْلِمُوْنَ ۞ وَالْمُؤْمِنُوْنَ وَالْمُؤْمِنٰتُ

بَعْضُهُمْ اَوْلِيَآءُ بَعْضٍ ۚ يَأْمُرُوْنَ

بِالْمَعْرُوْفِ وَيَنْهَوْنَ عَنِ الْمُنْكَرِ

وَيُقِيْمُوْنَ الصَّلٰوةَ وَيُؤْتُوْنَ

before you: they were mightier than you in power, and more flourishing in wealth and children. They had their enjoyment of their portion: and you have of yours, as did those before you; and you indulge in idle talk as they did. They! - their work are fruitless in this world and in the Hereafter, and they will lose (all spiritual good).

70. Has not the story reached them of those before them? -

قَبْلِكُمْ كَانُوْا أَشَدَّ مِنْكُمْ

قُوَّةً وَّ أَكْثَرَ أَمْوَالًا وَّ أَوْلَادًا

فَاسْتَمْتَعُوْا بِخَلَاقِهِمْ فَاسْتَمْتَعْتُمْ

بِخَلَاقِكُمْ كَمَا اسْتَمْتَعَ الَّذِيْنَ

مِنْ قَبْلِكُمْ بِخَلَاقِهِمْ وَخُضْتُمْ

كَالَّذِيْ خَاضُوْا أُولٰٓئِكَ حَبِطَتْ

أَعْمَالُهُمْ فِي الدُّنْيَا وَالْاٰخِرَةِ

وَأُولٰٓئِكَ هُمُ الْخٰسِرُوْنَ ۩ أَلَمْ

يَأْتِهِمْ نَبَأُ الَّذِيْنَ مِنْ قَبْلِهِمْ

and women, (have an understanding) with each other: they
enjoin evil, and forbid what is
just, and are close with their
hands. They have forgotten
Allah; so He has forgotten them.
Verily the Hypocrites are rebellious and per verse.

68. Allah has promised the
Hypocrites men and women, and
the rejecters, of Faith, the Fire of
Hell: therein shall they dwell:
sufficient is it for them: for them is
the curse of Allah, and an enduring punishment, -

69. As in the case of those

وَالْمُنٰفِقُتُ بَعْضُهُمْ مِّنْ بَعْضٍ ۚ

يَأْمُرُوْنَ بِالْمُنْكَرِ وَيَنْهَوْنَ عَنِ

الْمَعْرُوْفِ وَيَقْبِضُوْنَ اَيْدِيَهُمْ ۗ نَسُوا

اللّٰهَ فَنَسِيَهُمْ ۗ اِنَّ الْمُنٰفِقِيْنَ

هُمُ الْفٰسِقُوْنَ ۞ وَعَدَ اللّٰهُ

الْمُنٰفِقِيْنَ وَالْمُنٰفِقُتِ وَالْكُفَّارَ

نَارَ جَهَنَّمَ خٰلِدِيْنَ فِيْهَا ۗ هِيَ

حَسْبُهُمْ ۚ وَلَعَنَهُمُ اللّٰهُ ۚ وَلَهُمْ

عَذَابٌ مُّقِيْمٌ ۙ ۞ كَالَّذِيْنَ مِنْ

Say: "Mock you! But verily Allah will bring to light all that you fear (should be revealed).

65. If you question them, they declare (with emphasis): "We were only talking idly and in play." Say: "Was it at Allah, and His Signs, and His Apostle, that you were mocking?"

66. Make you no excuses: you have rejected Faith after you had accepted it. If We pardon some of you, We will punish others amongst you, for that they are sinners.

67. The Hypocrites, men

قُلِ اسْتَهْزِءُوا ۚ إِنَّ اللَّهَ مُخْرِجٌ

مَّا تَحْذَرُونَ ۞ وَلَئِن سَأَلْتَهُمْ

لَيَقُولُنَّ إِنَّمَا كُنَّا نَخُوضُ

وَنَلْعَبُ ۚ قُلْ أَبِاللَّهِ وَآيَتِهِ

وَرَسُولِهِ كُنتُمْ تَسْتَهْزِءُونَ ۞

لَا تَعْتَذِرُوا قَدْ كَفَرْتُم بَعْدَ

إِيمَانِكُمْ ۚ إِن نَّعْفُ عَن طَآئِفَةٍ

مِّنكُمْ نُعَذِّبْ طَآئِفَةً بِأَنَّهُمْ

كَانُوا مُجْرِمِينَ ۞ ٱلْمُنَٰفِقُونَ

62. To you they swear by Allah. In order to please you: but it is more fitting that they should please Allah and His Apostle, if they are believers.

63. Know they not that for those who oppose Allah and His Apostle, is the Fire of Hell?-wherein they shall dwell. That is the supreme disgrace.

64. The Hypocrites are afraid lest a Sura should be sent down about them, showing them what is (really passing) in their hearts.

اَلِيْمٌ ۞ يَحْلِفُوْنَ بِاللّٰهِ لَكُمْ

لِيُرْضُوْكُمْ ۚ وَاللّٰهُ وَرَسُوْلُهٗٓ

اَحَقُّ اَنْ يُّرْضُوْهُ اِنْ كَانُوْا

مُؤْمِنِيْنَ ۞ اَلَمْ يَعْلَمُوْٓا اَنَّهٗ

مَنْ يُّحَادِدِ اللّٰهَ وَرَسُوْلَهٗ فَاَنَّ

لَهٗ نَارَ جَهَنَّمَ خَالِدًا فِيْهَا ۚ

ذٰلِكَ الْخِزْيُ الْعَظِيْمُ ۞ يَحْذَرُ

الْمُنٰفِقُوْنَ اَنْ تُنَزَّلَ عَلَيْهِمْ

سُوْرَةٌ تُنَبِّئُهُمْ بِمَا فِيْ قُلُوْبِهِمْ ۚ

whose hearts have been (recently) reconciled (to Truth); for those in bondage and in debt; in the cause of Allah; and for the wayfarer: (thus is it) ordained by Allah, and Allah is full of knowledge and wisdom.

61. Among them are men who slander the Prophet and say, "He is (all) ear." Say, "He listens to what is best for you: he believes in Allah, has faith in the believers, and is a Mercy to those of you who believe." But those who slander the Apostle will have a grievous Chastisement.

قُلُوبُهُمْ وَفِي الرِّقَابِ وَالْغَارِمِيْنَ

وَفِيْ سَبِيْلِ اللَّهِ وَابْنِ السَّبِيْلِ

فَرِيْضَةً مِّنَ اللَّهِ ۗ وَاللَّهُ عَلِيْمٌ

حَكِيْمٌ ۞ وَمِنْهُمُ الَّذِيْنَ يُؤْذُوْنَ

النَّبِيَّ وَيَقُوْلُوْنَ هُوَ أُذُنٌ ۚ قُلْ

أُذُنُ خَيْرٍ لَّكُمْ يُؤْمِنُ بِاللَّهِ

وَيُؤْمِنُ لِلْمُؤْمِنِيْنَ وَرَحْمَةٌ

لِّلَّذِيْنَ اٰمَنُوْا مِنْكُمْ ۚ وَالَّذِيْنَ

يُؤْذُوْنَ رَسُوْلَ اللَّهِ لَهُمْ عَذَابٌ

are men who slander you in the matter of (the distribution of) the alms: if they are given part thereof, they are pleased, but if not, behold! they are indignant!

59. If only they had been content with what Allah and His Apostle gave them, and had said, "Sufficient unto us is Allah! Allah and His Apostle will soon give us of His Bounty: to Allah do we turn our hopes!" (that would have been the right course).

60. Alms are for the poor and the needy, and those employed to administer the (funds); for those

مَنْ يَلْمِزُكَ فِى الصَّدَقَٰتِ ۚ فَإِنْ

أُعْطُوا مِنْهَا رَضُوا وَإِن لَّمْ

يُعْطَوْا مِنْهَآ إِذَا هُمْ يَسْخَطُونَ ۝

وَلَوْ أَنَّهُمْ رَضُوا مَآ ءَاتَٮٰهُمُ اللَّهُ

وَرَسُولُهُۥ وَقَالُوا حَسْبُنَا اللَّهُ

سَيُؤْتِينَا اللَّهُ مِن فَضْلِهِۦ وَرَسُولُهُۥٓ

إِنَّآ إِلَى اللَّهِ رَٰغِبُونَ ۝ إِنَّمَا

الصَّدَقَٰتُ لِلْفُقَرَآءِ وَالْمَسَٰكِينِ

وَالْعَٰمِلِينَ عَلَيْهَا وَالْمُؤَلَّفَةِ

unwillingly.

55. Let not their wealth nor their (following in) sons dazzle you: in reality Allah's plan is to punish them with these things in this life, and that their souls may perish in their (very) denial of Allah.

56. They swear by Allah that they are indeed of you; but they are not of you: yet they are afraid (of you).

57. If they could find a place to flee to, or caves, or a place of concealment, they would turn straight way thereto, with an obstinate rush.

58. And among them

كِرِهُوْنَ ۞ فَلَا تُعْجِبْكَ اَمْوَالُهُمْ

وَلَآ اَوْلَادُهُمْ ۚ اِنَّمَا يُرِيْدُ اللّٰهُ

لِيُعَذِّبَهُمْ بِهَا فِي الْحَيٰوةِ الدُّنْيَا

وَتَزْهَقَ اَنْفُسُهُمْ وَهُمْ كٰفِرُوْنَ ۞

وَيَحْلِفُوْنَ بِاللّٰهِ اِنَّهُمْ لَمِنْكُمْ

وَمَا هُمْ مِّنْكُمْ وَلٰكِنَّهُمْ قَوْمٌ

يَّفْرَقُوْنَ ۞ لَوْ يَجِدُوْنَ مَلْجَاً

اَوْ مَغٰرٰتٍ اَوْ مُدَّخَلًا لَّوَلَّوْا

اِلَيْهِ وَهُمْ يَجْمَحُوْنَ ۞ وَمِنْهُمْ

from Himself, or by our hands. So wait (ex-pectant); we too will wait with you."

53. Say: "Spend (for the cause) willingly or unwillingly: not from you will it be accepted: for you are indeed a people rebellious and wicked."

54. The only reasons why their contributions are not accepted are: that they reject Allah and His Apostle; that they come to prayer without retuctantly and that they offer contributions

مِّنْ عِنْدِهٖ اَوْ بِاَيْدِيْنَا فَتَرَبَّصُوْا

اِنَّا مَعَكُمْ مُّتَرَبِّصُوْنَ ۞ قُلْ

اَنْفِقُوْا طَوْعًا اَوْ كَرْهًا لَّنْ

يُّتَقَبَّلَ مِنْكُمْ ط اِنَّكُمْ كُنْتُمْ

قَوْمًا فٰسِقِيْنَ ۞ وَمَا مَنَعَهُمْ

اَنْ تُقْبَلَ مِنْهُمْ نَفَقٰتُهُمْ اِلَّا

اَنَّهُمْ كَفَرُوْا بِاللّٰهِ وَبِرَسُوْلِهٖ

وَلَا يَاْتُوْنَ الصَّلٰوةَ اِلَّا وَهُمْ

كُسَالٰى وَلَا يُنْفِقُوْنَ اِلَّا وَهُمْ

a misfortune befalls you, they say, "We took indeed our precautions beforehand," and they turn away rejoicing.

51. Say: "Nothing will happen to us except what Allah has decreed for us: He is our Protector": and on Allah let the believers put their trust.

52. Say: "Can you expect for us (any fate) other than one of two glorious things - (martyrdom or victory)? But we can expect for you either that Allah will send His punishment

تُصِبْكَ مُصِيبَةٌ يَّقُوْلُوْا قَدْ

اَخَذْنَاۤ اَمْرَنَا مِنْ قَبْلُ

وَيَتَوَلَّوْا وَّهُمْ فَرِحُوْنَ ۞ قُلْ

لَّنْ يُّصِيْبَنَاۤ اِلَّا مَا كَتَبَ اللّٰهُ

لَنَا ۚ هُوَ مَوْلٰىنَا ۚ وَعَلَى اللّٰهِ

فَلْيَتَوَكَّلِ الْمُؤْمِنُوْنَ ۞ قُلْ

هَلْ تَرَبَّصُوْنَ بِنَاۤ اِلَّاۤ اِحْدَى

الْحُسْنَيَيْنِ ۚ وَنَحْنُ نَتَرَبَّصُ

بِكُمْ اَنْ يُّصِيْبَكُمُ اللّٰهُ بِعَذَابٍ

who would have listened to them. But Allah knows well those who do wrong.

48. Indeed they had plotted sedition before, and upset matters for you, until, - the Truth arrived, and the Decree of Allah became manifest much to their disgust.

49. Among them is (many) a man who says: "Grant me exemption and draw me not into trial." Have they not fallen into trial already? And indeed Hell surrounds the unbelievers (on all sides).

50. If good befalls you, it grieves them; but if

سَمّٰعُوْنَ لَهُمْ ۗ وَاللّٰهُ عَلِيْمٌۢ

بِالظّٰلِمِيْنَ ۞ لَقَدِ ابْتَغَوُا الْفِتْنَةَ

مِنْ قَبْلُ وَقَلَّبُوْا لَكَ الْاُمُوْرَ

حَتّٰى جَآءَ الْحَقُّ وَظَهَرَ اَمْرُ

اللّٰهِ وَهُمْ كٰرِهُوْنَ ۞ وَمِنْهُمْ

مَّنْ يَّقُوْلُ ائْذَنْ لِّيْ وَلَا

تَفْتِنِّيْ ۗ اَلَا فِي الْفِتْنَةِ سَقَطُوْا ۗ

وَاِنَّ جَهَنَّمَ لَمُحِيْطَةٌۢ بِالْكٰفِرِيْنَ ۞

اِنْ تُصِبْكَ حَسَنَةٌ تَسُؤْهُمْ ۚ وَاِنْ

who believe not in Allah and the Last Day, and whose hearts are in doubt, so that they are tossed in their doubts here and there.

46. If they had intended to come out, they would certainly have made some preparation therefor; but Allah was averse to their being sent forth; so He made them lag behind, and they were told, "Sit you among those who sit (inactive)."

47. If they had come out with you, they would not have added to your (strength) but only (made for) disorder, hurrying here and there in your midst and sowing sedition among you, and there would have been some among you

الَّذِينَ لَا يُؤْمِنُونَ بِاللهِ وَالْيَوْمِ

الْآخِرِ وَارْتَابَتْ قُلُوبُهُمْ فَهُمْ

فِى رَيْبِهِمْ يَتَرَدَّدُونَ ۞ وَلَوْ

اَرَادُوا الْخُرُوجَ لَاَعَدُّوا لَهُ

عُدَّةً وَّلٰكِنْ كَرِهَ اللهُ انْبِعَاثَهُمْ

فَثَبَّطَهُمْ وَقِيلَ اقْعُدُوا مَعَ

الْقٰعِدِينَ ۞ لَوْ خَرَجُوا فِيكُمْ مَّا

زَادُوكُمْ اِلَّا خَبَالًا وَّلَاَوْضَعُوا

خِلٰلَكُمْ يَبْغُونَكُمُ الْفِتْنَةَ وَفِيكُمْ

we should certainly have come out with you": they would destroy their own souls; for Allah does knows that they are certainly lying.

43. Allah give you grace! Why did you grant them exemption until those who told the truth were seen by you in a clear light, and you had proved the liars?

44. Those who believe in Allah and the Last Day ask you for no exemption from fighting with their goods and persons. And Allah knows well those who do their duty.

45. Only those ask you for exemption

لَخَرَجُوا مَعَكُمْ يُهْلِكُونَ أَنْفُسَهُمْ

وَاللّٰهُ يَعْلَمُ إِنَّهُمْ لَكَاذِبُونَ ۞

عَفَا اللّٰهُ عَنْكَ لِمَ أَذِنْتَ

لَهُمْ حَتّٰى يَتَبَيَّنَ لَكَ الَّذِينَ

صَدَقُوا وَتَعْلَمَ الْكَاذِبِينَ ۞ لَا

يَسْتَأْذِنُكَ الَّذِينَ يُؤْمِنُونَ بِاللّٰهِ

وَالْيَوْمِ الْاٰخِرِ أَنْ يُجَاهِدُوا

بِأَمْوَالِهِمْ وَأَنْفُسِهِمْ وَاللّٰهُ عَلِيمٌ

بِالْمُتَّقِينَ ۞ إِنَّمَا يَسْتَأْذِنُكَ

But the word of Allah is exalted to the heights: for Allah is Exalted in Might, Wise.

41. Go you forth, (whether equipped) lightly or heavily, and strive and struggle, with your goods and your persons, in the cause of Allah. That is best for you, if you (but) knew.

42. If there had been immediate gain (in sight), and the journey easy, they would (all) without doubt have followed you, but the distance was long, (and weighed) on them. They would indeed swear by Allah, "If we only could,

السُّفْلٰى ۚ وَكَلِمَةُ اللّٰهِ هِىَ

الْعُلْيَا ۗ وَاللّٰهُ عَزِيْزٌ حَكِيْمٌ ۞

اِنْفِرُوْا خِفَافًا وَّثِقَالًا وَّجَاهِدُوْا

بِاَمْوَالِكُمْ وَاَنْفُسِكُمْ فِىْ سَبِيْلِ

اللّٰهِ ۚ ذٰلِكُمْ خَيْرٌ لَّكُمْ اِنْ كُنْتُمْ

تَعْلَمُوْنَ ۞ لَوْ كَانَ عَرَضًا قَرِيْبًا

وَّسَفَرًا قَاصِدًا لَّاتَّبَعُوْكَ

وَلٰكِنْۢ بَعُدَتْ عَلَيْهِمُ الشُّقَّةُ ۗ

وَسَيَحْلِفُوْنَ بِاللّٰهِ لَوِ اسْتَطَعْنَا

in your place; but Him you would not harm in the least. For Allah has power over all things.

40. If you help not (your leader), (it is no matter): for Allah did indeed help him, when the unbelievers drove him out: he had no more than one companion; they two were in the cave, and he said to his companion, "Have no fear, for Allah is with us": then Allah sent down His peace upon him, and strengthened him with forces which you saw not, and humbled to the depths the word of the unbelievers.

غَيْرَكُمْ وَلَا تَضُرُّوهُ شَيْئًا ۗ

وَاللَّهُ عَلَىٰ كُلِّ شَيْءٍ قَدِيرٌ ۞

إِلَّا تَنْصُرُوهُ فَقَدْ نَصَرَهُ اللَّهُ

إِذْ أَخْرَجَهُ الَّذِينَ كَفَرُوا ثَانِيَ

اثْنَيْنِ إِذْ هُمَا فِى الْغَارِ إِذْ

يَقُولُ لِصَاحِبِهِ لَا تَحْزَنْ إِنَّ

اللَّهَ مَعَنَا ۖ فَأَنْزَلَ اللَّهُ سَكِينَتَهُ

عَلَيْهِ وَأَيَّدَهُ بِجُنُودٍ لَّمْ تَرَوْهَا

وَجَعَلَ كَلِمَةَ الَّذِينَ كَفَرُوا

guides not those who reject Faith.

38. O you who believe! What is the matter with you, that, when you are asked to go forth in the cause of Allah, you cling heavily to the earth? Do you prefer the life of this world to the Hereafter? But little is the comfort of this life, as compared with the Hereafter.

39. Unless you go forth, He will punish you with a grievous Chastisement, and put others

لَا يَهْدِى الْقَوْمَ الْكٰفِرِيْنَ ۞

يٰٓاَيُّهَا الَّذِيْنَ اٰمَنُوْا مَا لَكُمْ

اِذَا قِيْلَ لَكُمُ انْفِرُوْا فِيْ

سَبِيْلِ اللّٰهِ اثَّاقَلْتُمْ اِلَى

الْاَرْضِ ٱرَضِيْتُمْ بِالْحَيٰوةِ

الدُّنْيَا مِنَ الْاٰخِرَةِ ۚ فَمَا مَتَاعُ

الْحَيٰوةِ الدُّنْيَا فِي الْاٰخِرَةِ اِلَّا

قَلِيْلٌ ۞ اِلَّا تَنْفِرُوْا يُعَذِّبْكُمْ

عَذَابًا اَلِيْمًا ۙ وَّيَسْتَبْدِلْ قَوْمًا

yourselves therein, and fight the Pagans all together as they fight you all together. But know that Allah is with those who restrain themselves.

37. Verily the transposing (of a prohibited month) is an addition to Unbelief: the unbelievers are led to wrong thereby: for they make it lawful one year, and forbidden another year, in order to adjust the number of months forbidden by Allah and make such forbidden ones lawful. The evil of their course seems pleasing to them. But Allah

اَنْفُسِكُمْ وَ قَاتِلُوا الْمُشْرِكِيْنَ

كَآفَّةً كَمَا يُقَاتِلُوْنَكُمْ كَآفَّةً

وَاعْلَمُوْا اَنَّ اللّٰهَ مَعَ الْمُتَّقِيْنَ ۞

اِنَّمَا النَّسِيْٓءُ زِيَادَةٌ فِي الْكُفْرِ

يُضَلُّ بِهِ الَّذِيْنَ كَفَرُوْا

يُحِلُّوْنَهٗ عَامًا وَّيُحَرِّمُوْنَهٗ

عَامًا لِّيُوَاطِئُوْا عِدَّةَ مَا حَرَّمَ

اللّٰهُ فَيُحِلُّوْا مَا حَرَّمَ اللّٰهُ

زُيِّنَ لَهُمْ سُوْٓءُ اَعْمَالِهِمْ وَاللّٰهُ

of that (wealth) in the fire of Hell, and with it will be branded their foreheads, their flanks, and their backs - "This is the (treasure) which you hoarded for yourselves: taste you, then, the (treasures) you hoarded!"

36. The number of months in the sight of Allah is twelve (in a year) - so ordained by Him the day He created the heavens and the earth; of them four are sacred: that is the straight usage. So wrong not

عَلَيْهَا فِىْ نَارِ جَهَنَّمَ فَتُكْوٰى بِهَا

جِبَاهُهُمْ وَجُنُوْبُهُمْ وَظُهُوْرُهُمْ ۖ

هٰذَا مَا كَنَزْتُمْ لِاَنْفُسِكُمْ

فَذُوْقُوْا مَا كُنْتُمْ تَكْنِزُوْنَ ۞

اِنَّ عِدَّةَ الشُّهُوْرِ عِنْدَ اللّٰهِ

اثْنَا عَشَرَ شَهْرًا فِىْ كِتٰبِ اللّٰهِ

يَوْمَ خَلَقَ السَّمٰوٰتِ وَالْاَرْضَ

مِنْهَآ اَرْبَعَةٌ حُرُمٌ ۚ ذٰلِكَ الدِّيْنُ

الْقَيِّمُ ۙ فَلَا تَظْلِمُوْا فِيْهِنَّ

of Truth, to proclaim it over all religion, even though the Pagans may detest (it).

34. O you who believe! There are indeed many among the priests and anchorites, who in Falsehood devour the substance of men and hinder (them) from the way of Allah. And there are those who hoard gold and silver and spend it not in the way of Allah: announce unto them a most grievous Chastisement -

35. On the Day when heat will be produced out

الْحَقِّ لِيُظْهِرَهُ عَلَى الدِّينِ كُلِّهِ

وَلَوْ كَرِهَ الْمُشْرِكُونَ ۝ يَآ اَيُّهَا

الَّذِينَ اٰمَنُوٓا اِنَّ كَثِيرًا مِّنَ

الْاَحْبَارِ وَالرُّهْبَانِ لَيَأْكُلُونَ اَمْوَالَ

النَّاسِ بِالْبَاطِلِ وَيَصُدُّونَ عَنْ

سَبِيلِ اللهِ ۗ وَالَّذِينَ يَكْنِزُونَ

الذَّهَبَ وَالْفِضَّةَ وَلَا يُنْفِقُونَهَا

فِيْ سَبِيلِ اللهِ فَبَشِّرْهُمْ

بِعَذَابٍ اَلِيمٍ ۝ يَوْمَ يُحْمَىٰ

their priests and their anchorites to be their lords in derogation of Allah, and (they take as their Lord) Christ the son of Mary; yet they were commanded to worship but One Allah: there is no Allah but He. Praise and glory to Him: (far is He) from having the partners they associate (with Him).

32. They wish to extinguish Allah's light with their mouths, but Allah will not allow but that His light should be perfected, even though the unbelievers may detest (it).

33. It is He Who has sent His Apostle with guidance and the Religion

اَحْبَارَهُمْ وَرُهْبَانَهُمْ اَرْبَابًا مِّنْ

دُوْنِ اللهِ وَالْمَسِيْحَ ابْنَ مَرْيَمَ ۚ

وَمَا اُمِرُوْا اِلَّا لِيَعْبُدُوْا اِلٰهًا

وَّاحِدًا ۚ لَا اِلٰهَ اِلَّا هُوَ ۚ سُبْحٰنَهُ

عَمَّا يُشْرِكُوْنَ ۩ يُرِيْدُوْنَ اَنْ

يُّطْفِئُوْا نُوْرَ اللهِ بِاَفْوَاهِهِمْ

وَيَاْبَى اللهُ اِلَّا اَنْ يُّتِمَّ نُوْرَهٗ

وَلَوْ كَرِهَ الْكٰفِرُوْنَ ۩ هُوَ الَّذِيْ

اَرْسَلَ رَسُوْلَهٗ بِالْهُدٰى وَدِيْنِ

acknowledge the religion of Truth, (even if they are) of the People of the Book, until they pay the Jizya with willing submission, and feel themselves subdued.

30. The Jews call 'Uzair a son of Allah, and the Christians call Christ the son of Allah. That is a saying from their mouth;(in this) they but imitate what the unbelievers of old used to say. Allah's curse be on them: how they are deluded away from the Truth!

31. They take

يَدِينُوْنَ دِيْنَ الْحَقِّ مِنَ

الَّذِيْنَ أُوْتُوا الْكِتٰبَ حَتّٰى

يُعْطُوا الْجِزْيَةَ عَنْ يَّدٍ وَّهُمْ

صٰغِرُوْنَ ۩ وَقَالَتِ الْيَهُوْدُ عُزَيْرُ

ابْنُ اللّٰهِ وَقَالَتِ النَّصٰرَى

الْمَسِيْحُ ابْنُ اللّٰهِ ذٰلِكَ قَوْلُهُمْ

بِأَفْوَاهِهِمْ يُضَاهِئُوْنَ قَوْلَ

الَّذِيْنَ كَفَرُوْا مِنْ قَبْلُ قٰتَلَهُمُ

اللّٰهُ أَنّٰى يُؤْفَكُوْنَ ۩ اتَّخَذُوْا

who believe! Truly the Pagans are unclean; so let them not, after this year of theirs, approach the Sacred Mosque. And if you fear poverty, soon will Allah enrich you, if He wills, out of His bounty, for Allah is All-Knowing, All-Wise.

29.   Fight those who believe not in Allah nor the Last Day, nor hold that forbidden which has been forbidden by Allah and His Apostle, nor

الَّذِيْنَ اٰمَنُوْۤا اِنَّمَا الْمُشْرِكُوْنَ

نَجَسٌ فَلَا يَقْرَبُوا الْمَسْجِدَ

الْحَرَامَ بَعْدَ عَامِهِمْ هٰذَا ۚ وَاِنْ

خِفْتُمْ عَيْلَةً فَسَوْفَ يُغْنِيْكُمُ

اللّٰهُ مِنْ فَضْلِهٖۤ اِنْ شَآءَ ؕ

اِنَّ اللّٰهَ عَلِيْمٌ حَكِيْمٌ ۞ قَاتِلُوا

الَّذِيْنَ لَا يُؤْمِنُوْنَ بِاللّٰهِ وَلَا

بِالْيَوْمِ الْاٰخِرِ وَلَا يُحَرِّمُوْنَ

مَا حَرَّمَ اللّٰهُ وَرَسُوْلُهٗ وَلَا

the land, for all that it is wide, did constrain you, and you turned back in retreat.

26. But Allah did pour His calm on the Apostle and on the believers, and sent down forces which you saw not: He punished the unbelievers; thus does He reward those without Faith.

27. Again will Allah, after this, turn (in mercy) to whom He will: for Allah is Oft-Forgiving, Most Merciful.

28. O you

وَضَاقَتْ عَلَيْكُمُ الْأَرْضُ بِمَا

رَحُبَتْ ثُمَّ وَلَّيْتُمْ مُّدْبِرِينَ ۞

ثُمَّ اَنْزَلَ اللهُ سَكِينَتَهُ عَلَى

رَسُوْلِهِ وَعَلَى الْمُؤْمِنِيْنَ وَاَنْزَلَ

جُنُوْدًا لَّمْ تَرَوْهَا وَعَذَّبَ

الَّذِيْنَ كَفَرُوْا وَذٰلِكَ جَزَآءُ

الْكٰفِرِيْنَ ۞ ثُمَّ يَتُوْبُ اللهُ مِنْ

بَعْدِ ذٰلِكَ عَلَى مَنْ يَّشَآءُ

وَاللهُ غَفُوْرٌ رَّحِيْمٌ ۞ يٰٓاَيُّهَا

that you have gained; the commerce in which you fear a decline: or the dwellings in which you delight - are dearer to you than Allah, or His Apostle, or the striving in His cause; - then wait until Allah brings about His decision: and Allah guides not the rebellious.

25. Assuredly Allah did help you in many battle-fields and on the day of Hunain: behold! your great numbers elated you, but they availed you not:

اقْتَرَفْتُمُوْهَا وَتِجَارَةٌ تَخْشَوْنَ

كَسَادَهَا وَمَسٰكِنُ تَرْضَوْنَهَآ

اَحَبَّ اِلَيْكُمْ مِّنَ اللهِ وَرَسُوْلِهٖ

وَجِهَادٍ فِيْ سَبِيْلِهٖ فَتَرَبَّصُوْا

حَتّٰى يَأْتِيَ اللهُ بِاَمْرِهٖ ؕ وَاللهُ

لَا يَهْدِى الْقَوْمَ الْفٰسِقِيْنَ ۝

لَقَدْ نَصَرَكُمُ اللهُ فِيْ مَوَاطِنَ

كَثِيْرَةٍ ۙ وَّيَوْمَ حُنَيْنٍ ۙ اِذْ اَعْجَبَتْكُمْ

كَثْرَتُكُمْ فَلَمْ تُغْنِ عَنْكُمْ شَيْئًا

are delights that endure:

22. They will dwell therein for ever. Verily in Allah's presence is a reward, the greatest (of all).

23. O you who believe! Take not for protectors your fathers and your brothers if they love infidelity above Faith: if any of you do so, they do wrong.

24. Say: If it be that your fathers, your sons, your brothers, your mates, or your kindred; the wealth

نَعِيمٌ مُّقِيمٌ ۞ خٰلِدِيْنَ فِيْهَا
اَبَدًا ۭ اِنَّ اللّٰهَ عِنْدَهٗٓ اَجْرٌ
عَظِيْمٌ ۞ يٰٓاَيُّهَا الَّذِيْنَ اٰمَنُوْا
لَا تَتَّخِذُوْٓا اٰبَآءَكُمْ وَ اِخْوَانَكُمْ
اَوْلِيَآءَ اِنِ اسْتَحَبُّوا الْكُفْرَ عَلَى
الْاِيْمَانِ ۭ وَمَنْ يَّتَوَلَّهُمْ مِّنْكُمْ
فَاُولٰٓئِكَ هُمُ الظّٰلِمُوْنَ ۞ قُلْ اِنْ
كَانَ اٰبَآؤُكُمْ وَ اَبْنَآؤُكُمْ وَ اِخْوَانُكُمْ
وَ اَزْوَاجُكُمْ وَ عَشِيْرَتُكُمْ وَ اَمْوَالٌ

and strive with might and main in the cause of Allah? They are not comparable in the sight of Allah: and Allah guides not those who do wrong.

20. Those who believe, and suffer exile and strive with might and main, in Allah's cause, with their goods and their persons, have the highest rank in the sight of Allah: they are the people who will achieve (salvation).

21. Their Lord does give them glad tidings of a Mercy from Himself, of His good pleasure, and of Gardens for them, wherein

الْأَخِرِ وَجَاهَدَ فِي سَبِيلِ اللهِ
لَا يَسْتَوُونَ عِنْدَ اللهِ وَاللهُ
لَا يَهْدِي الْقَوْمَ الظَّالِمِينَ ۝

اَلَّذِينَ اٰمَنُوْا وَهَاجَرُوْا وَجَاهَدُوْا
فِي سَبِيلِ اللهِ بِأَمْوَالِهِمْ
وَأَنْفُسِهِمْ أَعْظَمُ دَرَجَةً عِنْدَ
اللهِ وَأُولٰئِكَ هُمُ الْفَائِزُوْنَ ۝

يُبَشِّرُهُمْ رَبُّهُمْ بِرَحْمَةٍ مِّنْهُ
وَرِضْوَانٍ وَجَنّٰتٍ لَّهُمْ فِيهَا

The works of such bear no fruit: in Fire shall they dwell.

18. The mosques of Allah shall be visited and maintained by such as believe in Allah and the Last Day, establish regular prayers, and practise regular charity, and fear none (at all) except Allah. It is they who are expected to be on true guidance.

19. Do you make the giving of drink to pilgrims, or the maintenance of the Sacred Mosque, equal to (the pious service of) those who believe in Allah and the Last Day,

حَبِطَتْ أَعْمَالُهُمْ وَفِي النَّارِ هُمْ

خَالِدُونَ ۝ إِنَّمَا يَعْمُرُ مَسَاجِدَ

اللهِ مَنْ آمَنَ بِاللهِ وَالْيَوْمِ

الْآخِرِ وَأَقَامَ الصَّلَوٰةَ وَآتَى

الزَّكَوٰةَ وَلَمْ يَخْشَ إِلَّا اللهَ

فَعَسَىٰ أُولَٰئِكَ أَنْ يَّكُونُوا مِنَ

الْمُهْتَدِينَ ۝ أَجَعَلْتُمْ سِقَايَةَ

الْحَاجِّ وَعِمَارَةَ الْمَسْجِدِ الْحَرَامِ

كَمَنْ آمَنَ بِاللهِ وَالْيَوْمِ

to whom He will; and Allah is All-Knowing, All-Wise.

16. Do you think that you shall be abandoned, as though Allah did not know those among you who strive with might and main, and take none for friends and protectors except Allah, His Apostle, and the (community of) believers? But Allah is Well-Acquainted with (all) that you do.

17. It is not for such as join gods with Allah, to visit or maintain the mosques of Allah while they witness against their own souls to infidelity.

اللهُ عَلَى مَنْ يَّشَاءُ ط وَاللهُ عَلِيْمٌ

حَكِيْمٌ ۝ اَمْ حَسِبْتُمْ اَنْ تُتْرَكُوْا

وَلَمَّا يَعْلَمِ اللهُ الَّذِيْنَ جَهَدُوْا

مِنْكُمْ وَلَمْ يَتَّخِذُوْا مِنْ دُوْنِ

اللهِ وَلَا رَسُوْلِهِ وَلَا الْمُؤْمِنِيْنَ

وَلِيْجَةً ط وَاللهُ خَبِيْرٌ بِمَا

تَعْمَلُوْنَ ۝ مَا كَانَ لِلْمُشْرِكِيْنَ

اَنْ يَّعْمُرُوْا مَسَاجِدَ اللهِ شٰهِدِيْنَ

عَلٰٓى اَنْفُسِهِمْ بِالْكُفْرِ ط اُولٰٓئِكَ

restrained.

13. Will you not fight people who violated their oaths, plotted to expel the Apostle, and took the aggressive by being the first (to assault) you? Do you fear them? No, it is Allah Whom you should more justly fear, if you believe!

14. Fight them, and Allah will punish them by your hands, cover them with shame, help you (to victory) over them, heal the breasts of believers,

15. And still the indignation of their hearts. For Allah will turn (in mercy)

يَنْتَهُوْنَ ۞ اَلَا تُقَاتِلُوْنَ قَوْمًا

نَّكَثُوْٓا اَيْمَانَهُمْ وَهَمُّوْا بِاِخْرَاجِ

الرَّسُوْلِ وَهُمْ بَدَءُوْكُمْ اَوَّلَ

مَرَّةٍ ۚ اَتَخْشَوْنَهُمْ ۚ فَاللّٰهُ اَحَقُّ اَنْ

تَخْشَوْهُ اِنْ كُنْتُمْ مُّؤْمِنِيْنَ ۞

قَاتِلُوْهُمْ يُعَذِّبْهُمُ اللّٰهُ بِاَيْدِيْكُمْ

وَيُخْزِهِمْ وَيَنْصُرْكُمْ عَلَيْهِمْ

وَيَشْفِ صُدُوْرَ قَوْمٍ مُّؤْمِنِيْنَ ۞

وَيُذْهِبْ غَيْظَ قُلُوْبِهِمْ ۗ وَيَتُوْبُ

the ties either of kinship or of covenant! It is they who have transgressed all bounds.

11. But (even so), if they repent, establish regular prayers, and practise regular charity, - then they are your brethren in Faith: (thus) do We explain the Signs in detail, for those who understand.

12. But if they violate their oaths after their covenant, and attack you for your Faith, - fight you the chiefs of Unfaith: for their oaths are nothing to them: that thus they may be

مُؤْمِنًا اِلًّا وَّلَا ذِمَّةً ۖ وَاُولٰٓئِكَ

هُمُ الْمُعْتَدُوْنَ ۞ فَاِنْ تَابُوْا

وَاَقَامُوا الصَّلٰوةَ وَاٰتَوُا الزَّكٰوةَ

فَاِخْوَانُكُمْ فِى الدِّيْنِ ۖ وَنُفَصِّلُ

الْاٰيٰتِ لِقَوْمٍ يَّعْلَمُوْنَ ۞ وَاِنْ

نَّكَثُوْٓا اَيْمَانَهُمْ مِّنْ بَعْدِ

عَهْدِهِمْ وَطَعَنُوْا فِيْ دِيْنِكُمْ

فَقَاتِلُوْٓا اَئِمَّةَ الْكُفْرِ ۙ اِنَّهُمْ

لَآ اَيْمَانَ لَهُمْ لَعَلَّهُمْ

stand you true to them: for Allah does love the righteous.

8. How (can there be such a covenant), seeing that if they get an advantage over you, they respect not in you the ties either of kinship or of covenant? With (fair words from) their mouths they please you, but their hearts are averse from you; and most of them are rebellious and wicked.

9. The Signs of Allah have they sold for a miserable price, and (many) have they hindered from His way: evil indeed are the deeds they have done.

10. In a believer they respect not

فَاسْتَقِيمُوا لَهُمْ ۚ إِنَّ اللّٰهَ يُحِبُّ

الْمُتَّقِينَ ۞ كَيْفَ وَإِنْ يَّظْهَرُوا

عَلَيْكُمْ لَا يَرْقُبُوا فِيكُمْ إِلًّا

وَّلَا ذِمَّةً ۚ يُرْضُونَكُمْ بِأَفْوَاهِهِمْ

وَتَأْبَىٰ قُلُوبُهُمْ ۚ وَأَكْثَرُهُمْ

فَاسِقُونَ ۞ اشْتَرَوْا بِآيَاتِ اللّٰهِ

ثَمَنًا قَلِيلًا فَصَدُّوا عَنْ

سَبِيلِهِ ۚ إِنَّهُمْ سَآءَ مَا كَانُوا

يَعْمَلُونَ ۞ لَا يَرْقُبُونَ فِيْ

Most Merciful.

6.   If one amongst the Pagans ask you for asylum, grant it to him, so that he may hear the word of Allah; and then escort him to where he can be secure. That is because they are men without knowledge.

7.   How can there be a Covenant of Allah and His Apostle, with the Pagans, except those with whom you made a treaty near the Sacred Mosque? As long as these stand true to you,

رَّحِيمٌ ۞ وَإِنْ أَحَدٌ مِّنَ

الْمُشْرِكِينَ اسْتَجَارَكَ فَأَجِرْهُ

حَتَّى يَسْمَعَ كَلَامَ اللهِ ثُمَّ

أَبْلِغْهُ مَأْمَنَهُ ذَٰلِكَ بِأَنَّهُمْ

قَوْمٌ لَّا يَعْلَمُونَ ۞ كَيْفَ

يَكُونُ لِلْمُشْرِكِينَ عَهْدٌ عِنْدَ

اللهِ وَعِنْدَ رَسُولِهِ إِلَّا

الَّذِينَ عَاهَدْتُّمْ عِنْدَ الْمَسْجِدِ

الْحَرَامِ فَمَا اسْتَقَامُوا لَكُمْ

any one against you. So fulfil your agreements with them to the end of their term: for Allah loves the righteous.

5. But when the forbidden months are past, then fight and slay the Pagans wherever you find them, an seize them, beleaguer them, and lie in wait for them in every stratagem (of war); but if they repent, and establish regular prayers and practise regular charity, then open the way for them: for Allah is Oft-Forgiving,

اَحَدًا فَاَتِمُّوْا اِلَيْهِمْ عَهْدَ هُمْ

اِلٰى مُدَّتِهِمْ ؕ اِنَّ اللّٰهَ يُحِبُّ

الْمُتَّقِيْنَ ۞ فَاِذَا انْسَلَخَ الْاَشْهُرُ

الْحُرُمُ فَاقْتُلُوا الْمُشْرِكِيْنَ

حَيْثُ وَجَدْتُّمُوْهُمْ وَخُذُوْهُمْ

وَاحْصُرُوْهُمْ وَاقْعُدُوْا لَهُمْ

كُلَّ مَرْصَدٍ ۚ فَاِنْ تَابُوْا وَاَقَامُوا

الصَّلٰوةَ وَ اٰتَوُا الزَّكٰوةَ فَخَلُّوْا

سَبِيْلَهُمْ ؕ اِنَّ اللّٰهَ غَفُوْرٌ

(assembled) on the day of the Great Pilgrimage, - that Allah and His Apostle dissolve (treaty) obligations with the Pagans. If then, you repent, it were best for you; but if you turn away, know you that you cannot frustrate Allah. And proclaim a grievous Chastisement to those who reject Faith.

4. (But the treaties are) not dissolved with those Pagans with whom you have entered into alliance and who have not subsequently failed you in any matter, nor aided

يَوْمَ الْحَجِّ الْأَكْبَرِ أَنَّ اللَّهَ

بَرِيٓءٌ مِّنَ الْمُشْرِكِينَ ۖ وَرَسُولُهُ ۚ

فَإِن تُبْتُمْ فَهُوَ خَيْرٌ لَّكُمْ ۚ

وَإِن تَوَلَّيْتُمْ فَاعْلَمُوٓا أَنَّكُمْ

غَيْرُ مُعْجِزِى اللَّهِ ۗ وَبَشِّرِ

الَّذِينَ كَفَرُوا بِعَذَابٍ أَلِيمٍ ۝

إِلَّا الَّذِينَ عَـٰهَدتُّم مِّنَ

الْمُشْرِكِينَ ثُمَّ لَمْ يَنقُصُوكُمْ

شَيْـًٔا وَلَمْ يُظَـٰهِرُوا عَلَيْكُمْ

Well-Acquainted with all things.

At-Tauba (Repentance)

1. A (declaration) of complete absolution on the part Allah and His Apostle, to those of the Pagans with whom you have contracted mutual alliances: -

2. Move about for four months, (as you will), throughout the land, but know that you cannot frustrate Allah (by your false-hood) but that Allah will cover with shame those who reject Him.

3. And an announcement from Allah and His Apostle, to the people

شَیْءٍ عَلِیْمٌ ۝

سُوْرَةُ التَّوْبَةِ مَدَنِیَّةٌ ١٦ اٰیَاتُهَا ١٢٩

بَرَآءَةٌ مِّنَ اللّٰهِ وَ رَسُوْلِهٖۤ

اِلَى الَّذِیْنَ عٰهَدْتُّمْ مِّنَ

الْمُشْرِكِیْنَ ۝ فَسِیْحُوْا فِی الْأَرْضِ

اَرْبَعَةَ اَشْهُرٍ وَّ اعْلَمُوْۤا اَنَّكُمْ

غَیْرُ مُعْجِزِی اللّٰهِ ۙ وَ اَنَّ اللّٰهَ

مُخْزِی الْكٰفِرِیْنَ ۝ وَ اَذَانٌ مِّنَ

اللّٰهِ وَ رَسُوْلِهٖۤ اِلَى النَّاسِ

74. Those who believe, and adopt exile, and fight for the Faith, in the cause of Allah as well as those who give (them) asylum and aid, - these are (all) in very truth the believers: for them is the forgiveness of sins and a provision most generous.

75. And those who accept Faith subsequently, and adopt exile, and fight for the Faith in your company, - they are of you. But kindred by blood have prior rights against each other in the Book of Allah. Verily Allah is

وَالَّذِيْنَ اٰمَنُوْا وَهَاجَرُوْا

وَجَاهَدُوْا فِيْ سَبِيْلِ اللّٰهِ

وَالَّذِيْنَ اٰوَوْا وَّنَصَرُوْا اُولٰٓئِكَ

هُمُ الْمُؤْمِنُوْنَ حَقًّا ۚ لَهُمْ مَّغْفِرَةٌ

وَّرِزْقٌ كَرِيْمٌ ۞ وَالَّذِيْنَ اٰمَنُوْا

مِنْ بَعْدُ وَهَاجَرُوْا وَجَاهَدُوْا

مَعَكُمْ فَاُولٰٓئِكَ مِنْكُمْ ۚ وَاُولُوا

الْاَرْحَامِ بَعْضُهُمْ اَوْلٰى بِبَعْضٍ

فِيْ كِتٰبِ اللّٰهِ ۚ اِنَّ اللّٰهَ بِكُلِّ

came not into exile, you owe no duty of protection to them until they come into exile; but if they seek your aid in religion, it is your duty to help them, except against a people with whom you have a treaty of mutual alliance. And (remember) Allah sees all that you do.

73. The unbelievers are protectors, one of another: unless you do this, (protect each other), there would be tumult and oppression on earth, and great mischief.

يُهَاجِرُوْا مَا لَكُمْ مِّنْ وَلَايَتِهِمْ
مِّنْ شَيْءٍ حَتّٰى يُهَاجِرُوْا ۚ
وَإِنِ اسْتَنْصَرُوْكُمْ فِى الدِّيْنِ
فَعَلَيْكُمُ النَّصْرُ إِلَّا عَلٰى قَوْمٍ
بَيْنَكُمْ وَبَيْنَهُمْ مِّيْثَاقٌ ۗ وَاللّٰهُ
بِمَا تَعْمَلُوْنَ بَصِيْرٌ ۞ وَالَّذِيْنَ
كَفَرُوْا بَعْضُهُمْ أَوْلِيَاءُ بَعْضٍ ۚ
إِلَّا تَفْعَلُوْهُ تَكُنْ فِتْنَةٌ فِى
الْأَرْضِ وَفَسَادٌ كَبِيْرٌ ۞

and He will forgive you: for Allah is Oft-Forgiving, Most Merciful."

71. But if they have treacherous designs against you,(O Apostle!), they have already been in treason against Allah, and so has He given (you) power over them. And Allah so He Who has (full) knowledge and wisdom.

72. Those who believed, and adopted exile, and fought for the Faith, with their property and their persons, in the cause of Allah, as well as those who gave (them) asylum and aid, - these are (all) friends and protectors, one of another. As to those who believed but

وَيَغْفِرْ لَكُمْ ۗ وَاللهُ غَفُوْرٌ رَّحِيْمٌ ۝

وَاِنْ يُّرِيْدُوْا خِيَانَتَكَ فَقَدْ

خَانُوا اللهَ مِنْ قَبْلُ فَاَمْكَنَ

مِنْهُمْ ۗ وَاللهُ عَلِيْمٌ حَكِيْمٌ ۝

اِنَّ الَّذِيْنَ اٰمَنُوْا وَهَاجَرُوْا

وَجَاهَدُوْا بِاَمْوَالِهِمْ وَاَنْفُسِهِمْ

فِيْ سَبِيْلِ اللهِ وَالَّذِيْنَ اٰوَوْا

وَّنَصَرُوْا اُولٰٓئِكَ بَعْضُهُمْ اَوْلِيَآءُ

بَعْضٍ ۗ وَالَّذِيْنَ اٰمَنُوْا وَلَمْ

and Allah is Exalted in might, Wise.

68. Had it not been for a previous ordainment from Allah, a severe penalty would have reached you for the (ransom) that you took.

69. But (now) enjoy what you took in war, lawful and good: but fear Allah: for Allah is Oft-Forgiving, Most Merciful.

70. O Apostle! Say to those who are captives in your hands: "If Allah findes any good in your hearts, He will give you something better than what has been taken from you,

وَاللهُ عَزِيزٌ حَكِيمٌ ۩ لَوْ لَا

كِتٰبٌ مِّنَ اللهِ سَبَقَ لَمَسَّكُمْ

فِيْمَآ أَخَذْتُمْ عَذَابٌ عَظِيْمٌ ۩

فَكُلُوْا مِمَّا غَنِمْتُمْ حَلٰلًا طَيِّبًا

وَّاتَّقُوا اللهَ ۗ إِنَّ اللهَ غَفُوْرٌ

رَّحِيْمٌ ۩ يٰٓأَيُّهَا النَّبِيُّ قُلْ لِّمَنْ

فِيْ أَيْدِيْكُمْ مِّنَ الْأَسْرٰىٓ ۙ إِنْ

يَّعْلَمِ اللهُ فِيْ قُلُوْبِكُمْ خَيْرًا

يُّؤْتِكُمْ خَيْرًا مِّمَّآ أُخِذَ مِنْكُمْ

your (task), for He knoweth that there is a weak spot in you: but (even so), if there are a hundred of you, patient and persevering, they will vanquish two hundred, and if a thousand, they will vanquish two thousand, with the leave of Allah: for Allah is with those who patiently persevere.

67. It is not fitting for a Apostle that he should have prisoners of war until he has thoroughly crushed the enemy in the battle field. You look for the temporal goods of this world; but Allah looks to the Hereafter:

اللهُ عَنْكُمْ وَ عَلِمَ اَنَّ فِيْكُمْ

ضَعْفًا ۚ فَاِنْ يَّكُنْ مِّنْكُمْ مِّائَةٌ

صَابِرَةٌ يَّغْلِبُوْا مِائَتَيْنِ ۚ وَاِنْ

يَّكُنْ مِّنْكُمْ اَلْفٌ يَّغْلِبُوْٓا

اَلْفَيْنِ بِاِذْنِ اللهِ ۚ وَاللهُ مَعَ

الصّٰبِرِيْنَ ۞ مَا كَانَ لِنَبِيٍّ اَنْ

يَّكُوْنَ لَهٗٓ اَسْرٰى حَتّٰى يُثْخِنَ

فِى الْاَرْضِ ۗ تُرِيْدُوْنَ عَرَضَ

الدُّنْيَا ۖ وَاللهُ يُرِيْدُ الْاٰخِرَةَ ۗ

is Exalted in Might, Wise.

64. O Apostle! Sufficient unto you is Allah, - (unto you) and unto those who follow you among the believers.

65. O Apostle! Rouse the believers to the fight. If there are twenty amongst you, patient and persevering, they will vanquish two hundred: if a hundred, they will vanquish a thousand of the unbelievers: for these are a people without understanding.

66. For the present, Allah has lightened

عَزِيزٌ حَكِيمٌ ۝ يَأَيُّهَا النَّبِيُّ

حَسْبُكَ اللَّهُ وَمَنِ اتَّبَعَكَ

مِنَ الْمُؤْمِنِينَ ۝ يَأَيُّهَا النَّبِيُّ

حَرِّضِ الْمُؤْمِنِينَ عَلَى الْقِتَالِ

إِن يَكُن مِّنكُمْ عِشْرُونَ

صَابِرُونَ يَغْلِبُوا مِائَتَيْنِ وَإِن

يَكُن مِّنكُم مِّائَةٌ يَغْلِبُوا أَلْفًا

مِّنَ الَّذِينَ كَفَرُوا بِأَنَّهُمْ

قَوْمٌ لَّا يَفْقَهُونَ ۝ الْئَنَ خَفَّفَ

do you (also) incline towards peace, and trust in Allah: for He is One that hears and knows (all things).

62. Should they intend to deceive you, - verily Allah suffices for you: He it is that has strengthened you with His aid and with (the company of) the believers;

63. And (moreover) He has put affection between their hearts: not if you had spent all that is in the earth, could you not have produced that affection, but Allah has done it: for He

فَاجْنَحْ لَهَا وَتَوَكَّلْ عَلَى اللّٰهِ

اِنَّهُ هُوَ السَّمِيعُ الْعَلِيمُ ۞

وَاِنْ يُّرِيْدُوْا اَنْ يَّخْدَعُوْكَ

فَاِنَّ حَسْبَكَ اللّٰهُ هُوَ الَّذِىْ

اَيَّدَكَ بِنَصْرِهِ وَبِالْمُؤْمِنِيْنَ ۞

وَاَلَّفَ بَيْنَ قُلُوْبِهِمْ لَوْ

اَنْفَقْتَ مَا فِى الْاَرْضِ جَمِيْعًا

مَّا اَلَّفْتَ بَيْنَ قُلُوْبِهِمْ

وَلٰكِنَّ اللّٰهَ اَلَّفَ بَيْنَهُمْ اِنَّهُ

will never frustrate (them).

60. Against them make ready your strength to the utmost of your power, including steeds of war, to strike terror into (the hearts of) the enemies of Allah and your enemies and others besides, whom you may not know, but whom Allah does know. Whatever you shall spend in the cause of Allah, shall be repaid unto you, and you shall not be treated unjustly.

61. But if the enemy incline towards peace,

لَا يُعْجِزُونَ ۞ وَأَعِدُّوا لَهُمْ

مَّا اسْتَطَعْتُمْ مِّنْ قُوَّةٍ وَّمِنْ

رِّبَاطِ الْخَيْلِ تُرْهِبُونَ بِهِ

عَدُوَّ اللهِ وَعَدُوَّكُمْ وَأخَرِينَ

مِنْ دُوْنِهِمْ لَا تَعْلَمُونَهُمْ

اللهُ يَعْلَمُهُمْ طُ وَمَا تُنْفِقُوا

مِنْ شَىْءٍ فِيْ سَبِيْلِ اللهِ

يُوَفَّ إِلَيْكُمْ وَأنْتُمْ لَا

تُظْلَمُونَ ۞ وَإِنْ جَنَحُوا لِلسَّلْمِ

their covenant every time, and they have not the fear (of Allah).

57. If you encounter them in a battle, deal severely with them so as to put terror in those who follow them, that they may remember.

58. If you fear treachery from any group, throw back (their covenant) to them, (so as to be) on equal terms: for Allah loves not the treacherous.

59. Let not the unbelievers think that they can get the better (of the godly): they

عَهْدَهُمْ فِى كُلِّ مَرَّةٍ وَّهُمْ

لَا يَتَّقُوْنَ ۞ فَاِمَّا تَثْقَفَنَّهُمْ

فِى الْحَرْبِ فَشَرِّدْ بِهِمْ مَّنْ

خَلْفَهُمْ لَعَلَّهُمْ يَذَّكَّرُوْنَ ۞

وَاِمَّا تَخَافَنَّ مِنْ قَوْمٍ

خِيَانَةً فَانْبِذْ اِلَيْهِمْ عَلٰى

سَوَآءٍ ۗ اِنَّ اللّٰهَ لَا يُحِبُّ

الْخَآئِنِيْنَ ۞ وَلَا يَحْسَبَنَّ

الَّذِيْنَ كَفَرُوْا سَبَقُوْا ۗ اِنَّهُمْ

Allah is He Who hears and knows (all things)."

54. (Deeds) after the manner of the people of Pharaoh and those before them": they treated as false the Signs of their Lord, so We destroyed them for their crimes, and We drowned the people of Pharaoh: for they were all oppressors and wrongdoers.

55. For the worst of all living creatures in the sight of Allah are those who reject Him: they will not believe.

56. They are those with whom you did make a covenant, but they break

اللَّهَ سَمِيعٌ عَلِيمٌ ۞ كَدَأْبِ

الِ فِرْعَوْنَ وَالَّذِينَ مِنْ

قَبْلِهِمْ كَذَّبُوا بِأَيَّتِ رَبِّهِمْ

فَأَهْلَكْنٰهُمْ بِذُنُوبِهِمْ وَأَغْرَقْنَا

الَ فِرْعَوْنَ وَكُلٌّ كَانُوا

ظٰلِمِينَ ۞ إِنَّ شَرَّ الدَّوَابِّ

عِنْدَ اللَّهِ الَّذِينَ كَفَرُوا

فَهُمْ لَا يُؤْمِنُونَ ۞ الَّذِينَ

عٰهَدْتَّ مِنْهُمْ ثُمَّ يَنْقُضُونَ

for Allah is never unjust to His servants:

52. "(Deeds) after the manner of the People of Pharaoh and of those before them: they rejected the Signs of Allah, and Allah punished them for their crimes: for Allah is Strong, and Strict in punishment:

53. "Because Allah will never change the grace which He has bestowed on a people until they change what is in their (own) souls, and surely

أَيْدِيكُمْ وَأَنَّ ٱللَّهَ لَيْسَ

بِظَلَّٰمٍ لِّلْعَبِيدِ ۞ كَدَأْبِ ءَالِ

فِرْعَوْنَ ۗ وَٱلَّذِينَ مِن قَبْلِهِمْ ۚ

كَفَرُوا۟ بِـَٔايَٰتِ ٱللَّهِ فَأَخَذَهُمُ

ٱللَّهُ بِذُنُوبِهِمْ ۗ إِنَّ ٱللَّهَ

قَوِىٌّ شَدِيدُ ٱلْعِقَابِ ۞

ذَٰلِكَ بِأَنَّ ٱللَّهَ لَمْ يَكُ مُغَيِّرًا

نِّعْمَةً أَنْعَمَهَا عَلَىٰ قَوْمٍ حَتَّىٰ

يُغَيِّرُوا۟ مَا بِأَنفُسِهِمْ ۙ وَأَنَّ

punishment."

49. Lo! The hypocrites say, and those in whose hearts is a disease: "These people, - their religion has misled them." But if any trust in Allah, behold! Allah is Exalted in might, Wise.

50. If you could see, when the angels take the souls of the unbelievers (at death), (how) they smite their faces and their backs, (saying): "Taste the Chastisement of the Blazing Fire -

51. "Because of (the deeds) which your (own) hands sent forth;

الْعِقَابِ ۞ اِذْ يَقُوْلُ الْمُنْفِقُوْنَ
وَ الَّذِيْنَ فِيْ قُلُوْبِهِمْ مَّرَضٌ
غَرَّ هٰٓؤُلَاءِ دِيْنُهُمْ ۚ وَ مَنْ
يَّتَوَكَّلْ عَلَى اللّٰهِ فَاِنَّ اللّٰهَ
عَزِيْزٌ حَكِيْمٌ ۞ وَ لَوْ تَرٰى
اِذْ يَتَوَفَّى الَّذِيْنَ كَفَرُوا
الْمَلٰٓئِكَةُ يَضْرِبُوْنَ وُجُوْهَهُمْ
وَ اَدْبَارَهُمْ ۚ وَ ذُوْقُوْا عَذَابَ
الْحَرِيْقِ ۞ ذٰلِكَ بِمَا قَدَّمَتْ

for Allah compasses round about all that they do.

48. Remember Satan made their (sinful) acts seem alluring to them, and said: "No one among men can overcome you this day, while I am near to you": but when the two forces came in sight of each other, he turned on his heels, and said: "Lo! I am clear of you; lo! I see what you see not; lo! I fear Allah: for Allah is strict in

وَاللّٰهُ بِمَا يَعْمَلُوْنَ مُحِيْطٌ ۩

وَإِذْ زَيَّنَ لَهُمُ الشَّيْطٰنُ

اَعْمَالَهُمْ وَقَالَ لَا غَالِبَ

لَكُمُ الْيَوْمَ مِنَ النَّاسِ

وَإِنِّيْ جَارٌ لَّكُمْ ۚ فَلَمَّا تَرَآءَتِ

الْفِئَتٰنِ نَكَصَ عَلٰى عَقِبَيْهِ

وَقَالَ اِنِّيْ بَرِيْٓءٌ مِّنْكُمْ

اِنِّيْٓ اَرٰى مَا لَا تَرَوْنَ اِنِّيْٓ

اَخَافُ اللّٰهَ ۚ وَاللّٰهُ شَدِيْدُ

When you meet a force, be firm, and call Allah in remembrance much (and often); that you may prosper:

46. And obey Allah and His Apostle; and fall into no disputes, lest you lose heart and your power depart; and be patient and persevering: for Allah is with those who patiently persevere:

47. And be not like those who started from their homes insolently and to be seen of men, and to hinder (men) from the path of Allah:

اِذَا لَقِيْتُمْ فِئَةً فَاثْبُتُوْا

وَاذْكُرُوا اللهَ كَثِيْرًا لَّعَلَّكُمْ

تُفْلِحُوْنَ ۞ وَاَطِيْعُوا اللهَ

وَرَسُوْلَهٗ وَلَا تَنَازَعُوْا فَتَفْشَلُوْا

وَتَذْهَبَ رِيْحُكُمْ وَاصْبِرُوْا

اِنَّ اللهَ مَعَ الصّٰبِرِيْنَ ۞ وَلَا

تَكُوْنُوْا كَالَّذِيْنَ خَرَجُوْا مِنْ

دِيَارِهِمْ بَطَرًا وَّرِئَآءَ النَّاسِ

وَيَصُدُّوْنَ عَنْ سَبِيْلِ اللهِ

if He had shown them to you as many, you would surely have been discouraged, and you would surely have disputed in (your) decision; but Allah saved (you): for He knows well the (secrets) of (all) hearts.

44. And remember when you met, He showed them to you as few in your eyes, and He made you appear as contemptible in their eyes: that Allah might accomplish a matter already decided. For to Allah do all questions go back (for decision).

45. O you who believe!

وَلَوْ اَرَاكَهُمْ كَثِيْرًا لَّفَشِلْتُمْ

وَلَتَنَازَعْتُمْ فِي الْأَمْرِ وَلٰكِنَّ

اللّٰهَ سَلَّمَ ۗ اِنَّهٗ عَلِيْمٌ بِذَاتِ

الصُّدُوْرِ ۞ وَاِذْ يُرِيْكُمُوْهُمْ

اِذِ الْتَقَيْتُمْ فِيْٓ اَعْيُنِكُمْ

قَلِيْلًا وَّيُقَلِّلُكُمْ فِيْٓ اَعْيُنِهِمْ

لِيَقْضِيَ اللّٰهُ اَمْرًا كَانَ

مَفْعُوْلًا ۗ وَاِلَى اللّٰهِ تُرْجَعُ

الْأُمُوْرُ ۞ يٰٓاَيُّهَا الَّذِيْنَ اٰمَنُوْٓا

and they on the farther side, and the caravan on lower ground than you. Even if you had made a mutual appointment to meet, you would certainly have failed in the appointment: but (thus you met), that Allah might accomplish a matter already decided; that those who died might die after a clear Sign (had been given), and those who lived might live after a clear Sign (had been given). And verily Allah is He Who hears and knows (all things).

43. Remember in your dream Allah showed them to you as few:

وَهُمْ بِالْعُدْوَةِ الْقُصْوَىٰ وَالرَّكْبُ

اَسْفَلَ مِنْكُمْ ۚ وَلَوْ تَوَاعَدْتُّمْ

لَاخْتَلَفْتُمْ فِي الْمِيْعَادِ ۙ وَلٰكِنْ

لِّيَقْضِيَ اللّٰهُ اَمْرًا كَانَ

مَفْعُوْلًا ۙ۬ لِّيَهْلِكَ مَنْ هَلَكَ

عَنْۢ بَيِّنَةٍ وَّيَحْيٰى مَنْ

حَيَّ عَنْۢ بَيِّنَةٍ ۗ وَاِنَّ اللّٰهَ

لَسَمِيْعٌ عَلِيْمٌ ۞ اِذْ يُرِيْكَهُمُ

اللّٰهُ فِيْ مَنَامِكَ قَلِيْلًا ۖ

41. And know that out of all the booty that you may acquire (in war), a fifth share is assigned to Allah, - and to the Apostle, and to near relatives, orphans, the needy, and the wayfarer, - if you do believe in Allah and in the revelation We sent down to Our servant on the Day of Discrimination, - the Day of the meeting of the two forces. For Allah has power over all things.

42. Remember you were on the hither side of the valley,

وَاعْلَمُوْٓا اَنَّمَا غَنِمْتُمْ مِّنْ شَيْءٍ

فَاَنَّ لِلّٰهِ خُمُسَهٗ وَلِلرَّسُوْلِ

وَلِذِى الْقُرْبٰى وَالْيَتٰمٰى

وَالْمَسٰكِيْنِ وَابْنِ السَّبِيْلِ

اِنْ كُنْتُمْ اٰمَنْتُمْ بِاللّٰهِ وَمَآ

اَنْزَلْنَا عَلٰى عَبْدِنَا يَوْمَ

الْفُرْقَانِ يَوْمَ الْتَقَى الْجَمْعٰنِ ۗ

وَاللّٰهُ عَلٰى كُلِّ شَيْءٍ قَدِيْرٌ ۞

اِذْ اَنْتُمْ بِالْعُدْوَةِ الدُّنْيَا

بتراك الكتب الاسلامية

پاره

وَاعْلَمُوْآ

(۱۰)

PART 11
Ya-'tadhiroon

His abounding grace on all who abound in merit! But if you turn away, then I fear for you the Chastisement of a great day:'

4.   'To Allah is your return, and He has power over all things.'"

5.   Behold! They fold up their hearts, that they may lie hid from Him! Ah even when they cover themselves with their garments, He knows what they conceal, and what they reveal: for He knows well the (inmost secrets) of the hearts.

كُلَّ ذِىْ فَضْلٍ فَضْلَهُ وَاِنْ

تَوَلَّوْا فَاِنِّىْٓ اَخَافُ عَلَيْكُمْ عَذَابَ

يَوْمٍ كَبِيْرٍ ۞ اِلَى اللّٰهِ مَرْجِعُكُمْ ۚ

وَهُوَ عَلٰى كُلِّ شَىْءٍ قَدِيْرٌ ۞

اَلَآ اِنَّهُمْ يَثْنُوْنَ صُدُوْرَهُمْ

لِيَسْتَخْفُوْا مِنْهُ ۗ اَلَا حِيْنَ

يَسْتَغْشُوْنَ ثِيَابَهُمْ ۙ يَعْلَمُ

مَا يُسِرُّوْنَ وَمَا يُعْلِنُوْنَ ۚ

اِنَّهُ عَلِيْمٌۢ بِذَاتِ الصُّدُوْرِ ۞

for He is the best to decide.

Hud (Prophet Hud)

Bismillahir-Rahmanir-Rahim

1. Alif. Lam. Raa. (This is) a Book, with verses basic or fundamental (of established meaning), further explained in detail, - from One Who is Wise and Well-Acquainted (with all things):

2. (It teaches) that you should worship none but Allah. (Say): "Verily I am (sent) unto you from Him to warn and to bring glad tidings:

3. "(And to preach thus), 'Seek you the forgiveness of your Lord, and turn to Him in repentance; that He may grant you enjoyment, good (and true), for a term appointed, and bestow

اللّٰهُ ۚ وَهُوَ خَيْرُ الْحٰكِمِيْنَ ۞

بِسْمِ اللّٰهِ الرَّحْمٰنِ الرَّحِيْمِ

الٓرٰ ۚ كِتٰبٌ اُحْكِمَتْ اٰيٰتُهٗ ثُمَّ

فُصِّلَتْ مِنْ لَّدُنْ حَكِيْمٍ

خَبِيْرٍ ۞ اَلَّا تَعْبُدُوْۤا اِلَّا اللّٰهَ ۚ

اِنَّنِيْ لَكُمْ مِّنْهُ نَذِيْرٌ وَّبَشِيْرٌ ۞

وَّاَنِ اسْتَغْفِرُوْا رَبَّكُمْ ثُمَّ

تُوْبُوْۤا اِلَيْهِ يُمَتِّعْكُمْ مَّتَاعًا

حَسَنًا اِلٰۤى اَجَلٍ مُّسَمًّى وَّيُؤْتِ

there is none can keep back His favour: He causes it to reach whomsoever of His servants He pleases. And He is the Oft-Forgiving, Most Merciful.

108. Say: "O you men! Now Truth has reached you from your Lord! Those who receive guidance, do so for the good of their own souls; those who stray, do so to their own loss: and I am not (set) over you to arrange your affairs."

109. Follow you the inspiration sent unto you, and be patient and constant, till Allah do decide:

فَلَا رَآدَّ لِفَضْلِهِ يُصِيبُ بِهِ
مَن يَشَآءُ مِنْ عِبَادِهِ وَهُوَ
الْغَفُورُ الرَّحِيمُ ۝ قُلْ يَٰٓأَيُّهَا
النَّاسُ قَدْ جَآءَكُمُ الْحَقُّ مِن
رَّبِّكُمْ فَمَنِ اهْتَدَىٰ فَإِنَّمَا
يَهْتَدِى لِنَفْسِهِ وَمَن ضَلَّ
فَإِنَّمَا يَضِلُّ عَلَيْهَا وَمَآ أَنَا۠
عَلَيْكُم بِوَكِيلٍ ۝ وَاتَّبِعْ مَا
يُوحَىٰٓ إِلَيْكَ وَاصْبِرْ حَتَّىٰ يَحْكُمَ

Allah - Who will take your souls (at death): I am commanded to be (in the ranks) of the believers,

105. "And further (thus): 'set your face towards religion with true piety, and never in any wise be of the unbelievers;'

106. 'Nor call on any, other than Allah; - such will neither profit you nor hurt you: if you do so, behold! you shall certainly be of those who do wrong.'"

107. If Allah do touch you with hurt, there is none can remove it but He: if He do design some benefit for you,

اللّٰهُ الَّذِىْ يَتَوَفّٰىكُمْ ۚ وَاُمِرْتُ

اَنْ اَكُوْنَ مِنَ الْمُؤْمِنِيْنَ ۙ ۰۱۰

وَاَنْ اَقِمْ وَجْهَكَ لِلدِّيْنِ حَنِيْفًا ۚ

وَلَا تَكُوْنَنَّ مِنَ الْمُشْرِكِيْنَ ۰۱۵

وَلَا تَدْعُ مِنْ دُوْنِ اللّٰهِ مَا لَا

يَنْفَعُكَ وَلَا يَضُرُّكَ ۚ فَاِنْ فَعَلْتَ

فَاِنَّكَ اِذًا مِّنَ الظّٰلِمِيْنَ ۰۱۹ وَاِنْ

يَّمْسَسْكَ اللّٰهُ بِضُرٍّ فَلَا كَاشِفَ

لَهٗٓ اِلَّا هُوَ ۚ وَاِنْ يُّرِدْكَ بِخَيْرٍ

but (what happened in) the days of the men who passed away before them? Say: "Wait you then: for I, too, will wait with you."

103. In the end We deliver Our Apostles and those who believe: thus is it fitting on Our part that We should deliver those who believe!

104. Say: "O you men! If you are in doubt as to my religion, (behold!) I worship not what you worship, other than Allah! But I worship

إِلَّا مِثْلَ أَيَّامِ الَّذِيْنَ خَلَوْا

مِنْ قَبْلِهِمْ ۚ قُلْ فَانْتَظِرُوْا

إِنِّيْ مَعَكُمْ مِّنَ الْمُنْتَظِرِيْنَ ۞

ثُمَّ نُنَجِّيْ رُسُلَنَا وَالَّذِيْنَ

اٰمَنُوْا ۚ كَذٰلِكَ ۚ حَقًّا عَلَيْنَا نُنْجِ

الْمُؤْمِنِيْنَ ۞ قُلْ يٰٓأَيُّهَا النَّاسُ

اِنْ كُنْتُمْ فِيْ شَكٍّ مِّنْ دِيْنِيْ

فَلَا أَعْبُدُ الَّذِيْنَ تَعْبُدُوْنَ

مِنْ دُوْنِ اللّٰهِ وَلٰكِنْ أَعْبُدُ

99.   If it had been your Lord's will, they would all have believed, - all who are on earth! Will you then compel mankind, against their will, to believe!

100.   No soul can believe, except by the Will of Allah, and He will place doubt (or obscurity) on those who will not understand.

101.   Say: "Behold all that is in the heavens and on earth"; but neither Signs nor Warners profit those who believe not.

102.   Do they then expect (any thing)

وَلَوْ شَآءَ رَبُّكَ لَاٰمَنَ مَنْ فِى الْاَرْضِ كُلُّهُمْ جَمِيْعًا ۚ اَفَاَنْتَ تُكْرِهُ النَّاسَ حَتّٰى يَكُوْنُوْا مُؤْمِنِيْنَ ۞

وَمَا كَانَ لِنَفْسٍ اَنْ تُؤْمِنَ اِلَّا بِاِذْنِ اللّٰهِ ۗ وَيَجْعَلُ الرِّجْسَ عَلَى الَّذِيْنَ لَا يَعْقِلُوْنَ ۞ قُلِ انْظُرُوْا مَاذَا فِى السَّمٰوٰتِ وَالْاَرْضِ ۚ وَمَا تُغْنِى الْاٰيٰتُ وَالنُّذُرُ عَنْ قَوْمٍ لَّا يُؤْمِنُوْنَ ۞ فَهَلْ يَنْتَظِرُوْنَ

or you shall be of those who perish.

96. Those against whom the Word of your Lord has been verified would not believe -

97. Even if every Sign was brought unto them, - until they see (for themselves) the grievous Chastisement.

98. Why was there not a single township (among those We warned), which believed, - so its faith should have profited it, - except the people of Jonah? When they believed, We removed from them the Chastisement of ignominy in the life of the present, and permitted them to enjoy (their life) for a while.

فَتَكُوْنَ مِنَ الْخٰسِرِيْنَ ۞ اِنَّ

الَّذِيْنَ حَقَّتْ عَلَيْهِمْ كَلِمَتُ

رَبِّكَ لَا يُؤْمِنُوْنَ ۞ وَلَوْ جَآءَتْهُمْ

كُلُّ اٰيَةٍ حَتّٰى يَرَوُا الْعَذَابَ

الْاَلِيْمَ ۞ فَلَوْلَا كَانَتْ قَرْيَةٌ

اٰمَنَتْ فَنَفَعَهَآ اِيْمَانُهَآ اِلَّا قَوْمَ

يُوْنُسَ ط لَمَّآ اٰمَنُوْا كَشَفْنَا عَنْهُمْ

عَذَابَ الْخِزْيِ فِي الْحَيٰوةِ

الدُّنْيَا وَمَتَّعْنٰهُمْ اِلٰى حِيْنٍ ۞

was after knowledge had been granted to them, that they fell into schisms. Verily Allah will judge between them as to the schisms amongst them, on the Day of Judgment.

94. If you were in doubt as to what We have revealed unto you, then ask those who have been reading the Book from before you: the Truth has indeed come to you from your Lord: so be in no wise of those in doubt.

95. Nor be of those who reject the Signs of Allah,

اخْتَلَفُوْا حَتّٰى جَآءَهُمُ الْعِلْمُ إِنَّ

رَبَّكَ يَقْضِيْ بَيْنَهُمْ يَوْمَ الْقِيٰمَةِ

فِيْمَا كَانُوْا فِيْهِ يَخْتَلِفُوْنَ ۞

فَاِنْ كُنْتَ فِيْ شَكٍّ مِّمَّآ اَنْزَلْنَآ

اِلَيْكَ فَسْئَلِ الَّذِيْنَ يَقْرَءُوْنَ

الْكِتٰبَ مِنْ قَبْلِكَ ۚ لَقَدْ جَآءَكَ

الْحَقُّ مِنْ رَّبِّكَ فَلَا تَكُوْنَنَّ

مِنَ الْمُمْتَرِيْنَ ۞ وَلَا تَكُوْنَنَّ

مِنَ الَّذِيْنَ كَذَّبُوْا بِاٰيٰتِ اللّٰهِ

Him Whom the Children of Israel believe in: I am of those who submit (to Allah in Islam)."

91. (It was said to him): "Ah now! - but a little while before, you were in rebellion! - and you did mischief (and violence)!

92. "This day shall We save you in the body, that you may be a Sign to those who come after you! But verily, many among mankind are heedless of Our Signs!"

93. We settled the Children of Israel in a beautiful dwelling-place, and provided for them sustenance of the best: it

الَّذِىٓ اٰمَنَتْ بِهٖ بَنُوٓا اِسْرَآءِيْلَ

وَاَنَا مِنَ الْمُسْلِمِيْنَ ۞ آٰلْئٰنَ

وَقَدْ عَصَيْتَ قَبْلُ وَكُنْتَ مِنَ

الْمُفْسِدِيْنَ ۞ فَالْيَوْمَ نُنَجِّيْكَ

بِبَدَنِكَ لِتَكُوْنَ لِمَنْ خَلْفَكَ

اٰيَةً ؕ وَاِنَّ كَثِيْرًا مِّنَ النَّاسِ

عَنْ اٰيٰتِنَا لَغٰفِلُوْنَ ۞ وَلَقَدْ

بَوَّاْنَا بَنِيْٓ اِسْرَآءِيْلَ مُبَوَّاَ صِدْقٍ

وَّرَزَقْنٰهُمْ مِّنَ الطَّيِّبٰتِ ۚ فَمَا

Deface our Lord, the features of their wealth, and send hardness to their hearts, so they will not believe until they see the grievous Chastisement."

89. Allah said: "Accepted is your prayer (O Moses and Aaron)! So stand you straight, and follow not the path of those who know not."

90. We took the Children of Israel across the sea: Pharaoh and his hosts followed them in insolence and spite. At length, when overwhelmed with the flood, he said: "I believe that there is no Allah except

اطْمِسْ عَلَى أَمْوَالِهِمْ وَاشْدُدْ عَلَى

قُلُوبِهِمْ فَلَا يُؤْمِنُوا حَتّٰى يَرَوُا

الْعَذَابَ الْأَلِيْمَ ۝ قَالَ قَدْ أُجِيْبَتْ

دَّعْوَتُكُمَا فَاسْتَقِيْمَا وَلَا تَتَّبِعٰنِّ

سَبِيْلَ الَّذِيْنَ لَا يَعْلَمُوْنَ ۝

وَجٰوَزْنَا بِبَنِي إِسْرَآءِيْلَ الْبَحْرَ

فَأَتْبَعَهُمْ فِرْعَوْنُ وَجُنُوْدُهُ بَغْيًا

وَّعَدْوًا حَتّٰى إِذَا أَدْرَكَهُ الْغَرَقُ

قَالَ اٰمَنْتُ أَنَّهُ لَا إِلٰهَ إِلَّا

a trial for those who practise oppression;"

86. "And deliver us by Your Mercy from those who reject (You)."

87. We inspired Moses and his brother with this Message: "Provide dwellings for your people in Egypt, make your dwellings into places of worship, and establish regular prayers: and give glad tidings to those who believe!"

88. Moses prayed: "Our Lord! You have indeed bestowed on Pharaoh and his chiefs splendour and wealth in the life of the present, and so, our Lord, they mislead (men) from Your Path.

فِتْنَةً لِّلْقَوْمِ الظّٰلِمِيْنَ ۞ وَ نَجِّنَا

بِرَحْمَتِكَ مِنَ الْقَوْمِ الْكٰفِرِيْنَ ۞

وَ اَوْحَيْنَاۤ اِلٰى مُوْسٰى وَ اَخِيْهِ اَنْ

تَبَوَّاٰ لِقَوْمِكُمَا بِمِصْرَ بُيُوْتًا وَّاجْعَلُوْا

بُيُوْتَكُمْ قِبْلَةً وَّ اَقِيْمُوا الصَّلٰوةَ ؕ

وَ بَشِّرِ الْمُؤْمِنِيْنَ ۞ وَ قَالَ مُوْسٰى

رَبَّنَاۤ اِنَّكَ اٰتَيْتَ فِرْعَوْنَ وَ مَلَاَهٗ

زِيْنَةً وَّ اَمْوَالًا فِى الْحَيٰوةِ الدُّنْيَا ۙ

رَبَّنَا لِيُضِلُّوْا عَنْ سَبِيْلِكَ ۚ رَبَّنَا

the sinners may hate it!"

83. But none believed in Moses except some children of his people, because of the fear of Pharaoh and his chiefs, lest they should persecute them; and certainly Pharaoh was mighty on the earth and one who transgressed all bounds.

84. Moses said: "O my people! If you do (really) believe in Allah, then in Him put your trust if you submit (your will to His)."

85. They said: "In Allah do we put out trust. Our Lord! Make us not

الْمُجْرِمُوْنَ ۝ فَمَاۤ اٰمَنَ لِمُوْسٰۤى

اِلَّا ذُرِّيَّةٌ مِّنْ قَوْمِهٖ عَلٰى

خَوْفٍ مِّنْ فِرْعَوْنَ وَمَلَائِهِمْ اَنْ

يَّفْتِنَهُمْ ؕ وَاِنَّ فِرْعَوْنَ لَعَالٍ فِى

الْاَرْضِ ۚ وَاِنَّهٗ لَمِنَ الْمُسْرِفِيْنَ ۝

وَقَالَ مُوْسٰى يٰقَوْمِ اِنْ كُنْتُمْ

اٰمَنْتُمْ بِاللّٰهِ فَعَلَيْهِ تَوَكَّلُوْۤا اِنْ

كُنْتُمْ مُّسْلِمِيْنَ ۝ فَقَالُوْا عَلَى

اللّٰهِ تَوَكَّلْنَا ۚ رَبَّنَا لَا تَجْعَلْنَا

in the land? But not we shall believe in you!"

79. Said Pharaoh: "Bring me every sorcerer well versed."

80. When the sorcerers came, Moses said to them: "Throw you what you (wish) to throw!"

81. When they had had their throw, Moses said: "What you have brought is sorcery: Allah will surely make it of no effect: for Allah prospereth not the work of those who make mischief.

82. "And Allah by His Words does prove and establish His truth, however much

فِى الْأَرْضِ ۚ وَمَا نَحْنُ لَكُمَا

بِمُؤْمِنِيْنَ ۞ وَقَالَ فِرْعَوْنُ ائْتُوْنِيْ

بِكُلِّ سٰحِرٍ عَلِيْمٍ ۞ فَلَمَّا جَآءَ

السَّحَرَةُ قَالَ لَهُمْ مُّوْسٰى أَلْقُوْا

مَآ أَنْتُمْ مُّلْقُوْنَ ۞ فَلَمَّآ أَلْقَوْا

قَالَ مُوْسٰى مَا جِئْتُمْ بِهِ السِّحْرُ ۚ

إِنَّ اللّٰهَ سَيُبْطِلُهُ ۚ إِنَّ اللّٰهَ لَا

يُصْلِحُ عَمَلَ الْمُفْسِدِيْنَ ۞ وَيُحِقُّ

اللّٰهُ الْحَقَّ بِكَلِمٰتِهِ وَلَوْ كَرِهَ

Moses and Aaron to Pharaoh and his chiefs with Our Signs. But they were arrogant: they were a people in sin.

76. When the Truth did come to them from Us, they said: "This is indeed evident sorcery!"

77. Said Moses: "Say you (this) about the truth when it has (actually) reached you? Is sorcery (like) this? But sorcerers will not prosper."

78. They said: "Have you come to us to turn us away from the ways we found our fathers following, - in order that you and your brother may have greatness

بَعْدِهِمْ مُّوْسٰى وَهٰرُوْنَ اِلٰى

فِرْعَوْنَ وَمَلَا۟ئِهٖ بِاٰيٰتِنَا فَاسْتَكْبَرُوْا

وَكَانُوْا قَوْمًا مُّجْرِمِيْنَ ۞ فَلَمَّا

جَآءَهُمُ الْحَقُّ مِنْ عِنْدِنَا قَالُوْٓا

اِنَّ هٰذَا لَسِحْرٌ مُّبِيْنٌ ۞ قَالَ

مُوْسٰىٓ اَتَقُوْلُوْنَ لِلْحَقِّ لَمَّا جَآءَكُمْ

اَسِحْرٌ هٰذَا ۗ وَلَا يُفْلِحُ السّٰحِرُوْنَ ۞

قَالُوْٓا اَجِئْتَنَا لِتَلْفِتَنَا عَمَّا وَجَدْنَا

عَلَيْهِ اٰبَآءَنَا وَتَكُوْنَ لَكُمَا الْكِبْرِيَآءُ

and those with him, in the Ark, and We made them inherit (the earth), while We overwhelmed in the flood those who rejected Our Signs. Then see what was the end of those who were warned (but heeded not)!

74. Then after him We sent (many) Apostles to their peoples: they brought them clear Signs, but they would not believe what they had already rejected before-hand. Thus do We seal the hearts of the transgressors.

75. Then after them sent We

وَمَن مَّعَهُ فِى الْفُلْكِ وَجَعَلْنَاهُمْ

خَلَآئِفَ وَأَغْرَقْنَا الَّذِيْنَ كَذَّبُوْا

بِـاٰيَاتِنَا فَانْظُرْ كَيْفَ كَانَ عَاقِبَةُ

الْمُنْذَرِيْنَ ۞ ثُمَّ بَعَثْنَا مِنْ

بَعْدِهِ رُسُلًا إِلَى قَوْمِهِمْ

فَجَآءُوْهُمْ بِالْبَيِّنَاتِ فَمَا كَانُوْا

لِيُؤْمِنُوْا بِمَا كَذَّبُوْا بِهِ مِنْ

قَبْلُ ۚ كَذٰلِكَ نَطْبَعُ عَلَى قُلُوْبِ

الْمُعْتَدِيْنَ ۞ ثُمَّ بَعَثْنَا مِنْ

"O my people, if it be hard on your (mind) that I should stay (with you) and commemorate the Signs of Allah, - yet I put my trust in Allah. Get you then an agreement about your plan and among your partners, so your plan be not to you dark and dubious. Then pass your sentence on me, and give me no respite."

72. "But if you turn back, (consider): no reward have I asked of you: my reward is only due from Allah, and I have been commanded to be of those who submit to Allah's Will (in Islam)."

73. They rejected Him, but We delivered him,

يٰقَوْمِ اِنْ كَانَ كَبُرَ عَلَيْكُمْ

مَّقَامِىْ وَتَذْكِيْرِىْ بِاٰيٰتِ اللّٰهِ

فَعَلَى اللّٰهِ تَوَكَّلْتُ فَاَجْمِعُوْٓا اَمْرَكُمْ

وَشُرَكَآءَكُمْ ثُمَّ لَا يَكُنْ اَمْرُكُمْ

عَلَيْكُمْ غُمَّةً ثُمَّ اقْضُوْٓا اِلَىَّ وَلَا

تُنْظِرُوْنِ ۞ فَاِنْ تَوَلَّيْتُمْ فَمَا

سَاَلْتُكُمْ مِّنْ اَجْرٍ ۖ اِنْ اَجْرِىَ

اِلَّا عَلَى اللّٰهِ ۖ وَاُمِرْتُ اَنْ اَكُوْنَ

مِنَ الْمُسْلِمِيْنَ ۞ فَكَذَّبُوْهُ فَنَجَّيْنٰهُ

and on earth! No warrant have you for this! Say you about Allah what you know not?

69. Say: "Those who invent a lie against Allah will never prosper."

70. A little enjoyment in this world! - and then, to Us will be their return, then shall We make them taste the severest Chastisement for their blasphemies.

71. Relate to them the story of Noah. Behold! He said to his people:

وَمَا فِي الْأَرْضِ ۚ إِنْ عِنْدَكُمْ

مِنْ سُلْطَنٍ بِهَذَا ۗ أَتَقُوْلُوْنَ

عَلَى اللّٰهِ مَا لَا تَعْلَمُوْنَ ۞ قُلْ

إِنَّ الَّذِيْنَ يَفْتَرُوْنَ عَلَى اللّٰهِ

الْكَذِبَ لَا يُفْلِحُوْنَ ۞ مَتَاعٌ

فِي الدُّنْيَا ثُمَّ إِلَيْنَا مَرْجِعُهُمْ

ثُمَّ نُذِيقُهُمُ الْعَذَابَ الشَّدِيْدَ

بِمَا كَانُوْا يَكْفُرُوْنَ ۞ وَاتْلُ

عَلَيْهِمْ نَبَأَ نُوْحٍ ۘ إِذْ قَالَ لِقَوْمِهٖ

and on earth. What do they follow who worship as His "partners" other than Allah? They follow nothing but fancy, and they do nothing but lie.

67. He it is that has made for you the night that you may rest therein, and the day to make things visible (to you). Verily in this are Signs for those who listen (to His Message).

68. They say: "Alalh has begotten a son!" - Glory be to Him! He is Self-Sufficient! His are all things in the heavens

وَمَنْ فِى الْاَرْضِ ۗ وَمَا يَتَّبِعُ

الَّذِيْنَ يَدْعُوْنَ مِنْ دُوْنِ اللّٰهِ

شُرَكَآءَ ۚ اِنْ يَّتَّبِعُوْنَ اِلَّا الظَّنَّ

وَاِنْ هُمْ اِلَّا يَخْرُصُوْنَ ۞ هُوَ

الَّذِىْ جَعَلَ لَكُمُ الَّيْلَ لِتَسْكُنُوْا

فِيْهِ وَالنَّهَارَ مُبْصِرًا ۗ اِنَّ فِىْ

ذٰلِكَ لَاٰيٰتٍ لِّقَوْمٍ يَّسْمَعُوْنَ ۞

قَالُوا اتَّخَذَ اللّٰهُ وَلَدًا سُبْحٰنَهٗ ۗ

هُوَ الْغَنِىُّ ۗ لَهٗ مَا فِى السَّمٰوٰتِ

62. Behold! Verily on the friends of Allah there is no fear, nor shall they grieve;

63. Those who believe and (constantly) guard against evil; -

64. For them are glad tidings, in the life of the present and in the Hereafter; no change can there be in the Words of Allah. This is indeed the supreme felicity.

65. Let not their speech grieve you: for all power and honour belong to Allah: it is He Who hears and knows (all things).

66. Behold! Verily to Allah belong all creatures, in the heavens

اَلَاۤ اِنَّ اَوْلِيَآءَ اللّٰهِ لَا خَوْفٌ

عَلَيْهِمْ وَلَا هُمْ يَحْزَنُوْنَ ۝

الَّذِيْنَ اٰمَنُوْا وَكَانُوْا يَتَّقُوْنَ ۝

لَهُمُ الْبُشْرٰى فِى الْحَيٰوةِ الدُّنْيَا

وَفِى الْاٰخِرَةِ ۗ لَا تَبْدِيْلَ لِكَلِمٰتِ

اللّٰهِ ۗ ذٰلِكَ هُوَ الْفَوْزُ الْعَظِيْمُ ۝

وَلَا يَحْزُنْكَ قَوْلُهُمْ ۘ اِنَّ الْعِزَّةَ

لِلّٰهِ جَمِيْعًا ۗ هُوَ السَّمِيْعُ الْعَلِيْمُ ۝

اَلَاۤ اِنَّ لِلّٰهِ مَنْ فِى السَّمٰوٰتِ

to mankind, but most of them are ungrateful.

61. In whatever business you may be, and whatever portion you may be reciting from the Qur'an, - and whatever deed you (mankind) may be doing, - We are Witnesses thereof when you are deeply engrossed therein. Nor is hidden from your Lord (so much as) the weight of an atom on the earth or in heaven. And not the least and not the greatest of these things but are recorded in a clear Record.

عَلَى النَّاسِ وَلٰكِنَّ اَكْثَرَهُمْ لَا

يَشْكُرُوْنَ ۞ وَمَا تَكُوْنُ فِيْ شَأْنٍ

وَمَا تَتْلُوْا مِنْهُ مِنْ قُرْاٰنٍ

وَلَا تَعْمَلُوْنَ مِنْ عَمَلٍ اِلَّا

كُنَّا عَلَيْكُمْ شُهُوْدًا اِذْ تُفِيْضُوْنَ

فِيْهِ ۚ وَمَا يَعْزُبُ عَنْ رَّبِّكَ مِنْ

مِّثْقَالِ ذَرَّةٍ فِي الْاَرْضِ وَلَا

فِي السَّمَآءِ وَلَا اَصْغَرَ مِنْ ذٰلِكَ

وَلَا اَكْبَرَ اِلَّا فِيْ كِتٰبٍ مُّبِيْنٍ ۞

58. Say: "In the Bounty of Allah, and in His Mercy, - in that let them rejoice": that is better than the (wealth) they hoard.

59. Say: "See you what things Allah has sent down to you for sustenance? Yet you hold forbidden some things thereof and (some things) lawful." Say: "Has Allah indeed permitted you, or do you invent (things) to attribute to Allah?"

60. And what think those who invent lies against Allah, of the Day of Judgment? Verily Allah is full of Bounty

قُلْ بِفَضْلِ اللّٰهِ وَبِرَحْمَتِهٖ

فَبِذٰلِكَ فَلْيَفْرَحُوْا ۚ هُوَ خَيْرٌ مِّمَّا

يَجْمَعُوْنَ ۞ قُلْ اَرَءَيْتُمْ مَّاۤ

اَنْزَلَ اللّٰهُ لَكُمْ مِّنْ رِّزْقٍ

فَجَعَلْتُمْ مِّنْهُ حَرَامًا وَّحَلٰلًا ۚ

قُلْ آٰللّٰهُ اَذِنَ لَكُمْ اَمْ عَلَى

اللّٰهِ تَفْتَرُوْنَ ۞ وَمَا ظَنُّ الَّذِيْنَ

يَفْتَرُوْنَ عَلَى اللّٰهِ الْكَذِبَ يَوْمَ

الْقِيٰمَةِ ؕ اِنَّ اللّٰهَ لَذُوْ فَضْلٍ

when they see the Chastisement: but the judgment between them will be with justice, and no wrong will be done unto them.

55. Is it not (the case) that to Allah belongs whatever is in the heavens and on earth? Is it not (the case) that Allah's promise is assuredly true? Yet most of them understand not.

56. It is He Who gives life and who takes it, and to Him shall you all be brought back.

57. O mankind! There has come to you a direction from your Lord and a healing for the (diseases) in your hearts, - and for those who believe, a Guidance and a Mercy.

لَمَّا رَاوُا الْعَذَابَ وَقُضِيَ بَيْنَهُمْ
بِالْقِسْطِ وَهُمْ لَا يُظْلَمُونَ ۝ اَلَآ
اِنَّ لِلّٰهِ مَا فِى السَّمٰوٰتِ وَالْاَرْضِ
اَلَآ اِنَّ وَعْدَ اللّٰهِ حَقٌّ وَّلٰكِنَّ
اَكْثَرَهُمْ لَا يَعْلَمُونَ ۝ هُوَ يُحْيٖ
وَيُمِيْتُ وَاِلَيْهِ تُرْجَعُوْنَ ۝ يٰٓاَيُّهَا
النَّاسُ قَدْ جَآءَتْكُمْ مَّوْعِظَةٌ مِّنْ
رَّبِّكُمْ وَشِفَآءٌ لِّمَا فِى الصُّدُوْرِ ۙ
وَهُدًى وَّرَحْمَةٌ لِّلْمُؤْمِنِيْنَ ۝

(It will then be said): 'Ah! now? And you wanted (aforetime) to hasten it on!'

52. "At length will be said to the wrong-doers: 'Taste you the enduring punishment! you get but the recompense of what you earned!'"

53. They seek to be informed by you: "Is that true?" Say: "Yes, by my Lord! it is the very truth and you cannot frustrat it!"

54. Every soul that has sinned, if it possessed all that is on earth, would gladly give it in ransom: they would declare (their) repentance

اٰمَنْتُمْ بِهٖٓ اٰلْـٰٔنَ وَقَدْ كُنْتُمْ بِهٖ

تَسْتَعْجِلُوْنَ ۞ ثُمَّ قِيْلَ لِلَّذِيْنَ

ظَلَمُوْا ذُوْقُوْا عَذَابَ الْخُلْدِ ۚ

هَلْ تُجْزَوْنَ اِلَّا بِمَا كُنْتُمْ

تَكْسِبُوْنَ ۞ وَيَسْتَنْۢبِـُٔوْنَكَ اَحَقٌّ

هُوَ ؕ قُلْ اِیْ وَرَبِّیْٓ اِنَّهٗ لَحَقٌّ ؕؔ

وَمَآ اَنْتُمْ بِمُعْجِزِيْنَ ۞ وَلَوْ اَنَّ

لِكُلِّ نَفْسٍ ظَلَمَتْ مَا فِی الْاَرْضِ

لَافْتَدَتْ بِهٖ ؕ وَاَسَرُّوا النَّدَامَةَ

will not be wronged.

48. They say: "When will this promise come to pass, - if you speak the truth?"

49. Say: "I have no power over any harm or profit to myself except as Allah wills. To every People is a term appointed: when their term is reached, not an hour can they cause delay, nor (an hour) can they advance (it in anticipation)."

50. Say: "Do you see, - if His punishment should come to you by night or by day, - what portion of it would the sinners wish to hasten?

51. "Would you then believe in it at last, when it actually comes to pass?

لَا يُظْلَمُوْنَ ۝ وَيَقُوْلُوْنَ مَتٰى هٰذَا

الْوَعْدُ اِنْ كُنْتُمْ صٰدِقِيْنَ ۝ قُلْ

لَّا اَمْلِكُ لِنَفْسِيْ ضَرًّا وَّلَا نَفْعًا

اِلَّا مَا شَاءَ اللّٰهُ لِكُلِّ اُمَّةٍ اَجَلٌ

اِذَا جَاءَ اَجَلُهُمْ فَلَا يَسْتَأْخِرُوْنَ

سَاعَةً وَّلَا يَسْتَقْدِمُوْنَ ۝ قُلْ

اَرَءَيْتُمْ اِنْ اَتٰكُمْ عَذَابُهٗ بَيَاتًا

اَوْ نَهَارًا مَّا ذَا يَسْتَعْجِلُ مِنْهُ

الْمُجْرِمُوْنَ ۝ اَثُمَّ اِذَا مَا وَقَعَ

(it will be) as if they had tarried but an hour of a day: they will recognise each other: assuredly those will be lost who denied the meeting with Allah and refused to receive true guidance.

46. Whether We show you (realised in your life-time) some part of what We promise them, - or We take your soul (to Our Mercy) (before that), - in any case, to Us is their return: ultimately Allah is Witness, to all that they do.

47. To every people (was sent) an Apostle: when their Apostle comes (before them), the matter will be judged between them with justice, and they

كَانَ لَّمْ يَلْبَثُوٓا إِلَّا سَاعَةً

مِّنَ النَّهَارِ يَتَعَارَفُونَ بَيْنَهُمْ ۚ

قَدْ خَسِرَ الَّذِينَ كَذَّبُوا بِلِقَآءِ

اللَّهِ وَمَا كَانُوا مُهْتَدِينَ ۞ وَإِمَّا

نُرِيَنَّكَ بَعْضَ الَّذِى نَعِدُهُمْ

أَوْ نَتَوَفَّيَنَّكَ فَإِلَيْنَا مَرْجِعُهُمْ ثُمَّ

اللَّهُ شَهِيدٌ عَلَىٰ مَا يَفْعَلُونَ ۞

وَلِكُلِّ أُمَّةٍ رَّسُولٌ ۖ فَإِذَا جَآءَ

رَسُولُهُمْ قُضِىَ بَيْنَهُم بِالْقِسْطِ وَهُمْ

are free from responsibility for what I do, and I for what you do!"

42.   Among them are some who (pretend to) listen to you: but cannot you make the deaf to hear, - even though they are without understanding?

43.   And among them are some who look at you: but cannot you guide the blind, - even though they will not see?

44.   Verily Allah will not deal unjustly with man in anything: it is man that wrongs his own soul.

45.   One day He will gather them together:

بَرِيْٓـُٔوْنَ مِمَّآ اَعْمَلُ وَاَنَا بَرِىْٓءٌ

مِّمَّا تَعْمَلُوْنَ ۞ وَمِنْهُمْ مَّنْ

يَّسْتَمِعُوْنَ اِلَيْكَ ۚ اَفَاَنْتَ تُسْمِعُ

الصُّمَّ وَلَوْ كَانُوْا لَا يَعْقِلُوْنَ ۞

وَمِنْهُمْ مَّنْ يَّنْظُرُ اِلَيْكَ ۚ اَفَاَنْتَ

تَهْدِى الْعُمْىَ وَلَوْ كَانُوْا لَا

يُبْصِرُوْنَ ۞ اِنَّ اللّٰهَ لَا يَظْلِمُ

النَّاسَ شَيْئًا وَّلٰكِنَّ النَّاسَ

اَنْفُسَهُمْ يَظْلِمُوْنَ ۞ وَيَوْمَ يَحْشُرُهُمْ

be you speak the truth!"

39. No, they charge with falsehood that whose knowledge they cannot compass, even before the elucidation thereof has reached them: thus did those before them make charges of falsehood: but see what was the end of those who did wrong!

40. Of them there are some who believe therein, and some who do not: and your Lord knows best those who are out for mischief.

41. If they charge you with falsehood, say: "My work to me, and yours to you! You

كُنْتُمْ صٰدِقِيْنَ ۞ بَلْ كَذَّبُوْا

بِمَا لَمْ يُحِيْطُوْا بِعِلْمِهٖ وَلَمَّا

يَأْتِهِمْ تَأْوِيْلُهٗ ۚ كَذٰلِكَ كَذَّبَ

الَّذِيْنَ مِنْ قَبْلِهِمْ فَانْظُرْ كَيْفَ

كَانَ عَاقِبَةُ الظّٰلِمِيْنَ ۞ وَمِنْهُمْ

مَّنْ يُّؤْمِنُ بِهٖ وَمِنْهُمْ مَّنْ

لَّا يُؤْمِنُ بِهٖ ۗ وَرَبُّكَ أَعْلَمُ

بِالْمُفْسِدِيْنَ ۞ وَإِنْ كَذَّبُوْكَ فَقُلْ

لِّيْ عَمَلِيْ وَلَكُمْ عَمَلُكُمْ ۚ أَنْتُمْ

can be of no avail against truth.
Verily Allah is Well Aware of all
that they do.

37. This Qur'an is not such as
can be produced by other than
Allah; on the contrary it is a
confirmation of (revelations) that
went before it, and a fuller
explanation of the Book - wherein
there is no doubt - from the Lord
of the Worlds.

38. Or do they say, "He forged
it"? Say: "Bring then a Sura like
unto it, and call (to your aid) anyone you can besides Allah, if it -

يُغْنِى مِنَ الْحَقِّ شَيْئًا ۚ إِنَّ اللّٰهَ

عَلِيْمٌ بِمَا يَفْعَلُوْنَ ۞ وَمَا كَانَ

هٰذَا الْقُرْاٰنُ اَنْ يُّفْتَرٰى مِنْ

دُوْنِ اللّٰهِ وَلٰكِنْ تَصْدِيْقَ الَّذِىْ

بَيْنَ يَدَيْهِ وَتَفْصِيْلَ الْكِتٰبِ لَا

رَيْبَ فِيْهِ مِنْ رَّبِّ الْعٰلَمِيْنَ ۞

اَمْ يَقُوْلُوْنَ افْتَرٰىهُ ۚ قُلْ فَأْتُوْا

بِسُوْرَةٍ مِّثْلِهٖ وَادْعُوْا مَنِ

اسْتَطَعْتُمْ مِّنْ دُوْنِ اللّٰهِ اِنْ

creation and repeat it?" Say: "It is Allah Who originates creation and repeats it: then how are you deluded away (from the truth)?"

35. Say: "Of your 'partners' is there any that can give any guidance towards truth?" Say: "It is Allah Who gives guidance towards truth, is then He Who gives guidance to truth more worthy to be followed, or he who finds not guidance (himself) unless he is guided? What then is the matter with you? How wrong judgments you make?"

36. But most of them follow nothing but conjecture: truly conjecture

الْخَلْقَ ثُمَّ يُعِيدُهُ قُلِ اللّٰهُ

يَبْدَؤُا الْخَلْقَ ثُمَّ يُعِيدُهُ فَأَنّٰى

تُؤْفَكُونَ ۞ قُلْ هَلْ مِنْ شُرَكَآئِكُمْ

مَّنْ يَّهْدِىٓ إِلَى الْحَقِّ قُلِ اللّٰهُ

يَهْدِىْ لِلْحَقِّ أَفَمَنْ يَّهْدِىٓ إِلَى

الْحَقِّ أَحَقُّ أَنْ يُّتَّبَعَ أَمَّنْ لَّا

يَهِدِّىٓ إِلَّآ أَنْ يُّهْدٰى فَمَا لَكُمْ

كَيْفَ تَحْكُمُونَ ۞ وَمَا يَتَّبِعُ

أَكْثَرُهُمْ إِلَّا ظَنًّا إِنَّ الظَّنَّ لَا

that brings out the living from the dead and the dead from the living? And who is it that rules and regulates all affairs?" They will soon say, "Allah". Say, "Will you not then show piety (to Him)?"

32. Such is Allah, your true Lord; apart from Truth, what (remains) but error? How then are you turned away?

33. Thus is the word of your Lord proved true against those who rebel: verily they will not believe.

34. Say: "Of your 'partners', can any originate

يُخۡرِجُ الۡحَىَّ مِنَ الۡمَيِّتِ وَيُخۡرِجُ

الۡمَيِّتَ مِنَ الۡحَىِّ وَمَنۡ يُّدَبِّرُ

الۡاَمۡرَ ۚ فَسَيَقُوۡلُوۡنَ اللّٰهُ ۚ فَقُلۡ اَفَلَا

تَتَّقُوۡنَ ۞ فَذٰلِكُمُ اللّٰهُ رَبُّكُمُ

الۡحَقُّ ۚ فَمَا ذَا بَعۡدَ الۡحَقِّ اِلَّا

الضَّلٰلُ ۚ فَاَنّٰى تُصۡرَفُوۡنَ ۞ كَذٰلِكَ

حَقَّتۡ كَلِمَتُ رَبِّكَ عَلَى الَّذِيۡنَ

فَسَقُوۡٓا اَنَّهُمۡ لَا يُؤۡمِنُوۡنَ ۞ قُلۡ

هَلۡ مِنۡ شُرَكَآئِكُمۡ مَّنۡ يَّبۡدَؤُا

us that you worshipped!"

29. "Enough is Allah for a witness between us and you: we certainly knew nothing of your worship of us!"

30. There will every soul prove (the fruits of) the deeds it sent before: they will be brought back to Allah their rightful Lord, and their invented falsehoods will leave them in the lurch.

31. Say: "Who is it that sustains you (in life) from the sky and from the earth? Or who is it that has power over hearing and sight? And who is it

كُنْتُمْ اِيَّانَا تَعْبُدُوْنَ ۞ فَكَفٰى

بِاللّٰهِ شَهِيْدًۢا بَيْنَنَا وَبَيْنَكُمْ اِنْ

كُنَّا عَنْ عِبَادَتِكُمْ لَغٰفِلِيْنَ ۞

هُنَالِكَ تَبْلُوْا كُلُّ نَفْسٍ مَّاۤ

اَسْلَفَتْ وَرُدُّوْۤا اِلَى اللّٰهِ مَوْلٰىهُمُ

الْحَقِّ وَضَلَّ عَنْهُمْ مَّا كَانُوْا

يَفْتَرُوْنَ ۞ قُلْ مَنْ يَّرْزُقُكُمْ

مِّنَ السَّمَآءِ وَالْاَرْضِ اَمَّنْ

يَّمْلِكُ السَّمْعَ وَالْاَبْصَارَ وَمَنْ

evil will have a reward of like evil: ignominy will cover their (faces): no defender will they have from (the wrath of) Allah: their faces will be covered, as it were, with pieces from the depth of the darkness of night : they are Companions of the Fire: they will abide therein (for ever)!

28. One day shall We gather them all together. Then shall We say to those who joined gods (with Us): "To your place! you and those who me you joined as 'partners' We shall separate them, and their "partners" shall say: "It was not

السَّيِّاٰتِ جَزَاءُ سَيِّئَةٍ بِمِثْلِهَا ۖ

وَتَرْهَقُهُمْ ذِلَّةٌ ۚ مَا لَهُمْ مِّنَ

اللّٰهِ مِنْ عَاصِمٍ ۖ كَأَنَّمَا أُغْشِيَتْ

وُجُوْهُهُمْ قِطَعًا مِّنَ الَّيْلِ

مُظْلِمًا ۚ أُولٰٓئِكَ أَصْحٰبُ النَّارِ ۖ هُمْ

فِيْهَا خٰلِدُوْنَ ۝ وَيَوْمَ نَحْشُرُهُمْ

جَمِيْعًا ثُمَّ نَقُوْلُ لِلَّذِيْنَ أَشْرَكُوْا

مَكَانَكُمْ أَنْتُمْ وَشُرَكَآؤُكُمْ ۚ فَزَيَّلْنَا

بَيْنَهُمْ وَقَالَ شُرَكَآؤُهُمْ مَّا

or by day, and We make it like a harvest clean-mown, as if it had not flourished only the day before! thus do We explain the Signs in detail for those who reflect.

25. But Allah does call to the Home of Peace: He guides those whom He pleases to a way that is straight.

26. To those who do right is a goodly (reward) - yes, more (than in measure)! No darkness nor shame shall cover their faces! They are Companions of the Garden; they will abide therein (for ever).

27. But those who have earned

اَوۡ نَهَارًا فَجَعَلۡنٰهَا حَصِيۡدًا كَاَنۡ

لَّمۡ تَغۡنَ بِالۡاَمۡسِ ؕ كَذٰلِكَ نُفَصِّلُ

الۡاٰيٰتِ لِقَوۡمٍ يَّتَفَكَّرُوۡنَ ۟ وَاللّٰهُ

يَدۡعُوۡۤا اِلٰى دَارِ السَّلٰمِ ؕ وَيَهۡدِىۡ

مَنۡ يَّشَآءُ اِلٰى صِرَاطٍ مُّسۡتَقِيۡمٍ

لِلَّذِيۡنَ اَحۡسَنُوا الۡحُسۡنٰى وَزِيَادَةٌ ؕ

وَلَا يَرۡهَقُ وُجُوۡهَهُمۡ قَتَرٌ وَّلَا

ذِلَّةٌ ؕ اُولٰٓئِكَ اَصۡحٰبُ الۡجَنَّةِ ۚ هُمۡ

فِيۡهَا خٰلِدُوۡنَ ۟ وَالَّذِيۡنَ كَسَبُوا

against your own souls, - an enjoyment of the life of the present: in the end, to Us is your return, and We shall show you the truth of all that you did.

24. The likeness of the life of the present is as the rain which We send down from the skies: by its mingling arises the produce of the earth - which provides food for men and animals: (it grows) till the earth is clad with its golden ornaments and is decked out (in beauty): the people to whom it belongs think they have all powers of disposal over it: there reaches it Our command by night

عَلٰۤى اَنْفُسِكُمْ مَّتَاعَ الْحَيٰوةِ الدُّنْيَا

ثُمَّ اِلَيْنَا مَرْجِعُكُمْ فَنُنَبِّئُكُمْ

بِمَا كُنْتُمْ تَعْمَلُوْنَ ۞ اِنَّمَا مَثَلُ

الْحَيٰوةِ الدُّنْيَا كَمَآءٍ اَنْزَلْنٰهُ مِنَ

السَّمَآءِ فَاخْتَلَطَ بِهٖ نَبَاتُ الْاَرْضِ

مِمَّا يَاْكُلُ النَّاسُ وَالْاَنْعَامُ

حَتّٰۤى اِذَآ اَخَذَتِ الْاَرْضُ زُخْرُفَهَا

وَازَّيَّنَتْ وَظَنَّ اَهْلُهَآ اَنَّهُمْ

قٰدِرُوْنَ عَلَيْهَآ اَتٰىهَآ اَمْرُنَا لَيْلًا

they sail with them with a favourable wind, and they rejoice thereat; then comes a stormy wind and the waves come to them from all sides, and they think they are being overwhelmed: they cry unto Allah, sincerely offering (their) duty unto Him saying, "If You does deliver us from this, we shall truly show our gratitude!"

23. But when He delivers them, behold! they transgress insolently through the earth in defiance of right! O mankind! your insolence is

وَجَرَيْنَ بِهِم بِرِيحٍ طَيِّبَةٍ

وَّفَرِحُوا بِهَا جَآءَتْهَا رِيحٌ

عَاصِفٌ وَّجَآءَهُمُ الْمَوْجُ مِن كُلِّ

مَكَانٍ وَّظَنُّوٓا أَنَّهُمْ أُحِيطَ بِهِمْ

دَعَوُا اللّٰهَ مُخْلِصِيْنَ لَهُ الدِّيْنَ ۚ

لَئِنْ أَنْجَيْتَنَا مِنْ هٰذِهٖ لَنَكُوْنَنَّ

مِنَ الشّٰكِرِيْنَ ۞ فَلَمَّآ أَنْجٰهُمْ

إِذَا هُمْ يَبْغُوْنَ فِي الْأَرْضِ بِغَيْرِ

الْحَقِّ ۗ يٰٓأَيُّهَا النَّاسُ إِنَّمَا بَغْيُكُمْ

from his Lord?" Say: "The Unseen is only for Allah (to know), then wait you: I too will wait with you."

21. When We make mankind taste of some mercy after adversity has touched them, behold! they take to plotting against Our Signs! Say: "Swifter to plan is Allah!" Verily, Our Angels record all the plots that you make.

22. He it is Who enables you to traverse through land and sea; so that you even board ships; -

اٰيَةٌ مِّنْ رَّبِّهٖ فَقُلْ اِنَّمَا

الْغَيْبُ لِلّٰهِ فَانْتَظِرُوْا اِنِّيْ مَعَكُمْ

مِّنَ الْمُنْتَظِرِيْنَ ۞ وَاِذَآ اَذَقْنَا

النَّاسَ رَحْمَةً مِّنْ بَعْدِ ضَرَّآءَ

مَسَّتْهُمْ اِذَا لَهُمْ مَّكْرٌ فِيْٓ اٰيَاتِنَا

قُلِ اللّٰهُ اَسْرَعُ مَكْرًا اِنَّ رُسُلَنَا

يَكْتُبُوْنَ مَا تَمْكُرُوْنَ ۞ هُوَ

الَّذِيْ يُسَيِّرُكُمْ فِي الْبَرِّ وَالْبَحْرِ

حَتّٰٓى اِذَا كُنْتُمْ فِي الْفُلْكِ

nor profit them, and they say: "These are our intercessors with Allah." Say: "Do you indeed inform Allah of something He knows not, in the heavens or on earth? - Glory to Him! and far is He above the partners they ascribe (to Him)!"

19. Mankind was but one nation, but differed (later). Had it not been for a word that went forth before from your Lord, their differences would have been settled between them.

20. They say: "Why is not a sign sent down to him

وَلَا يَنْفَعُهُمْ وَيَقُوْلُوْنَ هٰٓؤُلَاۤءِ

شُفَعَآؤُنَا عِنْدَ اللّٰهِ ؕ قُلْ اَتُنَبِّئُوْنَ

اللّٰهَ بِمَا لَا يَعْلَمُ فِى السَّمٰوٰتِ وَلَا

فِى الْاَرْضِ ؕ سُبْحٰنَهٗ وَتَعٰلٰى عَمَّا

يُشْرِكُوْنَ ۝ وَمَا كَانَ النَّاسُ

اِلَّاۤ اُمَّةً وَّاحِدَةً فَاخْتَلَفُوْا ؕ وَلَوْلَا

كَلِمَةٌ سَبَقَتْ مِنْ رَّبِّكَ لَقُضِىَ

بَيْنَهُمْ فِيْمَا فِيْهِ يَخْتَلِفُوْنَ ۝

وَيَقُوْلُوْنَ لَوْلَاۤ اُنْزِلَ عَلَيْهِ

to disobey my Lord, I should myself fear the Chastisement of a Great Day (to come)."

16.   Say: "If Allah had so willed, I should not have rehearsed it to you, nor would He have made it known to you. A whole life-time before this have I tarried amongst you: will you not then understand?"

17.   Who does more wrong than such as forge a lie against Allah, or deny His Signs? But never will prosper those who sin.

18.   They serve, besides Allah, things what hurt them not

اِنۡ عَصَيۡتُ رَبِّيۡ عَذَابَ يَوۡمٍ

عَظِيۡمٍ ۝ قُلۡ لَّوۡ شَآءَ اللّٰهُ مَا

تَلَوۡتُهٗ عَلَيۡكُمۡ وَلَاۤ اَدۡرٰىكُمۡ بِهٖ ۖ

فَقَدۡ لَبِثۡتُ فِيۡكُمۡ عُمُرًا مِّنۡ

قَبۡلِهٖ ؕ اَفَلَا تَعۡقِلُوۡنَ ۝ فَمَنۡ

اَظۡلَمُ مِمَّنِ افۡتَرٰى عَلَى اللّٰهِ

كَذِبًا اَوۡ كَذَّبَ بِاٰيٰتِهٖ ؕ اِنَّهٗ لَا

يُفۡلِحُ الۡمُجۡرِمُوۡنَ ۝ وَيَعۡبُدُوۡنَ

مِنۡ دُوۡنِ اللّٰهِ مَا لَا يَضُرُّهُمۡ

who sin!

14. Then We made you heirs in the land after them, to see how you would behave!

15. But when Our clear Signs are rehearsed unto them, those who rest not their hope on their meeting with Us, say: "Bring us a Qur'an other than this, or change this," Say: "It is not for me, of my own accord, to change it: I follow nothing but what is revealed unto me: if I were

الْمُجْرِمِينَ ﴿١٢﴾ ثُمَّ جَعَلْنَكُمْ خَلَـٰئِفَ

فِي الْاَرْضِ مِنْ بَعْدِهِمْ لِنَنْظُرَ

كَيْفَ تَعْمَلُوْنَ ﴿١٣﴾ وَ اِذَا تُتْلٰى

عَلَيْهِمْ اٰيَاتُنَا بَيِّنٰتٍ ۙ قَالَ

الَّذِيْنَ لَا يَرْجُوْنَ لِقَآءَنَا ائْتِ

بِقُرْاٰنٍ غَيْرِ هٰذَآ اَوْ بَدِّلْهُ ؕ

قُلْ مَا يَكُوْنُ لِيْ اَنْ اُبَدِّلَهٗ

مِنْ تِلْقَآئِ نَفْسِيْ ۚ اِنْ اَتَّبِعُ

اِلَّا مَا يُوْحٰى اِلَيَّ ۚ اِنِّيْ اَخَافُ

trouble touches a man, He cries unto Us (in all postures) - lying down on his side, or sitting, or standing. But when We have solved his trouble, he passeth on his way as if he had never cried to Us for a trouble that touched him! thus do the deeds of transgressors seem fair in their eyes!

13.   Generations before you We destroyed when they did wrong: their Apostles came to them with clear Signs, but they would not believe! thus do We requite those

مَسَّ الْإِنْسَانَ الضُّرُّ دَعَانَا

لِجَنْبِهٖٓ اَوْ قَاعِدًا اَوْ قَآئِمًا ۚ

فَلَمَّا كَشَفْنَا عَنْهُ ضُرَّهٗ مَرَّ

كَاَنْ لَّمْ يَدْعُنَآ اِلٰى ضُرٍّ مَّسَّهٗ ؕ

كَذٰلِكَ زُيِّنَ لِلْمُسْرِفِيْنَ مَا كَانُوْا

يَعْمَلُوْنَ ۞ وَلَقَدْ اَهْلَكْنَا الْقُرُوْنَ

مِنْ قَبْلِكُمْ لَمَّا ظَلَمُوْا ۙ وَجَآءَتْهُمْ

رُسُلُهُمْ بِالْبَيِّنٰتِ وَمَا كَانُوْا

لِيُؤْمِنُوْا ؕ كَذٰلِكَ نَجْزِى الْقَوْمَ

rivers in Gardens of Bliss.

10. (This will be) their prayer therein: "Glory to you, O Allah!" And "Peace" will be their greeting therein! and the close of their prayer will be: "Praise be to Allah, the Cherisher and Sustainer of the Worlds!"

11. If Allah were to hasten for men the ill (they have earned) as they would gladly hasten on the good, - then would their respite be settled at once. But We leave those who rest not their hope on their meeting with Us, in their trespasses, wandering in distraction here and there.

12. When

الۡاَنۡهٰرُ فِیۡ جَنّٰتِ النَّعِیۡمِ ۟

دَعۡوٰىهُمۡ فِیۡهَا سُبۡحٰنَكَ اللّٰهُمَّ

وَتَحِیَّتُهُمۡ فِیۡهَا سَلٰمٌ ۚ وَاٰخِرُ

دَعۡوٰىهُمۡ اَنِ الۡحَمۡدُ لِلّٰهِ رَبِّ

الۡعٰلَمِیۡنَ ۟ وَلَوۡ یُعَجِّلُ اللّٰهُ

لِلنَّاسِ الشَّرَّ اسۡتِعۡجَالَهُمۡ

بِالۡخَیۡرِ لَقُضِیَ اِلَیۡهِمۡ اَجَلُهُمۡ ؕ

فَنَذَرُ الَّذِیۡنَ لَا یَرۡجُوۡنَ لِقَآءَنَا

فِیۡ طُغۡیَانِهِمۡ یَعۡمَهُوۡنَ ۟ وَاِذَا

Allah has created, in the heavens and the earth, are Signs for those who fear Him.

7.   Those who rest not their hope on their meeting with Us, but are pleased and satisfied with the life of the present, and those who heed not Our Signs, -

8.   Their abode is the Fire, because of the (evil) they earned.

9.   Those who believe, and work righteousness, - their Lord will guide them because of their faith: beneath them will flow

خَلَقَ اللّٰهُ فِى السَّمٰوٰتِ وَالْاَرْضِ
لَاٰيٰتٍ لِّقَوْمٍ يَّتَّقُوْنَ ۞ اِنَّ الَّذِيْنَ
لَا يَرْجُوْنَ لِقَآءَنَا وَرَضُوْا
بِالْحَيٰوةِ الدُّنْيَا وَاطْمَاَنُّوْا بِهَا
وَالَّذِيْنَ هُمْ عَنْ اٰيٰتِنَا غٰفِلُوْنَ ۞
اُولٰٓئِكَ مَأْوٰىهُمُ النَّارُ بِمَا كَانُوْا
يَكْسِبُوْنَ ۞ اِنَّ الَّذِيْنَ اٰمَنُوْا
وَعَمِلُوا الصّٰلِحٰتِ يَهْدِيْهِمْ رَبُّهُمْ
بِاِيْمَانِهِمْ تَجْرِىْ مِنْ تَحْتِهِمُ

reject Him will have draughts of boiling fluids, and a Chastisement grievous, because they did reject Him.

5.   It is He Who made the sun to be a shining glory and the moon to be a light (of beauty), and measured out stages for it, that you might know the number of years and the count (of time). Nowise did Allah create this but in truth and righteousness. (Thus) does He explain His Signs in detail, for those who understand.

6.   Verily, in the alternation of the night and the day, and in all that

كَفَرُوا لَهُمْ شَرَابٌ مِّنْ حَمِيۡمٍ

وَّعَذَابٌ اَلِيۡمٌۢ بِمَا كَانُوۡا

يَكۡفُرُوۡنَ ۞ هُوَ الَّذِىۡ جَعَلَ

الشَّمۡسَ ضِيَآءً وَّالۡقَمَرَ نُوۡرًا

وَّقَدَّرَهٗ مَنَازِلَ لِتَعۡلَمُوۡا عَدَدَ

السِّنِيۡنَ وَالۡحِسَابَ ؕ مَا خَلَقَ

اللّٰهُ ذٰلِكَ اِلَّا بِالۡحَقِّ ۚ يُفَصِّلُ

الۡاٰيٰتِ لِقَوۡمٍ يَّعۡلَمُوۡنَ ۞ اِنَّ فِىۡ

اخۡتِلَافِ الَّيۡلِ وَالنَّهَارِ وَمَا

in six days, and is firmly established on the Throne (of authority), regulating and governing
all things. No intercessor (can
plead with Him) except after His
leave (has been obtained). This is
Allah your Lord; Him therefore
serve you: will you not receive
admonition?

4.   To Him will be your return -
of all of you. The promise of Allah
is true and sure. It is He Who
begins the process of creation,
and repeats it, that He may
reward with justice those who
believe and work righteousness;
but those who

فِىْ سِتَّةِ اَيَّامٍ ثُمَّ اسْتَوٰى

عَلَى الْعَرْشِ يُدَبِّرُ الْاَمْرَ مَا

مِنْ شَفِيْعٍ اِلَّا مِنْ بَعْدِ اِذْنِهِ

ذٰلِكُمُ اللّٰهُ رَبُّكُمْ فَاعْبُدُوْهُ

اَفَلَا تَذَكَّرُوْنَ ۞ اِلَيْهِ مَرْجِعُكُمْ

جَمِيْعًا ۚ وَعْدَ اللّٰهِ حَقًّا ۗ اِنَّهٗ

يَبْدَؤُا الْخَلْقَ ثُمَّ يُعِيْدُهٗ

لِيَجْزِىَ الَّذِيْنَ اٰمَنُوْا وَعَمِلُوا

الصّٰلِحٰتِ بِالْقِسْطِ ۚ وَالَّذِيْنَ

Yunus (Jonah)

Bismillahir-Rahmanir-Rahim

1.   Alif. Lam. Raa. These are the Ayats (Verses) of the Book of Wisdom.

2.   Is it a matter of wonderment to men that We have sent Our inspiration to a man from among themselves? - that he should warn mankind (of their danger), and give the good news to the believers that they have before their Lord the lofty rank of truth. (But) say the unbelievers: "This is indeed an evident sorcerer!"

3.   Verily your Lord is Allah, Who created the heavens and the earth

بِسْمِ اللهِ الرَّحْمٰنِ الرَّحِيْمِ

الٓرٰ ۚ تِلْكَ اٰيٰتُ الْكِتٰبِ الْحَكِيْمِ ۟

اَكَانَ لِلنَّاسِ عَجَبًا اَنْ اَوْحَيْنَآ

اِلٰى رَجُلٍ مِّنْهُمْ اَنْ اَنْذِرِ

النَّاسَ وَ بَشِّرِ الَّذِيْنَ اٰمَنُوْٓا

اَنَّ لَهُمْ قَدَمَ صِدْقٍ عِنْدَ

رَبِّهِمْ ۗ قَالَ الْكٰفِرُوْنَ اِنَّ هٰذَا

لَسٰحِرٌ مُّبِيْنٌ ۟ اِنَّ رَبَّكُمُ اللهُ

الَّذِيْ خَلَقَ السَّمٰوٰتِ وَ الْاَرْضَ

"Does anyone see you?" Then they turn aside: Allah has turned their hearts (from the light); for they are a people that understand not.

128. Now has come unto you an Apostle from amongst yourselves: it grieves him that you should perish: ardently anxious is he over you: to the believers is he most kind and merciful.

129. But if they turn away, say: "Allah is sufficient for me: there is no Allah but He: on Him is my trust, - He is the Lord of the Throne (of Glory) Supreme!"

هَلْ يَرَاكُمْ مِّنْ أَحَدٍ ثُمَّ

انْصَرَفُوْا صَرَفَ اللهُ قُلُوْبَهُمْ

بِأَنَّهُمْ قَوْمٌ لَّا يَفْقَهُوْنَ ۝ لَقَدْ

جَآءَكُمْ رَسُوْلٌ مِّنْ أَنْفُسِكُمْ

عَزِيْزٌ عَلَيْهِ مَا عَنِتُّمْ حَرِيْصٌ

عَلَيْكُمْ بِالْمُؤْمِنِيْنَ رَءُوْفٌ رَّحِيْمٌ ۝

فَإِنْ تَوَلَّوْا فَقُلْ حَسْبِيَ اللهُ

لَا إِلٰهَ إِلَّا هُوَ عَلَيْهِ تَوَكَّلْتُ

وَهُوَ رَبُّ الْعَرْشِ الْعَظِيْمِ ۝

those who believe,- their faith is increased and they do rejoice.

125. But those in whose hearts is a disease, - it will add doubt to their doubt, and they will die in a state of Unbelief.

126. See they not that they are tried every year once or twice? Yet they turn not in repentance, and they take no heed.

127. Whenever there comes down a Sura, they look at each other, (saying),

الَّذِيْنَ اٰمَنُوْا فَزَادَتْهُمْ اِيْمَانًا

وَّهُمْ يَسْتَبْشِرُوْنَ ۞ وَاَمَّا الَّذِيْنَ

فِيْ قُلُوْبِهِمْ مَّرَضٌ فَزَادَتْهُمْ

رِجْسًا اِلٰى رِجْسِهِمْ وَمَاتُوْا وَهُمْ

كٰفِرُوْنَ ۞ اَوَلَا يَرَوْنَ اَنَّهُمْ

يُفْتَنُوْنَ فِيْ كُلِّ عَامٍ مَّرَّةً اَوْ

مَرَّتَيْنِ ثُمَّ لَا يَتُوْبُوْنَ وَلَا هُمْ

يَذَّكَّرُوْنَ ۞ وَاِذَا مَآ اُنْزِلَتْ

سُوْرَةٌ نَّظَرَ بَعْضُهُمْ اِلٰى بَعْضٍ

A contingent from every expedition remained behind, they could devote themselves to studies in religion, and admonish the people when they return to them, - that thus they (may learn) to guard themselves (against evil).

123. O you who believe! Fight the unbelievers who gird you about, and let them find firmness in you: and know that Allah is with those who fear Him.

124. Whenever there comes down a Sura, some of them say: "Which of you has had his faith increased by it?" Yes,

نَفَرٌ مِّنْ كُلِّ فِرْقَةٍ مِّنْهُمْ طَآئِفَةٌ

لِّيَتَفَقَّهُوا فِى الدِّينِ وَلِيُنْذِرُوا

قَوْمَهُمْ إِذَا رَجَعُوا إِلَيْهِمْ لَعَلَّهُمْ

يَحْذَرُونَ ۩ يَآ أَيُّهَا الَّذِينَ ءَامَنُوا

قَاتِلُوا الَّذِينَ يَلُونَكُمْ مِّنَ الْكُفَّارِ

وَلْيَجِدُوا فِيكُمْ غِلْظَةً ۚ وَاعْلَمُوا

أَنَّ اللَّهَ مَعَ الْمُتَّقِينَ ۩ وَإِذَا مَآ

أُنْزِلَتْ سُورَةٌ فَمِنْهُمْ مَّنْ يَّقُولُ

أَيُّكُمْ زَادَتْهُ هَذِهِ إِيمَانًا ۚ فَأَمَّا

the unbelievers, or gain any gain on an enemy: for Allah suffers not the reward to be lost of those who do good; -

121. Nor could they spend anything (for the cause) - small or great - nor cut across a valley, but the deed is inscribed to their credit: that Allah may requite their deed with the best (reward).

122. Nor should the believers all go forth together: if

الْكُفَّارَ وَلَا يَنَالُوْنَ مِنْ عَدُوٍّ

نَّيْلًا اِلَّا كُتِبَ لَهُمْ بِهٖ عَمَلٌ

صَالِحٌ ۗ اِنَّ اللّٰهَ لَا يُضِيْعُ

اَجْرَ الْمُحْسِنِيْنَ ۙ وَلَا يُنْفِقُوْنَ

نَفَقَةً صَغِيْرَةً وَّلَا كَبِيْرَةً

وَّلَا يَقْطَعُوْنَ وَادِيًا اِلَّا كُتِبَ

لَهُمْ لِيَجْزِيَهُمُ اللّٰهُ اَحْسَنَ

مَا كَانُوْا يَعْمَلُوْنَ ۩ وَمَا كَانَ

الْمُؤْمِنُوْنَ لِيَنْفِرُوْا كَآفَّةً ۗ فَلَوْلَا

believe! Fear Allah and be with those who are true (in word and deed).

120. It was not fitting for the people of Medina and the desert Arabs of the neighbour-hood, to refuse to follow Allah's Apostle, nor to prefer their own lives to his: because nothing could they suffer or do, but was reckoned to their credit as a deed of righteousness, whether they suffered thirst, or fatigue, or hunger, in the cause of Allah, or trod paths to raise their of

أَمَنُوا اتَّقُوا اللَّهَ وَكُونُوا مَعَ

الصَّدِقِينَ ۞ مَا كَانَ لِأَهْلِ

الْمَدِينَةِ وَمَنْ حَوْلَهُمْ مِّنَ

الْأَعْرَابِ أَنْ يَّتَخَلَّفُوا عَنْ

رَّسُولِ اللَّهِ وَلَا يَرْغَبُوا

بِأَنْفُسِهِمْ عَنْ نَّفْسِهِ ذَٰلِكَ

بِأَنَّهُمْ لَا يُصِيبُهُمْ ظَمَأٌ وَّلَا

نَصَبٌ وَّلَا مَخْمَصَةٌ فِي سَبِيلِ

اللَّهِ وَلَا يَطَئُونَ مَوْطِئًا يَغِيظُ

the hearts of a part of them had nearly swerved (from duty); but He turned to them (also): for He is unto them Most Kind, Most Merciful.

118. (He turned in mercy also) to the three who were left behind; (they felt guilty) to such a degree that the earth seemed constrained to them, for all its spaciousness, and their (very) souls seemed straitened to them, - and they perceived that there is no fleeing from Allah (and no refuge) but to Himself. Then He turned to them, that they might repent: for Allah is Oft-Returning, Most Merciful.

119. O you who

قُلُوبُ فَرِيقٍ مِّنْهُمْ ثُمَّ تَابَ

عَلَيْهِمْ إِنَّهُ بِهِمْ رَءُوفٌ رَّحِيمٌ ۩

وَعَلَى الثَّلَثَةِ الَّذِينَ خُلِّفُوا حَتَّى

إِذَا ضَاقَتْ عَلَيْهِمُ الْأَرْضُ

بِمَا رَحُبَتْ وَضَاقَتْ عَلَيْهِمْ

أَنْفُسُهُمْ وَظَنُّوا أَنْ لَا مَلْجَأَ

مِنَ اللهِ إِلَّا إِلَيْهِ ثُمَّ تَابَ

عَلَيْهِمْ لِيَتُوبُوا إِنَّ اللهَ هُوَ

التَّوَّابُ الرَّحِيمُ ۩ يَأَيُّهَا الَّذِينَ

He has guided them, in order that He may make clear to them what to fear (and avoid) - for Allah has knowledge of all things.

116. Unto Allah belongeth the dominion of the heavens and the earth. He gives life and He takes it. Except for Him you have no protector nor helper.

117. Allah turned with favour to the Prophet, the Muhajirs, and the Ansar, - who followed him in a time of distress, after that

إِذْهَدَهُمْ حَتّٰى يُبَيِّنَ لَهُمْ مَّا

يَتَّقُوْنَ ۚ إِنَّ اللّٰهَ بِكُلِّ شَىْءٍ

عَلِيْمٌ ۞ إِنَّ اللّٰهَ لَهٗ مُلْكُ

السَّمٰوٰتِ وَالْأَرْضِ ۖ يُحْىٖ وَيُمِيْتُ ۚ

وَمَا لَكُمْ مِّنْ دُوْنِ اللّٰهِ مِنْ

وَّلِيٍّ وَّلَا نَصِيْرٍ ۞ لَقَدْ تَّابَ اللّٰهُ

عَلَى النَّبِيِّ وَالْمُهٰجِرِيْنَ وَالْأَنْصَارِ

الَّذِيْنَ اتَّبَعُوْهُ فِيْ سَاعَةِ

الْعُسْرَةِ مِنْ بَعْدِ مَا كَادَ يَزِيْغُ

that they should pray for forgiveness for Pagans, even though
they be of kin, after it is clear to
them that they are Companions
of the Fire.

114. And Abraham prayed for
his father's forgiveness only
because of a promise he had
made to him. But when it became
clear to him that he was an enemy
to Allah, he dissociated himself
from him: for Abraham was most
tender-hearted, forbearing.

115. And Allah will not mislead a
people after

اَنْ يَّسْتَغْفِرُوْا لِلْمُشْرِكِيْنَ وَلَوْ

كَانُوْٓا اُولِىْ قُرْبٰى مِنْۢ بَعْدِ

مَا تَبَيَّنَ لَهُمْ اَنَّهُمْ اَصْحٰبُ

الْجَحِيْمِ ۝ وَمَا كَانَ اسْتِغْفَارُ

اِبْرٰهِيْمَ لِاَبِيْهِ اِلَّا عَنْ مَّوْعِدَةٍ

وَّعَدَهَآ اِيَّاهُ ۚ فَلَمَّا تَبَيَّنَ لَهٗٓ

اَنَّهٗ عَدُوٌّ لِّلّٰهِ تَبَرَّاَ مِنْهُ ؕ اِنَّ

اِبْرٰهِيْمَ لَاَوَّاهٌ حَلِيْمٌ ۝ وَمَا

كَانَ اللّٰهُ لِيُضِلَّ قَوْمًۢا بَعْدَ

and the Qur'an: and who is more faithful to his covenant than Allah? Then rejoice in the bargain which you have concluded: that is the achievement supreme.

112. Those that turn (to Allah) in repentance; that serve Him, and praise Him; that wander in devotion to the cause of Allah; that bow down and prostrate themselves in prayer; that enjoin good and forbid evil; and observe the limit set by Allah; - (these do rejoice). So proclaim the glad tidings to the believers.

113. It is not fitting, for the Prophet and those who believe,

وَالْقُرْآنِ ۚ وَمَنْ أَوْفَىٰ بِعَهْدِهِ مِنَ

اللّٰهِ فَاسْتَبْشِرُوا بِبَيْعِكُمُ الَّذِى

بَايَعْتُمْ بِهِ ۚ وَذٰلِكَ هُوَ الْفَوْزُ

الْعَظِيمُ ۞ التَّآئِبُونَ الْعٰبِدُونَ

الْحٰمِدُونَ السَّآئِحُونَ الرَّاكِعُونَ

السّٰجِدُونَ الْآمِرُونَ بِالْمَعْرُوفِ

وَالنَّاهُونَ عَنِ الْمُنْكَرِ وَالْحٰفِظُونَ

لِحُدُودِ اللّٰهِ ۗ وَبَشِّرِ الْمُؤْمِنِينَ ۞

مَا كَانَ لِلنَّبِيِّ وَالَّذِينَ اٰمَنُوٓا

guides not people that do wrong.

110. The foundation of those who so build is never free from suspicion and shakiness in their hearts, until their hearts are cut to pieces. And Allah is All-Knowing, Wise.

111. Allah has purchased of the believers their persons and their goods; for theirs (in return) is the garden (of Paradise): they fight in His cause, and slay and are slain: a promise binding on Him in truth, through the Torah, the Gospel,

لَا يَهْدِى الْقَوْمَ الظّٰلِمِيْنَ ۞ لَا

يَزَالُ بُنْيَانُهُمُ الَّذِىْ بَنَوْا رِيْبَةً

فِىْ قُلُوْبِهِمْ اِلَّا اَنْ تَقَطَّعَ

قُلُوْبُهُمْ ط وَاللهُ عَلِيْمٌ حَكِيْمٌ ۞

اِنَّ اللهَ اشْتَرٰى مِنَ الْمُؤْمِنِيْنَ

اَنْفُسَهُمْ وَاَمْوَالَهُمْ بِاَنَّ لَهُمُ

الْجَنَّةَ ط يُقَاتِلُوْنَ فِىْ سَبِيْلِ اللهِ

فَيَقْتُلُوْنَ وَيُقْتَلُوْنَ وَعْدًا عَلَيْهِ

حَقًّا فِى التَّوْرٰىةِ وَالْاِنْجِيْلِ

whose foundation was laid from the first day on piety; it is more worthy of the standing forth (for prayer) therein. In it are men who love to be purified; and Allah loves those who make themselves pure.

109. Which then is best? - he that lays his foundation on piety to Allah and His good pleasure? - or he that lays his foundation on an undermined sand-cliff ready to crumble to pieces? And it does crumble to pieces with him, into the Fire of Hell. And Allah

اُسِّسَ عَلَى التَّقْوٰى مِنْ

اَوَّلِ يَوْمٍ اَحَقُّ اَنْ تَقُوْمَ

فِيْهِ ۚ فِيْهِ رِجَالٌ يُّحِبُّوْنَ

اَنْ يَّتَطَهَّرُوْا ۚ وَاللّٰهُ يُحِبُّ

الْمُطَّهِّرِيْنَ ۝ اَفَمَنْ اَسَّسَ

بُنْيَانَهٗ عَلٰى تَقْوٰى مِنَ اللّٰهِ

وَرِضْوَانٍ خَيْرٌ اَمْ مَّنْ اَسَّسَ

بُنْيَانَهٗ عَلٰى شَفَا جُرُفٍ هَارٍ

فَانْهَارَ بِهٖ فِيْ نَارِ جَهَنَّمَ ۗ وَاللّٰهُ

for the command of Allah, whether He will punish them, or turn in mercy to them: and Allah is All-Knowing, All-Wise.

107. And there are those who put up a mosque by way of mischief and infidelity - to disunite the believers - and in preparation for one who warred against Allah and His Apostle in the past. They will indeed swear that their intention is nothing but good; but Allah does declare that they are certainly liars.

108. You never stand you forth therein. There is a mosque

لِاَمْرِ اللّٰهِ اِمَّا يُعَذِّبُهُمْ وَاِمَّا

يَتُوبُ عَلَيْهِمْ ؕ وَاللّٰهُ عَلِيْمٌ

حَكِيْمٌ ۞ وَالَّذِيْنَ اتَّخَذُوْا

مَسْجِدًا ضِرَارًا وَّكُفْرًا وَّتَفْرِيْقًا

بَيْنَ الْمُؤْمِنِيْنَ وَاِرْصَادًا لِّمَنْ

حَارَبَ اللّٰهَ وَرَسُوْلَهٗ مِنْ قَبْلُ ؕ

وَلَيَحْلِفُنَّ اِنْ اَرَدْنَا اِلَّا الْحُسْنٰى ؕ

وَاللّٰهُ يَشْهَدُ اِنَّهُمْ لَكٰذِبُوْنَ ۞

لَا تَقُمْ فِيْهِ اَبَدًا ؕ لَمَسْجِدٌ

are a source of security for them: and Allah is One Who hears and knows.

104. Know they not that Allah does accept repentance from His votaries and receives their gifts of charity, and that Allah is verily He, the Oft-Returning, Most Merciful?

105. And say: "Work (righteousness): soon will Allah observe your work, and His Apostle, and the believers: soon will you be brought back to the knower of what is hidden and what is open: then will He show you the truth of all that you did."

106. There are (yet) others, held in suspense

سَكَنٌ لَّهُمْ وَاللّٰهُ سَمِيعٌ عَلِيمٌ ۩

اَلَمْ يَعْلَمُوٓا اَنَّ اللّٰهَ هُوَ يَقْبَلُ

التَّوْبَةَ عَنْ عِبَادِهٖ وَيَأْخُذُ

الصَّدَقٰتِ وَاَنَّ اللّٰهَ هُوَ التَّوَّابُ

الرَّحِيمُ ۩ وَقُلِ اعْمَلُوا فَسَيَرَى

اللّٰهُ عَمَلَكُمْ وَرَسُوْلُهُ وَالْمُؤْمِنُوْنَ

وَسَتُرَدُّوْنَ اِلٰى عٰلِمِ الْغَيْبِ

وَالشَّهَادَةِ فَيُنَبِّئُكُمْ بِمَا كُنْتُمْ

تَعْمَلُوْنَ ۩ وَاٰخَرُوْنَ مُرْجَوْنَ

you knows them not: We know them: twice shall We punish them: and in addition shall they be sent to a grievous Chastisement.

102.   Others (there are who) have acknowledged their wrong-doings: they have mixed an act that was good with another that was evil. Perhaps Allah will turn unto them (in Mercy): for Allah is Oft-Forgiving, Most Merciful.

103.   Of their goods, take alms, that so you might purify and sanctify them; and pray on their behalf. Verily your prayers

لَا تَعْلَمُهُمْ نَحْنُ نَعْلَمُهُمْ
سَنُعَذِّبُهُمْ مَّرَّتَيْنِ ثُمَّ يُرَدُّوْنَ
اِلٰى عَذَابٍ عَظِيْمٍ ۖ وَ اٰخَرُوْنَ
اعْتَرَفُوْا بِذُنُوبِهِمْ خَلَطُوْا عَمَلًا
صَالِحًا وَّ اٰخَرَ سَيِّئًا ۖ عَسَى اللّٰهُ
اَنْ يَّتُوْبَ عَلَيْهِمْ ۖ اِنَّ اللّٰهَ
غَفُوْرٌ رَّحِيْمٌ ۞ خُذْ مِنْ اَمْوَالِهِمْ
صَدَقَةً تُطَهِّرُهُمْ وَ تُزَكِّيْهِمْ
بِهَا وَ صَلِّ عَلَيْهِمْ ۖ اِنَّ صَلٰوتَكَ

Most Merciful.

100. The vanguard (of Islam)- the first of those who forsook (their homes) and of those who gave them aid, and (also) those who follow them in (all) good deeds,- well- pleased is Allah with them, as are they with Him: for them has He prepared Gardens under which rivers flow, to dwell therein for ever: that is the supreme felicity.

101. Certain of the desert Arabs round about you are hypocrites, as well as (desert Arabs) among the Medina folk: they are obstinate in hypocrisy:

رَّحِيْمٌ ۩ وَالسّٰبِقُوْنَ الْاَوَّلُوْنَ مِنَ
الْمُهٰجِرِيْنَ وَالْاَنْصَارِ وَالَّذِيْنَ
اتَّبَعُوْهُمْ بِاِحْسَانٍ ۙ رَّضِيَ اللّٰهُ
عَنْهُمْ وَرَضُوْا عَنْهُ وَاَعَدَّ لَهُمْ
جَنّٰتٍ تَجْرِيْ تَحْتَهَا الْاَنْهٰرُ
خٰلِدِيْنَ فِيْهَآ اَبَدًا ۚ ذٰلِكَ الْفَوْزُ
الْعَظِيْمُ ۩ وَمِمَّنْ حَوْلَكُمْ مِّنَ
الْاَعْرَابِ مُنٰفِقُوْنَ ۚ وَمِنْ اَهْلِ
الْمَدِيْنَةِ ۚ مَرَدُوْا عَلَى النِّفَاقِ ۚ

98. Some of the desert Arabs look upon their payments as a fine, and watch for disasters for you: on them be the disaster of evil: for Allah is He that hears and knows (all things).

99. But some of the desert Arabs believe in Allah and the Last Day, and look on their payments as pious gifts bringing them nearer to Allah and obtaining the prayers of the Apostle. Yes, indeed they bring them nearer (to Him): soon will Allah admit them to His Mercy: for Allah is Oft-Forgiving,

وَمِنَ الْاَعْرَابِ مَنْ يَّتَّخِذُ مَا

يُنْفِقُ مَغْرَمًا وَّيَتَرَبَّصُ بِكُمُ

الدَّوَآئِرَ عَلَيْهِمْ دَآئِرَةُ السَّوْءِ

وَاللّٰهُ سَمِيْعٌ عَلِيْمٌ ۞ وَمِنَ

الْاَعْرَابِ مَنْ يُّؤْمِنُ بِاللّٰهِ وَالْيَوْمِ

الْاٰخِرِ وَيَتَّخِذُ مَا يُنْفِقُ قُرُبٰتٍ

عِنْدَ اللّٰهِ وَصَلَوٰتِ الرَّسُوْلِ اَلَاۤ

اِنَّهَا قُرْبَةٌ لَّهُمْ سَيُدْخِلُهُمُ

اللّٰهُ فِيْ رَحْمَتِهٖ اِنَّ اللّٰهَ غَفُوْرٌ

So leave them alone: for they are an abomination, and Hell is their dwelling-place, - a fitting recompense for the (evil) that they did.

96. They will swear unto you, that you may be pleased with them. But if you are pleased with them, Allah is not pleased with those who disobey.

97. The Arabs of the desert are the worst in unbelief and hypocrisy, and most fitted to be in ignorance of the command which Allah has sent down to His Apostle: but Allah is All-Knowing, All-Wise.

فَاَعْرِضُوْا عَنْهُمْ ۖ اِنَّهُمْ رِجْسٌ ۗ

وَّمَاْوٰىهُمْ جَهَنَّمُ ۚ جَزَآءًۢ بِمَا كَانُوْا

يَكْسِبُوْنَ ۝ يَحْلِفُوْنَ لَكُمْ لِتَرْضَوْا

عَنْهُمْ ۚ فَاِنْ تَرْضَوْا عَنْهُمْ فَاِنَّ

اللّٰهَ لَا يَرْضٰى عَنِ الْقَوْمِ

الْفٰسِقِيْنَ ۝ اَلْاَعْرَابُ اَشَدُّ كُفْرًا

وَّنِفَاقًا وَّاَجْدَرُ اَلَّا يَعْلَمُوْا

حُدُوْدَ مَاْ اَنْزَلَ اللّٰهُ عَلٰى

رَسُوْلِهٖ ۗ وَاللّٰهُ عَلِيْمٌ حَكِيْمٌ ۝

94. They will present their excuses to you when you return to them. Say you: "Present no excuses: we shall not believe you: Allah has already informed us of the true state of matters concerning you: it is your actions that Allah and His Apostle will observe: in the end will you be brought back to Him Who knows what is hidden and what is open: then will He show you the truth of all that you did."

95. They will swear to you by Allah, when you return to them, that you may leave them alone.

يَعْتَذِرُوْنَ اِلَيْكُمْ اِذَا رَجَعْتُمْ
اِلَيْهِمْ ۚ قُلْ لَّا تَعْتَذِرُوْا وَلَنْ
نُّؤْمِنَ لَكُمْ قَدْ نَبَّأَنَا اللّٰهُ
مِنْ اَخْبَارِكُمْ ۚ وَسَيَرَى اللّٰهُ
عَمَلَكُمْ وَرَسُوْلُهٗ ثُمَّ تُرَدُّوْنَ
اِلٰى عٰلِمِ الْغَيْبِ وَالشَّهَادَةِ
فَيُنَبِّئُكُمْ بِمَا كُنْتُمْ تَعْمَلُوْنَ ۝
سَيَحْلِفُوْنَ بِاللّٰهِ لَكُمْ اِذَا
انْقَلَبْتُمْ اِلَيْهِمْ لِتُعْرِضُوْا عَنْهُمْ ۚ

بَرَكَاتُ الكُتُبِ السَّلَفِيَّة

پاره

يَعْتَذِرُوْنَ

(۱۱)

بَعْضُ الَّذِي أُنْزِلَ إِلَيْكَ

PART 12
Wama Min Daabbatin

is certainly Well Aware of their snare."

51. (The king) said (to the ladies): "What was your affair when you did seek to seduce Joseph from his (true) self?" The ladies said: "Allah preserve us! No evil know we against him!" Said the 'Aziz's wife: "Now is the truth manifest (to all): it was I who sought to seduce him from his (true) self: he is indeed of those who are (ever) true (and virtuous)."

52. "This (say I), in order that He may know that I have never been false to him in his absence, and that Allah will never guide the snare of the false ones.

بِكَيْدِهِنَّ عَلِيمٌ ۞ قَالَ مَا خَطْبُكُنَّ

اِذْ رَاوَدْتُّنَّ يُوسُفَ عَنْ نَّفْسِهِ ط

قُلْنَ حَاشَ لِلّٰهِ مَا عَلِمْنَا

عَلَيْهِ مِنْ سُوْٓءٍ ط قَالَتِ امْرَاَتُ

الْعَزِيزِ الْـٰٔنَ حَصْحَصَ الْحَقُّ زْ

اَنَا رَاوَدْتُّهٗ عَنْ نَّفْسِهِ وَاِنَّهٗ

لَمِنَ الصّٰدِقِيْنَ ۞ ذٰلِكَ لِيَعْلَمَ

اَنِّيْ لَمْ اَخُنْهُ بِالْغَيْبِ وَاَنَّ اللّٰهَ

لَا يَهْدِيْ كَيْدَ الْخَآئِنِيْنَ ۞

after that (period) seven dreadful
(years), which will devour what
you shall have laid by in advance
for them, - (all) except a little
which you shall have (specially)
guarded."

49.   "Then will come after that
(period) a year in which the
people will have abundant water,
and in which they will press
(wine and oil)."

50.   So the king said: "Bring you
him unto me." But when the
messenger came to him, (Joseph)
said: "Go you back to your lord,
and ask him, 'What is the state of
mind of the ladies who cut their
hands?' For my Lord

بَعْدِ ذَٰلِكَ سَبْعٌ شِدَادٌ يَّاكُلْنَ

مَا قَدَّمْتُمْ لَهُنَّ إِلَّا قَلِيلًا

مِّمَّا تُحْصِنُونَ ۞ ثُمَّ يَاتِى مِنْ

بَعْدِ ذَٰلِكَ عَامٌ فِيهِ يُغَاثُ

النَّاسُ وَفِيهِ يَعْصِرُونَ ۞ وَقَالَ

الْمَلِكُ ائْتُونِى بِهِ فَلَمَّا جَآءَهُ

الرَّسُولُ قَالَ ارْجِعْ إِلَىٰ رَبِّكَ

فَسْئَلْهُ مَا بَالُ النِّسْوَةِ الَّتِي

قَطَّعْنَ أَيْدِيَهُنَّ إِنَّ رَبِّى

send you me (therefore)."

46. "O Joseph!" (he said) "O man of truth! Expound to us (the dream) of seven fat kine whom seven lean ones devour, and of seven green ears of corn and (seven) others withered: that I may return to the people, and that they may understand."

47. (Joseph) said: "For seven years shall you diligently sow as is your wont: and the harvests that you reap, you shall leave them in the ear, - except a little, of which you shall eat."

48. "Then will come

فَأَرْسِلُونِ ۞ يُوسُفُ أَيُّهَا الصِّدِّيقُ

أَفْتِنَا فِي سَبْعِ بَقَرَاتٍ سِمَانٍ

يَأْكُلُهُنَّ سَبْعٌ عِجَافٌ وَّسَبْعِ

سُنْبُلَاتٍ خُضْرٍ وَّأُخَرَ يَبِسَاتٍ

لَّعَلِّي أَرْجِعُ إِلَى النَّاسِ لَعَلَّهُمْ

يَعْلَمُونَ ۞ قَالَ تَزْرَعُونَ سَبْعَ

سِنِينَ دَأَبًا فَمَا حَصَدْتُّمْ

فَذَرُوهُ فِي سُنْبُلِهِ إِلَّا قَلِيلًا

مِّمَّا تَأْكُلُونَ ۞ ثُمَّ يَأْتِي مِنْ

"I do see (in a vision) seven fat kine, whom seven lean ones devour, and seven green ears of corn, and seven (others) withered. O you chiefs! Expound to me my vision if it be that you can interpret visions."

44. They said: "A confused medley of dreams: and we are not skilled in the interpretation of dreams."

45. But the man who had been released, one of the two (who had been in prison) and who now remembered him after (so long) a space of time, said: "I will tell you the truth of its interpretation:

اِنِّیْۤ اَرٰی سَبْعَ بَقَرَاتٍ سِمَانٍ

یَّاْكُلُهُنَّ سَبْعٌ عِجَافٌ وَّ سَبْعَ

سُنْۢبُلٰتٍ خُضْرٍ وَّ اُخَرَ یٰبِسٰتٍؕ

یٰۤاَیُّهَا الْمَلَاُ اَفْتُوْنِیْ فِیْ رُءْیَایَ

اِنْ كُنْتُمْ لِلرُّءْیَا تَعْبُرُوْنَ ۞

قَالُوْۤا اَضْغَاثُ اَحْلَامٍ ۚ وَمَا نَحْنُ

بِتَاْوِیْلِ الْاَحْلَامِ بِعٰلِمِیْنَ ۞

وَقَالَ الَّذِیْ نَجَا مِنْهُمَا وَادَّكَرَ

بَعْدَ اُمَّةٍ اَنَا اُنَبِّئُكُمْ بِتَاْوِیْلِهٖ

understand not.

41. "O my two companions of the prison! As to one of you, he will pour out the wine for his lord to drink: as for the other, he will be hanged, and the birds will eat from off his head. (so) has been decreed that matter whereof you twain do enquire"...

42. And of the two, to that one whom he consider about to be saved, he said: "Mention me to your lord." But Satan made him forget to mention him to his lord: and (Joseph) lingered in prison a few (more) years.

43. The king (of Egypt) said:

لَا يَعْلَمُوْنَ ۞ يٰصَاحِبَيِ السِّجْنِ ءَاَ

اَحَدُكُمَا فَيَسْقِيْ رَبَّهٗ خَمْرًا ۚ وَاَمَّا

الْاٰخَرُ فَيُصْلَبُ فَتَأْكُلُ الطَّيْرُ

مِنْ رَّأْسِهٖ ۭ قُضِيَ الْاَمْرُ الَّذِيْ

فِيْهِ تَسْتَفْتِيٰنِ ۞ وَقَالَ لِلَّذِيْ

ظَنَّ اَنَّهٗ نَاجٍ مِّنْهُمَا اذْكُرْنِيْ

عِنْدَ رَبِّكَ ۡ فَاَنْسٰهُ الشَّيْطٰنُ

ذِكْرَ رَبِّهٖ فَلَبِثَ فِي السِّجْنِ

بِضْعَ سِنِيْنَ ۞ وَقَالَ الْمَلِكُ

men are not grateful.

39. "O my two companions of the prison! (I ask you): are many lords differing among themselves better, or the One Allah, Supreme and Irresistible?

40. "If not Him, you worship nothing but names which you have named, - you and your fathers, - for which Allah has sent down no authority: the command is for none but Allah: He has commanded that you worship none but Him: that is the right religion, but most men

النَّاسِ لَا يَشۡكُرُوۡنَ ۞ يٰصَاحِبَيِ

السِّجۡنِ ءَاَرۡبَابٌ مُّتَفَرِّقُوۡنَ خَيۡرٌ

اَمِ اللّٰهُ الۡوَاحِدُ الۡقَهَّارُ ۞ مَا

تَعۡبُدُوۡنَ مِنۡ دُوۡنِهٖۤ اِلَّاۤ اَسۡمَآءً

سَمَّيۡتُمُوۡهَاۤ اَنۡتُمۡ وَ اٰبَآؤُكُمۡ مَّاۤ

اَنۡزَلَ اللّٰهُ بِهَا مِنۡ سُلۡطٰنٍ ؕ

اِنِ الۡحُكۡمُ اِلَّا لِلّٰهِ ؕ اَمَرَ اَلَّا

تَعۡبُدُوۡۤا اِلَّاۤ اِيَّاهُ ؕ ذٰلِكَ الدِّيۡنُ

الۡقَيِّمُ وَ لٰكِنَّ اَكۡثَرَ النَّاسِ

I will surely reveal to you the truth and meaning of this before it befall you: that is part of the (duty) which my Lord has taught me. I have (I assure you) abandoned the ways of a people that believe not in Allah and that (even) deny the Hereafter.

38.   "And I follow the ways of my fathers, - Abraham, Isaac, and Jacob; and never could we attribute any partners whatever to Allah: that (comes) of the Grace of Allah to us and to mankind: yet most

اِلَّا نَبَّأْتُكُمَا بِتَأْوِيلِهِ قَبْلَ

اَنْ يَّأْتِيَكُمَا ۚ ذٰلِكُمَا مِمَّا عَلَّمَنِيْ

رَبِّيْ ؕ اِنِّيْ تَرَكْتُ مِلَّةَ قَوْمٍ لَّا

يُؤْمِنُوْنَ بِاللّٰهِ وَهُمْ بِالْاٰخِرَةِ هُمْ

كٰفِرُوْنَ ۞ وَاتَّبَعْتُ مِلَّةَ اٰبَآءِيْ

اِبْرٰهِيْمَ وَاِسْحٰقَ وَيَعْقُوْبَ ؕ مَا

كَانَ لَنَآ اَنْ نُّشْرِكَ بِاللّٰهِ مِنْ

شَيْءٍ ؕ ذٰلِكَ مِنْ فَضْلِ اللّٰهِ

عَلَيْنَا وَعَلَى النَّاسِ وَلٰكِنَّ اَكْثَرَ

it occurred to the men, after they had seen the signs, (that it was best) to imprison him for a time.

36. Now with him there came into the prison two young men. Said one of them: "I see myself (in a dream) pressing wine." said the other: "I see myself (in a dream) carrying bread on my head, and birds are eating, thereof." "Tell us" (they said) "The truth and meaning thereof: for we see you are one that does good (to all)."

37. He said: "Before any food comes (in due course) to feed either of you,

بَدَا لَهُمْ مِّنْ بَعْدِ مَا رَأَوُا

الْاٰيٰتِ لَيَسْجُنُنَّهُ حَتّٰى حِيْنٍ ۟

وَدَخَلَ مَعَهُ السِّجْنَ فَتَيٰنِ ۟

قَالَ اَحَدُ هُمَآ اِنِّىْ اَرٰنِىْٓ اَعْصِرُ

خَمْرًا ۚ وَقَالَ الْاٰخَرُ اِنِّىْٓ اَرٰنِىْٓ

اَحْمِلُ فَوْقَ رَأْسِىْ خُبْزًا تَأْكُلُ

الطَّيْرُ مِنْهُ ۟ نَبِّئْنَا بِتَأْوِيْلِهٖ ۟

اِنَّا نَرٰىكَ مِنَ الْمُحْسِنِيْنَ ۟

قَالَ لَا يَأْتِيْكُمَا طَعَامٌ تُرْزَقٰنِهٖٓ

I did seek to seduce him from his (true) self but he did firmly save himself guiltless!....and now, if he does not my bidding, he shall certainly be cast into prison, and (what is more) be of the company of the vilest!"

33. He said: "O my Lord! The prison is more to my liking than that to which they invite me: unless you turn away their snare from me, I should feel inclined towards them and join the ranks of the ignorant."

34. So his Lord heard to him (in his prayer), and turned away from him their snare: verily He hears and knows (all things).

35. Then

رَاوَدَتُّهُ عَنْ نَّفْسِهِ فَاسْتَعْصَمَ

وَلَئِنْ لَّمْ يَفْعَلْ مَا آمُرُهُ لَيُسْجَنَنَّ

وَلَيَكُونًا مِّنَ الصّٰغِرِينَ ۞ قَالَ

رَبِّ السِّجْنُ أَحَبُّ إِلَيَّ مِمَّا

يَدْعُونَنِي إِلَيْهِ وَ إِلَّا تَصْرِفْ

عَنِّي كَيْدَهُنَّ أَصْبُ إِلَيْهِنَّ وَ أَكُن

مِّنَ الْجَاهِلِينَ ۞ فَاسْتَجَابَ لَهُ

رَبُّهُ فَصَرَفَ عَنْهُ كَيْدَهُنَّ

إِنَّهُ هُوَ السَّمِيعُ الْعَلِيمُ ۞ ثُمَّ

31. When she heard of their malicious talk, she sent for them and prepared a banquet for them: she gave each of them a knife: and she said (to Joseph), "Come out before them." When they saw him, they did extol him, and (in their amazement) cut their hands: they said, "Allah preserve us! No mortal is this! This is none other than a noble angel!"

32. She said: "There before you is the man about whom you did blame me!

فَلَمَّا سَمِعَتْ بِمَكْرِهِنَّ أَرْسَلَتْ

إِلَيْهِنَّ وَ أَعْتَدَتْ لَهُنَّ مُتَّكَأً

وَّ آتَتْ كُلَّ وَاحِدَةٍ مِّنْهُنَّ

سِكِّينًا وَّ قَالَتِ اخْرُجْ عَلَيْهِنَّ

فَلَمَّا رَأَيْنَهُ أَكْبَرْنَهُ وَ قَطَّعْنَ

أَيْدِيَهُنَّ وَ قُلْنَ حَاشَ لِلّٰهِ

مَا هٰذَا بَشَرًا اِنْ هٰذَا اِلَّا

مَلَكٌ كَرِيمٌ ۝ قَالَتْ فَذٰلِكُنَّ

الَّذِي لُمْتُنَّنِي فِيهِ ۚ وَ لَقَدْ

his shirt, - that it was torn at the back, - (her husband) said: "Behold! It is a snare of you women! Truly, mighty is your snare!"

29.   "O Joseph, pass this over! (O wife), ask forgiveness for your sin, for truly you have been at fault!"

30.   Ladies said in the City: "The wife of the (great) 'Aziz is seeking to seduce her slave. Truly has he inspired her with violent love: we see she is evidently going astray."

قَمِيصُهُ قُدَّ مِنْ دُبُرٍ قَالَ

إِنَّهُ مِنْ كَيْدِكُنَّ إِنَّ كَيْدَكُنَّ

عَظِيمٌ ۞ يُوسُفُ أَعْرِضْ عَنْ

هٰذَا وَاسْتَغْفِرِى لِذَنبِكِ إِنَّكِ

كُنتِ مِنَ الْخَاطِئِينَ ۞ وَقَالَ

نِسْوَةٌ فِى الْمَدِينَةِ امْرَأَتُ

الْعَزِيزِ تُرَاوِدُ فَتَاهَا عَنْ

نَفْسِهِ قَدْ شَغَفَهَا حُبًّا إِنَّا

لَنَرَاهَا فِى ضَلَالٍ مُّبِينٍ ۞

formed an evil design against your wife, but prison or a grievous chastisement?"

26. He said: "It was she that sought to seduce me - from my (true) self." And one of her household saw (this) and bore witness, (thus): - "If it be that his shirt is torn from the front, then is her tale true, and he is a liar!"

27. "But if it be that his shirt is torn from the back, then is she the liar, and he is telling the truth!"

28. So when he saw

اَرَادَ بِاَهْلِكَ سُوٓءًا اِلَّآ اَنْ

يُّسْجَنَ اَوْ عَذَابٌ اَلِيْمٌ ۞

قَالَ هِيَ رَاوَدَتْنِيْ عَنْ نَّفْسِيْ

وَشَهِدَ شَاهِدٌ مِّنْ اَهْلِهَا ۚ

اِنْ كَانَ قَمِيْصُهٗ قُدَّ مِنْ

قُبُلٍ فَصَدَقَتْ وَهُوَ مِنَ

الْكٰذِبِيْنَ ۞ وَاِنْ كَانَ قَمِيْصُهٗ

قُدَّ مِنْ دُبُرٍ فَكَذَبَتْ وَهُوَ

مِنَ الصّٰدِقِيْنَ ۞ فَلَمَّا رَاٰ

truly (your husband) is my lord! he made my sojourn agreeable! truly to no good come those who do wrong!"

24.　And (with passion) did she desire him, and he would have desired her, but that he saw the evidence of his Lord: thus (did We order) that We might turn away from him (all) evil and shameful deeds: for he was one of Our servants, sincere and purified.

25.　So they both raced each other to the door, and she tore his shirt from the back: they both found her lord near the door. She said: "What is the (fitting) punishment for one who

اللهِ اِنَّهٗ رَبِّيْ اَحْسَنَ مَثْوَايَ

اِنَّهٗ لَا يُفْلِحُ الظّٰلِمُوْنَ ۞ وَلَقَدْ

هَمَّتْ بِهٖ ۚ وَهَمَّ بِهَا لَوْلَاۤ

اَنْ رَّاٰ بُرْهَانَ رَبِّهٖ ؕ كَذٰلِكَ

لِنَصْرِفَ عَنْهُ السُّوْٓءَ وَالْفَحْشَآءَ

اِنَّهٗ مِنْ عِبَادِنَا الْمُخْلَصِيْنَ ۞

وَاسْتَبَقَا الْبَابَ وَقَدَّتْ قَمِيْصَهٗ

مِنْ دُبُرٍ وَّاَلْفَيَا سَيِّدَهَا لَدَا

الْبَابِ ؕ قَالَتْ مَا جَزَآءُ مَنْ

Joseph in the land, that We might teach him the interpretation of stories (and events). And Allah has full power and control over His affairs; but most among mankind know it not.

22. When Joseph attained His full manhood, We gave him power and knowledge: thus do We reward those who do right.

23. But she in whose house he was, sought to seduce him from his (true) self: she fastened the doors, and said: "Now come, you (dear one)!" He said: "Allah forbid!

لِيُوْسُفَ فِى الْاَرْضِ وَلِنُعَلِّمَهٗ

مِنْ تَأْوِيْلِ الْاَحَادِيْثِ وَاللّٰهُ

غَالِبٌ عَلٰى اَمْرِهٖ وَلٰكِنَّ اَكْثَرَ

النَّاسِ لَا يَعْلَمُوْنَ ۞ وَلَمَّا بَلَغَ

اَشُدَّهٗ اٰتَيْنٰهُ حُكْمًا وَّعِلْمًا ۚ

وَكَذٰلِكَ نَجْزِى الْمُحْسِنِيْنَ ۞

وَرَاوَدَتْهُ الَّتِىْ هُوَ فِىْ بَيْتِهَا

عَنْ نَّفْسِهٖ وَغَلَّقَتِ الْاَبْوَابَ

وَقَالَتْ هَيْتَ لَكَ ۚ قَالَ مَعَاذَ

and he let down his bucket (into the well) ... He said: "Ah there! Good news! Here is a (fine) young man!" So they concealed him as a treasure! But Allah knows well all that they do!

20. The (Brethren) sold him for a miserable price, for a few dirhams counted out: in such low estimation did they hold him!

21. The man in Egypt who bought him, said to his wife: "Make his stay (among us) honourable: may be he will bring us much good, or we shall adopt him as a son." Thus did We establish

فَأَدْلَىٰ دَلْوَهُ ۖ قَالَ يَـٰبُشْرَىٰ

هَـٰذَا غُلَـٰمٌ ۚ وَأَسَرُّوهُ بِضَـٰعَةً ۚ

وَٱللَّهُ عَلِيمٌۢ بِمَا يَعْمَلُونَ ۝

وَشَرَوْهُ بِثَمَنٍۭ بَخْسٍ دَرَٰهِمَ

مَعْدُودَةٍ وَكَانُوا فِيهِ مِنَ

ٱلزَّٰهِدِينَ ۝ وَقَالَ ٱلَّذِى

ٱشْتَرَىٰهُ مِن مِّصْرَ لِٱمْرَأَتِهِ

أَكْرِمِى مَثْوَىٰهُ عَسَىٰ أَن يَنفَعَنَا

أَوْ نَتَّخِذَهُۥ وَلَدًا ۚ وَكَذَٰلِكَ مَكَّنَّا

"O our father! We went racing with one another, and left Joseph with our things; and the wolf devoured him. But you will never believe us even though we tell the truth."

18. They stained his shirt with false blood. He said: "No, but your minds have made up a tale (that may pass) with you, (for me) patience is most fitting: against that which you assert, it is Allah (alone) Whose help can be sought"..

19. Then there came a caravan of travellers: they sent their water-carrier (for water),

يَٰٓأَبَانَآ إِنَّا ذَهَبْنَا نَسْتَبِقُ وَتَرَكْنَا

يُوسُفَ عِنْدَ مَتَاعِنَا فَأَكَلَهُ

الذِّئْبُ وَمَآ أَنْتَ بِمُؤْمِنٍ لَّنَا

وَلَوْ كُنَّا صَٰدِقِينَ ۝ وَجَآءُو

عَلَىٰ قَمِيصِهِ بِدَمٍ كَذِبٍ قَالَ

بَلْ سَوَّلَتْ لَكُمْ أَنْفُسُكُمْ أَمْرًا

فَصَبْرٌ جَمِيلٌ وَاللَّهُ الْمُسْتَعَانُ

عَلَىٰ مَا تَصِفُونَ ۝ وَجَآءَتْ

سَيَّارَةٌ فَأَرْسَلُوا وَارِدَهُمْ

I fear lest the wolf should devour him while you attend not to him."

14. They said: "If the wolf were to devour him while we are (so large) a party, then should we indeed (first) have perished ourselves!"

15. So they did take him away, and they all agreed to throw him down to the bottom of the well: and We put into his heart (this Message): 'Of a surety you shall (one day) tell them the truth of this their affair while they know (you) not.'

16. Then they came to their father in the early part of the night, weeping.

17. They said:

بِهِ وَ اَخَافُ اَنْ يَّاْكُلَهُ الذِّئْبُ

وَ اَنْتُمْ عَنْهُ غٰفِلُوْنَ ۝ قَالُوْا

لَئِنْ اَكَلَهُ الذِّئْبُ وَ نَحْنُ

عُصْبَةٌ اِنَّاۤ اِذًا لَّخٰسِرُوْنَ ۝

فَلَمَّا ذَهَبُوْا بِهِ وَ اَجْمَعُوْۤا اَنْ

يَّجْعَلُوْهُ فِيْ غَيٰبَتِ الْجُبِّ ۚ

وَ اَوْحَيْنَاۤ اِلَيْهِ لَتُنَبِّئَنَّهُمْ بِاَمْرِهِمْ

هٰذَا وَ هُمْ لَا يَشْعُرُوْنَ ۝ وَ جَآءُوْ

اَبَاهُمْ عِشَآءً يَّبْكُوْنَ ۝ قَالُوْا

10.   Said one of them: "Slay not Joseph, but if you must do something, throw him down to the bottom of the well: he will be picked up by some caravan of travellers."

11.   They said: "O our father! Why do you not trust us with Joseph, - seeing we are indeed his sincere well-wishers?"

12.   "Send him with us tomorrow to enjoy himself and play, and we shall take every care of him."

13.   (Jacob) said: "Really it saddens me that you should take him away:

قَالَ قَآئِلٌ مِّنْهُمْ لَا تَقْتُلُوا

يُوسُفَ وَ أَلْقُوهُ فِي غَيَبَتِ

الْجُبِّ يَلْتَقِطْهُ بَعْضُ السَّيَّارَةِ

إِن كُنتُمْ فَاعِلِينَ ۝ قَالُوا

يَا أَبَانَا مَا لَكَ لَا تَأْمَنَّا عَلَى

يُوسُفَ وَإِنَّا لَهُ لَنَاصِحُونَ ۝

أَرْسِلْهُ مَعَنَا غَدًا يَرْتَعْ

وَيَلْعَبْ وَإِنَّا لَهُ لَحَافِظُونَ ۝

قَالَ إِنِّي لَيَحْزُنُنِي أَن تَذْهَبُوا

and Isaac aforetime! for Allah is full of knowledge and wisdom."

7.   Verily in Joseph and his brethren are Signs (or Symbols) for seekers (after Truth).

8.   They said: "Truly Joseph and his brother are loved more by our father than we: but we are a goodly body! really our father is obviously wandering (in his mind)!

9.   "Slay you Joseph or cast him out to some (unknown) land, so that the favour of your father may be given to you alone: (there will be time enough) for you to be righteous after that!"

وَ اِسْحٰقَ ۚ اِنَّ رَبَّكَ عَلِيْمٌ

حَكِيْمٌ ۞ لَقَدْ كَانَ فِيْ يُوْسُفَ

وَ اِخْوَتِهٖۤ اٰيٰتٌ لِّلسَّآئِلِيْنَ ۞ اِذْ

قَالُوْا لَيُوْسُفُ وَ اَخُوْهُ اَحَبُّ

اِلٰۤى اَبِيْنَا مِنَّا وَ نَحْنُ عُصْبَةٌ ؕ

اِنَّ اَبَانَا لَفِيْ ضَلٰلٍ مُّبِيْنِۨ ۞

اۨقْتُلُوْا يُوْسُفَ اَوِ اطْرَحُوْهُ اَرْضًا

يَّخْلُ لَكُمْ وَجْهُ اَبِيْكُمْ وَ تَكُوْنُوْا

مِنْۢ بَعْدِهٖ قَوْمًا صٰلِحِيْنَ ۞

and the sun and the moon: I saw them prostrate themselves to me!"

5.   Said (the father): "My (dear) little son! relate not your vision to your brothers, lest they concoct a plot against you: for Satan is to man an avowed enemy!"

6.   "Thus will your Lord choose you and teach you the interpretation of stories (and events) and perfect His favour to you and to the posterity of Jacob - even as He perfected it to your fathers Abraham

وَّالشَّمْسَ وَالْقَمَرَ رَأَيْتُهُمْ لِى

سَٰجِدِيْنَ ۝ قَالَ يٰبُنَىَّ لَا تَقْصُصْ

رُءْيَاكَ عَلٰى اِخْوَتِكَ فَيَكِيْدُوْا

لَكَ كَيْدًا ۚ اِنَّ الشَّيْطٰنَ لِلْاِنْسَانِ

عَدُوٌّ مُّبِيْنٌ ۝ وَكَذٰلِكَ يَجْتَبِيْكَ

رَبُّكَ وَيُعَلِّمُكَ مِنْ تَأْوِيْلِ

الْاَحَادِيْثِ وَيُتِمُّ نِعْمَتَهٗ عَلَيْكَ

وَعَلٰٓى اٰلِ يَعْقُوْبَ كَمَآ اَتَمَّهَا

عَلٰٓى اَبَوَيْكَ مِنْ قَبْلُ اِبْرٰهِيْمَ

Yusuf (Joseph)

Bismillahir-Rahmanir-Rahim

1. Alif. Lam. Raa. These are the Symbols (or Verses) of the perspicuous Book.

2. We have sent it down as an Arabic Qur'an, in order that you may learn wisdom.

3. We do relate unto you the most beautiful of stories, in that We reveal to you this (portion of the) Qur'an: before this, you too was among those who knew it not.

4. Behold! Joseph said to his father: "O my father! I did see eleven stars

بِسْمِ اللهِ الرَّحْمٰنِ الرَّحِيْمِ

الٓرٰ ۚ تِلْكَ اٰيٰتُ الْكِتٰبِ الْمُبِيْنِ ۟ ۚ

اِنَّآ اَنْزَلْنٰهُ قُرْءٰنًا عَرَبِيًّا لَّعَلَّكُمْ

تَعْقِلُوْنَ ۟ نَحْنُ نَقُصُّ عَلَيْكَ

اَحْسَنَ الْقَصَصِ بِمَآ اَوْحَيْنَآ

اِلَيْكَ هٰذَا الْقُرْاٰنَ ۖ وَاِنْ كُنْتَ

مِنْ قَبْلِهٖ لَمِنَ الْغٰفِلِيْنَ ۟

اِذْ قَالَ يُوْسُفُ لِاَبِيْهِ يٰٓاَبَتِ

اِنِّيْ رَاَيْتُ اَحَدَ عَشَرَ كَوْكَبًا

with it We make firm your heart:
in them there comes to you the
Truth, as well as an exhortation
and a message of remembrance to
those who believe.

121. Say to those who do not
believe: "Do whatever you can:
we shall do our part;"

122. "And wait you! We too shall
wait."

123. To Allah do belong the
Unseen (secrets) of the heavens
and the earth, and to Him goes
back every affair (for decision):
then worship Him, and put your
trust in Him: and your Lord is not
unmindful of anything that you
do.

نُثَبِّتُ بِهِ فُؤَادَكَ وَجَآءَكَ فِى
هٰذِهِ الْحَقُّ وَمَوْعِظَةٌ وَّذِكْرٰى
لِلْمُؤْمِنِينَ ۝ وَقُلْ لِّلَّذِينَ لَا
يُؤْمِنُونَ اعْمَلُوا عَلٰى مَكَانَتِكُمْ
اِنَّا عٰمِلُونَ ۝ وَانْتَظِرُوا اِنَّا
مُنْتَظِرُونَ ۝ وَلِلّٰهِ غَيْبُ السَّمٰوٰتِ
وَالْاَرْضِ وَاِلَيْهِ يُرْجَعُ الْاَمْرُ
كُلُّهُ فَاعْبُدْهُ وَتَوَكَّلْ عَلَيْهِ
وَمَا رَبُّكَ بِغَافِلٍ عَمَّا تَعْمَلُونَ ۝

would your Lord be the One to destroy communities for a single wrong-doing, if its members were likely to mend.

118. If your Lord had so willed, He could have made mankind one people: but they will not cease to dispute.

119. Except those on whom your Lord has bestowed His Mercy: and for this did He create them: and the Word of your Lord shall be fulfilled: "I will fill Hell with (disobedient) jinns and men all together."

120. All that We relate to you of the stories of the Apostles, -

كَانَ رَبُّكَ لِيُهۡلِكَ الۡقُرٰى

بِظُلۡمٍ وَّ اَهۡلُهَا مُصۡلِحُوۡنَ ۝ وَلَوۡ

شَآءَ رَبُّكَ لَجَعَلَ النَّاسَ اُمَّةً

وَّاحِدَةً وَّلَا يَزَالُوۡنَ مُخۡتَلِفِيۡنَ ۝

اِلَّا مَنۡ رَّحِمَ رَبُّكَ ؕ وَلِذٰلِكَ

خَلَقَهُمۡ ؕ وَتَمَّتۡ كَلِمَةُ رَبِّكَ

لَاَمۡلَئَنَّ جَهَنَّمَ مِنَ الۡجِنَّةِ

وَالنَّاسِ اَجۡمَعِيۡنَ ۝ وَكُلًّا نَّقُصُّ

عَلَيۡكَ مِنۡ اَنۡۢبَآءِ الرُّسُلِ مَا

the night: for those things, that are good remove those that are evil: be that the word of remembrance to those who remember (their Lord):

115. And be steadfast in patience; for verily Allah will not suffer the reward of the righteous to perish.

116. Why were there not, among the generations before you, persons possessed of balanced good sense, prohibiting (men) from mischief in the earth - except a few among them whom We saved (from harm)? But the wrong-doers pursued the enjoyment of the good things of life which were given them, and persisted in sin.

117. Nor

الَّيْلِ ۚ إِنَّ الْحَسَنَاتِ يُذْهِبْنَ

السَّيِّئَاتِ ۚ ذَٰلِكَ ذِكْرَىٰ لِلذَّاكِرِينَ ۝

وَاصْبِرْ فَإِنَّ اللَّهَ لَا يُضِيعُ أَجْرَ

الْمُحْسِنِينَ ۝ فَلَوْلَا كَانَ مِنَ

الْقُرُونِ مِنْ قَبْلِكُمْ أُولُوا بَقِيَّةٍ

يَنْهَوْنَ عَنِ الْفَسَادِ فِي الْأَرْضِ

إِلَّا قَلِيلًا مِّمَّنْ أَنْجَيْنَا مِنْهُمْ ۗ

وَاتَّبَعَ الَّذِينَ ظَلَمُوا مَا أُتْرِفُوا

فِيهِ وَكَانُوا مُجْرِمِينَ ۝ وَمَا

111. And, of a surety, to all will your Lord pay back (in full the recompense) of their deeds: for He knows well all that they do.

112. Therefore stand firm (in the straight Path) as you are commanded, - you and those who with you turn (unto Allah); and transgress not (from the Path): for He sees well all that you do.

113. And incline not to those who do wrong, or the Fire will seize you; and you have no protectors other than Allah, nor shall you be helped.

114. And establish regular prayers at the two ends of the day and at the approaches of

مُرِيْبٌ ۞ وَاِنَّ كُلًّا لَّمَّا لَيُوَفِّيَنَّهُمْ

رَبُّكَ اَعْمَالَهُمْ ؕ اِنَّهٗ بِمَا يَعْمَلُوْنَ

خَبِيْرٌ ۞ فَاسْتَقِمْ كَمَاۤ اُمِرْتَ

وَمَنْ تَابَ مَعَكَ وَلَا تَطْغَوْا ؕ اِنَّهٗ

بِمَا تَعْمَلُوْنَ بَصِيْرٌ ۞ وَلَا تَرْكَنُوْۤا

اِلَى الَّذِيْنَ ظَلَمُوْا فَتَمَسَّكُمُ النَّارُ ۙ

وَمَا لَكُمْ مِّنْ دُوْنِ اللّٰهِ مِنْ

اَوْلِيَآءَ ثُمَّ لَا تُنْصَرُوْنَ ۞ وَاَقِمِ

الصَّلٰوةَ طَرَفَيِ النَّهَارِ وَزُلَفًا مِّنَ

and the earth endure, except as your Lord wills: a gift without break.

109. Be not then in doubt as to what these men worship. They worship nothing but what their fathers worshipped before (them): but verily We shall pay them back (in full) their portion without (the least) abatement.

110. We certainly gave the Book to Moses, but differences arose therein: had it not been that a Word had gone forth before from your Lord, the matter would have been decided between them, but they are in suspicious doubt concerning it.

وَالْأَرْضُ إِلَّا مَا شَاءَ رَبُّكَ عَطَاءً

غَيْرَ مَجْذُوذٍ ۝ فَلَا تَكُ فِى مِرْيَةٍ

مِّمَّا يَعْبُدُ هَٰؤُلَاءِ ۚ مَا يَعْبُدُونَ

إِلَّا كَمَا يَعْبُدُ اٰبَاؤُهُم مِّن قَبْلُ ۚ

وَإِنَّا لَمُوَفُّوهُمْ نَصِيبَهُمْ غَيْرَ

مَنْقُوصٍ ۝ وَلَقَدْ اٰتَيْنَا مُوسَى

الْكِتَابَ فَاخْتُلِفَ فِيهِ ۗ وَلَوْلَا

كَلِمَةٌ سَبَقَتْ مِن رَّبِّكَ لَقُضِىَ

بَيْنَهُمْ ۚ وَإِنَّهُمْ لَفِى شَكٍّ مِّنْهُ

105. The day it arrives, no soul shall speak except by His leave: of those (gathered) some will be wretched and some will be blessed.

106. Those who are wretched shall be in the Fire: there will be for them therein (nothing but) the heaving of sighs and sobs:

107. They will dwell therein for all the time that the heavens and the earth endure, except as your Lord wills: for your Lord is the (sure) Accomplisher of what He plans.

108. And those who are blessed shall be in the Garden: they will dwell therein for all the time that the heavens

يَوْمَ يَاتِ لَا تَكَلَّمُ نَفْسٌ اِلَّا

بِاِذْنِهٖ ۚ فَمِنْهُمْ شَقِيٌّ وَّسَعِيْدٌ ۞

فَاَمَّا الَّذِيْنَ شَقُوْا فَفِى النَّارِ

لَهُمْ فِيْهَا زَفِيْرٌ وَّشَهِيْقٌ ۙ ۞

خٰلِدِيْنَ فِيْهَا مَا دَامَتِ السَّمٰوٰتُ

وَالْاَرْضُ اِلَّا مَا شَآءَ رَبُّكَ ۚ اِنَّ

رَبَّكَ فَعَّالٌ لِّمَا يُرِيْدُ ۞ وَاَمَّا

الَّذِيْنَ سُعِدُوْا فَفِى الْجَنَّةِ

خٰلِدِيْنَ فِيْهَا مَا دَامَتِ السَّمٰوٰتُ

other than Allah, whom they invoked, profited them no whit when there issued the Decree of your Lord: nor did they add anything (to their lot) but perdition!

102. Such is the chastisement of your Lord when He chastises communities in the midst of their wrong: grievous, indeed, and severe is His chastisement.

103. In that is a Sign for those who fear the Chastisement of the Hereafter: that is a Day for which mankind will be gathered together: that will be a Day of Testimony.

104. Nor shall We delay it but for a term appointed.

يَدْعُوْنَ مِنْ دُوْنِ اللّٰهِ مِنْ

شَىْءٍ ۚ لَمَّا جَآءَ اَمْرُ رَبِّكَ ۚ وَمَا

زَادُوْهُمْ غَيْرَ تَتْبِيْبٍ ۞ وَكَذٰلِكَ

اَخْذُ رَبِّكَ اِذَآ اَخَذَ الْقُرٰى وَهِىَ

ظَالِمَةٌ ۚ اِنَّ اَخْذَهٗٓ اَلِيْمٌ شَدِيْدٌ ۞

اِنَّ فِيْ ذٰلِكَ لَاٰيَةً لِّمَنْ خَافَ

عَذَابَ الْاٰخِرَةِ ۚ ذٰلِكَ يَوْمٌ مَّجْمُوْعٌ

لَّهُ النَّاسُ وَذٰلِكَ يَوْمٌ مَّشْهُوْدٌ ۞

وَمَا نُؤَخِّرُهٗٓ اِلَّا لِاَجَلٍ مَّعْدُوْدٍ ۞

Pharaoh and the command of Pharaoh was no right (guide).

98. He will go before his people on the Day of Judgment, and lead them into the Fire (as cattle are led to water): but woeful indeed will be the place to which they are led!

99. And they are followed by a curse in this (life) and on the Day of Judgment: and woeful is the gift which shall be given (unto them)!

100. These are some of the stories of communities which We relate unto you: of them some are standing, and some have been mown down (by the sickle of time).

101. It was not We that wronged them: they wronged their own souls: the deities,

فِرْعَوْنَ وَمَآ أَمْرُ فِرْعَوْنَ بِرَشِيْدٍ ۞

يَقْدُمُ قَوْمَهٗ يَوْمَ الْقِيٰمَةِ فَأَوْرَدَهُمُ

النَّارَ ۗ وَبِئْسَ الْوِرْدُ الْمَوْرُوْدُ ۞

وَأُتْبِعُوْا فِيْ هٰذِهٖ لَعْنَةً وَّيَوْمَ

الْقِيٰمَةِ ۗ بِئْسَ الرِّفْدُ الْمَرْفُوْدُ ۞

ذٰلِكَ مِنْ أَنْبَآءِ الْقُرٰى نَقُصُّهٗ

عَلَيْكَ مِنْهَا قَآئِمٌ وَّحَصِيْدٌ ۞ وَمَا

ظَلَمْنٰهُمْ وَلٰكِنْ ظَلَمُوْٓا أَنْفُسَهُمْ

فَمَآ أَغْنَتْ عَنْهُمْ اٰلِهَتُهُمُ الَّتِيْ

for I too am watching with you!"

94. When Our Decree issued, We saved Shu'aib and those who believed with him, by (special) Mercy from Ourselves: but the (mighty) blast did seize the wrong-doers, and they lay prostrate in their homes by the morning, -

95. As if they had never dwelt and flourished there! Behold! How the Madyan were cursed and destroyed as were the Thamud.

96. And we sent Moses, with Our clear (Signs) and an authority manifest,

97. Unto Pharaoh and his chiefs: but they followed the command of

اِنِّیْ مَعَکُمْ رَقِیْبٌ ۞ وَلَمَّا جَآءَ

اَمْرُنَا نَجَّیْنَا شُعَیْبًا وَّالَّذِیْنَ

اٰمَنُوْا مَعَهٗ بِرَحْمَةٍ مِّنَّا وَاَخَذَتِ

الَّذِیْنَ ظَلَمُوا الصَّیْحَةُ فَاَصْبَحُوْا

فِیْ دِیَارِهِمْ جٰثِمِیْنَ ۞ کَاَنْ لَّمْ

یَغْنَوْا فِیْهَا ۚ اَلَا بُعْدًا لِّمَدْیَنَ

کَمَا بَعِدَتْ ثَمُوْدُ ۞ وَلَقَدْ اَرْسَلْنَا

مُوْسٰی بِاٰیٰتِنَا وَسُلْطٰنٍ مُّبِیْنٍ ۞

اِلٰی فِرْعَوْنَ وَمَلَاۡئِهٖ فَاتَّبَعُوْۤا اَمْرَ

no strength! Were it not for your family, we should certainly have stoned you! For you have among us no great position!"

92. He said: "O my people! Is then my family of more consideration with you than Allah? For you cast Him away behind your backs (with contempt). But verily my Lord encompasseth on all sides all that you do!"

93. "And O my people! Do whatever you can: I will do (my part): soon will you know who it is on whom descends the Chastisement of ignominy; and who is a liar! and watch you!

فِينَا ضَعِيفًا ۖ وَلَوْلَا رَهْطُكَ

لَرَجَمْنَاكَ ۖ وَمَآ أَنْتَ عَلَيْنَا بِعَزِيزٍ ۝

قَالَ يَٰقَوْمِ أَرَهْطِيٓ أَعَزُّ عَلَيْكُم

مِّنَ اللَّهِ ۖ وَاتَّخَذْتُمُوهُ وَرَآءَكُمْ

ظِهْرِيًّا ۚ إِنَّ رَبِّي بِمَا تَعْمَلُونَ

مُحِيطٌ ۝ وَيَٰقَوْمِ اعْمَلُوا عَلَىٰ

مَكَانَتِكُمْ إِنِّي عَامِلٌ ۖ سَوْفَ

تَعْلَمُونَ ۙ مَن يَأْتِيهِ عَذَابٌ

يُخْزِيهِ وَمَنْ هُوَ كَاذِبٌ ۖ وَارْتَقِبُوٓا

my success (in my task) can only
come from Allah. In Him I trust,
and unto Him I look."

89. "And O my people! Let not
my dissent (from you) cause you
to sin, lest you suffer a fate similar
to that of the people of Noah or of
Hud or of Salih, nor are the
people of Lut far off from you!"

90. "But ask forgiveness of your
Lord, and turn unto Him (in
repentance): for my Lord is
indeed full of Mercy and Loving-
Kindness."

91. They said: "O Shu'aib! Much
of what you say we do not understand! In fact among us we see
that you have

تَوْفِيقِيْ اِلَّا بِاللّٰهِ ۚ عَلَيْهِ تَوَكَّلْتُ

وَاِلَيْهِ اُنِيْبُ ۞ وَيٰقَوْمِ لَا يَجْرِمَنَّكُمْ

شِقَاقِيْۤ اَنْ يُّصِيْبَكُمْ مِّثْلُ مَاۤ

اَصَابَ قَوْمَ نُوْحٍ اَوْ قَوْمَ هُوْدٍ

اَوْ قَوْمَ صٰلِحٍ ۚ وَمَا قَوْمُ لُوْطٍ مِّنْكُمْ

بِبَعِيْدٍ ۞ وَاسْتَغْفِرُوْا رَبَّكُمْ ثُمَّ

تُوْبُوْۤا اِلَيْهِ ۚ اِنَّ رَبِّيْ رَحِيْمٌ

وَّدُوْدٌ ۞ قَالُوْا يٰشُعَيْبُ مَا نَفْقَهُ

كَثِيْرًا مِّمَّا تَقُوْلُ وَاِنَّا لَنَرٰكَ

"O Shu'aib! Does your (religion of) prayer command you that we leave off the worship which our fathers practised, or that we leave off doing what we like with our property? Truly, you are the one that forbears with faults and is right-minded!"

88. He said: "O my people! See you whether I have a clear (Sign) from my Lord, and He has given me sustenance (pure and) good as from Himself? I wish not, in opposition to you, to do that which I forbid you to do. I only desire (your) betterment to the best of my power; and

يٰشُعَيْبُ اَصَلٰوتُكَ تَأْمُرُكَ اَنْ

نَّتْرُكَ مَا يَعْبُدُ اٰبَآؤُنَاۤ اَوْ اَنْ

نَّفْعَلَ فِيْ اَمْوَالِنَا مَا نَشٰٓؤُاْ اِنَّكَ

لَاَنْتَ الْحَلِيْمُ الرَّشِيْدُ ۝ قَالَ

يٰقَوْمِ اَرَءَيْتُمْ اِنْ كُنْتُ عَلٰى بَيِّنَةٍ

مِّنْ رَّبِّيْ وَرَزَقَنِيْ مِنْهُ رِزْقًا

حَسَنًا ؕ وَمَاۤ اُرِيْدُ اَنْ اُخَالِفَكُمْ

اِلٰى مَاۤ اَنْهٰىكُمْ عَنْهُ ؕ اِنْ اُرِيْدُ

اِلَّا الْاِصْلَاحَ مَا اسْتَطَعْتُ ؕ وَمَا

god but Him. And give not short measure or weight: I see you in prosperity, but I fear for you the Chastisement of a day that will compass (you) all round."

85. "And O my people! Give just measure and weight, nor with-hold from the people the things that are their due: commit not evil in the land with intent to do mischief."

86. "That which is left you by Allah is best for you, if you (but) believed! But I am not set over you to keep watch!"

87. They said:

اِلٰهٍ غَيْرُهُ ۖ وَلَا تَنْقُصُوا الْمِكْيَالَ

وَالْمِيزَانَ اِنِّيٓ اَرٰىكُمْ بِخَيْرٍ

وَاِنِّيٓ اَخَافُ عَلَيْكُمْ عَذَابَ يَوْمٍ

مُّحِيْطٍ ۞ وَيٰقَوْمِ اَوْفُوا الْمِكْيَالَ

وَالْمِيزَانَ بِالْقِسْطِ وَلَا تَبْخَسُوا

النَّاسَ اَشْيَآءَهُمْ وَلَا تَعْثَوْا فِى

الْاَرْضِ مُفْسِدِيْنَ ۞ بَقِيَّتُ اللّٰهِ

خَيْرٌ لَّكُمْ اِنْ كُنْتُمْ مُّؤْمِنِيْنَ ۚ

وَمَآ اَنَا۠ عَلَيْكُمْ بِحَفِيْظٍ ۞ قَالُوْا

to her will happen what happens to the people. Morning is their time appointed: is not the morning nigh?"

82. When Our Decree issued, We turned (the cities) upside down, and rained down on them brimstones hard as baked clay, spread, layer on layer, -

83. Marked as from your Lord: nor are they ever far from those who do wrong!

84. To the Madyan People (We sent) Shu'aib, one of their own brethren: he said: "O my people! Worship Allah: you have no other

إِنَّهُ مُصِيبُهَا مَآ أَصَابَهُمْ إِنَّ

مَوْعِدَهُمُ الصُّبْحُ أَلَيْسَ الصُّبْحُ

بِقَرِيبٍ ۞ فَلَمَّا جَآءَ أَمْرُنَا جَعَلْنَا

عَالِيَهَا سَافِلَهَا وَأَمْطَرْنَا عَلَيْهَا

حِجَارَةً مِّن سِجِّيلٍ مَّنضُودٍ ۞

مُّسَوَّمَةً عِندَ رَبِّكَ وَمَا هِيَ

مِنَ الظَّالِمِينَ بِبَعِيدٍ ۞ وَإِلَى

مَدْيَنَ أَخَاهُمْ شُعَيْبًا قَالَ

يَقَوْمِ اعْبُدُوا اللهَ مَا لَكُم مِّنْ

cover me not with shame about my guests! Is there not among you a single right-minded man?"

79. They said: "Well do you know we have no need of your daughters: indeed you know quite well what we want!"

80. He said: "Would that I had power to suppress you or that I could betake myself to some powerful support."

81. (The Messengers) said: "O Lut! We are Messengers from your Lord! By no means shall they reach you! Now travel with your family while yet a part of the night remains, and let not any of you look back: but your wife (will remain behind):

تَخۡزُوۡنِ فِیۡ ضَیۡفِیۡ ؕ اَلَیۡسَ مِنۡكُمۡ

رَجُلٌ رَّشِیۡدٌ ﴿۷۸﴾ قَالُوۡا لَقَدۡ عَلِمۡتَ

مَا لَنَا فِیۡ بَنَاتِكَ مِنۡ حَقٍّ ۚ وَاِنَّكَ

لَتَعۡلَمُ مَا نُرِیۡدُ ﴿۷۹﴾ قَالَ لَوۡ اَنَّ

لِیۡ بِكُمۡ قُوَّةً اَوۡ اٰوِیۡۤ اِلٰی رُكۡنٍ

شَدِیۡدٍ ﴿۸۰﴾ قَالُوۡا یٰلُوۡطُ اِنَّا رُسُلُ

رَبِّكَ لَنۡ یَّصِلُوۡۤا اِلَیۡكَ فَاَسۡرِ

بِاَهۡلِكَ بِقِطۡعٍ مِّنَ الَّیۡلِ وَلَا

یَلۡتَفِتۡ مِنۡكُمۡ اَحَدٌ اِلَّا امۡرَاَتَكَ

this. The decree of your Lord has gone forth: for them there comes a Chastisement that cannot be turned back!

77. When Our Messengers came to Lut, he was grieved on their account and felt himself power-less (to protect) them. He said: "This is a distressful day."

78. And his people came rushing towards him, and they had been long in the habit of practising abominations. He said: "O my people! Here are my daughters: they are purer for you (if you marry)! Now fear Allah, and

عَنۡ هٰذَاؕ اِنَّهٗ قَدۡ جَآءَ اَمۡرُ

رَبِّكَ وَاِنَّهُمۡ اٰتِيۡهِمۡ عَذَابٌ غَيۡرُ

مَرۡدُوۡدٍ ۞ وَلَمَّا جَآءَتۡ رُسُلُنَا

لُوۡطًا سِیْٓءَ بِهِمۡ وَضَاقَ بِهِمۡ

ذَرۡعًا وَّقَالَ هٰذَا يَوۡمٌ عَصِیۡبٌ ۞

وَجَآءَهٗ قَوۡمُهٗ يُهۡرَعُوۡنَ اِلَيۡهِ

وَمِنۡ قَبۡلُ كَانُوۡا يَعۡمَلُوۡنَ السَّيِّاٰتِ

قَالَ يٰقَوۡمِ هٰٓؤُلَآءِ بَنَاتِیۡ هُنَّ

اَطۡهَرُ لَكُمۡ فَاتَّقُوا اللّٰهَ وَلَا

Shall I bear a child, seeing I am an old woman, and my husband here is an old man? That would indeed be a wonderful thing!"

73. They said: "Do you wonder at Allah's Decree? The Grace of Allah and His blessings on you, o you people of the house! for He is indeed worthy of all praise, full of all glory!"

74. When fear had passed from (the mind of) Abraham and the glad tidings had reached him, he began to plead with us for Lut's people.

75. For Abraham was, without doubt, forbearing (of faults), compassionate, and given to look to Allah.

76. O Abraham! Seek not

ءَاَلِدُ وَ اَنَا عَجُوزٌ وَّ هٰذَا بَعْلِى

شَيْخًا ۖ اِنَّ هٰذَا لَشَىْءٌ عَجِيبٌ ۞

قَالُوٓا اَتَعْجَبِيْنَ مِنْ اَمْرِ اللّٰهِ

رَحْمَتُ اللّٰهِ وَ بَرَكٰتُهٗ عَلَيْكُمْ

اَهْلَ الْبَيْتِ ۖ اِنَّهٗ حَمِيْدٌ مَّجِيْدٌ ۞

فَلَمَّا ذَهَبَ عَنْ اِبْرٰهِيْمَ الرَّوْعُ

وَجَآءَتْهُ الْبُشْرٰى يُجَادِلُنَا فِىْ

قَوْمِ لُوْطٍ ۞ اِنَّ اِبْرٰهِيْمَ لَحَلِيْمٌ

اَوَّاهٌ مُّنِيْبٌ ۞ يٰٓاِبْرٰهِيْمُ اَعْرِضْ

Our Messengers (Angels) to Abraham with glad tidings. They said, "Peace!" He answered, "Peace!" and hastened to entertain them with a roasted calf.

70. But when he saw their hands went not reaching towards the (meal), he felt some mistrust of them, and conceived a fear of them. They said: "Fear not: We have been sent against the people of Lut."

71. And his wife was standing (there), and she laughed: but We gave her glad tidings of Isaac, and after him, of Jacob.

72. She said: "Alas for me!

رُسُلُنَآ اِبْرٰهِيْمَ بِالْبُشْرٰى قَالُوْا

سَلٰمًا قَالَ سَلٰمٌ فَمَا لَبِثَ اَنْ

جَآءَ بِعِجْلٍ حَنِيْذٍ ۞ فَلَمَّا رَاٰۤ

اَيْدِيَهُمْ لَا تَصِلُ اِلَيْهِ نَكِرَهُمْ

وَ اَوْجَسَ مِنْهُمْ خِيْفَةً ؕ قَالُوْا

لَا تَخَفْ اِنَّاۤ اُرْسِلْنَاۤ اِلٰى قَوْمِ

لُوْطٍ ؕ وَامْرَاَتُهٗ قَآئِمَةٌ فَضَحِكَتْ

فَبَشَّرْنٰهَا بِاِسْحٰقَ ۙ وَمِنْ وَّرَآءِ

اِسْحٰقَ يَعْقُوْبَ ۞ قَالَتْ يٰوَيْلَتٰۤى

(then will be your ruin): (behold) there is a promise not to be belied!"

66. When Our Decree issued, We saved Salih and those who believed with him, by (special) Grace from Ourselves - and from the Ignominy of that day. For your Lord - He is the Strong One, and able to enforce His Will.

67. The (mighty) Blast overtook the wrong-doers, and they lay prostrate in their homes before the morning, -

68. As if they had never dwelt and flourished there. Ah! Behold! For the Thamud rejected their Lord and Cherisher! and curse was on the Thamud!

69. There came

ذٰلِكَ وَعْدٌ غَيْرُ مَكْذُوبٍ ۞

فَلَمَّا جَآءَ أَمْرُنَا نَجَّيْنَا صٰلِحًا

وَّالَّذِيْنَ اٰمَنُوْا مَعَهٗ بِرَحْمَةٍ مِّنَّا

وَمِنْ خِزْيِ يَوْمِئِذٍ ؕ اِنَّ رَبَّكَ

هُوَ الْقَوِيُّ الْعَزِيْزُ ۞ وَاَخَذَ الَّذِيْنَ

ظَلَمُوا الصَّيْحَةُ فَاَصْبَحُوْا فِيْ

دِيَارِهِمْ جٰثِمِيْنَ ۙ كَاَنْ لَّمْ يَغْنَوْا

فِيْهَا ؕ اَلَآ اِنَّ ثَمُوْدَا۟ كَفَرُوْا رَبَّهُمْ ۙ

اَلَا بُعْدًا لِّثَمُوْدَ ۞ وَلَقَدْ جَآءَتْ

If I have a clear (Sign) from my Lord and He has sent Mercy unto me from Himself, - who then can help me against Allah if I were to disobey Him? What then would you add to my (portion) but perdition?

64. "And O my people! This she-camel of Allah is a Sign to you: leave her to feed on Allah's (free) earth, and inflict no harm on her, or a swift Chastisement will seize you!"

65. But they did hamstring her. so he said: "Enjoy yourselves in your homes for three days:

اِنْ كُنْتُ عَلٰى بَيِّنَةٍ مِّنْ رَّبِّيْ

وَاٰتٰنِيْ مِنْهُ رَحْمَةً فَمَنْ يَّنْصُرُنِيْ

مِنَ اللّٰهِ اِنْ عَصَيْتُهٗ ۖ فَمَا

تَزِيْدُوْنَنِيْ غَيْرَ تَخْسِيْرٍ ۝ وَيٰقَوْمِ

هٰذِهٖ نَاقَةُ اللّٰهِ لَكُمْ اٰيَةً

فَذَرُوْهَا تَأْكُلْ فِيْٓ اَرْضِ اللّٰهِ

وَلَا تَمَسُّوْهَا بِسُوْٓءٍ فَيَأْخُذَكُمْ

عَذَابٌ قَرِيْبٌ ۝ فَعَقَرُوْهَا فَقَالَ

تَمَتَّعُوْا فِيْ دَارِكُمْ ثَلٰثَةَ اَيَّامٍ

Salih, one of their own brethren. He said: "O my people! Worship Allah: You have no other god but Him. It is He Who has produced you from the earth and settled you therein: then ask for-giveness of Him, and turn to Him (in repentance): for my Lord is (always) near, ready to answer."

62. They said: "O Salih! You have been of us! a centre of our hopes hitherto! Do you (now) forbid us the worship of what our fathers worshipped? But we are really in suspicious (disquieting) doubt as to that to which you invited us."

63. He said: "O my people! Do you see?

صَٰلِحًا ۚ قَالَ يَٰقَوْمِ اعْبُدُوا اللّٰهَ

مَا لَكُم مِّنْ إِلٰهٍ غَيْرُهُۥ ۖ هُوَ أَنشَأَكُم

مِّنَ الْأَرْضِ وَاسْتَعْمَرَكُمْ فِيهَا

فَاسْتَغْفِرُوهُ ثُمَّ تُوبُوٓا إِلَيْهِ ۚ إِنَّ

رَبِّى قَرِيبٌ مُّجِيبٌ ۞ قَالُوا يَٰصَٰلِحُ

قَدْ كُنتَ فِينَا مَرْجُوًّا قَبْلَ هٰذَآ ۖ

أَتَنْهَىٰنَآ أَن نَّعْبُدَ مَا يَعْبُدُ ءَابَآؤُنَا

وَإِنَّنَا لَفِى شَكٍّ مِّمَّا تَدْعُونَآ إِلَيْهِ

مُرِيبٌ ۞ قَالَ يَٰقَوْمِ أَرَءَيْتُمْ

Our decree issued, We saved Hud and those who believed with him, by (special) Grace from Ourselves: We saved them from a severe Chastisement.

59. Such were the 'Ad People: they rejected the Signs of their Lord and Cherisher; disobeyed His Apostles; and followed the command of every powerful, obstinate transgressor.

60. And they were pursued by a Curse in this life, - and on the Day of Judgment. Ah! Behold! For the 'Ad rejected their Lord and Cherisher! And curse was on 'Ad the people of Hud!

61. To the Thamud People (We sent)

جَآءَ اَمْرُنَا نَجَّيْنَا هُوْدًا وَّالَّذِيْنَ

اٰمَنُوْا مَعَهٗ بِرَحْمَةٍ مِّنَّا ۚ وَنَجَّيْنٰهُمْ

مِّنْ عَذَابٍ غَلِيْظٍ ۞ وَتِلْكَ عَادٌ

جَحَدُوْا بِاٰيٰتِ رَبِّهِمْ وَعَصَوْا

رُسُلَهٗ وَاتَّبَعُوْۤا اَمْرَ كُلِّ جَبَّارٍ

عَنِيْدٍ ۞ وَاُتْبِعُوْا فِيْ هٰذِهِ الدُّنْيَا

لَعْنَةً وَّيَوْمَ الْقِيٰمَةِ ۚ اَلَاۤ اِنَّ عَادًا

كَفَرُوْا رَبَّهُمْ ۚ اَلَا بُعْدًا لِّعَادٍ

قَوْمِ هُوْدٍ ۞ وَاِلٰى ثَمُوْدَ اَخَاهُمْ

From the sin of ascribing, to Him,"

55. "Other gods as partners! so scheme (your worst) against me, all of you, and give me no respite."

56. "I put my trust in Allah, my Lord and your Lord! There is not a moving creature, but He has grasp of its fore-lock. Verily, it is my Lord that is on a straight Path.

57. "If you turn away, - I (at least) have conveyed the Message with which I was sent to you. My Lord will make another people to succeed you, and you will not harm Him in the least. For my Lord has care and watch over all things."

مِّمَّا تُشْرِكُونَ ۞ مِنْ دُونِهِ

فَكِيدُونِي جَمِيعًا ثُمَّ لَا تُنْظِرُونِ ۞

إِنِّي تَوَكَّلْتُ عَلَى اللهِ رَبِّي وَرَبِّكُمْ ۚ

مَا مِنْ دَآبَّةٍ إِلَّا هُوَ آخِذٌ بِنَاصِيَتِهَا ۚ

إِنَّ رَبِّي عَلَى صِرَاطٍ مُّسْتَقِيمٍ ۞ فَإِنْ

تَوَلَّوْا فَقَدْ أَبْلَغْتُكُمْ مَّا أُرْسِلْتُ

بِهِ إِلَيْكُمْ ۚ وَيَسْتَخْلِفُ رَبِّي قَوْمًا

غَيْرَكُمْ وَلَا تَضُرُّونَهُ شَيْئًا ۚ إِنَّ

رَبِّي عَلَى كُلِّ شَيْءٍ حَفِيظٌ ۞ وَلَمَّا

52. "And O my people! Ask forgiveness of your Lord, and turn to Him (in repentance): He will send you the skies pouring abundant rain, and add strength to your strength: so turn you not back in sin!"

53. They said: "O Hud! No clear (Sign) that have you brou-ght us, and we are not the ones to desert our gods on your word! Nor shall we believe in you!"

54. "We say nothing but that (perhaps) some of our gods may have seized you with imbecility." He said: "I call Allah to witness, and do you bear witness, that I am free

وَيَقَوْمِ اسْتَغْفِرُوْا رَبَّكُمْ ثُمَّ تُوْبُوْٓا

اِلَيْهِ يُرْسِلِ السَّمَآءَ عَلَيْكُمْ مِّدْرَارًا

وَّيَزِدْكُمْ قُوَّةً اِلٰى قُوَّتِكُمْ وَلَا

تَتَوَلَّوْا مُجْرِمِيْنَ ۞ قَالُوْا يٰهُوْدُ مَا

جِئْتَنَا بِبَيِّنَةٍ وَّمَا نَحْنُ بِتَارِكِيْٓ

اٰلِهَتِنَا عَنْ قَوْلِكَ وَمَا نَحْنُ لَكَ

بِمُؤْمِنِيْنَ ۞ اِنْ نَّقُوْلُ اِلَّا اعْتَرٰىكَ

بَعْضُ اٰلِهَتِنَا بِسُوْٓءٍ ۚ قَالَ اِنِّيْٓ

اُشْهِدُ اللّٰهَ وَاشْهَدُوْٓا اَنِّيْ بَرِيْٓءٌ

the stories of the Unseen, which We have revealed unto you: before this, neither you nor your people knew them. So persevere patiently: for the End is for those who are righteous.

50.   To the 'Ad People (We sent) Hud, one of their own brethren. He said: "O my people! Worship Allah! You have no other god but Him. (Your other gods) you do nothing but invent!"

51.   "O my people! I ask of you no reward for this (Message). My reward is from none but Him who created me: will you not then understand?"

أَنْۢبَآءِ الْغَيْبِ نُوْحِيْهَاۤ اِلَيْكَ ۚ مَا

كُنْتَ تَعْلَمُهَاۤ اَنْتَ وَلَا قَوْمُكَ مِنْ

قَبْلِ هٰذَا ۛ فَاصْبِرْ ۛ اِنَّ الْعَاقِبَةَ

لِلْمُتَّقِيْنَ ۞ وَاِلٰى عَادٍ اَخَاهُمْ هُوْدًا ۚ

قَالَ يٰقَوْمِ اعْبُدُوا اللّٰهَ مَا لَكُمْ

مِّنْ اِلٰهٍ غَيْرُهٗ ۚ اِنْ اَنْتُمْ اِلَّا

مُفْتَرُوْنَ ۞ يٰقَوْمِ لَاۤ اَسْـَٔلُكُمْ

عَلَيْهِ اَجْرًا ۚ اِنْ اَجْرِيَ اِلَّا عَلَى

الَّذِيْ فَطَرَنِيْ ۚ اَفَلَا تَعْقِلُوْنَ ۞

you have no knowledge! I give you counsel, lest you act like the ignorant!"

47. Noah said: "O my Lord! I do seek refuge with You, lest I ask You for that of which I have no knowledge. And unless You forgive me and have Mercy on me, I should indeed be lost!"

48. The word came: "O Noah! Come down (from the Ark) with peace from Us, and blessing on you and on some of the peoples (who will spring) from those with you: but (there will be other) peoples to whom We shall grant their pleasures (for a time), but in the end will a grievous Chastisement reach them from Us."

49. Such are some of

لَكَ بِهٖ عِلْمٌ ۚ اِنِّیۤ اَعِظُكَ اَنْ

تَكُوْنَ مِنَ الْجٰهِلِیْنَ ۞ قَالَ

رَبِّ اِنِّیۤ اَعُوْذُ بِكَ اَنْ اَسْئَلَكَ مَا

لَیْسَ لِیْ بِهٖ عِلْمٌ ؕ وَ اِلَّا تَغْفِرْ لِیْ

وَ تَرْحَمْنِیۤ اَكُنْ مِّنَ الْخٰسِرِیْنَ ۞

قِیْلَ یٰنُوْحُ اهْبِطْ بِسَلٰمٍ مِّنَّا

وَ بَرَكٰتٍ عَلَیْكَ وَ عَلٰۤی اُمَمٍ مِّمَّنْ

مَّعَكَ ؕ وَ اُمَمٌ سَنُمَتِّعُهُمْ ثُمَّ یَمَسُّهُمْ

مِّنَّا عَذَابٌ اَلِیْمٌ ۞ تِلْكَ مِنْ

your water, and O sky! withhold (your rain)!" And the water abated, and the matter was ended. The Ark rested on Mount Judi, and the word went forth: "Away with those who do wrong!"

45. And Noah called upon his Lord, and said: "O my Lord! Surely my son is of my family! And Your promise is true, and You are the Justest of Judges!"

46. He said: "O Noah! He is not of your family: for his conduct is unrighteous. So ask not of Me that of which

مَآؤُكِ وَيَسْمَآءُ أَقْلِعِي وَغِيضَ

الْمَآءُ وَقُضِيَ الْأَمْرُ وَاسْتَوَتْ عَلَى

الْجُودِيِّ وَقِيلَ بُعْدًا لِّلْقَوْمِ

الظَّالِمِينَ ۞ وَنَادَى نُوحٌ رَّبَّهُ

فَقَالَ رَبِّ إِنَّ ابْنِي مِنْ أَهْلِي

وَإِنَّ وَعْدَكَ الْحَقُّ وَأَنْتَ أَحْكَمُ

الْحَاكِمِينَ ۞ قَالَ يَٰنُوحُ إِنَّهُ

لَيْسَ مِنْ أَهْلِكَ إِنَّهُ عَمَلٌ

غَيْرُ صَالِحٍ فَلَا تَسْئَلْنِ مَالَيْسَ

Oft-Forgiving, Most Merciful!"

42. So the Ark floated with them on the waves (towering) like mountains, and Noah called out to his son, who had separated himself (from the rest): "O my son! Embark with us, and be not with the unbelievers!"

43. The son replied: "I will betake myself to some mountain: it will save me from the water." Noah said: "This day nothing can save, from the Command of Allah, any but those on whom He has mercy!" And the waves came between them, and the son was among those overwhelmed in the Flood.

44. Then the word went forth: "O earth! swallow up

لَغَفُوْرٌ رَّحِيْمٌ ۝ وَهِيَ تَجْرِيْ بِهِمْ فِيْ

مَوْجٍ كَالْجِبَالِ ۗ وَنَادٰى نُوْحُ ابْنَهُ

وَكَانَ فِيْ مَعْزِلٍ يّٰبُنَيَّ ارْكَبْ

مَّعَنَا وَلَا تَكُنْ مَّعَ الْكٰفِرِيْنَ ۝

قَالَ سَاٰوِيْ اِلٰى جَبَلٍ يَّعْصِمُنِيْ

مِنَ الْمَآءِ ۗ قَالَ لَا عَاصِمَ الْيَوْمَ

مِنْ اَمْرِ اللّٰهِ اِلَّا مَنْ رَّحِمَ ۚ

وَحَالَ بَيْنَهُمَا الْمَوْجُ فَكَانَ مِنَ

الْمُغْرَقِيْنَ ۝ وَقِيْلَ يٰٓاَرْضُ ابْلَعِيْ

39. "But soon will you know who it is on whom will descend a Chastisement that will cover them with shame, - on whom will be unloosed a Chastisement lasting:"

40. At length, behold! there came Our command, and the fountains of the earth gushed forth! We said: "Embark therein, of each kind two, male and female, and your family - except those against whom the word has already gone forth, - and the believers." But only a few believed with him.

41. So he said: "Embark you on the Ark, in the name of Allah, whether it move or be at rest! For my Lord is, be sure,

فَسَوْفَ تَعْلَمُوْنَ مَنْ يَّأْتِيْهِ عَذَابٌ

يُّخْزِيْهِ وَيَحِلُّ عَلَيْهِ عَذَابٌ

مُّقِيْمٌ ۞ حَتّٰى إِذَا جَآءَ أَمْرُنَا وَفَارَ

التَّنُّوْرُ ۙ قُلْنَا احْمِلْ فِيْهَا مِنْ

كُلٍّ زَوْجَيْنِ اثْنَيْنِ وَأَهْلَكَ إِلَّا

مَنْ سَبَقَ عَلَيْهِ الْقَوْلُ وَمَنْ

أٰمَنَ ۚ وَمَآ أٰمَنَ مَعَهُ إِلَّا قَلِيْلٌ ۞

وَقَالَ ارْكَبُوْا فِيْهَا بِسْمِ اللّٰهِ

مَجْرٰىهَا وَمُرْسٰىهَا ۚ إِنَّ رَبِّيْ

36. It was revealed to Noah: "None of your people will believe except those who have believed already! So grieve no longer over their (evil) deeds."

37. "But construct an Ark under Our eyes and Our inspiration, and address Me no (further) on behalf of those who are in sin: for they are about to be overwhelmed (in the Flood)."

38. Forthwith he (starts) constructing the Ark: every time that the chiefs of his people passed by him, they threw ridicule on him. He said: "If you ridicule us now, we (in our turn) can look down on you with ridicule likewise!"

وَأُوْحِىَ اِلٰى نُوْحٍ اَنَّهٗ لَنْ يُّؤْمِنَ

مِنْ قَوْمِكَ اِلَّا مَنْ قَدْ اٰمَنَ

فَلَا تَبْتَئِسْ بِمَا كَانُوْا يَفْعَلُوْنَ ۞

وَاصْنَعِ الْفُلْكَ بِاَعْيُنِنَا وَوَحْيِنَا

وَلَا تُخَاطِبْنِيْ فِى الَّذِيْنَ ظَلَمُوْا

اِنَّهُمْ مُّغْرَقُوْنَ ۞ وَيَصْنَعُ الْفُلْكَ

وَكُلَّمَا مَرَّ عَلَيْهِ مَلَاٌ مِّنْ قَوْمِهٖ

سَخِرُوْا مِنْهُ قَالَ اِنْ تَسْخَرُوْا مِنَّا

فَاِنَّا نَسْخَرُ مِنْكُمْ كَمَا تَسْخَرُوْنَ ۞

you speak the truth!?"

33. He said: "Truly, Allah will bring it on you if He wills, - and then, you will not be able to frustrate it!"

34. "Of no profit will be my counsel to you, much as I desire to give you (good) counsel, if it be that Allah wills to leave you astray: He is your Lord! and to Him will you return!"

35. Or do they say, "He has forged it"? Say: "If I had forged it, on me were my sin! And I am free of the sins of which you are guilty!

كُنْتَ مِنَ الصّٰدِقِيْنَ ۞ قَالَ

اِنَّمَا يَأْتِيْكُمْ بِهِ اللّٰهُ اِنْ شَآءَ

وَمَآ اَنْتُمْ بِمُعْجِزِيْنَ ۞ وَلَا

يَنْفَعُكُمْ نُصْحِيْٓ اِنْ اَرَدْتُّ اَنْ

اَنْصَحَ لَكُمْ اِنْ كَانَ اللّٰهُ يُرِيْدُ

اَنْ يُّغْوِيَكُمْ ۘ هُوَ رَبُّكُمْ ۗ وَاِلَيْهِ

تُرْجَعُوْنَ ۞ اَمْ يَقُوْلُوْنَ افْتَرٰىهُ ۗ

قُلْ اِنِ افْتَرَيْتُهٗ فَعَلَيَّ اِجْرَامِيْ

وَاَنَا بَرِيْٓءٌ مِّمَّا تُجْرِمُوْنَ ۞

Will you not then take heed?

31. "I tell you not that with me are the Treasures of Allah, nor do I know what is hidden, nor claim I to be an Angel. Nor yet do I say, of those whom your eyes do despise that Allah will not grant them (all) that is good: Allah knows best what is in their souls: I should, if I did, indeed be a wrong-doer."

32. They said: "O Noah! You have disputed with us, and (much) have you prolonged the dispute with us: now bring upon us what you threaten us with, if

أَفَلَا تَذَكَّرُوْنَ ۞ وَلَاۤ اَقُوْلُ لَكُمْ

عِنْدِىْ خَزَآئِنُ اللّٰهِ وَلَاۤ اَعْلَمُ

الْغَيْبَ وَلَاۤ اَقُوْلُ اِنِّىْ مَلَكٌ

وَّلَاۤ اَقُوْلُ لِلَّذِيْنَ تَزْدَرِىۤ

اَعْيُنُكُمْ لَنْ يُّؤْتِيَهُمُ اللّٰهُ خَيْرًا ؕ

اَللّٰهُ اَعْلَمُ بِمَا فِىۤ اَنْفُسِهِمْ ۚ

اِنِّىۤ اِذًا لَّمِنَ الظّٰلِمِيْنَ ۞ قَالُوْا

يٰنُوْحُ قَدْ جَادَلْتَنَا فَاَكْثَرْتَ

جِدَالَنَا فَأْتِنَا بِمَا تَعِدُنَاۤ اِنْ

See you if (it be that) I have a clear Sign from my Lord, and that He has sent Mercy unto me from His own presence, but that the Mercy has been obscured from your sight? Shall we compel you to accept it when you are averse to it?"

29. "And O my people! I ask you for no wealth in return: my reward is from none but Allah: but I will not drive away (in contempt) those who believe: for verily they are to meet their Lord, and you I see are the ignorant ones!"

30. "And O my people! Who would help me against Allah if I drove them away?

اَرَءَيْتُمْ اِنْ كُنْتُ عَلَى بَيِّنَةٍ مِّنْ

رَّبِّى وَ اٰتٰىنِىْ رَحْمَةً مِّنْ عِنْدِهٖ

فَعُمِّيَتْ عَلَيْكُمْ ؕ اَنُلْزِمُكُمُوْهَا وَاَنْتُمْ

لَهَا كٰرِهُوْنَ ۝ وَيٰقَوْمِ لَاۤ اَسْـَٔلُكُمْ

عَلَيْهِ مَالًا ؕ اِنْ اَجْرِىَ اِلَّا عَلَى

اللّٰهِ وَمَاۤ اَنَا بِطَارِدِ الَّذِيْنَ اٰمَنُوْا ؕ

اِنَّهُمْ مُّلٰقُوْا رَبِّهِمْ وَلٰكِنِّىْۤ اَرٰىكُمْ

قَوْمًا تَجْهَلُوْنَ ۝ وَيٰقَوْمِ مَنْ

يَّنْصُرُنِىْ مِنَ اللّٰهِ اِنْ طَرَدْتُّهُمْ ؕ

"I have come to you with a clear warning:"

26. "That you serve none but Allah: verily I do fear for you the Chastisement of a grievous day."

27. But the chiefs of the unbelievers among his people said: "We see (in) you nothing but a man like ourselves: nor do we see that any follow you but the meanest among us, in judgment immature: nor do we see in you (all) any merit above us: in fact we think you are liars!"

28. He said: "O my people!

اِنِّى لَكُمْ نَذِيرٌ مُّبِيْنٌ ۞ اَنْ لَّا

تَعْبُدُوْٓا اِلَّا اللّٰهَ اِنِّىٓ اَخَافُ

عَلَيْكُمْ عَذَابَ يَوْمٍ اَلِيْمٍ ۞ فَقَالَ

الْمَلَاُ الَّذِيْنَ كَفَرُوْا مِنْ قَوْمِهٖ

مَا نَرٰىكَ اِلَّا بَشَرًا مِّثْلَنَا وَمَا

نَرٰىكَ اتَّبَعَكَ اِلَّا الَّذِيْنَ هُمْ

اَرَاذِلُنَا بَادِىَ الرَّأْىِ ۚ وَمَا نَرٰى

لَكُمْ عَلَيْنَا مِنْ فَضْلٍ بَلْ

نَظُنُّكُمْ كٰذِبِيْنَ ۞ قَالَ يٰقَوْمِ

and the (fancies) they invented
have left them in the lurch!

22. Without a doubt, these are
the very ones who will lose most
in the Hereafter!

23. But those who believe and
work righteousness, and humble
themselves before their Lord, -
they will be Companions of the
Gardens, to dwell therein for ever!

24. These two kinds (of men)
may be compared to the blind
and deaf, and those who can see
and hear well. Are they equal
when compared? Will you not
then take heed?

25. We sent Noah to his people
(with a mission):

وَضَلَّ عَنْهُمْ مَّا كَانُوْا يَفْتَرُوْنَ ۞

لَا جَرَمَ اَنَّهُمْ فِى الْاٰخِرَةِ هُمُ

الْاَخْسَرُوْنَ ۞ اِنَّ الَّذِيْنَ اٰمَنُوْا

وَعَمِلُوا الصّٰلِحٰتِ وَاَخْبَتُوْۤا اِلٰى

رَبِّهِمْ اُولٰٓئِكَ اَصْحٰبُ الْجَنَّةِ هُمْ

فِيْهَا خٰلِدُوْنَ ۞ مَثَلُ الْفَرِيْقَيْنِ

كَالْاَعْمٰى وَالْاَصَمِّ وَالْبَصِيْرِ وَالسَّمِيْعِ ؕ

هَلْ يَسْتَوِيٰنِ مَثَلًا ؕ اَفَلَا تَذَكَّرُوْنَ ۞

وَلَقَدْ اَرْسَلْنَا نُوْحًا اِلٰى قَوْمِهٖۤ

those who do wrong! -

19. "Those who would hinder (men) from the path of Allah and would seek in it something crooked: these were they who denied the Hereafter!"

20. They will in no wise frustrate (His design) on earth, nor have they protectors besides Allah! Their Chastisement will be doubled! They lost the power to hear, and they did not see!

21. They are the ones who have lost their own souls:

ٱلظَّٰلِمِينَ ۝ ٱلَّذِينَ يَصُدُّونَ عَنْ

سَبِيلِ ٱللَّهِ وَيَبْغُونَهَا عِوَجًا

وَهُم بِٱلْءَاخِرَةِ هُمْ كَٰفِرُونَ ۝

أُوْلَٰٓئِكَ لَمْ يَكُونُوا۟ مُعْجِزِينَ فِى

ٱلْأَرْضِ وَمَا كَانَ لَهُم مِّن دُونِ

ٱللَّهِ مِنْ أَوْلِيَآءَ يُضَٰعَفُ لَهُمُ

ٱلْعَذَابُ مَا كَانُوا۟ يَسْتَطِيعُونَ

ٱلسَّمْعَ وَمَا كَانُوا۟ يُبْصِرُونَ ۝

أُوْلَٰٓئِكَ ٱلَّذِينَ خَسِرُوٓا۟ أَنفُسَهُمْ

therein; but those of the Sects that reject it, - the Fire will be their promised meeting-place. Be not then in doubt thereon: for it is the truth from your Lord: yet many among men do not believe!

18.   Who does more wrong than those who invent a life against Allah? They will be turned back to the presence of their Lord, and the witnesses will say, "These are the ones who lied against their Lord! Behold! The Curse of Allah is on

بِهٖ ۖ وَمَنْ يَّكْفُرْ بِهٖ مِنَ الْأَحْزَابِ

فَالنَّارُ مَوْعِدُهٗ ۚ فَلَا تَكُ فِيْ

مِرْيَةٍ مِّنْهُ ۚ إِنَّهُ الْحَقُّ مِنْ

رَّبِّكَ وَلٰكِنَّ أَكْثَرَ النَّاسِ لَا

يُؤْمِنُوْنَ ۞ وَمَنْ أَظْلَمُ مِمَّنِ

افْتَرٰى عَلَى اللّٰهِ كَذِبًا ۚ أُولٰٓئِكَ

يُعْرَضُوْنَ عَلٰى رَبِّهِمْ وَيَقُوْلُ

الْأَشْهَادُ هٰٓؤُلَآءِ الَّذِيْنَ كَذَبُوْا

عَلٰى رَبِّهِمْ ۚ أَلَا لَعْنَةُ اللّٰهِ عَلَى

and its glitter, - to them We shall pay (the price of) their deeds therein, - without diminution.

16. They are those for whom there is nothing in the Hereafter but the Fire: vain are the designs they frame therein, and of no effect and the deeds that they do!

17. Can they be (like) those who accept a clear (Sign) from their Lord, and whom a witness from Himself does teach, as did the Book of Moses before it, - a guide and a mercy? They believe

وَزَيَّنتَهَا نُوَفِّ إِلَيْهِمْ أَعْمَالَهُمْ

فِيهَا وَهُمْ فِيهَا لَا يُبْخَسُونَ ۝

أُولَٰٓئِكَ الَّذِينَ لَيْسَ لَهُمْ فِى

الْأَخِرَةِ إِلَّا النَّارُ ۖ وَحَبِطَ مَا

صَنَعُوا فِيهَا وَبَٰطِلٌ مَّا كَانُوا

يَعْمَلُونَ ۝ أَفَمَن كَانَ عَلَىٰ

بَيِّنَةٍ مِّن رَّبِّهِ وَيَتْلُوهُ شَاهِدٌ

مِّنْهُ وَمِن قَبْلِهِ كِتَٰبُ مُوسَىٰٓ

إِمَامًا وَّرَحْمَةً ۚ أُولَٰٓئِكَ يُؤْمِنُونَ

only to warn! it is Allah that arranges all affairs!

13. Or they may say, "He forged it. " Say, "Bring you then ten Suras forged, like unto it, and call (to your aid) whomsoever you can, other than Allah! - if you speak the truth!

14. "If then they (your false gods) answer not your (call), know you that this revelation is sent down (replete) with the knowledge of Allah, and that there is no god but He! will you even then not submit (to Islam)?"

15. Those who desire the life of the present

وَمَا مِنْ دَآبَّةٍ فِي الْأَرْضِ

إِلَّا عَلَى اللهِ رِزْقُهَا وَيَعْلَمُ

مُسْتَقَرَّهَا وَمُسْتَوْدَعَهَا كُلٌّ فِيْ

كِتٰبٍ مُّبِيْنٍ ۞ وَهُوَ الَّذِيْ خَلَقَ

السَّمٰوٰتِ وَالْأَرْضَ فِيْ سِتَّةِ

أَيَّامٍ وَّكَانَ عَرْشُهُ عَلَى الْمَآءِ

لِيَبْلُوَكُمْ أَيُّكُمْ أَحْسَنُ عَمَلًا ط

وَلَئِنْ قُلْتَ إِنَّكُمْ مَّبْعُوْثُوْنَ

مِنْ بَعْدِ الْمَوْتِ لَيَقُوْلَنَّ

ذٰلِكَ الْكِتٰبُ لَا رَيْبَ

پاره

وَمَا مِنْ دَآبَّةٍ

(۱۲)

6. There is no moving creature on earth but its sustenance depends on Allah: He knows the time and place of its definite abode and its temporary deposit: all is in a clear Record.

7. He it is Who created the heavens and the earth in six days - and His Throne was over the water - that He might try you, which of you is best in conduct. But if you were to say to them, "You shall indeed be raised up after death", the unbelievers would be sure to say,

الَّذِينَ كَفَرُوا إِنْ هَذَآ إِلَّا

سِحْرٌ مُّبِينٌ ۞ وَلَئِنْ أَخَّرْنَا

عَنْهُمُ الْعَذَابَ إِلَى أُمَّةٍ مَّعْدُودَةٍ

لَّيَقُولُنَّ مَا يَحْبِسُهُ ۚ أَلَا يَوْمَ

يَأْتِيهِمْ لَيْسَ مَصْرُوفًا عَنْهُمْ

وَحَاقَ بِهِم مَّا كَانُوا بِهِ

يَسْتَهْزِءُونَ ۞ وَلَئِنْ أَذَقْنَا

الْإِنْسَانَ مِنَّا رَحْمَةً ثُمَّ نَزَعْنَاهَا

مِنْهُ إِنَّهُ لَيَئُوسٌ كَفُورٌ ۞ وَلَئِنْ

like a goodly tree, whose root is firmly fixed, and its branches (reach) to the heavens.

25. It brings forth its fruit at all times, by the leave of its Lord. So Allah sets forth parables for men, in order that they may receive admonition.

26. And the parable of an evil word is that of an evil tree: it is torn up by the root from the surface of the earth: it has no stability.

27. Allah will establish in strength those who believe, with the word that stands firm,

فِى الْحَيٰوةِ الدُّنْيَا وَفِى الْاٰخِرَةِ

وَيُضِلُّ اللّٰهُ الظّٰلِمِيْنَ ۙ وَيَفْعَلُ

اللّٰهُ مَا يَشَآءُ ۟ أَلَمْ تَرَ إِلَى

الَّذِيْنَ بَدَّلُوْا نِعْمَتَ اللّٰهِ

كُفْرًا وَّأَحَلُّوْا قَوْمَهُمْ دَارَ

الْبَوَارِ ۙ جَهَنَّمَ ۚ يَصْلَوْنَهَا ۚ وَبِئْسَ

الْقَرَارُ ۞ وَجَعَلُوْا لِلّٰهِ أَنْدَادًا

لِّيُضِلُّوْا عَنْ سَبِيْلِهٖ ۗ قُلْ

تَمَتَّعُوْا فَإِنَّ مَصِيْرَكُمْ إِلَى

in this world and in the Hereafter; but Allah will leave, to stray, those who do wrong: Allah does what He will

28. Have you not turned your vision to those who have exchanged the favour of Allah. Into blasphemy and caused their people to descend to the House of Perdition? -

29. Into Hell? They will burn therein, - an evil place to stay in!

30. And they set up (idols) as equal to Allah, to mislead (men) from the Path! Say: "Enjoy (your brief power)! But verily you are making straight way for

النَّارِ ۞ قُلْ لِّعِبَادِيَ الَّذِيْنَ

اٰمَنُوْا يُقِيْمُوا الصَّلٰوةَ وَيُنْفِقُوْا

مِمَّا رَزَقْنٰهُمْ سِرًّا وَّعَلَانِيَةً

مِّنْ قَبْلِ اَنْ يَّاْتِيَ يَوْمٌ لَّا

بَيْعٌ فِيْهِ وَلَا خِلٰلٌ ۞ اَللّٰهُ

الَّذِيْ خَلَقَ السَّمٰوٰتِ وَالْاَرْضَ

وَاَنْزَلَ مِنَ السَّمَآءِ مَآءً فَاَخْرَجَ

بِهٖ مِنَ الثَّمَرٰتِ رِزْقًا لَّكُمْ ۚ

وَسَخَّرَ لَكُمُ الْفُلْكَ لِتَجْرِيَ فِى

Hell!"

31. Speak to My servants who have believed, that they may establish regular prayers, and spend (in charity) out of the sustenance We have given them, secretly and openly, before the coming of a Day in which there will be neither mutual bargaining nor befriending.

32. It is Allah Who has created the heavens and the earth and sendeth down rain from the skies, and with it bringeth out fruits wherewith to feed you; it is He Who have made the ships subject to you, that they may sail through

الْبَحْرَ بِأَمْرِهٖ ۚ وَسَخَّرَ لَكُمُ

الْأَنْهَارَ ۞ وَسَخَّرَ لَكُمُ الشَّمْسَ

وَالْقَمَرَ دَآئِبَيْنِ ۚ وَسَخَّرَ لَكُمُ

الَّيْلَ وَالنَّهَارَ ۞ وَاٰتٰىكُمْ مِّنْ

كُلِّ مَا سَاَلْتُمُوهُ ۚ وَاِنْ تَعُدُّوْا

نِعْمَتَ اللّٰهِ لَا تُحْصُوْهَا ۚ اِنَّ

الْاِنْسَانَ لَظَلُوْمٌ كَفَّارٌ ۞ وَاِذْ

قَالَ اِبْرٰهِيْمُ رَبِّ اجْعَلْ

هٰذَا الْبَلَدَ اٰمِنًا وَّاجْنُبْنِيْ

the sea by His Command; and the rivers (also) have He made subject to you.

33. And He has made subject to you the sun and the moon, both diligently pursuing their courses; and the night and the day has he (also) made subject to you.

34. And He gives you of all that you ask for. But if you count the favours of Allah, never will you be able to number them. Verily, man is given up to injustice and ingratitude.

35. Remember Abraham said: "O my Lord! Make this city one of peace and security: and preserve me

وَبَنِيَّ أَنْ نَّعْبُدَ الْأَصْنَامَ ۩

رَبِّ إِنَّهُنَّ أَضْلَلْنَ كَثِيرًا

مِنَ النَّاسِ ۚ فَمَنْ تَبِعَنِي

فَإِنَّهُ مِنِّي ۖ وَمَنْ عَصَانِي

فَإِنَّكَ غَفُورٌ رَّحِيمٌ ۩ رَّبَّنَآ

إِنِّيَ أَسْكَنتُ مِن ذُرِّيَّتِي

بِوَادٍ غَيْرِ ذِي زَرْعٍ عِندَ

بَيْتِكَ الْمُحَرَّمِ رَبَّنَا لِيُقِيمُوا

الصَّلَوٰةَ فَاجْعَلْ أَفْئِدَةً مِّنَ

and my sons from worshipping idols."

36. "O my Lord! They have indeed led astray many among mankind; he then who follows my (ways) is of me, and he that disobeys me, - but You are indeed Oft-Forgiving, Most Merciful.

37. "O our Lord! I have made some of my offspring to dwell in a valley without cultivation, by your Sacred House; in order, O our Lord, that they may establish regular prayer: so fill the hearts of some among

النَّاسِ تَهْوِىٓ اِلَيْهِمْ وَارْزُقْهُمْ

مِّنَ الثَّمَرٰتِ لَعَلَّهُمْ يَشْكُرُوْنَ ۞

رَبَّنَآ اِنَّكَ تَعْلَمُ مَا نُخْفِيْ

وَمَا نُعْلِنُ ۗ وَمَا يَخْفٰى عَلَى

اللّٰهِ مِنْ شَيْءٍ فِى الْاَرْضِ

وَلَا فِى السَّمَآءِ ۞ اَلْحَمْدُ لِلّٰهِ

الَّذِىْ وَهَبَ لِىْ عَلَى الْكِبَرِ

اِسْمٰعِيْلَ وَاِسْحٰقَ ۗ اِنَّ رَبِّىْ

لَسَمِيْعُ الدُّعَآءِ ۞ رَبِّ اجْعَلْنِيْ

men with love towards them, and feed them with fruits: so that they may give thanks."

38. "O our Lord! Truly you know what we conceal and what we reveal: for nothing whatever is hidden from Allah, whether on earth or in heaven."

39. "Praise be to Allah, Who has granted unto me in old age Isma'il and Isaac: for truly my Lord is He, the Hearer of Prayer!"

40. "O my Lord! Make me

مُقِيْمَ الصَّلٰوةِ وَمِنْ ذُرِّيَّتِيْ

رَبَّنَا وَتَقَبَّلْ دُعَآءِ ۞ رَبَّنَا

اغْفِرْلِيْ وَلِوَالِدَيَّ وَلِلْمُؤْمِنِيْنَ

يَوْمَ يَقُوْمُ الْحِسَابُ ۞ وَلَا

تَحْسَبَنَّ اللّٰهَ غَافِلًا عَمَّا

يَعْمَلُ الظّٰلِمُوْنَ ۬ؕ اِنَّمَا يُؤَخِّرُهُمْ

لِيَوْمٍ تَشْخَصُ فِيْهِ الْاَبْصَارُ ۞

مُهْطِعِيْنَ مُقْنِعِيْ رُءُوْسِهِمْ لَا

يَرْتَدُّ اِلَيْهِمْ طَرْفُهُمْ ۚ وَاَفْئِدَتُهُمْ

one who establishes regular prayer, and also (raise such) among my offspring O our Lord! and accept You my prayer."

41. "O our Lord! Cover (us) with Your Forgiveness - me, my parents, and (all) believers, on the Day that the reckoning will be established!"

42. Think not that Allah does not heed the deeds of those who do wrong. He but giveth them respite against a Day when the eyes will fixedly stare in horror, -

43. They running forward with necks outstretched, their heads uplifted, their gaze returning not towards them, and their hearts

وَاَنْذِرِ النَّاسَ يَوْمَ هٰوَاءٌ ۚ ۞ وَاَنْذِرِ النَّاسَ يَوْمَ

يَاْتِيْهِمُ الْعَذَابُ فَيَقُوْلُ الَّذِيْنَ

ظَلَمُوْا رَبَّنَآ اَخِّرْنَآ اِلٰٓى اَجَلٍ

قَرِيْبٍ نُّجِبْ دَعْوَتَكَ وَ نَتَّبِعِ

الرُّسُلَ ۗ اَوَلَمْ تَكُوْنُوْٓا اَقْسَمْتُمْ

مِّنْ قَبْلُ مَا لَكُمْ مِّنْ زَوَالٍ ۞

وَّسَكَنْتُمْ فِيْ مَسٰكِنِ الَّذِيْنَ

ظَلَمُوْٓا اَنْفُسَهُمْ وَتَبَيَّنَ لَكُمْ

كَيْفَ فَعَلْنَا بِهِمْ وَضَرَبْنَا لَكُمُ

a (gaping) void!

44. So warn mankind of the Day when the Wrath will reach them: then will the wrong-doers say: "Our Lord! Respite us (if only) for a short term: we will answer Your call, and follow the Apostles!" "What! Were you not wont to swear aforetime that you should suffer no decline?"

45. "And you dwelt in the dwellings of men who wronged their own souls; you were clearly shown how We dealt with them; and We put forth

الْأَمْثَالَ ۞ وَقَدْ مَكَرُوْا مَكْرَهُمْ

وَعِنْدَ اللّٰهِ مَكْرُهُمْ ۚ وَإِنْ كَانَ

مَكْرُهُمْ لِتَزُوْلَ مِنْهُ الْجِبَالُ ۞

فَلَا تَحْسَبَنَّ اللّٰهَ مُخْلِفَ

وَعْدِهٖ رُسُلَهٗ ۗ إِنَّ اللّٰهَ عَزِيْزٌ

ذُو انْتِقَامٍ ۖ يَوْمَ تُبَدَّلُ الْأَرْضُ

غَيْرَ الْأَرْضِ وَالسَّمٰوٰتُ وَبَرَزُوْا

لِلّٰهِ الْوَاحِدِ الْقَهَّارِ ۞ وَتَرَى

الْمُجْرِمِيْنَ يَوْمَئِذٍ مُّقَرَّنِيْنَ

ﺑﺬﻟﻚ ﺍﻟﻜﺘﺐ ﻻ ﺭﻳﺐ ﻓﻴﻪ

PART 13
Wamaa Ubarri'u

in fetters; -

50. Their garments of liquid pitch, and their faces covered with Fire;

51. That Allah may requite each soul according to its deserts; and verily Allah is swift in calling to account.

52. Here is a Message for mankind: let them take warning therefrom, and let them know that He is (no other than) One Allah: let men of understanding take heed.

Al-Hijr (The Rocky Tract)
Bismillahir-Rahmanir-Rahim

1. Alif . Lam . Raa. These are the Ayats of Revelation, - of a Qur'an that makes things clear.

We give him a taste of (Our) favours after adversity has touched him, he is sure to say, "All evil has departed from me:" Behold! He falls into exultation and pride.

11. Not so do those who show patience and constancy, and work righteousness; for them is forgiveness (of sins) and a great reward.

12. Perchance you may (feel the inclination) to give up a part of what is revealed unto you, and your heart feels straitened lest they say, "Why is not a treasure sent down unto him, or why does not an Angel come down with him?" But you are there

نَذِيرٌ ۗ وَ اللهُ عَلَى كُلِّ شَىْءٍ

وَكِيلٌ ۞ أَمْ يَقُولُونَ افْتَرَىٰهُ ۗ قُلْ

فَأْتُوا بِعَشْرِ سُوَرٍ مِّثْلِهِ مُفْتَرَيَاتٍ

وَّ ادْعُوا مَنِ اسْتَطَعْتُم مِّن

دُونِ اللهِ إِن كُنتُمْ صَادِقِينَ ۞

فَإِلَّمْ يَسْتَجِيبُوا لَكُمْ فَاعْلَمُوٓا أَنَّمَآ

أُنزِلَ بِعِلْمِ اللهِ وَ أَن لَّآ إِلَٰهَ

إِلَّا هُوَ ۖ فَهَلْ أَنتُم مُّسْلِمُونَ ۞

مَن كَانَ يُرِيدُ الْحَيَوٰةَ الدُّنْيَا

اَذَقۡنٰهُ نَعۡمَآءَ بَعۡدَ ضَرَّآءَ مَسَّتۡهُ

لَيَقُوۡلَنَّ ذَهَبَ السَّيِّاٰتُ عَنِّىۡ

اِنَّهٗ لَفَرِحٌ فَخُوۡرٌ ۙ اِلَّا الَّذِيۡنَ ﴿١٠﴾

صَبَرُوۡا وَعَمِلُوا الصّٰلِحٰتِ ؕ اُولٰٓئِكَ

لَهُمۡ مَّغۡفِرَةٌ وَّاَجۡرٌ كَبِيۡرٌ ﴿١١﴾

فَلَعَلَّكَ تَارِكٌۢ بَعۡضَ مَا يُوۡحٰٓى

اِلَيۡكَ وَضَآئِقٌۢ بِهٖ صَدۡرُكَ اَنۡ

يَّقُوۡلُوۡا لَوۡلَاۤ اُنۡزِلَ عَلَيۡهِ كَنۡزٌ

اَوۡ جَآءَ مَعَهٗ مَلَكٌ ؕ اِنَّمَاۤ اَنۡتَ

"This is nothing but obvious sorcery!"

8. If We delay the Chastisement for them for a definite term, they are sure to say, "What keeps it back?" Ah! On the day it (actually) reaches them, nothing will turn it away from them, and they will be completely encircled by that which they used to mock at!

9. If We give man a taste of Mercy from Ourselves, and then withdraw it from him, behold! he is in despair and (falls into) blasphemy.

10. But if

وَمَا مِنْ دَآبَّةٍ فِى الْأَرْضِ

إِلَّا عَلَى اللهِ رِزْقُهَا وَيَعْلَمُ

مُسْتَقَرَّهَا وَمُسْتَوْدَعَهَا كُلٌّ فِى

كِتَابٍ مُّبِيْنٍ ۞ وَهُوَ الَّذِى خَلَقَ

السَّمٰوٰتِ وَالْأَرْضَ فِى سِتَّةِ

أَيَّامٍ وَّكَانَ عَرْشُهُ عَلَى الْمَآءِ

لِيَبْلُوَكُمْ أَيُّكُمْ أَحْسَنُ عَمَلًا

وَلَئِنْ قُلْتَ إِنَّكُمْ مَّبْعُوْثُوْنَ

مِنْ بَعْدِ الْمَوْتِ لَيَقُوْلَنَّ

ذٰلِكَ الْكِتٰبُ لَا رَيْبَ

پاره

وَمَا مِنْ دَآبَّةٍ

(۱۲)

6. There is no moving creature on earth but its sustenance depends on Allah: He knows the time and place of its definite abode and its temporary deposit: all is in a clear Record.

7. He it is Who created the heavens and the earth in six days - and His Throne was over the water - that He might try you, which of you is best in conduct. But if you were to say to them, "You shall indeed be raised up after death", the unbelievers would be sure to say,

اَلَّذِیْنَ كَفَرُوۡۤا اِنۡ هٰذَاۤ اِلَّا

سِحۡرٌ مُّبِیۡنٌ ۞ وَلَئِنۡ اَخَّرۡنَا

عَنۡهُمُ الۡعَذَابَ اِلٰۤی اُمَّةٍ مَّعۡدُوۡدَةٍ

لَّیَقُوۡلُنَّ مَا یَحۡبِسُهٗ ؕ اَلَا یَوۡمَ

یَاۡتِیۡهِمۡ لَیۡسَ مَصۡرُوۡفًا عَنۡهُمۡ

وَحَاقَ بِهِمۡ مَّا كَانُوۡا بِهٖ

یَسۡتَهۡزِءُوۡنَ ۞ وَلَئِنۡ اَذَقۡنَا

الۡاِنۡسَانَ مِنَّا رَحۡمَةً ثُمَّ نَزَعۡنٰهَا

مِنۡهُ ؕ اِنَّهٗ لَیَـُٔوۡسٌ كَفُوۡرٌ ۞ وَلَئِنۡ

like a goodly tree, whose root is firmly fixed, and its branches (reach) to the heavens.

25. It brings forth its fruit at all times, by the leave of its Lord. So Allah sets forth parables for men, in order that they may receive admonition.

26. And the parable of an evil word is that of an evil tree: it is torn up by the root from the surface of the earth: it has no stability.

27. Allah will establish in strength those who believe, with the word that stands firm,

فِى الْحَيٰوةِ الدُّنْيَا وَفِى الْاٰخِرَةِ ۚ

وَيُضِلُّ اللّٰهُ الظّٰلِمِيْنَ ۙ وَيَفْعَلُ

اللّٰهُ مَا يَشَآءُ ۟ اَلَمْ تَرَ اِلَى

الَّذِيْنَ بَدَّلُوْا نِعْمَتَ اللّٰهِ

كُفْرًا وَّاَحَلُّوْا قَوْمَهُمْ دَارَ

الْبَوَارِ ۙ جَهَنَّمَ ۚ يَصْلَوْنَهَا ۚ وَبِئْسَ

الْقَرَارُ ۟ وَجَعَلُوْا لِلّٰهِ اَنْدَادًا

لِّيُضِلُّوْا عَنْ سَبِيْلِهٖ ۚ قُلْ

تَمَتَّعُوْا فَاِنَّ مَصِيْرَكُمْ اِلَى

in this world and in the Hereafter; but Allah will leave, to stray, those who do wrong: Allah does what He will

28.   Have you not turned your vision to those who have exchanged the favour of Allah. Into blasphemy and caused their people to descend to the House of Perdition? -

29.   Into Hell? They will burn therein, - an evil place to stay in!

30.   And they set up (idols) as equal to Allah, to mislead (men) from the Path! Say: "Enjoy (your brief power)! But verily you are making straight way for

النَّارِ ۞ قُلْ لِّعِبَادِيَ الَّذِيْنَ

اٰمَنُوْا يُقِيْمُوا الصَّلٰوةَ وَيُنْفِقُوْا

مِمَّا رَزَقْنٰهُمْ سِرًّا وَّعَلَانِيَةً

مِّنْ قَبْلِ اَنْ يَّاْتِيَ يَوْمٌ لَّا

بَيْعٌ فِيْهِ وَلَا خِلٰلٌ ۞ اَللّٰهُ

الَّذِيْ خَلَقَ السَّمٰوٰتِ وَالْاَرْضَ

وَاَنْزَلَ مِنَ السَّمَآءِ مَآءً فَاَخْرَجَ

بِهٖ مِنَ الثَّمَرٰتِ رِزْقًا لَّكُمْ

وَسَخَّرَ لَكُمُ الْفُلْكَ لِتَجْرِيَ فِي

Hell!"

31. Speak to My servants who have believed, that they may establish regular prayers, and spend (in charity) out of the sustenance We have given them, secretly and openly, before the coming of a Day in which there will be neither mutual bargaining nor befriending.

32. It is Allah Who has created the heavens and the earth and sendeth down rain from the skies, and with it bringeth out fruits wherewith to feed you; it is He Who have made the ships subject to you, that they may sail through

الْبَحْرَ بِأَمْرِهِ ۚ وَسَخَّرَ لَكُمُ

الْأَنْهَٰرَ ۞ وَسَخَّرَ لَكُمُ الشَّمْسَ

وَالْقَمَرَ دَآئِبَيْنِ ۖ وَسَخَّرَ لَكُمُ

الَّيْلَ وَالنَّهَارَ ۞ وَاٰتَىٰكُمْ مِّنْ

كُلِّ مَا سَأَلْتُمُوهُ ۚ وَإِنْ تَعُدُّوا

نِعْمَتَ اللهِ لَا تُحْصُوهَا ۗ إِنَّ

الْإِنْسَانَ لَظَلُومٌ كَفَّارٌ ۞ وَإِذْ

قَالَ إِبْرٰهِيمُ رَبِّ اجْعَلْ

هٰذَا الْبَلَدَ اٰمِنًا وَّاجْنُبْنِي

the sea by His Command; and the rivers (also) have He made subject to you.

33.   And He has made subject to you the sun and the moon, both diligently pursuing their courses; and the night and the day has he (also) made subject to you.

34.   And He gives you of all that you ask for. But if you count the favours of Allah, never will you be able to number them. Verily, man is given up to injustice and ingratitude.

35.   Remember Abraham said: "O my Lord! Make this city one of peace and security: and preserve me

وَبَنِيَّ أَنْ نَّعْبُدَ الْأَصْنَامَ ۞

رَبِّ إِنَّهُنَّ أَضْلَلْنَ كَثِيْرًا

مِّنَ النَّاسِ ۚ فَمَنْ تَبِعَنِي

فَإِنَّهُ مِنِّي ۖ وَمَنْ عَصَانِي

فَإِنَّكَ غَفُوْرٌ رَّحِيْمٌ ۞ رَبَّنَآ

إِنِّيْ أَسْكَنْتُ مِنْ ذُرِّيَّتِي

بِوَادٍ غَيْرِ ذِيْ زَرْعٍ عِنْدَ

بَيْتِكَ الْمُحَرَّمِ ۙ رَبَّنَا لِيُقِيْمُوا

الصَّلٰوةَ فَاجْعَلْ أَفْئِدَةً مِّنَ

and my sons from worshipping idols."

36. "O my Lord! They have indeed led astray many among mankind; he then who follows my (ways) is of me, and he that disobeys me, - but You are indeed Oft-Forgiving, Most Merciful.

37. "O our Lord! I have made some of my offspring to dwell in a valley without cultivation, by your Sacred House; in order, O our Lord, that they may establish regular prayer: so fill the hearts of some among

النَّاسِ تَهْوِىٓ إِلَيْهِمْ وَارْزُقْهُمْ

مِّنَ الثَّمَرٰتِ لَعَلَّهُمْ يَشْكُرُوْنَ ۞

رَبَّنَآ اِنَّكَ تَعْلَمُ مَا نُخْفِىْ

وَمَا نُعْلِنُ ۖ وَمَا يَخْفٰى عَلَى

اللهِ مِنْ شَىْءٍ فِى الْاَرْضِ

وَلَا فِى السَّمَآءِ ۞ اَلْحَمْدُ لِلّٰهِ

الَّذِىْ وَهَبَ لِىْ عَلَى الْكِبَرِ

اِسْمٰعِيْلَ وَاِسْحٰقَ ۚ اِنَّ رَبِّىْ

لَسَمِيْعُ الدُّعَآءِ ۞ رَبِّ اجْعَلْنِىْ

a (gaping) void!

44. So warn mankind of the Day when the Wrath will reach them: then will the wrong-doers say: "Our Lord! Respite us (if only) for a short term: we will answer Your call, and follow the Apostles!" "What! Were you not wont to swear aforetime that you should suffer no decline?"

45. "And you dwelt in the dwellings of men who wronged their own souls; you were clearly shown how We dealt with them; and We put forth

one who establishes regular prayer, and also (raise such) among my offspring O our Lord! and accept You my prayer."

41. "O our Lord! Cover (us) with Your Forgiveness - me, my parents, and (all) believers, on the Day that the reckoning will be established!"

42. Think not that Allah does not heed the deeds of those who do wrong. He but giveth them respite against a Day when the eyes will fixedly stare in horror, -

43. They running forward with necks outstretched, their heads uplifted, their gaze returning not towards them, and their hearts

اَلَمْ تَرَ اِلَى رَبِّكَ كَيْفَ مَدَّ الظِّلَّ ۞

وَلَوْ شَاءَ لَجَعَلَهُ سَاكِنًا ثُمَّ جَعَلْنَا

الشَّمْسَ عَلَيْهِ دَلِيلًا ۞ ثُمَّ قَبَضْنَاهُ اِلَيْنَا

قَبْضًا يَسِيرًا ۞ وَهُوَ الَّذِى جَعَلَ لَكُمُ

الَّيْلَ لِبَاسًا وَّالنَّوْمَ سُبَاتًا

وَّجَعَلَ النَّهَارَ نُشُورًا ۞ وَهُوَ الَّذِى

اَرْسَلَ الرِّيَاحَ بُشْرًا بَيْنَ يَدَىْ رَحْمَتِهِ

وَاَنْزَلْنَا مِنَ السَّمَاءِ مَاءً طَهُورًا ۞

لِّنُحْيِىَ بِهِ بَلْدَةً مَّيْتًا وَّنُسْقِيَهُ

men with love towards them, and feed them with fruits: so that they may give thanks."

38. "O our Lord! Truly you know what we conceal and what we reveal: for nothing whatever is hidden from Allah, whether on earth or in heaven."

39. "Praise be to Allah, Who has granted unto me in old age Isma'il and Isaac: for truly my Lord is He, the Hearer of Prayer!"

40. "O my Lord! Make me

(many) parables in your behalf!"

46. Mighty indeed were the plots which they made, but their plots were (well) within the sight of Allah, even though they were such as to shake the hills!

47. Never think that Allah would fail his Apostles in His promise: for Allah is Exalted in Power, - the Lord of Retribution.

48. One day the earth will be changed to a different earth, and so will be the heavens, and (men) will be marshalled forth, before Allah, the One, the Irresistible;

49. And you will see the sinners that day bound together

فِى الْأَصْفَادِ ۝ سَرَابِيلُهُمْ مِّنْ

قَطِرَانٍ وَّتَغْشٰى وُجُوهَهُمُ النَّارُ ۝

لِيَجْزِىَ اللّٰهُ كُلَّ نَفْسٍ مَّا كَسَبَتْ

اِنَّ اللّٰهَ سَرِيعُ الْحِسَابِ ۝

هٰذَا بَلٰغٌ لِّلنَّاسِ وَلِيُنْذَرُوْا

بِهٖ وَلِيَعْلَمُوْا اَنَّمَا هُوَ اِلٰهٌ وَّاحِدٌ

وَّلِيَذَّكَّرَ اُولُوا الْأَلْبَابِ ۝

بِسْمِ اللّٰهِ الرَّحْمٰنِ الرَّحِيْمِ سُورَةُ الْحِجْرِ مَكِّيَّةٌ ٩٩ آيَاتُهَا ٦ رُكُوعَاتُهَا

الۤرٰ تِلْكَ اٰيٰتُ الْكِتٰبِ وَقُرْاٰنٍ مُّبِيْنٍ ۝

كَشَجَرَةٍ طَيِّبَةٍ اَصْلُهَا ثَابِتٌ

وَّفَرْعُهَا فِى السَّمَآءِ ۞ تُؤْتِىۤ

اُكُلَهَا كُلَّ حِيْنٍ بِاِذْنِ رَبِّهَا

وَيَضْرِبُ اللّٰهُ الْاَمْثَالَ لِلنَّاسِ

لَعَلَّهُمْ يَتَذَكَّرُوْنَ ۞ وَمَثَلُ

كَلِمَةٍ خَبِيْثَةٍ كَشَجَرَةٍ خَبِيْثَةٍ

اجْتُثَّتْ مِنْ فَوْقِ الْاَرْضِ

مَا لَهَا مِنْ قَرَارٍ ۞ يُثَبِّتُ اللّٰهُ

الَّذِيْنَ اٰمَنُوْا بِالْقَوْلِ الثَّابِتِ

listen to your cries, nor can you listen to mine. I reject your former act in associating me with Allah. For wrong-doers there must be a grievous Chastisement."

23. But those who believe and work righteousness will be admitted to Gardens beneath which rivers flow, - to dwell therein for ever with the leave of their Lord. Their greeting therein will be: "Peace!"

24. Do you not see how Allah sets forth a parable? - a goodly word

بِمُصْرِخِكُمْ وَمَا أَنْتُمْ بِمُصْرِخِيَّ

إِنِّي كَفَرْتُ بِمَا أَشْرَكْتُمُونِ مِنْ

قَبْلُ ۚ إِنَّ الظَّٰلِمِينَ لَهُمْ عَذَابٌ

أَلِيمٌ ۞ وَأُدْخِلَ الَّذِينَ آمَنُوا

وَعَمِلُوا الصَّٰلِحَٰتِ جَنَّٰتٍ تَجْرِى

مِنْ تَحْتِهَا الْأَنْهَٰرُ خَٰلِدِينَ

فِيهَا بِإِذْنِ رَبِّهِمْ ۖ تَحِيَّتُهُمْ

فِيهَا سَلَٰمٌ ۞ أَلَمْ تَرَ كَيْفَ

ضَرَبَ اللَّهُ مَثَلًا كَلِمَةً طَيِّبَةً

They will reply, "If we had received the Guidance of Allah, we should have given it to you: to us it makes no difference (now) whether we rage, or bear (these torments) with patience: for ourselves there is no way of escape."

22. And Satan will say when the matter is decided: "It was Allah Who gave you a promise of Truth: I too promised, but I failed in my promise to you. I had no authority over you except to call you but you listened to me: then reproach not me, but reproach your own souls. I cannot

مِنْ شَيْءٍ ۚ قَالُوْا لَوْ هَدٰىنَا اللهُ

لَهَدَيْنٰكُمْ ؕ سَوَآءٌ عَلَيْنَآ اَجَزِعْنَآ

اَمْ صَبَرْنَا مَا لَنَا مِنْ مَّحِيْصٍ ۞

وَقَالَ الشَّيْطٰنُ لَمَّا قُضِيَ الْاَمْرُ

اِنَّ اللهَ وَعَدَكُمْ وَعْدَ الْحَقِّ

وَوَعَدْتُّكُمْ فَاَخْلَفْتُكُمْ ؕ وَمَا كَانَ

لِيَ عَلَيْكُمْ مِّنْ سُلْطٰنٍ اِلَّآ اَنْ

دَعَوْتُكُمْ فَاسْتَجَبْتُمْ لِيْ ۚ فَلَا

تَلُوْمُوْنِيْ وَلُوْمُوْٓا اَنْفُسَكُمْ ؕ مَآ اَنَا

that is the straying far, far (from the goal).

19. See you not that Allah created the heavens and the earth in Truth? If He so wills, He can remove you and put (in your place) a new creation?

20. Nor is that for Allah any great matter.

21. They will all be marshalled before Allah together: then will the weak say to those who were arrogant, "For us, we but followed you; can you then avail us to all against the Wrath of Allah?"

عَلَىٰ شَىْءٍ ذٰلِكَ هُوَ الضَّلٰلُ

الْبَعِيدُ ۝ اَلَمْ تَرَ اَنَّ اللهَ خَلَقَ

السَّمٰوٰتِ وَالْاَرْضَ بِالْحَقِّ اِنْ

يَّشَاْ يُذْهِبْكُمْ وَيَاْتِ بِخَلْقٍ

جَدِيدٍ ۝ وَّمَا ذٰلِكَ عَلَى اللهِ

بِعَزِيزٍ ۝ وَبَرَزُوْا لِلّٰهِ جَمِيْعًا فَقَالَ

الضُّعَفٰٓؤُا لِلَّذِيْنَ اسْتَكْبَرُوْٓا

اِنَّا كُنَّا لَكُمْ تَبَعًا فَهَلْ اَنْتُمْ

مُّغْنُوْنَ عَنَّا مِنْ عَذَابِ اللهِ

16. In front of such a one is Hell, and he is given, for drink, boiling fetid water.

17. In gulps will he sip it, but never will he be near swallowing it down his throat: death will come to him from every quarter, yet will he not die: and in front of him will be a Chastisement unrelenting.

18. The parable of those who reject their Lord is that their works are as ashes, on which the wind blows furiously on a tempestuous day: no power have they over anything that they have earned:

عَنِيدٌ ۝ مِّنْ وَّرَآئِهٖ جَهَنَّمُ

وَيُسْقٰى مِنْ مَّآءٍ صَدِيدٍ ۝

يَّتَجَرَّعُهٗ وَلَا يَكَادُ يُسِيغُهٗ

وَيَأْتِيهِ الْمَوْتُ مِنْ كُلِّ مَكَانٍ

وَّمَا هُوَ بِمَيِّتٍ ۚ وَمِنْ وَّرَآئِهٖ

عَذَابٌ غَلِيظٌ ۝ مَثَلُ الَّذِيْنَ

كَفَرُوْا بِرَبِّهِمْ أَعْمَالُهُمْ كَرَمَادٍ

اشْتَدَّتْ بِهِ الرِّيْحُ فِيْ يَوْمٍ

عَاصِفٍ ۚ لَا يَقْدِرُوْنَ مِمَّا كَسَبُوْا

all the hurt you may cause us. For those who put their trust should put their trust on Allah."

13. And the unbelievers said to their Apostles: "Be sure we shall drive you out of our land, or you shall return to our religion." But their Lord inspired (this Message) to them: "Verily We shall cause the wrong-doers to perish!

14. "And verily We shall cause you to abide in the land, and succeed them. This for such as fear the Time when they shall stand before My tribunal, - such as fear the punishment denounced."

15. But they sought victory and decision (there and then), and frustration was the lot of every powerful obstinate transgressor.

عَلَىٰ مَآ اٰذَيۡتُمُوۡنَا ۖ وَعَلَى اللّٰهِ
فَلۡيَتَوَكَّلِ الۡمُتَوَكِّلُوۡنَ ۞ وَقَالَ
الَّذِيۡنَ كَفَرُوۡا لِرُسُلِهِمۡ لَنُخۡرِجَنَّكُمۡ
مِّنۡ اَرۡضِنَآ اَوۡ لَتَعُوۡدُنَّ فِيۡ مِلَّتِنَا ۖ
فَاَوۡحٰىٓ اِلَيۡهِمۡ رَبُّهُمۡ لَنُهۡلِكَنَّ
الظّٰلِمِيۡنَ ۞ وَلَنُسۡكِنَنَّكُمُ الۡاَرۡضَ
مِنۡۢ بَعۡدِهِمۡ ۚ ذٰلِكَ لِمَنۡ
خَافَ مَقَامِيۡ وَخَافَ وَعِيۡدِ ۞
وَاسۡتَفۡتَحُوۡا وَخَابَ كُلُّ جَبَّارٍ

then bring us some clear authority."

11. Their Apostles said to them: "True, we are human like yourselves, but Allah does grant His grace to such of his servants as He pleases. It is not for us to bring you an authority except as Allah permits. And on Allah let all men of faith put their trust.

12. "No reason have we why we should not put our trust on Allah. Indeed He has guided us to the ways we (follow). We shall certainly bear with patience

اٰبَآؤُنَا فَأْتُوْنَا بِسُلْطٰنٍ مُّبِيْنٍ ۞

قَالَتْ لَهُمْ رُسُلُهُمْ اِنْ نَّحْنُ

اِلَّا بَشَرٌ مِّثْلُكُمْ وَلٰكِنَّ اللّٰهَ

يَمُنُّ عَلٰى مَنْ يَّشَآءُ مِنْ عِبَادِهٖ ط

وَمَا كَانَ لَنَآ اَنْ نَّأْتِيَكُمْ

بِسُلْطٰنٍ اِلَّا بِاِذْنِ اللّٰهِ ط وَعَلَى

اللّٰهِ فَلْيَتَوَكَّلِ الْمُؤْمِنُوْنَ ۞ وَمَا

لَنَآ اَلَّا نَتَوَكَّلَ عَلَى اللّٰهِ وَقَدْ

هَدٰىنَا سُبُلَنَا ط وَلَنَصْبِرَنَّ

up to their mouths, and said: "We do deny (the mission) on which you have been sent, and we are really in suspicious (disquieting) doubt as to that to which you invite us."

10. Their Apostles said: "Is there a doubt about Allah, the Creator of the heavens and the earth? It is He Who invites you, in order that He may forgive you your sins and give you respite for a term appointed!" They said: "Ah! You are no more than human, like ourselves! You wish to turn us away from the (gods) what our fathers used to worship:

فِىۡ أَفۡوَاهِهِمۡ وَ قَالُوۡۤا اِنَّا كَفَرۡنَا

بِمَاۤ اُرۡسِلۡتُمۡ بِهٖ وَ اِنَّا لَفِىۡ شَكٍّ

مِّمَّا تَدۡعُوۡنَنَاۤ اِلَيۡهِ مُرِيۡبٌ ۝

قَالَتۡ رُسُلُهُمۡ اَفِى اللّٰهِ شَكٌّ

فَاطِرِ السَّمٰوٰتِ وَالۡاَرۡضِ يَدۡعُوۡكُمۡ

لِيَغۡفِرَ لَكُمۡ مِّنۡ ذُنُوۡبِكُمۡ وَيُؤَخِّرَكُمۡ

اِلٰٓى اَجَلٍ مُّسَمًّى ؕ قَالُوۡۤا اِنۡ

اَنۡتُمۡ اِلَّا بَشَرٌ مِّثۡلُنَا ؕ تُرِيۡدُوۡنَ

اَنۡ تَصُدُّوۡنَا عَمَّا كَانَ يَعۡبُدُ

I will add more (favours) unto you; but if you show ingratitude, truly My Punishment is terrible indeed."

8.   And Moses said: "If you show ingratitude, you and all on earth together, yet is Allah free of all wants, worthy of all praise.

9.   Has not the story reached you, (O people!), of those who (went) before you? - of the people of Noah, and 'Ad, and Thamud? - and of those who (came) after them? None knows them but Allah. To them came Apostles with clear (Signs); but they put their hands

لَاَزِيْدَنَّكُمْ وَلَئِنْ كَفَرْتُمْ اِنَّ

عَذَابِيْ لَشَدِيْدٌ ۞ وَقَالَ مُوْسٰى

اِنْ تَكْفُرُوْٓا اَنْتُمْ وَمَنْ فِى

الْاَرْضِ جَمِيْعًا فَاِنَّ اللّٰهَ لَغَنِيٌّ

حَمِيْدٌ ۞ اَلَمْ يَاْتِكُمْ نَبَؤُا الَّذِيْنَ

مِنْ قَبْلِكُمْ قَوْمِ نُوْحٍ وَّعَادٍ

وَّثَمُوْدَ ۛ وَالَّذِيْنَ مِنْ بَعْدِهِمْ

لَا يَعْلَمُهُمْ اِلَّا اللّٰهُ ۛ جَآءَتْهُمْ

رُسُلُهُمْ بِالْبَيِّنٰتِ فَرَدُّوْٓا اَيْدِيَهُمْ

and teach them to remember the Days of Allah." Verily in this there are Signs for such as are firmly patient and constant, - grateful and appreciative.

6.   Remember! Moses said to his people: "Call to mind the favour of Allah to you when He delivered you from the people of Pharaoh: they set you hard tasks and punishments, slaughtered your sons, and let your women-folk live: therein was a tremendous trial from your Lord."

7.   And remember! Your Lord caused to be declared (publicly): "If you are grateful,

وَذَكِّرْهُمْ بِأَيَّامِ اللّٰهِ ۚ إِنَّ فِى

ذٰلِكَ لَأَيَٰتٍ لِّكُلِّ صَبَّارٍ شَكُورٍ ۝

وَإِذْ قَالَ مُوسٰى لِقَوْمِهِ اذْكُرُوا

نِعْمَةَ اللّٰهِ عَلَيْكُمْ إِذْ أَنْجَىٰكُمْ

مِّنْ اٰلِ فِرْعَوْنَ يَسُومُونَكُمْ سُوٓءَ

الْعَذَابِ وَيُذَبِّحُونَ أَبْنَآءَكُمْ

وَيَسْتَحْيُونَ نِسَآءَكُمْ ۚ وَفِى ذٰلِكُم

بَلَآءٌ مِّنْ رَّبِّكُمْ عَظِيمٌ ۝

وَإِذْ تَأَذَّنَ رَبُّكُمْ لَئِنْ شَكَرْتُمْ

who hinder (men) from the Path of Allah and seek therein something crooked: they are astray by a long distance.

4. We sent not an Apostle except (to teach) in the language of his (own) people, in order to make (things) clear to them. Now Allah leaves straying those whom He pleases and guides whom He pleases: and He is Exalted in Power, full of Wisdom.

5. We sent Moses with Our Signs (and the command). "Bring out your people from the depths of darkness into light,

وَيَصُدُّوْنَ عَنْ سَبِيْلِ اللهِ

وَيَبْغُوْنَهَا عِوَجًا ۚ أُولٰٓئِكَ فِيْ

ضَلٰلٍ بَعِيْدٍ ۞ وَمَآ اَرْسَلْنَا

مِنْ رَّسُوْلٍ اِلَّا بِلِسَانِ قَوْمِهٖ

لِيُبَيِّنَ لَهُمْ ۚ فَيُضِلُّ اللهُ مَنْ

يَّشَآءُ وَيَهْدِيْ مَنْ يَّشَآءُ ۚ

وَهُوَ الْعَزِيْزُ الْحَكِيْمُ ۞ وَلَقَدْ

اَرْسَلْنَا مُوْسٰى بِاٰيٰتِنَآ اَنْ اَخْرِجْ

قَوْمَكَ مِنَ الظُّلُمٰتِ اِلَى النُّوْرِ ۙ

Ibrahim (Abraham)

Bismillahir-Rahmanir-Rahim

1. Alif. Lam. Raa. A Book which We have revealed unto you, in order that you might lead mankind out of the depths of darkness into light - by the leave of their Lord - to the Way of (Him) the Exalted in power, worthy of all praise! -

2. Of Allah, to Whom do belong all things in the heavens and on earth! But alas for the unbelievers for a terrible Chastisement (their Unfaith will bring them)!-

3. Those who love the life of this world more than the Hereafter,

بِسْمِ اللَّهِ الرَّحْمَٰنِ الرَّحِيمِ

الٓرٰ ۚ كِتَٰبٌ أَنزَلْنَٰهُ إِلَيْكَ لِتُخْرِجَ النَّاسَ مِنَ الظُّلُمَٰتِ إِلَى النُّورِ بِإِذْنِ رَبِّهِمْ إِلَىٰ صِرَٰطِ الْعَزِيزِ الْحَمِيدِ ۞ اللَّهِ الَّذِى لَهُۥ مَا فِى السَّمَٰوَٰتِ وَمَا فِى الْأَرْضِ ۗ وَوَيْلٌ لِّلْكَٰفِرِينَ مِنْ عَذَابٍ شَدِيدٍ ۞ الَّذِينَ يَسْتَحِبُّونَ الْحَيَوٰةَ الدُّنْيَا عَلَى الْءَاخِرَةِ

(Where) Allah commands, there is none to put back His Command: and He is swift in calling to account.

42. Those before them did (also) devise plots; but in all things the master-planning is Allah's. He knows the doings of every soul: and soon will the unbelievers know who gets home in the end.

43. The unbelievers say: "No Apostle are you." Say: "Enough for a witness between me and you is Allah, and such as have knowledge of the Book."

وَاللّٰهُ يَحْكُمُ لَا مُعَقِّبَ لِحُكْمِهِ ۚ
وَهُوَ سَرِيعُ الْحِسَابِ ۞ وَقَدْ
مَكَرَ الَّذِينَ مِنْ قَبْلِهِمْ فَلِلّٰهِ
الْمَكْرُ جَمِيعًا ۖ يَعْلَمُ مَا تَكْسِبُ
كُلُّ نَفْسٍ ۗ وَسَيَعْلَمُ الْكُفَّارُ لِمَنْ
عُقْبَى الدَّارِ ۞ وَيَقُولُ الَّذِينَ
كَفَرُوا لَسْتَ مُرْسَلًا ۚ قُلْ كَفٰى
بِاللّٰهِ شَهِيدًۢا بَيْنِي وَبَيْنَكُمْ ۙ
وَمَنْ عِنْدَهُ عِلْمُ الْكِتٰبِ ۞

and children: and it was never the part of an Apostle to bring a Sign except as Allah permitted (or commanded). For each period is a Book (revealed).

39.   Allah does blot out or confirm what He pleases: with Him is the Mother of the Book.

40.   Whether We shall show you (within your life-time) part of what we promised them or take to ourselves your soul (before it is all accomplished), - your duty is to make (the Message) reach them: it is our part to call them to account.

41.   See they not that We gradually reduce the land (in their control) from its outlying borders?

وَذُرِّيَّةً ۚ وَمَا كَانَ لِرَسُولٍ اَنْ

يَّاتِيَ بِاٰيَةٍ اِلَّا بِاِذْنِ اللّٰهِ ۚ لِكُلِّ

اَجَلٍ كِتَابٌ ۞ يَمْحُوا اللّٰهُ مَا

يَشَآءُ وَيُثْبِتُ ۖ وَعِنْدَهٗٓ اُمُّ

الْكِتٰبِ ۞ وَاِنْ مَّا نُرِيَنَّكَ بَعْضَ

الَّذِيْ نَعِدُهُمْ اَوْ نَتَوَفَّيَنَّكَ

فَاِنَّمَا عَلَيْكَ الْبَلٰغُ وَعَلَيْنَا

الْحِسَابُ ۞ اَوَلَمْ يَرَوْا اَنَّا نَاْتِي

الْاَرْضَ نَنْقُصُهَا مِنْ اَطْرَافِهَا

those who reject a part thereof. Say: "I am commanded to worship Allah, and not to join partners with Him. Unto Him do I call, and unto Him is my return."

37. Thus have We revealed it to be a judgment of authority in Arabic. Were you to follow their (vain) desires after the knowledge which has reached you, then would you find neither protector nor defender against Allah.

38. We did send Apostles before you, and appointed for them wives

مَنْ يَّنْكِرُ بَعْضَهُ ۚ قُلْ اِنَّمَآ

اُمِرْتُ اَنْ اَعْبُدَ اللّٰهَ وَلَآ

اُشْرِكَ بِهٖ ۗ اِلَيْهِ اَدْعُوا وَاِلَيْهِ

مَاٰبِ ۩ وَكَذٰلِكَ اَنْزَلْنٰهُ حُكْمًا

عَرَبِيًّا ۗ وَلَئِنِ اتَّبَعْتَ اَهْوَآءَهُمْ

بَعْدَ مَا جَآءَكَ مِنَ الْعِلْمِ ۙ

مَا لَكَ مِنَ اللّٰهِ مِنْ وَّلِيٍّ وَّلَا

وَاقٍ ۩ وَلَقَدْ اَرْسَلْنَا رُسُلًا

مِّنْ قَبْلِكَ وَجَعَلْنَا لَهُمْ اَزْوَاجًا

in the life of this world, but harder, truly, is the Chastisement of the Hereafter: and defender have they none against Allah.

35.   The parable of the Garden which the righteous are promised! - beneath it flow rivers: perpetual is the enjoyment thereof and the shade therein: such is the end of the righteous; and the end of unbelievers in the Fire.

36.   Those to whom We have given the Book rejoice at what has been revealed unto you: but there are among the clans

فِى الْحَيَوةِ الدُّنْيَا ۚ وَلَعَذَابُ

الْأَخِرَةِ أَشَقُّ ۚ وَمَا لَهُمْ مِّنَ

اللّٰهِ مِنْ وَّاقٍ ۞ مَثَلُ الْجَنَّةِ

الَّتِى وُعِدَ الْمُتَّقُوْنَ ۘ تَجْرِىْ مِنْ

تَحْتِهَا الْأَنْهٰرُ ۘ أُكُلُهَا دَآئِمٌ

وَّظِلُّهَا ۚ تِلْكَ عُقْبَى الَّذِيْنَ

اتَّقَوْا ۗ وَّعُقْبَى الْكٰفِرِيْنَ النَّارُ ۞

وَالَّذِيْنَ اٰتَيْنٰهُمُ الْكِتٰبَ يَفْرَحُوْنَ

بِمَآ أُنْزِلَ إِلَيْكَ وَمِنَ الْأَحْزَابِ

I punished them: then how (terrible) was My requital!

33. Is then He Who stands over every soul (and knows) all that it does, (like any others)? And yet they ascribe partners to Allah. Say: "But name them! Is it that you will inform Him of something he knows not on earth, or is it (just) a show of words?" Nay! to those who believe not, their pretence seems pleasing, but they are kept back (thereby) from the path. And those whom Allah leaves to stray, no one can guide.

34. For them is a Chastisement

أَخَذْتُهُمْ ۖ فَكَيْفَ كَانَ عِقَابِ ﴿٣٢﴾

أَفَمَنْ هُوَ قَائِمٌ عَلَىٰ كُلِّ

نَفْسٍ بِمَا كَسَبَتْ ۗ وَجَعَلُوا لِلَّهِ

شُرَكَاءَ ۚ قُلْ سَمُّوهُمْ ۚ أَمْ تُنَبِّئُونَهُ

بِمَا لَا يَعْلَمُ فِي الْأَرْضِ أَمْ

بِظَاهِرٍ مِّنَ الْقَوْلِ ۗ بَلْ زُيِّنَ

لِلَّذِينَ كَفَرُوا مَكْرُهُمْ وَصُدُّوا

عَنِ السَّبِيلِ ۗ وَمَن يُضْلِلِ اللَّهُ

فَمَا لَهُ مِنْ هَادٍ ﴿٣٣﴾ لَّهُمْ عَذَابٌ

truly, the command is with Allah in all things! Do not the believers know, that, had Allah (so) willed, He could have guided all mankind (to the right)? But the unbelievers, - never will disaster cease to seize them for their (ill) deeds, or to settle close to their homes, until the promise of Allah come to pass, for, verily, Allah will not fail in His promise.

32. Mocked were (many) Apostles before you: but I granted respite to the unbelievers, and finally

لِلّٰهِ الْأَمْرُ جَمِيعًا ۗ أَفَلَمْ يَايْئَسِ

الَّذِيْنَ اٰمَنُوۤا أَنْ لَّوْ يَشَآءُ اللّٰهُ

لَهَدَى النَّاسَ جَمِيعًا ۗ وَلَا يَزَالُ

الَّذِيْنَ كَفَرُوْا تُصِيْبُهُمْ بِمَا

صَنَعُوْا قَارِعَةٌ أَوْ تَحُلُّ قَرِيْبًا

مِّنْ دَارِهِمْ حَتّٰى يَأْتِيَ وَعْدُ اللّٰهِ ۗ

إِنَّ اللّٰهَ لَا يُخْلِفُ الْمِيْعَادَ ۩ وَلَقَدِ

اسْتُهْزِئَ بِرُسُلٍ مِّنْ قَبْلِكَ

فَأَمْلَيْتُ لِلَّذِيْنَ كَفَرُوْا ثُمَّ

place of (final) return."

30. Thus have we sent you amongst a People before whom (long since) have (other) Peoples (gone and) passed away; in order that you might rehearse unto them what We send down unto you by inspiration; yet do they reject (Him), the Most Gracious! Say: "He is my Lord! There is no god but He! On Him is my trust, and to Him do I turn!"

31. If there were a Qur'an with which mountains were moved, or the earth were cloven asunder, or the dead were made to speak, (this would be the one!) But,

مَاٰبٍ ۞ كَذٰلِكَ اَرْسَلْنٰكَ فِيْ

اُمَّةٍ قَدْ خَلَتْ مِنْ قَبْلِهَآ

اُمَمٌ لِّتَتْلُوَا۟ عَلَيْهِمُ الَّذِيْٓ

اَوْحَيْنَآ اِلَيْكَ وَهُمْ يَكْفُرُوْنَ

بِالرَّحْمٰنِ ۚ قُلْ هُوَ رَبِّيْ لَآ اِلٰهَ

اِلَّا هُوَ ۚ عَلَيْهِ تَوَكَّلْتُ وَاِلَيْهِ

مَتَابِ ۞ وَلَوْ اَنَّ قُرْاٰنًا سُيِّرَتْ

بِهِ الْجِبَالُ اَوْ قُطِّعَتْ بِهِ

الْاَرْضُ اَوْ كُلِّمَ بِهِ الْمَوْتٰى ۚ بَلْ

but the life of this world is but
little comfort compard in the
Hereafter.

27. The unbelievers say: "Why
is not a Sign sent down to him
from his Lord?" Say: "Truly Allah
leaves, to stray, whom He will;
but He guides to Himself those
who turn to Him in penitence;

28. "Those who believe, and
whose hearts find satisfaction in
the remembrance of Allah: for
without doubt in the remembrance of Allah do hearts find
satisfaction."

29. "For those who believe and
work righteousness, is (every)
blessedness, and a beautiful

وَمَا الْحَيٰوةُ الدُّنْيَا فِى الْاٰخِرَةِ اِلَّا

مَتَاعٌ ۞ وَيَقُوْلُ الَّذِيْنَ كَفَرُوْا

لَوْلَاۤ اُنْزِلَ عَلَيْهِ اٰيَةٌ مِّنْ رَّبِّهٖ

قُلْ اِنَّ اللّٰهَ يُضِلُّ مَنْ يَّشَآءُ

وَيَهْدِيْۤ اِلَيْهِ مَنْ اَنَابَ ۞

الَّذِيْنَ اٰمَنُوْا وَتَطْمَئِنُّ قُلُوْبُهُمْ

بِذِكْرِ اللّٰهِ اَلَا بِذِكْرِ اللّٰهِ تَطْمَئِنُّ

الْقُلُوْبُ ۞ الَّذِيْنَ اٰمَنُوْا وَعَمِلُوا

الصّٰلِحٰتِ طُوْبٰى لَهُمْ وَحُسْنُ

unto them from every gate (with the salutation):

24. "Peace unto you for that you persevered in patience! Now how excellent is the final home!"

25. But those who break the Covenant of Allah, after having plighted their word thereto, and cut asunder those things which Allah has commanded to be joined, and work mischief in the land; - on them is the curse; for them is the terrible home!

26. Allah does enlarge, or grant by (strict) measure, the sustenance (which He giveth) to whomso He pleases. (The wordly) rejoice in the life of this world:

عَلَيْهِمْ مِّنْ كُلِّ بَابٍ ۞ سَلَامٌ

عَلَيْكُمْ بِمَا صَبَرْتُمْ فَنِعْمَ عُقْبَى

الدَّارِ ۞ وَالَّذِيْنَ يَنْقُضُوْنَ عَهْدَ

اللهِ مِنْ بَعْدِ مِيْثَاقِهِ وَيَقْطَعُوْنَ

مَآ أَمَرَ اللهُ بِهٖ أَنْ يُّوْصَلَ

وَيُفْسِدُوْنَ فِى الْأَرْضِ أُولٰٓئِكَ

لَهُمُ اللَّعْنَةُ وَلَهُمْ سُوْٓءُ الدَّارِ ۞

اللهُ يَبْسُطُ الرِّزْقَ لِمَنْ يَّشَآءُ

وَيَقْدِرُ ۚ وَفَرِحُوْا بِالْحَيٰوةِ الدُّنْيَا

joined, hold their Lord in awe, and fear the terrible reckoning;

22. Those who patiently persevere, seeking the countenance of their Lord; establish regular prayers; spend, out of (the gifts) We have bestowed for their sustenance, secretly and openly; and turn off evil with good: for such there is the final attainment of the (eternal) home, -

23. They shall enter the Gardens of perpetual bliss: as well as the righteous among their fathers, their spouses, and their offspring: and Angels shall enter

يُّوصَلَ وَيَخْشَوْنَ رَبَّهُمْ وَيَخَافُوْنَ

سُوْٓءَ الْحِسَابِ ۞ وَالَّذِيْنَ صَبَرُوا

ابْتِغَآءَ وَجْهِ رَبِّهِمْ وَاَقَامُوا

الصَّلٰوةَ وَاَنْفَقُوْا مِمَّا رَزَقْنٰهُمْ سِرًّا

وَّعَلَانِيَةً وَّيَدْرَءُوْنَ بِالْحَسَنَةِ

السَّيِّئَةَ اُولٰٓئِكَ لَهُمْ عُقْبَى الدَّارِ ۙ ۞

جَنّٰتُ عَدْنٍ يَّدْخُلُوْنَهَا وَمَنْ

صَلَحَ مِنْ اٰبَآئِهِمْ وَاَزْوَاجِهِمْ

وَذُرِّيّٰتِهِمْ وَالْمَلٰٓئِكَةُ يَدْخُلُوْنَ

and as much more, (in vain) would they offer it for ransom. For them will the reckoning be terrible: their abode will be Hell,- what a bed of misery!

19. Is then one who does know that that which has been revealed unto you from your Lord is the Truth, like one who is blind? It is those who are endued with understanding that receive admonition; -

20. Those who fulfil the Covenant of Allah and fail not in their plighted word;

21. Those who join together those things which Allah has commanded to be

وَمِثْلَهُ مَعَهُ لَافْتَدَوْا بِهِ ۚ أُولَٰئِكَ

لَهُمْ سُوٓءُ الْحِسَابِ ۚ وَمَأْوَاهُمْ

جَهَنَّمُ ۖ وَبِئْسَ الْمِهَادُ ۞ أَفَمَنْ

يَعْلَمُ أَنَّمَآ أُنْزِلَ إِلَيْكَ مِنْ

رَّبِّكَ الْحَقُّ كَمَنْ هُوَ أَعْمَىٰ ۚ

إِنَّمَا يَتَذَكَّرُ أُولُوا الْأَلْبَابِ ۞

الَّذِينَ يُوفُونَ بِعَهْدِ اللَّهِ وَلَا

يَنْقُضُونَ الْمِيثَاقَ ۞ وَالَّذِينَ

يَصِلُونَ مَآ أَمَرَ اللَّهُ بِهِ أَنْ

in the fire, to make ornaments or utensils therewith, there is a scum likewise. Thus does Allah (by parables) show forth Truth and Vanity. For the scum disap-pears like forth cast out; while that which is for the good of mankind remains on the earth. Thus does Allah set forth parables.

18. For those who respond to their Lord, are (all) good things. But those who respond not to Him, - even if they had all that is in the heavens and on earth,

عَلَيْهِ فِى النَّارِ ابْتِغَآءَ حِلْيَةٍ

أَوْ مَتَاعٍ زَبَدٌ مِّثْلُهُ ۚ كَذٰلِكَ

يَضْرِبُ اللّٰهُ الْحَقَّ وَ الْبَاطِلَ ۚ

فَأَمَّا الزَّبَدُ فَيَذْهَبُ جُفَآءً ۚ

وَأَمَّا مَا يَنْفَعُ النَّاسَ فَيَمْكُثُ

فِى الْأَرْضِ ۚ كَذٰلِكَ يَضْرِبُ اللّٰهُ

الْأَمْثَالَ ۞ لِلَّذِينَ اسْتَجَابُوا لِرَبِّهِمُ

الْحُسْنٰى ۚ وَالَّذِينَ لَمْ يَسْتَجِيبُوا لَهُ

لَوْ أَنَّ لَهُمْ مَّا فِى الْأَرْضِ جَمِيعًا

Say: "Are the blind equal with those who see? Or the depths of darkness equal with light?" Or do they assign to Allah partners who have created (anything) as He has created, so that the creation seemed to them similar? Say: "Allah is the Creator of all things: He is the One, the Supreme and Irresistible."

17.   He sends down water from the skies, and the cannals flow, each according to its measure: but the torrent bears away to foam that mounts up to the surface. Even so, from that (ore) which they heat

ضَرًّا ۚ قُلْ هَلْ يَسْتَوِى الْأَعْمٰى

وَالْبَصِيْرُ ۚ أَمْ هَلْ تَسْتَوِى الظُّلُمٰتُ

وَالنُّوْرُ ۚ أَمْ جَعَلُوْا لِلّٰهِ شُرَكَآءَ

خَلَقُوْا كَخَلْقِهٖ فَتَشَابَهَ الْخَلْقُ

عَلَيْهِمْ ۚ قُلِ اللّٰهُ خَالِقُ كُلِّ

شَىْءٍ وَّهُوَ الْوَاحِدُ الْقَهَّارُ ۝

أَنْزَلَ مِنَ السَّمَآءِ مَآءً فَسَالَتْ

أَوْدِيَةٌۢ بِقَدَرِهَا فَاحْتَمَلَ السَّيْلُ

زَبَدًا رَّابِيًا ۚ وَمِمَّا يُوْقِدُوْنَ

than if they were to stretch forth their hands for water to reach their mouths but it reaches them not: for the prayer of those without Faith is nothing but (futile) wandering (in the mind).

15. Whatever beings there are in the heavens and the earth do prostrate themselves to Allah (acknowledging subjection), - with good-will or in spite of themselves: so do their shadows in the morning and evenings.

16. Say: "Who is the Lord and Sustainer of the heavens and the earth?" Say: "(It is) Allah." Say: "Do you then take (for worship) protectors other than Him, such as have no power either for good or for harm to themselves?"

كَبَاسِطِ كَفَّيْهِ إِلَى الْمَاءِ لِيَبْلُغَ

فَاهُ وَمَا هُوَ بِبَالِغِهِ ۚ وَمَا

دُعَاءُ الْكَافِرِينَ إِلَّا فِي ضَلَالٍ ۝

وَلِلّٰهِ يَسْجُدُ مَنْ فِي السَّمٰوٰتِ

وَالْأَرْضِ طَوْعًا وَّكَرْهًا وَّظِلَالُهُمْ

بِالْغُدُوِّ وَالْآصَالِ ۩ قُلْ مَنْ

رَّبُّ السَّمٰوٰتِ وَالْأَرْضِ ۖ قُلِ اللّٰهُ ۚ

قُلْ أَفَاتَّخَذْتُمْ مِّنْ دُونِهِ أَوْلِيَاءَ

لَا يَمْلِكُونَ لِأَنْفُسِهِمْ نَفْعًا وَّلَا

Who does show you the lightning, by way both of fear and of hope: it is He Who does raise up the clouds, heavy with (fertilising) rain!

13. No, thunder repeats His praises, and so do the Angels, with awe: He flings the loud-voiced thunder-bolts, and therewith He strikes whomsoever He will ... Yet these (are the men) who (dare to) dispute about Allah, with the strength of His power (supreme)!

14. For Him (alone) is prayer in Truth: any others that they call upon besides Him hear them no more

الَّذِى يُرِيكُمُ الْبَرْقَ خَوْفًا

وَّطَمَعًا وَّيُنْشِئُ السَّحَابَ الثِّقَالَ ۱۲

وَيُسَبِّحُ الرَّعْدُ بِحَمْدِهِ وَالْمَلَٰئِكَةُ

مِنْ خِيفَتِهِ ۚ وَيُرْسِلُ الصَّوَاعِقَ

فَيُصِيبُ بِهَا مَن يَّشَاءُ وَهُمْ

يُجَادِلُونَ فِى اللهِ ۚ وَهُوَ شَدِيدُ

الْمِحَالِ ۱۳ لَهُ دَعْوَةُ الْحَقِّ

وَالَّذِينَ يَدْعُونَ مِن دُونِهِ

لَا يَسْتَجِيبُونَ لَهُم بِشَىْءٍ إِلَّا

whether any of you conceal his speech or declare it openly; whether he lie hid by night or walk forth freely by day.

11.   For each (such person) there are (Angels) in succession, before and behind him: they guard him by Command of Allah. Verily never will Allah change the condition of a people until they change it themselves (with their own souls). But when (once) Allah wills a people's punishment, there can be no turning it back, nor will they find, besides Him, any to protect.

12.   It is He

مِنْكُمْ مَّنْ أَسَرَّ الْقَوْلَ وَمَنْ جَهَرَ

بِهٖ وَمَنْ هُوَ مُسْتَخْفٍ بِالَّيْلِ

وَسَارِبٌ بِالنَّهَارِ ۞ لَهٗ مُعَقِّبٰتٌ

مِّنْۢ بَيْنِ يَدَيْهِ وَمِنْ خَلْفِهٖ

يَحْفَظُوْنَهٗ مِنْ أَمْرِ اللّٰهِ ؕ إِنَّ اللّٰهَ

لَا يُغَيِّرُ مَا بِقَوْمٍ حَتّٰى يُغَيِّرُوْا

مَا بِأَنْفُسِهِمْ ؕ وَإِذَآ أَرَادَ اللّٰهُ

بِقَوْمٍ سُوْٓءًا فَلَا مَرَدَّ لَهٗ ۚ وَمَا

لَهُمْ مِّنْ دُوْنِهٖ مِنْ وَّالٍ ۞ هُوَ

for mankind for their wrong-doing, and verily your Lord is (also) strict in punishment.

7.   And the unbelievers say: "Why is not a Sign sent down to him from his Lord?" But you are truly a warner, and to every people a guide.

8.   Allah does know what every female (womb) does bear, by how much the wombs fall short (of their time or number) or do exceed. Every single thing is before His sight, in (due) proportion.

9.   He knows the unseen and that which is open: He is the Great, the Most High.

10.   It is the same (to Him)

لِّلنَّاسِ عَلٰى ظُلْمِهِمْ ۗ وَاِنَّ رَبَّكَ
لَشَدِيْدُ الْعِقَابِ ۞ وَيَقُوْلُ الَّذِيْنَ
كَفَرُوْا لَوْ لَآ اُنْزِلَ عَلَيْهِ اٰيَةٌ
مِّنْ رَّبِّهٖ ۗ اِنَّمَآ اَنْتَ مُنْذِرٌ
وَّلِكُلِّ قَوْمٍ هَادٍ ۞ اَللّٰهُ يَعْلَمُ
مَا تَحْمِلُ كُلُّ اُنْثٰى وَمَا تَغِيْضُ
الْاَرْحَامُ وَمَا تَزْدَادُ ۗ وَكُلُّ شَيْءٍ
عِنْدَهٗ بِمِقْدَارٍ ۞ عٰلِمُ الْغَيْبِ
وَالشَّهَادَةِ الْكَبِيْرُ الْمُتَعَالِ ۞ سَوَآءٌ

who understand!

5. If you do marvel (at their want of faith), strange is their saying: "When we are (actually) dust, shall we indeed then be in a creation renewed?" They are those who deny their Lord! They are those round whose necks will be yokes (of servitude): they will be Companions of the Fire, to dwell therein (for ever)!

6. They ask you to hasten on the evil in preference to the good: yet have come to pass, before them, (many) exemplary punishments! But verily your Lord is full of forgiveness

يَّعْقِلُونَ ۞ وَإِنْ تَعْجَبْ فَعَجَبٌ

قَوْلُهُمْ ءَإِذَا كُنَّا تُرَابًا ءَإِنَّا لَفِى

خَلْقٍ جَدِيدٍ ۚ أُولَٰٓئِكَ الَّذِينَ

كَفَرُوا بِرَبِّهِمْ ۖ وَأُولَٰٓئِكَ الْأَغْلَٰلُ

فِىٓ أَعْنَاقِهِمْ ۖ وَأُولَٰٓئِكَ أَصْحَٰبُ

النَّارِ ۖ هُمْ فِيهَا خَٰلِدُونَ ۞

وَيَسْتَعْجِلُونَكَ بِالسَّيِّئَةِ قَبْلَ

الْحَسَنَةِ وَقَدْ خَلَتْ مِنْ قَبْلِهِمُ

الْمَثُلَٰتُ ۗ وَإِنَّ رَبَّكَ لَذُو مَغْفِرَةٍ

mountains standing firm and (flowing) rivers: and fruit of every kind He made in pairs, two and two: He draws the night as a veil over the day. Behold, verily in these things there are Signs for those who consider!

4.   And in the earth are tracts (diverse though) neighbouring, and gardens of vines and fields sown with corn, and palm trees - growing out of single roots or otherwise: watered with the same water, yet some of them We make more excellent than others to eat. Behold, verily in these things there are Signs for those

رَوَاسِيَ وَأَنْهَارًا ۖ وَمِنْ كُلِّ الثَّمَرٰتِ

جَعَلَ فِيهَا زَوْجَيْنِ اثْنَيْنِ

يُغْشِى الَّيْلَ النَّهَارَ ۚ إِنَّ فِى

ذٰلِكَ لَأيٰتٍ لِّقَوْمٍ يَّتَفَكَّرُونَ ۝ وَفِى

الْأَرْضِ قِطَعٌ مُّتَجٰوِرٰتٌ وَّجَنّٰتٌ

مِّنْ أَعْنَابٍ وَّزَرْعٌ وَّنَخِيلٌ

صِنْوَانٌ وَّغَيْرُ صِنْوَانٍ يُّسْقٰى بِمَآءٍ

وَّاحِدٍ ۗ وَنُفَضِّلُ بَعْضَهَا عَلٰى بَعْضٍ

فِى الْأُكُلِ ۚ إِنَّ فِى ذٰلِكَ لَأيٰتٍ لِّقَوْمٍ

has been revealed unto you from your Lord is the Truth; but most men believe not.

2. Allah is He Who raised the heavens without any pillars that you can see; is firmly established on the Throne (of Authority); He has subjected the sun and the moon (to his Law)! Each one runs (its course) for a term appointed. He does regulate all affairs, explaining the Signs in detail, that you may believe with certainty in the meeting with your Lord.

3. And it is He Who spread out the earth, and set thereon

أُنْزِلَ إِلَيْكَ مِنْ رَّبِّكَ الْحَقُّ

وَلٰكِنَّ أَكْثَرَ النَّاسِ لَا يُؤْمِنُونَ ۩

اللّٰهُ الَّذِى رَفَعَ السَّمٰوٰتِ بِغَيْرِ

عَمَدٍ تَرَوْنَهَا ثُمَّ اسْتَوٰى عَلَى

الْعَرْشِ وَسَخَّرَ الشَّمْسَ وَالْقَمَرَ

كُلٌّ يَّجْرِى لِأَجَلٍ مُّسَمًّى يُدَبِّرُ

الْأَمْرَ يُفَصِّلُ الْأٰيٰتِ لَعَلَّكُمْ

بِلِقَاءِ رَبِّكُمْ تُوقِنُونَ ۩ وَهُوَ

الَّذِى مَدَّ الْأَرْضَ وَجَعَلَ فِيْهَا

But never will be warded off our punish-ment from those who are in sin.

111. There is, in their stories, instruction for men endued with understanding. It is not a tale invented, but a confirmation of what went before it, - a detailed exposition of all things, and a guide and a mercy to any such as believe.

Ar-Ra'd (Thunder)

Bismillahir-Rahmanir-Rahim

1. Alif. Lam. Mim. Raa. These are the Signs (or Verses) of the Book: that which

مَنْ نَّشَاءُ ۚ وَلَا یُرَدُّ بَاْسُنَا عَنِ

الْقَوْمِ الْمُجْرِمِیْنَ ۞ لَقَدْ كَانَ

فِیْ قَصَصِهِمْ عِبْرَةٌ لِّاُولِی

الْاَلْبَابِ ؕ مَا كَانَ حَدِیْثًا

یُّفْتَرٰی وَلٰكِنْ تَصْدِیْقَ الَّذِیْ

بَیْنَ یَدَیْهِ وَتَفْصِیْلَ كُلِّ شَیْءٍ

وَّهُدًی وَّرَحْمَةً لِّقَوْمٍ یُّؤْمِنُوْنَ ۞

سُوْرَةُ الرَّعْدِ
مَدَنِیَّةٌ
بِسْمِ اللهِ الرَّحْمٰنِ الرَّحِیْمِ
اٰیَاتُهَا ٤٣
رُكُوْعَاتُهَا ٦

الٓمٓرٰ ۫ تِلْكَ اٰیٰتُ الْكِتٰبِ ؕ وَالَّذِیْۤ

before you (as Apostles) any but men, whom we did inspire, - (men) living in human habitations. Do they not travel through the earth, and see what was the end of those before them? But the home of the Hereafter is best, for those who do right. Will you not then understand?

110. (Respite will be granted) until, when the Apostles give up hope (of their people) and (come to) think that they were treated as liars, there reaches them Our help, and those whom We will are delivered into safety.

قَبْلِكَ إِلَّا رِجَالًا نُوحِي إِلَيْهِمْ

مِّنْ أَهْلِ الْقُرَىٰ أَفَلَمْ

يَسِيرُوا فِي الْأَرْضِ فَيَنظُرُوا

كَيْفَ كَانَ عَاقِبَةُ الَّذِينَ

مِن قَبْلِهِمْ وَلَدَارُ الْآخِرَةِ

خَيْرٌ لِّلَّذِينَ اتَّقَوْا ۗ أَفَلَا

تَعْقِلُونَ ۝ حَتَّىٰ إِذَا اسْتَيْـَٔسَ

الرُّسُلُ وَظَنُّوا أَنَّهُمْ قَدْ

كُذِبُوا جَاءَهُمْ نَصْرُنَا فَنُجِّيَ

turn (their faces) away from them!

106. And most of them believe not in Allah without associating (other as partners) with Him!

107. Do they then feel secure from the coming against them of the covering veil of the Wrath of Allah, - or of the coming against them of the (final) Hour all of a sudden while they perceive not?

108. Say you: "This is my way: I do invite to Allah, - on evidence clear as the seeing with one's eyes, - I and whoever follows me. Glory to Allah! And never will I join gods with Allah!"

109. Nor did We send

مُعْرِضُونَ ۝ وَمَا يُؤْمِنُ أَكْثَرُهُمْ

بِاللهِ إِلَّا وَهُمْ مُّشْرِكُونَ ۝ أَفَأَمِنُوٓا

أَنْ تَأْتِيَهُمْ غَاشِيَةٌ مِّنْ عَذَابِ

اللهِ أَوْ تَأْتِيَهُمُ السَّاعَةُ بَغْتَةً

وَهُمْ لَا يَشْعُرُونَ ۝ قُلْ هٰذِهٖ

سَبِيلِيٓ أَدْعُوٓا إِلَى اللهِ عَلَىٰ

بَصِيرَةٍ أَنَا وَمَنِ اتَّبَعَنِي

وَسُبْحَانَ اللهِ وَمَآ أَنَا مِنَ

الْمُشْرِكِينَ ۝ وَمَآ أَرْسَلْنَا مِنْ

as one submitting to your will (as a Muslim), and unite me with the righteous."

102. Such is one of the stories of what happened unseen, which We reveal by inspiration unto you; nor were you (present) with them then when they concerted their plans together in the process of weaving their plots.

103. Yet no faith will the greater part of mankind have, however ardently you does desire it.

104. And no reward do you ask of them for this: it is no less than a message for all creatures.

105. And how many Signs in the heavens and the earth do they pass by? Yet they

مُسْلِمًا وَّ أَلْحِقْنِى بِالصّٰلِحِينَ ۝

ذٰلِكَ مِنْ أَنْبَآءِ الْغَيْبِ نُوْحِيْهِ

اِلَيْكَ ۚ وَمَا كُنْتَ لَدَيْهِمْ اِذْ اَجْمَعُوْٓا

اَمْرَهُمْ وَهُمْ يَمْكُرُوْنَ ۝ وَمَآ اَكْثَرُ

النَّاسِ وَلَوْ حَرَصْتَ بِمُؤْمِنِيْنَ ۝

وَمَا تَسْئَلُهُمْ عَلَيْهِ مِنْ اَجْرٍ ۚ اِنْ

هُوَ اِلَّا ذِكْرٌ لِّلْعٰلَمِيْنَ ۝ وَكَاَيِّنْ

مِّنْ اٰيَةٍ فِى السَّمٰوٰتِ وَالْاَرْضِ

يَمُرُّوْنَ عَلَيْهَا وَهُمْ عَنْهَا

He took me out of prison and brought you (all here) out of the desert, (even) after Satan had sown enmity between me and my brothers. Verily my Lord understandeth best the mysteries of all that He plans to do, for verily He is full of knowledge and wisdom."

101. "O my Lord! You have indeed bestowed on me some power, and taught me something of the interpretation of dreams and events, - O you Creator of the heavens and the earth! you are my Protector in this world and in the Hereafter. Take you my soul (at death)

أَخْرَجَنِي مِنَ السِّجْنِ وَجَاءَ

بِكُمْ مِّنَ الْبَدْوِ مِنْ بَعْدِ أَنْ

نَّزَغَ الشَّيْطَنُ بَيْنِي وَبَيْنَ

إِخْوَتِي إِنَّ رَبِّي لَطِيفٌ لِّمَا

يَشَآءُ إِنَّهُ هُوَ الْعَلِيمُ الْحَكِيمُ ۝

رَبِّ قَدْ اتَيْتَنِي مِنَ الْمُلْكِ

وَعَلَّمْتَنِي مِنْ تَأْوِيلِ الْأَحَادِيثِ

فَاطِرَ السَّمَوَتِ وَالْأَرْضِ أَنْتَ

وَلِيِّي فِي الدُّنْيَا وَالْأَخِرَةِ تَوَفَّنِي

for He is indeed Oft-Forgiving, Most Merciful."

99. Then when they entered the presence of Joseph, he provided a home for his parents with himself, and said: "Enter you Egypt (all) in safety if it please Allah."

100. And he raised his parents high on the throne (of dignity), and they fell down in prostration, (all) before him. He said: "O my father! This is the fulfilment of my vision of old! Allah has made it come true! He was indeed good to me when

رَبِّيْ ۚ اِنَّهٗ هُوَ الْغَفُوْرُ الرَّحِيْمُ ۩

فَلَمَّا دَخَلُوْا عَلٰى يُوْسُفَ اٰوٰٓى

اِلَيْهِ اَبَوَيْهِ وَقَالَ ادْخُلُوْا

مِصْرَ اِنْ شَآءَ اللّٰهُ اٰمِنِيْنَ ۩

وَرَفَعَ اَبَوَيْهِ عَلَى الْعَرْشِ

وَخَرُّوْا لَهٗ سُجَّدًا ۚ وَقَالَ

يٰٓاَبَتِ هٰذَا تَاْوِيْلُ رُءْيَايَ

مِنْ قَبْلُ قَدْ جَعَلَهَا رَبِّيْ

حَقًّا ۚ وَقَدْ اَحْسَنَ بِيْ اِذْ

scent the presence of Joseph: no, think me not a dotard."

95. They said: "By Allah! Truly you are in your old wandering mind."

96. Then when the bearer of the good news came, he cast (the shirt) over his face, and he forthwith regained clear sight. He said: "Did I not say to you, 'I know from Allah that which you know not?'"

97. They said: "O our father! Ask for us forgiveness for our sins, for we were truly at fault."

98. He said: "Soon will I ask my Lord for forgiveness for you:

رِيحَ يُوسُفَ لَوْلَآ أَن تُفَنِّدُونِ ۝

قَالُوا تَاللهِ إِنَّكَ لَفِي ضَلٰلِكَ

الْقَدِيمِ ۝ فَلَمَّآ أَن جَآءَ

الْبَشِيرُ أَلْقٰهُ عَلٰى وَجْهِهِ

فَارْتَدَّ بَصِيرًا ۚ قَالَ أَلَمْ

أَقُل لَّكُمْ إِنِّي أَعْلَمُ مِنَ اللهِ

مَا لَا تَعْلَمُونَ ۝ قَالُوا يَآأَبَانَا

اسْتَغْفِرْ لَنَا ذُنُوبَنَآ إِنَّا كُنَّا

خٰطِئِينَ ۝ قَالَ سَوْفَ أَسْتَغْفِرُ لَكُمْ

of those who do right."

91. They said: "By Allah! Indeed has Allah preferred you above us, and we certainly have been guilty of sin!"

92. He said: "This day let no reproach be (cast) on you: Allah will forgive you, and He is the Most Merciful of those who show mercy!"

93. "Go with this my shirt, and cast it over the face of my father: he will come to see (clearly). Then come you (here) to me together with all your family."

94. When the caravan left (Egypt), their father said: "I do indeed

الْمُحْسِنِيْنَ ۝ قَالُوْا تَاللّٰهِ لَقَدْ

اٰثَرَكَ اللّٰهُ عَلَيْنَا وَ اِنْ كُنَّا

لَخٰطِئِيْنَ ۝ قَالَ لَا تَثْرِيْبَ

عَلَيْكُمُ الْيَوْمَ يَغْفِرُ اللّٰهُ لَكُمْ

وَ هُوَ اَرْحَمُ الرّٰحِمِيْنَ ۝ اِذْهَبُوْا

بِقَمِيْصِیْ هٰذَا فَاَلْقُوْهُ عَلٰی

وَجْهِ اَبِیْ يَأْتِ بَصِيْرًا وَّاْتُوْنِیْ

بِاَهْلِكُمْ اَجْمَعِيْنَ ۝ وَ لَمَّا فَصَلَتِ

الْعِيْرُ قَالَ اَبُوْهُمْ اِنِّیْ لَاَجِدُ

we have (now) brought but scanty capital: so pay us full measure, (we pray you), and treat it as charity to us: for Allah does reward the charitable."

89. He said: "Know you how you dealt with Joseph and his brother, not knowing (what you were doing)?"

90. They said: "Are you indeed Joseph?" He said, "I am Joseph, and this is my brother: Allah has indeed been gracious to us (all): behold, he that is righteous and patient, - never will Allah suffer the reward to be lost,

وَجِئْنَا بِبِضَاعَةٍ مُّزْجَاةٍ فَأَوْفِ

لَنَا الْكَيْلَ وَتَصَدَّقْ عَلَيْنَا ۖ

إِنَّ اللَّهَ يَجْزِى الْمُتَصَدِّقِينَ ۝

قَالَ هَلْ عَلِمْتُم مَّا فَعَلْتُم

بِيُوسُفَ وَأَخِيهِ إِذْ أَنتُمْ جَاهِلُونَ ۝

قَالُوا أَءِنَّكَ لَأَنتَ يُوسُفُ ۖ قَالَ

أَنَا يُوسُفُ وَهَٰذَآ أَخِى ۖ قَدْ مَنَّ

اللَّهُ عَلَيْنَا ۖ إِنَّهُۥ مَن يَتَّقِ

وَيَصْبِرْ فَإِنَّ اللَّهَ لَا يُضِيعُ أَجْرَ

die!"

86.　He said: "I only complain of
my distraction and anguish to
Allah, and I know from Allah that
which you know not …

87.　"O my sons! Go you and
enquire about Joseph and his
brother, and never give up hope
of Allah's Soothing Mercy: truly
no one despairs of Allah's
Soothing Mercy, except those
who have no faith."

88.　Then, when they came
(back) into (Joseph's) presence
they said: "O exalted one! Distress
has seized us and our family:

مِنَ الْهٰلِكِيْنَ ۝ قَالَ اِنَّمَآ

اَشْكُوْا بَثِّیْ وَحُزْنِیْ اِلَی اللّٰهِ

وَاَعْلَمُ مِنَ اللّٰهِ مَا لَا تَعْلَمُوْنَ ۝

یٰبَنِیَّ اذْهَبُوْا فَتَحَسَّسُوْا مِنْ

يُّوْسُفَ وَاَخِيْهِ وَلَا تَایْـَٔسُوْا مِنْ

رَّوْحِ اللّٰهِ ؕ اِنَّهٗ لَا يَایْـَٔسُ مِنْ

رَّوْحِ اللّٰهِ اِلَّا الْقَوْمُ الْكٰفِرُوْنَ ۝

فَلَمَّا دَخَلُوْا عَلَيْهِ قَالُوْا یٰۤاَيُّهَا

الْعَزِيْزُ مَسَّنَا وَاَهْلَنَا الضُّ

indeed telling the truth.'"

83. Jacob said: "No, but you have yourselves contrived a story (good enough) for you. So patience is most fitting (for me). May be Allah will bring them (back) all to me (in the end). For He is indeed full of knowledge and wisdom."

84. And he turned away from them, and said: "How great is my grief for Joseph!" And his eyes became white with sorrow, and he fell into silent melancholy.

85. They said: "By Allah! (Never) will you cease to remember Joseph until you reach the last extremity of illness, or until you

تَصۡدِقُوۡنَ ۞ قَالَ بَلۡ سَوَّلَتۡ

لَكُمۡ اَنۡفُسُكُمۡ اَمۡرًا ط فَصَبۡرٌ جَمِيۡلٌ

عَسَى اللّٰهُ اَنۡ يَّاۡتِيَنِیۡ بِهِمۡ

جَمِيۡعًا ط اِنَّهٗ هُوَ الۡعَلِيۡمُ الۡحَكِيۡمُ ۞

وَتَوَلّٰى عَنۡهُمۡ وَقَالَ يٰۤاَسَفٰى عَلٰى

يُوۡسُفَ وَابۡيَضَّتۡ عَيۡنٰهُ مِنَ

الۡحُزۡنِ فَهُوَ كَظِيۡمٌ ۞ قَالُوۡا

تَاللّٰهِ تَفۡتَؤُا تَذۡكُرُ يُوۡسُفَ

حَتّٰى تَكُوۡنَ حَرَضًا اَوۡ تَكُوۡنَ

before this, you did fail in your duty with Joseph? Therefore will I not leave this land until my father permits me, or Allah commands me; and He is the best to command.

81. "Turn you back to your father, and say, 'O our father! behold! your son committed theft! we bear witness only to what we know, and we could not well guard against the unseen!'

82. 'Ask at the town where we have been and the caravan in which we returned, and (you will find) we are

قَبْلُ مَا فَرَّطْتُمْ فِي يُوسُفَ

فَلَنْ أَبْرَحَ الْأَرْضَ حَتَّى يَأْذَنَ

لِي أَبِي أَوْ يَحْكُمَ اللهُ لِي وَهُوَ

خَيْرُ الْحَاكِمِينَ ۝ اِرْجِعُوا إِلَى

أَبِيكُمْ فَقُولُوا يَا أَبَانَا إِنَّ ابْنَكَ

سَرَقَ وَمَا شَهِدْنَا إِلَّا بِمَا عَلِمْنَا

وَمَا كُنَّا لِلْغَيْبِ حَافِظِينَ ۝

وَسْئَلِ الْقَرْيَةَ الَّتِي كُنَّا فِيهَا

وَالْعِيرَ الَّتِي أَقْبَلْنَا فِيهَا وَإِنَّا

78. They said: "O exalted one! Behold! He has a father, aged and venerable, (who will grieve for him); so take one of us in his place; for we see that you are (gracious) in doing good."

79. He said: "Allah forbid that we take other than him with whom we found our property: indeed (if we did so), we should be acting wrongfully.

80. Now when they saw no hope of his (yielding), they held a conference in private. The leader among them said: "Know you not that your father did take an oath from you in Allah's name, and how,

قَالُوْا يَآ اَيُّهَا الْعَزِيْزُ اِنَّ لَهٗٓ اَبًا

شَيْخًا كَبِيْرًا فَخُذْ اَحَدَنَا مَكَانَهٗ ۚ

اِنَّا نَرٰىكَ مِنَ الْمُحْسِنِيْنَ ۞

قَالَ مَعَاذَ اللّٰهِ اَنْ نَّاْخُذَ اِلَّا

مَنْ وَّجَدْنَا مَتَاعَنَا عِنْدَهٗٓ اِنَّآ

اِذًا لَّظٰلِمُوْنَ ۞ فَلَمَّا اسْتَيْـَٔسُوْا

مِنْهُ خَلَصُوْا نَجِيًّا ۚ قَالَ كَبِيْرُهُمْ

اَلَمْ تَعْلَمُوْٓا اَنَّ اَبَاكُمْ قَدْ اَخَذَ

عَلَيْكُمْ مَّوْثِقًا مِّنَ اللّٰهِ وَمِنْ

Thus did We plan for Joseph. He could not take his brother by the law of the king except that Allah willed it (so). We raise to degrees (of wisdom) whom We please: but over all endued with knowledge is one, the All-Knowing.

77.   They said: "If he steals, there was a brother of his who did steal before (him)." But these things did Joseph keep locked in his heart, revealing not the secrets to them. He (simply) said (to himself): "You are the worse situated; and Allah knows best the truth of what you assert!"

كَذٰلِكَ كِدْنَا لِيُوسُفَ ۖ مَا كَانَ

لِيَأْخُذَ أَخَاهُ فِي دِينِ الْمَلِكِ

إِلَّا أَنْ يَشَاءَ اللهُ ۚ نَرْفَعُ دَرَجٰتٍ

مَّنْ نَّشَاءُ ۗ وَفَوْقَ كُلِّ ذِي عِلْمٍ

عَلِيْمٌ ۩ قَالُوا إِنْ يَّسْرِقْ فَقَدْ

سَرَقَ أَخٌ لَّهُ مِنْ قَبْلُ ۚ فَأَسَرَّهَا

يُوسُفُ فِي نَفْسِهِ وَلَمْ يُبْدِهَا

لَهُمْ ۚ قَالَ أَنْتُمْ شَرٌّ مَّكَانًا ۖ

وَاللهُ أَعْلَمُ بِمَا تَصِفُونَ ۩

is (the reward of) a camel load; I will be bound by it."

73. (The brothers) said: "By Allah! Well you know that we came not to make mischief in the land, and we are no thieves!"

74. (The Egyptians) said: "What then shall be the penalty of this, if you are (proved) to have lied?"

75. They said: "The penalty should be that he in whose's saddle-bag it is found, should be held (as bondman) to atone for the (crime). Thus it is we punish the wrong-doers!"

76. So he began (the search) with their baggage, before (he came to) the baggage of his brother: at length he brought it out of his brother's baggage.

حِمْلُ بَعِيرٍ وَّأَنَا بِهِ زَعِيمٌ ۞

قَالُوا تَاللّٰهِ لَقَدْ عَلِمْتُمْ مَّا

جِئْنَا لِنُفْسِدَ فِى الْأَرْضِ وَمَا كُنَّا

سٰرِقِينَ ۞ قَالُوا فَمَا جَزَآؤُهٗۤ إِنْ

كُنْتُمْ كٰذِبِينَ ۞ قَالُوا جَزَآؤُهٗ

مَنْ وُّجِدَ فِىْ رَحْلِهٖ فَهُوَ جَزَآؤُهٗ

كَذٰلِكَ نَجْزِى الظّٰلِمِينَ ۞ فَبَدَأَ

بِأَوْعِيَتِهِمْ قَبْلَ وِعَآءِ أَخِيهِ

ثُمَّ اسْتَخْرَجَهَا مِنْ وِّعَآءِ أَخِيهِ

into Joseph's presence, he received his (full) brother to stay with him. He said (to him): "Behold! I am your (own) brother; so grieve not at anything of their doings."

70. At length when he had furnished them forth with provisions (suitable) for them, he put the measure pot into his brother's saddle-bag. Then shouted out a crier: "O you (in) the caravan! Behold! You are thieves, without doubt!"

71. They said, turning towards them: "What is it that you miss?"

72. They said: "We miss the measure pot of the king; for him who produces it,

عَلٰى يُوْسُفَ اٰوٰٓى اِلَيْهِ اَخَاهُ

قَالَ اِنِّيْٓ اَنَا اَخُوْكَ فَلَا

تَبْتَئِسْ بِمَا كَانُوْا يَعْمَلُوْنَ ۞

فَلَمَّا جَهَّزَهُمْ بِجَهَازِهِمْ جَعَلَ

السِّقَايَةَ فِيْ رَحْلِ اَخِيْهِ ثُمَّ

اَذَّنَ مُؤَذِّنٌ اَيَّتُهَا الْعِيْرُ اِنَّكُمْ

لَسَارِقُوْنَ ۞ قَالُوْا وَاَقْبَلُوْا عَلَيْهِمْ

مَّاذَا تَفْقِدُوْنَ ۞ قَالُوْا نَفْقِدُ

صُوَاعَ الْمَلِكِ وَلِمَنْ جَآءَ بِهٖ

I can profit you at all against Allah (with my advice): none can command except Allah: on Him do I put my trust: and let all that trust put their trust on Him."

68.   And when they entered in the manner their father had enjoined, it did not profit them in the least against (the plan of) Allah: it served only to satisfy Jacob's heart felt desire. For he was, by our instruction, full of knowledge (and experience): but most men know not.

69.   Now when they came

أُغْنِى عَنكُم مِّنَ اللهِ مِن شَىْءٍ

إِنِ الْحُكْمُ إِلَّا لِلهِ عَلَيْهِ تَوَكَّلْتُ

وَعَلَيْهِ فَلْيَتَوَكَّلِ الْمُتَوَكِّلُونَ ۞

وَلَمَّا دَخَلُوا مِنْ حَيْثُ أَمَرَهُمْ

أَبُوهُم مَّا كَانَ يُغْنِى عَنْهُم مِّنَ

اللهِ مِن شَىْءٍ إِلَّا حَاجَةً فِى

نَفْسِ يَعْقُوبَ قَضَاهَا وَإِنَّهُ لَذُو

عِلْمٍ لِّمَا عَلَّمْنَهُ وَلَكِنَّ أَكْثَرَ

النَّاسِ لَا يَعْلَمُونَ ۞ وَلَمَّا دَخَلُوا

our family; we shall take care of our brother; and add (at the same time) a full camel's load (of grain to our provisions). This is but a small quantity.

66. (Jacob) said: "Never will I send him with you until you swear a solemn oath to me, in Allah's name, that you will be sure to bring him back to me unless you are yourselves hemmed in (and made powerless). And when they had sworn their solemn oath, he said: "Over all that we say, be Allah the Witness and Guardian!"

67. Further he said: "O my sons! Enter not all by one gate: enter you by different gates. Not that

اَهۡلَنَا وَنَحۡفَظُ اَخَانَا وَنَزۡدَادُ

كَیۡلَ بَعِیۡرٍ ؕ ذٰلِكَ كَیۡلٌ یَّسِیۡرٌ ﴿٥٥﴾

قَالَ لَنۡ اُرۡسِلَهٗ مَعَكُمۡ حَتّٰی

تُؤۡتُوۡنِ مَوۡثِقًا مِّنَ اللّٰهِ لَتَاۡتُنَّنِیۡ

بِهٖۤ اِلَّاۤ اَنۡ یُّحَاطَ بِكُمۡ ۚ فَلَمَّاۤ

اٰتَوۡهُ مَوۡثِقَهُمۡ قَالَ اللّٰهُ عَلٰی

مَا نَقُوۡلُ وَكِیۡلٌ ﴿٦٦﴾ وَقَالَ یٰبَنِیَّ

لَا تَدۡخُلُوۡا مِنۡۢ بَابٍ وَّاحِدٍ

وَّادۡخُلُوۡا مِنۡ اَبۡوَابٍ مُّتَفَرِّقَةٍ ؕ وَمَاۤ

they said: "O our father! No more measure of grain shall we get (unless we take our brother): so send our brother with us, that we may get our measure; and we will indeed take every care of him."

64. He said: "Shall I trust you with him with any result other than when I trusted you with his brother aforetime? But Allah is the best to take care (of him), and He is the Most Merciful of those who show mercy!"

65. Then when they opened their baggage, they found their stock-in-trade had been returned to them. They said: "O our father! What (more) can we desire? This our stock-in-trade has been returned to us: so we shall get (more) food for

قَالُوا يَا أَبَانَا مُنِعَ مِنَّا الْكَيْلُ

فَأَرْسِلْ مَعَنَا أَخَانَا نَكْتَلْ وَإِنَّا

لَهُ لَحَافِظُونَ ۝ قَالَ هَلْ آمَنُكُمْ

عَلَيْهِ إِلَّا كَمَا أَمِنْتُكُمْ عَلَى أَخِيهِ

مِنْ قَبْلُ فَاللَّهُ خَيْرٌ حَافِظًا

وَهُوَ أَرْحَمُ الرَّاحِمِينَ ۝ وَلَمَّا

فَتَحُوا مَتَاعَهُمْ وَجَدُوا بِضَاعَتَهُمْ

رُدَّتْ إِلَيْهِمْ قَالُوا يَا أَبَانَا مَا نَبْغِي

هَذِهِ بِضَاعَتُنَا رُدَّتْ إِلَيْنَا وَنَمِيرُ

see you not that I pay out full measure, and that I do provide the best hospitality?

60. "Now if you bring him not to me, you shall have no measure (of corn) from me, nor shall you (even) come near me."

61. They said: "We shall certainly seek to get your wish about him from his father: indeed we shall do it."

62. And (Joseph) told his servants to put their stock-in-trade (with which they had bartered) into their saddle-bags, so they should know it only when they returned to their people, in order that they might come back.

63. Now when they returned to their father,

تَرَوۡنَ اَنِّىۡ اُوۡفِی الۡكَیۡلَ وَ اَنَا

خَیۡرُ الۡمُنۡزِلِیۡنَ ۝ فَاِنۡ لَّمۡ تَاۡتُوۡنِیۡ

بِهٖ فَلَا كَیۡلَ لَكُمۡ عِنۡدِیۡ وَلَا

تَقۡرَبُوۡنِ ۝ قَالُوۡا سَنُرَاوِدُ عَنۡهُ

اَبَاهُ وَ اِنَّا لَفٰعِلُوۡنَ ۝ وَ قَالَ

لِفِتۡیٰنِهِ اجۡعَلُوۡا بِضَاعَتَهُمۡ فِیۡ

رِحَالِهِمۡ لَعَلَّهُمۡ یَعۡرِفُوۡنَهَاۤ اِذَا

انۡقَلَبُوۡۤا اِلٰۤی اَهۡلِهِمۡ لَعَلَّهُمۡ

یَرۡجِعُوۡنَ ۝ فَلَمَّا رَجَعُوۡۤا اِلٰۤی اَبِیۡهِمۡ

in the land, to take possession therein as, when, or where he pleased. We bestow of our Mercy on whom We please, and We suffer not, to be lost, the reward of those who do good.

57. But verily the reward of the Hereafter is the best, for those who believe, and are constant in righteousness.

58. Then came Joseph's brethren: they entered his presence, and he knew them, but they knew him not.

59. And when he had furnished them forth with provisions (suitable) for them, he said: "Bring unto me a brother you have, of the same father as yourselves, (but a different mother):

فِى الْاَرْضِ يَتَبَوَّاُ مِنْهَا حَيْثُ

يَشَآءُ ۚ نُصِيْبُ بِرَحْمَتِنَا مَنْ نَّشَآءُ

وَلَا نُضِيْعُ اَجْرَ الْمُحْسِنِيْنَ ۝

وَلَاَجْرُ الْاٰخِرَةِ خَيْرٌ لِّلَّذِيْنَ

اٰمَنُوْا وَكَانُوْا يَتَّقُوْنَ ۝ وَجَآءَ

اِخْوَةُ يُوْسُفَ فَدَخَلُوْا عَلَيْهِ

فَعَرَفَهُمْ وَهُمْ لَهُ مُنْكِرُوْنَ ۝

وَلَمَّا جَهَّزَهُمْ بِجَهَازِهِمْ قَالَ

ائْتُوْنِىْ بِاَخٍ لَّكُمْ مِّنْ اَبِيْكُمْ ۚ اَلَا

53. "Nor do I absolve my own self (of blame): the (human) soul is certainly prone to evil, unless my Lord do bestow His Mercy: but surely my Lord is Oft-Forgiving, Most Merciful."

54. So the king said: "Bring him unto me; I will take him specially to serve about my own person." Therefore when he had spoken to him, he said: "Be assured this day, you are, of high standing with us, invested with all trust."

55. (Joseph) said: "Set me over the store-houses of the land: I will indeed guard them, as one that knows (their importance)."

56. Thus did We give established power to Joseph

وَمَآ أُبَرِّئُ نَفْسِىْ إِنَّ النَّفْسَ

لَأَمَّارَةٌ بِالسُّوْءِ إِلَّا مَا رَحِمَ

رَبِّىْ إِنَّ رَبِّىْ غَفُوْرٌ رَّحِيْمٌ ۞

وَ قَالَ الْمَلِكُ ائْتُوْنِىْ بِهٖ

أَسْتَخْلِصْهُ لِنَفْسِىْ فَلَمَّا كَلَّمَهٗ

قَالَ إِنَّكَ الْيَوْمَ لَدَيْنَا مَكِيْنٌ

أَمِيْنٌ ۞ قَالَ اجْعَلْنِىْ عَلٰى

خَزَآئِنِ الْأَرْضِ إِنِّىْ حَفِيْظٌ

عَلِيْمٌ ۞ وَ كَذٰلِكَ مَكَّنَّا لِيُوْسُفَ

ذٰلِكَ الْكِتٰبُ لَا رَيْبَ فِيْهِ

پارہ

وَمَآ أُبَرِّئُ

(۱۳)

PART 14
Rubama

His Path, and who receive guidance.

126. And if you do catch them out, catch them out no worse than they catch you out: but if you show patience, that is indeed the best (course) for those who are patient.

127. And do you be patient, for your patience is with the help from Allah; nor grieve over them and distress not yourself because of their plots.

128. For Allah is with those who restrain themselves, and those who do good.

سَبِيلِهِ ۖ وَهُوَ أَعْلَمُ بِالْمُهْتَدِينَ ۝

وَإِنْ عَاقَبْتُمْ فَعَاقِبُوا بِمِثْلِ

مَا عُوقِبْتُم بِهِ ۖ وَلَئِن صَبَرْتُمْ

لَهُوَ خَيْرٌ لِّلصَّابِرِينَ ۝ وَاصْبِرْ

وَمَا صَبْرُكَ إِلَّا بِاللَّهِ ۚ وَلَا

تَحْزَنْ عَلَيْهِمْ وَلَا تَكُ فِي

ضَيْقٍ مِّمَّا يَمْكُرُونَ ۝ إِنَّ

اللَّهَ مَعَ الَّذِينَ اتَّقَوا وَّالَّذِينَ

هُم مُّحْسِنُونَ ۝

and he joined not gods with Allah."

124. The Sabbath was only made (strict) for those who disagreed (as to its observance); but Allah will judge between them on the Day of Judgment, as to their differences.

125. Invite (all) to the Way of your Lord with wisdom and beautiful preaching; and argue with them in ways that are best and most gracious: for your Lord knows best, who have strayed from

وَمَا كَانَ مِنَ الْمُشْرِكِينَ ۝

إِنَّمَا جُعِلَ السَّبْتُ عَلَى الَّذِينَ

اخْتَلَفُوا فِيهِ ۚ وَإِنَّ رَبَّكَ لَيَحْكُمُ

بَيْنَهُمْ يَوْمَ الْقِيٰمَةِ فِيمَا

كَانُوا فِيهِ يَخْتَلِفُونَ ۝ أُدْعُ

إِلٰى سَبِيلِ رَبِّكَ بِالْحِكْمَةِ

وَالْمَوْعِظَةِ الْحَسَنَةِ وَجَادِلْهُمْ

بِالَّتِي هِيَ أَحْسَنُ ۚ إِنَّ رَبَّكَ

هُوَ أَعْلَمُ بِمَن ضَلَّ عَن

after all this, is Oft-Forgiving, Most Merciful.

120. Abraham was indeed a model, devoutly obedient to Allah, (and) true in Faith, and he joined not gods with Allah:

121. He showed his gratitude for the favours of Allah, Who chose him, and guided him to a Straight Way.

122. And We gave him Good in this world, and he will be, in the Hereafter, in the ranks of the Righteous.

123. So We have taught you the inspired (Message), "Follow the ways of Abraham, the True in Faith,

مِنْ بَعْدِهَا لَغَفُورٌ رَّحِيمٌ ۝

إِنَّ إِبْرَاهِيمَ كَانَ أُمَّةً قَانِتًا

لِلَّهِ حَنِيفًا ۗ وَلَمْ يَكُ مِنَ

الْمُشْرِكِينَ ۝ شَاكِرًا لِّأَنْعُمِهِ

اجْتَبَاهُ وَهَدَاهُ إِلَى صِرَاطٍ

مُّسْتَقِيمٍ ۝ وَآتَيْنَاهُ فِي الدُّنْيَا

حَسَنَةً ۖ وَإِنَّهُ فِي الْآخِرَةِ لَمِنَ

الصَّالِحِينَ ۝ ثُمَّ أَوْحَيْنَا إِلَيْكَ

أَنِ اتَّبِعْ مِلَّةَ إِبْرَاهِيمَ حَنِيفًا ۖ

false things to Allah, will never prosper.

117. (In such falsehood) is but a paltry profit; but they will have a most grievous Chastisement.

118. To the Jews We prohibited such things as We have mentioned to you before: We did them no wrong, but they were used to doing wrong to themselves.

119. But verily your Lord, - to those who do wrong in ignorance, but who thereafter repent and make amends, - your Lord,

اللّٰهِ الْكَذِبَ لَا يُفْلِحُوْنَ ۙ ۞

مَتَاعٌ قَلِيْلٌ ۖ وَّلَهُمْ عَذَابٌ

اَلِيْمٌ ۞ وَعَلَى الَّذِيْنَ هَادُوْا

حَرَّمْنَا مَا قَصَصْنَا عَلَيْكَ مِنْ

قَبْلُ ۚ وَمَا ظَلَمْنٰهُمْ وَلٰكِنْ

كَانُوْا اَنْفُسَهُمْ يَظْلِمُوْنَ ۞ ثُمَّ

اِنَّ رَبَّكَ لِلَّذِيْنَ عَمِلُوا السُّوْٓءَ

بِجَهَالَةٍ ثُمَّ تَابُوْا مِنْ بَعْدِ

ذٰلِكَ وَاَصْلَحُوْٓا اِنَّ رَبَّكَ

115. He has only forbidden you dead meat, and blood, and the flesh of swine, and any (food) over which the name of other than Allah has been invoked. But if one is forced by necessity, without wilful disobedience, nor transgressing due limits, - then Allah is Oft-Forgiving, Most Merciful.

116. But say not - for any false thing that your tongues may put forth, - "This is lawful, and this is forbidden," so as to ascribe false things to Allah. For those who ascribe

اِنَّمَا حَرَّمَ عَلَيْكُمُ الْمَيْتَةَ

وَالدَّمَ وَلَحْمَ الْخِنْزِيرِ وَمَآ

أُهِلَّ لِغَيْرِ اللهِ بِهِ ۚ فَمَنِ

اضْطُرَّ غَيْرَ بَاغٍ وَّلَا عَادٍ

فَاِنَّ اللهَ غَفُورٌ رَّحِيمٌ ۞ وَلَا

تَقُوْلُوْا لِمَا تَصِفُ اَلْسِنَتُكُمُ

الْكَذِبَ هٰذَا حَلٰلٌ وَّهٰذَا

حَرَامٌ لِّتَفْتَرُوْا عَلَى اللهِ الْكَذِبَ

اِنَّ الَّذِيْنَ يَفْتَرُوْنَ عَلَى

abundantly supplied with sustenance from every place: yet was it ungrateful for the favours of Allah: so Allah made it taste of hunger and terror (in extremes) (closing in on it) like a garment (from every side), because of the (evil) which (its people) wrought.

113. And there came to them an Apostle from among themselves, but they falsely rejected him; so the Wrath seized them even in the midst of their iniquities.

114. So eat of the sustenance which Allah has provided for you, lawful and good; and be grateful for the favours of Allah, if it is He Whom you serve.

يَأْتِيهَا رِزْقُهَا رَغَدًا مِّنْ كُلِّ مَكَانٍ فَكَفَرَتْ بِأَنْعُمِ اللَّهِ فَأَذَاقَهَا اللَّهُ لِبَاسَ الْجُوعِ وَالْخَوْفِ بِمَا كَانُوا يَصْنَعُونَ ۝ وَلَقَدْ جَاءَهُمْ رَسُولٌ مِّنْهُمْ فَكَذَّبُوهُ فَأَخَذَهُمُ الْعَذَابُ وَهُمْ ظَالِمُونَ ۝ فَكُلُوا مِمَّا رَزَقَكُمُ اللَّهُ حَلَالًا طَيِّبًا وَّاشْكُرُوا نِعْمَتَ اللَّهِ إِنْ كُنْتُمْ إِيَّاهُ تَعْبُدُونَ ۝

in the Hereafter they will perish.

110. But verily your Lord, - to those who leave their homes after trials and persecutions, - and who thereafter strive and fight for the faith and patiently persevere, - your Lord, after all this is Oft-Forgiving, Most Merciful.

111. One Day every soul will come up struggling for itself, and every soul will be recompensed (fully) for all its actions, and none will be unjustly dealt with.

112. Allah sets forth a parable: a city enjoying security and quiet,

أَنَّهُمْ فِي الْآخِرَةِ هُمُ الْخَاسِرُونَ ۝

ثُمَّ إِنَّ رَبَّكَ لِلَّذِينَ هَاجَرُوا

مِنْ بَعْدِ مَا فُتِنُوا ثُمَّ جَاهَدُوا

وَصَبَرُوا إِنَّ رَبَّكَ مِنْ بَعْدِهَا

لَغَفُورٌ رَّحِيمٌ ۝ يَوْمَ تَأْتِي كُلُّ

نَفْسٍ تُجَادِلُ عَنْ نَفْسِهَا وَتُوَفَّى

كُلُّ نَفْسٍ مَّا عَمِلَتْ وَهُمْ لَا

يُظْلَمُونَ ۝ وَضَرَبَ اللَّهُ مَثَلًا

قَرْيَةً كَانَتْ آمِنَةً مُّطْمَئِنَّةً

in Faith - but such as open their breast to Unbelief, on them is Wrath from Allah, and for them will be a dreadful Chastisement.

107. This because they love the life of this world better than the Hereafter: and Allah will not guide those who reject Faith.

108. Those are they whose hearts, ears, and eyes Allah has sealed up, and they take no heed.

109. Without doubt,

بِالْإِيْمَانِ وَلٰكِنْ مَّنْ شَرَحَ

بِالْكُفْرِ صَدْرًا فَعَلَيْهِمْ غَضَبٌ

مِّنَ اللّٰهِ وَلَهُمْ عَذَابٌ عَظِيْمٌ ۝

ذٰلِكَ بِأَنَّهُمُ اسْتَحَبُّوا الْحَيٰوةَ

الدُّنْيَا عَلَى الْاٰخِرَةِ وَاَنَّ اللّٰهَ

لَا يَهْدِى الْقَوْمَ الْكٰفِرِيْنَ ۝

اُولٰٓئِكَ الَّذِيْنَ طَبَعَ اللّٰهُ عَلٰى

قُلُوْبِهِمْ وَسَمْعِهِمْ وَاَبْصَارِهِمْ ۚ

وَاُولٰٓئِكَ هُمُ الْغٰفِلُوْنَ ۝ لَا جَرَمَ

they wickedly point to is notably foreign, while this is Arabic, pure and clear.

104. Those who believe not in the Signs of Allah, - Allah will not guide them, and theirs will be a grievous Chastisement.

105. It is those who believe not in the Signs of Allah, that forge falsehood: it is they who lie!

106. Any one who, after accepting faith in Allah, utters Unbelief, - except under compulsion, his heart remaining firm

يَلْحِدُوْنَ اِلَيْهِ اَعْجَمِيٌّ وَّهٰذَا

لِسَانٌ عَرَبِيٌّ مُّبِيْنٌ ۞ اِنَّ

الَّذِيْنَ لَا يُؤْمِنُوْنَ بِاٰيٰتِ اللّٰهِ

لَا يَهْدِيْهِمُ اللّٰهُ وَلَهُمْ عَذَابٌ

اَلِيْمٌ ۞ اِنَّمَا يَفْتَرِى الْكَذِبَ

الَّذِيْنَ لَا يُؤْمِنُوْنَ بِاٰيٰتِ اللّٰهِ

وَاُولٰٓئِكَ هُمُ الْكٰذِبُوْنَ ۞ مَنْ

كَفَرَ بِاللّٰهِ مِنْ بَعْدِ اِيْمَانِهٖ

اِلَّا مَنْ اُكْرِهَ وَقَلْبُهٗ مُطْمَئِنٌّ

join partners with Allah.

101. When We substitute one revelation for another, - and Allah knows best what He reveals (in stages), - they say, "You are but a forger": but most of them understand not.

102. Say, "The Holy Spirit has brought the revelation from your Lord in Truth, in order to strengthen those who believe, and as a Guide and Glad Tidings to Muslims."

103. We know indeed that they say, "It is a man that teaches him." The tongue of him

هُمْ بِهِ مُشْرِكُوْنَ ۝ وَإِذَا بَدَّلْنَآ

اٰيَةً مَّكَانَ اٰيَةٍ ۙ وَّاللّٰهُ اَعْلَمُ بِمَا

يُنَزِّلُ قَالُوْۤا اِنَّمَاۤ اَنْتَ مُفْتَرٍ ۚ

بَلْ اَكْثَرُهُمْ لَا يَعْلَمُوْنَ ۝ قُلْ

نَزَّلَهٗ رُوْحُ الْقُدُسِ مِنْ رَّبِّكَ

بِالْحَقِّ لِيُثَبِّتَ الَّذِيْنَ اٰمَنُوْا

وَهُدًى وَّبُشْرٰى لِلْمُسْلِمِيْنَ ۝

وَلَقَدْ نَعْلَمُ اَنَّهُمْ يَقُوْلُوْنَ اِنَّمَا

يُعَلِّمُهٗ بَشَرٌ ۗ لِسَانُ الَّذِيْ

righteousness, man or woman, and has Faith, verily, to him will We give a new Life, a life that is good and pure and We will bestow on such their reward according to the best of their actions.

98. When you read the Qur'an, seek Allah's protection from Satan the rejected one.

99. No authority has he over those who believe and put their trust in their Lord.

100. His authority is over those only, who take him as patron and who

صَالِحًا مِّنْ ذَكَرٍ اَوْ اُنْثٰى وَهُوَ

مُؤْمِنٌ فَلَنُحْيِيَنَّهٗ حَيٰوةً طَيِّبَةً ۚ

وَلَنَجْزِيَنَّهُمْ اَجْرَهُمْ بِاَحْسَنِ مَا

كَانُوْا يَعْمَلُوْنَ ۝ فَاِذَا قَرَأْتَ

الْقُرْاٰنَ فَاسْتَعِذْ بِاللّٰهِ مِنَ

الشَّيْطٰنِ الرَّجِيْمِ ۝ اِنَّهٗ لَيْسَ لَهٗ

سُلْطٰنٌ عَلَى الَّذِيْنَ اٰمَنُوْا وَعَلٰى

رَبِّهِمْ يَتَوَكَّلُوْنَ ۝ اِنَّمَا سُلْطٰنُهٗ

عَلَى الَّذِيْنَ يَتَوَلَّوْنَهٗ وَالَّذِيْنَ

with the result that someone's foot may slip after it was firmly planted, and you may have to taste the evil (consequences) of having hindered (men) from the Path of Allah, and a mighty Wrath descend on you.

95. Nor sell the Covenant of Allah for a miserable price: for with Allah is (a prize) far better for you, if you only knew.

96. What is with you must vanish: what is with Allah will endure. And We will certainly bestow, on those who patiently persevere, their reward according to the best of their actions.

97. Whoever works

فَتَزِلَّ قَدَمٌ بَعْدَ ثُبُوتِهَا وَتَذُوقُوا

السُّوْءَ بِمَا صَدَدْتُّمْ عَنْ سَبِيلِ

اللهِ وَلَكُمْ عَذَابٌ عَظِيمٌ ۞ وَلَا

تَشْتَرُوا بِعَهْدِ اللهِ ثَمَنًا قَلِيلًا ۚ

اِنَّمَا عِنْدَ اللهِ هُوَخَيْرٌ لَّكُمْ اِنْ

كُنْتُمْ تَعْلَمُوْنَ ۞ مَا عِنْدَكُمْ يَنْفَدُ

وَمَا عِنْدَ اللهِ بَاقٍ ۚ وَلَنَجْزِيَنَّ

الَّذِيْنَ صَبَرُوْا اَجْرَهُمْ بِاَحْسَنِ

مَا كَانُوْا يَعْمَلُوْنَ ۞ مَنْ عَمِلَ

your oaths to practise deception between yourselves, lest one party should be more numerous than another: for Allah will test you by this; and on the Day of Judgment He will certainly make clear to you (the truth of) that wherein you disagree.

93. If Allah so willed, He could make you all one People: but He leaves straying whom He pleases, and He guides whom He pleases: but you shall certainly be called to account for all your actions.

94. And take not your oaths, to practise deception between your-selves,

اَيْمَانَكُمْ دَخَلًا بَيْنَكُمْ اَنْ تَكُوْنَ

اُمَّةٌ هِيَ اَرْبٰى مِنْ اُمَّةٍ ؕ اِنَّمَا

يَبْلُوْكُمُ اللّٰهُ بِهٖ ؕ وَلَيُبَيِّنَنَّ

لَكُمْ يَوْمَ الْقِيٰمَةِ مَا كُنْتُمْ فِيْهِ

تَخْتَلِفُوْنَ ۝ وَلَوْ شَآءَ اللّٰهُ لَجَعَلَكُمْ

اُمَّةً وَّاحِدَةً وَّلٰكِنْ يُّضِلُّ مَنْ

يَّشَآءُ وَيَهْدِيْ مَنْ يَّشَآءُ ؕ

وَلَتُسْـَٔلُنَّ عَمَّا كُنْتُمْ تَعْمَلُوْنَ ۝

وَلَا تَتَّخِذُوْٓا اَيْمَانَكُمْ دَخَلًا بَيْنَكُمْ

and liberality to kith and kin, and He forbids all shameful deeds, and injustice and rebellion: He instructs you, that you may receive admonition.

91.   Fulfil the Covenant of Allah when you have entered into it, and break not your oaths after you have confirmed them; indeed you have made Allah your surety; for Allah knows all that you do.

92.   And be not like a woman who breaks into untwisted strands the yarn which she has spun, after it has become strong. Nor take

وَإِيتَآئِ ذِى الْقُرْبَى وَيَنْهَى عَنِ

الْفَحْشَآءِ وَالْمُنْكَرِ وَالْبَغْيِ يَعِظُكُمْ

لَعَلَّكُمْ تَذَكَّرُونَ ۞ وَأَوْفُوا بِعَهْدِ

اللهِ إِذَا عَاهَدْتُّمْ وَلَا تَنْقُضُوا

الْأَيْمَانَ بَعْدَ تَوْكِيدِهَا وَقَدْ

جَعَلْتُمُ اللهَ عَلَيْكُمْ كَفِيلًا إِنَّ

اللهَ يَعْلَمُ مَا تَفْعَلُونَ ۞ وَلَا

تَكُونُوا كَالَّتِى نَقَضَتْ غَزْلَهَا

مِنْ بَعْدِ قُوَّةٍ أَنْكَاثًا تَتَّخِذُونَ

the Path of Allah - for them will We add Chastisement to Chastisement; for that they used to spread mischief.

89. On that Day We shall raise from all Peoples a witness against them, from amongst themselves: and We shall bring you as a witness against these (your people): and We have sent down to you the Book explaining all things, a Guide, a Mercy, and Glad Tidings to Muslims.

90. Allah commands justice, the doing of good,

سَبِيلِ اللّٰهِ زِدْنٰهُمْ عَذَابًا

فَوْقَ الْعَذَابِ بِمَا كَانُوْا

يُفْسِدُوْنَ ۝ وَيَوْمَ نَبْعَثُ فِىْ

كُلِّ اُمَّةٍ شَهِيْدًا عَلَيْهِمْ مِّنْ

اَنْفُسِهِمْ وَجِئْنَا بِكَ شَهِيْدًا عَلٰى

هٰٓؤُلَآءِ ۗ وَنَزَّلْنَا عَلَيْكَ الْكِتٰبَ

تِبْيَانًا لِّكُلِّ شَىْءٍ وَّهُدًى

وَّرَحْمَةً وَّبُشْرٰى لِلْمُسْلِمِيْنَ ۝ اِنَّ

اللّٰهَ يَأْمُرُ بِالْعَدْلِ وَالْاِحْسَانِ

then will it in no way be mitigated, nor will they then receive respite.

86. When those who gave partners to Allah will see their "partners", they will say: "Our Lord! These are our 'partners,' those whom we used to invoke besides You." But they will throw back their word at them (and say): "Indeed you are liars!"

87. That Day shall they (openly) show (their) submission to Allah; and all their inventions shall leave them in the lurch.

88. Those who reject Allah and hinder (men) from

فَلَا يُخَفَّفُ عَنْهُمْ وَلَا هُمْ

يُنظَرُونَ ۝ وَإِذَا رَأَى الَّذِينَ

أَشْرَكُوا شُرَكَاءَهُمْ قَالُوا رَبَّنَا

هَٰؤُلَاءِ شُرَكَاؤُنَا الَّذِينَ كُنَّا

نَدْعُوا مِن دُونِكَ فَأَلْقَوْا إِلَيْهِمُ

الْقَوْلَ إِنَّكُمْ لَكَٰذِبُونَ ۝ وَأَلْقَوْا

إِلَى اللَّهِ يَوْمَئِذٍ السَّلَمَ وَضَلَّ

عَنْهُم مَّا كَانُوا يَفْتَرُونَ ۝

الَّذِينَ كَفَرُوا وَصَدُّوا عَنْ

on you, that you may bow to His Will (in Islam).

82.　But if they turn away, your duty is only to preach the clear Message.

83.　They recognise the favours of Allah; then they deny them; and most of them are (creatures) ungrateful.

84.　One Day We shall raise from all Peoples a witness: then will no excuse be accepted from unbelievers, nor will they receive any favours.

85.　When the wrong-doers (actually) see the Chastisement,

عَلَيْكُمْ لَعَلَّكُمْ تُسْلِمُونَ ۝

فَإِنْ تَوَلَّوْا فَإِنَّمَا عَلَيْكَ

الْبَلَاغُ الْمُبِينُ ۝ يَعْرِفُونَ

نِعْمَتَ اللّٰهِ ثُمَّ يُنْكِرُونَهَا

وَأَكْثَرُهُمُ الْكَافِرُونَ ۝ وَيَوْمَ

نَبْعَثُ مِنْ كُلِّ أُمَّةٍ شَهِيدًا

ثُمَّ لَا يُؤْذَنُ لِلَّذِينَ كَفَرُوا

وَلَا هُمْ يُسْتَعْتَبُونَ ۝ وَإِذَا

رَأَى الَّذِينَ ظَلَمُوا الْعَذَابَ

which you find so light (and handy) when you travel and when you stop (in your travels); and out of their wool, and their soft fibres (between wool and hair), and their hair, rich stuff and articles of convenience (to serve you) for a time.

81. It is Allah Who made out of the things He created, some things to give you shade; of the hills He made some for your shelter; He made you garments to protect you from heat, and coats of mail to protect you from your (mutual) violence. Thus does He complete His favours

تَسْتَخِفُّوْنَهَا يَوْمَ ظَعْنِكُمْ

وَيَوْمَ اِقَامَتِكُمْ وَمِنْ اَصْوَافِهَا

وَاَوْبَارِهَا وَاَشْعَارِهَآ اَثَاثًا

وَّمَتَاعًا اِلٰى حِيْنٍ ۞ وَاللّٰهُ

جَعَلَ لَكُمْ مِّمَّا خَلَقَ ظِلٰلًا

وَّجَعَلَ لَكُمْ مِّنَ الْجِبَالِ

اَكْنَانًا وَّجَعَلَ لَكُمْ سَرَابِيْلَ

تَقِيْكُمُ الْحَرَّ وَسَرَابِيْلَ تَقِيْكُمْ

بَأْسَكُمْ كَذٰلِكَ يُتِمُّ نِعْمَتَهٗ

of your mothers when you knew nothing; and He gave you hearing and sight and intelligence and affections: that you may give thanks (to Allah).

79. Do they not look at the birds, held poised in the midst of (the air and) the sky? Nothing holds them up but (the power of) Allah. Verily in this are Signs for those who believe.

80. It is Allah Who made your habitations homes of rest and quiet for you; and made for you, out of the skins of animals, (tents for) dwellings,

أُمَّهَٰتِكُمْ لَا تَعْلَمُونَ شَيْئًا

وَّجَعَلَ لَكُمُ السَّمْعَ وَالْأَبْصَارَ

وَالْأَفْـِٔدَةَ لَعَلَّكُمْ تَشْكُرُونَ ۝

أَلَمْ يَرَوْا إِلَى الطَّيْرِ مُسَخَّرَاتٍ

فِى جَوِّ السَّمَآءِ مَا يُمْسِكُهُنَّ

إِلَّا اللّٰهُ إِنَّ فِى ذٰلِكَ لَأَيَٰتٍ

لِّقَوْمٍ يُؤْمِنُونَ ۝ وَاللّٰهُ جَعَلَ

لَكُمْ مِّنْ بُيُوتِكُمْ سَكَنًا وَّجَعَلَ

لَكُمْ مِّنْ جُلُودِ الْأَنْعَامِ بُيُوتًا

any sort; a wearisome burden is he to his master; whichever way he directs him, he brings no good: is such a man equal with one who commands justice, and is on a Straight Way?

77. To Allah belongs the Mystery of the heavens and the earth. And the Decision of the Hour (of Judgment) is as the twinkling of an eye, or even quicker: for Allah has power over all things.

78. It is He Who brought you forth from the wombs

شَىْءٍ ۗ وَّهُوَ كُلٌّ عَلٰى مَوْلِهٖ

أَيْنَمَا يُوَجِّههُّ لَا يَأْتِ بِخَيْرٍ ۗ

هَلْ يَسْتَوِىْ هُوَ ۙ وَمَنْ يَّأْمُرُ

بِالْعَدْلِ ۙ وَهُوَ عَلٰى صِرَاطٍ

مُّسْتَقِيْمٍ ۞ وَلِلّٰهِ غَيْبُ السَّمٰوٰتِ

وَالْاَرْضِ ۗ وَمَاۤ اَمْرُ السَّاعَةِ

اِلَّا كَلَمْحِ الْبَصَرِ اَوْ هُوَ اَقْرَبُ ۗ

اِنَّ اللّٰهَ عَلٰى كُلِّ شَىْءٍ قَدِيْرٌ ۞

وَاللّٰهُ اَخْرَجَكُمْ مِّنْ بُطُوْنِ

for Allah knows, and you know not.

75.   Allah sets forth the parable (of two men: one) a slave under the dominion of another; he has no power of any sort; and (the other) a man on whom We have bestowed goodly favours from Ourselves, and he spends thereof (freely), privately and publicly: are the two equal? (By no means;) praise be to Allah. But most of them understand not.

76.   Allah sets forth (another) parable of two men: one of them dumb, with no power of

اِنَّ اللهَ يَعْلَمُ وَ اَنْتُمْ لَا

تَعْلَمُوْنَ ۞ ضَرَبَ اللهُ مَثَلًا

عَبْدًا مَّمْلُوْكًا لَّا يَقْدِرُ عَلٰى

شَيْءٍ وَّمَنْ رَّزَقْنٰهُ مِنَّا رِزْقًا

حَسَنًا فَهُوَ يُنْفِقُ مِنْهُ سِرًّا

وَّجَهْرًا ۖ هَلْ يَسْتَوٗنَ ۚ اَلْحَمْدُ

لِلّٰهِ ۚ بَلْ اَكْثَرُهُمْ لَا يَعْلَمُوْنَ ۞

وَضَرَبَ اللهُ مَثَلًا رَّجُلَيْنِ

اَحَدُهُمَآ اَبْكَمُ لَا يَقْدِرُ عَلٰى

has made for you mates (and companions) of your own nature, and made for you, out of them, sons and daughters and grandchildren, and provided for you sustenance of the best: will they then believe in vain things, and be ungrateful for Allah's favours? -

73. And worship others than Allah, - such as have no power of providing them, for sustenance, with anything in heavens or earth, and cannot possibly have such power?

74. Invent not similitudes for Allah:

جَعَلَ لَكُمْ مِّنْ اَنْفُسِكُمْ اَزْوَاجًا

وَّجَعَلَ لَكُمْ مِّنْ اَزْوَاجِكُمْ بَنِيْنَ

وَحَفَدَةً وَّرَزَقَكُمْ مِّنَ الطَّيِّبٰتِ

اَفَبِالْبَاطِلِ يُؤْمِنُوْنَ وَبِنِعْمَتِ

اللّٰهِ هُمْ يَكْفُرُوْنَ ۙ وَيَعْبُدُوْنَ

مِنْ دُوْنِ اللّٰهِ مَا لَا يَمْلِكُ

لَهُمْ رِزْقًا مِّنَ السَّمٰوٰتِ

وَالْاَرْضِ شَيْئًا وَّلَا يَسْتَطِيْعُوْنَ ۙ

فَلَا تَضْرِبُوْا لِلّٰهِ الْاَمْثَالَ

Who creates you and takes your souls at death; and of you there are some who are sent back to a feeble age, so that they know nothing after having known (much): for Allah is All-Knowing, All-Powerful.

71. Allah has bestowed His gifts of sustenance more freely on some of you than on others: those more favoured are not going to throw back their gifts to those whom their right hands possess, so as to be equal in that respect. Will they then deny the favours of Allah?

72. And Allah

خَلَقَكُمْ ثُمَّ يَتَوَفَّىٰكُمْ وَمِنْكُمْ

مَّن يُرَدُّ إِلَىٰ أَرْذَلِ الْعُمُرِ لِكَىْ

لَا يَعْلَمَ بَعْدَ عِلْمٍ شَيْئًا ۚ إِنَّ

اللَّهَ عَلِيمٌ قَدِيرٌ ۝ وَاللَّهُ

فَضَّلَ بَعْضَكُمْ عَلَىٰ بَعْضٍ فِي

الرِّزْقِ ۚ فَمَا الَّذِينَ فُضِّلُوا

بِرَآدِّي رِزْقِهِمْ عَلَىٰ مَا مَلَكَتْ

أَيْمَانُهُمْ فَهُمْ فِيهِ سَوَآءٌ ۚ

أَفَبِنِعْمَةِ اللَّهِ يَجْحَدُونَ ۝ وَاللَّهُ

in this also is a Sign for those who are wise.

68. And your Lord taught the Bee to build its cells in hills, on trees, and in (men's) habitations;

69. Then to eat of all the produce (of the earth), and find with skill the spacious paths of its Lord: there issues from within their bodies a drink of varying colours, wherein is healing for men: verily in this is a Sign for those who give thought.

70. It is Allah

فِىْ ذٰلِكَ لَاٰيَةً لِّقَوْمٍ يَّعْقِلُوْنَ ۞

وَ اَوْحٰى رَبُّكَ اِلَى النَّحْلِ اَنِ

اتَّخِذِىْ مِنَ الْجِبَالِ بُيُوْتًا وَّمِنَ

الشَّجَرِ وَمِمَّا يَعْرِشُوْنَ ۞ ثُمَّ

كُلِىْ مِنْ كُلِّ الثَّمَرٰتِ فَاسْلُكِىْ

سُبُلَ رَبِّكِ ذُلُلًا ۗ يَخْرُجُ مِنْ

بُطُوْنِهَا شَرَابٌ مُّخْتَلِفٌ اَلْوَانُهٗ

فِيْهِ شِفَآءٌ لِّلنَّاسِ ۗ اِنَّ فِىْ ذٰلِكَ

لَاٰيَةً لِّقَوْمٍ يَّتَفَكَّرُوْنَ ۞ وَ اللّٰهُ

to the earth after its death: verily in this is a Sign for those who listen.

66. And verily in cattle (too) will you find an instructive Sign. From what is within their bodies between excretions and blood, We produce, for your drink, milk, pure and agreeable to those who drink it.

67. And from the fruit of the date-palm and the vine, you get out strong drinks and wholesome food; behold,

بِهِ الْأَرْضَ بَعْدَ مَوْتِهَا ۗ

اِنَّ فِيْ ذٰلِكَ لَاٰيَةً لِّقَوْمٍ

يَّسْمَعُوْنَ ۞ وَاِنَّ لَكُمْ فِي

الْأَنْعَامِ لَعِبْرَةً ۗ نُّسْقِيْكُمْ مِّمَّا

فِيْ بُطُوْنِهٖ مِنْۢ بَيْنِ فَرْثٍ

وَّدَمٍ لَّبَنًا خَالِصًا سَآئِغًا

لِّلشّٰرِبِيْنَ ۞ وَمِنْ ثَمَرٰتِ

النَّخِيْلِ وَالْأَعْنَابِ تَتَّخِذُوْنَ

مِنْهُ سَكَرًا وَّرِزْقًا حَسَنًا ۗ اِنَّ

is the Fire, and they will be the first to be hastened on into it!

63. By Allah, We (also) sent (Our Apostles) to Peoples before you but Satan made, (to the wicked), their own acts seem alluring: he is also their patron today, but they shall have a most grievous Chastisement.

64. And We sent down the Book to you for the express purpose, that you should make clear to them those things in which they differ, and that it should be a guide and a mercy to those who believe.

65. And Allah sends down rain from the skies, and gives therewith life

النَّاسَ وَأَنَّهُمْ مُّفْرَطُونَ ۝ تَاللَّهِ

لَقَدْ أَرْسَلْنَا إِلَى أُمَمٍ مِّنْ

قَبْلِكَ فَزَيَّنَ لَهُمُ الشَّيْطَنُ

أَعْمَالَهُمْ فَهُوَ وَلِيُّهُمُ الْيَوْمَ

وَلَهُمْ عَذَابٌ أَلِيمٌ ۝ وَمَآ

أَنْزَلْنَا عَلَيْكَ الْكِتَبَ إِلَّا لِتُبَيِّنَ

لَهُمُ الَّذِى اخْتَلَفُوا فِيهِ وَهُدًى

وَرَحْمَةً لِّقَوْمٍ يُّؤْمِنُونَ ۝ وَاللَّهُ

أَنْزَلَ مِنَ السَّمَآءِ مَآءً فَأَحْيَا

for He is the Exalted in Power, full of Wisdom.

61. If Allah were to punish men for their wrong-doing, He would not leave, on the (earth), a single living creature: but He gives them respite for a stated Term: when their Term expires, they would not be able to delay (the punishment) for a single hour, just as they would not be able to advance it (for a single hour).

62. They attribute to Allah what they hate (for themselves), and their tongues assert the falsehood that all good things are for themselves: without doubt for them

وَهُوَ الْعَزِيزُ الْحَكِيمُ ۝ وَلَوْ

يُؤَاخِذُ اللَّهُ النَّاسَ بِظُلْمِهِمْ مَّا

تَرَكَ عَلَيْهَا مِنْ دَآبَّةٍ وَّلَٰكِنْ

يُؤَخِّرُهُمْ إِلَىٰٓ أَجَلٍ مُّسَمًّى ۚ

فَإِذَا جَآءَ أَجَلُهُمْ لَا يَسْتَأْخِرُونَ

سَاعَةً وَّلَا يَسْتَقْدِمُونَ ۝

وَيَجْعَلُونَ لِلَّهِ مَا يَكْرَهُونَ

وَتَصِفُ أَلْسِنَتُهُمُ الْكَذِبَ أَنَّ

لَهُمُ الْحُسْنَىٰ لَا جَرَمَ أَنَّ لَهُمُ

daughters for Allah! - Glory be to Him! - and for themselves (sons,- the issue) they desire!

58. When news is brought to one of them, of (the birth of) a female (child), his face darkens, and he is filled with inward grief!

59. With shame does he hide himself from his people, because of the bad news he has had! Shall he retain it on (sufferance and) contempt, or bury it in the dust? Ah! What an evil (choice) they decide on?

60. To those who believe not in the Hereafter, applies the similitude of evil: to Allah applies the highest similitude:

لِلّٰهِ الْبَنٰتِ سُبْحٰنَهٗ ۙ وَلَهُمْ مَّا
يَشْتَهُوْنَ ۞ وَاِذَا بُشِّرَ اَحَدُهُمْ
بِالْاُنْثٰى ظَلَّ وَجْهُهٗ مُسْوَدًّا
وَّهُوَ كَظِيْمٌ ۞ يَتَوَارٰى مِنَ الْقَوْمِ
مِنْ سُوْٓءِ مَا بُشِّرَ بِهٖ ؕ اَيُمْسِكُهٗ
عَلٰى هُوْنٍ اَمْ يَدُسُّهٗ فِى
التُّرَابِ ؕ اَلَا سَآءَ مَا يَحْكُمُوْنَ ۞
لِلَّذِيْنَ لَا يُؤْمِنُوْنَ بِالْاٰخِرَةِ
مَثَلُ السَّوْءِ ۚ وَلِلّٰهِ الْمَثَلُ الْاَعْلٰى ؕ

you have no good thing but is from Allah: and moreover, when you are touched by distress, unto Him you cry with groans;

54.   Yet, when He removes the distress from you, behold! some of you turn to other gods to join with their Lord -

55.   (As if) to show their ingratitude for the favours we have bestowed on them! Then enjoy (your brief day): but soon will you know (your folly)!

56.   And they (even) assign, to things they do not know, a portion out of that which We have bestowed for their sustenance! By Allah, you shall certainly be called to account for your false inventions.

57.   And they assign

بِكُمْ مِنْ نِعْمَةٍ فَمِنَ اللّٰهِ

ثُمَّ إِذَا مَسَّكُمُ الضُّرُّ فَإِلَيْهِ

تَجْـَٔرُوْنَ ۞ ثُمَّ إِذَا كَشَفَ الضُّرَّ

عَنْكُمْ إِذَا فَرِيْقٌ مِّنْكُمْ بِرَبِّهِمْ

يُشْرِكُوْنَ ۞ لِيَكْفُرُوْا بِمَاۤ اٰتَيْنٰهُمْ

فَتَمَتَّعُوْا فَسَوْفَ تَعْلَمُوْنَ ۞

وَيَجْعَلُوْنَ لِمَا لَا يَعْلَمُوْنَ نَصِيْبًا

مِّمَّا رَزَقْنٰهُمْ تَاللّٰهِ لَتُسْـَٔلُنَّ

عَمَّا كُنْتُمْ تَفْتَرُوْنَ ۞ وَيَجْعَلُوْنَ

all that is in the heavens and on earth, whether moving (living) creatures or the Angels: for none are arrogant (before their Lord).

50. They all revere their Lord, high above them, and they do all that they are commanded.

51. Allah has said: "Take not (for worship) two gods: for He is just One Allah: then fear Me (and Me alone)."

52. To Him belongs whatever is in the heavens and on earth, and to Him is duty due always: then will you fear other than Allah?

53. And

مَا فِى السَّمٰوٰتِ وَمَا فِى الْأَرْضِ

مِنْ دَآبَّةٍ وَّالْمَلٰٓئِكَةُ وَهُمْ لَا

يَسْتَكْبِرُوْنَ ۞ يَخَافُوْنَ رَبَّهُمْ مِّنْ

فَوْقِهِمْ وَيَفْعَلُوْنَ مَا يُؤْمَرُوْنَ ۞

وَقَالَ اللّٰهُ لَا تَتَّخِذُوْٓا اِلٰهَيْنِ

اثْنَيْنِ ۚ اِنَّمَا هُوَ اِلٰهٌ وَّاحِدٌ ۚ

فَاِيَّايَ فَارْهَبُوْنِ ۞ وَلَهٗ مَا فِى

السَّمٰوٰتِ وَالْأَرْضِ وَلَهُ الدِّيْنُ

وَاصِبًا ۚ اَفَغَيْرَ اللّٰهِ تَتَّقُوْنَ ۞ وَمَا

the earth to swallow them up, or that the Wrath will not seize them from directions they little perceive? -

46. Or that He may not call them to account in the midst of their goings to and fro, without a chance of their frustrating Him? -

47. Or that He may not call them to account by a process of slow wastage - for your Lord is indeed full of Kindness and Mercy.

48. Do they not look at Allah's creation, (even) among (inanimate) things, - how their (very) shadows turn round, from the right and the left, prostrating themselves to Allah, and that in the humblest manner?

49. And to Allah does obeisance

اللهُ بِهِمُ الْأَرْضَ أَوْ يَأْتِيَهُمُ

الْعَذَابُ مِنْ حَيْثُ لَا يَشْعُرُونَ ۝

أَوْ يَأْخُذَهُمْ فِي تَقَلُّبِهِمْ فَمَا

هُمْ بِمُعْجِزِينَ ۝ أَوْ يَأْخُذَهُمْ

عَلَى تَخَوُّفٍ فَإِنَّ رَبَّكُمْ لَرَءُوفٌ

رَّحِيمٌ ۝ أَوَلَمْ يَرَوْا إِلَى مَا خَلَقَ

اللهُ مِنْ شَيْءٍ يَتَفَيَّؤُا ظِلَالُهُ

عَنِ الْيَمِينِ وَالشَّمَآئِلِ سُجَّدًا

لِّلَّهِ وَهُمْ دَاخِرُونَ ۝ وَلِلَّهِ يَسْجُدُ

42. (They are) those who persevere in patience, and put their trust on their Lord.

43. And before you also the Apostles We sent were but men, to whom We granted inspiration: if you realise this not, ask of those who possess the Message.

44. (We sent them) with clear Signs and Scriptures and We have sent down unto you (also) the Message; that you may explain clearly to men what is sent for them, and that they may give thought.

45. Do then those who devise evil (plots) feel secure that Allah will not cause

الَّذِينَ صَبَرُوا وَعَلَى رَبِّهِمْ

يَتَوَكَّلُونَ ۞ وَمَآ أَرْسَلْنَا مِن

قَبْلِكَ إِلَّا رِجَالًا نُّوحِي إِلَيْهِمْ

فَسْـَٔلُوٓا أَهْلَ الذِّكْرِ إِن كُنتُمْ

لَا تَعْلَمُونَ ۞ بِالْبَيِّنَٰتِ وَالزُّبُرِ

وَأَنزَلْنَآ إِلَيْكَ الذِّكْرَ لِتُبَيِّنَ

لِلنَّاسِ مَا نُزِّلَ إِلَيْهِمْ وَلَعَلَّهُمْ

يَتَفَكَّرُونَ ۞ أَفَأَمِنَ الَّذِينَ

مَكَرُوا السَّيِّئَاتِ أَن يَخْسِفَ

39. (They must be raised up), in order that He may manifest to them the truth of that wherein they differ, and that the rejecters of Truth may realise that they had indeed (surrendered to) Falsehood.

40. For to anything which We have willed, We but say the word, "Be", and it is.

41. To those who leave their homes in the cause of Allah, after suffering oppression, - We will assuredly give a goodly home in this world; but truly the reward of the Hereafter will be greater. If they only realised (this)!

لِيُبَيِّنَ لَهُمُ الَّذِى يَخْتَلِفُونَ

فِيهِ وَلِيَعْلَمَ الَّذِينَ كَفَرُوٓا

أَنَّهُمْ كَانُوا كَذِبِينَ ۞ إِنَّمَا

قَوْلُنَا لِشَىْءٍ إِذَآ أَرَدْنَهُ أَن

نَّقُولَ لَهُ كُن فَيَكُونُ ۞

وَالَّذِينَ هَاجَرُوا فِى اللهِ مِنۢ

بَعْدِ مَا ظُلِمُوا لَنُبَوِّئَنَّهُمْ فِى

الدُّنْيَا حَسَنَةً وَلَأَجْرُ الْأَخِرَةِ

أَكْبَرُ لَوْ كَانُوا يَعْلَمُونَ ۞

So travel through the earth, and see what was the end of those who denied (the Truth).

37. If you are anxious for their guidance, yet Allah guides not such as He leaves to stray, and there is none to help them.

38. They swear their strongest oaths by Allah, that Allah will not raise up those who die: no, but it is a promise (binding) on Him in truth: but most among mankind realise it not.

الضَّلَلَةُ فَسِيرُوا فِي الْأَرْضِ

فَانْظُرُوا كَيْفَ كَانَ عَاقِبَةُ

الْمُكَذِّبِينَ ۝ إِنْ تَحْرِصْ عَلَى

هُدَاهُمْ فَإِنَّ اللهَ لَا يَهْدِى

مَنْ يُضِلُّ وَمَا لَهُمْ مِّنْ

نَّصِرِينَ ۝ وَأَقْسَمُوا بِاللهِ جَهْدَ

أَيْمَانِهِمْ لَا يَبْعَثُ اللهُ مَنْ

يَمُوتُ ۚ بَلَى وَعْدًا عَلَيْهِ حَقًّا

وَّلَكِنَّ أَكْثَرَ النَّاسِ لَا يَعْلَمُونَ ۝

aught but Him - neither we nor our fathers, - nor should we have prescribed prohibitions other than His." So did those who went before them. But what is the mission of Apostles but to preach the clear Message?

36. For We assuredly sent amongst every People an Apostle, (with the Command), "Serve Allah, and eschew Evil": of the People were some whom Allah guided, and some on whom error became inevitably (established).

مِنْ دُوْنِهٖ مِنْ شَىْءٍ نَّحْنُ

وَ لَاۤ اٰبَاۤؤُنَا وَ لَا حَرَّمْنَا مِنْ

دُوْنِهٖ مِنْ شَىْءٍ ۚ كَذٰلِكَ فَعَلَ

الَّذِيْنَ مِنْ قَبْلِهِمْ ۚ فَهَلْ عَلَى

الرُّسُلِ اِلَّا الْبَلٰغُ الْمُبِيْنُ ۞ وَلَقَدْ

بَعَثْنَا فِيْ كُلِّ اُمَّةٍ رَّسُوْلًا

اَنِ اعْبُدُوا اللّٰهَ وَ اجْتَنِبُوا

الطَّاغُوْتَ ۚ فَمِنْهُمْ مَّنْ هَدَى

اللّٰهُ وَ مِنْهُمْ مَّنْ حَقَّتْ عَلَيْهِ

they (ungodly) wait until the Angels come to them, or there comes the Command of your Lord (for their doom)? So did those who went before them. But Allah wronged them not: nay, they wronged their own souls.

34. But the evil results of their deeds overtook them, and that very (Wrath) at which they had scoffed hemmed them in.

35. The worshippers of false gods say: "If Allah had so willed, we should not have worshipped

يَنْظُرُونَ اِلَّا اَنْ تَاْتِيَهُمُ
الْمَلَٰٓئِكَةُ اَوْ يَاْتِيَ اَمْرُ رَبِّكَ
كَذٰلِكَ فَعَلَ الَّذِيْنَ مِنْ
قَبْلِهِمْ وَمَا ظَلَمَهُمُ اللّٰهُ وَلٰكِنْ
كَانُوْۤا اَنْفُسَهُمْ يَظْلِمُوْنَ ۝
فَاَصَابَهُمْ سَيِّاٰتُ مَا عَمِلُوْا
وَحَاقَ بِهِمْ مَّا كَانُوْا بِه
يَسْتَهْزِءُوْنَ ۝ وَقَالَ الَّذِيْنَ
اَشْرَكُوْا لَوْ شَآءَ اللّٰهُ مَا عَبَدْنَا

is good in this world, and the Home of the Hereafter is even better and excellent indeed is the Home of the righteous, -

31. Gardens of Eternity which they will enter: beneath them flow (pleasant) rivers: they will have therein all that they wish: thus does Allah reward the righteous, -

32. (Namely) those whose lives the Angels take in a state of purity, saying (to them), "Peace be on you; enter you the Garden, because of (the good) which you did (in the world)."

33. Do

الدُّنْيَا حَسَنَةٌ ۚ وَلَدَارُ الْآخِرَةِ
خَيْرٌ ۚ وَلَنِعْمَ دَارُ الْمُتَّقِينَ ۝
جَنَّاتُ عَدْنٍ يَدْخُلُونَهَا تَجْرِى
مِنْ تَحْتِهَا الْأَنْهَارُ ۖ لَهُمْ فِيهَا
مَا يَشَاءُونَ ۚ كَذَٰلِكَ يَجْزِى
اللَّهُ الْمُتَّقِينَ ۝ الَّذِينَ تَتَوَفَّاهُمُ
الْمَلَائِكَةُ طَيِّبِينَ ۙ يَقُولُونَ
سَلَامٌ عَلَيْكُمُ ادْخُلُوا الْجَنَّةَ
بِمَا كُنْتُمْ تَعْمَلُونَ ۝ هَلْ

28. "(Namely) those whose lives the Angels take in a state of wrong-doing to their own souls." Then would they offer submission (with the pretence), "We did no evil (knowingly)." (The Angels will reply,) "No, but verily Allah knows all that you did;

29. "So enter the gates of Hell, to dwell therein. Thus evil is indeed is the abode of the arrogant."

30. To the righteous (when) it is said, "What is it that your Lord has revealed?" They say, "All that is good." To those who do good, there

الَّذِيْنَ تَتَوَفَّىٰهُمُ الْمَلٰٓئِكَةُ

ظَالِمِيْٓ اَنْفُسِهِمْ ۖ فَاَلْقَوُا السَّلَمَ

مَا كُنَّا نَعْمَلُ مِنْ سُوْٓءٍ ۚ بَلٰٓى

اِنَّ اللّٰهَ عَلِيْمٌۢ بِمَا كُنْتُمْ

تَعْمَلُوْنَ ۞ فَادْخُلُوْٓا اَبْوَابَ جَهَنَّمَ

خٰلِدِيْنَ فِيْهَا ۚ فَلَبِئْسَ مَثْوَى

الْمُتَكَبِّرِيْنَ ۞ وَقِيْلَ لِلَّذِيْنَ

اتَّقَوْا مَاذَآ اَنْزَلَ رَبُّكُمْ ۚ قَالُوْا

خَيْرًا ۚ لِلَّذِيْنَ اَحْسَنُوْا فِيْ هٰذِهِ

but Allah took their structures from their foundations, and the roof fell down on them from above; and the Wrath seized them from directions they did not perceive.

27. Then, on the Day of Judgment, He will cover them with shame, and say: "Where are My 'partners' concerning whom you used to dispute (with the godly)?" Those endued with knowledge will say: "This Day, indeed, are the unbelievers covered with shame and misery, -

فَاَتَى اللهُ بُنْيَانَهُمْ مِّنَ

الْقَوَاعِدِ فَخَرَّ عَلَيْهِمُ السَّقْفُ

مِنْ فَوْقِهِمْ وَاَتٰهُمُ الْعَذَابُ

مِنْ حَيْثُ لَا يَشْعُرُوْنَ ۝ ثُمَّ

يَوْمَ الْقِيٰمَةِ يُخْزِيْهِمْ وَيَقُوْلُ

اَيْنَ شُرَكَآءِيَ الَّذِيْنَ كُنْتُمْ

تُشَآقُّوْنَ فِيْهِمْ ۚ قَالَ الَّذِيْنَ

اُوْتُوا الْعِلْمَ اِنَّ الْخِزْيَ

الْيَوْمَ وَالسُّوْٓءَ عَلَى الْكٰفِرِيْنَ ۝

Allah does know what they conceal, and what they reveal: verily He loves not the arrogant.

24. When it is said to them, "What is it that your Lord has revealed?" They say, "Tales of the ancients!"

25. Let them bear, on the Day of Judgment, their own burdens in full, and also (something) of the burdens of those without knowledge, whom they misled. Alas, how grievous the burdens they will bear!

26. Those before them did also plot (against Allah's Way):

أَنَّ اللهَ يَعْلَمُ مَا يُسِرُّونَ

وَمَا يُعْلِنُونَ إِنَّهُ لَا يُحِبُّ

الْمُسْتَكْبِرِينَ ۝ وَإِذَا قِيلَ لَهُمْ

مَاذَا أَنْزَلَ رَبُّكُمْ قَالُوٓا

أَسَاطِيرُ الْأَوَّلِينَ ۝ لِيَحْمِلُوٓا

أَوْزَارَهُمْ كَامِلَةً يَوْمَ الْقِيَٰمَةِ

وَمِنْ أَوْزَارِ الَّذِينَ يُضِلُّونَهُم

بِغَيْرِ عِلْمٍ أَلَا سَآءَ مَا يَزِرُونَ ۝

قَدْ مَكَرَ الَّذِينَ مِن قَبْلِهِمْ

would you be able to number them: for Allah is Oft-Forgiving, Most Merciful.

19.   And Allah does know what you conceal, and what you reveal.

20.   Those whom they invoke besides Allah create nothing and are themselves created.

21.   (They are things) dead, lifeless: nor do they know when they will be raised up.

22.   Your Allah is One Allah: as to those who believe not in the Hereafter, their hearts refuse to know, and they are arrogant.

23.   Undoubtedly

تُحْصُوهَا ۗ اِنَّ اللهَ لَغَفُوْرٌ

رَّحِيْمٌ ۝ وَاللهُ يَعْلَمُ مَا تُسِرُّوْنَ

وَمَا تُعْلِنُوْنَ ۝ وَالَّذِيْنَ يَدْعُوْنَ

مِنْ دُوْنِ اللهِ لَا يَخْلُقُوْنَ شَيْئًا

وَّهُمْ يُخْلَقُوْنَ ۝ اَمْوَاتٌ غَيْرُ اَحْيَاءٍ ۚ

وَمَا يَشْعُرُوْنَ ۙ اَيَّانَ يُبْعَثُوْنَ ۝

اِلٰهُكُمْ اِلٰهٌ وَّاحِدٌ ۚ فَالَّذِيْنَ لَا

يُؤْمِنُوْنَ بِالْاٰخِرَةِ قُلُوْبُهُمْ مُّنْكِرَةٌ

وَّهُمْ مُّسْتَكْبِرُوْنَ ۝ لَا جَرَمَ

to wear; and you see the ships therein that plough the waves, that you may seek (thus) of the Bounty of Allah and that you may be grateful.

15. And He has set up on the earth mountains standing firm, lest it should shake with you; and rivers and roads; that you may guide yourselves;

16. And marks and sign-posts; and by the stars (men) guide themselves.

17. Is then He Who creates like one that creates not? Will you not receive admonition?

18. If you would count up the favours of Allah, never

تَلْبَسُوْنَهَا ۚ وَتَرَى الْفُلْكَ مَوَاخِرَ

فِيْهِ وَلِتَبْتَغُوْا مِنْ فَضْلِهٖ

وَلَعَلَّكُمْ تَشْكُرُوْنَ ۝ وَأَلْقٰى فِى

الْأَرْضِ رَوَاسِىَ أَنْ تَمِيْدَ

بِكُمْ وَأَنْهَارًا وَّسُبُلًا لَّعَلَّكُمْ

تَهْتَدُوْنَ ۝ وَعَلٰمٰتٍ ۚ وَبِالنَّجْمِ

هُمْ يَهْتَدُوْنَ ۝ أَفَمَنْ يَّخْلُقُ

كَمَنْ لَّا يَخْلُقُ ۚ أَفَلَا تَذَكَّرُوْنَ ۝

وَإِنْ تَعُدُّوْا نِعْمَةَ اللّٰهِ لَا

for those who give thought.

12. He has made subject to you the night and the day; the sun and the moon; and the stars are in subjection by His Command: verily in this are Signs for men who are wise.

13. And the things on this earth which He has multiplied in varying colours (and qualities): verily in this is a Sign for men who celebrate the praises of Allah (in gratitude).

14. It is He Who has made the sea subject, that you may eat thereof flesh that is fresh and tender, and that you may extract therefrom ornaments

لِّقَوْمٍ يَّتَفَكَّرُوْنَ ۝ وَسَخَّرَ لَكُمُ

الَّيْلَ وَالنَّهَارَ وَالشَّمْسَ وَالْقَمَرَ

وَالنُّجُوْمُ مُسَخَّرَاتٌ بِأَمْرِهٖ ۚ اِنَّ

فِيْ ذٰلِكَ لَاٰيٰتٍ لِّقَوْمٍ يَّعْقِلُوْنَ ۝

وَمَا ذَرَاَ لَكُمْ فِى الْاَرْضِ مُخْتَلِفًا

اَلْوَانُهٗ ۗ اِنَّ فِيْ ذٰلِكَ لَاٰيَةً

لِّقَوْمٍ يَّذَّكَّرُوْنَ ۝ وَهُوَ الَّذِيْ

سَخَّرَ الْبَحْرَ لِتَأْكُلُوْا مِنْهُ لَحْمًا

طَرِيًّا وَّتَسْتَخْرِجُوْا مِنْهُ حِلْيَةً

and use for show; and He has created (other) things of which you have no knowledge.

9. And unto Allah leads straight the Way, but there are ways that turn aside: if Allah had willed, He could have guided all of you.

10. It is He Who sends down rain from the sky: from it you drink, and out of it (grows) the vegetation on which you feed your cattle.

11. With it He produces for you corn, olives, date-palms, grapes and every kind of fruit: verily in this is a Sign

وَزِينَةً ۚ وَيَخْلُقُ مَا لَا تَعْلَمُونَ ۝

وَعَلَى اللّٰهِ قَصْدُ السَّبِيلِ

وَمِنْهَا جَآئِرٌ ۚ وَلَوْ شَآءَ لَهَدَىٰكُمْ

أَجْمَعِينَ ۝ هُوَ الَّذِىٓ أَنْزَلَ مِنَ

السَّمَآءِ مَآءً ۖ لَكُمْ مِنْهُ شَرَابٌ

وَّمِنْهُ شَجَرٌ فِيهِ تُسِيمُونَ ۝

يُنْۢبِتُ لَكُمْ بِهِ الزَّرْعَ وَالزَّيْتُونَ

وَالنَّخِيلَ وَالْأَعْنَابَ وَمِنْ كُلِّ

الثَّمَرَٰتِ ۗ إِنَّ فِى ذَٰلِكَ لَآيَةً

from a sperm-drop; and behold this same (man) becomes an open disputer!

5.   And cattle He has created for you (men): from them you derive warmth, and numerous benefits, and of their (meat) you eat.

6.   And you have a sense of pride and beauty in them as you drive them home in the evening, and as you lead them forth to pasture in the morning.

7.   And they carry your heavy loads to lands that you could not (otherwise) reach except with souls distressed: for your Lord is indeed Most Kind, Most Merciful.

8.   And (He has created) horses, mules, and donkeys, for you to ride

مِنْ نُّطْفَةٍ فَإِذَا هُوَ خَصِيمٌ

مُّبِينٌ ۝ وَالْأَنْعَامَ خَلَقَهَا لَكُمْ

فِيهَا دِفْءٌ وَّمَنَافِعُ وَمِنْهَا

تَأْكُلُونَ ۝ وَلَكُمْ فِيهَا جَمَالٌ حِينَ

تُرِيحُونَ وَحِينَ تَسْرَحُونَ ۝

وَتَحْمِلُ أَثْقَالَكُمْ إِلَى بَلَدٍ لَّمْ

تَكُونُوا بَالِغِيهِ إِلَّا بِشِقِّ الْأَنْفُسِ

إِنَّ رَبَّكُمْ لَرَءُوفٌ رَّحِيمٌ ۝ وَالْخَيْلَ

وَالْبِغَالَ وَالْحَمِيرَ لِتَرْكَبُوهَا

An-Nahl (The Bee)

Bismillahir-Rahmanir-Rahim

1. (Inevitable) comes (to pass) the Command of Allah: seek you not then to hasten it: Glory to Him, and far is He above having the partners they ascribe unto Him!

2. He does send down His Angels with inspiration of His Command, to such of His servants as He pleases, (saying): "Warn (man) that there is no god but I: so do your duty unto Me."

3. He has created the heavens and the earth with truth. Far is He above having the partners they ascribe to Him!

4. He has created man

بِسْمِ اللهِ الرَّحْمٰنِ الرَّحِيمِ

اَتٰى اَمْرُ اللهِ فَلَا تَسْتَعْجِلُوهُ

سُبْحٰنَهٗ وَتَعٰلٰى عَمَّا يُشْرِكُونَ ۝

يُنَزِّلُ الْمَلٰٓئِكَةَ بِالرُّوحِ مِنْ

اَمْرِهٖ عَلٰى مَنْ يَّشَآءُ مِنْ

عِبَادِهٖۤ اَنْ اَنْذِرُوۤا اَنَّهٗ لَآ

اِلٰهَ اِلَّاۤ اَنَا فَاتَّقُونِ ۝ خَلَقَ

السَّمٰوٰتِ وَالْاَرْضَ بِالْحَقِّ تَعٰلٰى

عَمَّا يُشْرِكُونَ ۝ خَلَقَ الْاِنْسَانَ

what you are comman-ded, and turn away from those who join false gods with Allah.

95. For sufficient are We unto you against those who scoff,

96. Those who adopt, with Allah, another god: but soon will they come to know.

97. We do indeed know how your heart is distressed at what they say.

98. But celebrate the praises of your Lord, and be of those who prostrate themselves in adoration.

99. And serve your Lord until there come unto you the Hour that is Certain.

بِمَا تُؤْمَرُ وَأَعْرِضْ عَنِ

الْمُشْرِكِينَ ۞ إِنَّا كَفَيْنَاكَ

الْمُسْتَهْزِئِينَ ۞ الَّذِينَ يَجْعَلُونَ

مَعَ اللهِ إِلَهًا آخَرَ فَسَوْفَ

يَعْلَمُونَ ۞ وَلَقَدْ نَعْلَمُ أَنَّكَ

يَضِيقُ صَدْرُكَ بِمَا يَقُولُونَ ۞

فَسَبِّحْ بِحَمْدِ رَبِّكَ وَكُنْ

مِّنَ السَّاجِدِينَ ۞ وَاعْبُدْ رَبَّكَ

حَتَّى يَأْتِيَكَ الْيَقِينُ ۞

88. Strain not your eyes. (Wistfully) at what We have bestowed on certain classes of them, nor grieve over them: but lower your wing (in gentleness) to the believers.

89. And say: "I am indeed he that warns openly and without ambiguity," -

90. (Of just such wrath) as We sent down on those who divided (Scripture into arbitrary parts), -

91. (So also on such) as have made Qur'an into shreds (as they please).

92. Therefore, by the Lord, We will, of a surety, call them to account,

93. For all their deeds.

94. Therefore expound openly

لَا تَمُدَّنَّ عَيْنَيْكَ إِلَى مَا

مَتَّعْنَا بِهِ أَزْوَاجًا مِّنْهُمْ

وَلَا تَحْزَنْ عَلَيْهِمْ وَاخْفِضْ

جَنَاحَكَ لِلْمُؤْمِنِينَ ۞ وَقُلْ

إِنِّي أَنَا النَّذِيرُ الْمُبِينُ ۞

كَمَا أَنزَلْنَا عَلَى الْمُقْتَسِمِينَ ۞

الَّذِينَ جَعَلُوا الْقُرْآنَ عِضِينَ ۞

فَوَرَبِّكَ لَنَسْأَلَنَّهُمْ أَجْمَعِينَ ۞

عَمَّا كَانُوا يَعْمَلُونَ ۞ فَاصْدَعْ

(their) edifices, (feeling them-selves) secure.

83. But the (mighty) Blast seized them of a morning,

84. And of no avail to them was all that they did (with such art and care)!

85. We created not the heavens, the earth, and all between them, but for just ends. And the Hour is surely coming (when this will be manifest). So overlook (any human faults) with gracious forgiveness.

86. For verily it is your Lord Who is the Master-Creator, Knowing all things.

87. And We have bestowed upon you the Seven Oft-Repeated (Verses) and the Grand Qur'an.

بُيُوتًا اٰمِنِيْنَ ۞ فَاَخَذَتْهُمُ الصَّيْحَةُ

مُصْبِحِيْنَ ۞ فَمَاۤ اَغْنٰى عَنْهُمۡ

مَّا كَانُوْا يَكْسِبُوْنَ ۞ وَ خَلَقْنَا

السَّمٰوٰتِ وَالْاَرْضَ وَمَا بَيْنَهُمَاۤ

اِلَّا بِالْحَقِّ ۗ وَاِنَّ السَّاعَةَ لَاٰتِيَةٌ

فَاصْفَحِ الصَّفْحَ الْجَمِيْلَ ۞ اِنَّ

رَبَّكَ هُوَ الْخَلّٰقُ الْعَلِيْمُ ۞

وَلَقَدْ اٰتَيْنٰكَ سَبْعًا مِّنَ

الْمَثَانِيْ وَالْقُرْاٰنَ الْعَظِيْمَ ۞

this are Signs for those who by tokens do understand.

76. And the (cities were) right on the high-road.

77. Behold! In this is a Sign for those who believed.

78. And the Companions of the Wood were also wrong-doers;

79. So We exacted retribution from them. They were both on an open highway, plain to see.

80. The Companions of the Rocky Tract also rejected the Apostles:

81. We sent them Our Sings, but they persisted in turning away from them.

82. Out of the mountains did they hew

ذٰلِكَ لَاٰيٰتٍ لِّلْمُتَوَسِّمِيْنَ ۝ وَاِنَّهَا

لَبِسَبِيْلٍ مُّقِيْمٍ ۝ اِنَّ فِيْ ذٰلِكَ

لَاٰيَةً لِّلْمُؤْمِنِيْنَ ۝ وَاِنْ كَانَ

اَصْحٰبُ الْاَيْكَةِ لَظٰلِمِيْنَ ۝

فَانْتَقَمْنَا مِنْهُمْ ۚ وَاِنَّهُمَا لَبِاِمَامٍ

مُّبِيْنٍ ۝ وَلَقَدْ كَذَّبَ اَصْحٰبُ

الْحِجْرِ الْمُرْسَلِيْنَ ۝ وَاٰتَيْنٰهُمْ

اٰيٰتِنَا فَكَانُوْا عَنْهَا مُعْرِضِيْنَ ۝

وَكَانُوْا يَنْحِتُوْنَ مِنَ الْجِبَالِ

"These are my guests: disgrace me not:"

69. "But fear Allah, and shame me not."

70. They said: "Did we not forbid you (to speak) for all and sundry?"

71. He said: "There are my daughters (to marry), if you must act (so)."

72. Verily, by your life (O Prophet), in their wild intoxication, they wander in distraction, to and fro.

73. But the (mighty) Blast overtook them before morning,

74. And We turned (the cities) upside down, and rained down on them brimstones hard as baked clay.

75. Behold! In

هٰؤُلَاءِ ضَيْفِى فَلَا تَفْضَحُونِ ۞

وَاتَّقُوا اللَّهَ وَلَا تُخْزُونِ ۞ قَالُوٓا

أَوَلَمْ نَنْهَكَ عَنِ الْعٰلَمِينَ ۞

قَالَ هٰؤُلَاءِ بَنٰتِىٓ اِنْ كُنْتُمْ

فٰعِلِينَ ۞ لَعَمْرُكَ اِنَّهُمْ لَفِى

سَكْرَتِهِمْ يَعْمَهُونَ ۞ فَأَخَذَتْهُمُ

الصَّيْحَةُ مُشْرِقِينَ ۞ فَجَعَلْنَا

عَالِيَهَا سَافِلَهَا وَأَمْطَرْنَا عَلَيْهِمْ

حِجَارَةً مِّنْ سِجِّيلٍ ۞ اِنَّ فِى

"Yes, we have come to you to accomplish that of which they doubt."

64. "We have brought to you that which is inevitably due, and assuredly we tell the truth."

65. "Then travel by night with your household, when a portion of the night (yet remains), and do you bring up the rear: let no one amongst you look back, but pass on whither you are ordered."

66. And We made known this decree to him, that the last remnants of those (sinners) should be cut off by the morning.

67. The inhabitants of the city came in (mad) joy (at news of the young men).

68. Lut said:

بَلْ جِئْنَاكَ بِمَا كَانُوْا فِيْهِ

يَمْتَرُوْنَ ۞ وَاَتَيْنَاكَ بِالْحَقِّ وَاِنَّا

لَصَادِقُوْنَ ۞ فَاَسْرِ بِاَهْلِكَ بِقِطْعٍ

مِّنَ الَّيْلِ وَاتَّبِعْ اَدْبَارَهُمْ

وَلَا يَلْتَفِتْ مِنْكُمْ اَحَدٌ وَّامْضُوْا

حَيْثُ تُؤْمَرُوْنَ ۞ وَقَضَيْنَآ اِلَيْهِ

ذٰلِكَ الْاَمْرَ اَنَّ دَابِرَ هٰٓؤُلَآءِ

مَقْطُوْعٌ مُّصْبِحِيْنَ ۞ وَجَآءَ اَهْلُ

الْمَدِيْنَةِ يَسْتَبْشِرُوْنَ ۞ قَالَ اِنَّ

despairs of the Mercy of his Lord, but such as go astray?"

57. Abraham said: "What then is the business on which you (have come), O you Messengers (of Allah)?"

58. They said: "We have been sent to a people (deep) in sin,"

59. "Excepting the adherents of Lut: them we are certainly (charged) to save (from harm), - all -

60. "Except his wife, who, We have ascertained, will be among those who will lag behind."

61. At length when the Messengers arrived among the adherents of Lut,

62. He said: "You appear to be uncommon folk."

63. They said:

يَقْنَطُ مِنْ رَّحْمَةِ رَبِّهٖٓ اِلَّا

الضَّآلُّوْنَ ۞ قَالَ فَمَا خَطْبُكُمْ

اَيُّهَا الْمُرْسَلُوْنَ ۞ قَالُوْٓا اِنَّا

اُرْسِلْنَآ اِلٰى قَوْمٍ مُّجْرِمِيْنَ ۞

اِلَّآ اٰلَ لُوْطٍ ؕ اِنَّا لَمُنَجُّوْهُمْ

اَجْمَعِيْنَ ۞ اِلَّا امْرَاَتَهٗ قَدَّرْنَآ

اِنَّهَا لَمِنَ الْغٰبِرِيْنَ ۞ فَلَمَّا

جَآءَ اٰلَ لُوْطِ الْمُرْسَلُوْنَ ۞ قَالَ

اِنَّكُمْ قَوْمٌ مُّنْكَرُوْنَ ۞ قَالُوْا

My Chastisement will be indeed the most grievous Chastisement.

51. Tell them about the guests of Abraham.

52. When they entered his presence and said, "Peace!" He said, "We feel afraid of you!"

53. They said: "Fear not! We give you glad tidings of a son endowed with wisdom."

54. He said: "Do you give me glad tidings that old age has seized me? Of what, then, is your good news?"

55. They said: "We give your glad tidings in truth: be not then in despair!"

56. He said: "And who

عَذَابِيْ هُوَ الْعَذَابُ الْأَلِيْمُ ۞

وَنَبِّئْهُمْ عَنْ ضَيْفِ اِبْرَاهِيْمَ ۞

اِذْ دَخَلُوْا عَلَيْهِ فَقَالُوْا سَلَامًا

قَالَ اِنَّا مِنْكُمْ وَجِلُوْنَ ۞ قَالُوْا

لَا تَوْجَلْ اِنَّا نُبَشِّرُكَ بِغُلَامٍ

عَلِيْمٍ ۞ قَالَ اَبَشَّرْتُمُوْنِيْ عَلٰى اَنْ

مَّسَّنِيَ الْكِبَرُ فَبِمَ تُبَشِّرُوْنَ ۞

قَالُوْا بَشَّرْنٰكَ بِالْحَقِّ فَلَا

تَكُنْ مِّنَ الْقٰنِطِيْنَ ۞ قَالَ وَمَنْ

44. To it are seven gates: for each of those gates is a (special) class (of sinners) assigned.

45. The righteous (will be) amid Gardens and fountains (of clear-flowing water).

46. (Their greeting will be): "Enter you here in peace and security."

47. And We shall remove from their hearts any lurking sense of injury: (they will be) brothers (joyfully) facing each other on thrones (of dignity).

48. There no sense of fatigue shall touch them, nor shall they (ever) be asked to leave.

49. Tell My servants that I am indeed the Oft-Forgiving, Most Merciful;

50. And that

لَّهَا سَبْعَةُ اَبْوَابٍ ۚ لِكُلِّ بَابٍ

مِّنْهُمْ جُزْءٌ مَّقْسُوْمٌ ۞ اِنَّ

الْمُتَّقِيْنَ فِيْ جَنّٰتٍ وَّعُيُوْنٍ ۞

ادْخُلُوْهَا بِسَلٰمٍ اٰمِنِيْنَ ۞ وَنَزَعْنَا

مَا فِيْ صُدُوْرِهِمْ مِّنْ غِلٍّ

اِخْوَانًا عَلٰى سُرُرٍ مُّتَقٰبِلِيْنَ ۞

لَا يَمَسُّهُمْ فِيْهَا نَصَبٌ وَّمَا هُمْ

مِّنْهَا بِمُخْرَجِيْنَ ۞ نَبِّئْ عِبَادِيْٓ

اَنِّيْٓ اَنَا الْغَفُوْرُ الرَّحِيْمُ ۞ وَاَنَّ

38. "Till the Day of the Time appointed."

39. (Iblis) said: "O my Lord! Because You have put me in the wrong, I will make (wrong) fair-seeming to them on the earth, and I will put them all in the wrong," -

40. "Except your chosen servants among them, sincere and purified (by Your Grace)."

41. (Allah) said: "This (way of My sincere servants) is indeed a way that leads straight to Me."

42. "For over My servants no authority shall you have, except such as put themselves in the wrong and follow you."

43. And verily, Hell is the promised abode for them all!

اِلٰى يَوْمِ الْوَقْتِ الْمَعْلُوْمِ ۞ قَالَ

رَبِّ بِمَآ اَغْوَيْتَنِيْ لَاُزَيِّنَنَّ

لَهُمْ فِى الْاَرْضِ وَلَاُغْوِيَنَّهُمْ

اَجْمَعِيْنَ ۞ اِلَّا عِبَادَكَ مِنْهُمُ

الْمُخْلَصِيْنَ ۞ قَالَ هٰذَا صِرَاطٌ

عَلَيَّ مُسْتَقِيْمٌ ۞ اِنَّ عِبَادِيْ

لَيْسَ لَكَ عَلَيْهِمْ سُلْطٰنٌ اِلَّا

مَنِ اتَّبَعَكَ مِنَ الْغَاوِيْنَ ۞ وَاِنَّ

جَهَنَّمَ لَمَوْعِدُهُمْ اَجْمَعِيْنَ ۞

"O Iblis! What is your reason for not being among those who prostrated themselves?"

33. (Iblis) said: "I am not one to prostrate myself to man, whom You created from sounding clay, from mud moulded into shape."

34. (Allah) said: "Then get you out from here; for you are rejected, accursed."

35. "And the curse shall be on you till the Day of Judgment."

36. (Iblis) said: "O my Lord! Give me then respite till the Day the (dead) are raised."

37. (Allah) said: "Respite is granted to you -"

يَا بْلِيسُ مَا لَكَ اَلَّا تَكُوْنَ

مَعَ السّٰجِدِيْنَ ۝ قَالَ لَمْ اَكُنْ

لِّاَسْجُدَ لِبَشَرٍ خَلَقْتَهٗ مِنْ

صَلْصَالٍ مِّنْ حَمَاٍ مَّسْنُوْنٍ ۝

قَالَ فَاخْرُجْ مِنْهَا فَاِنَّكَ

رَجِيْمٌ ۝ وَّاِنَّ عَلَيْكَ اللَّعْنَةَ

اِلٰى يَوْمِ الدِّيْنِ ۝ قَالَ رَبِّ

فَاَنْظِرْنِيْۤ اِلٰى يَوْمِ يُبْعَثُوْنَ ۝

قَالَ فَاِنَّكَ مِنَ الْمُنْظَرِيْنَ ۝

before, from the fire of a scorching wind.

28. Behold! Your Lord said to the Angels: "I am about to create man, from sounding clay from mud moulded into shape;"

29. "When I have fashioned him (in due proportion) and breathed into him of My spirit, fall you down in obeisance unto him."

30. So the Angels prostrated themselves, all of them together:

31. Not so Iblis: he refused to be among those who prostrated themselves.

32. (Allah) said:

مِنْ قَبْلُ مِنْ نَّارِ السَّمُومِ ۞

وَاِذْ قَالَ رَبُّكَ لِلْمَلٰٓئِكَةِ اِنِّیْ

خَالِقٌ بَشَرًا مِّنْ صَلْصَالٍ

مِّنْ حَمَاٍ مَّسْنُوْنٍ ۞ فَاِذَا

سَوَّيْتُهٗ وَنَفَخْتُ فِيْهِ مِنْ

رُّوْحِیْ فَقَعُوْا لَهٗ سٰجِدِيْنَ ۞

فَسَجَدَ الْمَلٰٓئِكَةُ كُلُّهُمْ

اَجْمَعُوْنَ ۞ اِلَّاۤ اِبْلِيْسَ اَبٰۤى اَنْ

يَّكُوْنَ مَعَ السّٰجِدِيْنَ ۞ قَالَ

the sky, therewith providing you with water (in abundance), though you are not the guardians of its stores.

23.   And verily, it is We Who give life, and Who give death: it is We Who remain inheritors (after all else passes away).

24.   To Us are known those of you who hasten forward, and those who lag behind.

25.   Assuredly it is your Lord Who will gather them together: for He is perfect in Wisdom and Knowledge.

26.   We created man from sounding clay, from mud moulded into shape;

27.   And the Jinn race, We had created

السَّمَآءِ مَآءً فَاَسْقَيْنَاكُمُوهُ وَمَآ اَنْتُمْ

لَهُ بِخَازِنِيْنَ ۞ وَاِنَّا لَنَحْنُ نُحْى

وَنُمِيْتُ وَنَحْنُ الْوَارِثُوْنَ ۞ وَلَقَدْ

عَلِمْنَا الْمُسْتَقْدِمِيْنَ مِنْكُمْ

وَلَقَدْ عَلِمْنَا الْمُسْتَأْخِرِيْنَ

۞ وَاِنَّ رَبَّكَ هُوَ يَحْشُرُهُمْ اِنَّهُ

حَكِيْمٌ عَلِيْمٌ ۞ وَلَقَدْ خَلَقْنَا

الْاِنْسَانَ مِنْ صَلْصَالٍ مِّنْ

حَمَاٍ مَّسْنُوْنٍ ۞ وَالْجَآنَّ خَلَقْنَهُ

that gains a hearing by stealth, is pursued by a flaming fire, bright (to see).

19. And the earth We have spread out (like a carpet); set thereon mountains firm and immovable; and produced therein all kinds of things in due balance.

20. And We have provided therein means of subsistence, - for you and for those for whose sustenance you are not responsible.

21. And there is not a thing but its (sources and) treasures (inexhaustible) are with Us; but We only send down thereof in due and ascertainable measures.

22. And We send the fecundating winds, then cause the rain to descend from

اسْتَرَقَ السَّمْعَ فَأَتْبَعَهُ شِهَابٌ

مُبِينٌ ۝ وَالْأَرْضَ مَدَدْنَاهَا وَأَلْقَيْنَا

فِيهَا رَوَاسِيَ وَأَنْبَتْنَا فِيهَا مِنْ

كُلِّ شَيْءٍ مَوْزُونٍ ۝ وَجَعَلْنَا لَكُمْ

فِيهَا مَعَايِشَ وَمَنْ لَسْتُمْ لَهُ

بِرَازِقِينَ ۝ وَإِنْ مِنْ شَيْءٍ

إِلَّا عِنْدَنَا خَزَائِنُهُ وَمَا نُنَزِّلُهُ

إِلَّا بِقَدَرٍ مَعْلُومٍ ۝ وَأَرْسَلْنَا

الرِّيَاحَ لَوَاقِحَ فَأَنْزَلْنَا مِنَ

the hearts of the sinners

13. That they should not believe in the (Message); but the ways of the ancients have passed away.

14. Even if We opened out to them a gate from heaven, and they were to continue (all day) ascending therein,

15. They would only say: "Our eyes have been intoxicated: no, we have been bewitched by sorcery."

16. It is We Who have set out the zodiacal signs in the heavens, and made them fair-seeming to (all) beholders;

17. And (moreover) We have guarded them from every evil spirit accursed:

18. But any

قُلُوبُ الْمُجْرِمِينَ ۩ لَا يُؤْمِنُونَ

بِهِ وَقَدْ خَلَتْ سُنَّةُ الْأَوَّلِينَ ۩

وَلَوْ فَتَحْنَا عَلَيْهِمْ بَابًا مِنَ

السَّمَاءِ فَظَلُّوا فِيهِ يَعْرُجُونَ ۩

لَقَالُوا إِنَّمَا سُكِّرَتْ أَبْصَارُنَا

بَلْ نَحْنُ قَوْمٌ مَسْحُورُونَ ۩

وَلَقَدْ جَعَلْنَا فِي السَّمَاءِ بُرُوجًا

وَزَيَّنَّاهَا لِلنَّاظِرِينَ ۩ وَحَفِظْنَاهَا مِنْ

كُلِّ شَيْطَانٍ رَجِيمٍ ۩ إِلَّا مَنِ

the Angels to us if it be that you have the Truth?"

8.   We send not the Angels down except for just cause: if they came (to the ungodly), behold! no respite would they have!

9.   We have, without doubt, sent down the Message; and We will assuredly guard it (from corruption).

10.   We did send Apostles before you amongst the religious sects of old:

11.   But never came an Apostle to them but they mocked him.

12.   Even so do We let it creep into

بِالْمَلَٰٓئِكَةِ إِن كُنتَ مِنَ

الصَّٰدِقِينَ ۝ مَا نُنَزِّلُ الْمَلَٰٓئِكَةَ

إِلَّا بِالْحَقِّ وَمَا كَانُوٓا۟ إِذًا

مُّنظَرِينَ ۝ إِنَّا نَحْنُ نَزَّلْنَا

الذِّكْرَ وَإِنَّا لَهُۥ لَحَٰفِظُونَ ۝

وَلَقَدْ أَرْسَلْنَا مِن قَبْلِكَ

فِى شِيَعِ الْأَوَّلِينَ ۝ وَمَا

يَأْتِيهِم مِّن رَّسُولٍ إِلَّا كَانُوا۟ بِهِۦ

يَسْتَهْزِءُونَ ۝ كَذَٰلِكَ نَسْلُكُهُۥ فِى

2. Again and again will those who disbelieve, wish that they had bowed (to Allah's will) in Islam.

3. Leave them alone, to enjoy (the good things of this life) and to please themselves: let (false) hope amuse them: soon will knowledge (undeceive them).

4. Never did We destroy a population that had not a term decreed and assigned beforehand.

5. Neither can a people anticipate its term, nor delay it.

6. They say: "O you to whom the Message is being revealed! Truly you are mad (or possessed)!

7. "Why bring you not

رُبَمَا يَوَدُّ الَّذِينَ كَفَرُوا لَوْ
كَانُوا مُسْلِمِينَ ۝ ذَرْهُمْ يَأْكُلُوا
وَيَتَمَتَّعُوا وَيُلْهِهِمُ الْأَمَلُ فَسَوْفَ
يَعْلَمُونَ ۝ وَمَا أَهْلَكْنَا مِنْ
قَرْيَةٍ إِلَّا وَلَهَا كِتَابٌ مَعْلُومٌ
۝ مَا تَسْبِقُ مِنْ أُمَّةٍ أَجَلَهَا
وَمَا يَسْتَأْخِرُونَ ۝ وَقَالُوا يَا أَيُّهَا
الَّذِي نُزِّلَ عَلَيْهِ الذِّكْرُ
إِنَّكَ لَمَجْنُونٌ ۝ لَوْ مَا تَأْتِينَا

پارہ

رُبَمَا

(۱۴)

PART 15
Subhaanal-Ladhee

until, when they were in the boat, he scuttled it. Said Moses: "Have you scuttled it in order to drown those in it? Truly a strange thing have you done!"

72. He answered: "Did I not tell you that you can have no patience with me?"

73. Moses said: "Rebuke me not for forgetting, nor grieve me by raising difficulties in my case."

74. Then they proceeded: until, when they met a young man, he slew him. Moses said: "Have you slain an innocent person who had slain none? Truly a foul (unheard-of) thing have you done!"

حَتّىٰٓ إِذَا رَكِبَا فِى السَّفِينَةِ خَرَقَهَا

قَالَ أَخَرَقْتَهَا لِتُغْرِقَ أَهْلَهَا لَقَدْ

جِئْتَ شَيْئًا إِمْرًا ۝ قَالَ أَلَمْ أَقُلْ

إِنَّكَ لَن تَسْتَطِيعَ مَعِىَ صَبْرًا ۝

قَالَ لَا تُؤَاخِذْنِى بِمَا نَسِيتُ

وَلَا تُرْهِقْنِى مِنْ أَمْرِى عُسْرًا ۝

فَانطَلَقَا حَتّىٰٓ إِذَا لَقِيَا غُلَامًا فَقَتَلَهُ

قَالَ أَقَتَلْتَ نَفْسًا زَكِيَّةً بِغَيْرِ

نَفْسٍ لَّقَدْ جِئْتَ شَيْئًا نُّكْرًا ۝

66. Moses said to him: "May I follow you, on the footing that you teach me something of the (Higher) Truth which you has been taught?"

67. (The other) said: "Verily you will not be able to have patience with me!"

68. "And how can you have patience about things about which your understanding is not complete?"

69. Moses said: "You will find me, if Allah so will, (truly) patient: nor shall I disobey you in any matter."

70. The other said: "If then you would follow me, ask me no questions about anything until I myself speak to you concerning it."

71. So they both proceeded:

قَالَ لَهٗ مُوسٰى هَلْ اَتَّبِعُكَ عَلٰىٓ

اَنْ تُعَلِّمَنِ مِمَّا عُلِّمْتَ رُشْدًا ۝

قَالَ اِنَّكَ لَنْ تَسْتَطِيعَ مَعِىَ

صَبْرًا ۝ وَكَيْفَ تَصْبِرُ عَلٰى مَا لَمْ

تُحِطْ بِهٖ خُبْرًا ۝ قَالَ سَتَجِدُنِىٓ

اِنْ شَآءَ اللّٰهُ صَابِرًا وَّلَاۤ اَعْصِى

لَكَ اَمْرًا ۝ قَالَ فَاِنِ اتَّبَعْتَنِى

فَلَا تَسْـَٔلْنِى عَنْ شَىْءٍ حَتّٰى

اُحْدِثَ لَكَ مِنْهُ ذِكْرًا ۝ فَانْطَلَقَا

much fatigue at this (stage of) our journey."

63.   He replied: "Did you see (what happened) when we betook ourselves to the rock? I did indeed forget (about) the Fish: none but Satan made me forget to tell (you) about it: it took its course through the sea in a marvellous way!"

64.   Moses said: "That was what we were seeking after:" So they went back on their footsteps, following (the path they had come).

65.   So they found one of Our servants, on whom We had bestowed Mercy from Ourselves and whom We had taught knowledge from Our Own Presence.

مِّن سَفَرِنَا هٰذَا نَصَبًا ۞ قَالَ

اَرَءَيْتَ اِذْ اَوَيْنَآ اِلَى الصَّخْرَةِ

فَاِنِّىْ نَسِيْتُ الْحُوْتَ ۚ وَمَآ اَنْسٰنِيْهُ

اِلَّا الشَّيْطٰنُ اَنْ اَذْكُرَهٗ ۚ وَاتَّخَذَ

سَبِيْلَهٗ فِى الْبَحْرِ ۚ عَجَبًا ۞ قَالَ

ذٰلِكَ مَا كُنَّا نَبْغِ ۚ فَارْتَدَّا عَلٰى

اٰثَارِهِمَا قَصَصًا ۞ فَوَجَدَا عَبْدًا

مِّنْ عِبَادِنَآ اٰتَيْنٰهُ رَحْمَةً مِّنْ

عِنْدِنَا وَعَلَّمْنٰهُ مِنْ لَّدُنَّا عِلْمًا ۞

beyond which they will find no refuge.

59. Such were the populations we destroyed when they committed iniquities; but we fixed an appointed time for their destruction.

60. Behold, Moses said to his attendant, "I will not give up until I reach the junction of the two seas or (until) I spend years and years in travel."

61. But when they reached the Junction, they forgot (about) their Fish, which took its course through the sea (straight) as in a tunnel.

62. When they had passed on (some distance), Moses said to his attendant: "Bring us our early meal; truly we have suffered

يَّجِدُوا مِنْ دُوْنِهٖ مَوْئِلًا ۝ وَتِلْكَ

الْقُرٰى اَهْلَكْنٰهُمْ لَمَّا ظَلَمُوْا

وَجَعَلْنَا لِمَهْلِكِهِمْ مَّوْعِدًا ۝ وَاِذْ

قَالَ مُوْسٰى لِفَتٰىهُ لَاۤ اَبْرَحُ حَتّٰى

اَبْلُغَ مَجْمَعَ الْبَحْرَيْنِ اَوْ اَمْضِيَ

حُقُبًا ۝ فَلَمَّا بَلَغَا مَجْمَعَ بَيْنِهِمَا

نَسِيَا حُوْتَهُمَا فَاتَّخَذَ سَبِيْلَهٗ فِى

الْبَحْرِ سَرَبًا ۝ فَلَمَّا جَاوَزَا قَالَ

لِفَتٰىهُ اٰتِنَا غَدَآءَنَا ۖ لَقَدْ لَقِيْنَا

as a jest.

57. And who does more wrong than one who is reminded of the Signs of his Lord, but turns away from them, forgetting the (deeds) which his hands have sent forth? Verily We have set veils over their hearts lest they should understand this, and over their ears, deafness, if you call them to guidance, even then will they never accept guidance.

58. But your Lord is Most Forgiving, full of Mercy. If He were to call them (at once) to account for what they have earned, then surely He would have hastened their punishment: but they have their appointed time,

هُنُوْا ۞ وَمَنْ اَظْلَمُ مِمَّنْ ذُكِّرَ

بِاٰيٰتِ رَبِّهٖ فَاَعْرَضَ عَنْهَا

وَنَسِيَ مَا قَدَّمَتْ يَدٰهُ ۚ اِنَّا جَعَلْنَا

عَلٰى قُلُوْبِهِمْ اَكِنَّةً اَنْ يَّفْقَهُوْهُ

وَفِيْٓ اٰذَانِهِمْ وَقْرًا ۗ وَاِنْ تَدْعُهُمْ

اِلَى الْهُدٰى فَلَنْ يَّهْتَدُوْٓا اِذًا

اَبَدًا ۞ وَرَبُّكَ الْغَفُوْرُ ذُو الرَّحْمَةِ ۚ

لَوْ يُؤَاخِذُهُمْ بِمَا كَسَبُوْا لَعَجَّلَ

لَهُمُ الْعَذَابَ ۗ بَلْ لَّهُمْ مَّوْعِدٌ لَّنْ

in most things, contentious.

55. And what is there to keep back men from believing, now that Guidance has come to them, nor from praying for forgiveness from their Lord, but that (they ask that) the ways of the ancients be repeated with them, or the Wrath be brought to them face to face?

56. We only send the Apostles to give Glad Tidings and to give warnings; but the unbelievers dispute with vain argument, in order therewith to weaken the Truth, and they treat My Signs and warnings

اَكْثَرَ شَىْءٍ جَدَلًا ۞ وَمَا مَنَعَ

النَّاسَ اَنْ يُّؤْمِنُوْۤا اِذْ جَآءَهُمُ

الْهُدٰى وَيَسْتَغْفِرُوْا رَبَّهُمْ اِلَّاۤ

اَنْ تَاْتِيَهُمْ سُنَّةُ الْاَوَّلِيْنَ اَوْ

يَاْتِيَهُمُ الْعَذَابُ قُبُلًا ۞ وَمَا

نُرْسِلُ الْمُرْسَلِيْنَ اِلَّا مُبَشِّرِيْنَ

وَمُنْذِرِيْنَ وَيُجَادِلُ الَّذِيْنَ

كَفَرُوْا بِالْبَاطِلِ لِيُدْحِضُوْا بِهِ

الْحَقَّ وَاتَّخَذُوْۤا اٰيٰتِيْ وَمَاۤ اُنْذِرُوْا

is it for helpers such as Me to take as lead (men) astray!

52. One Day He will say, "Call on those whom you thought to be My partners," and they will call on them, but they will not listen to them; and We shall make for them a place of common perdition.

53. And the Sinful shall see the Fire and apprehend that they have to fall therein: no means will they find to turn away therefrom.

54. We have explained in detail in this Qur'an, for the benefit of mankind, every kind of similitude: but man is,

كُنْتُ مُتَّخِذَ الْمُضِلِّيْنَ عَضُدًا ۝

وَيَوْمَ يَقُوْلُ نَادُوْا شُرَكَآءِیَ

الَّذِيْنَ زَعَمْتُمْ فَدَعَوْهُمْ فَلَمْ

يَسْتَجِيْبُوْا لَهُمْ وَجَعَلْنَا بَيْنَهُمْ

مَّوْبِقًا ۝ وَرَاَ الْمُجْرِمُوْنَ النَّارَ

فَظَنُّوْٓا اَنَّهُمْ مُّوَاقِعُوْهَا وَلَمْ

يَجِدُوْا عَنْهَا مَصْرِفًا ۝ وَلَقَدْ

صَرَّفْنَا فِيْ هٰذَا الْقُرْاٰنِ لِلنَّاسِ

مِنْ كُلِّ مَثَلٍ ۛ وَكَانَ الْاِنْسَانُ

They will find all that they did, placed before them: and not one will your Lord treat with injustice.

50. Behold! We said to the Angels, "Bow down to Adam": they bowed down except Iblis. He was one of the Jinns, and he broke the Command of his Lord. Will you then take him and his progeny as protectors rather than Me? And they are enemies to you! Evil would be the exchange for the wrong-doers!

51. I called them not to witness the creation of the heavens and the earth, nor (even) their own creation: nor

وَوَجَدُوا مَا عَمِلُوا حَاضِرًا ۚ وَلَا

يَظْلِمُ رَبُّكَ أَحَدًا ۞ وَإِذْ قُلْنَا

لِلْمَلَائِكَةِ اسْجُدُوا لِآدَمَ فَسَجَدُوا

إِلَّا إِبْلِيسَ ۚ كَانَ مِنَ الْجِنِّ

فَفَسَقَ عَنْ أَمْرِ رَبِّهِ ۗ أَفَتَتَّخِذُونَهُ

وَذُرِّيَّتَهُ أَوْلِيَاءَ مِنْ دُونِي وَهُمْ

لَكُمْ عَدُوٌّ ۚ بِئْسَ لِلظَّالِمِينَ بَدَلًا ۞

مَا أَشْهَدْتُّهُمْ خَلْقَ السَّمَاوَاتِ

وَالْأَرْضِ وَلَا خَلْقَ أَنْفُسِهِمْ وَمَا

as a level stretch, and We shall gather them, all together, nor shall We leave out any one of them.

48. And they will be marshalled before your Lord in ranks, (with the announcement), "Now have you come to Us (bare) as We created you first instance; yes, you thought We shall not fulfil the appointment made to you to meet (Us)!":

49. And the Book (of Deeds) will be placed (before you); and you will see the sinful in great terror because of what is (recorded) therein; they will say, "Ah! Woe to us! What a Book is this! It leaves out nothing small or great, but takes account thereof!"

بَارِزَةً وَحَشَرْنَٰهُمْ فَلَمْ نُغَادِرْ مِنْهُمْ

أَحَدًا ۞ وَعُرِضُوا عَلَىٰ رَبِّكَ صَفًّا

لَّقَدْ جِئْتُمُونَا كَمَا خَلَقْنَٰكُمْ أَوَّلَ

مَرَّةٍ بَلْ زَعَمْتُمْ أَلَّن نَّجْعَلَ

لَكُم مَّوْعِدًا ۞ وَوُضِعَ الْكِتَٰبُ

فَتَرَى الْمُجْرِمِينَ مُشْفِقِينَ

مِمَّا فِيهِ وَيَقُولُونَ يَٰوَيْلَتَنَا

مَالِ هَٰذَا الْكِتَٰبِ لَا يُغَادِرُ

صَغِيرَةً وَلَا كَبِيرَةً إِلَّا أَحْصَىٰهَا

to give success.

45. Set forth to them the similitude of the life of this world: It is like the rain which We send down from the skies: the earth's vegetation absorbs it, but soon it becomes dry stubble, which the winds do scatter: it is (only) Allah Who prevails over all things.

46. Wealth and sons are allurements of the life of this world: but the things that endure, good deeds, are best in the sight of your Lord, as rewards, and best as (the foundation for) hopes.

47. One Day We shall remove the mountains, and you will see the earth

عُقْبًا ۞ وَاضْرِبْ لَهُمْ مَّثَلَ الْحَيٰوةِ

الدُّنْيَا كَمَآءٍ أَنْزَلْنٰهُ مِنَ السَّمَآءِ

فَاخْتَلَطَ بِهٖ نَبَاتُ الْأَرْضِ فَأَصْبَحَ

هَشِيْمًا تَذْرُوهُ الرِّيٰحُ ۗ وَكَانَ

اللهُ عَلٰى كُلِّ شَىْءٍ مُّقْتَدِرًا ۞

اَلْمَالُ وَالْبَنُوْنَ زِيْنَةُ الْحَيٰوةِ

الدُّنْيَا ۚ وَالْبٰقِيٰتُ الصّٰلِحٰتُ خَيْرٌ

عِنْدَ رَبِّكَ ثَوَابًا وَّخَيْرٌ أَمَلًا ۞

وَيَوْمَ نُسَيِّرُ الْجِبَالَ وَتَرَى الْأَرْضَ

the water of the garden will run off underground so that you will never be able to find it."

42. So his fruits (and enjoyment) were encompassed (with ruin), and he remained twisting and turning his hands over what he had spent on his property, which had (now) tumbled to pieces to its very foundations, and he could only say, "Woe is me! Would I had never ascribed partners to my Lord and Cherisher!"

43. Nor had he numbers to help him against Allah, nor was he able to deliver himself.

44. There, the (only) protection comes from Allah, the True One. He is the Best to reward, and the Best

مَآؤُهَا غَوْرًا فَلَنْ تَسْتَطِيعَ لَهُ

طَلَبًا ۝ وَأُحِيطَ بِثَمَرِهِ فَأَصْبَحَ

يُقَلِّبُ كَفَّيْهِ عَلَى مَآ أَنْفَقَ

فِيهَا وَهِيَ خَاوِيَةٌ عَلَى عُرُوشِهَا

وَيَقُولُ يَلَيْتَنِي لَمْ أُشْرِكْ بِرَبِّي

أَحَدًا ۝ وَلَمْ تَكُنْ لَّهُ فِئَةٌ

يَنْصُرُونَهُ مِنْ دُونِ اللّٰهِ وَمَا

كَانَ مُنْتَصِرًا ۝ هُنَالِكَ الْوَلَايَةُ

لِلّٰهِ الْحَقِّ هُوَ خَيْرٌ ثَوَابًا وَخَيْرٌ

dust, then out of a sperm-drop, then fashioned you into a man?"

38. "But (I think) for my part that He is Allah, my Lord, and none shall I associate with my Lord."

39. "Why did you not, as you went into your garden, say: 'Allah's Will (be done)! There is no power but with Allah! If you do see me less than you in wealth and sons,"

40. "It may be that my Lord will give me something better than your garden, and that He will send on your garden thunderbolts (by way of reckoning) from heaven, making it (but) slippery sand! -"

41. "Or

تُرَابٍ ثُمَّ مِنْ نُّطْفَةٍ ثُمَّ سَوّٰىكَ

رَجُلًا ۝ لّٰكِنَّا۠ هُوَ اللّٰهُ رَبِّيْ وَلَا

اُشْرِكُ بِرَبِّيْٓ اَحَدًا ۝ وَلَوْلَآ اِذْ

دَخَلْتَ جَنَّتَكَ قُلْتَ مَا شَآءَ اللّٰهُ

لَا قُوَّةَ اِلَّا بِاللّٰهِ ۚ اِنْ تَرَنِ اَنَا

اَقَلَّ مِنْكَ مَالًا وَّوَلَدًا ۝ فَعَسٰى

رَبِّيْٓ اَنْ يُّؤْتِيَنِ خَيْرًا مِّنْ جَنَّتِكَ

وَيُرْسِلَ عَلَيْهَا حُسْبَانًا مِّنَ السَّمَآءِ

فَتُصْبِحَ صَعِيْدًا زَلَقًا ۝ اَوْ يُصْبِحَ

34. (Abundant) was the produce this man had: he said to his companion, in the course of a mutual argument: "More wealth have I than you, and more honour and power in (my following of) men."

35. He went into his garden in a state (of mind) unjust to his soul: he said, "I deem not that this will ever perish,

36. "Nor do I deem that the Hour (of Judgment) will (ever) come: even if I am brought back to my Lord, I shall surely find (there) something better in exchange."

37. His companion said to him, in the course of the argument with him: "Do you deny Him Who created you out of

وَّكَانَ لَهٗ ثَمَرٌ ۚ فَقَالَ لِصَاحِبِهٖ

وَهُوَ يُحَاوِرُهٗٓ اَنَا اَكْثَرُ مِنْكَ مَالًا

وَّاَعَزُّ نَفَرًا ۝ وَدَخَلَ جَنَّتَهٗ وَهُوَ

ظَالِمٌ لِّنَفْسِهٖ ۚ قَالَ مَآ اَظُنُّ اَنْ

تَبِيْدَ هٰذِهٖۤ اَبَدًا ۝ وَّمَآ اَظُنُّ

السَّاعَةَ قَآئِمَةً ۙ وَّلَئِنْ رُّدِدْتُّ اِلٰى

رَبِّيْ لَاَجِدَنَّ خَيْرًا مِّنْهَا مُنْقَلَبًا ۝

قَالَ لَهٗ صَاحِبُهٗ وَهُوَ يُحَاوِرُهٗٓ

اَكَفَرْتَ بِالَّذِيْ خَلَقَكَ مِنْ

and they will wear green garments of fine silk and heavy brocade: they will recline therein on raised thrones. How good the recompense! How beautiful a couch to recline on!

32.   Set forth to them the parable of two men: for one of them We provided two gardens of grape-vines and surrounded them with date palms; in between the two We placed corn-fields.

33.   Each of those gardens brought forth its produce, and failed not in the least therein: in the midst of them We caused a river to flow.

وَيَلْبَسُونَ ثِيَابًا خُضْرًا مِّن سُنْدُسٍ

وَّاسْتَبْرَقٍ مُّتَّكِئِينَ فِيهَا عَلَى

الْأَرَائِكِ ۚ نِعْمَ الثَّوَابُ وَحَسُنَتْ

مُرْتَفَقًا ۞ وَاضْرِبْ لَهُم مَّثَلًا

رَّجُلَيْنِ جَعَلْنَا لِأَحَدِهِمَا جَنَّتَيْنِ

مِنْ أَعْنَابٍ وَّحَفَفْنَهُمَا بِنَخْلٍ

وَّجَعَلْنَا بَيْنَهُمَا زَرْعًا ۞ كِلْتَا

الْجَنَّتَيْنِ آتَتْ أُكُلَهَا وَلَمْ تَظْلِمْ

مِّنْهُ شَيْئًا ۚ وَّفَجَّرْنَا خِلَالَهُمَا نَهَرًا ۞

a Fire whose (smoke and flames), like the walls and roof of a tent, will hem them in: if they implore relief they will be granted water like melted brass, that will scald their faces. How dreadful the drink! How uncomfortable a couch to recline on!

30.　As to those who believe and work righteousness, verily We shall not suffer to perish the reward of any who do a (single) righteous deed.

31.　For them will be Gardens of Eternity; beneath them rivers will flow; they will be adorned therein with bracelets of gold,

لِلظّٰلِمِيْنَ نَارًا ۙ اَحَاطَ بِهِمْ

سُرَادِقُهَا ؕ وَاِنْ يَّسْتَغِيْثُوْا يُغَاثُوْا

بِمَآءٍ كَالْمُهْلِ يَشْوِى الْوُجُوْهَ ؕ

بِئْسَ الشَّرَابُ ؕ وَسَآءَتْ مُرْتَفَقًا ۞

اِنَّ الَّذِيْنَ اٰمَنُوْا وَعَمِلُوا الصّٰلِحٰتِ

اِنَّا لَا نُضِيْعُ اَجْرَ مَنْ اَحْسَنَ

عَمَلًا ۞ اُولٰٓئِكَ لَهُمْ جَنّٰتُ عَدْنٍ

تَجْرِىْ مِنْ تَحْتِهِمُ الْاَنْهٰرُ يُحَلَّوْنَ

فِيْهَا مِنْ اَسَاوِرَ مِنْ ذَهَبٍ

as a refuge other than Him.

28.　And keep your soul content with those who call on their Lord morning and evening, seeking His Face; and let not your eyes pass beyond them, seeking the pomp and glitter of this Life; no obey any whose heart We have permitted to neglect the rem embrance of Us, one who follows his own desires, whose case has gone beyond all bounds.

29.　Say, "The Truth is from your Lord": let him who will believe, and let him who will, reject (it): for the wrong-doers We have prepared

مُلْتَحَدًا ۞ وَاصْبِرْ نَفْسَكَ مَعَ

الَّذِينَ يَدْعُونَ رَبَّهُمْ بِالْغَدَوٰةِ

وَالْعَشِيِّ يُرِيدُونَ وَجْهَهُ وَلَا تَعْدُ

عَيْنَاكَ عَنْهُمْ تُرِيدُ زِينَةَ الْحَيَوٰةِ

الدُّنْيَا وَلَا تُطِعْ مَنْ أَغْفَلْنَا

قَلْبَهُ عَنْ ذِكْرِنَا وَاتَّبَعَ هَوَىٰهُ

وَكَانَ أَمْرُهُ فُرُطًا ۞ وَقُلِ الْحَقُّ

مِنْ رَبِّكُمْ فَمَنْ شَاءَ فَلْيُؤْمِنْ

وَّمَنْ شَاءَ فَلْيَكْفُرْ إِنَّا أَعْتَدْنَا

(even) than this to the right road."

25. So they stayed in their Cave three hundred years, and (some) add nine (more)

26. Say: "Allah knows best how long they stayed: with Him is (the knowledge of) the secrets of the heavens and the earth: how clearly He sees, how finely He hears (everything)! they have no protector other than Him; nor does He share His Command with any person whatsoever."

27. And recite (and teach) what has been revealed to you of the Book of your Lord: none can change His Words, and none will you find

مِنْ هٰذَا رَشَدًا ۞ وَلَبِثُوْا فِيْ

كَهْفِهِمْ ثَلٰثَ مِائَةٍ سِنِيْنَ

وَازْدَادُوْا تِسْعًا ۞ قُلِ اللّٰهُ اَعْلَمُ

بِمَا لَبِثُوْا ۚ لَهٗ غَيْبُ السَّمٰوٰتِ

وَالْاَرْضِ ۚ اَبْصِرْ بِهٖ وَاَسْمِعْ ۚ مَا لَهُمْ

مِّنْ دُوْنِهٖ مِنْ وَّلِيٍّ ۚ وَّلَا يُشْرِكُ

فِيْ حُكْمِهٖ اَحَدًا ۞ وَاتْلُ مَآ اُوْحِيَ

اِلَيْكَ مِنْ كِتَابِ رَبِّكَ ۚ لَا مُبَدِّلَ

لِكَلِمٰتِهٖ ۚ وَلَنْ تَجِدَ مِنْ دُوْنِهٖ

doubtfully guessing at the unknown; (yet others) say they were seven, the dog being the eighth. Say you: "My Lord knoweth best their number; it is but few that know their (real case)." Enter not, therefore, into controversies concerning them, except on a matter that is clear, nor consult any of them about (the affair of) the Sleepers.

23. Nor say of anything, "I shall be sure to do so and so tomorrow" -

24. Except, "If Allah so wills." And call your Lord to mind when you forget, and say, "I hope that my Lord will guide me ever closer

كَلْبُهُمْ رَجْمًا بِالْغَيْبِ وَيَقُولُونَ

سَبْعَةٌ وَّثَامِنُهُمْ كَلْبُهُمْ قُلْ رَّبِّى

أَعْلَمُ بِعِدَّتِهِمْ مَّا يَعْلَمُهُمْ إِلَّا

قَلِيلٌ فَلَا تُمَارِ فِيهِمْ إِلَّا مِرَآءً

ظَاهِرًا وَّلَا تَسْتَفْتِ فِيهِمْ مِّنْهُمْ

أَحَدًا ۞ وَلَا تَقُولَنَّ لِشَاىْءٍ إِنِّى

فَاعِلٌ ذٰلِكَ غَدًا ۞ إِلَّا أَنْ يَّشَاءَ

اللّٰهُ وَاذْكُرْ رَّبَّكَ إِذَا نَسِيتَ وَقُلْ

عَسَى أَنْ يَّهْدِيَنِ رَبِّى لِأَقْرَبَ

in that case you would never attain prosperity."

21. Thus did We make their case known to the people, that they might know that the promise of Allah is true, and that there can be no doubt about the Hour of Judgment. Behold, they disputed among themselves as to their affair. (Some) said, "Construct a building over them": Their Lord knows best about them: those who prevailed over their affair said, "Let us surely build a place of worship over them."

22. (Some) say they were three, the dog being the fourth among them; (others) say they were five, the dog being the sixth, -

تُفْلِحُوْٓا اِذًا اَبَدًا ۞ وَ كَذٰلِكَ

اَعْثَرْنَا عَلَيْهِمْ لِيَعْلَمُوْٓا اَنَّ وَعْدَ

اللّٰهِ حَقٌّ وَّ اَنَّ السَّاعَةَ لَا رَيْبَ

فِيْهَا ۚ اِذْ يَتَنَازَعُوْنَ بَيْنَهُمْ اَمْرَهُمْ

فَقَالُوا ابْنُوْا عَلَيْهِمْ بُنْيَانًا ؕ رَبُّهُمْ

اَعْلَمُ بِهِمْ ؕ قَالَ الَّذِيْنَ غَلَبُوْا

عَلٰٓى اَمْرِهِمْ لَنَتَّخِذَنَّ عَلَيْهِمْ

مَّسْجِدًا ۞ سَيَقُوْلُوْنَ ثَلٰثَةٌ رَّابِعُهُمْ

كَلْبُهُمْ وَيَقُوْلُوْنَ خَمْسَةٌ سَادِسُهُمْ

one of them, "How long have you stayed (here)?" They said, "We have stayed (perhaps) a day, or part of a day." (At length) they (all) said, "Allah (alone) knows best how long you have stayed here ... Now send you one of you with this money of yours to the town: let him find out which is the best food (to be had) and bring some to you, that (you may) satisfy your hunger therewith: and let him behave with care and courtesy, and let him not inform any one about you."

20. "For if they should come upon you, they would stone you or force you to return to their cult, and

قَآئِلٌ مِّنْهُمْ كَمْ لَبِثْتُمْ ۚ قَالُوا

لَبِثْنَا يَوْمًا أَوْ بَعْضَ يَوْمٍ ۚ قَالُوا

رَبُّكُمْ أَعْلَمُ بِمَا لَبِثْتُمْ فَابْعَثُوٓا

أَحَدَكُم بِوَرِقِكُمْ هَٰذِهٖٓ إِلَى الْمَدِينَةِ

فَلْيَنظُرْ أَيُّهَآ أَزْكَىٰ طَعَامًا

فَلْيَأْتِكُم بِرِزْقٍ مِّنْهُ وَلْيَتَلَطَّفْ

وَلَا يُشْعِرَنَّ بِكُمْ أَحَدًا ۝ إِنَّهُمْ

إِن يَظْهَرُوا عَلَيْكُمْ يَرْجُمُوكُمْ

أَوْ يُعِيدُوكُمْ فِي مِلَّتِهِمْ وَلَن

He whom Allah guides is rightly guided; but he whom Allah leaves to stray, - for him will you find no protector to lead him to the Right Way.

18. You will have thought them awake, whilst they were asleep, and We turned them on their right and on their left sides: their dog stretching forth his two fore-legs on the threshold: if you had come up on to them, you would have certainly turned back from them in flight, and would certainly have been filled with terror of them.

19. Such (being their state), we raised them up (from sleep), that they might question each other. Said

يَّهْدِ اللّٰهُ فَهُوَ الْمُهْتَدِ ۚ وَمَنْ

يُّضْلِلْ فَلَنْ تَجِدَ لَهٗ وَلِيًّا

مُّرْشِدًا ۞ وَتَحْسَبُهُمْ اَيْقَاظًا وَّهُمْ

رُقُوْدٌ ۚ وَنُقَلِّبُهُمْ ذَاتَ الْيَمِيْنِ

وَذَاتَ الشِّمَالِ ۖ وَكَلْبُهُمْ بَاسِطٌ

ذِرَاعَيْهِ بِالْوَصِيْدِ ؕ لَوِ اطَّلَعْتَ

عَلَيْهِمْ لَوَلَّيْتَ مِنْهُمْ فِرَارًا

وَّلَمُلِئْتَ مِنْهُمْ رُعْبًا ۞ وَكَذٰلِكَ

بَعَثْنٰهُمْ لِيَتَسَآءَلُوْا بَيْنَهُمْ ؕ قَالَ

16. "When you turn away from them and the things they worship other than Allah, betake yourselves to the Cave: your Lord will shower His mercies on you and disposes of your affair towards comfort and ease."

17. You would have seen the sun, when it rose, declining to the right from their Cave, and when it set, turning away from them to the left, while they lay in the open space in the midst of the Cave. Such are among the Signs of Allah:

كَذِبًا ۞ وَاِذِ اعْتَزَلْتُمُوْهُمْ وَمَا

يَعْبُدُوْنَ اِلَّا اللّٰهَ فَاْوٗۤا اِلَى

الْكَهْفِ يَنْشُرْ لَكُمْ رَبُّكُمْ مِّنْ

رَّحْمَتِهٖ وَيُهَيِّئْ لَكُمْ مِّنْ اَمْرِكُمْ

مِّرْفَقًا ۞ وَتَرَى الشَّمْسَ اِذَا

طَلَعَتْ تَّزٰوَرُ عَنْ كَهْفِهِمْ ذَاتَ

الْيَمِيْنِ وَاِذَا غَرَبَتْ تَّقْرِضُهُمْ

ذَاتَ الشِّمَالِ وَهُمْ فِيْ فَجْوَةٍ

مِّنْهُ ۚ ذٰلِكَ مِنْ اٰيٰتِ اللّٰهِ ۚ مَنْ

their story in truth: they were youths who believed in their Lord, and We advanced them in guidance:

14. We gave strength to their hearts: behold, they stood up and said: "Our Lord is the Lord of the heavens and of the earth: never shall we call upon any god other than Him: if we did, we should indeed have uttered an enormity!

15. "These our people have taken for worship gods other than Him: why do they not bring forward an authority clear (and convincing) for what they do? Who does more wrong than such as invent a falsehood against Allah?

نَبَاهُمْ بِالْحَقِّ اِنَّهُمْ فِتْيَةٌ اٰمَنُوْا

بِرَبِّهِمْ وَزِدْنٰهُمْ هُدًى ۞ وَّرَبَطْنَا

عَلٰى قُلُوْبِهِمْ اِذْ قَامُوْا فَقَالُوْا

رَبُّنَا رَبُّ السَّمٰوٰتِ وَالْاَرْضِ لَنْ

نَّدْعُوَا۟ مِنْ دُوْنِهٖٓ اِلٰهًا لَّقَدْ

قُلْنَاۤ اِذًا شَطَطًا ۞ هٰٓؤُلَاۤءِ قَوْمُنَا

اتَّخَذُوْا مِنْ دُوْنِهٖٓ اٰلِهَةً لَوْلَا

يَاْتُوْنَ عَلَيْهِمْ بِسُلْطٰنٍ بَيِّنٍ فَمَنْ

اَظْلَمُ مِمَّنِ افْتَرٰى عَلَى اللّٰهِ

of the Cave and of the Inscription were wonders among Our Signs?

10.　Behold, the youths betook themselves to the Cave: they said, "Our Lord! Bestow on us Mercy from Yourself, and dispose of our affair for us in the right way!"

11.　Then We draw (a veil) over their ears, for a number of years, in the Cave, (so that they heard not):

12.　Then We roused them, in order to test which of the two parties was best at calculating the term of years they had tarried!

13.　We relate to you

الْكَهْفِ وَ الرَّقِيْمِ كَانُوْا مِنْ

اٰيٰتِنَا عَجَبًا ۞ اِذْ اَوَى الْفِتْيَةُ

اِلَى الْكَهْفِ فَقَالُوْا رَبَّنَآ اٰتِنَا

مِنْ لَّدُنْكَ رَحْمَةً وَّهَيِّئْ لَنَا

مِنْ اَمْرِنَا رَشَدًا ۞ فَضَرَبْنَا

عَلٰٓى اٰذَانِهِمْ فِى الْكَهْفِ سِنِيْنَ

عَدَدًا ۞ ثُمَّ بَعَثْنٰهُمْ لِنَعْلَمَ

اَىُّ الْحِزْبَيْنِ اَحْصٰى لِمَا لَبِثُوْٓا

اَمَدًا ۞ نَحْنُ نَقُصُّ عَلَيْكَ

5. No knowledge have they of such a thing, nor had their fathers. It is a grievous thing that issues from their mouths as a saying what they say is nothing but falsehood!

6. You would only, perchance, fret yourself to death, following after them, in grief, if they believe not in this Message.

7. That which is on earth We have made but as a glittering show for the earth, in order that We may test them - as to which of them are best in conduct.

8. Verily what is on earth We shall make but as dust and dry soil (without growth or herbage).

9. Or do you reflect that the Companions

مَا لَهُمْ بِهٖ مِنْ عِلْمٍ وَّلَا لِاٰبَآئِهِمْ ۚ

كَبُرَتْ كَلِمَةً تَخْرُجُ مِنْ اَفْوَاهِهِمْ ؕ

اِنْ يَّقُوْلُوْنَ اِلَّا كَذِبًا ۝ فَلَعَلَّكَ

بَاخِعٌ نَّفْسَكَ عَلٰۤى اٰثَارِهِمْ اِنْ

لَّمْ يُؤْمِنُوْا بِهٰذَا الْحَدِيْثِ اَسَفًا

اِنَّا جَعَلْنَا مَا عَلَى الْاَرْضِ زِيْنَةً

لَّهَا لِنَبْلُوَهُمْ اَيُّهُمْ اَحْسَنُ عَمَلًا ۝

وَاِنَّا لَجٰعِلُوْنَ مَا عَلَيْهَا صَعِيْدًا

جُرُزًا ؕ اَمْ حَسِبْتَ اَنَّ اَصْحٰبَ

Al-Kahf (The Cave)

Bismillahir-Rahmanir-Rahim

1.   Praise be to Allah, Who has sent to His Servant the Book, and has allowed therein no crookedness:

2.   (He has made it) straight (and clear) in order that He may warn (the godless) of a terrible Punishment from Him, and that He may give Glad Tidings to the believers who work righteous deeds, that they shall have a goodly Reward,

3.   Wherein they shall remain for ever:

4.   Further, that He may warn those (also) who say, "Allah has begotten a son":

سورة الكهف مكية ١١٠ آياتها ١٢ ركوعاتها

بِسْمِ اللهِ الرَّحْمٰنِ الرَّحِيْمِ

اَلْحَمْدُ لِلّٰهِ الَّذِىْ اَنْزَلَ عَلٰى

عَبْدِهِ الْكِتٰبَ وَلَمْ يَجْعَلْ لَّهٗ

عِوَجًا ۜ قَيِّمًا لِّيُنْذِرَ بَأْسًا

شَدِيْدًا مِّنْ لَّدُنْهُ وَيُبَشِّرَ

الْمُؤْمِنِيْنَ الَّذِيْنَ يَعْمَلُوْنَ

الصّٰلِحٰتِ اَنَّ لَهُمْ اَجْرًا حَسَنًا ۙ

مَّاكِثِيْنَ فِيْهِ اَبَدًا ۙ وَّيُنْذِرَ

الَّذِيْنَ قَالُوا اتَّخَذَ اللهُ وَلَدًا ۗ

Allah, or call upon Rahman: by
whatever name you call upon
Him, (it is well): for to Him
belong the Most Beautiful
Names. Neither speak your
Prayer aloud, nor speak it in a low
tone, but seek a middle course
between."

111. Say: "Praise be to Allah,
Who begets no son, and has no
partner in (His) dominion: nor
(needs) He any to protect Him
from humiliation: yes, magnify
Him for His greatness and
glory!"

اللّٰهَ اَوِ ادْعُوا الرَّحْمٰنَ ؕ اَیًّا مَّا

تَدْعُوْا فَلَهُ الْاَسْمَآءُ الْحُسْنٰی ۚ

وَلَا تَجْهَرْ بِصَلَاتِكَ وَلَا تُخَافِتْ

بِهَا وَابْتَغِ بَیْنَ ذٰلِكَ سَبِیْلًا ۝

وَقُلِ الْحَمْدُ لِلّٰهِ الَّذِیْ لَمْ

یَتَّخِذْ وَلَدًا وَّلَمْ یَكُنْ لَّهٗ

شَرِیْكٌ فِی الْمُلْكِ وَلَمْ یَكُنْ

لَّهٗ وَلِیٌّ مِّنَ الذُّلِّ وَكَبِّرْهُ

تَكْبِیْرًا ۝

men at intervals: We have revealed it by stages.

107. Say: "Whether you believe in it or not, it is true that those who were given knowledge beforehand, when it is recited to them, fall down on their faces in humble prostration,

108. "And they say: 'Glory to our Lord! Truly has the promise of our Lord been fulfilled!'"

109. They fall down on their faces in tears, and it increases their (earnest) humility.

110. Say: "Call upon

النَّاسِ عَلَى مُكْثٍ وَّنَزَّلْنٰهُ

تَنْزِيْلًا ۞ قُلْ اٰمِنُوْا بِهٖ اَوْلَا

تُؤْمِنُوْا ۗ اِنَّ الَّذِيْنَ اُوْتُوا الْعِلْمَ

مِنْ قَبْلِهٖ اِذَا يُتْلٰى عَلَيْهِمْ

يَخِرُّوْنَ لِلْاَذْقَانِ سُجَّدًا ۞

وَّيَقُوْلُوْنَ سُبْحٰنَ رَبِّنَا اِنْ

كَانَ وَعْدُ رَبِّنَا لَمَفْعُوْلًا ۞

وَيَخِرُّوْنَ لِلْاَذْقَانِ يَبْكُوْنَ

وَيَزِيْدُهُمْ خُشُوْعًا ۩ قُلِ ادْعُوا

O Pharaoh, to be one doomed to destruction!"

103. So he resolved to remove them from the face of the earth: but We did drown him and all who were with him.

104. And We said thereafter to the Children of Israel, "Dwell securely in the land (of promise)": but when the second of the warnings came to pass, We gathered you together in a mingled crowd.

105. We sent down the (Qur'an) in Truth, and in Truth has it descended: and We sent you but to give Glad Tidings and to warn (sinners).

106. (It is) a Qur'an which We have divided (into parts from time to time), in order that you might recite it to

يُّفِرْعَوْنُ مَثْبُوْرًا ۞ فَاَرَادَ اَنْ

يَّسْتَفِزَّهُمْ مِّنَ الْاَرْضِ فَاَغْرَقْنٰهُ

وَمَنْ مَّعَهٗ جَمِيْعًا ۙ۞ وَّ قُلْنَا مِنْ

بَعْدِهٖ لِبَنِیْۤ اِسْرَآءِیْلَ اسْكُنُوا

الْاَرْضَ فَاِذَا جَآءَ وَعْدُ الْاٰخِرَةِ

جِئْنَا بِكُمْ لَفِيْفًا ؕ۞ وَبِالْحَقِّ

اَنْزَلْنٰهُ وَبِالْحَقِّ نَزَلَ ؕ وَمَاۤ

اَرْسَلْنٰكَ اِلَّا مُبَشِّرًا وَّ نَذِيْرًا ۞

وَقُرْاٰنًا فَرَقْنٰهُ لِتَقْرَاَهٗ عَلَی

the Mercy of my Lord, behold,
you would keep them back, for
fear of spending them: for man is
(every) niggardly!"

101. To Moses We did give Nine
Clear Sings: ask the Children of
Israel: when he came to them,
Pharaoh said to him: "O Moses! I
consider you, indeed, to have
been worked upon by sorcery!"

102. Moses said, "You knows
well that these things have been
sent down by none but the Lord
of the heavens and the earth as
eye-opening evidence: and I
consider you indeed,

رَحْمَةِ رَبِّى إِذًا لَّاَمْسَكْتُمْ

خَشْيَةَ الْاِنْفَاقِ ۖ وَكَانَ الْاِنْسَانُ

قَتُوْرًا ۟ وَلَقَدْ اٰتَيْنَا مُوْسٰى

تِسْعَ اٰيٰتٍ بَيِّنٰتٍ فَسْـَٔلْ بَنِىْٓ

اِسْرَآءِيْلَ اِذْ جَآءَهُمْ فَقَالَ لَهٗ

فِرْعَوْنُ اِنِّىْ لَاَظُنُّكَ يٰمُوْسٰى

مَسْحُوْرًا ۟ قَالَ لَقَدْ عَلِمْتَ مَاۤ

اَنْزَلَ هٰٓؤُلَآءِ اِلَّا رَبُّ السَّمٰوٰتِ

وَالْاَرْضِ بَصَآئِرَ ۚ وَاِنِّىْ لَاَظُنُّكَ

98. That is their recompense, because they rejected Our Signs, and said, "When we are reduced to bones and broken dust, should we really be raised up (to be) a new Creation?"

99. See they not that Allah, Who created the heavens and the earth, has power to create the like of them (anew)? Only He has decreed a term appointed, of which there is no doubt. But the unjust refuse (to receive it) except with ingratitude.

100. Say: "If you had control of the Treasures of

ذٰلِكَ جَزَآؤُهُمْ بِأَنَّهُمْ كَفَرُوا

بِـَٔايٰتِنَا وَقَالُوٓا ءَاِذَا كُنَّا عِظَامًا

وَّرُفَاتًا ءَاِنَّا لَمَبْعُوثُونَ خَلْقًا

جَدِيدًا ۞ اَوَلَمْ يَرَوْا اَنَّ اللهَ

الَّذِى خَلَقَ السَّمٰوٰتِ وَالْاَرْضَ

قَادِرٌ عَلٰٓى اَنْ يَّخْلُقَ مِثْلَهُمْ

وَجَعَلَ لَهُمْ اَجَلًا لَّا رَيْبَ فِيْهِ

فَاَبَى الظّٰلِمُونَ اِلَّا كُفُورًا ۞

قُلْ لَّوْ اَنْتُمْ تَمْلِكُونَ خَزَآئِنَ

from the heavens an Angel for an Apostle."

96. Say: "Enough is Allah for a Witness between me and you: for He is Well Acquainted with His servants, and He sees (all things).

97. It is he whom Allah guides, that is on true Guidance; but he whom He leaves astray - for such will you find no protector besides Him. On the Day of Judgment We shall gather, them together, prone on their faces, blind, dumb, and deaf: their abode will be Hell: every time it shows abatement, We shall increase for them the fierceness of the Fire.

مِنَ السَّمَاءِ مَلَكًا رَّسُوْلًا ۞

قُلْ كَفٰى بِاللّٰهِ شَهِيْدًا بَيْنِيْ

وَبَيْنَكُمْ ۗ اِنَّهٗ كَانَ بِعِبَادِهٖ خَبِيْرًۢا

بَصِيْرًا ۞ وَمَنْ يَّهْدِ اللّٰهُ فَهُوَ

الْمُهْتَدِ ۚ وَمَنْ يُّضْلِلْ فَلَنْ تَجِدَ

لَهُمْ اَوْلِيَآءَ مِنْ دُوْنِهٖ ۗ وَنَحْشُرُهُمْ

يَوْمَ الْقِيٰمَةِ عَلٰى وُجُوْهِهِمْ عُمْيًا

وَّبُكْمًا وَّصُمًّا ۗ مَأْوٰىهُمْ جَهَنَّمُ ۗ

كُلَّمَا خَبَتْ زِدْنٰهُمْ سَعِيْرًا ۞

gold, or you mount a ladder right into the skies. No, we shall not even believe in your moun-ting until you send down to us a book that we could read." Say: "Glory to my Lord! Am I not but a man, - an Apostle?"

94. What kept men back from belief when Guidance came to them, was nothing but this: they said, "Has Allah sent a man (like us) to be (His) Apostle?"

95. Say, "If there were settled, on earth, Angels walking about in peace and quiet, We should certainly have sent them down

زُخْرُفٍ اَوْ تَرْقٰى فِى السَّمَآءِ ؕ وَلَنْ

نُّؤْمِنَ لِرُقِيِّكَ حَتّٰى تُنَزِّلَ عَلَيْنَا

كِتٰبًا نَّقْرَؤُهٗ ؕ قُلْ سُبْحَانَ رَبِّىْ

هَلْ كُنْتُ اِلَّا بَشَرًا رَّسُوْلًا ۞

وَمَا مَنَعَ النَّاسَ اَنْ يُّؤْمِنُوۤا اِذْ

جَآءَهُمُ الْهُدٰۤى اِلَّاۤ اَنْ قَالُوۤا

اَبَعَثَ اللّٰهُ بَشَرًا رَّسُوْلًا ۞ قُلْ

لَّوْ كَانَ فِى الْاَرْضِ مَلٰٓئِكَةٌ

يَّمْشُوْنَ مُطْمَئِنِّيْنَ لَنَزَّلْنَا عَلَيْهِمْ

every kind of similitude: yet the greater part of men refuse (to receive it) except with ingratitude!

90. They say: "We shall not believe in you, until you cause a spring to gush forth for us from the earth,

91. "Or (until) you have a garden of date trees and vines, and cause rivers to gush forth in their midst, carrying abundant water;

92. "Or you cause the sky to fall in pieces, as you say (will happen), against us; or you bring Allah and the Angels before (us) face to face:

93. "Or you have a house adorned with

كُلِّ مَثَلٍ ۚ فَاَبٰى اَكْثَرُ النَّاسِ

اِلَّا كُفُوْرًا ۞ وَقَالُوْا لَنْ نُّؤْمِنَ

لَكَ حَتّٰى تَفْجُرَ لَنَا مِنَ الْاَرْضِ

يَنْبُوْعًا ۞ اَوْ تَكُوْنَ لَكَ جَنَّةٌ

مِّنْ نَّخِيْلٍ وَّعِنَبٍ فَتُفَجِّرَ

الْاَنْهٰرَ خِلٰلَهَا تَفْجِيْرًا ۞ اَوْ

تُسْقِطَ السَّمَآءَ كَمَا زَعَمْتَ عَلَيْنَا

كِسَفًا اَوْ تَأْتِىَ بِاللّٰهِ وَالْمَلٰٓئِكَةِ

قَبِيْلًا ۞ اَوْ يَكُوْنَ لَكَ بَيْتٌ مِّنْ

that which We have sent you by inspiration: then would you find none to plead your affair in that matter as against Us, -

87.   Except for Mercy from your Lord: for his bounty is to you (indeed) great.

88.   Say: "If the whole of mankind and Jinns were to gather together to produce the like of this Qur'an, they could not produce the like thereof, even if they backed up each other with help and support.

89.   And We have explained to man, in this Qur'an,

بِالَّذِيْۤ اَوْحَيْنَاۤ اِلَيْكَ ثُمَّ لَا

تَجِدُ لَكَ بِهٖ عَلَيْنَا وَكِيْلًا ۞

اِلَّا رَحْمَةً مِّنْ رَّبِّكَ ؕ اِنَّ فَضْلَهٗ

كَانَ عَلَيْكَ كَبِيْرًا ۞ قُلْ لَّئِنِ

اجْتَمَعَتِ الْاِنْسُ وَالْجِنُّ عَلٰۤى

اَنْ يَّاْتُوْا بِمِثْلِ هٰذَا الْقُرْاٰنِ لَا

يَاْتُوْنَ بِمِثْلِهٖ وَلَوْ كَانَ بَعْضُهُمْ

لِبَعْضٍ ظَهِيْرًا ۞ وَلَقَدْ صَرَّفْنَا

لِلنَّاسِ فِيْ هٰذَا الْقُرْاٰنِ مِنْ

to those who believe: to the unjust it causes nothing but loss after loss.

83. Yet when We bestow Our favours on man, he turns away and becomes remote on his side (instead of coming to Us), and when evil seizes him he gives himself up to despair.

84. Say: "Everyone acts according to his own disposition: but your Lord knows best who it is that is best guided on the Way."

85. They ask you concerning the Spirit (of inspiration). Say: "The Spirit (cometh) by command of my Lord: of knowledge it is only a little that is communicated to you, (O men!)"

86. If it were Our Will, We could take away

لِلْمُؤْمِنِيْنَ ۙ وَلَا يَزِيْدُ الظّٰلِمِيْنَ اِلَّا

خَسَارًا ۞ وَاِذَاۤ اَنْعَمْنَا عَلَى الْاِنْسَانِ

اَعْرَضَ وَنَاٰ بِجَانِبِهٖ ۚ وَاِذَا مَسَّهُ

الشَّرُّ كَانَ يَـُٔوْسًا ۞ قُلْ كُلٌّ يَّعْمَلُ

عَلٰى شَاكِلَتِهٖ ۖ فَرَبُّكُمْ اَعْلَمُ بِمَنْ

هُوَ اَهْدٰى سَبِيْلًا ۞ وَيَسْـَٔلُوْنَكَ

عَنِ الرُّوْحِ ۖ قُلِ الرُّوْحُ مِنْ اَمْرِ

رَبِّيْ وَمَاۤ اُوْتِيْتُمْ مِّنَ الْعِلْمِ اِلَّا

قَلِيْلًا ۞ وَلَئِنْ شِئْنَا لَنَذْهَبَنَّ

carry (Angels') testimony.

79. And as for the night keep awake a part of it as an additional prayer for you, soon will your Lord raise you to a Station of Praise and Glory!

80. Say: "O my Lord! Let my entry be by the Gate of Truth and Honour, and likewise my exit by the Gate of Truth and Honour; and grant me from Your Presence an authority to aid (me)."

81. And say: "Truth has (now) arrived, and Falsehood perished: for Falsehood is (by its nature) bound to perish."

82. We send down (stage by stage) in the Qur'an that which is a healing and a mercy

مَشْهُوْدًا ۞ وَمِنَ الَّيْلِ فَتَهَجَّدْ

بِهٖ نَافِلَةً لَّكَ ۖ عَسٰى اَنْ يَّبْعَثَكَ

رَبُّكَ مَقَامًا مَّحْمُوْدًا ۞ وَقُلْ رَّبِّ

اَدْخِلْنِيْ مُدْخَلَ صِدْقٍ وَّاَخْرِجْنِيْ

مُخْرَجَ صِدْقٍ وَّاجْعَلْ لِّيْ مِنْ

لَّدُنْكَ سُلْطٰنًا نَّصِيْرًا ۞ وَقُلْ

جَآءَ الْحَقُّ وَزَهَقَ الْبَاطِلُ ۚ اِنَّ

الْبَاطِلَ كَانَ زَهُوْقًا ۞ وَنُنَزِّلُ

مِنَ الْقُرْاٰنِ مَا هُوَ شِفَآءٌ وَّرَحْمَةٌ

you would have found none to help you against Us!

76. Their purpose was to scare you off the land, in order to expel you; but in that case they would not have stayed (therein) after you, except for a little while.

77. (This was Our) way with the Apostles We sent before you: you will find no change in Our ways.

78. Establish regular prayers at the sun's decline till the darkness of the night, and the recital of the Qur'an in morning prayer, for the recital in the morning

لَا تَجِدُ لَكَ عَلَيْنَا نَصِيْرًا ۞

وَاِنْ كَادُوْا لَيَسْتَفِزُّوْنَكَ مِنَ

الْاَرْضِ لِيُخْرِجُوْكَ مِنْهَا وَاِذًا لَّا

يَلْبَثُوْنَ خِلٰفَكَ اِلَّا قَلِيْلًا ۞

سُنَّةَ مَنْ قَدْ اَرْسَلْنَا قَبْلَكَ

مِنْ رُّسُلِنَا وَلَا تَجِدُ لِسُنَّتِنَا

تَحْوِيْلًا ۞ اَقِمِ الصَّلٰوةَ لِدُلُوْكِ

الشَّمْسِ اِلٰى غَسَقِ الَّيْلِ وَقُرْاٰنَ

الْفَجْرِ ۚ اِنَّ قُرْاٰنَ الْفَجْرِ كَانَ

in the least.

72. But those who were blind in this world, will be blind in the hereafter, and most astray from the Path.

73. And their purpose was to tempt you away from that which We had revealed unto you, to substitute in our name something quite different; (in that case), behold! they would certainly have made you (their) friend!

74. And had We not given you strength, you would nearly have inclined to them a little.

75. In that case We should have made you taste double portion (of punishment) in this life, and an equal portion in death: moreover

فَتِيلًا ۞ وَمَنْ كَانَ فِىْ هٰذِهٖ

اَعْمٰى فَهُوَ فِى الْاٰخِرَةِ اَعْمٰى

وَاَضَلُّ سَبِيْلًا ۞ وَاِنْ كَادُوْا

لَيَفْتِنُوْنَكَ عَنِ الَّذِىْ اَوْحَيْنَآ

اِلَيْكَ لِتَفْتَرِىَ عَلَيْنَا غَيْرَهٗ ۚ وَاِذًا

لَّا تَّخَذُوْكَ خَلِيْلًا ۞ وَلَوْلَاۤ اَنْ

ثَبَّتْنٰكَ لَقَدْ كِدْتَّ تَرْكَنُ اِلَيْهِمْ

شَيْئًا قَلِيْلًا ۞ اِذًا لَّاَذَقْنٰكَ ضِعْفَ

الْحَيٰوةِ وَضِعْفَ الْمَمَاتِ ثُمَّ

gale to drown you because of your ingratitude, so that you find no helper therein against Us?

70.   We have honoured the sons of Adam; provided them with transport on land and sea; given them for sustenance things good and pure; and conferred on them special favours, above a great part of our creation.

71.   One day We shall call together all human beings with their (respective) Imams: those who are given their record in their right hand will read it (with pleasure), and they will not be dealt with unjustly

الرِّيْحَ فَيُغْرِقَكُمْ بِمَا كَفَرْتُمْ ثُمَّ

لَا تَجِدُوْا لَكُمْ عَلَيْنَا بِهٖ تَبِيْعًا ۝

وَلَقَدْ كَرَّمْنَا بَنِىْ اٰدَمَ وَحَمَلْنٰهُمْ

فِى الْبَرِّ وَالْبَحْرِ وَرَزَقْنٰهُمْ مِّنَ

الطَّيِّبٰتِ وَفَضَّلْنٰهُمْ عَلٰى كَثِيْرٍ

مِّمَّنْ خَلَقْنَا تَفْضِيْلًا ۝ يَوْمَ

نَدْعُوْا كُلَّ اُنَاسٍ بِاِمَامِهِمْ ۚ فَمَنْ

اُوْتِىَ كِتٰبَهٗ بِيَمِيْنِهٖ فَاُولٰٓئِكَ

يَقْرَءُوْنَ كِتٰبَهُمْ وَلَا يُظْلَمُوْنَ

67. When distress seizes you at sea, those that you call upon - besides Himself - leave you in the lurch! But when He brings you back safe to land, you turn away (from Him). Most ungrateful is man!

68. Do you then feel secure that He will not cause you to be swallowed up beneath the Earth when you are on land, or that He will not send against you a violent tornado (with showers of stones) so that you shall find no protector?

69. Or do you feel secure that He will not send you back a second time to sea and send against you a heavy

وَ اِذَا مَسَّكُمُ الضُّرُّ فِى الْبَحْرِ

ضَلَّ مَنْ تَدْعُوْنَ اِلَّا اِيَّاهُ ۚ

فَلَمَّا نَجّٰكُمْ اِلَى الْبَرِّ اَعْرَضْتُمْ ؕ

وَكَانَ الْاِنْسَانُ كَفُوْرًا ۞ اَفَاَمِنْتُمْ

اَنْ يَّخْسِفَ بِكُمْ جَانِبَ الْبَرِّ اَوْ

يُرْسِلَ عَلَيْكُمْ حَاصِبًا ثُمَّ لَا

تَجِدُوْا لَكُمْ وَكِيْلًا ۞ اَمْ اَمِنْتُمْ

اَنْ يُّعِيْدَكُمْ فِيْهِ تَارَةً اُخْرٰى

فَيُرْسِلَ عَلَيْكُمْ قَاصِفًا مِّنَ

those whom you can among them, with your (seductive) voice; make assaults on them with your cavalry and your infantry; mutually share with them wealth and children; and make promises to them." But Satan promises them nothing but deceit.

65. "As for My servants, no authority shall you have over them:" Enough is your Lord for a Disposer of affairs.

66. Your Lord is He that makes the Ship go smoothly for you through the sea, in order that you may seek of His Bounty. For He is unto you Most Merciful.

مَنِ اسْتَطَعْتَ مِنْهُمْ بِصَوْتِكَ

وَاَجْلِبْ عَلَيْهِمْ بِخَيْلِكَ وَرَجِلِكَ

وَشَارِكْهُمْ فِى الْاَمْوَالِ وَالْاَوْلَادِ

وَعِدْهُمْ وَمَا يَعِدُهُمُ الشَّيْطٰنُ

اِلَّا غُرُوْرًا ۞ اِنَّ عِبَادِىْ لَيْسَ

لَكَ عَلَيْهِمْ سُلْطٰنٌ وَكَفٰى بِرَبِّكَ

وَكِيْلًا ۞ رَبُّكُمُ الَّذِىْ يُزْجِىْ لَكُمُ

الْفُلْكَ فِى الْبَحْرِ لِتَبْتَغُوْا مِنْ

فَضْلِهٖ اِنَّهٗ كَانَ بِكُمْ رَحِيْمًا ۞

inordinate transgression!

61.   Behold! We said to the Angels: "Bow down to Adam": they bowed down except Iblis: he said, "Shall I bow down to one whom You did create from clay?"

62.   He said: "Did You see? This is the one whom You have honoured above me! If you will but respite me to the Day of Judgment, I will surely bring his descendants under my sway - all but a few!"

63.   (Allah) said: "Go you away; if any of them follow you, verily Hell will be the recompense of you (all) - an ample recompense.

64.   "Lead to destruction

اِلَّا طُغْيَانًا كَبِيْرًا ۞ وَاِذْ قُلْنَا

لِلْمَلٰٓئِكَةِ اسْجُدُوْا لِاٰدَمَ فَسَجَدُوْٓا

اِلَّآ اِبْلِيْسَ قَالَ ءَاَسْجُدُ لِمَنْ

خَلَقْتَ طِيْنًا ۞ قَالَ اَرَءَيْتَكَ هٰذَا

الَّذِىْ كَرَّمْتَ عَلَىَّ لَئِنْ اَخَّرْتَنِ

اِلٰى يَوْمِ الْقِيٰمَةِ لَاَحْتَنِكَنَّ

ذُرِّيَّتَهٗٓ اِلَّا قَلِيْلًا ۞ قَالَ اذْهَبْ

فَمَنْ تَبِعَكَ مِنْهُمْ فَاِنَّ جَهَنَّمَ

جَزَآؤُكُمْ جَزَآءً مَّوْفُوْرًا ۞ وَاسْتَفْزِزْ

that is written in the (eternal) Record.

59. And We refrain from sending the Signs, only because the men of former generations treated them as false: We sent the she-camel to the Thamud to open their eyes, but they treated her wrongfully: We only send the Signs by way of terror (and warning from evil).

60. Behold! We told you that your Lord does encompass mankind round about: We granted the vision which We showed you, but as a trial for men, - as also the Cursed Tree (mentioned) in the Qur'an: We put terror (and warning) into them, but it only increases their

ذٰلِكَ فِی الْكِتٰبِ مَسْطُوْرًا ۞ وَ مَا

مَنَعَنَاۤ اَنْ نُّرْسِلَ بِالْاٰیٰتِ اِلَّاۤ اَنْ

كَذَّبَ بِهَا الْاَوَّلُوْنَ ۙ وَ اٰتَیْنَا ثَمُوْدَ

النَّاقَةَ مُبْصِرَةً فَظَلَمُوْا بِهَا ۙ وَ مَا

نُرْسِلُ بِالْاٰیٰتِ اِلَّا تَخْوِیْفًا ۞ وَ اِذْ

قُلْنَا لَكَ اِنَّ رَبَّكَ اَحَاطَ بِالنَّاسِ ۙ

وَ مَا جَعَلْنَا الرُّءْیَا الَّتِیْۤ اَرَیْنٰكَ اِلَّا

فِتْنَةً لِّلنَّاسِ وَ الشَّجَرَةَ الْمَلْعُوْنَةَ

فِی الْقُرْاٰنِ ۚ وَ نُخَوِّفُهُمْ ۙ فَمَا یَزِیْدُهُمْ

they have neither the power to remove your troubles from you nor to change them."

57.   Those whom they call upon do desire (for themselves) means of access to their Lord, - even those who are nearest: they hope for His Mercy and fear His Wrath: for the Wrath of your Lord is something to take heed of.

58.   There is not a population but We shall destroy it before the Day of Judgment or punish it with a dreadful Chastisement:

مِّنْ دُوْنِهٖ فَلَا يَمْلِكُوْنَ كَشْفَ

الضُّرِّ عَنْكُمْ وَلَا تَحْوِيْلًا ۞ اُولٰٓئِكَ

الَّذِيْنَ يَدْعُوْنَ يَبْتَغُوْنَ اِلٰى

رَبِّهِمُ الْوَسِيْلَةَ اَيُّهُمْ اَقْرَبُ

وَيَرْجُوْنَ رَحْمَتَهٗ وَيَخَافُوْنَ

عَذَابَهٗ ؕ اِنَّ عَذَابَ رَبِّكَ كَانَ

مَحْذُوْرًا ۞ وَاِنْ مِّنْ قَرْيَةٍ اِلَّا

نَحْنُ مُهْلِكُوْهَا قَبْلَ يَوْمِ الْقِيٰمَةِ

اَوْ مُعَذِّبُوْهَا عَذَابًا شَدِيْدًا ؕ كَانَ

for Satan does sow dissensions among them: for Satan is to man an avowed enemy.

54. It is your Lord that knows you best: if He please, He grants you mercy, or if He please, punishment: We have not sent you to be a disposer of their affairs for them.

55. And it is your Lord that knows best all beings that are in the heavens and on earth: We did bestow on some Prophets more (and other) gifts than on others: and We gave to David (the gift of) the Psalms.

56. Say: "Call on those - besides Him - whom you fancy:

اِنَّ الشَّيْطٰنَ يَنْزَغُ بَيْنَهُمْ اِنَّ

الشَّيْطٰنَ كَانَ لِلْاِنْسَانِ عَدُوًّا

مُّبِيْنًا ۞ رَبُّكُمْ اَعْلَمُ بِكُمْ اِنْ

يَّشَاْ يَرْحَمْكُمْ اَوْ اِنْ يَّشَاْ يُعَذِّبْكُمْ

وَمَاۤ اَرْسَلْنٰكَ عَلَيْهِمْ وَكِيْلًا ۞

وَرَبُّكَ اَعْلَمُ بِمَنْ فِى السَّمٰوٰتِ

وَالْاَرْضِ وَلَقَدْ فَضَّلْنَا بَعْضَ

النَّبِيّٖنَ عَلٰى بَعْضٍ وَّاٰتَيْنَا دَاوٗدَ

زَبُوْرًا ۞ قُلِ ادْعُوا الَّذِيْنَ زَعَمْتُمْ

iron,"

51. "Or any created matter which, in your minds, is hardest (to be raised up), - (yet shall you be raised up)!" Then will they say: "Who will cause us to return?" Say: "He who created you first!" Then will they wag their heads towards you, and say, "When will that be?" Say, "May be it will be quite soon!"

52. "It will be on a Day when He will call you, and you will answer (His call) with (words of) His praise, and you will think that you tarried but a little while!"

53. Say to My servants that they should (only) say those things that are best:

حَدِيْدًا ۙ اَوْ خَلْقًا مِّمَّا يَكْبُرُ

فِيْ صُدُوْرِكُمْ ۚ فَسَيَقُوْلُوْنَ مَنْ

يُّعِيْدُنَا ؕ قُلِ الَّذِيْ فَطَرَكُمْ اَوَّلَ

مَرَّةٍ ۚ فَسَيُنْغِضُوْنَ اِلَيْكَ رُءُوْسَهُمْ

وَيَقُوْلُوْنَ مَتٰى هُوَ ؕ قُلْ عَسٰۤى اَنْ

يَّكُوْنَ قَرِيْبًا ۟ يَوْمَ يَدْعُوْكُمْ

فَتَسْتَجِيْبُوْنَ بِحَمْدِهٖ وَتَظُنُّوْنَ

اِنْ لَّبِثْتُمْ اِلَّا قَلِيْلًا ۟ وَقُلْ

لِّعِبَادِيْ يَقُوْلُوا الَّتِيْ هِيَ اَحْسَنُ

their backs, fleeing (from the Truth).

47. We know best why it is they listen, when they listen to your and when they meet in private conference, behold, the wicked say, "You follow none other than a man bewitched!"

48. See what similes they strike for you: but they have gone astray, and never can they find a way.

49. They say: "What! When we are reduced to bones and dust, should we really be raised up (to be) a new creation?"

50. Say: "(No!) be you stones or

اَدْبَارِهِمْ نُفُوْرًا ۝ نَحْنُ اَعْلَمُ

بِمَا يَسْتَمِعُوْنَ بِهٖٓ اِذْ يَسْتَمِعُوْنَ

اِلَيْكَ وَاِذْهُمْ نَجْوٰٓى اِذْ يَقُوْلُ

الظّٰلِمُوْنَ اِنْ تَتَّبِعُوْنَ اِلَّا رَجُلًا

مَّسْحُوْرًا ۝ اُنْظُرْ كَيْفَ ضَرَبُوْا لَكَ

الْاَمْثَالَ فَضَلُّوْا فَلَا يَسْتَطِيْعُوْنَ

سَبِيْلًا ۝ وَقَالُوْٓا ءَاِذَا كُنَّا عِظَامًا

وَّرُفَاتًا ءَاِنَّا لَمَبْعُوْثُوْنَ خَلْقًا

جَدِيْدًا ۝ قُلْ كُوْنُوْا حِجَارَةً اَوْ

there is not a thing but celebrates His praise; and yet you understand not how they declare His glory! verily He is Oft-For-bearing, Most Forgiving!

45. When you do recite the Qur'an, We put, between you and those who believe not in the Hereafter, a veil invisible:

46. And We put coverings over their hearts (and minds) lest they should understand the Qur'an, and deafness into their ears: when you do commemorate your Lord and Him alone in the Qur'an, they turn on

وَمَنْ فِيْهِنَّ ۚ وَاِنْ مِّنْ شَىْءٍ اِلَّا

يُسَبِّحُ بِحَمْدِهٖ وَلٰكِنْ لَّا تَفْقَهُوْنَ

تَسْبِيْحَهُمْ ۗ اِنَّهٗ كَانَ حَلِيْمًا غَفُوْرًا ۞

وَاِذَا قَرَأْتَ الْقُرْاٰنَ جَعَلْنَا بَيْنَكَ

وَبَيْنَ الَّذِيْنَ لَا يُؤْمِنُوْنَ بِالْاٰخِرَةِ

حِجَابًا مَّسْتُوْرًا ۞ وَّجَعَلْنَا عَلٰى

قُلُوْبِهِمْ اَكِنَّةً اَنْ يَّفْقَهُوْهُ وَفِىْ

اٰذَانِهِمْ وَقْرًا ۗ وَاِذَا ذَكَرْتَ رَبَّكَ

فِى الْقُرْاٰنِ وَحْدَهٗ وَلَّوْا عَلٰى

daughters among the Angels? Truly you utter a most dreadful saying!

41. We have explained (things) in various (ways) in this Qur'an, in order that they may receive admonition, but it only increases their flight (from the Truth)!

42. Say: "If there had been (other) gods with Him, as they say, - behold, they would certainly have sought out a way to the Lord of the Throne!"

43. Glory to Him! He is high above all that they say! - Exalted and Great (beyond measure)!

44. The seven heavens and the earth, and all beings therein, declare His glory:

مِنَ الْمَلٰٓئِكَةِ اِنَاثًا ؕ اِنَّكُمْ

لَتَقُوْلُوْنَ قَوْلًا عَظِيْمًا ۰ وَلَقَدْ

صَرَّفْنَا فِىْ هٰذَا الْقُرْاٰنِ لِيَذَّكَّرُوْا ؕ

وَمَا يَزِيْدُهُمْ اِلَّا نُفُوْرًا ۰ قُلْ لَّوْ

كَانَ مَعَهٗۤ اٰلِهَةٌ كَمَا يَقُوْلُوْنَ

اِذًا لَّابْتَغَوْا اِلٰى ذِى الْعَرْشِ

سَبِيْلًا ۰ سُبْحٰنَهٗ وَتَعٰلٰى عَمَّا

يَقُوْلُوْنَ عُلُوًّا كَبِيْرًا ۰ تُسَبِّحُ

لَهُ السَّمٰوٰتُ السَّبْعُ وَالْاَرْضُ

37. Nor walk on the earth with insolence: for you can not rend the earth asunder, nor reach the mountains in height.

38. Of all such things the evil is hateful in the sight of your Lord.

39. These are among the (pre-cepts of) wisdom, which your Lord has revealed to you. Take not, with Allah, another object of worship, lest you should be thrown into Hell, blame-worthy and rejected.

40. Has then your Lord (O Pagans!) preferred for you sons, and taken for Himself

وَلَا تَمْشِ فِى الْاَرْضِ مَرَحًا

اِنَّكَ لَنْ تَخْرِقَ الْاَرْضَ وَلَنْ

تَبْلُغَ الْجِبَالَ طُوْلًا ۞ كُلُّ

ذٰلِكَ كَانَ سَيِّئُهٗ عِنْدَ رَبِّكَ

مَكْرُوْهًا ۞ ذٰلِكَ مِمَّآ اَوْحٰى

اِلَيْكَ رَبُّكَ مِنَ الْحِكْمَةِ ۚ وَلَا

تَجْعَلْ مَعَ اللّٰهِ اِلٰهًا اٰخَرَ فَتُلْقٰى

فِى جَهَنَّمَ مَلُوْمًا مَّدْحُوْرًا ۞

اَفَاَصْفٰىكُمْ رَبُّكُمْ بِالْبَنِيْنَ وَاتَّخَذَ

34. Come not near to the orphan's property except to improve it, until he attains the age of full strength; and fulfil (every) engagement, for (every) engagement will be enquired into (on the Day of Reckoning).

35. Give full measure when you measure, and weigh with a balance that is straight: that is the most fitting and the most advantageous in the final determination.

36. And pursue not that of which you have no knowledge; for every act of hearing, or of seeing or of (feeling in) the heart will be enquired into (on the Day of Reckoning).

وَلَا تَقْرَبُوْا مَالَ الْيَتِيْمِ اِلَّا
بِالَّتِىْ هِىَ اَحْسَنُ حَتّٰى يَبْلُغَ
اَشُدَّهٗ ۖ وَاَوْفُوْا بِالْعَهْدِ ۚ اِنَّ الْعَهْدَ
كَانَ مَسْـُٔوْلًا ۞ وَاَوْفُوا الْكَيْلَ اِذَا
كِلْتُمْ وَزِنُوْا بِالْقِسْطَاسِ الْمُسْتَقِيْمِ ؕ
ذٰلِكَ خَيْرٌ وَّاَحْسَنُ تَأْوِيْلًا ۞ وَلَا
تَقْفُ مَا لَيْسَ لَكَ بِهٖ عِلْمٌ ؕ
اِنَّ السَّمْعَ وَالْبَصَرَ وَالْفُؤَادَ كُلُّ
اُولٰٓئِكَ كَانَ عَنْهُ مَسْـُٔوْلًا ۞

31. Kill not your children for fear of want: We shall provide sustenance for them as well as for you. Verily the killing of them is a great sin.

32. Nor come near to adultery: for it is a shameful (deed) and an evil, opening the road (to other evils).

33. Nor take life - which Allah has made sacred - except for just cause. And if anyone is slain wrongfully, We have given his heir authority (to demand Qisas or to forgive): but let him nor exceed bounds in the matter of taking life; for he is helped (by the Law).

تَقْتُلُوٓا اَوْلَادَكُمْ خَشْيَةَ اِمْلَاقٍ

نَحْنُ نَرْزُقُهُمْ وَاِيَّاكُمْ ؕ اِنَّ

قَتْلَهُمْ كَانَ خِطْاً كَبِيْرًا ۝ وَلَا

تَقْرَبُوا الزِّنٓى اِنَّهٗ كَانَ فَاحِشَةً ؕ

وَسَآءَ سَبِيْلًا ۝ وَلَا تَقْتُلُوا

النَّفْسَ الَّتِىْ حَرَّمَ اللّٰهُ اِلَّا

بِالْحَقِّ ؕ وَمَنْ قُتِلَ مَظْلُوْمًا فَقَدْ

جَعَلْنَا لِوَلِيِّهٖ سُلْطَانًا فَلَا يُسْرِفْ

فِّى الْقَتْلِ ؕ اِنَّهٗ كَانَ مَنْصُوْرًا ۝

and the Evil One is to his Lord (himself) ungrateful.

28. And even if you have to turn away from them in pursuit of the Mercy from your Lord which you do expect, yet speak to them a word of easy kindness.

29. Make not your hand tied (like a niggard's) to your neck, nor stretch it forth to its utmost reach, so that you become blameworthy and destitute.

30. Surely your Lord does provide sustenance in abundance for whom He pleases, and He straiten it for whom he pleases, for He knows and regards all His servants.

وَكَانَ الشَّيْطٰنُ لِرَبِّهٖ كَفُوْرًا ۞

وَاِمَّا تُعْرِضَنَّ عَنْهُمُ ابْتِغَآءَ رَحْمَةٍ

مِّنْ رَّبِّكَ تَرْجُوْهَا فَقُلْ لَّهُمْ

قَوْلًا مَّيْسُوْرًا ۞ وَلَا تَجْعَلْ يَدَكَ

مَغْلُوْلَةً اِلٰى عُنُقِكَ وَلَا تَبْسُطْهَا

كُلَّ الْبَسْطِ فَتَقْعُدَ مَلُوْمًا

مَّحْسُوْرًا ۞ اِنَّ رَبَّكَ يَبْسُطُ

الرِّزْقَ لِمَنْ يَّشَآءُ وَيَقْدِرُ اِنَّهٗ

كَانَ بِعِبَادِهٖ خَبِيْرًا بَصِيْرًا ۞ وَلَا

in terms of honour.

24. And, out of kindness, lower to them the wing of humility, and say: "My Lord! Bestow on them Your Mercy even as they cherished me in childhood."

25. Your Lord knows best what is in your hearts: if you do deeds of righteousness, verily He is Most Forgiving to those who turn to Him again and again (in true penitence).

26. And render to the kindred their due rights, as (also) to those in want, and to the wayfarer: but squander not (your wealth) in the manner of a spendthrift.

27. Verily spendthrifts are brothers of the Evil Ones;

قَوْلًا كَرِيمًا ۞ وَاخْفِضْ لَهُمَا

جَنَاحَ الذُّلِّ مِنَ الرَّحْمَةِ وَقُلْ

رَّبِّ ارْحَمْهُمَا كَمَا رَبَّيَانِي صَغِيرًا ۞

رَّبُّكُمْ أَعْلَمُ بِمَا فِي نُفُوسِكُمْ

إِن تَكُونُوا صَالِحِينَ فَإِنَّهُ كَانَ

لِلْأَوَّابِينَ غَفُورًا ۞ وَآتِ ذَا

الْقُرْبَى حَقَّهُ وَالْمِسْكِينَ وَابْنَ

السَّبِيلِ وَلَا تُبَذِّرْ تَبْذِيرًا ۞ إِنَّ

الْمُبَذِّرِينَ كَانُوا إِخْوَانَ الشَّيَاطِينِ

We have bestowed more on some than on others; but verily the Hereafter is more in rank and gradation and more in excellence.

22. Take not with Allah another object of worship; or you (O man!) will sit in disgrace and destitution.

23. Your Lord has decreed that you worship none but Him, and that you be kind to parents. Whether one or both of them attain old age in your life, say not to them a word of contempt, nor repel them, but address them

فَضَّلْنَا بَعْضَهُمْ عَلَىٰ بَعْضٍ ۚ
وَلَلْأَخِرَةُ أَكْبَرُ دَرَجَٰتٍ وَّأَكْبَرُ
تَفْضِيلًا ۞ لَا تَجْعَلْ مَعَ اللَّهِ
إِلَٰهًا ءَاخَرَ فَتَقْعُدَ مَذْمُومًا
مَّخْذُولًا ۞ وَقَضَىٰ رَبُّكَ أَلَّا
تَعْبُدُوٓا إِلَّآ إِيَّاهُ وَبِالْوَٰلِدَيْنِ
إِحْسَٰنًا ۚ إِمَّا يَبْلُغَنَّ عِندَكَ الْكِبَرَ
أَحَدُهُمَآ أَوْ كِلَاهُمَا فَلَا تَقُل لَّهُمَآ
أُفٍّ وَّلَا تَنْهَرْهُمَا وَقُل لَّهُمَا

18. If any do wish for the transitory things (of this life), We readily grant them - such things as We will, to such person as We will: in the end have We provided Hell for them: they will burn therein, disgraced and rejected.

19. Those who do wish for the (things of) the Hereafter, and strive therefor with all due striving, and have Faith, - they are the ones whose striving is acceptable (to Allah).

20. Of the bounties of your Lord We bestow freely on all - these as well as those: the bounties of your Lord are not closed (to anyone)

21. See how

مَنْ كَانَ يُرِيْدُ الْعَاجِلَةَ عَجَّلْنَا

لَهٗ فِيْهَا مَا نَشَآءُ لِمَنْ نُّرِيْدُ

ثُمَّ جَعَلْنَا لَهٗ جَهَنَّمَ يَصْلٰىهَا

مَذْمُوْمًا مَّدْحُوْرًا ۝ وَمَنْ اَرَادَ

الْاٰخِرَةَ وَسَعٰى لَهَا سَعْيَهَا وَهُوَ

مُؤْمِنٌ فَاُولٰٓئِكَ كَانَ سَعْيُهُمْ

مَّشْكُوْرًا ۝ كُلًّا نُّمِدُّ هٰٓؤُلَآءِ وَهٰٓؤُلَآءِ

مِنْ عَطَآءِ رَبِّكَ وَمَا كَانَ عَطَآءُ

رَبِّكَ مَحْظُوْرًا ۝ اُنْظُرْ كَيْفَ

for his own benefit: who goes astray does so to his own loss: no bearer of burdens can bear the burden of another: nor would We visit with Our Wrath until We had sent an Apostle (to give warning).

16.   When We decide to destroy a population, We (first) send a definite order to those among them who are given the good things of this life and yet transgress; so that the word is proved true against them: then (it is) We destroy them utterly.

17.   How many generations have We destroyed after Noah? And enough is your Lord to note and see the sins of His servants.

لِنَفْسِهٖ ۚ وَمَنْ ضَلَّ فَاِنَّمَا يَضِلُّ

عَلَيْهَا ۗ وَلَا تَزِرُ وَازِرَةٌ وِّزْرَ اُخْرٰى ۗ

وَمَا كُنَّا مُعَذِّبِيْنَ حَتّٰى نَبْعَثَ

رَسُوْلًا ۝ وَاِذَآ اَرَدْنَآ اَنْ نُّهْلِكَ

قَرْيَةً اَمَرْنَا مُتْرَفِيْهَا فَفَسَقُوْا

فِيْهَا فَحَقَّ عَلَيْهَا الْقَوْلُ فَدَمَّرْنٰهَا

تَدْمِيْرًا ۝ وَكَمْ اَهْلَكْنَا مِنَ الْقُرُوْنِ

مِنْۢ بَعْدِ نُوْحٍ ۗ وَكَفٰى بِرَبِّكَ

بِذُنُوْبِ عِبَادِهٖ خَبِيْرًۢا بَصِيْرًا ۝

the Sign of the Day We have
made to enlighten you; that you
may seek bounty from your Lord,
and that you may know the
number and count of the years: all
things have We explained in
detail.

13. Every man's fate We have
fastened on his own neck: on the
Day of Judgment We shall bring
out for him a scroll, which he will
see spread open.

14. (It will be said to him:)
"Read your (own) record: sufficient is your soul this day to make
out an account against you."

15. Who receives guidance,
receives it

اٰیَةَ النَّهَارِ مُبْصِرَةً لِّتَبْتَغُوْا

فَضْلًا مِّنْ رَّبِّكُمْ وَلِتَعْلَمُوْا عَدَدَ

السِّنِیْنَ وَالْحِسَابَ ۚ وَكُلَّ شَیْءٍ

فَصَّلْنٰهُ تَفْصِیْلًا ۝ وَكُلَّ اِنْسَانٍ

اَلْزَمْنٰهُ طٰٓئِرَهٗ فِیْ عُنُقِهٖ ۚ وَنُخْرِجُ

لَهٗ یَوْمَ الْقِیٰمَةِ كِتٰبًا یَّلْقٰهُ

مَنْشُوْرًا ۝ اِقْرَأْ كِتٰبَكَ ۚ كَفٰی

بِنَفْسِكَ الْیَوْمَ عَلَیْكَ حَسِیْبًا ۝

مَنِ اهْتَدٰی فَاِنَّمَا یَهْتَدِیْ

9. Verily this Qur'an does guide to that which is most right (or stable), and gives the Glad Tidings to the believers who work deeds of righteousness, that they shall have a magnificent reward;

10. And to those who believe not in the Hereafter, (it announces) that We have prepared for them a grievous Chastisement (indeed).

11. The prayer that man should make for good, he makes for evil; for man is given to hasty (deeds).

12. We have made the Night and the Day as two (of Our) Signs: the Sign of the Night have We made dark, while

اِنَّ هٰذَا الْقُرْاٰنَ یَهْدِیْ لِلَّتِیْ هِیَ

اَقْوَمُ وَ یُبَشِّرُ الْمُؤْمِنِیْنَ الَّذِیْنَ

یَعْمَلُوْنَ الصّٰلِحٰتِ اَنَّ لَهُمْ اَجْرًا

كَبِیْرًا ۙ وَّ اَنَّ الَّذِیْنَ لَا یُؤْمِنُوْنَ

بِالْاٰخِرَةِ اَعْتَدْنَا لَهُمْ عَذَابًا

اَلِیْمًا ۠ وَ یَدْعُ الْاِنْسَانُ بِالشَّرِّ

دُعَآءَهٗ بِالْخَیْرِ ؕ وَ كَانَ الْاِنْسَانُ

عَجُوْلًا ۞ وَ جَعَلْنَا الَّیْلَ وَ النَّهَارَ

اٰیَتَیْنِ فَمَحَوْنَاۤ اٰیَةَ الَّیْلِ وَ جَعَلْنَا

in resources and sons, and made you the more nume-rous in man-power.

7.   If you did well, you did well for yourselves; if you did evil, (you did it) against yourselves. So when the second of the warnings came to pass, (We permitted your enemies) to disfigure your faces, and to enter your Temple as they had entered it before, and to visit with destruction all that fell into their power.

8.   It may be that your Lord may (yet) show Mercy unto you; but if you revert (to your sins), We shall revert (to Our punish-ments): and We have made Hell a prison for those who reject (all Faith).

بِاَمْوَالٍ وَّبَنِيْنَ وَجَعَلْنٰكُمْ اَكْثَرَ

نَفِيْرًا ۞ اِنْ اَحْسَنْتُمْ اَحْسَنْتُمْ

لِاَنْفُسِكُمْ ۚ وَاِنْ اَسَأْتُمْ فَلَهَا ۗ

فَاِذَا جَآءَ وَعْدُ الْاٰخِرَةِ لِيَسُوْٓءُوْا

وُجُوْهَكُمْ وَلِيَدْخُلُوا الْمَسْجِدَ كَمَا

دَخَلُوْهُ اَوَّلَ مَرَّةٍ وَّلِيُتَبِّرُوْا مَا

عَلَوْا تَتْبِيْرًا ۞ عَسٰى رَبُّكُمْ اَنْ

يَّرْحَمَكُمْ ۚ وَاِنْ عُدْتُّمْ عُدْنَا ۘ

وَجَعَلْنَا جَهَنَّمَ لِلْكٰفِرِيْنَ حَصِيْرًا ۞

Noah! Verily he was a devotee most grateful.

4. And We gave (clear) warning to the Children of Israel in the Book, that twice would they do mischief on the earth and be elated with mighty arrogance (and twice would they be punished)!

5. When the first of the warnings came to pass, We sent against you Our servants given to terrible warfare: they entered the very inmost parts of your homes; and it was a warning (completely) fulfilled.

6. Then did We grant you the Return as against them: We gave you increase

نُوْحٍ ؕ اِنَّهٗ كَانَ عَبْدًا شَكُوْرًا ۝

وَقَضَيْنَآ اِلٰى بَنِىٓ اِسْرَآءِیْلَ فِى

الْكِتٰبِ لَتُفْسِدُنَّ فِى الْاَرْضِ

مَرَّتَيْنِ وَلَتَعْلُنَّ عُلُوًّا كَبِيْرًا ۝

فَاِذَا جَآءَ وَعْدُ اُوْلٰىهُمَا بَعَثْنَا

عَلَيْكُمْ عِبَادًا لَّنَآ اُولِىْ بَاْسٍ

شَدِیْدٍ فَجَاسُوْا خِلٰلَ الدِّيَارِ ؕ

وَكَانَ وَعْدًا مَّفْعُوْلًا ۝ ثُمَّ رَدَدْنَا

لَكُمُ الْكَرَّةَ عَلَيْهِمْ وَاَمْدَدْنٰكُمْ

Bani-Isra'eel
(The Children of Israel)

Bismillahir-Rahmanir-Rahim

1. Glory to (Allah) Who did take His servant for a Journey by night from the Sacred Mosque to the Farthest Mosque, whose precincts We did bless, - in order that We might show him some of Our Signs: for He is the One Who hears and sees (all things).

2. We gave Moses the Book, and made it a Guide to the Children of Israel, (commanding): "Take not other than Me as Disposer of (your) affairs."

3. O you that are sprung from those whom We carried (in the Ark) with

بِسْمِ اللّٰهِ الرَّحْمٰنِ الرَّحِيْمِ

سُبْحٰنَ الَّذِيْۤ اَسْرٰى بِعَبْدِهٖ

لَيْلًا مِّنَ الْمَسْجِدِ الْحَرَامِ اِلَى

الْمَسْجِدِ الْاَقْصَا الَّذِيْ بٰرَكْنَا

حَوْلَهٗ لِنُرِيَهٗ مِنْ اٰيٰتِنَا ؕ اِنَّهٗ هُوَ

السَّمِيْعُ الْبَصِيْرُ ۝ وَ اٰتَيْنَا مُوْسَى

الْكِتٰبَ وَجَعَلْنٰهُ هُدًى لِّبَنِيْۤ

اِسْرَآءِيْلَ اَلَّا تَتَّخِذُوْا مِنْ دُوْنِيْ

وَكِيْلًا ؕ ۝ ذُرِّيَّةَ مَنْ حَمَلْنَا مَعَ

پاره

سُبْحٰنَ الَّذِى

(۱۵)

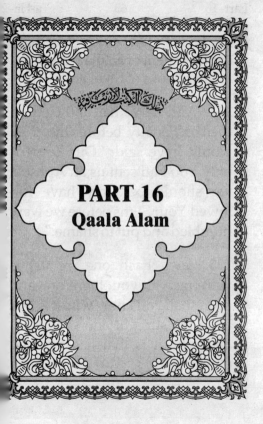

PART 16
Qaala Alam

his Lord?" Has not a clear Sign come to them of all that was in the former Books of revelation?

134. And if We had inflicted on them a Penalty before this, they would have said: "Our Lord! If only You had sent us an Apostle, we should certainly have followed Your Signs before we were humbled and put to shame."

135. Say: "Each one (of us) is waiting: wait you, therefore, and soon shall you know who it is that is on the straight and even way, and who it is that has received Guidance."

رَبِّهِ ۚ اَوَلَمْ تَأْتِهِمْ بَيِّنَةُ مَا

فِى الصُّحُفِ الْاُوْلٰى ۞ وَلَوْ اَنَّا

اَهْلَكْنٰهُمْ بِعَذَابٍ مِّنْ قَبْلِهٖ

لَقَالُوْا رَبَّنَا لَوْلَا اَرْسَلْتَ اِلَيْنَا

رَسُوْلًا فَنَتَّبِعَ اٰيٰتِكَ مِنْ قَبْلِ

اَنْ نَّذِلَّ وَنَخْزٰى ۞ قُلْ كُلٌّ

مُّتَرَبِّصٌ فَتَرَبَّصُوْا ۚ فَسَتَعْلَمُوْنَ

مَنْ اَصْحٰبُ الصِّرَاطِ السَّوِىِّ

وَمَنِ اهْتَدٰى ۞

yes, celebrate them for part of the hours of the night, and at the sides of the day: that you may have (spiritual) joy.

131. Nor strain your eyes in longing for the things We have given for enjoyment to parties of them, the splendour of the life of this world, through which We test them: but the provision of your Lord is better and more enduring.

132. Enjoin prayer on your people, and be constant therein. We ask you not to provide sustenance: We provide it for you. But the (fruit of) the Hereafter is for righteousness.

133. They say: "Why does he not bring us a Sign from

وَمِنْ اٰنَآئِ الَّيْلِ فَسَبِّحْ وَاَطْرَافَ

النَّهَارِ لَعَلَّكَ تَرْضٰى ۝ وَلَا تَمُدَّنَّ

عَيْنَيْكَ اِلٰى مَا مَتَّعْنَا بِهٖۤ اَزْوَاجًا

مِّنْهُمْ زَهْرَةَ الْحَيٰوةِ الدُّنْيَا ۙ

لِنَفْتِنَهُمْ فِيْهِ ۚ وَرِزْقُ رَبِّكَ خَيْرٌ

وَّاَبْقٰى ۝ وَاْمُرْ اَهْلَكَ بِالصَّلٰوةِ

وَاصْطَبِرْ عَلَيْهَا ۚ لَا نَسْـَٔلُكَ رِزْقًا ۗ

نَحْنُ نَرْزُقُكَ ۗ وَالْعَاقِبَةُ لِلتَّقْوٰى ۝

وَقَالُوْا لَوْلَا يَاْتِيْنَا بِاٰيَةٍ مِّنْ

in the Signs of his Lord: and the Chastisement of the Hereafter is far more grievous and more enduring.

128. Is it not a warning to such men (to call to mind) how many generations before them We destroyed, in whose haunts they (now) move? Verily, in this are Signs for men endued with understanding.

129. Had it not been for a Word that went forth before from your Lord, (their punishment) must necessarily have come; but there is a Term appointed (for respite).

130. Therefore be patient with what they say, and celebrate (constantly) the praises of your Lord, before the rising of the sun, and before its setting;

بِاٰيٰتِ رَبِّهٖ وَلَعَذَابُ الۡاٰخِرَةِ
اَشَدُّ وَاَبۡقٰی ۞ اَفَلَمۡ يَهۡدِ لَهُمۡ
كَمۡ اَهۡلَكۡنَا قَبۡلَهُمۡ مِّنَ الۡقُرُوۡنِ
يَمۡشُوۡنَ فِیۡ مَسٰكِنِهِمۡ ۗ اِنَّ فِیۡ ذٰلِكَ
لَاٰيٰتٍ لِّاُولِی النُّهٰی ۞ وَلَوۡلَا كَلِمَةٌ
سَبَقَتۡ مِنۡ رَّبِّكَ لَكَانَ لِزَامًا
وَّاَجَلٌ مُّسَمًّی ۞ فَاصۡبِرۡ عَلٰی مَا
يَقُوۡلُوۡنَ وَسَبِّحۡ بِحَمۡدِ رَبِّكَ قَبۡلَ
طُلُوۡعِ الشَّمۡسِ وَقَبۡلَ غُرُوۡبِهَا

Guidance from Me, whosoever follows My Guidance, will not lose his way, nor fall into misery."

124. "But whosoever turns away from My Message, verily for him is a life narrowed down, and We shall raise him up blind on the Day of Judgment."

125. He will say: "O my Lord! Why have you raised me up blind, while I had sight (before)?"

126. (Allah) will say: "Thus you, did when Our Signs came unto you, disregard them: so will you, this day, be disregarded."

127. And thus do We recompense him who transgresses beyond bounds and believes not

هُدًى ۚ فَمَنِ اتَّبَعَ هُدَاىَ فَلَا

يَضِلُّ وَلَا يَشْقٰى ۞ وَمَنْ اَعْرَضَ

عَنْ ذِكْرِىْ فَاِنَّ لَهٗ مَعِيْشَةً

ضَنْكًا وَّنَحْشُرُهٗ يَوْمَ الْقِيٰمَةِ

اَعْمٰى ۞ قَالَ رَبِّ لِمَ حَشَرْتَنِىْ

اَعْمٰى وَقَدْ كُنْتُ بَصِيْرًا ۞ قَالَ

كَذٰلِكَ اَتَتْكَ اٰيٰتُنَا فَنَسِيْتَهَا ۚ

وَكَذٰلِكَ الْيَوْمَ تُنْسٰى ۞ وَكَذٰلِكَ

نَجْزِىْ مَنْ اَسْرَفَ وَلَمْ يُؤْمِنْ

from the sun's heat."

120. But Satan whispered evil to him: he said, "O Adam! Shall I lead you to the Tree of Eternity and to a kingdom that never decays?"

121. In the result, they both ate of the tree, and so their nakedness appeared to them: they began to sew together, for their covering, leaves from the Garden: thus did Adam disobey his Lord, and allow himself to be seduced.

122. But his Lord chose him (for His Grace): He turned to him, and gave him Guidance.

123. He said: "Get you down, both of you, - all together, from the Garden, with enmity one to another: but if, as is sure, there comes to you

تَضْحٰى ۝ فَوَسْوَسَ اِلَيْهِ الشَّيْطٰنُ

قَالَ يٰٓاٰدَمُ هَلْ اَدُلُّكَ عَلٰى شَجَرَةِ

الْخُلْدِ وَمُلْكٍ لَّا يَبْلٰى ۝ فَاَكَلَا

مِنْهَا فَبَدَتْ لَهُمَا سَوْاٰتُهُمَا وَطَفِقَا

يَخْصِفٰنِ عَلَيْهِمَا مِنْ وَّرَقِ الْجَنَّةِ ۚ

وَعَصٰٓى اٰدَمُ رَبَّهٗ فَغَوٰى ۝ ثُمَّ

اجْتَبٰهُ رَبُّهٗ فَتَابَ عَلَيْهِ وَهَدٰى ۝

قَالَ اهْبِطَا مِنْهَا جَمِيعًۢا بَعْضُكُمْ

لِبَعْضٍ عَدُوٌّ ۚ فَاِمَّا يَاْتِيَنَّكُمْ مِّنِّيْ

in knowledge."

115. We had already, beforehand, taken the covenant of Adam, but he forgot: and We found on his part no firm resolve.

116. When We said to the Angels, "Prostrate yourselves to Adam", they prostrated themselves, but not Iblis: he refused.

117. Then We said: "O Adam! Verily, this is an enemy to you and your wife: so let him not get you both out of the Garden, so that you are landed in misery."

118. "There is therein (enough provision) for you not to go hungry nor to go naked,"

119. "Nor to suffer from thirst, nor

عِلْمًا ۞ وَلَقَدْ عَهِدْنَا إِلَى اٰدَمَ

مِنْ قَبْلُ فَنَسِىَ وَلَمْ نَجِدْ

لَهُ عَزْمًا ۞ وَإِذْ قُلْنَا لِلْمَلٰٓئِكَةِ

اسْجُدُوْا لِاٰدَمَ فَسَجَدُوْۤا اِلَّاۤ

اِبْلِيْسَ ؕ اَبٰى ۞ فَقُلْنَا يٰٓاٰدَمُ اِنَّ

هٰذَا عَدُوٌّ لَّكَ وَلِزَوْجِكَ فَلَا

يُخْرِجَنَّكُمَا مِنَ الْجَنَّةِ فَتَشْقٰى

۞ اِنَّ لَكَ اَلَّا تَجُوْعَ فِيْهَا وَلَا

تَعْرٰى ۞ وَاَنَّكَ لَا تَظْمَؤُا فِيْهَا وَلَا

112. But he who works deeds of righteousness, and has faith, will have no fear of harm nor of any curtailment (of what is his due).

113. Thus have We sent this down - an Arabic Qur'an - and explained therein in detail some of the warnings, in order that they may fear Allah, or that it may cause their remembrance (of Him).

114. High above all is Allah, the King, the Truth! Be not in haste with the Qur'an before its revelation to you is completed, but say, "O my Lord! Advance me

وَمَنْ يَّعْمَلْ مِنَ الصَّلِحٰتِ وَهُوَ

مُؤْمِنٌ فَلَا يَخٰفُ ظُلْمًا وَّلَا

هَضْمًا ۝ وَكَذٰلِكَ اَنْزَلْنٰهُ قُرْاٰنًا

عَرَبِيًّا وَّصَرَّفْنَا فِيهِ مِنَ

الْوَعِيدِ لَعَلَّهُمْ يَتَّقُوْنَ اَوْ

يُحْدِثُ لَهُمْ ذِكْرًا ۝ فَتَعٰلَى

اللّٰهُ الْمَلِكُ الْحَقُّ ۚ وَلَا تَعْجَلْ

بِالْقُرْاٰنِ مِنْ قَبْلِ اَنْ يُّقْضٰى

اِلَيْكَ وَحْيُهٗ ۖ وَقُلْ رَّبِّ زِدْنِيْ

108. On that Day will they follow the Caller (straight): no crookedness (can they show) him: all sounds shall humble themselves in the Presence of (Allah) Most Gracious: nothing shall you hear but the tramp of their feet (as they march).

109. On that Day shall no intercession avail except for those for whom permission has been granted by (Allah) Most Gracious and whose word is acceptable to Him.

110. He knows what (appears to His creatures as) before or after or behind them: but they shall not compass it with their knowledge.

111. (All) faces shall be humbled before (Him) - the Living, the Self-Subsisting, Eternal: hopeless indeed will be the man that carries iniquity (on his back).

يَوْمَئِذٍ يَّتَّبِعُونَ الدَّاعِى لَا عِوَجَ

لَهُ ۚ وَخَشَعَتِ الْاَصْوَاتُ لِلرَّحْمٰنِ

فَلَا تَسْمَعُ اِلَّا هَمْسًا ۩ يَوْمَئِذٍ

لَّا تَنْفَعُ الشَّفَاعَةُ اِلَّا مَنْ اَذِنَ

لَهُ الرَّحْمٰنُ وَرَضِىَ لَهُ قَوْلًا ۩

يَعْلَمُ مَا بَيْنَ اَيْدِيْهِمْ وَمَا

خَلْفَهُمْ وَلَا يُحِيْطُونَ بِهِ عِلْمًا ۩

وَعَنَتِ الْوُجُوهُ لِلْحَىِّ الْقَيُّوْمِ ۗ

وَقَدْ خَابَ مَنْ حَمَلَ ظُلْمًا ۩

the Trumpet will be sounded: that Day, We shall gather the sinful, blear-eyed (with terror).

103. In whispers will they consult each other: "You tarried not longer than ten (days);"

104. We know best what they will say, when their leader most eminent in conduct will say: "You tarried not longer than a day!"

105. They ask you concerning the Mountains: say, "My Lord will uproot them and scatter them as dust;"

106. "He will leave them as plains smooth and level;"

107. "Nothing crooked or curved will you see in their place."

فِى الصُّوْرِ وَنَحْشُرُ الْمُجْرِمِيْنَ

يَوْمَئِذٍ زُرْقًا ۙ يَّتَخَافَتُوْنَ بَيْنَهُمْ

اِنْ لَّبِثْتُمْ اِلَّا عَشْرًا ۙ نَحْنُ

اَعْلَمُ بِمَا يَقُوْلُوْنَ اِذْ يَقُوْلُ

اَمْثَلُهُمْ طَرِيْقَةً اِنْ لَّبِثْتُمْ اِلَّا

يَوْمًا ۧ وَيَسْـَٔلُوْنَكَ عَنِ الْجِبَالِ

فَقُلْ يَنْسِفُهَا رَبِّىْ نَسْفًا ۙ

فَيَذَرُهَا قَاعًا صَفْصَفًا ۙ لَّا

تَرٰى فِيْهَا عِوَجًا وَّلَآ اَمْتًا ۧ

and scatter it broadcast in the sea!"

98. But the god of you all is the One Allah: there is no god but He: all things He comprehends in His knowledge.

99. Thus do We relate to you some stories of what happened before: for We have sent you a Message from Our Own Presence.

100. If any do turn away therefrom, verily they will bear a burden on the Day of Judgment;

101. They will abide in this (state): and grievous will the burden be to them on that Day, -

102. The Day when

ثُمَّ لَنَنْسِفَنَّهُ فِي الْيَمِّ نَسْفًا ۝

اِنَّمَا اِلٰهُكُمُ اللّٰهُ الَّذِىْ لَآ اِلٰهَ

اِلَّا هُوَ ۚ وَسِعَ كُلَّ شَىْءٍ عِلْمًا ۝

كَذٰلِكَ نَقُصُّ عَلَيْكَ مِنْ اَنْبَآءِ

مَا قَدْ سَبَقَ ۚ وَقَدْ اٰتَيْنٰكَ

مِنْ لَّدُنَّا ذِكْرًا ۝ مَنْ اَعْرَضَ

عَنْهُ فَاِنَّهُ يَحْمِلُ يَوْمَ الْقِيٰمَةِ

وِزْرًا ۝ خٰلِدِيْنَ فِيْهِ ۚ وَسَآءَ لَهُمْ

يَوْمَ الْقِيٰمَةِ حِمْلًا ۝ يَوْمَ يُنْفَخُ

95. (Moses) said: "What then is your case, O Samiri?"

96. He replied: "I saw what they saw not: so I took a handful (of dust) from the footprint of the Messenger (Gabriel's Horse), and threw it (into the calf): thus did my soul suggest to me."

97. (Moses) said: "Get you gone! But your (punishment) in this life will be that you will say, 'Touch me not'; and moreover (for a future Chastisement) you have a promise that will not fail: now look at your god, of whom you have become a devoted worshipper: we will certainly (melt) it in a blazing fire

قَالَ فَمَا خَطْبُكَ يَا سَامِرِيُّ ۞

قَالَ بَصُرْتُ بِمَا لَمْ يَبْصُرُوا

بِهِ فَقَبَضْتُ قَبْضَةً مِّنْ أَثَرِ

الرَّسُولِ فَنَبَذْتُهَا وَكَذَٰلِكَ سَوَّلَتْ

لِى نَفْسِى ۞ قَالَ فَاذْهَبْ فَإِنَّ

لَكَ فِى الْحَيَوٰةِ أَن تَقُولَ لَا

مِسَاسَ وَإِنَّ لَكَ مَوْعِدًا لَّنْ

تُخْلَفَهُ وَانظُرْ إِلَىٰ إِلَٰهِكَ الَّذِى

ظَلْتَ عَلَيْهِ عَاكِفًا لَّنُحَرِّقَنَّهُ

is (Allah) Most Gracious; so follow me and obey my command."

91. They had said: "We will not cease to worship it, but we will devote ourselves to it until Moses returns to us."

92. (Moses) said: "O Aaron! What kept you back, when you saw them going wrong,"

93. "From following me? Did you then disobey my order?"

94. (Aaron) replied: "O son of my mother! Seize (me) not by my beard nor by (the hair of) my head! Truly I feared lest you should say, 'You has caused a division among the Children of Israel, and you did not respect my word!'"

الرَّحْمٰنُ فَاتَّبِعُونِي وَأَطِيعُوا أَمْرِي ۝

قَالُوا لَنْ نَّبْرَحَ عَلَيْهِ عٰكِفِينَ

حَتّٰى يَرْجِعَ إِلَيْنَا مُوسٰى ۝ قَالَ

يٰهٰرُونُ مَا مَنَعَكَ إِذْ رَأَيْتَهُمْ

ضَلُّوٓا ۝ أَلَّا تَتَّبِعَنِ ۖ أَفَعَصَيْتَ

أَمْرِي ۝ قَالَ يَبْنَؤُمَّ لَا تَأْخُذْ

بِلِحْيَتِي وَلَا بِرَأْسِي ۖ إِنِّي خَشِيتُ

أَن تَقُولَ فَرَّقْتَ بَيْنَ بَنِي

إِسْرَآءِيلَ وَلَمْ تَرْقُبْ قَوْلِي ۝

the weight of the ornaments of the (whole) people, and we threw them (into the fire), and that was what the Samiri suggested."

88.   "Then he brought out (of the fire) before the (people) the image of a calf: it seemed to low: so they said: this is your god, and the god of Moses, but (Moses) has forgotten!"

89.   Could they not see that it could not return them a word (for answer), and that it had no power either to harm them or to do them good?

90.   Aaron had already, before this said to them: "O my people! You are being tested in this: for verily your Lord

أَوۡزَارًا مِّنۡ زِينَةِ الۡقَوۡمِ فَقَذَفۡنَاهَا

فَكَذٰلِكَ أَلۡقَى السَّامِرِيُّ ﴿٨٧﴾ فَأَخۡرَجَ

لَهُمۡ عِجۡلًا جَسَدًا لَّهُ خُوَارٌ

فَقَالُوۡا هٰذَاۤ اِلٰهُكُمۡ وَاِلٰهُ مُوۡسٰى

فَنَسِيَ ﴿٨٨﴾ اَفَلَا يَرَوۡنَ اَلَّا يَرۡجِعُ

اِلَيۡهِمۡ قَوۡلًا ۙ وَّلَا يَمۡلِكُ لَهُمۡ

ضَرًّا وَّلَا نَفۡعًا ﴿٨٩﴾ وَلَقَدۡ قَالَ

لَهُمۡ هٰرُوۡنُ مِنۡ قَبۡلُ يٰقَوۡمِ

اِنَّمَا فُتِنۡتُمۡ بِهٖ ۚ وَاِنَّ رَبَّكُمُ

have tested your people in your absence: the Samiri has led them astray."

86. So Moses returned to his people in a state of indignation and sorrow. He said: "O my people! Did not your Lord make a handsome promise to you? Did then the promise seem to you long (in coming)? Or did you desire that Wrath should descend from your Lord on you, and so you broke your promise to me?"

87. They said: "We broke not the promise to you, as far as lay in our power: but we were made to carry

قَدْ فَتَنَّا قَوْمَكَ مِنْ بَعْدِكَ

وَأَضَلَّهُمُ السَّامِرِيُّ ۞ فَرَجَعَ

مُوسَىٰ إِلَىٰ قَوْمِهِ غَضْبَانَ أَسِفًا ۚ

قَالَ يَٰقَوْمِ أَلَمْ يَعِدْكُمْ رَبُّكُمْ

وَعْدًا حَسَنًا ۚ أَفَطَالَ عَلَيْكُمُ الْعَهْدُ

أَمْ أَرَدْتُّمْ أَن يَحِلَّ عَلَيْكُمْ

غَضَبٌ مِّن رَّبِّكُمْ فَأَخْلَفْتُم

مَّوْعِدِى ۞ قَالُوا مَآ أَخْلَفْنَا

مَوْعِدَكَ بِمَلْكِنَا وَلَٰكِنَّا حُمِّلْنَآ

to you Manna and quails:

81. (Saying): "Eat of the good things We have provided for your sustenance, but commit no excess therein, lest My Wrath should justly descend on you: and those on whom descends My Wrath do perish indeed!"

82. "But, without doubt, I am (also) He that forgives again and again, to those who repent, believe, and do right, - who, in fine, are ready to receive true guidance."

83. (When Moses was up on the Mount, Allah said:) "What made you hasten in advance of your people, O Moses?"

84. He replied: "Behold, they are close on my footsteps: I hastened to You, O my Lord, to please You."

85. (Allah) said: "We

عَلَيْكُمُ الْمَنَّ وَ السَّلْوٰى ۞ كُلُوْا

مِنْ طَيِّبٰتِ مَا رَزَقْنٰكُمْ وَ لَا تَطْغَوْا

فِيْهِ فَيَحِلَّ عَلَيْكُمْ غَضَبِيْ وَ مَنْ

يَّحْلِلْ عَلَيْهِ غَضَبِيْ فَقَدْ هَوٰى ۞

وَ اِنِّيْ لَغَفَّارٌ لِّمَنْ تَابَ وَ اٰمَنَ

وَ عَمِلَ صَالِحًا ثُمَّ اهْتَدٰى ۞ وَ مَا

اَعْجَلَكَ عَنْ قَوْمِكَ يٰمُوْسٰى

۞ قَالَ هُمْ اُولَاءِ عَلٰى اَثَرِيْ وَ عَجِلْتُ

اِلَيْكَ رَبِّ لِتَرْضٰى ۞ قَالَ فَاِنَّا

77. We sent an inspiration to Moses: "Travel by night with My servants, and strike a dry path for them through the sea, without fear of being overtaken (by Pharaoh) and without (any other) fear."

78. Then Pharaoh pursued them with his forces, but the waters completely overwhelmed them and covered them up.

79. Pharaoh led his people astray instead of leading them aright.

80. O you Children of Israel! We delivered you from your enemy, and We made a Covenant with you on the right side of Mount (Sinai), and We sent down

أَوْحَيْنَآ إِلَىٰ مُوسَىٰ أَنْ أَسْرِ
بِعِبَادِى فَاضْرِبْ لَهُمْ طَرِيقًا
فِى الْبَحْرِ يَبَسًا لَّا تَخَٰفُ دَرَكًا
وَّلَا تَخْشَىٰ ۝ فَأَتْبَعَهُمْ فِرْعَوْنُ
بِجُنُودِهِۦ فَغَشِيَهُم مِّنَ الْيَمِّ مَا
غَشِيَهُمْ ۝ وَأَضَلَّ فِرْعَوْنُ قَوْمَهُۥ
وَمَا هَدَىٰ ۝ يَٰبَنِىٓ إِسْرَآءِيلَ قَدْ
أَنجَيْنَٰكُم مِّنْ عَدُوِّكُمْ وَوَٰعَدْنَٰكُمْ
جَانِبَ الطُّورِ الْأَيْمَنَ وَنَزَّلْنَا

and the magic to which you did compel us: for Allah is Best and Most Abiding."

74.   Verily he who comes to his Lord as a sinner (at Judgment), - for him is Hell: therein shall he neither die nor live.

75.   But such as come to Him as believers who have worked righteous deeds, - for them are ranks exalted, -

76.   Gardens of Eternity, beneath which flow rivers: they will dwell therein for ever: such is the reward of those who purify themselves (from evil).

وَمَآ اَكْرَهْتَنَا عَلَيْهِ مِنَ السِّحْرِ

وَاللّٰهُ خَيْرٌ وَّاَبْقٰى ۝ اِنَّهُ مَنْ

يَّاْتِ رَبَّهُ مُجْرِمًا فَاِنَّ لَهُ

جَهَنَّمَ لَا يَمُوْتُ فِيْهَا وَلَا يَحْيٰى ۝

وَمَنْ يَّاْتِهِ مُؤْمِنًا قَدْ عَمِلَ

الصّٰلِحٰتِ فَاُولٰٓئِكَ لَهُمُ الدَّرَجٰتُ

الْعُلٰى ۝ جَنّٰتُ عَدْنٍ تَجْرِىْ مِنْ

تَحْتِهَا الْاَنْهٰرُ خٰلِدِيْنَ فِيْهَا

وَذٰلِكَ جَزٰٓؤُا مَنْ تَزَكّٰى ۝ وَلَقَدْ

Surely this must be your leader, who has taught you magic! Be sure I will cut off your hands and feet on opposite sides, and I will have you crucified on trunks of palm-trees: so shall you know for certain, which of us can give the more severe and the more lasting punishment!"

72. They said: "Never shall we regard you as more than the clear Sings that have come to us, or than Him Who created us! So decree whatever you desire to decree: for you can only decree (touching) the life of this world."

73. "For us, we have believed in our Lord: may He forgive us our faults,

إِنَّهُ لَكَبِيرُكُمُ الَّذِي عَلَّمَكُمُ السِّحْرَ

فَلَأُقَطِّعَنَّ أَيْدِيَكُمْ وَأَرْجُلَكُمْ مِّنْ

خِلَافٍ وَّلَأُصَلِّبَنَّكُمْ فِي جُذُوعِ

النَّخْلِ وَلَتَعْلَمُنَّ أَيُّنَا أَشَدُّ عَذَابًا

وَّأَبْقَى ۝ قَالُوا لَنْ نُّؤْثِرَكَ عَلَى

مَا جَاءَنَا مِنَ الْبَيِّنَاتِ وَالَّذِي

فَطَرَنَا فَاقْضِ مَا أَنتَ قَاضٍ

إِنَّمَا تَقْضِي هٰذِهِ الْحَيَوةَ الدُّنْيَا ۝

إِنَّا آمَنَّا بِرَبِّنَا لِيَغْفِرَ لَنَا خَطَايَانَا

so it seemed to him on account of their magic - began to be in lively motion!

67. So Moses conceived in his mind a (sort of) fear.

68. We said: "Fear not! For you have indeed the upper hand:"

69. "Throw that which is in your right hand: quickly will it swallow up that which they have faked what they have faked is but a magician's trick: and the magician thrives not, (no matter) where he goes."

70. So the magicians were thrown down to prostration: they said, "We believe in the Lord of Aaron and Moses".

71. (Pharaoh) said: "Believe you in Him before I give you permission?"

يُخَيَّلُ اِلَيْهِ مِنْ سِحْرِهِمْ اَنَّهَا

تَسْعٰى ۝ فَاَوْجَسَ فِىْ نَفْسِهٖ خِيْفَةً

مُّوْسٰى ۝ قُلْنَا لَا تَخَفْ اِنَّكَ اَنْتَ

الْاَعْلٰى ۝ وَاَلْقِ مَا فِىْ يَمِيْنِكَ

تَلْقَفْ مَا صَنَعُوْا ؕ اِنَّمَا صَنَعُوْا

كَيْدُ سٰحِرٍ ؕ وَلَا يُفْلِحُ السَّاحِرُ حَيْثُ

اَتٰى ۝ فَاُلْقِىَ السَّحَرَةُ سُجَّدًا قَالُوْۤا

اٰمَنَّا بِرَبِّ هٰرُوْنَ وَمُوْسٰى ۝ قَالَ

اٰمَنْتُمْ لَهٗ قَبْلَ اَنْ اٰذَنَ لَكُمْ ؕ

one with another, over their affair, but they kept their talk secret.

63. They said: "These two are certainly (expert) magicians: their object is to drive you out from your land with their magic, and to do away with your most cherished institutions."

64. "Therefore concert your plan, and then assemble in (serried) ranks: he wins (all along) today who gains the upper hand."

65. They said: "O Moses! Whether will you that you throw (first) or that we be the first to throw?"

66. He said, "No, throw you first!" Then behold their ropes and their rods –

أَمْرَهُمْ بَيْنَهُمْ وَأَسَرُّوا النَّجْوَى ۝

قَالُوٓا إِنْ هَٰذَٰنِ لَسَاحِرَانِ يُرِيدَانِ

أَن يُخْرِجَاكُم مِّنْ أَرْضِكُم بِسِحْرِهِمَا

وَيَذْهَبَا بِطَرِيقَتِكُمُ الْمُثْلَىٰ ۝ فَأَجْمِعُوا

كَيْدَكُمْ ثُمَّ ائْتُوا صَفًّا ۚ وَقَدْ

أَفْلَحَ الْيَوْمَ مَنِ اسْتَعْلَىٰ ۝ قَالُوا

يَٰمُوسَىٰٓ إِمَّآ أَن تُلْقِىَ وَإِمَّآ أَن

نَّكُونَ أَوَّلَ مَنْ أَلْقَىٰ ۝ قَالَ

بَلْ أَلْقُوا ۖ فَإِذَا حِبَالُهُمْ وَعِصِيُّهُمْ

O Moses?"

58.   "But we can surely produce magic to match your! So make a tryst between us and you, which we shall not fail to keep - neither we nor you - in a place where both shall have even chances."

59.   Moses said: "Your tryst is the Day of the Festival, and let the people be assembled when the sun is well up."

60.   So Pharaoh withdrew: he concerted his plan, and then came (back).

61.   Moses said to him: "Woe to you! Forge not you a lie against Allah, lest He destroy you (at once) utterly by Chastisement: the forger must suffer frustration!"

62.   So they disputed,

يُمُوسَى ۞ فَلَنَأْتِيَنَّكَ بِسِحْرٍ مِّثْلِهِ

فَاجْعَلْ بَيْنَنَا وَبَيْنَكَ مَوْعِدًا لَّا

نُخْلِفُهُ نَحْنُ وَلَا أَنتَ مَكَانًا

سُوًى ۞ قَالَ مَوْعِدُكُمْ يَوْمُ الزِّينَةِ

وَأَن يُّحْشَرَ النَّاسُ ضُحًى ۞ فَتَوَلَّى

فِرْعَوْنُ فَجَمَعَ كَيْدَهُ ثُمَّ أَتَى

۞ قَالَ لَهُم مُّوسَى وَيْلَكُمْ لَا تَفْتَرُوا

عَلَى اللَّهِ كَذِبًا فَيُسْحِتَكُم بِعَذَابٍ

وَقَدْ خَابَ مَنِ افْتَرَى ۞ فَتَنَازَعُوا

about therein by roads (and channels); and has sent down water from the sky." With it have We produced diverse pairs of plants each separate from the others.

54. Eat (for yourselves) and pasture your cattle: verily, in this are Signs for men endued with understanding.

55. From the (earth) did We create you, and into it shall We return you, and from it shall We bring you out once again.

56. And We showed Pharaoh all Our Signs, but he did reject and refuse.

57. He said: "Has you come to drive us out of our land with your magic,

لَكُمْ فِيهَا سُبُلًا وَّ اَنْزَلَ مِنَ

السَّمَآءِ مَآءً فَاَخْرَجْنَا بِهٖٓ اَزْوَاجًا

مِّنْ نَّبَاتٍ شَتّٰى ۞ كُلُوْا وَارْعَوْا

اَنْعَامَكُمْ ط اِنَّ فِيْ ذٰلِكَ لَاٰيٰتٍ

لِّاُولِى النُّهٰى ۞ مِنْهَا خَلَقْنٰكُمْ

وَفِيْهَا نُعِيْدُكُمْ وَمِنْهَا نُخْرِجُكُمْ

تَارَةً اُخْرٰى ۞ وَلَقَدْ اَرَيْنٰهُ اٰيٰتِنَا

كُلَّهَا فَكَذَّبَ وَاَبٰى ۞ قَالَ اَجِئْتَنَا

لِتُخْرِجَنَا مِنْ اَرْضِنَا بِسِحْرِكَ

guidance!"

48. "'Verily it has been revealed to us that the Chastisement (awaits) those who reject and turn away.'"

49. (When this message was delivered), (Pharaoh) said: "Who, then, O Moses, is the Lord of you two?"

50. He said: "Our Lord is He Who gave to each (created) thing its form and nature, and further, gave (it) guidance."

51. (Pharaoh) said: "What then is the condition of previous generations?"

52. He replied: "The knowledge of that is with my Lord, duly recorded: my Lord never errs, nor forgets," -

53. "He Who has, made for you the earth like a carpet spread out; has enabled you to go

الْهُدَىٰ ۞ إِنَّا قَدْ أُوحِيَ إِلَيْنَآ أَنَّ

الْعَذَابَ عَلَىٰ مَن كَذَّبَ وَتَوَلَّىٰ

۞ قَالَ فَمَن رَّبُّكُمَا يَٰمُوسَىٰ ۞ قَالَ

رَبُّنَا الَّذِىٓ أَعْطَىٰ كُلَّ شَىْءٍ

خَلْقَهُۥ ثُمَّ هَدَىٰ ۞ قَالَ فَمَا

بَالُ الْقُرُونِ الْأُولَىٰ ۞ قَالَ

عِلْمُهَا عِندَ رَبِّى فِى كِتَٰبٍ ۚ لَّا

يَضِلُّ رَبِّى وَلَا يَنسَى ۞ الَّذِى

جَعَلَ لَكُمُ الْأَرْضَ مَهْدًا وَّسَلَكَ

Pharaoh, for he has indeed transgressed all bounds;"

44. "But speak to him mildly; perchance he may take warning or fear (Allah)."

45. They (Moses and Aaron) said: "Our Lord! We fear lest he hasten with insolence against us, or lest he transgress all bounds."

46. He said: "Fear not: for I am with you: I hear and see (everything).

47. "So go you both to him, and say, 'Verily we are Apostles sent by your Lord: send forth, therefore, the Children of Israel with us, and afflict them not: with a Sign, indeed, have we come from your Lord! and peace to all who follow

فِرْعَوْنَ إِنَّهُ طَغَى ۞ فَقُولَا لَهُ قَوْلًا

لَيِّنًا لَعَلَّهُ يَتَذَكَّرُ أَوْ يَخْشَى ۞

قَالَا رَبَّنَا إِنَّنَا نَخَافُ أَن يَفْرُطَ

عَلَيْنَا أَوْ أَن يَطْغَى ۞ قَالَ لَا

تَخَافَا إِنَّنِي مَعَكُمَا أَسْمَعُ وَأَرَى

فَأْتِيَاهُ فَقُولَا إِنَّا رَسُولَا رَبِّكَ

فَأَرْسِلْ مَعَنَا بَنِي إِسْرَآءِيلَ وَلَا

تُعَذِّبْهُمْ قَدْ جِئْنَاكَ بِآيَةٍ مِّن

رَّبِّكَ وَالسَّلَامُ عَلَى مَنِ اتَّبَعَ

and says, 'Shall I show you one who will nurse and rear the (child)?' So We brought you back to your mother, that her eye might be cooled and she should not grieve. Then you did slay a man, but We saved you from trouble, and We tried you in various ways. Then did you tarry a number of years with the people of Midian. Then did you come hither as ordained, O Moses!"

41.   "And I have prepared you for Myself (for service)."

42.   "Go, you and your brother, with My Signs, and slacken not, either of you, in keeping Me in remembrance."

43.   "Go, both of you, to

اُخْتُكَ فَتَقُوْلُ هَلْ اَدُلُّكُمْ عَلٰى

مَنْ يَّكْفُلُهٗ ۚ فَرَجَعْنٰكَ اِلٰٓى اُمِّكَ

كَىْ تَقَرَّ عَيْنُهَا وَلَا تَحْزَنَ ۚ وَقَتَلْتَ

نَفْسًا فَنَجَّيْنٰكَ مِنَ الْغَمِّ وَفَتَنّٰكَ

فُتُوْنًا ۥ ڤ فَلَبِثْتَ سِنِيْنَ فِىْٓ اَهْلِ

مَدْيَنَ ۥ ثُمَّ جِئْتَ عَلٰى قَدَرٍ

يّٰمُوْسٰى ۞ وَاصْطَنَعْتُكَ لِنَفْسِىْ ۞

اِذْهَبْ اَنْتَ وَاَخُوْكَ بِاٰيٰتِىْ

وَلَا تَنِيَا فِىْ ذِكْرِىْ ۚ اِذْهَبَآ اِلٰى

34. "And remember You without stint:"

35. "For You are He that (ever) regards us."

36. (Allah) said: "Granted is your prayer, O Moses!"

37. "And indeed We conferred a favour on your another time (before).

38. "Behold! We sent to your mother, by inspiration, the message:"

39. "'Throw (the child) into the chest, and throw (the chest) into the river: the river will cast him up on the bank, and he will be taken up by one who is an enemy to Me and an enemy to him': but I cast (the garment of) love over you from Me: and (this) in order that you may be reared under Mine eye.

40. "Behold! Your sister goes forth

وَنَذْكُرَكَ كَثِيرًا ۞ اِنَّكَ كُنْتَ بِنَا

بَصِيرًا ۞ قَالَ قَدْ اُوتِيتَ سُؤْلَكَ

يٰمُوسٰى ۞ وَلَقَدْ مَنَنَّا عَلَيْكَ مَرَّةً

اُخْرٰى ۞ اِذْ اَوْحَيْنَا اِلٰى اُمِّكَ

مَا يُوحٰى ۞ اَنِ اقْذِفِيهِ فِى التَّابُوتِ

فَاقْذِفِيهِ فِى الْيَمِّ فَلْيُلْقِهِ الْيَمُّ

بِالسَّاحِلِ يَأْخُذْهُ عَدُوٌّ لِّى وَعَدُوٌّ

لَّهُ ۚ وَاَلْقَيْتُ عَلَيْكَ مَحَبَّةً مِّنِّى ۚ

وَلِتُصْنَعَ عَلٰى عَيْنِى ۞ اِذْ تَمْشِى

white (and shining), without harm (or stain), - as another Sign," -

23. "In order that We may show you (two) of Our Greater Signs."

24. "Go to Pharaoh, for he has indeed transgressed all bounds."

25. (Moses) said: "O my Lord! Expand me my breast;"

26. "Ease my task for me;"

27. "And remove the impediment from my speech,"

28. "So they may understand what I say:"

29. "And give me a Minister from my family,"

30. "Aaron, my brother;"

31. "Add to my strength through him,"

32. "And make him share my task:"

33. "That we may celebrate Your praise without stint,

بَيْضَاءَ مِنْ غَيْرِ سُوٓءٍ اٰيَةً اُخْرٰى ۞

لِنُرِيَكَ مِنْ اٰيٰتِنَا الْكُبْرٰى ۞ اِذْهَبْ

اِلٰى فِرْعَوْنَ اِنَّهٗ طَغٰى ۞ قَالَ

رَبِّ اشْرَحْ لِيْ صَدْرِيْ ۞ وَيَسِّرْ لِيْٓ

اَمْرِيْ ۞ وَاحْلُلْ عُقْدَةً مِّنْ

لِّسَانِيْ ۞ يَفْقَهُوْا قَوْلِيْ ۞ وَاجْعَلْ

لِّيْ وَزِيْرًا مِّنْ اَهْلِيْ ۞ هٰرُوْنَ اَخِي ۞

اشْدُدْ بِهٖٓ اَزْرِيْ ۞ وَاَشْرِكْهُ فِيْٓ

اَمْرِيْ ۞ كَيْ نُسَبِّحَكَ كَثِيْرًا ۞

such as believe not therein but follow their own lusts, divert you therefrom, lest you perish!"...

17. "And what is that in the right hand, O Moses?"

18. He said, "It is my rod: on it I lean; with it I beat down fodder for my flocks; and in it I find other uses."

19. (Allah) said, "Throw it, O Moses!"

20. He threw it, and behold! it was a snake, active in motion.

21. (Allah) said, "Seize it, and fear not: We shall return it at once to its former condition"...

22. "Now draw your hand close to your side: it shall come forth

عَنْهَا مَنْ لَا يُؤْمِنُ بِهَا وَاتَّبَعَ

هَوٰهُ فَتَرْدٰى ۞ وَمَا تِلْكَ بِيَمِيْنِكَ

يٰمُوْسٰى ۞ قَالَ هِىَ عَصَاىَ ۚ أَتَوَكَّؤُا

عَلَيْهَا وَأَهُشُّ بِهَا عَلٰى غَنَمِىْ

وَلِىَ فِيْهَا مَآرِبُ أُخْرٰى ۞ قَالَ

أَلْقِهَا يٰمُوْسٰى ۞ فَأَلْقٰىهَا فَإِذَا هِىَ

حَيَّةٌ تَسْعٰى ۞ قَالَ خُذْهَا وَلَا

تَخَفْ ۖ سَنُعِيْدُهَا سِيْرَتَهَا الْأُوْلٰى ۞

وَاضْمُمْ يَدَكَ إِلٰى جَنَاحِكَ تَخْرُجْ

some burning brand therefrom, or find some guidance at the fire."

11. But when he came to the fire, a voice was heard: "O Moses!"

12. "Verily I am your Lord! Therefore (in My presence) put off your shoes: you are in the sacred valley Tuwa."

13. "I have chosen you: listen, then, to the inspiration (sent to you)."

14. "Verily, I am Allah: there is no god but I: so serve you Me (only), and establish regular prayer for celebrating My praise."

15. "Verily the Hour is coming - I have kept it hidden - for every soul to receive its reward by the measure of its Endeavour."

16. "Therefore let not

بِقَبَسٍ اَوْ اَجِدُ عَلَى النَّارِ هُدًى ۝

فَلَمَّآ اَتٰىهَا نُوْدِىَ يٰمُوْسٰى ۝ اِنِّىْٓ

اَنَا رَبُّكَ فَاخْلَعْ نَعْلَيْكَ اِنَّكَ

بِالْوَادِ الْمُقَدَّسِ طُوًى ۝ وَ اَنَا

اخْتَرْتُكَ فَاسْتَمِعْ لِمَا يُوْحٰى ۝ اِنَّنِىْٓ

اَنَا اللّٰهُ لَآ اِلٰهَ اِلَّآ اَنَا فَاعْبُدْنِىْ

وَ اَقِمِ الصَّلٰوةَ لِذِكْرِىْ ۝ اِنَّ

السَّاعَةَ اٰتِيَةٌ اَكَادُ اُخْفِيْهَا لِتُجْزٰى

كُلُّ نَفْسٍ بِمَا تَسْعٰى ۝ فَلَا يَصُدَّنَّكَ

on high.

5. (Allah) Most Gracious is firmly established on the Throne (of Authority).

6. To Him belongs what is in the heavens and on earth, and all between them, and all beneath the soil.

7. If you pronounce the word aloud, (it is no matter): for verily He knows what is secret and what is yet more hidden.

8. Allah! There is no god but He! To Him belong the most Beautiful Names.

9. Has the story of Moses reached you?

10. Behold, he saw a fire: so he said to his family, "Tarry you; I perceive a fire; perhaps I can bring you

الْعُلَى ۞ اَلرَّحْمٰنُ عَلَى الْعَرْشِ

اسْتَوٰى ۞ لَهُ مَا فِى السَّمٰوٰتِ وَمَا

فِى الْاَرْضِ وَمَا بَيْنَهُمَا وَمَا تَحْتَ

الثَّرٰى ۞ وَاِنْ تَجْهَرْ بِالْقَوْلِ فَاِنَّهُ

يَعْلَمُ السِّرَّ وَاَخْفٰى ۞ اَللّٰهُ لَا اِلٰهَ

اِلَّا هُوَ لَهُ الْاَسْمَاءُ الْحُسْنٰى ۞

وَهَلْ اَتٰىكَ حَدِيْثُ مُوْسٰى ۞ اِذْ

رَاٰ نَارًا فَقَالَ لِاَهْلِهِ امْكُثُوْا

اِنِّىْ اٰنَسْتُ نَارًا لَّعَلِّىْ اٰتِيْكُمْ مِّنْهَا

will (Allah) Most Gracious bestow love.

97. So have We made the (Qur'an) easy in your own tongue, that with it you may give Glad Tidings to the righteous, and warnings to people given to contention

98. But how many (countless) generations before them have We destroyed? Can you find a single one of them (now) or hear (so much as) a whisper of them?

Ta-Ha

Bismillahir-Rahmanir-Rahim

1. Ta-Ha. **2.** We have not sent down the Qur'an to you to be (an occasion) for your distress,

3. But only as an admonition to those who fear (Allah), -

4. A revelation from Him Who created the earth and the heavens

سَيَجْعَلُ لَهُمُ الرَّحْمٰنُ وُدًّا ۞ فَاِنَّمَا

يَسَّرْنٰهُ بِلِسَانِكَ لِتُبَشِّرَ بِهِ الْمُتَّقِيْنَ

وَتُنْذِرَ بِهٖ قَوْمًا لُّدًّا ۞ وَكَمْ اَهْلَكْنَا

قَبْلَهُمْ مِّنْ قَرْنٍ ۗ هَلْ تُحِسُّ مِنْهُمْ

مِّنْ اَحَدٍ اَوْ تَسْمَعُ لَهُمْ رِكْزًا ۞

بِسْمِ اللهِ الرَّحْمٰنِ الرَّحِيْمِ

طٰهٰ ۞ مَآ اَنْزَلْنَا عَلَيْكَ الْقُرْاٰنَ

لِتَشْقٰى ۞ اِلَّا تَذْكِرَةً لِّمَنْ يَّخْشٰى ۞

تَنْزِيْلًا مِّمَّنْ خَلَقَ الْاَرْضَ وَالسَّمٰوٰتِ

89. Indeed you have put forth a thing most monstrous!

90. At it the skies are ready to burst, the earth to split asunder, and the mountains to fall down in utter ruin,

91. That they should invoke a son for (Allah) Most Gracious.

92. For it is not consonant with the majesty of (Allah) Most Gracious that He should beget a son.

93. Not one of the beings in the heavens and the earth but must come to (Allah) Most Gracious as a servant.

94. He does take an account of them (all), and has numbered them (all) exactly.

95. And everyone of them will come to Him singly on the Day of Judgment.

96. On those who believe and work deeds of righteousness,

لَقَدْ جِئْتُمْ شَيْئًا إِدًّا ۞ تَكَادُ السَّمٰوٰتُ

يَتَفَطَّرْنَ مِنْهُ وَتَنْشَقُّ الْأَرْضُ

وَتَخِرُّ الْجِبَالُ هَدًّا ۞ اَنْ دَعَوْا

لِلرَّحْمٰنِ وَلَدًا ۞ وَمَا يَنْبَغِيْ لِلرَّحْمٰنِ

اَنْ يَّتَّخِذَ وَلَدًا ۞ اِنْ كُلُّ مَنْ فِي

السَّمٰوٰتِ وَالْأَرْضِ اِلَّا اٰتِي الرَّحْمٰنِ

عَبْدًا ۞ لَقَدْ اَحْصٰهُمْ وَعَدَّهُمْ عَدًّا ۞

وَكُلُّهُمْ اٰتِيْهِ يَوْمَ الْقِيٰمَةِ فَرْدًا ۞

اِنَّ الَّذِيْنَ اٰمَنُوْا وَعَمِلُوا الصّٰلِحٰتِ

adversaries against them.

83. Do you see not that We have set the Evil Ones on against the unbelievers, to incite them with fury?

84. So make no haste against them, for We but count out to them a (limited) number (of days).

85. The day We shall gather the righteous to (Allah) Most Gracious, like a band presented before a king for honours,

86. And We shall drive the sinners to Hell, like thirsty cattle driven down to water, -

87. None shall have the power of intercession but such a one as has received permission (or promise) from (Allah) Most Gracious.

88. They say: "(Allah) Most Gracious has begotten a son!"

عَلَيْهِمْ ضِدًّا ۩ اَلَمْ تَرَ اَنَّا

اَرْسَلْنَا الشَّيَاطِيْنَ عَلَى الْكَفِرِيْنَ

تَؤُزُّهُمْ اَزًّا ۞ فَلَا تَعْجَلْ عَلَيْهِمْ

اِنَّمَا نَعُدُّ لَهُمْ عَدًّا ۞ يَوْمَ نَحْشُرُ

الْمُتَّقِيْنَ اِلَى الرَّحْمٰنِ وَفْدًا

۞ وَنَسُوْقُ الْمُجْرِمِيْنَ اِلٰى جَهَنَّمَ

وِرْدًا ۞ لَا يَمْلِكُوْنَ الشَّفَاعَةَ اِلَّا

مَنِ اتَّخَذَ عِنْدَ الرَّحْمٰنِ عَهْدًا ۞

وَقَالُوا اتَّخَذَ الرَّحْمٰنُ وَلَدًا ۞

77. Have you then seen the (sort of) man who rejects Our Signs, yet says: "I shall certainly be given wealth and children?"

78. Has he penetrated to the Unseen, or has he taken a contract with (Allah) Most Gracious?

79. No! We shall record what he says, and We shall add and add to his punishment.

80. To Us shall return all that he talks of and he shall appear before Us bare and alone.

81. And they have taken (for worship) gods other than Allah, to give them power and glory!

82. Instead, they shall reject their worship, and become

أَفَرَءَيْتَ الَّذِیْ كَفَرَ بِاٰیٰتِنَا

وَ قَالَ لَاُوْتَیَنَّ مَالًا وَّ وَلَدًاﻭ

اَطَّلَعَ الْغَیْبَ اَمِ اتَّخَذَ عِنْدَ

الرَّحْمٰنِ عَهْدًاﻭ كَلَّا سَنَكْتُبُ

مَا یَقُوْلُ وَ نَمُدُّ لَهٗ مِنَ الْعَذَابِ

مَدًّاﻭ وَّ نَرِثُهٗ مَا یَقُوْلُ وَ یَاْتِیْنَا

فَرْدًاﻭ وَاتَّخَذُوْا مِنْ دُوْنِ اللهِ

اٰلِهَةً لِّیَكُوْنُوْا لَهُمْ عِزًّاﻭ كَلَّا

سَیَكْفُرُوْنَ بِعِبَادَتِهِمْ وَ یَكُوْنُوْنَ

who were even better in equipment and in glitter to the eye?

75. Say: "If any men go astray, (Allah) Most Gracious extends (the rope) to them, until, when they see the warning of Allah (being fulfilled) - either in punishment or in (the approach of) the Hour, - they will at length realise who is worst in position, and (who) weakest in forces!"

76. "And Allah does advance in guidance those who seek guidance: and the things that endure, Good Deeds, are best in the sight of your Lord, as rewards, and best in respect of (their) eventual return."

هُمْ أَحْسَنُ أَثَاثًا وَّرِءْيًا ۞ قُلْ

مَنْ كَانَ فِي الضَّلٰلَةِ فَلْيَمْدُدْ

لَهُ الرَّحْمٰنُ مَدًّا ۚ حَتّٰى إِذَا رَأَوْا

مَا يُوعَدُونَ إِمَّا الْعَذَابَ وَإِمَّا

السَّاعَةَ ۗ فَسَيَعْلَمُونَ مَنْ هُوَ

شَرٌّ مَّكَانًا وَّأَضْعَفُ جُنْدًا ۞

وَيَزِيدُ اللهُ الَّذِينَ اهْتَدَوْا

هُدًى ۗ وَالْبَاقِيَاتُ الصّٰلِحٰتُ خَيْرٌ

عِنْدَ رَبِّكَ ثَوَابًا وَّخَيْرٌ مَّرَدًّا ۞

those who are most worthy of being burned therein.

71. Not one of you but will pass over it: this is, with your Lord, a Decree which must be accomplished.

72. But We shall save those who guarded against evil, and We shall leave the wrong-doers therein, (humbled) to their knees.

73. When Our clear Signs are rehearsed to them, the unbelievers say to those who believe, "Which of the two sides is best in point of position? Which makes the best show in council?"

74. But how many (countless) generations before them have We destroyed,

بِالَّذِينَ هُمْ اَوْلَى بِهَا صِلِيًّا ۞

وَاِنْ مِّنْكُمْ اِلَّا وَارِدُهَا ۚ كَانَ عَلٰى

رَبِّكَ حَتْمًا مَّقْضِيًّا ۞ ثُمَّ نُنَجِّى

الَّذِينَ اتَّقَوْا وَّنَذَرُ الظّٰلِمِينَ

فِيهَا جِثِيًّا ۞ وَاِذَا تُتْلٰى عَلَيْهِمْ

اٰيٰتُنَا بَيِّنٰتٍ قَالَ الَّذِينَ كَفَرُوا

لِلَّذِينَ اٰمَنُوْا ۚ اَىُّ الْفَرِيقَيْنِ

خَيْرٌ مَّقَامًا وَّاَحْسَنُ نَدِيًّا ۞

وَكَمْ اَهْلَكْنَا قَبْلَهُمْ مِّنْ قَرْنٍ

in His worship: do you of any who is worthy of the same Name as He?"

66. Man says: "What! When I am dead, shall I then be raised up alive?"

67. But does not man call to mind that We created him before out of nothing?

68. So, by your Lord, without doubt, We shall gather them together, and (also) the Evil Ones (with them); then shall We bring them forth on their knees round about Hell;

69. Then shall We certainly drag out from every sect all those who were worst in obstinate rebellion against (Allah) Most Gracious.

70. And certainly We know best

لِعِبَادَتِهِ هَلْ تَعْلَمُ لَهُ سَمِيًّا ۝

وَيَقُوْلُ الْإِنْسَانُ ءَاِذَا مَا مِتُّ

لَسَوْفَ اُخْرَجُ حَيًّا ۝ اَوَلَا يَذْكُرُ

الْإِنْسَانُ اَنَّا خَلَقْنٰهُ مِنْ قَبْلُ وَلَمْ

يَكُ شَيْئًا ۝ فَوَرَبِّكَ لَنَحْشُرَنَّهُمْ

وَالشَّيٰطِيْنَ ثُمَّ لَنُحْضِرَنَّهُمْ حَوْلَ

جَهَنَّمَ جِثِيًّا ۝ ثُمَّ لَنَنْزِعَنَّ مِنْ

كُلِّ شِيْعَةٍ اَيُّهُمْ اَشَدُّ عَلَى

الرَّحْمٰنِ عِتِيًّا ۝ ثُمَّ لَنَحْنُ اَعْلَمُ

62. They will not there hear any vain discourse, but only salutations of Peace: and they will have therein their sustenance, morning and evening.

63. Such is the Garden which We give as an inheritance to those of Our servants who guard against Evil.

64. (The Angels say:) "We descend not but by command of your Lord: to Him belongs what is before us and what is behind us, and what is between: and your Lord never does forget," -

65. "Lord of the heavens and of the earth, and of all that is between them; so worship Him, and be constant and patient

يَّسْمَعُوْنَ فِيْهَا لَغْوًا اِلَّا سَلٰمًا ۗ وَلَهُمْ

رِزْقُهُمْ فِيْهَا بُكْرَةً وَّعَشِيًّا ۞

تِلْكَ الْجَنَّةُ الَّتِيْ نُوْرِثُ مِنْ

عِبَادِنَا مَنْ كَانَ تَقِيًّا ۞ وَمَا

نَتَنَزَّلُ اِلَّا بِاَمْرِ رَبِّكَ ۚ لَهٗ مَا

بَيْنَ اَيْدِيْنَا وَمَا خَلْفَنَا وَمَا

بَيْنَ ذٰلِكَ ۚ وَمَا كَانَ رَبُّكَ

نَسِيًّا ۞ رَبُّ السَّمٰوٰتِ وَالْاَرْضِ

وَمَا بَيْنَهُمَا فَاعْبُدْهُ وَاصْطَبِرْ

the Signs of (Allah) Most Gracious were rehearsed to them, they would fall down in prostrate adoration and in tears.

59. But after them there followed a posterity who missed prayers and followed after lusts soon, then, will they face Destruction, -

60. Except those who repent and believe, and work righteousness: for these will enter the Garden and will not be wronged in the least, -

61. Gardens of Eternity, those which (Allah) Most Gracious has promised to His servants in the Unseen: for His promise must (necessarily) come to pass.

عَلَيْهِمْ اٰيٰتُ الرَّحْمٰنِ خَرُّوْا سُجَّدًا

وَّبُكِيًّا ۩ فَخَلَفَ مِنْ بَعْدِهِمْ

خَلْفٌ اَضَاعُوا الصَّلٰوةَ وَاتَّبَعُوا

الشَّهَوٰتِ فَسَوْفَ يَلْقَوْنَ غَيًّا ۙ

اِلَّا مَنْ تَابَ وَاٰمَنَ وَعَمِلَ

صَالِحًا فَاُولٰٓئِكَ يَدْخُلُوْنَ الْجَنَّةَ

وَلَا يُظْلَمُوْنَ شَيْئًا ۙ جَنّٰتِ عَدْنِ

الَّتِيْ وَعَدَ الرَّحْمٰنُ عِبَادَهٗ بِالْغَيْبِ

اِنَّهٗ كَانَ وَعْدُهٗ مَأْتِيًّا ۙ لَا

Prayer and Charity, and he was most acceptable in the sight of his Lord.

56.   Also mention in the Book the case of Idris: he was a man of truth (and sincerity), (and) a Prophet:

57.   And We raised him to a lofty station.

58.   Those were some of the Prophets on whom Allah did bestow His Grace, - of the posterity of Adam, and of those who We carried (in the Ark) with Noah, and of the posterity of Abraham and Israel of those whom We guided and chose. Whenever

بِالصَّلٰوةِ وَالزَّكٰوةِ ۚ وَكَانَ عِنْدَ

رَبِّهٖ مَرْضِيًّا ۞ وَاذْكُرْ فِى الْكِتٰبِ

اِدْرِيْسَ ۫ اِنَّهٗ كَانَ صِدِّيْقًا نَّبِيًّا ۙ ۞

وَّرَفَعْنٰهُ مَكَانًا عَلِيًّا ۞ اُولٰٓئِكَ

الَّذِيْنَ اَنْعَمَ اللّٰهُ عَلَيْهِمْ مِّنَ

النَّبِيّٖنَ مِنْ ذُرِّيَّةِ اٰدَمَ وَمِمَّنْ

حَمَلْنَا مَعَ نُوْحٍ ۫ وَّمِنْ ذُرِّيَّةِ

اِبْرٰهِيْمَ وَاِسْرَآئِيْلَ ۫ وَمِمَّنْ

هَدَيْنَا وَاجْتَبَيْنَا ۗ اِذَا تُتْلٰى

them lofty honour on the tongue of truth.

51.   Also mention in the Book (the story of) Moses: for he was specially chosen, and he was an Apostle (and) a Prophet.

52.   And We called him from the right side of Mount (Sinai), and made him draw near to Us, for mystic (converse).

53.   And, out of Our Mercy, We gave him his brother Aaron, (also) a Prophet.

54.   Also mention in the Book (the story of) Isma'il: he was (strictly) true to what he promised, and he was an Apostle (and) a Prophet.

55.   He used to enjoin on his people

لَهُمْ لِسَانَ صِدْقٍ عَلِيًّا ۞ وَاذْكُرْ

فِي الْكِتٰبِ مُوسٰى ۖ اِنَّهٗ كَانَ

مُخْلَصًا وَّكَانَ رَسُوْلًا نَّبِيًّا ۞

وَنَادَيْنٰهُ مِنْ جَانِبِ الطُّوْرِ

الْاَيْمَنِ وَقَرَّبْنٰهُ نَجِيًّا ۞ وَوَهَبْنَا

لَهٗ مِنْ رَّحْمَتِنَا أَخَاهُ هٰرُوْنَ

نَبِيًّا ۞ وَاذْكُرْ فِي الْكِتٰبِ اِسْمٰعِيْلَ ۖ

اِنَّهٗ كَانَ صَادِقَ الْوَعْدِ وَكَانَ

رَسُوْلًا نَّبِيًّا ۞ وَكَانَ يَأْمُرُ اَهْلَهٗ

for a good long while!"

47. (Abraham) said: "Peace be on you: I will pray to my Lord for your forgiveness: for He is to me Most Gracious."

48. "And I will turn away from you (all) and from those whom you invoke besides Allah: I will call on my Lord: perhaps, by my prayer to my Lord, I shall be not unblessed."

49. When he had turned away from them and from those whom they worshipped besides Allah, We bestowed on him Isaac and Jacob, and each one of them We made a Prophet.

50. And We bestowed of Our Mercy on them, and We granted

مَلِيًّا ۞ قَالَ سَلٰمٌ عَلَيْكَ سَاَسْتَغْفِرُ

لَكَ رَبِّیۡ ؕ اِنَّهٗ كَانَ بِیۡ حَفِیًّا ۞

وَ اَعْتَزِلُكُمْ وَ مَا تَدْعُوْنَ مِنْ

دُوْنِ اللّٰهِ وَ اَدْعُوْا رَبِّیۡ ۖ عَسٰۤى

اَلَّاۤ اَكُوْنَ بِدُعَآءِ رَبِّیۡ شَقِیًّا ۞

فَلَمَّا اعْتَزَلَهُمْ وَ مَا يَعْبُدُوْنَ

مِنْ دُوْنِ اللّٰهِ ۙ وَهَبْنَا لَهٗۤ اِسْحٰقَ

وَيَعْقُوْبَ ؕ وَكُلًّا جَعَلْنَا نَبِيًّا ۞

وَوَهَبْنَا لَهُمْ مِّنْ رَّحْمَتِنَا وَجَعَلْنَا

43. "O my father! To me has come knowledge which has not reached you: so follow me: I will guide you to a way that is even and straight."

44. "O my father! Serve not Satan: for Satan is a rebel against (Allah) Most Gracious."

45. "O my father! I fear lest a Chastisement afflict you from (Allah) Most Gracious, so that you become to Satan a friend."

46. (The father) replied: "Do you hate my gods, O Abraham? If you forbear not, I will indeed stone you: now get away from me

يٰۤاَبَتِ اِنِّیۡ قَدۡ جَآءَنِیۡ مِنَ الۡعِلۡمِ

مَا لَمۡ یَاۡتِكَ فَاتَّبِعۡنِیۡۤ اَهۡدِكَ

صِرَاطًا سَوِیًّا ۞ یٰۤاَبَتِ لَا تَعۡبُدِ

الشَّیۡطٰنَ ؕ اِنَّ الشَّیۡطٰنَ كَانَ

لِلرَّحۡمٰنِ عَصِیًّا ۞ یٰۤاَبَتِ اِنِّیۡۤ اَخَافُ

اَنۡ یَّمَسَّكَ عَذَابٌ مِّنَ الرَّحۡمٰنِ

فَتَكُوۡنَ لِلشَّیۡطٰنِ وَلِیًّا ۞ قَالَ

اَرَاغِبٌ اَنۡتَ عَنۡ اٰلِهَتِیۡ یٰۤاِبۡرٰهِیۡمُ ۚ

لَئِنۡ لَّمۡ تَنۡتَهِ لَاَرۡجُمَنَّكَ وَاهۡجُرۡنِیۡ

are in error manifest!

39.   But warn them of the Day of Distress, when the matter will be determined: for (behold,) they are negligent and they do not believe!

40.   It is We Who will inherit the earth, and all beings thereon: to Us will they all be returned.

41.   (Also mention in the Book (the story of) Abraham: he was a man of Truth, a Prophet.

42.   Behold, he said to his father: "O my father! Why worship that which hears not and sees not, and can profit you nothing?"

فِىْ ضَلٰلٍ مُّبِيْنٍ ۞ وَاَنْذِرْهُمْ يَوْمَ

الْحَسْرَةِ اِذْ قُضِىَ الْاَمْرُ وَهُمْ

فِىْ غَفْلَةٍ وَّهُمْ لَا يُؤْمِنُوْنَ ۞

اِنَّا نَحْنُ نَرِثُ الْاَرْضَ وَمَنْ

عَلَيْهَا وَاِلَيْنَا يُرْجَعُوْنَ ۞ وَاذْكُرْ

فِى الْكِتٰبِ اِبْرٰهِيْمَ ۚ اِنَّهٗ كَانَ

صِدِّيْقًا نَّبِيًّا ۞ اِذْ قَالَ لِاَبِيْهِ

يٰٓاَبَتِ لِمَ تَعْبُدُ مَا لَا يَسْمَعُ

وَلَا يُبْصِرُ وَلَا يُغْنِىْ عَنْكَ شَيْئًا ۞

35. It is not befitting to (the majesty of) Allah that He should beget a son. Glory be to Him! When He determines a matter, He only says to it, "Be", and it is.

36. Verily Allah is my Lord and your Lord: Him therefore serve you: this is a way that is straight.

37. But the sects differ among themselves: and woe to the unbelievers because of the (coming) Judgment of a momentous Day!

38. How plainly will they see and hear, the Day that they will appear before Us! But the unjust today

مَا كَانَ لِلّٰهِ اَنْ يَّتَّخِذَ مِنْ

وَّلَدٍ سُبْحٰنَهٗ ؕ اِذَا قَضٰى اَمْرًا

فَاِنَّمَا يَقُوْلُ لَهٗ كُنْ فَيَكُوْنُ ۟ؕ

وَاِنَّ اللّٰهَ رَبِّيْ وَرَبُّكُمْ فَاعْبُدُوْهُ ؕ

هٰذَا صِرَاطٌ مُّسْتَقِيْمٌ ۝ فَاخْتَلَفَ

الْاَحْزَابُ مِنْ بَيْنِهِمْ ۚ فَوَيْلٌ

لِّلَّذِيْنَ كَفَرُوْا مِنْ مَّشْهَدِ يَوْمٍ

عَظِيْمٍ ۝ اَسْمِعْ بِهِمْ وَاَبْصِرْ ۙ يَوْمَ

يَاْتُوْنَنَا لٰكِنِ الظّٰلِمُوْنَ الْيَوْمَ

30. He said: "I am indeed a servant of Allah: He has given me revelation and made me a Prophet;"

31. "And He has made me blessed wheresoever I be, and has enjoined on me Prayer and Charity as long as I live;"

32. "(He) has made me kind to my mother, and not overbearing or miserable;"

33. "So peace is on me the day I was born, the day that I die, and the day that I shall be raised up to life (again)"!

34. Such (was) Jesus the son of Mary: (it is) a statement of truth, about which they (vainly) dispute.

قَالَ اِنِّیْ عَبْدُ اللّٰهِ ۟ اٰتٰىنِیَ الْكِتٰبَ

وَجَعَلَنِیْ نَبِیًّا ۟ ۙ وَّجَعَلَنِیْ مُبٰرَكًا

اَیْنَ مَا كُنْتُ ۚ وَاَوْصٰنِیْ بِالصَّلٰوةِ

وَالزَّكٰوةِ مَا دُمْتُ حَیًّا ۟ ۙ وَبَرًّۢا

بِوَالِدَتِیْ ۫ وَلَمْ یَجْعَلْنِیْ جَبَّارًا

شَقِیًّا ۟ وَالسَّلٰمُ عَلَیَّ یَوْمَ وُلِدْتُّ

وَیَوْمَ اَمُوْتُ وَیَوْمَ اُبْعَثُ حَیًّا ۟

ذٰلِكَ عِیْسَی ابْنُ مَرْیَمَ ۚ قَوْلَ

الْحَقِّ الَّذِیْ فِیْهِ یَمْتَرُوْنَ ۟

and if you see any man, say, 'I have vowed a fast to (Allah) Most Gracious, and this day will I enter into not talk with any human being.'"

27. At length she brought the (babe) to her people, carrying him (in her arms). They said: "O Mary! Truly an amazing thing have you brought!"

28. "O sister of Aaron! Your father was not a man of evil, nor your mother a woman unchaste!"

29. But she pointed to the babe. They said: "How can we talk to one who is a child in the cradle?"

فَإِمَّا تَرَيِنَّ مِنَ الْبَشَرِ أَحَدًا

فَقُولِي إِنِّي نَذَرْتُ لِلرَّحْمَنِ صَوْمًا

فَلَنْ أُكَلِّمَ الْيَوْمَ إِنْسِيًّا ۝ فَأَتَتْ

بِهِ قَوْمَهَا تَحْمِلُهُ ۖ قَالُوا يَا مَرْيَمُ

لَقَدْ جِئْتِ شَيْئًا فَرِيًّا ۝ يَا أُخْتَ

هَارُونَ مَا كَانَ أَبُوكِ امْرَأَ

سَوْءٍ وَمَا كَانَتْ أُمُّكِ بَغِيًّا ۝

فَأَشَارَتْ إِلَيْهِ ۖ قَالُوا كَيْفَ نُكَلِّمُ

مَنْ كَانَ فِي الْمَهْدِ صَبِيًّا ۝

22. So she conceived him, and she retired with him to a remote place.

23. And the pains of childbirth drove her to the trunk of a palm-tree: she cried (in her anguish): "Ah! Would that I had died before this! Would that I had been a thing forgotten and out of sight!"

24. But (a voice) cried to her from beneath the (palm-tree): "Grieve not! For your Lord has provided a rivulet beneath you";

25. "And shake towards thyself the trunk of the palm-tree: it will let fall fresh ripe dates upon you."

26. "So eat and drink and cool (your) eye.

فَحَمَلَتْهُ فَانْتَبَذَتْ بِهِ مَكَانًا

قَصِيًّا ۞ فَأَجَاءَهَا الْمَخَاضُ إِلَى

جِذْعِ النَّخْلَةِ قَالَتْ يَا لَيْتَنِي مِتُّ

قَبْلَ هَذَا وَكُنْتُ نَسْيًا مَنْسِيًّا ۞

فَنَادَاهَا مِنْ تَحْتِهَا أَلَّا تَحْزَنِي

قَدْ جَعَلَ رَبُّكِ تَحْتَكِ سَرِيًّا ۞

وَهُزِّي إِلَيْكِ بِجِذْعِ النَّخْلَةِ

تُسَاقِطْ عَلَيْكِ رُطَبًا جَنِيًّا ۞

فَكُلِي وَاشْرَبِي وَقَرِّي عَيْنًا

and he appeared before her as a man in all respects.

18.   She said: "I seek refuge from you to (Allah) Most Gracious: (come not near) if you do fear Allah."

19.   He said: "No, I am only a Messenger from your Lord, (to announce) to you the gift of a holy son."

20.   She said: "How shall I have a son, seeing that no man has touched me, and I am not unchaste?"

21.   He said: "So (it will be): your Lord says 'that is easy for Me: and (We wish) to appoint him as a Sign unto men and a Mercy from Us': it is a matter (so) decreed."

فَتَمَثَّلَ لَهَا بَشَرًا سَوِيًّا ۝ قَالَتْ

اِنِّى اَعُوْذُ بِالرَّحْمٰنِ مِنْكَ اِنْ

كُنْتَ تَقِيًّا ۝ قَالَ اِنَّمَا اَنَا رَسُوْلُ

رَبِّكِ لِاَهَبَ لَكِ غُلٰمًا زَكِيًّا ۝

قَالَتْ اَنّٰى يَكُوْنُ لِيْ غُلٰمٌ وَّلَمْ

يَمْسَسْنِيْ بَشَرٌ وَّلَمْ اَكُ بَغِيًّا ۝

قَالَ كَذٰلِكِ ۚ قَالَ رَبُّكِ هُوَ عَلَيَّ

هَيِّنٌ ۚ وَلِنَجْعَلَهٗ اٰيَةً لِّلنَّاسِ

وَرَحْمَةً مِّنَّا ۚ وَكَانَ اَمْرًا مَّقْضِيًّا ۝

and We gave him Wisdom even as a youth,

13. And piety (for all creatures) as from Us, and purity: he was devout,

14. And kind to his parents, and he was not overbearing or rebellious.

15. So Peace on him the day he was born, the day that he dies, and the day that he will be raised up to life (again)!

16. Relate in the Book (the story of) Mary, when she withdrew from her family to a place in the East.

17. She placed a screen (to screen herself) from them; then We sent to her Our Angel,

وَاٰتَيْنٰهُ الْحُكْمَ صَبِيًّا ۟ وَّحَنَانًا

مِّنْ لَّدُنَّا وَزَكٰوةً ۖ وَكَانَ تَقِيًّا ۟

وَّبَرًّۢا بِوَالِدَيْهِ وَلَمْ يَكُنْ

جَبَّارًا عَصِيًّا ۟ وَسَلٰمٌ عَلَيْهِ يَوْمَ

وُلِدَ وَيَوْمَ يَمُوْتُ وَيَوْمَ يُبْعَثُ

حَيًّا ۟ وَاذْكُرْ فِي الْكِتٰبِ مَرْيَمَ ۘ

اِذِ انْتَبَذَتْ مِنْ اَهْلِهَا مَكَانًا

شَرْقِيًّا ۟ فَاتَّخَذَتْ مِنْ دُوْنِهِمْ

حِجَابًا ۪ فَاَرْسَلْنَآ اِلَيْهَا رُوْحَنَا

I have grown quite decrepit from old age?"

9. He said: "So (it will be) your Lord says, 'That is easy for Me: I did indeed create you before, when you had been nothing!'"

10. (Zakariya) said: "O my Lord! Give me a Sign." "Your Sign," was the answer, "Shall be that you shall speak to no man for three nights, although you are not dumb."

11. So Zakariya came out to his people from his chamber: he told them by signs to celebrate Allah's praises in the morning and in the evening.

12. (To his son came the command): "O Yahya! Take hold of the Book with might,"

بَلَغْتُ مِنَ الْكِبَرِ عِتِيًّا ۞ قَالَ

كَذٰلِكَ قَالَ رَبُّكَ هُوَ عَلَىَّ هَيِّنٌ

وَّقَدْ خَلَقْتُكَ مِنْ قَبْلُ وَلَمْ

تَكُ شَيْئًا ۞ قَالَ رَبِّ اجْعَلْ

لِّيْ اٰيَةً ۚ قَالَ اٰيَتُكَ اَلَّا تُكَلِّمَ

النَّاسَ ثَلٰثَ لَيَالٍ سَوِيًّا ۞

فَخَرَجَ عَلٰى قَوْمِهٖ مِنَ الْمِحْرَابِ

فَاَوْحٰى اِلَيْهِمْ اَنْ سَبِّحُوْا بُكْرَةً

وَّعَشِيًّا ۞ يٰيَحْيٰى خُذِ الْكِتٰبَ بِقُوَّةٍ

5.   "Now I fear (what) my relatives (and colleagues) (will do) after me: but my wife is barren: so give me an heir as from Yourself,"

6.   "(One that) will (truly) represent me, and represent the posterity of Jacob; and make him, O my Lord! one with whom You are well-pleased!"

7.   (His prayer was answered): "O Zakariya! We give you good news of a son: his name shall be Yahya: on none by that name have We conferred distinction before."

8.   He said: "O my Lord! How shall I have a son, when my wife is barren and

شَقِيًّا ۞ وَاِنِّى خِفْتُ الْمَوَالِىَ مِنْ

وَّرَآءِى وَكَانَتِ امْرَاَتِىْ عَاقِرًا

فَهَبْ لِىْ مِنْ لَّدُنْكَ وَلِيًّا ۞

يَّرِثُنِىْ وَيَرِثُ مِنْ اٰلِ يَعْقُوبَ

وَاجْعَلْهُ رَبِّ رَضِيًّا ۞ يٰزَكَرِيَّآ اِنَّا

نُبَشِّرُكَ بِغُلٰمِ اسْمُهٗ يَحْيٰى لَمْ

نَجْعَلْ لَّهٗ مِنْ قَبْلُ سَمِيًّا ۞

قَالَ رَبِّ اَنّٰى يَكُوْنُ لِىْ غُلٰمٌ

وَّكَانَتِ امْرَاَتِىْ عَاقِرًا وَّقَدْ

expects to meet his Lord, let him work righteousness, and, in the worship of his Lord, admit no one as partner.

Maryam (Mary)

Bismillahir-Rahmanir-Rahim

1. Kaf. Ha. Ya. 'Ain. Sad.

2. (This is) a recital of the Mercy of your Lord to His servant Zakariya.

3. Behold! He cried to his Lord in secret,

4. Praying: "O my Lord! Infirm indeed are my bones, and the hair of my head does glisten with grey: but never am I unblest, O my Lord, in my prayer to You!

يَرْجُوا۟ لِقَآءَ رَبِّهِۦ فَلْيَعْمَلْ

عَمَلًا صَالِحًا وَّلَا يُشْرِكْ بِعِبَادَةِ

رَبِّهِۦٓ أَحَدًا ۝

بِسْمِ اللَّهِ الرَّحْمَٰنِ الرَّحِيمِ

كٓهيعٓصٓ ۝ ذِكْرُ رَحْمَتِ رَبِّكَ

عَبْدَهُۥ زَكَرِيَّآ ۝ إِذْ نَادَىٰ رَبَّهُۥ

نِدَآءً خَفِيًّا ۝ قَالَ رَبِّ إِنِّى وَهَنَ

ٱلْعَظْمُ مِنِّى وَٱشْتَعَلَ ٱلرَّأْسُ

شَيْبًا وَّلَمْ أَكُنۢ بِدُعَآئِكَ رَبِّ

107. As to those who believe and work righteous deeds, they have, for their entertainment, the Gardens of Paradise,

108. Wherein they shall dwell (for ever), no change will they wish for from them.

109. Say: "If the ocean were ink (wherewith to write out) the Words of my Lord, sooner would the ocean be exhausted than would the Words of my Lord, even if we added another ocean like it, for its aid."

110. Say: "I am but a man like yourselves, (but) the inspiration has come to me, that your Allah is one Allah: whoever

اِنَّ الَّذِيْنَ اٰمَنُوْا وَعَمِلُوا الصَّلِحٰتِ

كَانَتْ لَهُمْ جَنّٰتُ الْفِرْدَوْسِ نُزُلًا ۝

خٰلِدِيْنَ فِيْهَا لَا يَبْغُوْنَ عَنْهَا

حِوَلًا ۝ قُلْ لَّوْ كَانَ الْبَحْرُ مِدَادًا

لِّكَلِمٰتِ رَبِّيْ لَنَفِدَ الْبَحْرُ قَبْلَ

اَنْ تَنْفَدَ كَلِمٰتُ رَبِّيْ وَلَوْ جِئْنَا

بِمِثْلِهٖ مَدَدًا ۝ قُلْ اِنَّمَاۤ اَنَا

بَشَرٌ مِّثْلُكُمْ يُوْحٰىۤ اِلَيَّ اَنَّمَاۤ

اِلٰهُكُمْ اِلٰهٌ وَّاحِدٌ ۚ فَمَنْ كَانَ

103. Say: "Shall we tell you of those who lose most in respect of their deeds?" -

104. "Those whose efforts have been wasted in this life, while they thought that they were acquiring good by their works?"

105. They are those who deny the Signs of their Lord and the fact of their having to meet Him (in the Hereafter): vain will be their works, nor shall We, on the Day of Judgment, give them any weight.

106. That is their reward, Hell, because they rejected Faith, and took My Signs and My Messengers by way of jest.

قُلْ هَلْ نُنَبِّئُكُمْ بِالْأَخْسَرِينَ

أَعْمَالًا ۟ اَلَّذِينَ ضَلَّ سَعْيُهُمْ

فِى الْحَيَوٰةِ الدُّنْيَا وَهُمْ يَحْسَبُونَ

أَنَّهُمْ يُحْسِنُونَ صُنْعًا ۟ أُولَٰٓئِكَ

الَّذِينَ كَفَرُوا بِآيَٰتِ رَبِّهِمْ

وَلِقَآئِهِ فَحَبِطَتْ أَعْمَالُهُمْ فَلَا

نُقِيمُ لَهُمْ يَوْمَ الْقِيٰمَةِ وَزْنًا ۟

ذَٰلِكَ جَزَآؤُهُمْ جَهَنَّمُ بِمَا كَفَرُوا

وَاتَّخَذُوٓا اٰيَٰتِى وَرُسُلِى هُزُوًا ۟

them to surge like waves on one another: the trumpet will be blown, and We shall collect them all together.

100. And We shall present Hell that day for unbelievers to see, all spread out, -

101. (Unbelievers) whose eyes had been under a veil from remembrance of Me, and who had been unable even to hear.

102. Do the unbelievers think that they can take My servants as protectors besides Me? Verily We have prepared Hell for the unbelievers for (their) entertainment.

بَعْضُهُمْ يَوْمَئِذٍ يَمُوجُ فِيْ بَعْضٍ
وَّنُفِخَ فِي الصُّوْرِ فَجَمَعْنٰهُمْ جَمْعًا ۞
وَّعَرَضْنَا جَهَنَّمَ يَوْمَئِذٍ لِّلْكٰفِرِيْنَ
عَرْضًا ۞ اَلَّذِيْنَ كَانَتْ اَعْيُنُهُمْ
فِيْ غِطَاءٍ عَنْ ذِكْرِيْ وَكَانُوْا لَا
يَسْتَطِيْعُوْنَ سَمْعًا ۞ اَفَحَسِبَ
الَّذِيْنَ كَفَرُوْۤا اَنْ يَّتَّخِذُوْا
عِبَادِيْ مِنْ دُوْنِيْۤ اَوْلِيَاءَ اِنَّاۤ
اَعْتَدْنَا جَهَنَّمَ لِلْكٰفِرِيْنَ نُزُلًا ۞

I will erect a strong barrier between you and them:"

96. "Bring me blocks of iron." At length, when he had filled up the space between the two steep mountain-sides, He said, "Blow (with your bellows)" then, when he had made it (red) as fire, he said: "Bring me, that I may pour over it, molten copper."

97. Thus were they made powerless to scale it or to dig through it.

98. He said: "This is a mercy from my Lord: but when the promise of my Lord comes to pass, He will make it into dust; and the promise of my Lord is true."

99. On that day We shall leave

اَجْعَلْ بَيْنَكُمْ وَ بَيْنَهُمْ رَدْمًا ۝

اٰتُونِيْ زُبَرَ الْحَدِيْدِ ۖ حَتّٰى اِذَا

سَاوٰى بَيْنَ الصَّدَفَيْنِ قَالَ انْفُخُوْا ۖ

حَتّٰى اِذَا جَعَلَهٗ نَارًا ۙ قَالَ اٰتُوْنِيْ

اُفْرِغْ عَلَيْهِ قِطْرًا ۝ فَمَا اسْطَاعُوْا

اَنْ يَّظْهَرُوْهُ وَ مَا اسْتَطَاعُوْا لَهٗ

نَقْبًا ۝ قَالَ هٰذَا رَحْمَةٌ مِّنْ رَّبِّيْ ۖ

فَاِذَا جَآءَ وَعْدُ رَبِّيْ جَعَلَهٗ دَكَّآءَ ۖ

وَكَانَ وَعْدُ رَبِّيْ حَقًّا ۝ وَتَرَكْنَا

92.   Then followed he (another) way,

93.   Until, when he reached (a tract) between two mountains, he found, beneath them, a people who scarcely understood a word.

94.   They said: "O Zul-qarnain! The Gog and Magog (People) do great mischief on earth: shall we then render you tribute in order that you might erect a barrier between us and them?"

95.   He said: "(The power) in which my Lord has established me is better (than tribute): help me therefore with strength (and labour):

خُبْرًا ۝ ثُمَّ اَتْبَعَ سَبَبًا ۝ حَتّٰى

اِذَا بَلَغَ بَيْنَ السَّدَّيْنِ وَجَدَ

مِنْ دُوْنِهِمَا قَوْمًا لَّا يَكَادُوْنَ

يَفْقَهُوْنَ قَوْلًا ۝ قَالُوْا يٰذَا الْقَرْنَيْنِ

اِنَّ يَأْجُوْجَ وَمَأْجُوْجَ مُفْسِدُوْنَ

فِى الْاَرْضِ فَهَلْ نَجْعَلُ لَكَ

خَرْجًا عَلٰٓى اَنْ تَجْعَلَ بَيْنَنَا

وَبَيْنَهُمْ سَدًّا ۝ قَالَ مَا مَكَّنِّيْ

فِيْهِ رَبِّيْ خَيْرٌ فَاَعِيْنُوْنِيْ بِقُوَّةٍ

does wrong, him shall we punish; then shall he be sent back to his Lord; and He will punish him with a punishment unheard-of (before)."

88. "But whoever believes, and works righteousness, - he shall have a goodly reward, and easy will be his task as we order it by our Command."

89. Then followed he (another) way,

90. Until, when he came to the rising of the sun, he found it rising on a people for whom We had provided no covering protection against the sun.

91. (He left them) as they were: We completely understood what was before him.

ظَلَمَ فَسَوْفَ نُعَذِّبُهُ ثُمَّ يُرَدُّ إِلَى

رَبِّهِ فَيُعَذِّبُهُ عَذَابًا نُّكْرًا ۞

وَأَمَّا مَنْ أَمَنَ وَعَمِلَ صَالِحًا

فَلَهُ جَزَآءً الْحُسْنَى وَسَنَقُولُ لَهُ

مِنْ أَمْرِنَا يُسْرًا ۞ ثُمَّ أَتْبَعَ

سَبَبًا ۞ حَتَّى إِذَا بَلَغَ مَطْلِعَ

الشَّمْسِ وَجَدَهَا تَطْلُعُ عَلَى قَوْمٍ

لَّمْ نَجْعَل لَّهُم مِّن دُونِهَا سِتْرًا ۞

كَذَٰلِكَ ۖ وَقَدْ أَحَطْنَا بِمَا لَدَيْهِ

Zul-qarnain. Say, "I will rehearse to you something of his story."

84. Verily We established his power on earth, and We gave him the ways and the means to all ends.

85. One (such) way he followed,

86. Until, when he reached the setting of the sun, he found it set in a spring of murky water: near it he found a people: We said: "O Zul-qarnain! (You have authority,) either to punish them, or to treat them with kindness."

87. He said: "Whoever

ذِى الْقَرْنَيْنِ ۗ قُلْ سَاَتْلُوْا عَلَيْكُمْ
مِّنْهُ ذِكْرًا ۞ اِنَّا مَكَّنَّا لَهٗ فِى
الْاَرْضِ وَ اٰتَيْنٰهُ مِنْ كُلِّ شَىْءٍ
سَبَبًا ۙ فَاَتْبَعَ سَبَبًا ۞ حَتّٰى اِذَا
بَلَغَ مَغْرِبَ الشَّمْسِ وَجَدَهَا
تَغْرُبُ فِىْ عَيْنٍ حَمِئَةٍ وَّ وَجَدَ
عِنْدَهَا قَوْمًا ۗ قُلْنَا يٰذَا الْقَرْنَيْنِ
اِمَّاۤ اَنْ تُعَذِّبَ وَاِمَّاۤ اَنْ تَتَّخِذَ
فِيْهِمْ حُسْنًا ۞ قَالَ اَمَّا مَنْ

(a son) better in purity (of conduct) and closer in affection."

82. "As for the wall, it belonged to two youths, orphans, in the Town; there was, beneath it, a buried treasure, to which they were entitled: their father had been a righteous man: so your Lord desired that they should attain their age of full strength and get out their treasure - a mercy (and favour) from your Lord. I did it not of my own accord. Such is the interpretation of (those things) over which you were unable to hold patience."

83. They ask you concerning

بَّهُمَا خَيْرًا مِّنْهُ زَكٰوةً وَّاَقْرَبَ

رُحْمًا ۞ وَاَمَّا الْجِدَارُ فَكَانَ

لِغُلٰمَيْنِ يَتِيْمَيْنِ فِى الْمَدِيْنَةِ

وَكَانَ تَحْتَهٗ كَنْزٌ لَّهُمَا وَكَانَ

اَبُوْهُمَا صَالِحًا ۚ فَاَرَادَ رَبُّكَ اَنْ

يَّبْلُغَاۤ اَشُدَّهُمَا وَيَسْتَخْرِجَا كَنْزَهُمَا

رَحْمَةً مِّنْ رَّبِّكَ ۚ وَمَا فَعَلْتُهٗ عَنْ

اَمْرِىْ ۚ ذٰلِكَ تَاْوِيْلُ مَا لَمْ تَسْطِعْ

عَلَيْهِ صَبْرًا ۞ وَيَسْـَٔلُوْنَكَ عَنْ

78. He answered: "This is the parting between me and you: now will I tell you the interpretation of (those things) over which you were unable to hold patience."

79. "As for the boat, it belonged to certain men in dire want: they plied on the water: I but wished to render it unserviceable, for there was after them a certain king who seized on every boat by force."

80. "As for the youth, his parents were people of Faith, and we feared that he would grieve them by obstinate rebellion and ingratitude (to Allah)."

81. "So we desired that their Lord would give them in exchange

قَالَ هٰذَا فِرَاقُ بَيْنِي وَبَيْنِكَ

سَأُنَبِّئُكَ بِتَأْوِيلِ مَا لَمْ تَسْتَطِعْ

عَلَيْهِ صَبْرًا ۞ أَمَّا السَّفِينَةُ

فَكَانَتْ لِمَسَاكِينَ يَعْمَلُونَ فِي الْبَحْرِ

فَأَرَدْتُ أَنْ أَعِيبَهَا وَكَانَ وَرَآءَهُمْ

مَلِكٌ يَأْخُذُ كُلَّ سَفِينَةٍ غَصْبًا ۞

وَأَمَّا الْغُلٰمُ فَكَانَ أَبَوَاهُ مُؤْمِنَيْنِ

فَخَشِينَآ أَنْ يُرْهِقَهُمَا طُغْيَانًا

وَكُفْرًا ۞ فَأَرَدْنَآ أَنْ يُبْدِلَهُمَا

75. He answered: "Did I not tell you that you can have no patience with me?"

76. (Moses) said: "If ever I ask you about anything after this, keep me not in your company: then would you have received (full) excuse from my side."

77. Then they proceeded: until, when they came to the inhabitants of a town, they asked them for food, but they refused them hospitality. They found there a wall on the point of falling down, but he set it up straight. (Moses) said: "If you had wished, surely you could have exacted some recompense for it!"

قَالَ اَلَمْ اَقُلْ لَّكَ اِنَّكَ لَنْ

تَسْتَطِيعَ مَعِىَ صَبْرًا ۞ قَالَ اِنْ

سَاَلْتُكَ عَنْ شَيْءٍ بَعْدَهَا فَلَا

تُصٰحِبْنِى ۖ قَدْ بَلَغْتَ مِنْ لَّدُنِّى

عُذْرًا ۞ فَانْطَلَقَا ۚ حَتّٰى اِذَآ اَتَيَآ

اَهْلَ قَرْيَةِ ۨ اسْتَطْعَمَآ اَهْلَهَا فَاَبَوْا

اَنْ يُّضَيِّفُوهُمَا فَوَجَدَا فِيهَا جِدَارًا

يُّرِيْدُ اَنْ يَّنْقَضَّ فَاَقَامَهٗ ۚ قَالَ

لَوْ شِئْتَ لَتَّخَذْتَ عَلَيْهِ اَجْرًا ۞

ذٰلِكَ الْكِتٰبُ لَا رَيْبَ فِيهِ

پارہ

قَالَ اَلَمْ

(۱۶)

PART 17
Iqtaraba Linnaasi

and has imposed no difficulties on you in religion; it is the cult of your father Abraham. It is He Who has named you Muslims, both before and in this (Revelation); that the Apostle may be a witness for you, and you be witnesses for mankind! So establish regular Prayer, give regular Charity, and hold fast to Allah! He is your Protector - the Best to protect and the Best to help!

وَمَا جَعَلَ عَلَيْكُمْ فِي الدِّينِ
مِنْ حَرَجٍ مِّلَّةَ أَبِيكُمْ إِبْرَاهِيمَ
هُوَ سَمَّاكُمُ الْمُسْلِمِينَ مِنْ
قَبْلُ وَفِي هٰذَا لِيَكُونَ الرَّسُولُ
شَهِيدًا عَلَيْكُمْ وَتَكُونُوا شُهَدَاءَ
عَلَى النَّاسِ ۚ فَأَقِيمُوا الصَّلٰوةَ
وَآتُوا الزَّكٰوةَ وَاعْتَصِمُوا بِاللَّهِ
هُوَ مَوْلٰىكُمْ ۚ فَنِعْمَ الْمَوْلٰى
وَنِعْمَ النَّصِيرُ ۩

chooses messengers from Angels and from men for Allah is He Who hears and sees (all things).

76. He knows what is before them and what is behind them: and to Allah go back all questions (for decision).

77. O you who believe! Bow down, prostrate yourselves, and adore your Lord; and do good; that you may prosper.

78. And strive in His cause as you ought to strive, (with sincerity and under discipline). He has chosen you,

يَصْطَفِى مِنَ الْمَلَٰٓئِكَةِ رُسُلًا

وَّمِنَ النَّاسِ ۗ إِنَّ اللَّهَ سَمِيعٌ

بَصِيرٌ ۞ يَعْلَمُ مَا بَيْنَ أَيْدِيهِمْ

وَمَا خَلْفَهُمْ ۗ وَإِلَى اللَّهِ تُرْجَعُ

الْأُمُورُ ۞ يَٰٓأَيُّهَا الَّذِينَ آمَنُوا

ارْكَعُوا وَاسْجُدُوا وَاعْبُدُوا

رَبَّكُمْ وَافْعَلُوا الْخَيْرَ لَعَلَّكُمْ

تُفْلِحُونَ ۩ وَجَاهِدُوا فِي اللَّهِ

حَقَّ جِهَادِهِ ۚ هُوَ اجْتَبَٰكُمْ

73. O men! Here is a parable set forth! Listen to it! Those on whom, besides Allah, you call, cannot create (even) a fly, if they all met together for the purpose! And if the fly should snatch away anything from them, they would have no power to release it from the fly. Feeble are those who petition and those whom they petition!

74. No just estimate have they made of Allah: for Allah is He Who is strong and able to carry out His Will.

75. Allah

يَـٰٓأَيُّهَا النَّاسُ ضُرِبَ مَثَلٌ

فَٱسْتَمِعُوا۟ لَهُۥٓ ۚ إِنَّ ٱلَّذِينَ

تَدْعُونَ مِن دُونِ ٱللَّهِ لَن

يَخْلُقُوا۟ ذُبَابًا وَلَوِ ٱجْتَمَعُوا۟

لَهُۥ ۖ وَإِن يَسْلُبْهُمُ ٱلذُّبَابُ

شَيْـًٔا لَّا يَسْتَنقِذُوهُ مِنْهُ ۚ

ضَعُفَ ٱلطَّالِبُ وَٱلْمَطْلُوبُ ۝

مَا قَدَرُوا۟ ٱللَّهَ حَقَّ قَدْرِهِۦٓ ۗ

إِنَّ ٱللَّهَ لَقَوِىٌّ عَزِيزٌ ۝ ٱللَّهُ

and of which they have (really) no knowledge: for those that do wrong there is no helper.

72. When Our clear Signs are rehearsed to them, you will notice a denial on the faces of the unbelievers! They nearly attack with violence those who rehearse Our Signs to them. Say, "Shall I tell you of something (far) worse than these Signs? It is the Fire (of Hell)! Allah has promised it to the unbelievers! And evil is that destination!"

وَّمَا لَيْسَ لَهُمْ بِهِ عِلْمٌ

وَمَا لِلظَّالِمِيْنَ مِنْ نَّصِيْرٍ ۞

وَإِذَا تُتْلَى عَلَيْهِمْ اٰيٰتُنَا

بَيِّنٰتٍ تَعْرِفُ فِيْ وُجُوْهِ الَّذِيْنَ

كَفَرُوا الْمُنْكَرَ ۖ يَكَادُوْنَ يَسْطُوْنَ

بِالَّذِيْنَ يَتْلُوْنَ عَلَيْهِمْ اٰيٰتِنَا ۗ

قُلْ اَفَاُنَبِّئُكُمْ بِشَرٍّ مِّنْ

ذٰلِكُمْ ۗ اَلنَّارُ ۗ وَعَدَهَا اللّٰهُ

الَّذِيْنَ كَفَرُوْا ۗ وَبِئْسَ الْمَصِيْرُ ۞

they do wrangle with you, say, "Allah knows best what it is you are doing."

69. "Allah will judge between you on the Day of Judgment concerning the matters in which you differ."

70. Do you not Know that Allah knows all that is in heaven and on earth? Indeed it is all in a Record, and that is easy for Allah.

71. Yet they worship, besides Allah, things for which no authority has been sent down to them,

جَادَلُوكَ فَقُلِ اللهُ أَعْلَمُ بِمَا

تَعْمَلُونَ ۞ اللهُ يَحْكُمُ بَيْنَكُمْ

يَوْمَ الْقِيمَةِ فِيمَا كُنْتُمْ فِيهِ

تَخْتَلِفُونَ ۞ أَلَمْ تَعْلَمْ أَنَّ

اللهَ يَعْلَمُ مَا فِى السَّمَآءِ

وَالْأَرْضِ ۗ إِنَّ ذٰلِكَ فِى كِتٰبٍ

إِنَّ ذٰلِكَ عَلَى اللهِ يَسِيرٌ ۞

وَيَعْبُدُونَ مِنْ دُونِ اللهِ

مَا لَمْ يُنَزِّلْ بِهِ سُلْطٰنًا

the sky (rain) from failing on the earth except by His leave: for Allah is Most Kind and Most Merciful to man.

66.   It is He Who gave you life, will cause you to die, and will again give you life: truly man is a most ungrateful creature!

67.   To every people have We appointed rites and ceremonies which they must follow: let them not then dispute with you on the matter, but do you invite (them) to your Lord: for you are assuredly on the Right Way.

68.   If

السَّمَآءُ اَنْ تَقَعَ عَلَى الْاَرْضِ

اِلَّا بِاِذْنِهٖ ۚ اِنَّ اللّٰهَ بِالنَّاسِ

لَرَءُوْفٌ رَّحِيْمٌ ۞ وَهُوَ الَّذِيْۤ

اَحْيَاكُمْ ثُمَّ يُمِيْتُكُمْ ثُمَّ يُحْيِيْكُمْ ؕ

اِنَّ الْاِنْسَانَ لَكَفُوْرٌ ۞ لِكُلِّ

اُمَّةٍ جَعَلْنَا مَنْسَكًا هُمْ

نَاسِكُوْهُ فَلَا يُنَازِعُنَّكَ فِى

الْاَمْرِ وَادْعُ اِلٰى رَبِّكَ ؕ اِنَّكَ

لَعَلٰى هُدًى مُّسْتَقِيْمٍ ۞ وَاِنْ

Allah is He, Most High, Most Great.

63. See you not that Allah sends down rain from the sky, and forthwith the earth becomes clothed with green? For Allah is He Who understands the finest mysteries, and is Well-Acquainted (with them).

64. To Him belongs all that is in the heavens and on earth: for verily Allah, - He is free of all wants, Worthy of all Praise.

65. Do you not see that Allah has made subject to you (men) all that is on the earth, and the ships that sail through the sea by His Command? He withholds

اللهُ هُوَ الْعَلِيُّ الْكَبِيرُ ۝ اَلَمْ تَرَ

اَنَّ اللهَ اَنْزَلَ مِنَ السَّمَآءِ

مَآءً فَتُصْبِحُ الْاَرْضُ مُخْضَرَّةً ۚ

اِنَّ اللهَ لَطِيفٌ خَبِيرٌ ۝ لَهُ مَا

فِى السَّمٰوٰتِ وَمَا فِى الْاَرْضِ ۚ

وَاِنَّ اللهَ لَهُوَ الْغَنِيُّ الْحَمِيدُ ۝

اَلَمْ تَرَ اَنَّ اللهَ سَخَّرَ لَكُمْ مَّا

فِى الْاَرْضِ وَالْفُلْكَ تَجْرِى

فِى الْبَحْرِ بِاَمْرِهِ ۗ وَيُمْسِكُ

All-Knowing, Most Forbearing.

60. That (is so). And if one has retaliated to no greater extent than the injury he received, and is again set upon inordinately, Allah will help him: for Allah is One that blots out (sins) and forgives (again and again).

61. That is because Allah merges night into day, and He merges day into night, and verily it is Allah Who hears and sees (all things).

62. That is because Allah - He is the Reality; and those besides Him whom they invoke, - they are but vain Falsehood: verily

لَعَلِيمٌ حَلِيمٌ ۝ ذَٰلِكَ وَمَنْ عَاقَبَ

بِمِثْلِ مَا عُوقِبَ بِهِ ثُمَّ بُغِيَ

عَلَيْهِ لَيَنْصُرَنَّهُ اللَّهُ إِنَّ اللَّهَ

لَعَفُوٌّ غَفُورٌ ۝ ذَٰلِكَ بِأَنَّ اللَّهَ

يُولِجُ الَّيْلَ فِي النَّهَارِ وَيُولِجُ

النَّهَارَ فِي الَّيْلِ وَأَنَّ اللَّهَ

سَمِيعٌ بَصِيرٌ ۝ ذَٰلِكَ بِأَنَّ اللَّهَ

هُوَ الْحَقُّ وَأَنَّ مَا يَدْعُونَ

مِنْ دُونِهِ هُوَ الْبَاطِلُ وَأَنَّ

so those who believe and work righteous deeds will be in Gardens of Delight.

57. And for those who reject Faith and deny Our Signs, there will be a humiliating Punishment.

58. Those who leave their homes in the cause of Allah, and are then slain or die, - on them will Allah bestow verily a goodly Provision: truly Allah is He Who bestows the best provision.

59. Verily He will admit them to a place with which they shall be well pleased: for Allah

فَالَّذِيْنَ اٰمَنُوْا وَعَمِلُوا الصّٰلِحٰتِ

فِيْ جَنّٰتِ النَّعِيْمِ ۞ وَالَّذِيْنَ

كَفَرُوْا وَكَذَّبُوْا بِاٰيٰتِنَا فَأُولٰٓئِكَ

لَهُمْ عَذَابٌ مُّهِيْنٌ ۞ وَالَّذِيْنَ

هَاجَرُوْا فِيْ سَبِيْلِ اللّٰهِ ثُمَّ

قُتِلُوْٓا اَوْ مَاتُوْا لَيَرْزُقَنَّهُمُ اللّٰهُ

رِزْقًا حَسَنًا ۗ وَإِنَّ اللّٰهَ لَهُوَ

خَيْرُ الرّٰزِقِيْنَ ۞ لَيُدْخِلَنَّهُمْ

مُّدْخَلًا يَّرْضَوْنَهٗ ۗ وَإِنَّ اللّٰهَ

that the (Qur'an) is the Truth from your Lord, and that they may believe therein, and their hearts may be made humbly (open) to it: for verily Allah is the Guide of those who believe, to the Straight Way.

55. Those who reject Faith will not cease to be in doubt concerning (Revelation) until the Hour (of Judgment) comes suddenly upon them, or there comes to them the Chastisement of a Day of Disaster.

56. On that Day the Dominion will be that of Allah: He will judge between them:

الْعِلْمَ اَنَّهُ الْحَقُّ مِنْ رَّبِّكَ

فَيُؤْمِنُوْا بِهٖ فَتُخْبِتَ لَهٗ

قُلُوْبُهُمْ وَاِنَّ اللّٰهَ لَهَادِ الَّذِيْنَ

اٰمَنُوْا اِلٰى صِرَاطٍ مُّسْتَقِيْمٍ ۩

وَلَا يَزَالُ الَّذِيْنَ كَفَرُوْا

فِيْ مِرْيَةٍ مِّنْهُ حَتّٰى تَأْتِيَهُمُ

السَّاعَةُ بَغْتَةً اَوْ يَأْتِيَهُمْ

عَذَابُ يَوْمٍ عَقِيْمٍ ۞ اَلْمُلْكُ

يَوْمَئِذٍ لِّلّٰهِ ۚ يَحْكُمُ بَيْنَهُمْ

but, when he framed a desire, Satan threw some (vanity) into his desire: but Allah will cancel anything (vain) that Satan throws in, and Allah will confirm (and establish) His Signs: for Allah is full of Knowledge and Wisdom:

53. That He may make the suggestions thrown in by Satan, but a trial for those in whose hearts is a disease and who are hardened of heart: verily the wrong-doers are in a schism far (from the Truth):

54. And that those on whom knowledge has been bestowed may learn

إِلَّا إِذَا تَمَنَّى أَلْقَى الشَّيْطَنُ

فِي أُمْنِيَّتِهِ فَيَنْسَخُ اللهُ مَا

يُلْقِى الشَّيْطَنُ ثُمَّ يُحْكِمُ اللهُ

ءَايَتِهِ ط وَاللهُ عَلِيمٌ حَكِيمٌ ۝

لِّيَجْعَلَ مَا يُلْقِى الشَّيْطَنُ

فِتْنَةً لِّلَّذِينَ فِي قُلُوبِهِم

مَّرَضٌ وَالْقَاسِيَةِ قُلُوبُهُم ط

وَإِنَّ الظَّلِمِينَ لَفِي شِقَاقٍ

بَعِيدٍ ۝ وَلِيَعْلَمَ الَّذِينَ أُوتُوا

were given to wrong-doing? In the end I punished them. To me is the destination (of all).

49. Say: "O men! I am (sent) to you only to give a clear warning:"

50. "Those who believe and work righteousness, for them is forgiveness and a sustenance most generous."

51. "But those who strive against Our Signs, to frustrate them, - they will be Companions of the Fire."

52. Never did We send an Apostle or a Prophet before you,

ظَالِمَةٌ ثُمَّ اَخَذْتُهَا ۚ وَاِلَى

الْمَصِيرُ ۞ قُلْ يٰٓاَيُّهَا النَّاسُ

اِنَّمَاۤ اَنَا لَكُمْ نَذِيرٌ مُّبِينٌ ۞

فَالَّذِيْنَ اٰمَنُوْا وَعَمِلُوا الصّٰلِحٰتِ

لَهُمْ مَّغْفِرَةٌ وَّرِزْقٌ كَرِيْمٌ ۞

وَالَّذِيْنَ سَعَوْا فِيْۤ اٰيٰتِنَا

مُعٰجِزِيْنَ اُولٰٓئِكَ اَصْحٰبُ

الْجَحِيْمِ ۞ وَمَاۤ اَرْسَلْنَا مِنْ

قَبْلِكَ مِنْ رَّسُوْلٍ وَّلَا نَبِيٍّ

their hearts (and minds) may thus learn wisdom and their ears may thus learn to hear? Truly it is not their eyes that are blind, but their hearts which are in their breasts.

47. Yet they ask you to hasten on the Punishment! But Allah will not fail in His Promise. Verily a Day in the sight of your Lord is like a thousand years of your reckoning.

48. And to how many populations did I give respite, which

لَهُمْ قُلُوبٌ يَعْقِلُونَ بِهَا

أَوْ اٰذَانٌ يَسْمَعُونَ بِهَا فَإِنَّهَا

لَا تَعْمَى الْأَبْصَارُ وَلٰكِنْ تَعْمَى

الْقُلُوبُ الَّتِي فِي الصُّدُورِ ۝

وَيَسْتَعْجِلُونَكَ بِالْعَذَابِ وَلَنْ

يُخْلِفَ اللّٰهُ وَعْدَهُ ۚ وَإِنَّ يَوْمًا

عِنْدَ رَبِّكَ كَأَلْفِ سَنَةٍ

مِّمَّا تَعُدُّونَ ۝ وَكَأَيِّنْ مِّنْ

قَرْيَةٍ أَمْلَيْتُ لَهَا وَهِيَ

and 'Ad and Thamud;

43. Those of Abraham and Lut;

44. And the Companions of the Madyan People; and Moses was rejected (in the same way). But I granted respite to the unbelievers, and (only) after that did I punish them: but how (terrible) was my rejection (of them)!

45. How many populations have We destroyed, which were given to wrong-doing? They tumbled down on their roofs. And how many wells are lying idle and neglected, and castles lofty and well-built?

46. Do they not travel through the land, so that

وَعَادٌ وَّثَمُوْدُ ۞ وَقَوْمُ اِبْرٰهِيْمَ

وَقَوْمُ لُوْطٍ ۞ وَّاَصْحٰبُ مَدْيَنَ ۚ

وَكُذِّبَ مُوْسٰى فَاَمْلَيْتُ لِلْكٰفِرِيْنَ

ثُمَّ اَخَذْتُهُمْ ۚ فَكَيْفَ كَانَ

نَكِيْرِ ۞ فَكَاَيِّنْ مِّنْ قَرْيَةٍ

اَهْلَكْنٰهَا وَهِيَ ظَالِمَةٌ فَهِيَ

خَاوِيَةٌ عَلٰى عُرُوْشِهَا وَبِئْرٍ

مُّعَطَّلَةٍ وَّقَصْرٍ مَّشِيْدٍ ۞ اَفَلَمْ

يَسِيْرُوْا فِي الْاَرْضِ فَتَكُوْنَ

and mosques, in which the name of Allah is commemorated in abundant measure. Allah will certainly aid those who aid his (cause); - for verily Allah is full of Strength, Exalted in Might, (able to enforce His Will).

41. (They are) those who, if We establish them in the land, establish regular Prayer and give regular Charity, enjoin the right and forbid wrong: with Allah rests the end (and decision) of (all) affairs.

42. If they disbelieve you so did the peoples before them (with their Prophets), - the People of Noah,

وَّ مَسَاجِدُ يُّذْكَرُ فِيْهَا اسْمُ

اللّٰهِ كَثِيْرًا ۗ وَلَيَنْصُرَنَّ

مَنْ يَّنْصُرُهٗ ؕ اِنَّ اللّٰهَ لَقَوِيٌّ

عَزِيْزٌ ۞ اَلَّذِيْنَ اِنْ مَّكَّنّٰهُمْ

فِى الْاَرْضِ اَقَامُوا الصَّلٰوةَ

وَاٰتَوُا الزَّكٰوةَ وَاَمَرُوْا بِالْمَعْرُوْفِ

وَنَهَوْا عَنِ الْمُنْكَرِ ؕ وَلِلّٰهِ عَاقِبَةُ

الْاُمُوْرِ ۞ وَاِنْ يُّكَذِّبُوْكَ فَقَدْ

كَذَّبَتْ قَبْلَهُمْ قَوْمُ نُوْحٍ

those who believe: verily, Allah loves not any that is a traitor to faith, or show ingratitude.

39.   To those against whom war is made, permission is given (to fight), because they are wronged; - and verily, Allah is Most Powerful for their aid; -

40.   (They are) those who have been expelled from their homes in defiance of right, - (for no cause) except that they say, "Our Lord is Allah". Did not Allah check one set of people by means of another, there would surely have been pulled down monasteries, churches, synagogues,

عَنِ الَّذِينَ اٰمَنُوْا ۗ اِنَّ اللّٰهَ

لَا يُحِبُّ كُلَّ خَوَّانٍ كَفُوْرٍ ۞

اُذِنَ لِلَّذِينَ يُقَاتَلُوْنَ بِاَنَّهُمْ

ظُلِمُوْا ۗ وَاِنَّ اللّٰهَ عَلٰى نَصْرِهِمْ

لَقَدِيْرُۨ ۞ الَّذِيْنَ اُخْرِجُوْا مِنْ

دِيَارِهِمْ بِغَيْرِ حَقٍّ اِلَّاۤ اَنْ

يَّقُوْلُوْا رَبُّنَا اللّٰهُ ۗ وَلَوْلَا دَفْعُ

اللّٰهِ النَّاسَ بَعْضَهُمْ بِبَعْضٍ

لَّهُدِّمَتْ صَوَامِعُ وَبِيَعٌ وَّصَلَوٰتٌ

over them as they line up (for sacrifice): when they are down on their sides (after slaughter), eat you thereof, and feed such as (beg not but) live in contentment, and such as beg with due humility: thus have We made animals subject to you, that you may be grateful.

37. It is not their meat nor their blood, that reaches Allah: it is your piety that reaches Him: He has thus made them subject to you, that you may glorify Allah for His Guidance to you and proclaim the good news to all who do right.

38. Verily Allah will defend (from ill)

عَلَيْهَا صَوَآفَّ ۚ فَإِذَا وَجَبَتْ

جُنُوْبُهَا فَكُلُوْا مِنْهَا وَأَطْعِمُوا

الْقَانِعَ وَالْمُعْتَرَّ ۚ كَذٰلِكَ سَخَّرْنٰهَا

لَكُمْ لَعَلَّكُمْ تَشْكُرُوْنَ ۝ لَنْ

يَّنَالَ اللّٰهَ لُحُوْمُهَا وَلَا دِمَآؤُهَا

وَلٰكِنْ يَّنَالُهُ التَّقْوٰى مِنْكُمْ ۚ

كَذٰلِكَ سَخَّرَهَا لَكُمْ لِتُكَبِّرُوا

اللّٰهَ عَلٰى مَا هَدٰىكُمْ ۗ وَبَشِّرِ

الْمُحْسِنِيْنَ ۝ اِنَّ اللّٰهَ يُدٰفِعُ

the sustenance He gave them from animals (fit for food). But your Allah is One Allah: submit then your wills to Him (in Islam): and give you the good news to those who humble themselves, -

35. To those whose hearts when Allah is mentioned, are filled with fear, who show patient perseverance over their afflictions, keep up regular prayer, and spend (in charity) out of what We have bestowed upon them.

36. The sacrificial camels We have made for you as among the Symbols from Allah: in them is (much) good for you: then pronounce the name of Allah

رَزَقَهُمْ مِّنْ بَهِيمَةِ الْاَنْعَامِ
فَاِلٰهُكُمْ اِلٰهٌ وَّاحِدٌ فَلَهٗۤ اَسْلِمُوْا ۗ
وَبَشِّرِ الْمُخْبِتِيْنَ ۙ الَّذِيْنَ اِذَا
ذُكِرَ اللّٰهُ وَجِلَتْ قُلُوْبُهُمْ
وَالصّٰبِرِيْنَ عَلٰى مَاۤ اَصَابَهُمْ
وَالْمُقِيْمِى الصَّلٰوةِ ۙ وَمِمَّا رَزَقْنٰهُمْ
يُنْفِقُوْنَ ۝ وَالْبُدْنَ جَعَلْنٰهَا
لَكُمْ مِّنْ شَعَآئِرِ اللّٰهِ لَكُمْ
فِيْهَا خَيْرٌ ۖ فَاذْكُرُوا اسْمَ اللّٰهِ

from heaven and been snatched up by birds, or the wind had swooped (like a bird on its prey) and thrown him into a far-distant place.

32. Such (is his state): and whoever holds in honour the Symbols of Allah, (in the sacrifice of animals), such (honour) should come truly from piety of heart.

33. In them you have benefits for a term appointed: in the end their place of sacrifice is near the Ancient House.

34. To every people did We appoint rites (of sacrifice), that they might celebrate the name of Allah over

مِنَ السَّمَآءِ فَتَخْطَفُهُ الطَّيْرُ

أَوْ تَهْوِىْ بِهِ الرِّيحُ فِىْ

مَكَانٍ سَحِيْقٍ ۞ ذٰلِكَ وَمَنْ

يُّعَظِّمْ شَعَآئِرَ اللّٰهِ فَإِنَّهَا مِنْ

تَقْوَى الْقُلُوْبِ ۞ لَكُمْ فِيْهَا

مَنَافِعُ إِلٰى أَجَلٍ مُّسَمًّى ثُمَّ

مَحِلُّهَا إِلَى الْبَيْتِ الْعَتِيْقِ ۞

وَلِكُلِّ أُمَّةٍ جَعَلْنَا مَنْسَكًا

لِّيَذْكُرُوا اسْمَ اللّٰهِ عَلٰى مَا

perform their vows, and (again) circumambulate the Ancient House."

30. Such (is the Pilgrimage): whoever honours the sacred rites of Allah, for him it is good in the Sight of his Lord. Lawful to you (for food in Pilgrimage) are cattle, except those mentioned to you (as exception): but shun the abomination of idols, and shun the word that is false, -

31. Being true in faith to Allah, and never assigning partners to Him: if anyone assigns partners to Allah, is as if he had fallen

وَلْيُوْفُوْا نُذُوْرَهُمْ وَلْيَطَّوَّفُوْا

بِالْبَيْتِ الْعَتِيْقِ ۞ ذٰلِكَ ۚ وَمَنْ

يُّعَظِّمْ حُرُمٰتِ اللّٰهِ فَهُوَ خَيْرٌ

لَّهٗ عِنْدَ رَبِّهٖ ؕ وَاُحِلَّتْ لَكُمُ

الْاَنْعَامُ اِلَّا مَا يُتْلٰى عَلَيْكُمْ

فَاجْتَنِبُوا الرِّجْسَ مِنَ الْاَوْثَانِ

وَاجْتَنِبُوْا قَوْلَ الزُّوْرِ ۞ حُنَفَآءَ

لِلّٰهِ غَيْرَ مُشْرِكِيْنَ بِهٖ ؕ وَمَنْ

يُّشْرِكْ بِاللّٰهِ فَكَاَنَّمَا خَرَّ

or prostrate themselves (therein in prayer)."

27. "And proclaim the Pilgrimage among men: they will come to you on foot and (mounted) on every kind of camel, lean on account of journeys through deep and distant mountain highways;"

28. "That they may witness the benefits (provided) for them, and celebrate the name of Allah, through the days appointed, over the cattle which He has provided for them (for sacrifice): then eat you thereof and feed the distressed ones in want."

29. "Then let them complete the rites prescribed for them,

السُّجُودُ ۩ وَاَذِّنْ فِى النَّاسِ

بِالْحَجِّ يَاْتُوْكَ رِجَالًا وَّعَلٰى

كُلِّ ضَامِرٍ يَّاْتِيْنَ مِنْ كُلِّ

فَجٍّ عَمِيْقٍ ۙ لِّيَشْهَدُوْا مَنَافِعَ

لَهُمْ وَيَذْكُرُوا اسْمَ اللّٰهِ

فِىْ اَيَّامٍ مَّعْلُوْمٰتٍ عَلٰى مَا

رَزَقَهُمْ مِّنْۢ بَهِيْمَةِ الْاَنْعَامِ ۚ

فَكُلُوْا مِنْهَا وَاَطْعِمُوا الْبَآئِسَ

الْفَقِيْرَ ۙ ثُمَّ لْيَقْضُوْا تَفَثَهُمْ

those who have rejected (Allah), and would keep back (men) from the Way of Allah, and from the Sacred Mosque, which We have made (open) to (all) men - equal is the dweller there and the visitor from the country - and any whose purpose therein is profanity or wrong-doing - them will We cause to taste of a most grievous Chastisement.

26. Behold! We gave the site, to Abraham, of the (Sacred) House, (saying): "Associate not anything (in worship) with Me; and sanctify My House for those who compass it round, or stand up, or bow,

اَلَّذِيۡنَ كَفَرُوۡا وَ يَصُدُّوۡنَ عَنۡ

سَبِيۡلِ اللّٰهِ وَ الۡمَسۡجِدِ الۡحَرَامِ

الَّذِىۡ جَعَلۡنٰهُ لِلنَّاسِ سَوَآءَ

الۡعَاكِفُ فِيۡهِ وَ الۡبَادِ ؕ وَ مَنۡ يُّرِدۡ

فِيۡهِ بِاِلۡحَادٍۭ بِظُلۡمٍ نُّذِقۡهُ

مِنۡ عَذَابٍ اَلِيۡمٍ ۩ وَ اِذۡ بَوَّاۡنَا

لِاِبۡرٰهِيۡمَ مَكَانَ الۡبَيۡتِ اَنۡ

لَّا تُشۡرِكۡ بِیۡ شَیۡئًا وَّ طَهِّرۡ بَيۡتِیَ

لِلطَّآئِفِيۡنَ وَ الۡقَآئِمِيۡنَ وَ الرُّكَّعِ

from anguish, they will be forced back therein, and (it will be said), "Taste you the Chastisement of Burning!"

23. Allah will admit those who believe and work righteous deeds, to Gardens beneath which rivers flow: they shall be adorned therein with bracelets of gold and pearls; and their garments there will be of silk.

24. For they have been guided (in this life) to the purest of speeches; they have been guided to the Path of Him Who is Worthy of (all) Praise.

25. As to

مِنْ غَمٍّ أُعِيْدُوْا فِيْهَا وَذُوْقُوْا

عَذَابَ الْحَرِيْقِ ۝ اِنَّ اللّٰهَ

يُدْخِلُ الَّذِيْنَ اٰمَنُوْا وَعَمِلُوا

الصّٰلِحٰتِ جَنّٰتٍ تَجْرِىْ مِنْ

تَحْتِهَا الْاَنْهٰرُ يُحَلَّوْنَ فِيْهَا

مِنْ اَسَاوِرَ مِنْ ذَهَبٍ وَّلُؤْلُؤًا ۚ

وَلِبَاسُهُمْ فِيْهَا حَرِيْرٌ ۝ وَهُدُوْٓا

اِلَى الطَّيِّبِ مِنَ الْقَوْلِ ۚ وَهُدُوْٓا

اِلٰى صِرَاطِ الْحَمِيْدِ ۝ اِنَّ

Allah shall disgrace, - none can raise to honour: for Allah carries out all that He wills.

19. These two antagonists dispute with each other about their Lord: but those who deny (their Lord), - for them will be cut out a garment of Fire: over their heads will be poured out boiling water.

20. With it will be scalded what is within their bodies, as well as (their) skins.

21. In addition there will be maces of iron (to punish) them.

22. Every time they wish to get away therefrom,

يُهِنِ اللهُ فَمَا لَهُ مِنْ مُكْرِمٍ

اِنَّ اللهَ يَفْعَلُ مَا يَشَآءُ ۩

هٰذٰنِ خَصْمٰنِ اخْتَصَمُوْا فِيْ

رَبِّهِمْ فَالَّذِيْنَ كَفَرُوْا قُطِّعَتْ

لَهُمْ ثِيَابٌ مِّنْ نَّارٍ ۭ يُصَبُّ مِنْ

فَوْقِ رُءُوْسِهِمُ الْحَمِيْمُ ۙ يُصْهَرُ

بِهٖ مَا فِيْ بُطُوْنِهِمْ وَالْجُلُوْدُ ۖ

وَلَهُمْ مَّقَامِعُ مِنْ حَدِيْدٍ ۩

كُلَّمَآ اَرَادُوْٓا اَنْ يَّخْرُجُوْا مِنْهَا

Polytheists, - Allah will judge between them on the Day of Judgment: for Allah is Witness of all things.

18. Do you not see that to Allah bow down in worship all things that are in the heavens and on earth, - the sun, the moon, the stars; the hills, the trees, the animals; and a great number among mankind? But a great number are (also) such as are fit for Punishment: and such as

أَشْرِكُوا ۗ إِنَّ اللّٰهَ يَفْصِلُ بَيْنَهُمْ

يَوْمَ الْقِيٰمَةِ ۗ إِنَّ اللّٰهَ عَلٰى

كُلِّ شَىْءٍ شَهِيْدٌ ۞ أَلَمْ تَرَ

أَنَّ اللّٰهَ يَسْجُدُ لَهٗ مَنْ فِى

السَّمٰوٰتِ وَمَنْ فِى الْأَرْضِ

وَالشَّمْسُ وَالْقَمَرُ وَالنُّجُوْمُ

وَالْجِبَالُ وَالشَّجَرُ وَالدَّوَآبُّ

وَكَثِيْرٌ مِّنَ النَّاسِ ۚ وَكَثِيْرٌ

حَقَّ عَلَيْهِ الْعَذَابُ ۗ وَمَنْ

think that Allah will not help him (His Apostle) in this world and the Hereafter, let him stretch out a rope to the ceiling and cut (himself) off: then let him see whether his plan will remove that which enrages (him)!

16. Thus have We sent down clear Signs; and verily Allah does guide whom He will!

17. Those who believe (in the Qur'an), those who follow the Jewish (scriptures), and the Sabians, Christians, Magians, and

كَانَ يَظُنُّ أَنْ لَّنْ يَّنْصُرَهُ

اللهُ فِي الدُّنْيَا وَ الْآخِرَةِ

فَلْيَمْدُدْ بِسَبَبٍ إِلَى السَّمَآءِ ثُمَّ

لِيَقْطَعْ فَلْيَنْظُرْ هَلْ يُذْهِبَنَّ

كَيْدُهُ مَا يَغِيظُ ۞ وَ كَذٰلِكَ

أَنْزَلْنٰهُ اٰيٰتٍۭ بَيِّنٰتٍ وَّ أَنَّ اللهَ

يَهْدِى مَنْ يُّرِيْدُ ۞ اِنَّ الَّذِيْنَ

اٰمَنُوْا وَالَّذِيْنَ هَادُوْا وَالصّٰبِئِيْنَ

وَ النَّصٰرٰى وَالْمَجُوْسَ وَالَّذِيْنَ

for all to see!

12. They call on such deities, besides Allah, as can neither hurt nor profit them: that is straying far indeed (from the Way)!

13. (Perhaps) they call on one whose hurt is nearer than his god: evil, indeed, is the patron, and evil the companion (for help)!

14. Verily Allah will admit those who believe and work righteous deeds, to Gardens, beneath which rivers flow: for Allah carries out all that He plans.

15. If any

الْمُبِينُ ۞ يَدْعُوا مِنْ دُونِ اللهِ

مَا لَا يَضُرُّهُ وَمَا لَا يَنْفَعُهُ

ذٰلِكَ هُوَ الضَّلَلُ الْبَعِيدُ ۞

يَدْعُوا لَمَنْ ضَرُّهُ أَقْرَبُ مِنْ

نَّفْعِهِ لَبِئْسَ الْمَوْلَى وَلَبِئْسَ

الْعَشِيرُ ۞ إِنَّ اللهَ يُدْخِلُ

الَّذِينَ آمَنُوا وَعَمِلُوا الصَّلِحَتِ

جَنَّتٍ تَجْرِي مِنْ تَحْتِهَا الْأَنْهٰرُ

إِنَّ اللهَ يَفْعَلُ مَا يُرِيدُ ۞ مَنْ

there is disgrace in this life, and on the Day of Judgment We shall make him taste the Chastisement of burning (Fire).

10. (It will be said): "This is because of the deeds which your hands sent forth, for verily Allah is not unjust to His servants.

11. There are among men some who serve Allah, as it were, on the verge: if good befalls them, they are, therewith, well content; but if a trial comes to them, they turn on their faces: they lose both this world and the Hereafter: that is loss

فِى الدُّنْيَا خِزْىٌ وَّنُذِيْقُهٗ يَوْمَ

الْقِيٰمَةِ عَذَابَ الْحَرِيْقِ ۝ ذٰلِكَ

بِمَا قَدَّمَتْ يَدٰكَ وَاَنَّ اللهَ

لَيْسَ بِظَلَّامٍ لِّلْعَبِيْدِ ۝ وَمِنَ

النَّاسِ مَنْ يَّعْبُدُ اللهَ عَلٰى

حَرْفٍ ۚ فَاِنْ اَصَابَهٗ خَيْرُ

اطْمَاَنَّ بِهٖ ۚ وَاِنْ اَصَابَتْهُ فِتْنَةُ

انْقَلَبَ عَلٰى وَجْهِهٖ ۚ خَسِرَ الدُّنْيَا

وَالْاٰخِرَةَ ۚ ذٰلِكَ هُوَ الْخُسْرَانُ

beautiful growth (in pairs).

6. This is so, because Allah is the Reality: it is He Who gives life to the dead, and it is He Who has power over all things.

7. And verily the Hour will come: there can be no doubt about it, or about (the fact) that Allah will raise up all who are in the graves.

8. Yet there is among men such a one as disputes about Allah, without Knowledge, without Guidance, and without a Book of Enlightenment, -

9. (Disdainfully) bending his side, in order to lead (men) astray from the Path of Allah: for him

بَهِيجٌ ۞ ذَلِكَ بِأَنَّ اللَّهَ هُوَ الْحَقُّ وَأَنَّهُ يُحْيِ الْمَوْتَى وَأَنَّهُ عَلَى كُلِّ شَيْءٍ قَدِيرٌ ۞ وَأَنَّ السَّاعَةَ اتِيَةٌ لَا رَيْبَ فِيهَا وَأَنَّ اللَّهَ يَبْعَثُ مَنْ فِي الْقُبُورِ ۞ وَمِنَ النَّاسِ مَنْ يُجَادِلُ فِي اللَّهِ بِغَيْرِ عِلْمٍ وَلَا هُدًى وَلَا كِتَابٍ مُنِيرٍ ۞ ثَانِيَ عِطْفِهِ لِيُضِلَّ عَنْ سَبِيلِ اللَّهِ لَهُ

to you; and We cause whom We will to rest in the wombs for an appoin-ted term, then do We bring you out as babes, then (foster you) that you may reach your age of full strength; and some of you are called to die, and some are sent back to the feeblest old age, so that they know nothing after having known (much), and (further), you see the earth barren and lifeless, but when We pour down rain on it, it is stirred (to life), it swells, and it puts forth every kind of

لَكُمْ ۖ وَنُقِرُّ فِى الْأَرْحَامِ مَا نَشَآءُ

إِلَىٰٓ أَجَلٍ مُّسَمًّى ثُمَّ نُخْرِجُكُمْ

طِفْلًا ثُمَّ لِتَبْلُغُوٓا أَشُدَّكُمْ ۖ

وَمِنكُم مَّن يُتَوَفَّىٰ وَمِنكُم مَّن

يُرَدُّ إِلَىٰٓ أَرْذَلِ الْعُمُرِ لِكَيْلَا

يَعْلَمَ مِنۢ بَعْدِ عِلْمٍ شَيْـًٔا ۚ

وَتَرَى الْأَرْضَ هَامِدَةً فَإِذَآ

أَنزَلْنَا عَلَيْهَا الْمَآءَ اهْتَزَّتْ

وَرَبَتْ وَأَنۢبَتَتْ مِن كُلِّ زَوْجٍ

without knowledge, and follow every evil one obstinate in rebellion!

4.　About the (Evil One) it is decreed that whoever turns to him for friendship, him will he lead astray, and he will guide him to the Chastisement of the Fire.

5.　O mankind! If you have a doubt about the Resurrection, (consider) that We created you out of dust, then out of sperm, then out of a leech-like clot, then out of a morsel of flesh, partly formed and partly unformed, in order that We may manifest (our power)

بِغَيْرِ عِلْمٍ وَّيَتَّبِعُ كُلَّ شَيْطٰنٍ

مَرِيْدٍ ۞ كُتِبَ عَلَيْهِ اَنَّهٗ مَنْ

تَوَلَّاهُ فَاَنَّهٗ يُضِلُّهٗ وَيَهْدِيْهِ

اِلٰى عَذَابِ السَّعِيْرِ ۞ يٰٓاَيُّهَا

النَّاسُ اِنْ كُنْتُمْ فِيْ رَيْبٍ

مِّنَ الْبَعْثِ فَاِنَّا خَلَقْنٰكُمْ مِّنْ

تُرَابٍ ثُمَّ مِنْ نُّطْفَةٍ ثُمَّ

مِنْ عَلَقَةٍ ثُمَّ مِنْ مُّضْغَةٍ

مُّخَلَّقَةٍ وَّغَيْرِ مُخَلَّقَةٍ لِّنُبَيِّنَ

Al-Hajj (The Pilgrimage)

Bismillahir-Rahmanir-Rahim

1. O mankind! Fear your Lord! For the convulsion of the Hour (of Judgment) will be a thing terrible!

2. The Day you shall see it, every mother giving suck shall forget her suckling-babe, and every pregnant female shall drop her load (unformed): you shall see mankind as in a drunken riot, yet not drunk: but dreadful will be the Chastisement of Allah.

3. And yet among men there are such as dispute about Allah,

بِسْمِ اللهِ الرَّحْمٰنِ الرَّحِيمِ

يٰٓاَيُّهَا النَّاسُ اتَّقُوْا رَبَّكُمْ ۚ اِنَّ زَلْزَلَةَ السَّاعَةِ شَيْءٌ عَظِيْمٌ ۝

يَوْمَ تَرَوْنَهَا تَذْهَلُ كُلُّ مُرْضِعَةٍ عَمَّآ اَرْضَعَتْ وَتَضَعُ كُلُّ ذَاتِ حَمْلٍ حَمْلَهَا وَتَرَى النَّاسَ سُكٰرٰى وَمَا هُمْ بِسُكٰرٰى وَلٰكِنَّ عَذَابَ اللهِ شَدِيْدٌ ۝ وَمِنَ النَّاسِ مَنْ يُّجَادِلُ فِي اللهِ

therefore bow to His Will (in Islam)?"

109. But if they turn back, say: "I have proclaimed the Message to you all alike and in truth; but I know not whether that which you are promised is near or far.

110. "It is He Who knows what is open in speech and what you hide (in your hearts).

111. "I know not but that it may be a trial for you, and a grant of (worldly) livelihood (to you) for a time."

112. Say: "O my Lord! Judge You in truth!" "Our Lord Most Gracious is the One Whose assistance should be sought against the blasphemies you utter!"

مُّسْلِمُوْنَ ۝ فَاِنْ تَوَلَّوْا فَقُلْ

اٰذَنْتُكُمْ عَلٰى سَوَآءٍ ۖ وَاِنْ

اَدْرِيْٓ اَقَرِيْبٌ اَمْ بَعِيْدٌ مَّا

تُوْعَدُوْنَ ۝ اِنَّهٗ يَعْلَمُ الْجَهْرَ

مِنَ الْقَوْلِ وَيَعْلَمُ مَا تَكْتُمُوْنَ ۝

وَاِنْ اَدْرِيْ لَعَلَّهٗ فِتْنَةٌ لَّكُمْ

وَمَتَاعٌ اِلٰى حِيْنٍ ۝ قٰلَ رَبِّ

احْكُمْ بِالْحَقِّ ۗ وَرَبُّنَا الرَّحْمٰنُ

الْمُسْتَعَانُ عَلٰى مَا تَصِفُوْنَ ۝

We produced the first creation, so shall We produce a new one: a promise We have undertaken: truly shall We fulfil it.

105. Before this We wrote in the Psalms, after the Message (given to Moses): "My servants the righteous, shall inherit the earth."

106. Verily in this (Qur'an) is a Message for people who would (truly) worship Allah.

107. We sent you not, but as a Mercy for all creatures.

108. Say: "What has come to me by inspiration is that your Allah is One Allah: will you

بَدَأْنَآ اَوَّلَ خَلْقٍ نُّعِيْدُهٗ ۚ وَعْدًا

عَلَيْنَا ۚ اِنَّا كُنَّا فٰعِلِيْنَ ۞ وَلَقَدْ

كَتَبْنَا فِى الزَّبُوْرِ مِنْۢ بَعْدِ الذِّكْرِ

اَنَّ الْاَرْضَ يَرِثُهَا عِبَادِىَ

الصّٰلِحُوْنَ ۞ اِنَّ فِىْ هٰذَا لَبَلٰغًا

لِّقَوْمٍ عٰبِدِيْنَ ۞ وَمَآ اَرْسَلْنٰكَ

اِلَّا رَحْمَةً لِّلْعٰلَمِيْنَ ۞ قُلْ

اِنَّمَا يُوْحٰٓى اِلَيَّ اَنَّمَآ اِلٰهُكُمْ

اِلٰهٌ وَّاحِدٌ ۚ فَهَلْ اَنْتُمْ

101. Those for whom the good (record) from Us has gone before, will be removed far therefrom.

102. Not the slightest sound will they hear of Hell: what their souls desired, in that will they dwell.

103. The Great Terror will bring them no grief: but the Angels will meet them (with mutual greetings): "This is your Day, - (the Day) that you were promised."

104. The Day that We roll up the heavens like a scroll rolled up for books (completed), - even as

اِنَّ الَّذِيْنَ سَبَقَتْ لَهُمْ

مِّنَّا الْحُسْنٰٓ اُولٰٓئِكَ عَنْهَا

مُبْعَدُوْنَ ۞ لَا يَسْمَعُوْنَ

حَسِيْسَهَا ۚ وَهُمْ فِيْ مَا اشْتَهَتْ

اَنْفُسُهُمْ خٰلِدُوْنَ ۞ لَا يَحْزُنُهُمُ

الْفَزَعُ الْاَكْبَرُ وَتَتَلَقّٰهُمُ

الْمَلٰٓئِكَةُ ۚ هٰذَا يَوْمُكُمُ الَّذِيْ

كُنْتُمْ تُوْعَدُوْنَ ۞ يَوْمَ نَطْوِى

السَّمَآءَ كَطَىِّ السِّجِلِّ لِلْكُتُبِ ۚ كَمَا

then behold! the eyes of the unbelievers will fixedly stare in horror: "Ah! Woe to us! We were indeed heedless of this; no, we truly did wrong!"

98. Verily you, (unbelievers), and the (false) gods that you worship besides Allah, are (but) fuel for Hell! To it will you (surely) come!

99. If these had been gods, they would not have got there! But each one will abide therein.

100. There, sobbing will be their lot, nor will they there hear (anything else).

الْحَقُّ فَإِذَا هِيَ شَاخِصَةٌ أَبْصَارُ

الَّذِينَ كَفَرُوا يَا وَيْلَنَا قَدْ كُنَّا

فِي غَفْلَةٍ مِّنْ هَٰذَا بَلْ كُنَّا

ظَالِمِينَ ۝ إِنَّكُمْ وَمَا تَعْبُدُونَ

مِنْ دُونِ اللَّهِ حَصَبُ جَهَنَّمَ

أَنْتُمْ لَهَا وَارِدُونَ ۝ لَوْ كَانَ

هَٰؤُلَاءِ آلِهَةً مَّا وَرَدُوهَا ۖ وَكُلٌّ

فِيهَا خَالِدُونَ ۝ لَهُمْ فِيهَا

زَفِيرٌ وَهُمْ فِيهَا لَا يَسْمَعُونَ ۝

93. But (later generations) cut off their affair (of unity), one from another: (yet) will they all return to Us.

94. Whoever works any act of righteousness and has faith, - his endeavour will not be rejected: We shall record it in his favour.

95. But there is a ban on any population which We have destroyed: that they shall not return,

96. Until the Gog and Magog (people) are let through (their barrier), and they swiftly swarm from every hill.

97. Then will the true promise draw near (of fulfilment):

وَتَقَطَّعُوٓا أَمْرَهُم بَيْنَهُمْ ۖ كُلٌّ

إِلَيْنَا رَٰجِعُونَ ۝ فَمَن يَعْمَلْ

مِنَ ٱلصَّٰلِحَٰتِ وَهُوَ مُؤْمِنٌ

فَلَا كُفْرَانَ لِسَعْيِهِۦ وَإِنَّا لَهُۥ

كَٰتِبُونَ ۝ وَحَرَٰمٌ عَلَىٰ قَرْيَةٍ

أَهْلَكْنَٰهَآ أَنَّهُمْ لَا يَرْجِعُونَ ۝

حَتَّىٰٓ إِذَا فُتِحَتْ يَأْجُوجُ

وَمَأْجُوجُ وَهُم مِّن كُلِّ حَدَبٍ

يَنسِلُونَ ۝ وَٱقْتَرَبَ ٱلْوَعْدُ

Yahya: We cured his wife's (barrenness) for him. These (three) were ever quick in emulation in good works; they used to call on Us with love and reverence, and humble themselves before Us.

91. And (remember) her who guarded her chastity: We breathed into her of Our Spirit, and We made her and her son a Sign for all peoples.

92. Verily, this brotherhood of yours is a single brotherhood, and I am your Lord and Cherisher: therefore serve Me (and no other).

يَحْيَى وَأَصْلَحْنَا لَهُ زَوْجَهُ

إِنَّهُمْ كَانُوا يُسَارِعُونَ فِي

الْخَيْرَاتِ وَيَدْعُونَنَا رَغَبًا

وَّرَهَبًا ۚ وَكَانُوا لَنَا خَاشِعِينَ ۞

وَالَّتِي أَحْصَنَتْ فَرْجَهَا فَنَفَخْنَا

فِيهَا مِنْ رُّوحِنَا وَجَعَلْنَاهَا

وَابْنَهَا آيَةً لِّلْعَالَمِينَ ۞ إِنَّ

هٰذِهِ أُمَّتُكُمْ أُمَّةً وَّاحِدَةً ۖ

وَّأَنَا رَبُّكُمْ فَاعْبُدُونِ ۞

We had no power over him! But he cried through the depths of darkness, "There is no god but You: Glory to You: I was indeed wrong!"

88. So We listened to him: and delivered him from distress: and thus do We deliver those who have faith.

89. And (remember) Zakariya, when he cried to his Lord: "O my Lord! Leave me not without offspring, though You are the best of inheritors."

90. So We listened to him: and We granted him

نَقْدِرَ عَلَيْهِ فَنَادَى فِي

الظُّلُمَتِ أَنْ لَّا إِلٰهَ إِلَّا أَنْتَ

سُبْحٰنَكَ ۖ إِنِّي كُنْتُ مِنَ

الظّٰلِمِينَ ۙ فَاسْتَجَبْنَا لَهُ ۙ

وَنَجَّيْنٰهُ مِنَ الْغَمِّ ۚ وَكَذٰلِكَ

نُـۨجِي الْمُؤْمِنِينَ ۩ وَزَكَرِيَّا ۖ إِذْ

نَادٰى رَبَّهُ رَبِّ لَا تَذَرْنِي

فَرْدًا وَّأَنْتَ خَيْرُ الْوٰرِثِينَ ۙ

فَاسْتَجَبْنَا لَهُ ۙ وَوَهَبْنَا لَهُ

84.   So We listened to him: We removed the distress that was on him, and We restored his people to him, and doubled their number, - as a Grace from Ourselves, and a thing for commemoration, for all who serve Us.

85.   And (remember) Isma'il, Idris, and Zul-kifl, all (men) of constancy and patience;

86.   We admitted them to Our Mercy: for they were of the righteous ones.

87.   And remember Zun-nun, when he departed in wrath: he imagined that

فَاسْتَجَبْنَا لَهُ فَكَشَفْنَا مَا

بِهِ مِنْ ضُرٍّ وَّاٰتَيْنٰهُ اَهْلَهُ

وَمِثْلَهُمْ مَّعَهُمْ رَحْمَةً مِّنْ

عِنْدِنَا وَذِكْرٰى لِلْعٰبِدِيْنَ ۞

وَاِسْمٰعِيْلَ وَاِدْرِيْسَ وَذَا الْكِفْلِ ۗ

كُلٌّ مِّنَ الصّٰبِرِيْنَ ۞ وَاَدْخَلْنٰهُمْ

فِيْ رَحْمَتِنَا اِنَّهُمْ مِّنَ

الصّٰلِحِيْنَ ۞ وَذَا النُّوْنِ اِذْ

ذَّهَبَ مُغَاضِبًا فَظَنَّ اَنْ لَّنْ

you then be grateful?

81. (It was Our power that made) the violent (unruly) wind flow (tamely) for Solomon, to his order, to the land which We had blessed: for We do know all things.

82. And of the evil ones, were some who dived for him, and did other work besides; and it was We Who guarded them.

83. And (remember) Job, when He cried to his Lord, "Truly distress has seized me, but You are the Most Merciful of those that are merciful."

اَنْتُمْ شٰكِرُوْنَ ۞ وَلِسُلَيْمٰنَ

الرِّيْحَ عَاصِفَةً تَجْرِيْ بِاَمْرِهٖٓ

اِلَى الْاَرْضِ الَّتِيْ بٰرَكْنَا فِيْهَا ۚ

وَكُنَّا بِكُلِّ شَيْءٍ عٰلِمِيْنَ ۞

وَمِنَ الشَّيٰطِيْنِ مَنْ يَّغُوْصُوْنَ

لَهٗ وَيَعْمَلُوْنَ عَمَلًا دُوْنَ ذٰلِكَ ۚ

وَكُنَّا لَهُمْ حٰفِظِيْنَ ۞ وَاَيُّوْبَ

اِذْ نَادٰى رَبَّهٗٓ اَنِّيْ مَسَّنِيَ

الضُّرُّ وَاَنْتَ اَرْحَمُ الرّٰحِمِيْنَ ۞

78. And remember David and Solomon, when they gave judgment in the matter of the field into which the sheep of certain people had strayed by night: We did witness their judgment.

79. To Solomon We inspired the (right) understanding of the matter: to each (of them) We gave Judgment and Knowledge; it was Our power that made the hills and the birds celebrate Our praises, with David: it was We Who did (all these things).

80. It was We Who taught him the making of coats of mail for your benefit, to guard you from each other's violence: will

وَدَاوُدَ وَسُلَيْمَٰنَ إِذْ يَحْكُمَٰنِ

فِى الْحَرْثِ إِذْ نَفَشَتْ فِيهِ

غَنَمُ الْقَوْمِ ۚ وَكُنَّا لِحُكْمِهِمْ

شَٰهِدِينَ ۝ فَفَهَّمْنَٰهَا سُلَيْمَٰنَ ۚ

وَكُلًّا ءَاتَيْنَا حُكْمًا وَّعِلْمًا ۚ

وَسَخَّرْنَا مَعَ دَاوُدَ الْجِبَالَ

يُسَبِّحْنَ وَالطَّيْرَ ۚ وَكُنَّا فَٰعِلِينَ ۝

وَعَلَّمْنَٰهُ صَنْعَةَ لَبُوسٍ لَّكُمْ

لِتُحْصِنَكُم مِّنۢ بَأْسِكُمْ ۖ فَهَلْ

practised abominations: truly they were a people given to evil, a rebellious people.

75. And We admitted him to Our Mercy: for he was one of the righteous.

76. (Remember) Noah, when he cried (to Us) aforetime: We listened to his (prayer) and delivered him and his family from great distress.

77. We helped him against people who rejected Our Signs: truly they were a people given to evil: so We drowned them (in the Flood) all together.

تَعْمَلُ الْخَبٰٓئِثَ ۚ اِنَّهُمْ كَانُوْا قَوْمَ

سَوْءٍ فٰسِقِيْنَ ۞ وَاَدْخَلْنٰهُ فِيْ

رَحْمَتِنَا ۚ اِنَّهٗ مِنَ الصّٰلِحِيْنَ ۞

وَنُوْحًا اِذْ نَادٰى مِنْ قَبْلُ

فَاسْتَجَبْنَا لَهٗ فَنَجَّيْنٰهُ وَاَهْلَهٗ

مِنَ الْكَرْبِ الْعَظِيْمِ ۞ وَنَصَرْنٰهُ

مِنَ الْقَوْمِ الَّذِيْنَ كَذَّبُوْا

بِاٰيٰتِنَا ۚ اِنَّهُمْ كَانُوْا قَوْمَ

سَوْءٍ فَاَغْرَقْنٰهُمْ اَجْمَعِيْنَ ۞

for the nations.

72. And We bestowed on him Isaac and, as an additional gift, (a grandson), Jacob, and We made righteous men of every one (of them).

73. And We made them leaders, guiding (men) by Our Command, and We sent them inspiration to do good deeds, to establish regular Prayers, and to practise regular Charity; and they constantly served Us (and Us only).

74. And to Lut, too, We gave Judgment and Knowledge, and We saved him from the town which

فِيهَا لِلْعَلَمِينَ ۝ وَوَهَبْنَا لَهُ

اِسْحَقَ ۖ وَيَعْقُوبَ نَافِلَةً ۖ وَكُلًّا

جَعَلْنَا صَلِحِينَ ۝ وَجَعَلْنَهُمْ

اَئِمَّةً يَّهْدُوْنَ بِاَمْرِنَا

وَاَوْحَيْنَآ اِلَيْهِمْ فِعْلَ الْخَيْرَتِ

وَاِقَامَ الصَّلٰوةِ وَاِيْتَآءَ الزَّكٰوةِ ۚ

وَكَانُوْا لَنَا عٰبِدِيْنَ ۝ وَلُوْطًا

اٰتَيْنٰهُ حُكْمًا وَّعِلْمًا وَّنَجَّيْنٰهُ

مِنَ الْقَرْيَةِ الَّتِيْ كَانَتْ

nor do you harm?"

67. "Fie upon you, and upon the things that you worship besides Allah! Have you no sense?"...

68. They said, "Burn him and protect your gods, if you do (anything at all)!"

69. We said, "O Fire! Be you cool, and (a means of) safety for Abraham!"

70. Then they planned against him: but We made them the ones that lost most!

71. But We delivered him and (his nephew) Lut (and directed them) to the land which We have blessed

وَلَا يَضُرُّكُمْ ۚ اُفٍّ لَّكُمْ وَلِمَا

تَعْبُدُوْنَ مِنْ دُوْنِ اللّٰهِ ۚ

اَفَلَا تَعْقِلُوْنَ ۝ قَالُوْا حَرِّقُوْهُ

وَانْصُرُوْٓا اٰلِهَتَكُمْ اِنْ كُنْتُمْ

فٰعِلِيْنَ ۝ قُلْنَا يٰنَارُ كُوْنِيْ

بَرْدًا وَّسَلٰمًا عَلٰٓى اِبْرٰهِيْمَ ۙ۝

وَاَرَادُوْا بِهٖ كَيْدًا فَجَعَلْنٰهُمُ

الْاَخْسَرِيْنَ ۝ وَنَجَّيْنٰهُ وَلُوْطًا

اِلَى الْاَرْضِ الَّتِيْ بٰرَكْنَا

this with our gods, O Abraham?"

63. He said: "Nay, this was done by - this is their biggest one! Ask them, if they can speak intelligently!"

64. So they turned to themselves and said, "Surely you are the ones in the wrong!"

65. Then were they confounded with shame: (they said), "You know full well that these (idols) do not speak!"

66. (Abraham) said, "Do you then worship, besides Allah, things that can neither be of any good to you

هٰذَا بِاٰلِهَتِنَا يَـٰٓإِبْرٰهِيمُ ۩

قَالَ بَلْ فَعَلَهٗ كَبِيرُهُمْ

هٰذَا فَسْـَٔلُوهُمْ إِنْ كَانُوْا

يَنْطِقُوْنَ ۝ فَرَجَعُوْٓا إِلٰٓى أَنْفُسِهِمْ

فَقَالُوْٓا إِنَّكُمْ أَنْتُمُ الظّٰلِمُوْنَ ۝

ثُمَّ نُكِسُوْا عَلٰى رُءُوْسِهِمْ لَقَدْ

عَلِمْتَ مَا هٰٓؤُلَآءِ يَنْطِقُوْنَ ۝

قَالَ أَفَتَعْبُدُوْنَ مِنْ دُوْنِ

اللّٰهِ مَا لَا يَنْفَعُكُمْ شَيْـًٔا

after you go away and turn your backs".

58. So he broke them to pieces, (all) but the biggest of them, that they might turn (and address themselves) to it.

59. They said, "Who has done this to our gods? He must indeed be some man of impiety!"

60. They said, "We heard a youth talk of them: he is called Abraham."

61. They said, "Then bring him before the eyes of the people, that they may bear witness."

62. They said, "Are you the one that did

بَعْدَ اَنْ تُوَلُّوْا مُدْبِرِيْنَ ۝

فَجَعَلَهُمْ جُذَاذًا اِلَّا كَبِيْرًا

لَّهُمْ لَعَلَّهُمْ اِلَيْهِ يَرْجِعُوْنَ ۝

قَالُوْا مَنْ فَعَلَ هٰذَا بِاٰلِهَتِنَآ

اِنَّهٗ لَمِنَ الظّٰلِمِيْنَ ۝ قَالُوْا

سَمِعْنَا فَتًى يَّذْكُرُهُمْ يُقَالُ

لَهٗٓ اِبْرٰهِيْمُ ۝ قَالُوْا فَاْتُوْا

بِهٖ عَلٰٓى اَعْيُنِ النَّاسِ لَعَلَّهُمْ

يَشْهَدُوْنَ ۝ قَالُوْٓا ءَاَنْتَ فَعَلْتَ

are (so assiduously) devoted?"

53. They said, "We found our fathers worshipping them."

54. He said, "Indeed you have been in manifest error - you and your fathers."

55. They said, "Have you brought us the Truth, or are you one of those who jest?"

56. He said, "No, your Lord is the Lord of the heavens and the earth, He Who created them (from nothing): and I am a witness to this (Truth)."

57. "And by Allah, I have a plan for your idols -

عٰكِفُوْنَ ۞ قَالُوْا وَجَدْنَآ اٰبَآءَنَا

لَهَا عٰبِدِيْنَ ۞ قَالَ لَقَدْ كُنْتُمْ

اَنْتُمْ وَاٰبَآؤُكُمْ فِيْ ضَلٰلٍ

مُّبِيْنٍ ۞ قَالُوْٓا اَجِئْتَنَا بِالْحَقِّ

اَمْ اَنْتَ مِنَ اللّٰعِبِيْنَ ۞ قَالَ

بَلْ رَّبُّكُمْ رَبُّ السَّمٰوٰتِ

وَالْاَرْضِ الَّذِيْ فَطَرَهُنَّ ۖ وَاَنَا

عَلٰى ذٰلِكُمْ مِّنَ الشّٰهِدِيْنَ ۞

وَ تَاللّٰهِ لَاَكِيْدَنَّ اَصْنَامَكُمْ

and a Message for those who would do right, -

49. Those who fear their Lord in their most secret thoughts, and who hold the Hour (of Judgment) in awe.

50. And this is a blessed Message which We have sent down: will you then reject it?

51. We bestowed aforetime on Abraham his rectitude of conduct, and We were Well Acquainted with him.

52. Behold! He said to his father and his people, "What are these images, to which you

وَذِكْرٌ لِّلْمُتَّقِينَ ۞ الَّذِينَ

يَخْشَوْنَ رَبَّهُم بِالْغَيْبِ وَهُم

مِّنَ السَّاعَةِ مُشْفِقُونَ ۞ وَهَٰذَا

ذِكْرٌ مُّبَارَكٌ أَنزَلْنَٰهُ ۚ أَفَأَنتُمْ

لَهُ مُنكِرُونَ ۞ وَلَقَدْ ءَاتَيْنَآ

إِبْرَٰهِيمَ رُشْدَهُ مِن قَبْلُ

وَكُنَّا بِهِ عَٰلِمِينَ ۞ إِذْ قَالَ

لِأَبِيهِ وَقَوْمِهِ مَا هَٰذِهِ

التَّمَاثِيلُ الَّتِىٓ أَنتُمْ لَهَا

they are warned!

46. If but a breath of the Wrath of your Lord do touch them, they will then say, "Woe to us! We did wrong indeed!"

47. We shall set up scales of justice for the Day of Judgment, so that not a soul will be dealt with unjustly in the least, and if there be (no more than) the weight of a mustard seed, We will bring it (to account): and enough are We to take account.

48. In the past We granted to Moses and Aaron the criterion (for judgment), and a Light

يُنذَرُونَ ۞ وَلَئِن مَّسَّتْهُمْ

نَفْحَةٌ مِّنْ عَذَابِ رَبِّكَ

لَيَقُولُنَّ يَٰوَيْلَنَآ إِنَّا كُنَّا ظَٰلِمِينَ ۞

وَنَضَعُ ٱلْمَوَٰزِينَ ٱلْقِسْطَ لِيَوْمِ

ٱلْقِيَٰمَةِ فَلَا تُظْلَمُ نَفْسٌ شَيْـًٔا

وَإِن كَانَ مِثْقَالَ حَبَّةٍ مِّنْ

خَرْدَلٍ أَتَيْنَا بِهَا وَكَفَىٰ بِنَا

حَٰسِبِينَ ۞ وَلَقَدْ ءَاتَيْنَا مُوسَىٰ

وَهَٰرُونَ ٱلْفُرْقَانَ وَضِيَآءً

they gods that can guard them from Us? They have no power to aid themselves, nor can they be defended from Us.

44. No, We gave the good things of this life to these men and their fathers until the period grew long for them; see they not that We gradually reduce the land (in their control) from its outlying borders? Is it then they who will win?

45. Say, "I do but warn you according to revelation": but the deaf will not hear the call, (even) when

لَهُمْ اٰلِهَةٌ تَمْنَعُهُمْ مِّنْ دُوْنِنَاؕ

لَا يَسْتَطِيْعُوْنَ نَصْرَ اَنْفُسِهِمْ

وَلَا هُمْ مِّنَّا يُصْحَبُوْنَ ۞ بَلْ

مَتَّعْنَا هٰٓؤُلَاءِ وَاٰبَآءَهُمْ حَتّٰى

طَالَ عَلَيْهِمُ الْعُمُرُؕ اَفَلَا يَرَوْنَ

اَنَّا نَأْتِى الْاَرْضَ نَنْقُصُهَا مِنْ

اَطْرَافِهَاؕ اَفَهُمُ الْغٰلِبُوْنَ ۞ قُلْ

اِنَّمَآ اُنْذِرُكُمْ بِالْوَحْىِۖ وَلَا

يَسْمَعُ الصُّمُّ الدُّعَآءَ اِذَا مَا

40. Nay, it may come to them all of a sudden and confound them: no power will they have then to avert it, nor will they (then) get respite.

41. Mocked were (many) Apostle before you; but their scoffers were hemmed in by the thing that they mocked.

42. Say: "Who can keep you safe by night and by day from (the Wrath of) Allah) Most Gracious?" Yet they turn away from the mention of their Lord.

43. Or have

بَلْ تَأْتِيْهِمْ بَغْتَةً فَتَبْهَتُهُمْ

فَلَا يَسْتَطِيْعُوْنَ رَدَّهَا وَلَا

هُمْ يُنْظَرُوْنَ ۞ وَلَقَدِ اسْتُهْزِئَ

بِرُسُلٍ مِّنْ قَبْلِكَ فَحَاقَ

بِالَّذِيْنَ سَخِرُوْا مِنْهُمْ مَّا

كَانُوْا بِهٖ يَسْتَهْزِءُوْنَ ۞ قُلْ

مَنْ يَّكْلَؤُكُمْ بِالَّيْلِ وَالنَّهَارِ

مِنَ الرَّحْمٰنِ بَلْ هُمْ عَنْ

ذِكْرِ رَبِّهِمْ مُّعْرِضُوْنَ ۞ أَمْ

(they say), "the one who talks of your gods?" And they blaspheme at the mention of (Allah) Most Gracious!

37.   Man is a creature of haste: soon (enough) will I show you My Signs; then you will not ask Me to hasten them!

38.   They say: "When will this promise come to pass, if you are telling the truth?"

39.   If only the unbelievers knew (the time) when they will not be able to ward off the fire from their faces, nor yet from their backs, and (when) no help can reach them!

الَّذِىْ يَذْكُرُ اٰلِهَتَكُمْ وَهُمْ

بِذِكْرِ الرَّحْمٰنِ هُمْ كٰفِرُوْنَ ۞

خُلِقَ الْاِنْسَانُ مِنْ عَجَلٍ ۗ

سَاُوْرِيْكُمْ اٰيٰتِىْ فَلَا تَسْتَعْجِلُوْنِ ۞

وَيَقُوْلُوْنَ مَتٰى هٰذَا الْوَعْدُ

اِنْ كُنْتُمْ صٰدِقِيْنَ ۞ لَوْ يَعْلَمُ

الَّذِيْنَ كَفَرُوْا حِيْنَ لَا يَكُفُّوْنَ

عَنْ وُّجُوْهِهِمُ النَّارَ وَلَا عَنْ

ظُهُوْرِهِمْ وَلَا هُمْ يُنْصَرُوْنَ ۞

and the Day, and the sun and the moon: all (the celestial bodies) swim along, each in its rounded course.

34. We granted not to any man before you permanent life (here): if then you should die, would they live permanently?

35. Every soul shall have a taste of death: and We test you by evil and by good by way of trial. to Us must you return.

36. When the unbelievers see you, they treat you not except with ridicule. "Is this,"

وَالنَّهَارَ وَالشَّمْسَ وَالْقَمَرَ

كُلٌّ فِى فَلَكٍ يَّسْبَحُوْنَ ۝ وَمَا

جَعَلْنَا لِبَشَرٍ مِّنْ قَبْلِكَ

الْخُلْدَ ۚ أَفَإِنْ مِّتَّ فَهُمُ

الْخَٰلِدُوْنَ ۝ كُلُّ نَفْسٍ ذَآئِقَةُ

الْمَوْتِ ۗ وَنَبْلُوْكُمْ بِالشَّرِّ وَالْخَيْرِ

فِتْنَةً ۗ وَإِلَيْنَا تُرْجَعُوْنَ ۝

وَإِذَا رَاٰكَ الَّذِيْنَ كَفَرُوٓا إِنْ

يَّتَّخِذُوْنَكَ إِلَّا هُزُوًا ۗ أَهٰذَا

the heavens and the earth were joined together (as one unit of creation), before We clove them asunder? We made from water every living thing. Will they not then believe?

31. And We have set on the earth mountains standing firm, lest it should shake with them, and We have made therein broad highways (between mountains) for them to pass through: that they may receive guidance.

32. And We have made the heavens as a canopy well guarded: yet do they turn away from the Signs which these things (point to)!

33. It is He Who created the Night

السَّمٰوٰتِ وَالْأَرْضَ كَانَتَا رَتْقًا

فَفَتَقْنٰهُمَا ۖ وَجَعَلْنَا مِنَ الْمَآءِ

كُلَّ شَيْءٍ حَيٍّ ۗ أَفَلَا يُؤْمِنُوْنَ ۝

وَجَعَلْنَا فِي الْأَرْضِ رَوَاسِيَ أَنْ

تَمِيدَ بِهِمْ وَجَعَلْنَا فِيْهَا فِجَاجًا

سُبُلًا لَّعَلَّهُمْ يَهْتَدُوْنَ ۝

وَجَعَلْنَا السَّمَآءَ سَقْفًا مَّحْفُوْظًا ۖ

وَّهُمْ عَنْ اٰيٰتِهَا مُعْرِضُوْنَ ۝

وَهُوَ الَّذِيْ خَلَقَ الَّيْلَ

27. They speak not before He speaks, and they act (in all things) by His Command.

28. He knows what is before them, and what is behind them, and they offer no intercession except for those who are acceptable, and they stand in awe and reverence of His (Glory).

29. If any of them should say, "I am a god besides Him", such a one We should reward with Hell: thus do We reward those who do wrong.

30. Do not the unbelievers see that

لَا يَسْبِقُونَهُ بِالْقَوْلِ وَهُمْ

بِأَمْرِهِ يَعْمَلُونَ ۝ يَعْلَمُ مَا

بَيْنَ أَيْدِيهِمْ وَمَا خَلْفَهُمْ

وَلَا يَشْفَعُونَ إِلَّا لِمَنِ ارْتَضَى

وَهُمْ مِّنْ خَشْيَتِهِ مُشْفِقُونَ ۝

وَمَنْ يَّقُلْ مِنْهُمْ إِنِّيٓ إِلٰهٌ

مِّنْ دُونِهِ فَذٰلِكَ نَجْزِيهِ

جَهَنَّمَ كَذٰلِكَ نَجْزِى الظّٰلِمِينَ ۝

أَوَلَمْ يَرَ الَّذِينَ كَفَرُوٓا أَنَّ

(other) gods besides him? Say, "Bring your convincing proof: this is the Message of those with me and the Message of those before me." But most of them know not the Truth, and so turn away.

25. Not an Apostle did We send before you without this inspiration sent by Us to him: that there is no god but I; therefore worship and serve Me.

26. And they say: "(Allah) Most Gracious has begotten offspring." Glory to Him! They are (but) servants raised to honour.

دُونِهِ اٰلِهَةً ۗ قُلْ هَاتُوا بُرْهَانَكُمْ ۚ

هٰذَا ذِكْرُ مَنْ مَّعِيَ وَذِكْرُ

مَنْ قَبْلِيْ ۗ بَلْ اَكْثَرُهُمْ لَا

يَعْلَمُوْنَ الْحَقَّ فَهُمْ مُّعْرِضُوْنَ ۩

وَمَآ اَرْسَلْنَا مِنْ قَبْلِكَ مِنْ

رَّسُوْلٍ اِلَّا نُوْحِيْ اِلَيْهِ اَنَّهٗ

لَآ اِلٰهَ اِلَّا اَنَا فَاعْبُدُوْنِ ۩

وَقَالُوا اتَّخَذَ الرَّحْمٰنُ وَلَدًا ۗ

سُبْحٰنَهٗ ۗ بَلْ عِبَادٌ مُّكْرَمُوْنَ ۩

serve Him, nor are they (ever) weary (of His service):

20. They celebrate His praises night and day, nor do they ever flag or intermit.

21. Or have they taken (for worship) gods from the earth who can raise (the dead)?

22. If there were, in the heavens and the earth, other gods besides Allah, there would have been confusion in both! But Glory to Allah, the Lord of the Throne: (high is He) above what they attribute to Him!

23. He cannot be questioned for His acts, but they will be questioned (for theirs).

24. Or have they taken for worship

عِبَادَتِهِ وَلَا يَسْتَحْسِرُوْنَ ۝

يُسَبِّحُوْنَ الَّيْلَ وَالنَّهَارَ لَا

يَفْتُرُوْنَ ۝ اَمِ اتَّخَذُوْٓا اٰلِهَةً

مِّنَ الْاَرْضِ هُمْ يُنْشِرُوْنَ ۝

لَوْ كَانَ فِيْهِمَآ اٰلِهَةٌ اِلَّا

اللّٰهُ لَفَسَدَتَا ۚ فَسُبْحٰنَ اللّٰهِ

رَبِّ الْعَرْشِ عَمَّا يَصِفُوْنَ ۝

لَا يُسْئَلُ عَمَّا يَفْعَلُ وَهُمْ

يُسْئَلُوْنَ ۝ اَمِ اتَّخَذُوْا مِنْ

and all that is between!

17. If it had been Our wish to take (just) a pastime, We should surely have taken it from the things nearest to Us, if We would do (such a thing)!

18. No, We hurl the Truth against falsehood, and it knocks out its brain, and behold, falsehood does perish! Ah! woe be to you for the (false) things you ascribe (to Us).

19. To Him belong all (creatures) in the heavens and on earth: even those who are in His (very) Presence are not too proud to

وَمَا بَيْنَهُمَا لَعِبِيْنَ ۞ لَوْ

اَرَدْنَآ اَنْ نَّتَّخِذَ لَهْوًا

لَّاتَّخَذْنٰهُ مِنْ لَّدُنَّآ ۖ اِنْ

كُنَّا فٰعِلِيْنَ ۞ بَلْ نَقْذِفُ

بِالْحَقِّ عَلَى الْبَاطِلِ فَيَدْمَغُهٗ

فَاِذَا هُوَ زَاهِقٌ ۖ وَلَكُمُ الْوَيْلُ

مِمَّا تَصِفُوْنَ ۞ وَلَهٗ مَنْ

فِى السَّمٰوٰتِ وَالْاَرْضِ ۚ وَمَنْ

عِنْدَهٗ لَا يَسْتَكْبِرُوْنَ عَنْ

setting up in their places other peoples?

12. Yet, when they felt Our Punishment (coming), behold, they (tried to) flee from it.

13. Flee not, but return to the good things of this life which were given you, and to your homes in order that you may be called to account.

14. They said: "Ah! Woe to us! We were indeed wrong-doers!"

15. And that cry of theirs ceased not, till We made them as a field that is mown, as ashes silent and quenched.

16. Not for (idle) sport did We create the heavens and the earth

وَاَنْشَاْنَا بَعْدَهَا قَوْمًا اٰخَرِيْنَ ۞

فَلَمَّآ اَحَسُّوْا بَاْسَنَآ اِذَا هُمْ

مِّنْهَا يَرْكُضُوْنَ ۞ لَا تَرْكُضُوْا

وَارْجِعُوْٓا اِلٰى مَآ اُتْرِفْتُمْ فِيْهِ

وَمَسٰكِنِكُمْ لَعَلَّكُمْ تُسْئَلُوْنَ ۞

قَالُوْا يٰوَيْلَنَآ اِنَّا كُنَّا ظٰلِمِيْنَ ۞

فَمَا زَالَتْ تِّلْكَ دَعْوٰىهُمْ حَتّٰى

جَعَلْنٰهُمْ حَصِيْدًا خٰمِدِيْنَ ۞

وَمَا خَلَقْنَا السَّمَآءَ وَالْاَرْضَ

if you realise this not, ask of those who possess the Message.

8.   Nor did We give them bodies that ate no food, nor were they exempt from death.

9.   In the end We fulfilled to them Our Promise, and We saved them and those whom We pleased, but We destroyed those who transgressed beyond bounds.

10.   We have revealed for you (O men!) a book in which is a Message for you: will you not then understand?

11.   How many were the populations We utterly destroyed because of their iniquities,

فَسْـَٔلُوٓا أَهْلَ الذِّكْرِ إِن كُنتُمْ

لَا تَعْلَمُونَ ۞ وَمَا جَعَلْنَٰهُمْ

جَسَدًا لَّا يَأْكُلُونَ الطَّعَامَ وَمَا

كَانُوا خَٰلِدِينَ ۞ ثُمَّ صَدَقْنَٰهُمُ

الْوَعْدَ فَأَنجَيْنَٰهُمْ وَمَن نَّشَآءُ

وَأَهْلَكْنَا الْمُسْرِفِينَ ۞ لَقَدْ

أَنزَلْنَآ إِلَيْكُمْ كِتَٰبًا فِيهِ

ذِكْرُكُمْ ۚ أَفَلَا تَعْقِلُونَ ۞ وَكَمْ

قَصَمْنَا مِن قَرْيَةٍ كَانَتْ ظَالِمَةً

4. Say: "My Lord knows (every) word (spoken) in the heavens and on earth: He is the One that hears and knows (all things)."

5. "No," they say, "(these are) medleys of dream! - No, he forged it! - No, he is (but) a poet! Let him then bring us a Sign like the ones that were sent to (Prophets) of old!"

6. (As to those) before them, not one of the populations which We destroyed believed: will these believe?

7. Before you, also, the Apostles We sent were but men, to whom we granted inspiration:

قُلْ رَّبِّى يَعْلَمُ الْقَوْلَ فِى
السَّمَآءِ وَالْأَرْضِ وَهُوَ السَّمِيعُ
الْعَلِيمُ ۞ بَلْ قَالُوٓا أَضْغَاثُ
أَحْلَامٍ بَلِ افْتَرَىٰهُ بَلْ
هُوَ شَاعِرٌ فَلْيَأْتِنَا بِآيَةٍ كَمَآ
أُرْسِلَ الْأَوَّلُونَ ۞ مَآ آمَنَتْ
قَبْلَهُمْ مِّن قَرْيَةٍ أَهْلَكْنَاهَآ
أَفَهُمْ يُؤْمِنُونَ ۞ وَمَآ أَرْسَلْنَا
قَبْلَكَ إِلَّا رِجَالًا نُّوحِىٓ إِلَيْهِمْ

Al-Ambiya (The Prophets)

Bismillahir-Rahmanir-Rahim

1. Closer and closer to mankind comes their Reckoning: yet they heed not and they turn away.

2. Never comes (aught) to them of a renewed Message from their Lord, but they listen to it as in jest, -

3. Their hearts toying as with trifles. The wrong-doers conceal their private counsels, (saying), "Is this (one) more than a man like yourselves? Will you go to witchcraft with your eyes open?"

بِسْمِ اللهِ الرَّحْمٰنِ الرَّحِيْمِ

اِقْتَرَبَ لِلنَّاسِ حِسَابُهُمْ

وَهُمْ فِيْ غَفْلَةٍ مُّعْرِضُوْنَ ۝

مَا يَأْتِيْهِمْ مِّنْ ذِكْرٍ مِّنْ

رَّبِّهِمْ مُّحْدَثٍ اِلَّا اسْتَمَعُوْهُ

وَهُمْ يَلْعَبُوْنَ ۝ لَاهِيَةً قُلُوْبُهُمْ

وَاَسَرُّوا النَّجْوَى الَّذِيْنَ ظَلَمُوْا

هَلْ هٰذَا اِلَّا بَشَرٌ مِّثْلُكُمْ

اَفَتَأْتُوْنَ السِّحْرَ وَاَنْتُمْ تُبْصِرُوْنَ ۝

ذٰلِكَ الْكِتٰبُ لَا رَيْبَ فِيهِ

پارہ

اِقْتَرَبَ لِلنَّاسِ

(۱۷)

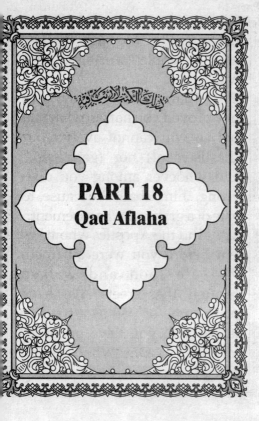

بتلك الكتب الاسلامية

PART 18
Qad Aflaha

they forgot the Message: for they were a people (worthless and) lost."

19. (Allah will say): "Now have they proved you liars in what you say: so you cannot avert (your Chastisement) nor (get) help." And whoever among you does wrong, him shall We cause to taste of a grievous Chastisement.

20. And the Apostles whom We sent before you were all (men) who ate food and walked through the streets: We have made some of you as a trial for others: will you have patience? For Allah is One Who sees (all things).

نَسُوا الذِّكۡرَ ۚ وَكَانُوۡا قَوۡمًۢا بُوۡرًا ۞

فَقَدۡ كَذَّبُوۡكُمۡ بِمَا تَقُوۡلُوۡنَ ۙ

فَمَا تَسۡتَطِيۡعُوۡنَ صَرۡفًا وَّلَا نَصۡرًا ۚ

وَمَنۡ يَّظۡلِمۡ مِّنۡكُمۡ نُذِقۡهُ عَذَابًا

كَبِيۡرًا ۞ وَمَاۤ اَرۡسَلۡنَا قَبۡلَكَ مِنَ

الۡمُرۡسَلِيۡنَ اِلَّاۤ اِنَّهُمۡ لَيَاۡكُلُوۡنَ

الطَّعَامَ وَيَمۡشُوۡنَ فِى الۡاَسۡوَاقِ ؕ

وَجَعَلۡنَا بَعۡضَكُمۡ لِبَعۡضٍ فِتۡنَةً ؕ

اَتَصۡبِرُوۡنَ ۚ وَكَانَ رَبُّكَ بَصِيۡرًا ۞

as well as a goal (of attainment)."

16. "For them there will be therein all that they wish for: they will dwell (there) for ever: a promise binding upon your Lord."

17. The Day He will gather them together as well as those whom they worship besides Allah, He will ask: "Was it you who let these My servants astray, or did they stray from the Path them-selves?"

18. They will say: "Glory to You! Not meet was it for us that we should take for protectors others besides You: but You did bestow, on them and their fathers, good things (in life), until

وَّمَصِيْرًا ۞ لَّهُمْ فِيْهَا مَا يَشَآءُوْنَ

خٰلِدِيْنَ ۗ كَانَ عَلٰى رَبِّكَ وَعْدًا

مَّسْـُٔوْلًا ۞ وَيَوْمَ يَحْشُرُهُمْ وَمَا

يَعْبُدُوْنَ مِنْ دُوْنِ اللّٰهِ فَيَقُوْلُ

ءَاَنْتُمْ اَضْلَلْتُمْ عِبَادِيْ هٰٓؤُلَآءِ

اَمْ هُمْ ضَلُّوا السَّبِيْلَ ۞ قَالُوْا

سُبْحٰنَكَ مَا كَانَ يَنْۢبَغِيْ لَنَآ اَنْ

نَّتَّخِذَ مِنْ دُوْنِكَ مِنْ اَوْلِيَآءَ

وَلٰكِنْ مَّتَّعْتَهُمْ وَاٰبَآءَهُمْ حَتّٰى

but We have prepared a blazing fire for such as deny the Hour:

12. When it sees them from a place far off, they will hear its fury and its ranging sigh.

13. And when they are cast, bound together into a constricted place therein, they will plead for destruction there and then!

14. "This day plead not for a single destruction: plead for destruction oft-repeated!"

15. Say: "Is that best, or the eternal Garden, promised to the righteous? For them, that is a reward

وَأَعْتَدْنَا لِمَنْ كَذَّبَ بِالسَّاعَةِ

سَعِيرًا ۝ إِذَا رَأَتْهُمْ مِّن مَّكَانٍ

بَعِيدٍ سَمِعُوا لَهَا تَغَيُّظًا وَّزَفِيرًا ۝

وَإِذَآ أُلْقُوا مِنْهَا مَكَانًا ضَيِّقًا

مُّقَرَّنِينَ دَعَوْا هُنَالِكَ ثُبُورًا ۝

لَا تَدْعُوا الْيَوْمَ ثُبُورًا وَّاحِدًا

وَّادْعُوا ثُبُورًا كَثِيرًا ۝ قُلْ أَذَلِكَ

خَيْرٌ أَمْ جَنَّةُ الْخُلْدِ الَّتِي وُعِدَ

الْمُتَّقُونَ ۚ كَانَتْ لَهُمْ جَزَآءً

(why) has not a treasure been bestowed on him, or why has he (not) a garden for enjoyment?" The wicked say: "You follow none other than a man bewitched."

9. See what kinds of comparisons they make for you! But they have gone astray, and never a way will they be able to find!

10. Blessed is He Who, if that were His will, could give you better (things) than those,- Gardens beneath which rivers flow; and He could give you palaces (secure to dwell in).

11. Nay, they deny the Hour (of the Judgment to come):

يُلۡقَىٰٓ اِلَيۡهِ كَنۡزٌ اَوۡ تَكُوۡنُ لَهٗ

جَنَّةٌ يَّاۡكُلُ مِنۡهَا ۚ وَقَالَ الظّٰلِمُوۡنَ

اِنۡ تَتَّبِعُوۡنَ اِلَّا رَجُلًا مَّسۡحُوۡرًا ۝

اُنۡظُرۡ كَيۡفَ ضَرَبُوۡا لَكَ الۡاَمۡثَالَ

فَضَلُّوۡا فَلَا يَسۡتَطِيۡعُوۡنَ سَبِيۡلًا ۝

تَبٰرَكَ الَّذِىۡٓ اِنۡ شَآءَ جَعَلَ لَكَ

خَيۡرًا مِّنۡ ذٰلِكَ جَنّٰتٍ تَجۡرِىۡ

مِنۡ تَحۡتِهَا الۡاَنۡهٰرُ ۙ وَيَجۡعَلۡ لَّكَ

قُصُوۡرًا ۝ بَلۡ كَذَّبُوۡا بِالسَّاعَةِ ۚ

In truth it is they who have put forward an iniquity and a falsehood.

5. And they say: "Tales of the ancients, which he has caused to be written: and they are dictated before him morning and evening."

6. Say: "The (Qur'an) was sent down by Him Who knows the mystery (that is) in the heavens and the earth: verily He is Oft-Forgiving, Most Merciful."

7. And they say: "What sort of an Apostle is this, who eats food, and walks through the streets? Why has not an Angel been sent down to him to give admonition with him?"

8. "Or

اخَرُوْنَ ۚ فَقَدْ جَآءُوْ ظُلْمًا وَّ زُوْرًا ۝

وَ قَالُوْۤا اَسَاطِيْرُ الْاَوَّلِيْنَ اكْتَتَبَهَا

فَهِيَ تُمْلٰى عَلَيْهِ بُكْرَةً وَّ اَصِيْلًا ۝

قُلْ اَنْزَلَهُ الَّذِيْ يَعْلَمُ السِّرَّ

فِى السَّمٰوٰتِ وَ الْاَرْضِ ۚ اِنَّهٗ كَانَ

غَفُوْرًا رَّحِيْمًا ۝ وَ قَالُوْا مَالِ هٰذَا

الرَّسُوْلِ يَاْكُلُ الطَّعَامَ وَ يَمْشِيْ

فِى الْاَسْوَاقِ ۭ لَوْ لَاۤ اُنْزِلَ اِلَيْهِ

مَلَكٌ فَيَكُوْنَ مَعَهٗ نَذِيْرًا ۝ اَوْ

has He a partner in His dominion: it is He who created all things, and ordered them in due proportions.

3.   Yet have they taken, besides him, gods that can create nothing but are themselves created; that have no control of hurt or good to themselves; nor can they control death nor life nor resurrection.

4.   But the misbelievers say: "Nothing is this but a lie which he has forged, and others have helped him at it."

يَكُنْ لَّهُ شَرِيكٌ فِى الْمُلْكِ وَخَلَقَ
كُلَّ شَىْءٍ فَقَدَّرَهُ تَقْدِيرًا ۞
وَاتَّخَذُوْا مِنْ دُوْنِهٖ اٰلِهَةً لَّا
يَخْلُقُوْنَ شَيْئًا وَّهُمْ يُخْلَقُوْنَ
وَلَا يَمْلِكُوْنَ لِاَنْفُسِهِمْ ضَرًّا
وَّلَا نَفْعًا وَّلَا يَمْلِكُوْنَ مَوْتًا
وَّلَا حَيٰوةً وَّلَا نُشُوْرًا ۞ وَقَالَ
الَّذِيْنَ كَفَرُوْا اِنْ هٰذَآ اِلَّآ
اِفْكُِ افْتَرٰىهُ وَاَعَانَهٗ عَلَيْهِ قَوْمٌ

sure that to Allah belong whatever is in the heavens and on earth. Well does He know what you are intent upon: and the day they will be brought back to Him, and He will tell them the truth of what they did: for Allah does know all things.

Al-Furqan (The Criterion)

Bismillahir-Rahmanir-Rahim

1. Blessed is He Who sent down the criterion to His servant, that it may be an admonition to all creatures; -

2. He to Whom belongs the dominion of the heavens and the earth: no son has He begotten, nor

اِنَّ لِلّٰهِ مَا فِى السَّمٰوٰتِ وَ الْاَرْضِ

قَدْ يَعْلَمُ مَاۤ اَنْتُمْ عَلَيْهِ ۚ وَيَوْمَ

يُرْجَعُوْنَ اِلَيْهِ فَيُنَبِّئُهُمْ بِمَا

عَمِلُوْا ؕ وَاللّٰهُ بِكُلِّ شَىْءٍ عَلِيْمٌ ۟ ۖ

بِسْمِ اللّٰهِ الرَّحْمٰنِ الرَّحِيْمِ

تَبٰرَكَ الَّذِىْ نَزَّلَ الْفُرْقَانَ

عَلٰى عَبْدِهٖ لِيَكُوْنَ لِلْعٰلَمِيْنَ

نَذِيْرَا ۙ ۟ الَّذِىْ لَهٗ مُلْكُ السَّمٰوٰتِ

وَالْاَرْضِ وَلَمْ يَتَّخِذْ وَلَدًا وَّلَمْ

so when they ask for your leave, for some business of theirs, give leave to those of them whom you will, and ask Allah for their forgiveness: for Allah is Oft-Forgiving, Most Merciful.

63. Deem not the summons of the Apostle among yourselves like the summons of one of you to another: Allah does know those of you who slip away under shelter of some excuse: then let those beware who withstand the Apostle's order, lest some trial befall them, or a grievous Chastisement be inflicted on them.

64. Be quite

فَإِذَا اسْتَأْذَنُوكَ لِبَعْضِ شَأْنِهِمْ

فَأْذَنْ لِّمَن شِئْتَ مِنْهُمْ وَاسْتَغْفِرْ

لَهُمُ اللَّهَ إِنَّ اللَّهَ غَفُورٌ رَّحِيمٌ ۝

لَا تَجْعَلُوا دُعَآءَ الرَّسُولِ بَيْنَكُمْ

كَدُعَآءِ بَعْضِكُم بَعْضًا قَدْ يَعْلَمُ

اللَّهُ الَّذِينَ يَتَسَلَّلُونَ مِنكُمْ

لِوَاذًا فَلْيَحْذَرِ الَّذِينَ يُخَالِفُونَ

عَنْ أَمْرِهِ أَن تُصِيبَهُمْ فِتْنَةٌ

أَوْ يُصِيبَهُمْ عَذَابٌ أَلِيمٌ ۝ أَلَا

houses, salute each other - a greeting of blessing and purity as from Allah. Thus does Allah make clear the Signs to you: that you may understand.

62. Only those are believers, who believe in Allah and His Apostle: when they are with him on a matter requiring collective action, they do not depart until they have asked for his leave; those who ask for your leave are those who believe in Allah and His Apostle;

بُيُوتًا فَسَلِّمُوا عَلَى اَنْفُسِكُمْ تَحِيَّةً

مِّنْ عِنْدِ اللّٰهِ مُبٰرَكَةً طَيِّبَةً

كَذٰلِكَ يُبَيِّنُ اللّٰهُ لَكُمُ الْاٰيٰتِ

لَعَلَّكُمْ تَعْقِلُونَ ۞ اِنَّمَا الْمُؤْمِنُونَ

الَّذِينَ اٰمَنُوا بِاللّٰهِ وَرَسُولِهٖ

وَاِذَا كَانُوا مَعَهٗ عَلَى اَمْرٍ جَامِعٍ

لَّمْ يَذْهَبُوا حَتّٰى يَسْتَأْذِنُوهُ

اِنَّ الَّذِينَ يَسْتَأْذِنُونَكَ اُولٰئِكَ

الَّذِينَ يُؤْمِنُونَ بِاللّٰهِ وَرَسُولِهٖ

one afflicted with illness, nor in yourselves, that you should eat in your own houses, or those of your fathers, or your mothers, or your brothers, or your sisters, or your father's brothers or your father's sisters, or your mohter's brothers, or your mother's sisters, or in houses of which the keys are in your possession, or in the house of a sincere friend of yours: there is no blame on you, whether you eat in company or separately. But if you enter

الْمَرِيضِ حَرَجٌ وَّلَا عَلٰى أَنْفُسِكُمْ

أَنْ تَأْكُلُوْا مِنْ بُيُوْتِكُمْ أَوْ بُيُوْتِ

اٰبَائِكُمْ أَوْ بُيُوْتِ أُمَّهٰتِكُمْ أَوْ بُيُوْتِ

إِخْوَانِكُمْ أَوْ بُيُوْتِ أَخَوٰتِكُمْ أَوْ بُيُوْتِ

أَعْمَامِكُمْ أَوْ بُيُوْتِ عَمّٰتِكُمْ أَوْ بُيُوْتِ

أَخْوَالِكُمْ أَوْ بُيُوْتِ خٰلٰتِكُمْ أَوْ مَا

مَلَكْتُمْ مَّفَاتِحَهٗٓ أَوْ صَدِيْقِكُمْ ۚ

لَيْسَ عَلَيْكُمْ جُنَاحٌ أَنْ تَأْكُلُوْا

جَمِيْعًا أَوْ أَشْتَاتًا ۚ فَإِذَا دَخَلْتُمْ

do those senior to them (in age): thus does Allah make clear His Signs to you: for Allah is full of knowledge and wisdom.

60.   Such elderly women as are past the prospect of marriage, - there is no blame on them if they lay aside their (outer) garments, provided they make not a wanton display of their beauty: but it is best for them to be modest: and Allah is One Who sees and knows all things.

61.   It is no fault in the blind nor in one born lame, nor in

اسْتَأْذَنَ الَّذِينَ مِنْ قَبْلِهِمْ

كَذَلِكَ يُبَيِّنُ اللهُ لَكُمُ اٰيٰتِهِ

وَاللهُ عَلِيمٌ حَكِيمٌ ۞ وَالْقَوَاعِدُ

مِنَ النِّسَاءِ الّٰتِي لَا يَرْجُونَ نِكَاحًا

فَلَيْسَ عَلَيْهِنَّ جُنَاحٌ أَنْ يَّضَعْنَ

ثِيَابَهُنَّ غَيْرَ مُتَبَرِّجٰتٍ بِزِينَةٍ وَأَنْ

يَّسْتَعْفِفْنَ خَيْرٌ لَّهُنَّ وَاللهُ سَمِيعٌ

عَلِيمٌ ۞ لَيْسَ عَلَى الْأَعْمٰى حَرَجٌ

وَّلَا عَلَى الْأَعْرَجِ حَرَجٌ وَّلَا عَلٰى

on three occasions: before morning prayer; the while you doff your clothes for the noonday heat; and after the late-night prayer: these are your three times of undress: outside those times it is not wrong for you or for them to move about attending to each other: thus does Allah make clear the Signs to you: for Allah is full of knowledge and wisdom.

59. But when the children among you come of age, let them (also) ask for permission, as

ثَلَثَ مَرَّتٍ مِّنْ قَبْلِ صَلَوةِ

الْفَجْرِ وَحِينَ تَضَعُونَ ثِيَابَكُمْ مِّنَ

الظَّهِيرَةِ وَمِنْ بَعْدِ صَلَوةِ الْعِشَآءِ

ثَلَثُ عَوْرَاتٍ لَّكُمْ لَيْسَ عَلَيْكُمْ

وَلَا عَلَيْهِمْ جُنَاحٌ بَعْدَهُنَّ طَوَّفُونَ

عَلَيْكُمْ بَعْضُكُمْ عَلَى بَعْضٍ كَذَلِكَ

يُبَيِّنُ اللَّهُ لَكُمُ الْأَيَتِ وَاللَّهُ

عَلِيمٌ حَكِيمٌ ۞ وَإِذَا بَلَغَ الْأَطْفَالُ

مِنكُمُ الْحُلُمَ فَلْيَسْتَأْذِنُوا كَمَا

any one with Me.' If any do reject Faith after this, they are rebellious and wicked.

56. So establish regular Prayer and give regular Charity; and obey the Apostle; that you may receive mercy.

57. Never think you that the unbelievers are going to frustrate (Allah's Plan) on earth: their abode is the Fire, - and it is indeed an evil refuge!

58. O you who believe! Let those whom your right hands possess, and the (children) among you who have not come of age ask your permission (before they come to your presence),

بِي شَيْئًا ۚ وَمَنْ كَفَرَ بَعْدَ ذٰلِكَ

فَأُولٰٓئِكَ هُمُ الْفٰسِقُونَ ۞ وَأَقِيمُوا

الصَّلٰوةَ وَآتُوا الزَّكٰوةَ وَأَطِيعُوا

الرَّسُولَ لَعَلَّكُمْ تُرْحَمُونَ ۞ لَا

تَحْسَبَنَّ الَّذِينَ كَفَرُوا مُعْجِزِينَ

فِي الْأَرْضِ ۚ وَمَأْوٰىهُمُ النَّارُ ۚ وَلَبِئْسَ

الْمَصِيرُ ۞ يٰٓأَيُّهَا الَّذِينَ اٰمَنُوا

لِيَسْتَأْذِنْكُمُ الَّذِينَ مَلَكَتْ أَيْمَانُكُمْ

وَالَّذِينَ لَمْ يَبْلُغُوا الْحُلُمَ مِنْكُمْ

for the duty placed on him and you for that placed on you. If you obey him, you shall be on right guidance. The Apostle's duty is only to preach the clear (Message).

55.   Allah has promised, to those among you who believe and work righteous deeds, that He will, of a surety, grant them in the land, inheritance (of power), as He granted it to those before them; that He will establish in authority their religion - the one which He has chosen for them; and that He will change (their state), after the fear in which they (lived), to one of security and peace: 'They will worship Me (alone) and not associate

مَا حُمِّلَ وَعَلَيْكُمْ مَّا حُمِّلْتُمْ ۖ

وَاِنْ تُطِيعُوهُ تَهْتَدُوْا ۚ وَمَا عَلَى

الرَّسُوْلِ اِلَّا الْبَلٰغُ الْمُبِيْنُ ۞

وَعَدَ اللّٰهُ الَّذِيْنَ اٰمَنُوْا مِنْكُمْ

وَعَمِلُوا الصّٰلِحٰتِ لَيَسْتَخْلِفَنَّهُمْ فِى

الْاَرْضِ كَمَا اسْتَخْلَفَ الَّذِيْنَ مِنْ

قَبْلِهِمْ ۖ وَلَيُمَكِّنَنَّ لَهُمْ دِيْنَهُمُ الَّذِى

ارْتَضٰى لَهُمْ وَلَيُبَدِّلَنَّهُمْ مِّنْ بَعْدِ

خَوْفِهِمْ اَمْنًا ۚ يَعْبُدُوْنَنِيْ لَا يُشْرِكُوْنَ

"We hear and we obey": it is such as these that will attain felicity.

52. It is such as obey Allah and His Apostle, and fear Allah and do right, that will win (in the end),

53. They swear their strongest oaths by Allah that, if only you would command them, they would leave (their homes). Say: "Swear you not; obedience is (more) reasonable; verily, Allah is Well Acquainted with all that you do."

54. Say: "Obey Allah, and obey the Apostle: but if you turn away, he is only responsible

سَمِعْنَا وَ اَطَعْنَا وَ اُولٰٓئِكَ هُمُ
الْمُفْلِحُوْنَ ۞ وَمَنْ يُّطِعِ اللهَ
وَرَسُوْلَهٗ وَيَخْشَ اللهَ وَيَتَّقْهِ
فَاُولٰٓئِكَ هُمُ الْفَآئِزُوْنَ ۞ وَاَقْسَمُوْا
بِاللهِ جَهْدَ اَيْمَانِهِمْ لَئِنْ اَمَرْتَهُمْ
لَيَخْرُجُنَّ ۗ قُلْ لَّا تُقْسِمُوْا ۚ طَاعَةٌ
مَّعْرُوْفَةٌ ۗ اِنَّ اللهَ خَبِيْرٌۢ بِمَا
تَعْمَلُوْنَ ۞ قُلْ اَطِيْعُوا اللهَ وَاَطِيْعُوا
الرَّسُوْلَ ۚ فَاِنْ تَوَلَّوْا فَاِنَّمَا عَلَيْهِ

and His Apostle, in order that He may judge between them, behold some of them decline (to come).

49. But if the right is on their side, they come to him with all submission.

50. Is it that there is a disease in their hearts? Or do they doubt, or are they in fear, that Allah and His Apostle will deal unjustly with them? No, it is they themselves who do wrong.

51. The answer of the believers, when summoned to Allah and His Apostle, in order that He may judge between them, is no other than this: they say,

وَرَسُولِهِ لِيَحْكُمَ بَيْنَهُمْ إِذَا فَرِيقٌ

مِّنْهُمْ مُّعْرِضُونَ ۞ وَإِنْ يَّكُنْ لَّهُمُ

الْحَقُّ يَأْتُوا إِلَيْهِ مُذْعِنِينَ ۞

أَفِيْ قُلُوبِهِمْ مَّرَضٌ أَمِ ارْتَابُوا

أَمْ يَخَافُونَ أَنْ يَّحِيفَ اللهُ

عَلَيْهِمْ وَرَسُولُهُ ۚ بَلْ أُولَٰئِكَ

هُمُ الظّٰلِمُونَ ۞ إِنَّمَا كَانَ قَوْلَ

الْمُؤْمِنِينَ إِذَا دُعُوا إِلَى اللهِ

وَرَسُولِهِ لِيَحْكُمَ بَيْنَهُمْ أَنْ يَّقُولُوا

and some that walk on four. Allah creates what He wills; for verily Allah has power over all things.

46. We have indeed sent down Signs that make things manifest: and Allah guides whom He wills to a way that is straight.

47. They say, "We believe in Allah and in the Apostle, and we obey": but even after that, some of them turn away: they are not (really) believers.

48. When they are summoned to Allah

وَمِنْهُمْ مَّنْ يَّمْشِىْ عَلٰى اَرْبَعٍ ؕ

يَخْلُقُ اللّٰهُ مَا يَشَآءُ ؕ اِنَّ اللّٰهَ

عَلٰى كُلِّ شَىْءٍ قَدِيْرٌ ۞ لَقَدْ اَنْزَلْنَا

اٰيٰتٍ مُّبَيِّنٰتٍ ؕ وَاللّٰهُ يَهْدِىْ

مَنْ يَّشَآءُ اِلٰى صِرَاطٍ مُّسْتَقِيْمٍ ۞

وَيَقُوْلُوْنَ اٰمَنَّا بِاللّٰهِ وَبِالرَّسُوْلِ

وَاَطَعْنَا ثُمَّ يَتَوَلّٰى فَرِيْقٌ مِّنْهُمْ

مِّنْۢ بَعْدِ ذٰلِكَ ؕ وَمَاۤ اُولٰٓئِكَ

بِالْمُؤْمِنِيْنَ ۞ وَاِذَا دُعُوْۤا اِلَى اللّٰهِ

the sky mountain masses (of clouds) wherein is hail: He strikes therewith whom He pleases and He turns it away from whom He pleases, the vivid flash of His lightning well-nigh blinds the sight.

44. It is Allah Who alternates the Night and the Day: verily in these things is an instructive example for those who have vision!

45. And Allah has created every animal from water: of them there are some that creep on their bellies; some that walk on two legs;

السَّمَآءِ مِنْ جِبَالٍ فِيْهَا مِنْ

بَرَدٍ فَيُصِيْبُ بِهٖ مَنْ يَّشَآءُ

وَيَصْرِفُهٗ عَنْ مَّنْ يَّشَآءُ يَكَادُ

سَنَا بَرْقِهٖ يَذْهَبُ بِالْاَبْصَارِ ۞

يُقَلِّبُ اللّٰهُ الَّيْلَ وَ النَّهَارَ اِنَّ

فِيْ ذٰلِكَ لَعِبْرَةً لِّاُولِى الْاَبْصَارِ ۞

وَاللّٰهُ خَلَقَ كُلَّ دَآبَّةٍ مِّنْ مَّآءٍ

فَمِنْهُمْ مَّنْ يَّمْشِيْ عَلٰى بَطْنِهٖ

وَمِنْهُمْ مَّنْ يَّمْشِيْ عَلٰى رِجْلَيْنِ

Whose praises all beings in the heavens and on earth do celebrate, and the birds (of the air) with wings outspread? Each one knows its own (mode of) prayer and praise. And Allah knows well all that they do.

42. Yes, to Allah belongs the dominion of the heavens and the earth; and to Allah is the final goal (of all).

43. See you not that Allah makes the clouds move gently, then joins them together, then makes them into a heap? - then will you see rain issue forth from their midst. And He sends down from

يُسَبِّحُ لَهُ مَن فِى السَّمٰوٰتِ
وَالْأَرْضِ وَالطَّيْرُ صٰٓفّٰتٍ ۚ كُلٌّ قَدْ
عَلِمَ صَلَاتَهُۥ وَتَسْبِيحَهُۥ ۗ وَاللَّهُ
عَلِيمٌۢ بِمَا يَفْعَلُونَ ﴿٤١﴾ وَلِلَّهِ مُلْكُ
السَّمٰوٰتِ وَالْأَرْضِ ۖ وَإِلَى اللَّهِ
الْمَصِيرُ ﴿٤٢﴾ أَلَمْ تَرَ أَنَّ اللَّهَ يُزْجِى
سَحَابًا ثُمَّ يُؤَلِّفُ بَيْنَهُۥ ثُمَّ
يَجْعَلُهُۥ رُكَامًا فَتَرَى الْوَدْقَ
يَخْرُجُ مِنْ خِلٰلِهِۦ وَيُنَزِّلُ مِن

he comes up to it, he finds it to be nothing: but he finds Allah (ever) with him, and Allah will pay him his account: and Allah is swift in taking account.

40. Or (the unbelievers' state) is like the depths of darkness in a vast deep ocean, overwhelmed with billow topped by billow, topped by (dark) clouds: depths of darkness, one above another: if a man stretches out his hands, he can hardly see it! for any to whom Allah gives not light, there is no light!

41. See you not that it is Allah

جَآءَهُ لَمْ يَجِدْهُ شَيْئًا وَّوَجَدَ اللَّهَ
عِنْدَهُ فَوَفَّىٰهُ حِسَابَهُ ۗ وَاللَّهُ
سَرِيعُ الْحِسَابِ ۞ أَوْ كَظُلُمَٰتٍ
فِى بَحْرٍ لُّجِّىٍّ يَغْشَىٰهُ مَوْجٌ مِّن
فَوْقِهِ مَوْجٌ مِّن فَوْقِهِ سَحَابٌ ۚ
ظُلُمَٰتٌ بَعْضُهَا فَوْقَ بَعْضٍ ۗ إِذَآ
أَخْرَجَ يَدَهُ لَمْ يَكَدْ يَرَىٰهَا ۗ وَمَن
لَّمْ يَجْعَلِ اللَّهُ لَهُ نُورًا فَمَا
لَهُ مِن نُّورٍ ۞ أَلَمْ تَرَ أَنَّ اللَّهَ

whom neither traffic nor merchandise can divert from the Remembrance of Allah, nor from regular Prayer, nor from paying Zakat; their (only) fear is for the Day when hearts and eyes will be turned about,

38. That Allah may reward them according to the best of their deeds, and add even more for them out of His Grace: for Allah does provide for those whom He will, without measure.

39. But the unbelievers, - their deeds are like a mirage in sandy deserts, which the man parched with thirst mistakes for water; until when

لَا تُلْهِيهِمْ تِجَارَةٌ وَّلَا بَيْعٌ عَنْ

ذِكْرِ اللّٰهِ وَإِقَامِ الصَّلٰوةِ وَإِيْتَآءِ

الزَّكٰوةِ ۙ يَخَافُوْنَ يَوْمًا تَتَقَلَّبُ

فِيْهِ الْقُلُوْبُ وَالْأَبْصَارُ ۙ لِيَجْزِيَهُمُ

اللّٰهُ أَحْسَنَ مَا عَمِلُوْا وَيَزِيْدَهُمْ

مِّنْ فَضْلِهٖ ۗ وَاللّٰهُ يَرْزُقُ مَنْ

يَّشَآءُ بِغَيْرِ حِسَابٍ ۞ وَالَّذِيْنَ

كَفَرُوْا أَعْمَالُهُمْ كَسَرَابٍۢ بِقِيْعَةٍ

يَّحْسَبُهُ الظَّمْاٰنُ مَآءً ۚ حَتّٰى إِذَا

from a blessed Tree, an Olive, neither of the east nor of the west, whose oil is well-nigh luminous, though fire scarce touched it: Light upon Light! Allah does guide whom He will to His Light: Allah does set forth parables for men: and Allah does know all things.

36. (Lit is such a Light) in houses, which Allah has permitted to be raised to honour; for the celebration, in them, of His name: In them is He glorified in the mornings and in the evenings, (again and again), -

37. By men

مِنْ شَجَرَةٍ مُّبٰرَكَةٍ زَيْتُوْنَةٍ لَّا

شَرْقِيَّةٍ وَّلَا غَرْبِيَّةٍ يَّكَادُ زَيْتُهَا

يُضِيْٓءُ وَلَوْ لَمْ تَمْسَسْهُ نَارٌ �‘

نُوْرٌ عَلٰى نُوْرٍ ؕ يَهْدِى اللّٰهُ لِنُوْرِهٖ

مَنْ يَّشَآءُ ؕ وَيَضْرِبُ اللّٰهُ الْاَمْثَالَ

لِلنَّاسِ ؕ وَاللّٰهُ بِكُلِّ شَىْءٍ عَلِيْمٌ ۙ ۞

فِىْ بُيُوْتٍ اَذِنَ اللّٰهُ اَنْ تُرْفَعَ

وَيُذْكَرَ فِيْهَا اسْمُهٗ ۙ يُسَبِّحُ لَهٗ

فِيْهَا بِالْغُدُوِّ وَالْاٰصَالِ ۙ ۞ رِجَالٌ ۙ

of this life. But if anyone compels them, yet, after such compulsion, is Allah Oft-Forgiving, Most Merciful (to them).

34. We have already sent down to you verses making things clear, an illustration from (the story of) people who passed away before you, and an admonition for those who fear (Allah).

35. Allah is the Light of the heavens and the earth. The parable of His Light is as if there were a Niche and within it a Lamp: the Lamp enclosed in Glass: the Glass as it were a brilliant star: lit

الْحَيٰوةِ الدُّنْيَا وَمَنْ يُّكْرِهُّهُنَّ

فَاِنَّ اللّٰهَ مِنْ بَعْدِ اِكْرَاهِهِنَّ

غَفُوْرٌ رَّحِيْمٌ ۞ وَلَقَدْ اَنْزَلْنَا

اِلَيْكُمْ اٰيٰتٍ مُّبَيِّنٰتٍ وَّمَثَلًا مِّنَ

الَّذِيْنَ خَلَوْا مِنْ قَبْلِكُمْ وَمَوْعِظَةً

لِّلْمُتَّقِيْنَ ۞ اَللّٰهُ نُوْرُ السَّمٰوٰتِ

وَالْاَرْضِ مَثَلُ نُوْرِهٖ كَمِشْكٰوةٍ فِيْهَا

مِصْبَاحٌ اَلْمِصْبَاحُ فِيْ زُجَاجَةٍ

اَلزُّجَاجَةُ كَاَنَّهَا كَوْكَبٌ دُرِّيٌّ يُّوْقَدُ

in poverty, Allah will give them means out of His Grace: for Allah encompasses all, and he knows all things.

33.   Let those who find not the wherewithal for marriage keep themselves chaste, until Allah gives them means out of His Grace. And if any of your slaves ask for a deed in writing (to enable them to earn their freedom for a certain sum), give them such a deed if you know any good in them: yes, give them something yourselves out of the means which Allah has given to you. But force not your maids to prostitution when they desire chastity, in order that you may make a gain in the goods

فُقَرَآءَ يُغْنِهِمُ اللّٰهُ مِنْ فَضْلِهٖ ۗ وَاللّٰهُ

وَاسِعٌ عَلِيْمٌ ۞ وَلْيَسْتَعْفِفِ الَّذِيْنَ

لَا يَجِدُوْنَ نِكَاحًا حَتّٰى يُغْنِيَهُمُ

اللّٰهُ مِنْ فَضْلِهٖ ۗ وَالَّذِيْنَ يَبْتَغُوْنَ

الْكِتٰبَ مِمَّا مَلَكَتْ اَيْمَانُكُمْ فَكَاتِبُوْهُمْ

اِنْ عَلِمْتُمْ فِيْهِمْ خَيْرًا ۖ وَّاٰتُوْهُمْ

مِّنْ مَّالِ اللّٰهِ الَّذِيْٓ اٰتٰىكُمْ ۗ وَلَا

تُكْرِهُوْا فَتَيٰتِكُمْ عَلَى الْبِغَآءِ اِنْ

اَرَدْنَ تَحَصُّنًا لِّتَبْتَغُوْا عَرَضَ

or male servants free of sexual urge, or small children who have no sense of the shame of sex; and that they should not strike their feet in order to draw attention to their hidden ornaments. And O you believers! Turn you all together towards Allah, that you may attain Bliss.

32. Marry those among you who are single, or the virtuous ones among yourselves, male or female: if they are

اَيْمَانُهُنَّ اَوِ التّٰبِعِيْنَ غَيْرِ اُولِى

الْاِرْبَةِ مِنَ الرِّجَالِ اَوِ الطِّفْلِ

الَّذِيْنَ لَمْ يَظْهَرُوْا عَلٰى عَوْرٰتِ

النِّسَاءِ ۖ وَلَا يَضْرِبْنَ بِاَرْجُلِهِنَّ

لِيُعْلَمَ مَا يُخْفِيْنَ مِنْ زِيْنَتِهِنَّ ۗ

وَتُوْبُوْٓا اِلَى اللّٰهِ جَمِيْعًا اَيُّهَ

الْمُؤْمِنُوْنَ لَعَلَّكُمْ تُفْلِحُوْنَ ۝

وَاَنْكِحُوا الْاَيَامٰى مِنْكُمْ وَالصّٰلِحِيْنَ

مِنْ عِبَادِكُمْ وَاِمَآئِكُمْ ۚ اِنْ يَّكُوْنُوْا

that they should lower their gaze and guard their modesty; that they should not display their beauty and ornaments except what (must ordinarily) appear thereof; that they should draw their veils over their bosoms and not display their beauty except to their husbands, their fathers, their husband's fathers, their sons, their husbands' sons, their brothers or their brothers' sons, or their sisters' sons, or their women, or the slaves whom their right hands possess,

يَغْضُضْنَ مِنْ اَبْصَارِهِنَّ وَيَحْفَظْنَ

فُرُوجَهُنَّ وَلَا يُبْدِينَ زِينَتَهُنَّ

اِلَّا مَا ظَهَرَ مِنْهَا وَلْيَضْرِبْنَ

بِخُمُرِهِنَّ عَلٰى جُيُوبِهِنَّ وَلَا

يُبْدِينَ زِينَتَهُنَّ اِلَّا لِبُعُوْلَتِهِنَّ

اَوْ اٰبَآئِهِنَّ اَوْ اٰبَآءِ بُعُوْلَتِهِنَّ اَوْ

اَبْنَآئِهِنَّ اَوْ اَبْنَآءِ بُعُوْلَتِهِنَّ اَوْ

اِخْوَانِهِنَّ اَوْ بَنِيٓ اِخْوَانِهِنَّ اَوْ بَنِيٓ

اَخَوَاتِهِنَّ اَوْ نِسَآئِهِنَّ اَوْ مَا مَلَكَتْ

go back: that makes for greater purity for yourselves: and Allah knows well all that you do.

29. It is no fault on your part to enter houses not used for living in, which serve some (other) use for you: and Allah has knowledge of what you reveal and what you conceal.

30. Say to the believing men that they should lower their gaze and guard their modesty: that will make for greater purity for them: and Allah is Well Acquainted with all that they do.

31. And say to the believing women

فَارْجِعُوا هُوَ اَزْكٰى لَكُمْ ۚ وَاللّٰهُ

بِمَا تَعْمَلُوْنَ عَلِيْمٌ ۞ لَيْسَ

عَلَيْكُمْ جُنَاحٌ اَنْ تَدْخُلُوْا بُيُوْتًا

غَيْرَ مَسْكُوْنَةٍ فِيْهَا مَتَاعٌ لَّكُمْ ۚ

وَاللّٰهُ يَعْلَمُ مَا تُبْدُوْنَ وَمَا

تَكْتُمُوْنَ ۞ قُلْ لِّلْمُؤْمِنِيْنَ يَغُضُّوْا

مِنْ اَبْصَارِهِمْ وَيَحْفَظُوْا فُرُوْجَهُمْ ۚ

ذٰلِكَ اَزْكٰى لَهُمْ ۗ اِنَّ اللّٰهَ خَبِيْرٌۢ

بِمَا يَصْنَعُوْنَ ۞ وَقُلْ لِّلْمُؤْمِنٰتِ

these are not affected by what people say: for them there is forgiveness, and a provision honourable.

27. O you who believe! Enter not houses other than your own, until you have asked permission and saluted those in them: that is best for you, in order that you may heed (what is seemly).

28. If you find no one in the house, enter not until permission is given to you: if you are asked to go back,

اُولٰٓئِكَ مُبَرَّءُوْنَ مِمَّا يَقُوْلُوْنَ

لَهُمْ مَّغْفِرَةٌ وَّ رِزْقٌ كَرِيْمٌ ۞

يٰٓاَيُّهَا الَّذِيْنَ اٰمَنُوْا لَا تَدْخُلُوْا

بُيُوْتًا غَيْرَ بُيُوْتِكُمْ حَتّٰى تَسْتَأْنِسُوْا

وَ تُسَلِّمُوْا عَلٰٓى اَهْلِهَا ذٰلِكُمْ

خَيْرٌ لَّكُمْ لَعَلَّكُمْ تَذَكَّرُوْنَ ۞

فَاِنْ لَّمْ تَجِدُوْا فِيْهَآ اَحَدًا

فَلَا تَدْخُلُوْهَا حَتّٰى يُؤْذَنَ

لَكُمْ وَ اِنْ قِيْلَ لَكُمُ ارْجِعُوْا

but believing, are cursed in this life and in the Hereafter: for them is a grievous Chastisement, -

24. On the Day when their tongues, their hands, and their feet will bear witness against them as to their actions.

25. On that Day Allah will pay them back (all) their just dues, and they will realise that Allah is the (very) Truth, that makes all things manifest.

26. Women impure are for men impure, and men impure for women impure and women of purity are for men of purity, and men of purity are for women of purity:

الْمُؤْمِنَاتِ لُعِنُوا فِى الدُّنْيَا وَالْآخِرَةِ

وَلَهُمْ عَذَابٌ عَظِيمٌ ۞ يَوْمَ

تَشْهَدُ عَلَيْهِمْ أَلْسِنَتُهُمْ وَأَيْدِيهِمْ

وَأَرْجُلُهُمْ بِمَا كَانُوا يَعْمَلُونَ ۞

يَوْمَئِذٍ يُوَفِّيهِمُ اللَّهُ دِينَهُمُ الْحَقَّ

وَيَعْلَمُونَ أَنَّ اللَّهَ هُوَ الْحَقُّ

الْمُبِينُ ۞ الْخَبِيثَاتُ لِلْخَبِيثِينَ

وَالْخَبِيثُونَ لِلْخَبِيثَاتِ وَالطَّيِّبَاتُ

لِلطَّيِّبِينَ وَالطَّيِّبُونَ لِلطَّيِّبَاتِ

but Allah does purify whom He pleases: and Allah is One Who hears and knows (all things).

22. Let not those among you who are endued with grace and amplitude of means resolve by oath against helping their kinsmen, those in want, and those who have left their homes in Allah's cause: let them forgive and overlook, do you not wish that Allah should forgive you? For Allah is Oft-Forgiving, Most Merciful.

23. Those who slander chaste women, indiscreet

مِّنْ اَحَدٍ اَبَدًا وَّلٰكِنَّ اللهَ

يُزَكِّىْ مَنْ يَّشَآءُ وَاللهُ سَمِيْعٌ

عَلِيْمٌ ۞ وَلَا يَاْتَلِ اُولُوا الْفَضْلِ

مِنْكُمْ وَالسَّعَةِ اَنْ يُّؤْتُوْۤا اُولِى

الْقُرْبٰى وَالْمَسٰكِيْنَ وَالْمُهٰجِرِيْنَ فِىْ

سَبِيْلِ اللهِ وَلْيَعْفُوْا وَلْيَصْفَحُوْا

اَلَا تُحِبُّوْنَ اَنْ يَّغْفِرَ اللهُ لَكُمْ

وَاللهُ غَفُوْرٌ رَّحِيْمٌ ۞ اِنَّ الَّذِيْنَ

يَرْمُوْنَ الْمُحْصَنٰتِ الْغٰفِلٰتِ

in this life and in the Hereafter: Allah knows, and you know not.

20. Were it not for the Grace and Mercy of Allah on you, and that Allah is full of kindness and mercy, (you. would be ruined indeed).

21. O you who believe! Follow not Satan's footsteps: if any will follow the footsteps of Satan, he will (but) command what is shameful and wrong: and were it not for the Grace and Mercy of Allah on you, not one of you would ever have been pure:

فِى الدُّنْيَا وَالْأَخِرَةِ ۖ وَاللّٰهُ

يَعْلَمُ وَأَنْتُمْ لَا تَعْلَمُوْنَ ۝ وَلَوْ

لَا فَضْلُ اللّٰهِ عَلَيْكُمْ وَرَحْمَتُهُ

وَأَنَّ اللّٰهَ رَءُوْفٌ رَّحِيْمٌ ۝ يٰٓأَيُّهَا

الَّذِيْنَ اٰمَنُوْا لَا تَتَّبِعُوْا خُطُوٰتِ

الشَّيْطٰنِ ۚ وَمَنْ يَّتَّبِعْ خُطُوٰتِ

الشَّيْطٰنِ فَإِنَّهُ يَأْمُرُ بِالْفَحْشَاءِ

وَالْمُنْكَرِ ۚ وَلَوْلَا فَضْلُ اللّٰهِ

عَلَيْكُمْ وَرَحْمَتُهُ مَا زَكٰى مِنْكُمْ

most serious in the sight of Allah.

16. And why did you not, when you heard it, say? - "It is not right of us to speak of this: Glory to Allah! This is a most serious slander!"

17. Allah does admonish you, that you may never repeat such (conduct), if you are (true) believers.

18. And Allah makes the Signs plain to you: for Allah is full of knowledge and wisdom.

19. Those who love (to see) scandal published broadcast among the believers, will have a grievous Chastisement

اللهِ عَظِيْمٌ ۞ وَلَوْلَا اِذْ سَمِعْتُمُوْهُ

قُلْتُمْ مَّا يَكُوْنُ لَنَا آنْ نَّتَكَلَّمَ

بِهٰذَا ۙ سُبْحٰنَكَ هٰذَا بُهْتَانٌ

عَظِيْمٌ ۞ يَعِظُكُمُ اللهُ آنْ تَعُوْدُوْا

لِمِثْلِهٖ اَبَدًا اِنْ كُنْتُمْ مُّؤْمِنِيْنَ ۞

وَيُبَيِّنُ اللهُ لَكُمُ الْاٰيٰتِ ۚ وَاللهُ

عَلِيْمٌ حَكِيْمٌ ۞ اِنَّ الَّذِيْنَ

يُحِبُّوْنَ آنْ تَشِيْعَ الْفَاحِشَةُ فِي

الَّذِيْنَ اٰمَنُوْا لَهُمْ عَذَابٌ اَلِيْمٌ

four witnesses to prove it? When they have not brought the witnesses, such men, in the sight of Allah, (stand forth) themselves as liars!

14. Were it not for the Grace and Mercy of Allah on you, in this world and the Hereafter, a grievous Chastisement would have seized you in that you rushed glibly into this affair.

15. Behold, you received it on your tongues, and said out of your mouths things of which you had no knowledge; and you thought it to be a light matter, while it was

عَلَيْهِ بِاَرْبَعَةِ شُهَدَآءَ فَاِذْ لَمْ

يَاْتُوْا بِالشُّهَدَآءِ فَاُولٰٓئِكَ عِنْدَ

اللّٰهِ هُمُ الْكٰذِبُوْنَ ۱۳ وَلَوْ لَا

فَضْلُ اللّٰهِ عَلَيْكُمْ وَرَحْمَتُهٗ فِي

الدُّنْيَا وَالْاٰخِرَةِ لَمَسَّكُمْ فِيْ مَاۤ

اَفَضْتُمْ فِيْهِ عَذَابٌ عَظِيْمٌ ۱۴

اِذْ تَلَقَّوْنَهٗ بِاَلْسِنَتِكُمْ وَتَقُوْلُوْنَ

بِاَفْوَاهِكُمْ مَّا لَيْسَ لَكُمْ بِهٖ

عِلْمٌ وَّتَحْسَبُوْنَهٗ هَيِّنًا وَّهُوَ عِنْدَ

Oft-Returning, full of Wisdom, - (you would be ruined indeed).

11.   Those who brought forward the lie are a body among yourselves: think it not to be an evil to you; on the contrary it is good for you: to every man among them (will come the punishment) of the sin that he earned, and for him who took on himself the lead among them, will be a Chastisement grievous.

12.   Why did not the believers - men and women - when you heard of the affair, - thought well of their people and say, "This (charge) is an obvious lie"?

13.   Why did they not bring

تَوَّابٌ حَكِيمٌ ۝ إِنَّ الَّذِينَ

جَآءُو بِالْإِفْكِ عُصْبَةٌ مِّنْكُمْ

لَا تَحْسَبُوهُ شَرًّا لَّكُمْ بَلْ هُوَ

خَيْرٌ لَّكُمْ لِكُلِّ امْرِئٍ مِّنْهُم مَّا

اكْتَسَبَ مِنَ الْإِثْمِ وَالَّذِي تَوَلَّى

كِبْرَهُ مِنْهُمْ لَهُ عَذَابٌ عَظِيمٌ ۝

لَّوْلَا إِذْ سَمِعْتُمُوهُ ظَنَّ الْمُؤْمِنُونَ

وَالْمُؤْمِنَاتُ بِأَنْفُسِهِمْ خَيْرًا وَّقَالُوا

هَٰذَا إِفْكٌ مُّبِينٌ ۝ لَّوْلَا جَآءُو

that they are solemnly telling the truth;

7.   And the fifth (oath) (should be) that they solemnly invoke the Curse of Allah on themselves if they tell a lie.

8.   But it would avert the punishment from the wife, if she bears witness four times (with an oath) by Allah, that (her husband) is telling a lie;

9.   And the fifth (oath) should be that she solemnly invokes the Wrath of Allah on herself if (her accuser) is telling the truth.

10.   If it were not for Allah's Grace and Mercy on you, and that Allah is

إِنَّهٗ لَمِنَ الصّٰدِقِيْنَ ۝ وَالْخَامِسَةُ

أَنَّ لَعْنَتَ اللّٰهِ عَلَيْهِ اِنْ كَانَ

مِنَ الْكٰذِبِيْنَ ۝ وَيَدْرَؤُا عَنْهَا

الْعَذَابَ اَنْ تَشْهَدَ اَرْبَعَ

شَهٰدٰتٍ بِاللّٰهِ ۙ اِنَّهٗ لَمِنَ

الْكٰذِبِيْنَ ۝ وَالْخَامِسَةَ اَنَّ

غَضَبَ اللّٰهِ عَلَيْهَآ اِنْ كَانَ

مِنَ الصّٰدِقِيْنَ ۝ وَلَوْلَا فَضْلُ

اللّٰهِ عَلَيْكُمْ وَرَحْمَتُهٗ وَاَنَّ اللّٰهَ

four witnesses (to support their allegations), - flog them with eighty stripes; and reject their evidence ever after: for such men are wicked transgressors; -

5.   Unless they repent thereafter and mend (their conduct); for Allah is Oft-Forgiving, Most Merciful.

6.   And for those who launch a charge against their spouses, (or wives) and have (in support) no evidence but their own, - their solitary evidence (can be received) if they bear witness four times (with an oath) by Allah

بِأَرْبَعَةِ شُهَدَآءَ فَاجْلِدُوْهُمْ

ثَمٰنِيْنَ جَلْدَةً وَّلَا تَقْبَلُوْا لَهُمْ

شَهَادَةً اَبَدًا ۚ وَاُولٰٓئِكَ هُمُ

الْفٰسِقُوْنَ ۙ اِلَّا الَّذِيْنَ تَابُوْا

مِنْۢ بَعْدِ ذٰلِكَ وَاَصْلَحُوْا ۚ فَاِنَّ

اللّٰهَ غَفُوْرٌ رَّحِيْمٌ ۞ وَالَّذِيْنَ

يَرْمُوْنَ اَزْوَاجَهُمْ وَلَمْ يَكُنْ لَّهُمْ

شُهَدَآءُ اِلَّآ اَنْفُسُهُمْ فَشَهَادَةُ

اَحَدِهِمْ اَرْبَعُ شَهٰدٰتٍۭ بِاللّٰهِ

stripes: let not compassion move you in their case, in a matter prescribed by Allah, if you believe in Allah and the Last Day: and let a party of the believers witness their punishment.

3.　Let no man guilty of adultery or fornication marry any but a woman similarly guilty, or an unbeliever: nor let any but such a man or an unbeliever marry such a woman: to the believers such a thing is forbidden.

4.　And those who launch a charge against chaste women, and produce not

جَلْدَةٍ وَّلَا تَأْخُذْكُمْ بِهِمَا رَأْفَةٌ

فِيْ دِيْنِ اللّٰهِ اِنْ كُنْتُمْ تُؤْمِنُوْنَ

بِاللّٰهِ وَالْيَوْمِ الْاٰخِرِ وَلْيَشْهَدْ

عَذَابَهُمَا طَآئِفَةٌ مِّنَ الْمُؤْمِنِيْنَ ۞

اَلزَّانِيْ لَا يَنْكِحُ اِلَّا زَانِيَةً اَوْ

مُشْرِكَةً وَّالزَّانِيَةُ لَا يَنْكِحُهَا

اِلَّا زَانٍ اَوْ مُشْرِكٌ وَحُرِّمَ

ذٰلِكَ عَلَى الْمُؤْمِنِيْنَ ۞ وَالَّذِيْنَ

يَرْمُوْنَ الْمُحْصَنٰتِ ثُمَّ لَمْ يَأْتُوْا

he has no authority therefor; and his reckoning will be only with his Lord! and verily the unbelievers shall not prosper!

118. So say: "O my Lord! Grant us forgiveness and mercy! For You are the Best of those who show mercy!"

An-Noor (The Light)
Bismillahir-Rahmanir-Rahim

1. A Surah which We have sent down and which We have ordained: in it have We sent down clear Signs, in order that you may receive admonition.

2. The woman and the man guilty of adultery or fornication, - flog each of them with a hundred

لَا بُرْهَانَ لَهُ بِهِ فَإِنَّمَا حِسَابُهُ

عِنْدَ رَبِّهِ إِنَّهُ لَا يُفْلِحُ الْكَافِرُونَ ۝

وَقُلْ رَّبِّ اغْفِرْ وَارْحَمْ وَأَنْتَ

خَيْرُ الرَّاحِمِينَ ۝

بِسْمِ اللهِ الرَّحْمٰنِ الرَّحِيمِ

سُورَةٌ أَنْزَلْنَاهَا وَفَرَضْنَاهَا

وَأَنْزَلْنَا فِيهَا آيَاتٍ بَيِّنَاتٍ لَّعَلَّكُمْ

تَذَكَّرُونَ ۝ الزَّانِيَةُ وَالزَّانِي

فَاجْلِدُوا كُلَّ وَاحِدٍ مِّنْهُمَا مِائَةَ

number of years did you stay on earth?"

113. They will say: "We stayed a day or part of a day: but ask those who keep account."

114. He will say: "You stayed not but a little, - if you had only known!"

115. "Did you then think that We had created you in jest, and that you would not be brought back to Us (for account)?"

116. Therefore exalted be Allah, the King, the Reality: there is no god but He, the Lord of the Throne of Honour!

117. If anyone invokes, besides Allah, any other god,

لَبِثْتُمْ فِى الْاَرْضِ عَدَدَ سِنِيْنَ ۝

قَالُوْا لَبِثْنَا يَوْمًا اَوْ بَعْضَ

يَوْمٍ فَسْئَلِ الْعَآدِّيْنَ ۝ قُلْ اِنْ

لَّبِثْتُمْ اِلَّا قَلِيْلًا لَّوْ اَنَّكُمْ كُنْتُمْ

تَعْلَمُوْنَ ۝ اَفَحَسِبْتُمْ اَنَّمَا خَلَقْنٰكُمْ

عَبَثًا وَّ اَنَّكُمْ اِلَيْنَا لَا تُرْجَعُوْنَ ۝

فَتَعٰلَى اللّٰهُ الْمَلِكُ الْحَقُّ لَا اِلٰهَ

اِلَّا هُوَ رَبُّ الْعَرْشِ الْكَرِيْمِ ۝

وَمَنْ يَّدْعُ مَعَ اللّٰهِ اِلٰهًا اٰخَرَ

of this: if ever we return (to Evil), then shall we be wrong-doers indeed!"

108. He will say: "Be you driven into it (with ignominy)! And speak you not to Me!

109. "A part of My servants there was, who used to pray, 'Our Lord! We believe; then do You forgive us, and have mercy upon us: for You are the Best of those who show mercy!"

110. "But you treated them with ridicule, so much so that (ridicule of) them made you forget My Message while you were laughing at them!"

111. "I have rewarded them this Day for their patience and constancy: they are indeed the ones that have achieved Bliss..."

112. He will say: "What

مِنْهَا فَإِنْ عُدْنَا فَإِنَّا ظَلِمُوْنَ ۝

قَالَ اخْسَئُوْا فِيْهَا وَلَا تُكَلِّمُوْنِ ۝

اِنَّهٗ كَانَ فَرِيْقٌ مِّنْ عِبَادِيْ

يَقُوْلُوْنَ رَبَّنَا اٰمَنَّا فَاغْفِرْ لَنَا

وَارْحَمْنَا وَاَنْتَ خَيْرُ الرَّاحِمِيْنَ ۝

فَاتَّخَذْتُمُوْهُمْ سِخْرِيًّا حَتّٰى اَنْسَوْكُمْ

ذِكْرِيْ وَكُنْتُمْ مِّنْهُمْ تَضْحَكُوْنَ ۝

اِنِّيْ جَزَيْتُهُمُ الْيَوْمَ بِمَا صَبَرُوْٓا

اَنَّهُمْ هُمُ الْفَآئِزُوْنَ ۝ قٰلَ كَمْ

they will attain salvation:

103. But those whose balance is light, will be those who have lost their souls, in Hell will they abide.

104. The Fire will burn their faces, and they will therein grin, with their lips displaced.

105. "Were not My Signs rehearsed to you, and you but treated them as falsehood?"

106. They will say: "Our Lord! Our misfortune overwhelmed us, and we became a people astray!"

107. "Our Lord! Bring us out

مَوَازِينُهُ فَأُولَٰئِكَ هُمُ الْمُفْلِحُونَ ۞

وَمَنْ خَفَّتْ مَوَازِينُهُ فَأُولَٰئِكَ

الَّذِينَ خَسِرُوا أَنْفُسَهُمْ فِي

جَهَنَّمَ خَالِدُونَ ۞ تَلْفَحُ وُجُوهَهُمُ

النَّارُ وَهُمْ فِيهَا كَالِحُونَ ۞ أَلَمْ

تَكُنْ آيَاتِي تُتْلَىٰ عَلَيْكُمْ فَكُنْتُمْ

بِهَا تُكَذِّبُونَ ۞ قَالُوا رَبَّنَا

غَلَبَتْ عَلَيْنَا شِقْوَتُنَا وَكُنَّا

قَوْمًا ضَالِّينَ ۞ رَبَّنَا أَخْرِجْنَا

the Evil Ones."

98. "And I seek refuge with You O my Lord! Lest they should come near me."

99. (In Falsehood will they be) until, when death comes to one of them, he says: "O my Lord! Send me back (to life)," -

100. "In order that I may work righteousness in the things I neglected." - "By no means! It is but a word he says." - Before them is a Partition till the Day they are raised up.

101. Then when the Trumpet is blown, there will be no more relationships between them that Day, nor will one ask after another!

102. Then those whose balance (of good deeds) is heavy, -

الشَّيْطِينِ ۞ وَأَعُوذُ بِكَ رَبِّ أَنْ

يَّحْضُرُونِ ۞ حَتّى إِذَا جَآءَ أَحَدَهُمُ

الْمَوْتُ قَالَ رَبِّ ارْجِعُونِ ۞

لَعَلِّى أَعْمَلُ صَالِحًا فِيمَا تَرَكْتُ

كَلَّا ۚ إِنَّهَا كَلِمَةٌ هُوَ قَآئِلُهَا ۗ

وَمِنْ وَّرَآئِهِمْ بَرْزَخٌ إِلَى يَوْمِ

يُبْعَثُونَ ۞ فَإِذَا نُفِخَ فِى الصُّورِ

فَلَا أَنْسَابَ بَيْنَهُمْ يَوْمَئِذٍ

وَّلَا يَتَسَآءَلُونَ ۞ فَمَنْ ثَقُلَتْ

(He is free) from the (sort of) things they attribute to Him!

92. He knows what is hidden and what is open: too high is He for the partners they attribute to Him!

93. Say: "O my Lord! If You will show me (in my lifetime) that which they are warned against," -

94. "Then, O my Lord! Put me not amongst the people who do wrong!"

95. And We are certainly able to show you (in fulfilment) that against which they are warned.

96. Repel evil with that which is best: We are well acquainted with the things they say.

97. And say "O my Lord! I seek refuge with You from the suggestions of

عَمَّا يَصِفُوْنَ ۞ عٰلِمِ الْغَيْبِ

وَالشَّهَادَةِ فَتَعٰلٰى عَمَّا يُشْرِكُوْنَ ۞

قُلْ رَّبِّ إِمَّا تُرِيَنِّيْ مَا يُوْعَدُوْنَ ۞

رَبِّ فَلَا تَجْعَلْنِيْ فِي الْقَوْمِ

الظّٰلِمِيْنَ ۞ وَإِنَّا عَلٰى أَنْ نُّرِيَكَ

مَا نَعِدُهُمْ لَقٰدِرُوْنَ ۞ اِدْفَعْ

بِالَّتِيْ هِيَ أَحْسَنُ السَّيِّئَةَ ۖ نَحْنُ

أَعْلَمُ بِمَا يَصِفُوْنَ ۞ وَقُلْ

رَّبِّ أَعُوْذُ بِكَ مِنْ هَمَزٰتِ

is the governance of all things, - who protects (all), but is not protected (of any)? (Say) If you know."

89. They will say, "(It belongs) to Allah." Say: "Then how are you deluded?"

90. We have sent them the Truth: but they indeed practise falsehood!

91. No son did Allah beget, nor is there any god along with Him: (if there were many gods), behold, each god would have taken away what he had created, and some would have lorded it over others! Glory to Allah!

مَلَكُوْتُ كُلِّ شَىْءٍ وَّهُوَ يُجِيْرُ

وَلَا يُجَارُ عَلَيْهِ اِنْ كُنْتُمْ

تَعْلَمُوْنَ ۞ سَيَقُوْلُوْنَ لِلّٰهِ قُلْ

فَاَنّٰى تُسْحَرُوْنَ ۞ بَلْ اٰتَيْنٰهُمْ

بِالْحَقِّ وَاِنَّهُمْ لَكٰذِبُوْنَ ۞ مَا

اتَّخَذَ اللّٰهُ مِنْ وَّلَدٍ وَّمَا كَانَ

مَعَهُ مِنْ اِلٰهٍ اِذًا لَّذَهَبَ

كُلُّ اِلٰهٍ بِمَا خَلَقَ وَلَعَلَا

بَعْضُهُمْ عَلٰى بَعْضٍ سُبْحٰنَ اللّٰهِ

83. "Such things have been promised to us and to our fathers before! They are nothing but tales of the ancients!"

84. Say: "To whom belong the earth and all beings therein? (Say) If you know!"

85. They will say, "To Allah!" say: "Yet will you not receive admonition?"

86. Say: "Who is the Lord of the seven heavens, and the Lord of the Throne (of Glory) Supreme?"

87. They will say, "(They belong) to Allah." Say: "Will you not then fear?"

88. Say: "Who is it in whose hands

لَقَدْ وُعِدْنَا نَحْنُ وَ اٰبَآؤُنَا

هٰذَا مِنْ قَبْلُ اِنْ هٰذَآ اِلَّا

اَسَاطِيْرُ الْاَوَّلِيْنَ ۝ قُلْ لِّمَنِ

الْاَرْضُ وَمَنْ فِيْهَآ اِنْ كُنْتُمْ

تَعْلَمُوْنَ ۝ سَيَقُوْلُوْنَ لِلّٰهِ ۚ قُلْ

اَفَلَا تَذَكَّرُوْنَ ۝ قُلْ مَنْ رَّبُّ

السَّمٰوٰتِ السَّبْعِ وَرَبُّ الْعَرْشِ

الْعَظِيْمِ ۝ سَيَقُوْلُوْنَ لِلّٰهِ ۚ قُلْ

اَفَلَا تَتَّقُوْنَ ۝ قُلْ مَنْ بِيَدِهٖ

for you (the faculties of) hearing, sight, feeling and understanding: but little thanks it is you give!

79. And He has multiplied you through the earth, and to Him shall you be gathered back.

80. It is He Who gives life and death, and to Him (is due) the alternation of Night and Day: will you not then understand?

81. On the contrary they say things similar to what the ancients said.

82. They say: "What! When we die and become dust and bones, could we really be raised up again?"

لَكُمُ السَّمْعَ وَالْأَبْصَارَ وَالْأَفْئِدَةَ

قَلِيلًا مَّا تَشْكُرُونَ ۞ وَهُوَ

الَّذِى ذَرَأَكُمْ فِى الْأَرْضِ وَإِلَيْهِ

تُحْشَرُونَ ۞ وَهُوَ الَّذِى يُحْيِ

وَيُمِيتُ وَلَهُ اخْتِلَافُ الَّيْلِ

وَالنَّهَارِ أَفَلَا تَعْقِلُونَ ۞ بَلْ

قَالُوا مِثْلَ مَا قَالَ الْأَوَّلُونَ ۞

قَالُوا أَءِذَا مِتْنَا وَكُنَّا تُرَابًا

وَّعِظَامًا أَءِنَّا لَمَبْعُوثُونَ ۞

those who believe not in the Hereafter are deviating from that Way.

75. If We had mercy on them and removed the distress which is on them, they would obstinately persist in their transgression, wandering in distraction to and fro.

76. We inflicted Punishment on them, but they humbled not themselves to their Lord, nor do they submissively entreat (Him)! -

77. Until We open on them a gate leading to a severe Punishment: then lo! they will be plunged in despair therein!

78. It is He Who has created

اَلَّذِيْنَ لَا يُؤْمِنُوْنَ بِالْاٰخِرَةِ عَنِ

الصِّرَاطِ لَنَاكِبُوْنَ ۝ وَلَوْ رَحِمْنَاهُمْ

وَكَشَفْنَا مَا بِهِمْ مِّنْ ضُرٍّ

لَّلَجُّوْا فِيْ طُغْيَانِهِمْ يَعْمَهُوْنَ ۝

وَلَقَدْ اَخَذْنَاهُمْ بِالْعَذَابِ فَمَا

اسْتَكَانُوْا لِرَبِّهِمْ وَمَا يَتَضَرَّعُوْنَ ۝

حَتّٰى اِذَا فَتَحْنَا عَلَيْهِمْ بَابًا ذَا

عَذَابٍ شَدِيْدٍ اِذَا هُمْ فِيْهِ

مُبْلِسُوْنَ ۝ وَهُوَ الَّذِيْ اَنْشَأَ

No, he has brought them the Truth, but most of them hate the Truth.

71.   If the Truth had been in accord with their desires, truly the heavens and the earth, and all beings therein would have been in confusion and corruption! No, We have sent them their admonition, but they turn away from their admonition.

72.   Or is it that you ask them for some recompense? But the recompense of your Lord is best: He is the Best of those who give sustenance.

73.   But verily you call them to the Straight Way;

74.   And verily

بَلْ جَآءَهُمْ بِالْحَقِّ وَاَكْثَرُهُمْ

لِلْحَقِّ كَارِهُوْنَ ۞ وَلَوِ اتَّبَعَ الْحَقُّ

اَهْوَآءَهُمْ لَفَسَدَتِ السَّمٰوٰتُ

وَالْاَرْضُ وَمَنْ فِيْهِنَّ ۚ بَلْ

اَتَيْنٰهُمْ بِذِكْرِهِمْ فَهُمْ عَنْ

ذِكْرِهِمْ مُّعْرِضُوْنَ ۞ اَمْ تَسْـَٔلُهُمْ

خَرْجًا فَخَرَاجُ رَبِّكَ خَيْرٌ ۖ وَّهُوَ

خَيْرُ الرّٰزِقِيْنَ ۞ وَاِنَّكَ لَتَدْعُوْهُمْ

اِلٰى صِرَاطٍ مُّسْتَقِيْمٍ ۞ وَاِنَّ

behold, they will groan in supplication!

65. (It will be said): "Groan not in supplication this day: for you shall certainly not be helped by Us."

66. "My Signs used to be rehearsed to you, but you used to turn back on your heels" -

67. "In arrogance: talking nonsense about the (Qur'an), like one telling fables by night."

68. Do they not ponder over the Word (of Allah), or has anything (new) come to them that did not come to their fathers of old?

69. Or do they not recognise their Apostle, that they deny him?

70. Or do they say, "He is possessed"?

اِذَا هُمْ يَجْـَٔرُوْنَ ۞ لَا تَجْـَٔرُوا

الْيَوْمَ اِنَّكُمْ مِّنَّا لَا تُنْصَرُوْنَ ۞

قَدْ كَانَتْ اٰيٰتِيْ تُتْلٰى عَلَيْكُمْ

فَكُنْتُمْ عَلٰى اَعْقَابِكُمْ تَنْكِصُوْنَ ۞

مُسْتَكْبِرِيْنَ بِهٖ سٰمِرًا تَهْجُرُوْنَ ۞

اَفَلَمْ يَدَّبَّرُوا الْقَوْلَ اَمْ جَآءَهُمْ

مَّا لَمْ يَاْتِ اٰبَآءَهُمُ الْاَوَّلِيْنَ ۞

اَمْ لَمْ يَعْرِفُوْا رَسُوْلَهُمْ فَهُمْ لَهٗ

مُنْكِرُوْنَ ۞ اَمْ يَقُوْلُوْنَ بِهٖ جِنَّةٌ ۭ

full of fear, because they will return to their Lord; -

61. It is these who hasten in every good work, and these who are foremost in them.

62. On no soul do We place a burden greater than it can bear: before Us is a record which clearly speaks the truth: they will never be wronged.

63. But their hearts are in confused ignorance of this; and there are, besides that, deeds of theirs, which they will (continue) to do, -

64. Until, when We seize in Punishment those of them who received the good things of this world,

وَجِلَةٌ أَنَّهُمْ إِلَىٰ رَبِّهِمْ رَاجِعُوْنَ ۝

أُولَٰئِكَ يُسَارِعُوْنَ فِى الْخَيْرَٰتِ

وَهُمْ لَهَا سَابِقُوْنَ ۝ وَلَا نُكَلِّفُ

نَفْسًا إِلَّا وُسْعَهَا وَلَدَيْنَا كِتَٰبٌ

يَنْطِقُ بِالْحَقِّ وَهُمْ لَا يُظْلَمُوْنَ ۝

بَلْ قُلُوْبُهُمْ فِى غَمْرَةٍ مِّنْ

هَٰذَا وَلَهُمْ أَعْمَالٌ مِّنْ دُوْنِ

ذَٰلِكَ هُمْ لَهَا عَامِلُوْنَ ۝ حَتَّىٰ

إِذَآ أَخَذْنَا مُتْرَفِيْهِمْ بِالْعَذَابِ

54. But leave them in their confused ignorance for a time.

55. Do they think that because We have granted them abundance of wealth and sons,

56. We would hasten them on in every good? No, they do not understand.

57. Verily those who live in awe for fear of their Lord;

58. Those who believe in the Signs of their Lord;

59. Those who join not (in worship) partners with their Lord;

60. And those who dispense their charity with their hearts

فَرِحُوْنَ ۝ فَذَرْهُمْ فِیْ غَمْرَتِهِمْ

حَتّٰی حِیْنٍ ۝ اَیَحْسَبُوْنَ اَنَّمَا

نُمِدُّهُمْ بِهٖ مِنْ مَّالٍ وَّبَنِیْنَ ۝

نُسَارِعُ لَهُمْ فِی الْخَیْرٰتِ بَلْ لَّا

یَشْعُرُوْنَ ۝ اِنَّ الَّذِیْنَ هُمْ مِّنْ

خَشْیَةِ رَبِّهِمْ مُّشْفِقُوْنَ ۝ وَالَّذِیْنَ

هُمْ بِاٰیٰتِ رَبِّهِمْ یُؤْمِنُوْنَ ۝

وَالَّذِیْنَ هُمْ بِرَبِّهِمْ لَا یُشْرِكُوْنَ ۝

وَالَّذِیْنَ یُؤْتُوْنَ مَآ اٰتَوْا وَّقُلُوْبُهُمْ

Moses the Book, in order that they might receive guidance.

50. And We made the son of Mary and his mother as a Sign: We gave them both shelter on high ground, affording rest and security and furnished with springs.

51. O you Apostles! Enjoy (all) things good and pure, and work righteousness: for I am Well-Acquainted with (all) that you do.

52. And verily this Brotherhood of yours is a single (Ummah) or Brotherhood, and I am your Lord and Cherisher: therefore fear Me (and no other).

53. But people have cut off their affair (of unity), between them, into sects: each party rejoices in that which is with itself.

مُوسَى الْكِتٰبَ لَعَلَّهُمْ يَهْتَدُوْنَ ۝

وَجَعَلْنَا ابْنَ مَرْيَمَ وَاُمَّهُ اٰيَةً

وَّاٰوَيْنٰهُمَآ اِلٰى رَبْوَةٍ ذَاتِ قَرَارٍ

وَّمَعِيْنٍ ۝ يٰٓاَيُّهَا الرُّسُلُ كُلُوْا

مِنَ الطَّيِّبٰتِ وَاعْمَلُوْا صَالِحًا ۗ

اِنِّيْ بِمَا تَعْمَلُوْنَ عَلِيْمٌ ۝ وَاِنَّ

هٰذِهٖٓ اُمَّتُكُمْ اُمَّةً وَّاحِدَةً ۖ وَّاَنَا

رَبُّكُمْ فَاتَّقُوْنِ ۝ فَتَقَطَّعُوْٓا اَمْرَهُمْ

بَيْنَهُمْ زُبُرًا ۖ كُلُّ حِزْبٍۭ بِمَا لَدَيْهِمْ

each other (in punishment): We made them as a tale (that is told): so away with a people that will not believe!

45. Then We sent Moses and his brother Aaron, with Our Signs and authority manifest,

46. To Pharaoh and his chiefs: but these behaved insolently: they were an arrogant people.

47. They said: "Shall we believe in two men like ourselves? And their people are subject to us!"

48. So they (rejected) and accused them of falsehood, and they became of those who were destroyed.

49. And We gave

بَعْضًا وَّجَعَلْنٰهُمْ اَحَادِيْثَ ۚ فَبُعْدًا

لِّقَوْمٍ لَّا يُؤْمِنُوْنَ ۝ ثُمَّ اَرْسَلْنَا

مُوْسٰى وَاَخَاهُ هٰرُوْنَ ۙ بِاٰيٰتِنَا

وَسُلْطٰنٍ مُّبِيْنٍ ۝ اِلٰى فِرْعَوْنَ

وَمَلَإِيْهِ فَاسْتَكْبَرُوْا وَكَانُوْا

قَوْمًا عَالِيْنَ ۝ فَقَالُوْٓا اَنُؤْمِنُ

لِبَشَرَيْنِ مِثْلِنَا وَقَوْمُهُمَا لَنَا

عٰبِدُوْنَ ۝ فَكَذَّبُوْهُمَا فَكَانُوْا

مِنَ الْمُهْلَكِيْنَ ۝ وَلَقَدْ اٰتَيْنَا

40. (Alalh) said: "In but a little while, they are sure to be sorry!"

41. Then the Blast overtook them with justice, and We made them as rubbish of dead leaves (floating on the stream of Time)! So away with the people who do wrong!

42. Then We raised after them other generations.

43. No people can hasten their term, nor can they delay (it).

44. Then We sent Our Apostles in succession: every time there came to a people their Apostle, they accused him of falsehood: so We made them follow

قَالَ عَمَّا قَلِيْلٍ لَّيُصْبِحُنَّ

نَدِمِيْنَ ۝ فَاَخَذَتْهُمُ الصَّيْحَةُ

بِالْحَقِّ فَجَعَلْنٰهُمْ غُثَآءً ۚ فَبُعْدًا

لِّلْقَوْمِ الظّٰلِمِيْنَ ۝ ثُمَّ اَنْشَأْنَا

مِنْۢ بَعْدِهِمْ قُرُوْنًا اٰخَرِيْنَ ۝

مَا تَسْبِقُ مِنْ اُمَّةٍ اَجَلَهَا

وَمَا يَسْتَأْخِرُوْنَ ۝ ثُمَّ اَرْسَلْنَا

رُسُلَنَا تَتْرَا ۚ كُلَّ مَا جَآءَ اُمَّةً

رَّسُوْلُهَا كَذَّبُوْهُ فَاَتْبَعْنَا بَعْضَهُمْ

like yourselves, behold, it is certain you will be lost."

35. "Does he promise that when you die and become dust and bones, you shall be brought forth (again)?"

36. "Far, very far is that which you are promised!"

37. "There is nothing but our life in this world! We shall die and we live! But we shall never be raised up again!"

38. "He is only a man who invents a lie against Allah, but we are not the ones to believe in him!"

39. (The Prophet) said: "O my Lord! Help me: for that they accuse me of falsehood."

مِثْلُكُمْ اِنَّكُمْ اِذًا لَّخٰسِرُوْنَ ۞

اَيَعِدُكُمْ اَنَّكُمْ اِذَا مِتُّمْ وَكُنْتُمْ

تُرَابًا وَّعِظَامًا اَنَّكُمْ مُّخْرَجُوْنَ ۞

هَيْهَاتَ هَيْهَاتَ لِمَا تُوْعَدُوْنَ ۞

اِنْ هِيَ اِلَّا حَيَاتُنَا الدُّنْيَا نَمُوْتُ

وَنَحْيَا وَمَا نَحْنُ بِمَبْعُوْثِيْنَ ۞

اِنْ هُوَ اِلَّا رَجُلٌ اِفْتَرٰى عَلَى اللّٰهِ

كَذِبًا وَّمَا نَحْنُ لَهٗ بِمُؤْمِنِيْنَ ۞

قَالَ رَبِّ انْصُرْنِيْ بِمَا كَذَّبُوْنِ ۞

32. And We sent to them an Apostle from among themselves, (saying), "Worship Allah! You have no other god but Him. Will you not fear (Him)?"

33. And the chiefs of his people, who disbelieved and denied the Meeting in the Hereafter, and on whom We had bestowed the good things of this life, said: "He is no more than a man like yourselves: he eats of that of which you eat, and drinks of what you drink.

34. "If you obey a man

اٰخِرِیۡنَ ۲ فَاَرۡسَلۡنَا فِیۡهِمۡ رَسُوۡلًا

مِّنۡهُمۡ اَنِ اعۡبُدُوا اللّٰهَ مَا لَكُمۡ

مِّنۡ اِلٰهٍ غَیۡرُهٗ ؕ اَفَلَا تَتَّقُوۡنَ ۳

وَ قَالَ الۡمَلَاُ مِنۡ قَوۡمِهِ الَّذِیۡنَ

كَفَرُوۡا وَ كَذَّبُوۡا بِلِقَآءِ الۡاٰخِرَةِ

وَ اَتۡرَفۡنٰهُمۡ فِی الۡحَیٰوةِ الدُّنۡیَا ۙ

مَا هٰذَاۤ اِلَّا بَشَرٌ مِّثۡلُكُمۡ ۙ یَاۡكُلُ

مِمَّا تَاۡكُلُوۡنَ مِنۡهُ وَ یَشۡرَبُ مِمَّا

تَشۡرَبُوۡنَ ۳ وَ لَئِنۡ اَطَعۡتُمۡ بَشَرًا

of them against whom the Word has already gone forth: and address Me not in favour of the wrong-doers; for they shall be drowned (in the Flood).

28. And when you have embarked on the Ark - you and those with you, - say: "Praise be to Allah, Who has saved us from the people who do wrong."

29. And say: "O my Lord! Enable me to disembark with Your blessing: for You are the Best to enable (us) to disembark."

30. Verily in this there are Signs (for men to understand); (thus) do We try (men).

31. Then We raised after them another generation.

عَلَيۡهِ الۡقَوۡلُ مِنۡهُمۡ وَلَا تُخَاطِبۡنِيۡ

فِي الَّذِيۡنَ ظَلَمُوۡا اِنَّهُمۡ مُّغۡرَقُوۡنَ ۲۷

فَاِذَا اسۡتَوَيۡتَ اَنۡتَ وَمَنۡ مَّعَكَ

عَلَى الۡفُلۡكِ فَقُلِ الۡحَمۡدُ لِلّٰهِ

الَّذِيۡ نَجّٰنَا مِنَ الۡقَوۡمِ الظّٰلِمِيۡنَ ۲۸

وَقُلۡ رَّبِّ اَنۡزِلۡنِيۡ مُنۡزَلًا مُّبَٰرَكًا

وَّاَنۡتَ خَيۡرُ الۡمُنۡزِلِيۡنَ ۲۹ اِنَّ فِيۡ

ذٰلِكَ لَاٰيٰتٍ وَّاِنۡ كُنَّا لَمُبۡتَلِيۡنَ ۳۰

ثُمَّ اَنۡشَاۡنَا مِنۡ بَعۡدِهِمۡ قَرۡنًا

Angels; never did we hear such a thing (as he says), among our ancestors of old."

25. (And some said): "He is only a man possessed; wait (and have patience) with him for a time."

26. (Noah) said: "O my Lord! Help me: for that they accuse me of falsehood!"

27. So We inspired him (with this message): "Construct the Ark within Our Sight and under Our Guidance: then when comes Our Command, and the fountains of the earth gush forth, take you on board pairs of every species, male and female, and your family-except those

مَلَـٰٓئِكَةٌ مَّا سَمِعْنَا بِهَـٰذَا فِىٓ

ءَابَآئِنَا الْأَوَّلِينَ ۞ إِنْ هُوَ إِلَّا

رَجُلٌۢ بِهِۦ جِنَّةٌ فَتَرَبَّصُوا۟ بِهِۦ

حَتَّىٰ حِينٍ ۞ قَالَ رَبِّ انصُرْنِى

بِمَا كَذَّبُونِ ۞ فَأَوْحَيْنَآ إِلَيْهِ أَنِ

اصْنَعِ الْفُلْكَ بِأَعْيُنِنَا وَوَحْيِنَا

فَإِذَا جَآءَ أَمْرُنَا وَفَارَ التَّنُّورُ

فَاسْلُكْ فِيهَا مِن كُلٍّ زَوْجَيْنِ

اثْنَيْنِ وَأَهْلَكَ إِلَّا مَن سَبَقَ

and of their (meat) you eat;

22. And on them, as well as in ships, you ride.

23. We sent Noah to his people: he said, "O my people; worship Allah, you have no other god but Him. Will you not fear (Him)?"

24. The chiefs of the unbelievers among his people said: "He is no more than a man like yourselves: his wish is to assert his superiority over you. If Allah had wished (to send Messengers), He could have sent down

كَثِيرَةٌ وَّمِنْهَا تَأْكُلُونَ ۞ وَعَلَيْهَا

وَعَلَى الْفُلْكِ تُحْمَلُونَ ۞ وَلَقَدْ

اَرْسَلْنَا نُوحًا اِلٰى قَوْمِهٖ فَقَالَ

يٰقَوْمِ اعْبُدُوا اللّٰهَ مَا لَكُمْ

مِّنْ اِلٰهٍ غَيْرُهٗ ط اَفَلَا تَتَّقُوْنَ ۞

فَقَالَ الْمَلَؤُا الَّذِيْنَ كَفَرُوْا

مِنْ قَوْمِهٖ مَا هٰذَآ اِلَّا بَشَرٌ

مِّثْلُكُمْ يُرِيْدُ اَنْ يَّتَفَضَّلَ

عَلَيْكُمْ ط وَلَوْ شَآءَ اللّٰهُ لَاَنْزَلَ

in the soil; and We certainly are able to drain it off (with ease).

19. With it We grow for you gardens of date-palms and vines: in them have you abundant fruits: and of them you eat (and have enjoyment), -

20. Also a tree springing out of Mount Sinai, which produces oil, and relish for those who use it for food.

21. And in cattle (too) you have an instructive example: from within their bodies We produce (milk) for you to drink; there are, in them, (besides), numerous (other) benefits for you;

فِي الْاَرْضِ ۚ وَاِنَّا عَلٰى ذَهَابٍ

بِهٖ لَقٰدِرُوْنَ ۞ فَاَنْشَاْنَا لَكُمْ

بِهٖ جَنّٰتٍ مِّنْ نَّخِيْلٍ وَّاَعْنَابٍ ۘ

لَكُمْ فِيْهَا فَوَاكِهُ كَثِيْرَةٌ وَّمِنْهَا

تَاْكُلُوْنَ ۞ وَشَجَرَةً تَخْرُجُ مِنْ

طُوْرِ سَيْنَآءَ تَنْبُتُ بِالدُّهْنِ

وَصِبْغٍ لِّلْاٰكِلِيْنَ ۞ وَاِنَّ لَكُمْ فِي

الْاَنْعَامِ لَعِبْرَةً ۚ نُّسْقِيْكُمْ مِّمَّا

فِيْ بُطُوْنِهَا وَلَكُمْ فِيْهَا مَنَافِعُ

a (foetus) lump; then We made out of that lump bones and clothed the bones with flesh; then We developed out of it another creature. So blessed be Allah, the best to create!

15. After that, at length you will die.

16. Again, on the Day of Judgment, will you be raised up.

17. And We have made, above you, seven tracts; and We are never unmindful of (Our) Creation.

18. And We send down water from the sky according to (due) measure, and We cause it to soak

مُضْغَةً فَخَلَقْنَا الْمُضْغَةَ عِظَامًا

فَكَسَوْنَا الْعِظَامَ لَحْمًا ثُمَّ أَنْشَأْنَاهُ

خَلْقًا اخَرَ فَتَبَارَكَ اللَّهُ أَحْسَنُ

الْخَالِقِينَ ۞ ثُمَّ إِنَّكُمْ بَعْدَ ذَلِكَ

لَمَيِّتُونَ ۞ ثُمَّ إِنَّكُمْ يَوْمَ الْقِيَامَةِ

تُبْعَثُونَ ۞ وَلَقَدْ خَلَقْنَا فَوْقَكُمْ

سَبْعَ طَرَائِقَ وَمَا كُنَّا عَنِ

الْخَلْقِ غَافِلِينَ ۞ وَأَنْزَلْنَا مِنَ

السَّمَاءِ مَاءً بِقَدَرٍ فَأَسْكَنَّاهُ

transgressors; -

8. Those who faithfully observe their trusts and their covenants;

9. And who (strictly) guard their Prayers;-

10. These will be the heirs,

11. Who will inherit Paradise: they will dwell therein (for ever).

12. Man We did create from a quintessence (of clay);

13. Then We placed him as (a drop of) sperm in a place of rest, firmly fixed;

14. Then We made the sperm into a clot of congealed blood; then of that clot We made

قَبْلَهُمْ قَوْمُ نُوحٍ وَّالْاَحْزَابُ

مِنْ بَعْدِهِمْ وَهَمَّتْ كُلُّ اُمَّةٍ

بِرَسُوْلِهِمْ لِيَاْخُذُوْهُ وَجَادَلُوْا

بِالْبَاطِلِ لِيُدْحِضُوْا بِهِ الْحَقَّ

فَاَخَذْتُهُمْ فَكَيْفَ كَانَ عِقَابِ ۞

وَكَذٰلِكَ حَقَّتْ كَلِمَتُ رَبِّكَ عَلَى

الَّذِيْنَ كَفَرُوْا اَنَّهُمْ اَصْحٰبُ

النَّارِ ۞ اَلَّذِيْنَ يَحْمِلُوْنَ الْعَرْشَ

وَمَنْ حَوْلَهُ يُسَبِّحُوْنَ بِحَمْدِ

Al-Mu'min (The Believer)

Bismillahir-Rahmanir-Rahim

1. Ha. Mim.

2. The Revelation of this Book is from Allah, Exalted in Power, full of Knowledge, -

3. Who forgives sin, accepts repentance, is strict in punishment, and has a long reach (in all things). There is no god but He: to Him is the final Goal.

4. None can dispute about the Signs of Allah but the unbelievers. Let not, then, their strutting about through the land deceive you!

5. But (there were people) before them, who denied (the Signs),-

بِسۡمِ اللّٰهِ الرَّحۡمٰنِ الرَّحِيۡمِ

حٰمٓ ۚ تَنۡزِيۡلُ الۡكِتٰبِ مِنَ اللّٰهِ الۡعَزِيۡزِ الۡعَلِيۡمِ ۙ غَافِرِ الذَّنۡۢبِ وَقَابِلِ التَّوۡبِ شَدِيۡدِ الۡعِقَابِ ذِى الطَّوۡلِ ؕ لَاۤ اِلٰهَ اِلَّا هُوَ ؕ اِلَيۡهِ الۡمَصِيۡرُ ۞ مَا يُجَادِلُ فِىۡۤ اٰيٰتِ اللّٰهِ اِلَّا الَّذِيۡنَ كَفَرُوۡا فَلَا يَغۡرُرۡكَ تَقَلُّبُهُمۡ فِى الۡبِلَادِ ۞ كَذَّبَتۡ

"Peace be upon you! Well have you done! Enter you here, to dwell therein."

74. They will say: "Praise be to Allah, Who has truly fulfilled His Promise to us, and has given us (this) land in heritage: we can dwell in the Garden as we will: how excellent a reward for those who work (righteousness)!"

75. And you will see the Angels surrounding the Throne (Divine) on all sides, singing Glory and Praise to their Lord. The Decision between them (at Judgment) will be in (perfect) justice, and the cry (on all sides) will be, "Praise be to Allah, the Lord of the Worlds!"

سَلَٰمٌ عَلَيْكُمْ طِبْتُمْ فَادْخُلُوهَا

خَٰلِدِينَ ۩ وَقَالُوا الْحَمْدُ لِلَّهِ

الَّذِي صَدَقَنَا وَعْدَهُ وَأَوْرَثَنَا

الْأَرْضَ نَتَبَوَّأُ مِنَ الْجَنَّةِ حَيْثُ

نَشَاءُ ۚ فَنِعْمَ أَجْرُ الْعَٰمِلِينَ ۩

وَتَرَى الْمَلَٰئِكَةَ حَآفِّينَ مِنْ

حَوْلِ الْعَرْشِ يُسَبِّحُونَ بِحَمْدِ

رَبِّهِمْ ۖ وَقُضِيَ بَيْنَهُم بِالْحَقِّ وَقِيلَ

الْحَمْدُ لِلَّهِ رَبِّ الْعَٰلَمِينَ ۩

your Lord, and warning you of the Meeting of this Day of yours?" The answer will be: "True: but the Decree of Punishment has been proved true against the unbelievers!"

72. (To them) will be said: "Enter you the gates of Hell, to dwell therein: and evil is (this) abode of the arrogant!"

73. And those who feared their Lord will be led to the Garden in crowds: until behold, they arrive there; its gates will be opened; and its keepers will say:

رَبِّكُمْ وَيُنْذِرُونَكُمْ لِقَآءَ يَوْمِكُمْ

هٰذَا ۗ قَالُوا بَلٰى وَلٰكِنْ حَقَّتْ

كَلِمَةُ الْعَذَابِ عَلَى الْكٰفِرِينَ ۞

قِيلَ ادْخُلُوٓا أَبْوَابَ جَهَنَّمَ

خٰلِدِينَ فِيهَا ۖ فَبِئْسَ مَثْوَى

الْمُتَكَبِّرِينَ ۞ وَسِيقَ الَّذِينَ

اتَّقَوْا رَبَّهُمْ إِلَى الْجَنَّةِ زُمَرًا ۖ

حَتّٰى إِذَا جَآءُوهَا وَفُتِحَتْ

أَبْوَابُهَا وَقَالَ لَهُمْ خَزَنَتُهَا

the Prophets and the witnesses will be brought forward and a just decision pronounced between them; and they will not be wronged (in the least).

70. And to every soul will be paid in full (the fruit) of its deeds; and (Allah) knows best all that they do.

71. The unbelievers will be led to Hell in crowd: until, when they arrive, there, its gates will be opened. And its keepers will say, "Did not Apostles come to you from among yourselves, rehearsing to you the Signs of

وَجِاىٓءَ بِالنَّبِيِّنَ وَالشُّهَدَآءِ

وَقُضِيَ بَيْنَهُمْ بِالْحَقِّ وَهُمْ لَا

يُظْلَمُونَ ۞ وَوُفِّيَتْ كُلُّ نَفْسٍ

مَّا عَمِلَتْ وَهُوَ أَعْلَمُ بِمَا

يَفْعَلُونَ ۞ وَسِيقَ الَّذِينَ كَفَرُوٓا

إِلَى جَهَنَّمَ زُمَرًا ۗ حَتَّىٰٓ إِذَا

جَآءُوهَا فُتِحَتْ أَبْوَابُهَا وَقَالَ

لَهُمْ خَزَنَتُهَآ أَلَمْ يَأْتِكُمْ رُسُلٌ

مِّنكُمْ يَتْلُونَ عَلَيْكُمْ ءَايَٰتِ

but His handful, and the heavens will be rolled up in His right hand: Glory to Him! High is He above the partners they attribute to Him!

68. The Trumpet will (just) be sounded, when all that are in the heavens and on earth will swoon, except such as it will please Allah (to exempt). Then will a second one be sounded, when, behold, they will be standing and looking on!

69. And the earth will shine with the Glory of its Lord: the Record (of Deeds) will be placed (open);

قَبْضَتُهٗ يَوْمَ الْقِيٰمَةِ وَالسَّمٰوٰتُ

مَطْوِيّٰتٌ بِيَمِيْنِهٖ ۚ سُبْحٰنَهٗ

وَتَعٰلٰى عَمَّا يُشْرِكُوْنَ ۞ وَنُفِخَ

فِى الصُّوْرِ فَصَعِقَ مَنْ فِى

السَّمٰوٰتِ وَمَنْ فِى الْاَرْضِ

اِلَّا مَنْ شَآءَ اللّٰهُ ۖ ثُمَّ نُفِخَ

فِيْهِ اُخْرٰى فَاِذَا هُمْ قِيَامٌ

يَنْظُرُوْنَ ۞ وَاَشْرَقَتِ الْاَرْضُ

بِنُوْرِ رَبِّهَا وَوُضِعَ الْكِتٰبُ

Allah, - it is they who will be in loss.

64. Say: "Is it some one other than Allah that you order me to worship, O you ignorant ones?"

65. But it has already been revealed to you, - as it was to those before you, - "If you were to join (gods with Allah), truly fruitless will be your work (in life), and you will surely be in the ranks of those who lose (all spiritual good)".

66. No, but worship Allah, and be of those who give thanks.

67. No just estimate have they made of Allah, such as is due to Him: on the Day of Judgment the whole of the earth will be

اللهِ أُولَٰئِكَ هُمُ الْخَٰسِرُونَ ۝

قُلْ أَفَغَيْرَ اللهِ تَأْمُرُونِّي أَعْبُدُ

أَيُّهَا الْجَٰهِلُونَ ۝ وَلَقَدْ أُوحِيَ

إِلَيْكَ وَإِلَى الَّذِينَ مِن قَبْلِكَ

لَئِنْ أَشْرَكْتَ لَيَحْبَطَنَّ عَمَلُكَ

وَلَتَكُونَنَّ مِنَ الْخَٰسِرِينَ ۝

بَلِ اللهَ فَاعْبُدْ وَكُن مِّنَ

الشَّٰكِرِينَ ۝ وَمَا قَدَرُوا اللهَ

حَقَّ قَدْرِهِ وَالْأَرْضُ جَمِيعًا

Judgment will you see those who told lies against Allah; - their faces will be turned black; is there not in Hell an abode for the haughty?

61. But Allah will deliver the righteous to their place of salvation: no evil shall touch them, nor shall they grieve.

62. Allah is the Creator of all things, and He is the Guardian and Disposer of all affairs.

63. To Him belong the keys of the heavens and the earth: and those who reject the Signs of

الْقِيمَةِ تَرَى الَّذِينَ كَذَبُوا عَلَى

اللهِ وُجُوهُهُمْ مُسْوَدَّةٌ ٱلَيْسَ

فِى جَهَنَّمَ مَثْوًى لِّلْمُتَكَبِّرِينَ ۞

وَيُنَجِّى اللهُ الَّذِينَ اتَّقَوْا

بِمَفَازَتِهِمْ لَا يَمَسُّهُمُ السُّوٓءُ

وَلَا هُمْ يَحْزَنُونَ ۞ اللهُ خَالِقُ

كُلِّ شَىْءٍ وَّهُوَ عَلَى كُلِّ شَىْءٍ

وَّكِيلٌ ۞ لَهُ مَقَالِيدُ السَّمٰوٰتِ

وَالْأَرْضِ ۗ وَالَّذِينَ كَفَرُوا بِـَٔايٰتِ

'Ah! Woe is me! - in that I neglected (my duty) towards Allah, and was but among those who mocked!'" -

57. "Or (lest) it should say: 'If only Allah had guided me, I should certainly have been among the righteous!'"

58. "Or (lest) it should say when it (actually) sees the Chastisement: 'If only I had another chance, I should certainly be among those who do good!'"

59. "(The reply will be:) 'No, but there came to you my Signs, and you did reject them: you were haughty, and became one of those who reject Faith!'"

60. On the Day of

يَحَسْرَتَى عَلَى مَا فَرَّطْتُ فِي

جَنبِ اللهِ وَإِن كُنتُ لَمِنَ

السَّاخِرِينَ ۝ أَوْ تَقُولَ لَوْ أَنَّ اللهَ

هَدَانِي لَكُنتُ مِنَ الْمُتَّقِينَ ۝

أَوْ تَقُولَ حِينَ تَرَى الْعَذَابَ

لَوْ أَنَّ لِي كَرَّةً فَأَكُونَ مِنَ

الْمُحْسِنِينَ ۝ بَلَى قَدْ جَاءَتْكَ

ءَايَتِي فَكَذَّبْتَ بِهَا وَاسْتَكْبَرْتَ

وَكُنتَ مِنَ الْكَافِرِينَ ۝ وَيَوْمَ

the Mercy of Allah: for Allah forgives all sins: for He is Oft-Forgiving, Most Merciful."

54. "Turn you to your Lord (in repentance) and bow to His (Will), before the Chastisement comes on you: after that you shall not be helped."

55. "And follow the best of (the courses) revealed to you from your Lord, before the Chastisement comes on you - of a sudden while you perceive not!" -

56. "Lest the soul should (then) say:

رَّحْمَةِ اللهِ ۚ إِنَّ اللهَ يَغْفِرُ

الذُّنُوبَ جَمِيعًا ۚ إِنَّهُ هُوَ الْغَفُورُ

الرَّحِيمُ ۞ وَأَنِيبُوٓا إِلَىٰ رَبِّكُمْ

وَأَسْلِمُوا لَهُ مِنْ قَبْلِ أَنْ

يَأْتِيَكُمُ الْعَذَابُ ثُمَّ لَا تُنصَرُونَ

۞ وَاتَّبِعُوٓا أَحْسَنَ مَآ أُنزِلَ إِلَيْكُم

مِّن رَّبِّكُم مِّن قَبْلِ أَن يَأْتِيَكُمُ

الْعَذَابُ بَغْتَةً وَّأَنتُمْ لَا

تَشْعُرُونَ ۞ أَن تَقُولَ نَفْسٌ

51. No, the evil results of their deeds overtook them. And the wrong-doers of this (generation) - the evil results of their deeds will soon overtake them (too), and they shall never escape.

52. Do they not know that Allah enlarges the provision or restricts it, for any He pleases? Verily, in this are Signs for those who believe!

53. Say: "O my servants who have transgressed against their souls! Despair not of

يَكْسِبُونَ ۝ فَأَصَابَهُمْ سَيِّئَاتُ

مَا كَسَبُوا ۚ وَالَّذِينَ ظَلَمُوا مِنْ

هَٰؤُلَاءِ سَيُصِيبُهُمْ سَيِّئَاتُ مَا

كَسَبُوا ۚ وَمَا هُم بِمُعْجِزِينَ ۝

أَوَلَمْ يَعْلَمُوا أَنَّ اللَّهَ يَبْسُطُ

الرِّزْقَ لِمَن يَشَاءُ وَيَقْدِرُ ۚ إِنَّ

فِي ذَٰلِكَ لَآيَاتٍ لِّقَوْمٍ يُؤْمِنُونَ ۝

قُلْ يَا عِبَادِيَ الَّذِينَ أَسْرَفُوا

عَلَىٰ أَنفُسِهِمْ لَا تَقْنَطُوا مِنْ

counted upon!

48. For the evils of their deeds will confront them, and they will be (completely) encircled by that which they used to mock at!

49. Now, when trouble touches man, he cries to Us: but when We bestow a favour upon him as from Ourselves, he says, "This has been given to me because of a certain knowledge (I have)!" No, but this is but a trial, but most of them understand not!

50. Thus did the (generations) before them say! But all that they did was of no profit to them.

يَحۡتَسِبُوۡنَ ۝ وَبَدَالَهُمۡ سَيِّاٰتُ

مَا كَسَبُوۡا وَحَاقَ بِهِمۡ مَّا كَانُوۡا

بِهٖ يَسۡتَهۡزِءُوۡنَ ۝ فَاِذَا مَسَّ

الۡاِنۡسَانَ ضُرٌّ دَعَانَا ثُمَّ اِذَا

خَوَّلۡنٰهُ نِعۡمَةً مِّنَّا قَالَ اِنَّمَاۤ

اُوۡتِيۡتُهٗ عَلٰى عِلۡمٍ ؕ بَلۡ هِيَ فِتۡنَةٌ

وَّلٰكِنَّ اَكۡثَرَهُمۡ لَا يَعۡلَمُوۡنَ ۝

قَدۡ قَالَهَا الَّذِيۡنَ مِنۡ قَبۡلِهِمۡ

فَمَاۤ اَغۡنٰى عَنۡهُمۡ مَّا كَانُوۡا

behold, they are filled with joy!

46. Say: "O Allah! Creator of the heavens and the earth! Knower of all that is hidden and open! It is you that will judge between your Servants in those matters about which they have differed."

47. Even if the wrong-doers had all that there is on earth, and as much more, (in vain) would they offer it for ransom from the pain of the Chastisement on the Day of Judgment: but something will confront them from Allah, which they could never have

اِذَا هُمْ يَسْتَبْشِرُوْنَ ۞ قُلِ

اللّٰهُمَّ فَاطِرَ السَّمٰوٰتِ وَالْاَرْضِ

عٰلِمَ الْغَيْبِ وَالشَّهَادَةِ اَنْتَ

تَحْكُمُ بَيْنَ عِبَادِكَ فِيْ مَا كَانُوْا

فِيْهِ يَخْتَلِفُوْنَ ۞ وَلَوْ اَنَّ لِلَّذِيْنَ

ظَلَمُوْا مَا فِي الْاَرْضِ جَمِيْعًا

وَّمِثْلَهٗ مَعَهٗ لَافْتَدَوْا بِهٖ

مِنْ سُوْٓءِ الْعَذَابِ يَوْمَ الْقِيٰمَةِ ۚ

وَبَدَا لَهُمْ مِّنَ اللّٰهِ مَا لَمْ يَكُوْنُوْا

are Signs for those who reflect.

43. What! Do they take for intercessors others besides Allah? Say: "Even if they have no power whatever and no intelligence?"

44. Say: "To Allah belongs exclusively (the right to grant) intercession: to Him belongs the dominion of the heavens and the earth: in the End, it is to Him that you shall be brought back."

45. When Allah, the One and Only, is mentioned, the hearts of those who believe not in the Hereafter are filled with disgust and horror; but when (gods) other than He are mentioned,

لَايَتٍ لِّقَوْمٍ يَّتَفَكَّرُوْنَ ۞ أَمِ

اتَّخَذُوْا مِنْ دُوْنِ اللّٰهِ شُفَعَآءَ

قُلْ أَوَلَوْ كَانُوْا لَا يَمْلِكُوْنَ شَيْئًا

وَّلَا يَعْقِلُوْنَ ۞ قُلْ لِّلّٰهِ الشَّفَاعَةُ

جَمِيْعًا لَهُ مُلْكُ السَّمٰوٰتِ وَالْأَرْضِ

ثُمَّ اِلَيْهِ تُرْجَعُوْنَ ۞ وَاِذَا ذُكِرَ

اللّٰهُ وَحْدَهُ اشْمَأَزَّتْ قُلُوْبُ

الَّذِيْنَ لَا يُؤْمِنُوْنَ بِالْاٰخِرَةِ

وَاِذَا ذُكِرَ الَّذِيْنَ مِنْ دُوْنِهٖ

the Book to you in Truth, for (instructing) mankind. He, then, that receives guidance benefits his own soul: but he that strays injures his own soul. Nor you are set over them to dispose of their affairs.

42. It is Allah that takes the souls (of men) at death; and those that die not (He takes) during their sleep: those on whom He has passed the decree of death, He keeps back (from returning to life), but the rest He sends (to their bodies) for a term appointed. Verily in this

عَلَيْكَ الْكِتَبَ لِلنَّاسِ بِالْحَقِّ

فَمَنِ اهْتَدَى فَلِنَفْسِهِ وَمَنْ

ضَلَّ فَإِنَّمَا يَضِلُّ عَلَيْهَا وَمَآ

أَنْتَ عَلَيْهِمْ بِوَكِيلٍ ۞ اَللّٰهُ

يَتَوَفَّى الْأَنْفُسَ حِينَ مَوْتِهَا

وَالَّتِي لَمْ تَمُتْ فِي مَنَامِهَا

فَيُمْسِكُ الَّتِي قَضَى عَلَيْهَا

الْمَوْتَ وَيُرْسِلُ الْأُخْرَى إِلَى

أَجَلٍ مُسَمًّى إِنَّ فِي ذٰلِكَ

Allah, - can they, if Allah wills some Penalty for me, remove His Penalty? - Or if He wills some Grace for me, can they keep back his Grace?" Say: "Sufficient is Allah for me! In Him trust those who put their trust."

39. Say: "O my People! Do whatever you can: I will do (my part): but soon will you know" -

40. "Who it is to whom comes a Chastisement of ignominy, and on whom descends a Penalty that abides."

41. Verily We have revealed

اللهِ ۗ إِنْ أَرَادَنِيَ اللهُ بِضُرٍّ

هَلْ هُنَّ كَاشِفَاتُ ضُرِّهِ أَوْ

أَرَادَنِي بِرَحْمَةٍ هَلْ هُنَّ مُمْسِكَاتُ

رَحْمَتِهِ ۚ قُلْ حَسْبِيَ اللهُ ۖ عَلَيْهِ

يَتَوَكَّلُ الْمُتَوَكِّلُونَ ۝ قُلْ يَا قَوْمِ

اعْمَلُوا عَلَى مَكَانَتِكُمْ إِنِّي عَامِلٌ ۖ

فَسَوْفَ تَعْلَمُونَ ۝ مَنْ يَأْتِيهِ

عَذَابٌ يُخْزِيهِ وَيَحِلُّ عَلَيْهِ

عَذَابٌ مُقِيمٌ ۝ إِنَّا أَنْزَلْنَا

they have done.

36. Is not Allah enough for his servant? But they try to frighten you with other (gods) besides Him! For such as Allah leaves to stray, there can be no guide.

37. And such as Allah does guide there can be none to lead astray. Is not Allah Exalted in Power, (Able to enforce His Will), Lord of Retribution?

38. If indeed you ask them who it is that created the heavens and the earth, they would be sure to say, "Allah". Say: "See you then? The things that you invoke besides

كَانُوا يَعْمَلُونَ ۞ أَلَيْسَ اللّٰهُ

بِكَافٍ عَبْدَهُ ۖ وَيُخَوِّفُونَكَ بِالَّذِينَ

مِنْ دُونِهٖ ۖ وَمَنْ يُّضْلِلِ اللّٰهُ

فَمَا لَهٗ مِنْ هَادٍ ۞ وَمَنْ يَّهْدِ

اللّٰهُ فَمَا لَهٗ مِنْ مُّضِلٍّ ۗ أَلَيْسَ

اللّٰهُ بِعَزِيزٍ ذِى انْتِقَامٍ ۞ وَلَئِنْ

سَاَلْتَهُمْ مَّنْ خَلَقَ السَّمٰوٰتِ

وَالْاَرْضَ لَيَقُولُنَّ اللّٰهُ ۚ قُلْ

اَفَرَءَيْتُمْ مَّا تَدْعُونَ مِنْ دُونِ

32. Who, then, does more wrong than one who utters a lie concerning Allah, and rejects the Truth when it comes to him; is there not in Hell an abode for blasphemers?

33. And he who brings the Truth and he who confirms (and supports) it - such are the men who do right.

34. They shall have all that they wish for, in the presence of their Lord: such is the reward of those who do good:

35. So that Allah will turn off from them (even) the worst in their deeds and give them their reward according to the best of what

الجزء الرابع والعشرون (٢٤)

فَمَنْ أَظْلَمُ مِمَّن كَذَبَ عَلَى

اللَّهِ وَكَذَّبَ بِالصِّدْقِ إِذْ

جَآءَهُۥ ۚ أَلَيْسَ فِى جَهَنَّمَ مَثْوًى

لِّلْكَٰفِرِينَ ﴿٣٢﴾ وَالَّذِى جَآءَ بِالصِّدْقِ

وَصَدَّقَ بِهِۦٓ ۚ أُوْلَٰٓئِكَ هُمُ الْمُتَّقُونَ ﴿٣٣﴾

لَهُم مَّا يَشَآءُونَ عِندَ رَبِّهِمْ ۚ

ذَٰلِكَ جَزَآءُ الْمُحْسِنِينَ ﴿٣٤﴾ لِيُكَفِّرَ

اللَّهُ عَنْهُمْ أَسْوَأَ الَّذِى عَمِلُوا۟

وَيَجْزِيَهُمْ أَجْرَهُم بِأَحْسَنِ الَّذِى

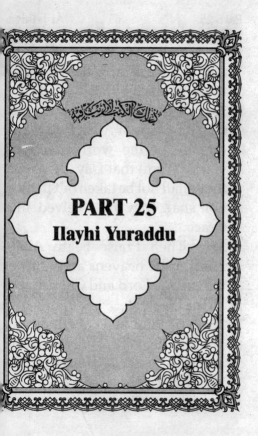

PART 25
Ilayhi Yuraddu

the Meeting of this Day of yours!
And your abode is the Fire, and
no helpers have you!"

35. "This, because you used to
take the Signs of Allah in jest, and
the life of the world deceived
you:" (From) that Day, therefore,
they shall not be taken out thence,
nor shall they be received into
Grace.

36. Then Praise be to Allah,
Lord of the heavens and Lord of
the earth, - Lord and Cherisher of
all the Worlds!

37. To Him be Glory throughout the heavens and the earth:
and He is Exalted in Power, full of
Wisdom!

لِقَآءَ يَوْمِكُمْ هٰذَا ۚ وَمَأْوٰىكُمُ

النَّارُ وَمَا لَكُمْ مِّنْ نّٰصِرِيْنَ ۞

ذٰلِكُمْ بِأَنَّكُمُ اتَّخَذْتُمْ اٰيٰتِ اللّٰهِ

هُزُوًا وَّغَرَّتْكُمُ الْحَيٰوةُ الدُّنْيَا ۚ

فَالْيَوْمَ لَا يُخْرَجُوْنَ مِنْهَا وَلَا هُمْ

يُسْتَعْتَبُوْنَ ۞ فَلِلّٰهِ الْحَمْدُ رَبِّ

السَّمٰوٰتِ وَرَبِّ الْأَرْضِ رَبِّ

الْعٰلَمِيْنَ ۞ وَلَهُ الْكِبْرِيَآءُ فِى السَّمٰوٰتِ

وَالْأَرْضِ ۖ وَهُوَ الْعَزِيْزُ الْحَكِيْمُ ۞

Our Signs rehearsed to you? But you were arrogant, and were a people given to sin!"

32.   "And when it was said that the Promise of Allah was true, and that the Hour - there was no doubt about its (coming), you used to say, 'We know not what is the hour: we only think it is an idea, and we have no firm assurance.'"

33.   Then will appear to them the evil (fruits) of what they did, and they will be completely encircled by that which they used to mock at!

34.   It will also be said: "This Day We will forget you as you forgot

اٰیٰتِیۡ تُتۡلٰی عَلَیۡکُمۡ فَاسۡتَکۡبَرۡتُمۡ

وَکُنۡتُمۡ قَوۡمًا مُّجۡرِمِیۡنَ ۞ وَاِذَا

قِیۡلَ اِنَّ وَعۡدَ اللّٰهِ حَقٌّ وَّالسَّاعَةُ

لَا رَیۡبَ فِیۡهَا قُلۡتُمۡ مَّا نَدۡرِیۡ

مَا السَّاعَةُ ۙ اِنۡ نَّظُنُّ اِلَّا ظَنًّا

وَّمَا نَحۡنُ بِمُسۡتَیۡقِنِیۡنَ ۞ وَبَدَا لَهُمۡ

سَیِّاٰتُ مَا عَمِلُوۡا وَحَاقَ بِهِمۡ

مَّا کَانُوۡا بِهٖ یَسۡتَهۡزِءُوۡنَ ۞ وَقِیۡلَ

الۡیَوۡمَ نَنۡسٰکُمۡ کَمَا نَسِیۡتُمۡ

nation bowing the knee: every nation will be called to its Record: "This Day shall you be recompensed for all that you did!"

29. "This Our Record speaks about you with truth: for We were wont to put on Record all that you did."

30. Then, as to those who believed and did righteous deeds, their Lord will admit them to His Mercy that will be the achievement for all to see.

31. But as to those who rejected Allah, (to them will be said): "Were not

أُمَّةٍ جَاثِيَةً ۚ كُلُّ أُمَّةٍ تُدْعَى

إِلَىٰ كِتٰبِهَا ۚ ٱلْيَوْمَ تُجْزَوْنَ مَا

كُنْتُمْ تَعْمَلُونَ ۞ هٰذَا كِتٰبُنَا

يَنْطِقُ عَلَيْكُمْ بِالْحَقِّ ۚ إِنَّا كُنَّا

نَسْتَنْسِخُ مَا كُنْتُمْ تَعْمَلُونَ ۞

فَأَمَّا الَّذِينَ آمَنُوا وَعَمِلُوا

الصّٰلِحٰتِ فَيُدْخِلُهُمْ رَبُّهُمْ فِى

رَحْمَتِهِ ۚ ذٰلِكَ هُوَ الْفَوْزُ الْمُبِينُ ۞

وَأَمَّا الَّذِينَ كَفَرُوا ۗ أَفَلَمْ تَكُنْ

Signs are rehearsed to them their argument is nothing but this: they say, "Bring (back) our fore-fathers, if what you say is true!"

26. Say: "It is Allah Who gives you life, then gives you death; then He will gather you together for the Day of Judgment about which there is no doubt": but most men do not understand.

27. To Allah belongs the dominion of the heavens and the earth, and the Day that the Hour of Judgment is established, - that Day will the dealers in Falsehood perish!

28. And you will see every

اٰيٰتُنَا بَيِّنٰتٍ مَّا كَانَ حُجَّتَهُمْ اِلَّاۤ

اَنْ قَالُوا ائْتُوا بِاٰبَآئِنَاۤ اِنْ كُنْتُمْ

صٰدِقِيْنَ ۝ قُلِ اللّٰهُ يُحْيِيْكُمْ

ثُمَّ يُمِيْتُكُمْ ثُمَّ يَجْمَعُكُمْ اِلٰى

يَوْمِ الْقِيٰمَةِ لَا رَيْبَ فِيْهِ

وَلٰكِنَّ اَكْثَرَ النَّاسِ لَا يَعْلَمُوْنَ ۝

وَلِلّٰهِ مُلْكُ السَّمٰوٰتِ وَالْاَرْضِ ۭ

وَيَوْمَ تَقُوْمُ السَّاعَةُ يَوْمَئِذٍ

يَّخْسَرُ الْمُبْطِلُوْنَ ۝ وَتَرٰى كُلَّ

as his god his own vain desire? Allah has, knowing (him as such), left him astray, and sealed his hearing and his heart (and understanding), and put a cover on his sight. Who, then, will guide him after Allah (has withdrawn Guidance)? Will you not then receive admonition?

24. And they say: "What is there but our life in this world? We shall die and we live, and nothing but time can destroy us." But of that they have no knowledge: they merely conjecture:

25. And when Our clear

إِلَهَهُ هَوَهُ وَأَضَلَّهُ اللَّهُ عَلَى

عِلْمٍ وَّخَتَمَ عَلَى سَمْعِهِ وَقَلْبِهِ

وَجَعَلَ عَلَى بَصَرِهِ غِشَوَةً فَمَنْ

يَّهْدِيهِ مِنْ بَعْدِ اللَّهِ أَفَلَا

تَذَكَّرُونَ ۝ وَقَالُوا مَا هِيَ إِلَّا

حَيَاتُنَا الدُّنْيَا نَمُوتُ وَنَحْيَا

وَمَا يُهْلِكُنَا إِلَّا الدَّهْرُ وَمَا

لَهُمْ بِذَلِكَ مِنْ عِلْمٍ إِنْ هُمْ

إِلَّا يَظُنُّونَ ۝ وَإِذَا تُتْلَى عَلَيْهِمْ

20. These are clear evidences to men and a Guidance and Mercy to those of assured Faith.

21. What! Do those who seek after evil ways think that We shall hold them equal with those who believe and do righteous deeds, - that equal will be their life and their death? Ill is the judgment that they make.

22. Allah created the heavens and the earth for just ends, and in order that each soul may find the recompense of what it has earned, and none of them be wronged.

23. Do you see such a one as takes

هٰذَا بَصَآئِرُ لِلنَّاسِ وَ هُدًى

وَّرَحْمَةٌ لِّقَوْمٍ يُّوْقِنُوْنَ ۝ أَمْ

حَسِبَ الَّذِيْنَ اجْتَرَحُوا السَّيِّاٰتِ

أَنْ نَّجْعَلَهُمْ كَالَّذِيْنَ اٰمَنُوْا وَعَمِلُوا

الصّٰلِحٰتِ سَوَآءً مَّحْيَاهُمْ وَمَمَاتُهُمْ

سَآءَ مَا يَحْكُمُوْنَ ۝ وَخَلَقَ اللّٰهُ

السَّمٰوٰتِ وَالْأَرْضَ بِالْحَقِّ وَلِتُجْزٰى

كُلُّ نَفْسٍ بِمَا كَسَبَتْ وَهُمْ لَا

يُظْلَمُوْنَ ۝ أَفَرَءَيْتَ مَنِ اتَّخَذَ

knowledge had been granted to them that they fell into schisms, through insolent envy among themselves. Verily your Lord will judge between them on the Day of Judgment as to those matters in which they set up differences.

18. Then We put you on the (right) Way of Religion: so follow you that (Way), and follow not the desires of those who know not.

19. They will be of no use to you in the sight of Allah: it is only wrong-doers (that stand as) protectors, one to another: but Allah is the Protector of the Righteous.

مَا جَآءَهُمُ الْعِلْمُ بَغْيًا بَيْنَهُمْ ۚ اِنَّ

رَبَّكَ يَقْضِىْ بَيْنَهُمْ يَوْمَ الْقِيٰمَةِ

فِيْمَا كَانُوْا فِيْهِ يَخْتَلِفُوْنَ ۞ ثُمَّ جَعَلْنٰكَ عَلٰى شَرِيْعَةٍ مِّنَ

الْاَمْرِ فَاتَّبِعْهَا وَلَا تَتَّبِعْ اَهْوَآءَ

الَّذِيْنَ لَا يَعْلَمُوْنَ ۞ اِنَّهُمْ لَنْ

يُّغْنُوْا عَنْكَ مِنَ اللّٰهِ شَيْئًا ۚ

وَاِنَّ الظّٰلِمِيْنَ بَعْضُهُمْ اَوْلِيَآءُ

بَعْضٍ ۚ وَاللّٰهُ وَلِىُّ الْمُتَّقِيْنَ ۞

of Allah: it is for Him to recompense (for good or ill) each People according to what they have earned.

15. If any one does a righteous deed, it ensures to the benefit of his own soul; if he does evil, it works against (his own soul). In the End will you (all) be brought back to your Lord.

16. We did aforetime grant to the Children of Israel the Book, the Power of Command, and Prophethood; We gave them, for Sustenance, things good and pure; and We favoured them above the nations.

17. And We granted them clear Signs in affairs (of Religion): it was only after

اللهِ لِيَجْزِيَ قَوْمًا بِمَا كَانُوا

يَكْسِبُونَ ۞ مَنْ عَمِلَ صَالِحًا

فَلِنَفْسِهِ ۚ وَمَنْ أَسَاءَ فَعَلَيْهَا

ثُمَّ إِلَىٰ رَبِّكُمْ تُرْجَعُونَ ۞ وَلَقَدْ

اٰتَيْنَا بَنِيْ إِسْرَآءِيْلَ الْكِتٰبَ

وَالْحُكْمَ وَالنُّبُوَّةَ وَرَزَقْنٰهُمْ

مِّنَ الطَّيِّبٰتِ وَفَضَّلْنٰهُمْ عَلَى

الْعٰلَمِيْنَ ۞ وَاٰتَيْنٰهُمْ بَيِّنٰتٍ مِّنَ

الْأَمْرِ ۚ فَمَا اخْتَلَفُوا إِلَّا مِنْ بَعْدِ

of abomination.

12. It is Allah Who has subjected the sea to you, that ships may sail through it by His Command, that you may seek of His Bounty, and that you may be grateful.

13. And He has subjected to you, as from Him, all that is in the heavens and on earth: behold, in that are Signs indeed for those who reflect.

14. Tell those who believe, to forgive those who do not look forward to the Days

مِنْ رِّجْزٍ اَلِيمٌ ۞ اَللّٰهُ الَّذِى

سَخَّرَ لَكُمُ الْبَحْرَ لِتَجْرِىَ الْفُلْكُ

فِيْهِ بِاَمْرِهٖ وَلِتَبْتَغُوْا مِنْ

فَضْلِهٖ وَلَعَلَّكُمْ تَشْكُرُوْنَ ۞

وَسَخَّرَ لَكُمْ مَّا فِى السَّمٰوٰتِ

وَمَا فِى الْاَرْضِ جَمِيْعًا مِّنْهُ

اِنَّ فِىْ ذٰلِكَ لَاٰيٰتٍ لِّقَوْمٍ

يَّتَفَكَّرُوْنَ ۞ قُلْ لِّلَّذِيْنَ اٰمَنُوْا

يَغْفِرُوْا لِلَّذِيْنَ لَا يَرْجُوْنَ اَيَّامَ

as if he had not heard them: then announce to him a Chastisement grievous!

9. And when he learns something of Our Signs, he takes them in jest: for such there will be a humiliating Penalty.

10. In front of them is Hell: and of no profit to them is anything they may have earned, nor any protectors they may have taken to themselves besides Allah: for them is a tremendous Chastisement.

11. This is (true) Guidance and for those who reject the Signs of their Lord, is a grievous Chastisement

كَانَ لَّمْ يَسْمَعْهَا فَبَشِّرْهُ بِعَذَابٍ

اَلِيمٍ ۝ وَاِذَا عَلِمَ مِنْ اٰيٰتِنَا

شَيْئًا اتَّخَذَهَا هُزُوًا ۚ اُولٰٓئِكَ

لَهُمْ عَذَابٌ مُّهِينٌ ۚ مِّنْ وَّرَآئِهِمْ

جَهَنَّمُ ۚ وَلَا يُغْنِي عَنْهُمْ مَّا كَسَبُوْا

شَيْئًا وَّلَا مَا اتَّخَذُوْا مِنْ

دُوْنِ اللّٰهِ اَوْلِيَآءَ ۚ وَلَهُمْ عَذَابٌ

عَظِيمٌ ۝ هٰذَا هُدًى ۚ وَالَّذِيْنَ

كَفَرُوْا بِاٰيٰتِ رَبِّهِمْ لَهُمْ عَذَابٌ

Night and Day, and the fact that Allah sends down Sustenance from the sky, and revives there with the earth after its death, and in the change of the winds, - are Signs for those that are wise.

6.   Such are the Signs of Allah, which We rehearse to you in Truth; then in what exposition will they believe after (rejecting) Allah and His Signs?

7.   Woe to each sinful dealer in Falsehoods:

8.   He hears the Signs of Allah rehearsed to him, yet is obstinate and lofty,

الَّيْلِ وَ النَّهَارِ وَ مَآ اَنْزَلَ اللهُ

مِنَ السَّمَآءِ مِنْ رِّزْقٍ فَاَحْيَا بِهِ

الْاَرْضَ بَعْدَ مَوْتِهَا وَ تَصْرِيْفِ

الرِّيحِ اٰيٰتٌ لِّقَوْمٍ يَّعْقِلُوْنَ ۞

تِلْكَ اٰيٰتُ اللهِ نَتْلُوْهَا عَلَيْكَ

بِالْحَقِّ ۚ فَبِاَيِّ حَدِيْثٍ بَعْدَ اللهِ

وَ اٰيٰتِه يُؤْمِنُوْنَ ۞ وَيْلٌ لِّكُلِّ

اَفَّاكٍ اَثِيْمٍ ۙ يَّسْمَعُ اٰيٰتِ اللهِ

تُتْلٰى عَلَيْهِ ثُمَّ يُصِرُّ مُسْتَكْبِرًا

will be the supreme achievement!
58. Verily, We have made this (Qur'an) easy, in your tongue, in order that they may give heed.
59. So wait you and watch; for they (too) are waiting.

Al-Jathiya
(Bowing the Knee)

Bismillahir-Rahmanir-Rahim

1. Ha-Mim.
2. The Revelation of the Book is from Allah the Exalted in Power, full of Wisdom.
3. Verily in the heavens and the earth, are Signs for those who believe.
4. And in the creation of yourselves and the fact that animals are scattered (through the earth), are Signs for those of assured Faith.
5. And in the alternation of

هُوَ الْفَوْزُ الْعَظِيمُ ۞ فَأَنَّمَا يَسَّرْنَٰهُ

بِلِسَانِكَ لَعَلَّهُمْ يَتَذَكَّرُونَ ۞

فَارْتَقِبْ إِنَّهُم مُّرْتَقِبُونَ ۞

سُورَةُ الْجَاثِيَةِ مَكِّيَّةٌ ٣٧ بِسْمِ اللهِ الرَّحْمَٰنِ الرَّحِيمِ ٣٠ آيَاتُهَا ٤ رُكُوعَاتُهَا

حمٓ ۞ تَنزِيلُ الْكِتَٰبِ مِنَ اللهِ

الْعَزِيزِ الْحَكِيمِ ۞ إِنَّ فِى السَّمَٰوَٰتِ

وَالْأَرْضِ لَأَيَٰتٍ لِّلْمُؤْمِنِينَ ۞ وَفِى

خَلْقِكُمْ وَمَا يَبُثُّ مِن دَآبَّةٍ

ءَايَٰتٌ لِّقَوْمٍ يُوقِنُونَ ۞ وَاخْتِلَٰفِ

what you used to doubt!"

51. As to the Righteous (they will be) in a position of Security,

52. Among Gardens and Springs;

53. Dressed in fine silk and in rich brocade, they will face each other;

54. So; and We shall join them to Companions with beautiful, big, and lustrous eyes.

55. There can they call for every kind of fruit in peace and security;

56. Nor will they there taste Death, except the first death; and He will preserve them from the Chastisement of the Blazing Fire,

57. As a Bounty from your Lord! That

مَا كُنْتُمْ بِهِ تَمْتَرُونَ ۝ اِنَّ

الْمُتَّقِينَ فِي مَقَامٍ اَمِينٍ ۝ فِي

جَنّٰتٍ وَّعُيُونٍ ۙ يَلْبَسُونَ مِنْ

سُنْدُسٍ وَّاِسْتَبْرَقٍ مُّتَقٰبِلِينَ ۝

كَذٰلِكَ ۚ وَزَوَّجْنٰهُمْ بِحُورٍ عِينٍ ۝

يَدْعُونَ فِيْهَا بِكُلِّ فَاكِهَةٍ

اٰمِنِينَ ۝ لَا يَذُوقُونَ فِيْهَا الْمَوْتَ

اِلَّا الْمَوْتَةَ الْاُولٰى ۚ وَوَقٰهُمْ عَذَابَ

الْجَحِيْمِ ۝ فَضْلًا مِّنْ رَّبِّكَ ۚ ذٰلِكَ

help can they receive,

42. Except such as receive Allah's Mercy: for He is Exalted in Might, Most Merciful.

43. Verily the tree of Zaqqum

44. Will be the food of the Sinful, -

45. Like molten brass; it will boil in their insides.

46. Like the boiling of scalding water.

47. (A voice will cry: "Seize you him and drag him into the midst of the Blazing Fire!"

48. "Then pour over his head the Chastisement of Boiling Water,"

49. "Taste you (this)! Truly were you mighty, full of honour!"

50. "Truly this is

يَنْصَرُوْنَ ۞ اِلَّا مَنْ رَّحِمَ اللّٰهُ

اِنَّهُ هُوَ الْعَزِيْزُ الرَّحِيْمُ ۞

اِنَّ شَجَرَتَ الزَّقُّوْمِ ۞ طَعَامُ

الْاَثِيْمِ ۞ كَالْمُهْلِ يَغْلِيْ فِى

الْبُطُوْنِ ۞ كَغَلْيِ الْحَمِيْمِ ۞ خُذُوْهُ

فَاعْتِلُوْهُ اِلٰى سَوَآءِ الْجَحِيْمِ ۞

ثُمَّ صُبُّوْا فَوْقَ رَاْسِهٖ مِنْ

عَذَابِ الْحَمِيْمِ ۞ ذُقْ اِنَّكَ

اَنْتَ الْعَزِيْزُ الْكَرِيْمُ ۞ اِنَّ هٰذَا

what you say is true!"

37. What! Are they better than the people of Tubba and those who were before them? We destroyed them because they were guilty of sin.

38. We created not the heavens, the earth, and all between them, merely in (idle) sport:

39. We created them not except for just ends: but most of them do not understand.

40. Verily the Day of Sorting out is the time appointed for all of them, -

41. The Day when no protector can avail his client in any thing, and no

كُنْتُمْ صَٰدِقِينَ ۞ اَهُمْ خَيْرٌ اَمْ

قَوْمُ تُبَّعٍ وَّالَّذِيْنَ مِنْ قَبْلِهِمْ

اَهْلَكْنٰهُمْ اِنَّهُمْ كَانُوْا مُجْرِمِيْنَ ۞

وَمَا خَلَقْنَا السَّمٰوٰتِ وَالْاَرْضَ

وَمَا بَيْنَهُمَا لٰعِبِيْنَ ۞ مَا خَلَقْنٰهُمَا

اِلَّا بِالْحَقِّ وَلٰكِنَّ اَكْثَرَهُمْ لَا

يَعْلَمُوْنَ ۞ اِنَّ يَوْمَ الْفَصْلِ

مِيْقَاتُهُمْ اَجْمَعِيْنَ ۞ يَوْمَ لَا يُغْنِيْ

مَوْلًى عَنْ مَّوْلًى شَيْئًا وَّلَا هُمْ

were they given a respite (again).

30. We did deliver aforetime the Children of Israel from humiliating Punishment,

31. Inflicted by Pharaoh, for he was arrogant (even) among inordinate transgressors.

32. And We chose them aforetime above the nations, knowingly,

33. And granted them Signs in which there was a manifest trial.

34. As to these (Quraish), they say forsooth:

35. "There is nothing beyond our first death, and we shall not be raised again."

36. "Then bring (back) our forefathers, if

كَانُوا مُنْظِرِينَ ۞ وَلَقَدْ نَجَّيْنَا بَنِي

اِسْرَآءِيلَ مِنَ الْعَذَابِ الْمُهِينِ ۞

مِنْ فِرْعَوْنَ اِنَّهُ كَانَ عَالِيًا مِنَ

الْمُسْرِفِينَ ۞ وَلَقَدِ اخْتَرْنٰهُمْ عَلٰى

عِلْمٍ عَلَى الْعٰلَمِينَ ۞ وَاٰتَيْنٰهُمْ

مِنَ الْاٰيٰتِ مَا فِيهِ بَلٰٓؤُا مُّبِينٌ ۞

اِنَّ هٰٓؤُلَآءِ لَيَقُوْلُوْنَ ۞ اِنْ هِيَ

اِلَّا مَوْتَتُنَا الْاُوْلٰى وَمَا نَحْنُ

بِمُنْشَرِينَ ۞ فَاْتُوْا بِاٰبَآئِنَا اِنْ

at least keep yourselves away from me."

22. (But they were aggressive:) then he cried to his Lord: "These are indeed a people given to sin."

23. (The reply came:) "March forth with My servants by night: for you are sure to be pursued."

24. "And leave the sea as a furrow (divided): for they are a host (destined) to be drowned."

25. How many were the gardens and springs they left behind,

26. And corn-fields and noble buildings,

27. And wealth (and conveniences of life), wherein they had taken such delight! **28.** T h u s (was their end)! And We made other people inherit (those things)!

29. And neither heaven nor earth shed a tear over them: nor

فَاعْتَزِلُونِ ۞ فَدَعَا رَبَّهُۥٓ اَنَّ

هٰٓؤُلَآءِ قَوْمٌ مُّجْرِمُوْنَ ۞ فَاَسْرِ

بِعِبَادِىْ لَيْلًا اِنَّكُمْ مُّتَّبَعُوْنَ ۞

وَاتْرُكِ الْبَحْرَ رَهْوًا ۭ اِنَّهُمْ جُنْدٌ

مُّغْرَقُوْنَ ۞ كَمْ تَرَكُوْا مِنْ جَنّٰتٍ

وَّعُيُوْنٍ ۞ وَّزُرُوْعٍ وَّمَقَامٍ كَرِيْمٍ ۞

وَّنَعْمَةٍ كَانُوْا فِيْهَا فٰكِهِيْنَ ۞ كَذٰلِكَ

وَاَوْرَثْنٰهَا قَوْمًا اٰخَرِيْنَ ۞ فَمَا

بَكَتْ عَلَيْهِمُ السَّمَآءُ وَالْاَرْضُ وَمَا

the Chastisement for a while, (but) truly you will revert (to your ways).

16. One day We shall seize you with a mighty onslaught: We will indeed (then) exact Retribution!

17. We did, before them, try the people of Pharaoh: there came to them an Apostle most honourable,

18. Saying: "Restore to me the servants of Allah: I am to you an Apostle worthy of all trust;"

19. "And be not arrogant as against Allah: for I come to you with authority manifest.

20. "For me, I have sought safety with my Lord and your Lord, against your injuring me."

21. "If you believe me not,

الْعَذَابَ قَلِيْلًا اِنَّكُمْ عَآئِدُوْنَ ۞

يَوْمَ نَبْطِشُ الْبَطْشَةَ الْكُبْرٰى اِنَّا

مُنْتَقِمُوْنَ ۞ وَلَقَدْ فَتَنَّا قَبْلَهُمْ قَوْمَ

فِرْعَوْنَ وَجَآءَهُمْ رَسُوْلٌ كَرِيْمٌ ۞

اَنْ اَدُّوْا اِلَيَّ عِبَادَ اللّٰهِ اِنِّیْ لَكُمْ

رَسُوْلٌ اَمِيْنٌ ۞ وَّاَنْ لَّا تَعْلُوْا عَلَى

اللّٰهِ اِنِّیْ اٰتِيْكُمْ بِسُلْطٰنٍ مُّبِيْنٍ ۞

وَاِنِّیْ عُذْتُ بِرَبِّیْ وَرَبِّكُمْ اَنْ

تَرْجُمُوْنِ ۞ وَاِنْ لَّمْ تُؤْمِنُوْا لِیْ

He: it is He Who gives life and gives death, - the Lord and Cherisher to you and your earliest ancestors.

9. Yet they play about in doubt.

10. Then watch you for the Day that the sky will bring forth a kind of smoke (or mist) plainly visible,

11. Enveloping the people: this will be a Chastisement grievous.

12. (They will say:) "Our Lord! Remove the Chastisement from us, for we do really believe!"

13. How shall the message be (effectual) for them, seeing that an Apostle explaining things clearly has (already) come to them, -

14. Yet they turn away from him and say: "Tutored (by others), a man possessed!"

15. We shall indeed remove

هُوَ يُحْيٖ وَيُمِيتُ ۖ رَبُّكُمْ وَرَبُّ

اٰبَآئِكُمُ الْاَوَّلِيْنَ ۞ بَلْ هُمْ فِيْ

شَكٍّ يَّلْعَبُوْنَ ۞ فَارْتَقِبْ يَوْمَ تَاْتِى

السَّمَآءُ بِدُخَانٍ مُّبِيْنٍ ۞ يَّغْشَى

النَّاسَ ۖ هٰذَا عَذَابٌ اَلِيْمٌ ۞ رَبَّنَا

اكْشِفْ عَنَّا الْعَذَابَ اِنَّا مُؤْمِنُوْنَ ۞

اَنّٰى لَهُمُ الذِّكْرٰى وَقَدْ جَآءَهُمْ

رَسُوْلٌ مُّبِيْنٌ ۞ ثُمَّ تَوَلَّوْا عَنْهُ

وَقَالُوْا مُعَلَّمٌ مَّجْنُوْنٌ ۞ اِنَّا كَاشِفُوا

Ad-Dukhan (Smoke)

Bismillahir-Rahmanir-Rahim

1. Ha-Mim.

2. By the Book that makes things clear; -

3. We sent it down during a Blessed Night: for We (ever) wish to warn (against Evil).

4. In the (Night) is made distinct every affair of wisdom,

5. By command, from Our Presence. For We (ever) send (revelations),

6. As Mercy from your Lord: for He hears and knows (all things);

7. The Lord of the heavens and the earth and all between them, if you (but) have an assured faith.

8. There is no god but

بِسْمِ اللهِ الرَّحْمٰنِ الرَّحِيْمِ

حٰمٓ ۚ ۝ وَالْكِتٰبِ الْمُبِيْنِ ۙ ۝ اِنَّاۤ

اَنْزَلْنٰهُ فِيْ لَيْلَةٍ مُّبٰرَكَةٍ اِنَّا

كُنَّا مُنْذِرِيْنَ ۝ فِيْهَا يُفْرَقُ كُلُّ

اَمْرٍ حَكِيْمٍ ۙ ۝ اَمْرًا مِّنْ عِنْدِنَا ؕ

اِنَّا كُنَّا مُرْسِلِيْنَ ۝ رَحْمَةً مِّنْ

رَّبِّكَ ؕ اِنَّهٗ هُوَ السَّمِيْعُ الْعَلِيْمُ ۙ ۝

رَبِّ السَّمٰوٰتِ وَالْاَرْضِ وَمَا بَيْنَهُمَا ۘ

اِنْ كُنْتُمْ مُّوْقِنِيْنَ ۝ لَاۤ اِلٰهَ اِلَّا

is the Knowledge of the Hour (of Judgment): and to Him shall you be brought back.

86. And those whom they invoke besides Allah have no power of intercession; - only he who bears witness to the Truth, and they know (him).

87. If you ask them, who created them, they will certainly say, Allah: how then are they deluded away (from the Truth)?

88. (Allah has knowledge) of the (Prophet's) cry, "O my Lord! Truly these are people who will not believe!"

89. But turn away from them, and say "Peace!" But soon shall they know!

بِسْمِ عِلْمُ السَّاعَةِ وَإِلَيْهِ تُرْجَعُوْنَ ۞

وَلَا يَمْلِكُ الَّذِيْنَ يَدْعُوْنَ مِنْ

دُوْنِهِ الشَّفَاعَةَ إِلَّا مَنْ شَهِدَ

بِالْحَقِّ وَهُمْ يَعْلَمُوْنَ ۞ وَلَئِنْ

سَأَلْتَهُمْ مَّنْ خَلَقَهُمْ لَيَقُوْلُنَّ اللهُ

فَأَنَّى يُؤْفَكُوْنَ ۞ وَقِيْلِهِ يٰرَبِّ

إِنَّ هٰؤُلَآءِ قَوْمٌ لَّا يُؤْمِنُوْنَ ۞

فَاصْفَحْ عَنْهُمْ وَقُلْ سَلٰمٌ

فَسَوْفَ يَعْلَمُوْنَ ۞

the first to worship."

82. Glory to the Lord of the heavens and the earth, the Lord of the Throne (of Authority)! (He is free) from the things they attribute (to him)!

83. So leave them to babble and play (with vanities) until they meet that Day of theirs, which they have been promised.

84. It is He Who is Allah in heaven and Allah on earth; and He is full of Wisdom and Knowledge.

85. And blessed is He to Whom belongs the dominion of the heavens and the earth, and all between them: with Him

أَوَّلُ الْعَٰبِدِيْنَ ۝ سُبْحٰنَ رَبِّ
السَّمٰوٰتِ وَالْأَرْضِ رَبِّ الْعَرْشِ
عَمَّا يَصِفُوْنَ ۝ فَذَرْهُمْ يَخُوْضُوْا
وَيَلْعَبُوْا حَتّٰى يُلٰقُوْا يَوْمَهُمُ
الَّذِيْ يُوْعَدُوْنَ ۝ وَهُوَ الَّذِيْ
فِى السَّمَاءِ اِلٰهٌ وَّفِى الْأَرْضِ
اِلٰهٌ ۚ وَهُوَ الْحَكِيْمُ الْعَلِيْمُ
۝ وَتَبٰرَكَ الَّذِيْ لَهٗ مُلْكُ السَّمٰوٰتِ
وَالْأَرْضِ وَمَا بَيْنَهُمَا ۚ وَعِنْدَهٗ

it is they who have been unjust themselves.

77. They will cry: "O Malik! Would that your Lord put an end to us!" He will say, "No, but you shall abide!"

78. Verily We have brought the Truth to you: but most of you have a hatred for Truth.

79. What! Have they settled some plan (among themselves)? But it is We Who settle things.

80. Or do they think that We hear not their secrets and their private counsels? Indeed (We do), and Our Messengers are by them, to record.

81. Say: "If (Allah) Most Gracious had a son, I would be

كَانُوْا هُمُ الظّٰلِمِيْنَ ۞ وَ نَادَوْا

يٰمٰلِكُ لِيَقْضِ عَلَيْنَا رَبُّكَ ۚ قَالَ

اِنَّكُمْ مّٰكِثُوْنَ ۞ لَقَدْ جِئْنٰكُمْ

بِالْحَقِّ وَ لٰكِنَّ اَكْثَرَكُمْ لِلْحَقِّ

كٰرِهُوْنَ ۞ اَمْ اَبْرَمُوْٓا اَمْرًا فَاِنَّا

مُبْرِمُوْنَ ۞ اَمْ يَحْسَبُوْنَ اَنَّا لَا

نَسْمَعُ سِرَّهُمْ وَ نَجْوٰىهُمْ ۚ بَلٰى

وَ رُسُلُنَا لَدَيْهِمْ يَكْتُبُوْنَ ۞ قُلْ

اِنْ كَانَ لِلرَّحْمٰنِ وَلَدٌ ۖ فَاَنَا

of gold: there will be there all that the souls could desire, all that their ayes could delight in: and you shall abide therein (for ever).

72. Such will be the Garden of which you are made heirs for your (good) deeds (in life).

73. You shall have therein abundance of fruit, from which you shall have satisfaction.

74. The sinners will be in the Punishment of Hell, to dwell therein (for ever):

75. Nowise will the (Punishment) be lightened for them, and in despair will they be there overwhelmed.

76. Nowise shall We be unjust to them: but

مِّنۡ ذَهَبٍ وَّاَكۡوَابٌ ۚ وَفِيۡهَا مَا

تَشۡتَهِيۡهِ الۡاَنۡفُسُ وَتَلَذُّ الۡاَعۡيُنُ ۚ

وَاَنۡتُمۡ فِيۡهَا خٰلِدُوۡنَ ۞ وَتِلۡكَ

الۡجَنَّةُ الَّتِيۡۤ اُوۡرِثۡتُمُوۡهَا بِمَا كُنۡتُمۡ

تَعۡمَلُوۡنَ ۞ لَكُمۡ فِيۡهَا فَاكِهَةٌ

كَثِيۡرَةٌ مِّنۡهَا تَاۡكُلُوۡنَ ۞ اِنَّ

الۡمُجۡرِمِيۡنَ فِيۡ عَذَابِ جَهَنَّمَ

خٰلِدُوۡنَ ۟ۖ لَا يُفَتَّرُ عَنۡهُمۡ وَهُمۡ

فِيۡهِ مُبۡلِسُوۡنَ ۞ وَمَا ظَلَمۡنٰهُمۡ وَلٰكِنۡ

from the Chastisement of a Grievous Day!

66. Do they only wait for the Hour - that it should come on them all of a sudden, while they perceive not?

67. Friends on that Day will be foes, one to another, - except the Righteous.

68. My devotees! No fear shall be on you that Day, nor shall you grieve,-

69. (Being) those who have believed in Our Signs and bowed (their wills to Ours) in Islam.

70. Enter you the Garden, you and your wives, in (beauty and) rejoicing.

71. To them will be passed round, dishes and goblets

مِنْ عَذَابِ يَوْمٍ أَلِيمٍ ۝ هَلْ

يَنْظُرُوْنَ اِلَّا السَّاعَةَ اَنْ تَاْتِيَهُمْ

بَغْتَةً وَّهُمْ لَا يَشْعُرُوْنَ ۝ اَلْاَخِلَّآءُ

يَوْمَئِذٍ بَعْضُهُمْ لِبَعْضٍ عَدُوٌّ اِلَّا

الْمُتَّقِيْنَ ۝ يٰعِبَادِ لَاخَوْفٌ عَلَيْكُمُ

الْيَوْمَ وَلَا اَنْتُمْ تَحْزَنُوْنَ ۝ اَلَّذِيْنَ

اٰمَنُوْا بِاٰيٰتِنَا وَكَانُوْا مُسْلِمِيْنَ ۝

اُدْخُلُوا الْجَنَّةَ اَنْتُمْ وَاَزْوَاجُكُمْ

تُحْبَرُوْنَ ۝ يُطَافُ عَلَيْهِمْ بِصِحَافٍ

62. Let not the Evil One hinder you: for he is to you an enemy avowed.

63. When Jesus came with clear Signs, he said: "Now have I come to you with Wisdom, and in order to make clear to you some of the (points) on which you dispute: therefore fear Allah and obey me."

64. "For Allah, He is my Lord and your Lord: so worship you Him: this is a Straight Way."

65. But sects from among themselves fell into disagreement: then woe to the wrong-doers,

وَلَا يَصُدَّنَّكُمُ الشَّيْطَانُ إِنَّهُ لَكُمْ

عَدُوٌّ مُّبِينٌ ۝ وَلَمَّا جَاءَ عِيسَى

بِالْبَيِّنَاتِ قَالَ قَدْ جِئْتُكُم

بِالْحِكْمَةِ وَلِأُبَيِّنَ لَكُم بَعْضَ

الَّذِي تَخْتَلِفُونَ فِيهِ فَاتَّقُوا اللَّهَ

وَأَطِيعُونِ ۝ إِنَّ اللَّهَ هُوَ رَبِّي

وَرَبُّكُمْ فَاعْبُدُوهُ هَٰذَا صِرَاطٌ

مُّسْتَقِيمٌ ۝ فَاخْتَلَفَ الْأَحْزَابُ

مِنۢ بَيْنِهِمْ فَوَيْلٌ لِّلَّذِينَ ظَلَمُوا

raise a clamour thereat (in ridicule)!

58. And they say, "Are our gods best, or he?" This they set forth to you, only by way of disputation: yes, they are a contentious people.

59. He was no more than a servant: We granted Our favour to him, and We made him an example to the Children of Israel.

60. And if it were Our Will, We could make Angels from amongst you, succeeding each other on the earth.

61. And (Jesus) shall be a Sign (for the coming of) the Hour (of Judgment): therefore have no doubt about the (Hour), but follow you Me: this is a Straight Way.

يَصِدُّوْنَ ۞ وَقَالُوْۤا ءَاٰلِهَتُنَا خَيْرٌ

اَمْ هُوَ ۚ مَا ضَرَبُوْهُ لَكَ اِلَّا جَدَلًا ۚ

بَلْ هُمْ قَوْمٌ خَصِمُوْنَ ۞ اِنْ هُوَ

اِلَّا عَبْدٌ اَنْعَمْنَا عَلَيْهِ وَجَعَلْنٰهُ

مَثَلًا لِّبَنِيْۤ اِسْرَآءِيْلَ ۞ وَلَوْ

نَشَآءُ لَجَعَلْنَا مِنْكُمْ مَّلٰٓئِكَةً

فِى الْاَرْضِ يَخْلُفُوْنَ ۞ وَاِنَّهٗ

لَعِلْمٌ لِّلسَّاعَةِ فَلَا تَمْتَرُنَّ بِهَا

وَاتَّبِعُوْنِ ۚ هٰذَا صِرَاطٌ مُّسْتَقِيْمٌ ۞

a contemptible wretch and can scarcely express himself clearly?"

53. "Then why are not gold bracelets bestowed on him, or (why) come (not) with him Angels accompanying him in procession?"

54. Thus did he make fools of his people, and they obeyed him: truly were they a people rebellious (against Allah).

55. When at length they provoked Us, We exacted retribution from them, and We drowned them all.

56. And We made them (a people) of the Past and an Example to later ages.

57. When (Jesus) the son of Mary is held up as an example, behold, your people

مَهِيْنٌ ۗ وَّلَا يَكَادُ يُبِيْنُ ۞ فَلَوْلَاۤ

اُلْقِىَ عَلَيْهِ اَسْوِرَةٌ مِّنْ ذَهَبٍ

اَوْ جَآءَ مَعَهُ الْمَلَآئِكَةُ مُقْتَرِنِيْنَ ۞

فَاسْتَخَفَّ قَوْمَهٗ فَاَطَاعُوْهُ ۚ اِنَّهُمْ

كَانُوْا قَوْمًا فٰسِقِيْنَ ۞ فَلَمَّاۤ

اٰسَفُوْنَا انْتَقَمْنَا مِنْهُمْ فَاَغْرَقْنٰهُمْ

اَجْمَعِيْنَ ۙ فَجَعَلْنٰهُمْ سَلَفًا وَّمَثَلًا

لِّلْاٰخِرِيْنَ ۞ وَلَمَّا ضُرِبَ ابْنُ

مَرْيَمَ مَثَلًا اِذَا قَوْمُكَ مِنْهُ

in order that they might turn (to Us).

49. And they said, "O you sorcerer! Invoke your Lord for us according to His covenant with you; for we shall truly accept guidance."

50. But when We removed the Penalty from them, behold, they broke their word.

51. And Pharaoh proclaimed among his people, saying: "O my people! Does not the dominion of Egypt belong to me, (witness) these streams flowing underneath my (palace)? Do you not see then?"

52. "Am I not better than this (Moses), who is

لَعَلَّهُمْ يَرْجِعُوْنَ ۝ وَقَالُوْا يٰٓاَيُّهَ

السّٰحِرُ ادْعُ لَنَا رَبَّكَ بِمَا عَهِدَ

عِنْدَكَ اِنَّنَا لَمُهْتَدُوْنَ ۝ فَلَمَّا

كَشَفْنَا عَنْهُمُ الْعَذَابَ اِذَا هُمْ

يَنْكُثُوْنَ ۝ وَنَادٰى فِرْعَوْنُ فِيْ

قَوْمِهٖ قَالَ يٰقَوْمِ اَلَيْسَ لِيْ

مُلْكُ مِصْرَ وَهٰذِهِ الْاَنْهٰرُ تَجْرِيْ

مِنْ تَحْتِيْۤ اَفَلَا تُبْصِرُوْنَ ۝ اَمْ

اَنَا خَيْرٌ مِّنْ هٰذَا الَّذِيْ هُوَ

Our Apostles whom We sent before you; did We appoint any deities other than (Allah) Most Gracious, to be worshipped?

46. We did send Moses afore-time, with Our Signs, to Pharaoh and his chiefs: he said, "I am an Apostle of the Lord of the Worlds."

47. But when he came to them with Our Signs, behold they ridiculed them.

48. We showed them Sign after Sign, each greater than its fellow, and We seized them with Punishment,

مَنْ أَرْسَلْنَا مِنْ قَبْلِكَ مِنْ

رُّسُلِنَا أَجَعَلْنَا مِنْ دُونِ الرَّحْمٰنِ

اٰلِهَةً يُّعْبَدُونَ ۞ وَلَقَدْ أَرْسَلْنَا

مُوسٰى بِاٰيٰتِنَآ إِلٰى فِرْعَوْنَ

وَمَلَإِيْهِ فَقَالَ إِنِّي رَسُولُ رَبِّ

الْعٰلَمِينَ ۞ فَلَمَّا جَآءَهُمْ بِاٰيٰتِنَآ

إِذَا هُمْ مِّنْهَا يَضْحَكُونَ ۞ وَمَا

نُرِيْهِمْ مِّنْ اٰيَةٍ إِلَّا هِيَ أَكْبَرُ

مِنْ أُخْتِهَا وَأَخَذْنٰهُمْ بِالْعَذَابِ

40.   Can you then make the deaf to hear, or give direction to the blind or to such as (wander) in manifest error?

41.   Even if We take you away, We shall be sure to exact retribution from them,

42.   Or We shall show you that (accomplished) which We have promised them: for verily We shall prevail over them.

43.   So hold you fast to the Revelation sent down to you; verily you are on a Straight Way.

44.   The (Qur'an) is indeed the message, for you and for your people; and soon shall you (all) be brought to account.

45.   And question you

أَفَأَنتَ تُسۡمِعُ الصُّمَّ أَوۡ تَهۡدِى

الۡعُمۡىَ وَمَن كَانَ فِىۡ ضَلٰلٍ

مُّبِيۡنٍ ۞ فَإِمَّا نَذۡهَبَنَّ بِكَ فَإِنَّا

مِنۡهُمۡ مُّنۡتَقِمُوۡنَ ۞ أَوۡ نُرِيَنَّكَ

الَّذِىۡ وَعَدۡنٰهُمۡ فَإِنَّا عَلَيۡهِمۡ

مُّقۡتَدِرُوۡنَ ۞ فَاسۡتَمۡسِكۡ بِالَّذِىۡٓ

أُوۡحِىَ إِلَيۡكَ ۚ إِنَّكَ عَلٰى صِرَاطٍ

مُّسۡتَقِيۡمٍ ۞ وَإِنَّهٗ لَذِكۡرٌ لَّكَ

وَلِقَوۡمِكَ ۚ وَسَوۡفَ تُسۡئَلُوۡنَ ۞ وَسۡئَلۡ

in the sight of your Lord is for the righteous.

36. If anyone withdraws himself from remembrance of (Allah) Most Gracious, We appoint for him an evil one, to be an intimate companion to him.

37. Such (evil ones) really hinder them from the Path, but they think that they are being guided aright!

38. At length, when (such a one) comes to Us, he says (to his evil companion): "Would that between me and you were the distance of East and West!" Ah! Evil is the companion (indeed)!

39. When you have done wrong, it will avail you nothing, that Day, that you shall be partners in Punishment!

عِنْدَ رَبِّكَ لِلْمُتَّقِيْنَ ۩ وَمَنْ

يَّعْشُ عَنْ ذِكْرِ الرَّحْمٰنِ نُقَيِّضْ

لَهٗ شَيْطٰنًا فَهُوَ لَهٗ قَرِيْنٌ ۩

وَإِنَّهُمْ لَيَصُدُّوْنَهُمْ عَنِ السَّبِيْلِ

وَيَحْسَبُوْنَ اَنَّهُمْ مُّهْتَدُوْنَ ۩ حَتّٰى

اِذَا جَآءَنَا قَالَ يٰلَيْتَ بَيْنِيْ وَبَيْنَكَ

بُعْدَ الْمَشْرِقَيْنِ فَبِئْسَ الْقَرِيْنُ ۩

وَلَنْ يَّنْفَعَكُمُ الْيَوْمَ اِذْ ظَّلَمْتُمْ

اَنَّكُمْ فِى الْعَذَابِ مُشْتَرِكُوْنَ ۩

in ranks, so that some may command work from others. But the Mercy of your Lord is better than the (wealth) which they amass.

33. And were it not that (all) men might become of one community, We would provide, for everyone that blasphemes against (Allah) Most Gracious, silver roofs for their houses and (silver) stair-ways on which to go up,

34. And (silver) doors to their houses, and thrones (of silver) on which they could recline,

35. And also adornments of gold. But all this were nothing but enjoyment of the present life: the Hereafter,

دَاجَتْ لِيَتَّخِذَ بَعْضُهُمْ بَعْضًا

سُخْرِيًّا ۗ وَرَحْمَتُ رَبِّكَ خَيْرٌ مِّمَّا

يَجْمَعُونَ ۞ وَلَوْلَا أَنْ يَّكُونَ النَّاسُ

أُمَّةً وَّاحِدَةً لَّجَعَلْنَا لِمَنْ يَّكْفُرُ

بِالرَّحْمٰنِ لِبُيُوتِهِمْ سُقُفًا مِّنْ

فِضَّةٍ وَّمَعَارِجَ عَلَيْهَا يَظْهَرُونَ ۞

وَلِبُيُوتِهِمْ أَبْوَابًا وَّسُرُرًا عَلَيْهَا

يَتَّكِئُونَ ۞ وَزُخْرُفًا ۚ وَإِنْ كُلُّ ذٰلِكَ

لَمَّا مَتَاعُ الْحَيٰوةِ الدُّنْيَا ۚ وَالْاٰخِرَةُ

to these (men) and their fathers, until the Truth has come to them, and an Apostle making things clear.

30. But when the Truth came to them, they said: "This is sorcery, and we do reject it."

31. Also, they say: "Why is not this Qur'an sent down to some leading man in either of the two (chief) cities?"

32. Is it they who would portion out the Mercy of your Lord? It is We Who portion out between them their livelihood in the life of this world: and We raise some of them above others

هٰٓؤُلَآءِ وَ اٰبَآءَهُمْ حَتّٰى جَآءَهُمُ

الْحَقُّ وَ رَسُوْلٌ مُّبِيْنٌ ۩ وَلَمَّا

جَآءَهُمُ الْحَقُّ قَالُوْا هٰذَا سِحْرٌ

وَّاِنَّا بِهٖ كٰفِرُوْنَ ۩ وَقَالُوْا لَوْلَا

نُزِّلَ هٰذَا الْقُرْاٰنُ عَلٰى رَجُلٍ مِّنَ

الْقَرْيَتَيْنِ عَظِيْمٍ ۩ اَهُمْ يَقْسِمُوْنَ

رَحْمَتَ رَبِّكَ ۚ نَحْنُ قَسَمْنَا بَيْنَهُمْ

مَّعِيْشَتَهُمْ فِى الْحَيٰوةِ الدُّنْيَا

وَرَفَعْنَا بَعْضَهُمْ فَوْقَ بَعْضٍ

I brought you better guidance than that which you found your fathers following?" They said: "For us, we deny that you (Prophets) are sent (on a mission at all)."

25. So We exacted retribution from them: now see what was the end of those who rejected (Truth)!

26. Behold! Abraham said to his father and his people: "I do indeed clear myself of what you worship:"

27. "(I worship) only Him Who made me, and He will certainly guide me."

28. And he left it as a Word to endure among those who came after him, that they may turn back (to Allah).

29. Yes, I have given the good things of this life

جِئْتُكُمْ بِأَهْدَى مِمَّا وَجَدْتُمْ عَلَيْهِ

أَبَاءَكُمْ قَالُوٓا إِنَّا بِمَآ أُرْسِلْتُمْ بِهِ

كَفِرُونَ ۞ فَانْتَقَمْنَا مِنْهُمْ فَانْظُرْ

كَيْفَ كَانَ عَاقِبَةُ الْمُكَذِّبِينَ ۞

وَإِذْ قَالَ إِبْرَاهِيمُ لِأَبِيهِ وَقَوْمِهِ

إِنَّنِي بَرَآءٌ مِّمَّا تَعْبُدُونَ ۞ اِلَّا

الَّذِى فَطَرَنِى فَإِنَّهُ سَيَهْدِينِ ۞

وَجَعَلَهَا كَلِمَةً بَاقِيَةً فِى عَقِبِهِ

لَعَلَّهُمْ يَرْجِعُونَ ۞ بَلْ مَتَّعْتُ

They do nothing but lie!

21. ·What! Have We given them a Book before this, to which they are holding fast?

22. No! They say: "We found our fathers following a certain reli-gion, and we do guide ourselves by their footsteps."

23. Just in the same way, when-ever We sent a warner before you to any people, the wealthy ones among them said: "We found our fathers following a certain religion, and we will certainly follow in their footsteps."

24. He said: "What! Even if

هُمْ لَا يُخْرَصُوْنَ ۞ اَمْ اٰتَيْنٰهُمْ

كِتٰبًا مِّنْ قَبْلِهٖ فَهُمْ بِهٖ

مُسْتَمْسِكُوْنَ ۞ بَلْ قَالُوْٓا اِنَّا

وَجَدْنَآ اٰبَآءَنَا عَلٰٓى اُمَّةٍ وَّاِنَّا عَلٰٓى

اٰثٰرِهِمْ مُّهْتَدُوْنَ ۞ وَكَذٰلِكَ مَآ

اَرْسَلْنَا مِنْ قَبْلِكَ فِىْ قَرْيَةٍ مِّنْ

نَّذِيْرٍ اِلَّا قَالَ مُتْرَفُوْهَآ اِنَّا

وَجَدْنَآ اٰبَآءَنَا عَلٰٓى اُمَّةٍ وَّاِنَّا

عَلٰٓى اٰثٰرِهِمْ مُّقْتَدُوْنَ ۞ قُلْ اَوَلَوْ

news is brought to one of them of (the birth of) what he sets up as a likeness to (Allah) Most Gracious, his face darkens, and he is filled with inward grief!

18. Is then one brought up among trinkets, and unable to give a clear account in a dispute (to be associated with Allah)?

19. And they make into female Angels who themselves serve Allah. Did they witness their creation? Their evidence will be recorded, and they will be called to account!

20. ("Ah!") they say, "If it had been the will of (Allah) Most Gracious, we should not have worshipped such (deities)!" Of that they have no knowledge!

بُشِّرَ أَحَدُهُم بِمَا ضَرَبَ لِلرَّحْمٰنِ

مَثَلًا ظَلَّ وَجْهُهُ مُسْوَدًّا وَّهُوَ

كَظِيمٌ ۝ أَوَمَن يُنَشَّؤُا فِى الْحِلْيَةِ

وَهُوَ فِى الْخِصَامِ غَيْرُ مُبِينٍ ۝

وَجَعَلُوا الْمَلٰئِكَةَ الَّذِينَ هُمْ عِبٰدُ

الرَّحْمٰنِ إِنَاثًا أَشَهِدُوا خَلْقَهُمْ

سَتُكْتَبُ شَهَادَتُهُمْ وَيُسْئَلُونَ ۝

وَقَالُوا لَوْ شَآءَ الرَّحْمٰنُ مَا عَبَدْنٰهُم

مَّا لَهُم بِذٰلِكَ مِنْ عِلْمٍ إِنْ

on which you ride,

13. In order that you may sit firm and square on their backs, and when so seated, you may celebrate the (kind) favour of your Lord, and say, "Glory to Him Who has subjected these to our (use), for we could never have accomplished this (by ourselves),"

14. "And to our Lord, surely, must we turn back!"

15. Yet they attribute to some of His servants a share with Him (in His godhead)! Truly is man a blasphemous ingrate avowed!

16. What! Has He taken daughters out of what He himself creates, and granted to you sons for choice?

17. When

مَا تَرْكَبُونَ ۝ لِتَسْتَوُوا عَلَى ظُهُورِهِ

ثُمَّ تَذْكُرُوا نِعْمَةَ رَبِّكُمْ إِذَا

اسْتَوَيْتُمْ عَلَيْهِ وَتَقُولُوا سُبْحَانَ

الَّذِى سَخَّرَ لَنَا هَذَا وَمَا كُنَّا

لَهُ مُقْرِنِينَ ۝ وَإِنَّا إِلَى رَبِّنَا

لَمُنْقَلِبُونَ ۝ وَجَعَلُوا لَهُ مِنْ

عِبَادِهِ جُزْءًا إِنَّ الْإِنْسَانَ لَكَفُورٌ

مُبِينٌ ۝ أَمِ اتَّخَذَ مِمَّا يَخْلُقُ

بَنَاتٍ وَأَصْفَاكُمْ بِالْبَنِينَ ۝ وَإِذَا

9. If you were to question them, 'Who created the heavens and the earth?' They would be sure to reply, 'They were created by (Him), the Exalted in Power, full of Knowledge'; -

10. (Yes, the same that) has made for you the earth (like a carpet) spread out, and has made for you roads (and channels) therein, in order that you may find guidance (on the way);

11. We sends down (from time to time) rain from the sky in due measure; - and We raise to life therewith a land that is dead; even so will you be raised (from the dead); -

12. That has created pairs in all things, and has made for you ships and cattle

وَلَئِنْ سَأَلْتَهُمْ مَّنْ خَلَقَ السَّمٰوٰتِ

وَالْأَرْضَ لَيَقُولُنَّ خَلَقَهُنَّ الْعَزِيزُ

الْعَلِيمُ ۙ الَّذِيْ جَعَلَ لَكُمُ الْأَرْضَ

مَهْدًا وَّجَعَلَ لَكُمْ فِيْهَا سُبُلًا

لَّعَلَّكُمْ تَهْتَدُوْنَ ۙ وَالَّذِيْ نَزَّلَ

مِنَ السَّمَآءِ مَآءًۢ بِقَدَرٍ ۚ فَأَنْشَرْنَا بِهٖ

بَلْدَةً مَّيْتًا ۚ كَذٰلِكَ تُخْرَجُوْنَ ۙ

وَالَّذِيْ خَلَقَ الْأَزْوَاجَ كُلَّهَا

وَجَعَلَ لَكُمْ مِّنَ الْفُلْكِ وَالْأَنْعَامِ

have made it a Qur'an in Arabic, that you may be able to understand (and learn wisdom).

4. And verily, it is in the Mother of the Book, in Our Presence, high (in dignity), full of wisdom.

5. Shall We then take away the Message from you all together for that you are a people transgressing beyond bounds?

6. But how many were the Prophets We sent amongst the peoples of old?

7. And never came there a Prophet to them but they mocked him.

8. So We destroyed (them) - stronger in power than these; - and (thus) has passed on the parable of the peoples of old.

جَعَلْنٰهُ قُرْءٰنًا عَرَبِيًّا لَّعَلَّكُمْ

تَعْقِلُوْنَ ۞ وَاِنَّهٗ فِيْۤ اُمِّ الْكِتٰبِ

لَدَيْنَا لَعَلِيٌّ حَكِيْمٌ ۞ اَفَنَضْرِبُ

عَنْكُمُ الذِّكْرَ صَفْحًا اَنْ كُنْتُمْ

قَوْمًا مُّسْرِفِيْنَ ۞ وَكَمْ اَرْسَلْنَا

مِنْ نَّبِيٍّ فِى الْاَوَّلِيْنَ ۞ وَمَا

يَاْتِيْهِمْ مِّنْ نَّبِيٍّ اِلَّا كَانُوْا بِهٖ

يَسْتَهْزِءُوْنَ ۞ فَاَهْلَكْنَاۤ اَشَدَّ مِنْهُمْ

بَطْشًا وَّمَضٰى مَثَلُ الْاَوَّلِيْنَ ۞

you know not (before) what was Revelation, and what was Faith; but We have made the (Qur'an) a Light, wherewith We guide such of Our servants as We will; and verily you does guide (men) to the Straight Way, -

53. The Way of Allah, to Whom belongs whatever is in the heavens and whatever is on earth. Behold (how) all affairs tend towards Allah!

Az-Zukhruf
(Gold Adornments)

Bismillahir-Rahmanir-Rahim

1. Ha-Mim. **2.** By the Book that makes things clear, -
3. We

أَمۡرِنَا مَا كُنتَ تَدۡرِى مَا الۡكِتَٰبُ

وَلَا الۡإِيمَٰنُ وَلَٰكِن جَعَلۡنَٰهُ نُورًا

نَّهۡدِى بِهِۦ مَن نَّشَآءُ مِنۡ

عِبَادِنَا ۚ وَإِنَّكَ لَتَهۡدِىٓ إِلَىٰ صِرَٰطٍ

مُّسۡتَقِيمٍ ۞ صِرَٰطِ اللَّهِ الَّذِى لَهُۥ

مَا فِى السَّمَٰوَٰتِ وَمَا فِى الۡأَرۡضِ ۗ

أَلَآ إِلَى اللَّهِ تَصِيرُ الۡأُمُورُ ۞

بِسۡمِ اللَّهِ الرَّحۡمَٰنِ الرَّحِيمِ

سُورَةُ الدُّخَان مَكِّيَّة ٨٩ آياتها ٥٧

حمٓ ۞ وَالۡكِتَٰبِ الۡمُبِينِ ۞ إِنَّآ

He bestows (children) male or female according to His Will (and Plan),

50. Or He bestows both males and females, and He leaves barren whom He wills: for He is full of Knowledge and Power.

51. It is not fitting for a man that Allah should speak to him except by inspiration, or from behind a veil, or by the sending of a messenger to reveal, with Allah's permission, what Allah wills: for He is Most High, Most Wise.

52. And thus have We, by Our Command, sent inspiration to you:

يَهَبُ لِمَنْ يَّشَآءُ اِنَاثًا وَّيَهَبُ

لِمَنْ يَّشَآءُ الذُّكُوْرَ ۙ اَوْ يُزَوِّجُهُمْ

ذُكْرَانًا وَّاِنَاثًا ۚ وَيَجْعَلُ مَنْ

يَّشَآءُ عَقِيْمًا ؕ اِنَّهٗ عَلِيْمٌ قَدِيْرٌ ۩

وَمَا كَانَ لِبَشَرٍ اَنْ يُّكَلِّمَهُ اللّٰهُ

اِلَّا وَحْيًا اَوْ مِنْ وَّرَآئِ حِجَابٍ

اَوْ يُرْسِلَ رَسُوْلًا فَيُوْحِيَ بِاِذْنِهٖ

مَا يَشَآءُ ؕ اِنَّهٗ عَلِيٌّ حَكِيْمٌ ۩

وَكَذٰلِكَ اَوْحَيْنَآ اِلَيْكَ رُوْحًا مِّنْ

because of (the ordainment of) Allah! That Day there will be for you no place of refuge nor will there be for you any room for denial (of your sins)!

48. If then they run away, We have not sent you as a guard over them. Your duty is but to convey (the Message). And truly, when We give man a taste of a Mercy from Ourselves, he does exult thereat, but when some ill happens to him, on account of the deeds which his hands have sent forth, truly then is man ungrateful!

49. To Allah belongs the dominion of the heavens and the earth. He creates what He wills (and plans).

لَهٗ مِنَ اللّٰهِ مَا لَكُمْ مِّنْ مَّلْجَاٍ

يَّوْمَئِذٍ وَّمَا لَكُمْ مِّنْ نَّكِيْرٍ ۞ فَاِنْ

اَعْرَضُوْا فَمَآ اَرْسَلْنٰكَ عَلَيْهِمْ

حَفِيْظًا ۭ اِنْ عَلَيْكَ اِلَّا الْبَلٰغُ

وَاِنَّآ اِذَآ اَذَقْنَا الْاِنْسَانَ مِنَّا

رَحْمَةً فَرِحَ بِهَا ۚ وَاِنْ تُصِبْهُمْ

سَيِّئَةٌۢ بِمَا قَدَّمَتْ اَيْدِيْهِمْ

فَاِنَّ الْاِنْسَانَ كَفُوْرٌ ۞ لِلّٰهِ مُلْكُ

السَّمٰوٰتِ وَالْاَرْضِ ۚ يَخْلُقُ مَا يَشَآءُ

with a stealthy glance. And the believers will say: "Those are indeed in loss, who have given to perdition their own selves and those belonging to them on the Day of Judgment. Behold! Truly the wrong-doers are in a lasting Chastisement!"

46. And no protectors have they to help them, other than Allah. and for any whom Allah leaves to stray, there is no way (to the Goal).

47. Respond your Lord, before there come a Day which there will be no putting back,

مِنْ طَرْفٍ خَفِيٍّ ۚ وَقَالَ الَّذِيْنَ

اٰمَنُوْۤا اِنَّ الْخٰسِرِيْنَ الَّذِيْنَ

خَسِرُوْۤا اَنْفُسَهُمْ وَاَهْلِيْهِمْ يَوْمَ

الْقِيٰمَةِ ۗ اَلَاۤ اِنَّ الظّٰلِمِيْنَ فِيْ

عَذَابٍ مُّقِيْمٍ ۞ وَمَا كَانَ لَهُمْ

مِّنْ اَوْلِيَآءَ يَنْصُرُوْنَهُمْ مِّنْ دُوْنِ

اللّٰهِ ۗ وَمَنْ يُّضْلِلِ اللّٰهُ فَمَا لَهٗ

مِنْ سَبِيْلٍ ۞ اِسْتَجِيْبُوْا لِرَبِّكُمْ

مِّنْ قَبْلِ اَنْ يَّاْتِيَ يَوْمٌ لَّا مَرَدَّ

and insolently transgress beyond bounds through the land, defying right and justice: for such there will be a Chastisement grievous.

43. But indeed if any show patience and forgive, that would truly be an affair of great resolution.

44. For any whom Allah leaves astray, there is no protector thereafter. And you will see the wrong-doers, when in sight of the Penalty, say: "Is there any way (to effect) a return?"

45. And you will see them brought forward to the Chastisement, in a humble frame of mind because of (their) disgrace, (and) looking

وَيَبْغُونَ فِى الْأَرْضِ بِغَيْرِ الْحَقِّ

أُولَٰئِكَ لَهُمْ عَذَابٌ أَلِيمٌ ۞ وَلَمَنْ

صَبَرَ وَغَفَرَ إِنَّ ذَٰلِكَ لَمِنْ عَزْمِ

الْأُمُورِ ۞ وَمَنْ يُضْلِلِ اللَّهُ فَمَا

كَ مِنْ وَلِيٍّ مِنْ بَعْدِهِ وَتَرَى

الظَّالِمِينَ لَمَّا رَأَوُا الْعَذَابَ

يَقُولُونَ هَلْ إِلَى مَرَدٍّ مِنْ

سَبِيلٍ ۞ وَتَرَاهُمْ يُعْرَضُونَ عَلَيْهَا

خَاشِعِينَ مِنَ الذُّلِّ يَنْظُرُونَ

who (conduct) their affairs by mutual Consultation; who spend out of what We bestow on them for Sustenance;

39. And those who, when an oppressive wrong is inflicted on them, (are not cowed but) help and defend themselves.

40. The recompense for an injury is an injury equal thereto (in degree): but if a person forgives and makes reconciliation, his reward is due from Allah: for (Allah) loves not those who do wrong.

41. But indeed if any do help and defend themselves after a wrong (done) to them, against such there is no cause of blame.

42. The blame is only against those who oppress men with wrong-doing

وَأَمْرُهُمْ شُوْرىٰ بَيْنَهُمْ وَمِمَّا

رَزَقْنٰهُمْ يُنْفِقُوْنَ ۞ وَالَّذِيْنَ اِذَآ

اَصَابَهُمُ الْبَغْيُ هُمْ يَنْتَصِرُوْنَ ۞

وَجَزٰٓؤُا سَيِّئَةٍ سَيِّئَةٌ مِّثْلُهَا ۚ

فَمَنْ عَفَا وَاَصْلَحَ فَاَجْرُهٗ عَلَى اللّٰهِ ۚ

اِنَّهٗ لَا يُحِبُّ الظّٰلِمِيْنَ ۞ وَلَمَنِ

انْتَصَرَ بَعْدَ ظُلْمِهٖ فَاُولٰٓئِكَ مَا

عَلَيْهِمْ مِّنْ سَبِيْلٍ ۞ اِنَّمَا السَّبِيْلُ

عَلَى الَّذِيْنَ يَظْلِمُوْنَ النَّاسَ

35. But let those know, who dispute about Our Signs, that there is for them no way of escape.

36. Whatever you are given (here) is (but) a convenience of this life: but that which is with Allah is better and more lasting: (it is) for those who believe and put their trust in their Lord:

37. Those who avoid the greater crimes and shameful deeds, and, when they are angry even then forgive;

38. Those who hearken to their Lord, and establish regular Prayer;

وَيَعْلَمَ الَّذِيْنَ يُجَادِلُوْنَ فِيْ

اٰيٰتِنَا مَا لَهُمْ مِّنْ مَّحِيْصٍ ۞ فَمَآ

اُوْتِيْتُمْ مِّنْ شَيْءٍ فَمَتَاعُ الْحَيٰوةِ

الدُّنْيَا وَ مَا عِنْدَ اللّٰهِ خَيْرٌ

وَّ اَبْقٰى لِلَّذِيْنَ اٰمَنُوْا وَعَلٰى رَبِّهِمْ

يَتَوَكَّلُوْنَ ۞ وَالَّذِيْنَ يَجْتَنِبُوْنَ

كَبٰٓئِرَ الْاِثْمِ وَالْفَوَاحِشَ وَاِذَا مَا

غَضِبُوْا هُمْ يَغْفِرُوْنَ ۞ وَالَّذِيْنَ

اسْتَجَابُوْا لِرَبِّهِمْ وَ اَقَامُوا الصَّلٰوةَ

your hands have wrought, and for many (a sin) He grants forgiveness.

31. Nor can you escape (aught), (fleeing) through the earth; nor have you, besides Allah, any one to protect or to help.

32. And among His Signs are the ships, smooth-running through the ocean, (tall) as mountains.

33. If it be His Will He can still the Wind: then would they become motionless on the back of the (ocean). Verily in this are Signs for everyone who patiently perseveres and is grateful.

34. Or He can cause them to perish because of the (evil) which (the men) have earned; but much does He forgive.

أَيْدِيكُمْ وَيَعْفُوا عَنْ كَثِيرٍ ۝ وَمَآ

أَنْتُمْ بِمُعْجِزِيْنَ فِي الْأَرْضِ ۚ وَمَا

لَكُمْ مِّنْ دُوْنِ اللهِ مِنْ وَّلِيٍّ

وَّلَا نَصِيرٍ ۝ وَمِنْ اٰيٰتِهِ الْجَوَارِ

فِي الْبَحْرِ كَالْأَعْلَامِ ۝ اِنْ يَّشَأْ

يُسْكِنِ الرِّيْحَ فَيَظْلَلْنَ رَوَاكِدَ

عَلٰى ظَهْرِهٖ ۚ اِنَّ فِي ذٰلِكَ لَأيٰتٍ

لِّكُلِّ صَبَّارٍ شَكُوْرٍ ۝ اَوْ يُوْبِقْهُنَّ

بِمَا كَسَبُوْا وَيَعْفُ عَنْ كَثِيرٍ ۝

for His servants, they would indeed transgress beyond all bounds through the earth; but He sends (it) down in due measure as He pleases. For He is with His servants Well-Acquainted, Watchful.

28. He is the One that sends down rain (even) after (men) have given up all hope, and scatters His Mercy (far and wide). And He is the Protector, Worthy of all Praise.

29. And among His Signs is the Creation of the heavens and the earth, and the living creatures that He has scattered through them: and He has power to gather them together when He wills.

30. Whatever misfortune happens to you, is because on the things

لِعِبَادِهِ لَبَغَوْا فِى الْاَرْضِ وَلٰكِنْ

يُنَزِّلُ بِقَدَرٍ مَّا يَشَآءُ اِنَّهُ بِعِبَادِهِ

خَبِيْرٌ بَصِيْرٌ ۞ وَهُوَ الَّذِىْ يُنَزِّلُ

الْغَيْثَ مِنْ بَعْدِ مَا قَنَطُوْا وَيَنْشُرُ

رَحْمَتَهُ وَهُوَ الْوَلِىُّ الْحَمِيْدُ ۞ وَمِنْ

اٰيٰتِهِ خَلْقُ السَّمٰوٰتِ وَالْاَرْضِ وَمَا

بَثَّ فِيْهِمَا مِنْ دَآبَّةٍ وَهُوَ عَلٰى

جَمْعِهِمْ اِذَا يَشَآءُ قَدِيْرٌ ۞ وَمَآ

اَصَابَكُمْ مِّنْ مُّصِيْبَةٍ فَبِمَا كَسَبَتْ

He could seal up your heart. And Allah blots out Vanity, and proves the Truth by His Words. For He knows well the secrets of all hearts.

25. He is the One that accepts repentance from His servants and forgives sins: and He knows all that you do.

26. And He listens to those who believe and do deeds of righteousness, and gives them increase of His Bounty: but for the unbelievers their is a terrible Chastisement.

27. If Allah were to enlarge the provision

يَخْتِمْ عَلَىٰ قَلْبِكَ ۚ وَيَمْحُ اللهُ

الْبَاطِلَ وَيُحِقُّ الْحَقَّ بِكَلِمَاتِهِ ۚ إِنَّهُ

عَلِيمٌۢ بِذَاتِ الصُّدُوْرِ ۝ وَهُوَ

الَّذِيْ يَقْبَلُ التَّوْبَةَ عَنْ عِبَادِهِ

وَيَعْفُوْا عَنِ السَّيِّاٰتِ وَيَعْلَمُ مَا

تَفْعَلُوْنَ ۝ وَيَسْتَجِيْبُ الَّذِيْنَ اٰمَنُوْا

وَعَمِلُوا الصّٰلِحٰتِ وَيَزِيْدُهُمْ مِّنْ

فَضْلِهِ ۚ وَالْكٰفِرُوْنَ لَهُمْ عَذَابٌ

شَدِيْدٌ ۝ وَلَوْ بَسَطَ اللهُ الرِّزْقَ

before their Lord, all that they wish for. That will indeed be the magnificent Bounty (of Allah).

23. That is (the Bounty) whereof Allah gives Glad Tidings to His servants who believe and do righteous deeds. Say: "No reward do I ask of you for this except the love of those near of kin." And if any one earns any good, We shall give him an increase of good in respect thereof: for Allah is Oft-Forgiving, Most Ready to appreciate (service).

24. What! Do they say, "He has forged a falsehood against God"? But if Allah willed,

يَشَاءُوْنَ عِنْدَ رَبِّهِمْ ذٰلِكَ هُوَ

الْفَضْلُ الْكَبِيْرُ ۞ ذٰلِكَ الَّذِىْ

يُبَشِّرُ اللهُ عِبَادَهُ الَّذِيْنَ اٰمَنُوْا

وَعَمِلُوا الصّٰلِحٰتِ ۭ قُلْ لَّا اَسْئَلُكُمْ

عَلَيْهِ اَجْرًا اِلَّا الْمَوَدَّةَ فِى الْقُرْبٰى ۭ

وَمَنْ يَّقْتَرِفْ حَسَنَةً نَّزِدْ لَهُ

فِيْهَا حُسْنًا ۭ اِنَّ اللهَ غَفُوْرٌ

شَكُوْرٌ ۞ اَمْ يَقُوْلُوْنَ افْتَرٰى

عَلَى اللهِ كَذِبًا ۚ فَاِنْ يَّشَاِ اللهُ

but he has no share or lot in the Hereafter.

21. What! Have they partners (in godhead), who have established for them some religion without the permission of Allah? Had it not been for the Decree of Judgment, the matter would have been decided between them (at once). But verily the wrong-doers will have a grievous Chastisement.

22. You will see the wrong-doers in fear on account of what they have earned, and (the burden of) that must (necessarily) fall on them. But those who believe and work righteous deeds will be in the luxuriant meads of the Gardens: they shall have,

وَمَا لَهُ فِي الْأَخِرَةِ مِنْ نَصِيبٍ ۞

أَمْ لَهُمْ شُرَكَؤُا شَرَعُوا لَهُمْ مِنَ

الدِّينِ مَا لَمْ يَأْذَنْ بِهِ اللّٰهُ ۚ

وَلَوْلَا كَلِمَةُ الْفَصْلِ لَقُضِيَ

بَيْنَهُمْ ۚ وَإِنَّ الظّٰلِمِينَ لَهُمْ عَذَابٌ

أَلِيمٌ ۞ تَرَى الظّٰلِمِينَ مُشْفِقِينَ

مِمَّا كَسَبُوا وَهُوَ وَاقِعٌ بِهِمْ ۗ

وَالَّذِينَ أٰمَنُوا وَعَمِلُوا الصّٰلِحٰتِ

فِي رَوْضَاتِ الْجَنّٰتِ ۚ لَهُمْ مَّا

believe not in it: those who believe hold it in awe, and know that it is the Truth. Behold, verily those that dispute concerning the Hour are far astray.

19. Gracious is Allah to His servants: He gives sustenance to whom He pleases: and He is Strong, the Mighty.

20. To any that desires the tilth of the Hereafter, We give increase in his tilth, and to any that desires the tilth of this world, We grant somewhat thereof,

لَا يُؤْمِنُوْنَ بِهَا ۚ وَالَّذِيْنَ اٰمَنُوْا

مُشْفِقُوْنَ مِنْهَا وَيَعْلَمُوْنَ اَنَّهَا

الْحَقُّ ۗ اَلَا اِنَّ الَّذِيْنَ يُمَارُوْنَ

فِى السَّاعَةِ لَفِىْ ضَلٰلٍ بَعِيْدٍ ۝

اَللّٰهُ لَطِيْفٌ بِعِبَادِهٖ يَرْزُقُ مَنْ

يَّشَاءُ ۚ وَهُوَ الْقَوِىُّ الْعَزِيْزُ ۝

مَنْ كَانَ يُرِيْدُ حَرْثَ الْاٰخِرَةِ

نَزِدْ لَهٗ فِىْ حَرْثِهٖ ۚ وَمَنْ كَانَ

يُرِيْدُ حَرْثَ الدُّنْيَا نُؤْتِهٖ مِنْهَا

There is no contention between us and you. Allah will bring us together, and to Him is (our) Final Goal.

16.   But those who dispute concerning Allah after He has been accepted, - futile is their dispute in the Sight of their Lord: on them is Wrath, and for them will be a Chastisement terrible.

17.   It is Allah Who has sent down the Book in Truth, and the Balance (by which to weigh conduct). And what will make you realise that perhaps the Hour is close at hand?

18.   Only those wish to hasten it who

لَاحُجَّةَ بَيْنَنَا وَبَيْنَكُمُ ۗ اللهُ

يَجْمَعُ بَيْنَنَا ۚ وَإِلَيْهِ الْمَصِيْرُ ۝

وَالَّذِيْنَ يُحَآجُّوْنَ فِى اللهِ مِنْ

بَعْدِ مَا اسْتُجِيْبَ لَهٗ حُجَّتُهُمْ

دَاحِضَةٌ عِنْدَ رَبِّهِمْ وَعَلَيْهِمْ

غَضَبٌ وَّلَهُمْ عَذَابٌ شَدِيْدٌ ۝

اللهُ الَّذِيْ أَنْزَلَ الْكِتٰبَ بِالْحَقِّ

وَالْمِيْزَانَ ۗ وَمَا يُدْرِيْكَ لَعَلَّ السَّاعَةَ

قَرِيْبٌ ۝ يَسْتَعْجِلُ بِهَا الَّذِيْنَ

for a Word that went forth before from your Lord, (tending) to a Term appointed, the matter would have been settled between them: but truly those who have inherited the Book after them are in suspicious (disquieting) doubt concerning it.

15. Now then, for that (reason), call (them to the Faith), and stand steadfast as you are commanded, nor follow you their vain desires; but say: "I believe in the Book which Allah has sent down; and I am commanded to judge justly between you. Allah is our Lord and your Lord: for us (is the responsibility for) our deeds, and for you for your deeds.

كَلِمَةٌ سَبَقَتْ مِنْ رَّبِّكَ اِلٰى

اَجَلٍ مُّسَمًّى لَّقُضِيَ بَيْنَهُمْ وَاِنَّ

الَّذِيْنَ اُوْرِثُوا الْكِتٰبَ مِنْ بَعْدِهِمْ

لَفِيْ شَكٍّ مِّنْهُ مُرِيْبٍ ۩ فَلِذٰلِكَ

فَادْعُ وَاسْتَقِمْ كَمَا اُمِرْتَ وَلَا

تَتَّبِعْ اَهْوَآءَهُمْ وَقُلْ اٰمَنْتُ

بِمَآ اَنْزَلَ اللّٰهُ مِنْ كِتٰبٍ

وَاُمِرْتُ لِاَعْدِلَ بَيْنَكُمْ اَللّٰهُ رَبُّنَا

وَرَبُّكُمْ لَنَآ اَعْمَالُنَا وَلَكُمْ اَعْمَالُكُمْ

as that which He enjoined on Noah - the which We have sent by inspiration to you - and that which We enjoined on Abraham, Moses, and Jesus: namely, that you should remain steadfast in religion, and make no divisions therein: to those who worship other things than Allah, hard is the (way) to which you call them. Allah chooses to Himself those whom He pleases, and guides to Himself those who turn (to Him).

14. And they became divided only after knowledge reached them, - through selfish envy as between themselves. Had it not been

اَلدِّيْنِ مَا وَصّٰى بِهٖ نُوْحًا

وَّالَّذِىْٓ اَوْحَيْنَآ اِلَيْكَ وَمَا وَصَّيْنَا

بِهٖٓ اِبْرٰهِيْمَ وَمُوْسٰى وَعِيْسٰٓى اَنْ

اَقِيْمُوا الدِّيْنَ وَلَا تَتَفَرَّقُوْا فِيْهِ

كَبُرَ عَلَى الْمُشْرِكِيْنَ مَا تَدْعُوْهُمْ

اِلَيْهِ ۗ اَللّٰهُ يَجْتَبِىْٓ اِلَيْهِ مَنْ يَّشَآءُ

وَيَهْدِىْٓ اِلَيْهِ مَنْ يُّنِيْبُ ۞

وَمَا تَفَرَّقُوْٓا اِلَّا مِنْۢ بَعْدِ مَا

جَآءَهُمُ الْعِلْمُ بَغْيًۢا بَيْنَهُمْ ۗ وَلَوْلَا

Allah my Lord: in Him I trust, and to Him I turn.

11. (He is) the Creator of the heavens and the earth: He has made for you pairs from among yourselves, and pairs among cattle: by this means does He multiply you: there is nothing whatever like unto Him, and He is the One that hears and sees (all things).

12. To Him belong the keys of the heavens and the earth: He enlarges and restricts the Sustenance to whom He wills: for He knows full well all things.

13. The same religion has He established for you

اللهُ رَبِّي عَلَيْهِ تَوَكَّلْتُ وَاِلَيْهِ

اُنِيبُ ۞ فَاطِرُ السَّمٰوٰتِ وَالْاَرْضِ

جَعَلَ لَكُمْ مِّنْ اَنْفُسِكُمْ اَزْوَاجًا

وَّمِنَ الْاَنْعَامِ اَزْوَاجًا يَذْرَؤُكُمْ

فِيهِ لَيْسَ كَمِثْلِهِ شَيْءٌ وَهُوَ

السَّمِيعُ الْبَصِيرُ ۞ لَهُ مَقَالِيدُ

السَّمٰوٰتِ وَالْاَرْضِ يَبْسُطُ الرِّزْقَ

لِمَنْ يَّشَآءُ وَيَقْدِرُ اِنَّهُ بِكُلِّ

شَيْءٍ عَلِيمٌ ۞ شَرَعَ لَكُمْ مِّنَ

and some in the Blazing Fire.

8.   If Allah had so willed, He could have made them a single people; but He admits whom He will to His Mercy; and the wrong-doers will have no protector nor helper.

9.   What! Have they taken (for worship) protectors besides Him? But it is Allah, - He is the Protector, and it is He Who gives life to the dead: it is He Who has power over all things,

10.   Whatever it be wherein you differ, the decision thereof is with Allah: such is

وَفَرِيْقٌ فِى السَّعِيْرِ ۞ وَلَوْ شَآءَ

اللهُ لَجَعَلَهُمْ اُمَّةً وَّاحِدَةً وَّلٰكِنْ

يُّدْخِلُ مَنْ يَّشَآءُ فِىْ رَحْمَتِهٖ

وَالظّٰلِمُوْنَ مَا لَهُمْ مِّنْ وَّلِىٍّ وَّلَا

نَصِيْرٍ ۞ اَمِ اتَّخَذُوْا مِنْ دُوْنِهٖ

اَوْلِيَآءَ ۚ فَاللهُ هُوَ الْوَلِىُّ وَهُوَ

يُحْىِ الْمَوْتٰى ۚ وَهُوَ عَلٰى كُلِّ شَىْءٍ

قَدِيْرٌ ۞ وَمَا اخْتَلَفْتُمْ فِيْهِ مِنْ

شَىْءٍ فَحُكْمُهٗ اِلَى اللهِ ۚ ذٰلِكُمُ

celebrate the Praises of their Lord, and pray for forgiveness for (all) beings on earth: behold! verily Allah is He, the Oft-Forgiving, Most Merciful.

6. And those who take as protectors others besides Him, - Allah does watch over them; and you are not the disposer of their affairs.

7. Thus have We sent by inspiration to you an Arabic Qur'an: that you may warn the Mother of Cities and all around her, - and warn (them) of the Day of Assembly, of which there is no doubt: (when) some will be in the Garden,

يُسَبِّحُونَ بِحَمْدِ رَبِّهِمْ وَيَسْتَغْفِرُونَ

لِمَنْ فِي الْأَرْضِ أَلَا إِنَّ اللّٰهَ

هُوَ الْغَفُورُ الرَّحِيمُ ۞ وَالَّذِينَ

اتَّخَذُوا مِنْ دُونِهِ أَوْلِيَآءَ اللّٰهُ

حَفِيظٌ عَلَيْهِمْ وَمَا أَنْتَ عَلَيْهِمْ

بِوَكِيلٍ ۞ وَكَذٰلِكَ أَوْحَيْنَا إِلَيْكَ

قُرْآنًا عَرَبِيًّا لِتُنْذِرَ أُمَّ الْقُرٰى

وَمَنْ حَوْلَهَا وَتُنْذِرَ يَوْمَ الْجَمْعِ

لَا رَيْبَ فِيهِ فَرِيقٌ فِي الْجَنَّةِ

doubt concerning the Meeting with their Lord? Ah indeed! It is He that does encompass all things!

Ash-Shura (Consultation)

Bismillahir-Rahmanir-Rahim

1.   Ha-Mim.

2.   'Ain. Sin. Qaf.

3.   Thus does (He) send inspiration to you as (He did) to those before you, - Allah, Exalted in Power, full of Wisdom.

4.   To Him belongs all that is in the heavens and on earth: and He is Most High, Most Great.

5.   The heavens are almost rent asunder from above them (by Him Glory): and the Angels

مِرْيَةٍ مِّنْ لِّقَاءِ رَبِّهِمْ اَلَآ اِنَّهٗ بِكُلِّ شَىْءٍ مُّحِيْطٌ ۞

بِسْمِ اللّٰهِ الرَّحْمٰنِ الرَّحِيْمِ

حٰمٓ ۞ عٓسٓقٓ ۞ كَذٰلِكَ يُوْحِىْٓ اِلَيْكَ وَاِلَى الَّذِيْنَ مِنْ قَبْلِكَ اللّٰهُ الْعَزِيْزُ الْحَكِيْمُ ۞ لَهٗ مَا فِى السَّمٰوٰتِ وَمَا فِى الْاَرْضِ وَهُوَ الْعَلِىُّ الْعَظِيْمُ ۞ تَكَادُ السَّمٰوٰتُ يَتَفَطَّرْنَ مِنْ فَوْقِهِنَّ وَالْمَلٰٓئِكَةُ

and when evil seizes him, (he comes) full of prolonged prayer!

52. Say: "See you if the (Revelation) is (really) from Allah, and yet do you reject it? Who is more astray than one who is in a schism far (from any purpose)?"

53. Soon will We show them Our Signs in the (furthest) regions (of the earth), and in their own souls, until it becomes manifest to them that this is the Truth. Is it not enough that your Lord does witness all things?

54. Ah indeed! Are they in

وَإِذَا مَسَّهُ الشَّرُّ فَذُوْ دُعَآءٍ

عَرِيْضٍ ۞ قُلْ اَرَءَيْتُمْ اِنْ كَانَ

مِنْ عِنْدِ اللّٰهِ ثُمَّ كَفَرْتُمْ بِهٖ

مَنْ اَضَلُّ مِمَّنْ هُوَ فِيْ شِقَاقٍ

بَعِيْدٍ ۞ سَنُرِيْهِمْ اٰيٰتِنَا فِي

الْاٰفَاقِ وَفِيْٓ اَنْفُسِهِمْ حَتّٰى

يَتَبَيَّنَ لَهُمْ اَنَّهُ الْحَقُّ اَوَلَمْ

يَكْفِ بِرَبِّكَ اَنَّهُ عَلٰى كُلِّ

شَيْءٍ شَهِيْدٌ ۞ اَلَآ اِنَّهُمْ فِيْ

but if ill touches him, he gives up all hope (and) is lost in despair.

50. When We give him a taste of some Mercy from Ourselves, after some adversity has touched him, he is sure to say, "This is due to my (merit): I think not that the Hour (of Judgment) will (ever) be established; but if I am brought back to my Lord, I have (much) good (stored) in His sight!" But We will show the unbelievers the truth of all that they did, and We shall give them the taste of a severe Chastisement.

51. When We bestow favours on man, he turns away, and gets himself remote on his side (instead of coming to Us);

وَاِنْ مَّسَّهُ الشَّرُّ فَيَؤُسٌ قَنُوْطٌ ۞

وَلَئِنْ اَذَقْنٰهُ رَحْمَةً مِّنَّا مِنْ

بَعْدِ ضَرَّآءَ مَسَّتْهُ لَيَقُوْلَنَّ هٰذَا

لِيْ ۙ وَمَاۤ اَظُنُّ السَّاعَةَ قَآئِمَةً ۙ

وَّلَئِنْ رُّجِعْتُ اِلٰى رَبِّيْۤ اِنَّ لِيْ

عِنْدَهٗ لَلْحُسْنٰى ۚ فَلَنُنَبِّئَنَّ الَّذِيْنَ

كَفَرُوْا بِمَا عَمِلُوْا ۖ وَلَنُذِيْقَنَّهُمْ

مِّنْ عَذَابٍ غَلِيْظٍ ۞ وَاِذَاۤ اَنْعَمْنَا

عَلَى الْاِنْسَانِ اَعْرَضَ وَنَاٰ بِجَانِبِهٖ

47. To Him is referred the Knowledge of the Hour (of Judgment: He knows all): no date-fruit comes out of its sheath, nor does a female conceive (within her womb) nor bring forth the (young), but by his knowledge. The Day that (Allah) will propound to them the (question), "Where are the partners (you attributed) to Me?" They will say, "We do assure you not one of us can bear witness!"

48. The (deities) they used to invoke aforetime will leave them in the lurch, and they will perceive that they have no way of escape.

49. Man does not weary of asking for good (things),

اِلَیْهِ یُرَدُّ عِلْمُ السَّاعَةِ ۚ وَمَا

تَخْرُجُ مِنْ ثَمَرَاتٍ مِّنْ اَکْمَامِهَا

وَمَا تَحْمِلُ مِنْ اُنْثٰی وَلَا تَضَعُ

اِلَّا بِعِلْمِهٖ ۚ وَیَوْمَ یُنَادِیْهِمْ اَیْنَ

شُرَکَآءِیْ ۙ قَالُوْۤا اٰذَنّٰکَ ۙ مَا مِنَّا

مِنْ شَهِیْدٍ ۚ وَضَلَّ عَنْهُمْ مَّا

کَانُوْا یَدْعُوْنَ مِنْ قَبْلُ وَظَنُّوْا

مَا لَهُمْ مِّنْ مَّحِیْصٍ ۞ لَا

یَسْئَمُ الْاِنْسَانُ مِنْ دُعَآءِ الْخَیْرِ ۫

پاره

اَلَيْهِ يُرَدُّ

(۲۵)

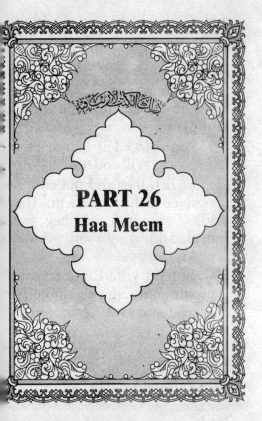

PART 26
Haa Meem

"Peace!" (and thought, "These seem) unusual people."

26. Then he turned quickly to his household, brought out a fatted calf,

27. And placed it before them … he said, "Will you not eat?"

28. (When they did not eat), he conceived a fear of them. They said, "Fear not," and they gave him glad tidings of a son endowed with knowledge.

29. But his wife came forward (laughing) aloud: she smote her forehead and said: "A barren old woman!"

30. They said, "Even so has your Lord spoken: and He is full of Wisdom and Knowledge."

سَلٰمٌ قَوْمٌ مُّنْكَرُوْنَ ۞ فَرَاغَ اِلٰى

اَهْلِهٖ فَجَآءَ بِعِجْلٍ سَمِيْنٍ ۞

فَقَرَّبَهٗۤ اِلَيْهِمْ قَالَ اَلَا تَاْكُلُوْنَ ۞

فَاَوْجَسَ مِنْهُمْ خِيْفَةً ؕ قَالُوْا

لَا تَخَفْ ؕ وَبَشَّرُوْهُ بِغُلٰمٍ عَلِيْمٍ ۞

فَاَقْبَلَتِ امْرَاَتُهٗ فِيْ صَرَّةٍ

فَصَكَّتْ وَجْهَهَا وَقَالَتْ عَجُوْزٌ

عَقِيْمٌ ۞ قَالُوْا كَذٰلِكِ ۙ قَالَ

رَبُّكِ ؕ اِنَّهٗ هُوَ الْحَكِيْمُ الْعَلِيْمُ ۞

19. And in their wealth and possessions (was remembered) the right of the (needy,) him who asked, and him who (for some reason) was prevented (from asking).

20. On the earth are Signs for those of assured Faith,

21. As also in your own selves: will you not then see?

22. And in heaven is your Sustenance, as (also) that which you are promised.

23. Then, by the Lord of heaven and earth, this is the very Truth, as much as the fact that you can speak intelligently to each other.

24. Has the story reached you, of the honoured guests of Abraham?

25. Behold, they entered his presence, and said: "Peace!" He said,

وَفِىۡٓ اَمۡوَالِهِمۡ حَقٌّ لِّلسَّآئِلِ

وَالۡمَحۡرُوۡمِ ۝ وَفِى الۡاَرۡضِ اٰيٰتٌ

لِّلۡمُوۡقِنِيۡنَ ۝ وَفِىۡٓ اَنۡفُسِكُمۡ ؕ اَفَلَا

تُبۡصِرُوۡنَ ۝ وَفِى السَّمَآءِ رِزۡقُكُمۡ

وَمَا تُوۡعَدُوۡنَ ۝ فَوَرَبِّ السَّمَآءِ

وَالۡاَرۡضِ اِنَّهٗ لَحَقٌّ مِّثۡلَ مَآ اَنَّكُمۡ

تَنۡطِقُوۡنَ ۝ هَلۡ اَتٰىكَ حَدِيۡثُ

ضَيۡفِ اِبۡرٰهِيۡمَ الۡمُكۡرَمِيۡنَ ۝ اِذۡ

دَخَلُوۡا عَلَيۡهِ فَقَالُوۡا سَلٰمًا ؕ قَالَ

12. They ask, "When will be the Day of Judgment and Justice?"

13. (It will be) a Day when they will be tried (and tested) over the Fire!

14. "Taste you your trial! This is what you used to ask to be hastened!"

15. As to the Righteous, they will be in the midst of Gardens and Springs,

16. Taking joy in the things which their Lord gives them, because, before then, they lived a good life.

17. They were in the habit of sleeping but little by night,

18. And in the hours of early dawn, they (were found) praying for Forgiveness;

يَسْئَلُوْنَ اَيَّانَ يَوْمُ الدِّيْنِ ۩ يَوْمَ

هُمْ عَلَى النَّارِ يُفْتَنُوْنَ ۩ ذُوْقُوْا

فِتْنَتَكُمْ ۗ هٰذَا الَّذِيْ كُنْتُمْ بِهٖ

تَسْتَعْجِلُوْنَ ۩ اِنَّ الْمُتَّقِيْنَ فِيْ

جَنّٰتٍ وَّعُيُوْنٍ ۙ اٰخِذِيْنَ مَآ

اٰتٰىهُمْ رَبُّهُمْ ؕ اِنَّهُمْ كَانُوْا

قَبْلَ ذٰلِكَ مُحْسِنِيْنَ ۩ كَانُوْا

قَلِيْلًا مِّنَ الَّيْلِ مَا يَهْجَعُوْنَ

۩ وَبِالْاَسْحَارِ هُمْ يَسْتَغْفِرُوْنَ ۩

Az-Zariyat
(The Winds that Scatter)

Bismillahir-Rahmanir-Rahim

1. By the (Winds) that scatter broadcast; **2.** And those that lift and bear away heavy weights;

3. And those that flow with ease and gentleness;

4. And those that distribute and apportion by Command;

5. Verily that which you are promised is true;

6. And verily Judgment and Justice must indeed come to pass.

7. By the Sky with (its) numerous Paths, **8.** Truly you are in a doctrine discordant,

9. Through which are deluded (away from the Truth) such as would be deluded. **10.** Woe to the falsehood-mongers, -

11. Those who (flounder) heedless in a flood of confusion:

سورة الذاريٰت مكية بِسْمِ اللّٰهِ الرَّحْمٰنِ الرَّحِيْمِ ٦٠ اٰياتها ٦٠ ركوعاتها ٣

وَالذَّارِيٰتِ ذَرْوًا ۙ فَالْحٰمِلٰتِ وِقْرًا ۙ

فَالْجٰرِيٰتِ يُسْرًا ۙ فَالْمُقَسِّمٰتِ

اَمْرًا ۙ اِنَّمَا تُوْعَدُوْنَ لَصَادِقٌ ۙ

وَّاِنَّ الدِّيْنَ لَوَاقِعٌ ؕ وَالسَّمَآءِ

ذَاتِ الْحُبُكِ ۙ اِنَّكُمْ لَفِيْ قَوْلٍ

مُّخْتَلِفٍ ۙ يُّؤْفَكُ عَنْهُ مَنْ

اُفِكَ ؕ قُتِلَ الْخَرّٰصُوْنَ ۙ الَّذِيْنَ

هُمْ فِيْ غَمْرَةٍ سَاهُوْنَ ۙ

when the Caller will call out from a place quiet near, -

42.   The Day when they will hear a (mighty) Blast in (very) truth: that will be the Day of Resurrection.

43.   Verily it is We Who give Life and Death; and to Us is the Final Goal -

44.   The Day when the Earth will be rent asunder, from (men) hurrying out: that will be a gathering together, - quite easy for Us.

45.   We know best what they say; and you are not one to overawe them by force. So admonish with the Qur'an such as fear My Warning!

يُنَادِ الْمُنَادِ مِنْ مَّكَانٍ قَرِيبٍ ۙ ﴿٤١﴾

يَوْمَ يَسْمَعُونَ الصَّيْحَةَ بِالْحَقِّ ۚ

ذٰلِكَ يَوْمُ الْخُرُوجِ ﴿٤٢﴾ إِنَّا نَحْنُ

نُحْيٖ وَنُمِيتُ وَإِلَيْنَا الْمَصِيرُ ﴿٤٣﴾

يَوْمَ تَشَقَّقُ الْأَرْضُ عَنْهُمْ سِرَاعًا ۚ

ذٰلِكَ حَشْرٌ عَلَيْنَا يَسِيرٌ ﴿٤٤﴾ نَحْنُ

أَعْلَمُ بِمَا يَقُولُونَ ۖ وَمَا أَنْتَ

عَلَيْهِمْ بِجَبَّارٍ ۖ فَذَكِّرْ بِالْقُرْآنِ

مَنْ يَخَافُ وَعِيدِ ﴿٤٥﴾

in this is a Message for any that has a heart and understanding or who gives ear and earnestly witnesses (the truth).

38.   We created the heavens and the earth and all between them in Six Days, nor did any sense of weariness touch Us.

39.   Bear, then, with patience, all that they say, and celebrate the praises of your Lord, before the rising of the sun and before (its) setting.

40.   And during part of the night, (also,) celebrate His praises, and (so likewise) after the postures of adoration.

41.   And listen for the Day

إِنَّ فِي ذَٰلِكَ لَذِكْرَىٰ لِمَن كَانَ لَهُ

قَلْبٌ أَوْ أَلْقَى السَّمْعَ وَهُوَ شَهِيدٌ ۝

وَلَقَدْ خَلَقْنَا السَّمَاوَاتِ وَالْأَرْضَ

وَمَا بَيْنَهُمَا فِي سِتَّةِ أَيَّامٍ

وَمَا مَسَّنَا مِن لُّغُوبٍ ۝ فَاصْبِرْ

عَلَىٰ مَا يَقُولُونَ وَسَبِّحْ بِحَمْدِ

رَبِّكَ قَبْلَ طُلُوعِ الشَّمْسِ وَقَبْلَ

الْغُرُوبِ ۝ وَمِنَ الَّيْلِ فَسَبِّحْهُ

وَأَدْبَارَ السُّجُودِ ۝ وَاسْتَمِعْ يَوْمَ

to the Righteous, - no more a thing distant.

32. (A voice will say:) "This is what was promised for you, - for every one who turned (to Allah) in sincere repentance, who kept (His Law)",

33. "Who feared (Allah) Most Gracious unseen, and brought a heart turned in devotion (to Him):"

34. "Enter you therein in Peace and Security; this is a Day of Eternal Life!"

35. There will be for them therein all that they wish, - and more besides in Our Presence.

36. But how many generations before them did We destroy (for their sins), - stronger in power than they? Then did they wander through the land: was there any place of escape (for them)?

37. Verily

لِّلْمُتَّقِينَ غَيْرَ بَعِيدٍ ۞ هٰذَا مَا

تُوعَدُونَ لِكُلِّ أَوَّابٍ حَفِيظٍ ۞

مَّنْ خَشِيَ الرَّحْمٰنَ بِالْغَيْبِ وَجَاءَ

بِقَلْبٍ مُّنِيبٍ ۞ ادْخُلُوهَا بِسَلَامٍ

ذٰلِكَ يَوْمُ الْخُلُودِ ۞ لَهُم مَّا

يَشَاءُونَ فِيهَا وَلَدَيْنَا مَزِيدٌ ۞

وَكَمْ أَهْلَكْنَا قَبْلَهُم مِّن قَرْنٍ

هُمْ أَشَدُّ مِنْهُم بَطْشًا فَنَقَّبُوا فِي

الْبِلَادِ هَلْ مِن مَّحِيصٍ ۞ إِنَّ

throw him into a severe Chastisement."

27. His Companion will say: "Our Lord! I did not make him transgress, but he was (himself) far astray."

28. He will say: "Dispute not with each other in My Presence: I had already in advance sent you Warning."

29. "The Word changes not before Me, and I do not the least injustice to My servants."

30. That Day We will ask Hell, "Are you filled to the full?" It will say, "Are there any more (to come)?"

31. And the Garden will be brought near

فَأَلْقِيَاهُ فِى الْعَذَابِ الشَّدِيدِ ۝

قَالَ قَرِينُهُ رَبَّنَا مَآ أَطْغَيْتُهُ

وَلَكِنْ كَانَ فِى ضَلَلٍ بَعِيدٍ ۝

قَالَ لَا تَخْتَصِمُوا لَدَىَّ وَقَدْ

قَدَّمْتُ إِلَيْكُمْ بِالْوَعِيدِ ۝ مَا

يُبَدَّلُ الْقَوْلُ لَدَىَّ وَمَآ أَنَا

بِظَلَّامٍ لِّلْعَبِيدِ ۝ يَوْمَ نَقُولُ

لِجَهَنَّمَ هَلِ امْتَلَأْتِ وَتَقُولُ هَلْ

مِن مَّزِيدٍ ۝ وَأُزْلِفَتِ الْجَنَّةُ

that will be the Day whereof Warning (had been given).

21. And there will come forth every soul: with each will be an (Angel) to drive, and an (Angel) to bear witness.

22. (It will be said:) "You were heedless of this; now have We removed your veil, and sharp is your sight this Day!"

23. And his Companion will say: "Here is (his Record) ready with me!"

24. (The sentence will be:) "Throw, both of you into Hell every contumacious Rejecter (of Allah)!" -

25. "Who forbade what was good, transgressed all bounds, cast doubts and suspicions;".

26. "Who set up another god beside Allah:

ذٰلِكَ يَوْمُ الْوَعِيدِ ۞ وَجَآءَتْ كُلُّ

نَفْسٍ مَّعَهَا سَآئِقٌ وَّشَهِيدٌ ۞

لَقَدْ كُنْتَ فِيْ غَفْلَةٍ مِّنْ هٰذَا

فَكَشَفْنَا عَنْكَ غِطَآءَكَ فَبَصَرُكَ

الْيَوْمَ حَدِيْدٌ ۞ وَقَالَ قَرِيْنُهٗ

هٰذَا مَا لَدَيَّ عَتِيْدٌ ۞ اَلْقِيَا

فِيْ جَهَنَّمَ كُلَّ كَفَّارٍ عَنِيْدٍ

۞ مَّنَّاعٍ لِّلْخَيْرِ مُعْتَدٍ مُّرِيْبِ

الَّذِيْ جَعَلَ مَعَ اللهِ اِلٰهًا اٰخَرَ

16. It was We Who created man, and We know what dark suggestions his soul makes to him: for We are nearer to him than (his) jugular vein.

17. Behold, two (guardian Angels) appointed to learn (his doings and noted them), one sitting on the right and one on the left.

18. Not a word does he utter but there is a sentinel by him, ready (to note it).

19. And the stupor of death will bring Truth (before his eyes): "This was the thing which you were trying to escape!"

20. And the Trumpet shall be blown:

وَلَقَدْ خَلَقْنَا الْإِنسَانَ وَنَعْلَمُ

مَا تُوَسْوِسُ بِهِ نَفْسُهُ ۖ وَنَحْنُ

أَقْرَبُ إِلَيْهِ مِنْ حَبْلِ الْوَرِيدِ ۞

إِذْ يَتَلَقَّى الْمُتَلَقِّيَانِ عَنِ الْيَمِينِ

وَعَنِ الشِّمَالِ قَعِيدٌ ۞ مَا

يَلْفِظُ مِن قَوْلٍ إِلَّا لَدَيْهِ

رَقِيبٌ عَتِيدٌ ۞ وَجَاءَتْ سَكْرَةُ

الْمَوْتِ بِالْحَقِّ ۚ ذَٰلِكَ مَا كُنتَ

مِنْهُ تَحِيدُ ۞ وَنُفِخَ فِي الصُّورِ

with shoots of fruit-stalks, piled one over another; -

11. As sustenance for (Allah's) servants; - and We give (new) life therewith to land that is dead: thus will be the Resurrection.

12. Before them was denied (the Hereafter) by the People of Noah, the Companions of the Rass, the Thamud,

13. The 'Ad, Pharaoh, the Brethren of Lut,

14. The Companions of the Wood, and the People of Tubba'; each one (of them) rejected the Apostles, and My Warning was duly fulfilled (in them).

15. Were We then weary with the first Creation, that they should be in confused doubt about a new Creation?

لَّهَا طَلْعٌ نَّضِيدٌ ۞ رِّزْقًا لِّلْعِبَادِ

وَأَحْيَيْنَا بِهِ بَلْدَةً مَّيْتًا ۚ كَذَٰلِكَ

الْخُرُوجُ ۞ كَذَّبَتْ قَبْلَهُمْ قَوْمُ

نُوحٍ وَّأَصْحَابُ الرَّسِّ وَثَمُودُ

وَعَادٌ وَّفِرْعَوْنُ وَإِخْوَانُ لُوطٍ

وَّأَصْحَابُ الْأَيْكَةِ وَقَوْمُ تُبَّعٍ ۚ كُلٌّ

كَذَّبَ الرُّسُلَ فَحَقَّ وَعِيدِ ۞

أَفَعَيِينَا بِالْخَلْقِ الْأَوَّلِ ۚ بَلْ هُمْ

فِي لَبْسٍ مِّنْ خَلْقٍ جَدِيدٍ ۞

6. Do they not look at the sky above them? - How We have made it and adorned it, and there are no flaws in it?

7. And the earth - We have spread it out, and set thereon mountains standing firm, and produced therein every kind of beautiful growth (in pairs) -

8. To be observed and commemorated by every devotee turning (to Allah).

9. And We send down from the sky rain charged with blessing, and We produce therewith gardens and grain for harvests;

10. And tall (and stately) palm-trees,

اَفَلَمْ يَنْظُرُوۡۤا اِلَى السَّمَآءِ فَوْقَهُمْ

كَيْفَ بَنَيۡنٰهَا وَزَيَّنّٰهَا وَمَا لَهَا

مِنْ فُرُوۡجٍ ۞ وَالْاَرْضَ مَدَدْنٰهَا

وَاَلْقَيۡنَا فِيۡهَا رَوَاسِىَ وَاَنۡبَتۡنَا

فِيۡهَا مِنْ كُلِّ زَوۡجٍۭ بَهِيۡجٍ ۞

تَبۡصِرَةً وَّذِكۡرٰى لِكُلِّ عَبۡدٍ

مُّنِيۡبٍ ۞ وَنَزَّلۡنَا مِنَ السَّمَآءِ

مَآءً مُّبٰرَكًا فَاَنۡبَتۡنَا بِهٖ جَنّٰتٍ

وَّحَبَّ الْحَصِيۡدِ ۞ وَالنَّخۡلَ بٰسِقٰتٍ

Qaaf

Bismillahir-Rahmanir-Rahim

1.　Qaf: by the Glorious Qur'an (You are Allha's Apostle).

2.　But they wonder that there has come to them a warner from among themselves. So the unbelievers say: "This is a wonderful thing!"

3.　"What! When we die and become dust, (shall we live again?) That is a (sort of) return far (from our understanding)."

4.　We already know how much of them the earth takes away: with Us is a record guarding (the full account).

5.　But they deny the Truth when it comes to them: so they are in a confused state.

بِسْمِ اللهِ الرَّحْمٰنِ الرَّحِيمِ

قٓ ۚ وَالْقُرْاٰنِ الْمَجِيدِ ۙ بَلْ عَجِبُوْا

اَنْ جَآءَهُمْ مُّنْذِرٌ مِّنْهُمْ فَقَالَ

الْكٰفِرُوْنَ هٰذَا شَيْءٌ عَجِيْبٌ ۚ

ءَاِذَا مِتْنَا وَكُنَّا تُرَابًا ۚ ذٰلِكَ رَجْعٌ

بَعِيْدٌ ۚ قَدْ عَلِمْنَا مَا تَنْقُصُ

الْاَرْضُ مِنْهُمْ ۚ وَعِنْدَنَا كِتٰبٌ

حَفِيْظٌ ۚ بَلْ كَذَّبُوْا بِالْحَقِّ لَمَّا

جَآءَهُمْ فَهُمْ فِيْٓ اَمْرٍ مَّرِيْجٍ ۚ

But Allah knows all that is in the heavens and on earth: He has full knowledge of all things.

17. They impress on you as a favour that they have embraced Islam. Say, "Count not your Islam as a favour upon me: No, Allah has conferred a favour upon you that He has guided you to the faith, if you be true and sincere."

18. "Verily Allah knows the secrets of the heavens and the earth: and Allah sees well all that you do."

وَاللّٰهُ يَعْلَمُ مَا فِى السَّمٰوٰتِ

وَمَا فِى الْاَرْضِ ۗ وَاللّٰهُ بِكُلِّ

شَىْءٍ عَلِيْمٌ ۰۱ يَمُنُّوْنَ عَلَيْكَ

اَنْ اَسْلَمُوْا ۗ قُلْ لَّا تَمُنُّوْا عَلَىَّ

اِسْلَامَكُمْ ۚ بَلِ اللّٰهُ يَمُنُّ عَلَيْكُمْ

اَنْ هَدٰىكُمْ لِلْاِيْمَانِ اِنْ كُنْتُمْ

صٰدِقِيْنَ ۰۱ اِنَّ اللّٰهَ يَعْلَمُ غَيْبَ

السَّمٰوٰتِ وَالْاَرْضِ ۗ وَاللّٰهُ بَصِيْرٌ

بِمَا تَعْمَلُوْنَ ۰۱

has Faith entered your hearts. But if you obey Allah and His Apostle, He will not belittle any of your deeds: for Allah is Oft-Forgiving, Most Merciful."

15. Only those are believers who have believed in Allah and His Apostle, and have never since doubted, but have striven with their belongings and their persons in the Cause of Allah: such are the sincere ones.

16. Say: "What! Will you instruct Allah about your religion?

يَدْخُلِ الْإِيْمَانُ فِىْ قُلُوْبِكُمْ ۚ

وَإِنْ تُطِيْعُوا اللّٰهَ وَرَسُوْلَهٗ

لَا يَلِتْكُمْ مِّنْ اَعْمَالِكُمْ شَيْئًا ۗ

إِنَّ اللّٰهَ غَفُوْرٌ رَّحِيْمٌ ۞ إِنَّمَا

الْمُؤْمِنُوْنَ الَّذِيْنَ اٰمَنُوْا بِاللّٰهِ

وَرَسُوْلِهٖ ثُمَّ لَمْ يَرْتَابُوْا وَجَاهَدُوْا

بِاَمْوَالِهِمْ وَاَنْفُسِهِمْ فِىْ سَبِيْلِ

اللّٰهِ ۗ اُولٰٓئِكَ هُمُ الصّٰدِقُوْنَ ۞

قُلْ اَتُعَلِّمُوْنَ اللّٰهَ بِدِيْنِكُمْ ۗ

to eat the flesh of his dead brother? No, you would abhor it … But fear Allah: for Allah is Oft-Returning, Most Merciful.

13. O mankind! We created you from a single (pair) of a male and a female, and made you into nations and tribes, that you may know each other (not that you may despise each other). Verily the most honoured of you in the sight of Allah is (he who is) the most righteous of you. And Allah has full Knowledge and is Well Acquainted (with all things).

14. The desert Arabs say, "We believe." Say, "You have no faith; but you (only)say, 'We have submitted our wills to Allah,' for not yet

أَحَدُكُمْ أَنْ يَّأْكُلَ لَحْمَ أَخِيهِ

مَيْتًا فَكَرِهْتُمُوهُ ۚ وَاتَّقُوا اللّٰهَ ۚ

إِنَّ اللّٰهَ تَوَّابٌ رَّحِيمٌ ۝ يٰٓأَيُّهَا

النَّاسُ إِنَّا خَلَقْنٰكُمْ مِّنْ ذَكَرٍ

وَّأُنْثٰى وَجَعَلْنٰكُمْ شُعُوبًا وَّقَبَآئِلَ

لِتَعَارَفُوا ۚ إِنَّ أَكْرَمَكُمْ عِنْدَ اللّٰهِ

أَتْقٰكُمْ ۚ إِنَّ اللّٰهَ عَلِيمٌ خَبِيرٌ ۝

قَالَتِ الْأَعْرَابُ أٰمَنَّا ۖ قُلْ لَّمْ

تُؤْمِنُوا وَلٰكِنْ قُولُوا أَسْلَمْنَا وَلَمَّا

at others: it may be that the (latter are better than the (former): nor defame nor be sarcastic to each other, nor call each other by (offensive) nicknames: ill-seeming is a name connoting wickedness, (to be used of one) after he has believed: and those who do not desist are (indeed) doing wrong.

12. O you who believe! Avoid suspicion as much (as possible): for suspicion in some cases is a sin: and spy not on each other behind their backs. Would any of you like

مِّن نِّسَآءٍ عَسَىٰ أَن يَّكُنَّ خَيْرًا

مِّنْهُنَّ ۖ وَلَا تَلْمِزُوٓا أَنفُسَكُمْ وَلَا

تَنَابَزُوا بِالْأَلْقَابِ ۖ بِئْسَ الِاسْمُ

الْفُسُوقُ بَعْدَ الْإِيمَانِ ۚ وَمَن لَّمْ

يَتُبْ فَأُولَٰئِكَ هُمُ الظَّٰلِمُونَ ﴿١١﴾

يَٰٓأَيُّهَا الَّذِينَ آمَنُوا اجْتَنِبُوا

كَثِيرًا مِّنَ الظَّنِّ إِنَّ بَعْضَ

الظَّنِّ إِثْمٌ ۖ وَلَا تَجَسَّسُوا وَلَا

يَغْتَب بَّعْضُكُم بَعْضًا ۚ أَيُحِبُّ

then fight you (all) against the one that transgresses until it complies with the Command of Allah; but if it complies, then make peace between them with justice, and be fair: for Allah loves those who are fair (and just).

10. The believers are but a single brotherhood: so make peace and reconciliation between your two (contending) brothers; and fear Allah, that you may receive Mercy.

11. O you who believe! Let not some men among you laugh at others: it may be that the (latter) are better than the (former): nor let some women laugh

فَقَاتِلُوا الَّتِي تَبْغِي حَتّٰى تَفِيٓءَ
إِلٰٓى أَمْرِ اللّٰهِ ۚ فَإِنْ فَآءَتْ فَأَصْلِحُوا
بَيْنَهُمَا بِالْعَدْلِ وَأَقْسِطُوا ۖ إِنَّ
اللّٰهَ يُحِبُّ الْمُقْسِطِينَ ۝ إِنَّمَا
الْمُؤْمِنُونَ إِخْوَةٌ فَأَصْلِحُوا بَيْنَ
أَخَوَيْكُمْ ۚ وَاتَّقُوا اللّٰهَ لَعَلَّكُمْ
تُرْحَمُونَ ۝ يٰٓأَيُّهَا الَّذِينَ ءَامَنُوا
لَا يَسْخَرْ قَوْمٌ مِّنْ قَوْمٍ عَسٰىٓ
أَن يَكُونُوا خَيْرًا مِّنْهُمْ وَلَا نِسَآءٌ

you would certainly fall into misfortune: but Allah has endeared the Faith to you, and has made it beautiful in your hearts, and He has made hateful to you Unbelief, wickedness, and rebellion: such indeed are those who walk in righteousness; -

8. A Grace and Favour from Allah; and Allah is full of Knowledge and Wisdom.

9. If two parties among the believers fall into a quarrel, make you peace between them: but if one of them transgresses beyond bounds against the other,

مِنَ الْاَمْرِ لَعَنِتُّمْ وَلٰكِنَّ اللّٰهَ

حَبَّبَ اِلَيْكُمُ الْاِيْمَانَ وَزَيَّنَهٗ

فِيْ قُلُوْبِكُمْ وَكَرَّهَ اِلَيْكُمُ الْكُفْرَ

وَالْفُسُوْقَ وَالْعِصْيَانَ ؕ اُولٰٓئِكَ هُمُ

الرّٰشِدُوْنَ ۙ فَضْلًا مِّنَ اللّٰهِ

وَنِعْمَةً ؕ وَاللّٰهُ عَلِيْمٌ حَكِيْمٌ ۝

وَاِنْ طَآئِفَتٰنِ مِنَ الْمُؤْمِنِيْنَ

اقْتَتَلُوْا فَاَصْلِحُوْا بَيْنَهُمَا ۚ فَاِنْ

بَغَتْ اِحْدٰىهُمَا عَلَى الْاُخْرٰى

the inner apartments - most of them lack understanding.

5.   If only they had patience until you could come out to them, it would be best for them: but Allah is Oft-Forgiving, Most Merciful.

6.   O you who believe! If a wicked person comes to you with any news, ascertain the truth, lest you harm people unwittingly, and afterwards become full of repentance for what you have done.

7.   And know that among you is Allah's Apostle: were he, in many matters, to follow your (wishes)

الْحُجُرٰتِ اَكْثَرُهُمْ لَا يَعْقِلُوْنَ ۝

وَلَوْ اَنَّهُمْ صَبَرُوْا حَتّٰى تَخْرُجَ

اِلَيْهِمْ لَكَانَ خَيْرًا لَّهُمْ ۗ وَاللهُ

غَفُوْرٌ رَّحِيْمٌ ۝ يٰٓاَيُّهَا الَّذِيْنَ

اٰمَنُوْۤا اِنْ جَاۤءَكُمْ فَاسِقٌۢ بِنَبَاٍ

فَتَبَيَّنُوْۤا اَنْ تُصِيْبُوْا قَوْمًا

بِجَهَالَةٍ فَتُصْبِحُوْا عَلٰى مَا فَعَلْتُمْ

نٰدِمِيْنَ ۝ وَاعْلَمُوْۤا اَنَّ فِيْكُمْ

رَسُوْلَ اللهِ ۗ لَوْ يُطِيْعُكُمْ فِيْ كَثِيْرٍ

your voices above the voice of the Prophet, nor speak aloud to him in talk, as you may speak aloud to one another, lest your deeds become vain and you perceive not.

3.   Those that lower their voices in the presence of Allah's Apostle, - their hearts has Allah tested for piety: for them is Forgiveness and a great Reward.

4.   Those who shout out to you from without

أَصْوَاتَكُمْ فَوْقَ صَوْتِ النَّبِيِّ

وَلَا تَجْهَرُوا لَهُ بِالْقَوْلِ كَجَهْرِ

بَعْضِكُمْ لِبَعْضٍ أَنْ تَحْبَطَ

أَعْمَالُكُمْ وَأَنْتُمْ لَا تَشْعُرُونَ ۝

إِنَّ الَّذِينَ يَغُضُّونَ أَصْوَاتَهُمْ

عِنْدَ رَسُولِ اللّٰهِ أُولٰئِكَ الَّذِينَ

امْتَحَنَ اللّٰهُ قُلُوبَهُمْ لِلتَّقْوٰى

لَهُمْ مَغْفِرَةٌ وَأَجْرٌ عَظِيمٌ ۝ إِنَّ

الَّذِينَ يُنَادُونَكَ مِنْ وَّرَاءِ

its own stem, (filling) the sowers with wonder and delight. As a result, it fills the unbelievers with rage at them. Allah has promised those among them who believe and do righteous deeds forgiveness, and a great Reward.

Al-Hujurat
(The Inner Apartments)

Bismillahir-Rahmanir-Rahim

1. O You who believe! Put not yourselves forward before Allah and His Apostle; but fear Allah: for Allah is He Who hears and knows all things.

2. O you who believe! Raise not

سُوقِهِ يُعْجِبُ الزُّرَّاعَ لِيَغِيظَ

بِهِمُ الْكُفَّارَ ۗ وَعَدَ اللَّهُ الَّذِينَ

ءَامَنُوا وَعَمِلُوا الصَّلِحَٰتِ مِنْهُم

مَّغْفِرَةً وَأَجْرًا عَظِيمًا ۝

سُورَةُ الحُجُرَاتِ مَدَنِيَّةٌ ۝ بِسْمِ اللَّهِ الرَّحْمَٰنِ الرَّحِيمِ ءَايَاتُهَا ١٨ وَرُكُوعَاتُهَا ٢

يَٰٓأَيُّهَا الَّذِينَ ءَامَنُوا لَا تُقَدِّمُوا

بَيْنَ يَدَيِ اللَّهِ وَرَسُولِهِ ۖ وَاتَّقُوا

اللَّهَ ۚ إِنَّ اللَّهَ سَمِيعٌ عَلِيمٌ ۝

يَٰٓأَيُّهَا الَّذِينَ ءَامَنُوا لَا تَرْفَعُوٓا

and enough is Allah for a Witness.

29.   Muhammad is the Apostle of Allah; and those who are with him are strong against unbelievers, (but) compassionate amongst each other. You will see them bow and prostrate themselves (in prayer), seeking Grace from Allah and (His) Good Pleasure. On their faces are their marks, (being) the traces of their prostration. This is their similitude in the Taurat; and their similitude in the Gospel is: like a seed which sends forth its blade, then makes it strong; it then becomes thick, and it stands on

كُلِّهِ ۖ وَكَفٰى بِاللّٰهِ شَهِيْدًا ۗ مُحَمَّدٌ

رَّسُوْلُ اللّٰهِ ۚ وَالَّذِيْنَ مَعَهٗٓ

اَشِدَّآءُ عَلَى الْكُفَّارِ رُحَمَآءُ بَيْنَهُمْ

تَرٰىهُمْ رُكَّعًا سُجَّدًا يَّبْتَغُوْنَ

فَضْلًا مِّنَ اللّٰهِ وَرِضْوَانًا ۖ سِيْمَاهُمْ

فِيْ وُجُوْهِهِمْ مِّنْ اَثَرِ السُّجُوْدِ ؕ

ذٰلِكَ مَثَلُهُمْ فِى التَّوْرٰىةِ ؚۖ وَمَثَلُهُمْ

فِى الْاِنْجِيْلِ ۚ كَزَرْعٍ اَخْرَجَ شَطْاَهٗ

فَاٰزَرَهٗ فَاسْتَغْلَظَ فَاسْتَوٰى عَلٰى

Allah has full knowledge of all things.

27. Truly did Allah fulfil the vision for His Apostle: you shall enter the Sacred Mosque, if Allah wills, with minds secure, heads shaved, hair cut short, and without fear. For He knew what you knew not, and He granted, besides this, a speedy victory.

28. It is He Who has sent His Apostle with Guidance and the Religion of Truth, to proclaim it over all religion:

اللهُ بِكُلِّ شَيْءٍ عَلِيْمًا ۞ لَقَدْ

صَدَقَ اللهُ رَسُوْلَهُ الرُّءْيَا بِالْحَقِّ ۚ

لَتَدْخُلُنَّ الْمَسْجِدَ الْحَرَامَ اِنْ

شَاءَ اللهُ اٰمِنِيْنَ مُحَلِّقِيْنَ

رُءُوْسَكُمْ وَمُقَصِّرِيْنَ لَا تَخَافُوْنَ ۗ

فَعَلِمَ مَا لَمْ تَعْلَمُوْا فَجَعَلَ مِنْ

دُوْنِ ذٰلِكَ فَتْحًا قَرِيْبًا ۞ هُوَ

الَّذِيْٓ اَرْسَلَ رَسُوْلَهُ بِالْهُدٰى

وَدِيْنِ الْحَقِّ لِيُظْهِرَهُ عَلَى الدِّيْنِ

and on whose account a crime would have accrued to you without (your) knowledge, (Allah would have allowed you to force your way, but He held back your hands) that He may admit to His Mercy whom He wills. If they had been apart, We should certainly have punished the unbelievers among them with a grievous Punishment.

26.   While the unbelievers got up in their hearts heat and cant - the heat and cant of ignorance, - Allah sent down His Tranquillity to His Apostle and to the believers, and made them stick close to the command of self-restraint; and well were they entitled to it and worthy of it. And

فَتُصِيبَكُم مِّنْهُم مَّعَرَّةٌ بِغَيْرِ عِلْمٍ

لِّيُدْخِلَ اللّهُ فِي رَحْمَتِهِ مَن

يَشَاءُ لَوْ تَزَيَّلُوا لَعَذَّبْنَا الَّذِينَ

كَفَرُوا مِنْهُمْ عَذَابًا أَلِيمًا ۝ إِذْ

جَعَلَ الَّذِينَ كَفَرُوا فِي قُلُوبِهِمُ

الْحَمِيَّةَ حَمِيَّةَ الْجَاهِلِيَّةِ فَأَنزَلَ

اللّهُ سَكِينَتَهُ عَلَى رَسُولِهِ وَعَلَى

الْمُؤْمِنِينَ وَأَلْزَمَهُمْ كَلِمَةَ التَّقْوَى

وَكَانُوا أَحَقَّ بِهَا وَأَهْلَهَا وَكَانَ

in the practice (approved) of Allah.

24.   And it is He Who has restrained their hands from you and your hands from them in the midst of Makka, after that He gave you the victory over them. And Allah sees well all that you do.

25.   They are the ones who denied Revelation and hindered you from the Sacred Mosque and obstructed the sacrificial animals, detained from reaching their place of sacrifice. Had there not been believing men and believing women whom you did not know that you were trampling down

لِسُنَّةِ اللّٰهِ تَبۡدِيۡلًا ۞ وَهُوَ الَّذِىۡ

كَفَّ اَيۡدِيَهُمۡ عَنۡكُمۡ وَ اَيۡدِيَكُمۡ

عَنۡهُمۡ بِبَطۡنِ مَكَّةَ مِنۡۢ بَعۡدِ اَنۡ

اَظۡفَرَكُمۡ عَلَيۡهِمۡ ؕ وَكَانَ اللّٰهُ بِمَا

تَعۡمَلُوۡنَ بَصِيۡرًا ۞ هُمُ الَّذِيۡنَ كَفَرُوۡا

وَصَدُّوۡكُمۡ عَنِ الۡمَسۡجِدِ الۡحَرَامِ

وَالۡهَدۡىَ مَعۡكُوۡفًا اَنۡ يَّبۡلُغَ مَحِلَّهٗ ؕ

وَلَوۡلَا رِجَالٌ مُّؤۡمِنُوۡنَ وَنِسَآءٌ

مُّؤۡمِنٰتٌ لَّمۡ تَعۡلَمُوۡهُمۡ اَنۡ تَطَـُٔوۡهُمۡ

these beforehand; and He has restrained the hands of men from you; that it may be a Sign for the believers, and that He may guide you to a Straight Path;

21. And other gains (there are), which are not within your power, but which Allah has compassed and Allah has power over all things.

22. If the unbelievers should fight you, they would certainly turn their backs; then would they find neither protector nor helper.

23. (Such has been) the practice (approved) of Allah already in the past: no change will you find

هٰذِهٖ وَكَفَّ أَيْدِىَ النَّاسِ عَنْكُمْ ۚ

وَلِتَكُوْنَ اٰيَةً لِّلْمُؤْمِنِيْنَ وَيَهْدِيَكُمْ

صِرَاطًا مُّسْتَقِيْمًا ۙ وَّأُخْرٰى لَمْ

تَقْدِرُوْا عَلَيْهَا قَدْ أَحَاطَ اللّٰهُ

بِهَا ۚ وَكَانَ اللّٰهُ عَلٰى كُلِّ شَىْءٍ

قَدِيْرًا ۝ وَلَوْ قَاتَلَكُمُ الَّذِيْنَ كَفَرُوْا

لَوَلَّوُا الْأَدْبَارَ ثُمَّ لَا يَجِدُوْنَ

وَلِيًّا وَّلَا نَصِيْرًا ۝ سُنَّةَ اللّٰهِ الَّتِىْ

قَدْ خَلَتْ مِنْ قَبْلُ ۖ وَلَنْ تَجِدَ

rivers flow; and he who turns back, (Allah) will punish him with a grievous Chastisement.

18. Allah's Good Pleasure was on the believers when they swore fealty to you under the Tree: He knew what was in their hearts, and He sent down tranquillity to them; and He rewarded them with a speedy victory;

19. And many gains will they acquire (besides): and Allah is Exalted in Power, full of Wisdom.

20. Allah has promised you many gains that you shall acquire, and He has given you

الْآثَهُمْ وَمَنْ يَّتَوَلَّ يُعَذِّبْهُ عَذَابًا
أَلِيمًا ۝ لَقَدْ رَضِيَ اللّٰهُ عَنِ
الْمُؤْمِنِيْنَ اِذْ يُبَايِعُوْنَكَ تَحْتَ
الشَّجَرَةِ فَعَلِمَ مَا فِيْ قُلُوبِهِمْ
فَأَنْزَلَ السَّكِيْنَةَ عَلَيْهِمْ وَأَثَابَهُمْ
فَتْحًا قَرِيْبًا ۝ وَّمَغَانِمَ كَثِيْرَةً
يَّأْخُذُوْنَهَا ۗ وَكَانَ اللّٰهُ عَزِيْزًا
حَكِيْمًا ۝ وَعَدَكُمُ اللّٰهُ مَغَانِمَ
كَثِيْرَةً تَأْخُذُوْنَهَا فَعَجَّلَ لَكُمْ

"You shall be summoned (to fight) against a people given to vehement war: then shall you fight, or they shall submit. Then if you show obedience, Allah will grant you a goodly reward, but if you turn back as you did before, He will punish you with a grievous Chastisement."

17. No blame is there on the blind, nor is there blame on the lame, nor on one ill (if he joins not the war): but he that obeys Allah and His Apostle, - (Allah) will admit him to Gardens beneath which

سَتُدْعَوْنَ اِلٰى قَوْمٍ اُولِى بَاْسٍ

شَدِيْدٍ تُقَاتِلُوْنَهُمْ اَوْ يُسْلِمُوْنَ فَاِنْ

تُطِيْعُوْا يُؤْتِكُمُ اللّٰهُ اَجْرًا حَسَنًا

وَاِنْ تَتَوَلَّوْا كَمَا تَوَلَّيْتُمْ مِّنْ

قَبْلُ يُعَذِّبْكُمْ عَذَابًا اَلِيْمًا ۞

لَيْسَ عَلَى الْاَعْمٰى حَرَجٌ وَّلَا عَلَى

الْاَعْرَجِ حَرَجٌ وَّلَا عَلَى الْمَرِيْضِ

حَرَجٌ وَمَنْ يُّطِعِ اللّٰهَ وَرَسُوْلَهُ

يُدْخِلْهُ جَنّٰتٍ تَجْرِيْ مِنْ تَحْتِهَا

whom He wills: but Allah is Oft-Forgiving, Most Merciful.

15. Those who lagged behind (will say), when you (are free to) march and take booty (in war): "Permit us to follow you." They wish to change Allah's Decree: Say: "Not thus will you follow us: Allah has already declared (this) beforehand": then they will say, "But you are jealous of us." No, but little do they understand (such things).

16. Say to the desert Arabs who lagged behind:

مَن يَشَآءُ ۚ وَكَانَ اللّٰهُ غَفُوْرًا

رَّحِيْمًا ۞ سَيَقُوْلُ الْمُخَلَّفُوْنَ اِذَا

انْطَلَقْتُمْ اِلَىٰ مَغَانِمَ لِتَأْخُذُوْهَا

ذَرُوْنَا نَتَّبِعْكُمْ ۚ يُرِيْدُوْنَ اَنْ

يُّبَدِّلُوْا كَلٰمَ اللّٰهِ ۚ قُلْ لَّنْ تَتَّبِعُوْنَا

كَذٰلِكُمْ قَالَ اللّٰهُ مِنْ قَبْلُ ۚ

فَسَيَقُوْلُوْنَ بَلْ تَحْسُدُوْنَنَا ۚ بَلْ

كَانُوْا لَا يَفْقَهُوْنَ اِلَّا قَلِيْلًا ۞

قُلْ لِّلْمُخَلَّفِيْنَ مِنَ الْاَعْرَابِ

or to give you some profit? But Allah is Well Acquainted with all that you do.

12. "No, you thought that the Apostle and the believers would never return to their families; this seemed pleasing in your hearts, and you conceived an evil thought, for you are a people lost (in wickedness)."

13. And if any believe not in Allah and His Apostle, We have prepared, for those who reject Allah, a Blazing Fire!

14. To Allah belongs the dominion of the heavens and the earth: He forgives whom He wills, and He punishes

اَوۡ اَرَادَ بِكُمۡ نَفۡعًا ۚ بَلۡ كَانَ اللّٰهُ

بِمَا تَعۡمَلُوۡنَ خَبِيۡرًا ۞ بَلۡ ظَنَنۡتُمۡ

اَنۡ لَّنۡ يَّنۡقَلِبَ الرَّسُوۡلُ وَالۡمُؤۡمِنُوۡنَ

اِلٰۤى اَهۡلِيۡهِمۡ اَبَدًا وَّزُيِّنَ ذٰلِكَ فِيۡ

قُلُوۡبِكُمۡ وَظَنَنۡتُمۡ ظَنَّ السَّوۡءِ ۚ وَكُنۡتُمۡ

قَوۡمًۢا بُوۡرًا ۞ وَمَنۡ لَّمۡ يُؤۡمِنۡۢ بِاللّٰهِ

وَرَسُوۡلِهٖ فَاِنَّاۤ اَعۡتَدۡنَا لِلۡكٰفِرِيۡنَ

سَعِيۡرًا ۞ وَلِلّٰهِ مُلۡكُ السَّمٰوٰتِ

وَالۡاَرۡضِ ۚ يَغۡفِرُ لِمَنۡ يَّشَآءُ وَيُعَذِّبُ

Allah: the Hand of Allah is over their hands: then any one who violates his oath, does so to the harm of his own soul, and any one who fulfils what he has covenanted with Allah, - Allah will soon grant him a great Reward.

11. The desert Arabs who lagged behind will say to you: "We were engaged in (looking after) our flocks and herds, and our families: do you then ask forgiveness for us." They say with their tongues what is not in their hearts. Say: "Who then has any power at all (to intervene) on your behalf with Allah, if His Will is to give you some loss

اللهِ يَدُ اللهِ فَوْقَ اَيْدِيهِمْ فَمَنْ

نَّكَثَ فَاِنَّمَا يَنْكُثُ عَلَى نَفْسِهٖ

وَمَنْ اَوْفَىٰ بِمَا عَاهَدَ عَلَيْهُ اللهَ

فَسَيُؤْتِيهِ اَجْرًا عَظِيمًا ۞ سَيَقُوْلُ

لَكَ الْمُخَلَّفُوْنَ مِنَ الْاَعْرَابِ

شَغَلَتْنَآ اَمْوَالُنَا وَاَهْلُوْنَا فَاسْتَغْفِرْ

لَنَا يَقُوْلُوْنَ بِاَلْسِنَتِهِمْ مَّا لَيْسَ

فِيْ قُلُوْبِهِمْ ۗ قُلْ فَمَنْ يَّمْلِكُ لَكُمْ

مِّنَ اللهِ شَيْئًا اِنْ اَرَادَ بِكُمْ ضَرًّا

an evil opinion of Allah. On them is a round of Evil: the Wrath of Allah is on them: He has cursed them and got Hell ready for them: and evil is it for a destination.

7. For to Allah belong the Forces of the heavens and the earth; and Allah is Exalted in Power, full of Wisdom.

8. We have truly sent you as a witness, as a bringer of Glad Tidings, and as a warner:

9. In order that you (O men) may believe in Allah and His Apostle, that you may assist and honour Him, and celebrate His praise morning and evening.

10. Verily those who plight their fealty to you do no less than plight their fealty to

بِٱللَّهِ ظَنَّ ٱلسَّوْءِ ۚ عَلَيْهِمْ دَآئِرَةُ

ٱلسَّوْءِ ۖ وَغَضِبَ ٱللَّهُ عَلَيْهِمْ وَلَعَنَهُمْ

وَأَعَدَّ لَهُمْ جَهَنَّمَ ۖ وَسَآءَتْ مَصِيرًا ۝

وَلِلَّهِ جُنُودُ ٱلسَّمَٰوَٰتِ وَٱلْأَرْضِ ۚ وَكَانَ

ٱللَّهُ عَزِيزًا حَكِيمًا ۝ إِنَّآ أَرْسَلْنَٰكَ

شَٰهِدًا وَمُبَشِّرًا وَنَذِيرًا ۝ لِّتُؤْمِنُوا۟

بِٱللَّهِ وَرَسُولِهِۦ وَتُعَزِّرُوهُ وَتُوَقِّرُوهُ

وَتُسَبِّحُوهُ بُكْرَةً وَأَصِيلًا ۝ إِنَّ

ٱلَّذِينَ يُبَايِعُونَكَ إِنَّمَا يُبَايِعُونَ

the hearts of the believers, that they may add faith to their faith; - for to Allah belong the Forces of the heavens and the earth; and Allah is full of Knowledge and Wisdom; -

5. That He may admit the men and women who believe, to Gardens beneath which rivers flow, to dwell therein for ever, and remove their ills from them; - and that is, in the sight of Allah, the highest achievement (for man), -

6. And that He may punish the Hypocrites, men and women, and the Polytheists men and women, who imagine

قُلُوبُ الْمُؤْمِنِينَ لِيَزْدَادُوا إِيمَانًا

مَّعَ إِيمَانِهِمْ وَلِلَّهِ جُنُودُ السَّمَوَاتِ

وَالْأَرْضِ وَكَانَ اللَّهُ عَلِيمًا حَكِيمًا ۝

لِّيُدْخِلَ الْمُؤْمِنِينَ وَالْمُؤْمِنَاتِ

جَنَّاتٍ تَجْرِي مِن تَحْتِهَا الْأَنْهَارُ

خَالِدِينَ فِيهَا وَيُكَفِّرَ عَنْهُمْ سَيِّئَاتِهِمْ

وَكَانَ ذَلِكَ عِندَ اللَّهِ فَوْزًا عَظِيمًا ۝

وَيُعَذِّبَ الْمُنَافِقِينَ وَالْمُنَافِقَاتِ

وَالْمُشْرِكِينَ وَالْمُشْرِكَاتِ الظَّانِّينَ

If you turn back (from the Path), He will substitute in your stead another people; then they would not be like you!

Al-Fat-h (Victory)

Bismillahir-Rahmanir-Rahim

1.   Verily We have granted you a manifest Victory:

2.   That Allah may forgive you your faults of the past and those to follow; fulfil His favour to you; and guide you on the Straight Way;

3.   And that Allah may help you with powerful help.

4.   It is He Who sent down tranquillity into

وَإِن تَتَوَلَّوْا يَسْتَبْدِلْ قَوْمًا

غَيْرَكُمْ ثُمَّ لَا يَكُونُوٓا أَمْثَالَكُم ۝

بِسْمِ اللَّهِ الرَّحْمَٰنِ الرَّحِيمِ

إِنَّا فَتَحْنَا لَكَ فَتْحًا مُّبِينًا ۝

لِّيَغْفِرَ لَكَ اللَّهُ مَا تَقَدَّمَ مِن

ذَنبِكَ وَمَا تَأَخَّرَ وَيُتِمَّ نِعْمَتَهُ

عَلَيْكَ وَيَهْدِيَكَ صِرَاطًا مُّسْتَقِيمًا ۝

وَيَنصُرَكَ اللَّهُ نَصْرًا عَزِيزًا ۝

هُوَ الَّذِيٓ أَنزَلَ السَّكِينَةَ فِي

36. The life of this world is but play and amusement: and if you believe and guard against Evil, He will grant you your recompense, and will not ask you (to give up) your possessions.

37. If He were to ask you for all of them, and press you, you would covetously withhold, and He would bring out all your ill-feeling.

38. Behold, you are those invited to spend (of your substance) in the Way of Allah: but among you are some that are niggardly. But any who are niggardly are so at the expense of their own souls. But Allah is free of all wants, and it is you that are needy.

إِنَّمَا الْحَيٰوةُ الدُّنْيَا لَعِبٌ وَّلَهْوٌ ۚ

وَإِنْ تُؤْمِنُوْا وَتَتَّقُوْا يُؤْتِكُمْ

أُجُوْرَكُمْ وَلَا يَسْئَلْكُمْ أَمْوَالَكُمْ ۞

إِنْ يَّسْئَلْكُمُوْهَا فَيُحْفِكُمْ تَبْخَلُوْا

وَيُخْرِجْ أَضْغَانَكُمْ ۞ هٰٓأَنْتُمْ

هٰٓؤُلَآءِ تُدْعَوْنَ لِتُنْفِقُوْا فِيْ

سَبِيْلِ اللّٰهِ ۚ فَمِنْكُمْ مَّنْ يَّبْخَلُ ۚ

وَمَنْ يَّبْخَلْ فَإِنَّمَا يَبْخَلُ عَنْ

نَّفْسِهٖ ۚ وَاللّٰهُ الْغَنِيُّ وَأَنْتُمُ الْفُقَرَآءُ ۚ

Allah in the least, but He will make their deeds of no effect.

33. O you who believe! Obey Allah, and obey the A postle, and make not vain your deeds!

34. Those who reject Allah, and hinder (men) from the Path of Allah, then as a disbeliever Allah, - Allah will not forgive them.

35. Be not weary and faint-hearted, crying for peace, when you should be uppermost: for Allah is with you, and will never put you in loss for your (good) deeds.

اللهُ شَيْئًا وَسَيُحْبِطُ أَعْمَالَهُمْ ۞

يَا أَيُّهَا الَّذِينَ آمَنُوا أَطِيعُوا اللهَ

وَأَطِيعُوا الرَّسُولَ وَلَا تُبْطِلُوا

أَعْمَالَكُمْ ۞ إِنَّ الَّذِينَ كَفَرُوا

وَصَدُّوا عَنْ سَبِيلِ اللهِ ثُمَّ

مَاتُوا وَهُمْ كُفَّارٌ فَلَنْ يَغْفِرَ

اللهُ لَهُمْ ۞ فَلَا تَهِنُوا وَتَدْعُوا

إِلَى السَّلْمِ وَأَنْتُمُ الْأَعْلَوْنَ وَاللهُ

مَعَكُمْ وَلَنْ يَتِرَكُمْ أَعْمَالَكُمْ ۞

Allah will not bring to light all their rancour?

30. Had We so willed, We could have shown them up to you, and you should have known them by their marks: but surely you will know them by the tone of their speech! And Allah knows all that you do.

31. And We shall try you until We test those among you who strive their utmost and persevere in patience; and We shall try your reported (mettle).

32. Those who reject Allah, hinder (men) from the Path of Allah, and resist the Apostle, after Guidance has been clearly shown to them, will not injure

اللهُ اَضْغَانَهُمْ ۞ وَلَوْ نَشَآءُ

لَاَرَيْنٰكَهُمْ فَلَعَرَفْتَهُمْ بِسِيمٰهُمْ

وَلَتَعْرِفَنَّهُمْ فِيْ لَحْنِ الْقَوْلِ ۗ وَاللهُ

يَعْلَمُ اَعْمَالَكُمْ ۞ وَلَنَبْلُوَنَّكُمْ

حَتّٰى نَعْلَمَ الْمُجٰهِدِيْنَ مِنْكُمْ

وَالصّٰبِرِيْنَ ۙ وَنَبْلُوَا۟ اَخْبَارَكُمْ ۞ اِنَّ

الَّذِيْنَ كَفَرُوْا وَصَدُّوْا عَنْ سَبِيْلِ

اللهِ وَشَآقُّوا الرَّسُوْلَ مِنْ بَعْدِ

مَا تَبَيَّنَ لَهُمُ الْهُدٰى ۙ لَنْ يَّضُرُّوا

because they said to those who hate what Allah has revealed, "We will obey you in part of (this) matter"; but Allah knows their (inner) secrets.

27. But how (will it be) when the Angels take their souls at death, and smite their faces and their backs?

28. This because they followed that which called forth the Wrath of Allah, and they hated Allah's good pleasure; so He made their deeds of no effect.

29. Or do those in whose hearts is a disease, think that

بِأَنَّهُمْ قَالُوا لِلَّذِينَ كَرِهُوا مَا

نَزَّلَ اللهُ سَنُطِيعُكُمْ فِى بَعْضِ

الْأَمْرِ ۚ وَاللهُ يَعْلَمُ إِسْرَارَهُمْ ۞

فَكَيْفَ إِذَا تَوَفَّتْهُمُ الْمَلٰٓئِكَةُ

يَضْرِبُونَ وُجُوهَهُمْ وَأَدْبَارَهُمْ ۞

ذٰلِكَ بِأَنَّهُمُ اتَّبَعُوا مَا أَسْخَطَ

اللهَ وَكَرِهُوا رِضْوَانَهُ فَأَحْبَطَ

أَعْمَالَهُمْ ۞ أَمْ حَسِبَ الَّذِينَ فِى

قُلُوبِهِمْ مَرَضٌ أَنْ لَّنْ يُخْرِجَ

22. Then, is it to be expected of you, if you were put in authority, that you will do mischief in the land, and break your ties of kith and kin?

23. Such are the men whom Allah has cursed, for He has made them deaf and blinded their sight.

24. Do they not then earnestly seek to understand the Qur'an, or are their hearts locked up by them?

25. Those who turn back as apostates after Guidance was clearly shown to them, - the Evil One has instigated them and buoyed them up with false hopes.

26. This,

لَهُمْ ۞ فَهَلْ عَسَيْتُمْ اِنْ تَوَلَّيْتُمْ

اَنْ تُفْسِدُوْا فِي الْاَرْضِ وَتُقَطِّعُوْۤا

اَرْحَامَكُمْ ۞ اُولٰٓئِكَ الَّذِيْنَ لَعَنَهُمُ

اللّٰهُ فَاَصَمَّهُمْ وَاَعْمٰۤى اَبْصَارَهُمْ ۞

اَفَلَا يَتَدَبَّرُوْنَ الْقُرْاٰنَ اَمْ عَلٰى

قُلُوْبٍ اَقْفَالُهَا ۞ اِنَّ الَّذِيْنَ

ارْتَدُّوْا عَلٰۤى اَدْبَارِهِمْ مِّنْۢ بَعْدِ

مَا تَبَيَّنَ لَهُمُ الْهُدَى ۙ الشَّيْطٰنُ

سَوَّلَ لَهُمْ ۖ وَاَمْلٰى لَهُمْ ۞ ذٰلِكَ

and women who believe: for Allah knows how you move about and how you dwell in your homes.

20. Those who believe say, "Why is not a sura sent down (for us)?" But when a sura of basic or categorical meaning is revealed, and fighting is mentioned therein, you will see those in whose hearts is a disease looking at you with a look of one in swoon at the approach of death. But more fitting for them -

21. Were it to obey and say what is just, and when a matter is resolved on, it were best for them if they were true to Allah.

وَالْمُؤْمِنٰتِ ۗ وَاللّٰهُ يَعْلَمُ مُتَقَلَّبَكُمْ

وَمَثْوٰىكُمْ ۞ وَيَقُوْلُ الَّذِيْنَ اٰمَنُوْا

لَوْلَا نُزِّلَتْ سُوْرَةٌ ۚ فَاِذَآ اُنْزِلَتْ

سُوْرَةٌ مُّحْكَمَةٌ وَّذُكِرَ فِيْهَا الْقِتَالُ ۙ

رَاَيْتَ الَّذِيْنَ فِيْ قُلُوْبِهِمْ مَّرَضٌ

يَنْظُرُوْنَ اِلَيْكَ نَظَرَ الْمَغْشِيِّ عَلَيْهِ

مِنَ الْمَوْتِ ۗ فَاَوْلٰى لَهُمْ ۞ طَاعَةٌ

وَّقَوْلٌ مَّعْرُوْفٌ ۚ فَاِذَا عَزَمَ الْاَمْرُ ۙ

فَلَوْ صَدَقُوا اللّٰهَ لَكَانَ خَيْرًا

"What is it he said just then?"
Such are men whose hearts Allah
has sealed, and who follow their
own lusts.

17. But to those who receive
Guidance, He increases the (light
of) Guidance, and bestows on
them their Piety and Restraint
(from evil).

18. Do they then only wait for
the Hour, - that it should come on
them of a sudden? But already
have come some tokens thereof,
and when it (actually) is on them,
how can they benefit then by their
admonition?

19. Know, therefore, that there
is no god but Allah, and ask
forgiveness for your fault, and for
the men

مَاذَا قَالَ اٰنِفًا ؕ اُولٰٓئِكَ الَّذِيْنَ

طَبَعَ اللّٰهُ عَلٰى قُلُوْبِهِمْ وَاتَّبَعُوْۤا

اَهْوَآءَهُمْ ۞ وَالَّذِيْنَ اهْتَدَوْا زَادَهُمْ

هُدًى وَّاٰتٰهُمْ تَقْوٰىهُمْ ۞ فَهَلْ

يَنْظُرُوْنَ اِلَّا السَّاعَةَ اَنْ تَاْتِيَهُمْ

بَغْتَةً ۚ فَقَدْ جَآءَ اَشْرَاطُهَا ۚ فَاَنّٰى

لَهُمْ اِذَا جَآءَتْهُمْ ذِكْرٰىهُمْ ۞

فَاعْلَمْ اَنَّهٗ لَاۤ اِلٰهَ اِلَّا اللّٰهُ

وَاسْتَغْفِرْ لِذَنْبِكَ وَلِلْمُؤْمِنِيْنَ

rivers of milk of which the taste never changes; rivers of wine, a joy to those who drink; and rivers of honey pure and clear. In it there are for them all kinds of fruits; and Grace from their Lord. (Can those in such Bliss) be compared to such as shall dwell for ever in the Fire, and be given, to drink, boiling water, so that it cuts up their bowels (to pieces)?

16. And among them are men who listen to you, but in the end, when they go out from you, they say to those who have received knowledge,

وَاَنْهٰرٌ مِّنْ لَّبَنٍ لَّمْ يَتَغَيَّرْ طَعْمُهٗ ۖ

وَاَنْهٰرٌ مِّنْ خَمْرٍ لَّذَّةٍ لِّلشّٰرِبِيْنَ ۚ

وَاَنْهٰرٌ مِّنْ عَسَلٍ مُّصَفًّى ۖ وَلَهُمْ

فِيْهَا مِنْ كُلِّ الثَّمَرٰتِ وَمَغْفِرَةٌ

مِّنْ رَّبِّهِمْ ۖ كَمَنْ هُوَ خَالِدٌ فِى

النَّارِ وَسُقُوْا مَآءً حَمِيْمًا فَقَطَّعَ

اَمْعَآءَهُمْ ۞ وَمِنْهُمْ مَّنْ يَّسْتَمِعُ

اِلَيْكَ ۚ حَتّٰى اِذَا خَرَجُوْا مِنْ

عِنْدِكَ قَالُوْا لِلَّذِيْنَ اُوْتُوا الْعِلْمَ

will enjoy (this world) and eat as cattle eat; and the Fire will be their abode.

13. And how many cities, with more power than your city which has driven you out, have We destroyed (for their sins)? And there was none to aid them.

14. Is then one who is on a clear (Path) from his Lord, no better than one to whom the evil of his conduct seems pleasing, and such as follow their own lusts?

15. (Here is) a description of the Garden which the righteous are promised: in it are rivers of water incorruptible;

يَتَمَتَّعُونَ وَيَأْكُلُونَ كَمَا تَأْكُلُ

الْأَنْعَامُ وَالنَّارُ مَثْوًى لَّهُمْ ۝ وَكَأَيِّنْ

مِّنْ قَرْيَةٍ هِيَ أَشَدُّ قُوَّةً مِّنْ

قَرْيَتِكَ الَّتِيٓ أَخْرَجَتْكَ أَهْلَكْنٰهُمْ

فَلَا نَاصِرَ لَهُمْ ۝ أَفَمَنْ كَانَ عَلٰى

بَيِّنَةٍ مِّنْ رَّبِّهٖ كَمَنْ زُيِّنَ لَهٗ

سُوٓءُ عَمَلِهٖ وَاتَّبَعُوٓا أَهْوَآءَهُمْ ۝

مَثَلُ الْجَنَّةِ الَّتِيْ وُعِدَ الْمُتَّقُونَ ۗ

فِيْهَآ أَنْهٰرٌ مِّنْ مَّآءٍ غَيْرِ اٰسِنٍ

their deeds fruitless.

10. Do they not travel through the earth, and see what was the end of those before them (who did evil)? Allah brought utter destruction on them, and similar (fates await) those who reject Allah.

11. That is because Allah is the Protector of those who believe, but those who reject Allah have no protector.

12. Verily Allah will admit those who believe and do righteous deeds, to Gardens beneath which rivers flow; while those who reject Allah

أَعْمَالَهُمْ ۞ أَفَلَمْ يَسِيْرُوْا فِي

الْأَرْضِ فَيَنْظُرُوْا كَيْفَ كَانَ عَاقِبَةُ

الَّذِيْنَ مِنْ قَبْلِهِمْ ۗ دَمَّرَ اللّٰهُ

عَلَيْهِمْ ۖ وَلِلْكٰفِرِيْنَ أَمْثَالُهَا ۞ ذٰلِكَ

بِأَنَّ اللّٰهَ مَوْلَى الَّذِيْنَ اٰمَنُوْا وَأَنَّ

الْكٰفِرِيْنَ لَا مَوْلٰى لَهُمْ ۞ إِنَّ اللّٰهَ

يُدْخِلُ الَّذِيْنَ اٰمَنُوْا وَعَمِلُوا

الصّٰلِحٰتِ جَنّٰتٍ تَجْرِيْ مِنْ

تَحْتِهَا الْأَنْهٰرُ ۗ وَالَّذِيْنَ كَفَرُوْا

some with others. But those who are slain in the Way of Allah, - He will never let their deeds be lost.

5.　Soon will He guide them and improve their condition,

6.　And admit them to the Garden which He has announced for them.

7.　O you who believe! If you will aid (the cause of) Allah, He will aid you, and plant your feet firmly.

8.　But those who reject (Allah), - for them is destruction, and (Allah) will render their deeds worthless.

9.　That is because they hate the Revelation of Allah; so He has made

بَعْضَكُمْ بِبَعْضٍ ۗ وَالَّذِينَ قُتِلُوا

فِي سَبِيلِ اللّٰهِ فَلَنْ يُضِلَّ

أَعْمَالَهُمْ ۞ سَيَهْدِيهِمْ وَيُصْلِحُ

بَالَهُمْ ۞ وَيُدْخِلُهُمُ الْجَنَّةَ عَرَّفَهَا

لَهُمْ ۞ يَا أَيُّهَا الَّذِينَ آمَنُوا إِنْ

تَنْصُرُوا اللّٰهَ يَنْصُرْكُمْ وَيُثَبِّتْ

أَقْدَامَكُمْ ۞ وَالَّذِينَ كَفَرُوا فَتَعْسًا

لَّهُمْ وَأَضَلَّ أَعْمَالَهُمْ ۞ ذَٰلِكَ بِأَنَّهُمْ

كَرِهُوا مَا أَنْزَلَ اللّٰهُ فَأَحْبَطَ

follow falsehood, while those who believe follow the Truth from their Lord: thus does Allah set forth for men their lessons by similitudes.

4.   Therefore, when you meet the unbelievers (in fight), smite at their necks; at length, when you have thoroughly subdued them, bind a bond firmly (on them): thereafter (is the time for) either generosity or ransom: until the war lays down its burdens. Thus (are you commanded): but if it had been Allah's Will, He could certainly have exacted retri-bution from them (Himself); but (He lets you fight) in order to test you,

اتَّبَعُوا الْبَاطِلَ وَاَنَّ الَّذِينَ اٰمَنُوا

اتَّبَعُوا الْحَقَّ مِنْ رَّبِّهِمْ ۖ كَذٰلِكَ

يَضْرِبُ اللهُ لِلنَّاسِ اَمْثَالَهُمْ ۝

فَاِذَا لَقِيْتُمُ الَّذِينَ كَفَرُوْا فَضَرْبَ

الرِّقَابِ ۖ حَتّٰى اِذَآ اَثْخَنْتُمُوْهُمْ

فَشُدُّوا الْوَثَاقَ ۙ فَاِمَّا مَنًّا بَعْدُ

وَاِمَّا فِدَآءً حَتّٰى تَضَعَ الْحَرْبُ

اَوْزَارَهَا ۛ ذٰلِكَ ۛ وَلَوْ يَشَآءُ اللهُ

لَانْتَصَرَ مِنْهُمْ وَلٰكِنْ لِّيَبْلُوَا۟

more than an hour in a single day.
(Yours but) to proclaim the
Message: but shall any be
destroyed except those who
transgress?

Muhammad
Bismillahir-Rahmanir-Rahim

1. Those who reject Allah and
hinder (men) from the Path of
Allah, - their deeds will Allah
render astray (from their mark).

2. But those who believe and
work deeds of righteousness, and
believe in the (Revelation) sent
down to Muhammad - for it is the
Truth from their Lord, - He will
remove from them their ills and
improve their condition.

3. This because those who
reject Allah

اِلَّا سَاعَةً مِّنْ نَّهَارٍ ۢ بَلَٰغٌ ۚ فَهَلْ

يُهْلَكُ اِلَّا الْقَوْمُ الْفٰسِقُوْنَ ۞

بِسْمِ اللّٰهِ الرَّحْمٰنِ الرَّحِيْمِ

اَلَّذِيْنَ كَفَرُوْا وَصَدُّوْا عَنْ سَبِيْلِ

اللّٰهِ اَضَلَّ اَعْمَالَهُمْ ۞ وَالَّذِيْنَ

اٰمَنُوْا وَعَمِلُوا الصّٰلِحٰتِ وَاٰمَنُوْا بِمَا

نُزِّلَ عَلٰى مُحَمَّدٍ وَّهُوَ الْحَقُّ مِنْ

رَّبِّهِمْ ۙ كَفَّرَ عَنْهُمْ سَيِّاٰتِهِمْ وَاَصْلَحَ

بَالَهُمْ ۞ ذٰلِكَ بِاَنَّ الَّذِيْنَ كَفَرُوْا

give life to the dead? Yes, verily He has power over all things.

34. And on the Day that the unbelievers will be placed before the Fire, (they will be asked,) "Is this not the Truth?" They will say, "Yes, by our Lord!" (One will say:) "Then taste you the Chastisement, for that you were wont to deny (Truth)!"

35. Therefore patiently persevere, as did (all) Apostles of inflexible purpose; and be in no haste about the (unbelievers). On the Day that they see the (Punishment) promised them, (it will be) as if they had not tarried

اَنْ يُّحْيِ الْمَوْتٰى ط بَلٰى اِنَّهٗ عَلٰى

كُلِّ شَىْءٍ قَدِيْرٌ ۞ وَيَوْمَ يُعْرَضُ

الَّذِيْنَ كَفَرُوْا عَلَى النَّارِ اَلَيْسَ

هٰذَا بِالْحَقِّ ط قَالُوْا بَلٰى وَرَبِّنَا

قَالَ فَذُوْقُوا الْعَذَابَ بِمَا كُنْتُمْ

تَكْفُرُوْنَ ۞ فَاصْبِرْ كَمَا صَبَرَ

اُولُوا الْعَزْمِ مِنَ الرُّسُلِ وَلَا

تَسْتَعْجِلْ لَّهُمْ ط كَاَنَّهُمْ يَوْمَ

يَرَوْنَ مَا يُوْعَدُوْنَ لَمْ يَلْبَثُوْٓا

31. "O our people, hearken to the one who invites (you) to Allah, and believe in him: He will forgive you your faults, and deliver you from a Chastisement grievous."

32. "If any does not hearken to the one who invites (us) to Allah, he can not frustrate (Allah's Plan) on earth, and no protectors can he have besides Allah: such men (wander) in manifest error."

33. See they not that Allah, Who created the heavens and the earth, and never wearied with their creation, is able to

يٰقَوْمَنَآ اَجِيْبُوْا دَاعِىَ اللّٰهِ وَاٰمِنُوْا بِهٖ

يَغْفِرْ لَكُمْ مِّنْ ذُنُوْبِكُمْ وَيُجِرْكُمْ

مِّنْ عَذَابٍ اَلِيْمٍ ۞ وَمَنْ لَّا

يُّجِبْ دَاعِىَ اللّٰهِ فَلَيْسَ بِمُعْجِزٍ

فِى الْاَرْضِ وَلَيْسَ لَهٗ مِنْ

دُوْنِهٖٓ اَوْلِيَآءُ ۖ اُولٰٓئِكَ فِىْ ضَلٰلٍ

مُّبِيْنٍ ۞ اَوَلَمْ يَرَوْا اَنَّ اللّٰهَ

الَّذِىْ خَلَقَ السَّمٰوٰتِ وَالْاَرْضَ

وَلَمْ يَعْىَ بِخَلْقِهِنَّ بِقٰدِرٍ عَلٰٓى

but that was their falsehood and their invention.

29. Behold, We turned towards you a company of Jinns (quietly) listening to the Qur'an: when they stood in the presence thereof, they said, "Listen in silence!" When the (reading) was finished, they returned to their people, to warn (them of their sins).

30. They said, "O our people! We have heard a Book revealed after Moses, confirming what came before it: it guides (men) to the Truth and to a Straight Path."

وَذٰلِكَ اِفْكُهُمْ وَمَا كَانُوْا يَفْتَرُوْنَ ۞

وَاِذْ صَرَفْنَاۤ اِلَيْكَ نَفَرًا مِّنَ

الْجِنِّ يَسْتَمِعُوْنَ الْقُرْاٰنَ ۚ فَلَمَّا

حَضَرُوْهُ قَالُوْۤا اَنْصِتُوْا ۚ فَلَمَّا قُضِيَ

وَلَّوْا اِلٰى قَوْمِهِمْ مُّنْذِرِيْنَ ۞

قَالُوْا يٰقَوْمَنَاۤ اِنَّا سَمِعْنَا كِتٰبًا

اُنْزِلَ مِنْۢ بَعْدِ مُوْسٰى مُصَدِّقًا

لِّمَا بَيْنَ يَدَيْهِ يَهْدِيْۤ اِلَى

الْحَقِّ وَاِلٰى طَرِيْقٍ مُّسْتَقِيْمٍ ۞

profit to them were their (faculties of) hearing, sight, and heart and intellect, when they went on rejecting the Signs of Allah; and they were (completely) encircled by that which they used to mock at!

27. We destroyed afore time populations round about you; and We have shown the Signs in various ways, that they may turn (to Us).

28. Why then was no help forthcoming to them from those whom they worshiped as gods, besides Allah, as a means of access (to Allah)? No, they left them in the lurch:

اَغْنٰى عَنْهُمْ سَمْعُهُمْ وَلَا

اَبْصَارُهُمْ وَلَا اَفْئِدَتُهُمْ مِّنْ

شَىْءٍ اِذْ كَانُوْا يَجْحَدُوْنَ بِاٰيٰتِ

اللّٰهِ وَحَاقَ بِهِمْ مَّا كَانُوْا بِهٖ

يَسْتَهْزِءُوْنَ ۞ وَلَقَدْ اَهْلَكْنَا مَا

حَوْلَكُمْ مِّنَ الْقُرٰى وَصَرَّفْنَا الْاٰيٰتِ

لَعَلَّهُمْ يَرْجِعُوْنَ ۞ فَلَوْلَا نَصَرَهُمُ

الَّذِيْنَ اتَّخَذُوْا مِنْ دُوْنِ اللّٰهِ

قُرْبَانًا اٰلِهَةً ؕ بَلْ ضَلُّوْا عَنْهُمْ

towards their valleys, they said, "This cloud will give us rain!" "No, it is the (calamity) you were asking to be hastened, - a wind wherein is a grievous Chastisement!"

25. "Everything will it destroy by the Command of its Lord!" Then by the morning nothing was to be seen but (the ruins of) their houses! Thus do We recompense those given to sin!

26. And We had firmly established them in a (prosperity and) power which We have not given to you (you Quraish!) and We had endowed them with (faculties of) hearing, seeing, heart and intellect: but of no

مُّسْتَقْبِلَ اَوْدِيَتِهِمْ قَالُوْا هٰذَا

عَارِضٌ مُّمْطِرُنَا ۚ بَلْ هُوَ مَا

اسْتَعْجَلْتُمْ بِهٖ ۚ رِيْحٌ فِيْهَا

عَذَابٌ اَلِيْمٌ ۙ تُدَمِّرُ كُلَّ شَيْءٍ

بِاَمْرِ رَبِّهَا فَاَصْبَحُوْا لَا يُرٰى

اِلَّا مَسٰكِنُهُمْ ۚ كَذٰلِكَ نَجْزِى الْقَوْمَ

الْمُجْرِمِيْنَ ۞ وَلَقَدْ مَكَّنّٰهُمْ فِيْمَا

اِنْ مَّكَّنّٰكُمْ فِيْهِ وَجَعَلْنَا لَهُمْ

سَمْعًا وَّاَبْصَارًا وَّاَفْئِدَةً ۖ فَمَا

before him and after him: "Worship you none other than Allah: truly I fear for you the Chastisement of a Mighty Day."

22. They said: "Have you come in order to turn us aside from our gods? Then bring upon us the (calamity) with which you do threaten us, if you are telling the truth?"

23. He said: "The Knowledge (of when it will come) is only with Allah: I proclaim to you the mission on which I have been sent: but I see that you are a people in ignorance!" ...

24. Then, when they saw a cloud advancing

مِنْ بَيْنِ يَدَيْهِ وَمِنْ خَلْفِهۦ

اَلَّا تَعْبُدُوٓا اِلَّا اللّٰهَ اِنِّيٓ اَخَافُ

عَلَيْكُمْ عَذَابَ يَوْمٍ عَظِيمٍ ۝

قَالُوٓا اَجِئْتَنَا لِتَأْفِكَنَا عَنْ

اٰلِهَتِنَا فَأْتِنَا بِمَا تَعِدُنَآ اِنْ

كُنْتَ مِنَ الصّٰدِقِينَ ۝ قَالَ

اِنَّمَا الْعِلْمُ عِنْدَ اللّٰهِ وَاُبَلِّغُكُمْ

مَّآ اُرْسِلْتُ بِهٖ وَلٰكِنِّيٓ اَرٰىكُمْ قَوْمًا

تَجْهَلُونَ ۝ فَلَمَّا رَاَوْهُ عَارِضًا

their deeds, and no injustice be done to them.

20. And on the Day that the unbelievers will be placed before the Fire, (it will be said to them): "You received your good things in the life of the world, and you took your pleasure out of them: but today shall you be recompensed with a Chastisement of humiliation: for that you were arrogant on earth without just cause, and that you (ever) transgressed."

21. Mention (Hud) one of 'Ad's (own) brethren: behold, he warned his people about the winding Sand-tracts: but there have been warners

أَعْمَالَهُمْ وَهُمْ لَا يُظْلَمُونَ ۝ وَيَوْمَ

يُعْرَضُ الَّذِينَ كَفَرُوا عَلَى النَّارِ

أَذْهَبْتُمْ طَيِّبَاتِكُمْ فِي حَيَاتِكُمُ

الدُّنْيَا وَاسْتَمْتَعْتُمْ بِهَا ۖ فَالْيَوْمَ

تُجْزَوْنَ عَذَابَ الْهُونِ بِمَا كُنْتُمْ

تَسْتَكْبِرُونَ فِي الْأَرْضِ بِغَيْرِ

الْحَقِّ وَبِمَا كُنْتُمْ تَفْسُقُونَ ۝

وَاذْكُرْ أَخَا عَادٍ إِذْ أَنْذَرَ قَوْمَهُ

بِالْأَحْقَافِ وَقَدْ خَلَتِ النُّذُرُ

generations have passed before me (without rising again)?" And they two seek Allah's aid, (and rebuke the son): "Woe to you Have faith! For the Promise of Allah is true." But he says, "This is nothing but tales of the ancients!"

18. Such are they against whom is proved the sentence among the previous generations of Jinns and men, that have passed away; for they will be (utterly) lost.

19. And to all are (assigned) degrees according to the deeds which they (have done), and in order that (Allah) may recompense

خَلَتِ الْقُرُونُ مِنْ قَبْلِىْ وَهُمَا

يَسْتَغِيْثٰنِ اللّٰهَ وَيْلَكَ اٰمِنْ

اِنَّ وَعْدَ اللّٰهِ حَقٌّ فَيَقُوْلُ مَا

هٰذَآ اِلَّاۤ اَسَاطِيْرُ الْاَوَّلِيْنَ ۝

اُولٰٓئِكَ الَّذِيْنَ حَقَّ عَلَيْهِمُ

الْقَوْلُ فِيْۤ اُمَمٍ قَدْ خَلَتْ مِنْ

قَبْلِهِمْ مِّنَ الْجِنِّ وَالْاِنْسِ

اِنَّهُمْ كَانُوْا خٰسِرِيْنَ ۝ وَلِكُلٍّ

دَرَجٰتٌ مِّمَّا عَمِلُوْا وَلِيُوَفِّيَهُمْ

and that I may work righteousness such as You may approve;
and be gracious to me in my
issue. Truly have I turned to You
and truly do I bow (to You) in
Islam."

16. Such are they from whom
We shall accept the best of their
deeds and pass by their ill deeds:
(they shall be) among the Companions of the Garden: a promise
of truth, which was made to them
(in this life).

17. But (there is one) who says
to his parents, "Fie on you! Do
you hold out the promise to me
that I shall be raised up, even
though

وَ اَنْ اَعْمَلَ صَالِحًا تَرْضٰهُ

وَاَصْلِحْ لِيْ فِيْ ذُرِّيَّتِيْ ۚ اِنِّيْ تُبْتُ

اِلَيْكَ وَ اِنِّيْ مِنَ الْمُسْلِمِيْنَ ۞

اُولٰٓئِكَ الَّذِيْنَ نَتَقَبَّلُ عَنْهُمْ

اَحْسَنَ مَا عَمِلُوْا وَ نَتَجَاوَزُ عَنْ

سَيِّاٰتِهِمْ فِيْۤ اَصْحٰبِ الْجَنَّةِ ۚ وَعْدَ

الصِّدْقِ الَّذِيْ كَانُوْا يُوْعَدُوْنَ ۞

وَ الَّذِيْ قَالَ لِوَالِدَيْهِ اُفٍّ

لَّكُمَاۤ اَتَعِدٰنِنِيْۤ اَنْ اُخْرَجَ وَقَدْ

14. Such shall be Companions of the Gardens, dwelling therein (for ever): a recompense for their (good) deeds.

15. We have enjoined on man kindness to his parents: in pain did his mother bear him, and in pain did she give him birth. The carrying of the (child) to his weaning is (a period of) thirty months. At length, when he reaches the age of full strength and attains forty years, he says, "O my Lord! Grant me that I may be grateful for Your favour which You has bestowed upon me, and upon both my parents,

أُولَٰئِكَ أَصْحَٰبُ الْجَنَّةِ خَٰلِدِينَ

فِيهَا جَزَآءًۢ بِمَا كَانُوا۟ يَعْمَلُونَ ۝

وَوَصَّيْنَا الْإِنسَٰنَ بِوَٰلِدَيْهِ إِحْسَٰنًا

حَمَلَتْهُ أُمُّهُۥ كُرْهًا وَّوَضَعَتْهُ

كُرْهًا وَحَمْلُهُۥ وَفِصَٰلُهُۥ ثَلَٰثُونَ

شَهْرًا حَتَّىٰٓ إِذَا بَلَغَ أَشُدَّهُۥ

وَبَلَغَ أَرْبَعِينَ سَنَةً قَالَ

رَبِّ أَوْزِعْنِىٓ أَنْ أَشْكُرَ نِعْمَتَكَ

الَّتِىٓ أَنْعَمْتَ عَلَىَّ وَعَلَىٰ وَٰلِدَىَّ

a good thing, (such men) would not have gone to it first, before us!" And seeing that they guide not themselves thereby, they will say, "This is an (old,) falsehood!"

12. And before this, was the Book of Moses as a guide and a mercy: and this Book confirms (it) in the Arabic tongue; to admonish the unjust, and as glad tidings to those who do right.

13. Verily those who say, "Our Lord is Allah," and remain firm (on that Path), - on them shall be no fear, nor shall they grieve.

خَيْرًا مَّا سَبَقُوْنَاۤ اِلَيْهِ ۚ وَاِذْ لَمْ

يَهْتَدُوْا بِهٖ فَسَيَقُوْلُوْنَ هٰذَاۤ

اِفْكٌ قَدِيْمٌ ۞ وَمِنْ قَبْلِهٖ كِتٰبُ

مُوْسٰۤى اِمَامًا وَّرَحْمَةً ۗ وَهٰذَا

كِتٰبٌ مُّصَدِّقٌ لِّسَانًا عَرَبِيًّا

لِّيُنْذِرَ الَّذِيْنَ ظَلَمُوْا ۖ وَبُشْرٰى

لِلْمُحْسِنِيْنَ ۞ اِنَّ الَّذِيْنَ قَالُوْا

رَبُّنَا اللّٰهُ ثُمَّ اسْتَقَامُوْا فَلَا

خَوْفٌ عَلَيْهِمْ وَلَا هُمْ يَحْزَنُوْنَ ۞

what will be done with me or with you. I follow but that which is revealed to me by inspiration; I am but a warner open and clear."

10. Say: "See you? If (this teaching) be from Allah, and you reject it, and a witness from among the Children of Israel testifies to its similarity (with earlier scripture), and has believed while you are arrogant, (how unjust you are!) truly, Allah guides not a people unjust."

11. The unbelievers say of those who believe: "If (this Message) were

مَا يُفْعَلُ بِيْ وَلَا بِكُمْ ۚ اِنْ اَتَّبِعُ

اِلَّا مَا يُوْحٰى اِلَيَّ وَمَا اَنَا اِلَّا

نَذِيْرٌ مُّبِيْنٌ ۞ قُلْ اَرَءَيْتُمْ اِنْ

كَانَ مِنْ عِنْدِ اللّٰهِ وَكَفَرْتُمْ

بِهٖ وَشَهِدَ شَاهِدٌ مِّنْ بَنِيْۤ

اِسْرَآءِيْلَ عَلٰى مِثْلِهٖ فَاٰمَنَ

وَاسْتَكْبَرْتُمْ ۚ اِنَّ اللّٰهَ لَا يَهْدِى

الْقَوْمَ الظّٰلِمِيْنَ ۞ وَقَالَ الَّذِيْنَ

كَفَرُوْا لِلَّذِيْنَ اٰمَنُوْا لَوْ كَانَ

Our clear Signs are rehearsed to them, the unbelievers say, of the Truth when it comes to them: "This is evident sorcery!"

8.　Or do they say, "He has forged it"? Say: "Had I forged it, then you will not at all be able to save me from the wrath of Allah. He knows best of that whereof you talk (so glibly)! Enough is He for a witness between me and you! And he is Oft-Forgiving, Most Merciful."

9.　Say: "I am no bringer of new-fangled doctrine among the Apostles, nor do I know

عَلَيْهِمْ اٰيَاتُنَا بَيِّنٰتٍ قَالَ الَّذِيْنَ

كَفَرُوْا لِلْحَقِّ لَمَّا جَآءَهُمْ هٰذَا

سِحْرٌ مُّبِيْنٌ ۙ اَمْ يَقُوْلُوْنَ

افْتَرٰىهُ ۗ قُلْ اِنِ افْتَرَيْتُهٗ فَلَا

تَمْلِكُوْنَ لِيْ مِنَ اللّٰهِ شَيْئًا ۗ هُوَ

اَعْلَمُ بِمَا تُفِيْضُوْنَ فِيْهِ ۗ كَفٰى

بِهٖ شَهِيْدًۢا بَيْنِيْ وَبَيْنَكُمْ ۗ وَهُوَ

الْغَفُوْرُ الرَّحِيْمُ ۝ قُلْ مَا كُنْتُ

بِدْعًا مِّنَ الرُّسُلِ وَمَآ اَدْرِيْ

have they a share in the heavens bring me a book (revealed) before this, or any remnant of know-ledge (you may have), if you are telling the truth!

5. And who is more astray than one who invokes besides Allah, such as will not answer him to the Day of Judgment, and who (in fact) are unconscious of their call (to them)?

6. And when mankind are gathered together (at the Resur-rection), they will be hostile to them and reject their worship (altogether)!

7. When

لَهُمْ شِرْكٌ فِى السَّمٰوٰتِ ۖ اِيْتُوْنِىْ

بِكِتٰبٍ مِّنْ قَبْلِ هٰذَاۤ اَوْ اَثٰرَةٍ

مِّنْ عِلْمٍ اِنْ كُنْتُمْ صٰدِقِيْنَ ۝

وَمَنْ اَضَلُّ مِمَّنْ يَّدْعُوْا مِنْ

دُوْنِ اللّٰهِ مَنْ لَّا يَسْتَجِيْبُ لَهٗۤ

اِلٰى يَوْمِ الْقِيٰمَةِ وَهُمْ عَنْ

دُعَآئِهِمْ غٰفِلُوْنَ ۝ وَاِذَا حُشِرَ

النَّاسُ كَانُوْا لَهُمْ اَعْدَآءً وَّكَانُوْا

بِعِبَادَتِهِمْ كٰفِرِيْنَ ۝ وَاِذَا تُتْلٰى

Al-Ahqaf
(Winding Sand-Tracts)

Bismillahir-Rahmanir-Rahim

1. Ha-Mim.

2. The Revelation of the Book is from Allah, the Exalted in Power, full of Wisdom.

3. We created not the heavens and the earth and all between them but for just ends, and for a Term appointed. But those who reject Faith turn away from that whereof they are warned.

4. Say: "Do you see what it is you invoke besides Allah? Show me what it is they have created on earth, or

بِسْمِ اللهِ الرَّحْمٰنِ الرَّحِيْمِ

حٰمٓ ۚ﴿١﴾ تَنْزِيْلُ الْكِتٰبِ مِنَ

اللهِ الْعَزِيْزِ الْحَكِيْمِ ﴿٢﴾ مَا خَلَقْنَا

السَّمٰوٰتِ وَالْأَرْضَ وَمَا بَيْنَهُمَآ

اِلَّا بِالْحَقِّ وَأَجَلٍ مُّسَمًّى ۚ

وَالَّذِيْنَ كَفَرُوْا عَمَّآ أُنْذِرُوْا

مُعْرِضُوْنَ ﴿٣﴾ قُلْ أَرَءَيْتُمْ مَّا

تَدْعُوْنَ مِنْ دُوْنِ اللهِ أَرُوْنِيْ

مَاذَا خَلَقُوْا مِنَ الْأَرْضِ أَمْ

مكتبة الكتب الإسلامية

پاره

حم

(۲۶)

قَالَ فَمَا خَطْبُكُمْ أَيُّهَا

الْمُرْسَلُونَ ۝ قَالُوٓا إِنَّآ أُرْسِلْنَآ إِلَىٰ

قَوْمٍ مُّجْرِمِينَ ۝ لِنُرْسِلَ عَلَيْهِمْ

حِجَارَةً مِّن طِينٍ ۝ مُّسَوَّمَةً

عِندَ رَبِّكَ لِلْمُسْرِفِينَ ۝ فَأَخْرَجْنَا

مَن كَانَ فِيهَا مِنَ الْمُؤْمِنِينَ ۝

فَمَا وَجَدْنَا فِيهَا غَيْرَ بَيْتٍ مِّنَ

الْمُسْلِمِينَ ۝ وَتَرَكْنَا فِيهَآ ءَايَةً

لِّلَّذِينَ يَخَافُونَ الْعَذَابَ الْأَلِيمَ ۝

تلك الكتب الإسلامية

پاره

قَالَ فَمَا خَطْبُكُمْ

(۲۷)

31. (Abraham) said: "And what, O you Messengers, is your errand (now)?"

32. They said, "We have been sent to a people (deep) in sin; -

33. "To bring on, on them, (a shower of) stones of clay (brimstone),"

34. "Marked as from your Lord for those who trespass beyond bounds."

35. Then We evacuated those of the believers who were there,

36. But We found not there any just (Muslim) persons except in one house:

37. And We left there a Sign for such as fear the grievous Chastisement.

وَفِىْ مُوْسٰۤى اِذْ اَرْسَلْنٰهُ اِلٰى

فِرْعَوْنَ بِسُلْطٰنٍ مُّبِیْنٍ ۟ فَتَوَلّٰى

بِرُكْنِهٖ وَقَالَ سٰحِرٌ اَوْ مَجْنُوْنٌ ۟

فَاَخَذْنٰهُ وَجُنُوْدَهٗ فَنَبَذْنٰهُمْ فِی

الْیَمِّ وَهُوَ مُلِیْمٌ ۟ وَفِىْ عَادٍ اِذْ

اَرْسَلْنَا عَلَیْهِمُ الرِّیْحَ الْعَقِیْمَ ۟

مَا تَذَرُ مِنْ شَیْءٍ اَتَتْ عَلَیْهِ

اِلَّا جَعَلَتْهُ كَالرَّمِیْمِ ۟ وَفِىْ ثَمُوْدَ

اِذْ قِیْلَ لَهُمْ تَمَتَّعُوْا حَتّٰى حِیْنٍ ۟

38. And in Moses (was another Sign): behold, We sent him to Pharaoh, with authority manifest.

39. But (Pharaoh) turned back with his chiefs, and said, "A sorcerer, or one possessed!"

40. So We took him and his forces, and threw them into the sea; and his was the cursed.

41. And in the 'Ad (People) (was another Sign): behold, We sent against them the devastating Wind:

42. It left nothing whatever that it came up against, but reduced it to ruin and rottenness.

43. And in the Thamud (was another Sign): behold, they were told, "Enjoy (your brief day) for a little while!"

فَعَتَوْا عَنْ أَمْرِ رَبِّهِمْ فَأَخَذَتْهُمُ

الصَّاعِقَةُ وَهُمْ يَنْظُرُونَ ۝ فَمَا

اسْتَطَاعُوا مِنْ قِيَامٍ وَّمَا كَانُوا

مُنْتَصِرِينَ ۝ وَقَوْمَ نُوحٍ مِّن

قَبْلُ ۚ إِنَّهُمْ كَانُوا قَوْمًا فَاسِقِينَ ۝

وَالسَّمَاءَ بَنَيْنَاهَا بِأَيْيْدٍ وَّإِنَّا

لَمُوسِعُونَ ۝ وَالْأَرْضَ فَرَشْنَاهَا

فَنِعْمَ الْمَاهِدُونَ ۝ وَمِنْ كُلِّ

شَيْءٍ خَلَقْنَا زَوْجَيْنِ لَعَلَّكُمْ

44. But they insolently defied the Command of their Lord: so the stunning noise (of an earth-quake) seized them, even while they were looking on.

45. Then they could not even stand (on their feet), nor could they help themselves.

46. So were the People of Noah before them, for they wickedly transgressed.

47. With power and skill did We construct the Firmament: for it is We Who create the vastness of space.

48. And We have spread out the (spacious) earth: how excellently We do spread out!

49. And of every thing We have created pairs: that you may

تَذَكَّرُوْنَ ۞ فَفِرُّوْۤا اِلَى اللّٰهِ ۖ

اِنِّيْ لَكُمْ مِّنْهُ نَذِيْرٌ مُّبِيْنٌ ۞

وَلَا تَجْعَلُوْا مَعَ اللّٰهِ اِلٰهًا اٰخَرَ ؕ

اِنِّيْ لَكُمْ مِّنْهُ نَذِيْرٌ مُّبِيْنٌ ۞

كَذٰلِكَ مَاۤ اَتَى الَّذِيْنَ مِنْ

قَبْلِهِمْ مِّنْ رَّسُوْلٍ اِلَّا قَالُوْا

سَاحِرٌ اَوْ مَجْنُوْنٌ ۞ اَتَوَاصَوْا بِهٖ ۚ

بَلْ هُمْ قَوْمٌ طَاغُوْنَ ۞ فَتَوَلَّ

عَنْهُمْ فَمَاۤ اَنْتَ بِمَلُوْمٍ ۞ وَّذَكِّرْ

receive instruction.

50. Then you Hasten (at once) to Allah: I am from Him a warner to you, clear and open!

51. And make not another an object of worship with Allah: I am from Him a warner to you, clear and open!

52. Similarly, no Apostle came to the Peoples before them, but they said (of him) in like manner, "A sorcerer, or one possessed!"

53. Is this the legacy they have transmitted, one to another? No, they are themselves a people transgressing beyond bounds!

54. So turn away from them: not blame on you.

55. But teach (your Message),

فَإِنَّ الذِّكْرٰى تَنْفَعُ الْمُؤْمِنِيْنَ ۝

وَمَا خَلَقْتُ الْجِنَّ وَالْاِنْسَ اِلَّا

لِيَعْبُدُوْنِ ۝ مَآ اُرِيْدُ مِنْهُمْ مِّنْ

رِّزْقٍ وَّمَآ اُرِيْدُ اَنْ يُّطْعِمُوْنِ ۝

اِنَّ اللّٰهَ هُوَ الرَّزَّاقُ ذُو الْقُوَّةِ

الْمَتِيْنُ ۝ فَإِنَّ لِلَّذِيْنَ ظَلَمُوْا

ذَنُوْبًا مِّثْلَ ذَنُوْبِ اَصْحٰبِهِمْ فَلَا

يَسْتَعْجِلُوْنِ ۝ فَوَيْلٌ لِّلَّذِيْنَ كَفَرُوْا

مِنْ يَّوْمِهِمُ الَّذِيْ يُوْعَدُوْنَ ۝

for teaching benefits the believers.

56. I have only created Jinns and men, that they may serve Me.

57. No Sustenance do I require of them, nor do I require that they should feed Me.

58. For Allah is He Who gives (all) Sustenance, - Lord of Power, - Steadfast (for ever).

59. For the wrong-doers, their portion is like unto the portion of their fellows (of earlier generations): then let them not ask Me to hasten (that portion)!

60. Woe, then, to the unbelievers, on account of that Day of theirs which they have been promised!

بِسْمِ اللّٰهِ الرَّحْمٰنِ الرَّحِيْمِ

وَالطُّوْرِ ۙ وَكِتٰبٍ مَّسْطُوْرٍ ۙ فِيْ

رَقٍّ مَّنْشُوْرٍ ۙ وَّالْبَيْتِ الْمَعْمُوْرِ ۙ

وَالسَّقْفِ الْمَرْفُوْعِ ۙ وَالْبَحْرِ

الْمَسْجُوْرِ ۙ اِنَّ عَذَابَ رَبِّكَ

لَوَاقِعٌ ۙ مَّا لَهٗ مِنْ دَافِعٍ ۙ

يَّوْمَ تَمُوْرُ السَّمَآءُ مَوْرًا ۙ وَّتَسِيْرُ

الْجِبَالُ سَيْرًا ۙ فَوَيْلٌ يَّوْمَئِذٍ

لِّلْمُكَذِّبِيْنَ ۙ الَّذِيْنَ هُمْ فِيْ

At-Tur (The Mount)

Bismillahir-Rahmanir-Rahim

1.　By the Mount (of Revelation);

2.　By a Decree inscribed,

3.　In a Scroll unfolded;

4.　By the much-frequented Fane;

5.　By the Canopy raised High;

6.　And by the Ocean filled with Swell; -

7.　Verily, the Doom of your Lord will indeed come to pass; -

8.　There is none can avert it; -

9.　On the Day when the firmament will be in dreadful commotion. **10.**　And the mountains will fly hither and thither.

11.　Then woe that Day to those that treat (Truth) as Falsehood; -

12.　That play (and paddle) in

خَوْضٍ يَّلْعَبُوْنَ ۞ يَوْمَ يُدَعُّوْنَ

اِلٰى نَارِ جَهَنَّمَ دَعًّا ۞ هٰذِهِ النَّارُ

الَّتِيْ كُنْتُمْ بِهَا تُكَذِّبُوْنَ ۞ اَفَسِحْرٌ

هٰذَآ اَمْ اَنْتُمْ لَا تُبْصِرُوْنَ ۞

اِصْلَوْهَا فَاصْبِرُوْۤا اَوْ لَا تَصْبِرُوْا

سَوَآءٌ عَلَيْكُمْ ۗ اِنَّمَا تُجْزَوْنَ مَا

كُنْتُمْ تَعْمَلُوْنَ ۞ اِنَّ الْمُتَّقِيْنَ فِيْ

جَنّٰتٍ وَّنَعِيْمٍ ۞ فٰكِهِيْنَ بِمَآ اٰتٰىهُمْ

رَبُّهُمْ ۚ وَوَقٰىهُمْ رَبُّهُمْ عَذَابَ

shallow trifles.

13. That Day shall they be thrust down to the Fire of Hell, irresistibly.

14. "This", it will be said, "is the Fire, - which you were wont to deny!

15. "Is this then a fake, or is it you that do not see?"

16. "Burn you therein: the same is it to you whether you bear it with patience, or not: you but receive the recompense of your (own) deeds."

17. As to the Righteous, they will be in Gardens, and in Happiness, -

18. Enjoying the (Bliss) which their Lord has bestowed on them, and their Lord shall deliver them from the Chastisement

الْجَحِيمِ ۝ كُلُوا وَاشْرَبُوا هَنِيئًا

بِمَا كُنْتُمْ تَعْمَلُونَ ۝ مُتَّكِئِينَ

عَلَى سُرُرٍ مَّصْفُوفَةٍ وَزَوَّجْنَاهُمْ

بِحُورٍ عِينٍ ۝ وَالَّذِينَ آمَنُوا

وَاتَّبَعَتْهُمْ ذُرِّيَّتُهُمْ بِإِيمَانٍ أَلْحَقْنَا

بِهِمْ ذُرِّيَّتَهُمْ وَمَا أَلَتْنَاهُمْ مِّنْ

عَمَلِهِمْ مِّنْ شَيْءٍ كُلُّ امْرِئٍ

بِمَا كَسَبَ رَهِينٌ ۝ وَأَمْدَدْنَاهُمْ

بِفَاكِهَةٍ وَلَحْمٍ مِّمَّا يَشْتَهُونَ ۝

of the Fire.

19.   (To them will be said:) "Eat and drink you, with good pleasure, because of your (good) deeds."

20.   They will recline (with ease) on thrones (of dignity) arranged in ranks; and We shall join them to Companions, with beautiful, big and lustrous eyes.

21.   And those who believe and whose families follow them in Faith, - to them shall We join their families: nor shall We deprive them (of the fruit) of any of their works: (yet) is each individual in pledge for his deeds.

22.   And We shall bestow on them, of fruit and meat, anything they shall desire.

يَتَنَازَعُونَ فِيهَا كَأْسًا لَّا لَغْوٌ

فِيهَا وَلَا تَأْثِيمٌ ۝ وَيَطُوفُ عَلَيْهِمْ

غِلْمَانٌ لَّهُمْ كَأَنَّهُمْ لُؤْلُؤٌ مَّكْنُونٌ ۝

وَأَقْبَلَ بَعْضُهُمْ عَلَىٰ بَعْضٍ

يَتَسَآءَلُونَ ۝ قَالُوٓا إِنَّا كُنَّا قَبْلُ

فِىٓ أَهْلِنَا مُشْفِقِينَ ۝ فَمَنَّ اللَّهُ

عَلَيْنَا وَوَقَىٰنَا عَذَابَ السَّمُومِ ۝

إِنَّا كُنَّا مِن قَبْلُ نَدْعُوهُ إِنَّهُ

هُوَ الْبَرُّ الرَّحِيمُ ۝ فَذَكِّرْ فَمَآ

23. They shall there exchange, one with another, a (loving) cup free of frivolity, free of all taint of ill.

24. Round about them will serve, (devoted) to them, Youths (handsome) as Pearls well-guarded.

25. They will advance to each other, engaging in mutual enquiry.

26. They will say: "Aforetime, we were not without fear for the sake of our people."

27. "But Allah has been good to us, and has delivered us from the Penalty of the Scorching Wind."

28. "Truly, we did call unto Him from of old: truly it is He, the Beneficent, the Merciful!"

29. Therefore proclaim you the praises (of your Lord): for

اَنْتَ بِنِعْمَتِ رَبِّكَ بِكَاهِنٍ وَّلَا

مَجْنُوْنٍ ۚ اَمْ يَقُوْلُوْنَ شَاعِرٌ

نَّتَرَبَّصُ بِهٖ رَيْبَ الْمَنُوْنِ ۞

قُلْ تَرَبَّصُوْا فَاِنِّيْ مَعَكُمْ مِّنَ

الْمُتَرَبِّصِيْنَ ۚ اَمْ تَأْمُرُهُمْ

اَحْلَامُهُمْ بِهٰذَآ اَمْ هُمْ قَوْمٌ

طَاغُوْنَ ۚ اَمْ يَقُوْلُوْنَ تَقَوَّلَهٗ ۚ

بَلْ لَّا يُؤْمِنُوْنَ ۞ فَلْيَأْتُوْا بِحَدِيْثٍ

مِّثْلِهٖ اِنْ كَانُوْا صٰدِقِيْنَ ۚ اَمْ

By the Grace of your Lord, you are no (vulgar) soothsayer, nor are you one possessed.

30.   Or do they say: - "A Poet! We await for him some calamity (hatched) by Time!"

31.   Say: "Await you! - I too will wait along with you!"

32.   Is it that their faculties of understanding urge them to this, or are they but a people transgressing beyond bounds?

33.   Or do they say, "He fabricated the (Message)"? No, they have no faith!

34.   Let them then produce a recital like it, - if (it be) they speak the truth!

35.   Were

خُلِقُوْا مِنْ غَيْرِ شَيْءٍ اَمْ هُمُ

الْخٰلِقُوْنَ ۝ اَمْ خَلَقُوا السَّمٰوٰتِ

وَالْاَرْضَ ۚ بَلْ لَّا يُوْقِنُوْنَ ۝ اَمْ

عِنْدَهُمْ خَزَآئِنُ رَبِّكَ اَمْ هُمُ

الْمُصَۜيْطِرُوْنَ ۝ اَمْ لَهُمْ سُلَّمٌ

يَّسْتَمِعُوْنَ فِيْهِ ۚ فَلْيَأْتِ مُسْتَمِعُهُمْ

بِسُلْطٰنٍ مُّبِيْنٍ ۝ اَمْ لَهُ الْبَنٰتُ

وَلَكُمُ الْبَنُوْنَ ۝ اَمْ تَسْئَلُهُمْ اَجْرًا

فَهُمْ مِّنْ مَّغْرَمٍ مُّثْقَلُوْنَ ۝ اَمْ

they created of nothing, or were they themselves the creators?

36. Or did they create the heavens and the earth? No, they have no firm belief.

37. Or are the Treasures of your Lord with them, or are they the managers (of affairs)?

38. Or have they a ladder, by which they can (climb up to heaven and) listen (to its secrets)? Then let (such a) listener of theirs produce a manifest proof.

39. Or has He only daughters and you have sons?

40. Or is it that you do ask for a reward, so that they are burdened with a load of debt? –

41. Or

عِنْدَهُمُ الْغَيْبُ فَهُمْ يَكْتُبُونَ ۞

أَمْ يُرِيدُونَ كَيْدًا ۖ فَالَّذِينَ

كَفَرُوا هُمُ الْمَكِيدُونَ ۞ أَمْ لَهُمْ

إِلَٰهٌ غَيْرُ اللَّهِ ۚ سُبْحَانَ اللَّهِ عَمَّا

يُشْرِكُونَ ۞ وَإِن يَرَوْا كِسْفًا مِّنَ

السَّمَاءِ سَاقِطًا يَّقُولُوا سَحَابٌ

مَّرْكُومٌ ۞ فَذَرْهُمْ حَتَّىٰ يُلَاقُوا

يَوْمَهُمُ الَّذِي فِيهِ يُصْعَقُونَ ۞

يَوْمَ لَا يُغْنِي عَنْهُمْ كَيْدُهُمْ شَيْئًا

that the Unseen is in their hands,
and they write it down?

42. Or do they intend a plot
(against you)? But those who
defy Allah are themselves invol-
ved in a Plot!

43. Or have they a god other
than Allah? Exalted is Allah far
above the things they associate
with Him!

44. Were they to see a piece of
the sky falling (on them), they
would (only) say: "Clouds gathered in heaps!"

45. So leave them alone until
they encounter that Day of theirs,
wherein they shall (perforce)
swoon (with terror), -

46. The Day when their plotting
will avail them nothing

وَّلَا هُمْ يُنْصَرُوْنَ ۞ وَاِنَّ لِلَّذِيْنَ

ظَلَمُوْا عَذَابًا دُوْنَ ذٰلِكَ وَلٰكِنَّ

اَكْثَرَهُمْ لَا يَعْلَمُوْنَ ۞ وَاصْبِرْ

لِحُكْمِ رَبِّكَ فَاِنَّكَ بِاَعْيُنِنَا وَسَبِّحْ

بِحَمْدِ رَبِّكَ حِيْنَ تَقُوْمُ ۙ ۞ وَمِنَ

الَّيْلِ فَسَبِّحْهُ وَاِدْبَارَ النُّجُوْمِ ۞

سُوْرَةُ النَّجْم   بِسْمِ اللهِ الرَّحْمٰنِ الرَّحِيْمِ

وَالنَّجْمِ اِذَا هَوٰى ۙ ۞ مَا ضَلَّ

صَاحِبُكُمْ وَمَا غَوٰى ۙ ۞ وَمَا يَنْطِقُ

and no help shall be given them.

47. And verily, for those who do wrong, there is another punishment besides this: but most of them understand not.

48. Now await in patience the command of your Lord: for verily you are in Our eyes: and celebrate the praises of your Lord the while you stand forth,

49. And for part of the night also praise you Him, - and at the retreat of the stars!

An-Najm (The Star)

Bismillahir-Rahmanir-Rahim

1. By the Star when it goes down, -

2. Your Companion is neither astray nor being misled.

3. Nor does he say

عَنِ الْهَوٰى ۚ اِنْ هُوَ اِلَّا وَحْيٌ ۙ

يُّوْحٰى ۙ عَلَّمَهٗ شَدِيْدُ الْقُوٰى ۙ

ذُوْ مِرَّةٍ ۗ فَاسْتَوٰى ۙ وَهُوَ بِالْاُفُقِ

الْاَعْلٰى ۗ ثُمَّ دَنَا فَتَدَلّٰى ۙ فَكَانَ

قَابَ قَوْسَيْنِ اَوْ اَدْنٰى ۚ فَاَوْحٰى

اِلٰى عَبْدِهٖ مَاۤ اَوْحٰى ۗ مَا كَذَبَ

الْفُؤَادُ مَا رَاٰى ۙ اَفَتُمٰرُوْنَهٗ عَلٰى

مَا يَرٰى ۙ وَلَقَدْ رَاٰهُ نَزْلَةً

اُخْرٰى ۙ عِنْدَ سِدْرَةِ الْمُنْتَهٰى ۙ

(anything) of (his own) Desire.

4.   It is no less than Inspiration sent down to him: **5.** He was taught by one Mighty in Power,

6.   Endued with Wisdom: for he appeared (in stately form);

7.   While he was in the highest part of the horizon: **8.** Then he approached and came closer,

9.   And was at a distance of but two bow-lengths or (even) nearer;

10. So did (Allah) convey the inspiration to His servant - (conveyed) what He (meant) to convey.

11. The (Prophet's) (mind and) heart in no way falsified that which he saw. **12.** Will you then dispute with him concerning what he saw?

13. For indeed he saw him at a second descent, **14.** Near the Lote-tree beyond which none may pass:

عِنْدَهَا جَنَّةُ الْمَأْوَى ۞ إِذْ يَغْشَى

السِّدْرَةَ مَا يَغْشَى ۞ مَا زَاغَ الْبَصَرُ

وَمَا طَغَى ۞ لَقَدْ رَأَى مِنْ آيَاتِ

رَبِّهِ الْكُبْرَى ۞ أَفَرَأَيْتُمُ اللَّاتَ

وَالْعُزَّى ۞ وَمَنَاةَ الثَّالِثَةَ الْأُخْرَى

۞ أَلَكُمُ الذَّكَرُ وَلَهُ الْأُنْثَى ۞ تِلْكَ

إِذًا قِسْمَةٌ ضِيزَى ۞ إِنْ هِيَ إِلَّا

أَسْمَاءٌ سَمَّيْتُمُوهَا أَنْتُمْ وَآبَاؤُكُمْ

مَا أَنْزَلَ اللَّهُ بِهَا مِنْ سُلْطَانٍ

15. Near it is the Garden of Abode.

16. Behold, the Lote-tree was shrouded (in mystery unspeakable!)

17. (His) sight never swerved, nor did it go wrong!

18. For truly did he see, of the Signs of his Lord, the Greatest!

19. Have you seen Lat, and 'Uzza,

20. And another, the third (goddess), Manat?

21. What! For you the male sex, and for Him, the female?

22. Behold, such would be indeed a division most unfair!

23. These are nothing but names which you have devised, - you and your fathers, - for which Allah has sent down no authority (whatever).

اِنْ يَّتَّبِعُوْنَ اِلَّا الظَّنَّ وَمَا تَهْوَى

الْاَنْفُسُ وَلَقَدْ جَآءَهُمْ مِّنْ رَّبِّهِمُ

الْهُدٰى ۛ اَمْ لِلْاِنْسَانِ مَا تَمَنّٰى ۗ

فَلِلّٰهِ الْاٰخِرَةُ وَالْاُوْلٰى ۞ وَكَمْ

مِّنْ مَّلَكٍ فِى السَّمٰوٰتِ لَا تُغْنِىْ

شَفَاعَتُهُمْ شَيْئًا اِلَّا مِنْۢ بَعْدِ اَنْ

يَّاْذَنَ اللّٰهُ لِمَنْ يَّشَآءُ وَيَرْضٰى ۞

اِنَّ الَّذِيْنَ لَا يُؤْمِنُوْنَ بِالْاٰخِرَةِ

لَيُسَمُّوْنَ الْمَلٰٓئِكَةَ تَسْمِيَةَ

They follow nothing but conjecture and what their own souls desire! - even though there has already come to them Guidance from their Lord!

24. No, shall man have (just) anything he hankers after?

25. But it is to Allah that the End and the Beginning (of all things) belong.

26. How many-so-ever be the Angels in the heavens, their intercession will avail nothing except after Allah has given leave for whom He pleases and that he is acceptable to Him.

27. Those who believe not in the Hereafter, name the Angels with

الْأُنْثَىٰ ۝ وَمَا لَهُمْ بِهِ مِنْ عِلْمٍ

إِنْ يَتَّبِعُونَ إِلَّا الظَّنَّ وَإِنَّ الظَّنَّ

لَا يُغْنِي مِنَ الْحَقِّ شَيْئًا ۝ فَأَعْرِضْ

عَنْ مَّنْ تَوَلَّىٰ عَنْ ذِكْرِنَا وَلَمْ

يُرِدْ إِلَّا الْحَيَوٰةَ الدُّنْيَا ۝ ذَٰلِكَ

مَبْلَغُهُمْ مِّنَ الْعِلْمِ إِنَّ رَبَّكَ

هُوَ أَعْلَمُ بِمَنْ ضَلَّ عَنْ سَبِيلِهِ

وَهُوَ أَعْلَمُ بِمَنِ اهْتَدَىٰ ۝ وَلِلَّهِ

مَا فِي السَّمَاوَاتِ وَمَا فِي الْأَرْضِ

female names.

28. But they have no knowledge therein. They follow nothing but conjecture; and conjecture avails nothing against Truth.

29. Therefore shun those who turn away from Our Message and desire nothing but the life of this world.

30. That is as far as knowledge will reach them. Verily your Lord knows best those who stray from His Path, and He knows best those who receive guidance.

31. Yes, to Allah belongs all that is in the heavens and on earth:

لِيَجْزِيَ الَّذِيْنَ اَسَاۤءُوْا بِمَا عَمِلُوْا

وَيَجْزِيَ الَّذِيْنَ اَحْسَنُوْا بِالْحُسْنٰى ۚ ۝

اَلَّذِيْنَ يَجْتَنِبُوْنَ كَبٰٓئِرَ الْاِثْمِ

وَالْفَوَاحِشَ اِلَّا اللَّمَمَ ۚ اِنَّ رَبَّكَ

وَاسِعُ الْمَغْفِرَةِ ۗ هُوَ اَعْلَمُ بِكُمْ اِذْ

اَنْشَاَكُمْ مِّنَ الْاَرْضِ وَاِذْ اَنْتُمْ

اَجِنَّةٌ فِيْ بُطُوْنِ اُمَّهٰتِكُمْ ۚ فَلَا

تُزَكُّوْٓا اَنْفُسَكُمْ ۗ هُوَ اَعْلَمُ بِمَنِ

اتَّقٰى ۝ اَفَرَءَيْتَ الَّذِيْ تَوَلّٰى ۝

so that He rewards those who do evil, according to their deeds, and He rewards those who do good, with what is best.

32. Those who avoid great sins and shameful deeds, only (falling into) small faults, - verily your Lord is ample in forgiveness. He knows you well when He brings you out of the earth, and when you are hidden in your mothers' wombs. Therefore justify not yourselves: He knows best who it is that guards against evil.

33. Do you see one who turns back,

وَاَعْطٰى قَلِيْلًا وَّاَكْدٰى ۞ اَعِنْدَهٗ

عِلْمُ الْغَيْبِ فَهُوَ يَرٰى ۞ اَمْ لَمْ

يُنَبَّأْ بِمَا فِيْ صُحُفِ مُوْسٰى ۞

وَاِبْرٰهِيْمَ الَّذِيْ وَفّٰى ۞ اَلَّا تَزِرُ

وَازِرَةٌ وِّزْرَ اُخْرٰى ۞ وَاَنْ لَّيْسَ

لِلْاِنْسَانِ اِلَّا مَا سَعٰى ۞ وَاَنَّ

سَعْيَهٗ سَوْفَ يُرٰى ۞ ثُمَّ يُجْزٰهُ

الْجَزَآءَ الْاَوْفٰى ۞ وَاَنَّ اِلٰى رَبِّكَ

الْمُنْتَهٰى ۞ وَاَنَّهٗ هُوَ اَضْحَكَ

Part–27   19   An-Najm–53

34. Gives a little, then hardens (his heart)?

35. What! Has he knowledge of the Unseen so that he can see?

36. No, is he not acquainted with what is in the Books of Moses -

37. And of Abraham who fulfilled his engagements?' -

38. Namely, that no bearer of burdens can bear the burden of another; **39.** That man can have nothing but what he strives for;

40. That (the fruit of) his striving will soon come in sight:

41. Then will he be rewarded with a reward complete;

42. That to your Lord is the final Goal;   **43.** That it is He Who grants Laughter

وَأَبْكٰى ۞ وَأَنَّهُ هُوَ أَمَاتَ وَأَحْيَا ۞

وَأَنَّهُ خَلَقَ الزَّوْجَيْنِ الذَّكَرَ

وَالْأُنْثٰى ۞ مِنْ نُّطْفَةٍ إِذَا تُمْنٰى ۞

وَأَنَّ عَلَيْهِ النَّشْأَةَ الْأُخْرٰى ۞

وَأَنَّهُ هُوَ أَغْنٰى وَأَقْنٰى ۞

وَأَنَّهُ هُوَ رَبُّ الشِّعْرٰى ۞

وَأَنَّهُ أَهْلَكَ عَادَا الْأُولٰى ۞

وَثَمُودَا فَمَا أَبْقٰى ۞ وَقَوْمَ نُوحٍ

مِنْ قَبْلُ ۗ إِنَّهُمْ كَانُوا هُمْ أَظْلَمَ

and Tears;   **44.**   That it is He Who grants Death and Life;

45.   That He did create in pairs, - male and female,

46.   From a seed when lodged (in its place);

47.   That He has promised a Second Creation (raising of the Dead);

48.   That it is He Who gives wealth and satisfaction;

49.   That He is the Lord of Sirius (the Mighty Star);

50.   And that it is He Who destroyed the (powerful) ancient 'Ad (People),

51.   And the Thamud, nor gave them a lease of perpetual life.

52.   And before them, the People of Noah, for that they were (all) most unjust

وَأَطْغَى ۞ وَالْمُؤْتَفِكَةَ أَهْوَى ۞

فَغَشّٰهَا مَا غَشّٰى ۞ فَبِأَيِّ اٰلَآءِ

رَبِّكَ تَتَمَارٰى ۞ هٰذَا نَذِيْرٌ مِّنَ

النُّذُرِ الْأُوْلٰى ۞ أَزِفَتِ الْاٰزِفَةُ ۞

لَيْسَ لَهَا مِنْ دُوْنِ اللّٰهِ

كَاشِفَةٌ ۞ أَفَمِنْ هٰذَا الْحَدِيْثِ

تَعْجَبُوْنَ ۞ وَتَضْحَكُوْنَ وَلَا

تَبْكُوْنَ ۞ وَأَنْتُمْ سٰمِدُوْنَ ۞

فَاسْجُدُوْا لِلّٰهِ وَاعْبُدُوْا ۩ ۞

and most insolent transgressors,

53. And He destroyed the Overthrown Cities (of Sodom and Gomorrah).

54. So that (ruins unknown) have covered them up.

55. Then which of the gifts of your Lord, (O man,) will you dispute about?

56. This is a warner, of the (series of) warners of old!

57. The (Judgment) ever approaching draws closer:

58. No (soul) but Allah can lay it bare. **59.** Do you then wonder at this recital?

60. And will you laugh and not weep, - **61.** Wasting your time in vanities?

62. But you fall down in prostration to Allah, and adore (Him)

بِسۡمِ اللهِ الرَّحۡمٰنِ الرَّحِيۡمِ

اِقۡتَرَبَتِ السَّاعَةُ وَانۡشَقَّ الۡقَمَرُ ۝

وَاِنۡ يَّرَوۡا اٰيَةً يُّعۡرِضُوۡا وَيَقُوۡلُوۡا

سِحۡرٌ مُّسۡتَمِرٌّ ۝ وَكَذَّبُوۡا وَاتَّبَعُوۡۤا

اَهۡوَآءَهُمۡ وَكُلُّ اَمۡرٍ مُّسۡتَقِرٌّ ۝

وَلَقَدۡ جَآءَهُمۡ مِّنَ الۡاَنۡبَآءِ مَا

فِيۡهِ مُزۡدَجَرٌ ۝ حِكۡمَةٌ بَالِغَةٌ فَمَا

تُغۡنِ النُّذُرُ ۝ فَتَوَلَّ عَنۡهُمۡ يَوۡمَ

يَدۡعُ الدَّاعِ اِلٰى شَىۡءٍ نُّكُرٍ ۝

Al-Qamar (The Moon)

Bismillahir-Rahmanir-Rahim

1. The Hour (of Judgment) is nigh, and the moon is cleft asunder.

2. But if they see a Sign, they turn away, and say, "This is (but) transient magic."

3. They reject (the warning) and follow their (own) lusts but every matter has its appointed time.

4. There have already come to them such tidings as contain a deterrent – **5.** Mature wisdom; - but (the preaching of) warners profits them not.

6. Therefore, (O Prophet,) turn away from them. The Day that the Caller will call (them) to a terrible affair,

خُشَّعًا اَبْصَارُهُمْ يَخْرُجُونَ مِنَ
الْاَجْدَاثِ كَاَنَّهُمْ جَرَادٌ مُّنْتَشِرٌ ۙ
مُّهْطِعِيْنَ اِلَى الدَّاعِ ۗ يَقُوْلُ
الْكٰفِرُوْنَ هٰذَا يَوْمٌ عَسِرٌ ۞ كَذَّبَتْ
قَبْلَهُمْ قَوْمُ نُوْحٍ فَكَذَّبُوْا عَبْدَنَا
وَقَالُوْا مَجْنُوْنٌ وَّازْدُجِرَ ۞ فَدَعَا
رَبَّهٗۤ اَنِّيْ مَغْلُوْبٌ فَانْتَصِرْ ۞
فَفَتَحْنَاۤ اَبْوَابَ السَّمَاءِ بِمَاءٍ
مُّنْهَمِرٍ ۙ وَّفَجَّرْنَا الْاَرْضَ عُيُوْنًا

7. They will come forth, - their eyes humbled - from (their) graves, (torpid) like locusts scattered abroad,

8. Hastening, with eyes transfixed, towards the Caller! - "Hard is this Day!", the unbelievers will say.

9. Before them the People of Noah rejected (their Apostle): they rejected Our servant, and said, "Here is one possessed!", and he was driven out.

10. Then he called on his Lord: "I am one overcome: do You then help (me)!"

11. So We opened the gates of heaven, with water pouring forth.

12. And We caused the earth to gush forth with springs,

فَالْتَقَى الْمَاءُ عَلَى أَمْرٍ قَدْ قُدِرَ ۞

وَحَمَلْنَهُ عَلَى ذَاتِ أَلْوَاحٍ وَّدُسُرٍ ۞

تَجْرِى بِأَعْيُنِنَا جَزَآءً لِّمَن كَانَ

كُفِرَ ۞ وَلَقَد تَّرَكْنَهَآ ءَايَةً فَهَلْ مِن

مُّدَّكِرٍ ۞ فَكَيْفَ كَانَ عَذَابِى وَنُذُرِ ۞

وَلَقَدْ يَسَّرْنَا الْقُرْءَانَ لِلذِّكْرِ فَهَلْ

مِن مُّدَّكِرٍ ۞ كَذَّبَتْ عَادٌ فَكَيْفَ

كَانَ عَذَابِى وَنُذُرِ ۞ إِنَّآ أَرْسَلْنَا

عَلَيْهِمْ رِيحًا صَرْصَرًا فِى يَوْمِ نَحْسٍ

so the waters met (and rose) to the extent decreed.

13. But We bore him on an (Ark) made of broad planks and caulked with palm- fibre:

14. She floats under our eyes (and care): a recompense to one who had been rejected (with scorn)!

15. And We have left this as a Sign (for all time): then is there any that will receive admonition?

16. But how (terrible) was My Chastisement and My Warning?

17. And We have indeed made the Qur'an easy to understand and remember: then is there any that will receive admonition?

18. The 'Ad (People) (too) rejected (Truth): then how terrible was My Chastisement and My Warning?

19. For We sent against them a furi- ous wind, on a Day of violent

مُّسْتَمِرٌّ ۱۹ تَنْزِعُ النَّاسَ ۙ كَأَنَّهُمْ

أَعْجَازُ نَخْلٍ مُّنْقَعِرٍ ۲۰ فَكَيْفَ كَانَ

عَذَابِيْ وَنُذُرِ ۲۱ وَلَقَدْ يَسَّرْنَا الْقُرْآنَ

لِلذِّكْرِ فَهَلْ مِنْ مُّدَّكِرٍ ۲۲ كَذَّبَتْ

ثَمُوْدُ بِالنُّذُرِ ۲۳ فَقَالُوْا أَبَشَرًا مِّنَّا

وَاحِدًا نَّتَّبِعُهٗ ۙ إِنَّا إِذًا لَّفِيْ ضَلٰلٍ

وَّسُعُرٍ ۲۴ ءَأُلْقِيَ الذِّكْرُ عَلَيْهِ مِنْ

بَيْنِنَا بَلْ هُوَ كَذَّابٌ أَشِرٌ ۲۵

سَيَعْلَمُوْنَ غَدًا مَّنِ الْكَذَّابُ

Disaster,

20. Plucking out men as if they were roots of palm-trees torn up (from the ground).

21. Yes, how (terrible) was My Chastisement and My Warning!

22. But We have indeed made the Qur'an easy to understand and remember: then is there any that will receive admonition?

23. The Thamud (also) rejected (their) warners.

24. For they said: "What! A man! a solitary one from among ourselves! Shall we follow such a one? Truly should we then be straying in mind, and mad!"

25. "Is it that the Message is sent to him, of all people amongst us? No, he is a liar, an insolent one!"

26. Ah! They will know on the morrow, which is the liar,

الْأَشِرُ ۞ إِنَّا مُرْسِلُوا النَّاقَةِ فِتْنَةً

لَّهُمْ فَارْتَقِبْهُمْ وَاصْطَبِرْ ۞ وَنَبِّئْهُمْ

أَنَّ الْمَآءَ قِسْمَةٌ بَيْنَهُمْ كُلُّ

شِرْبٍ مُّحْتَضَرٌ ۞ فَنَادَوْا صَاحِبَهُمْ

فَتَعَاطَى فَعَقَرَ ۞ فَكَيْفَ كَانَ عَذَابِي

وَنُذُرِ ۞ إِنَّا أَرْسَلْنَا عَلَيْهِمْ صَيْحَةً

وَاحِدَةً فَكَانُوا كَهَشِيمِ الْمُحْتَظِرِ ۞

وَلَقَدْ يَسَّرْنَا الْقُرْآنَ لِلذِّكْرِ فَهَلْ

مِن مُّدَّكِرٍ ۞ كَذَّبَتْ قَوْمُ لُوطٍ

The insolent one!

27. For We will send the she-camel by way of trial for them. So watch them, (O Salih), and possess yourself in patience!

28. And tell them that the water is to be divided between them: each one's right to drink being brought forward (by suitable turns).

29. But they called to their companion, and he took a sword in hand, and hamstrung (her).

30. Ah! How (terrible) was My Chastisement and My Warning!

31. For We sent against them a single Mighty Blast, and they became like the dry stubble used by one who pens cattle.

32. And We have indeed made the Qur'an easy to understand and remember: then is there any that will receive admonition?

33. The people of Lut rejected

بِالنُّذُرِ ۝ إِنَّا أَرْسَلْنَا عَلَيْهِمْ

حَاصِبًا إِلَّا آلَ لُوطٍ نَجَّيْنَاهُمْ

بِسَحَرٍ ۝ نِّعْمَةً مِّنْ عِنْدِنَا

كَذَٰلِكَ نَجْزِي مَنْ شَكَرَ ۝ وَلَقَدْ

أَنْذَرَهُمْ بَطْشَتَنَا فَتَمَارَوْا

بِالنُّذُرِ ۝ وَلَقَدْ رَاوَدُوهُ عَنْ

ضَيْفِهِ فَطَمَسْنَا أَعْيُنَهُمْ فَذُوقُوا

عَذَابِي وَنُذُرِ ۝ وَلَقَدْ صَبَّحَهُمْ

بُكْرَةً عَذَابٌ مُّسْتَقِرٌّ ۝ فَذُوقُوا

(his) warning.

34. We sent against them a violent tornado with showers of stones, (which destroyed them), except Lut's household: them We delivered by early Dawn, -

35. As a Grace from Us: thus do We reward those who give thanks.

36. And (Lut) did warn them of Our Punishment, but they disputed about the Warning.

37. And they even sought to snatch away his guests from him, but We blinded their eyes. (They heard:) "Now taste you My Wrath and My Warning."

38. Early on the morrow an abiding Punishment seized them:

39. "So taste you

عَذَابِي وَنُذُرِ ۞ وَلَقَدْ يَسَّرْنَا

الْقُرْآنَ لِلذِّكْرِ فَهَلْ مِنْ مُّدَّكِرٍ ۞

وَلَقَدْ جَآءَ الَ فِرْعَوْنَ النُّذُرُ ۞

كَذَّبُوا بِأَيْتِنَا كُلِّهَا فَأَخَذْنَٰهُمْ

أَخْذَ عَزِيزٍ مُّقْتَدِرٍ ۞ أَكُفَّارُكُمْ

خَيْرٌ مِّنْ أُولَٰٓئِكُمْ أَمْ لَكُمْ

بَرَآءَةٌ فِى الزُّبُرِ ۞ أَمْ يَقُولُونَ

نَحْنُ جَمِيعٌ مُّنْتَصِرٌ ۞ سَيُهْزَمُ

الْجَمْعُ وَيُوَلُّونَ الدُّبُرَ ۞ بَلِ

My Wrath and My Warning."

40.   And We have indeed made the Qur'an easy to understand and remember: then is there any that will receive admonition?

41.   To the People of Pharaoh, too, aforetime, came warners (from Allah).

42.   The (people) rejected all Our Signs; but We seized them with such Chastisement (as comes) from One Exalted in Power, able to carry out His Will.

43.   Are your unbelievers, (O Quraish), better than they? Or have you an immunity in the Sacred Books?

44.   Or do they say: "We acting together can defend ourselves"?

45.   Soon will their multitude be put to flight, and they will show their backs.   **46.**   No,

السَّاعَةُ مَوْعِدُهُمْ وَالسَّاعَةُ

أَدْهَىٰ وَأَمَرُّ ۞ إِنَّ الْمُجْرِمِينَ

فِى ضَلَلٍ وَسُعُرٍ ۞ يَوْمَ يُسْحَبُونَ

فِى النَّارِ عَلَىٰ وُجُوهِهِمْ ذُوقُوا

مَسَّ سَقَرَ ۞ إِنَّا كُلَّ شَىْءٍ

خَلَقْنَٰهُ بِقَدَرٍ ۞ وَمَآ أَمْرُنَآ

إِلَّا وَاحِدَةٌ كَلَمْحٍ بِالْبَصَرِ ۞

وَلَقَدْ أَهْلَكْنَآ أَشْيَاعَكُمْ فَهَلْ

مِن مُّدَّكِرٍ ۞ وَكُلُّ شَىْءٍ فَعَلُوهُ

the Hour (of Judgment) is the time promised them (for their full recompense): and that Hour will be most grievous and most bitter.

47. Truly those in sin are the ones straying in mind, and mad.

48. The Day they will be dragged through the Fire on their faces, (they will hear:) "Taste you the touch of Hell!"

49. Verily, all things have We created in proportion and measure.

50. And Our Command is but a single (Act), - like the twinkling of an eye.

51. And (oft) in the past, have We destroyed gangs like you: then is there any that will receive admonition?

52. All that they do is noted

فِى الزُّبُرِ ۞ وَكُلُّ صَغِيرٍ وَّكَبِيرٍ

مُّسْتَطَرٌ ۞ اِنَّ الْمُتَّقِينَ فِى

جَنّٰتٍ وَّنَهَرٍ ۞ فِى مَقْعَدِ صِدْقٍ

عِنْدَ مَلِيكٍ مُّقْتَدِرٍ ۞

بِسْمِ اللهِ الرَّحْمٰنِ الرَّحِيمِ

اَلرَّحْمٰنُ ۞ عَلَّمَ الْقُرْاٰنَ ۞ خَلَقَ

الْاِنْسَانَ ۞ عَلَّمَهُ الْبَيَانَ ۞

اَلشَّمْسُ وَالْقَمَرُ بِحُسْبَانٍ ۞

وَالنَّجْمُ وَالشَّجَرُ يَسْجُدَانِ ۞

in (their) Books (of Deeds):

53. Every matter, small and great, is on record.

54. As to the Righteous, they will be in the midst of Gardens and Rivers,

55. In an Assembly of Truth, in the Presence of a Sovereign Omnipotent.

Ar-Rahman (Most Gracious)

Bismillahir-Rahmanir-Rahim

1. (Allah) Most Gracious!

2. It is He Who has taught the Qur'an. **3.** He has created man:

4. He has taught him speech (and intelligence).

5. The sun and the moon follow courses (exactly) computed;

6. And the herbs and the trees - both (alike) bow in adoration.

وَالسَّمَآءَ رَفَعَهَا وَوَضَعَ الْمِيزَانَ ۞

اَلَّا تَطْغَوْا فِى الْمِيزَانِ ۞ وَاَقِيمُوا

الْوَزْنَ بِالْقِسْطِ وَلَا تُخْسِرُوا

الْمِيزَانَ ۞ وَالْاَرْضَ وَضَعَهَا

لِلْاَنَامِ ۞ فِيْهَا فَاكِهَةٌ وَّالنَّخْلُ

ذَاتُ الْاَكْمَامِ ۞ وَالْحَبُّ ذُو الْعَصْفِ

وَالرَّيْحَانُ ۞ فَبِاَىِّ اٰلَآءِ رَبِّكُمَا

تُكَذِّبٰنِ ۞ خَلَقَ الْاِنْسَانَ مِنْ

صَلْصَالٍ كَالْفَخَّارِ ۞ وَخَلَقَ الْجَآنَّ

7.   And the Firmament has He raised high, and He has set up the Balance (of Justice),

8.   In order that you may not transgress (due) balance.

9.   So establish weight with justice and fall not short in the balance.

10.   It is He Who has spread out the earth for (His) creatures:

11.   Therein is fruit and date-palms, producing spathes (enclosing dates);

12.   Also corn, with (its) leaves and stalk for fodder, and sweet-smelling plants.

13.   Then which of the favours of your Lord will you deny?

14.   He created man from sounding clay like unto pottery,

15.   And He created Jinns

مِن مَّارِجٍ مِّن نَّارٍ ۝ فَبِأَيِّ

الَآءِ رَبِّكُمَا تُكَذِّبَانِ ۝ رَبُّ

الْمَشْرِقَيْنِ وَرَبُّ الْمَغْرِبَيْنِ ۝

فَبِأَيِّ الَآءِ رَبِّكُمَا تُكَذِّبَانِ ۝ مَرَجَ

الْبَحْرَيْنِ يَلْتَقِيَانِ ۝ بَيْنَهُمَا

بَرْزَخٌ لَّا يَبْغِيَانِ ۝ فَبِأَيِّ الَآءِ

رَبِّكُمَا تُكَذِّبَانِ ۝ يَخْرُجُ مِنْهُمَا

اللُّؤْلُؤُ وَالْمَرْجَانُ ۝ فَبِأَيِّ الَآءِ

رَبِّكُمَا تُكَذِّبَانِ ۝ وَلَهُ الْجَوَارِ

from fire free of smoke:

16. Then which of the favours of your Lord will you deny?

17. (He is) Lord of the two Easts and Lord of the two Wests:

18. Then which of the favours of your Lord will you deny?

19. He has let free the two seas of flowing water, meeting together:

20. Between them is a Barrier which they do not transgress:

21. Then which of the favours of your Lord will you deny?

22. Out of them come Pearls and Coral:

23. Then which of the favours of your Lord will you deny?

24. And His are the ships

وَالْمُنْشَئَاتُ فِي الْبَحْرِ كَالْأَعْلَامِ ۚ ۞

فَبِأَيِّ آلَاءِ رَبِّكُمَا تُكَذِّبَانِ ۞ كُلُّ

مَنْ عَلَيْهَا فَانٍ ۞ وَّيَبْقٰى وَجْهُ

رَبِّكَ ذُو الْجَلَالِ وَالْإِكْرَامِ ۞ فَبِأَيِّ

آلَاءِ رَبِّكُمَا تُكَذِّبَانِ ۞ يَسْـَٔلُهٗ

مَنْ فِي السَّمٰوٰتِ وَالْأَرْضِ ۚ كُلَّ

يَوْمٍ هُوَ فِي شَأْنٍ ۞ فَبِأَيِّ آلَاءِ

رَبِّكُمَا تُكَذِّبَانِ ۞ سَنَفْرُغُ لَكُمْ

أَيُّهَ الثَّقَلَانِ ۞ فَبِأَيِّ آلَاءِ رَبِّكُمَا

sailing smoothly through the seas, lofty as mountains:

25. Then which of the favours of your Lord will you deny?

26. All that is on earth will perish:

27. But will abide (for ever) the Face of your Lord, - full of Majesty, Bounty and Honour.

28. Then which of the favours of your Lord will you deny?

29. Of Him seeks (its need) every creature in the heavens and on earth: every day in (new) Splendour does He (shine)!

30. Then which of the favours of your Lord will you deny?

31. Soon shall We settle your affairs, O burden of the world.

32. Then which of the favours of your Lord

تُكَذِّبَانِ ۞ يَمَعْشَرَ الْجِنِّ وَالْإِنْسِ

إِنِ اسْتَطَعْتُمْ أَنْ تَنْفُذُوا مِنْ

أَقْطَارِ السَّمٰوٰتِ وَالْأَرْضِ فَانْفُذُوا ۗ

لَا تَنْفُذُونَ إِلَّا بِسُلْطٰنٍ ۞ فَبِأَيِّ

اٰلَاءِ رَبِّكُمَا تُكَذِّبَانِ ۞ يُرْسَلُ عَلَيْكُمَا

شُوَاظٌ مِّنْ نَّارٍ ۙ وَّنُحَاسٌ فَلَا

تَنْتَصِرَانِ ۞ فَبِأَيِّ اٰلَاءِ رَبِّكُمَا

تُكَذِّبَانِ ۞ فَإِذَا انْشَقَّتِ السَّمَاءُ

فَكَانَتْ وَرْدَةً كَالدِّهَانِ ۞ فَبِأَيِّ

will you deny?

33. O you assembly of Jinns and men! If it be you can pass beyond the zones of the heavens and the earth, pass you! Not without authority shall you be able to pass!

34. Then which of the favours of your Lord will you deny?

35. On you will be sent (O you evil ones twain) a flame of fire (to burn) and a smoke (to choke): no defence will you have:

36. Then which of the favours of your Lord will you deny?

37. When the sky is rent asunder, and it becomes red like ointment:

38. Then which of

اٰلَاۤءِ رَبِّكُمَا تُكَذِّبٰنِ ۞ فَيَوْمَىِٕذٍ

لَّا يُسْـَٔلُ عَنْ ذَنْۢبِهٖۤ اِنْسٌ وَّلَا

جَآنٌّ ۞ فَبِاَىِّ اٰلَاۤءِ رَبِّكُمَا تُكَذِّبٰنِ ۞

يُعْرَفُ الْمُجْرِمُوْنَ بِسِيْمٰهُمْ فَيُؤْخَذُ

بِالنَّوَاصِيْ وَالْاَقْدَامِ ۞ فَبِاَىِّ اٰلَاۤءِ

رَبِّكُمَا تُكَذِّبٰنِ ۞ هٰذِهٖ جَهَنَّمُ

الَّتِيْ يُكَذِّبُ بِهَا الْمُجْرِمُوْنَ ۞

يَطُوْفُوْنَ بَيْنَهَا وَبَيْنَ حَمِيْمٍ اٰنٍ ۞

فَبِاَىِّ اٰلَاۤءِ رَبِّكُمَا تُكَذِّبٰنِ ۞ وَلِمَنْ

the favours of your Lord will you deny?

39. On that Day no question will be asked of man or Jinn as to his sin.

40. Then which of the favours of your Lord will you deny?

41. (For) the sinners will be known by their marks: and they will be seized by their forelocks and their feet.

42. Then which of the favours of your Lord will you deny?

43. This is the Hell which the Sinners deny:

44. In its midst and in the midst of boiling hot water will they wander round!

45. Then which of the favours of your Lord will you deny?

46. But for such as

خَافَ مَقَامَ رَبِّهِ جَنَّتَانِ ۞

فَبِأَىِّ آلَاءِ رَبِّكُمَا تُكَذِّبَانِ ۞

ذَوَاتَا أَفْنَانٍ ۞ فَبِأَىِّ آلَاءِ رَبِّكُمَا

تُكَذِّبَانِ ۞ فِيهِمَا عَيْنَانِ تَجْرِيَانِ ۞

فَبِأَىِّ آلَاءِ رَبِّكُمَا تُكَذِّبَانِ ۞

فِيهِمَا مِنْ كُلِّ فَاكِهَةٍ زَوْجَانِ ۞

فَبِأَىِّ آلَاءِ رَبِّكُمَا تُكَذِّبَانِ ۞

مُتَّكِئِينَ عَلَى فُرُشٍ بَطَائِنُهَا مِنْ

إِسْتَبْرَقٍ وَجَنَا الْجَنَّتَيْنِ دَانٍ ۞

fear the time when they will stand before (the Judgment Seat of) their Lord, there will be two Gardens -

47. Then which of the favours of your Lord will you deny? -

48. Containing all kinds (of trees and delights); -

49. Then which of the favours of your Lord will you deny? -

50. In them (each) will be two springs flowing (free);

51. Then which of the favours of your Lord will you deny? -

52. In them will be Fruits of every kind, two and two.

53. Then which of the favours of your Lord will you deny?

54. They will recline on carpets, whose inner linings will be of rich brocade: the Fruit of the Gardens will be near (and easy of reach).

فَبِأَيِّ اٰلَاۤءِ رَبِّكُمَا تُكَذِّبٰنِ ۩ فِيْهِنَّ

قٰصِرٰتُ الطَّرْفِ لَمْ يَطْمِثْهُنَّ اِنْسٌ

قَبْلَهُمْ وَلَا جَآنٌّ ۩ فَبِأَيِّ اٰلَاۤءِ

رَبِّكُمَا تُكَذِّبٰنِ ۩ كَأَنَّهُنَّ الْيَاقُوْتُ

وَالْمَرْجَانُ ۩ فَبِأَيِّ اٰلَاۤءِ رَبِّكُمَا

تُكَذِّبٰنِ ۩ هَلْ جَزَآءُ الْاِحْسَانِ

اِلَّا الْاِحْسَانُ ۩ فَبِأَيِّ اٰلَاۤءِ رَبِّكُمَا

تُكَذِّبٰنِ ۩ وَمِنْ دُوْنِهِمَا جَنَّتٰنِ ۩

فَبِأَيِّ اٰلَاۤءِ رَبِّكُمَا تُكَذِّبٰنِ ۩

55. Then which of the favours of your Lord will you deny?

56. In them will be (Maidens), chaste, restraining their glances, whom no man or Jinn before them has touched; -

57. Then which of the favours of your Lord will you deny? -

58. Like unto Rubies and coral.

59. Then which of the favours of your Lord will you deny?

60. Is there any Reward for Good - other than Good?

61. Then which of the favours of your Lord will you deny?

62. And besides these two, there are two other Gardens, -

63. Then which of the favours of your Lord will you deny? -

مُدْهَآمَّتَانِ ۝ فَبِأَيِّ آلَآءِ رَبِّكُمَا

تُكَذِّبَانِ ۝ فِيهِمَا عَيْنَانِ نَضَّاخَتَانِ ۝

فَبِأَيِّ آلَآءِ رَبِّكُمَا تُكَذِّبَانِ ۝ فِيهِمَا

فَاكِهَةٌ وَّنَخْلٌ وَّرُمَّانٌ ۝ فَبِأَيِّ

آلَآءِ رَبِّكُمَا تُكَذِّبَانِ ۝ فِيهِنَّ

خَيْرَاتٌ حِسَانٌ ۝ فَبِأَيِّ آلَآءِ رَبِّكُمَا

تُكَذِّبَانِ ۝ حُورٌ مَّقْصُورَاتٌ فِي

الْخِيَامِ ۝ فَبِأَيِّ آلَآءِ رَبِّكُمَا

تُكَذِّبَانِ ۝ لَمْ يَطْمِثْهُنَّ إِنْسٌ

64. Dark-green in colour (from plentiful watering).

65. Then which of the favours of your Lord will you deny?

66. In them (each) will be two springs pouring forth water in continuous abundance:

67. Then which of the favours of your Lord will you deny?

68. In them will be Fruits, and dates and pomegranates:

69. Then which of the favours of your Lord will you deny?

70. In them will be fair (Companions), good, beautiful; -

71. Then which of the favours of your Lord will you deny? -

72. Companions restrained (as to their glances), in (goodly) pavilions; -

73. Then which of the favours of your Lord will you deny? -

74. Whom no man

قَبْلَهُمْ وَلَا جَآنٌّ ۝ فَبِأَىِّ اٰلَآءِ

رَبِّكُمَا تُكَذِّبٰنِ ۝ مُتَّكِئِيْنَ عَلٰى

رَفْرَفٍ خُضْرٍ وَّعَبْقَرِيٍّ حِسَانٍ ۝

فَبِأَىِّ اٰلَآءِ رَبِّكُمَا تُكَذِّبٰنِ ۝ تَبٰرَكَ

اسْمُ رَبِّكَ ذِى الْجَلٰلِ وَالْإِكْرَامِ ۝

بِسْمِ اللهِ الرَّحْمٰنِ الرَّحِيْمِ

اِذَا وَقَعَتِ الْوَاقِعَةُ ۝ لَيْسَ

لِوَقْعَتِهَا كَاذِبَةٌ ۝ خَافِضَةٌ

رَّافِعَةٌ ۝ اِذَا رُجَّتِ الْأَرْضُ

or Jinn before them has touched; -

75. Then which of the favours of your Lord will you deny? -

76. Reclining on green cushions and rich carpets of beauty.

77. Then which of the favours of your Lord will you deny?

78. Blessed be the name of your Lord, full of Majesty, Bounty and Honour.

Al-Waqi'a
(The Inevitable Event)

Bismillahir-Rahmanir-Rahim

1. When the inevitable event comes to pass,

2. Then will no (soul) deny its coming.

3. (Many) will it bring low; (many) will it exalt;

4. When the Earth shall be shaken

هَاجًا ۞ وَّبُسَّتِ الْجِبَالُ بَسًّا ۞ فَكَانَتْ هَبَاءً مُّنْبَثًّا ۞ وَّكُنْتُمْ أَزْوَاجًا ثَلٰثَةً ۞ فَأَصْحٰبُ الْمَيْمَنَةِ مَا أَصْحٰبُ الْمَيْمَنَةِ ۞ وَأَصْحٰبُ الْمَشْئَمَةِ مَا أَصْحٰبُ الْمَشْئَمَةِ ۞ وَالسّٰبِقُونَ السّٰبِقُونَ ۞ أُولٰئِكَ الْمُقَرَّبُونَ ۞ فِى جَنّٰتِ النَّعِيمِ ۞ ثُلَّةٌ مِّنَ الْأَوَّلِينَ ۞ وَقَلِيلٌ مِّنَ الْأٰخِرِينَ ۞ عَلٰى سُرُرٍ مَّوْضُونَةٍ ۞

to its depths,

5. And the mountains shall be crumbled to atoms,

6. Becoming dust scattered abroad, **7.** And you shall be sorted out into three classes.

8. Then (there will be) the People of the Right Hand; –What will be the People of the Right Hand? **9.** And the People of the Left Hand, – what will be the People of the Left Hand?

10. And those foremost (in Faith) will be foremost (in the Hereafter).

11. These will be those Nearest to Allah: **12.** In Gardens of Bliss:

13. A number of people from those of old,

14. And a few from those of later times. **15.** (They will be) on Thrones encrusted (with gold and precious stones),

مُتَّكِئِيْنَ عَلَيْهَا مُتَقَابِلِيْنَ ۝ يَطُوْفُ

عَلَيْهِمْ وِلْدَانٌ مُّخَلَّدُوْنَ ۝ بِأَكْوَابٍ

وَّأَبَارِيْقَ ۙ وَكَأْسٍ مِّنْ مَّعِيْنٍ ۝

لَّا يُصَدَّعُوْنَ عَنْهَا وَلَا يُنْزِفُوْنَ ۝

وَفَاكِهَةٍ مِّمَّا يَتَخَيَّرُوْنَ ۝ وَلَحْمِ

طَيْرٍ مِّمَّا يَشْتَهُوْنَ ۝ وَحُوْرٌ

عِيْنٌ ۝ كَأَمْثَالِ اللُّؤْلُؤِ الْمَكْنُوْنِ ۝

جَزَاءً بِمَا كَانُوْا يَعْمَلُوْنَ ۝ لَا

يَسْمَعُوْنَ فِيْهَا لَغْوًا وَّلَا تَأْثِيْمًا ۝

16. Reclining on them, facing each other.

17. Round about them will (serve) youths of perpetual (freshness),

18. With goblets, (shining) beakers, and cups (filled) out of clear-flowing fountains:

19. No after-ache will they receive therefrom, nor will they suffer intoxication:

20. And with fruits, any that they may select:

21. And the flesh of fowls, any that they may desire.

22. And (there will be) Companions with beautiful, big, and lustrous eyes, -

23. Like unto Pearls well-guarded. **24.** A Reward for the deeds of their past (life).

25. Not frivolity will they hear therein, nor any taint of ill, -

إِلَّا قِيلًا سَلٰمًا سَلٰمًا ۞ وَأَصْحٰبُ

الْيَمِيْنِ ۙ مَآ أَصْحٰبُ الْيَمِيْنِ ۞ فِيْ

سِدْرٍ مَّخْضُوْدٍ ۞ وَّطَلْحٍ مَّنْضُوْدٍ ۞

وَّظِلٍّ مَّمْدُوْدٍ ۞ وَّمَآءٍ مَّسْكُوْبٍ ۞

وَّفَاكِهَةٍ كَثِيْرَةٍ ۞ لَّا مَقْطُوْعَةٍ

وَّلَا مَمْنُوْعَةٍ ۞ وَّفُرُشٍ مَّرْفُوْعَةٍ ۞

إِنَّآ أَنْشَأْنٰهُنَّ إِنْشَآءً ۞ فَجَعَلْنٰهُنَّ

أَبْكَارًا ۞ عُرُبًا أَتْرَابًا ۞ لِّأَصْحٰبِ

الْيَمِيْنِ ۞ ثُلَّةٌ مِّنَ الْأَوَّلِيْنَ ۞

26. Only the saying, "Peace! Peace".

27. The Companions of the Right Hand, - what will be the Companions of the Right Hand?

28. (They will be) among Lote-trees without thorns,

29. Among Talh trees with flowers (or fruits) piled one above another, -

30. In shade long-extended,

31. By water flowing constantly,

32. And fruit in abundance.

33. Whose season is not limited, nor (supply) forbidden,

34. And on Thrones (of Dignity), raised high.

35. We have created (their Companions) of special creation.

36. And made them virgin-pure (and undefiled), **37.** Beloved (by nature), equal in age, - **38.** For the Companions of the Right Hand.

39. A (goodly) number from those of old,

وَثُلَّةٌ مِّنَ الْأَخِرِينَ ۞ وَأَصْحَبُ

الشِّمَالِ ۙ مَآ أَصْحَبُ الشِّمَالِ ۞

فِى سَمُومٍ وَّحَمِيمٍ ۞ وَّظِلٍّ مِّنْ

يَّحْمُومٍ ۞ لَّا بَارِدٍ وَّلَا كَرِيمٍ ۞

إِنَّهُمْ كَانُوا قَبْلَ ذَلِكَ مُتْرَفِينَ ۞

وَكَانُوا يُصِرُّونَ عَلَى الْحِنْثِ

الْعَظِيمِ ۞ وَكَانُوا يَقُولُونَ ۙ أَئِذَا

مِتْنَا وَكُنَّا تُرَابًا وَّعِظَامًا ءَإِنَّا

لَمَبْعُوثُونَ ۞ أَوَ ءَابَآؤُنَا الْأَوَّلُونَ ۞

40. And a (goodly) number from those of later times.

41. The Companions of the Left Hand, - what will be the Companions of the Left Hand?

42. (They will be) in the midst of a fierce Blast of Fire and in Boiling Water,

43. And in the shades of Black Smoke: **44.** Nothing (will there be) to refresh, nor to please:

45. For that they were wont to be indulged, before that, in sinful and luxury,

46. And persisted obstinately in wickedness supreme!

47. And they used to say, "What! When we die and become dust and bones, shall we then indeed be raised up again? -

48. "(We) and our fathers of old?"

قُلْ اِنَّ الْاَوَّلِيْنَ وَالْاٰخِرِيْنَ ۞

لَمَجْمُوْعُوْنَ ۙ اِلٰى مِيْقَاتِ يَوْمٍ

مَّعْلُوْمٍ ۞ ثُمَّ اِنَّكُمْ اَيُّهَا الضَّآلُّوْنَ

الْمُكَذِّبُوْنَ ۙ لَاٰكِلُوْنَ مِنْ شَجَرٍ

مِّنْ زَقُّوْمٍ ۞ فَمَالِئُوْنَ مِنْهَا

الْبُطُوْنَ ۞ فَشَارِبُوْنَ عَلَيْهِ مِنَ

الْحَمِيْمِ ۞ فَشَارِبُوْنَ شُرْبَ الْهِيْمِ ۞

هٰذَا نُزُلُهُمْ يَوْمَ الدِّيْنِ ۞ نَحْنُ

خَلَقْنٰكُمْ فَلَوْلَا تُصَدِّقُوْنَ ۞

49. Say: "Yes, those of old and those of later times,"

50. "All will certainly be gathered together for the Meeting appointed for a Day well-known."

51. "Then will you truly,- O you that go wrong, and treat (Truth) as Falsehood! -

52. "You will surely taste of the tree of Zaqqum."

53. "Then will you fill your insides therewith,"

54. "And drink Boiling Water on top of it:"

55. "Indeed you shall drink like diseased camels raging with thirst!" **56.** Such will be their entertainment on the Day of Requital! **57.** It is We Who have created you: why will you not witness the Truth?

أَفَرَءَيْتُمْ مَّا تُمْنُونَ ۞ ءَأَنتُمْ

تَخْلُقُونَهُ أَمْ نَحْنُ الْخَالِقُونَ ۞

نَحْنُ قَدَّرْنَا بَيْنَكُمُ الْمَوْتَ

وَمَا نَحْنُ بِمَسْبُوقِينَ ۞ عَلَى

أَن نُّبَدِّلَ أَمْثَالَكُمْ وَنُنشِئَكُمْ

فِي مَا لَا تَعْلَمُونَ ۞ وَلَقَدْ

عَلِمْتُمُ النَّشْأَةَ الْأُولَى فَلَوْلَا

تَذَكَّرُونَ ۞ أَفَرَءَيْتُم مَّا تَحْرُثُونَ ۞

ءَأَنتُمْ تَزْرَعُونَهُ أَمْ نَحْنُ

58. Do you then see? - The (human seed) that you throw out, -

59. Is it you who create it, or are We the Creators?

60. We have decreed Death to be your common lot, and We are not to be frustrated

61. from changing your Forms and creating you (again) in (Forms) that you know not.

62. And you certainly know already the first form of creation: why then do you not celebrate His praises?

63. See you the seed that you sow in the ground?

64. Is it you that cause it to grow, or are We

الزَّرِعُوْنَ ۞ لَوْ نَشَاءُ لَجَعَلْنٰهُ

حُطَامًا فَظَلْتُمْ تَفَكَّهُوْنَ ۞ إِنَّا

لَمُغْرَمُوْنَ ۞ بَلْ نَحْنُ مَحْرُوْمُوْنَ ۞

اَفَرَءَيْتُمُ الْمَاءَ الَّذِيْ تَشْرَبُوْنَ ۞

ءَاَنْتُمْ اَنْزَلْتُمُوْهُ مِنَ الْمُزْنِ

اَمْ نَحْنُ الْمُنْزِلُوْنَ ۞ لَوْ نَشَاءُ

جَعَلْنٰهُ اُجَاجًا فَلَوْلَا تَشْكُرُوْنَ ۞

اَفَرَءَيْتُمُ النَّارَ الَّتِيْ تُوْرُوْنَ ۞

ءَاَنْتُمْ اَنْشَأْتُمْ شَجَرَتَهَا اَمْ

the Cause?

65. Were it Our Will, We could crumble it to dry powder, and you would be left in wonderment,

66. (Saying), "We are indeed left with debts (for nothing):"

67. "Indeed are we shut out (of the fruits of our labour)".

68. See you the water which you drink?

69. Do you bring it down (in rain) from the cloud or do We?

70. Were it Our Will, We could make it salt (and unpalatable): then why do you not give thanks?

71. See you the Fire which you kindle?

72. Is it you who grow the tree which feeds the fire, or

نَحْنُ الْمُنْشِئُونَ ۞ نَحْنُ جَعَلْنَاهَا

تَذْكِرَةً وَّ مَتَاعًا لِّلْمُقْوِينَ ۞

فَسَبِّحْ بِاسْمِ رَبِّكَ الْعَظِيمِ ۞

فَلَا أُقْسِمُ بِمَوَاقِعِ النُّجُومِ ۞

وَ إِنَّهُ لَقَسَمٌ لَّوْ تَعْلَمُونَ

عَظِيمٌ ۞ إِنَّهُ لَقُرْآنٌ كَرِيمٌ ۞

فِي كِتَابٍ مَّكْنُونٍ ۞ لَّا يَمَسُّهُ

إِلَّا الْمُطَهَّرُونَ ۞ تَنْزِيلٌ مِّنْ

رَّبِّ الْعَالَمِينَ ۞ أَفَبِهَذَا الْحَدِيثِ

do We grow it?

73. We have made it a memorial (of Our handiwork), and an article of comfort and convenience for the denizens of deserts.

74. Then celebrate with praises the name of your Lord, the Supreme!

75. Furthermore I call to witness the setting of the Stars, -

76. And that is indeed a mighty adjuration if you but knew, -

77. That this is indeed a Qur'an, Most Honourable,

78. In a Book well-guarded,

79. Which none shall touch but those who are clean:

80. A Revelation from the Lord of the Worlds.

81. Is it such a Message

أَنْتُمْ مُّدْهِنُوْنَ ۞ وَتَجْعَلُوْنَ

رِزْقَكُمْ أَنَّكُمْ تُكَذِّبُوْنَ ۞ فَلَوْلَا

إِذَا بَلَغَتِ الْحُلْقُوْمَ ۞ وَأَنْتُمْ

حِيْنَئِذٍ تَنْظُرُوْنَ ۞ وَنَحْنُ أَقْرَبُ

إِلَيْهِ مِنْكُمْ وَلٰكِنْ لَّا تُبْصِرُوْنَ ۞

فَلَوْلَا إِنْ كُنْتُمْ غَيْرَ مَدِيْنِيْنَ ۞

تَرْجِعُوْنَهَا إِنْ كُنْتُمْ صٰدِقِيْنَ ۞

فَأَمَّا إِنْ كَانَ مِنَ الْمُقَرَّبِيْنَ ۞

فَرَوْحٌ وَّرَيْحَانٌ ۙ وَّجَنَّتُ نَعِيْمٍ ۞ وَأَمَّا

that you would hold in light esteem?

82. And is it only this of your thanksgiving that you declare it false?

83. Then why do you not (intervene) when (the soul of the dying man) reaches the throat, -

84. And you the while (sit) looking on, -

85. But We are nearer to him than you, and yet see not, -

86. Then why do you not, - if you are exempt from (future) account, -

87. Call back the soul, if you are true (in the claim of independence)?

88. Thus, then, if he be of those Nearest to Allah,

89. (There is for him) Rest and Satisfaction, and a Garden of Delights.

90. And

إِنْ كَانَ مِنْ أَصْحَبِ الْيَمِينِ ۞

فَسَلَمٌ لَّكَ مِنْ أَصْحَبِ الْيَمِينِ ۞

وَأَمَّا إِنْ كَانَ مِنَ الْمُكَذِّبِينَ

الضَّالِّينَ ۞ فَنُزُلٌ مِّنْ حَمِيمٍ ۞

وَّتَصْلِيَةُ جَحِيمٍ ۞ إِنَّ هَذَا

لَهُوَ حَقُّ الْيَقِينِ ۞ فَسَبِّحْ بِاسْمِ

رَبِّكَ الْعَظِيمِ ۞

سُورَةُ الْحَدِيدِ مَدَنِيَّةٌ بِسْمِ اللهِ الرَّحْمٰنِ الرَّحِيمِ ٢٩ آيَاتُهَا رُكُوعَاتُهَا ٤

سَبَّحَ لِلَّهِ مَا فِي السَّمٰوٰتِ وَالْأَرْضِ

if he be of the Companions of the Right Hand,

91. (For him is the salutation), "Peace be unto you", from the Companions of the Right Hand.

92. And if he be of those who treat (Truth) as Falsehood, who go wrong,

93. For him is Entertainment with Boiling Water.

94. And burning in Hell-Fire.

95. Verily, this is the very Truth of assured certainty.

96. So celebrate with praises the name of your Lord, the Supreme.

Al-Hadid (Iron)

Bismillahir-Rahmanir-Rahim

1. Whatever is in the heavens and on earth, - let it declare the Praises and Glory of Allah:

وَهُوَ الْعَزِيزُ الْحَكِيمُ ۞ لَهُ مُلْكُ

السَّمٰوٰتِ وَالْأَرْضِ يُحْيٖ وَيُمِيتُ

وَهُوَ عَلٰى كُلِّ شَيْءٍ قَدِيرٌ ۞ هُوَ

الْأَوَّلُ وَالْآخِرُ وَالظَّاهِرُ وَالْبَاطِنُ

وَهُوَ بِكُلِّ شَيْءٍ عَلِيمٌ ۞ هُوَ

الَّذِيْ خَلَقَ السَّمٰوٰتِ وَالْأَرْضَ

فِيْ سِتَّةِ أَيَّامٍ ثُمَّ اسْتَوٰى

عَلَى الْعَرْشِ يَعْلَمُ مَا يَلِجُ

فِي الْأَرْضِ وَمَا يَخْرُجُ مِنْهَا

for He is the Exalted in Might, the Wise.

2.   To Him belongs the dominion of the heavens and the earth: it is He Who gives Life and Death; and He has Power over all things.

3.   He is the First and the Last, the Evident and the Hidden: and He has full knowledge of all things.

4.   He it is Who created the heavens and the earth in Six Days, and is moreover firmly established on the Throne (of Authority). He knows what enters within the earth and what comes forth out of it,

وَمَا يَنْزِلُ مِنَ السَّمَاءِ وَمَا
يَعْرُجُ فِيهَا ۖ وَهُوَ مَعَكُمْ أَيْنَ
مَا كُنْتُمْ ۚ وَاللّٰهُ بِمَا تَعْمَلُونَ
بَصِيرٌ ۞ لَهُ مُلْكُ السَّمٰوٰتِ
وَالْأَرْضِ ۚ وَإِلَى اللّٰهِ تُرْجَعُ
الْأُمُورُ ۞ يُولِجُ الَّيْلَ فِي النَّهَارِ
وَيُولِجُ النَّهَارَ فِي الَّيْلِ ۚ وَهُوَ
عَلِيمٌ بِذَاتِ الصُّدُورِ ۞ آمِنُوا
بِاللّٰهِ وَرَسُولِهِ وَأَنْفِقُوا مِمَّا

what comes down from heaven and what mounts up to it. And He is with you wheresoever you may be. And Allah sees well all that you do.

5. To Him belongs the dominion of the heavens and the earth: and all affairs are referred back to Allah.

6. He merges Night into Day, and He merges Day into Night; and He has full knowledge of the secrets of (all) hearts.

7. Believe in Allah and His Apostle, and spend (in charity) out of the (substance)

جَعَلَكُمْ مُّسْتَخْلَفِيْنَ فِيْهِ

فَالَّذِيْنَ اٰمَنُوْا مِنْكُمْ وَ اَنْفَقُوْا

لَهُمْ اَجْرٌ كَبِيْرٌ ۞ وَ مَا لَكُمْ

لَا تُؤْمِنُوْنَ بِاللّٰهِ وَ الرَّسُوْلُ

يَدْعُوْكُمْ لِتُؤْمِنُوْا بِرَبِّكُمْ وَقَدْ

اَخَذَ مِيْثَاقَكُمْ اِنْ كُنْتُمْ

مُّؤْمِنِيْنَ ۞ هُوَ الَّذِيْ يُنَزِّلُ

عَلٰى عَبْدِهٖ اٰيٰتٍۭ بَيِّنٰتٍ لِّيُخْرِجَكُمْ

مِّنَ الظُّلُمٰتِ اِلَى النُّوْرِ وَاِنَّ

whereof He has made you heirs.
For, those of you who believe and
spend (in charity), - for them is a
great Reward.

8. What cause have you why
you should not believe in
Allah? - And the Apostle invites
you to believe in your Lord, and
has indeed taken your Covenant,
if you are men of Faith.

9. He is the One Who sends to
His servant manifest Signs, that
He may lead you from the depths
of Darkness into the Light. And
verily

اللهُ بِكُمْ لَرَءُوفٌ رَّحِيمٌ ۞ وَمَا

لَكُمْ اَلَّا تُنْفِقُوا فِىْ سَبِيلِ اللهِ

وَلِلّٰهِ مِيْرَاثُ السَّمٰوٰتِ وَالْاَرْضِ ۚ

لَا يَسْتَوِىْ مِنْكُمْ مَّنْ اَنْفَقَ مِنْ

قَبْلِ الْفَتْحِ وَقَاتَلَ ۚ اُولٰٓئِكَ

اَعْظَمُ دَرَجَةً مِّنَ الَّذِيْنَ

اَنْفَقُوْا مِنْۢ بَعْدُ وَقَاتَلُوْا ۚ وَكُلًّا

وَّعَدَ اللهُ الْحُسْنٰى ۚ وَاللهُ بِمَا

تَعْمَلُوْنَ خَبِيْرٌ ۞ مَنْ ذَا الَّذِىْ

Allah is to you Most Kind and Merciful.

10. And what cause have you why you should not spend in the cause of Allah? For to Allah belongs the heritage of the heavens and the earth. Not equal among you are those who spent (freely) and fought, before the Victory, (with those who did so later). Those are higher in rank than those who spent (freely) and fought afterwards. But to all has Allah promised a goodly (reward). And Allah is Well Acquainted with all that you do.

11. Who is he that

يُقْرِضُ اللَّهَ قَرْضًا حَسَنًا فَيُضَعِفَهُ
لَهُ وَلَهُ أَجْرٌ كَرِيمٌ ۞ يَوْمَ تَرَى
الْمُؤْمِنِينَ وَالْمُؤْمِنَاتِ يَسْعَى نُورُهُم
بَيْنَ أَيْدِيهِمْ وَبِأَيْمَانِهِمْ بُشْرَىٰكُمُ
الْيَوْمَ جَنَّاتٌ تَجْرِى مِن تَحْتِهَا
الْأَنْهَارُ خَالِدِينَ فِيهَا ذَٰلِكَ هُوَ
الْفَوْزُ الْعَظِيمُ ۞ يَوْمَ يَقُولُ
الْمُنَافِقُونَ وَالْمُنَافِقَاتُ لِلَّذِينَ
ءَامَنُوا انظُرُونَا نَقْتَبِسْ مِن نُّورِكُمْ

will Loan to Allah a beautiful loan? For (Allah) will increase it manifold to his credit, and he will have (besides) a liberal Reward.

12. One Day shall you see the believing men and the believing women - how their Light runs forward before them and by their right hands: (their greeting will be): "Good News for you this Day! Gardens beneath which flow rivers! To dwell therein for ever! This is indeed the highest Achievement!"

13. One Day will the Hypocrites - men and women - say to the believers: "Wait for us! Let us borrow (a light) from your Light!"

قِيلَ ارْجِعُوا وَرَآءَكُمْ فَالْتَمِسُوا

نُوْرًا ۙ فَضُرِبَ بَيْنَهُمْ بِسُوْرٍ

لَّهٗ بَابٌ ۙ بَاطِنُهٗ فِيْهِ الرَّحْمَةُ

وَظَاهِرُهٗ مِنْ قِبَلِهِ الْعَذَابُ ۗ ۱۳

يُنَادُوْنَهُمْ اَلَمْ نَكُنْ مَّعَكُمْ ۖ قَالُوْا

بَلٰى وَلٰكِنَّكُمْ فَتَنْتُمْ اَنْفُسَكُمْ

وَتَرَبَّصْتُمْ وَارْتَبْتُمْ وَغَرَّتْكُمُ

الْاَمَانِيُّ حَتّٰى جَآءَ اَمْرُ اللّٰهِ

وَغَرَّكُمْ بِاللّٰهِ الْغَرُوْرُ ۱۴ فَالْيَوْمَ

It will be said: "Turn you back to your rear! Then seek a light (where you can)!" So a wall will be put up between them, with a gate therein. Within it will be Mercy throughout, and without it, all alongside, will be (Wrath and) Punishment!

14. (Those without) will call out, "Were we not with you?" (The others) will reply, "True! But you led yourselves into temptation; you looked forward (to our ruin); you doubted (Allah's Promise); and (your false) desires deceived you; until there issued the Command of Allah. And the Deceiver deceived you in respect of Allah.

15. "This Day

لَا يُؤْخَذُ مِنْكُمْ فِدْيَةٌ وَّلَا

مِنَ الَّذِيْنَ كَفَرُوْا ۚ مَأْوٰىكُمُ

النَّارُ ۚ هِىَ مَوْلٰىكُمْ ۚ وَبِئْسَ

الْمَصِيْرُ ۞ اَلَمْ يَأْنِ لِلَّذِيْنَ

اٰمَنُوْا اَنْ تَخْشَعَ قُلُوْبُهُمْ لِذِكْرِ

اللهِ وَمَا نَزَلَ مِنَ الْحَقِّ ۚ وَلَا

يَكُوْنُوْا كَالَّذِيْنَ اُوْتُوا الْكِتٰبَ

مِنْ قَبْلُ فَطَالَ عَلَيْهِمُ الْاَمَدُ

فَقَسَتْ قُلُوْبُهُمْ ۚ وَكَثِيْرٌ مِّنْهُمْ

shall no ransom be accepted of you, nor of those who rejected Allah. Your abode is the Fire: that is the proper place to claim you: and an evil refuge it is!"

16. Has not the time arrived for the believers that their hearts in all humility should engage in the remembrance of Allah and of the Truth which has been revealed (to them), and that they should not become like those to whom was given Revelation aforetime, but long ages passed over them and their hearts grew hard? For many among them

فَسِقُّوْنَ ۞ اعْلَمُوْٓا اَنَّ اللّٰهَ يُحْيِ الْاَرْضَ بَعْدَ مَوْتِهَا ؕ قَدْ بَيَّنَّا لَكُمُ الْاٰيٰتِ لَعَلَّكُمْ تَعْقِلُوْنَ ۞ اِنَّ الْمُصَّدِّقِيْنَ وَالْمُصَّدِّقٰتِ وَاَقْرَضُوا اللّٰهَ قَرْضًا حَسَنًا يُّضٰعَفُ لَهُمْ وَلَهُمْ اَجْرٌ كَرِيْمٌ ۞ وَالَّذِيْنَ اٰمَنُوْا بِاللّٰهِ وَرُسُلِهٖٓ اُولٰٓئِكَ هُمُ الصِّدِّيْقُوْنَ ۚ وَالشُّهَدَآءُ عِنْدَ رَبِّهِمْ ؕ لَهُمْ اَجْرُهُمْ وَنُوْرُهُمْ

are rebellious transgressors.

17. Know you (all) that Allah gives life to the earth after its death! Already have We shown the Signs plainly to you, that you may learn wisdom.

18. For those who give in Charity, men and women, and loan to Allah a beautiful loan, it shall be increased manifold (to their credit), and they shall have (besides) a liberal reward.

19. And those who believe in Allah and His Apostles - they are the sincere (lovers of Truth), and the witnesses (who testify), in the eyes of their Lord: they shall have their Reward and their Light.

وَالَّذِيْنَ كَفَرُوْا وَكَذَّبُوْا بِاٰيٰتِنَآ

اُولٰٓئِكَ اَصْحٰبُ الْجَحِيْمِ ۩ اِعْلَمُوْٓا

اَنَّمَا الْحَيٰوةُ الدُّنْيَا لَعِبٌ وَّلَهْوٌ

وَّزِيْنَةٌ وَّتَفَاخُرٌ بَيْنَكُمْ وَتَكَاثُرٌ

فِى الْاَمْوَالِ وَالْاَوْلَادِ ۗ كَمَثَلِ

غَيْثٍ اَعْجَبَ الْكُفَّارَ نَبَاتُهٗ ثُمَّ

يَهِيْجُ فَتَرٰىهُ مُصْفَرًّا ثُمَّ

يَكُوْنُ حُطَامًا ۗ وَفِى الْاٰخِرَةِ

عَذَابٌ شَدِيْدٌ وَّمَغْفِرَةٌ مِّنَ

But those who reject Allah and deny Our Signs, - they are the Companions of Hell-Fire.

20. Know you (all), that the life of this world is but play and amusement, pomp and mutual boasting and multiplying, (in rivalry) among yourselves, riches and children. Here is a similitude: How rain and the growth which it brings forth, delight (the hearts of) the tillers; soon it withers; you will see it grow yellow; then it becomes dry and crumbles away. But in the Hereafter is a Chastisement severe (for the devotees of wrong). And Forgiveness from

اللهِ وَرِضْوَانٌ ۚ وَمَا الْحَيٰوةُ

الدُّنْيَآ اِلَّا مَتَاعُ الْغُرُورِ ۞

سَابِقُوْٓا اِلٰى مَغْفِرَةٍ مِّنْ رَّبِّكُمْ

وَجَنَّةٍ عَرْضُهَا كَعَرْضِ السَّمَآءِ

وَالْاَرْضِ ۙ اُعِدَّتْ لِلَّذِيْنَ اٰمَنُوْا

بِاللهِ وَرُسُلِهٖ ۚ ذٰلِكَ فَضْلُ

اللهِ يُؤْتِيْهِ مَنْ يَّشَآءُ ۚ وَاللهُ

ذُو الْفَضْلِ الْعَظِيْمِ ۞ مَآ اَصَابَ

مِنْ مُّصِيْبَةٍ فِى الْاَرْضِ وَلَا

Allah and (His) Good Pleasure (for the devotees of Allah). And what is the life of this world, but goods and chattels of deception?

21. Be you foremost (in seeking) Forgiveness from your Lord, and a Garden (of Bliss), the width whereof is as the width of heaven and earth, prepared for those who believe in Allah and His Apostles: that is the Grace of Allah, which He bestows on whom he pleases: and Allah is the Lord of Grace abounding.

22. No misfortune can happen on earth or

فِىٓ اَنْفُسِكُمْ اِلَّا فِىْ كِتٰبٍ مِّنْ

قَبْلِ اَنْ نَّبْرَاَهَا ۚ اِنَّ ذٰلِكَ عَلَى

اللّٰهِ يَسِيْرٌ ۚ ۝ لِّكَيْلَا تَاْسَوْا عَلٰى

مَا فَاتَكُمْ وَلَا تَفْرَحُوْا بِمَآ اٰتٰىكُمْ ۗ

وَاللّٰهُ لَا يُحِبُّ كُلَّ مُخْتَالٍ فَخُوْرِ ۝

الَّذِيْنَ يَبْخَلُوْنَ وَيَاْمُرُوْنَ

النَّاسَ بِالْبُخْلِ ۗ وَمَنْ يَّتَوَلَّ فَاِنَّ

اللّٰهَ هُوَ الْغَنِىُّ الْحَمِيْدُ ۝ لَقَدْ

اَرْسَلْنَا رُسُلَنَا بِالْبَيِّنٰتِ وَاَنْزَلْنَا

in your souls but is recorded in a decree before We bring it into existence: That is truly easy for Allah:

23. In order that you may not despair over matters that pass you by, nor exult over favours bestowed upon you. For Allah loves not any vainglorious boaster, -

24. Such persons as are covetous and commend covetousness to men. And if any turn back (from Allah's Way), verily Allah is Free of all needs, Worthy of all praise.

25. We sent aforetime Our Apostles with clear Signs and sent down

مَعَهُمُ الْكِتَبَ وَالْمِيزَانَ لِيَقُوْمَ

النَّاسُ بِالْقِسْطِ ۚ وَاَنْزَلْنَا الْحَدِيْدَ

فِيْهِ بَأْسٌ شَدِيْدٌ وَّمَنَافِعُ

لِلنَّاسِ وَلِيَعْلَمَ اللّٰهُ مَنْ يَّنْصُرُهُ

وَرُسُلَهُ بِالْغَيْبِ ؕ اِنَّ اللّٰهَ قَوِيٌّ

عَزِيْزٌ ۞ وَلَقَدْ اَرْسَلْنَا نُوْحًا

وَّاِبْرٰهِيْمَ وَجَعَلْنَا فِيْ ذُرِّيَّتِهِمَا

النُّبُوَّةَ وَالْكِتٰبَ فَمِنْهُمْ مُّهْتَدٍ ۚ

وَكَثِيْرٌ مِّنْهُمْ فٰسِقُوْنَ ۞ ثُمَّ قَفَّيْنَا

with them the Book and the Balance (of Right and Wrong), that men may stand forth in justice; and We sent down Iron, in which is (material for) mighty war, as well as many benefits for mankind, that Allah may test who it is that will help, Unseen, Him and His Apostles: for Allah is full of Strength, Exalted in Might (and able to enforce His Will).

26. And We sent Noah and Abraham, and established in their line Prophethood and Revelation: and some among progeny were on right guidance. But many of them became rebellious transgressors.

27. Then, in their wake, We followed them

عَلَىٰٓ اٰثَارِهِمۡ بِرُسُلِنَا وَقَفَّيۡنَا بِعِيۡسَى

ابۡنِ مَرۡيَمَ وَاٰتَيۡنٰهُ الۡاِنۡجِيۡلَ ۙ

وَجَعَلۡنَا فِىۡ قُلُوۡبِ الَّذِيۡنَ اتَّبَعُوۡهُ

رَاۡفَةً وَّرَحۡمَةً ؕ وَرَهۡبَانِيَّةَ

ۨابۡتَدَعُوۡهَا مَا كَتَبۡنٰهَا عَلَيۡهِمۡ

اِلَّا ابۡتِغَآءَ رِضۡوَانِ اللّٰهِ فَمَا

رَعَوۡهَا حَقَّ رِعَايَتِهَا ۚ فَاٰتَيۡنَا

الَّذِيۡنَ اٰمَنُوۡا مِنۡهُمۡ اَجۡرَهُمۡ ؕ

وَكَثِيۡرٌ مِّنۡهُمۡ فٰسِقُوۡنَ ۝ يٰۤاَيُّهَا

up with (others of) Our Apostles: We sent after them Jesus the son of Mary, and bestowed on him the Gospel; and We ordained in the hearts of those who followed him Compassion and Mercy. But the Monasticism which they invented for them-selves, We did not prescribe for them: (We commanded) only the seeking for the Good Pleasure of Allah; but that they did not foster as they should have done. Yet We bestowed, on those among them who believed, their (due) reward, but many of them are rebellious transgressors.

28. O you

اَلَّذِيْنَ اٰمَنُوا اتَّقُوا اللّٰهَ وَ اٰمِنُوْا

بِرَسُوْلِهٖ يُؤْتِكُمْ كِفْلَيْنِ مِنْ

رَّحْمَتِهٖ وَ يَجْعَلْ لَّكُمْ نُوْرًا

تَمْشُوْنَ بِهٖ وَ يَغْفِرْ لَكُمْ ۗ وَ اللّٰهُ

غَفُوْرٌ رَّحِيْمٌ ۙ لِّئَلَّا يَعْلَمَ اَهْلُ

الْكِتٰبِ اَلَّا يَقْدِرُوْنَ عَلٰى شَيْءٍ

مِّنْ فَضْلِ اللّٰهِ وَ اَنَّ الْفَضْلَ

بِيَدِ اللّٰهِ يُؤْتِيْهِ مَنْ يَّشَآءُ ۗ

وَ اللّٰهُ ذُو الْفَضْلِ الْعَظِيْمِ ۝

that believe! Fear Allah, and believe in His Apostle, and He will bestow on you a double portion of His Mercy: He will provide for you a Light by which you shall walk (straight in your path), and He will forgive you (your past): for Allah is Oft-Forgiving, Most Merciful.

29. That the People of the Book may know that they have no power whatever over the Grace of Allah, that (His) Grace is (entirely) in His Hand, to bestow it on whomsoever He wills. For Allah is the Lord of Grace abounding.

PART 27
Qaala Fama Khatbukum

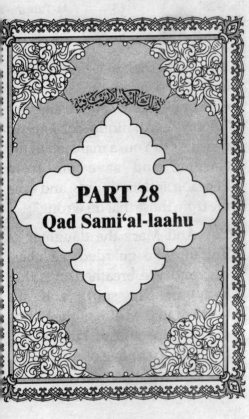

PART 28
Qad Sami'al-laahu

(others) that enter!"

11. And Allah sets forth, as an example to those who believe the wife of Pharaoh: behold she said: "O my Lord! Build for me, in nearness to You, a mansion in the Garden, and save me from Pharaoh and his doings, and save me from those that do wrong";

12. And Mary the daughter of 'Imran, who guarded her chastity; and We breathed into (her body) of Our spirit; and she testified to the truth of the words of her Lord and of His Revelations, and was one of the devout (servants).

الدَّاخِلِينَ ۝ وَضَرَبَ اللَّهُ مَثَلًا

لِّلَّذِينَ آمَنُوا امْرَأَتَ فِرْعَوْنَ إِذْ

قَالَتْ رَبِّ ابْنِ لِي عِنْدَكَ بَيْتًا فِي

الْجَنَّةِ وَنَجِّنِي مِنْ فِرْعَوْنَ وَعَمَلِهِ

وَنَجِّنِي مِنَ الْقَوْمِ الظَّالِمِينَ ۝

وَمَرْيَمَ ابْنَتَ عِمْرَانَ الَّتِي

أَحْصَنَتْ فَرْجَهَا فَنَفَخْنَا فِيهِ مِنْ

رُّوحِنَا وَصَدَّقَتْ بِكَلِمَاتِ رَبِّهَا

وَكُتُبِهِ وَكَانَتْ مِنَ الْقَانِتِينَ ۝

power over all things."

9. O Prophet! Strive hard against the unbelievers and the Hypocrites, and be firm against them. Their abode is Hell, - an evil refuge (indeed).

10. Allah sets forth, for an example to the unbelievers, the wife of Noah and the wife of Lut: they were (respectively) under two of Our righteous servants, but they were false to their (husbands), and they profited nothing before Allah on their account, but were told: "Enter you the Fire along with

كُلِّ شَيْءٍ قَدِيرٌ ۞ يَاۤ أَيُّهَا النَّبِيُّ

جَاهِدِ الْكُفَّارَ وَالْمُنَافِقِينَ

وَاغْلُظْ عَلَيْهِمْ ۚ وَمَأْوَاهُمْ جَهَنَّمُ ۖ

وَبِئْسَ الْمَصِيرُ ۞ ضَرَبَ اللهُ

مَثَلًا لِّلَّذِينَ كَفَرُوا امْرَأَتَ نُوحٍ

وَّامْرَأَتَ لُوطٍ ۖ كَانَتَا تَحْتَ عَبْدَيْنِ

مِنْ عِبَادِنَا صَالِحَيْنِ فَخَانَتَاهُمَا

فَلَمْ يُغْنِيَا عَنْهُمَا مِنَ اللهِ

شَيْئًا وَّقِيلَ ادْخُلَا النَّارَ مَعَ

8. O you who believe! Turn to Allah with sincere repentance: in the hope that your Lord will remove from you your ills and admit you to Gardens beneath which rivers flow, - the Day that Allah will not permit to be humiliated the Prophet and those who believe with him. Their Light will run forward before them and by their right hands, while they say, "Our Lord! Perfect our Light for us, and grant us Forgiveness: for you have

يَـٰٓأَيُّهَا الَّذِينَ ءَامَنُوا تُوبُوٓا إِلَى

اللَّهِ تَوْبَةً نَّصُوحًا عَسَىٰ رَبُّكُمْ

أَن يُكَفِّرَ عَنكُمْ سَيِّـَٔاتِكُمْ

وَيُدْخِلَكُمْ جَنَّـٰتٍ تَجْرِى مِن

تَحْتِهَا ٱلْأَنْهَـٰرُ يَوْمَ لَا يُخْزِى

اللَّهُ النَّبِىَّ وَالَّذِينَ ءَامَنُوا مَعَهُۥ

نُورُهُمْ يَسْعَىٰ بَيْنَ أَيْدِيهِمْ

وَبِأَيْمَـٰنِهِمْ يَقُولُونَ رَبَّنَآ أَتْمِمْ

لَنَا نُورَنَا وَاغْفِرْ لَنَآ إِنَّكَ عَلَىٰ

who submit (their wills), who believe, who are devout, who turn to Allah in repentance, who worship (in humility), who travel (for Faith) and fast, - previously married or virgins.

6.　O you who believe! Save yourselves and your families from a Fire whose fuel is Men and Stones, over which are (appointed) Angels stern (and) severe, who flinch not (from executing) the Commands they receive from Allah, but do (precisely) what they are commanded.

7.　(They will say), "O you unbelievers! Make no excuses this Day! You are being but requited for all that you did!"

مُّسْلِمَٰتٍ مُّؤْمِنَٰتٍ قَٰنِتَٰتٍ تَٰٓئِبَٰتٍ

عَٰبِدَٰتٍ سَٰٓئِحَٰتٍ ثَيِّبَٰتٍ وَّأَبْكَارًا ۞

يَٰٓأَيُّهَا الَّذِينَ ءَامَنُوا قُوٓا أَنفُسَكُمْ

وَأَهْلِيكُمْ نَارًا وَّقُودُهَا النَّاسُ

وَالْحِجَارَةُ عَلَيْهَا مَلَٰٓئِكَةٌ غِلَاظٌ

شِدَادٌ لَّا يَعْصُونَ اللهَ مَآ أَمَرَهُمْ

وَيَفْعَلُونَ مَا يُؤْمَرُونَ ۞ يَٰٓأَيُّهَا

الَّذِينَ كَفَرُوا لَا تَعْتَذِرُوا الْيَوْمَ

إِنَّمَا تُجْزَوْنَ مَا كُنتُمْ تَعْمَلُونَ ۞

a part. Then when he told her
thereof, she said, "Who told you
this? "He said, "He told me Who
knows and is Well-Acquainted
(with all things)."

4.   If you two turn in repentance to Him, your hearts are
indeed so inclined; but if you
back up each other against him,
truly Allah is his Protector, and
Gabriel, and (every) righteous
one among those who believe, -
and furthermore, the Angels -
will back (him) up.

5.   It may be, if he divorced you
(all), that Allah will give him in
exchange consorts better than
you, -

عَنْ بَعْضٍ فَلَمَّا نَبَّاهَا بِهِ قَالَتْ

مَنْ أَنْبَأَكَ هَذَا قَالَ نَبَّانِي

الْعَلِيمُ الْخَبِيرُ ۝ إِنْ تَتُوبَا إِلَى

اللهِ فَقَدْ صَغَتْ قُلُوبُكُمَا وَإِنْ

تَظَهَرَا عَلَيْهِ فَإِنَّ اللهَ هُوَ مَوْلَهُ

وَجِبْرِيلُ وَصَالِحُ الْمُؤْمِنِينَ

وَالْمَلَئِكَةُ بَعْدَ ذَلِكَ ظَهِيرٌ ۝ عَسَى رَبُّهُ إِنْ طَلَّقَكُنَّ أَنْ

يُبْدِلَهُ أَزْوَاجًا خَيْرًا مِنْكُنَّ

At-Tahrim (Holding - Something - to be Forbidden

Bismillahir-Rahmanir-Rahim

1. O Prophet! Why holds you to be forbidden that which Allah has made lawful to you? You seek to please your consorts. But Allah is Oft-Forgiving, Most Merciful.

2. Allah has already ordained for you, (O men), the absolution of your oaths (in some cases): and Allah is your Protector, and He is full of Knowledge and Wisdom.

3. When the Prophet disclosed a matter in confidence to one of his consorts, and she then divulged it (to another), and Allah made it known to him, he confirmed part thereof and repudiated

بِسْمِ اللّٰهِ الرَّحْمٰنِ الرَّحِيمِ

يَٰٓأَيُّهَا النَّبِيُّ لِمَ تُحَرِّمُ مَآ أَحَلَّ

اللّٰهُ لَكَ تَبْتَغِي مَرْضَاتَ أَزْوَاجِكَ

وَاللّٰهُ غَفُورٌ رَّحِيمٌ ۝ قَدْ فَرَضَ

اللّٰهُ لَكُمْ تَحِلَّةَ أَيْمَانِكُمْ وَاللّٰهُ

مَوْلَٰكُمْ وَهُوَ الْعَلِيمُ الْحَكِيمُ ۝ وَإِذْ

أَسَرَّ النَّبِيُّ إِلَىٰ بَعْضِ أَزْوَاجِهِ

حَدِيثًا فَلَمَّا نَبَّأَتْ بِهِ وَأَظْهَرَهُ

اللّٰهُ عَلَيْهِ عَرَّفَ بَعْضَهُ وَأَعْرَضَ

And those who believe in Allah and work righteousness, He will admit to Gardens beneath which rivers flow, to dwell therein for ever: Allah has indeed granted for them a most excellent Provision.

12. Allah is He Who created seven Firmaments and of the earth a similar number. Through the midst of them (all) descends His Command: that you may know that Allah has power over all things, and that Allah comprehends, all things in (His) Knowledge.

وَمَنْ يُّؤْمِنْ بِاللّٰهِ وَيَعْمَلْ صَالِحًا

يُّدْخِلْهُ جَنّٰتٍ تَجْرِيْ مِنْ تَحْتِهَا

الْاَنْهٰرُ خٰلِدِيْنَ فِيْهَآ اَبَدًا ۚ قَدْ

اَحْسَنَ اللّٰهُ لَهٗ رِزْقًا ۞ اَللّٰهُ

الَّذِيْ خَلَقَ سَبْعَ سَمٰوٰتٍ وَّمِنَ

الْاَرْضِ مِثْلَهُنَّ ۖ يَتَنَزَّلُ الْاَمْرُ

بَيْنَهُنَّ لِتَعْلَمُوْٓا اَنَّ اللّٰهَ عَلٰى

كُلِّ شَيْءٍ قَدِيْرٌ ۙ وَّاَنَّ اللّٰهَ

قَدْ اَحَاطَ بِكُلِّ شَيْءٍ عِلْمًا ۞

to severe account? - and We imposed on them an exemplary Punishment.

9. Then did they taste the evil result of their conduct, and the End of their conduct was Perdition.

10. Allah has prepared for them a severe Punishment (in the Hereafter). Therefore fear Allah, O you men of understanding - who have believed! - for Allah has indeed sent down to you a Message, -

11. An Apostle, who rehearses to you the Signs of Allah containing clear explanations, that he may lead forth those who believe and do righteous deeds from the depths of Darkness into Light.

شَدِيدًا ۙ وَّذَاقَتْ وَبَالَ اَمْرِهَا عَذَابًا نُّكْرًا ۞

فَذَاقَتْ وَبَالَ اَمْرِهَا وَكَانَ عَاقِبَةُ

اَمْرِهَا خُسْرًا ۞ اَعَدَّ اللهُ لَهُمْ

عَذَابًا شَدِيدًا ۙ فَاتَّقُوا اللهَ يٰۤاُولِى

الْاَلْبَابِ ۬ ۙ الَّذِيْنَ اٰمَنُوْا ۘ قَدْ

اَنْزَلَ اللهُ اِلَيْكُمْ ذِكْرًا ۞ رَّسُوْلًا

يَّتْلُوْا عَلَيْكُمْ اٰيٰتِ اللهِ مُبَيِّنٰتٍ

لِّيُخْرِجَ الَّذِيْنَ اٰمَنُوْا وَعَمِلُوا

الصّٰلِحٰتِ مِنَ الظُّلُمٰتِ اِلَى النُّوْرِ ۬ ؕ

their recompense: and take mutual counsel together, according to what is just and reasonable. And if you find yourselves in difficulties, let another woman suckle (the child) on the (father's) behalf.

7.   Let the man of means spend according to his means: and the man whose resources are restricted, let him spend according to what Allah has given him. Allah puts no burden on any person beyond what He has given him. After a difficulty, Allah will soon grant relief.

8.   How many populations that insolently opposed the Command of their Lord and of His Apostles, did We not then call to account, -

أُجُورَهُنَّ وَأْتَمِرُوا بَيْنَكُم بِمَعْرُوفٍ ۖ

وَإِن تَعَاسَرْتُمْ فَسَتُرْضِعُ لَهُۥٓ

أُخْرَىٰ ۞ لِيُنفِقْ ذُو سَعَةٍ مِّن

سَعَتِهِۦ ۖ وَمَن قُدِرَ عَلَيْهِ رِزْقُهُۥ

فَلْيُنفِقْ مِمَّآ ءَاتَىٰهُ ٱللَّهُ ۚ لَا يُكَلِّفُ

ٱللَّهُ نَفْسًا إِلَّا مَآ ءَاتَىٰهَا ۚ سَيَجْعَلُ

ٱللَّهُ بَعْدَ عُسْرٍ يُسْرًا ۞ وَكَأَيِّن

مِّن قَرْيَةٍ عَتَتْ عَنْ أَمْرِ رَبِّهَا

وَرُسُلِهِۦ فَحَاسَبْنَٰهَا حِسَابًا

and for those who fear Allah, He will make their path easy.

5. That is the Command of Allah, which He has sent down to you: and if any one fears Allah, He will remove his ills, from him, and will enlarge his reward.

6. Let the women live (in *'iddat*) in the same style as you live, according to your means: Annoy them not, so as to restrict them. And if they carry (life in their wombs), then spend (your substance) on them until they deliver their burden: and if they suckle your (offspring), give them

وَمَنْ يَّتَّقِ اللّٰهَ يَجْعَلْ لَّهٗ مِنْ

اَمْرِهٖ يُسْرًا ۞ ذٰلِكَ اَمْرُ اللّٰهِ اَنْزَلَهٗۤ

اِلَيْكُمْ ۗ وَمَنْ يَّتَّقِ اللّٰهَ يُكَفِّرْ

عَنْهُ سَيِّاٰتِهٖ وَيُعْظِمْ لَهٗۤ اَجْرًا ۞

اَسْكِنُوْهُنَّ مِنْ حَيْثُ سَكَنْتُمْ

مِّنْ وُّجْدِكُمْ وَلَا تُضَآرُّوْهُنَّ

لِتُضَيِّقُوْا عَلَيْهِنَّ ۗ وَاِنْ كُنَّ اُولَاتِ

حَمْلٍ فَاَنْفِقُوْا عَلَيْهِنَّ حَتّٰى يَضَعْنَ

حَمْلَهُنَّ ۚ فَاِنْ اَرْضَعْنَ لَكُمْ فَاٰتُوْهُنَّ

He (ever) prepares a way out,

3.   And He provides for him from (sources) he never could imagine. And if any one puts his trust in Allah, sufficient is (Allah) for him. For Allah will surely accomplish His purpose: verily, for all things has Allah appointed a due proportion.

4.   Such of your women as have passed the age of monthly courses, for them the prescribed period, if you have any doubts, is three months, and for those who have no courses (it is the same): for those who carry (life within their wombs), their period is until they deliver their burdens:

يَجْعَلْ لَّهُ مَخْرَجًا ۙ وَّيَرْزُقْهُ

مِنْ حَيْثُ لَا يَحْتَسِبُ ؕ وَمَنْ

يَّتَوَكَّلْ عَلَى اللّٰہِ فَهُوَ حَسْبُهٗ ؕ اِنَّ

اللّٰہَ بَالِغُ اَمْرِهٖ ؕ قَدْ جَعَلَ اللّٰہُ

لِكُلِّ شَيْءٍ قَدْرًا ۟ وَالّٰٓئِیْ یَئِسْنَ

مِنَ الْمَحِیْضِ مِنْ نِّسَآئِكُمْ اِنِ

ارْتَبْتُمْ فَعِدَّتُهُنَّ ثَلٰثَةُ اَشْهُرٍ ۙ

وَّالّٰٓئِیْ لَمْ یَحِضْنَ ؕ وَاُولَاتُ الْاَحْمَالِ

اَجَلُهُنَّ اَنْ یَّضَعْنَ حَمْلَهُنَّ ؕ

transgresses the limits of Allah, does verily wrong his (own) soul: you knows not if perchance Allah will bring about thereafter some new situation.

2. Thus when they fulfil their term appointed, either take them back on equitable terms or part with them on equitable terms; and take for witness two persons from among you, endued with justice, and establish the evidence (as) before Allah. Such is the admonition given to him who believes in Allah and the Last Day. And for those who fear Allah,

يَّتَعَدَّ حُدُوْدَ اللهِ فَقَدْ ظَلَمَ

نَفْسَهٗ ۚ لَا تَدْرِیْ لَعَلَّ اللهَ

یُحْدِثُ بَعْدَ ذٰلِكَ اَمْرًا ۝ فَاِذَا

بَلَغْنَ اَجَلَهُنَّ فَاَمْسِكُوْهُنَّ

بِمَعْرُوْفٍ اَوْ فَارِقُوْهُنَّ بِمَعْرُوْفٍ

وَّاَشْهِدُوْا ذَوَیْ عَدْلٍ مِّنْكُمْ

وَاَقِیْمُوا الشَّهَادَةَ لِلّٰهِ ؕ ذٰلِكُمْ

یُوْعَظُ بِهٖ مَنْ كَانَ یُؤْمِنُ بِاللهِ

وَالْیَوْمِ الْاٰخِرِ ۚ وَمَنْ یَّتَّقِ اللهَ

18. Knower of what is hidden and what is open, Exalted in Might, full of Wisdom.

At-Talaq (The Divorce)

Bismillahir-Rahmanir-Rahim

1. O Prophet! When you do divorce women, divorce them at their prescribed periods, and count (accurately), their prescribed periods: and fear Allah your Lord: and turn them not out of their houses, nor shall they (themselves) leave, except it case they are guilty of some open lewdness, those are limits set by Allah: and any who

عٰلِمُ الْغَيْبِ وَ الشَّهَادَةِ الْعَزِيزُ

الْحَكِيمُ ۝

يٰاَيُّهَا النَّبِيُّ اِذَا طَلَّقْتُمُ النِّسَآءَ

فَطَلِّقُوْهُنَّ لِعِدَّتِهِنَّ وَ اَحْصُوا

الْعِدَّةَ وَ اتَّقُوا اللهَ رَبَّكُمْ لَا

تُخْرِجُوْهُنَّ مِنْ بُيُوْتِهِنَّ وَ لَا

يَخْرُجْنَ اِلَّا اَنْ يَّاْتِيْنَ بِفَاحِشَةٍ

مُّبَيِّنَةٍ وَ تِلْكَ حُدُوْدُ اللهِ وَ مَنْ

Oft-Forgiving, Most Merciful.

15. Your riches and your children may be but a trial: but in the Presence of Allah, is the highest, Reward.

16. So fear Allah as much as you can; listen and obey and spend in charity for the benefit of your own soul and those saved from the covetousness of their own souls, - they are the ones that achieve prosperity.

17. If you loan to Allah, a beautiful loan, He will double it to your (credit), and He will grant you Forgiveness: for Allah is most ready to appreciate (service), Most Forbearing, -

غَفُوٌّ رَّحِيمٌ ۞ اِنَّمَاۤ اَمۡوَالُكُمۡ

وَاَوۡلَادُكُمۡ فِتۡنَةٌ ۗ وَاللّٰهُ عِنۡدَهٗۤ

اَجۡرٌ عَظِيمٌ ۞ فَاتَّقُوا اللّٰهَ مَا

اسۡتَطَعۡتُمۡ وَاسۡمَعُوۡا وَاَطِيۡعُوۡا

وَاَنۡفِقُوۡا خَيۡرًا لِّاَنۡفُسِكُمۡ ۗ وَمَنۡ

يُّوۡقَ شُحَّ نَفۡسِهٖ فَاُولٰٓئِكَ هُمُ

الۡمُفۡلِحُوۡنَ ۞ اِنۡ تُقۡرِضُوا اللّٰهَ

قَرۡضًا حَسَنًا يُّضٰعِفۡهُ لَكُمۡ

وَيَغۡفِرۡ لَكُمۡ ۗ وَاللّٰهُ شَكُوۡرٌ حَلِيۡمٌ ۞

his heart (aright): for Allah knows all things.

12. So obey Allah, and obey His Apostle: but if you turn back, the duty of Our Apostle is but to proclaim (the Message) clearly and openly.

13. Allah! There is no god but He: and on Allah, therefore, let the believers put their trust.

14. O you who believe! Truly, among your wives and your children are (some that are) enemies to yourselves: so beware of them! but if you forgive and overlook, and cover up (their faults), verily Allah is

قَلْبَهُ ۚ وَاللّٰهُ بِكُلِّ شَىْءٍ عَلِيْمٌ ۞

وَاَطِيْعُوا اللّٰهَ وَاَطِيْعُوا الرَّسُوْلَ ۚ

فَاِنْ تَوَلَّيْتُمْ فَاِنَّمَا عَلٰى رَسُوْلِنَا

الْبَلٰغُ الْمُبِيْنُ ۞ اَللّٰهُ لَآ اِلٰهَ

اِلَّا هُوَ ۗ وَعَلَى اللّٰهِ فَلْيَتَوَكَّلِ

الْمُؤْمِنُوْنَ ۞ يٰٓاَيُّهَا الَّذِيْنَ اٰمَنُوْۤا

اِنَّ مِنْ اَزْوَاجِكُمْ وَاَوْلَادِكُمْ عَدُوًّا

لَّكُمْ فَاحْذَرُوْهُمْ ۚ وَاِنْ تَعْفُوْا

وَتَصْفَحُوْا وَتَغْفِرُوْا فَاِنَّ اللّٰهَ

and work righteousness, - He will remove from them their ills, and He will admit them to Gardens beneath which rivers flow, to dwell therein for ever: that will be the supreme Achievement.

10. But those who reject Faith and treat Our Signs as falsehoods, they will be Companions of the Fire, to dwell therein for ever: and evil is that Goal.

11. No kind of calamity can occur, except by the leave of Allah: and if any one believes in Allah, (Allah) guides

وَيَعْمَلْ صَالِحًا يُكَفِّرْ عَنْهُ

سَيِّئَاتِهِ وَيُدْخِلْهُ جَنَّتٍ تَجْرِى

مِنْ تَحْتِهَا الْأَنْهَرُ خَالِدِينَ

فِيهَآ أَبَدًا ذَلِكَ الْفَوْزُ الْعَظِيمُ ۞

وَالَّذِينَ كَفَرُوا وَكَذَّبُوا بِأَيَاتِنَآ

أُولَئِكَ أَصْحَبُ النَّارِ خَالِدِينَ

فِيهَا وَبِئْسَ الْمَصِيرُ ۞ مَآ

أَصَابَ مِنْ مُّصِيبَةٍ إِلَّا بِإِذْنِ

اللهِ وَمَنْ يُؤْمِنْ بِاللهِ يَهْدِ

and Allah is Free of all needs, Worthy of all praise.

7.   The unbelievers think that they will not be raised up (for Judgment). Say: "Yes, By my Lord, You shall surely be raised up: then shall you be told (the truth) of all that you did. And that is easy for Allah."

8.   Believe, therefore, in Allah and His Apostle, and in the Light which We have sent down. And Allah is Well Acquainted with all that you do.

9.   The Day that He assembles you (all) for a Day of Assembly, - that will be a Day of mutual loss and gain (among you), and those who believe in Allah

وَاللهُ غَنِيٌّ حَمِيدٌ ۞ زَعَمَ

الَّذِينَ كَفَرُوا أَن لَّن يُبْعَثُوا ۚ

قُلْ بَلَى وَرَبِّى لَتُبْعَثُنَّ ثُمَّ

لَتُنَبَّؤُنَّ بِمَا عَمِلْتُمْ ۚ وَذَٰلِكَ

عَلَى اللهِ يَسِيرٌ ۞ فَـَامِنُوا بِاللهِ

وَرَسُولِهِ وَالنُّورِ الَّذِى أَنزَلْنَا ۚ

وَاللهُ بِمَا تَعْمَلُونَ خَبِيرٌ ۞ يَوْمَ

يَجْمَعُكُمْ لِيَوْمِ الْجَمْعِ ۖ ذَٰلِكَ

يَوْمُ التَّغَابُنِ ۗ وَمَن يُؤْمِن بِاللهِ

the heavens and on earth; and He knows what you conceal and what you reveal: yes, Allah knows well the (secrets) of (all) hearts.

5.   Has not the story reached you, of those who rejected Faith aforetime? So they tasted the evil result of their conduct; and they had a grievous Chastisement.

6.   That was because there came to them Apostles with clear Signs, but they said: "Shall (mere) human beings direct us?" So they rejected (the Message) and turned away. But Allah can do without (them):

السَّمٰوٰتِ وَالْاَرْضِ وَيَعْلَمُ مَا

تُسِرُّوْنَ وَمَا تُعْلِنُوْنَ ۗ وَاللهُ

عَلِيْمٌۢ بِذَاتِ الصُّدُوْرِ ۞ اَلَمْ

يَاْتِكُمْ نَبَؤُا الَّذِيْنَ كَفَرُوْا مِنْ

قَبْلُ ۫ فَذَاقُوْا وَبَالَ اَمْرِهِمْ

وَلَهُمْ عَذَابٌ اَلِيْمٌ ۞ ذٰلِكَ

بِاَنَّهٗ كَانَتْ تَّاْتِيْهِمْ رُسُلُهُمْ

بِالْبَيِّنٰتِ فَقَالُوْٓا اَبَشَرٌ يَّهْدُوْنَنَا

فَكَفَرُوْا وَتَوَلَّوْا وَّاسْتَغْنَى اللهُ

At-Taghabun (The Mutual Loss and Gain)

Bismillahir-Rahmanir-Rahim

1. Whatever is in the heavens and on earth, does declare the Praises and Glory of Allah: to Him belongs Dominion, and to Him belongs Praise: and He has power over all things.

2. It is He Who has created you; and of you are some that are unbelievers, and some that are believers: and Allah sees well all that you do.

3. He has created the heavens and the earth in just proportions, and has given you shape, and made your shapes beautiful: and to Him is the Final Goal.

4. He knows what is in

بِسْمِ اللهِ الرَّحْمٰنِ الرَّحِيمِ

يُسَبِّحُ لِلّٰهِ مَا فِى السَّمٰوٰتِ وَمَا فِى

الْأَرْضِ لَهُ الْمُلْكُ وَلَهُ الْحَمْدُ

وَهُوَ عَلٰى كُلِّ شَىْءٍ قَدِيْرٌ ۞

هُوَ الَّذِيْ خَلَقَكُمْ فَمِنْكُمْ كَافِرٌ

وَّمِنْكُمْ مُّؤْمِنٌ ۚ وَاللهُ بِمَا تَعْمَلُوْنَ

بَصِيْرٌ ۞ خَلَقَ السَّمٰوٰتِ وَالْأَرْضَ

بِالْحَقِّ وَصَوَّرَكُمْ فَأَحْسَنَ صُوَرَكُمْ ۚ

وَإِلَيْهِ الْمَصِيْرُ ۞ يَعْلَمُ مَا فِى

from the remembrance of Allah. If any act thus, the loss is their own.

10. And spend something (in charity) out of the substance which We have bestowed on you, before Death should come to any of you and he should say, "O my Lord! Why did You not give me respite for a little while? I should then have given (largely) in charity, and I should have been one of the doers of good".

11. But to no soul will Allah grant respite when the time appointed (for it) has come; and Allah is Well Acquainted with (all) that you do.

عَنْ ذِكْرِ اللّٰهِ ۚ وَمَنْ يَّفْعَلْ

ذٰلِكَ فَأُولٰٓئِكَ هُمُ الْخٰسِرُوْنَ ۞

وَأَنْفِقُوْا مِنْ مَّا رَزَقْنٰكُمْ مِّنْ

قَبْلِ أَنْ يَّأْتِيَ أَحَدَكُمُ الْمَوْتُ

فَيَقُوْلَ رَبِّ لَوْلَآ أَخَّرْتَنِيْ إِلٰى

أَجَلٍ قَرِيْبٍ ۙ فَأَصَّدَّقَ وَأَكُنْ

مِّنَ الصّٰلِحِيْنَ ۞ وَلَنْ يُّؤَخِّرَ

اللّٰهُ نَفْسًا إِذَا جَآءَ أَجَلُهَا ۚ وَاللّٰهُ

خَبِيْرٌۢ بِمَا تَعْمَلُوْنَ ۞

"Spend nothing on those who are with Allah's Apostle, to the end that they may disperse (and quit Medina)." But to Allah belong the treasures of the heavens and the earth; but the Hypocrites understand not.

8.   They say, "If we return to Medina, surely the more honourable (element) will expel therefrom the meaner." But honour belongs to Allah and His Apostle, and the Believers; but the Hypocrites know not.

9.   O you who believe! Let not your riches or your children divert you

لَا تُنْفِقُوا عَلَى مَنْ عِنْدَ رَسُولِ

اللَّهِ حَتَّى يَنْفَضُّوا ۗ وَلِلَّهِ خَزَآئِنُ

السَّمَوَاتِ وَالْأَرْضِ وَلَٰكِنَّ الْمُنَافِقِينَ

لَا يَفْقَهُونَ ۞ يَقُولُونَ لَئِن رَّجَعْنَا

إِلَى الْمَدِينَةِ لَيُخْرِجَنَّ الْأَعَزُّ مِنْهَا

الْأَذَلَّ ۚ وَلِلَّهِ الْعِزَّةُ وَلِرَسُولِهِ

وَلِلْمُؤْمِنِينَ وَلَٰكِنَّ الْمُنَافِقِينَ لَا

يَعْلَمُونَ ۞ يَا أَيُّهَا الَّذِينَ آمَنُوا

لَا تُلْهِكُمْ أَمْوَالُكُمْ وَلَا أَوْلَادُكُمْ

against them. They are the enemies; so beware of them. The curse of Allah be on them! How are they deluded (away from the Truth)!

5.   And when it is said to them, "Come, the Apostle of Allah will pray for your forgiveness", they turn aside their heads, and you would see them turning away their faces in arrogance.

6.   It is equal to them whether you pray for their forgiveness or not. Allah will not forgive them. Truly Allah guides not rebellious transgressors.

7.   They are the ones who say,

عَلَيْهِمْ هُمُ الْعَدُوُّ فَاحْذَرْهُمْ

قٰتَلَهُمُ اللّٰهُ ۖ اَنّٰى يُؤْفَكُوْنَ ۞ وَاِذَا

قِيْلَ لَهُمْ تَعَالَوْا يَسْتَغْفِرْ لَكُمْ

رَسُوْلُ اللّٰهِ لَوَّوْا رُءُوْسَهُمْ وَرَاَيْتَهُمْ

يَصُدُّوْنَ وَهُمْ مُّسْتَكْبِرُوْنَ ۞

سَوَآءٌ عَلَيْهِمْ اَسْتَغْفَرْتَ لَهُمْ اَمْ

لَمْ تَسْتَغْفِرْ لَهُمْ ۚ لَنْ يَّغْفِرَ اللّٰهُ

لَهُمْ ۗ اِنَّ اللّٰهَ لَا يَهْدِى الْقَوْمَ

الْفٰسِقِيْنَ ۞ هُمُ الَّذِيْنَ يَقُوْلُوْنَ

the Hypocrites are indeed liars.

2.   They have made their oaths a screen (for their misdeeds): thus they obstruct (men) from the Path of Allah: truly evil are their deeds.

3.   That is because they believed, then they rejected Faith: so a seal was set on their hearts: therefore they understand not.

4.   When you look at them, their exteriors please you; and when they speak, you listen to their words. They are as (worthless as hollow) pieces of timber propped up, (unable to stand on their own). They think that every cry is

الْمُنٰفِقِيْنَ لَكٰذِبُوْنَ ۞ اِتَّخَذُوْۤا

اَيْمَانَهُمْ جُنَّةً فَصَدُّوْا عَنْ

سَبِيْلِ اللّٰهِ ؕ اِنَّهُمْ سَآءَ مَا كَانُوْا

يَعْمَلُوْنَ ۞ ذٰلِكَ بِاَنَّهُمْ اٰمَنُوْا

ثُمَّ كَفَرُوْا فَطُبِعَ عَلٰى قُلُوْبِهِمْ

فَهُمْ لَا يَفْقَهُوْنَ ۞ وَاِذَا رَاَيْتَهُمْ

تُعْجِبُكَ اَجْسَامُهُمْ ؕ وَاِنْ يَّقُوْلُوْا

تَسْمَعْ لِقَوْلِهِمْ ؕ كَاَنَّهُمْ خُشُبٌ

مُّسَنَّدَةٌ ؕ يَحْسَبُوْنَ كُلَّ صَيْحَةٍ

Allah often (and without stint): that you may prosper.

11. But when they see some bargain or some amusement, they disperse headlong to it, and leave you standing. Say: "The (blessing) from the Presence of Allah is better than any amusement or bargain! And Allah is the Best to provide (for all needs)."

Al-Munafiqun
(The Hypocrites)

Bismillahir-Rahmanir-Rahim

1. When the Hypocrites come to you, they say, "We bear witness that you are indeed the Apostle of Allah." Yes, Allah knows that you are indeed His Apostle, and Allah bears witness that

اللّٰهَ كَثِيرًا لَّعَلَّكُمْ تُفْلِحُونَ ۞

وَإِذَا رَأَوْا تِجَارَةً أَوْ لَهْوًا ۨانْفَضُّوۤا

إِلَيْهَا وَتَرَكُوكَ قَآئِمًا ۗ قُلْ مَا

عِنْدَ اللّٰهِ خَيْرٌ مِّنَ اللَّهْوِ وَمِنَ

التِّجَارَةِ ۗ وَاللّٰهُ خَيْرُ الرّٰزِقِينَ ۞

سُورَةُ المُنٰفِقُونَ مَدَنِيَّةٌ - بِسْمِ اللّٰهِ الرَّحْمٰنِ الرَّحِيمِ - آيَاتُهَا ١١ رُكُوعَاتُهَا ٢

إِذَا جَآءَكَ الْمُنٰفِقُونَ قَالُوا نَشْهَدُ

إِنَّكَ لَرَسُولُ اللّٰهِ ۗ وَاللّٰهُ يَعْلَمُ

إِنَّكَ لَرَسُولُهُ ۗ وَاللّٰهُ يَشْهَدُ إِنَّ

will truly overtake you: then will you be sent back to the Knower of things secret and open: and He will tell you (the truth of) the things that you did!"

9. O you who believe! When the call is proclaimed to Prayer on Friday (the Day of Assembly), hasten earnestly to the Remembrance of Allah, and leave off business (and traffic): that is best for you if you but knew!

10. And when the Prayer is finished, then may you disperse through the land, and seek of the Bounty of Allah: and celebrate the Praises of

فَإِنَّهُ مُلَاقِيكُمْ ثُمَّ تُرَدُّوْنَ اِلٰى عٰلِمِ الْغَيْبِ وَالشَّهَادَةِ فَيُنَبِّئُكُمْ بِمَا كُنْتُمْ تَعْمَلُوْنَ ۞ يٰٓاَيُّهَا الَّذِيْنَ اٰمَنُوْٓا اِذَا نُوْدِيَ لِلصَّلٰوةِ مِنْ يَّوْمِ الْجُمُعَةِ فَاسْعَوْا اِلٰى ذِكْرِ اللّٰهِ وَذَرُوا الْبَيْعَ ذٰلِكُمْ خَيْرٌ لَّكُمْ اِنْ كُنْتُمْ تَعْلَمُوْنَ ۞ فَاِذَا قُضِيَتِ الصَّلٰوةُ فَانْتَشِرُوْا فِى الْاَرْضِ وَابْتَغُوْا مِنْ فَضْلِ اللّٰهِ وَاذْكُرُوا

the Signs of Allah: and Allah guides not people who do wrong.

6. Say: "O you that stand on Judaism! If you think that you are friends to Allah, to the exclusion of (other) men, then express your desire for Death, if you are truthful!"

7. But never will they express their desire (for Death), because of the (deeds) their hands have sent on before them! And Allah knows well those that do wrong!

8. Say: "The Death from which you flee

بِاٰيٰتِ اللهِ ۖ وَاللهُ لَا يَهْدِى

الْقَوْمَ الظّٰلِمِيْنَ ۞ قُلْ يٰاَيُّهَا

الَّذِيْنَ هَادُوْا اِنْ زَعَمْتُمْ اَنَّكُمْ

اَوْلِيَاۤءُ لِلّٰهِ مِنْ دُوْنِ النَّاسِ

فَتَمَنَّوُا الْمَوْتَ اِنْ كُنْتُمْ

صٰدِقِيْنَ ۞ وَلَا يَتَمَنَّوْنَهٗٓ اَبَدًا

بِمَا قَدَّمَتْ اَيْدِيْهِمْ ۚ وَاللهُ

عَلِيْمٌۢ بِالظّٰلِمِيْنَ ۞ قُلْ اِنَّ

الْمَوْتَ الَّذِيْ تَفِرُّوْنَ مِنْهُ

although they had been, before, in manifest error; -

3.   As well as (to confer all these benefits upon) others of them, who have not already joined them: and He is Exalted in Might, Wise.

4.   Such is the Bounty of Allah, which He bestows on whom He wills: and Allah is the Lord of the highest Bounty.

5.   The similitude of those who were charged with the (obligations of the) Mosaic Law, but who subsequently failed in those (obligations), is that of a donkey which carries huge tomes (but understands them not). Evil is the similitude of people who falsify

وَإِنْ كَانُوا مِنْ قَبْلُ لَفِى

ضَلَالٍ مُّبِينٍ ۞ وَّاٰخَرِينَ مِنْهُمْ

لَمَّا يَلْحَقُوا بِهِمْ ۚ وَهُوَ الْعَزِيزُ

الْحَكِيمُ ۞ ذٰلِكَ فَضْلُ اللهِ

يُؤْتِيهِ مَنْ يَّشَآءُ ۚ وَاللهُ ذُو

الْفَضْلِ الْعَظِيمِ ۞ مَثَلُ الَّذِينَ

حُمِّلُوا التَّوْرَاةَ ثُمَّ لَمْ يَحْمِلُوهَا

كَمَثَلِ الْحِمَارِ يَحْمِلُ أَسْفَارًا ۚ

بِئْسَ مَثَلُ الْقَوْمِ الَّذِينَ كَذَّبُوا

but We gave power to those who believed, against their enemies, and they became the ones that prevailed.

Al-Jumu'a
(The Friday Prayer)

Bismillahir-Rahmanir-Rahim

1. Whatever is in the heavens and on earth, does declare the Praises and Glory of Allah, - the Sovereign, the Holy One, the Exalted in Might, the Wise.

2. It is He Who has sent amongst the Unlettered an Apostle from among themselves, to rehearse to them His Signs, to purify them, and to instruct them in Scripture and Wisdom, -

طَآئِفَةٌ ۚ فَأَيَّدْنَا الَّذِينَ آمَنُوا

عَلَى عَدُوِّهِمْ فَأَصْبَحُوا ظَاهِرِينَ ۞

سُورَةُ الجُمُعَةِ مَدَنِيَّةٌ ۞ بِسْمِ اللهِ الرَّحْمٰنِ الرَّحِيمِ

يُسَبِّحُ لِلّٰهِ مَا فِي السَّمٰوٰتِ وَمَا

فِي الْأَرْضِ الْمَلِكِ الْقُدُّوسِ

الْعَزِيزِ الْحَكِيمِ ۞ هُوَ الَّذِى

بَعَثَ فِي الْأُمِّيِّنَ رَسُولًا مِّنْهُمْ

يَتْلُوا عَلَيْهِمْ آيٰتِهِ وَيُزَكِّيهِمْ

وَيُعَلِّمُهُمُ الْكِتٰبَ وَالْحِكْمَةَ

that is indeed the supreme Achievement.

13. And another (favour will He bestow,) which you do love, - help from Allah and a speedy victory. So give the Glad Tidings to the believers.

14. O you who believe! Be you helpers of Allah: as said Jesus the son of Mary to the Disciples, "Who will be my helpers to (the work of) Allah?" Said the disciples, "We are Allah's helpers!" Then a portion of the Children of Israel believed, and a portion disbelieved:

ذٰلِكَ الْفَوْزُ الْعَظِيْمُ ۞ وَأُخْرٰى

تُحِبُّوْنَهَا ۚ نَصْرٌ مِّنَ اللّٰهِ وَفَتْحٌ

قَرِيْبٌ ۗ وَبَشِّرِ الْمُؤْمِنِيْنَ ۞ يٰٓأَيُّهَا

الَّذِيْنَ اٰمَنُوْا كُوْنُوْٓا أَنْصَارَ اللّٰهِ

كَمَا قَالَ عِيْسَى ابْنُ مَرْيَمَ

لِلْحَوَارِيّٖنَ مَنْ أَنْصَارِيْٓ إِلَى

اللّٰهِ ۗ قَالَ الْحَوَارِيُّوْنَ نَحْنُ

أَنْصَارُ اللّٰهِ فَاٰمَنَتْ طَّآئِفَةٌ

مِّنْ بَنِيْٓ إِسْرَآءِيْلَ وَكَفَرَتْ

who believe! Shall I lead you to a bargain that will save you from a grievous Chastisement? -

11. That you believe in Allah and His Apostle, and that you strive (your utmost) in the Cause of Allah, with your property and your persons: that will be best for you, if you but knew!

12. He will forgive you your sins, and admit you to Gardens beneath which rivers flow, and to beautiful mansions in Gardens of Eternity:

اَلَّذِيْنَ اٰمَنُوْا هَلْ اَدُلُّكُمْ عَلٰى

تِجَارَةٍ تُنْجِيْكُمْ مِّنْ عَذَابٍ

اَلِيْمٍ ۝ تُؤْمِنُوْنَ بِاللّٰهِ وَرَسُوْلِهٖ

وَتُجَاهِدُوْنَ فِيْ سَبِيْلِ اللّٰهِ

بِاَمْوَالِكُمْ وَاَنْفُسِكُمْ ذٰلِكُمْ خَيْرٌ

لَّكُمْ اِنْ كُنْتُمْ تَعْلَمُوْنَ ۝ يَغْفِرْ

لَكُمْ ذُنُوْبَكُمْ وَيُدْخِلْكُمْ جَنّٰتٍ

تَجْرِيْ مِنْ تَحْتِهَا الْاَنْهٰرُ

وَمَسٰكِنَ طَيِّبَةً فِيْ جَنّٰتِ عَدْنٍ

invents falsehood against Allah, even as he is being invited to Islam? And Allah guides not those who do wrong.

8. Their intention is to extinguish Allah's Light (by blowing) with their mouths: but Allah will complete (the revelation of) His Light, even though the unbelievers may detest (it).

9. It is He Who has sent His Apostle with Guidance and the Religion of Truth, that he may proclaim it over all religion, even though the Pagans may detest (it).

10. O you

افْتَرَى عَلَى اللهِ الْكَذِبَ وَهُوَ

يُدْعَى إِلَى الْإِسْلَامِ ۗ وَاللهُ

لَا يَهْدِى الْقَوْمَ الظّٰلِمِينَ ۝

يُرِيدُونَ لِيُطْفِئُوا نُورَ اللهِ

بِأَفْوَاهِهِمْ وَاللهُ مُتِمُّ نُورِهٖ

وَلَوْ كَرِهَ الْكٰفِرُونَ ۝ هُوَ الَّذِىٓ

أَرْسَلَ رَسُولَهٗ بِالْهُدٰى وَدِينِ

الْحَقِّ لِيُظْهِرَهٗ عَلَى الدِّينِ كُلِّهٖ

وَلَوْ كَرِهَ الْمُشْرِكُونَ ۝ يٰٓأَيُّهَا

they went wrong, Allah let their hearts go wrong. For Allah guides not those who are rebellious transgressors.

6. And remember, Jesus, the son of Mary, said: "O Children of Israel! I am the Apostle of Allah (sent) to you, confirming the Law (which came) before me, and giving Glad Tidings of an Apostle to come after me, whose name shall be Ahmad." But when he came to them with clear Signs, they said, "This is evident sorcery!"

7. Who does greater wrong than one who

زَاغُوا أَزَاغَ اللَّهُ قُلُوبَهُمْ وَاللَّهُ

لَا يَهْدِى الْقَوْمَ الْفَاسِقِينَ ۝

وَإِذْ قَالَ عِيسَى ابْنُ مَرْيَمَ يَبَنِى

إِسْرَآءِيلَ إِنِّى رَسُولُ اللَّهِ إِلَيْكُم

مُّصَدِّقًا لِّمَا بَيْنَ يَدَىَّ مِنَ

التَّوْرَاةِ وَمُبَشِّرًا بِرَسُولٍ يَأْتِى

مِنْ بَعْدِى اسْمُهُ أَحْمَدُ فَلَمَّا

جَآءَهُم بِالْبَيِّنَاتِ قَالُوا هَٰذَا

سِحْرٌ مُّبِينٌ ۝ وَمَنْ أَظْلَمُ مِمَّنِ

for He is the Exalted in Might, the Wise.

2. O you who believe, why say you that which you do not?

3. Grievously odious is it in the sight of Allah that you say that which you do not.

4. Truly Allah loves those who fight in His Cause in battle array, as if they were a solid cemented structure.

5. And remember, Moses said to his people: "O my people! Why do you vex and insult me, though you know that I am the Apostle of Allah (sent) to you?" Then when

الْأَرْضِ ۚ وَهُوَ الْعَزِيزُ الْحَكِيمُ ۞

يَا أَيُّهَا الَّذِينَ اٰمَنُوا لِمَ تَقُولُونَ

مَا لَا تَفْعَلُونَ ۞ كَبُرَ مَقْتًا عِنْدَ

اللهِ أَنْ تَقُولُوا مَا لَا تَفْعَلُونَ ۞

إِنَّ اللهَ يُحِبُّ الَّذِينَ يُقَاتِلُونَ

فِي سَبِيلِهِ صَفًّا كَأَنَّهُمْ بُنْيَانٌ

مَّرْصُوصٌ ۞ وَإِذْ قَالَ مُوسَى لِقَوْمِهِ

يَا قَوْمِ لِمَ تُؤْذُونَنِي وَقَدْ تَعْلَمُونَ

أَنِّي رَسُولُ اللهِ إِلَيْكُمْ ۖ فَلَمَّا

intentionally forging falsehood, and that they will not disobey you in any just matter, - then do you receive their fealty, and pray to Allah for the forgiveness (of their sins): for Allah is Oft-Forgiving, Most Merciful.

13.   O you who believe! Turn not (for friendship) to people on whom is the Wrath of Allah, of the Hereafter they are already in despair, just as the unbelievers are in despair about those (buried) in graves.

As-Saff (Battle Array)

Bismillahir-Rahmanir-Rahim

1.   Whatever is in the heavens and on earth, let it declare the Praises and Glory of Allah:

يَفْتَرِيْنَهٗ بَيْنَ اَيْدِيْهِنَّ وَاَرْجُلِهِنَّ

وَلَا يَعْصِيْنَكَ فِيْ مَعْرُوْفٍ فَبَايِعْهُنَّ

وَاسْتَغْفِرْ لَهُنَّ اللهَ اِنَّ اللهَ غَفُوْرٌ

رَّحِيْمٌ ۞ يٰٓاَيُّهَا الَّذِيْنَ اٰمَنُوْا

لَا تَتَوَلَّوْا قَوْمًا غَضِبَ اللهُ عَلَيْهِمْ

قَدْ يَئِسُوْا مِنَ الْاٰخِرَةِ كَمَا يَئِسَ

الْكُفَّارُ مِنْ اَصْحٰبِ الْقُبُوْرِ ۞

مُقْدِمَةٌ الصَّفُّ اٰيَاتُهَا ١٣ مَدَنِيَّةٌ رُكُوْعَاتُهَا ٢ بِسْمِ اللهِ الرَّحْمٰنِ الرَّحِيْمِ

سَبَّحَ لِلّٰهِ مَا فِي السَّمٰوٰتِ وَمَا فِي

and Wisdom.

11. And if any of your wives deserts you to the unbelievers, and you have an accession (by the coming over of a woman from the other side), then pay to those whose wives have deserted the equivalent of what they had spent (on their dower). And fear Allah, in Whom you believe.

12. O Prophet! When believing women come to you to take the oath of fealty to you, that they will not associate in worship any other thing whatever with Allah, that they will not steal, that they will not commit adultery (or fornication), that they will not kill their children, that they will not utter slander,

حَكِيمٌ ۝ وَإِنْ فَاتَكُمْ شَيْءٌ مِّنْ

أَزْوَاجِكُمْ إِلَى الْكُفَّارِ فَعَاقَبْتُمْ فَاتُوا

الَّذِيْنَ ذَهَبَتْ أَزْوَاجُهُمْ مِّثْلَ

مَآ أَنْفَقُوْا ۗ وَاتَّقُوا اللهَ الَّذِيٓ أَنْتُمْ

بِهٖ مُؤْمِنُوْنَ ۝ يَآيُّهَا النَّبِيُّ إِذَا

جَآءَكَ الْمُؤْمِنٰتُ يُبَايِعْنَكَ عَلٰى

أَنْ لَّا يُشْرِكْنَ بِاللهِ شَيْئًا وَّلَا

يَسْرِقْنَ وَلَا يَزْنِيْنَ وَلَا يَقْتُلْنَ

أَوْلَادَهُنَّ وَلَا يَأْتِيْنَ بِبُهْتَانٍ

Allah knows best as to their Faith:
if you ascertain that they are
believers, then send them not back
to the unbelievers. They are not
lawful (wives) for the unbelievers, nor are the (unbelievers)
lawful (husbands) for them. But
pay the unbelievers what they
have spent (on their dower), and
there will be no blame on you if
you marry them on payment of
their dower to them. But hold not
to the guardianship of unbelieving women: ask for what you
have spent on their dowers, and let
the (unbelievers) ask for what they
have spent (on the dowers of
women who come over to you).
Such is the command of Allah: He
judges (with justice) between you.
And Allah is full of Knowledge

اللّٰهُ أَعْلَمُ بِإِيْمَانِهِنَّ فَإِنْ

عَلِمْتُمُوْهُنَّ مُؤْمِنَاتٍ فَلَا تَرْجِعُوْهُنَّ

إِلَى الْكُفَّارِ لَا هُنَّ حِلٌّ لَّهُمْ وَلَا

هُمْ يَحِلُّوْنَ لَهُنَّ وَاٰتُوْهُمْ مَّا أَنْفَقُوْا

وَلَا جُنَاحَ عَلَيْكُمْ أَنْ تَنْكِحُوْهُنَّ

إِذَا اٰتَيْتُمُوْهُنَّ أُجُوْرَهُنَّ وَلَا تُمْسِكُوْا

بِعِصَمِ الْكَوَافِرِ وَسْئَلُوْا مَا أَنْفَقْتُمْ

وَلْيَسْئَلُوْا مَا أَنْفَقُوْا ذٰلِكُمْ حُكْمُ

اللّٰهِ يَحْكُمُ بَيْنَكُمْ وَاللّٰهُ عَلِيْمٌ

from dealing kindly and justly with them: for Allah loves those who are just.

9.   Allah only forbids you, with regard to those who fight you for (your) Faith, and drive you out of your homes, and support (others) in driving you out, from turning to them (for friendship and protection). It is such as turn to them (in these circumstances), that do wrong.

10. O you who believe! When there come to you believing women refugees, examine (and test) them:

أَنْ تَبَرُّوهُمْ وَتُقْسِطُوا إِلَيْهِمْ

إِنَّ اللهَ يُحِبُّ الْمُقْسِطِينَ ۞

إِنَّمَا يَنْهَىٰكُمُ اللهُ عَنِ الَّذِينَ

قَاتَلُوكُمْ فِي الدِّينِ وَأَخْرَجُوكُمْ

مِّنْ دِيَارِكُمْ وَظَاهَرُوا عَلَىٰ

إِخْرَاجِكُمْ أَنْ تَوَلَّوْهُمْ وَمَنْ

يَتَوَلَّهُمْ فَأُولَٰئِكَ هُمُ الظَّالِمُونَ ۞

يَٰأَيُّهَا الَّذِينَ آمَنُوا إِذَا جَاءَكُمُ

الْمُؤْمِنَاتُ مُهَاجِرَاتٍ فَامْتَحِنُوهُنَّ

for those whose hope is in Allah and in the Last Day. But if any turn away, truly Allah is Free of all wants, Worthy of all praise.

7. It may be that Allah will grant love (and friendship) between you and those whom you (now) hold as enemies. For Allah has power (over all things); and Allah is Oft-Forgiving, Most Merciful.

8. Allah forbids you not, with regard to those who fight you not for (your) Faith nor drive you out of your homes,

لِّمَنۡ كَانَ يَرۡجُوا اللّٰهَ وَالۡيَوۡمَ

الۡاٰخِرَ ۚ وَمَنۡ يَّتَوَلَّ فَاِنَّ اللّٰهَ

هُوَ الۡغَنِيُّ الۡحَمِيۡدُ ۞ عَسَى اللّٰهُ

اَنۡ يَّجۡعَلَ بَيۡنَكُمۡ وَبَيۡنَ

الَّذِيۡنَ عَادَيۡتُمۡ مِّنۡهُمۡ مَّوَدَّةً ؕ

وَاللّٰهُ قَدِيۡرٌ ؕ وَاللّٰهُ غَفُوۡرٌ

رَّحِيۡمٌ ۞ لَا يَنۡهٰىكُمُ اللّٰهُ عَنِ

الَّذِيۡنَ لَمۡ يُقَاتِلُوۡكُمۡ فِى الدِّيۡنِ

وَلَمۡ يُخۡرِجُوۡكُمۡ مِّنۡ دِيَارِكُمۡ

and hatred for ever, - unless you believe in Allah and Him alone": but not when Abraham said to his father: "I will pray for forgiveness for you, though I have no power (to get) aught on you behalf from Allah." (They prayed): "Our Lord! In You do we trust, and to You do we turn in repentance: to You is (our) Final Goal.

5. "Our Lord! Make us not a (test and) trial for the unbelievers, but forgive us, our Lord! for You are the Exalted in Might, the Wise."

6. There was indeed in them an excellent example for you to follow, -

وَالْبَغْضَآءُ اَبَدًا حَتّٰى تُؤْمِنُوْا

بِاللهِ وَحْدَهٗ اِلَّا قَوْلَ اِبْرٰهِيْمَ

لِاَبِيْهِ لَاَسْتَغْفِرَنَّ لَكَ وَمَآ

اَمْلِكُ لَكَ مِنَ اللهِ مِنْ شَيْءٍ ۗ

رَبَّنَا عَلَيْكَ تَوَكَّلْنَا وَاِلَيْكَ اَنَبْنَا

وَاِلَيْكَ الْمَصِيْرُ ۞ رَبَّنَا لَا تَجْعَلْنَا

فِتْنَةً لِّلَّذِيْنَ كَفَرُوْا وَاغْفِرْ لَنَا

رَبَّنَا ۚ اِنَّكَ اَنْتَ الْعَزِيْزُ الْحَكِيْمُ ۞

لَقَدْ كَانَ لَكُمْ فِيْهِمْ اُسْوَةٌ حَسَنَةٌ

for evil: and they desire that you should reject the Truth.

3. Of no profit to you will be your relatives and your children on the Day of Judgment: He will judge between you: for Allah sees well all that you do.

4. There is for you an excellent example (to follow) in Abraham and those with him, when they said to their people: "We are clear of you and of whatever you worship besides Allah: we have rejected you, and there has arisen, between us and you, enmity

بِالسُّوٓءِ ۖ وَوَدُّوْا لَوْ تَكْفُرُوْنَ ۞ لَنْ

تَنْفَعَكُمْ اَرْحَامُكُمْ وَلَاۤ اَوْلَادُكُمْ ۚ

يَوْمَ الْقِيٰمَةِ ۚ يَفْصِلُ بَيْنَكُمْ ۚ وَاللّٰهُ

بِمَا تَعْمَلُوْنَ بَصِيْرٌ ۞ قَدْ كَانَتْ

لَكُمْ اُسْوَةٌ حَسَنَةٌ فِيْۤ اِبْرٰهِيْمَ

وَالَّذِيْنَ مَعَهٗ ۚ اِذْ قَالُوْا لِقَوْمِهِمْ

اِنَّا بُرَءٰٓؤُا مِنْكُمْ وَمِمَّا تَعْبُدُوْنَ

مِنْ دُوْنِ اللّٰهِ ۖ كَفَرْنَا بِكُمْ

وَبَدَا بَيْنَنَا وَبَيْنَكُمُ الْعَدَاوَةُ

the Prophet and yourselves (from your homes), (simply) because you believe in Allah your Lord! If you have come out to strive in My Way and to seek My Good Pleasure, (take them not as friends), holding secret conclave of love (and friendship) with them: for I know full well all that you conceal and all that you reveal. And any of you that does this has strayed from the Straight Path.

2.   If they were to get the better of you, they would behave to you as enemies, and stretch forth their hands and their tongues against you

الرَّسُولَ وَ اِيَّاكُمْ اَنْ تُؤْمِنُوا بِاللّٰهِ

رَبِّكُمْ اِنْ كُنْتُمْ خَرَجْتُمْ جِهَادًا

فِى سَبِيلِى وَابْتِغَاءَ مَرْضَاتِى

تُسِرُّوْنَ اِلَيْهِمْ بِالْمَوَدَّةِ وَ اَنَا

اَعْلَمُ بِمَا اَخْفَيْتُمْ وَمَا اَعْلَنْتُمْ

وَمَنْ يَّفْعَلْهُ مِنْكُمْ فَقَدْ ضَلَّ

سَوَآءَ السَّبِيلِ ۞ اِنْ يَّثْقَفُوكُمْ

يَكُوْنُوا لَكُمْ اَعْدَآءً وَّيَبْسُطُوْا

اِلَيْكُمْ اَيْدِيَهُمْ وَاَلْسِنَتَهُمْ

the Creator, the Evolver, (the Fashioner) the Bestower of Forms (or Colours). To Him belong the Most Beautiful Names: whatever is in the heavens and on earth, does declare His Praises and Glory: and He is the Exalted in Might, the Wise.

Al-Mumtahina (The Woman to be Examined)

Bismillahir-Rahmanir-Rahim

1.   O you who believe! Take not my enemies and yours as friends (or protectors), - offering them (your) love, even though they have rejected the Truth that has come to you, and have (on the contrary) driven out

ٱلْخَالِقُ ٱلْبَارِئُ ٱلْمُصَوِّرُ لَهُ
ٱلْأَسْمَآءُ ٱلْحُسْنَىٰ يُسَبِّحُ لَهُ مَا
فِى ٱلسَّمَٰوَٰتِ وَٱلْأَرْضِ وَهُوَ ٱلْعَزِيزُ
ٱلْحَكِيمُ ۞

سُورَةُ ٱلْمُمْتَحِنَةِ مَدَنِيَّة ﴿ءَايَٰتُهَا ١٣﴾ ﴿رُكُوعَاتُهَا ٢﴾

بِسْمِ ٱللَّهِ ٱلرَّحْمَٰنِ ٱلرَّحِيمِ

يَٰٓأَيُّهَا ٱلَّذِينَ ءَامَنُوا۟ لَا تَتَّخِذُوا۟
عَدُوِّى وَعَدُوَّكُمْ أَوْلِيَآءَ تُلْقُونَ
إِلَيْهِم بِٱلْمَوَدَّةِ وَقَدْ كَفَرُوا۟ بِمَا
جَآءَكُم مِّنَ ٱلْحَقِّ يُخْرِجُونَ

and cleave asunder for fear of Allah. Such are the similitudes which We propound to men, that they may reflect.

22. Allah is He, than Whom there is no other god; - Who knows (all things) both secret and open; He, Most Gracious, Most Merciful.

23. Allah is He, than Whom there is no other god; - the Sovereign, the Holy One, the Source of Peace (and Perfection), the Guardian of Faith, the Preserver of Safety, the Exalted in Might, the Irresistible, the Supreme: Glory to Allah! (High is He) above the partners they attribute to Him.

24. He is Allah,

مُّتَصَدِّعًا مِّنْ خَشْيَةِ اللّٰهِ ۚ وَتِلْكَ

الْأَمْثَالُ نَضْرِبُهَا لِلنَّاسِ لَعَلَّهُمْ

يَتَفَكَّرُونَ ۞ هُوَ اللّٰهُ الَّذِي لَآ

إِلٰهَ إِلَّا هُوَ ۚ عٰلِمُ الْغَيْبِ وَالشَّهَادَةِ ۖ

هُوَ الرَّحْمٰنُ الرَّحِيمُ ۞ هُوَ اللّٰهُ

الَّذِي لَآ إِلٰهَ إِلَّا هُوَ ۚ الْمَلِكُ

الْقُدُّوسُ السَّلٰمُ الْمُؤْمِنُ الْمُهَيْمِنُ

الْعَزِيزُ الْجَبَّارُ الْمُتَكَبِّرُ ۚ سُبْحٰنَ

اللّٰهِ عَمَّا يُشْرِكُونَ ۞ هُوَ اللّٰهُ

who believe! Fear Allah, and let every soul look to what (pro-vision) He has sent forth for the morrow. Yes, fear Allah: for Allah is Well-Acquainted with (all) that you do.

19.   And be you not like those who forgot Allah; and He made them forget their own souls! such are the rebellious transgressors!

20.   Not equal are the Compa-nions of the Fire and the Compa-nions of the Garden: it is the Companions of the Garden, that will achieve Felicity.

21.   Had We sent down this Qur'an on a mountain, verily, you would have seen it humble itself

الَّذِيْنَ اٰمَنُوا اتَّقُوا اللّٰهَ وَلْتَنْظُرْ

نَفْسٌ مَّا قَدَّمَتْ لِغَدٍ ۚ وَاتَّقُوا اللّٰهَ ۚ

اِنَّ اللّٰهَ خَبِيْرٌۢ بِمَا تَعْمَلُوْنَ ۝

وَلَا تَكُوْنُوْا كَالَّذِيْنَ نَسُوا اللّٰهَ

فَاَنْسٰهُمْ اَنْفُسَهُمْ ۚ اُولٰٓئِكَ هُمُ

الْفٰسِقُوْنَ ۝ لَا يَسْتَوِيْٓ اَصْحٰبُ النَّارِ

وَاَصْحٰبُ الْجَنَّةِ ۚ اَصْحٰبُ الْجَنَّةِ

هُمُ الْفَآئِزُوْنَ ۝ لَوْ اَنْزَلْنَا هٰذَا

الْقُرْاٰنَ عَلٰى جَبَلٍ لَّرَاَيْتَهٗ خَاشِعًا

that is because they are a people devoid of wisdom.

15. Like those who lately preceded them, they have tasted the evil result of their conduct; and (in the Hereafter there is) for them a grievous Chastisement; -

16. (Their allies deceived them), like the Evil One, when he says to man, "Deny Allah": but when (man) denies Allah, (the Evil One) says, "I am free of you: I do fear Allah, the Lord of the Worlds!"

17. The end of both will be that they will go into the Fire, dwelling therein for ever. Such is the reward of the wrong-doers.

18. O you

ذَٰلِكَ بِأَنَّهُمْ قَوْمٌ لَّا يَعْقِلُونَ ۞

كَمَثَلِ الَّذِينَ مِن قَبْلِهِمْ قَرِيبًا

ذَاقُوا وَبَالَ أَمْرِهِمْ وَلَهُمْ عَذَابٌ

أَلِيمٌ ۞ كَمَثَلِ الشَّيْطَانِ إِذْ قَالَ

لِلْإِنسَانِ اكْفُرْ فَلَمَّا كَفَرَ قَالَ

إِنِّي بَرِيءٌ مِّنكَ إِنِّي أَخَافُ اللَّهَ

رَبَّ الْعَالَمِينَ ۞ فَكَانَ عَاقِبَتَهُمَا

أَنَّهُمَا فِي النَّارِ خَالِدَيْنِ فِيهَا

وَذَٰلِكَ جَزَاءُ الظَّالِمِينَ ۞ يَا أَيُّهَا

never will they go out with them;
and if they are attacked (in fight),
they will never help them; and if
they do help them, they will turn
their backs; so they will receive
no help.

13. Of a truth you are stronger
(than they) because of the terror
in their hearts, (sent) by Allah.
This is because they are men
devoid of understanding.

14. They will not fight you
(even) together, except in fortified
townships, or from behind walls.
Strong is their fighting (spirit)
amongst themselves: you would
think they were united, but their
hearts are divided:

لَا يَخْرُجُونَ مَعَهُمْ وَلَئِنْ قُوتِلُوا

لَا يَنْصُرُونَهُمْ وَلَئِنْ نَّصَرُوهُمْ

لَيُوَلُّنَّ الْأَدْبَارَ ثُمَّ لَا يُنْصَرُونَ ۝

لَأَنْتُمْ أَشَدُّ رَهْبَةً فِي صُدُورِهِمْ

مِّنَ اللّٰهِ ذٰلِكَ بِأَنَّهُمْ قَوْمٌ لَّا

يَفْقَهُونَ ۝ لَا يُقَاتِلُونَكُمْ جَمِيعًا

إِلَّا فِي قُرًى مُّحَصَّنَةٍ أَوْ مِنْ

وَّرَاءِ جُدُرٍ بَأْسُهُمْ بَيْنَهُمْ شَدِيدٌ

تَحْسَبُهُمْ جَمِيعًا وَّقُلُوبُهُمْ شَتَّى

came before us into the Faith, and leave not, in our hearts, rancour (or sense of injury) against those who have believed. Our Lord! You are indeed full of Kindness, Most Merciful."

11.   Have you not observed the Hypocrites say to their misbelieving brethren among the People of the Book? - "If you are expelled, we too will go out with you, and we will never hearken to any one in your affair; and if you are attacked (in fight) we will help you". But Allah is Witness that they are indeed liars.

12.   If they are expelled,

سَبَقُونَا بِالْإِيمَانِ وَلَا تَجْعَلْ فِى

قُلُوبِنَا غِلًّا لِّلَّذِينَ آمَنُوا رَبَّنَا

إِنَّكَ رَءُوفٌ رَّحِيمٌ ۞ أَلَمْ تَرَ إِلَى

الَّذِينَ نَافَقُوا يَقُولُونَ لِإِخْوَانِهِمُ

الَّذِينَ كَفَرُوا مِنْ أَهْلِ الْكِتَٰبِ

لَئِنْ أُخْرِجْتُمْ لَنَخْرُجَنَّ مَعَكُمْ وَلَا

نُطِيعُ فِيكُمْ أَحَدًا أَبَدًا وَّإِن

قُوتِلْتُمْ لَنَنصُرَنَّكُمْ وَاللَّهُ يَشْهَدُ

إِنَّهُمْ لَكَٰذِبُونَ ۞ لَئِنْ أُخْرِجُوا

indeed the sincere ones: -

9. But those who before them, had homes (in Medina) and had adopted the Faith, - show their affection to such as came to them for refuge, and entertain no desire in their hearts for things given to the (latter), but give them preference over themselves, even though poverty was their (own lot). And those saved from the covetousness of their own souls, - they are the ones that achieve prosperity.

10. And those who came after them say: "Our Lord! Forgive us, and our brethren who

هُمُ الصَّادِقُونَ ۝ وَالَّذِينَ تَبَوَّءُو الدَّارَ

وَالْإِيمَانَ مِنْ قَبْلِهِمْ يُحِبُّونَ

مَنْ هَاجَرَ إِلَيْهِمْ وَلَا يَجِدُونَ

فِي صُدُورِهِمْ حَاجَةً مِّمَّا أُوتُوا

وَيُؤْثِرُونَ عَلَى أَنْفُسِهِمْ وَلَوْ كَانَ

بِهِمْ خَصَاصَةٌ ۚ وَمَنْ يُوقَ شُحَّ

نَفْسِهِ فَأُولَٰئِكَ هُمُ الْمُفْلِحُونَ ۝

وَالَّذِينَ جَاءُو مِنْ بَعْدِهِمْ يَقُولُونَ

رَبَّنَا اغْفِرْ لَنَا وَلِإِخْوَانِنَا الَّذِينَ

and orphans, the needy and the wayfarer; in order that it may not (merely) make a circuit between the wealthy among you. So take what the Apostle assigns to you, and deny yourselves that which he withholds from you. And fear Allah; for Allah is strict in Punishment.

8.   (Some part is due) to the indigent Muhajirs, those who were expelled from their homes and their property, while seeking Grace from Allah and (His) Good Pleasure, and aiding Allah and His Apostle: such are

وَالْيَتٰمٰى وَالْمَسٰكِيْنِ وَابْنِ السَّبِيْلِ ۙ

كَيْ لَا يَكُوْنَ دُوْلَةً ۢ بَيْنَ الْاَغْنِيَآءِ

مِنْكُمْ ۚ وَمَآ اٰتٰىكُمُ الرَّسُوْلُ فَخُذُوْهُ ۚ

وَمَا نَهٰىكُمْ عَنْهُ فَانْتَهُوْا ۚ وَاتَّقُوا

اللّٰهَ ؕ اِنَّ اللّٰهَ شَدِيْدُ الْعِقَابِ ۘ ۚ

لِلْفُقَرَآءِ الْمُهٰجِرِيْنَ الَّذِيْنَ

اُخْرِجُوْا مِنْ دِيَارِهِمْ وَاَمْوَالِهِمْ

يَبْتَغُوْنَ فَضْلًا مِّنَ اللّٰهِ وَرِضْوَانًا

وَّيَنْصُرُوْنَ اللّٰهَ وَرَسُوْلَهٗ ؕ اُولٰٓئِكَ

or you left them standing on their roots, it was by leave of Allah, and in order that He might cover with shame the rebellious transgressors.

6.   What Allah has bestowed on His Apostle (and taken away) from them - for this you made no expedition with either cavalry or camelry: but Allah gives power to His Apostles over any He pleases: and Allah has power over all things.

7.   What Allah has bestowed on His Apostle (and taken away) from the people of the townships, -belongs to Allah, - to His Apostle and to kindred

اَوْ تَرَكْتُمُوهَا قَآئِمَةً عَلٰى اُصُوْلِهَا

فَبِاِذْنِ اللّٰهِ وَلِيُخْزِيَ الْفٰسِقِيْنَ ۞

وَمَاۤ اَفَآءَ اللّٰهُ عَلٰى رَسُوْلِهٖ مِنْهُمْ

فَمَاۤ اَوْجَفْتُمْ عَلَيْهِ مِنْ خَيْلٍ

وَّلَا رِكَابٍ وَّلٰكِنَّ اللّٰهَ يُسَلِّطُ

رُسُلَهٗ عَلٰى مَنْ يَّشَآءُ ۚ وَاللّٰهُ عَلٰى

كُلِّ شَيْءٍ قَدِيْرٌ ۞ مَاۤ اَفَآءَ اللّٰهُ

عَلٰى رَسُوْلِهٖ مِنْ اَهْلِ الْقُرٰى

فَلِلّٰهِ وَلِلرَّسُوْلِ وَلِذِى الْقُرْبٰى

terror into their hearts, so that they destroyed their dwellings by their own hands and the hands of the believers. Take warning, then, O you with eyes (to see)!

3. And had it not been that Allah had decreed banishment for them, He would certainly have punished them in this world: and in the Hereafter they shall (certainly) have the Punishment of the Fire.

4. That is because they resisted Allah and His Apostle: and if any one resists Allah, verily Allah is severe in Punishment.

5. Whether you cut down (O you Muslim!) the tender palm-trees,

فِى قُلُوبِهِمُ الرُّعْبَ يُخْرِبُونَ بُيُوتَهُمْ

بِأَيْدِيهِمْ وَأَيْدِى الْمُؤْمِنِينَ

فَاعْتَبِرُوا يَا أُولِى الْأَبْصَارِ ۞ وَلَوْلَا

أَنْ كَتَبَ اللَّهُ عَلَيْهِمُ الْجَلَاءَ

لَعَذَّبَهُمْ فِى الدُّنْيَا وَلَهُمْ فِى

الْآخِرَةِ عَذَابُ النَّارِ ۞ ذَلِكَ

بِأَنَّهُمْ شَاقُّوا اللَّهَ وَرَسُولَهُ وَمَنْ

يُشَاقِّ اللَّهَ فَإِنَّ اللَّهَ شَدِيدُ

الْعِقَابِ ۞ مَا قَطَعْتُمْ مِنْ لِينَةٍ

Al-Hashr (The Gathering)

Bismillahir-Rahmanir-Rahim

1. Whatever is in the heavens and on earth, let it declare the Praises and Glory of Allah: for He is the Exalted in Might, the Wise.

2. It is He Who got out the unbelievers among the People of the Book from their homes at the first gathering (of the forces). Little did you think that they would get out: and they thought that their fortresses would defend them from Allah! But the (Wrath of) Allah came to them from quarters from which they little expected (it), and cast

بِسْمِ اللهِ الرَّحْمٰنِ الرَّحِيْمِ

سَبَّحَ لِلّٰهِ مَا فِى السَّمٰوٰتِ وَمَا

فِى الْاَرْضِ ۚ وَهُوَ الْعَزِيْزُ الْحَكِيْمُ ۝

هُوَ الَّذِىْۤ اَخْرَجَ الَّذِيْنَ كَفَرُوْا

مِنْ اَهْلِ الْكِتٰبِ مِنْ دِيَارِهِمْ

لِاَوَّلِ الْحَشْرِ ؕ مَا ظَنَنْتُمْ اَنْ

يَّخْرُجُوْا وَظَنُّوْۤا اَنَّهُمْ مَّانِعَتُهُمْ

حُصُوْنُهُمْ مِّنَ اللهِ فَاَتٰىهُمُ اللهُ

مِنْ حَيْثُ لَمْ يَحْتَسِبُوْا ۫ وَقَذَفَ

resist Allah and His Apostle, even though they were their fathers or their sons, or their brothers, or their kindred. For such He has written Faith in their hearts, and strengthened them with a spirit from Himself. And He will admit them to Gardens beneath which rivers flow, to dwell therein (for ever). Allah will be well pleased with them, and they with Him. They are the Party of Allah. Truly, it is the Party of Allah that will achieve Felicity.

حَآدَّ اللَّهَ وَرَسُولَهُ وَلَوْ كَانُوٓا

اٰبَآءَهُمْ اَوْ اَبْنَآءَهُمْ اَوْ اِخْوَانَهُمْ

اَوْ عَشِيْرَتَهُمْ اُولٰٓئِكَ كَتَبَ فِيْ

قُلُوْبِهِمُ الْاِيْمَانَ وَاَيَّدَهُمْ بِرُوْحٍ

مِّنْهُ وَيُدْخِلُهُمْ جَنّٰتٍ تَجْرِيْ

مِنْ تَحْتِهَا الْاَنْهٰرُ خٰلِدِيْنَ فِيْهَا

رَضِيَ اللَّهُ عَنْهُمْ وَرَضُوْا عَنْهُ

اُولٰٓئِكَ حِزْبُ اللَّهِ اَلَآ اِنَّ حِزْبَ

اللَّهِ هُمُ الْمُفْلِحُوْنَ ۝

No, indeed! they are but liars!

19. The Evil One has got the better of them: so he has made them lose the remembrance of Allah. They are the Party of the Evil One. Truly, it is the Party of the Satan that will perish!

20. Those who resist Allah and His Apostle will be among those most humiliated.

21. Allah has decreed: "It is I and My Apostles who must prevail": For Allah is One full of Strength, able to enforce His Will.

22. You will not find any people who believe in Allah and the Last Day, loving those who

أَلَا إِنَّهُمْ هُمُ الْكَٰذِبُونَ ۝ اِسْتَحْوَذَ

عَلَيْهِمُ الشَّيْطٰنُ فَأَنسٰىهُمْ ذِكْرَ اللّٰهِ

أُولٰٓئِكَ حِزْبُ الشَّيْطٰنِ ۚ أَلَا إِنَّ

حِزْبَ الشَّيْطٰنِ هُمُ الْخٰسِرُونَ ۝

إِنَّ الَّذِينَ يُحَآدُّونَ اللّٰهَ وَرَسُولَهُ

أُولٰٓئِكَ فِي الْأَذَلِّينَ ۝ كَتَبَ اللّٰهُ

لَأَغْلِبَنَّ أَنَا وَرُسُلِيٓ ۚ إِنَّ اللّٰهَ قَوِيٌّ

عَزِيزٌ ۝ لَا تَجِدُ قَوْمًا يُؤْمِنُونَ

بِاللّٰهِ وَالْيَوْمِ الْآخِرِ يُوَآدُّونَ مَنْ

evil indeed are their deeds.

16. They have made their oaths a screen (for their misdeeds): thus .they obstruct (men) from the Path of Allah: therefore shall they have a humiliating Chastisement.

17. Of no profit whatever to them, against Allah, will be their riches nor their sons: they will be Companions of the Fire, to dwell therein (for ever)!

18. One day will Allah raise them all up (for Judgment): then will they swear to Him as they swear to you: and they think that they have something (to stand upon).

شَدِيدًا ٱ إِنَّهُمْ سَآءَ مَا كَانُوا

يَعْمَلُونَ ۝ اتَّخَذُوٓا أَيْمَانَهُمْ جُنَّةً

فَصَدُّوا عَنْ سَبِيلِ اللّٰهِ فَلَهُمْ

عَذَابٌ مُّهِينٌ ۝ لَّن تُغْنِىَ عَنْهُمْ

أَمْوَالُهُمْ وَلَآ أَوْلَادُهُم مِّنَ اللّٰهِ

شَيْئًا أُولَٰٓئِكَ أَصْحَابُ النَّارِ هُمْ

فِيهَا خَالِدُونَ ۝ يَوْمَ يَبْعَثُهُمُ اللّٰهُ

جَمِيعًا فَيَحْلِفُونَ لَهُ كَمَا يَحْلِفُونَ

لَكُمْ وَيَحْسَبُونَ أَنَّهُمْ عَلَىٰ شَىْءٍ

13. Is it that you are afraid of spending sums in charity before your private consultation (with him)? If, then, you do not so, and Allah forgives you, then (at least) establish regular prayer; practise regular charity; and obey Allah and His Apostle. And Allah is Well-Acquainted with all that you do.

14. Turn you not your attention to those who turn (in friendship) to such as have the Wrath of Allah upon them? They are neither of you nor of them, and the swear to falsehood knowingly.

15. Allah has prepared for them a severe Chastisement:

ءَاَشْفَقْتُمْ اَنْ تُقَدِّمُوْا بَيْنَ يَدَىْ

نَجْوٰىكُمْ صَدَقٰتٍ ۚ فَاِذْ لَمْ تَفْعَلُوْا

وَتَابَ اللّٰهُ عَلَيْكُمْ فَاَقِيْمُوا الصَّلٰوةَ

وَاٰتُوا الزَّكٰوةَ وَاَطِيْعُوا اللّٰهَ وَرَسُوْلَهٗ ۚ

وَاللّٰهُ خَبِيْرٌۢ بِمَا تَعْمَلُوْنَ ۞ اَلَمْ تَرَ

اِلَى الَّذِيْنَ تَوَلَّوْا قَوْمًا غَضِبَ

اللّٰهُ عَلَيْهِمْ ۗ مَا هُمْ مِّنْكُمْ وَلَا مِنْهُمْ ۙ

وَيَحْلِفُوْنَ عَلَى الْكَذِبِ وَهُمْ

يَعْلَمُوْنَ ۞ اَعَدَّ اللّٰهُ لَهُمْ عَذَابًا

(ample) room will Allah provide for you. And when you are told to rise up, rise up: Allah will raise up, to (suitable) ranks (and degrees) those of you who believe and who have been granted (mystic) Knowledge. And Allah is Well-Acquainted with all you do.

12. O you who believe! When you consult the Apostle in private, spend something in charity before your private consultation. That will be best for you, and most conducive to purity (of conduct). But if you find not (the wherewithal), Allah is Oft-Forgiving, Most Merciful.

يَفْسَحِ ٱللَّهُ لَكُمْ وَإِذَا قِيلَ

ٱنشُزُوا فَٱنشُزُوا يَرْفَعِ ٱللَّهُ

ٱلَّذِينَ ءَامَنُوا مِنكُمْ وَٱلَّذِينَ أُوتُوا

ٱلْعِلْمَ دَرَجَٰتٍ وَٱللَّهُ بِمَا تَعْمَلُونَ

خَبِيرٌ ۝ يَٰٓأَيُّهَا ٱلَّذِينَ ءَامَنُوٓا

إِذَا نَٰجَيْتُمُ ٱلرَّسُولَ فَقَدِّمُوا

بَيْنَ يَدَيْ نَجْوَىٰكُمْ صَدَقَةً ۚ

ذَٰلِكَ خَيْرٌ لَّكُمْ وَأَطْهَرُ ۚ فَإِن لَّمْ

تَجِدُوا فَإِنَّ ٱللَّهَ غَفُورٌ رَّحِيمٌ ۝

and hostility, and disobedience to the Prophet; but do it for righteousness and self-restraint; and fear Allah, to Whom you shall be brought back.

10. Secret counsels are only (inspired) by the Evil One, in order that he may cause grief to the believers; but he can not harm them in the least, except as Allah permits; and on Allah let the believers put their trust.

11. O you who believe! When you are told to make room in the assemblies, (spread out and) make room:

وَالْعُدْوَانِ وَمَعْصِيَتِ الرَّسُولِ

وَتَنَاجَوْا بِالْبِرِّ وَالتَّقْوَىٰ وَاتَّقُوا

اللَّهَ الَّذِيٓ إِلَيْهِ تُحْشَرُونَ ۝

إِنَّمَا النَّجْوَىٰ مِنَ الشَّيْطٰنِ

لِيَحْزُنَ الَّذِينَ أَمَنُوا وَلَيْسَ

بِضَآرِّهِمْ شَيْئًا إِلَّا بِإِذْنِ اللَّهِ

وَعَلَى اللَّهِ فَلْيَتَوَكَّلِ الْمُؤْمِنُونَ ۝

يَٰٓأَيُّهَا الَّذِينَ أَمَنُوٓا إِذَا قِيلَ لَكُمْ

تَفَسَّحُوا فِى الْمَجَالِسِ فَافْسَحُوا

were forbidden secret counsels
yet revert to that which they were
forbidden (to do)? And they hold
secret counsels among themselves
for iniquity and hostility, and
disobedience to the Apostle. And
when they come to you, they
salute you, not as Allah salutes
you, (but in crooked ways): and
they say to themselves, "Why
does not Allah punish us for our
words?" Enough for them is Hell:
in it will they burn, and evil is that
destination!

9.   O you who believe! When
you hold secret counsel, do it not
for iniquity

نُهُوا عَنِ النَّجْوٰى ثُمَّ يَعُودُونَ

لِمَا نُهُوا عَنْهُ وَيَتَنَاجَوْنَ بِالْإِثْمِ

وَالْعُدْوَانِ وَمَعْصِيَتِ الرَّسُولِ

وَإِذَا جَآءُوكَ حَيَّوْكَ بِمَا لَمْ يُحَيِّكَ

بِهِ اللهُ وَيَقُولُونَ فِيٓ أَنْفُسِهِمْ

لَوْلَا يُعَذِّبُنَا اللهُ بِمَا نَقُولُ

حَسْبُهُمْ جَهَنَّمُ يَصْلَوْنَهَا فَبِئْسَ

الْمَصِيرُ ۝ يٰٓأَيُّهَا الَّذِينَ اٰمَنُوٓا

إِذَا تَنَاجَيْتُمْ فَلَا تَتَنَاجَوْا بِالْإِثْمِ

7. Do you see not that Allah does know (all) that is in the heavens and on earth? There is not a secret consultation between three, but He makes the fourth among them, - nor between five but He makes the sixth, - nor between fewer nor more, but He is in their midst, wheresoever they be: in the end will He tell them the truth of their conduct, on the Day of Judgment. For Allah has full knowledge of all things.

8. Turn you not your sight towards those who

شَهِيدٌ ۞ اَلَمْ تَرَ اَنَّ اللهَ يَعْلَمُ

مَا فِي السَّمٰوٰتِ وَمَا فِي الْاَرْضِ

مَا يَكُوْنُ مِنْ نَّجْوٰى ثَلٰثَةٍ اِلَّا

هُوَ رَابِعُهُمْ وَلَا خَمْسَةٍ اِلَّا هُوَ

سَادِسُهُمْ وَلَاۤ اَدْنٰى مِنْ ذٰلِكَ

وَلَاۤ اَكْثَرَ اِلَّا هُوَ مَعَهُمْ اَيْنَ مَا

كَانُوْا ثُمَّ يُنَبِّئُهُمْ بِمَا عَمِلُوْا

يَوْمَ الْقِيٰمَةِ اِنَّ اللهَ بِكُلِّ شَيْءٍ

عَلِيْمٌ ۞ اَلَمْ تَرَ اِلَى الَّذِيْنَ

that you may show your faith in Allah and His Apostle. Those are limits (set by) Allah. For those who reject (Him), there is a grievous Chastisement.

5.   Those who resist Allah and His Apostle will be humbled to dust, as were those before them: for We have already sent down clear Signs. And the unbelievers (will have) a humiliating Chastisement, -

6.   On the Day that Allah will raise them all up (again) and show them the Truth (and meaning) of their conduct. Allah has reckoned its (value), though they may have forgotten it, for Allah is Witness to all things.

لِتُؤْمِنُوا بِاللّٰهِ وَرَسُوْلِهٖ ۖ وَتِلْكَ

حُدُوْدُ اللّٰهِ ۚ وَلِلْكٰفِرِيْنَ عَذَابٌ

اَلِيْمٌ ۞ اِنَّ الَّذِيْنَ يُحَآدُّوْنَ

اللّٰهَ وَرَسُوْلَهٗ كُبِتُوْا كَمَا كُبِتَ

الَّذِيْنَ مِنْ قَبْلِهِمْ وَقَدْ اَنْزَلْنَا

اٰيٰتٍ بَيِّنٰتٍ ۚ وَلِلْكٰفِرِيْنَ عَذَابٌ

مُّهِيْنٌ ۞ يَوْمَ يَبْعَثُهُمُ اللّٰهُ جَمِيْعًا

فَيُنَبِّئُهُمْ بِمَا عَمِلُوْا ۗ اَحْصٰهُ اللّٰهُ

وَنَسُوْهُ ۗ وَاللّٰهُ عَلٰى كُلِّ شَيْءٍ

and false: but truly Allah is One that blots out (sins), and forgives (again and again).

3.   But those who divorce their wives by Zihar, then wish to go back on the words they uttered, - (it is ordained that such a one) should free a slave before they touch each other: this are you admonished to perform: and Allah is Well-Acquainted with (all) that you do.

4.   And if any has not (the wherewithal), he should fast for two months consecutively before they touch each other. But if any is unable to do so, he should feed sixty indigent ones, this,

وَزُوْرًا ۚ وَإِنَّ اللَّهَ لَعَفُوٌّ غَفُوْرٌ ۞

وَالَّذِيْنَ يُظٰهِرُوْنَ مِنْ نِّسَآئِهِمْ

ثُمَّ يَعُوْدُوْنَ لِمَا قَالُوْا فَتَحْرِيْرُ

رَقَبَةٍ مِّنْ قَبْلِ أَنْ يَّتَمَآسَّا ۚ

ذٰلِكُمْ تُوْعَظُوْنَ بِهٖ ۚ وَاللَّهُ بِمَا

تَعْمَلُوْنَ خَبِيْرٌ ۞ فَمَنْ لَّمْ يَجِدْ

فَصِيَامُ شَهْرَيْنِ مُتَتَابِعَيْنِ مِنْ

قَبْلِ أَنْ يَّتَمَآسَّا ۚ فَمَنْ لَّمْ يَسْتَطِعْ

فَإِطْعَامُ سِتِّيْنَ مِسْكِيْنًا ۚ ذٰلِكَ

Al-Mujadila
(The Women who pleads)

Bismillahir-Rahmanir-Rahim

1. Allah has indeed heard (and accepted) the statement of the woman who pleads with you concerning her husband and carries her complaint (in prayer) to Allah: and Allah (always) heard the arguments between both sides among you: for Allah hears and sees (all things).

2. If any men among you divorce their wives by Zihar (calling them mothers), they can not be their mothers: none can be their mothers except those who gave them birth. And in fact they use words (both) iniquitous

بِسۡمِ اللهِ الرَّحۡمٰنِ الرَّحِيۡمِ

قَدۡ سَمِعَ اللهُ قَوۡلَ الَّتِىۡ

تُجَادِلُكَ فِىۡ زَوۡجِهَا وَ تَشۡتَكِىۡۤ اِلَى

اللهِ ۖ وَاللهُ يَسۡمَعُ تَحَاوُرَكُمَا ؕ اِنَّ

اللهَ سَمِيۡعٌۢ بَصِيۡرٌ ۞ اَلَّذِيۡنَ

يُظٰهِرُوۡنَ مِنۡكُمۡ مِّنۡ نِّسَآئِهِمۡ

مَّا هُنَّ اُمَّهٰتِهِمۡ ؕ اِنۡ اُمَّهٰتُهُمۡ

اِلَّا الّٰٓـئِىۡ وَلَدۡنَهُمۡ ؕ وَاِنَّهُمۡ

لَيَقُوۡلُوۡنَ مُنۡكَرًا مِّنَ الۡقَوۡلِ

پاره

قَدْ سَمِعَ اللّٰهُ

(۲۸)

PART 29
Tabaarakal-Ladhi

all they desire.

43. "Eat you and drink you to your heart's content: for that you worked (Righteousness).

44. Thus do We certainly reward the Doers of Good.

45. Ah woe, that Day, to the Rejecters of Truth!

46. (O you unjust!) Eat you and enjoy yourselves (but) a little while, for that you are Sinners.

47. Ah woe, that Day, to the Rejecters of Truth!

48. And when it is said to them, "Prostrate yourselves!" they do not so.

49. Ah woe, that Day, to the Rejecters of Truth!

50. Then what Message, after that, will they believe in?

مِمَّا يَشْتَهُوْنَ ۚ كُلُوْا وَاشْرَبُوْا

هَنِيْئًا بِمَا كُنْتُمْ تَعْمَلُوْنَ ۚ اِنَّا

كَذٰلِكَ نَجْزِى الْمُحْسِنِيْنَ ۚ وَيْلٌ

يَّوْمَئِذٍ لِّلْمُكَذِّبِيْنَ ۚ كُلُوْا وَتَمَتَّعُوْا

قَلِيْلًا اِنَّكُمْ مُّجْرِمُوْنَ ۚ وَيْلٌ

يَّوْمَئِذٍ لِّلْمُكَذِّبِيْنَ ۚ وَاِذَا قِيْلَ

لَهُمُ ارْكَعُوْا لَا يَرْكَعُوْنَ ۚ وَيْلٌ

يَّوْمَئِذٍ لِّلْمُكَذِّبِيْنَ ۚ فَبِاَىِّ

حَدِيْثٍ بَعْدَهٗ يُؤْمِنُوْنَ ۚ

(huge) as Forts,"　　**33.**　　"As if there were (a string of) yellow camels (marching swiftly)."

34.　Ah woe, that Day, to the Rejecters of Truth!

35.　That will be a Day when they shall not be able to speak.

36.　Nor will it be open to them to put forth pleas.　**37.**　Ah woe, that Day, to the Rejecters of Truth!

38.　That will be a Day of Sorting out! We shall gather you together and those before (you)!

39.　Now, if you have a trick (or plot), use it against Me!

40.　Ah woe, that Day, to the Rejecters of Truth!

41.　As to the Righteous, they shall be amidst (cool) shades and springs (of water).

42.　And (they shall have) fruits, -

كَالْقَصْرِ ۞ كَاَنَّهٗ جِمٰلَتٌ صُفْرٌ ۞

وَيْلٌ يَّوْمَئِذٍ لِّلْمُكَذِّبِيْنَ ۞

هٰذَا يَوْمُ لَا يَنْطِقُوْنَ ۞ وَلَا

يُؤْذَنُ لَهُمْ فَيَعْتَذِرُوْنَ ۞ وَيْلٌ

يَّوْمَئِذٍ لِّلْمُكَذِّبِيْنَ ۞ هٰذَا يَوْمُ

الْفَصْلِ ۚ جَمَعْنٰكُمْ وَالْاَوَّلِيْنَ ۞

فَاِنْ كَانَ لَكُمْ كَيْدٌ فَكِيْدُوْنِ ۞

وَيْلٌ يَّوْمَئِذٍ لِّلْمُكَذِّبِيْنَ ۞ اِنَّ

الْمُتَّقِيْنَ فِيْ ظِلٰلٍ وَّعُيُوْنٍ ۞ وَّفَوَاكِهَ

that Day, to the rejecters of Truth!

25. Have We not made the earth (as a place) to draw together.

26. The living and the dead,

27. And made therein mountains standing firm, lofty (in stature); and provided for you water sweet (and wholesome)?

28. Ah woe, that Day, to the Rejecters of Truth!

29. (It will be said:) "Depart you to that which you used to reject as false!" **30.** "Depart you to a Shadow (of smoke ascending) in three columns,"

31. "(Which yields) no shade of coolness, and is of no use against the fierce Blaze."

32. "Indeed it throws about sparks

يَوْمَئِذٍ لِّلْمُكَذِّبِيْنَ ۞ اَلَمْ نَجْعَلِ

الْاَرْضَ كِفَاتًا ۞ اَحْيَآءً وَّاَمْوَاتًا ۞

وَّجَعَلْنَا فِيْهَا رَوَاسِىَ شَامِخٰتٍ

وَّاَسْقَيْنٰكُمْ مَّآءً فُرَاتًا ۞ وَيْلٌ

يَّوْمَئِذٍ لِّلْمُكَذِّبِيْنَ ۞ اِنْطَلِقُوْٓا

اِلٰى مَا كُنْتُمْ بِهٖ تُكَذِّبُوْنَ ۞

اِنْطَلِقُوْٓا اِلٰى ظِلٍّ ذِىْ ثَلٰثِ

شُعَبٍ ۞ لَّا ظَلِيْلٍ وَّلَا يُغْنِىْ

مِنَ اللَّهَبِ ۞ اِنَّهَا تَرْمِىْ بِشَرَرٍ

are these (portents) deferred?

13. For the Day of Sorting out.

14. And what will explain to you what is the Day of Sorting out?

15. Ah woe, that Day, to the Rejecters of Truth!

16. Did We not destroy the men of old (for their evil)?

17. So shall We make later (generations) follow them.

18. Thus do We deal with men of sin. **19.** Ah, woe that Day, to the Rejecters of Truth!

20. Have We not created you from a fluid (held) despicable?

21. The which We placed in a place of rest, firmly fixed,

22. For a period (of gestation), determined (according to need)?

23. For We do determine (according to need); for We are the best to determine (things). **24.** Ah woe,

اُجِّلَتْ ۞ لِيَوْمِ الْفَصْلِ ۞ وَمَاۤ

اَدْرٰىكَ مَا يَوْمُ الْفَصْلِ ۞ وَيْلٌ

يَّوْمَئِذٍ لِّلْمُكَذِّبِيْنَ ۞ اَلَمْ نُهْلِكِ

الْاَوَّلِيْنَ ۞ ثُمَّ نُتْبِعُهُمُ الْاٰخِرِيْنَ ۞

كَذٰلِكَ نَفْعَلُ بِالْمُجْرِمِيْنَ ۞ وَيْلٌ

يَّوْمَئِذٍ لِّلْمُكَذِّبِيْنَ ۞ اَلَمْ نَخْلُقْكُّمْ

مِّنْ مَّآءٍ مَّهِيْنٍ ۞ فَجَعَلْنٰهُ فِيْ

قَرَارٍ مَّكِيْنٍ ۞ اِلٰى قَدَرٍ مَّعْلُوْمٍ ۞

فَقَدَرْنَا ۖ فَنِعْمَ الْقٰدِرُوْنَ ۞ وَيْلٌ

Al-Mursalat
(Those Sent Forth)

Bismillahir-Rahmanir-Rahim

1.   By the (Winds) sent forth one after another (to man's profit);

2.   Which then blow violently in tempestuous gusts,

3.   And scatter (things) far and wide;   **4.**   Then separate them, one from another,

5.   Then spread abroad a Message,

6.   Whether of Justification or of Warning; - **7.** Assuredly, what you are promised must come to pass.

8.   Then when the stars become dim;   **9.**   When the heaven is cleft asunder;

10.   When the mountains are scattered (to the winds) as dust;

11. And when the time fixed for the gathering of all Apostles comes.

12.   For what Day

بِسْمِ اللهِ الرَّحْمٰنِ الرَّحِيْمِ

وَالْمُرْسَلٰتِ عُرْفًا ۙ فَالْعٰصِفٰتِ

عَصْفًا ۙ وَّالنّٰشِرٰتِ نَشْرًا ۙ

فَالْفٰرِقٰتِ فَرْقًا ۙ فَالْمُلْقِيٰتِ

ذِكْرًا ۙ عُذْرًا اَوْ نُذْرًا ۙ اِنَّمَا

تُوْعَدُوْنَ لَوَاقِعٌ ؕ فَاِذَا النُّجُوْمُ

طُمِسَتْ ۙ وَاِذَا السَّمَآءُ فُرِجَتْ ۙ

وَاِذَا الْجِبَالُ نُسِفَتْ ۙ وَاِذَا

الرُّسُلُ اُقِّتَتْ ؕ لِاَیِّ يَوْمٍ

(that will be) hard.

28. It is We Who created them, and We have made their joints strong; but, when We will, We can substitute the like of them by a complete change.

29. This is an admonition: whosoever will, let him take a (straight) Path to his Lord.

30. But you will not, except as Allah wills; for Allah is full of Knowledge and Wisdom.

31. He will admit to His Mercy whom He wills; but the wrong-doers, - for them has He prepared a grievous Chastisement.

ثَقِيلًا ۝ نَحْنُ خَلَقْنَاهُمْ وَشَدَدْنَا

أَسْرَهُمْ ۚ وَإِذَا شِئْنَا بَدَّلْنَا

أَمْثَالَهُمْ تَبْدِيلًا ۝ إِنَّ هَٰذِهِ

تَذْكِرَةٌ ۖ فَمَنْ شَاءَ اتَّخَذَ إِلَىٰ

رَبِّهِ سَبِيلًا ۝ وَمَا تَشَاءُونَ إِلَّا

أَنْ يَشَاءَ اللَّهُ ۚ إِنَّ اللَّهَ كَانَ

عَلِيمًا حَكِيمًا ۝ يُدْخِلُ مَنْ يَشَاءُ

فِي رَحْمَتِهِ ۚ وَالظَّالِمِينَ أَعَدَّ لَهُمْ

عَذَابًا أَلِيمًا ۝

a Reward for you, and your Endeavour is accepted and recognised."

23. It is We Who have sent down the Qur'an to you by stages.

24. Therefore be patient with constancy to the Command of your Lord, and hearken not to the sinner or the ingrate among them.

25. And celebrate the name or your Lord morning and evening,

26. And part of the night, prostrate yourself to Him; and glorify Him a long night through.

27. As to these, they love the fleeting life, and put away behind them a Day

لَكُمْ جَزَآءً وَّ كَانَ سَعْيُكُمْ

مَّشْكُوْرًا ۞ إِنَّا نَحْنُ نَزَّلْنَا

عَلَيْكَ الْقُرْاٰنَ تَنْزِيْلًا ۞ فَاصْبِرْ

لِحُكْمِ رَبِّكَ وَلَا تُطِعْ مِنْهُمْ

اٰثِمًا اَوْ كَفُوْرًا ۞ وَاذْكُرِ اسْمَ

رَبِّكَ بُكْرَةً وَّاَصِيْلًا ۞ وَمِنَ

الَّيْلِ فَاسْجُدْ لَهُ وَسَبِّحْهُ

لَيْلًا طَوِيْلًا ۞ اِنَّ هٰٓؤُلَآءِ يُحِبُّوْنَ

الْعَاجِلَةَ وَيَذَرُوْنَ وَرَآءَهُمْ يَوْمًا

a cup (of wine) mixed with Zanjabil, -

18. A fountain there, called Salsabil.

19. And round about them will (serve) youths of perpetual (freshness): if you see them, you would think them scattered Pearls.

20. And when you look, it is there you will see a Bliss and a Realm Magnificent.

21. Upon them will be green garments of fine silk and heavy brocade, and they will be adorned with bracelets of silver; and their Lord will give to them to drink of a wine pure and holy.

22. "Verily this is

كَأْسًا كَانَ مِزَاجُهَا زَنْجَبِيلًا ۞

عَيْنًا فِيهَا تُسَمَّى سَلْسَبِيلًا ۞ وَيَطُوفُ

عَلَيْهِمْ وِلْدَانٌ مُّخَلَّدُونَ ۖ إِذَا

رَأَيْتَهُمْ حَسِبْتَهُمْ لُؤْلُؤًا مَّنثُورًا ۞

وَإِذَا رَأَيْتَ ثَمَّ رَأَيْتَ نَعِيمًا

وَّمُلْكًا كَبِيرًا ۞ عَلِيَهُمْ ثِيَابُ

سُنْدُسٍ خُضْرٌ وَّإِسْتَبْرَقٌ ۖ وَحُلُّوٓا

أَسَاوِرَ مِنْ فِضَّةٍ وَسَقَاهُمْ رَبُّهُمْ

شَرَابًا طَهُورًا ۞ إِنَّ هَٰذَا كَانَ

Day, and will shed over them a Light of Beauty and (blissful) Joy.

12. And because they were patient and constant, He will reward them with a Garden and (garments of) silk.

13. Reclining in the (Garden) on raised thrones, they will see there neither the sun's (excessive heat) nor (the moon's) excessive cold.

14. And the shades of the (Garden) will come low over them, and the bunche (of fruit), there, will hang low in humility.

15. And amongst them will be passed round vessels of silver and goblets of crystal, -

16. Crystal-clear, made of silver: they will determine the measure thereof (according to their wishes). 17. And they will be given to drink there of

اَلْيَوْمَ وَلَقَّهُمْ نَضْرَةً وَّسُرُوْرًا ۞

وَّجَزٰهُمْ بِمَا صَبَرُوْا جَنَّةً وَّحَرِيْرًا ۞

مُّتَّكِئِيْنَ فِيْهَا عَلَى الْاَرَآئِكِ ۚ لَا

يَرَوْنَ فِيْهَا شَمْسًا وَّلَا زَمْهَرِيْرًا ۞

وَّدَانِيَةً عَلَيْهِمْ ظِلٰلُهَا وَذُلِّلَتْ

قُطُوْفُهَا تَذْلِيْلًا ۞ وَيُطَافُ عَلَيْهِمْ

بِاٰنِيَةٍ مِّنْ فِضَّةٍ وَّاَكْوَابٍ كَانَتْ

قَوَارِيْرَا۠ ۞ قَوَارِيْرَا۠ مِنْ فِضَّةٍ

قَدَّرُوْهَا تَقْدِيْرًا ۞ وَيُسْقَوْنَ فِيْهَا

(of wine) mixed with *Kafur*,-

6. A Fountain where the Devotees of Allah do drink, making it flow in unstinted abundance.

7. They perform (their) vows, and they fear a Day whose evil flies far and wide.

8. And they feed, for the love of Allah, the indigent, the orphan, and the captive, -

9. (Saying),"We feed you for the sake of Allah alone: no reward do we desire from you, nor thanks."

10. "We only fear a Day of distressful Wrath from the side of our Lord."

11. But Allah will deliver them from the evil of that

كَانَ مِزَاجُهَا كَافُوْرًا ۞ عَيْنًا يَّشْرَبُ

بِهَا عِبَادُ اللهِ يُفَجِّرُوْنَهَا تَفْجِيْرًا ۞

يُوْفُوْنَ بِالنَّذْرِ وَيَخَافُوْنَ يَوْمًا

كَانَ شَرُّهُ مُسْتَطِيْرًا ۞ وَيُطْعِمُوْنَ

الطَّعَامَ عَلَى حُبِّهٖ مِسْكِيْنًا وَّيَتِيْمًا

وَّأَسِيْرًا ۞ اِنَّمَا نُطْعِمُكُمْ لِوَجْهِ اللهِ

لَا نُرِيْدُ مِنْكُمْ جَزَآءً وَّلَا شُكُوْرًا ۞

اِنَّا نَخَافُ مِنْ رَّبِّنَا يَوْمًا عَبُوْسًا

قَمْطَرِيْرًا ۞ فَوَقَىٰهُمُ اللهُ شَرَّ ذٰلِكَ

Ad-Dahr (Time)

Bismillahir-Rahmanir-Rahim

1.   Has there not been over Man a long period of Time, when he was nothing - (not even) mentioned?

2.   Verily We created Man from a drop of mingled sperm, in order to try him: so We gave him (the gifts), of Hearing and Sight.

3.   We showed him the Way: whether he be grateful or un-grateful (rests on his will).

4.   For the Rejecters We have prepared Chains, Yokes, and a Blazing Fire.

5.   As to the Righteous, they shall drink of a cup

بِسْمِ اللهِ الرَّحْمٰنِ الرَّحِيمِ

هَلْ أَتٰى عَلَى الْإِنْسَانِ حِيْنٌ مِّنَ

الدَّهْرِ لَمْ يَكُنْ شَيْئًا مَّذْكُوْرًا ۞

إِنَّا خَلَقْنَا الْإِنْسَانَ مِنْ نُّطْفَةٍ

أَمْشَاجٍ نَّبْتَلِيْهِ فَجَعَلْنٰهُ سَمِيْعًا

بَصِيْرًا ۞ إِنَّا هَدَيْنٰهُ السَّبِيْلَ إِمَّا

شَاكِرًا وَّإِمَّا كَفُوْرًا ۞ إِنَّا أَعْتَدْنَا

لِلْكٰفِرِيْنَ سَلٰسِلَا۟ وَأَغْلٰلًا وَّسَعِيْرًا ۞

إِنَّ الْأَبْرَارَ يَشْرَبُوْنَ مِنْ كَأْسٍ

and turned away!

33. Then did he stalk to his family in full conceit!

34. Woe to you, (O man!), yes, woe!

35. Again, Woe to thee, (O man!), yes, woe!

36. Does man think that he will be left uncontrolled, (without purpose)?

37. Was he not a drop of sperm emitted (in lowly form)?

38. Then did he become a leech-like clot; then did (Allah) make and fashion (him) in due proportion.

39. And of him He made two sexes, male and female.

40. Has not He, (the same), the power to give life to the dead.

وَتَوَلّٰى ۞ ثُمَّ ذَهَبَ اِلٰٓى اَهۡلِهٖ

يَتَمَطّٰى ۞ اَوۡلٰى لَكَ فَاَوۡلٰى ۞ ثُمَّ

اَوۡلٰى لَكَ فَاَوۡلٰى ۞ اَيَحۡسَبُ

الۡاِنۡسَانُ اَنۡ يُّتۡرَكَ سُدًى ۞

اَلَمۡ يَكُ نُطۡفَةً مِّنۡ مَّنِيٍّ يُّمۡنٰى ۞

ثُمَّ كَانَ عَلَقَةً فَخَلَقَ فَسَوّٰى ۞

فَجَعَلَ مِنۡهُ الزَّوۡجَيۡنِ الذَّكَرَ

وَالۡاُنۡثٰى ۞ اَلَيۡسَ ذٰلِكَ بِقٰدِرٍ عَلٰٓى

اَنۡ يُّحۡـِۧيَ الۡمَوۡتٰى ۞

the fleeting life,

21. And leave alone the Hereafter.

22. Some faces, that Day, will beam (in brightness and beauty); -

23. Looking towards their Lord;

24. And some faces, that Day, will be sad and dismal,

25. In the thought that some back-breaking calamity was about to be inflicted on them;

26. Yes, when (the soul) reaches to the collar-bone (in its exit),

27. And there will be a cry, "Who is a magician (to restore him)?"

28. And he will conclude that it was (the Time) of Parting;

29. And one leg will be joined with another: **30.** That Day the Drive will be (all) to your Lord!

31. So he gave nothing in charity, nor did he pray! - **32.** But on the contrary, he rejected Truth

الْعَاجِلَةَ ۞ وَتَذَرُونَ الْأَخِرَةَ ۞

وُجُوهٌ يَوْمَئِذٍ نَّاضِرَةٌ ۞ إِلَىٰ رَبِّهَا

نَاظِرَةٌ ۞ وَوُجُوهٌ يَوْمَئِذٍ بَاسِرَةٌ ۞

تَظُنُّ أَن يُفْعَلَ بِهَا فَاقِرَةٌ ۞

كَلَّا إِذَا بَلَغَتِ التَّرَاقِيَ ۞ وَقِيلَ

مَنْ رَاقٍ ۞ وَظَنَّ أَنَّهُ الْفِرَاقُ ۞

وَالْتَفَّتِ السَّاقُ بِالسَّاقِ ۞ إِلَىٰ

رَبِّكَ يَوْمَئِذٍ الْمَسَاقُ ۞ فَلَا

صَدَّقَ وَلَا صَلَّىٰ ۞ وَلَٰكِن كَذَّبَ

10. That Day will Man say: "Where is the refuge?" **11.** By no means! No place of safety!

12. Before your Lord (alone), that Day will be the place of rest.

13. That Day will Man be told (all) that he put forward, and all that he put back.

14. No, man will be evidence against himself,

15. Even though he were to put up his excuses.

16. Move not your tongue concerning the (Qur'an) to make haste therewith.

17. It is for Us to collect it and to promulgate it: **18.** But when We have promulgated it, follow you its recital (as promulgated):

19. No more, it is for Us to explain it (and make it clear):

20. No, (you men!) but you love

اَلْاِنْسَانُ يَوْمَئِذٍ اَيْنَ الْمَفَرُّ ۞ كَلَّا

لَا وَزَرَ ۞ اِلٰى رَبِّكَ يَوْمَئِذِ الْمُسْتَقَرُّ ۞

يُنَبَّؤُا الْاِنْسَانُ يَوْمَئِذٍ بِمَا قَدَّمَ

وَاَخَّرَ ۞ بَلِ الْاِنْسَانُ عَلٰى نَفْسِهٖ

بَصِيْرَةٌ ۞ وَّلَوْ اَلْقٰى مَعَاذِيْرَهٗ ۞ لَا

تُحَرِّكْ بِهٖ لِسَانَكَ لِتَعْجَلَ بِهٖ ۞

اِنَّ عَلَيْنَا جَمْعَهٗ وَقُرْاٰنَهٗ ۞ فَاِذَا

قَرَاْنَاهُ فَاتَّبِعْ قُرْاٰنَهٗ ۞ ثُمَّ اِنَّ

عَلَيْنَا بَيَانَهٗ ۞ كَلَّا بَلْ تُحِبُّوْنَ

Al-Qiyamah (The Resurrection)

Bismillahir-Rahmanir-Rahim

1.   I do call to witness the Resurrection Day;

2. And I do call to witness the self-reproaching soul (Eschew Evil).

3.   Does man think that We can not assemble his bones?

4.   No, We are able to put together in perfect order the very tips of his fingers.

5.   But man wishes to do wrong (even) in the time in front of him.

6.   He questions: "When is the Day of Resurrection?"

7.   At length, when the sight is dazed,   **8.**   And the moon is buried in darkness.

9.   And the sun and moon are joined together, -

49. Then what is the matter with them that they turn away from admonition?

50. As if they were affrighted asses,

51. Fleeing from a lion!

52. Forsooth, each one of them wants to be given scrolls (of revelation) spread out!

53. By no means! But they fear not the Hereafter,

54. No, this surely is an admonition:

55. Let any who will, keep it in remembrance!

56. But none will keep it in remembrance except as Allah wills: He is the Lord of Righteousness, and the Lord of Forgiveness.

فَمَا لَهُمْ عَنِ التَّذْكِرَةِ مُعْرِضِينَ ۝

كَأَنَّهُمْ حُمُرٌ مُّسْتَنْفِرَةٌ ۝ فَرَّتْ

مِنْ قَسْوَرَةٍ ۝ بَلْ يُرِيدُ كُلُّ

امْرِئٍ مِّنْهُمْ أَنْ يُؤْتَى صُحُفًا

مُّنَشَّرَةً ۝ كَلَّا ۖ بَلْ لَّا يَخَافُونَ

الْآخِرَةَ ۝ كَلَّا إِنَّهُ تَذْكِرَةٌ ۝

فَمَنْ شَاءَ ذَكَرَهُ ۝ وَمَا يَذْكُرُونَ

إِلَّا أَنْ يَشَاءَ اللَّهُ ۚ هُوَ أَهْلُ التَّقْوَى

وَأَهْلُ الْمَغْفِرَةِ ۝

38. Every soul will be (held) in pledge for its deeds.

39. Except the Companions of the Right Hand.

40. (They will be) in Gardens (of Delight): they will question each other,

41. And (ask) of the Sinners:

42. "What led you into Hell Fire?"

43. They will say: "We were not of those who prayed;"

44. "Nor were we of those who fed the indigent;"

45. "But we used to talk vanities with vain talkers;"

46. "And we used to deny the Day of Judgment,"

47. "Until there came to us (the Hour) that is certain."

48. Then will no intercession of (any) intercessors profit them.

كُلُّ نَفْسٍ بِمَا كَسَبَتْ رَهِينَةٌ ۞

إِلَّا أَصْحَابَ الْيَمِينِ ۞ فِى جَنّٰتٍ

يَتَسَآءَلُونَ ۞ عَنِ الْمُجْرِمِينَ ۞ مَا

سَلَكَكُمْ فِى سَقَرَ ۞ قَالُوا لَمْ نَكُ

مِنَ الْمُصَلِّينَ ۞ وَلَمْ نَكُ نُطْعِمُ

الْمِسْكِينَ ۞ وَكُنَّا نَخُوضُ مَعَ

الْخَآئِضِينَ ۞ وَكُنَّا نُكَذِّبُ بِيَوْمِ

الدِّينِ ۞ حَتّٰى أَتَانَا الْيَقِينُ ۞

فَمَا تَنْفَعُهُمْ شَفَاعَةُ الشَّافِعِينَ ۞

and that those in whose hearts is a disease and the unbelievers may say, "What symbol does Allah intend by this ?" Thus does Allah leave to stray whom He pleases, and guide whom He pleases: and none can know the forces of your Lord, except He. And this is no other than a warning to mankind.

32. No, verily: by the Moon,

33. And by the Night as it retreats,

34. And by the Dawn as it shines forth, -

35. This is but one of the mighty (portents),

36. A warning to mankind, -

37. To any of you that chooses to press forward, or to follow behind; -

وَلِيَقُوْلَ الَّذِيْنَ فِيْ قُلُوْبِهِمْ مَّرَضٌ

وَّالْكٰفِرُوْنَ مَاذَاۤ اَرَادَ اللّٰهُ بِهٰذَا

مَثَلًا ۚ كَذٰلِكَ يُضِلُّ اللّٰهُ مَنْ يَّشَآءُ

وَيَهْدِيْ مَنْ يَّشَآءُ ۗ وَمَا يَعْلَمُ جُنُوْدَ

رَبِّكَ اِلَّا هُوَ ۗ وَمَا هِيَ اِلَّا ذِكْرٰى

لِلْبَشَرِ ۞ كَلَّا وَالْقَمَرِ ۞ وَالَّيْلِ اِذْ

اَدْبَرَ ۞ وَالصُّبْحِ اِذَاۤ اَسْفَرَ ۞ اِنَّهَا

لَاِحْدَى الْكُبَرِ ۞ نَذِيْرًا لِّلْبَشَرِ ۞ لِمَنْ

شَآءَ مِنْكُمْ اَنْ يَّتَقَدَّمَ اَوْ يَتَاَخَّرَ ۞

of a mortal!"

26. Soon will I cast him into Hell-Fire!

27. And what will explain to you what Hell-Fire is?

28. Nothing does it permit to endure, and nothing does it leave alone! -

29. Darkening and changing the colour of man!

30. Over it are Nineteen.

31. And We have set none but Angels as Guardians of the Fire; and We have fixed their number only as a trial for unbelievers, - in order that the People of the Book may arrive at certainty, and the believers may increase in Faith, - and that no doubts may be left for the People of the Book and the believers,

الْبَشَرِ ۞ سَاُصْلِيْهِ سَقَرَ ۞ وَمَآ

اَدْرٰىكَ مَا سَقَرُ ۞ لَا تُبْقِيْ وَلَا

تَذَرُ ۞ لَوَّاحَةٌ لِّلْبَشَرِ ۞ عَلَيْهَا تِسْعَةَ

عَشَرَ ۞ وَمَا جَعَلْنَآ اَصْحٰبَ النَّارِ

اِلَّا مَلٰٓئِكَةً ۖ وَّمَا جَعَلْنَا عِدَّتَهُمْ

اِلَّا فِتْنَةً لِّلَّذِيْنَ كَفَرُوْا لِيَسْتَيْقِنَ

الَّذِيْنَ اُوْتُوا الْكِتٰبَ وَيَزْدَادَ

الَّذِيْنَ اٰمَنُوْآ اِيْمَانًا وَّلَا يَرْتَابَ

الَّذِيْنَ اُوْتُوا الْكِتٰبَ وَالْمُؤْمِنُوْنَ

12. To whom I granted resources in abundance,

13. And sons to be by his side! -

14. To whom I made (life) smooth and comfortable!

15. Yet is he greedy - that I should add (yet more); -

16. By no means! For to Our Signs he has been refractory!

17. Soon will I visit him with a mount of calamities!

18. For he thought and he plotted; - **19.** And woe to him! How he plotted! - **20.** Yes, Woe to him; how he plotted! -

21. Then he looked round;

22. Then he frowned and he scowled; **23.** Then he turned back and was haughty;

24. Then said he: "This is nothing but magic, derived from of old;"

25. "This is nothing but the word

وَجَعَلْتُ لَهُ مَالًا مَّمْدُودًا ۞ وَبَنِينَ

شُهُودًا ۞ وَمَهَّدْتُ لَهُ تَمْهِيدًا ۞

ثُمَّ يَطْمَعُ أَنْ أَزِيدَ ۞ كَلَّا ۖ إِنَّهُ

كَانَ لِآيَاتِنَا عَنِيدًا ۞ سَأُرْهِقُهُ

صَعُودًا ۞ إِنَّهُ فَكَّرَ وَقَدَّرَ ۞ فَقُتِلَ

كَيْفَ قَدَّرَ ۞ ثُمَّ قُتِلَ كَيْفَ قَدَّرَ ۞

ثُمَّ نَظَرَ ۞ ثُمَّ عَبَسَ وَبَسَرَ ۞ ثُمَّ

أَدْبَرَ وَاسْتَكْبَرَ ۞ فَقَالَ إِنْ هَٰذَا

إِلَّا سِحْرٌ يُؤْثَرُ ۞ إِنْ هَٰذَا إِلَّا قَوْلُ

Allah: for Allah is Oft-Forgiving, Most Merciful.

Al-Muddaththir (The One Wrapped Up)

Bismillahir-Rahmanir-Rahim

1. O you wrapped up (in the mantle)!

2. Arise and deliver your warning!

3. And your Lord do you magnify!

4. And your garments keep free from stain!

5. And all abomination shun!

6. Nor expect, in giving, any increase (for yourself)!

7. But, for your Lord's (Cause), be patient and constant!

8. Finally, when the Trumpet is sounded, 9. That will be - that Day - a Day of Distress, -

10. Far from easy for those without Faith. 11. Leave Me alone, (to deal) with the (creature) whom I created (bare and) alone!-

اللّٰهِ ۗ اِنَّ اللّٰهَ غَفُوْرٌ رَّحِيْمٌ ۞

بِسْمِ اللّٰهِ الرَّحْمٰنِ الرَّحِيْمِ

يٰٓاَيُّهَا الْمُدَّثِّرُ ۞ قُمْ فَاَنْذِرْ ۞

وَرَبَّكَ فَكَبِّرْ ۞ وَثِيَابَكَ فَطَهِّرْ ۞

وَالرُّجْزَ فَاهْجُرْ ۞ وَلَا تَمْنُنْ

تَسْتَكْثِرُ ۞ وَلِرَبِّكَ فَاصْبِرْ ۞ فَاِذَا

نُقِرَ فِى النَّاقُوْرِ ۞ فَذٰلِكَ يَوْمَئِذٍ

يَوْمٌ عَسِيْرٌ ۞ عَلَى الْكٰفِرِيْنَ غَيْرُ

يَسِيْرٍ ۞ ذَرْنِىْ وَمَنْ خَلَقْتُ وَحِيْدًا ۞

of the Qur'an as much as may be easy for you. He knows that there may be (some) among you in ill-health; others travelling through the land, seeking of Allah's Bounty; yet others fighting in Allah's Cause, read you, therefore, as much of the Qur'an as may be easy (for you); and establish regular Prayer and give regular Charity; and loan to Allah, a beautiful loan. And whatever good you send forth for your souls, you shall find it in Allah's Presence, - yes, better and greater, in Reward. And seek you the Grace of

مَا تَيَسَّرَ مِنَ الْقُرْاٰنِ ۚ عَلِمَ اَنْ

سَيَكُوْنُ مِنْكُمْ مَّرْضٰى ۙ وَاٰخَرُوْنَ

يَضْرِبُوْنَ فِى الْاَرْضِ يَبْتَغُوْنَ مِنْ

فَضْلِ اللّٰهِ وَاٰخَرُوْنَ يُقَاتِلُوْنَ فِىْ

سَبِيْلِ اللّٰهِ ۖ فَاقْرَءُوْا مَا تَيَسَّرَ

مِنْهُ ۙ وَاَقِيْمُوا الصَّلٰوةَ وَاٰتُوا الزَّكٰوةَ

وَاَقْرِضُوا اللّٰهَ قَرْضًا حَسَنًا ۚ وَمَا تُقَدِّمُوْا

لِاَنْفُسِكُمْ مِّنْ خَيْرٍ تَجِدُوْهُ عِنْدَ اللّٰهِ

هُوَ خَيْرًا وَّاَعْظَمَ اَجْرًا ۚ وَاسْتَغْفِرُوا

Against a Day that will make children hoary-headed? -

18. Whereon the sky will be cleft asunder? His Promise needs must be accomplished.

19. Verily this is an Admonition: therefore, whoso will, let him take a (straight) path to his Lord!

20. Thy Lord does know that you stands forth (to prayer) nearly two-thirds of the night, or half the night, or a third of the night, and so does a party of those with you. But Allah does appoint night and day in due measure. He knows that you are unable to keep count thereof. So He has turned to you (in mercy): read you, therefore,

كَفَرْتُمْ يَوْمًا يَّجْعَلُ الْوِلْدَانَ شِيبًا ۞

السَّمَآءُ مُنْفَطِرٌ بِهِ ۚ كَانَ وَعْدُهُ

مَفْعُولًا ۞ اِنَّ هٰذِهِ تَذْكِرَةٌ ۖ فَمَنْ

شَآءَ اتَّخَذَ اِلٰى رَبِّهِ سَبِيلًا ۞

اِنَّ رَبَّكَ يَعْلَمُ اَنَّكَ تَقُوْمُ اَدْنٰى

مِنْ ثُلُثَيِ الَّيْلِ وَنِصْفَهُ وَثُلُثَهُ

وَطَآئِفَةٌ مِّنَ الَّذِيْنَ مَعَكَ ۚ وَاللّٰهُ

يُقَدِّرُ الَّيْلَ وَالنَّهَارَ ۚ عَلِمَ اَنْ

لَّنْ تُحْصُوْهُ فَتَابَ عَلَيْكُمْ فَاقْرَءُوْا

of the good things of life, who
(yet) deny the Truth; and bear
with them for a little while.

12. With Us are Fetters (to bind
them), and a Fire (to burn them),

13. And a Food that chokes, and
a Chastisement grievous.

14. One Day the earth and the
mountains will be in violent
commotion. And the mountains
will be as a heap of sand poured
out and flowing down.

15. We have sent to you, (O
men!) an Apostle, to be a witness
concerning you, even as We sent
an Apostle to Pharaoh.

16. But Pharaoh disobeyed the
Apostle; so We seized him with a
heavy Punishment.

17. Then how shall you, if you
deny (Allah), guard yourselves

أُولِى النِّعْمَةِ وَمَهِّلْهُمْ قَلِيلًا ۝ إِنَّ

لَدَيْنَآ أَنْكَالًا وَّجَحِيمًا ۝ وَّطَعَامًا

ذَا غُصَّةٍ وَّعَذَابًا أَلِيمًا ۝ يَوْمَ

تَرْجُفُ الْأَرْضُ وَالْجِبَالُ وَكَانَتِ

الْجِبَالُ كَثِيبًا مَّهِيلًا ۝ إِنَّآ أَرْسَلْنَآ

إِلَيْكُمْ رَسُولًا ەۙ شَاهِدًا عَلَيْكُمْ كَمَآ

أَرْسَلْنَآ إِلَى فِرْعَوْنَ رَسُولًا ۝

فَعَصَى فِرْعَوْنُ الرَّسُولَ فَأَخَذْنٰهُ

أَخْذًا وَّبِيلًا ۝ فَكَيْفَ تَتَّقُونَ إِنْ

measured rhythmic tones.

5.   Soon shall We send down to you a weighty Message.

6.   Truly the rising by night is most potent for governing (the soul), and most suitable for (framing) the Word (of Prayer and Praise).

7.   True, there is for you by day prolonged occupation with ordinary duties:

8.   But keep in remembrance the name of your Lord and devote thyself to Him whole-heartedly.

9.   (He is) Lord of the East and the West: there is no god but He: take Him therefore for (your) Disposer of Affairs.

10.   And have patience with what they say, and leave them with noble (dignity).

11.   And leave Me (alone to deal with) those in possession

تَرْتِيلًا ۗ اِنَّا سَنُلْقِى عَلَيْكَ قَوْلًا

ثَقِيلًا ۞ اِنَّ نَاشِئَةَ الَّيْلِ هِىَ

اَشَدُّ وَطْأً وَّ اَقْوَمُ قِيلًا ۞ اِنَّ

لَكَ فِى النَّهَارِ سَبْحًا طَوِيلًا ۗ

وَاذْكُرِ اسْمَ رَبِّكَ وَتَبَتَّلْ اِلَيْهِ

تَبْتِيلًا ۞ رَبُّ الْمَشْرِقِ وَالْمَغْرِبِ

لَا اِلٰهَ اِلَّا هُوَ فَاتَّخِذْهُ وَكِيلًا ۞

وَاصْبِرْ عَلٰى مَا يَقُوْلُوْنَ وَاهْجُرْهُمْ

هَجْرًا جَمِيلًا ۞ وَذَرْنِى وَالْمُكَذِّبِيْنَ

an Apostle whom He has chosen: and then He makes a band of watchers march before him and behind him,"

28. "That He may know that they have (truly) brought and delivered the Messages of their Lord: and He surrounds (all the mysteries) that are with them, and takes account of every single thing."

Al-Muzzammil
(Folded in Garments)

Bismillahir-Rahmanir-Rahim

1. O you folded in garments!

2. Stand (to prayer) by night, but not all night, -

3. Half of it,- or a little less,

4. Or a little more; and recite the Qur'an in slow,

اِرْتَضٰى مِنْ رَّسُوْلٍ فَاِنَّهٗ يَسْلُكُ

مِنْۢ بَيْنِ يَدَيْهِ وَمِنْ خَلْفِهٖ

رَصَدًا ۟ لِّيَعْلَمَ اَنْ قَدْ اَبْلَغُوْا

رِسٰلٰتِ رَبِّهِمْ وَاَحَاطَ بِمَا لَدَيْهِمْ

وَاَحْصٰى كُلَّ شَىْءٍ عَدَدًا ۟

بِسْمِ اللّٰهِ الرَّحْمٰنِ الرَّحِيْمِ

يٰۤاَيُّهَا الْمُزَّمِّلُ ۟ قُمِ الَّيْلَ اِلَّا

قَلِيْلًا ۙ نِّصْفَهٗۤ اَوِ انْقُصْ مِنْهُ

قَلِيْلًا ۙ اَوْ زِدْ عَلَيْهِ وَرَتِّلِ الْقُرْاٰنَ

refuge except in Him,"

23. "Unless I proclaim what I receive from Allah and His Messages: for any that disobey Allah and His Apostle, - for them is Hell: they shall dwell therein for ever."

24. At length, when they see (with their own eyes) that which they are promised, - then will they know who it is that is weakest in (his) helper and least important in point of numbers.

25. Say: "I know not whether the (Punishment) which you are promised is near, or whether my Lord will appoint for it a distant term."

26. "He (alone) knows the Unseen, nor does He make any one acquainted with His Mysteries, -   **27.** "Except

مُلْتَحَدًا ۞ اِلَّا بَلَٰغًا مِّنَ اللّٰهِ

وَرِسَٰلَٰتِهٖ ؕ وَمَنْ يَّعْصِ اللّٰهَ وَرَسُوْلَهٗ

فَاِنَّ لَهٗ نَارَ جَهَنَّمَ خٰلِدِيْنَ فِيْهَاۤ

اَبَدًا ۞ حَتّٰٓى اِذَا رَاَوْا مَا يُوْعَدُوْنَ

فَسَيَعْلَمُوْنَ مَنْ اَضْعَفُ نَاصِرًا

وَّاَقَلُّ عَدَدًا ۞ قُلْ اِنْ اَدْرِیۡۤ

اَقَرِيْبٌ مَّا تُوْعَدُوْنَ اَمْ يَجْعَلُ لَهٗ

رَبِّیْۤ اَمَدًا ۞ عٰلِمُ الْغَيْبِ فَلَا

يُظْهِرُ عَلٰى غَيْبِهٖۤ اَحَدًا ۞ اِلَّا مَنِ

the remembrance of his Lord, He will cause him to undergo a severe Chastisement."

18. "And the places of worship are for Allah (alone): so invoke not any one along with Allah;"

19. "Yet when the devotee of Allah stands forth to invoke Him, they just make round him a dense crowd."

20. Say: "I do no more than invoke my Lord, and I join not with Him any (false Allah)."

21. Say: "It is not in my power to cause you harm, or to bring you to right conduct."

22. Say: "No one can deliver me from Allah (if I were to disobey Him), nor should I find

ذِكْرًا ۚ رَّبِّهٖ يَسْلُكْهُ عَذَابًا صَعَدًا ۙ ۞

وَّاَنَّ الْمَسٰجِدَ لِلّٰهِ فَلَا تَدْعُوْا مَعَ

اللّٰهِ اَحَدًا ۙ ۞ وَّاَنَّهٗ لَمَّا قَامَ

عَبْدُ اللّٰهِ يَدْعُوْهُ كَادُوْا يَكُوْنُوْنَ

عَلَيْهِ لِبَدًا ۚ ۞ قُلْ اِنَّمَاۤ اَدْعُوْا رَبِّيْ

وَلَاۤ اُشْرِكُ بِهٖۤ اَحَدًا ۞ قُلْ اِنِّيْ

لَاۤ اَمْلِكُ لَكُمْ ضَرًّا وَّلَا رَشَدًا ۞

قُلْ اِنِّيْ لَنْ يُّجِيْرَنِيْ مِنَ اللّٰهِ

اَحَدٌ ۙ ۙ وَّلَنْ اَجِدَ مِنْ دُوْنِهٖ

nor can we frustrate Him by flight.

13. 'And as for us, since we have listened to the Guidance, we have accepted it: and any who believes in his Lord has no fear, either of a short (account) or of any injustice.'

14. 'Amongst us are some that submit their wills (to Allah), and some that swerve from justice. Now those who submit their wills - they have sought out (the path) of right conduct:'

15. 'But those who swerve, - they are (but) fuel for Hell-fire' -

16. (And Allah's Message is): "If they (the Pagans) had (only) remained on the (right) Way, We should certainly have bestowed on them Rain in abundance."

17. "That We might try them by that (means). But if any turns away from

وَلَنْ نُّعْجِزَهٗ هَرَبًا ۞ وَّاَنَّا لَمَّا

سَمِعْنَا الْهُدٰى اٰمَنَّا بِهٖ ؕ فَمَنْ يُّؤْمِنْ

بِرَبِّهٖ فَلَا يَخَافُ بَخْسًا وَّلَا رَهَقًا

۞ وَّاَنَّا مِنَّا الْمُسْلِمُوْنَ وَمِنَّا الْقٰسِطُوْنَ ؕ

فَمَنْ اَسْلَمَ فَاُولٰٓئِكَ تَحَرَّوْا رَشَدًا

۞ وَاَمَّا الْقٰسِطُوْنَ فَكَانُوْا لِجَهَنَّمَ

حَطَبًا ۞ وَّاَنْ لَّوِ اسْتَقَامُوْا عَلَى

الطَّرِيْقَةِ لَاَسْقَيْنٰهُمْ مَّآءً غَدَقًا

۞ لِّنَفْتِنَهُمْ فِيْهِ ؕ وَمَنْ يُّعْرِضْ عَنْ

pried into the secrets of heaven; but we found it filled with stern guards and flaming fires.'

9. 'We used, indeed, to sit there in (hidden) stations, to (steal) a hearing; but any who listen now will find a flaming fire watching him in ambush.'

10. 'And we understand not whether ill is intended to those on earth, or whether their Lord (really) intends to guide them to right conduct.'

11. 'There are among us some that are righteous, and some the contrary: we follow divergent paths.'

12. 'But we think that we can by no means frustrate Allah throughout the earth,

لَّمَسْنَا السَّمَاءَ فَوَجَدْنَاهَا مُلِئَتْ حَرَسًا

شَدِيدًا وَّشُهُبًا ۙ وَّأَنَّا كُنَّا نَقْعُدُ

مِنْهَا مَقَاعِدَ لِلسَّمْعِ ۚ فَمَنْ يَّسْتَمِعِ

الْآنَ يَجِدْ لَهُ شِهَابًا رَّصَدًا ۙ

وَّأَنَّا لَا نَدْرِىٓ أَشَرٌّ أُرِيدَ بِمَنْ فِى

الْأَرْضِ أَمْ أَرَادَ بِهِمْ رَبُّهُمْ رَشَدًا ۙ

وَّأَنَّا مِنَّا الصَّالِحُونَ وَمِنَّا دُونَ

ذَٰلِكَ ۖ كُنَّا طَرَائِقَ قِدَدًا ۙ وَّأَنَّا ظَنَنَّآ

أَن لَّن نُّعْجِزَ اللهَ فِى الْأَرْضِ

3.   'And Exalted is the Majesty of our Lord: He has taken neither a wife nor a son.'

4.   'There were some foolish ones among us, who used to utter extravagant lies against Allah;'

5.   'But we do think that no man or spirit should say anything that untrue against Allah.'

6.   'True, there were persons among mankind who took shelter with persons among the Jinns, but they increased them in folly.'

7.   'And they (came to) think as you thought, that Allah would not raise up any one (to Judgment).'

8.   'And we

أَحَدًا ۞ وَّأَنَّهُ تَعَالَى جَدُّ رَبِّنَا مَا
اتَّخَذَ صَاحِبَةً وَّلَا وَلَدًا ۞ وَّأَنَّهُ
كَانَ يَقُوْلُ سَفِيْهُنَا عَلَى اللّٰهِ
شَطَطًا ۞ وَّأَنَّا ظَنَنَّآ أَنْ لَّنْ تَقُوْلَ
الْإِنْسُ وَالْجِنُّ عَلَى اللّٰهِ كَذِبًا ۞
وَّأَنَّهُ كَانَ رِجَالٌ مِّنَ الْإِنْسِ
يَعُوْذُوْنَ بِرِجَالٍ مِّنَ الْجِنِّ فَزَادُوْهُمْ
رَهَقًا ۞ وَّأَنَّهُمْ ظَنُّوْا كَمَا ظَنَنْتُمْ
أَنْ لَّنْ يَّبْعَثَ اللّٰهُ أَحَدًا ۞ وَّأَنَّا

but wicked ungrateful ones."

28. "O my Lord! Forgive me, my parents, all who enter my house in Faith, and (all) believing men and believing women: and to the wrong-doers grant You no increase but in perdition!"

Al-Jinn

Bismillahir-Rahmanir-Rahim

1. Say: It has been revealed to me that a company of Jinns listened (to the Qur'an). They said, 'We have really heard a wonderful Recital!'

2. 'It gives guidance to the Right, and we have believed therein: we shall not join (in worship) any (gods) with our Lord.

اِلَّا فَاجِرًا كَفَّارًا ۞ رَبِّ اغْفِرْلِى

وَلِوَالِدَىَّ وَلِمَنْ دَخَلَ بَيْتِىَ

مُؤْمِنًا وَّلِلْمُؤْمِنِينَ وَالْمُؤْمِنٰتِ

وَلَا تَزِدِ الظّٰلِمِينَ اِلَّا تَبَارًا ۞

سُورَةُ الْجِنِّ مَكِّيَّةٌ
اٰيَاتُهَا ٢٨
رُكُوعَاتُهَا ٢
بِسْمِ اللهِ الرَّحْمٰنِ الرَّحِيمِ

قُلْ اُوحِىَ اِلَىَّ اَنَّهُ اسْتَمَعَ نَفَرٌ

مِّنَ الْجِنِّ فَقَالُوٓا اِنَّا سَمِعْنَا

قُرْاٰنًا عَجَبًا ۞ يَهْدِىٓ اِلَى الرُّشْدِ

فَاٰمَنَّا بِه ۖ وَلَنْ نُّشْرِكَ بِرَبِّنَآ

abandon neither Wadd nor Suwa', neither Yaguth nor Ya'uq, nor Nasr'; -

24. "They have already misled many; and grant You no increase to the wrong-doers but in straying (from their mark)."

25. Because of their sins they were drowned (in the flood), and were made to enter the Fire (of Punishment): and they found - in lieu of Allah - none to help them.

26. And Noah said: "O my Lord! Leave not of the unbelievers, a single one on earth!"

27. "For, if You does leave (any of) them, they will but mislead Your devotees, and they will breed none

تَذَرُنَّ وَدًّا وَّلَا سُوَاعًا ۬ وَّلَا يَغُوثَ
وَيَعُوقَ وَنَسْرًا ۬ ۞ وَقَدْ اَضَلُّوْا
كَثِيْرًا ۬ وَّلَا تَزِدِ الظّٰلِمِيْنَ اِلَّا
ضَلٰلًا ۞ مِمَّا خَطِيْٓئٰتِهِمْ اُغْرِقُوْا
فَاُدْخِلُوْا نَارًا ۬ فَلَمْ يَجِدُوْا لَهُمْ
مِّنْ دُوْنِ اللّٰهِ اَنْصَارًا ۞ وَقَالَ
نُوْحٌ رَّبِّ لَا تَذَرْ عَلَى الْاَرْضِ
مِنَ الْكٰفِرِيْنَ دَيَّارًا ۞ اِنَّكَ اِنْ
تَذَرْهُمْ يُضِلُّوْا عِبَادَكَ وَلَا يَلِدُوْٓا

as a (Glorious) Lamp? **17.** "'And Allah has produced you from the earth growing (gradually),'

18. 'And in the End He will return you into the (earth), and raise you forth (again at the Resurrection)?'

19. 'And Allah has made the earth for you as a carpet (spread out),'

20. 'That you may go about therein, in spacious roads.'"

21. Noah said: "O my Lord! They have disobeyed me, but they follow (men) whose wealth and children give them no increase but only Loss."

22. "And they have devised a tremendous Plot."

23. "And they have said (to each other), 'Abandon not your gods:

سَرَاجًا ۝ وَاللَّهُ أَنْبَتَكُمْ مِّنَ

الْأَرْضِ نَبَاتًا ۝ ثُمَّ يُعِيدُكُمْ فِيهَا

وَيُخْرِجُكُمْ إِخْرَاجًا ۝ وَاللَّهُ جَعَلَ

لَكُمُ الْأَرْضَ بِسَاطًا ۝ لِّتَسْلُكُوا

مِنْهَا سُبُلًا فِجَاجًا ۝ قَالَ نُوحٌ

رَّبِّ إِنَّهُمْ عَصَوْنِي وَاتَّبَعُوا مَن

لَّمْ يَزِدْهُ مَالُهُ وَوَلَدُهُ إِلَّا

خَسَارًا ۝ وَمَكَرُوا مَكْرًا كُبَّارًا ۝

وَقَالُوا لَا تَذَرُنَّ آلِهَتَكُمْ وَلَا

10. "Saying, 'Ask forgiveness from your Lord; for He is Oft-Forgiving;"

11. 'He will send rain to you in abundance;'

12. 'Give you increase in wealth and sons; and bestow on you gardens and bestow on you rivers (of flowing water).'

13. 'What is the matter with you, that you are not mindful of Allah's Majesty.'

14. 'Seeing that it is He that has created you in diverse stages?'

15. 'See you not how Allah has created the seven heavens one above another,'

16. 'And made the moon a light in their midst, and made the sun

فَقُلْتُ اسْتَغْفِرُوْا رَبَّكُمْ إِنَّهُ كَانَ

غَفَّارًا ۙ ١٠ يُرْسِلِ السَّمَآءَ عَلَيْكُمْ

مِّدْرَارًا ۙ ١١ وَّيُمْدِدْكُمْ بِأَمْوَالٍ وَّبَنِيْنَ

وَيَجْعَلْ لَّكُمْ جَنّٰتٍ وَّيَجْعَلْ لَّكُمْ

أَنْهٰرًا ۭ ١٢ مَا لَكُمْ لَا تَرْجُوْنَ لِلّٰهِ

وَقَارًا ۙ ١٣ وَقَدْ خَلَقَكُمْ أَطْوَارًا ١٤

أَلَمْ تَرَوْا كَيْفَ خَلَقَ اللّٰهُ سَبْعَ

سَمٰوٰتٍ طِبَاقًا ۙ ١٥ وَّجَعَلَ الْقَمَرَ

فِيْهِنَّ نُوْرًا وَّجَعَلَ الشَّمْسَ

is accomplished, it cannot be put forward: if you only knew."

5. He said: "O my Lord! I have called to my People night and day:"

6. "But my call only increases (their) flight (from the Right)."

7. "And every time I have called to them, that you might forgive them, they have (only) thrust their fingers into their ears, covered themselves up with their garments, grown obstinate, and given themselves up to arrogance."

8. "So I have called to them aloud;"

9. "Further I have spoken to them in public and secretly in private,"

وَقَالُوا

جَآءَ لَا يُؤَخَّرُ لَوْ كُنْتُمْ تَعْلَمُوْنَ ۞

قَالَ رَبِّ اِنِّى دَعَوْتُ قَوْمِى لَيْلًا

وَّنَهَارًا ۞ فَلَمْ يَزِدْهُمْ دُعَآءِىْ

اِلَّا فِرَارًا ۞ وَاِنِّى كُلَّمَا دَعَوْتُهُمْ

لِتَغْفِرَ لَهُمْ جَعَلُوْا اَصَابِعَهُمْ فِىْٓ

اٰذَانِهِمْ وَاسْتَغْشَوْا ثِيَابَهُمْ وَاَصَرُّوْا

وَاسْتَكْبَرُوْا اسْتِكْبَارًا ۞ ثُمَّ اِنِّىْ

دَعَوْتُهُمْ جِهَارًا ۞ ثُمَّ اِنِّىْٓ اَعْلَنْتُ

لَهُمْ وَاَسْرَرْتُ لَهُمْ اِسْرَارًا ۞

they are promised!

Nuh (Noah)

Bismillahir-Rahmanir-Rahim

1. We sent Noah to his People (with the Command): "Do you warn your People before there comes to them a grievous Chastisement."

2. He said: "O my People! I am to you a Warner, clear and open:"

3. "That you should worship Allah, fear Him and obey me:"

4. "So that He may forgive you your sins and give you respite for a stated Term: for when the Term given by Allah

كَانُوْا يُوْعَدُوْنَ ۞

بِسْمِ اللهِ الرَّحْمٰنِ الرَّحِيْمِ

اِنَّاۤ اَرْسَلْنَا نُوْحًا اِلٰى قَوْمِهٖۤ اَنْ

اَنْذِرْ قَوْمَكَ مِنْ قَبْلِ اَنْ يَّاْتِيَهُمْ

عَذَابٌ اَلِيْمٌ ۞ قَالَ يٰقَوْمِ اِنِّيْ

لَكُمْ نَذِيْرٌ مُّبِيْنٌ ۞ اَنِ اعْبُدُوا

اللهَ وَاتَّقُوْهُ وَاَطِيْعُوْنِ ۞ يَغْفِرْ

لَكُمْ مِّنْ ذُنُوْبِكُمْ وَيُؤَخِّرْكُمْ اِلٰۤى

اَجَلٍ مُّسَمًّى ۗ اِنَّ اَجَلَ اللهِ اِذَا

they know about.

40. Now I do call to witness the Lord of all points in the East and the West that We can certainly -

41. Substitute for them better (men) than they; and We are not to be defeated (in Our Plan).

42. So leave them to plunge in vain talk and play about, until they encounter that Day of theirs which they have been promised! -

43. The Day whereon they will issue from their sepulchres in sudden haste as if they were rushing to a goal-post (fixed for them), -

44. Their eyes lowered in dejection,- ignominy covering them (all over)! Such is the Day the which

يَعْلَمُونَ ۝ فَلَا أُقْسِمُ بِرَبِّ الْمَشَارِقِ

وَالْمَغَارِبِ إِنَّا لَقَادِرُونَ ۝ عَلَى أَنْ

نُّبَدِّلَ خَيْرًا مِّنْهُمْ ۙ وَمَا نَحْنُ

بِمَسْبُوقِينَ ۝ فَذَرْهُمْ يَخُوضُوا

وَيَلْعَبُوا حَتَّى يُلَاقُوا يَوْمَهُمُ الَّذِى

يُوعَدُونَ ۝ يَوْمَ يَخْرُجُونَ مِنَ

الْأَجْدَاثِ سِرَاعًا كَأَنَّهُمْ إِلَى نُصُبٍ

يُوفِضُونَ ۝ خَاشِعَةً أَبْصَارُهُمْ

تَرْهَقُهُمْ ذِلَّةٌ ۚ ذَٰلِكَ الْيَوْمُ الَّذِى

32. And those who respect their trusts and covenants;

33. And those who stand firm in their testimonies;

34. And those who guard (the sacredness) of their worship; -

35. Such will be the honoured ones in the Gardens (of Bliss).

36. Now what is the matter with the unbelievers that they rush madly before you –

37. From the right and from the left, in crowds?

38. Does every man of them long to enter the Garden of Bliss?

39. By no means! For We have created them out of the (base matter)

وَالَّذِينَ هُمْ لِأَمٰنٰتِهِمْ وَعَهْدِهِمْ

رَاعُونَ ۞ وَالَّذِينَ هُمْ بِشَهٰدٰتِهِمْ

قَآئِمُونَ ۞ وَالَّذِينَ هُمْ عَلٰى صَلَاتِهِمْ

يُحَافِظُونَ ۞ أُولٰٓئِكَ فِيْ جَنّٰتٍ

مُّكْرَمُونَ ۞ فَمَالِ الَّذِينَ كَفَرُوْا

قِبَلَكَ مُهْطِعِيْنَ ۞ عَنِ الْيَمِيْنِ

وَعَنِ الشِّمَالِ عِزِيْنَ ۞ أَيَطْمَعُ كُلُّ

امْرِئٍ مِّنْهُمْ أَنْ يُّدْخَلَ جَنَّةَ

نَعِيْمٍ ۞ كَلَّا ۗ إِنَّا خَلَقْنٰهُمْ مِّمَّا

whose wealth is a recognised right.

25. For the (needy) who asks and him who is prevented (for some reason from asking);

26. And those who hold to the truth of the Day of Judgment;

27. And those who fear the displeasure of their Lord, -

28. For their Lord's displeasure is the opposite of Peace and Tranquillity; -

29. And those who guard their chastity,

30. Except with their wives and the (captives) whom their right hands possess, - for (then) they are not to be blamed,

31. But those who trespass beyond this are transgressors;

أَمْوَالِهِمْ حَقٌّ مَّعْلُومٌ ۝ لِّلسَّائِلِ

وَالْمَحْرُومِ ۝ وَالَّذِينَ يُصَدِّقُونَ

بِيَوْمِ الدِّينِ ۝ وَالَّذِينَ هُم مِّنْ

عَذَابِ رَبِّهِم مُّشْفِقُونَ ۝ إِنَّ عَذَابَ

رَبِّهِمْ غَيْرُ مَأْمُونٍ ۝ وَالَّذِينَ

هُمْ لِفُرُوجِهِمْ حَافِظُونَ ۝ إِلَّا عَلَىٰ

أَزْوَاجِهِمْ أَوْ مَا مَلَكَتْ أَيْمَانُهُمْ

فَإِنَّهُمْ غَيْرُ مَلُومِينَ ۝ فَمَنِ ابْتَغَىٰ

وَرَآءَ ذَٰلِكَ فَأُولَٰئِكَ هُمُ الْعَادُونَ ۝

and his brother, **13.** His kindred who sheltered him,

14. And all, all that is on earth, - so it could deliver him:

15. By no means! For it would be the Fire of Hell! -

16. Plucking out (his being) right to the skull! -

17. Inviting (all) such as turn their backs and turn away their faces (from the Right),

18. And collect (wealth) and hide it (from use)!

19. Truly man was created very impatient; -

20. Fretful when evil touches him;

21. And niggardly when good reaches him; -

22. Not so those devoted to Prayer; - **23.** Those who remain steadfast to their prayer;

24. And those in

وَأَخِيهِ ۝ وَفَصِيلَتِهِ الَّتِى تُؤْوِيهِ ۝

وَمَنْ فِى الْأَرْضِ جَمِيعًا ثُمَّ

يُنْجِيهِ ۝ كَلَّا إِنَّهَا لَظَى ۝ نَزَّاعَةً

لِّلشَّوَى ۝ تَدْعُوا مَنْ أَدْبَرَ وَتَوَلَّى ۝

وَجَمَعَ فَأَوْعَى ۝ إِنَّ الْإِنْسَانَ

خُلِقَ هَلُوعًا ۝ إِذَا مَسَّهُ الشَّرُّ

جَزُوعًا ۝ وَإِذَا مَسَّهُ الْخَيْرُ مَنُوعًا ۝

إِلَّا الْمُصَلِّينَ ۝ الَّذِينَ هُمْ عَلَى

صَلَاتِهِمْ دَآئِمُونَ ۝ وَالَّذِينَ فِى

4. The Angels and the Spirit ascend unto him in a Day the measure where-of is (as) fifty thousand years:

5. Therefore do you hold patience, - a patience of beautiful (contentment).

6. They see the (Day) indeed as a far-off (event):

7. But We see it (quite) near.

8. The Day that the sky will be like molten brass,

9. And the mountains will be like wool,

10. And no friend will ask after a friend, **11.** Though they will be put in sight of each other, - the sinner's desire will be: would that he could redeem himself from the Penalty of that Day by (sacrificing) his children,

12. His wife

الْمَلٰٓئِكَةُ وَالرُّوحُ اِلَيْهِ فِىْ يَوْمٍ

كَانَ مِقْدَارُهٗ خَمْسِيْنَ اَلْفَ سَنَةٍ ۚ

فَاصْبِرْ صَبْرًا جَمِيْلًا ۞ اِنَّهُمْ

يَرَوْنَهٗ بَعِيْدًا ۞ وَّنَرٰىهُ قَرِيْبًا ۞

يَوْمَ تَكُوْنُ السَّمَآءُ كَالْمُهْلِ ۞

وَتَكُوْنُ الْجِبَالُ كَالْعِهْنِ ۞ وَلَا

يَسْـَٔلُ حَمِيْمٌ حَمِيْمًا ۞ يُّبَصَّرُوْنَهُمْ

يَوَدُّ الْمُجْرِمُ لَوْ يَفْتَدِىْ مِنْ

عَذَابِ يَوْمِئِذٍ بِبَنِيْهِ ۞ وَصَاحِبَتِهٖ

withhold him (from Our wrath).

48. But verily this is a Message for the God-fearing.

49. And We certainly know that there are amongst you those that reject (it).

50. But truly (Revelation) is a cause of sorrow for the unbelievers.

51. But verily it is Truth of assured certainty.

52. So glorify the name of your Lord Most High.

Al-Ma'arij
(The Ways of Ascent)
Bismillahir-Rahmanir-Rahim

1. A questioner asked about a Chastisement to befall -

2. The unbelievers, the which there is none to ward off,-

3. (A Penalty) from Allah, Lord of the Ways of Ascent.

عَنْهُ حٰجِزِيْنَ ۞ وَاِنَّهٗ لَتَذْكِرَةٌ

لِّلْمُتَّقِيْنَ ۞ وَاِنَّا لَنَعْلَمُ اَنَّ مِنْكُمْ

مُّكَذِّبِيْنَ ۞ وَاِنَّهٗ لَحَسْرَةٌ عَلَى

الْكٰفِرِيْنَ ۞ وَاِنَّهٗ لَحَقُّ الْيَقِيْنِ ۞

فَسَبِّحْ بِاسْمِ رَبِّكَ الْعَظِيْمِ ۞

بِسْمِ اللّٰهِ الرَّحْمٰنِ الرَّحِيْمِ

سَاَلَ سَآئِلٌۢ بِعَذَابٍ وَّاقِعٍ ۞

لِّلْكٰفِرِيْنَ لَيْسَ لَهٗ دَافِعٌ ۞ مِّنَ

اللّٰهِ ذِى الْمَعَارِجِ ۞ تَعْرُجُ

to witness what you see,

39. And what you see not,

40. That this is verily the word of an honoured Apostle;

41. It is not the word of a poet: little it is you believe!

42. Nor is it the word of a soothsayer: little admonition it is you receive.

43. (This is) a Message sent down from the Lord of the Worlds.

44. And if the Apostle were to invent any sayings in Our name,

45. We should certainly seize him by his right hand,

46. And We should certainly then cut off the artery of his heart:

47. Nor could any of you

بِمَا تُبْصِرُونَ ۞ وَمَا لَا تُبْصِرُونَ ۞

اِنَّهٗ لَقَوْلُ رَسُوْلٍ كَرِيْمٍ ۞ وَّمَا هُوَ

بِقَوْلِ شَاعِرٍ ۗ قَلِيْلًا مَّا تُؤْمِنُوْنَ ۞

وَلَا بِقَوْلِ كَاهِنٍ ۗ قَلِيْلًا مَّا

تَذَكَّرُوْنَ ۞ تَنْزِيْلٌ مِّنْ رَّبِّ

الْعٰلَمِيْنَ ۞ وَلَوْ تَقَوَّلَ عَلَيْنَا

بَعْضَ الْاَقَاوِيْلِ ۞ لَاَخَذْنَا مِنْهُ

بِالْيَمِيْنِ ۞ ثُمَّ لَقَطَعْنَا مِنْهُ

الْوَتِيْنَ ۞ فَمَا مِنْكُمْ مِّنْ اَحَدٍ

profit to me has been my wealth!"

29. "My power has perished from me!"...

30. (The stern command will say): "Seize you him, and bind you him,"

31. "And burn you him in the Blazing Fire."

32. "Further, make him march in a chain, whereof the length is seventy cubits!

33. "This was he that would not believe in Allah Most High."

34. "And would not encourage the feeding of the indigent!"

35. "So no friend has he here this Day. **36.** "Nor has he any food except the corruption from the washing of wounds,"

37. "Which none do eat but those in sin." **38.** So I do call

اَغْنٰى عَنِّىْ مَالِيَهْ ۚ ۝ هَلَكَ عَنِّىْ

سُلْطٰنِيَهْ ۚ ۝ خُذُوْهُ فَغُلُّوْهُ ۙ ۝ ثُمَّ

الْجَحِيْمَ صَلُّوْهُ ۙ ۝ ثُمَّ فِىْ سِلْسِلَةٍ

ذَرْعُهَا سَبْعُوْنَ ذِرَاعًا فَاسْلُكُوْهُ ۚ ۝

اِنَّهٗ كَانَ لَا يُؤْمِنُ بِاللّٰهِ الْعَظِيْمِ ۙ ۝

وَلَا يَحُضُّ عَلٰى طَعَامِ الْمِسْكِيْنِ ۚ ۝

فَلَيْسَ لَهُ الْيَوْمَ هٰهُنَا حَمِيْمٌ ۙ ۝

وَّلَا طَعَامٌ اِلَّا مِنْ غِسْلِيْنٍ ۙ ۝ لَّا

يَاْكُلُهٗ اِلَّا الْخَاطِـُٔوْنَ ۝ فَلَا اُقْسِمُ

Read you my Record!"

20. "I did really understand that my Account would (One Day) reach me!"

21. And he will be in a life of Bliss,

22. In a Garden on high,

23. The Fruits whereof (will hang in bunches) low and near.

24. "Eat you and drink you, with full satisfaction; because of the (good) that you sent before you, in the days that are gone!"

25. And he that will be given his Record in his left hand, will say: "Ah! Would that my Record had not been given to me!"

26. "And that I had never realised how my account (stood)!

27. "Ah! Would that (Death) had made an end of me!"

28. "Of no

اقْرَءُوا كِتَابِيَهْ ۝ إِنِّى ظَنَنْتُ أَنِّى

مُلَاقٍ حِسَابِيَهْ ۝ فَهُوَ فِى عِيشَةٍ

رَّاضِيَةٍ ۝ فِى جَنَّةٍ عَالِيَةٍ ۝

قُطُوفُهَا دَانِيَةٌ ۝ كُلُوا وَاشْرَبُوا

هَنِيئًا بِمَا أَسْلَفْتُمْ فِى الْأَيَّامِ

الْخَالِيَةِ ۝ وَأَمَّا مَنْ أُوتِىَ كِتَابَهُ

بِشِمَالِهِ فَيَقُولُ يَالَيْتَنِى لَمْ أُوتَ

كِتَابِيَهْ ۝ وَلَمْ أَدْرِ مَا حِسَابِيَهْ ۝

يَالَيْتَهَا كَانَتِ الْقَاضِيَةَ ۝ مَآ

one Blast is sounded on the Trumpet,

14. And the earth is moved, and its mountains, and they are crushed to powder at one stroke,-

15. On that Day shall the (Great) Event come to pass.

16. And the sky will be rent asunder, for it will that Day be flimsy,

17. And the Angels will be on its sides, and eight will, that Day, bear the Throne of your Lord above them.

18. That Day shall you be brought to Judgment: not an act of yours that you hide will be hidden.

19. Then he that will be given his Record in his right hand will say: "Ah here!

فِى الصُّوْرِ نَفْخَةٌ وَّاحِدَةٌ ۙ ﴿١٣﴾

وَّحُمِلَتِ الْاَرْضُ وَالْجِبَالُ فَدُكَّتَا

دَكَّةً وَّاحِدَةً ۙ ﴿١٤﴾ فَيَوْمَئِذٍ وَّقَعَتِ

الْوَاقِعَةُ ۙ ﴿١٥﴾ وَانْشَقَّتِ السَّمَآءُ فَهِىَ

يَوْمَئِذٍ وَّاهِيَةٌ ۙ ﴿١٦﴾ وَّالْمَلَكُ عَلٰى

اَرْجَآئِهَا ۚ وَيَحْمِلُ عَرْشَ رَبِّكَ فَوْقَهُمْ

يَوْمَئِذٍ ثَمٰنِيَةٌ ۗ ﴿١٧﴾ يَوْمَئِذٍ تُعْرَضُوْنَ

لَا تَخْفٰى مِنْكُمْ خَافِيَةٌ ﴿١٨﴾ فَاَمَّا مَنْ

اُوْتِىَ كِتٰبَهٗ بِيَمِيْنِهٖ ۙ فَيَقُوْلُ هَآؤُمُ

nights and eight days in succession: so that you could see the (whole) people lying prostrate in its (path), as they had been roots of hollow palm-trees tumbled down!

8. Then do you see any of them left surviving?

9. And Pharaoh, and those before him, and the Cities Overthrown, committed habitual Sin.

10. And disobeyed (each) the Apostle of their Lord; so He punished them with an abundant Chastisement. **11.** We, when the water (of Noah's Flood) overflowed beyond its limits, carried you (mankind), in the floating (Ark),

12. That We might make it a Message unto you, and that ears (that should hear the tale and) retain its memory should bear its (lessons) in remembrance.

13. Then, when

لَيَالٍ وَّ ثَمٰنِيَةَ اَيَّامٍ حُسُوْمًا فَتَرَى

الْقَوْمَ فِيْهَا صَرْعٰى كَاَنَّهُمْ اَعْجَازُ

نَخْلٍ خَاوِيَةٍ ۞ فَهَلْ تَرٰى لَهُمْ

مِّنْ بَاقِيَةٍ ۞ وَجَاءَ فِرْعَوْنُ وَمَنْ

قَبْلَهٗ وَالْمُؤْتَفِكٰتُ بِالْخَاطِئَةِ ۚ

فَعَصَوْا رَسُوْلَ رَبِّهِمْ فَاَخَذَهُمْ اَخْذَةً

رَّابِيَةً ۞ اِنَّا لَمَّا طَغَا الْمَاءُ حَمَلْنٰكُمْ

فِى الْجَارِيَةِ ۞ لِنَجْعَلَهَا لَكُمْ تَذْكِرَةً

وَّتَعِيَهَآ اُذُنٌ وَّاعِيَةٌ ۞ فَاِذَا نُفِخَ

with their eyes when they hear the Message; and they say: "Surely he is possessed!"

52. But it is nothing less than a Message to all the worlds.

Al-Haaqqa
(The Sure Reality)

Bismillahir-Rahmanir-Rahim

1. The Sure Reality!

2. What is the Sure Reality?

3. And what will make you realise what the Sure Reality is?

4. The Thamud and the 'Ad People (branded) as false the Stunning Calamity!

5. But the Thamud, - they were destroyed by a terrible Storm of thunder and lightning!

6. And the 'Ad, they were destroyed by a furious Wind, exceedingly violent; 7. He made it rage against them seven

بِأَبْصَارِهِمْ لَمَّا سَمِعُوا الذِّكْرَ وَيَقُولُونَ إِنَّهُ لَمَجْنُونٌ ۞ وَمَا هُوَ إِلَّا ذِكْرٌ لِّلْعَالَمِينَ ۞

بِسْمِ اللَّهِ الرَّحْمَنِ الرَّحِيمِ

الْحَاقَّةُ ۞ مَا الْحَاقَّةُ ۞ وَمَا أَدْرَاكَ مَا الْحَاقَّةُ ۞ كَذَّبَتْ ثَمُودُ وَعَادٌ بِالْقَارِعَةِ ۞ فَأَمَّا ثَمُودُ فَأُهْلِكُوا بِالطَّاغِيَةِ ۞ وَأَمَّا عَادٌ فَأُهْلِكُوا بِرِيحٍ صَرْصَرٍ عَاتِيَةٍ ۞ سَخَّرَهَا عَلَيْهِمْ سَبْعَ

powerful is My Plan.

46. Or is it that you does ask them for a reward, so that they are burdened with a load of debt? -

47. Or that the Unseen is in their hands, so that they can write it down?

48. So wait with patience for the Command of your Lord, and be not like the Companion of the Fish, - when he cried out in agony.

49. Had not Grace from his Lord reached him, he would indeed have been cast off on the naked shore, in disgrace.

50. Thus did his Lord choose him and make him of the company of the righteous.

51. And the unbelievers would almost trip you up

مَّتِيْنٌ ۞ اَمْ تَسْـَٔلُهُمْ اَجْرًا فَهُمْ

مِّنْ مَّغْرَمٍ مُّثْقَلُوْنَ ۞ اَمْ عِنْدَهُمُ

الْغَيْبُ فَهُمْ يَكْتُبُوْنَ ۞ فَاصْبِرْ لِحُكْمِ

رَبِّكَ وَلَا تَكُنْ كَصَاحِبِ الْحُوْتِ ۚ

اِذْ نَادٰى وَهُوَ مَكْظُوْمٌ ۞ لَوْلَاۤ اَنْ

تَدٰرَكَهٗ نِعْمَةٌ مِّنْ رَّبِّهٖ لَنُبِذَ

بِالْعَرَآءِ وَهُوَ مَذْمُوْمٌ ۞ فَاجْتَبٰهُ

رَبُّهٗ فَجَعَلَهٗ مِنَ الصّٰلِحِيْنَ ۞ وَاِنْ

يَّكَادُ الَّذِيْنَ كَفَرُوْا لَيُزْلِقُوْنَكَ

Then let them produce their "partners", if they are truthful!

42. The Day that the shin shall be laid bare, and they shall be summoned to bow in adoration, but they shall not be able, -

43. Their eyes will be cast down, - ignominy will cover them; seeing that they had been summoned aforetime to bow in adoration, while they were hale and hearty, (and had refused).

44. Then leave Me alone with such as reject this Message: by degrees shall We punish them from directions they perceive not.

45. A (long) respite will I grant them: truly

فَلْيَأْتُوا بِشُرَكَآبِهِمْ إِن كَانُوا

صَٰدِقِينَ ۞ يَوْمَ يُكْشَفُ عَن

سَاقٍ وَيُدْعَوْنَ إِلَى السُّجُودِ فَلَا

يَسْتَطِيعُونَ ۞ خَاشِعَةً أَبْصَارُهُمْ

تَرْهَقُهُمْ ذِلَّةٌ وَقَدْ كَانُوا يُدْعَوْنَ

إِلَى السُّجُودِ وَهُمْ سَٰلِمُونَ ۞ فَذَرْنِي

وَمَن يُكَذِّبُ بِهَٰذَا الْحَدِيثِ

سَنَسْتَدْرِجُهُم مِّنْ حَيْثُ لَا

يَعْلَمُونَ ۞ وَأُمْلِي لَهُمْ إِنَّ كَيْدِي

knew!

34. Verily, for the Righteous, are Gardens of Delight, in the Presence of their Lord.

35. Shall We then treat the People of Faith like the People of Sin?

36. What is the matter with you? How judge you?

37. Or have you a book through which you learn -

38. That you shall have, through it whatever you choose?

39. Or have you Covenants with Us to oath, reaching to the Day of Judgment, (providing) that you shall have whatever you shall demand?

40. Ask you of them, which of them will stand surety for that!

41. Or have they some "partners" (in Godhead)?

يَعْلَمُوْنَ ۞ اِنَّ لِلْمُتَّقِيْنَ عِنْدَ

رَبِّهِمْ جَنّٰتِ النَّعِيْمِ ۞ اَفَنَجْعَلُ

الْمُسْلِمِيْنَ كَالْمُجْرِمِيْنَ ۞ مَا لَكُمْ

كَيْفَ تَحْكُمُوْنَ ۞ اَمْ لَكُمْ كِتٰبٌ

فِيْهِ تَدْرُسُوْنَ ۞ اِنَّ لَكُمْ فِيْهِ

لَمَا تَخَيَّرُوْنَ ۞ اَمْ لَكُمْ اَيْمَانٌ

عَلَيْنَا بَالِغَةٌ اِلٰى يَوْمِ الْقِيٰمَةِ اِنَّ

لَكُمْ لَمَا تَحْكُمُوْنَ ۞ سَلْهُمْ اَيُّهُمْ

بِذٰلِكَ زَعِيْمٌ ۞ اَمْ لَهُمْ شُرَكَاءُ

they said: "We have surely lost our way:"

27. "Indeed we are shut out (of the fruits of our labour)!"

28. Said one of them, more just (than the rest): "Did I not say to you, 'Why not glorify (Allah)?'"

29. They said: "Glory to our Lord! Verily we have been doing wrong!"

30. Then they turned, one against another, in reproach.

31. They said: "Alas for us! We have indeed transgressed!"

32. "It may be that our Lord will give us in exchange a better (garden) than this: for we do turn to Him (in repentance)!"

33. Such is the Punishment (in this life); but greater is the Punishment in the Hereafter,- if only they

قَالُوٓا اِنَّا لَضَآلُّوۡنَ ۞ بَلۡ نَحۡنُ

مَحۡرُوۡمُوۡنَ ۞ قَالَ اَوۡسَطُهُمۡ اَلَمۡ

اَقُلۡ لَّكُمۡ لَوۡلَا تُسَبِّحُوۡنَ ۞ قَالُوۡا

سُبۡحٰنَ رَبِّنَاۤ اِنَّا كُنَّا ظٰلِمِيۡنَ ۞ فَاَقۡبَلَ

بَعۡضُهُمۡ عَلٰى بَعۡضٍ يَّتَلَاوَمُوۡنَ ۞

قَالُوۡا يٰوَيۡلَنَاۤ اِنَّا كُنَّا طٰغِيۡنَ ۞ عَسٰى

رَبُّنَاۤ اَنۡ يُّبۡدِلَنَا خَيۡرًا مِّنۡهَاۤ اِنَّاۤ

اِلٰى رَبِّنَا رٰغِبُوۡنَ ۞ كَذٰلِكَ الۡعَذَابُ

وَلَعَذَابُ الۡاٰخِرَةِ اَكۡبَرُ لَوۡ كَانُوۡا

when they resolved to gather the fruits of the (garden) in the morning.

18. But made no reservation, ("If it be Allah's Will").

19. Then there came on the (garden) a visitation from your Lord, (which swept away) all around, while they were asleep.

20. So the (garden) became, by the morning, like a dark and desolate spot, (whose fruit had been gathered).

21. As the morning broke, they called out, one to another, -

22. "Go you to your tilth (betimes) in the morning, if you would gather the fruits."

23. So they departed, conversing in secret low tones, (saying) -

24. "Let not a single indigent person break in upon you into the (garden) this day."

25. And they opened the morning, strong in an (unjust) resolve.

26. But when they saw the (garden),

إِذْ أَقْسَمُوا لَيَصْرِمُنَّهَا مُصْبِحِينَ ۝

وَلَا يَسْتَثْنُونَ ۝ فَطَافَ عَلَيْهَا

طَآئِفٌ مِّنْ رَّبِّكَ وَهُمْ نَآئِمُونَ ۝

فَأَصْبَحَتْ كَالصَّرِيمِ ۝ فَتَنَادَوْا

مُصْبِحِينَ ۝ أَنِ اغْدُوا عَلَى حَرْثِكُمْ

إِنْ كُنْتُمْ صَارِمِينَ ۝ فَانْطَلَقُوا

وَهُمْ يَتَخَافَتُونَ ۝ أَنْ لَّا يَدْخُلَنَّهَا

الْيَوْمَ عَلَيْكُمْ مِّسْكِينٌ ۝ وَغَدَوْا

عَلَى حَرْدٍ قَادِرِينَ ۝ فَلَمَّا رَأَوْهَا

to those who deny (the Truth).

9. Their desire is that you should be pliant: so would they be pliant.

10. Do not obey every mean swearer; **11.** A slanderer, going about with calumnies,

12. (Habitually) hindering (all) good, transgressing beyond bounds, deep in sin,

13. Violent (and cruel), - with all that, base-born, -

14. Because he possesses wealth and (numerous) sons.

15. When to him are rehearsed Our Signs, "Tales of the ancients", he cries!

16. Soon shall We brand (the beast) on the snout!

17. Verily We have tried them as We tried the People of the Garden,

الْمُكَذِّبِيْنَ ۝ وَدُّوْا لَوْ تُدْهِنُ

فَيُدْهِنُوْنَ ۝ وَلَا تُطِعْ كُلَّ حَلَّافٍ

مَّهِيْنٍ ۝ هَمَّازٍ مَّشَّاءٍ بِنَمِيْمٍ ۝

مَّنَّاعٍ لِّلْخَيْرِ مُعْتَدٍ أَثِيْمٍ ۝ عُتُلٍّ

بَعْدَ ذَٰلِكَ زَنِيْمٍ ۝ أَنْ كَانَ ذَا

مَالٍ وَّبَنِيْنَ ۝ إِذَا تُتْلَى عَلَيْهِ

اٰيَاتُنَا قَالَ أَسَاطِيْرُ الْأَوَّلِيْنَ ۝

سَنَسِمُهُ عَلَى الْخُرْطُوْمِ ۝ إِنَّا

بَلَوْنَاهُمْ كَمَا بَلَوْنَا أَصْحَابَ الْجَنَّةِ

who then can supply you with clear-flowing water?"

Al-Qalam (The Pen)

Bismillahir-Rahmanir-Rahim

1.   Nun. By the Pen and the (Record) which (men) write, -

2.   You are not, by the Grace of your Lord, mad or possessed.

3.   No, verily for you is a Reward unfailing:

4.   And you (stand) on an exalted standard of character.

5.   Soon will you see, and they will see, **6.** Which of you is afflicted with madness.

7.   Verily it is your Lord that knows best, which (among men) have strayed from His Path: and He knows best those who receive (true) Guidance.

8.   So hearken not

فَمَنْ يَّأْتِيكُمْ بِمَآءٍ مَّعِينٍ ۝

سُورَةُ القَلَمِ مَكِّيَّةٌ بِسْمِ اللهِ الرَّحْمٰنِ الرَّحِيمِ آيَاتُهَا ٥٢ رُكُوعُهَا ٢

نٓ وَالْقَلَمِ وَمَا يَسْطُرُونَ ۝ مَآ أَنْتَ

بِنِعْمَةِ رَبِّكَ بِمَجْنُونٍ ۝ وَإِنَّ لَكَ

لَأَجْرًا غَيْرَ مَمْنُونٍ ۝ وَإِنَّكَ لَعَلٰى

خُلُقٍ عَظِيمٍ ۝ فَسَتُبْصِرُ وَيُبْصِرُونَ ۝

بِأَيِّكُمُ الْمَفْتُونُ ۝ إِنَّ رَبَّكَ هُوَ

أَعْلَمُ بِمَنْ ضَلَّ عَنْ سَبِيلِهِ وَهُوَ

أَعْلَمُ بِالْمُهْتَدِينَ ۝ فَلَا تُطِعِ

only to warn plainly in public."

27. At length, when they see it close at hand, grieved will be the faces of the unbelievers, and it will be said (to them): "This is (the promise fulfilled), which you were calling for!"

28. Say: "See you? - If Allah were to destroy me, and those with me, or if He bestows His Mercy on us, - yet who can deliver the unbelievers from a grievous Chastisement?"

29. Say: "He is (Allah) Most Gracious: we have believed in Him, and on Him have we put our trust: so, soon will you know which (of us) it is that is in manifest error."

30. Say: "Don't you see? - If your stream be some morning lost (in the underground earth),

نَذِيرٌ مُّبِينٌ ۞ فَلَمَّا رَاَوْهُ زُلْفَةً

سِيئَتْ وُجُوهُ الَّذِينَ كَفَرُوا وَقِيلَ

هٰذَا الَّذِى كُنْتُمْ بِهٖ تَدَّعُونَ ۞

قُلْ اَرَءَيْتُمْ اِنْ اَهْلَكَنِىَ اللّٰهُ وَمَنْ

مَّعِىَ اَوْ رَحِمَنَا فَمَنْ يُّجِيرُ الْكٰفِرِينَ

مِنْ عَذَابٍ اَلِيمٍ ۞ قُلْ هُوَ الرَّحْمٰنُ

اٰمَنَّا بِهٖ وَعَلَيْهِ تَوَكَّلْنَا فَسَتَعْلَمُونَ

مَنْ هُوَ فِى ضَلٰلٍ مُّبِينٍ ۞ قُلْ

اَرَءَيْتُمْ اِنْ اَصْبَحَ مَاؤُكُمْ غَوْرًا

and flight (from the Truth).

22. Is then one who walks headlong, with his face grovelling, better guided, - or one who walks evenly on a Straight Way?

23. Say: "It is He Who has created you (and made you grow), and made for you the faculties of hearing, seeing, feeling and understanding: little thanks it is you give.

24. Say: "It is He Who has multiplied you through the earth, and to Him shall you be gathered together."

25. They ask: When will this promise be (fulfilled)? - If you are telling the truth.

26. Say: "As to the knowledge of the time, it is with Allah alone: I am (sent)

وَنُفُورٍ ۞ أَفَمَنْ يَمْشِى مُكِبًّا عَلَى

وَجْهِهِ أَهْدَى أَمَّنْ يَمْشِى سَوِيًّا عَلَى

صِرَاطٍ مُّسْتَقِيمٍ ۞ قُلْ هُوَ الَّذِى

أَنْشَأَكُمْ وَجَعَلَ لَكُمُ السَّمْعَ وَالْأَبْصَارَ

وَالْأَفْئِدَةَ قَلِيلًا مَّا تَشْكُرُونَ ۞ قُلْ

هُوَ الَّذِى ذَرَأَكُمْ فِى الْأَرْضِ وَإِلَيْهِ

تُحْشَرُونَ ۞ وَيَقُولُونَ مَتَى هٰذَا

الْوَعْدُ إِنْ كُنْتُمْ صَادِقِينَ ۞ قُلْ

إِنَّمَا الْعِلْمُ عِنْدَ اللهِ وَإِنَّمَا أَنَا

18. But indeed men before them rejected (My warning): then how (terrible) was My rejection (of them)?

19. Do they not observe the birds above them, spreading their wings and folding them in? None can uphold them except (Allah) Most Gracious: truly it is He that watches over all things.

20. No, who is there that can help you, (even as) an army, besides (Allah) Most Merciful? In nothing but delusion are the unbelievers.

21. Or who is there that can provide you with Sustenance if He were to withhold His provision? No, they obstinately persist in insolent impiety

وَلَقَدْ كَذَّبَ الَّذِيْنَ مِنْ قَبْلِهِمْ

فَكَيْفَ كَانَ نَكِيْرِ ۞ اَوَلَمْ يَرَوْا

اِلَى الطَّيْرِ فَوْقَهُمْ صٰٓفّٰتٍ وَّيَقْبِضْنَ ۗ

مَا يُمْسِكُهُنَّ اِلَّا الرَّحْمٰنُ ۘ اِنَّهٗ بِكُلِّ

شَيْءٍ بَصِيْرٌ ۞ اَمَّنْ هٰذَا الَّذِىْ

هُوَ جُنْدٌ لَّكُمْ يَنْصُرُكُمْ مِّنْ دُوْنِ

الرَّحْمٰنِ ۚ اِنِ الْكٰفِرُوْنَ اِلَّا فِىْ غُرُوْرٍ ۞

اَمَّنْ هٰذَا الَّذِىْ يَرْزُقُكُمْ اِنْ

اَمْسَكَ رِزْقَهٗ ۚ بَلْ لَّجُّوْا فِىْ عُتُوِّ

(full) knowledge, of the secrets of (all) hearts.

14. Should He not know, - He that created? And He is the One that understands the finest mysteries (and) is Well-Acquainted (with them).

15. It is He Who has made the earth manageable for you, so traverse you through its tracts and enjoy of the Sustenance which He furnishes: but unto Him is the Resurrection.

16. Do you feel secure that He Who is in heaven will not cause you to be swallowed up by the earth even it shakes (as in an earthquake)? **17.** Or do you feel secure that He Who is in heaven will not send against you a violent tornado (with showers of stones), so that you shall know how (terrible) was My warning?

عَلِيمٌۢ بِذَاتِ الصُّدُورِ ۝ اَلَا يَعْلَمُ

مَنْ خَلَقَ ۗ وَهُوَ اللَّطِيفُ الْخَبِيرُ ۝

هُوَ الَّذِىْ جَعَلَ لَكُمُ الْاَرْضَ ذَلُوْلًا

فَامْشُوْا فِىْ مَنَاكِبِهَا وَكُلُوْا مِنْ

رِّزْقِهٖ ۗ وَاِلَيْهِ النُّشُوْرُ ۝ ءَاَمِنْتُمْ

مَّنْ فِى السَّمَآءِ اَنْ يَّخْسِفَ بِكُمُ

الْاَرْضَ فَاِذَا هِىَ تَمُوْرُ ۝ اَمْ اَمِنْتُمْ

مَّنْ فِى السَّمَآءِ اَنْ يُّرْسِلَ عَلَيْكُمْ

حَاصِبًا ۗ فَسَتَعْلَمُوْنَ كَيْفَ نَذِيْرِ ۝

"Did no warner come to you?"

9. They will say: "Yes indeed; a warner did come to us, but we rejected him and said, 'Allah never sent down any (Message): you are nothing but an egregious delusion!'"

10. They will further say: "Had we but listened or used our intelligence, we should not (now) be among the Companions of the Blazing Fire!"

11. They will then confess their sins: but far will be (Forgiveness) from the Companions of the Blazing Fire!

12. As for those who fear their Lord unseen, for them is Forgiveness and a great Reward.

13. And whether you hide your word or publish it, He certainly has

اَلَمْ يَأْتِكُمْ نَذِيْرٌ ۞ قَالُوْا بَلٰى قَدْ

جَآءَنَا نَذِيْرٌ ەۣ فَكَذَّبْنَا وَ قُلْنَا مَا نَزَّلَ

اللهُ مِنْ شَىْءٍ ۚ اِنْ اَنْتُمْ اِلَّا فِىْ

ضَلٰلٍ كَبِيْرٍ ۞ وَ قَالُوْا لَوْ كُنَّا نَسْمَعُ

اَوْ نَعْقِلُ مَا كُنَّا فِىْٓ اَصْحٰبِ السَّعِيْرِ

۞ فَاعْتَرَفُوْا بِذَنْبِهِمْ ۚ فَسُحْقًا لِّاَصْحٰبِ

السَّعِيْرِ ۞ اِنَّ الَّذِيْنَ يَخْشَوْنَ رَبَّهُمْ

بِالْغَيْبِ لَهُمْ مَّغْفِرَةٌ وَّ اَجْرٌ كَبِيْرٌ

۞ وَ اَسِرُّوْا قَوْلَكُمْ اَوِ اجْهَرُوْا بِهٖ ۚ اِنَّهٗ

a second time: (your) vision will come back to you dull and discomfited, in a state worn out.

5.　　And We have, (from of old), adorned the lowest heaven with Lamps, and We have made such (Lamps) (as) missiles to drive away the Evil Ones, and have prepared for them the Chastisement of the Blazing Fire.

6.　　For those who reject their Lord (and Cherisher) is the Penalty of Hell: and evil is (such), Destination.

7.　　When they are cast therein, they will hear the (terrible) drawing in of its breath even as it blazes forth,

8.　　Almost bursting with fury: every time a Group is cast therein, its Keepers will ask,

كَرَّتَيْنِ يَنْقَلِبْ إِلَيْكَ الْبَصَرُ خَاسِئًا

وَّهُوَ حَسِيرٌ ۞ وَلَقَدْ زَيَّنَّا السَّمَآءَ

الدُّنْيَا بِمَصَابِيحَ وَجَعَلْنَاهَا رُجُومًا

لِّلشَّيَاطِينِ وَأَعْتَدْنَا لَهُمْ عَذَابَ

السَّعِيرِ ۞ وَلِلَّذِينَ كَفَرُوا بِرَبِّهِمْ

عَذَابُ جَهَنَّمَ وَبِئْسَ الْمَصِيرُ ۞

إِذَآ أُلْقُوا فِيهَا سَمِعُوا لَهَا شَهِيقًا

وَّهِيَ تَفُورُ ۞ تَكَادُ تَمَيَّزُ مِنَ الْغَيْظِ

كُلَّمَا أُلْقِيَ فِيهَا فَوْجٌ سَأَلَهُمْ خَزَنَتُهَا

Al-Mulk (Dominion)

Bismillahir-Rahmanir-Rahim

1. Blessed be He in Whose hands is Dominion; and He over all things has Power; -

2. He Who created Death and Life, that He may try which of you is best in deed: and He is the Exalted in Might, Oft-Forgiving; -

3. He Who created the seven heavens one above another: no want of proportion will you see in the Creation of (Allah) Most Gracious. So turn your vision again: do you see any flaw?

4. Again turn your vision

بِسْمِ اللهِ الرَّحْمٰنِ الرَّحِيْمِ

تَبٰرَكَ الَّذِىْ بِيَدِهِ الْمُلْكُ وَهُوَ

عَلٰى كُلِّ شَىْءٍ قَدِيْرُ ۙ الَّذِىْ خَلَقَ

الْمَوْتَ وَالْحَيٰوةَ لِيَبْلُوَكُمْ اَيُّكُمْ

اَحْسَنُ عَمَلًا ؕ وَهُوَ الْعَزِيْزُ الْغَفُوْرُ ۙ

الَّذِىْ خَلَقَ سَبْعَ سَمٰوٰتٍ طِبَاقًا ؕ

مَا تَرٰى فِىْ خَلْقِ الرَّحْمٰنِ مِنْ

تَفٰوُتٍ ؕ فَارْجِعِ الْبَصَرَ ۙ هَلْ تَرٰى

مِنْ فُطُوْرٍ ۙ ثُمَّ ارْجِعِ الْبَصَرَ

ذٰلِكَ الْكِتٰبُ لَا رَيْبَ فِيْهِ

پاره

تَبٰرَكَ الَّذِیْ

(۲۹)

PART 30
'Amma

دُعَاءُ خَتْمِ الْقُرْآنِ

اللَّهُمَّ ارْحَمْنِي حَشْيِ فِي فَهْمِي اللَّهُمَّ ارْحَمْنِي بِالْقُرْآنِ الْعَظِيمِ وَاجْعَلْهُ لِي إِمَامًا وَنُورًا وَهُدًى وَرَحْمَةً اللَّهُمَّ ذَكِّرْنِي مِنْهُ مَا نَسِيتُ وَعَلِّمْنِي مِنْهُ مَا جَهِلْتُ وَارْزُقْنِي تِلَاوَتَهُ آنَاءَ اللَّيْلِ وَأَطْرَافَ النَّهَارِ وَاجْعَلْهُ لِي حُجَّةً يَا رَبَّ الْعَالَمِينَ

the mischief of Darkness as it over-spreads; 4. From the mischief of those who blow on knots;

5. And from the mischief of the envious one as he practises envy.

An-Naas (Mankind)

Bismillahir-Rahmanir-Rahim

1. Say: I seek refuge with the Lord and Cherisher of Mankind,

2. The King (or Ruler) of Mankind,

3. The God (Allah) (or Judge) of Mankind,-

4. From the mischief of the whisperer (of Evil), who with-draws (after his whisper), -

5. (The same) who whispers into the hearts of Mankind, -

6. Among Jinns and among men.

شَرِّ غَاسِقٍ إِذَا وَقَبَ ۞ وَمِنْ

شَرِّ النَّفَّثَاتِ فِي الْعُقَدِ ۞ وَمِنْ

شَرِّ حَاسِدٍ إِذَا حَسَدَ ۞

بِسْمِ اللهِ الرَّحْمٰنِ الرَّحِيمِ

قُلْ أَعُوذُ بِرَبِّ النَّاسِ ۞ مَلِكِ

النَّاسِ ۞ إِلٰهِ النَّاسِ ۞ مِنْ شَرِّ

الْوَسْوَاسِ الْخَنَّاسِ ۞ الَّذِي

يُوَسْوِسُ فِي صُدُورِ النَّاسِ ۞

مِنَ الْجِنَّةِ وَالنَّاسِ ۞

the (crackling) wood - as fuel! -

5.   A twisted rope of palm-leaf fibre round her (own) neck!

Al-Ikhlas (Purity of Faith)

Bismillahir-Rahmanir-Rahim

1.   Say: He is Allah, the One and Only;

2.   Allah, the Eternal, Absolute;

3.   He begets not, nor is He begotten;

4.   And there is none like unto Him.

Al-Falaq (The Dawn)

Bismillahir-Rahmanir-Rahim

1.   Say: I seek refuge with the Lord of the Dawn.

2.   From the mischief of created things;

3.   From

الْحَطَبِ ۞ فِىْ جِيْدِهَا حَبْلٌ

مِّنْ مَّسَدٍ ۞

بِسْمِ اللهِ الرَّحْمٰنِ الرَّحِيْمِ

قُلْ هُوَ اللهُ أَحَدٌ ۞ اللهُ

الصَّمَدُ ۞ لَمْ يَلِدْ وَلَمْ يُوْلَدْ

۞ وَلَمْ يَكُنْ لَّهٗ كُفُوًا أَحَدٌ ۞

بِسْمِ اللهِ الرَّحْمٰنِ الرَّحِيْمِ

قُلْ أَعُوْذُ بِرَبِّ الْفَلَقِ ۞

مِنْ شَرِّ مَا خَلَقَ ۞ وَمِنْ

2. And you does see the people enter Allah's Religion in crowds,

3. Celebrate the praises of your Lord, and pray for His Forgiveness: for He is Oft-Returning (in Grace and Mercy).

Al-Lahab
(The Father of Flame)
Bismillahir-Rahmanir-Rahim

1. Perish the hands of the Father of Flame! Perish he!

2. No benefit to him all his wealth, and all he accumulated!

3. Burnt soon will he be in a Fire of Blazing Flame!

4. And his wife shall carry

وَرَاَيْتَ النَّاسَ يَدْخُلُوْنَ فِيْ

دِيْنِ اللّٰهِ اَفْوَاجًا ۙ۝ فَسَبِّحْ

بِحَمْدِ رَبِّكَ وَاسْتَغْفِرْهُ ؕ اِنَّهٗ

كَانَ تَوَّابًا ۩۝

بِسْمِ اللّٰهِ الرَّحْمٰنِ الرَّحِيْمِ

تَبَّتْ يَدَاۤ اَبِيْ لَهَبٍ وَّتَبَّ ؕ۝

مَاۤ اَغْنٰى عَنْهُ مَالُهٗ وَمَا

كَسَبَ ؕ۝ سَيَصْلٰى نَارًا ذَاتَ

لَهَبٍ ۙ۝ وَّامْرَاَتُهٗ ؕ حَمَّالَةَ

Al-Kafirun
(Those Who reject Faith)

Bismillahir-Rahmanir-Rahim

1.   Say : O you that reject Faith!

2.   I worship not that which you worship,

3.   Nor will you worship that which I worship.

4.   And I will not worship that which you have been wont to worship,

5.   Nor will you worship that which I worship.

6.   To you be your Way, and to me mine.

An-Nasr (The Help)

Bismillahir-Rahmanir-Rahim

1.   When comes the Help of Allah, and Victory,

3. And encourages not the feeding of the indigent.

4. So woe to the worshippers

5. Who are neglectful of their Prayers,

6. Those who (want but) to be seen (of men),

7. But refuse (to supply) (even) neighbourly needs

Al-Kauthar
(The Abundance)

Bismillahir-Rahmanir-Rahim

1. To you have We granted the Fount (of Abundance).

2. Therefore to your Lord turn in Prayer and Sacrifice.

3. For he who hates you, he will be cut off (from Future Hope).

وَلَا يَحُضُّ عَلَىٰ طَعَامِ الْمِسْكِينِ ۚ

فَوَيْلٌ لِّلْمُصَلِّينَ ۙ الَّذِينَ

هُمْ عَن صَلَاتِهِمْ سَاهُونَ ۙ

الَّذِينَ هُمْ يُرَاءُونَ ۙ وَيَمْنَعُونَ

الْمَاعُونَ ۚ

بِسْمِ اللَّهِ الرَّحْمَٰنِ الرَّحِيمِ

إِنَّا أَعْطَيْنَاكَ الْكَوْثَرَ ۚ فَصَلِّ

لِرَبِّكَ وَانْحَرْ ۚ إِنَّ شَانِئَكَ

هُوَ الْأَبْتَرُ ۚ

Quraish
Bismillahir-Rahmanir-Rahim

1. For the covenants (of security and safeguard enjoyed) by the Quraish,

2. Their covenants (covering safe) journeys by winter and summer, -

3. Let them adore the Lord of this House,

4. Who provides them with food against hunger, and with security against fear (of danger).

Al-Ma'un
(The Neighbourly Needs)
Bismillahir-Rahmanir-Rahim

1. Did you see one who denies the Judgment (to come)?

2. Then such is the (man) who repulses the orphan (with harshness),

بِسۡمِ اللّٰهِ الرَّحۡمٰنِ الرَّحِيۡمِ

لِإِيۡلٰفِ قُرَيۡشٍ ۙ ١ إٖلٰفِهِمۡ رِحۡلَةَ

الشِّتَآءِ وَالصَّيۡفِ ۚ ٢ فَلۡيَعۡبُدُوۡا

رَبَّ هٰذَا الۡبَيۡتِ ۙ ٣ الَّذِىۡٓ

أَطۡعَمَهُمۡ مِّنۡ جُوۡعٍ ۙ ٤ وَّاٰمَنَهُمۡ

مِّنۡ خَوۡفٍ ۖ ٥

بِسۡمِ اللّٰهِ الرَّحۡمٰنِ الرَّحِيۡمِ

أَرَءَيۡتَ الَّذِىۡ يُكَذِّبُ بِالدِّيۡنِ ۚ ١

فَذٰلِكَ الَّذِىۡ يَدُعُّ الۡيَتِيۡمَ ۙ ٢

8.   It shall be made into a vault over them,

9.   In columns outstretched.

Al-Fil (The Elephant)

Bismillahir-Rahmanir-Rahim

1.   Do you see not how your Lord dealt with the Companions of the Elephant?

2.   Did He not make their treacherous plan go astray?

3.   And He sent against them flights of Birds,

4.   Striking them with stones of baked clay.

5.   Then did He make them like an empty field of stalks and straw, (of which the corn) has been eaten up.

إِنَّهَا عَلَيْهِمْ مُّؤْصَدَةٌ ۞ فِىْ

عَمَدٍ مُّمَدَّدَةٍ ۞

بِسْمِ اللّٰهِ الرَّحْمٰنِ الرَّحِيْمِ

أَلَمْ تَرَ كَيْفَ فَعَلَ رَبُّكَ

بِأَصْحٰبِ الْفِيْلِ ۞ أَلَمْ يَجْعَلْ

كَيْدَهُمْ فِىْ تَضْلِيْلٍ ۞ وَّأَرْسَلَ

عَلَيْهِمْ طَيْرًا أَبَابِيْلَ ۞ تَرْمِيْهِمْ

بِحِجَارَةٍ مِّنْ سِجِّيْلٍ ۞ فَجَعَلَهُمْ

كَعَصْفٍ مَّأْكُوْلٍ ۞

righteous deeds, and (join together) in the mutual teaching of Truth, and of Patience and Constancy.

Al-Humaza
(The Scandal-Monger)

Bismillahir-Rahmanir-Rahim

1. Woe to every (kind of) scandal-monger and backbiter,

2. Who piles up wealth and lays it by counting (penny by penny),

3. Thinking that his wealth would make him last for ever!

4. By no means! He will be sure to be thrown into that which breaks to pieces,

5. And what will explain to you that which breaks to pieces?

6. (It is) the Fire of (the Wrath of) Allah kindled (to a blaze),

7. The which does mount (right) up to the Hearts:

الصّٰلِحٰتِ وَتَوَاصَوْا بِالْحَقِّ ۙ

وَتَوَاصَوْا بِالصَّبْرِ ۟

بِسْمِ اللّٰهِ الرَّحْمٰنِ الرَّحِيمِ

وَيْلٌ لِّكُلِّ هُمَزَةٍ لُّمَزَةِۨ ۙ الَّذِيْ

جَمَعَ مَالًا وَّعَدَّدَهٗ ۙ يَحْسَبُ

اَنَّ مَالَهٗۤ اَخْلَدَهٗ ۚ كَلَّا لَيُنۢبَذَنَّ

فِي الْحُطَمَةِ ۖ وَمَاۤ اَدْرٰىكَ مَا

الْحُطَمَةُ ۗ نَارُ اللّٰهِ الْمُوْقَدَةُ ۙ

الَّتِيْ تَطَّلِعُ عَلَى الْاَفْئِدَةِ ۗ

the graves.   **3.**   But nay, you soon shall know (the reality).

4.   Again, you soon shall know!

5.   No, were you to know with certainty of mind, (you would beware!)

6.   You shall certainly see Hell-Fire!

7.   Again, you shall see it with certainty of sight!

8.   Then, shall you be questioned that Day about the joy (you indulged in!).

Al-'Asr
(Time Through the Ages)

Bismillahir-Rahmanir-Rahim

1.   By (the Token of) Time (through the ages),

2.   Verily Man is in loss,

3.   Except such as have Faith, and do

الْمَقَابِرَ ۞ كَلَّا سَوْفَ تَعْلَمُوْنَ ۞

ثُمَّ كَلَّا سَوْفَ تَعْلَمُوْنَ ۞ كَلَّا

لَوْ تَعْلَمُوْنَ عِلْمَ الْيَقِيْنِ ۞

لَتَرَوُنَّ الْجَحِيْمَ ۞ ثُمَّ لَتَرَوُنَّهَا

عَيْنَ الْيَقِيْنِ ۞ ثُمَّ لَتُسْئَلُنَّ

يَوْمَئِذٍ عَنِ النَّعِيْمِ ۞

بِسْمِ اللهِ الرَّحْمٰنِ الرَّحِيْمِ

وَالْعَصْرِ ۞ اِنَّ الْاِنْسَانَ لَفِيْ

خُسْرٍ ۞ اِلَّا الَّذِيْنَ اٰمَنُوْا وَعَمِلُوا

men will be like moths scattered about,

5.   And the mountains will be like carded wool.

6.   Then, he whose balance (of good deeds) will be (found) heavy,

7.   Will be in a life of good pleasure and satisfaction.

8.   But he whose balance (of good deeds) will be (found) light, -

9.   Will have his home in a (bottomless) Pit.

10.   And what will explain to you what this is?

11.   (It is) a Fire Blazing fiercely!

At-Takathur (The Piling Up)

Bismillahir-Rahmanir-Rahim

1.   The mutual rivalry for piling up (the good things of this world) diverts you (from the more serious things),   2. Until you visit

النَّاسُ كَالْفَرَاشِ الْمَبْثُوثِ ۙ

وَتَكُونُ الْجِبَالُ كَالْعِهْنِ

الْمَنْفُوشِ ۚ فَاَمَّا مَنْ ثَقُلَتْ

مَوَازِينُهُ ۙ فَهُوَ فِيْ عِيْشَةٍ

رَّاضِيَةٍ ۗ وَاَمَّا مَنْ خَفَّتْ

مَوَازِينُهُ ۙ فَاُمُّهُ هَاوِيَةٌ ۗ وَمَآ

اَدْرٰىكَ مَاهِيَهْ ۗ نَارٌ حَامِيَةٌ ۠

بِسْمِ اللّٰهِ الرَّحْمٰنِ الرَّحِيْمِ

اَلْهٰىكُمُ التَّكَاثُرُ ۙ حَتّٰى زُرْتُمُ

ungrateful;   **7**.   And to that (fact) he bears witness (by his deeds);

8.   And violent is he in his love of wealth.

9.   Does he not know, - when that which is in the graves is scattered abroad.

10.   And that which is (locked up) in (human) breasts is made manifest -

11.   That their Lord had been Well-Acquainted with them, (even to) that Day?

Al-Qari'ah (The Day of Noise and Clamour)

Bismillahir-Rahmanir-Rahim

1.   The (Day) of Noise and Clamour: **2**.   What is the (Day) of Noise and Clamour?

3.   And what will explain to you what the (Day) of Noise and Clamour is?

4.   (It is) a Day whereon

لَكَنُودٌ ۞ وَاِنَّهُ عَلَىٰ ذَٰلِكَ

لَشَهِيدٌ ۞ وَاِنَّهُ لِحُبِّ الْخَيْرِ

لَشَدِيدٌ ۞ اَفَلَا يَعْلَمُ اِذَا بُعْثِرَ

مَا فِي الْقُبُورِ ۞ وَحُصِّلَ مَا فِي

الصُّدُورِ ۞ اِنَّ رَبَّهُمْ بِهِمْ

يَوْمَئِذٍ لَخَبِيرٌ ۞

سُورَةُ الْقَارِعَةِ مَكِّيَّةٌ
بِسْمِ اللّٰهِ الرَّحْمٰنِ الرَّحِيمِ
اٰيَاتُهَا ١١ رُكُوعُهَا

اَلْقَارِعَةُ ۞ مَا الْقَارِعَةُ ۞ وَمَآ

اَدْرَاكَ مَا الْقَارِعَةُ ۞ يَوْمَ يَكُونُ

men proceed in companies sorted out, to be shown the deeds that they (had done).

7.   Then anyone who has done an atom's weight of good, shall see it!

8.   And anyone who has done an atom's weight of evil, shall see it.

Al-'Adiyat (Those That Run)

Bismillahir-Rahmanir-Rahim

1.   By the (Steeds) that run, with panting (breath),

2.   And strike sparks of fire,

3.   And push home the charge in the morning,   4.   And raise the dust in clouds the while,

5.   And penetrate forthwith into the midst (of the foe) en masse; -

6.   Truly man is to his Lord,

النَّاسُ أَشْتَاتًا ۙ لِّيُرَوْا أَعْمَالَهُمْ ۖ ۞

فَمَنْ يَّعْمَلْ مِثْقَالَ ذَرَّةٍ خَيْرًا

يَّرَهُ ۞ وَمَنْ يَّعْمَلْ مِثْقَالَ ذَرَّةٍ

شَرًّا يَّرَهُ ۞

۞ بِسْمِ اللّٰهِ الرَّحْمٰنِ الرَّحِيْمِ ۞

وَالْعٰدِيٰتِ ضَبْحًا ۙ ۞ فَالْمُوْرِيٰتِ

قَدْحًا ۙ ۞ فَالْمُغِيْرٰتِ صُبْحًا ۙ ۞

فَأَثَرْنَ بِهٖ نَقْعًا ۙ ۞ فَوَسَطْنَ

بِهٖ جَمْعًا ۙ ۞ إِنَّ الْإِنْسَانَ لِرَبِّهٖ

beneath which rivers flow; they will dwell therein for ever; Allah well-pleased with them, and they with Him: all this is for such as fear their Lord and Cherisher.

Az-Zilzal (The Convulsion)

Bismillahir-Rahmanir-Rahim

1.   When the earth is shaken to her (utmost) convulsion,

2.   And the earth throws up her burdens (from within),

3.   And man cries (distressed): 'What is the matter with her?'

4.   On that Day will she declare her tidings:

5.   For that your Lord will have given her inspiration.

6.   On that Day will

مِنْ تَحْتِهَا الْأَنْهَرُ خَلِدِيْنَ فِيْهَآ

اَبَدًا ۚ رَضِيَ اللّٰهُ عَنْهُمْ وَرَضُوْا

عَنْهُ ۚ ذٰلِكَ لِمَنْ خَشِيَ رَبَّهُ ۞

الزلزال ۝ بِسْمِ اللّٰهِ الرَّحْمٰنِ الرَّحِيْمِ

اِذَا زُلْزِلَتِ الْأَرْضُ زِلْزَالَهَا ۞

وَاَخْرَجَتِ الْأَرْضُ اَثْقَالَهَا ۞

وَقَالَ الْإِنْسَانُ مَا لَهَا ۞ يَوْمَئِذٍ

تُحَدِّثُ اَخْبَارَهَا ۞ بِاَنَّ رَبَّكَ

اَوْحٰى لَهَا ۚ يَوْمَئِذٍ يَّصْدُرُ

devotion, being true (in faith); to establish regular Prayer; and to practise regular Charity; and that is the religion right and straight.

6. Those who reject (Truth), among the People of the Book and among the Polytheists, will be in Hell-Fire, to dwell therein (for ever). They are the worst of creatures.

7. Those who have faith and do righteous deeds, - they are the best of creatures.

8. Their reward is with Allah: Gardens of Eternity,

لَهُ الدِّينَ ۙ حُنَفَآءَ وَيُقِيْمُوا
الصَّلٰوةَ وَيُؤْتُوا الزَّكٰوةَ وَذٰلِكَ
دِيْنُ الْقَيِّمَةِ ۝ اِنَّ الَّذِيْنَ كَفَرُوْا
مِنْ اَهْلِ الْكِتٰبِ وَالْمُشْرِكِيْنَ فِيْ
نَارِ جَهَنَّمَ خٰلِدِيْنَ فِيْهَا ۚ اُولٰٓئِكَ
هُمْ شَرُّ الْبَرِيَّةِ ۝ اِنَّ الَّذِيْنَ
اٰمَنُوْا وَعَمِلُوا الصّٰلِحٰتِ اُولٰٓئِكَ
هُمْ خَيْرُ الْبَرِيَّةِ ۝ جَزَآؤُهُمْ
عِنْدَ رَبِّهِمْ جَنّٰتُ عَدْنٍ تَجْرِيْ

Al-Bayyinah
(The Clear Evidence)

Bismillahir-Rahmanir-Rahim

1. Those who reject (Truth), among the People of the Book and among the Polytheists, were not going to depart (from their ways) until there should come to them Clear Evidence, -

2. An Apostle from Allah, rehearsing scriptures kept pure and holy:

3. Wherein are laws (or decrees) right and straight.

4. Nor did the People of the Book make schisms, until after there came to them Clear Evidence.

5. And they have been commanded no more than this: to worship Allah, offering Him sincere

بِسْمِ اللهِ الرَّحْمٰنِ الرَّحِيْمِ

لَمْ يَكُنِ الَّذِيْنَ كَفَرُوْا مِنْ اَهْلِ
الْكِتٰبِ وَالْمُشْرِكِيْنَ مُنْفَكِّيْنَ
حَتّٰى تَاْتِيَهُمُ الْبَيِّنَةُ ۙ رَسُوْلٌ
مِّنَ اللهِ يَتْلُوْا صُحُفًا مُّطَهَّرَةً ۙ
فِيْهَا كُتُبٌ قَيِّمَةٌ ؕ وَمَا تَفَرَّقَ
الَّذِيْنَ اُوْتُوا الْكِتٰبَ اِلَّا مِنْ بَعْدِ
مَا جَآءَتْهُمُ الْبَيِّنَةُ ؕ وَمَاۤ اُمِرُوْۤا
اِلَّا لِيَعْبُدُوا اللهَ مُخْلِصِيْنَ

pay no heed to him but bow down in adoration, and bring yourself the closer (to Allah)!

Al-Qadr (The Honour)

Bismillahir-Rahmanir-Rahim

1. We have indeed revealed this (Message) in the Night of Power:

2. And what will explain to you what the Night of Power is?

3. The Night of Power is better than a thousand months.

4. Therein come down the Angels and the Spirit by Allah's permission, on every errand:

5. Peace! ... This until the rise Morn!

لَا تُطِعْهُ وَاسْجُدْ وَاقْتَرِبْ ۩ ﴿١٩﴾

بِسْمِ اللهِ الرَّحْمٰنِ الرَّحِيمِ

إِنَّا أَنْزَلْنٰهُ فِيْ لَيْلَةِ الْقَدْرِ ۚ ﴿١﴾

وَمَا أَدْرٰىكَ مَا لَيْلَةُ الْقَدْرِ ۚ ﴿٢﴾

لَيْلَةُ الْقَدْرِ ۙ خَيْرٌ مِّنْ أَلْفِ

شَهْرٍ ۚ تَنَزَّلُ الْمَلٰٓئِكَةُ وَالرُّوْحُ

فِيْهَا بِإِذْنِ رَبِّهِمْ ۚ مِّنْ كُلِّ

أَمْرٍ ۙ سَلٰمٌ ۛ هِيَ حَتّٰى مَطْلَعِ

الْفَجْرِ ۚ ﴿٥﴾

to your Lord is the return (of all).

9 .   Do you see one who forbids -

10.   A votary when he (turns) to pray?

11.   Do you see if he is on (the road of) Guidance? -

12.   Or enjoins Righteousness?

13.   Do you see if he denies (Truth) and turns away?

14.   Knows he not that Allah does see?

15.   Let him beware! If he desist not, We will drag him by the forelock, -

16.   A lying, sinful forelock!

17.   Then, let him call (for help) to his council (of comrades):

18.   We will call on the Angels of punishment (to deal with him)!

19.   No,

اِلَى رَبِّكَ الرُّجْعَى ۞ اَرَءَيْتَ

الَّذِى يَنْهَى ۞ عَبْدًا اِذَا صَلَّى ۞

اَرَءَيْتَ اِنْ كَانَ عَلَى الْهُدَى ۞

اَوْ اَمَرَ بِالتَّقْوَى ۞ اَرَءَيْتَ اِنْ

كَذَّبَ وَتَوَلَّى ۞ اَلَمْ يَعْلَمْ بِاَنَّ

اللهَ يَرَى ۞ كَلَّا لَئِنْ لَّمْ

يَنْتَهِ ۵ لَنَسْفَعًا بِالنَّاصِيَةِ ۞

نَاصِيَةٍ كَاذِبَةٍ خَاطِئَةٍ ۞ فَلْيَدْعُ

نَادِيَهُ ۞ سَنَدْعُ الزَّبَانِيَةَ ۞ كَلَّا

as to the judgment (to come)?

8.   Is not Allah the Wisest of judges?

Al-'Alaq
(The Clot of Congealed Blood)

Bismillahir-Rahmanir-Raheem

1.   Proclaim! (Or read!) in the name of your Lord and Cherisher, Who created -

2.   Created man, out of a (mere) clot of congealed blood:

3.   Proclaim! And your Lord is Most Bountiful, -

4.   He Who taught (the use of) the pen, -

5.   Taught man that which he knew not.   6.   No, but man does transgress all bounds,

7.   In that he looks upon himself as self-sufficient.   8.   Verily,

بَعْدُ بِالدِّينِ ۛ أَلَيْسَ اللهُ

بِأَحْكَمِ الْحَٰكِمِينَ ۛ

بِسْمِ اللهِ الرَّحْمٰنِ الرَّحِيمِ

اقْرَأْ بِاسْمِ رَبِّكَ الَّذِى خَلَقَ ۛ

خَلَقَ الْإِنْسَانَ مِنْ عَلَقٍ ۛ اقْرَأْ

وَرَبُّكَ الْأَكْرَمُ ۛ الَّذِى عَلَّمَ

بِالْقَلَمِ ۛ عَلَّمَ الْإِنْسَانَ مَا لَمْ

يَعْلَمْ ۛ كَلَّا إِنَّ الْإِنْسَانَ

لَيَطْغَىٰٓ ۛ أَنْ رَّءَاهُ اسْتَغْنَىٰٓ ۛ إِنَّ

still labour hard,   **8.** And to your Lord turn (all) your attention.

At-Tin (The Fig)

Bismillahir-Rahmanir-Rahim

1.   By the Fig and the Olive,

2.   And the Mount of Sinai,

3.   And this City of security, -

4.   We have indeed created man in the best of moulds,

5.   Then do We abase him (to be) the lowest of the low, -

6.   Except such as believe and do righteous deeds: for they shall have a reward unfailing.

7.   Then what can, after this, contradict you,

فَانْصَبْ ۞ وَإِلَى رَبِّكَ فَارْغَبْ ۞

سُورَةُ التِّينِ مَكِّيَّةٌ ٨ بِسْمِ اللهِ الرَّحْمٰنِ الرَّحِيمِ وَرُكُوعُهَا ١ آيَاتُهَا

وَالتِّينِ وَالزَّيْتُونِ ۞ وَطُورِ

سِينِينَ ۞ وَهٰذَا الْبَلَدِ الْأَمِينِ ۞

لَقَدْ خَلَقْنَا الْإِنْسَانَ فِي أَحْسَنِ

تَقْوِيمٍ ۞ ثُمَّ رَدَدْنَاهُ أَسْفَلَ

سَافِلِينَ ۞ إِلَّا الَّذِينَ آمَنُوا

وَعَمِلُوا الصَّالِحَاتِ فَلَهُمْ أَجْرٌ

غَيْرُ مَمْنُونٍ ۞ فَمَا يُكَذِّبُكَ

and made you independent.

9. Therefore, treat not the orphan with harshness,

10. Nor repulse the petitioner (unheard);

11. But the Bounty of the Lord - rehearse and proclaim!

Alam-Nashrah
(The Expansion)

Bismillahir-Rahmanir-Rahim

1. Have We not expanded for you your breast? - **2.** And removed from you your burden,

3. The which did gall your back? -

4. And raised high the esteem (in which) you (are held)?

5. So, verily, with every difficulty, there is relief:

6. Verily, with every difficulty there is relief.

7. Therefore, when you are free (from your immediate task),

فَأَغْنٰى ۗ فَأَمَّا الْيَتِيْمَ فَلَا تَقْهَرْ ۗ

وَأَمَّا السَّآئِلَ فَلَا تَنْهَرْ ۗ وَأَمَّا

بِنِعْمَةِ رَبِّكَ فَحَدِّثْ ۗ

بِسْمِ اللهِ الرَّحْمٰنِ الرَّحِيْمِ

اَلَمْ نَشْرَحْ لَكَ صَدْرَكَ ۗ وَوَضَعْنَا

عَنْكَ وِزْرَكَ ۗ الَّذِيْٓ اَنْقَضَ

ظَهْرَكَ ۗ وَرَفَعْنَا لَكَ ذِكْرَكَ ۗ

فَاِنَّ مَعَ الْعُسْرِ يُسْرًا ۗ اِنَّ

مَعَ الْعُسْرِ يُسْرًا ۗ فَاِذَا فَرَغْتَ

20. But only the desire to seek for the Countenance of their Lord Most High;   **21.** And soon will they attain (complete) satisfaction.

Az-Zuha
(The Glorious Morning Light)

Bismillahir-Rahmanir-Rahim

1. By the Glorious Morning Light,   **2.** And by the Night when it is still, -

3. Your Guardian-Lord has not forsaken you, nor is He displeased.

4. And verily the Hereafter will be better for you than the present.

5. And soon will your Guardian-Lord give you (that wherewith) you shall be well-pleased.

6. Did He not find you an orphan and give you shelter (and care)?

7. And He found you wandering, and He gave you guidance.

8. And He found you in need,

إِلَّا ابْتِغَآءَ وَجْهِ رَبِّهِ الْأَعْلٰى ۚ ۝

وَلَسَوْفَ يَرْضٰى ۝

بِسْمِ اللهِ الرَّحْمٰنِ الرَّحِيْمِ

وَالضُّحٰى ۝ وَالَّيْلِ إِذَا سَجٰى ۝ مَا

وَدَّعَكَ رَبُّكَ وَمَا قَلٰى ۝ وَلَلْآخِرَةُ

خَيْرٌ لَّكَ مِنَ الْأُوْلٰى ۝ وَلَسَوْفَ

يُعْطِيْكَ رَبُّكَ فَتَرْضٰى ۝ أَلَمْ

يَجِدْكَ يَتِيْمًا فَآوٰى ۝ وَوَجَدَكَ

ضَآلًّا فَهَدٰى ۝ وَوَجَدَكَ عَآئِلًا

and thinks himself self-sufficient,

9. And gives the lie to the best, -

10. We will indeed make smooth for him the path to Misery;

11. Nor will his wealth profit him when he falls headlong (into the Pit). **12.** Verily We take upon Ourselves to guide,

13. And verily unto Us (belong) the End and the Beginning.

14. Therefore do I warn you of a Fire blazing fiercely;

15. None shall reach it but those most unfortunate ones

16. Who give the lie to Truth and turn their backs.

17. But those most devoted to Allah shall be removed far from it, -

18. Those who spend their wealth for increase in self-purification,

19. And have in their minds no favour from anyone for which a reward is expected in return,

وَاسْتَغْنَىٰ ۞ وَكَذَّبَ بِالْحُسْنَىٰ ۞

فَسَنُيَسِّرُهُ لِلْعُسْرَىٰ ۞ وَمَا يُغْنِىٰ

عَنْهُ مَالُهُ إِذَا تَرَدَّىٰ ۞ إِنَّ عَلَيْنَا

لَلْهُدَىٰ ۞ وَإِنَّ لَنَا لَلْآخِرَةَ

وَالْأُولَىٰ ۞ فَأَنذَرْتُكُمْ نَارًا تَلَظَّىٰ ۞

لَا يَصْلَاهَا إِلَّا الْأَشْقَى ۞ الَّذِى

كَذَّبَ وَتَوَلَّىٰ ۞ وَسَيُجَنَّبُهَا الْأَتْقَى ۞

الَّذِى يُؤْتِى مَالَهُ يَتَزَكَّىٰ ۞ وَمَا

لِأَحَدٍ عِندَهُ مِن نِّعْمَةٍ تُجْزَىٰ ۞

and they hamstrung her. So their Lord, on account of their crime, obliterated their traces and made them equal (in destruction, high and low)!

15. And for Him is no fear of its consequences.

Al-Lail (The Night)

Bismillahir-Rahmanir-Rahim

1. By the Night as it conceals (the light); **2**. By the Day as it appears in glory;

3. By (the mystery of) the creation of male and female; -

4. Verily, (the ends) you strive for are diverse. **5**. So he who gives (in charity) and fears (Allah),

6. And (in all sincerity) testifies to the best, - **7**. We will indeed make smooth for him the path to Bliss. **8**. But he who is a greedy miser

فَعَقَرُوهَا ۖ فَدَمْدَمَ عَلَيْهِمْ

رَبُّهُمْ بِذَنْۢبِهِمْ فَسَوّٰىهَا ۙ ۞ وَلَا

يَخَافُ عُقْبٰهَا ۞

بِسْمِ اللّٰهِ الرَّحْمٰنِ الرَّحِيمِ

وَالَّيْلِ اِذَا يَغْشٰى ۙ ۞ وَالنَّهَارِ اِذَا

تَجَلّٰى ۙ ۞ وَمَا خَلَقَ الذَّكَرَ وَالْاُنْثٰى ۙ ۞

اِنَّ سَعْيَكُمْ لَشَتّٰى ۗ ۞ فَاَمَّا مَنْ

اَعْطٰى وَاتَّقٰى ۙ ۞ وَصَدَّقَ بِالْحُسْنٰى ۙ ۞

فَسَنُيَسِّرُهٗ لِلْيُسْرٰى ۗ ۞ وَاَمَّا مَنْ بَخِلَ

4. By the Night as it conceals it;

5. By the Firmament and its (wonderful) structure;

6. By the Earth and its (wide) expanse:

7. By the Soul, and the proportion and order given to it.

8. And its enlightenment as to its wrong and its right; -

9. Truly he succeeds that purifies it,

10. And he fails that corrupts it!

11. The Thamud (People) rejected (their Prophet) through their inordinate wrong-doing,

12. Behold, the most wicked man among them was deputed (for impiety).

13. But the Apostle of Allah said to them: "It is a She-camel of Allah! And (bar her not from) having her drink!"

14. Then they rejected him (as a false Prophet),

وَالَّيْلِ اِذَا يَغْشٰهَا ۙ ۛ وَالسَّمَآءِ

وَمَا بَنٰهَا ۙ ۛ وَالْاَرْضِ وَمَا

طَحٰهَا ۙ ۛ وَنَفْسٍ وَّمَا سَوّٰهَا ۙ ۛ

فَاَلْهَمَهَا فُجُوْرَهَا وَتَقْوٰهَا ۙ ۛ

قَدْ اَفْلَحَ مَنْ زَكّٰهَا ۙ ۛ وَقَدْ

خَابَ مَنْ دَسّٰهَا ؕ ۛ كَذَّبَتْ

ثَمُوْدُ بِطَغْوٰهَآ ۙ ۛ اِذِ انْۢبَعَثَ

اَشْقٰهَا ۙ ۛ فَقَالَ لَهُمْ رَسُوْلُ اللّٰهِ

نَاقَةَ اللّٰهِ وَسُقْيٰهَا ؕ ۛ فَكَذَّبُوْهُ

to the indigent (down) in the dust.

17. Then will he be of those who believe, and enjoin patience, (constancy, and self-restraint), and enjoin deeds of kindness and compassion.

18. Such are the Companions of the Right Hand.

19. But those who reject Our Signs, they are the (unhappy) Companions of the Left Hand.

20. On them will be Fire vaulted over (all round).

Ash-Shams (The Sun)

Bismillahir-Rahmanir-Rahim

1. By the Sun and his (glorious) splendour;

2. By the Moon as she follows him; **3.** By the Day as it shows up (the Sun's) glory;

مِسْكِينًا ذَا مَتْرَبَةٍ ۩ ثُمَّ كَانَ

مِنَ الَّذِينَ أٰمَنُوْا وَ تَوَاصَوْا

بِالصَّبْرِ وَ تَوَاصَوْا بِالْمَرْحَمَةِ ۩

أُولٰئِكَ أَصْحٰبُ الْمَيْمَنَةِ ۩ وَالَّذِينَ

كَفَرُوْا بِاٰيٰتِنَا هُمْ أَصْحٰبُ الْمَشْئَمَةِ ۩

عَلَيْهِمْ نَارٌ مُّؤْصَدَةٌ ۩

بِسْمِ اللهِ الرَّحْمٰنِ الرَّحِيْمِ

وَالشَّمْسِ وَضُحٰهَا ۩ وَالْقَمَرِ اِذَا

تَلٰهَا ۩ وَالنَّهَارِ اِذَا جَلّٰهَا ۩

toil and struggle.   **5**.   Thinks he, that none has power over him?

6.   He may say (boastfully); wealth have I squandered in abundance!

7.   Thinks he that none beholds him?

8.   Have We not made for him a pair of eyes? -

9.   And a tongue, and a pair of lips?-   **10**. And shown him the two highways?

11. But he has made no haste on the path that is steep.

12. And what will explain to you the path that is steep? -

13. (It is:) freeing the bondman;

14. Or the giving of food in a day of privation.   **15**. To the orphan with claims of relationship,

16. Or

وَقَضَيْنَا

كَبَدٍ ۚ أَيَحْسَبُ أَن لَّن يَقْدِرَ

عَلَيْهِ أَحَدٌ ۚ يَقُولُ أَهْلَكْتُ مَالًا

لُّبَدًا ۚ أَيَحْسَبُ أَن لَّمْ يَرَهُ

أَحَدٌ ۚ أَلَمْ نَجْعَل لَّهُ عَيْنَيْنِ ۚ

وَلِسَانًا وَّشَفَتَيْنِ ۚ وَهَدَيْنَاهُ

النَّجْدَيْنِ ۚ فَلَا اقْتَحَمَ الْعَقَبَةَ ۚ

وَمَا أَدْرَاكَ مَا الْعَقَبَةُ ۚ فَكُّ

رَقَبَةٍ ۚ أَوْ إِطْعَامٌ فِي يَوْمٍ ذِى

مَسْغَبَةٍ ۚ يَتِيمًا ذَا مَقْرَبَةٍ ۚ أَوْ

His Chastisement will be such as none (else) can inflict,

26. And His bonds will be such as none (other) can bind.

27. (To the righteous soul will be said:) "O (you) soul, in (complete) rest and satisfaction!"

28. "Come back you to your Lord,- well-pleased (yourself), and well-pleasing unto Him!"

29. "Enter you, then, among My devotees!"

30. "Yes, enter you My Heaven!"

Al-Balad (The City)

Bismillahir-Rahmanir-Rahim

1. I do call to witness this City; -

2. And you are a freeman of this City; - **3**. And (the mystic ties of) parent and child;-

4. Verily We have created man into

يُعَذِّبُ عَذَابَهُ أَحَدٌ ۝ وَّلَا يُوْثِقُ

وَثَاقَهُ أَحَدٌ ۝ يَآيَّتُهَا النَّفْسُ

الْمُطْمَئِنَّةُ ۝ ارْجِعِىْ اِلٰى رَبِّكِ

رَاضِيَةً مَّرْضِيَّةً ۝ فَادْخُلِىْ فِىْ

عِبٰدِىْ ۝ وَادْخُلِىْ جَنَّتِىْ ۝

بِسْمِ اللهِ الرَّحْمٰنِ الرَّحِيْمِ

لَآ أُقْسِمُ بِهٰذَا الْبَلَدِ ۝ وَأَنْتَ

حِلٌّ بِهٰذَا الْبَلَدِ ۝ وَوَالِدٍ وَّمَا

وَلَدَ ۝ لَقَدْ خَلَقْنَا الْإِنْسَانَ فِىْ

the orphans!

18. Nor do you encourage one another to feed the poor! -

19. And you devour inheritance - all with greed,

20. And you love wealth with inordinate love!

21. No! When the earth is pounded to powder,

22. And your Lord comes, and His Angels, rank upon rank,

23. And Hell, that Day, is brought (face to face), - on that Day will man remember, but how will that remembrance profit him?

24. He will say: "Ah! Would that I had sent forth (good deeds) for (this) my (Future) Life!"

25. For, that Day,

الْيَتِيمَ ۝ وَلَا تَحَٰضُّونَ عَلَىٰ طَعَامِ

الْمِسْكِينِ ۝ وَتَأْكُلُونَ التُّرَاثَ

أَكْلًا لَّمًّا ۝ وَتُحِبُّونَ الْمَالَ حُبًّا

جَمًّا ۝ كَلَّا إِذَا دُكَّتِ الْأَرْضُ

دَكًّا دَكًّا ۝ وَجَاءَ رَبُّكَ وَالْمَلَكُ

صَفًّا صَفًّا ۝ وَجِا۟ىٓءَ يَوْمَئِذٍ

بِجَهَنَّمَ ۚ يَوْمَئِذٍ يَتَذَكَّرُ الْإِنسَانُ

وَأَنَّىٰ لَهُ الذِّكْرَىٰ ۝ يَقُولُ يَٰلَيْتَنِى

قَدَّمْتُ لِحَيَاتِى ۝ فَيَوْمَئِذٍ لَّا

10. And with Pharaoh, lord of stakes?

11. (All) these transgressed beyond bounds in the lands,

12. And heaped therein mischief (on mischief).

13. Therefore did your Lord pour on them a scourge of diverse Chastisements:

14. For your Lord is (as a Guardian) on a watch-tower.

15. Now, as for man, when his Lord tries him, giving him honour and gifts, then says he, (puffed up), "My Lord has honoured me."

16. But when He tries him, restricting his subsistence for him, then says he (in despair), "My Lord has humiliated me!"

17. No, nay! But you honour not

وَفِرْعَوْنَ ذِى الْأَوْتَادِ ﴿۱۰﴾ الَّذِيْنَ

طَغَوْا فِى الْبِلَادِ ﴿۱۱﴾ فَأَكْثَرُوْا فِيْهَا

الْفَسَادَ ﴿۱۲﴾ فَصَبَّ عَلَيْهِمْ رَبُّكَ سَوْطَ

عَذَابٍ ﴿۱۳﴾ اِنَّ رَبَّكَ لَبِالْمِرْصَادِ ﴿۱۴﴾

فَأَمَّا الْاِنْسَانُ اِذَا مَا ابْتَلَاهُ رَبُّهُ

فَأَكْرَمَهُ وَ نَعَّمَهُ ۙ فَيَقُوْلُ رَبِّيْ

أَكْرَمَنِ ﴿۱۵﴾ وَ أَمَّا اِذَا مَا ابْتَلَاهُ

فَقَدَرَ عَلَيْهِ رِزْقَهُ ۙ فَيَقُوْلُ رَبِّيْ

أَهَانَنِ ﴿۱۶﴾ كَلَّا بَلْ لَّا تُكْرِمُوْنَ

will be their return;   **26.**   Then it will be for Us to call them to account.

Al-Fajr (The Break of Day)

Bismillahir-Rahmanir-Rahim

1.   By the Break of Day;

2.   By the Ten Nights.

3.   By the even and odd (contrasted);   **4.**   And by the Night when it passes away; -

5.   Is there (not) in these an adjuration (or evidence) for those who understand?

6.   Do you not see how your Lord dealt with the 'Ad (People),

7.   Of the (city of) Iram, with lofty pillars,

8.   The like of which were not produced in (all) the land?

9.   And with the Thamud (People), who cut out (huge) rocks in the valley? -

إِيَابَهُمْ ۝ ثُمَّ اِنَّ عَلَيْنَا حِسَابَهُمْ ۝

سُورَةُ الْفَجْرِ مَكِّيَّةٌ ۞ بِسْمِ اللهِ الرَّحْمٰنِ الرَّحِيْمِ ۞ اٰیَاتُهَا ۳۰ وَرُكُوْعُهَا ۱

وَالْفَجْرِ ۝ وَلَيَالٍ عَشْرٍ ۝ وَّالشَّفْعِ

وَالْوَتْرِ ۝ وَّالَّيْلِ اِذَا يَسْرِ ۝ هَلْ

فِيْ ذٰلِكَ قَسَمٌ لِّذِيْ حِجْرٍ ۝ اَلَمْ

تَرَ كَيْفَ فَعَلَ رَبُّكَ بِعَادٍ ۝

اِرَمَ ذَاتِ الْعِمَادِ ۝ الَّتِيْ لَمْ

يُخْلَقْ مِثْلُهَا فِى الْبِلَادِ ۝ وَثَمُوْدَ

الَّذِيْنَ جَابُوا الصَّخْرَ بِالْوَادِ ۝

set in rows,

16. And rich carpets (all) spread out.

17. Do they not look at the Camels, how they are made? -

18. And at the Sky, how it is raised high? -

19. And at the Mountains, how they are fixed firm? -

20. And at the Earth, how it is spread out?

21. Therefore you do give re-mind, for you are one to remind.

22. You are not one to manage (men's) affairs.

23. But if any turn away and reject Allah, -

24. Allah will punish him with a mighty Punishment,

25. For to Us

مَصْفُوفَةٌ ۝ وَزَرَابِيُّ مَبْثُوثَةٌ ۝

اَفَلَا يَنْظُرُوْنَ اِلَى الْاِبِلِ كَيْفَ

خُلِقَتْ ۝ وَاِلَى السَّمَآءِ كَيْفَ

رُفِعَتْ ۝ وَاِلَى الْجِبَالِ كَيْفَ

نُصِبَتْ ۝ وَاِلَى الْاَرْضِ كَيْفَ

سُطِحَتْ ۝ فَذَكِّرْ اِنَّمَآ اَنْتَ

مُذَكِّرٌ ۝ لَسْتَ عَلَيْهِمْ بِمُصَيْطِرٍ ۝

اِلَّا مَنْ تَوَلَّى وَكَفَرَ ۝ فَيُعَذِّبُهُ

اللّٰهُ الْعَذَابَ الْاَكْبَرَ ۝ اِنَّ اِلَيْنَا

Weary, - **4**.   The while they enter the Blazing Fire, -

5.   The while they are given, to drink, of a boiling hot spring,

6.   No food will there be for them but a bitter *Dhari'*,

7.   Which will neither nourish nor satisfy hunger.

8.   (Other) faces that Day will be joyful,

9.   Pleased with their striving, -

10.   In a Garden on high,

11.   Where they shall hear no (word) of vanity:

12.   Therein will be a bubbling spring:

13.   Therein will be couches (of dignity), raised on high,

14.   Goblets placed (ready),

15.   And cushions

نَاصِبَةٌ ۞ تَصْلَى نَارًا حَامِيَةً ۞

تُسْقَى مِنْ عَيْنٍ آنِيَةٍ ۞ لَيْسَ

لَهُمْ طَعَامٌ إِلَّا مِنْ ضَرِيعٍ ۞ لَا

يُسْمِنُ وَلَا يُغْنِي مِنْ جُوعٍ ۞

وُجُوهٌ يَوْمَئِذٍ نَّاعِمَةٌ ۞ لِسَعْيِهَا

رَاضِيَةٌ ۞ فِي جَنَّةٍ عَالِيَةٍ ۞ لَا

تَسْمَعُ فِيهَا لَاغِيَةً ۞ فِيهَا عَيْنٌ

جَارِيَةٌ ۞ فِيهَا سُرُرٌ مَّرْفُوعَةٌ ۞

وَأَكْوَابٌ مَّوْضُوعَةٌ ۞ وَنَمَارِقُ

13. In which they will then neither die nor live.

14. But those will prosper who purify themselves,

15. And glorify the name of their Guardian-Lord, and (lift their hearts) in prayer.

16. No, you prefer the life of this world;   **17.** But the Hereafter is better and more enduring.

18. And this is in the Books of the earliest (Revelation),-

19. The Books of Abraham and Moses.

Al-Ghashiya
(The Overwhelming Event)
Bismillahir-Rahmanir-Rahim

1. Has the story reached you of the overwhelming (Event)?

2. Some faces, that Day, will be humiliated,

3. Labouring (hard),

ثُمَّ لَا يَمُوتُ فِيهَا وَلَا يَحْيَىٰ ۝

قَدْ أَفْلَحَ مَن تَزَكَّىٰ ۝ وَذَكَرَ

اسْمَ رَبِّهِ فَصَلَّىٰ ۝ بَلْ تُؤْثِرُونَ

الْحَيَوٰةَ الدُّنْيَا ۝ وَالْآخِرَةُ خَيْرٌ

وَأَبْقَىٰ ۝ إِنَّ هَٰذَا لَفِي الصُّحُفِ

الْأُولَىٰ ۝ صُحُفِ إِبْرَاهِيمَ وَمُوسَىٰ ۝

بِسْمِ اللَّهِ الرَّحْمَٰنِ الرَّحِيمِ

هَلْ أَتَاكَ حَدِيثُ الْغَاشِيَةِ ۝

وُجُوهٌ يَوْمَئِذٍ خَاشِعَةٌ ۝ عَامِلَةٌ

has created, and further, given order and proportion;

3. Who has ordained laws, and granted guidance;

4. And Who brings out the (green and luscious) pasture,

5. And then does make it (but) swarthy stubble. **6**. By degrees shall We teach you to declare (the Message), so you shall not forget,

7. Except as Allah wills: for He knows what is manifest and what is hidden.

8. And We will make it easy for you (to follow) the simple (Path).

9. Therefore give admonition in case the admonition profits (the hearer). **10**. The admonition will be recei-ved by those who fear (Allah): **11**. But it will be avoided by those most unfortunate ones,

12. Who will enter the Great Fire,

الَّذِى خَلَقَ فَسَوّٰى ۙ وَالَّذِى قَدَّرَ

فَهَدٰى ۙ وَالَّذِىٓ أَخْرَجَ الْمَرْعٰى ۙ

فَجَعَلَهٗ غُثَآءً أَحْوٰى ۙ سَنُقْرِئُكَ

فَلَا تَنْسٰىٓ ۙ إِلَّا مَا شَآءَ اللّٰهُ

إِنَّهٗ يَعْلَمُ الْجَهْرَ وَمَا يَخْفٰى ۙ

وَنُيَسِّرُكَ لِلْيُسْرٰى ۚ فَذَكِّرْ إِنْ

نَّفَعَتِ الذِّكْرٰى ۙ سَيَذَّكَّرُ مَنْ

يَّخْشٰى ۙ وَيَتَجَنَّبُهَا الْأَشْقَى ۙ

الَّذِى يَصْلَى النَّارَ الْكُبْرٰى ۚ

that (all) things secret will be tested,   **10**.   (Man) will have no power, and no helper.

11. By the Firmament which gives recurring rain,

12.   And by the Earth which opens out (for the gushing of springs or the sprouting of vegetation), -

13.   Behold this is the Word that distinguishes (Good from Evil):

14. It is not a thing for amusement.

15. As for them, they are but plotting a scheme,

16.   And I am planning a scheme.

17.   Therefore grant a delay to the unbelievers: give respite to them gently (for a while).

Al-A'la (The Most High)

Bismillahir-Rahmanir-Rahim

1.   Glorify the name of your Guardian-Lord Most High,

2.   Who

تُبْلَى السَّرَائِرُ ۞ فَمَا لَهُ مِنْ

قُوَّةٍ وَّلَا نَاصِرٍ ۞ وَالسَّمَاءِ ذَاتِ

الرَّجْعِ ۞ وَالْأَرْضِ ذَاتِ الصَّدْعِ ۞

إِنَّهُ لَقَوْلٌ فَصْلٌ ۞ وَمَا هُوَ

بِالْهَزْلِ ۞ إِنَّهُمْ يَكِيدُوْنَ كَيْدًا ۞

وَّأَكِيدُ كَيْدًا ۞ فَمَهِّلِ الْكَافِرِيْنَ

أَمْهِلْهُمْ رُوَيْدًا ۞

بِسْمِ اللهِ الرَّحْمٰنِ الرَّحِيْمِ

سَبِّحِ اسْمَ رَبِّكَ الْأَعْلَى ۞ الَّذِيْ

22. (Inscribed) in a Tablet Preserved.

At-Tariq (The Night-Visitant)

Bismillahir-Rahmanir-Rahim

1. By the Sky and the Night-Visitant (therein); -

2. And what will explain to you what the Night-Visitant is?

3. (It is) the Star of piercing brightness; -

4. There is no soul but has a protector over it.

5. Now let man but think from what he is created!

6. He is created from a drop emitted -

7. Proceeding from between the backbone and the ribs:

8. Surely (Allah) is able to bring him back (to life)!

9. The Day

فِى لَوْحٍ مَّحْفُوظٍ ۞

وَالسَّمَاءِ وَالطَّارِقِ ۞ وَمَا أَدْرَاكَ

مَا الطَّارِقُ ۞ النَّجْمُ الثَّاقِبُ ۞

إِنْ كُلُّ نَفْسٍ لَّمَّا عَلَيْهَا حَافِظٌ ۞

فَلْيَنْظُرِ الْإِنْسَانُ مِمَّ خُلِقَ ۞

خُلِقَ مِنْ مَّاءٍ دَافِقٍ ۞ يَخْرُجُ

مِنْ بَيْنِ الصُّلْبِ وَالتَّرَائِبِ ۞

إِنَّهُ عَلَى رَجْعِهِ لَقَادِرٌ ۞ يَوْمَ

beneath which rivers flow: that is the great Salvation, (the fulfilment of all desires),

12. Truly strong is the Grip (and Power) of your Lord.

13. It is He Who creates from the very beginning, and He can restore (life).

14. And He is the Oft-Forgiving, full of Loving-Kindness,

15. Lord of the Throne of Glory,

16. Doer (without let) of all that He intends. **17**. Has the story reached you, of the Forces -

18. Of Pharaoh and the Thamud?

19. And yet the unbelievers (persist) in rejecting (the Truth)!

20. But Allah does encompass them from behind!

21. No, this is a Glorious Qur'an,

تَجْرِيْ مِنْ تَحْتِهَا الْاَنْهٰرُ ۘ ذٰلِكَ

الْفَوْزُ الْكَبِيْرُ ۞ اِنَّ بَطْشَ رَبِّكَ

لَشَدِيْدٌ ۞ اِنَّهٗ هُوَ يُبْدِئُ وَيُعِيْدُ ۞

وَهُوَ الْغَفُوْرُ الْوَدُوْدُ ۞ ذُو الْعَرْشِ

الْمَجِيْدُ ۞ فَعَّالٌ لِّمَا يُرِيْدُ ۞ هَلْ

اَتٰىكَ حَدِيْثُ الْجُنُوْدِ ۞ فِرْعَوْنَ

وَثَمُوْدَ ۞ بَلِ الَّذِيْنَ كَفَرُوْا فِيْ

تَكْذِيْبٍ ۞ وَّاللّٰهُ مِنْ وَّرَآئِهِمْ

مُّحِيْطٌ ۞ بَلْ هُوَ قُرْاٰنٌ مَّجِيْدٌ ۞

7.　And they witnessed (all) that they were doing against the believers.

8.　And they ill-treated them for no other reason than that they believed in Allah, Exalted in Power, Worthy of all Praise! -

9.　Him to Whom belongs the dominion of the heavens and the earth! And Allah is Witness to all things.

10.　Those who persecute (or draw into temptation) the believers, men and women, and do not turn in repentance, will have the Chastisement of Hell: they will have the Chastisement of the Burning Fire.

11.　For those who believe and do righteous deeds, will be in the Gardens;

وَهُمْ عَلَى مَا يَفْعَلُونَ بِالْمُؤْمِنِينَ

شُهُودٌ ۗ وَمَا نَقَمُوا مِنْهُمْ إِلَّا أَن

يُؤْمِنُوا بِاللّٰهِ الْعَزِيزِ الْحَمِيدِ ۙ

الَّذِي لَهُ مُلْكُ السَّمٰوٰتِ وَالْأَرْضِ ۚ

وَاللّٰهُ عَلَىٰ كُلِّ شَيْءٍ شَهِيدٌ ۗ إِنَّ

الَّذِينَ فَتَنُوا الْمُؤْمِنِينَ وَالْمُؤْمِنٰتِ

ثُمَّ لَمْ يَتُوبُوا فَلَهُمْ عَذَابُ جَهَنَّمَ

وَلَهُمْ عَذَابُ الْحَرِيقِ ۗ إِنَّ الَّذِينَ

اٰمَنُوا وَعَمِلُوا الصَّالِحٰتِ لَهُمْ جَنّٰتٌ

Has full knowledge of what they secrete (in their breasts).

24. So announce to them a Chastisement grievous,

25. Except to those who believe and work righteous deeds: for them is a Reward that will never fail.

Al-Buruj (The Zodiacal Signs)

Bismillahir-Rahmanir-Rahim

1.   By the sky, with its constellations.   **2**.   By the promised Day (of Judgment);

3.   By one that witnesses, and the subject of the witness; -

4.   Woe to the makers of the pit (of fire),   **5**.   Fire supplied (abundantly) with fuel:

6.   Behold! They sat over against the (fire),

أَعْلَمُ بِمَا يُوعُونَ ۞ فَبَشِّرْهُمْ

بِعَذَابٍ أَلِيمٍ ۞ إِلَّا الَّذِينَ

آمَنُوا وَعَمِلُوا الصَّالِحَاتِ لَهُمْ

أَجْرٌ غَيْرُ مَمْنُونٍ ۞

بِسْمِ اللهِ الرَّحْمٰنِ الرَّحِيمِ

وَالسَّمَاءِ ذَاتِ الْبُرُوجِ ۞ وَالْيَوْمِ

الْمَوْعُودِ ۞ وَشَاهِدٍ وَمَشْهُودٍ ۞

قُتِلَ أَصْحَابُ الْأُخْدُودِ ۞ النَّارِ

ذَاتِ الْوَقُودِ ۞ إِذْ هُمْ عَلَيْهَا قُعُودٌ ۞

go about among his people, rejoicing!

14. Truly, did he think that he would not have to return (to Us)!

15. No, no! For his Lord was (ever) watchful of him!

16. So I do call to witness the ruddy glow of Sunset;

17. The Night and its Homing;

18. And the Moon in her fullness:

19. You shall surely travel from stage to stage.

20. What then is the matter with them, that they believe not? -

21. And when the Qur'an is read to them, they fall not prostrate,

22. But on the contrary the unbelievers reject (it).

23. But Allah

فِى أَهْلِهِ مَسْرُورًا ۞ إِنَّهُ ظَنَّ

أَن لَّن يَحُورَ ۞ بَلَىٰ إِنَّ رَبَّهُ

كَانَ بِهِ بَصِيرًا ۞ فَلَآ أُقْسِمُ

بِالشَّفَقِ ۞ وَالَّيْلِ وَمَا وَسَقَ ۞

وَالْقَمَرِ إِذَا اتَّسَقَ ۞ لَتَرْكَبُنَّ

طَبَقًا عَن طَبَقٍ ۞ فَمَا لَهُمْ لَا

يُؤْمِنُونَ ۞ وَإِذَا قُرِئَ عَلَيْهِمُ

الْقُرْآنُ لَا يَسْجُدُونَ ۩ ۞ بَلِ

الَّذِينَ كَفَرُوا يُكَذِّبُونَ ۞ وَاللَّهُ

is flattened out, **4.** And casts forth what is within it and becomes (clean) empty,

5. And obeys to (the Command of) its Lord, - and it must needs (do so); - (then will come home the full Reality). **6.** O you man! Verily you are ever toiling on towards your Lord - painfully toiling, - but you shall meet Him.

7. Then he who is given his Record in his right hand,

8. Soon will his account be taken by an easy reckoning,

9. And he will turn to his people, rejoicing!

10. But he who is given his Record behind his back, -

11. Soon will he cry for perdition,

12. And he will enter a Blazing Fire.

13. Truly, did he

مُدَّتْ ۞ وَاَلْقَتْ مَا فِيهَا وَتَخَلَّتْ ۞

وَاَذِنَتْ لِرَبِّهَا وَحُقَّتْ ۞ يٰٓاَيُّهَا

الْاِنْسَانُ اِنَّكَ كَادِحٌ اِلٰى رَبِّكَ

كَدْحًا فَمُلٰقِيهِ ۞ فَاَمَّا مَنْ اُوْتِيَ

كِتٰبَهُ بِيَمِيْنِهِ ۞ فَسَوْفَ يُحَاسَبُ

حِسَابًا يَّسِيْرًا ۞ وَّيَنْقَلِبُ اِلٰٓى اَهْلِهٖ

مَسْرُوْرًا ۞ وَاَمَّا مَنْ اُوْتِيَ كِتٰبَهُ

وَرَآءَ ظَهْرِهٖ ۞ فَسَوْفَ يَدْعُوْا

ثُبُوْرًا ۞ وَّيَصْلٰى سَعِيْرًا ۞ اِنَّهُ كَانَ

they saw them, they would say, "Behold! These are the people truly astray!"

33.   But they had not been sent as keepers over them!

34.   But on this Day the believers will laugh at the unbelievers:

35.   On thrones (of dignity) they will command (a sight) (of all things).

36.   Will not the unbelievers have been paid back for what they did?

Al-Inshiqaq
(The Rending Asunder)

Bismillahir-Rahmanir-Rahim

1.   When the sky is rend asunder,   **2**.   And obeys to (the Command of) its Lord, - and it must needs (do so); -

3.   And when the earth

رَاَوْهُمْ قَالُوٓا اِنَّ هٰٓؤُلَاءِ لَضَالُّوْنَ ۞

وَمَآ اُرْسِلُوْا عَلَيْهِمْ حٰفِظِيْنَ ۞

فَالْيَوْمَ الَّذِيْنَ اٰمَنُوْا مِنَ الْكُفَّارِ

يَضْحَكُوْنَ ۞ عَلَى الْاَرَآئِكِ

يَنْظُرُوْنَ ۞ هَلْ ثُوِّبَ الْكُفَّارُ

مَا كَانُوْا يَفْعَلُوْنَ ۞

بِسْمِ اللّٰهِ الرَّحْمٰنِ الرَّحِيْمِ

اِذَا السَّمَآءُ انْشَقَّتْ ۞ وَاَذِنَتْ

لِرَبِّهَا وَحُقَّتْ ۞ وَاِذَا الْاَرْضُ

24. You will recognise in their faces the beaming brightness of Bliss.

25. Their thirst will be slaked with Pure Wine sealed:

26. The seal thereof will be Musk: and for this let those aspire, who have aspirations:

27. With it will be (given) a mixture of Tasnim:

28. A spring, from (the waters) whereof drink those Nearest to Allah.

29. Those in sin used to laugh at those who believed,

30. And whenever they passed by them, used to wink at each other (in mockery);

31. And when they returned to their own people, they would return jesting; **32**. And whenever

تَعْرِفُ فِى وُجُوهِهِمْ نَضْرَةَ النَّعِيمِ ۝

يُسْقَوْنَ مِن رَّحِيقٍ مَّخْتُومٍ ۝ خِتَمُهُۥ

مِسْكٌ ۚ وَفِى ذَٰلِكَ فَلْيَتَنَافَسِ

الْمُتَنَافِسُونَ ۝ وَمِزَاجُهُۥ مِن تَسْنِيمٍ ۝

عَيْنًا يَشْرَبُ بِهَا الْمُقَرَّبُونَ ۝ إِنَّ

الَّذِينَ أَجْرَمُوا كَانُوا مِنَ الَّذِينَ

ءَامَنُوا يَضْحَكُونَ ۝ وَإِذَا مَرُّوا بِهِمْ

يَتَغَامَزُونَ ۝ وَإِذَا انقَلَبُوٓا إِلَىٰٓ

أَهْلِهِمُ انقَلَبُوا فَكِهِينَ ۝ وَإِذَا

which they do!

15. Verily, from (the Light of) their Lord, that Day, will they be veiled.

16. Further, they will enter the Fire of Hell.

17. Further, it will be said to them: "This is the (reality) which you rejected as false!"

18. No, verily the Record of the Righteous is (preserved) in 'Illiyin.

19. And what will explain to you what 'Illiyun is?

20. (There is) a Register (fully) inscribed,

21. To which bear witness those Nearest (to Allah).

22. Truly the Righteous will be in Bliss:

23. On Thrones (of Dignity) will they command a sight (of all things):

مَّا كَانُوا يَكْسِبُونَ ۝ كَلَّا إِنَّهُمْ

عَن رَّبِّهِمْ يَوْمَئِذٍ لَّمَحْجُوبُونَ ۝

ثُمَّ إِنَّهُمْ لَصَالُوا الْجَحِيمِ ۝ ثُمَّ

يُقَالُ هَٰذَا الَّذِي كُنتُم بِهِ

تُكَذِّبُونَ ۝ كَلَّا إِنَّ كِتَابَ الْأَبْرَارِ

لَفِي عِلِّيِّينَ ۝ وَمَا أَدْرَاكَ مَا

عِلِّيُّونَ ۝ كِتَابٌ مَّرْقُومٌ ۝ يَشْهَدُهُ

الْمُقَرَّبُونَ ۝ إِنَّ الْأَبْرَارَ لَفِي

نَعِيمٍ ۝ عَلَى الْأَرَائِكِ يَنظُرُونَ ۝

5.   On a Mighty Day,

6.   A Day when (all) mankind will stand before the Lord of the Worlds?

7.   No! Surely the record of the wicked is (preserved) in Sijjin.

8.   And what will explain to you what Sijjin is?

9.   (There is) a Register (fully) inscribed.

10.   Woe, that Day, to those that deny -

11.   Those that deny the Day of Judgment.

12.   And none can deny it but the Transgressor beyond bounds, the Sinner!

13.   When Our Signs are rehearsed to him, he says, "Tales of the Ancients!"

14.   By no means! But on their hearts is the stain of the (ill)

لِيَوْمٍ عَظِيمٍ ۝ يَّوْمَ يَقُومُ النَّاسُ

لِرَبِّ الْعَالَمِينَ ۝ كَلَّا إِنَّ كِتَابَ

الْفُجَّارِ لَفِي سِجِّينٍ ۝ وَمَا أَدْرَاكَ

مَا سِجِّينٌ ۝ كِتَابٌ مَّرْقُومٌ ۝ وَيْلٌ

يَّوْمَئِذٍ لِّلْمُكَذِّبِينَ ۝ الَّذِينَ

يُكَذِّبُونَ بِيَوْمِ الدِّينِ ۝ وَمَا

يُكَذِّبُ بِهِ إِلَّا كُلُّ مُعْتَدٍ أَثِيمٍ ۝

إِذَا تُتْلَى عَلَيْهِ آيَاتُنَا قَالَ أَسَاطِيرُ

الْأَوَّلِينَ ۝ كَلَّا بَلْ رَانَ عَلَى قُلُوبِهِم

be able to keep away therefrom.

17. And what will explain to you what the Day of Judgment is?

18. Again, what will explain to you what the Day of Judgment is?

19. (It will be) the Day when no soul shall have power (to do) anything for another: for that Command, that Day, will be (wholly) with Allah.

Al-Mutaffifin
(The Dealers in Fraud)

Bismillahir-Rahmanir-Rahim

1. Woe to those that deal in fraud,- **2**. Those who, when they have to receive by measure from men, exact full measure,

3. But when they have to give by measure or weight to men, give less than due.

4. Do they not think that they will be called to account? -

بِغَآئِبِيْنَ ۞ وَمَآ أَدْرَاكَ مَا يَوْمُ

الدِّيْنِ ۞ ثُمَّ مَآ أَدْرَاكَ مَا يَوْمُ

الدِّيْنِ ۞ يَوْمَ لَا تَمْلِكُ نَفْسٌ

لِنَفْسٍ شَيْئًا ۗ وَالْأَمْرُ يَوْمَئِذٍ لِّلّٰهِ ۞

سُوْرَةُ الطففين مَكِّيَّةٌ بِسْمِ اللّٰهِ الرَّحْمٰنِ الرَّحِيْمِ

وَيْلٌ لِّلْمُطَفِّفِيْنَ ۞ الَّذِيْنَ اِذَا

اكْتَالُوْا عَلَى النَّاسِ يَسْتَوْفُوْنَ ۞ وَاِذَا

كَالُوْهُمْ اَوْ وَّزَنُوْهُمْ يُخْسِرُوْنَ ۞

اَلَا يَظُنُّ اُولٰٓئِكَ اَنَّهُمْ مَّبْعُوْثُوْنَ ۞

6. O man! What has seduced you from your Lord Most Beneficent? -

7. Him Who created you. Fashioned you in due proportion, and gave you a just bias;

8. In whatever form He wills, does He put you together.

9. No, but you reject Right and Judgment!

10. But verily over you (are appointed Angels) to protect you, -

11. Kind and honourable, - writing down (your deeds):

12. They know (and understand) all that you do.

13. As for the Righteous, they will be in Bliss;

14. And the Wicked - they will be in the Fire,

15. Which they will enter on the Day of Judgment,

16. And they will not

يَا أَيُّهَا الْإِنْسَانُ مَا غَرَّكَ بِرَبِّكَ

الْكَرِيمِ ۝ الَّذِى خَلَقَكَ فَسَوَّاكَ

فَعَدَلَكَ ۝ فِى أَيِّ صُورَةٍ مَّا شَآءَ

رَكَّبَكَ ۝ كَلَّا بَلْ تُكَذِّبُونَ بِالدِّينِ

وَإِنَّ عَلَيْكُمْ لَحَافِظِينَ ۝ كِرَامًا

كَاتِبِينَ ۝ يَعْلَمُونَ مَا تَفْعَلُونَ

إِنَّ الْأَبْرَارَ لَفِى نَعِيمٍ ۝ وَإِنَّ

الْفُجَّارَ لَفِى جَحِيمٍ ۝ يَصْلَوْنَهَا

يَوْمَ الدِّينِ ۝ وَمَا هُمْ عَنْهَا

26. Then whither go you?

27. Verily this is no less than a Message to (all) the Worlds:

28. (With profit) to whoever among you wills to go straight:

29. But you shall not will except as Allah wills, - the Cherisher of the Worlds.

Al-Infitar
(The Cleaving Asunder)
Bismillahir-Rahmanir-Rahim

1. When the Sky is cleft asunder;

2. When the Stars are scattered;

3. When the Oceans are suffered to burst forth;

4. And when the Graves are turned upside down; -

5. (Then) shall each soul know what it has sent forward and (what it has) kept back.

فَاَيْنَ تَذْهَبُوْنَ ۞ اِنْ هُوَ اِلَّا ذِكْرٌ

لِّلْعٰلَمِيْنَ ۞ لِمَنْ شَآءَ مِنْكُمْ

اَنْ يَّسْتَقِيْمَ ۞ وَمَا تَشَآءُوْنَ اِلَّا

اَنْ يَّشَآءَ اللّٰهُ رَبُّ الْعٰلَمِيْنَ ۞

بِسْمِ اللّٰهِ الرَّحْمٰنِ الرَّحِيْمِ

اِذَا السَّمَآءُ انْفَطَرَتْ ۞ وَاِذَا

الْكَوَاكِبُ انْتَثَرَتْ ۞ وَاِذَا الْبِحَارُ

فُجِّرَتْ ۞ وَاِذَا الْقُبُوْرُ بُعْثِرَتْ ۞

عَلِمَتْ نَفْسٌ مَّا قَدَّمَتْ وَاَخَّرَتْ ۞

I call to witness the Planets - that recede,

16. Go straight, or hide;

17. And the Night as it dissipates;

18. And the Dawn as it breathes away the darkness; -

19. Verily this is the word of a most honourable Messenger,

20. Endued with Power, held in honour by the Lord of the Throne,

21. With authority there, (and) faithful to his trust.

22. And (O people!) your companion is not one possessed;

23. And without doubt he saw him in the clear horizon.

24. Neither does he withhold grudgingly a knowledge of the Unseen. **25**. Nor is it the word of an evil spirit accursed.

فَلَا أُقْسِمُ بِالْخُنَّسِ ﴿١٥﴾ الْجَوَارِ الْكُنَّسِ ﴿١٦﴾

وَالَّيْلِ إِذَا عَسْعَسَ ﴿١٧﴾ وَالصُّبْحِ

إِذَا تَنَفَّسَ ﴿١٨﴾ إِنَّهُ لَقَوْلُ رَسُولٍ

كَرِيمٍ ﴿١٩﴾ ذِى قُوَّةٍ عِنْدَ ذِى

الْعَرْشِ مَكِينٍ ﴿٢٠﴾ مُّطَاعٍ ثَمَّ

أَمِينٍ ﴿٢١﴾ وَمَا صَاحِبُكُمْ بِمَجْنُونٍ ﴿٢٢﴾

وَلَقَدْ رَآهُ بِالْأُفُقِ الْمُبِينِ ﴿٢٣﴾

وَمَا هُوَ عَلَى الْغَيْبِ بِضَنِينٍ ﴿٢٤﴾

وَمَا هُوَ بِقَوْلِ شَيْطَانٍ رَّجِيمٍ ﴿٢٥﴾

fall, losing their lustre;

3.   When the mountains vanish (like a mirage);

4.   When the she-camels, ten months with young, are left untended; 5. When the wild beasts are herded together (in the human habitations);

6.   When the oceans boil over with a swell;

7.   When the souls are sorted out, (being joined, like with like);

8.   When the female (infant), buried alive, is questioned -

9.   For what crime she was killed;

10.   When the scrolls are laid open;

11.   When the sky is unveiled;

12.   When the Blazing Fire is kindled to fierce heat;

13.   And when the Garden is brought near; - 14. (Then) shall each soul know what it has put forward. 15. So verily

انْكَدَرَتْ ۞ وَإِذَا الْجِبَالُ سُيِّرَتْ ۞

وَإِذَا الْعِشَارُ عُطِّلَتْ ۞ وَإِذَا

الْوُحُوشُ حُشِرَتْ ۞ وَإِذَا الْبِحَارُ

سُجِّرَتْ ۞ وَإِذَا النُّفُوسُ زُوِّجَتْ ۞

وَإِذَا الْمَوْءُودَةُ سُئِلَتْ ۞ بِأَيِّ ذَنْبٍ

قُتِلَتْ ۞ وَإِذَا الصُّحُفُ نُشِرَتْ ۞ وَإِذَا

السَّمَاءُ كُشِطَتْ ۞ وَإِذَا الْجَحِيمُ

سُعِّرَتْ ۞ وَإِذَا الْجَنَّةُ أُزْلِفَتْ ۞

عَلِمَتْ نَفْسٌ مَّا أَحْضَرَتْ ۞ فَلَا

from his own brother,
35.   And from his mother and his father,   **36**.   And from his wife and his children.   **37**. Each one of them, that Day, will have enough concern (of his own) to make him unmindful to the others.
38. Some faces that Day will be beaming, **39**. Laughing, rejoicing.
40.   And other faces that Day will be dust-stained,
41.   Blackness will cover them:
42.   Such will be the rejecters of Allah, the doers of iniquity.

At-Takwir (The Folding Up)

Bismillahir-Rahmanir-Rahim

1.   When the sun (with its spacious light) is folded up;
2.   When the stars

الْمَرْءُ مِنْ أَخِيهِ ۙ وَأُمِّهِ وَأَبِيهِ ۙ

وَصَاحِبَتِهِ وَبَنِيهِ ۗ لِكُلِّ امْرِئٍ

مِّنْهُمْ يَوْمَئِذٍ شَأْنٌ يُغْنِيهِ ۗ

وُجُوهٌ يَوْمَئِذٍ مُّسْفِرَةٌ ۙ ضَاحِكَةٌ

مُّسْتَبْشِرَةٌ ۚ وَوُجُوهٌ يَوْمَئِذٍ عَلَيْهَا

غَبَرَةٌ ۙ تَرْهَقُهَا قَتَرَةٌ ۘ أُولٰئِكَ

هُمُ الْكَفَرَةُ الْفَجَرَةُ ۠

بِسْمِ اللهِ الرَّحْمٰنِ الرَّحِيمِ

إِذَا الشَّمْسُ كُوِّرَتْ ۙ وَإِذَا النُّجُومُ

21. Then He causes him to die, and puts him in his grave;

22. Then, when it is His Will, He will raise him up (again).

23. By no means has he fulfilled what Allah has commanded him.

24. Then let man look at his food, (and how We provide it):

25. For that We pour forth water in abundance, **26.** And We split the earth in fragments,

27. And produce therein corn,

28. And Grapes and nutritious plants, **29.** And Olives and Dates,

30. And enclosed Gardens, dense with lofty trees,

31. And fruits and fodder, -

32. For use and convenience to you and your cattle.

33. At length, when there comes the Deafening Noise, -

34. That Day shall a man flee

ثُمَّ أَمَاتَهُ فَأَقْبَرَهُ ۞ ثُمَّ إِذَا شَآءَ

أَنْشَرَهُ ۞ كَلَّا لَمَّا يَقْضِ مَآ أَمَرَهُ ۞

فَلْيَنْظُرِ الْإِنْسَانُ إِلَى طَعَامِهِ ۞ أَنَّا

صَبَبْنَا الْمَآءَ صَبًّا ۞ ثُمَّ شَقَقْنَا

الْأَرْضَ شَقًّا ۞ فَأَنْبَتْنَا فِيهَا

حَبًّا ۞ وَعِنَبًا وَقَضْبًا ۞ وَزَيْتُونًا

وَنَخْلًا ۞ وَحَدَآئِقَ غُلْبًا ۞ وَفَاكِهَةً

وَأَبًّا ۞ مَتَاعًا لَكُمْ وَلِأَنْعَامِكُمْ ۞

فَإِذَا جَآءَتِ الصَّآخَّةُ ۞ يَوْمَ يَفِرُّ

to you if he grow not (in spiritual understanding).

8. But as to him who came to you striving earnestly,

9. And with fear (in his heart),

10. Of him were you unmindful.

11. By no means (should it be so)! For it is indeed a Message of instruction: **12**. Therefore let who so will, keep it in remembrance.

13. (It is) in Books held (greatly) in honour, **14.** Exalted (in dignity), kept pure and holy,

15. (Written) by the hands of scribes - **16.** (Honourable and Pious and Just. **17.** (Woe to man! What has made him reject Allah;

18. From what stuff has He created him? **19.** From a sperm-drop: He has created him, and then moulded him in due proportion;

20. Then does He make His path smooth for him;

عَلَيْكَ اَلَّا يَزَّكّٰى ۞ وَاَمَّا مَنْ جَآءَكَ

يَسْعٰى ۞ وَهُوَ يَخْشٰى ۞ فَاَنْتَ عَنْهُ

تَلَهّٰى ۞ كَلَّا اِنَّهَا تَذْكِرَةٌ ۞ فَمَنْ

شَآءَ ذَكَرَهُ ۞ فِىْ صُحُفٍ مُّكَرَّمَةٍ ۞

مَّرْفُوعَةٍ مُّطَهَّرَةٍ ۞ بِاَيْدِىْ

سَفَرَةٍ ۞ كِرَامٍ بَرَرَةٍ ۞ قُتِلَ

الْاِنْسَانُ مَآ اَكْفَرَهُ ۞ مِنْ اَىِّ

شَىْءٍ خَلَقَهُ ۞ مِنْ نُّطْفَةٍ خَلَقَهُ

فَقَدَّرَهُ ۞ ثُمَّ السَّبِيْلَ يَسَّرَهُ ۞

you (concerned) with the declaration thereof?

44. With your Lord is the time fixed therefor.

45. You are but a warner for such as fear it. **46**. The Day they see it, (it will be) as if they had tarried but a single evening, or (at most till) the following morn!

'Abasa (He Frowned)

Bismillahir-Rahmanir-Rahim

1. (The Prophet) frowned and turned away,

2. Because there came to him the blind man (interrupting).

3. But what could tell you but that perchance he might grow (in spiritual understanding)? -

4. Or that he might receive admonition, and the teaching might profit him? **5**. As to one who regards himself as self-sufficient,

6. To him do you attend;

7. Though it is no blame

اَنْتَ مِنْ ذِكْرٰىهَا ۝ اِلٰى رَبِّكَ

مُنْتَهٰىهَا ۝ اِنَّمَاۤ اَنْتَ مُنْذِرُ مَنْ

يَّخْشٰىهَا ۝ كَاَنَّهُمْ يَوْمَ يَرَوْنَهَا لَمْ

يَلْبَثُوۤا اِلَّا عَشِيَّةً اَوْ ضُحٰىهَا ۝

بِسْمِ اللّٰهِ الرَّحْمٰنِ الرَّحِيْمِ

عَبَسَ وَتَوَلّٰۤى ۝ اَنْ جَآءَهُ الْاَعْمٰى ۝

وَمَا يُدْرِيْكَ لَعَلَّهُ يَزَّكّٰٓى ۝ اَوْ

يَذَّكَّرُ فَتَنْفَعَهُ الذِّكْرٰى ۝ اَمَّا مَنِ

اسْتَغْنٰى ۝ فَاَنْتَ لَهُ تَصَدّٰى ۝ وَمَا

there comes the great, over-whelming (Event), -

35. The Day when man shall remember (all) that he strove for,

36. And Hell-Fire shall be placed in full view for (all) to see, -

37. Then, for such as had trans-gressed all bounds,

38. And had preferred the life of this world,

39. The Abode will be Hell-Fire;

40. And for such as had enter-tained the fear of standing before their Lord's (tribunal) and had restrained (their) soul from lower desires,

41. Their Abode will be the Garden.

42. They ask you about the Hour, -'When will be its appointed time?'

43. Wherein are

جَآءَتِ الطَّآمَّةُ الْكُبْرَىٰ ۞ يَوْمَ

يَتَذَكَّرُ الْإِنْسَانُ مَا سَعَىٰ ۞ وَبُرِّزَتِ

الْجَحِيمُ لِمَنْ يَرَىٰ ۞ فَأَمَّا مَنْ

طَغَىٰ ۞ وَ اٰثَرَ الْحَيٰوةَ الدُّنْيَا ۞

فَإِنَّ الْجَحِيمَ هِيَ الْمَأْوَىٰ ۞ وَأَمَّا

مَنْ خَافَ مَقَامَ رَبِّهِ وَ نَهَى

النَّفْسَ عَنِ الْهَوَىٰ ۞ فَإِنَّ

الْجَنَّةَ هِيَ الْمَأْوَىٰ ۞ يَسْئَلُونَكَ

عَنِ السَّاعَةِ أَيَّانَ مُرْسَٰهَا ۞ فِيمَ

Most High". **25**. But Allah did punish him, (and made an) example of him, - in the Hereafter, as in this life. **26**. Verily in this is an instructive warning for whosoever fears (Allah).

27. What! Are you the more difficult to create or the heaven (above)? (Allah) has constructed it:

28. On high has He raised its canopy, and He has given it order and perfection.

29. Its night does He endow with darkness, and its splendour does He bring out (with light).

30. And the earth, moreover, has He extended (to a wide expanse);

31. He draws out therefrom its moisture and its pasture;

32. And the mountains has He firmly fixed. **33**. A provision for you and your cattle.

34. Therefore, when

الْأَعْلَىٰ ۞ فَأَخَذَهُ اللّٰهُ نَكَالَ

الْأَخِرَةِ وَالْأُولَىٰ ۞ اِنَّ فِي ذٰلِكَ

لَعِبْرَةً لِّمَنْ يَخْشَىٰ ۞ ءَاَنْتُمْ اَشَدُّ

خَلْقًا اَمِ السَّمَآءُ بَنٰهَا ۞ رَفَعَ سَمْكَهَا

فَسَوّٰىٰهَا ۞ وَاَغْطَشَ لَيْلَهَا وَاَخْرَجَ

ضُحٰىهَا ۞ وَالْاَرْضَ بَعْدَ ذٰلِكَ

دَحٰىهَا ۞ اَخْرَجَ مِنْهَا مَآءَهَا

وَمَرْعٰىهَا ۞ وَالْجِبَالَ اَرْسٰىهَا ۞

مَتَاعًا لَّكُمْ وَلِاَنْعَامِكُمْ ۞ فَاِذَا

14. When, behold, they will be in the (full) awakening (to Judgment).

15. Has the story of Moses reached you?

16. Behold, your Lord did call to him in the sacred valley of Tuwa: -

17. "Go you to Pharaoh for he has indeed transgressed all bounds:"

18. "And say to him, 'Do you wish to be purified (from sin)?' -

19. 'And that I guide you to your Lord, so you should fear Him?'"

20. Then did (Moses) show him the Great Sign.

21. But (Pharaoh) rejected it and disobeyed (guidance);

22. Further, he turned his back, striving hard (against Allah).

23. Then he collected (his men) and made a proclamation,

24. Saying, "I am your Lord,

وَاحِدَةٌ ۞ فَإِذَا هُم بِالسَّاهِرَةِ ۞

هَلْ أَتَاكَ حَدِيثُ مُوسَى ۞ إِذْ

نَادَاهُ رَبُّهُ بِالْوَادِ الْمُقَدَّسِ

طُوًى ۞ اذْهَبْ إِلَى فِرْعَوْنَ إِنَّهُ

طَغَى ۞ فَقُلْ هَل لَّكَ إِلَى أَن

تَزَكَّى ۞ وَأَهْدِيَكَ إِلَى رَبِّكَ

فَتَخْشَى ۞ فَأَرَاهُ الْآيَةَ الْكُبْرَى ۞

فَكَذَّبَ وَعَصَى ۞ ثُمَّ أَدْبَرَ يَسْعَى ۞

فَحَشَرَ فَنَادَى ۞ فَقَالَ أَنَا رَبُّكُمُ

(the souls of the blessed);

3. And by those who glide along (on errands of mercy),

4. Then press forward as in a race,

5. Then arrange to do (the Commands of their Lord),

6. On that day everything that can be in commotion will be in violent commotion,

7. Followed by oft-repeated (commotions):

8. Hearts that Day will be in agitation; **9.** Cast down will be (their owners') eyes.

10. They say (now): "What! Shall we indeed be returned to (our) former state?"

11. "What! - when we shall have become rotten bones?"

12. They say: "It would, in that case, be a return with loss!"

13. But verily, it will be but a single (compelling) Cry,

نَّشْطًا ۞ وَّ السّٰبِحٰتِ سَبْحًا ۞

فَالسّٰبِقٰتِ سَبْقًا ۞ فَالْمُدَبِّرٰتِ

اَمْرًا ۞ يَوْمَ تَرْجُفُ الرَّاجِفَةُ ۞

تَتْبَعُهَا الرَّادِفَةُ ۞ قُلُوبٌ يَّوْمَئِذٍ

وَّاجِفَةٌ ۞ اَبْصَارُهَا خَاشِعَةٌ ۞

يَقُوْلُوْنَ ءَاِنَّا لَمَرْدُوْدُوْنَ فِى

الْحَافِرَةِ ۞ ءَاِذَا كُنَّا عِظَامًا

نَّخِرَةً ۞ قَالُوْا تِلْكَ اِذًا كَرَّةٌ

خَاسِرَةٌ ۞ فَاِنَّمَا هِىَ زَجْرَةٌ

none shall speak except any who is permitted by (Allah) Most Gracious, and he will say what is right.

39. That Day will be the sure Reality: therefore, whoso will, let him take a (straight) return to his Lord!

40. Verily, We have warned you of a Chastisement near, the Day when man will see (the deeds) which his hands have sent forth, and the unbeliever will say, "Woe unto me! Would that I were (mere) dust!"

An-Nazi'at
(Those Who Tear Out)

Bismillahir-Rahmanir-Rahim

1. By the (Angels) who tear out (the souls of the wicked) with violence;

2. By those who gently draw out

لَا يَتَكَلَّمُونَ اِلَّا مَنْ اَذِنَ لَهُ
الرَّحْمٰنُ وَ قَالَ صَوَابًا ۞ ذٰلِكَ
الْيَوْمُ الْحَقُّ ۚ فَمَنْ شَآءَ اتَّخَذَ
اِلٰى رَبِّهٖ مَاٰبًا ۞ اِنَّآ اَنْذَرْنٰكُمْ
عَذَابًا قَرِيْبًا ۚ يَّوْمَ يَنْظُرُ الْمَرْءُ
مَا قَدَّمَتْ يَدٰهُ وَيَقُوْلُ الْكٰفِرُ
يٰلَيْتَنِيْ كُنْتُ تُرٰبًا ۞

سُورَةُ النَّازِعَاتِ مَكِّيَّةٌ ٤٦ ٰايَاتُهَا بِسْمِ اللهِ الرَّحْمٰنِ الرَّحِيْمِ رُكُوعَاتُهَا ٢

وَالنّٰزِعٰتِ غَرْقًا ۞ وَّالنّٰشِطٰتِ

increase shall We grant you, except in Punishment."

31. Verily for the Righteous there will be a fulfilment of (the heart's) desires;

32. Gardens enclosed, and grapevines;

33. Companions of equal age;

34. And a cup full (to the brim).

35. No loose talk shall they hear therein, nor Untruth: -

36. Recompense from your Lord, a gift, (amply) sufficient,

37. (From) the Lord of the heavens and the earth, and all between, (Allah) Most Gracious: none shall have power to argue with Him.

38. The Day that the Spirit and the Angels will stand forth in ranks,

نَزِيدَكُمْ إِلَّا عَذَابًا ۝ إِنَّ

لِلْمُتَّقِينَ مَفَازًا ۝ حَدَائِقَ

وَأَعْنَابًا ۝ وَكَوَاعِبَ أَتْرَابًا ۝

وَكَأْسًا دِهَاقًا ۝ لَا يَسْمَعُونَ فِيهَا

لَغْوًا وَّلَا كِذَّابًا ۝ جَزَآءً مِّن رَّبِّكَ

عَطَآءً حِسَابًا ۝ رَّبِّ السَّمَوَٰتِ

وَالْأَرْضِ وَمَا بَيْنَهُمَا الرَّحْمَٰنِ

لَا يَمْلِكُونَ مِنْهُ خِطَابًا ۝ يَوْمَ

يَقُومُ الرُّوحُ وَالْمَلَٰٓئِكَةُ صَفًّا

as if they were a mirage.

21. Truly Hell is as a place of ambush,

22. For the transgressors a place of destination:

23. They will dwell therein for ages.

24. Nothing cool shall they taste therein, nor any drink,

25. Save a boiling fluid and a fluid, dark, murky, intensely cold,

26. A fitting recompense (for them).

27. For that they used not to fear any account (for their deeds),

28. But they (impudently) treated Our Signs as false.

29. And all things have We preserved on record.

30. "So taste you (the fruits of your deeds); for no

الْجِبَالُ فَكَانَتْ سَرَابًا ۝

إِنَّ جَهَنَّمَ كَانَتْ مِرْصَادًا ۝

لِلطَّاغِينَ مَآبًا ۝ لَّبِثِينَ فِيهَا

أَحْقَابًا ۝ لَا يَذُوقُونَ فِيهَا

بَرْدًا وَّلَا شَرَابًا ۝ إِلَّا حَمِيمًا

وَغَسَّاقًا ۝ جَزَآءً وِّفَاقًا ۝ إِنَّهُمْ

كَانُوا لَا يَرْجُونَ حِسَابًا ۝ وَكَذَّبُوا

بِأٰيٰتِنَا كِذَّابًا ۝ وَكُلَّ شَىْءٍ

أَحْصَيْنٰهُ كِتٰبًا ۝ فَذُوقُوا فَلَنْ

as a means of subsistence?

12. And (have We not) built over you the seven firmaments,

13. And placed (therein) a Light of Splendour?

14. And do We not send down from the clouds water in abundance,

15. That We may produce therewith corn and vegetables,

16. And gardens of luxurious growth?

17. Verily the Day of Sorting out is a thing appointed,

18. The Day that the Trumpet shall be sounded, and you will come forth in crowds;

19. And the heavens shall be opened as if there were doors,

20. And the mountains shall vanish,

مَعَاشًا ۝ وَّبَنَيْنَا فَوْقَكُمْ سَبْعًا

شِدَادًا ۝ وَّجَعَلْنَا سِرَاجًا وَّهَّاجًا ۝

وَّ اَنْزَلْنَا مِنَ الْمُعْصِرٰتِ مَآءً

ثَجَّاجًا ۝ لِّنُخْرِجَ بِهٖ حَبًّا

وَّ نَبَاتًا ۝ وَّ جَنّٰتٍ اَلْفَافًا ۝ اِنَّ

يَوْمَ الْفَصْلِ كَانَ مِيْقَاتًا ۝ يَّوْمَ

يُنْفَخُ فِى الصُّوْرِ فَتَاْتُوْنَ

اَفْوَاجًا ۝ وَّ فُتِحَتِ السَّمَآءُ

فَكَانَتْ اَبْوَابًا ۝ وَّ سُيِّرَتِ

An-Nabaa (The Great News)

Bismillahir-Rahmanir-Rahim

1.   Concerning what are they disputing?

2.   Concerning the Great News,

3.   About which they can not agree.

4.   Verily, they shall soon (come to) know!

5.   Verily, verily they shall soon (come to) know!

6.   Have We not made the earth as a wide expanse,

7.   And the mountains as pegs?

8.   And (have We not) created you in pairs,

9.   And made your sleep for rest,

10.   And made the night as a covering,

11.   And made the day

بِسْمِ اللهِ الرَّحْمٰنِ الرَّحِيمِ

عَمَّ يَتَسَآءَلُونَ ۞ عَنِ النَّبَإِ

الْعَظِيمِ ۞ الَّذِى هُمْ فِيهِ

مُخْتَلِفُونَ ۞ كَلَّا سَيَعْلَمُونَ ۞

ثُمَّ كَلَّا سَيَعْلَمُونَ ۞ أَلَمْ نَجْعَلِ

الْأَرْضَ مِهَادًا ۞ وَّالْجِبَالَ

أَوْتَادًا ۞ وَّخَلَقْنٰكُمْ أَزْوَاجًا ۞

وَّجَعَلْنَا نَوْمَكُمْ سُبَاتًا ۞ وَّجَعَلْنَا

الَّيْلَ لِبَاسًا ۞ وَّجَعَلْنَا النَّهَارَ

مكتبة الله الرحمة

پارہ

عمّ

(۳۰)

الْعَدُونَ ۞ وَالَّذِينَ هُمْ لِأَمَنَٰتِهِمْ

وَعَهْدِهِمْ رَاعُونَ ۞ وَالَّذِينَ هُمْ

عَلَىٰ صَلَوَٰتِهِمْ يُحَافِظُونَ ۞ أُو۟لَٰٓئِكَ

هُمُ الْوَٰرِثُونَ ۞ الَّذِينَ يَرِثُونَ

الْفِرْدَوْسَ هُمْ فِيهَا خَٰلِدُونَ ۞

وَلَقَدْ خَلَقْنَا الْإِنسَٰنَ مِن سُلَٰلَةٍ

مِّن طِينٍ ۞ ثُمَّ جَعَلْنَٰهُ نُطْفَةً

فِى قَرَارٍ مَّكِينٍ ۞ ثُمَّ خَلَقْنَا

النُّطْفَةَ عَلَقَةً فَخَلَقْنَا الْعَلَقَةَ

Al-Mu'minoon
(The Believers)

Bismillahir-Rahmanir-Rahim

1.   The believers must (eventually) win through, -

2.   Those who humble themselves in their Prayers;

3.   Who avoid vain talk;

4.   Who are active in deeds of Charity;

5.   Who abstain from sex,

6.   Except with those joined to them in the marriage bond, or (the captives) whom their right hands possess, - for (in their case) they are free from blame,

7.   But those whose desires exceed those limits are

بِسْمِ اللهِ الرَّحْمٰنِ الرَّحِيْمِ   سُوْرَةُ الْمُؤْمِنُوْنَ مَكِّيَّةٌ   اٰيَاتُهَا ١١٨ رُكُوْعَاتُهَا ٦

قَدْ اَفْلَحَ الْمُؤْمِنُوْنَ ۙ الَّذِيْنَ

هُمْ فِيْ صَلَاتِهِمْ خَاشِعُوْنَ ۙ وَالَّذِيْنَ

هُمْ عَنِ اللَّغْوِ مُعْرِضُوْنَ ۙ وَالَّذِيْنَ

هُمْ لِلزَّكٰوةِ فَاعِلُوْنَ ۙ وَالَّذِيْنَ

هُمْ لِفُرُوْجِهِمْ حٰفِظُوْنَ ۙ اِلَّا عَلٰى

اَزْوَاجِهِمْ اَوْ مَا مَلَكَتْ اَيْمَانُهُمْ

فَاِنَّهُمْ غَيْرُ مَلُوْمِيْنَ ۚ فَمَنِ

ابْتَغٰى وَرَآءَ ذٰلِكَ فَاُولٰٓئِكَ هُمُ

پاره

قَدْ اَفْلَحَ

(۱۸)

PART 19
Wa Qaalal-Ladhina

(grossly) ignorant!"

56. But his people gave no other answer but this: they said, "Drive out the followers of Lut from your city: these are indeed men who want to be clean and pure!"

57. But We saved him and his family, except his wife; her We destined to be of those who lagged behind.

58. And We rained down on them a shower (of brimstone): and evil was the shower on those who were admonished (but heeded not)!

59. Say: Praise be to Allah, and Peace on His servants whom He has chosen (for His Message). (Who) is better? - Allah or the false gods they associate (with Him)?

تَجْهَلُونَ ۞ فَمَا كَانَ جَوَابَ

قَوْمِهِ إِلَّا أَنْ قَالُوْۤا أَخْرِجُوْۤا اٰلَ

لُوْطٍ مِّنْ قَرْيَتِكُمْ ۚ إِنَّهُمْ أُنَاسٌ

يَّتَطَهَّرُوْنَ ۞ فَأَنْجَيْنٰهُ وَأَهْلَهٗۤ إِلَّا

امْرَأَتَهٗ ۖ قَدَّرْنٰهَا مِنَ الْغٰبِرِيْنَ ۞

وَأَمْطَرْنَا عَلَيْهِمْ مَّطَرًا ۚ فَسَآءَ

مَطَرُ الْمُنْذَرِيْنَ ۞ قُلِ الْحَمْدُ

لِلّٰهِ وَسَلٰمٌ عَلٰى عِبَادِهِ الَّذِيْنَ

اصْطَفٰى ۗ آٰللّٰهُ خَيْرٌ أَمَّا يُشْرِكُوْنَ ۞

Was the end of their plot! - this, that We destroyed them and their people, all (of them).

52. Now such were their houses, - in utter ruin, - because they practised wrong-doing. Verily in this is a Sign for people of knowledge.

53. And We saved those who believed and practised righteousness.

54. (We also sent) Lut (as an Apostle): behold, He said to his people, "Do you do what is shameful though you see (its iniquity)?"

55. "Would you really approach men in your lusts rather than women? No, you are a people

كَانَ عَاقِبَةُ مَكْرِهِمْ أَنَّا دَمَّرْنَاهُمْ

وَقَوْمَهُمْ أَجْمَعِيْنَ ۞ فَتِلْكَ بُيُوتُهُمْ

خَاوِيَةً بِمَا ظَلَمُوْا ۗ إِنَّ فِيْ ذَٰلِكَ

لَآيَةً لِّقَوْمٍ يَّعْلَمُوْنَ ۞ وَأَنْجَيْنَا

الَّذِيْنَ أَمَنُوْا وَكَانُوْا يَتَّقُوْنَ ۞

وَلُوْطًا إِذْ قَالَ لِقَوْمِهٖٓ أَتَأْتُوْنَ

الْفَاحِشَةَ وَأَنْتُمْ تُبْصِرُوْنَ ۞ أَئِنَّكُمْ

لَتَأْتُوْنَ الرِّجَالَ شَهْوَةً مِّنْ

دُوْنِ النِّسَآءِ ۚ بَلْ أَنْتُمْ قَوْمٌ

He said: "Your ill omen is with Allah; yes, you are a people under trial."

48. There were in the city nine men of a family, who made mischief in the land, and would not reform.

49. They said: "Swear a mutual oath by Allah that we shall make a secret night attack on him and his people, and that we shall then say to his heir (when he seeks vengeance): 'We were not present at the slaughter of his people, and we are positively telling the truth.'"

50. They plotted and planned, but We too planned, even while they perceived it not.

51. Then see what

قَالَ طَائِرُكُمْ عِنْدَ اللهِ بَلْ

أَنْتُمْ قَوْمٌ تُفْتَنُوْنَ ۝ وَكَانَ فِى

الْمَدِيْنَةِ تِسْعَةُ رَهْطٍ يُفْسِدُوْنَ

فِى الْأَرْضِ وَلَا يُصْلِحُوْنَ ۝ قَالُوْا

تَقَاسَمُوْا بِاللهِ لَنُبَيِّتَنَّهٗ وَأَهْلَهٗ

ثُمَّ لَنَقُوْلَنَّ لِوَلِيِّهٖ مَا شَهِدْنَا

مَهْلِكَ أَهْلِهٖ وَإِنَّا لَصَادِقُوْنَ ۝

وَمَكَرُوْا مَكْرًا وَّمَكَرْنَا مَكْرًا

وَّهُمْ لَا يَشْعُرُوْنَ ۝ فَانْظُرْ كَيْفَ

She said: "O my Lord! I have indeed wronged my soul: I do (now) submit (in Islam), with Solomon, to the Lord of the Worlds."

45. We sent (aforetime), to the Thamud, their brother Salih, saying, "Serve Allah": but behold, they became two factions quarrelling with each other.

46. He said: "O my people! Why ask you to hasten on the evil in preference to the good? If only you ask Allah for forgiveness, you may hope to receive mercy."

47. They said: "Ill omen do we augur from you and those that are with you."

قَالَتْ رَبِّ إِنِّي ظَلَمْتُ نَفْسِي

وَأَسْلَمْتُ مَعَ سُلَيْمَٰنَ لِلَّهِ رَبِّ

الْعَٰلَمِينَ ۝ وَلَقَدْ أَرْسَلْنَا إِلَىٰ ثَمُودَ

أَخَاهُمْ صَٰلِحًا أَنِ اعْبُدُوا اللَّهَ

فَإِذَا هُمْ فَرِيقَانِ يَخْتَصِمُونَ ۝

قَالَ يَٰقَوْمِ لِمَ تَسْتَعْجِلُونَ

بِالسَّيِّئَةِ قَبْلَ الْحَسَنَةِ لَوْلَا

تَسْتَغْفِرُونَ اللَّهَ لَعَلَّكُمْ تُرْحَمُونَ ۝

قَالُوا اطَّيَّرْنَا بِكَ وَبِمَن مَّعَكَ

she arrived, she was asked, "Is this your throne?" She said, "It was just like this; and knowledge was bestowed on us in advance of this, and we have submitted to Allah (in Islam)."

43. And he diverted her from the worship of others besides Allah: for she was (sprung) of a people that had no faith.

44. She was asked to enter the lofty palace: but when she saw it, she thought it was a lake of water, and she (tucked up her skirts), uncovering her legs. He said: "This is but a palace paved smooth with slabs of glass."

جَآءَتْ قِيلَ أَهَٰكَذَا عَرْشُكِ

قَالَتْ كَأَنَّهُ هُوَ وَأُوتِينَا الْعِلْمَ

مِن قَبْلِهَا وَكُنَّا مُسْلِمِينَ ۝

وَصَدَّهَا مَا كَانَت تَّعْبُدُ مِن

دُونِ اللَّهِ إِنَّهَا كَانَتْ مِن

قَوْمٍ كَٰفِرِينَ ۝ قِيلَ لَهَا ادْخُلِي

الصَّرْحَ فَلَمَّا رَأَتْهُ حَسِبَتْهُ

لُجَّةً وَكَشَفَتْ عَن سَاقَيْهَا قَالَ

إِنَّهُ صَرْحٌ مُّمَرَّدٌ مِّن قَوَارِيرَ

"I will bring it to you within the twinkling of an eye!" Then when (Solomon) saw it placed firmly before him, he said: "This is by the Grace of my Lord! - to test me whether I am grateful or ungrateful! and if any is grateful, truly his gratitude is (a gain) for his own soul; but if any is ungrateful, truly my Lord is Free of all Needs, Supreme in Honour!"

41. He said: "Disguise her throne, let us see whether she is guided (to the truth) or is one of those who receive no guidance."

42. So when

اٰنَا اٰتِيْكَ بِهٖ قَبْلَ اَنْ يَّرْتَدَّ

اِلَيْكَ طَرْفُكَ ۚ فَلَمَّا رَاٰهُ مُسْتَقِرًّا

عِنْدَهٗ قَالَ هٰذَا مِنْ فَضْلِ

رَبِّيْ ۚ لِيَبْلُوَنِيْ ءَاَشْكُرُ اَمْ اَكْفُرُ ۗ

وَمَنْ شَكَرَ فَاِنَّمَا يَشْكُرُ لِنَفْسِهٖ ۚ

وَمَنْ كَفَرَ فَاِنَّ رَبِّيْ غَنِيٌّ

كَرِيْمٌ ۞ قَالَ نَكِّرُوْا لَهَا عَرْشَهَا

نَنْظُرْ اَتَهْتَدِيْۤ اَمْ تَكُوْنُ مِنَ

الَّذِيْنَ لَا يَهْتَدُوْنَ ۞ فَلَمَّا

to them, and be sure we shall come to them with such hosts as they will never be able to meet: we shall expel them from there in disgrace, and they will feel humbled (indeed)."

38. He said (to his own men): "You chiefs! Which of you can bring me her throne before they come to me in submission?"

39. Said an 'Ifrit, of the Jinns: "I will bring it to you before you rise from your council: indeed I have full strength for the purpose, and may be trusted."

40. Said one who had knowledge of the Book:

اِلَيْهِمْ فَلَنَأْتِيَنَّهُمْ بِجُنُودٍ لَّا قِبَلَ

لَهُمْ بِهَا وَلَنُخْرِجَنَّهُمْ مِّنْهَآ اَذِلَّةً

وَّهُمْ صٰغِرُوْنَ ۞ قَالَ يٰٓاَيُّهَا

الْمَلَؤُا اَيُّكُمْ يَأْتِيْنِيْ بِعَرْشِهَا

قَبْلَ اَنْ يَّأْتُوْنِيْ مُسْلِمِيْنَ ۞ قَالَ

عِفْرِيْتٌ مِّنَ الْجِنِّ اَنَا اٰتِيْكَ

بِهٖ قَبْلَ اَنْ تَقُوْمَ مِنْ مَّقَامِكَ

وَاِنِّيْ عَلَيْهِ لَقَوِيٌّ اَمِيْنٌ ۞ قَالَ

الَّذِيْ عِنْدَهٗ عِلْمٌ مِّنَ الْكِتٰبِ

you will command."

34. She said: "Kings, when they enter a country, despoil it, and make the noblest of its people its meanest; thus do they behave."

35. "But I am going to send him a present, and (wait) to see with what (answer) return (my) ambassadors."

36. Now when (the embassy) came to Solomon, he said: "Will you give me abundance in wealth? But that which Allah has given me is better than that which He has given you! No it is you who rejoice in your gift!"

37. "Go back

تَامُرِيْنَ ۩ قَالَتْ اِنَّ الْمُلُوْكَ اِذَا

دَخَلُوْا قَرْيَةً اَفْسَدُوْهَا وَجَعَلُوْا

اَعِزَّةَ اَهْلِهَا اَذِلَّةً ۚ وَكَذٰلِكَ

يَفْعَلُوْنَ ۩ وَاِنِّيْ مُرْسِلَةٌ اِلَيْهِمْ

بِهَدِيَّةٍ فَنٰظِرَةٌۢ بِمَ يَرْجِعُ

الْمُرْسَلُوْنَ ۩ فَلَمَّا جَآءَ سُلَيْمٰنَ

قَالَ اَتُمِدُّوْنَنِ بِمَالٍ فَمَآ اٰتٰىنَ

اللّٰهُ خَيْرٌ مِّمَّآ اٰتٰىكُمْ ۚ بَلْ

اَنْتُمْ بِهَدِيَّتِكُمْ تَفْرَحُوْنَ ۩ اِرْجِعْ

"You chiefs! Here is - delivered to me - a letter worthy of respect."

30. "It is from Solomon, and is (as follows): 'In the name of Allah, Most Gracious, Most Merciful:'

31. 'Be you not arrogant against me, but come to me in submission (to the true Religion).''

32. She said: "You chiefs! Advise me in (this) my affair: no affair have I decided except in your presence."

33. They said: "We are endued with strength, and given to vehement war: but the command is with you; so consider what

يَآيُّهَا الْمَلَؤُا اِنِّيٓ اُلْقِيَ اِلَيَّ كِتٰبٌ

كَرِيْمٌ ۲۹ اِنَّهٗ مِنْ سُلَيْمٰنَ وَاِنَّهٗ

بِسْمِ اللّٰهِ الرَّحْمٰنِ الرَّحِيْمِ ۳۰

اَلَّا تَعْلُوْا عَلَيَّ وَاْتُوْنِيْ مُسْلِمِيْنَ ۳۱

قَالَتْ يَآيُّهَا الْمَلَؤُا اَفْتُوْنِيْ فِيْ

اَمْرِيْ مَا كُنْتُ قَاطِعَةً اَمْرًا

حَتّٰى تَشْهَدُوْنِ ۳۲ قَالُوْا نَحْنُ

اُولُوْا قُوَّةٍ وَّاُولُوْا بَأْسٍ شَدِيْدٍ ۙ

وَّالْاَمْرُ اِلَيْكِ فَانْظُرِيْ مَاذَا

receive no guidance, -

25. "(Kept them away from the path), that they should not worship Allah, Who brings to light what is hidden in the heavens and the earth, and knows what you hide and what you reveal."

26. "Allah! - there is no god but He! - Lord of the Throne Supreme!"

27. (Solomon) said: "Soon shall we see whether you have told the truth or lied!"

28. "Go you, with this letter of mine, and deliver it to them: then draw back from them, and (wait to) see what answer they return".

29. (The queen) said:

لَا يَهْتَدُونَ ۩ أَلَّا يَسْجُدُوا لِلَّهِ

الَّذِي يُخْرِجُ الْخَبْءَ فِي السَّمَاوَاتِ

وَالْأَرْضِ وَيَعْلَمُ مَا تُخْفُونَ وَمَا

تُعْلِنُونَ ۩ اللَّهُ لَا إِلَهَ إِلَّا هُوَ

رَبُّ الْعَرْشِ الْعَظِيمِ ۩ قَالَ

سَنَنْظُرُ أَصَدَقْتَ أَمْ كُنْتَ مِنَ

الْكَاذِبِينَ ۩ اذْهَبْ بِكِتَابِي هَذَا

فَأَلْقِهْ إِلَيْهِمْ ثُمَّ تَوَلَّ عَنْهُمْ

فَانْظُرْ مَاذَا يَرْجِعُونَ ۩ قَالَتْ

he bring me a clear reason (for absence)."

22. But the Hoopoe tarried not far: he (came up and) said: "I have compassed (territory) which you have not compassed, and I have come to you from Saba with tidings true."

23. "I found (there) a woman ruling over them and provided with every requisite; and she has a magnificent throne."

24. "I found her and her people worshipping the sun besides Allah: Satan has made their deeds seem pleasing in their eyes, and has kept them away from the path, - so they

لَيَأْتِيَنِّيْ بِسُلْطٰنٍ مُّبِيْنٍ ۞ فَمَكَثَ

غَيْرَ بَعِيْدٍ فَقَالَ اَحَطْتُّ بِمَا لَمْ

تُحِطْ بِهٖ وَجِئْتُكَ مِنْ سَبَاٍ

بِنَبَاٍ يَّقِيْنٍ ۞ اِنِّيْ وَجَدْتُّ امْرَاَةً

تَمْلِكُهُمْ وَاُوْتِيَتْ مِنْ كُلِّ شَىْءٍ

وَّلَهَا عَرْشٌ عَظِيْمٌ ۞ وَجَدْتُّهَا

وَقَوْمَهَا يَسْجُدُوْنَ لِلشَّمْسِ مِنْ

دُوْنِ اللّٰهِ وَزَيَّنَ لَهُمُ الشَّيْطٰنُ

اَعْمَالَهُمْ فَصَدَّهُمْ عَنِ السَّبِيْلِ فَهُمْ

without knowing it."

19. So he smiled, amused at her speech; and he said: "O my Lord! So order me that I may be grateful for Your favours, which You have bestowed on me and on my parents, and that I may work the righteousness that will please You: and admit me, by Your Grace, to the ranks of Your righteous servants."

20. And he took a muster of the Birds; and he said: "Why is it I see not the Hoopoe? Or is he among the absentees?"

21. "I will certainly punish him with a severe penalty or execute him, unless

لَا يَشْعُرُونَ ۞ فَتَبَسَّمَ ضَاحِكًا

مِّن قَوْلِهَا وَقَالَ رَبِّ أَوْزِعْنِي

أَنْ أَشْكُرَ نِعْمَتَكَ الَّتِي أَنْعَمْتَ

عَلَيَّ وَعَلَى وَالِدَيَّ وَأَنْ أَعْمَلَ

صَالِحًا تَرْضَاهُ وَأَدْخِلْنِي بِرَحْمَتِكَ

فِي عِبَادِكَ الصَّالِحِينَ ۞ وَتَفَقَّدَ

الطَّيْرَ فَقَالَ مَا لِيَ لَا أَرَى الْهُدْهُدَ

أَمْ كَانَ مِنَ الْغَائِبِينَ ۞ لَأُعَذِّبَنَّهُ

عَذَابًا شَدِيدًا أَوْ لَأَاذْبَحَنَّهُ أَوْ

16.   And Solomon was David's heir. He said: "O you people! We have been taught the speech of birds, and on us has been bestowed (a little) of all things: this is indeed Grace manifest (from Allah.)"

17.   And before Solomon were marshalled his hosts, - of Jinns and men and birds, and they were all kept in order and ranks.

18.   At length, when they came to a (lowly) valley of ants, one of the ants said: "O ants, get into your habitations, lest Solomon and his hosts crush you (under foot)

وَوَرِثَ سُلَيْمَٰنُ دَاوُۥدَ وَقَالَ يَٰٓأَيُّهَا
النَّاسُ عُلِّمْنَا مَنطِقَ الطَّيْرِ
وَأُوتِينَا مِن كُلِّ شَىْءٍ إِنَّ هَٰذَا
لَهُوَ الْفَضْلُ الْمُبِينُ ۝ وَحُشِرَ
لِسُلَيْمَٰنَ جُنُودُهُۥ مِنَ الْجِنِّ وَالْإِنسِ
وَالطَّيْرِ فَهُمْ يُوزَعُونَ ۝ حَتَّىٰٓ إِذَآ
أَتَوْا عَلَىٰ وَادِ النَّمْلِ قَالَتْ نَمْلَةٌ
يَٰٓأَيُّهَا النَّمْلُ ادْخُلُوا مَسَٰكِنَكُمْ لَا
يَحْطِمَنَّكُمْ سُلَيْمَٰنُ وَجُنُودُهُۥ وَهُمْ

and his people: for they are a people rebellious in transgression."

13. But when Our Signs came to them, that should have opened their eyes, they said: "This is sorcery manifest!"

14. And they rejected those Signs in iniquity and arrogance, though their souls were convinced thereof: so see what was the end of those who acted corruptly!

15. We gave (in the past) knowledge to David and Solomon: and they both said: "Praise be to Allah, Who has favoured us above many of his servants who believe!"

وَقَوْمَهُ اِنَّهُمْ كَانُوا قَوْمًا فٰسِقِينَ ۞

فَلَمَّا جَآءَتْهُمْ اٰيٰتُنَا مُبْصِرَةً

قَالُوْا هٰذَا سِحْرٌ مُّبِيْنٌ ۞

وَجَحَدُوْا بِهَا وَاسْتَيْقَنَتْهَآ

اَنْفُسُهُمْ ظُلْمًا وَّعُلُوًّا ۖ فَانْظُرْ

كَيْفَ كَانَ عَاقِبَةُ الْمُفْسِدِيْنَ ۞

وَلَقَدْ اٰتَيْنَا دَاوٗدَ وَسُلَيْمٰنَ عِلْمًا ۖ

وَقَالَا الْحَمْدُ لِلّٰهِ الَّذِيْ فَضَّلَنَا

عَلٰى كَثِيْرٍ مِّنْ عِبَادِهِ الْمُؤْمِنِيْنَ ۞

I am Allah, the Exalted in Might, the Wise!.

10. "Now do you throw your rod!" But when he saw it moving (of its own accord) as if it had been a snake, he turned back in retreat, and retraced not his steps: "O Moses!" (it was said), "Fear not: truly, in My presence, those called as Apostles have no fear," -

11. "But if any have done wrong and have thereafter substituted good to take the place of evil, truly, I am Oft-Forgiving, Most Merciful."

12. "Now put your hand into your bosom, and it will come forth white without stain (or harm): (these are) among the nine Signs (you will take) to Pharaoh

اَنَا اللّٰهُ الْعَزِيزُ الْحَكِيمُ ۞ وَ اَلْقِ

عَصَاكَ ۚ فَلَمَّا رَاٰهَا تَهْتَزُّ كَاَنَّهَا

جَآنٌّ وَّلّٰى مُدْبِرًا وَّلَمْ يُعَقِّبْ

يٰمُوسٰى لَا تَخَفْ ۙ اِنِّى لَا يَخَافُ

لَدَىَّ الْمُرْسَلُوْنَ ۞ اِلَّا مَنْ ظَلَمَ

ثُمَّ بَدَّلَ حُسْنًا بَعْدَ سُوْٓءٍ فَاِنِّى

غَفُوْرٌ رَّحِيْمٌ ۞ وَ اَدْخِلْ يَدَكَ فِى

جَيْبِكَ تَخْرُجْ بَيْضَآءَ مِنْ غَيْرِ

سُوْٓءٍ ۚ فِى تِسْعِ اٰيٰتٍ اِلٰى فِرْعَوْنَ

and in the Hereafter theirs will be the greatest loss.

6.   As to you, the Qur'an is bestowed upon you from the presence of One Who is Wise and All-Knowing.

7.   Behold! Moses said to his family: "I perceive a fire; soon will I bring you from there some information, or I will bring you a burning brand to light our fuel, that you may warm yourselves.

8.   But when he came to the (fire), a voice was heard: "Blessed are those in the fire and those around: and Glory to Allah, the Lord of the Worlds.

9.   "O Moses! Verily,

وَهُمْ فِي الْأَخِرَةِ هُمُ الْأَخْسَرُونَ ۞

وَإِنَّكَ لَتُلَقَّى الْقُرْآنَ مِنْ لَدُنْ

حَكِيمٍ عَلِيمٍ ۞ إِذْ قَالَ مُوسَى

لِأَهْلِهِ إِنِّي آنَسْتُ نَارًا سَآتِيكُمْ

مِنْهَا بِخَبَرٍ أَوْ آتِيكُمْ بِشِهَابٍ

قَبَسٍ لَّعَلَّكُمْ تَصْطَلُونَ ۞ فَلَمَّا

جَاءَهَا نُودِيَ أَنْ بُورِكَ مَنْ

فِي النَّارِ وَمَنْ حَوْلَهَا وَسُبْحَانَ

اللهِ رَبِّ الْعَالَمِينَ ۞ يَا مُوسَى إِنَّهُ

An-Naml (The Ants)

Bismillahir-Rahmanir-Rahim

1.　　Ta. Sin. These are verses of the Qur'an, - a book that makes (things) clear;

2.　　A guide: and glad tidings for the believers, -

3.　　Those who establish regular Prayers and give in regular Charity, and also have (full) assurance of the Hereafter.

4.　　As to those who believe not in the Hereafter, We have made their deeds pleasing in their eyes; and so they wander about in distraction.

5.　Such are they for whom a grievous Chastisement is (waiting);

سُوْرَةُ النَّمْل مَكِّيَّةٌ اٰيَاتُهَا ٩٣ رُكُوْعَاتُهَا ٧
بِسْمِ اللّٰهِ الرَّحْمٰنِ الرَّحِيْمِ

طٰسٓ ۛ تِلْكَ اٰيٰتُ الْقُرْاٰنِ

وَكِتَابٍ مُّبِيْنٍ ۙ هُدًى وَّبُشْرٰى

لِلْمُؤْمِنِيْنَ ۙ الَّذِيْنَ يُقِيْمُوْنَ

الصَّلٰوةَ وَيُؤْتُوْنَ الزَّكٰوةَ وَهُمْ

بِالْاٰخِرَةِ هُمْ يُوْقِنُوْنَ ۞ اِنَّ

الَّذِيْنَ لَا يُؤْمِنُوْنَ بِالْاٰخِرَةِ زَيَّنَّا

لَهُمْ اَعْمَالَهُمْ فَهُمْ يَعْمَهُوْنَ ۞

اُولٰٓئِكَ الَّذِيْنَ لَهُمْ سُوْٓءُ الْعَذَابِ

223. (Into whose ears) they pour hearsay vanities, and most of them are liars.

224. And the Poets, - it is those straying in Evil, who follow them:

225. Do you see not that they wander distracted in every valley? -

226. And that they say what they practise not? -

227. Except those who believe, work righteousness, engage much in the remembrance of Allah, and defend themselves only after they are unjustly attacked. And soon will the unjust assailants know what vicissitudes their affairs will take!

يُلْقُونَ السَّمْعَ وَأَكْثَرُهُمْ كَذِبُونَ ۝

وَالشُّعَرَاءُ يَتَّبِعُهُمُ الْغَاوُونَ ۝ أَلَمْ تَرَ

أَنَّهُمْ فِي كُلِّ وَادٍ يَهِيمُونَ ۝ وَأَنَّهُمْ

يَقُولُونَ مَا لَا يَفْعَلُونَ ۝ إِلَّا

الَّذِينَ آمَنُوا وَعَمِلُوا الصَّالِحَاتِ

وَذَكَرُوا اللَّهَ كَثِيرًا وَّانْتَصَرُوا

مِنْ بَعْدِ مَا ظُلِمُوا ۚ وَسَيَعْلَمُ

الَّذِينَ ظَلَمُوا أَيَّ مُنْقَلَبٍ

يَنْقَلِبُونَ ۝

your wing to the believers who follow you.

216. Then if they disobey you, say: "I am free (of responsibility) for what you do!"

217. And put your trust on the Exalted in Might, the Merciful, -

218. Who sees you standing forth (in prayer),

219. And your movements among those who prostrate themselves,

220. For it is He Who hears and knows all things.

221. Shall I inform you, (O people!), on whom it is that the evil ones descend?

222. They descend on every lying, wicked person,

جَنَاحَكَ لِمَنِ اتَّبَعَكَ مِنَ

الْمُؤْمِنِينَ ۞ فَإِنْ عَصَوْكَ فَقُلْ

إِنِّي بَرِيٓءٌ مِّمَّا تَعْمَلُونَ ۞

وَتَوَكَّلْ عَلَى الْعَزِيزِ الرَّحِيمِ ۞

الَّذِي يَرَاكَ حِينَ تَقُومُ ۞

وَتَقَلُّبَكَ فِي السَّاجِدِينَ ۞ إِنَّهُ هُوَ

السَّمِيعُ الْعَلِيمُ ۞ هَلْ أُنَبِّئُكُمْ

عَلَى مَنْ تَنَزَّلُ الشَّيَاطِينُ ۞

تَنَزَّلُ عَلَى كُلِّ أَفَّاكٍ أَثِيمٍ ۞

they enjoyed (this life)!

208. Never did We destroy a town, but had its warners –

209. By way of reminder; and We never are unjust.

210. No evil ones have brought down this (Revelation):

211. It would neither suit them nor would they be able (to produce it).

212. Indeed they have been removed far from even (a chance of) hearing it.

213. So call not on any other god with Allah, or you will be among those under the Penalty.

214. And admonish your nearest kinsmen,

215. And lower

كَانُوا يَمْتَعُونَ ۞ وَمَا أَهْلَكْنَا

مِنْ قَرْيَةٍ إِلَّا لَهَا مُنْذِرُونَ ۞

ذِكْرَى ۞ وَمَا كُنَّا ظَالِمِينَ ۞ وَمَا

تَنَزَّلَتْ بِهِ الشَّيَاطِينُ ۞ وَمَا

يَنْبَغِي لَهُمْ وَمَا يَسْتَطِيعُونَ ۞

إِنَّهُمْ عَنِ السَّمْعِ لَمَعْزُولُونَ ۞

فَلَا تَدْعُ مَعَ اللهِ إِلَهًا أَخَرَ

فَتَكُونَ مِنَ الْمُعَذَّبِينَ ۞ وَأَنْذِرْ

عَشِيرَتَكَ الْأَقْرَبِينَ ۞ وَاخْفِضْ

to them, they would not have believed in it.

200. Thus have We caused it to enter the hearts of the sinners.

201. They will not believe in it until they see the grievous Chastisement;

202. But the (Chastisement) will come to them of a sudden, while they perceive it not;

203. Then they will say: "Shall we be respited?"

204. Do they then ask for Our Chastisement to be hastened on?

205. See you? If We do let them enjoy (this life) for a few years,

206. Yet there comes to them at length the (Punishment) which they were promised!

207. It will profit them not that

عَلَيْهِمْ مَّا كَانُوْا بِهِ مُؤْمِنِيْنَ ۞

كَذٰلِكَ سَلَكْنٰهُ فِيْ قُلُوْبِ

الْمُجْرِمِيْنَ ۞ لَا يُؤْمِنُوْنَ بِهِ حَتّٰى

يَرَوُا الْعَذَابَ الْأَلِيْمَ ۞ فَيَأْتِيَهُمْ

بَغْتَةً وَّهُمْ لَا يَشْعُرُوْنَ ۞ فَيَقُوْلُوْا

هَلْ نَحْنُ مُنْظَرُوْنَ ۞ أَفَبِعَذَابِنَا

يَسْتَعْجِلُوْنَ ۞ أَفَرَءَيْتَ اِنْ مَّتَّعْنٰهُمْ

سِنِيْنَ ۞ ثُمَّ جَآءَهُمْ مَّا كَانُوْا

يُوْعَدُوْنَ ۞ مَآ أَغْنٰى عَنْهُمْ مَّا

believe.

191. And verily your Lord is He, the Exalted in Might, Most Merciful.

192. Verily this is a Revelation from the Lord of the Worlds:

193. With it came down the spirit of Faith and Truth -

194. To your heart and mind, that you may admonish.

195. In the perspicuous Arabic tongue.

196. Without doubt it is (announced) in the mystic Books of former peoples.

197. Is it not a Sign to them that the Learned of the Children of Israel knew it (as true)?

198. Had We revealed it to any of the non-Arabs,

199. And had he recited it

مُؤْمِنِينَ ۝ وَإِنَّ رَبَّكَ لَهُوَ الْعَزِيزُ

الرَّحِيمُ ۝ وَإِنَّهُ لَتَنْزِيلُ رَبِّ

الْعَالَمِينَ ۝ نَزَلَ بِهِ الرُّوحُ

الْأَمِينُ ۝ عَلَى قَلْبِكَ لِتَكُونَ

مِنَ الْمُنْذِرِينَ ۝ بِلِسَانٍ عَرَبِيٍّ

مُبِينٍ ۝ وَإِنَّهُ لَفِي زُبُرِ الْأَوَّلِينَ

أَوَلَمْ يَكُنْ لَهُمْ آيَةً أَنْ يَعْلَمَهُ

عُلَمَاءُ بَنِي إِسْرَائِيلَ ۝ وَلَوْ نَزَّلْنَاهُ

عَلَى بَعْضِ الْأَعْجَمِينَ ۝ فَقَرَأَهُ

before (you)."

185. They said: "You are only one of those bewitched!"

186. "You are no more than a mortal like us, and indeed we think you are a liar!"

187. "Now cause a piece of the sky to fall on us, if you are truthful!"

188. He said: "My Lord knows best what you do."

189. But they rejected him. Then the punishment of a day of over-shadowing gloom seized them, and that was the Chastisement of a Great Day.

190. Verily in that is a Sign: but most of them do not

الْأَوَّلِينَ ۞ قَالُوٓا إِنَّمَآ أَنتَ مِنَ

الْمُسَحَّرِينَ ۞ وَمَآ أَنتَ إِلَّا بَشَرٌ

مِّثْلُنَا وَإِن نَّظُنُّكَ لَمِنَ الْكَٰذِبِينَ ۞

فَأَسْقِطْ عَلَيْنَا كِسَفًا مِّنَ السَّمَآءِ

إِن كُنتَ مِنَ الصَّٰدِقِينَ ۞ قَالَ

رَبِّىٓ أَعْلَمُ بِمَا تَعْمَلُونَ ۞ فَكَذَّبُوهُ

فَأَخَذَهُمْ عَذَابُ يَوْمِ الظُّلَّةِ إِنَّهُۥ

كَانَ عَذَابَ يَوْمٍ عَظِيمٍ ۞ إِنَّ

فِى ذَٰلِكَ لَءَايَةً وَمَا كَانَ أَكْثَرُهُم

178. "I am to you an Apostle worthy of all trust."

179. "So fear Allah and obey me.

180. "No reward do I ask of you for it: my reward is only from the Lord of the Worlds."

181. "Give just measure, and cause no loss (to others by fraud).

182. "And weigh with scales true and upright."

183. "And withhold not things justly due to men, nor do evil in the land, working mischief."

184. "And fear Him Who created you and (Who created) the generations

إِنِّي لَكُمْ رَسُولٌ أَمِينٌ ۝ فَاتَّقُوا

اللَّهَ وَأَطِيعُونِ ۝ وَمَا أَسْئَلُكُمْ

عَلَيْهِ مِنْ أَجْرٍ ۖ إِنْ أَجْرِيَ إِلَّا

عَلَىٰ رَبِّ الْعَٰلَمِينَ ۝ أَوْفُوا الْكَيْلَ

وَلَا تَكُونُوا مِنَ الْمُخْسِرِينَ ۝

وَزِنُوا بِالْقِسْطَاسِ الْمُسْتَقِيمِ ۝

وَلَا تَبْخَسُوا النَّاسَ أَشْيَاءَهُمْ وَلَا

تَعْثَوْا فِي الْأَرْضِ مُفْسِدِينَ ۝

وَاتَّقُوا الَّذِي خَلَقَكُمْ وَالْجِبِلَّةَ

and my family from such things as they do!"

170. So We delivered him and his family, - all

171. Except an old woman who lingered behind.

172. But the rest We destroyed utterly.

173. We rained down on them a shower (of brimstone): and evil was the shower on those who were admonished (but heeded not)!

174. Verily in this is a Sign: but most of them do not believe.

175. And verily your Lord is He, the Exalted in Might Most Merciful.

176. The Companions of the Wood rejected the Apostles.

177. Behold, Shu'aib said to them: "Will you not fear (Allah)?"

وَأَهْلِى مِمَّا يَعْمَلُونَ ۞ فَنَجَّيْنٰهُ

وَأَهْلَهُ أَجْمَعِينَ ۞ إِلَّا عَجُوزًا فِى

الْغٰبِرِينَ ۞ ثُمَّ دَمَّرْنَا الْأٰخَرِينَ ۞

وَأَمْطَرْنَا عَلَيْهِمْ مَّطَرًا ۚ فَسَآءَ مَطَرُ

الْمُنْذَرِينَ ۞ إِنَّ فِى ذٰلِكَ لَأٰيَةً ۖ

وَمَا كَانَ أَكْثَرُهُمْ مُّؤْمِنِينَ ۞

وَإِنَّ رَبَّكَ لَهُوَ الْعَزِيزُ الرَّحِيمُ ۞

كَذَّبَ أَصْحٰبُ لْئَيْكَةِ الْمُرْسَلِينَ ۞

إِذْ قَالَ لَهُمْ شُعَيْبٌ أَلَا تَتَّقُونَ ۞

Allah and obey me."

164. "No reward do I ask of you for it: my reward is only from the Lord of the Worlds."

165. "Of all the creatures in the world, will you approach males,"

166. "And leave those whom Allah has created for you to be your mates? No, you are a people transgressing (all limits)!"

167. They said: "If you desist not, O Lut! you will assuredly be cast out!"

168. He said: "I do detest your doings."

169. "O my Lord! Deliver me

اللهَ وَ اَطِيعُونِ ۞ وَمَاۤ اَسْئَلُكُمْ

عَلَيْهِ مِنْ اَجْرٍ ۚ اِنْ اَجْرِىَ اِلَّا

عَلَىٰ رَبِّ الْعٰلَمِيْنَ ۞ اَتَاْتُوْنَ

الذُّكْرَانَ مِنَ الْعٰلَمِيْنَ ۞ وَتَذَرُوْنَ

مَا خَلَقَ لَكُمْ رَبُّكُمْ مِّنْ اَزْوَاجِكُمْ ؕ

بَلْ اَنْتُمْ قَوْمٌ عٰدُوْنَ ۞ قَالُوْا

لَئِنْ لَّمْ تَنْتَهِ يٰلُوْطُ لَتَكُوْنَنَّ

مِنَ الْمُخْرَجِيْنَ ۞ قَالَ اِنِّى لِعَمَلِكُمْ

مِّنَ الْقَالِيْنَ ؕ رَبِّ نَجِّنِى

with harm, lest the Chastisement of a Great Day seize you."

157. But they ham-strung her: then did they become full of regrets.

158. But the Chastisement seized them. Verily in this is a Sign: but most of them do not believe.

159. And verily your Lord is He, the Exalted in Might, Most Merciful.

160. The people of Lut rejected the Apostles.

161. Behold, their brother Lut said to them: "Will you not fear (Allah)?"

162. "I am to you an Apostle worthy of all trust."

163. "So fear

بِسُوٓءٍ فَيَأْخُذَكُمْ عَذَابُ يَوْمٍ

عَظِيمٍ ۞ فَعَقَرُوهَا فَأَصْبَحُوا

نَادِمِينَ ۞ فَأَخَذَهُمُ الْعَذَابُ

إِنَّ فِي ذَٰلِكَ لَأَيَةً ۗ وَمَا كَانَ

أَكْثَرُهُمْ مُؤْمِنِينَ ۞ وَإِنَّ رَبَّكَ

لَهُوَ الْعَزِيزُ الرَّحِيمُ ۞ كَذَّبَتْ

قَوْمُ لُوطٍ الْمُرْسَلِينَ ۞ إِذْ قَالَ

لَهُمْ أَخُوهُمْ لُوطٌ أَلَا تَتَّقُونَ ۞

إِنِّي لَكُمْ رَسُولٌ أَمِينٌ ۞ فَاتَّقُوا

with great skill."

150. "But fear Allah and obey me;"

151. "And follow not the bidding of those who are extravagant,"-

152. "Who make mischief in the land, and mend not (their ways)."

153. They said: "You are only one of those bewitched!"

154. "You are no more than a mortal like us: then bring us a Sign, if you tell the truth!"

155. He said: "Here is a she-camel: she has a right of watering, and you have a right of watering, (severally) on a day appointed."

156. "Touch her not

بُيُوتًا فَرِهِينَ ۞ فَاتَّقُوا اللَّهَ

وَأَطِيعُونِ ۞ وَلَا تُطِيعُوا أَمْرَ

الْمُسْرِفِينَ ۞ الَّذِينَ يُفْسِدُونَ

فِي الْأَرْضِ وَلَا يُصْلِحُونَ ۞ قَالُوا

إِنَّمَا أَنْتَ مِنَ الْمُسَحَّرِينَ ۞ مَا

أَنْتَ إِلَّا بَشَرٌ مِثْلُنَا فَأْتِ بِآيَةٍ

إِنْ كُنْتَ مِنَ الصَّادِقِينَ ۞ قَالَ

هَٰذِهِ نَاقَةٌ لَهَا شِرْبٌ وَلَكُمْ

شِرْبُ يَوْمٍ مَعْلُومٍ ۞ وَلَا تَمَسُّوهَا

the Apostles.

142. Behold, their brother Salih said to them: "Will you not fear (Allah)?"

143. "I am to you an Apostle worthy of all trust."

144. "So fear Allah, and obey me."

145. "No reward do I ask of you for it: my reward is only from the Lord of the Worlds."

146. "Will you be left secure, in (the enjoyment of) all that you have here?" -

147. "Gardens and Springs,"

148. "And corn-fields and date-palms with spathes near breaking (with the weight of fruit)?"

149. "And you carve houses out of (rocky) mountains

ثَمُودُ الْمُرْسَلِينَ ۝ إِذْ قَالَ لَهُمْ

أَخُوهُمْ صَلِحٌ أَلَا تَتَّقُونَ ۝ إِنِّي

لَكُمْ رَسُولٌ أَمِينٌ ۝ فَاتَّقُوا اللَّهَ

وَأَطِيعُونِ ۝ وَمَا أَسْئَلُكُمْ عَلَيْهِ

مِنْ أَجْرٍ إِنْ أَجْرِيَ إِلَّا عَلَى

رَبِّ الْعَلَمِينَ ۝ أَتُتْرَكُونَ فِي

مَا هَهُنَا آمِنِينَ ۝ فِي جَنَّاتٍ

وَعُيُونٍ ۝ وَزُرُوعٍ وَنَخْلٍ طَلْعُهَا

هَضِيمٌ ۝ وَتَنْحِتُونَ مِنَ الْجِبَالِ

cattle and sons,"-

134. "And gardens and springs."

135. "Truly I fear for you the Chastisement of a Great Day,"

136. They said: "It is the same to us whether you admonish us or be not among (our) admonishers!"

137. "This is no other than a customary device of the ancients,"

138. "And we are not the ones to receive Pains and Penalties!"

139. So they rejected him, and We destroyed them. Verily in this is a Sign: but most of them do not believe.

140. And verily your Lord is He, the Exalted in Might, Most Merciful.

141. The Thamud (people) rejected

بِاَنْعَامٍ وَّبَنِيْنَ ۞ وَجَنّٰتٍ وَّعُيُوْنٍ ۞

اِنِّيْٓ اَخَافُ عَلَيْكُمْ عَذَابَ يَوْمٍ

عَظِيْمٍ ۞ قَالُوْا سَوَآءٌ عَلَيْنَآ اَوَعَظْتَ

اَمْ لَمْ تَكُنْ مِّنَ الْوٰعِظِيْنَ ۞

اِنْ هٰذَآ اِلَّا خُلُقُ الْاَوَّلِيْنَ ۞

وَمَا نَحْنُ بِمُعَذَّبِيْنَ ۞ فَكَذَّبُوْهُ

فَاَهْلَكْنٰهُمْ ط اِنَّ فِيْ ذٰلِكَ لَاٰيَةً ط

وَمَا كَانَ اَكْثَرُهُمْ مُّؤْمِنِيْنَ ۞ وَاِنَّ

رَبَّكَ لَهُوَ الْعَزِيْزُ الرَّحِيْمُ ۞ كَذَّبَتْ

fear (Allah)?"

125. "I am to you an Apostle worthy of all trust:"

126. "So fear Allah and obey me."

127. "No reward do I ask of you for it: my reward is only from the Lord of the Worlds."

128. "Do you build a landmark on every high place to amuse yourselves?"

129. "And do you get for yourselves fine buildings in the hope of living therein (for ever)?"

130. "And when you strike, you strike like tyrants."

131. "Now fear Allah, and obey me."

132. "Yes, fear Him Who has bestowed on you freely all that you know."

133. "Freely has He bestowed on you

تَتَّقُوْنَ ۝ اِنِّیْ لَکُمْ رَسُوْلٌ اَمِیْنٌ ۝

فَاتَّقُوا اللّٰهَ وَاَطِیْعُوْنِ ۝ وَمَاۤ

اَسْـَٔلُکُمْ عَلَیْهِ مِنْ اَجْرٍ اِنْ اَجْرِیَ

اِلَّا عَلٰی رَبِّ الْعٰلَمِیْنَ ۝ اَتَبْنُوْنَ

بِکُلِّ رِیْعٍ اٰیَةً تَعْبَثُوْنَ ۝ وَتَتَّخِذُوْنَ

مَصَانِعَ لَعَلَّکُمْ تَخْلُدُوْنَ ۝ وَاِذَا

بَطَشْتُمْ بَطَشْتُمْ جَبَّارِیْنَ ۝ فَاتَّقُوا

اللّٰهَ وَاَطِیْعُوْنِ ۝ وَاتَّقُوا الَّذِیْۤ

اَمَدَّکُمْ بِمَا تَعْلَمُوْنَ ۝ اَمَدَّکُمْ

stoned (to death)."

117. He said: "O my Lord! Truly my people have rejected me."

118. "Judge You, then, between me and them openly, and deliver me and those of the believers who are with me."

119. So We delivered him and those with him, in the Ark filled (with all creatures).

120. Thereafter We drowned those who remained behind.

121. Verily in this is a Sign: but most of them do not believe.

122. And verily your Lord is He, the Exalted in Might, Most Merciful.

123. The 'Ad (people) rejected the Apostles.

124. Behold, their brother Hud said to them: "Will you not

الْمَرْجُومِينَ ۱۱۶ قَالَ رَبِّ إِنَّ قَوْمِي

كَذَّبُونِ ۱۱۷ فَافْتَحْ بَيْنِي وَبَيْنَهُمْ فَتْحًا

وَنَجِّنِي وَمَنْ مَعِيَ مِنَ الْمُؤْمِنِينَ ۱۱۸

فَأَنْجَيْنَاهُ وَمَنْ مَعَهُ فِي الْفُلْكِ

الْمَشْحُونِ ۱۱۹ ثُمَّ أَغْرَقْنَا بَعْدُ الْبَاقِينَ

۱۲۰ إِنَّ فِي ذَلِكَ لَآيَةً وَمَا كَانَ أَكْثَرُهُمْ

مُؤْمِنِينَ ۱۲۱ وَإِنَّ رَبَّكَ لَهُوَ الْعَزِيزُ

الرَّحِيمُ ۱۲۲ كَذَّبَتْ عَادٌ الْمُرْسَلِينَ

۱۲۳ إِذْ قَالَ لَهُمْ أَخُوهُمْ هُودٌ أَلَا

for it: my reward is only from the Lord of the Worlds:"

110. "So fear Allah, and obey me."

111. They said: "Shall we believe in you when it is the meanest that follow you?"

112. He said: "And what do I know as to what they do?"

113. "Their account is only with my Lord, if you could (but) understand."

114. "I am not one to drive away those who believe."

115. "I am sent only to warn plainly in public."

116. They said: "If you desist not, O Noah! you shall be

عَلَيْهِ مِنْ أَجْرٍ إِنْ أَجْرِيَ إِلَّا عَلَى

رَبِّ الْعَالَمِينَ ۞ فَاتَّقُوا اللَّهَ

وَأَطِيعُونِ ۞ قَالُوا أَنُؤْمِنُ لَكَ

وَاتَّبَعَكَ الْأَرْذَلُونَ ۞ قَالَ وَمَا

عِلْمِي بِمَا كَانُوا يَعْمَلُونَ ۞ إِنْ

حِسَابُهُمْ إِلَّا عَلَى رَبِّي لَوْ تَشْعُرُونَ ۞

وَمَا أَنَا بِطَارِدِ الْمُؤْمِنِينَ ۞ إِنْ أَنَا

إِلَّا نَذِيرٌ مُبِينٌ ۞ قَالُوا لَئِنْ

لَّمْ تَنْتَهِ يَا نُوحُ لَتَكُونَنَّ مِنَ

those who were steeped in guilt."

100. "Now, then, we have none to intercede (for us),"

101. "Nor a single friend to feel (for us)."

102. "Now if we only had a chance of return we shall truly be of those who believe!"

103. Verily in this is a Sign but most of them do not believe.

104. "And verily your Lord is He, the Exalted in Might, Most Merciful.

105. The people of Noah rejected the Apostles.

106. Behold, their brother Noah said to them: "Will you not fear (Allah)?"

107. "I am to you an Apostle worthy of all trust:"

108. "So fear Allah, and obey me."

109. "No reward do I ask of you

الْمُجْرِمُونَ ۞ فَمَا لَنَا مِن شَافِعِينَ ۞

وَلَا صَدِيقٍ حَمِيمٍ ۞ فَلَوْ أَنَّ لَنَا

كَرَّةً فَنَكُونَ مِنَ الْمُؤْمِنِينَ ۞ إِنَّ

فِى ذَٰلِكَ لَآيَةً وَمَا كَانَ أَكْثَرُهُم

مُّؤْمِنِينَ ۞ وَإِنَّ رَبَّكَ لَهُوَ الْعَزِيزُ

الرَّحِيمُ ۞ كَذَّبَتْ قَوْمُ نُوحٍ الْمُرْسَلِينَ ۞

إِذْ قَالَ لَهُمْ أَخُوهُمْ نُوحٌ أَلَا

تَتَّقُونَ ۞ إِنِّى لَكُمْ رَسُولٌ أَمِينٌ ۞

فَاتَّقُوا اللَّهَ وَأَطِيعُونِ ۞ وَمَا أَسْئَلُكُمْ

90. "To the righteous, the Garden will be brought near,"

91. "And to those straying in Evil, the Fire will be placed in full view;

92. "And it shall be said to them: 'Where are the (gods) you worshipped -

93. 'Besides Allah? Can they help you or help themselves?'

94. "Then they will be thrown headlong into the (Fire), - they and those straying in Evil,

95. "And the whole hosts of Iblis together.

96. "They will say there in their mutual bickerings:

97. "'By Allah, we were truly in an error manifest,

98. "'When we held you as equals with the Lord of the Worlds;

99. "'And our seducers were only

الْجَنَّةُ لِلْمُتَّقِينَ ۞ وَبُرِّزَتِ الْجَحِيمُ

لِلْغَاوِينَ ۞ وَقِيلَ لَهُمْ أَيْنَمَا كُنْتُمْ

تَعْبُدُونَ ۞ مِنْ دُونِ اللّٰهِ هَلْ

يَنْصُرُونَكُمْ أَوْ يَنْتَصِرُونَ ۞ فَكُبْكِبُوا

فِيهَا هُمْ وَالْغَاوُونَ ۞ وَجُنُودُ

إِبْلِيسَ أَجْمَعُونَ ۞ قَالُوا وَهُمْ

فِيهَا يَخْتَصِمُونَ ۞ تَاللّٰهِ إِنْ كُنَّا

لَفِي ضَلَالٍ مُبِينٍ ۞ إِذْ نُسَوِّيكُمْ

بِرَبِّ الْعَالَمِينَ ۞ وَمَا أَضَلَّنَا إِلَّا

will forgive me my faults on the Day of Judgment.

83. "O my Lord! Bestow wisdom on me, and join me with the righteous;"

84. "Grant me honourable mention on the tongue of truth among the latest (generations);"

85. "Make me one of the inheritors of the Garden of Bliss;"

86. "Forgive my father, for that he is among those astray;"

87. "And let me not be in disgrace on the Day when (men) will be raised up;" -

88. "The Day whereon neither wealth nor sons will avail,"

89. "But only he (will prosper) that brings to Allah a sound heart;"

يَغْفِرُ لِى خَطِيٓئَتِى يَوْمَ الدِّينِ ۞

رَبِّ هَبْ لِى حُكْمًا وَّأَلْحِقْنِى بِالصَّالِحِينَ ۞ وَاجْعَل لِّى لِسَانَ صِدْقٍ فِى الْآخِرِينَ ۞ وَاجْعَلْنِى مِن وَرَثَةِ جَنَّةِ النَّعِيمِ ۞ وَاغْفِرْ لِأَبِىٓ إِنَّهُ كَانَ مِنَ الضَّالِّينَ ۞ وَلَا تُخْزِنِى يَوْمَ يُبْعَثُونَ ۞ يَوْمَ لَا يَنفَعُ مَالٌ وَّلَا بَنُونَ ۞ إِلَّا مَنْ أَتَى اللَّهَ بِقَلْبٍ سَلِيمٍ ۞ وَأُزْلِفَتِ

or harm?"

74. They said: "No, but we found our fathers doing thus (what we do)."

75. He said: "Do you then see whom you have been worshipping, -

76. "You and your fathers before you?" -

77. "For they are enemies to me; not so the Lord and Cherisher of the Worlds;"

78. "Who created me, and it is He Who guides me;"

79. "Who gives me food and drink,"

80. "And when I am ill, it is He Who cures me;"

81. "Who will cause me to die, and then to live (again);"

82. "And who, I hope,

أَوْيُضُرُّونَ ۞ قَالُوا بَلْ وَجَدْنَا

آبَآءَنَا كَذَٰلِكَ يَفْعَلُونَ ۞ قَالَ

أَفَرَءَيْتُمْ مَّا كُنْتُمْ تَعْبُدُونَ ۞

أَنْتُمْ وَآبَآؤُكُمُ الْأَقْدَمُونَ ۞ فَإِنَّهُمْ

عَدُوٌّ لِّي إِلَّا رَبَّ الْعَٰلَمِينَ ۞ الَّذِي

خَلَقَنِي فَهُوَ يَهْدِينِ ۞ وَالَّذِي هُوَ

يُطْعِمُنِي وَيَسْقِينِ ۞ وَإِذَا مَرِضْتُ

فَهُوَ يَشْفِينِ ۞ وَالَّذِي يُمِيتُنِي

ثُمَّ يُحْيِينِ ۞ وَالَّذِي أَطْمَعُ أَنْ

Moses and all who were with him;

66. But We drowned the others.

67. Verily in this is a Sign: but most of them do not believe.

68. And verily your Lord is He, the Exalted in Might, Most Merciful.

69. And rehearse to them (something of) Abraham's story.

70. Behold, he said to his father and his people: "Whome do you worship?"

71. They said: "We worship idols, and we remain constantly in attendance on them."

72. He said: "Do they listen to you when you call (on them),"

73. "Or do you good

مُوسَى وَمَنْ مَّعَهُ أَجْمَعِينَ ۝

ثُمَّ أَغْرَقْنَا الْآخَرِينَ ۝ إِنَّ فِي

ذَلِكَ لَآيَةً ۚ وَمَا كَانَ أَكْثَرُهُم

مُّؤْمِنِينَ ۝ وَإِنَّ رَبَّكَ لَهُوَ الْعَزِيزُ

الرَّحِيمُ ۝ وَاتْلُ عَلَيْهِمْ نَبَأَ

إِبْرَاهِيمَ ۝ إِذْ قَالَ لِأَبِيهِ وَقَوْمِهِ

مَا تَعْبُدُونَ ۝ قَالُوا نَعْبُدُ أَصْنَامًا

فَنَظَلُّ لَهَا عَاكِفِينَ ۝ قَالَ هَلْ

يَسْمَعُونَكُمْ إِذْ تَدْعُونَ ۝ أَوْ يَنفَعُونَكُمْ

and every kind of honourable position;

59. Thus it was, but We made the Children of Israel inheritors of such things.

60. So they pursued them at sunrise.

61. And when the two bodies saw each other, the people of Moses said: "We are sure to be overtaken."

62. (Moses) said: "By no means! My Lord is with me! Soon will He guide me!"

63. Then We told Moses by inspiration: "Strike the sea with your rod." So it divided, and each separate part became like the huge, firm mass of a mountain.

64. And We made the other party approach there.

65. We delivered

وَّمَقَامٍ كَرِيْمٍ ۝ كَذٰلِكَ وَاَوْرَثْنٰهَا

بَنِىْۤ اِسْرَآءِيْلَ ۝ فَاَتْبَعُوْهُمْ

مُّشْرِقِيْنَ ۝ فَلَمَّا تَرَآءَ الْجَمْعٰنِ

قَالَ اَصْحٰبُ مُوْسٰۤى اِنَّا لَمُدْرَكُوْنَ ۝

قَالَ كَلَّاۤ اِنَّ مَعِىَ رَبِّىْ سَيَهْدِيْنِ ۝

فَاَوْحَيْنَاۤ اِلٰى مُوْسٰۤى اَنِ اضْرِبْ

بِّعَصَاكَ الْبَحْرَ فَانْفَلَقَ فَكَانَ

كُلُّ فِرْقٍ كَالطَّوْدِ الْعَظِيْمِ ۝

وَاَزْلَفْنَا ثَمَّ الْاٰخَرِيْنَ ۝ وَاَنْجَيْنَا

return to our Lord!"

51. "Only, our desire is that our Lord will forgive us our faults, that we may become foremost among the believers!"

52. By inspiration We told Moses: "Travel by night with my servants; for surely you shall be pursued."

53. Then Pharaoh sent heralds to (all) the Cities,

54. (Saying): "These (Israelites) are but a small band,"

55. "And they are raging furiously against us;"

56. "But we are a multitude amply fore-warned."

57. So We expelled them from gardens, springs,

58. Treasures,

مُنقَلِبُونَ ۞ إِنَّا نَطْمَعُ أَن يَغْفِرَ

لَنَا رَبُّنَا خَطَايَانَا أَن كُنَّا أَوَّلَ

الْمُؤْمِنِينَ ۞ وَأَوْحَيْنَا إِلَىٰ مُوسَىٰ

أَنْ أَسْرِ بِعِبَادِي إِنَّكُم مُّتَّبَعُونَ ۞

فَأَرْسَلَ فِرْعَوْنُ فِي الْمَدَائِنِ

حَاشِرِينَ ۞ إِنَّ هَٰؤُلَاءِ لَشِرْذِمَةٌ

قَلِيلُونَ ۞ وَإِنَّهُمْ لَنَا لَغَائِظُونَ ۞

وَإِنَّا لَجَمِيعٌ حَاذِرُونَ ۞ فَأَخْرَجْنَاهُم

مِّن جَنَّاتٍ وَعُيُونٍ ۞ وَكُنُوزٍ

swallows up all the falsehoods
which they fake!

46. Then did the sorcerers fall
down, prostrate in adoration,

47. Saying: "We believe in the
Lord of the Worlds,"

48. "The Lord of Moses and
Aaron."

49. Said (Pharaoh): "Believe
you in Him before I give you permission? Surely he is your leader,
who has taught you sorcery! But
soon shall you know! Be sure I
will cut off your hands and your
feet on opposite sides, and I will
cause you all to die on the cross!"

50. They said: "No matter! For
us, we shall but

تَلْقَفُ مَا يَأْفِكُونَ ۩ فَأُلْقِيَ

السَّحَرَةُ سٰجِدِينَ ۝ قَالُوْا اٰمَنَّا

بِرَبِّ الْعٰلَمِيْنَ ۝ رَبِّ مُوْسٰى

وَهٰرُوْنَ ۝ قَالَ اٰمَنْتُمْ لَهُ قَبْلَ

اَنْ اٰذَنَ لَكُمْ اِنَّهُ لَكَبِيْرُكُمُ الَّذِيْ

عَلَّمَكُمُ السِّحْرَ فَلَسَوْفَ تَعْلَمُوْنَ ۛ

لَاُقَطِّعَنَّ اَيْدِيَكُمْ وَاَرْجُلَكُمْ مِّنْ

خِلَافٍ وَّلَاُوصَلِّبَنَّكُمْ اَجْمَعِيْنَ ۝

قَالُوْا لَا ضَيْرَ اِنَّا اِلٰى رَبِّنَا

the sorcerers (in religion) if they win?"

41. So when the sorcerers arrived, they said to Pharaoh: "Of course - shall we have a (suitable) reward if we win?"

42. He said: "Yes, (and more), - for you shall in that case be (raised to posts) nearest (to my person)."

43. Moses said to them: "Throw you - that which you are about to throw!"

44. So they threw their ropes and their rods, and said: "By the might of Pharaoh, it is we who will certainly win!"

45. Then Moses threw his rod, when, behold, it

السَّحَرَةَ اِنْ كَانُوا هُمُ الْغٰلِبِينَ ۝

فَلَمَّا جَآءَ السَّحَرَةُ قَالُوا لِفِرْعَوْنَ

اَئِنَّ لَنَا لَاَجْرًا اِنْ كُنَّا نَحْنُ

الْغٰلِبِينَ ۝ قَالَ نَعَمْ وَاِنَّكُمْ اِذًا

لَّمِنَ الْمُقَرَّبِينَ ۝ قَالَ لَهُمْ مُّوسَى

اَلْقُوا مَآ اَنْتُمْ مُّلْقُونَ ۝ فَاَلْقَوْا

حِبَالَهُمْ وَعِصِيَّهُمْ وَقَالُوا بِعِزَّةِ

فِرْعَوْنَ اِنَّا لَنَحْنُ الْغٰلِبُونَ ۝

فَاَلْقَى مُوسَى عَصَاهُ فَاِذَا هِيَ

white to all beholders!

34. (Pharaoh) said to the Chiefs around him: "This is indeed a sorcerer well-versed:"

35. "His plan is to get you out of your land by his sorcery; then what is it you counsel?"

36. They said: "Keep him and his brother in suspense (for a while), and dispatch to the Cities heralds to collect"-

37. "And bring up to you all (our) sorcerers well-versed."

38. So the sorcerers were got together for the appointment of a day well-known,

39. And the people were told: "Are you (now) assembled?"-

40. "That we may follow

بَيْضَآءُ لِلنّٰظِرِيْنَ ۞ قَالَ لِلْمَلَاِ حَوْلَهٗٓ

اِنَّ هٰذَا لَسٰحِرٌ عَلِيْمٌ ۞ يُّرِيْدُ

اَنْ يُّخْرِجَكُمْ مِّنْ اَرْضِكُمْ بِسِحْرِهٖ

فَمَاذَا تَاْمُرُوْنَ ۞ قَالُوْٓا اَرْجِهْ

وَ اَخَاهُ وَابْعَثْ فِي الْمَدَآئِنِ

حٰشِرِيْنَ ۞ يَاْتُوْكَ بِكُلِّ سَحَّارٍ

عَلِيْمٍ ۞ فَجُمِعَ السَّحَرَةُ لِمِيْقَاتِ

يَوْمٍ مَّعْلُوْمٍ ۞ وَّقِيْلَ لِلنَّاسِ هَلْ

اَنْتُمْ مُّجْتَمِعُوْنَ ۞ لَعَلَّنَا نَتَّبِعُ

is a veritable madman!"

28. (Moses) said: "Lord of the East and the West, and all between! if you only had sense!"

29. (Pharaoh) said: "If you do put forward any god other than me, I will certainly put you in prison!"

30. (Moses) said: "Even if I showed you something clear (and) convincing?"

31. (Pharaoh) said: "Show it then, if you tell the truth!"

32. So (Moses) threw his rod, and behold, it was a serpent, plain (for all to see)!

33. And he drew out his hand, and behold, it was

لَمَجْنُوْنٌ ۞ قَالَ رَبُّ الْمَشْرِقِ
وَالْمَغْرِبِ وَمَا بَيْنَهُمَا إِنْ كُنْتُمْ
تَعْقِلُوْنَ ۞ قَالَ لَئِنِ اتَّخَذْتَ
اِلٰهًا غَيْرِىْ لَاَجْعَلَنَّكَ مِنَ
الْمَسْجُوْنِيْنَ ۞ قَالَ اَوَلَوْ جِئْتُكَ
بِشَىْءٍ مُّبِيْنٍ ۞ قَالَ فَأْتِ بِهٖ
اِنْ كُنْتَ مِنَ الصّٰدِقِيْنَ ۞
فَاَلْقٰى عَصَاهُ فَإِذَا هِىَ ثُعْبَانٌ
مُّبِيْنٌ ۞ وَّنَزَعَ يَدَهُ فَإِذَا هِىَ

as one of the Apostles."

22. "And this is the favour with which you do reproach me, - that you have enslaved the Children of Israel!"

23. Pharaoh said: "And who is the 'Lord and Cherisher of the worlds'?"

24. (Moses) said: "The Lord and Cherisher of the heavens and the earth, and all between, - if you want to be quite sure."

25. (Pharaoh) said to those around: "Did you not listen (to what he says)?"

26. (Moses) said: "Your Lord and the Lord of your fathers from the beginning!"

27. (Pharaoh) said: "Truly your Apostle who has been sent to you

مِنَ الْمُرْسَلِيْنَ ۞ وَتِلْكَ نِعْمَةٌ

تَمُنُّهَا عَلَيَّ اَنْ عَبَّدْتَّ بَنِيٓ

اِسْرَآءِيْلَ ۞ قَالَ فِرْعَوْنُ وَمَا رَبُّ

الْعٰلَمِيْنَ ۞ قَالَ رَبُّ السَّمٰوٰتِ

وَالْاَرْضِ وَمَا بَيْنَهُمَا ۘ اِنْ كُنْتُمْ

مُّوْقِنِيْنَ ۞ قَالَ لِمَنْ حَوْلَهٗٓ

اَلَا تَسْتَمِعُوْنَ ۞ قَالَ رَبُّكُمْ وَرَبُّ

اٰبَآئِكُمُ الْاَوَّلِيْنَ ۞ قَالَ اِنَّ

رَسُوْلَكُمُ الَّذِيٓ اُرْسِلَ اِلَيْكُمْ

the Lord and Cherisher of the worlds;'

17. 'Send you with us the Children of Israel.'"

18. (Pharaoh) said: "Did we not cherish your as a child among us, and did you not stay in our midst many years of your life?"

19. "And you did a deed of yours which (you know) you did, and you are an ungrateful (wretch)!"

20. Moses said: "I did it then, when I was in error.

21. "So I fled from you (all) when I feared you; but my Lord has (since) invested me with judgment (and wisdom) and appointed me

رَبِّ الْعٰلَمِيْنَ ۞ اَنْ اَرْسِلْ

مَعَنَا بَنِىٓ اِسْرَآءِيْلَ ۞ قَالَ

اَلَمْ نُرَبِّكَ فِيْنَا وَلِيْدًا وَّلَبِثْتَ

فِيْنَا مِنْ عُمُرِكَ سِنِيْنَ ۞

وَ فَعَلْتَ فَعْلَتَكَ الَّتِىْ فَعَلْتَ

وَ اَنْتَ مِنَ الْكٰفِرِيْنَ ۞ قَالَ

فَعَلْتُهَآ اِذًا وَّ اَنَا مِنَ الضَّآلِّيْنَ ۞

فَفَرَرْتُ مِنْكُمْ لَمَّا خِفْتُكُمْ

فَوَهَبَ لِىْ رَبِّىْ حُكْمًا وَّ جَعَلَنِىْ

10. Behold, your Lord called Moses: "Go to the people of iniquity," -

11. "The people of the Pharaoh: will they not fear Allah?"

12. He said: "O my Lord! I do fear that they will charge me with falsehood:"

13. "My breast will be straitened. And my speech may not go (smoothly): so send unto Aaron."

14. "And (further), they have a charge of crime against me; and I fear they may slay me."

15. Allah said: "By no means! Proceed then, both of you, with Our Signs; We are with you, and will listen (to your call).

16. "So go forth, both of you, to Pharaoh, and say: 'We have been sent by

وَإِذْ نَادَىٰ رَبُّكَ مُوْسَىٰ أَنِ ائْتِ

الْقَوْمَ الظَّالِمِيْنَ ۞ قَوْمَ فِرْعَوْنَ

أَلَا يَتَّقُوْنَ ۞ قَالَ رَبِّ إِنِّيْ أَخَافُ

أَنْ يُّكَذِّبُوْنِ ۞ وَيَضِيْقُ صَدْرِيْ

وَلَا يَنْطَلِقُ لِسَانِيْ فَأَرْسِلْ إِلَىٰ

هَارُوْنَ ۞ وَلَهُمْ عَلَيَّ ذَنْبٌ فَأَخَافُ

أَنْ يَّقْتُلُوْنِ ۞ قَالَ كَلَّا فَاذْهَبَا

بِآيَاتِنَا إِنَّا مَعَكُمْ مُّسْتَمِعُوْنَ ۞

فَأْتِيَا فِرْعَوْنَ فَقُوْلَا إِنَّا رَسُوْلُ

in humility.

5.   But there comes not to them a newly-revealed Message from (Allah) Most Gracious, but they turn away therefrom.

6.   They have indeed rejected (the Message): so they will know soon (enough) the truth of what they mocked at!

7.   Do they not look at the earth, - how many noble things of all kinds We have produced therein?

8.   Verily, in this is a Sign: but most of them do not believe.

9.   And verily, your Lord is He, the Exalted in Might, Most Merciful.

لَهَا خَاضِعِينَ ۞ وَمَا يَأْتِيهِمْ مِّنْ

ذِكْرٍ مِّنَ الرَّحْمٰنِ مُحْدَثٍ إِلَّا

كَانُوا عَنْهُ مُعْرِضِينَ ۞ فَقَدْ

كَذَّبُوا فَسَيَأْتِيهِمْ أَنْبٰؤُا مَا كَانُوا

بِهِ يَسْتَهْزِءُونَ ۞ أَوَلَمْ يَرَوْا إِلَى

الْأَرْضِ كَمْ أَنْبَتْنَا فِيهَا مِنْ كُلِّ

زَوْجٍ كَرِيمٍ ۞ إِنَّ فِي ذٰلِكَ لَآيَةً

وَمَا كَانَ أَكْثَرُهُمْ مُؤْمِنِينَ ۞

وَإِنَّ رَبَّكَ لَهُوَ الْعَزِيزُ الرَّحِيمُ ۞

76. Dwelling therein; - how beautiful an abode and place of rest!

77. Say (to the rejecters): "My Lord would not concern Himself with you if you call not on Him: but you have indeed rejected (Him), and soon will come the inevitable (punishment)!"

Ash-Shu'ara (The Poets)

Bismillahir-Rahmanir-Rahim

1. Ta. Sin. Mim.

2. These are verses of the Book that makes (things) clear.

3. It may be you will kill yourself with grief, that they do not become believers.

4. If (such) were Our Will, We could send down to them from the sky a Sign, to which they would bend their necks

خٰلِدِينَ فِيهَا حَسُنَتْ مُسْتَقَرًّا

وَّمُقَامًا ۝ قُلْ مَا يَعْبَؤُا بِكُمْ

رَبِّي لَوْلَا دُعَاؤُكُمْ فَقَدْ كَذَّبْتُمْ

فَسَوْفَ يَكُونُ لِزَامًا ۝

بِسْمِ اللهِ الرَّحْمٰنِ الرَّحِيمِ

طٰسٓمّٓ ۝ تِلْكَ اٰيٰتُ الْكِتٰبِ الْمُبِينِ

لَعَلَّكَ بَاخِعٌ نَّفْسَكَ اَلَّا يَكُونُوا

مُؤْمِنِينَ ۝ اِنْ نَّشَأْ نُنَزِّلْ عَلَيْهِمْ

مِّنَ السَّمَاءِ اٰيَةً فَظَلَّتْ اَعْنَاقُهُمْ

who witness no falsehood, and, if they pass by futility, they pass by it with honourable (avoidance);

73. Those who, when they are admonished with the Signs of their Lord, droop not down at them as if they were deaf or blind;

74. And those who pray, "Our Lord! Grant unto us wives and offspring who will be the comfort of our eyes, and give us (the grace) to lead the righteous."

75. Those are the ones who will be rewarded with the highest place in heaven, because of their patient constancy: therein shall they be met with salutations and peace,

لَا يَشْهَدُونَ الزُّورَ وَإِذَا مَرُّوا
بِاللَّغْوِ مَرُّوا كِرَامًا ۝ وَالَّذِينَ إِذَا
ذُكِّرُوا بِآيَٰتِ رَبِّهِمْ لَمْ يَخِرُّوا
عَلَيْهَا صُمًّا وَعُمْيَانًا ۝ وَالَّذِينَ
يَقُولُونَ رَبَّنَا هَبْ لَنَا مِنْ
أَزْوَاجِنَا وَذُرِّيَّاتِنَا قُرَّةَ أَعْيُنٍ
وَاجْعَلْنَا لِلْمُتَّقِينَ إِمَامًا ۝ أُولَٰئِكَ
يُجْزَوْنَ الْغُرْفَةَ بِمَا صَبَرُوا
وَيُلَقَّوْنَ فِيهَا تَحِيَّةً وَسَلَامًا ۝

as Allah has made sacred except for just cause, nor commit fornication; - and any that does this (not only) meets punishment.

69. (But) the Chastisement on the Day of Judgment will be doubled to him, and he will dwell therein in ignominy, -

70. Unless he repents, believes, and works righteous deeds, for Allah will change the evil of such persons into good, and Allah is Oft-Forgiving, Most Merciful,

71. And whoever repents and does good has truly turned to Allah with an (acceptable) conversion; -

72. Those

الَّتِي حَرَّمَ اللهُ إِلَّا بِالْحَقِّ وَلَا

يَزْنُونَ وَمَنْ يَّفْعَلْ ذٰلِكَ يَلْقَ

أَثَامًا ۖ ﴿٦٨﴾ يُّضٰعَفْ لَهُ الْعَذَابُ يَوْمَ

الْقِيٰمَةِ وَيَخْلُدْ فِيهِ مُهَانًا ﴿٦٩﴾

إِلَّا مَنْ تَابَ وَآمَنَ وَعَمِلَ عَمَلًا

صَالِحًا فَأُولٰٓئِكَ يُبَدِّلُ اللهُ سَيِّئٰتِهِمْ

حَسَنٰتٍ ۗ وَكَانَ اللهُ غَفُورًا رَّحِيمًا

﴿٧٠﴾ وَمَنْ تَابَ وَعَمِلَ صَالِحًا فَإِنَّهُ

يَتُوبُ إِلَى اللهِ مَتَابًا ﴿٧١﴾ وَالَّذِينَ

64. Those who spend the night in adoration of their Lord prostrate and standing;

65. Those who say, "Our Lord! Avert from us the Wrath of Hell, for its Wrath is indeed an affliction grievous, -

66. "Evil indeed is it as an abode, and as a place to rest in";

67. Those who, when they spend, are not extravagant and not niggardly, but hold a just (balance) between those (extremes);

68. Those who invoke not, with Allah, any other god, nor slay such life

وَالَّذِيْنَ يَبِيْتُوْنَ لِرَبِّهِمْ سُجَّدًا

وَّقِيَامًا ۞ وَالَّذِيْنَ يَقُوْلُوْنَ رَبَّنَا

اصْرِفْ عَنَّا عَذَابَ جَهَنَّمَ ۚ إِنَّ

عَذَابَهَا كَانَ غَرَامًا ۞ إِنَّهَا

سَاءَتْ مُسْتَقَرًّا وَّمُقَامًا ۞ وَالَّذِيْنَ

إِذَآ أَنْفَقُوْا لَمْ يُسْرِفُوْا وَلَمْ

يَقْتُرُوْا وَكَانَ بَيْنَ ذٰلِكَ قَوَامًا ۞

وَالَّذِيْنَ لَا يَدْعُوْنَ مَعَ اللهِ

إِلٰهًا اٰخَرَ وَلَا يَقْتُلُوْنَ النَّفْسَ

"And what is (Allah) Most Gracious? Shall we adore that which you command us?" And it increases their flight (from the Truth).

61. Blessed is He Who made constellations in the skies, and placed therein a Lamp and a Moon giving light;

62. And it is He Who made the Night and the Day to follow each other: for such as desire to be mindful or to show their gratitude.

63. And the servants of (Allah) Most Gracious are those who walk on the earth in humility, and when the ignorant address them, they say, "Peace!";

وَمَا الرَّحْمَٰنُ أَنَسْجُدُ لِمَا تَأْمُرُنَا

وَزَادَهُمْ نُفُورًا ۩ تَبَارَكَ الَّذِى

جَعَلَ فِى السَّمَاءِ بُرُوجًا وَجَعَلَ

فِيهَا سِرَاجًا وَقَمَرًا مُّنِيرًا ۞ وَهُوَ

الَّذِى جَعَلَ الَّيْلَ وَالنَّهَارَ خِلْفَةً

لِّمَنْ أَرَادَ أَن يَذَّكَّرَ أَوْ أَرَادَ

شُكُورًا ۞ وَعِبَادُ الرَّحْمَٰنِ الَّذِينَ

يَمْشُونَ عَلَى الْأَرْضِ هَوْنًا وَإِذَا

خَاطَبَهُمُ الْجَاهِلُونَ قَالُوا سَلَامًا ۞

reward do I ask of you for it but this: that each one who will may take a (straight) path to his Lord."

58. And put your trust in Him Who lives and dies not; and celebrate his praise; and enough is He to be acquainted with the faults of His servants; -

59. He Who created the heavens and the earth and all that is between, in six days, and is firmly established on the Throne (of Authority): Allah Most Gracious: ask you, then, about Him of any acquainted (with such things).

60. When it is said to them, "Adore you (Allah) Most Gracious!", they say,

أَسْئَلُكُمْ عَلَيْهِ مِنْ أَجْرٍ اِلَّا مَنْ

شَآءَ أَنْ يَّتَّخِذَ اِلٰى رَبِّهٖ سَبِيْلًا ۞

وَتَوَكَّلْ عَلَى الْحَيِّ الَّذِىْ لَا يَمُوْتُ

وَسَبِّحْ بِحَمْدِهٖ ۙ وَكَفٰى بِهٖ بِذُنُوْبِ

عِبَادِهٖ خَبِيْرًا ۞ اَلَّذِىْ خَلَقَ

السَّمٰوٰتِ وَالْاَرْضَ وَمَا بَيْنَهُمَا فِىْ

سِتَّةِ اَيَّامٍ ثُمَّ اسْتَوٰى عَلَى الْعَرْشِ ۚ

الرَّحْمٰنُ فَسْئَلْ بِهٖ خَبِيْرًا ۞ وَاِذَا

قِيْلَ لَهُمُ اسْجُدُوْا لِلرَّحْمٰنِ قَالُوْا

the two bodies of flowing water: one palatable and sweet, and the other salt and bitter; yet has He made a barrier between them, a partition that is forbidden to be passed.

54. It is He Who has created man from water: then has He established relationships of lineage and marriage: for your Lord has power (over all things).

55. Yet do they worship, besides Allah, things that can neither profit them nor harm them: and the misbeliever is a helper (of Evil), against his own Lord!

56. But you We only sent to give glad tidings and admonition.

57. Say: "No

الْبَحْرَيْنِ هٰذَا عَذْبٌ فُرَاتٌ وَهٰذَا

مِلْحٌ أُجَاجٌ وَجَعَلَ بَيْنَهُمَا بَرْزَخًا

وَّحِجْرًا مَّحْجُورًا ۞ وَهُوَ الَّذِى

خَلَقَ مِنَ الْمَآءِ بَشَرًا فَجَعَلَهٗ

نَسَبًا وَّصِهْرًا ۗ وَكَانَ رَبُّكَ قَدِيرًا ۞

وَيَعْبُدُونَ مِنْ دُونِ اللّٰهِ مَا لَا

يَنْفَعُهُمْ وَلَا يَضُرُّهُمْ ۗ وَكَانَ الْكَافِرُ

عَلٰى رَبِّهٖ ظَهِيرًا ۞ وَمَآ اَرْسَلْنٰكَ

اِلَّا مُبَشِّرًا وَّنَذِيرًا ۞ قُلْ مَآ

going before His Mercy, and We send down pure water from the sky, -

49. That with it We may give life to a dead land, and slake the thirst of things We have created, - cattle and men in great numbers.

50. And We have distributed the (water) amongst them, in order that they may celebrate (our) praises, but most men are averse (to anything) but (rank) ingratitude.

51. Had it been Our Will, We could have sent a warner to every centre of population.

52. Therefore listen not to the unbelievers, but strive against them with the utmost strenuousness, with the (Qur'an).

53. It is He Who has let free

بَيْنَ يَدَىْ رَحْمَتِهِ وَأَنْزَلْنَا مِنَ
السَّمَاءِ مَاءً طَهُورًا ۞ لِنُحْيِۦ بِهِ
بَلْدَةً مَّيْتًا وَّنُسْقِيَهُ مِمَّا خَلَقْنَا
أَنْعَامًا وَّأَنَاسِىَّ كَثِيرًا ۞ وَلَقَدْ
صَرَّفْنٰهُ بَيْنَهُمْ لِيَذَّكَّرُوا ۗ فَأَبَىٰ
أَكْثَرُ النَّاسِ إِلَّا كُفُورًا ۞ وَلَوْ شِئْنَا
لَبَعَثْنَا فِى كُلِّ قَرْيَةٍ نَّذِيرًا ۞
فَلَا تُطِعِ الْكٰفِرِينَ وَجَاهِدْهُمْ بِهِ
جِهَادًا كَبِيرًا ۞ وَهُوَ الَّذِىْ مَرَجَ

understand? They are only like cattle; - nay, they are worse astray in path.

45. Have you not turned your vision to your Lord? - How He does prolong the shadow! If He willed, He could make it stationary! Then do We make the sun its guide;

46. Then We draw it in towards Ourselves, - a contraction by easy stages.

47. And He it is Who makes the Night as a robe for you, and sleep as repose, and makes the Day (as it were) a resurrection.

48. And He it is Who sends the winds as heralds of glad tidings,

يَعْقِلُوْنَ ۚ اِنْ هُمْ اِلَّا كَالْاَنْعَامِ

بَلْ هُمْ اَضَلُّ سَبِيْلًا ۞ اَلَمْ تَرَ

اِلٰى رَبِّكَ كَيْفَ مَدَّ الظِّلَّ ۚ وَلَوْ

شَاءَ لَجَعَلَهُ سَاكِنًا ۚ ثُمَّ جَعَلْنَا

الشَّمْسَ عَلَيْهِ دَلِيْلًا ۞ ثُمَّ

قَبَضْنٰهُ اِلَيْنَا قَبْضًا يَّسِيْرًا ۞ وَهُوَ

الَّذِيْ جَعَلَ لَكُمُ الَّيْلَ لِبَاسًا وَّالنَّوْمَ

سُبَاتًا وَّ جَعَلَ النَّهَارَ نُشُوْرًا ۞

وَهُوَ الَّذِيْ اَرْسَلَ الرِّيٰحَ بُشْرًا

the Resurrection.

41. When they see you, they treat you no otherwise than in mockery: "Is this the one whom Allah has sent as an Apostle?"

42. "He indeed would well-nigh have misled us from our gods, had it not been that we were constant to them!" - Soon will they know, when they see the Chastisement, who it is that is most misled in Path!

43. Do you see such a one as takes for his god his own passion (or impulse)? Could you be a disposer of affairs for him?

44. Or do you think that most of them listen or

نُشُورًا ۞ وَاِذَا رَاَوْكَ اِنْ يَّتَّخِذُوْنَكَ

اِلَّا هُزُوًا ۗ اَهٰذَا الَّذِىْ بَعَثَ اللّٰهُ

رَسُوْلًا ۞ اِنْ كَادَ لَيُضِلُّنَا عَنْ

اٰلِهَتِنَا لَوْ لَا اَنْ صَبَرْنَا عَلَيْهَا ۗ

وَسَوْفَ يَعْلَمُوْنَ حِيْنَ يَرَوْنَ

الْعَذَابَ مَنْ اَضَلُّ سَبِيْلًا ۞

اَرَءَيْتَ مَنِ اتَّخَذَ اِلٰهَهٗ هَوٰىهُ ۗ

اَفَاَنْتَ تَكُوْنُ عَلَيْهِ وَكِيْلًا ۞ اَمْ

تَحْسَبُ اَنَّ اَكْثَرَهُمْ يَسْمَعُوْنَ اَوْ

Noah, - when they rejected the Apostles, We drowned them, and We made them as a Sign for mankind; and We have prepared for (all) wrong-doers a grievous Chastisement; -

38. As also 'Ad and Thamud, and the Companions of the Rass, and many a generation between them.

39. To each one We set forth parables and examples; and each one We broke to utter annihilation (for their sins).

40. And the (unbelievers) must indeed have passed by the town on which was rained a shower of evil: did they not then see it (with their own eyes)? But they fear not

نُوحٍ لَّمَّا كَذَّبُوا الرُّسُلَ أَغْرَقْنٰهُمْ

وَجَعَلْنٰهُمْ لِلنَّاسِ اٰيَةً ۖ وَأَعْتَدْنَا

لِلظّٰلِمِينَ عَذَابًا أَلِيمًا ۞ وَّعَادًا

وَّثَمُودَا۟ وَأَصْحٰبَ الرَّسِّ وَقُرُونًۢا

بَيْنَ ذٰلِكَ كَثِيرًا ۞ وَكُلًّا ضَرَبْنَا

لَهُ الْأَمْثَالَ ۖ وَكُلًّا تَبَّرْنَا تَتْبِيرًا

۞ وَلَقَدْ أَتَوْا عَلَى الْقَرْيَةِ الَّتِىٓ

أُمْطِرَتْ مَطَرَ السَّوْءِ ۚ أَفَلَمْ يَكُونُوا

يَرَوْنَهَا ۚ بَلْ كَانُوا لَا يَرْجُونَ

well-arranged stages, gradually.

33.   And no question do they bring to you but We reveal to you the truth and the best explanation (thereof).

34.   Those who will be gathered to Hell (prone) on their faces, - they will be in an evil plight, and, as to Path, most astray.

35.   (Before this,) We sent Moses the Book, and appointed his brother Aaron with him as minister;

36.   And We command: "Go you both, to the people who have rejected our Signs:" and those (people) We destroyed with utter destruction.

37.   And the people of

تَرْتِيلًا ۝ وَلَا يَأْتُونَكَ بِمَثَلٍ إِلَّا

جِئْنَاكَ بِالْحَقِّ وَأَحْسَنَ تَفْسِيرًا ۝

الَّذِينَ يُحْشَرُونَ عَلَى وُجُوهِهِمْ

إِلَى جَهَنَّمَ أُولَٰئِكَ شَرٌّ مَّكَانًا

وَأَضَلُّ سَبِيلًا ۝ وَلَقَدْ اٰتَيْنَا

مُوسَى الْكِتَابَ وَجَعَلْنَا مَعَهُ أَخَاهُ

هَارُونَ وَزِيرًا ۝ فَقُلْنَا اذْهَبَا

إِلَى الْقَوْمِ الَّذِينَ كَذَّبُوا بِاٰيٰتِنَا

فَدَمَّرْنَاهُمْ تَدْمِيرًا ۝ وَقَوْمَ

after it had come to me! Ah! The Evil One is but a traitor to man!"

30. Then the Apostle will say: "O my Lord! Truly my people took this Qur'an for just foolish nonsense."

31. Thus have We made for every Prophet an enemy among the sinners: but enough is your Lord to guide and to help.

32. Those who reject Faith say: "Why is not the Qur'an revealed to him all at once? Thus (is it revealed), that We may strengthen your heart thereby, and We have rehearsed it to you in slow,

بَعْدَ اِذْ جَاءَنِیْ ۗ وَكَانَ الشَّيْطٰنُ

لِلْاِنْسَانِ خَذُوْلًا ۝ وَقَالَ الرَّسُوْلُ

يٰرَبِّ اِنَّ قَوْمِی اتَّخَذُوْا هٰذَا

الْقُرْاٰنَ مَهْجُوْرًا ۝ وَكَذٰلِكَ جَعَلْنَا

لِكُلِّ نَبِیٍّ عَدُوًّا مِّنَ الْمُجْرِمِيْنَ ۗ

وَكَفٰى بِرَبِّكَ هَادِيًا وَّنَصِيْرًا ۝

وَقَالَ الَّذِيْنَ كَفَرُوْا لَوْلَا نُزِّلَ

عَلَيْهِ الْقُرْاٰنُ جُمْلَةً وَّاحِدَةً ۚ

كَذٰلِكَ ۛ لِنُثَبِّتَ بِهٖ فُؤَادَكَ وَرَتَّلْنٰهُ

in their abode, and have the fairest of places for repose.

25. The Day the heaven shall be rent asunder with clouds, and Angels shall be sent down, descending (in ranks), -

26. That Day, the dominion as of right and truth, shall be (wholly) for (Allah) Most Merciful: it will be a Day of dire difficulty for the misbelievers.

27. The Day that the wrong-doer will bite at his hands, he will say, "Oh! Would that I had taken a (straight) path with the Apostle!"

28. "Ah! Woe is me! Would that I had never taken such a one for a friend!"

29. "He did lead me astray from the Message (of Allah)

خَيْرٌ مُّسْتَقَرًّا وَّاَحْسَنُ مَقِيلًا ۞

وَيَوْمَ تَشَقَّقُ السَّمَآءُ بِالْغَمَامِ وَنُزِّلَ

الْمَلَٰٓئِكَةُ تَنْزِيلًا ۞ اَلْمُلْكُ يَوْمَئِذٍ

الْحَقُّ لِلرَّحْمَٰنِ ۚ وَكَانَ يَوْمًا عَلَى

الْكَٰفِرِينَ عَسِيرًا ۞ وَيَوْمَ يَعَضُّ

الظَّالِمُ عَلَىٰ يَدَيْهِ يَقُولُ يَٰلَيْتَنِي

اتَّخَذْتُ مَعَ الرَّسُولِ سَبِيلًا ۞

يَٰوَيْلَتَىٰ لَيْتَنِي لَمْ اَتَّخِذْ فُلَانًا

خَلِيلًا ۞ لَّقَدْ اَضَلَّنِي عَنِ الذِّكْرِ

21. Such as fear not the meeting with Us (for Judgment) say: "Why are not the Angels sent down to us, or (why) do we not see our Lord?" Indeed they have an arrogant conceit of themselves, and mighty is the insolence of their impiety!

22. The Day they see the Angels, - no joy will there be to the sinners that Day: the (Angels) will say: "There is a barrier forbidden (to you) altogether!"

23. And We shall turn to whatever deeds they did (in this life), and We shall make such deeds as floating dust scattered about.

24. The Companions of the Garden will be well, that Day,

وَقَالَ الَّذِيْنَ لَا يَرْجُوْنَ لِقَآءَنَا

لَوْلَا اُنْزِلَ عَلَيْنَا الْمَلٰٓئِكَةُ اَوْ

نَرٰى رَبَّنَا لَقَدِ اسْتَكْبَرُوْا فِيْٓ

اَنْفُسِهِمْ وَعَتَوْ عُتُوًّا كَبِيْرًا ۞

يَوْمَ يَرَوْنَ الْمَلٰٓئِكَةَ لَا بُشْرٰى

يَوْمَئِذٍ لِّلْمُجْرِمِيْنَ وَيَقُوْلُوْنَ

حِجْرًا مَّحْجُوْرًا ۞ وَقَدِمْنَآ اِلٰى

مَا عَمِلُوْا مِنْ عَمَلٍ فَجَعَلْنٰهُ هَبَآءً

مَّنْثُوْرًا ۞ اَصْحٰبُ الْجَنَّةِ يَوْمَئِذٍ

پاره

وَقَالَ الَّذِينَ

(۱۹)

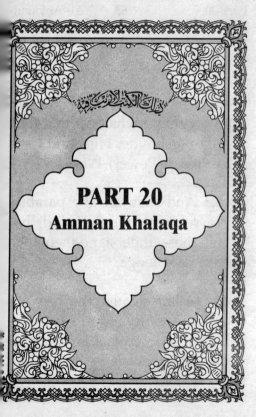

بذلك الكتاب لا ريب فيه

PART 20
Amman Khalaqa

of houses is the spider's house; - if they but knew.

42. Verily Allah does know of (every thing) whatever that they call upon besides Him: and He is Exalted (in Power), Wise.

43. And such are the parables We set forth for mankind, but only those understand them who have knowledge.

44. Allah created the heavens and the earth in true (proportions): verily in that is a Sign for those who believe.

الْبُيُوتِ لَبَيْتُ الْعَنْكَبُوتِ

لَوْ كَانُوا يَعْلَمُونَ ۞ إِنَّ اللّٰهَ

يَعْلَمُ مَا يَدْعُونَ مِنْ دُوْنِهِ

مِنْ شَيْءٍ ﳲ وَ هُوَ الْعَزِيزُ

الْحَكِيمُ ۞ وَ تِلْكَ الْاَمْثَالُ

نَضْرِبُهَا لِلنَّاسِ ۚ وَ مَا يَعْقِلُهَا

اِلَّا الْعٰلِمُوْنَ ۞ خَلَقَ اللّٰهُ

السَّمٰوٰتِ وَالْاَرْضَ بِالْحَقِّ ۚ إِنَّ

فِيْ ذٰلِكَ لَاٰيَةً لِّلْمُؤْمِنِيْنَ ۞

a violent tornado (with showers of stones); some were caught by a (mighty) Blast; some We caused the earth to swallow up; and some We drowned (in the waters): it was not Allah Who injured (or oppressed) them: they wronged themselves.

41. The parable of those who take protectors other than Allah is that of the spider, who builds (to itself) a house; but truly the flimsiest

عَلَيۡهِ حَاصِبًا ۚ وَمِنۡهُمۡ مَّنۡ

اَخَذَتۡهُ الصَّيۡحَةُ ۚ وَمِنۡهُمۡ مَّنۡ

خَسَفۡنَا بِهِ الۡاَرۡضَ ۚ وَمِنۡهُمۡ

مَّنۡ اَغۡرَقۡنَا ۚ وَمَا كَانَ

اللّٰهُ لِيَظۡلِمَهُمۡ وَلٰكِنۡ كَانُوۡۤا

اَنۡفُسَهُمۡ يَظۡلِمُوۡنَ ۞ مَثَلُ

الَّذِيۡنَ اتَّخَذُوۡا مِنۡ دُوۡنِ

اللّٰهِ اَوۡلِيَآءَ كَمَثَلِ الۡعَنۡكَبُوۡتِ ۖ

اِتَّخَذَتۡ بَيۡتًا ۚ وَاِنَّ اَوۡهَنَ

and the Thamud (people): clearly will appear to you from (the traces) of their buildings (their fate): the Evil One made their deeds alluring to them, and kept them back from the Path, though they were gifted with intelligence and skill.

39. (Remember also) Qarun, Pharaoh, and Haman: there came to them Moses with clear Signs, but they behaved with insolence on the earth; yet they could not overreach (Us).

40. Each one of them We seized for his crime: of them, against some We sent

وَثَمُودَا۟ وَقَد تَّبَيَّنَ لَكُم

مِّن مَّسٰكِنِهِمْ وَزَيَّنَ لَهُمُ

الشَّيْطٰنُ أَعْمَالَهُمْ فَصَدَّهُمْ عَنِ

السَّبِيلِ وَكَانُوا۟ مُسْتَبْصِرِينَ ۞

وَقَارُونَ وَفِرْعَوْنَ وَهَامٰنَ ۖ

وَلَقَدْ جَاءَهُم مُّوسٰى بِالْبَيِّنٰتِ

فَاسْتَكْبَرُوا۟ فِي الْأَرْضِ وَمَا

كَانُوا۟ سٰبِقِينَ ۞ فَكُلًّا أَخَذْنَا

بِذَنبِهِ ۖ فَمِنْهُم مَّنْ أَرْسَلْنَا

heaven, because they have been wickedly rebellious."

35. And We have left thereof an evident Sign, for any people who (care to) understand.

36. To the Madyan (people) (We sent) their brother Shu'aib. Then he said: "O my people! Serve Allah, and fear the Last Day: nor commit evil on the earth, with intent to do mischief."

37. But they rejected him: then the mighty Blast seized them, and they lay prostrate in their homes by the morning.

38. (Remember also) the 'Ad

السَّمَاءِ بِمَا كَانُوْا يَفْسُقُوْنَ ۞

وَلَقَدْ تَّرَكْنَا مِنْهَا ايَةًۢ

بَيِّنَةً لِّقَوْمٍ يَّعْقِلُوْنَ ۞ وَاِلٰى

مَدْيَنَ اَخَاهُمْ شُعَيْبًا فَقَالَ

يٰقَوْمِ اعْبُدُوا اللّٰهَ وَارْجُوا

الْيَوْمَ الْاٰخِرَ وَلَا تَعْثَوْا فِى

الْاَرْضِ مُفْسِدِيْنَ ۞ فَكَذَّبُوْهُ

فَاَخَذَتْهُمُ الرَّجْفَةُ فَاَصْبَحُوْا

فِىْ دَارِهِمْ جٰثِمِيْنَ ۞ وَعَادًا

is there : we will certainly save him and his followrs, - except his wife: she is of those who lag behind!"

33. And when Our Messengers came to Lut, he was grieved on their account, and felt himself powerless (to protect) them: but they said: "Fear you not, nor grieve: we are (here) to save you and your kinsfolk, except your wife: she is of those who lag behind."

34. "For we are going to bring down on the people of this township a Punishment from

فِيهَا لَنُنَجِّيَنَّهُ وَأَهْلَهُ إِلَّا

امْرَأَتَهُ كَانَتْ مِنَ الْغٰبِرِينَ

۞ وَلَمَّآ أَن جَآءَتْ رُسُلُنَا

لُوطًا سِيٓءَ بِهِمْ وَضَاقَ بِهِمْ

ذَرْعًا وَقَالُوا لَا تَخَفْ وَلَا

تَحْزَنْ إِنَّا مُنَجُّوكَ وَأَهْلَكَ

إِلَّا امْرَأَتَكَ كَانَتْ مِنَ

الْغٰبِرِينَ ۞ إِنَّا مُنزِلُونَ عَلَىٰ

أَهْلِ هٰذِهِ الْقَرْيَةِ رِجْزًا مِّنَ

but this: they said: "Bring us the Wrath of Allah if you tell the truth."

30. He said: "O my Lord! Help you me against people who do mischief!"

31. When Our Messengers came to Abraham with the good news, they said: "We are indeed going to destroy the people of this township: for truly they are (addicted to) crime."

32. He said: "But there is Lut there." They said: "Well do we know who

قَوْمِهِ إِلَّا أَن قَالُوا ائْتِنَا

بِعَذَابِ اللَّهِ إِن كُنتَ مِنَ

الصَّادِقِينَ ۞ قَالَ رَبِّ انصُرْنِي

عَلَى الْقَوْمِ الْمُفْسِدِينَ ۞ وَلَمَّا

جَآءَتْ رُسُلُنَآ إِبْرَٰهِيمَ بِالْبُشْرَىٰ

قَالُوٓا إِنَّا مُهْلِكُوٓا أَهْلِ هَٰذِهِ

الْقَرْيَةِ إِنَّ أَهْلَهَا كَانُوا

ظَٰلِمِينَ ۞ قَالَ إِنَّ فِيهَا

لُوطًا قَالُوا نَحْنُ أَعْلَمُ بِمَن

Prophethood and Revelation, and We granted him his reward in this life; and he will be in the Hereafter (of the company) of the righteous.

28. And (remember) Lut: behold, he said to his people: "You do commit lewdness, such as no people in creation (ever) committed before you."

29. "Do you indeed approach men, and cut off the highway? - and practise wickedness (even) in your councils?" But his people gave no answer

النُّبُوَّةَ وَالْكِتٰبَ وَاٰتَيْنٰهُ أَجْرَهُ
فِي الدُّنْيَا ۚ وَإِنَّهُ فِي الْاٰخِرَةِ
لَمِنَ الصّٰلِحِيْنَ ۞ وَلُوْطًا اِذْ
قَالَ لِقَوْمِهٖ اِنَّكُمْ لَتَأْتُوْنَ
الْفَاحِشَةَ ۖ مَا سَبَقَكُمْ بِهَا مِنْ
اَحَدٍ مِّنَ الْعٰلَمِيْنَ ۞ اَئِنَّكُمْ
لَتَأْتُوْنَ الرِّجَالَ وَتَقْطَعُوْنَ
السَّبِيْلَ ۙ وَتَأْتُوْنَ فِيْ نَادِيْكُمُ
الْمُنْكَرَ ۗ فَمَا كَانَ جَوَابَ

out of mutual love and regard
between yourselves in this life;
but on the Day of Judgment you
shall disown each other and curse
each other: and your abode will
be the Fire, and you shall have
none to help."

26.   But Lut had faith in Him: he
said: "I will leave home for the
sake of my Lord: for He is Exalted
in Might, and Wise."

27.   And We gave (Abraham)
Isaac and Jacob, and ordained
among his progeny

أَوْثَانًا مَّوَدَّةَ بَيْنِكُمْ فِي

الْحَيْوةِ الدُّنْيَا ثُمَّ يَوْمَ الْقِيْمَةِ

يَكْفُرُ بَعْضُكُمْ بِبَعْضٍ وَّيَلْعَنُ

بَعْضُكُمْ بَعْضًا وَّمَأْوَاكُمُ النَّارُ

وَمَا لَكُمْ مِّنْ نَّصِرِيْنَ ۞ فَاٰمَنَ

لَهُ لُوْطٌ وَقَالَ اِنِّيْ مُهَاجِرٌ

اِلٰى رَبِّيْ اِنَّهُ هُوَ الْعَزِيْزُ

الْحَكِيْمُ ۞ وَوَهَبْنَا لَهٗٓ اِسْحٰقَ

وَيَعْقُوْبَ وَجَعَلْنَا فِيْ ذُرِّيَّتِهِ

reject the Signs of Allah and the Meeting with Him (in the Hereafter), - it is they who shall despair of My Mercy: it is they who will (suffer) a most grievous Chastisement.

24. So nothing was the answer of (Abraham's) people except that they said: "Slay him or burn him." But Allah did save him from the Fire. Verily in this are Signs for people who believe.

25. And he said: "For you, you have taken (for worship) idols besides Allah,

كَفَرُوا بِـَايَتِ اللّٰهِ وَلِقَآئِهٖ

أُولٰٓئِكَ يَئِسُوا مِنْ رَّحْمَتِىْ

وَأُولٰٓئِكَ لَهُمْ عَذَابٌ أَلِيْمٌ ۝

فَمَا كَانَ جَوَابَ قَوْمِهٖٓ

إِلَّآ أَنْ قَالُوا اقْتُلُوهُ أَوْ

حَرِّقُوهُ فَأَنْجَىٰهُ اللّٰهُ مِنَ

النَّارِ ۚ إِنَّ فِىْ ذٰلِكَ لَأَيٰتٍ

لِّقَوْمٍ يُّؤْمِنُوْنَ ۝ وَقَالَ إِنَّمَا

اتَّخَذْتُمْ مِّنْ دُوْنِ اللّٰهِ

Allah did originate creation; so will Allah produce a later creation: for Allah has power over all things."

21. "He punishes whom He pleases, and He grants Mercy to whom He pleases, and towards Him are you turned."

22. "Not on earth nor in heaven will you be able (fleeing) to frustrate (His Plan), nor have you, besides Allah, any protector or helper."

23. Those who

بَدَاَ الْخَلْقَ ثُمَّ اللهُ يُنْشِئُ

النَّشْاَةَ الْاٰخِرَةَ ۚ اِنَّ اللهَ

عَلٰى كُلِّ شَىْءٍ قَدِيْرٌ ۩

يُعَذِّبُ مَنْ يَّشَاءُ وَيَرْحَمُ

مَنْ يَّشَاءُ ۚ وَاِلَيْهِ تُقْلَبُوْنَ ۩

وَمَاۤ اَنْتُمْ بِمُعْجِزِيْنَ فِى

الْاَرْضِ وَلَا فِى السَّمَاءِ ۚ وَمَا

لَكُمْ مِّنْ دُوْنِ اللهِ مِنْ

وَّلِيٍّ وَّلَا نَصِيْرٍ ۩ وَالَّذِيْنَ

serve Him, and be grateful to Him: to Him will be your return."

18. "And if you reject (the Message), so did generations before you: and the duty of the Apostle is only to preach publicly (and clearly)."

19. See they not how Allah originates creation, then repeats it: truly that is easy for Allah.

20. Say: "Travel through the earth and see how

الرِّزْقَ وَاعْبُدُوْهُ وَاشْكُرُوْا

لَهٗ ؕ اِلَيْهِ تُرْجَعُوْنَ ۞ وَاِنْ

تُكَذِّبُوْا فَقَدْ كَذَّبَ اُمَمٌ

مِّنْ قَبْلِكُمْ ؕ وَمَا عَلَى الرَّسُوْلِ

اِلَّا الْبَلٰغُ الْمُبِيْنُ ۞ اَوَلَمْ

يَرَوْا كَيْفَ يُبْدِئُ اللّٰهُ

الْخَلْقَ ثُمَّ يُعِيْدُهٗ ؕ اِنَّ ذٰلِكَ

عَلَى اللّٰهِ يَسِيْرٌ ۞ قُلْ سِيْرُوْا

فِى الْاَرْضِ فَانْظُرُوْا كَيْفَ

and We made the (Ark) a Sign for all peoples!

16. And (We also saved) Abraham: behold, he said to his people, "Serve Allah and fear Him: that will be best for you - if you understand!"

17. "For you do worship idols besides Allah, and you invent falsehood. The things that you worship besides Allah have no power to give you sustenance: then seek sustenance from Allah,

وَجَعَلْنَاهَآ اٰيَةً لِّلْعٰلَمِيْنَ ۝

وَاِبْرٰهِيْمَ اِذْ قَالَ لِقَوْمِهِ

اعْبُدُوا اللّٰهَ وَاتَّقُوهُ ذٰلِكُمْ

خَيْرٌ لَّكُمْ اِنْ كُنْتُمْ تَعْلَمُوْنَ ۝

اِنَّمَا تَعْبُدُوْنَ مِنْ دُوْنِ

اللّٰهِ اَوْثَانًا وَّتَخْلُقُوْنَ اِفْكًا

اِنَّ الَّذِيْنَ تَعْبُدُوْنَ مِنْ

دُوْنِ اللّٰهِ لَا يَمْلِكُوْنَ لَكُمْ

رِزْقًا فَابْتَغُوْا عِنْدَ اللّٰهِ

in fact they are liars!

13. They will bear their own burdens, and (other) burdens along with their own, and on the Day of Judgments they will be called to account for their falsehoods.

14. We (once) sent Noah to his people, and he tarried among them a thousand years less fifty: but the Deluge overwhelmed them while they (persisted in) sin.

15. But We saved him and the companions of the Ark,

مِنْ شَىْءٍ ۚ إِنَّهُمْ لَكٰذِبُوْنَ ۞

وَلَيَحْمِلُنَّ أَثْقَالَهُمْ وَأَثْقَالًا

مَّعَ أَثْقَالِهِمْ ۖ وَلَيُسْـَٔلُنَّ يَوْمَ

الْقِيٰمَةِ عَمَّا كَانُوْا يَفْتَرُوْنَ ۞

وَلَقَدْ أَرْسَلْنَا نُوْحًا إِلٰى قَوْمِهٖ

فَلَبِثَ فِيْهِمْ أَلْفَ سَنَةٍ إِلَّا

خَمْسِيْنَ عَامًا ۖ فَأَخَذَهُمُ

الطُّوْفَانُ وَهُمْ ظٰلِمُوْنَ ۞

فَأَنْجَيْنٰهُ وَأَصْحٰبَ السَّفِيْنَةِ

Allah! and if help comes (to you) from your Lord, they are sure to say, "We have (always) been with you!" Does not Allah know best all that is in the hearts of all creation?

11. And Allah most certainly knows those who believe, and as certainly those who are Hypocrites.

12. And the unbelievers say to those who believe: "Follow our path, and we will bear (the consequences) of your faults." Never in the least will they bear their faults:

اللهُ وَلَئِنْ جَاءَ نَصْرٌ مِّنْ

رَّبِّكَ لَيَقُولُنَّ إِنَّا كُنَّا مَعَكُمْ

أَوَ لَيْسَ اللهُ بِأَعْلَمَ بِمَا فِي

صُدُورِ الْعُلَمِينَ ۝ وَلَيَعْلَمَنَّ

اللهُ الَّذِينَ أَمَنُوا وَلَيَعْلَمَنَّ

الْمُنْفِقِينَ ۝ وَقَالَ الَّذِينَ

كَفَرُوا لِلَّذِينَ أَمَنُوا اتَّبِعُوا

سَبِيلَنَا وَلْنَحْمِلْ خَطَيكُمْ وَمَا

هُمْ بِحْمِلِينَ مِنْ خَطَيهُمْ

but if they (either of them) strive (to force) you to join with Me (in worship) anything of which you have no knowledge, obey them not. You have (all) to return to me, and I will tell you (the truth) of all that you did.

9.   And those who believe and work righteous deeds, - them shall We admit to the company of the Righteous.

10.   Then there are among men such as say, "We believe in Allah"; but when they suffer affliction in (the cause of) Allah, they treat men's oppression as if it were the Wrath of

حُسْنًا ۚ وَإِنْ جَاهَدَاكَ لِتُشْرِكَ

بِى مَا لَيْسَ لَكَ بِهِ عِلْمٌ

فَلَا تُطِعْهُمَا ۚ إِلَىَّ مَرْجِعُكُمْ

فَأُنَبِّئُكُمْ بِمَا كُنْتُمْ تَعْمَلُونَ ۝

وَالَّذِينَ آمَنُوا وَعَمِلُوا الصَّالِحَاتِ

لَنُدْخِلَنَّهُمْ فِى الصَّالِحِينَ ۝

وَمِنَ النَّاسِ مَن يَقُولُ آمَنَّا

بِاللَّهِ فَإِذَآ أُوذِىَ فِى اللَّهِ

جَعَلَ فِتْنَةَ النَّاسِ كَعَذَابِ

hopes are in the meeting with Allah (in the Hereafter, let them strive); for the term (appointed) by Allah is surely coming and He hears and knows (all things).

6. And if any strive (with might and main), they do so for their own souls: for Allah is free of all needs from all creation.

7. Those who believe and work righteous deeds, - from them shall We blot out all evil (that may be) in them, and We shall reward them according to the best of their deeds.

8. We have enjoined on man kindness to parents:

يَرْجُوا لِقَآءَ اللّٰهِ فَاِنَّ اَجَلَ

اللّٰهِ لَاٰتٍ ؕ وَهُوَ السَّمِيْعُ الْعَلِيْمُ ۝

وَمَنْ جَاهَدَ فَاِنَّمَا يُجَاهِدُ

لِنَفْسِهٖ ؕ اِنَّ اللّٰهَ لَغَنِيٌّ عَنِ

الْعٰلَمِيْنَ ۝ وَالَّذِيْنَ اٰمَنُوْا

وَعَمِلُوا الصّٰلِحٰتِ لَنُكَفِّرَنَّ

عَنْهُمْ سَيِّاٰتِهِمْ وَلَنَجْزِيَنَّهُمْ

اَحْسَنَ الَّذِيْ كَانُوْا يَعْمَلُوْنَ ۝

وَوَصَّيْنَا الْاِنْسَانَ بِوَالِدَيْهِ

Al-'Ankabut (The Spider)
Bismillahir-Rahmanir-Rahim

1.   Alif. Lam. Mim.

2.   Do men think that they will be left alone on saying, "We believe", and that they will not be tested?

3.   We did test those before them, and Allah will certainly know those who are true from those who are false.

4.   Do those who practise evil think that they will get the better of Us? Evil is their judgment!

5.   For those whose

بِسْمِ اللهِ الرَّحْمٰنِ الرَّحِيمِ

الٓمّٓ ۚ اَحَسِبَ النَّاسُ اَنْ يُّتْرَكُوٓا

اَنْ يَّقُوْلُوٓا اٰمَنَّا وَهُمْ لَا

يُفْتَنُوْنَ ۞ وَلَقَدْ فَتَنَّا الَّذِيْنَ

مِنْ قَبْلِهِمْ فَلَيَعْلَمَنَّ اللهُ

الَّذِيْنَ صَدَقُوْا وَلَيَعْلَمَنَّ

الْكٰذِبِيْنَ ۞ اَمْ حَسِبَ الَّذِيْنَ

يَعْمَلُوْنَ السَّيِّاٰتِ اَنْ يَّسْبِقُوْنَا ۗ

سَآءَ مَا يَحْكُمُوْنَ ۞ مَنْ كَانَ

as a Mercy from your Lord: therefore lend not you support in any way to those who reject (Allah's Message).

87. And let nothing keep you back from the Signs of Allah after they have been revealed to you: and invite (men) to your Lord, and be not of the company of those who join gods with Allah.

88. And call not, besides Allah, on another god. There is no god but He. Everything (that exists) will perish except His Own Face. To Him belongs the Command, and to Him will you (all) be brought back.

رَحْمَةً مِّن رَّبِّكَ فَلَا تَكُونَنَّ

ظَهِيرًا لِّلْكَافِرِينَ ۞ وَلَا يَصُدُّنَّكَ

عَنْ اٰيَاتِ اللّٰهِ بَعْدَ اِذْ اُنزِلَتْ

اِلَيْكَ وَادْعُ اِلٰى رَبِّكَ وَلَا

تَكُونَنَّ مِنَ الْمُشْرِكِينَ ۞ وَلَا

تَدْعُ مَعَ اللّٰهِ اِلٰهًا اٰخَرَ ۘ

لَا اِلٰهَ اِلَّا هُوَ ۚ كُلُّ شَيْءٍ

هَالِكٌ اِلَّا وَجْهَهُ ۚ لَهُ الْحُكْمُ

وَاِلَيْهِ تُرْجَعُونَ ۞

good, the reward to him is better than his deed; but if any does evil, the doers of evil are only punished (to the extent) of their deeds.

85. Verily He Who ordained the Qur'an for you, will bring you back to the Place of Return. Say: "My Lord knows best who it is that brings true guidance, and who is in manifest error."

86. And you had not expected that the Book would be sent to you except

بِالْحَسَنَةِ فَلَهُ خَيْرٌ مِّنْهَا ۚ وَمَنْ

جَآءَ بِالسَّيِّئَةِ فَلَا يُجْزَى

الَّذِينَ عَمِلُوا السَّيِّاٰتِ اِلَّا

مَا كَانُوا يَعْمَلُوْنَ ۝ اِنَّ الَّذِيْ

فَرَضَ عَلَيْكَ الْقُرْاٰنَ لَرَآدُّكَ

اِلٰى مَعَادٍ ۚ قُلْ رَّبِّيْ اَعْلَمُ مَنْ

جَآءَ بِالْهُدٰى وَمَنْ هُوَ فِيْ

ضَلٰلٍ مُّبِيْنٍ ۝ وَمَا كُنْتَ تَرْجُوْا

اَنْ يُّلْقٰى اِلَيْكَ الْكِتٰبُ اِلَّا

had envied his position the day before began to say on the morrow: "Ah! It is indeed Allah Who enlarges the provision or restricts it, to any of His servants He pleases! Had it not been that Allah was gracious to us, He could have caused the earth to swallow us up! Ah! Those who reject Allah will assuredly never prosper."

83.   That Home of the Hereafter We shall give to those who intend not high-handedness or mischief on earth: and the end is (best) for the righteous.

84.   If any does

تَمَنَّوْا مَكَانَهُ بِالْأَمْسِ يَقُولُونَ

وَيْكَأَنَّ اللهَ يَبْسُطُ الرِّزْقَ

لِمَنْ يَشَاءُ مِنْ عِبَادِهِ وَيَقْدِرُ ۚ

لَوْلَا أَنْ مَنَّ اللهُ عَلَيْنَا

لَخَسَفَ بِنَا ۚ وَيْكَأَنَّهُ لَا يُفْلِحُ

الْكَافِرُونَ ۞ تِلْكَ الدَّارُ الْأَخِرَةُ

نَجْعَلُهَا لِلَّذِينَ لَا يُرِيدُونَ

عُلُوًّا فِي الْأَرْضِ وَلَا فَسَادًا ۚ

وَالْعَاقِبَةُ لِلْمُتَّقِينَ ۞ مَنْ جَاءَ

Qarun has got! For he is truly a lord of mighty good fortune!"

80. But those who had been granted (true) knowledge said: "Alas for you! The reward of Allah (in the Hereafter) is best for those who believe and work righteousness: but this none shall attain, save those who steadfastly persevere (in good)."

81. Then We caused the earth to swallow up him and his house; and he had not (the least little) party to help him against Allah, nor could he defend himself.

82. And those who

أُوتِيَ قَارُونُ إِنَّهُ لَذُو حَظٍّ

عَظِيمٍ ۞ وَقَالَ الَّذِينَ أُوتُوا

الْعِلْمَ وَيْلَكُمْ ثَوَابُ اللهِ خَيْرٌ

لِّمَنْ أَمَنَ وَعَمِلَ صَالِحًا وَلَا

يُلَقَّاهَا إِلَّا الصَّابِرُونَ ۞ فَخَسَفْنَا

بِهِ وَبِدَارِهِ الْأَرْضَ فَمَا

كَانَ لَهُ مِنْ فِئَةٍ يَنْصُرُونَهُ

مِنْ دُونِ اللهِ وَمَا كَانَ مِنَ

الْمُنْتَصِرِينَ ۞ وَأَصْبَحَ الَّذِينَ

78. He said: "This has been given to me because of a certain knowledge which I have." Did he not know that Allah had destroyed, before him, (whole) generations, - which were superior to him in strength and greater in the amount (of riches) they had collected? But the wicked are not called (immediately) to account for their sins.

79. So he went forth among his people in the (pride of his wordly) glitter. Said those whose aim is the Life of this World: "Oh! That we had the like of what

قَالَ اِنَّمَآ اُوْتِيْتُهٗ عَلٰى عِلْمٍ

عِنْدِيْ ۚ اَوَلَمْ يَعْلَمْ اَنَّ اللّٰهَ

قَدْ اَهْلَكَ مِنْ قَبْلِهٖ مِنَ

الْقُرُوْنِ مَنْ هُوَ اَشَدُّ مِنْهُ

قُوَّةً وَّ اَكْثَرُ جَمْعًا ۚ وَ لَا يُسْئَلُ

عَنْ ذُنُوْبِهِمُ الْمُجْرِمُوْنَ ۝

فَخَرَجَ عَلٰى قَوْمِهٖ فِيْ زِيْنَتِهٖ ۚ

قَالَ الَّذِيْنَ يُرِيْدُوْنَ الْحَيٰوةَ

الدُّنْيَا يٰلَيْتَ لَنَا مِثْلَ مَآ

that their very keys would have been a burden to a body of strong men, behold, his people said to him: "Exult not, for Allah loves not those who exult (in riches)."

77. "But seek, with the (wealth) which Allah has bestowed on you, the Home of the Hereafter, nor forget your portion in this world: but do you good, as Allah has been good to you, and seek not (occasions for) mischief in the land: for Allah loves not those who do mischief."

مَآ اِنَّ مَفَاتِحَهُ لَتَنُوٓأُ بِالْعُصْبَةِ
أُولِى الْقُوَّةِ اِذْ قَالَ لَهُ قَوْمُهُ
لَا تَفْرَحْ اِنَّ اللّٰهَ لَا يُحِبُّ
الْفَرِحِيْنَ ۝ وَابْتَغِ فِيْمَآ اٰتٰىكَ
اللّٰهُ الدَّارَ الْاٰخِرَةَ وَلَا تَنْسَ
نَصِيْبَكَ مِنَ الدُّنْيَا وَاَحْسِنْ
كَمَآ اَحْسَنَ اللّٰهُ اِلَيْكَ وَلَا
تَبْغِ الْفَسَادَ فِى الْاَرْضِ اِنَّ
اللّٰهَ لَا يُحِبُّ الْمُفْسِدِيْنَ ۝

of His Grace;- and in order that you may be grateful.

74. The Day that He will call on them, He will say: "Where are my 'partners'? Whom you imagined (to be such)?"

75. And from each people shall We draw a witness, and We shall say: "Produce your Proof": then shall they know that the Truth is in Allah (alone), and the (lies) which they invented will leave them in lurch.

76. Qarun was doubtless, of the people of Moses; but he acted insolently towards them: such were the treasures We had bestowed on him

مِنْ فَضْلِهِ وَلَعَلَّكُمْ تَشْكُرُوْنَ ۞

وَيَوْمَ يُنَادِيْهِمْ فَيَقُوْلُ اَيْنَ

شُرَكَآءِيَ الَّذِيْنَ كُنْتُمْ تَزْعُمُوْنَ ۞

وَنَزَعْنَا مِنْ كُلِّ اُمَّةٍ شَهِيْدًا

فَقُلْنَا هَاتُوْا بُرْهَانَكُمْ فَعَلِمُوْٓا

اَنَّ الْحَقَّ لِلّٰهِ وَضَلَّ عَنْهُمْ مَّا

كَانُوْا يَفْتَرُوْنَ ۞ اِنَّ قَارُوْنَ

كَانَ مِنْ قَوْمِ مُوْسٰى فَبَغٰى

عَلَيْهِمْ ۖ وَاٰتَيْنٰهُ مِنَ الْكُنُوْزِ

to the Day of Judgment, what god is there other than Allah, who can give you enlighten-ment? Will you not then hearken?

72. Say, do you see? If Allah were to make the day perpetual over you to the Day of Judgment, what god is there other than Allah, who can give you a night in which you can rest? Will you not then see?

73. It is out of His Mercy that He has made for you Night and Day, - that you may rest therein, and that you may seek

اِلٰى يَوْمِ الْقِيٰمَةِ مَنْ اِلٰهٌ

غَيْرُ اللّٰهِ يَأْتِيكُمْ بِضِيَاءٍ ۗ

اَفَلَا تَسْمَعُوْنَ ۞ قُلْ اَرَءَيْتُمْ

اِنْ جَعَلَ اللّٰهُ عَلَيْكُمُ النَّهَارَ

سَرْمَدًا اِلٰى يَوْمِ الْقِيٰمَةِ مَنْ

اِلٰهٌ غَيْرُ اللّٰهِ يَأْتِيكُمْ بِلَيْلٍ

تَسْكُنُوْنَ فِيْهِ ۗ اَفَلَا تُبْصِرُوْنَ ۞

وَمِنْ رَّحْمَتِهٖ جَعَلَ لَكُمُ الَّيْلَ

وَالنَّهَارَ لِتَسْكُنُوْا فِيْهِ وَلِتَبْتَغُوْا

does create and choose as He pleases: no choice have they (in the matter): Glory to Allah! and far is He above the partners they ascribe (to Him)!

69. And your Lord knows all that their hearts conceal and all that they reveal.

70. And He is Allah: there is no god but He. To Him be praise, at the first and at the last: for Him is the Command, and to Him shall you (all) be brought back.

71. Say, do you see? If Allah were to make the night perpetual over you

يَخۡلُقُ مَا يَشَآءُ وَيَخۡتَارُ مَا

كَانَ لَهُمُ الۡخِيَرَةُ سُبۡحَٰنَ اللّٰهِ

وَتَعَٰلَىٰ عَمَّا يُشۡرِكُونَ ۞ وَرَبُّكَ

يَعۡلَمُ مَا تُكِنُّ صُدُورُهُمۡ وَمَا

يُعۡلِنُونَ ۞ وَهُوَ اللّٰهُ لَآ إِلَٰهَ

إِلَّا هُوَ لَهُ الۡحَمۡدُ فِى الۡأُولَىٰ

وَالۡأَخِرَةِ وَلَهُ الۡحُكۡمُ وَإِلَيۡهِ

تُرۡجَعُونَ ۞ قُلۡ أَرَءَيۡتُمۡ إِنۡ

جَعَلَ اللّٰهُ عَلَيۡكُمُ الَّيۡلَ سَرۡمَدًا

"Call upon your 'partners' (for help)": they will call upon them, but they will not listen to them; and they will see the Chastisement (before them); (how they will wish) 'if only they had been open to guidance!'

65. That Day (Allah) will call to them, and say: "What was the answer you gave to the Apostles?"

66. Then the (whole) story that Day will seem obscure to them (like light to the blind) and they will not be able (even) to question each other.

67. But any that (in this life) had repented, believed, and worked righteousness, happily he shall be one of the successful.

68. Your Lord

ادْعُوا شُرَكَاءَكُمْ فَدَعَوْهُمْ فَلَمْ

يَسْتَجِيبُوا لَهُمْ وَرَأَوُا الْعَذَابَ

لَوْ أَنَّهُمْ كَانُوا يَهْتَدُونَ ۞

وَيَوْمَ يُنَادِيهِمْ فَيَقُولُ مَاذَا

أَجَبْتُمُ الْمُرْسَلِينَ ۞ فَعَمِيَتْ

عَلَيْهِمُ الْأَنبَاءُ يَوْمَئِذٍ فَهُمْ

لَا يَتَسَاءَلُونَ ۞ فَأَمَّا مَن تَابَ

وَآمَنَ وَعَمِلَ صَالِحًا فَعَسَى أَن

يَكُونَ مِنَ الْمُفْلِحِينَ ۞ وَرَبُّكَ

is going to reach its (fulfilment), and one to whom We have given the good things of this life, but who, on the Day of Judgment, is to be among those brought up (for punishment)?

62. That Day (Allah) will call to them, and say "Where are my 'partners?' - whom you imagined (to be such)?"

63. Those against whom the charge will be proved, will say: "Our Lord! These are the ones whom we led astray: we led them astray, as we were astray ourselves: we free ourselves (from them) in Your presence: it was not us they worshipped."

64. It will be said (to them):

لَاقِيهِ كَمَنْ مَّتَّعْنَٰهُ مَتَاعَ

الْحَيَوٰةِ الدُّنْيَا ثُمَّ هُوَ يَوْمَ

الْقِيٰمَةِ مِنَ الْمُحْضَرِينَ ۝ وَيَوْمَ

يُنَادِيهِمْ فَيَقُولُ اَيْنَ شُرَكَآءِىَ

الَّذِينَ كُنْتُمْ تَزْعُمُونَ ۝ قَالَ

الَّذِينَ حَقَّ عَلَيْهِمُ الْقَوْلُ رَبَّنَا

هٰٓؤُلَآءِ الَّذِينَ اَغْوَيْنَا اَغْوَيْنٰهُمْ

كَمَا غَوَيْنَا تَبَرَّأْنَا اِلَيْكَ مَا

كَانُوٓا اِيَّانَا يَعْبُدُونَ ۝ وَقِيلَ

59. Nor was your Lord the one to destroy a population until He had sent to its centre an Apostle, rehearsing to them Our Signs; nor are We going to destroy a population except when its members practise iniquity.

60. The (material) things which you are given are but the conveniences of this life and the glitter thereof; but that which is with Allah is better and more enduring: will you not then be wise?

61. Are (these two) alike? - one to whom We have made a goodly promise, and who

وَمَا كَانَ رَبُّكَ مُهْلِكَ الْقُرَى

حَتَّى يَبْعَثَ فِيٓ أُمِّهَا رَسُولًا

يَتْلُوا عَلَيْهِمْ اٰيٰتِنَا وَمَا كُنَّا

مُهْلِكِي الْقُرَىٰ إِلَّا وَأَهْلُهَا

ظٰلِمُونَ ۞ وَمَآ أُوتِيتُمْ مِّنْ

شَىْءٍ فَمَتَاعُ الْحَيٰوةِ الدُّنْيَا

وَزِينَتُهَا وَمَا عِنْدَ اللّٰهِ خَيْرٌ

وَّأَبْقَىٰ أَفَلَا تَعْقِلُونَ ۞ أَفَمَنْ

وَّعَدْنٰهُ وَعْدًا حَسَنًا فَهُوَ

57. They say: "If we were to follow the guidance with you, we should be snatched away from our land." Have We not established for them a secure sanctuary, to which are brought as tribute fruits of all kinds, - a provision from Ourselves? But most of them understand not.

58. And how many populations We destroyed, which exulted in their life (of ease and plenty)! Now those habitations of theirs, after them, are deserted, - all but a (miserable) few! and We are their heirs!

وَقَالُوٓا اِنْ نَّتَّبِعِ الْهُدٰى مَعَكَ

نُتَخَطَّفْ مِنْ اَرْضِنَا ۗ اَوَلَمْ

نُمَكِّنْ لَّهُمْ حَرَمًا اٰمِنًا يُّجْبٰۤى

اِلَيْهِ ثَمَرٰتُ كُلِّ شَىْءٍ رِّزْقًا

مِّنْ لَّدُنَّا وَلٰكِنَّ اَكْثَرَهُمْ لَا

يَعْلَمُوْنَ ۞ وَكَمْ اَهْلَكْنَا مِنْ

قَرْيَةٍۭ بَطِرَتْ مَعِيْشَتَهَا ۚ فَتِلْكَ

مَسٰكِنُهُمْ لَمْ تُسْكَنْ مِّنْۢ بَعْدِهِمْ

اِلَّا قَلِيْلًا ۗ وَكُنَّا نَحْنُ الْوٰرِثِيْنَ ۞

54. Twice will they be given their reward, for that they have persevered, that they avert Evil with Good, and that they spend (in charity) out of what We have given them.

55. And when they hear vain talk, they turn away therefrom and say: "To us our deeds, and to you yours; peace be to you: we seek not the ignorant."

56. It is true you will not be able to guide every one, whom you love; but Allah guides those whom He wills. And He knows best those who receive guidance.

أُولَٰئِكَ يُؤْتَوْنَ أَجْرَهُم مَّرَّتَيْنِ

بِمَا صَبَرُوا وَيَدْرَءُونَ بِالْحَسَنَةِ

السَّيِّئَةَ وَمِمَّا رَزَقْنَاهُمْ يُنفِقُونَ ۝

وَإِذَا سَمِعُوا اللَّغْوَ أَعْرَضُوا

عَنْهُ وَقَالُوا لَنَا أَعْمَالُنَا وَلَكُمْ

أَعْمَالُكُمْ سَلَامٌ عَلَيْكُمْ لَا نَبْتَغِي

الْجَاهِلِينَ ۝ إِنَّكَ لَا تَهْدِي مَنْ

أَحْبَبْتَ وَلَٰكِنَّ اللَّهَ يَهْدِي مَن

يَشَاءُ وَهُوَ أَعْلَمُ بِالْمُهْتَدِينَ ۝

than one who follow his own lusts, devoid of guidance From Allah? For Allah guides not people given to wrong-doing.

51. Now have We caused the Word to reach them themselves, in order that they may receive admonition.

52. Those to whom We sent the Book before this, - they do believe in this (revelation):

53. And when it is recited to them, they say: "We believe therein, for it is the Truth from our Lord: indeed we have been Muslims (bowing to Allah's Will) from before this.

مِمَّنِ اتَّبَعَ هَوٰهُ بِغَيْرِ هُدًى

مِّنَ اللهِ ؕ اِنَّ اللهَ لَا يَهْدِى

الْقَوْمَ الظّٰلِمِيْنَ ۞ وَلَقَدْ وَصَّلْنَا

لَهُمُ الْقَوْلَ لَعَلَّهُمْ يَتَذَكَّرُوْنَ ۞

اَلَّذِيْنَ اٰتَيْنٰهُمُ الْكِتٰبَ مِنْ

قَبْلِهٖ هُمْ بِهٖ يُؤْمِنُوْنَ ۞

وَاِذَا يُتْلٰى عَلَيْهِمْ قَالُوْٓا اٰمَنَّا

بِهٖۤ اِنَّهُ الْحَقُّ مِنْ رَّبِّنَآ اِنَّا

كُنَّا مِنْ قَبْلِهٖ مُسْلِمِيْنَ ۞

they say, "Why are not (Signs) sent to him, like those which were sent to Moses?" Do they not then reject (the Signs) which were formerly sent to Moses? They say: "Two kinds of sorcery , each assisting the other!" And they say: "For us, we reject all (such things)!"

49.   Say: "Then bring you a Book from Allah, which is a better guide than either of them, that I may follow it! (do), if you are truthful!"

50.   But if they hearken not to you, know that they only follow their own lusts: and who is more astray

قَالُوا لَوْلَا أُوتِيَ مِثْلَ مَا أُوتِيَ

مُوسَى أَوَلَمْ يَكْفُرُوا بِمَا أُوتِيَ

مُوسَى مِنْ قَبْلُ قَالُوا سِحْرَانِ

تَظَاهَرَا وَقَالُوا إِنَّا بِكُلٍّ كَافِرُونَ ۝

قُلْ فَأْتُوا بِكِتَابٍ مِنْ عِنْدِ

اللهِ هُوَ أَهْدَى مِنْهُمَا أَتَّبِعْهُ

إِنْ كُنْتُمْ صَادِقِينَ ۝ فَإِنْ لَّمْ

يَسْتَجِيبُوا لَكَ فَاعْلَمْ أَنَّمَا

يَتَّبِعُونَ أَهْوَاءَهُمْ وَمَنْ أَضَلُّ

We called (to Moses). Yet (are you sent) as Mercy from your Lord, to give warning to a people to whom no warner had come before you: in order that they may receive admonition.

47. If (We had) not (sent you to the Quraish), - in case a calamity should seize them for (the deeds) that their hands have sent forth, they might say: "Our Lord! Why did You not sent us an Apostle? We should then have followed Your Signs and been amongst those who believe!"

48. But (now), when the Truth has come to them from Ourselves,

نَادَيْنَا وَلٰكِنْ رَّحْمَةً مِّنْ رَّبِّكَ

لِتُنْذِرَ قَوْمًا مَّا آتٰهُمْ مِّنْ

نَّذِيرٍ مِّنْ قَبْلِكَ لَعَلَّهُمْ

يَتَذَكَّرُوْنَ ۞ وَلَوْ لَآ اَنْ تُصِيْبَهُمْ

مُّصِيْبَةٌ ۢ بِمَا قَدَّمَتْ اَيْدِيْهِمْ

فَيَقُوْلُوْا رَبَّنَا لَوْ لَآ اَرْسَلْتَ

اِلَيْنَا رَسُوْلًا فَنَتَّبِعَ اٰيٰتِكَ

وَنَكُوْنَ مِنَ الْمُؤْمِنِيْنَ ۞ فَلَمَّا

جَآءَهُمُ الْحَقُّ مِنْ عِنْدِنَا

and Guidance and Mercy, that they might receive admonition.

44. You were not on the Western side when We decreed the Commission to Moses, nor were you a witness (of those events).

45. But We raised up (new) generations, and long were the ages that passed over them; but you were not a dweller among the people of Madyan, rehearsing Our Signs to them; but it is We Who send Apostles (with inspiration).

46. Nor were you at the side of (the Mountain of) Tur when

وَ هُدًى وَّ رَحْمَةً لَّعَلَّهُمْ

يَتَذَكَّرُوْنَ ۞ وَ مَا كُنْتَ بِجَانِبِ

الْغَرْبِيِّ اِذْ قَضَيْنَاۤ اِلَى مُوْسَى

الْاَمْرَ وَ مَا كُنْتَ مِنَ الشّٰهِدِيْنَ ۞

وَ لٰكِنَّاۤ اَنْشَاْنَا قُرُوْنًا فَتَطَاوَلَ

عَلَيْهِمُ الْعُمُرُ وَ مَا كُنْتَ ثَاوِيًا

فِيْۤ اَهْلِ مَدْيَنَ تَتْلُوْا عَلَيْهِمْ

اٰيٰتِنَا وَ لٰكِنَّا كُنَّا مُرْسِلِيْنَ ۞

وَ مَا كُنْتَ بِجَانِبِ الطُّوْرِ اِذْ

and We flung them into the sea: now behold what was the end of those who did wrong!

41. And We made them (but) leaders inviting to the Fire; and on the Day of Judgment no help shall they find.

42. In this world We made a Curse to follow them and on the Day of Judgment they will be among the loathed (and despised).

43. We did reveal to Moses the Book after We had destroyed the earlier generations, (to give) Insight to men,

فَنَبَذْنٰهُمْ فِي الْيَمِّ ۖ فَانْظُرْ

كَيْفَ كَانَ عَاقِبَةُ الظّٰلِمِيْنَ ۞

وَجَعَلْنٰهُمْ اَئِمَّةً يَّدْعُوْنَ اِلَى النَّارِ ۖ

وَيَوْمَ الْقِيٰمَةِ لَا يُنْصَرُوْنَ ۞

وَاَتْبَعْنٰهُمْ فِيْ هٰذِهِ الدُّنْيَا

لَعْنَةً ۖ وَيَوْمَ الْقِيٰمَةِ هُمْ مِّنَ

الْمَقْبُوْحِيْنَ ۞ وَلَقَدْ اٰتَيْنَا مُوْسَى

الْكِتٰبَ مِنْ بَعْدِ مَاۤ اَهْلَكْنَا

الْقُرُوْنَ الْاُوْلٰى بَصَآئِرَ لِلنَّاسِ

38. Pharaoh said: "O chiefs! No god do I know for you but myself: therefore, O Haman! Light me a (kiln to bake bricks) out of clay, and build me a lofty palace, that I may mount up to the god of Moses: but as far as I am concerned, I think (Moses) is a liar!"

39. And he was arrogant and insolent in the land, beyond reason, - he and his hosts: they thought that they would not have to return to Us!

40. So We seized him and his hosts,

وَ قَالَ فِرْعَوْنُ يَآ أَيُّهَا الْمَلَأُ مَا
عَلِمْتُ لَكُمْ مِّنْ إِلٰهٍ غَيْرِى
فَأَوْقِدْ لِى يَا هَامٰنُ عَلَى الطِّينِ
فَاجْعَلْ لِّى صَرْحًا لَّعَلِّى أَطَّلِعُ
إِلَى إِلٰهِ مُوسَى وَ إِنِّى لَأَظُنُّهُ
مِنَ الْكٰذِبِينَ ۝ وَاسْتَكْبَرَ هُوَ
وَ جُنُودُهُ فِي الْأَرْضِ بِغَيْرِ
الْحَقِّ وَ ظَنُّوٓا أَنَّهُمْ إِلَيْنَا لَا
يُرْجَعُونَ ۝ فَأَخَذْنٰهُ وَ جُنُودَهُ

with Our Signs shall you triumph, - you two as well as those who follow you."

36. When Moses came to them with Our clear Signs, they said: "This is nothing but sorcery faked up: never did we hear the like among our fathers of old!"

37. Moses said: "My Lord knows best who it is that comes with guidance from Him and whose end will be best in the Hereafter: certain it is that the wrong-doers will not prosper."

بِاٰيَتِنَآ اَنْتُمَا وَمَنِ اتَّبَعَكُمَا الْغٰلِبُوْنَ ۞ فَلَمَّا جَآءَهُمْ مُّوْسٰى بِاٰيَتِنَا بَيِّنٰتٍ قَالُوْا مَا هٰذَآ اِلَّا سِحْرٌ مُّفْتَرًى وَّمَا سَمِعْنَا بِهٰذَا فِىْٓ اٰبَآئِنَا الْاَوَّلِيْنَ ۞ وَقَالَ مُوْسٰى رَبِّىْٓ اَعْلَمُ بِمَنْ جَآءَ بِالْهُدٰى مِنْ عِنْدِهٖ وَمَنْ تَكُوْنُ لَهٗ عَاقِبَةُ الدَّارِ اِنَّهٗ لَا يُفْلِحُ الظّٰلِمُوْنَ ۞

and his chiefs: for truly they are a people rebellious and wicked."

33. He said: "O my Lord! I have slain a man among them, and I fear lest they slay me."

34. "And my brother Aaron - he is more eloquent in speech than I: so send him with me as a helper, to confirm (and streng-then) me: for I fear that they may accuse me of falsehood."

35. He said: "We will certainly strengthen your arm through your brother, and invest you both with authority, so they shall not be able to touch you:

وَمَلَاۡئِهٖ اِنَّهُمْ كَانُوۡا قَوۡمًا

فٰسِقِيۡنَ ۞ قَالَ رَبِّ اِنِّيۡ

قَتَلْتُ مِنْهُمْ نَفْسًا فَاَخَافُ

اَنۡ يَّقۡتُلُوۡنِ ۞ وَاَخِيۡ هٰرُوۡنُ

هُوَ اَفۡصَحُ مِنِّيۡ لِسَانًا فَاَرۡسِلْهُ

مَعِيَ رِدۡءًا يُّصَدِّقُنِيۡۤ اِنِّيۡۤ اَخَافُ

اَنۡ يُّكَذِّبُوۡنِ ۞ قَالَ سَنَشُدُّ

عَضُدَكَ بِاَخِيۡكَ وَنَجْعَلُ لَكُمَا

سُلۡطٰنًا فَلَا يَصِلُوۡنَ اِلَيۡكُمَا ۚ

the Worlds ..."

31. "Now do you throw your
rod!" But when he saw it moving
(of its own accord) as if it had
been a snake, he turned back in
retreat, and retraced not his steps:
"O Moses!" (it was said), "Draw
near, and fear not: for you are of
those who are secure."

32. "Move your hand into your
bosom, and it will come forth
white without stain (or harm),
and draw your hand close to your
side (to guard) against fear. Those
are the two credentials from your
Lord to Pharaoh

الْعٰلَمِيْنَ ۞ وَاَنْ اَلْقِ عَصَاكَ

فَلَمَّا رَاٰهَا تَهْتَزُّ كَاَنَّهَا

جَانٌّ وَّلّٰى مُدْبِرًا وَّلَمْ يُعَقِّبْ

يٰمُوْسٰٓى اَقْبِلْ وَلَا تَخَفْ اِنَّكَ

مِنَ الْاٰمِنِيْنَ ۞ اُسْلُكْ يَدَكَ

فِيْ جَيْبِكَ تَخْرُجْ بَيْضَآءَ مِنْ

غَيْرِ سُوْٓءٍ وَّاضْمُمْ اِلَيْكَ

جَنَاحَكَ مِنَ الرَّهْبِ فَذٰنِكَ

بُرْهَانَانِ مِنْ رَّبِّكَ اِلٰى فِرْعَوْنَ

Moses had fulfilled the term, and was travelling with his family, he perceived a fire in the direction of Mount Tur. He said to his family: "Tarry you; I perceive a fire; I hope to bring you from there some information, or a burning firebrand, that you may warm yourselves."

30. But when he came to the (fire), a voice was heard from the right bank of the valley, from a tree in hallowed ground: "O Moses! Verily I am Allah, the Lord of

قَضَى مُوسَى الْأَجَلَ وَسَارَ بِأَهْلِهِ

أَنَسَ مِنْ جَانِبِ الطُّورِ نَارًا

قَالَ لِأَهْلِهِ امْكُثُوا إِنِّي آنَسْتُ

نَارًا لَّعَلِّي آتِيكُمْ مِّنْهَا بِخَبَرٍ

أَوْ جَذْوَةٍ مِّنَ النَّارِ لَعَلَّكُمْ

تَصْطَلُونَ ۞ فَلَمَّا أَتَاهَا نُودِيَ

مِنْ شَاطِئِ الْوَادِ الْأَيْمَنِ فِي

الْبُقْعَةِ الْمُبَارَكَةِ مِنَ الشَّجَرَةِ

أَنْ يَّا مُوسَى إِنِّي أَنَا اللَّهُ رَبُّ

intend to wed one of these my daughters to you, on condition that you serve me for eight years; but if you complete ten years, it will be (grace) from you. But I intend not to place you under a difficulty: you will find me, in deed, if Allah wills, one of the righteous."

28. He said: "Be that (the agreement) between me and you: whichever of the two terms I fulfil, let there be no ill-will to me. Be Allah a Witness to what we say."

29. Now when

أُرِيدُ أَنْ أُنْكِحَكَ إِحْدَى

ابْنَتَيَّ هَاتَيْنِ عَلَى أَنْ تَأْجُرَنِي

ثَمَانِيَ حِجَجٍ فَإِنْ أَتْمَمْتَ عَشْرًا

فَمِنْ عِنْدِكَ وَمَا أُرِيدُ أَنْ أَشُقَّ

عَلَيْكَ سَتَجِدُنِي إِنْ شَاءَ اللّٰهُ

مِنَ الصَّالِحِينَ ۝ قَالَ ذَٰلِكَ

بَيْنِي وَ بَيْنَكَ أَيَّمَا الْأَجَلَيْنِ

قَضَيْتُ فَلَا عُدْوَانَ عَلَيَّ وَاللّٰهُ

عَلَى مَا نَقُولُ وَكِيلٌ ۝ فَلَمَّا

25. Afterwards one of the (damsels) came (back) to him, walking bashfully. She said: "My father invites you that he may reward you for having watered (our flocks) for us." So when he came to him and narrated the story, he said: "Fear you not: (well) have you escaped from unjust people."

26. Said one of the (damsels): "O my (dear) father! Engage him on wages: truly the best of men for you to employ is the (man) who is strong and trustworthy."

27. He said: "I

فَقِيرٌ ۞ فَجَآءَتْهُ اِحْدٰىهُمَا

تَمْشِىْ عَلَى اسْتِحْيَآءٍ قَالَتْ

اِنَّ اَبِىْ يَدْعُوْكَ لِيَجْزِيَكَ اَجْرَ

مَا سَقَيْتَ لَنَا فَلَمَّا جَآءَهٗ

وَقَصَّ عَلَيْهِ الْقَصَصَ قَالَ

لَا تَخَفْ نَجَوْتَ مِنَ الْقَوْمِ

الظّٰلِمِيْنَ ۞ قَالَتْ اِحْدٰىهُمَا يٰٓاَبَتِ

اسْتَأْجِرْهُ اِنَّ خَيْرَ مَنِ اسْتَأْجَرْتَ

الْقَوِىُّ الْاَمِيْنُ ۞ قَالَ اِنِّىْ

the smooth and straight path."

23. And when he arrived at the watering (place) in Madyan, he found there a group of men watering (their flocks), and besides them he found two women who were keeping back (their flocks). He said: "What is the matter with you?" They said: "We can not water (our flocks) until the shepherds take back (their flocks): and our father is a very old man."

24. So he watered (their flocks) for them; then he turned back to the shade, and said:"O my Lord! Truly am I in (desperate) need of any good that You send me!"

سَوَآءَ السَّبِيلِ ۩ وَلَمَّا وَرَدَ

مَآءَ مَدْيَنَ وَجَدَ عَلَيْهِ أُمَّةً

مِّنَ النَّاسِ يَسْقُونَ ۦ وَوَجَدَ

مِنْ دُونِهِمُ امْرَاَتَيْنِ تَذُودَانِ ۖ

قَالَ مَا خَطْبُكُمَا ۖ قَالَتَا لَا نَسْقِي

حَتّٰى يُصْدِرَ الرِّعَآءُ ۖ وَاَبُونَا

شَيْخٌ كَبِيرٌ ۩ فَسَقٰى لَهُمَا ثُمَّ

تَوَلّٰى اِلَى الظِّلِّ فَقَالَ رَبِّ

اِنِّي لِمَآ اَنْزَلْتَ اِلَيَّ مِنْ خَيْرٍ

one who sets things right!"

20. And there came a man, running, from the furthest end of the City. He said: "O Moses! The chiefs are taking counsel together about you, to slay you: so get you away, for I do give you sincere advice."

21. He therefore got away therefrom, looking about, in a state of fear. He prayed "O my Lord! Save me from people given to wrong-doing."

22. Then, when he turned his face towards (the land of) Madyan, he said: "I do hope that my Lord will show me

مِنَ الْمُصْلِحِينَ ۝ وَجَآءَ رَجُلٌ

مِّنْ اَقْصَا الْمَدِيْنَةِ يَسْعٰى ۙ

قَالَ يٰمُوْسٰى اِنَّ الْمَلَاَ يَأْتَمِرُوْنَ

بِكَ لِيَقْتُلُوْكَ فَاخْرُجْ اِنِّيْ لَكَ

مِنَ النّٰصِحِيْنَ ۝ فَخَرَجَ مِنْهَا

خَآئِفًا يَّتَرَقَّبُ ۖ قَالَ رَبِّ

نَجِّنِيْ مِنَ الْقَوْمِ الظّٰلِمِيْنَ

۝

وَلَمَّا تَوَجَّهَ تِلْقَآءَ مَدْيَنَ

قَالَ عَسٰى رَبِّيْٓ اَنْ يَّهْدِيَنِيْ

and vigilant, when he saw, the man who had, the day before, sought his help called aloud for his help (again). Moses said to him: "You are truly, it is clear, a quarrelsome fellow!"

19. Then, when he was about to lay his hands on their enemy, that man said: "O Moses! Is it your intention to slay me as you slew a man yesterday? Your intention is none other than to become a powerful violent man in the land, and not to be

يَتَرَقَّبُ فَاِذَا الَّذِى اسْتَنْصَرَهٗ

بِالْاَمْسِ يَسْتَصْرِخُهٗ ۚ قَالَ لَهٗ

مُوْسٰۤى اِنَّكَ لَغَوِىٌّ مُّبِيْنٌ ۞

فَلَمَّاۤ اَنْ اَرَادَ اَنْ يَّبْطِشَ

بِالَّذِىْ هُوَ عَدُوٌّ لَّهُمَا ۙ قَالَ

يٰمُوْسٰۤى اَتُرِيْدُ اَنْ تَقْتُلَنِيْ

كَمَا قَتَلْتَ نَفْسًۢا بِالْاَمْسِ ۖ اِنْ

تُرِيْدُ اِلَّاۤ اَنْ تَكُوْنَ جَبَّارًا فِى

الْاَرْضِ وَمَا تُرِيْدُ اَنْ تَكُوْنَ

against his foe, and Moses struck him with his fist and made an end of him. He said: "This is a work of Evil (Satan): for he is an enemy that manifestly misleads!"

16. He prayed: "O my Lord! I have indeed wronged my soul! Do You then forgive me!" So (Allah) forgave him: for He is the Oft-Forgiving, Most Merciful.

17. He said: "O my Lord! For that You have bestowed Your Grace on me, never shall I be a help to those who sin!"

18. In the morning, he was in the city, fearful

عَلَى الَّذِى مِنْ عَدُوِّهٖ فَوَكَزَهٗ

مُوْسٰى فَقَضٰى عَلَيْهِ ۗ قَالَ هٰذَا

مِنْ عَمَلِ الشَّيْطٰنِ ۗ اِنَّهٗ عَدُوٌّ

مُّضِلٌّ مُّبِيْنٌ ۝ قَالَ رَبِّ اِنِّى

ظَلَمْتُ نَفْسِىْ فَاغْفِرْ لِىْ فَغَفَرَ

لَهٗ ۗ اِنَّهٗ هُوَ الْغَفُوْرُ الرَّحِيْمُ ۝

قَالَ رَبِّ بِمَآ اَنْعَمْتَ عَلَىَّ

فَلَنْ اَكُوْنَ ظَهِيْرًا لِّلْمُجْرِمِيْنَ ۝

فَاَصْبَحَ فِى الْمَدِيْنَةِ خَآئِفًا

the promise of Allah is true: but most of them do not understand.

14.   When he reached full age, and was firmly established (in life), We bestowed on him wisdom and knowledge: for thus do We reward those who do good.

15.   And he entered the city at a time when its people were not watching: and he found there two men fighting, - one of his own religion, and the other, of his foes. Now the man of his own religion appealed to him

وَعْدَ اللّٰهِ حَقًّا وَّلٰكِنَّ اَكْثَرَهُمْ

لَا يَعْلَمُوْنَ ۞ وَلَمَّا بَلَغَ اَشُدَّهٗ

وَاسْتَوٰۤى اٰتَيْنٰهُ حُكْمًا وَّعِلْمًا ؕ

وَكَذٰلِكَ نَجْزِى الْمُحْسِنِيْنَ ۞

وَدَخَلَ الْمَدِيْنَةَ عَلٰى حِيْنِ

غَفْلَةٍ مِّنْ اَهْلِهَا فَوَجَدَ فِيْهَا

رَجُلَيْنِ يَقْتَتِلٰنِ ۫ هٰذَا مِنْ

شِيْعَتِهٖ وَهٰذَا مِنْ عَدُوِّهٖ ۚ

فَاسْتَغَاثَهُ الَّذِيْ مِنْ شِيْعَتِهٖ

strengthened her heart (with faith), so that she might remain a (firm) believer.

11. And she said to the sister of (Moses), "Follow him." So she (the sister) watched him in the character of a stranger. And they knew not.

12. And we ordained that he refused suck at first, until (His sister came up and) said: "Shall I point out to you the people of a house that will nourish and bring him up for you and be sincerely attached to him?"...

13. Thus did We restore him to his mother, that her eye might be comforted, that she might not grieve, and that she might know that

اَنْ رَّبَطْنَا عَلٰى قَلْبِهَا لِتَكُوْنَ

مِنَ الْمُؤْمِنِيْنَ ۞ وَقَالَتْ لِاُخْتِهٖ

قُصِّيْهِ ۚ فَبَصُرَتْ بِهٖ عَنْ جُنُبٍ

وَّهُمْ لَا يَشْعُرُوْنَ ۞ وَحَرَّمْنَا

عَلَيْهِ الْمَرَاضِعَ مِنْ قَبْلُ فَقَالَتْ

هَلْ اَدُلُّكُمْ عَلٰى اَهْلِ بَيْتٍ

يَّكْفُلُوْنَهٗ لَكُمْ وَهُمْ لَهٗ نٰصِحُوْنَ

۞ فَرَدَدْنٰهُ اِلٰى اُمِّهٖ كَيْ تَقَرَّ

عَيْنُهَا وَلَا تَحْزَنَ وَلِتَعْلَمَ اَنَّ

8. Then the people of Pharaoh picked him up (from the river): (it was intended) that (Moses) should be to them an adversary and a cause of sorrow: for Pharaoh and Haman and (all) their hosts were men of sin.

9. The wife of Pharaoh said: "(Here is) joy of the eye, for me and for you: slay him not. It may be that he will be of use to us, or we may adopt him as a son." And they perceived not (what they were doing)!

10. But there came to be a void in the heart of the mother of Moses: she was going almost to disclose his (case), had We not

فَالْتَقَطَهٗٓ اٰلُ فِرْعَوْنَ لِيَكُوْنَ

لَهُمْ عَدُوًّا وَّ حَزَنًا ۗ اِنَّ فِرْعَوْنَ

وَهَامٰنَ وَجُنُوْدَهُمَا كَانُوْا

خٰطِـٔيْنَ ۞ وَقَالَتِ امْرَاَتُ فِرْعَوْنَ

قُرَّتُ عَيْنٍ لِّيْ وَلَكَ ۖ لَا تَقْتُلُوْهُ ۖ

عَسٰٓى اَنْ يَّنْفَعَنَاۤ اَوْ نَتَّخِذَهٗ

وَلَدًا وَّهُمْ لَا يَشْعُرُوْنَ ۞

وَاَصْبَحَ فُؤَادُ اُمِّ مُوْسٰى فٰرِغًا ۗ

اِنْ كَادَتْ لَتُبْدِيْ بِهٖ لَوْلَاۤ

leaders (in Faith) and make them heirs,

6.   To establish a firm place for them in the land, and to show Pharaoh, Haman, and their hosts, at their hands, the very things against which they were taking precautions.

7.   So We sent this inspiration to the mother of Moses: "Suckle (your child), but when you have fears about him, cast him into the river, but fear not nor grieve: for We shall restore him to you, and We shall make him one of Our Apostles."

أَىِّمَّةً وَّنَجْعَلَهُمُ الْوَارِثِيْنَ ۞

وَنُمَكِّنَ لَهُمْ فِى الْاَرْضِ وَنُرِيَ

فِرْعَوْنَ وَهَامَانَ وَجُنُوْدَهُمَا

مِنْهُمْ مَّا كَانُوْا يَحْذَرُوْنَ ۞

وَاَوْحَيْنَا اِلٰى اُمِّ مُوْسٰى اَنْ

اَرْضِعِيْهِ ۚ فَاِذَا خِفْتِ عَلَيْهِ

فَاَلْقِيْهِ فِى الْيَمِّ وَلَا تَخَافِيْ

وَلَا تَحْزَنِيْ ۚ اِنَّا رَآدُّوْهُ اِلَيْكِ

وَجَاعِلُوْهُ مِنَ الْمُرْسَلِيْنَ ۞

that makes (things) clear.

3.   We rehearse to you some of the story of Moses and Pharaoh in Truth, for people who believe.

4.   Truly Pharaoh elated himself in the land and broke up its people into sections, depressing a small group among them: their sons he slew, but he kept alive their females: for he was indeed a maker of mischief.

5.   And We wished to be gracious to those who were being depressed in the land, to make them

الْمُبِينُ ۞ نَتْلُوا عَلَيْكَ مِنْ نَبَإِ

مُوسَى وَفِرْعَوْنَ بِالْحَقِّ لِقَوْمٍ

يُؤْمِنُونَ ۞ إِنَّ فِرْعَوْنَ عَلَا

فِي الْأَرْضِ وَجَعَلَ أَهْلَهَا

شِيَعًا يَّسْتَضْعِفُ طَآئِفَةً مِّنْهُمْ

يُذَبِّحُ أَبْنَاءَهُمْ وَيَسْتَحْىِ نِسَاءَهُمْ

إِنَّهُ كَانَ مِنَ الْمُفْسِدِينَ

۞ وَنُرِيدُ أَن نَّمُنَّ عَلَى الَّذِينَ

اسْتُضْعِفُوا فِي الْأَرْضِ وَنَجْعَلَهُمْ

to be of those who bow in Islam to Allah's Will, -

92.   And to rehearse the Qur'an: and if any accept guidance, they do it for the good of their own souls, and if any stray, say: "I am only a Warner".

93.   And say: "Praise be to Allah, Who will soon show you His Signs, so that you shall know them"; and your Lord is not unmindful of all that you do.

Al-Qasas (The Narration)

Bismillahhir-Rahmanir-Rahim

1.   Ta. Sin. Mim.

اَنْ اَكُوْنَ مِنَ الْمُسْلِمِيْنَ ۝ وَاَنْ

اَتْلُوَا الْقُرْاٰنَ فَمَنِ اهْتَدٰى

فَاِنَّمَا يَهْتَدِيْ لِنَفْسِهٖ وَمَنْ

ضَلَّ فَقُلْ اِنَّمَاۤ اَنَا مِنَ

الْمُنْذِرِيْنَ ۝ وَقُلِ الْحَمْدُ لِلّٰهِ

سَيُرِيْكُمْ اٰيٰتِهٖ فَتَعْرِفُوْنَهَا ۗ وَمَا

رَبُّكَ بِغَافِلٍ عَمَّا تَعْمَلُوْنَ ۝

سُوْرَةُ الْقَصَص مَكِّيَّةٌ   بِسْمِ اللّٰهِ الرَّحْمٰنِ الرَّحِيْمِ   اٰيَاتُهَا ٨٨ رُكُوْعَاتُهَا ٩

طٰسٓمّٓ ۝ تِلْكَ اٰيٰتُ الْكِتٰبِ

for He is Well Acquainted with all that you do.

89. If any do good, good will (accrue) to them therefrom; and they will be secure from terror that Day.

90. And if any do evil, their faces will be thrown headlong into the Fire: "Do you receive a reward other than that which you have earned by your deeds?"

91. For me, I have been commanded to serve the Lord of this city, Him Who has sanctified it and to Whom (belong) all things: and I am commanded

شَىْءٍ ۚ إِنَّهُ خَبِيرٌ بِمَا تَفْعَلُونَ ۩

مَنْ جَآءَ بِالْحَسَنَةِ فَلَهُ خَيْرٌ

مِّنْهَا ۚ وَهُمْ مِّنْ فَزَعٍ يَّوْمَئِذٍ

ءَامِنُونَ ۩ وَمَنْ جَآءَ بِالسَّيِّئَةِ

فَكُبَّتْ وُجُوهُهُمْ فِى النَّارِ ۚ

هَلْ تُجْزَوْنَ إِلَّا مَا كُنْتُمْ

تَعْمَلُونَ ۩ إِنَّمَآ أُمِرْتُ أَنْ

أَعْبُدَ رَبَّ هَٰذِهِ الْبَلْدَةِ الَّذِى

حَرَّمَهَا وَلَهُ كُلُّ شَىْءٍ ۖ وَأُمِرْتُ

have made the Night for them to rest in and the Day to give them light? Verily in this are Signs for any people that believe!

87. And the Day that the Trumpet will be sounded - then will be smitten with terror those who are in the heavens, and those who are on earth, except such as Allah will please (to exempt): and all shall come to His (Presence) as beings conscious of their lowliness.

88. You see the mountains and think them firmly fixed: but they shall pass away as the clouds pass away: (such is) the artistry of Allah, Who disposes of all things in perfect order:

جَعَلْنَا الَّيْلَ لِيَسْكُنُوا فِيهِ

وَالنَّهَارَ مُبْصِرًا ۚ اِنَّ فِى ذٰلِكَ

لَاٰيٰتٍ لِّقَوْمٍ يُّؤْمِنُوْنَ ۞ وَيَوْمَ

يُنْفَخُ فِى الصُّوْرِ فَفَزِعَ مَنْ

فِى السَّمٰوٰتِ وَمَنْ فِى الْاَرْضِ

اِلَّا مَنْ شَآءَ اللّٰهُ ۚ وَكُلٌّ اَتَوْهُ

دٰخِرِيْنَ ۞ وَتَرَى الْجِبَالَ تَحْسَبُهَا

جَامِدَةً وَّهِىَ تَمُرُّ مَرَّ السَّحَابِ ۚ

صُنْعَ اللّٰهِ الَّذِىْ اَتْقَنَ كُلَّ

for that mankind did not believe with assurance in Our Signs.

83.   One day We shall gather together from every people a troop of those who reject Our Signs, and they shall be kept in ranks, -

84.   Until, when they come (before the Judgment-seat), (Allah) will say: "Did you reject My Signs, though you comprehended them not in knowledge, or what was it you did?"

85.   And the Word will be fulfilled against them, because of their wrong-doing, and they will be unable to speak (in plea).

86.   See they not that We

اَنَّ النَّاسَ كَانُوا بِاٰيٰتِنَا لَا

يُوقِنُونَ ۞ وَيَوْمَ نَحْشُرُ مِنْ

كُلِّ اُمَّةٍ فَوْجًا مِّمَّنْ يُّكَذِّبُ

بِاٰيٰتِنَا فَهُمْ يُوزَعُونَ ۞ حَتّٰى

اِذَا جَآءُو قَالَ اَكَذَّبْتُمْ بِاٰيٰتِي

وَلَمْ تُحِيْطُوا بِهَا عِلْمًا اَمَّا

ذَا كُنْتُمْ تَعْمَلُونَ ۞ وَوَقَعَ

الْقَوْلُ عَلَيْهِمْ بِمَا ظَلَمُوا فَهُمْ

لَا يَنْطِقُونَ ۞ اَلَمْ يَرَوْا اَنَّا

79. So put your trust in Allah: for you are on (the path of) manifest Truth.

80. Truly you cannot cause the dead to listen, nor can you cause the deaf to hear the call, (especially) when they turn back in retreat.

81. Nor can you be a guide to the blind, (to prevent them) from straying: only those will you get to listen who believe in Our Signs, and they will bow in Islam.

82. And when the Word is fulfilled against them (the unjust), We shall produce from the earth a beast to (face) them: he will speak to them,

فَتَوَكَّلْ عَلَى اللهِ ۖ اِنَّكَ عَلَى

الْحَقِّ الْمُبِيْنِ ۝ اِنَّكَ لَا تُسْمِعُ

الْمَوْتٰى وَلَا تُسْمِعُ الصُّمَّ الدُّعَآءَ

اِذَا وَلَّوْا مُدْبِرِيْنَ ۝ وَمَآ اَنْتَ

بِهٰدِى الْعُمْىِ عَنْ ضَلٰلَتِهِمْ ۖ

اِنْ تُسْمِعُ اِلَّا مَنْ يُّؤْمِنُ بِاٰيٰتِنَا

فَهُمْ مُّسْلِمُوْنَ ۝ وَاِذَا وَقَعَ

الْقَوْلُ عَلَيْهِمْ اَخْرَجْنَا لَهُمْ

دَآبَّةً مِّنَ الْاَرْضِ تُكَلِّمُهُمْ

all that their hearts do hide, as well as all that they reveal.

75.   Nor is there aught of the Unseen, in heaven or earth, but is (recorded) in a clear Record.

76.   Verily this Qur'an does explain to the Children of Israel most of the matters in which they disagree.

77.   And it certainly is a Guide and a Mercy to those who believe.

78.   Verily your Lord will decide between them by His Decree: and He is Exalted in Might, All-Knowing.

مَا تُكِنُّ صُدُورُهُمْ وَمَا يُعْلِنُونَ ۝

وَمَا مِنْ غَآئِبَةٍ فِى السَّمَآءِ
وَالْأَرْضِ إِلَّا فِى كِتَبٍ مُّبِينٍ ۝

إِنَّ هَذَا الْقُرْآنَ يَقُصُّ عَلَى
بَنِىٓ إِسْرَآءِيلَ أَكْثَرَ الَّذِى
هُمْ فِيهِ يَخْتَلِفُونَ ۝ وَإِنَّهُ
لَهُدًى وَّرَحْمَةٌ لِّلْمُؤْمِنِينَ ۝

إِنَّ رَبَّكَ يَقْضِى بَيْنَهُمْ
بِحُكْمِهِ وَهُوَ الْعَزِيزُ الْعَلِيمُ ۝

of those guilty (of sin)."

70. But grieve not over them, nor distress yourself because of their plots.

71. They also say: "When will this promise (come to pass)? (Say) if you are truthful."

72. Say: "It may be that some of the events which you wish to hasten on may be (close) in your pursuit!"

73. But verily your Lord is full of grace to mankind: yet most of them are ungrateful.

74. And verily your Lord knows

الْمُجْرِمِينَ ۞ وَلَا تَحْزَنْ عَلَيْهِمْ

وَلَا تَكُنْ فِى ضَيْقٍ مِّمَّا

يَمْكُرُونَ ۞ وَيَقُولُونَ مَتَى هٰذَا

الْوَعْدُ اِنْ كُنْتُمْ صٰدِقِينَ ۞

قُلْ عَسَى اَنْ يَّكُونَ رَدِفَ

لَكُمْ بَعْضُ الَّذِىْ تَسْتَعْجِلُونَ ۞

وَاِنَّ رَبَّكَ لَذُوْ فَضْلٍ عَلَى

النَّاسِ وَلٰكِنَّ اَكْثَرَهُمْ لَا

يَشْكُرُونَ ۞ وَاِنَّ رَبَّكَ لَيَعْلَمُ

the Here-after; no, they are in doubt and uncertainty thereat; no, they are blind thereto.

67.   The unbelievers say: "What! When we become dust, - we and our fathers, - shall we really be raised (from the dead)?

68.   "It is true we were promised this, - we and our fathers before (us): these are nothing but tales of the ancients."

69.   Say: "Go you through the earth and see what has been the end

فِي الْاٰخِرَةِ ۛ بَلْ هُمْ فِي شَكٍّ

مِّنْهَا ۛ بَلْ هُمْ مِّنْهَا عَمُوْنَ ۞

وَقَالَ الَّذِيْنَ كَفَرُوْۤا ءَاِذَا

كُنَّا تُرٰبًا وَّاٰبَآؤُنَاۤ اَئِنَّا

لَمُخْرَجُوْنَ ۞ لَقَدْ وُعِدْنَا هٰذَا

نَحْنُ وَاٰبَآؤُنَا مِنْ قَبْلُ اِنْ

هٰذَاۤ اِلَّاۤ اَسَاطِيْرُ الْاَوَّلِيْنَ ۞

قُلْ سِيْرُوْا فِي الْاَرْضِ

فَانْظُرُوْا كَيْفَ كَانَ عَاقِبَةُ

High is Allah above what they associate with Him!

64. Or, who originates creation, then repeats it, and who gives you sustenance from heaven and earth? (Can there be another) god besides Allah? Say, "Bring forth your argument, if you are telling the truth!"

65. Say: None in the heavens or on earth, except Allah, knows what is hidden: nor can they perceive when they shall be raised up (for Judgment).

66. No, but their knowledge fails to comprehend

تَعَلَى اللهُ عَمَّا يُشْرِكُونَ ۞

اَمَّنْ يَّبْدَؤُا الْخَلْقَ ثُمَّ يُعِيْدُهٗ

وَمَنْ يَّرْزُقُكُمْ مِّنَ السَّمَاءِ

وَالْاَرْضِ ءَاِلٰهٌ مَّعَ اللهِ ۚ قُلْ

هَاتُوْا بُرْهَانَكُمْ اِنْ كُنْتُمْ

صٰدِقِيْنَ ۞ قُلْ لَّا يَعْلَمُ مَنْ

فِى السَّمٰوٰتِ وَالْاَرْضِ الْغَيْبَ

اِلَّا اللهُ ۗ وَمَا يَشْعُرُوْنَ اَيَّانَ

يُبْعَثُوْنَ ۞ بَلِ ادّٰرَكَ عِلْمُهُمْ

(Can there be another) god besides Allah? No, most of them know not.

62. Or, who listens to the (soul) distressed when it calls on Him, and who relieves its suffering, and makes you (mankind) inheritors of the earth? (Can there be another) god besides Allah? Little it is that you heed.

63. Or, who guides you through the depths of darkness on land and sea, and who sends the winds as heralds of glad tidings, going before His Mercy? (Can there be another) god besides Allah? -

حَاجِزًا ءَاِلَهٌ مَّعَ اللهِ ۚ بَلْ

أَكْثَرُهُمْ لَا يَعْلَمُونَ ۩ أَمَّنْ

يُّجِيبُ الْمُضْطَرَّ إِذَا دَعَاهُ

وَيَكْشِفُ السُّوٓءَ وَيَجْعَلُكُمْ خُلَفَآءَ

الْأَرْضِ ۚ ءَاِلَهٌ مَّعَ اللهِ ۚ قَلِيلًا

مَّا تَذَكَّرُونَ ۩ أَمَّنْ يَّهْدِيكُمْ

فِي ظُلُمَاتِ الْبَرِّ وَالْبَحْرِ وَمَنْ

يُّرْسِلُ الرِّيَاحَ بُشْرًۢا بَيْنَ

يَدَىْ رَحْمَتِهِ ۚ ءَاِلَهٌ مَّعَ اللهِ

60. Or, who has created the heavens and the earth, and who sends you down rain from the sky? Yes, with it We cause to grow well-planted orchards full of beauty of delight: it is not in your power to cause the growth of the trees in them. (Can there be another) god besides Allah? No, they are a people who swerve from justice.

61. Or, who has made the earth firm to live in; made rivers in its midst; set thereon mountains immovable; and made a separating bar between the two bodies of flowing water?

اَمَّنْ خَلَقَ السَّمٰوٰتِ وَالْاَرْضِ

وَاَنْزَلَ لَكُمْ مِّنَ السَّمَاءِ مَآءً

فَاَنْۢبَتْنَا بِهٖ حَدَآئِقَ ذَاتَ بَهْجَةٍ

مَا كَانَ لَكُمْ اَنْ تُنْۢبِتُوْا

شَجَرَهَا ؕ ءَاِلٰهٌ مَّعَ اللّٰهِ ؕ بَلْ

هُمْ قَوْمٌ يَّعْدِلُوْنَ ۞ اَمَّنْ

جَعَلَ الْاَرْضَ قَرَارًا وَّجَعَلَ

خِلٰلَهَا اَنْهٰرًا وَّجَعَلَ لَهَا

رَوَاسِيَ وَجَعَلَ بَيْنَ الْبَحْرَيْنِ

پارہ

اَمَّنْ خَلَقَ

(۲۰)

بِسْمِ اللهِ الكِتَابِ الأَرْضِيَّةِ

PART 21
Utlu Maa Oohiya

and its glitter, - then come! I will provide for your enjoyment and set you free in a handsome manner."

29. "But if you seek Allah and His Apostle, and the Home of the Hereafter, verily Allah has prepared for the well-doers amongst you a great reward."

30. O consorts of the Prophet! If any of you were guilty of evident unseemly conduct, the Punishment would be doubled to her, and that is easy for Allah.

وَزِينَتِهَا فَتَعَالَيْنَ أُمَتِّعْكُنَّ

وَأُسَرِّحْكُنَّ سَرَاحًا جَمِيلًا ۞ وَإِن

كُنْتُنَّ تُرِدْنَ اللَّهَ وَرَسُولَهُ

وَالدَّارَ الْآخِرَةَ فَإِنَّ اللَّهَ

أَعَدَّ لِلْمُحْسِنَاتِ مِنكُنَّ أَجْرًا

عَظِيمًا ۞ يَنِسَاءَ النَّبِيِّ مَن

يَأْتِ مِنكُنَّ بِفَاحِشَةٍ مُّبَيِّنَةٍ

يُضَاعَفْ لَهَا الْعَذَابُ ضِعْفَيْنِ

وَكَانَ ذَلِكَ عَلَى اللَّهِ يَسِيرًا ۞

those of the People of the Book who aided them - Allah did take them down from their strongholds and cast terror into their hearts. (So that) some you slew, and some you made prisoners.

27. And He made you heirs of their lands, their houses, and their goods, and of a land which you had not frequented (before). And Allah has Power over all things.

28. O Prophet! Say to your consorts: "If it be that you desire the life of this world,

وَالَّذِينَ ظَاهَرُوهُم مِّنْ أَهْلِ

الْكِتَابِ مِن صَيَاصِيهِمْ وَقَذَفَ

فِى قُلُوبِهِمُ الرُّعْبَ فَرِيقًا

تَقْتُلُونَ وَتَأْسِرُونَ فَرِيقًا ۞

وَأَوْرَثَكُمْ أَرْضَهُمْ وَدِيَارَهُمْ

وَأَمْوَالَهُمْ وَأَرْضًا لَّمْ تَطَئُوهَا ۗ وَكَانَ

اللَّهُ عَلَىٰ كُلِّ شَىْءٍ قَدِيرًا ۞

يَا أَيُّهَا النَّبِىُّ قُل لِّأَزْوَاجِكَ إِن

كُنتُنَّ تُرِدْنَ الْحَيَوٰةَ الدُّنْيَا

their vow (to the extreme), and some (still) wait: but they have never changed (their determination) in the least:

24. That Allah may reward the men of Truth for their Truth, and punish the Hypocrites if that be His Will, or turn to them in Mercy: for Allah is Oft-Forgiving, Most Merciful.

25. And Allah turned back the unbelievers for (all) their fury, no advantage did they gain; and enough is Allah for the believers in their fight. And Allah is full of Strength, able to enforce His Will.

26. And

نَحْبَهُ وَمِنْهُمْ مَّنْ يَّنْتَظِرُ ۖ وَمَا

بَدَّلُوْا تَبْدِيْلًا ۞ لِّيَجْزِىَ اللّٰهُ

الصّٰدِقِيْنَ بِصِدْقِهِمْ وَيُعَذِّبَ

الْمُنٰفِقِيْنَ اِنْ شَآءَ اَوْ يَتُوْبَ

عَلَيْهِمْ ۚ اِنَّ اللّٰهَ كَانَ غَفُوْرًا

رَّحِيْمًا ۞ وَرَدَّ اللّٰهُ الَّذِيْنَ كَفَرُوْا

بِغَيْظِهِمْ لَمْ يَنَالُوْا خَيْرًا ۚ وَكَفَى

اللّٰهُ الْمُؤْمِنِيْنَ الْقِتَالَ ۚ وَكَانَ

اللّٰهُ قَوِيًّا عَزِيْزًا ۞ وَاَنْزَلَ

21. You have indeed in the Apostle of Allah a beautiful pattern (of conduct) for any one whose hope is in Allah and the Final Day, and who engages much in the Praise of Allah.

22. When the believers saw the Confederate forces, they said: "This is what Allah and His Apostle had promised us, and Allah and His Apostle told us what was true." And it only added to their faith and their zeal in obedience.

23. Among the believers are men who have been true to their covenant with Allah: of them some have completed

كَانَ لَكُمْ فِى رَسُولِ اللهِ أُسْوَةٌ

حَسَنَةٌ لِّمَنْ كَانَ يَرْجُوا اللهَ

وَالْيَوْمَ الْاٰخِرَ وَذَكَرَ اللهَ كَثِيْرًا ۝

وَلَمَّا رَاَ الْمُؤْمِنُوْنَ الْاَحْزَابَ قَالُوْا

هٰذَا مَا وَعَدَنَا اللهُ وَرَسُوْلُهُ

وَصَدَقَ اللهُ وَرَسُوْلُهُ ۚ وَمَا زَادَهُمْ

اِلَّا اِيْمَانًا وَّتَسْلِيْمًا ۝ مِنَ الْمُؤْمِنِيْنَ

رِجَالٌ صَدَقُوْا مَا عَاهَدُوا

اللهَ عَلَيْهِ ۚ فَمِنْهُمْ مَّنْ قَضٰى

but when the fear is past, they will smite you with sharp tongues, covetous of goods. Such men have no faith, and so Allah has made their deeds of none effect: and that is easy for Allah.

20. They think that the Confederates have not withdrawn; and if the Confederates should come (again), they would wish they were in the deserts (wandering) among the Bedouins, and seeking news about you (from a safe distance); and if they were in your midst, they would fight but little.

فَإِذَا ذَهَبَ الْخَوْفُ سَلَقُوكُمْ

بِأَلْسِنَةٍ حِدَادٍ أَشِحَّةً عَلَى الْخَيْرِ ۚ

أُولَٰئِكَ لَمْ يُؤْمِنُوا فَأَحْبَطَ اللَّهُ

أَعْمَالَهُمْ ۚ وَكَانَ ذَٰلِكَ عَلَى اللَّهِ

يَسِيرًا ۝ يَحْسَبُونَ الْأَحْزَابَ لَمْ

يَذْهَبُوا ۖ وَإِن يَأْتِ الْأَحْزَابُ يَوَدُّوا

لَوْ أَنَّهُم بَادُونَ فِي الْأَعْرَابِ

يَسْأَلُونَ عَنْ أَنبَائِكُمْ ۖ وَلَوْ كَانُوا

فِيكُم مَّا قَاتَلُوا إِلَّا قَلِيلًا ۝ لَّقَدْ

it be His wish to give you punishment or to give you Mercy?" Nor will they find for themselves, besides Allah, any protector or helper.

18. Verily Allah knows those among you who keep back (men) and those who say to their brethren, "Come along to us", but come not to the fight except for just a little while.

19. Covetous over you. Then when fear comes, you will see them looking to you, their eyes revolving, like (those of) one over whom hovers death:

اَرَادَ بِکُمْ سُوْٓءًا اَوْ اَرَادَ بِکُمْ رَحْمَةً ؕ

وَلَا یَجِدُوْنَ لَهُمْ مِّنْ دُوْنِ اللّٰهِ

وَلِیًّا وَّلَا نَصِیْرًا ۞ قَدْ یَعْلَمُ

اللّٰهُ الْمُعَوِّقِیْنَ مِنْکُمْ وَالْقَآئِلِیْنَ

لِاِخْوَانِهِمْ هَلُمَّ اِلَیْنَا ۚ وَلَا یَاْتُوْنَ

الْبَاْسَ اِلَّا قَلِیْلًا ۙ ۞ اَشِحَّةً

عَلَیْکُمْ ۚۖ فَاِذَا جَآءَ الْخَوْفُ رَاَیْتَهُمْ

یَنْظُرُوْنَ اِلَیْکَ تَدُوْرُ اَعْیُنُهُمْ

کَالَّذِیْ یُغْشٰی عَلَیْهِ مِنَ الْمَوْتِ ۚ

To them from the sides of the (city), and they had been incited to sedition, they would certainly have brought it to pass, with none but a brief delay!

15. And yet they had already covenanted with Allah not to turn their backs, and a covenant with Allah must (surely) be answered for.

16. Say: "Running away will not profit you if you are running away from death or slaughter; and even if (you do escape), no more than a brief (respite) will you be allowed to enjoy!"

17. Say: "Who is it that can screen you from Allah if

عَلَیْهِمْ مِّنْ اَقْطَارِهَا ثُمَّ سُئِلُوا

الْفِتْنَةَ لَاٰتَوْهَا وَمَا تَلَبَّثُوْا بِهَا

اِلَّا یَسِیْرًا ۝ وَلَقَدْ کَانُوْا عَاهَدُوا

اللّٰهَ مِنْ قَبْلُ لَا یُوَلُّوْنَ الْاَدْبَارَ

وَکَانَ عَهْدُ اللّٰهِ مَسْئُوْلًا ۝ قُلْ

لَّنْ یَّنْفَعَکُمُ الْفِرَارُ اِنْ فَرَرْتُمْ

مِّنَ الْمَوْتِ اَوِ الْقَتْلِ وَ اِذًا لَّا

تُمَتَّعُوْنَ اِلَّا قَلِیْلًا ۝ قُلْ مَنْ ذَا

الَّذِیْ یَعْصِمُکُمْ مِّنَ اللّٰهِ اِنْ

they were shaken as by a tremendous shaking.

12. And behold! The Hypocrites and those in whose hearts is a disease (even) say: "Allah and His Apostle promised us nothing but delusion."

13. Behold! A party among them said: "O men of Yathrib! You cannot stand (the attack)! Therefore go back!" And a band of them ask for leave of the Prophet, saying, "Truly our houses are bare and exposed:," though they were not exposed: they intended nothing but to run away.

14. And if an entry had been effected

وَزُلْزِلُوا زِلْزَالًا شَدِيدًا ۞ وَإِذْ

يَقُولُ الْمُنَافِقُونَ وَالَّذِينَ فِي

قُلُوبِهِمْ مَرَضٌ مَّا وَعَدَنَا اللهُ

وَرَسُولُهُ إِلَّا غُرُورًا ۞ وَإِذْ قَالَتْ

طَّائِفَةٌ مِّنْهُمْ يَا أَهْلَ يَثْرِبَ لَا

مُقَامَ لَكُمْ فَارْجِعُوا ۚ وَيَسْتَأْذِنُ

فَرِيقٌ مِّنْهُمُ النَّبِيَّ يَقُولُونَ إِنَّ

بُيُوتَنَا عَوْرَةٌ ۚ وَمَا هِيَ بِعَوْرَةٍ ۖ إِنْ

يُرِيدُونَ إِلَّا فِرَارًا ۞ وَلَوْ دُخِلَتْ

for the unbelievers a grievous Chastisement.

9.   O you who believe! Remember the Grace of Allah, (bestowed) on you, when there came down on you hosts (to overwhelm you): but We sent against them a hurricane and forces that you saw not: but Allah sees (clearly) all that you do.

10.   Behold! They came on you from above you and from below you, and behold, the eyes became dim and the hearts gaped up to the throats, and you imagined various (vain) thoughts about Allah!

11.   In that situation were the believers tried:

لِلْكَٰفِرِينَ عَذَابًا أَلِيمًا ۝ يَـٰٓأَيُّهَا

الَّذِينَ ءَامَنُوا اذْكُرُوا نِعْمَةَ اللَّهِ

عَلَيْكُمْ إِذْ جَآءَتْكُمْ جُنُودٌ فَأَرْسَلْنَا

عَلَيْهِمْ رِيحًا وَجُنُودًا لَّمْ تَرَوْهَا ۚ

وَكَانَ اللَّهُ بِمَا تَعْمَلُونَ بَصِيرًا ۝

إِذْ جَآءُوكُم مِّن فَوْقِكُمْ وَمِنْ أَسْفَلَ

مِنكُمْ وَإِذْ زَاغَتِ الْأَبْصَٰرُ وَبَلَغَتِ

الْقُلُوبُ الْحَنَاجِرَ وَتَظُنُّونَ بِاللَّهِ

الظُّنُونَا۠ ۝ هُنَالِكَ ابْتُلِيَ الْمُؤْمِنُونَ

have closer personal ties, in the Decree of Allah, than (the brotherhood of) believers and Muhajirs: nevertheless do you what is just to your closest friends: such is the writing in the Decree (of Allah).

7.   And remember We took from the Prophets their covenant: as (We did) from you: from Noah, Abraham, Moses, and Jesus the son of Mary: We took from them a solemn covenant:

8.   So that (Allah) may question the (custodians) of Truth concerning the Truth they (were charged with): and He has prepared

أُولَى بِبَعْضٍ فِى كِتَبِ اللهِ مِنَ

الْمُؤْمِنِينَ وَالْمُهَٰجِرِينَ إِلَّا أَنْ

تَفْعَلُوٓا إِلَىٰ أَوْلِيَآئِكُم مَّعْرُوفًا كَانَ

ذَٰلِكَ فِى الْكِتَٰبِ مَسْطُورًا ۞ وَإِذْ

أَخَذْنَا مِنَ النَّبِيِّـۧنَ مِيثَٰقَهُمْ

وَمِنكَ وَمِن نُّوحٍ وَإِبْرَٰهِيمَ

وَمُوسَىٰ وَعِيسَى ابْنِ مَرْيَمَ وَأَخَذْنَا

مِنْهُم مِّيثَٰقًا غَلِيظًا ۞ لِّيَسْـَٔلَ

الصَّٰدِقِينَ عَن صِدْقِهِمْ وَأَعَدَّ

the (right) way.

5.   Call them by (the names of) their fathers: that is juster in the sight of Allah. But if you know not their father's (names, call them) your Brothers in faith, or your Maulas. But there is no blame on you if you make a mistake therein: (what counts is) the intention of your hearts: and Allah is Oft-Returning, Most Merciful.

6.   The Prophet is closer to the believers than their own selves, and his wives are their mothers. Blood-relations among each other

السَّبِيلَ ۞ اُدْعُوهُمْ لِاٰبَآئِهِمْ

هُوَ اَقْسَطُ عِنْدَ اللّٰهِ ۚ فَاِنْ لَّمْ

تَعْلَمُوْٓا اٰبَآءَهُمْ فَاِخْوَانُكُمْ فِى

الدِّيْنِ وَمَوَالِيْكُمْ ۚ وَلَيْسَ عَلَيْكُمْ

جُنَاحٌ فِيْمَآ اَخْطَاْتُمْ بِهٖ ۙ وَلٰكِنْ

مَّا تَعَمَّدَتْ قُلُوْبُكُمْ ۚ وَكَانَ اللّٰهُ

غَفُوْرًا رَّحِيْمًا ۞ اَلنَّبِيُّ اَوْلٰى

بِالْمُؤْمِنِيْنَ مِنْ اَنْفُسِهِمْ وَاَزْوَاجُهٗٓ

اُمَّهٰتُهُمْ ۗ وَاُولُوا الْاَرْحَامِ بَعْضُهُمْ

comes to you by inspiration from your Lord: for Allah is Well Acquainted with (all) that you do.

3. And put your trust in Allah, and enough is Allah as a Disposer of affairs.

4. Allah has not made for any man two hearts in his (one) body: nor has He made your wives whom you divorce by Zihar your mothers: nor has He made your adopted sons your sons. Such is (only) your (manner of) speech by your mouths. But Allah tells (you) the Truth, and He shows

یُوْحٰۤی اِلَیْكَ مِنْ رَّبِّكَ ؕ اِنَّ اللّٰهَ

كَانَ بِمَا تَعْمَلُوْنَ خَبِیْرًا ۙ

وَّتَوَكَّلْ عَلَی اللّٰهِ ؕ وَكَفٰی بِاللّٰهِ

وَكِیْلًا ۟ مَا جَعَلَ اللّٰهُ لِرَجُلٍ

مِّنْ قَلْبَیْنِ فِیْ جَوْفِهٖ ۚ وَمَا جَعَلَ

اَزْوَاجَكُمُ الّٰٓـِیْ تُظٰهِرُوْنَ مِنْهُنَّ

اُمَّهٰتِكُمْ ۚ وَمَا جَعَلَ اَدْعِیَآءَكُمْ

اَبْنَآءَكُمْ ؕ ذٰلِكُمْ قَوْلُكُمْ بِاَفْوَاهِكُمْ ؕ

وَاللّٰهُ یَقُوْلُ الْحَقَّ وَهُوَ یَهْدِی

will this decision be, if you are telling the truth?"

29. Say: "On the Day of Decision, no profit will it be to unbelievers if they (then) believe! Nor will they be granted a respite."

30. So turn away from them, and wait: they too are waiting.

Al-Ahzab
(The Confederates)
Bismillahir-Rahmanir-Rahim

1. O Prophet! Fear Allah, and hearken not to the unbelievers and the Hypocrites: verily Allah is full of Knowledge and Wisdom.

2. But follow that which

هٰذَا الْفَتْحُ إِنْ كُنْتُمْ صٰدِقِيْنَ ۞

قُلْ يَوْمَ الْفَتْحِ لَا يَنْفَعُ الَّذِيْنَ

كَفَرُوْٓا اِيْمَانُهُمْ وَلَا هُمْ يُنْظَرُوْنَ ۞

فَاَعْرِضْ عَنْهُمْ وَانْتَظِرْ اِنَّهُمْ

مُنْتَظِرُوْنَ ۞

بِسْمِ اللّٰهِ الرَّحْمٰنِ الرَّحِيْمِ

يٰٓاَيُّهَا النَّبِيُّ اتَّقِ اللّٰهَ وَلَا تُطِعِ

الْكٰفِرِيْنَ وَالْمُنٰفِقِيْنَ اِنَّ اللّٰهَ

كَانَ عَلِيْمًا حَكِيْمًا ۞ وَّاتَّبِعْ مَا

on the Day of Judgment, in the matters wherein they differ (among themselves).

26. Does it not teach them a lesson, how many generations We destroyed before them, in whose dwellings they (now) go to and fro? Verily in that are Signs: Do they not then listen?

27. And do they not see that We do drive rain to parched soil (bare of herbage), and produce therewith crops, providing food for their cattle and themselves? Have they not the vision?

28. They say: "When

يَوْمَ الْقِيْمَةِ فِيْمَا كَانُوْا فِيْهِ

يَخْتَلِفُوْنَ ۞ اَوَلَمْ يَهْدِ لَهُمْ كَمْ

اَهْلَكْنَا مِنْ قَبْلِهِمْ مِّنَ الْقُرُوْنِ

يَمْشُوْنَ فِيْ مَسٰكِنِهِمْ ط اِنَّ فِيْ

ذٰلِكَ لَاٰيٰتٍ ط اَفَلَا يَسْمَعُوْنَ ۞

اَوَلَمْ يَرَوْا اَنَّا نَسُوْقُ الْمَآءَ اِلَى

الْاَرْضِ الْجُرُزِ فَنُخْرِجُ بِهٖ زَرْعًا

تَاْكُلُ مِنْهُ اَنْعَامُهُمْ وَاَنْفُسُهُمْ ط

اَفَلَا يُبْصِرُوْنَ ۞ وَيَقُوْلُوْنَ مَتٰى

22.   And who does more wrong than one to whom are recited the Signs of his Lord, and who then turns away therefrom? Verily from those who transgress We shall exact (due) Retribution.

23.   We did indeed before this give the Book to Moses: be not then in doubt of its reaching (you): and We made it a guide to the Children of Israel.

24.   And We appointed, from among them, leaders, giving guidance under Our Command, so long as they persevered with patience and continued to have faith in Our Signs.

25.   Verily your Lord will judge between them

وَمَنْ اَظْلَمُ مِمَّنْ ذُكِّرَ بِاٰيٰتِ

رَبِّهٖ ثُمَّ اَعْرَضَ عَنْهَا ؕ اِنَّا مِنَ

الْمُجْرِمِيْنَ مُنْتَقِمُوْنَ ۩ وَلَقَدْ

اٰتَيْنَا مُوْسَى الْكِتٰبَ فَلَا تَكُنْ

فِيْ مِرْيَةٍ مِّنْ لِّقَآئِهٖ وَجَعَلْنٰهُ

هُدًى لِّبَنِيْٓ اِسْرَآءِيْلَ ۩ وَجَعَلْنَا

مِنْهُمْ اَئِمَّةً يَّهْدُوْنَ بِاَمْرِنَا لَمَّا

صَبَرُوْا ؕ وَكَانُوْا بِاٰيٰتِنَا يُوْقِنُوْنَ ۩

اِنَّ رَبَّكَ هُوَ يَفْصِلُ بَيْنَهُمْ

believe and do righteous deeds, are Gardens as hospitable homes, for their (good) deeds.

20. As to those who are rebellious and wicked, their abode will be the Fire: every time they wish to get away therefrom, they will be forced back thereinto, and it will be said to them: "Taste you the Chastisement of the Fire, which you were wont to reject as false."

21. And indeed We will make them taste of the Chastisement of this (life) prior to the supreme Chastisement, in order that they may (repent and) return.

ءَامَنُوا وَعَمِلُوا الصَّلِحْتِ فَلَهُمْ

جَنَّتُ الْمَأْوٰى نُزُلًا ۢ بِمَا كَانُوا

يَعْمَلُونَ ۞ وَأَمَّا الَّذِينَ فَسَقُوا

فَمَأْوٰىهُمُ النَّارُ ۖ كُلَّمَا أَرَادُوٓا أَنْ

يَّخْرُجُوا مِنْهَآ أُعِيدُوا فِيهَا وَقِيلَ

لَهُمْ ذُوقُوا عَذَابَ النَّارِ الَّذِى

كُنْتُمْ بِهٖ تُكَذِّبُونَ ۞ وَلَنُذِيقَنَّهُمْ

مِّنَ الْعَذَابِ الْأَدْنٰى دُونَ

الْعَذَابِ الْأَكْبَرِ لَعَلَّهُمْ يَرْجِعُونَ ۞

fall down in adoration, and celebrate the praises of their Lord, nor are they (ever) puffed up with pride.

16. Their limbs do forsake their beds of sleep, the while they call on their Lord, in Fear and Hope: and they spend (in charity) out of the sustenance which We have bestowed on them.

17. Now no person knows what delights of the eye are kept hidden (in reserve) for them - as a reward for their (good) deeds.

18. Is then the man who believes no better than the man who is rebellious and wicked? Not equal are they.

19. For those who

خَرُّوْا سُجَّدًا وَّسَبَّحُوْا بِحَمْدِ رَبِّهِمْ

وَهُمْ لَا يَسْتَكْبِرُوْنَ ۩ تَتَجَافٰى

جُنُوْبُهُمْ عَنِ الْمَضَاجِعِ يَدْعُوْنَ

رَبَّهُمْ خَوْفًا وَّطَمَعًا ۙ وَّمِمَّا

رَزَقْنٰهُمْ يُنْفِقُوْنَ ۞ فَلَا تَعْلَمُ

نَفْسٌ مَّا أُخْفِيَ لَهُمْ مِّنْ قُرَّةِ

أَعْيُنٍ ۚ جَزَآءًۢ بِمَا كَانُوْا يَعْمَلُوْنَ ۞

أَفَمَنْ كَانَ مُؤْمِنًا كَمَنْ كَانَ

فَاسِقًا ۚ لَا يَسْتَوُوْنَ ۞ أَمَّا الَّذِيْنَ

we will work righteousness: for we do indeed (now) believe."

13. If We had so willed, We could certainly have brought every soul its true guidance: but the Word from Me will come true, "I will fill Hell with Jinns and men all together."

14. "Taste you then - for you forgot the Meeting of this Day of yours, and We too will forget you - taste you the Chastisement of Eternity for your (evil) deeds!"

15. Only those believe in Our Signs, who, when these are recited to them,

نَعْمَلْ صَالِحًا إِنَّا مُوقِنُونَ ۝

وَلَوْ شِئْنَا لَآتَيْنَا كُلَّ نَفْسٍ

هُدٰىهَا وَلٰكِنْ حَقَّ الْقَوْلُ مِنِّي

لَأَمْلَأَنَّ جَهَنَّمَ مِنَ الْجِنَّةِ

وَالنَّاسِ أَجْمَعِينَ ۝ فَذُوقُوا بِمَا

نَسِيتُمْ لِقَاءَ يَوْمِكُمْ هٰذَا إِنَّا

نَسِينٰكُمْ وَذُوقُوا عَذَابَ الْخُلْدِ

بِمَا كُنْتُمْ تَعْمَلُونَ ۝ إِنَّمَا يُؤْمِنُ

بِآيٰتِنَا الَّذِينَ إِذَا ذُكِّرُوا بِهَا

(the faculties of) hearing and sight and feeling (and understanding): little thanks do you give!

10. And they say: "What! When we lie, hidden and lost, in the earth, shall we indeed be in a Creation renewed? No, they deny the Meeting with their Lord.

11. Say: "The Angel of Death, put in charge of you, will (duly) take your souls: then shall you be brought back to your Lord."

12. If only you could see when the guilty ones will bend low their heads before their Lord, (saying:) "Our Lord! We have seen and we have heard: now then send us back (to the world):

السَّمْعَ وَالْاَبْصَارَ وَالْاَفْـِٕدَةَ ۖ قَلِيْلًا

مَّا تَشْكُرُوْنَ ۝ وَقَالُوْٓا ءَاِذَا ضَلَلْنَا

فِى الْاَرْضِ ءَاِنَّا لَفِىْ خَلْقٍ جَدِيْدٍ ۖ

بَلْ هُمْ بِلِقَآئِ رَبِّهِمْ كٰفِرُوْنَ ۝

قُلْ يَتَوَفّٰىكُمْ مَّلَكُ الْمَوْتِ

الَّذِىْ وُكِّلَ بِكُمْ ثُمَّ اِلٰى رَبِّكُمْ

تُرْجَعُوْنَ ۝ وَلَوْ تَرٰىٓ اِذِ الْمُجْرِمُوْنَ

نَاكِسُوْا رُءُوْسِهِمْ عِنْدَ رَبِّهِمْ ۖ

رَبَّنَآ اَبْصَرْنَا وَسَمِعْنَا فَارْجِعْنَا

the earth: in the end will (all affairs) go up to Him, on a Day, the space whereof will be (as) a thousand years of your reckoning.

6.   Such is He, the Knower of all things, hidden and open, the Exalted (in Power), the Merciful; -

7.   He Who has made everything which He has created most good: He began the creation of man with (nothing more than) clay,

8.   And made his progeny from a quintessence of the nature of a fluid despised:

9.   But He fashioned him in due proportion, and breathed into him something of His spirit. And He gave you

الْاَرْضِ ثُمَّ يَعْرُجُ اِلَيْهِ فِیْ يَوْمٍ

كَانَ مِقْدَارُهٗۤ اَلْفَ سَنَةٍ مِّمَّا

تَعُدُّوْنَ ۞ ذٰلِكَ عٰلِمُ الْغَيْبِ

وَالشَّهَادَةِ الْعَزِيْزُ الرَّحِيْمُ ۙ الَّذِیْۤ

اَحْسَنَ كُلَّ شَیْءٍ خَلَقَهٗ وَبَدَاَ

خَلْقَ الْاِنْسَانِ مِنْ طِيْنٍ ۚ ثُمَّ

جَعَلَ نَسْلَهٗ مِنْ سُلٰلَةٍ مِّنْ

مَّآءٍ مَّهِيْنٍ ۚ ثُمَّ سَوّٰىهُ وَنَفَخَ

فِيْهِ مِنْ رُّوْحِهٖ وَجَعَلَ لَكُمُ

"He has forged it"? No, it is the Truth from your Lord, that you may admonish a people to whom no warner has come before you: in order that they may receive guidance.

4. It is Allah Who has created the heavens and the earth, and all between them, in six Days, and is firmly established on the Throne (of Authority): you have none, besides Him, to protect or intercede (for you): will you not then receive admonition?

5. He rules (all) affairs from the heavens to

اَفْتَرٰىهُ بَلْ هُوَ الْحَقُّ مِنْ

رَّبِّكَ لِتُنْذِرَ قَوْمًا مَّآ اَتٰىهُمْ

مِّنْ نَّذِيْرٍ مِّنْ قَبْلِكَ لَعَلَّهُمْ

يَهْتَدُوْنَ ۞ اَللّٰهُ الَّذِيْ خَلَقَ

السَّمٰوٰتِ وَالْاَرْضَ وَمَا بَيْنَهُمَا

فِيْ سِتَّةِ اَيَّامٍ ثُمَّ اسْتَوٰى عَلَى

الْعَرْشِ ۖ مَا لَكُمْ مِّنْ دُوْنِهٖ مِنْ

وَّلِيٍّ وَّلَا شَفِيْعٍ ۚ اَفَلَا تَتَذَكَّرُوْنَ ۞

يُدَبِّرُ الْاَمْرَ مِنَ السَّمَآءِ اِلَى

34. Verily the knowledge of the Hour is with Allah (alone). It is He Who sends down rain, and He Who knows what is in the wombs. Nor does any one know what it is that he will earn on the morrow: nor does any one know in what land he is to die. Verily with Allah is full of Knowledge and He is Acquainted (with all things).

As-Sajda (Adoration)

Bismillahir-Rahmanir-Rahim

1. Alif. Lam. Mim.

2. (This is) the Revelation of the Book in which there is no doubt, - from the Lord of the Worlds.

3. Or do they say,

الْغُرُوْرُ ۞ اِنَّ اللّٰهَ عِنْدَهٗ عِلْمُ

السَّاعَةِ ۚ وَيُنَزِّلُ الْغَيْثَ ۚ وَيَعْلَمُ

مَا فِى الْاَرْحَامِ ۗ وَمَا تَدْرِىْ

نَفْسٌ مَّا ذَا تَكْسِبُ غَدًا ۗ وَمَا

تَدْرِىْ نَفْسٌ بِاَىِّ اَرْضٍ تَمُوْتُ ۗ

اِنَّ اللّٰهَ عَلِيْمٌ خَبِيْرٌ ۞

بِسْمِ اللّٰهِ الرَّحْمٰنِ الرَّحِيْمِ

الٓمّٓ ۞ تَنْزِيْلُ الْكِتٰبِ لَا رَيْبَ فِيْهِ

مِنْ رَّبِّ الْعٰلَمِيْنَ ۞ اَمْ يَقُوْلُوْنَ

Allah, offering Him sincere devotion. But when He has delivered them safely to land, there are among them those that falter between (right and wrong). But none reject Our Signs except only a perfidious ungrateful (wretch)!

33. O mankind! Do your duty to your Lord, and fear (the coming of) a Day when no father can avail aught for his son, nor a son avail aught for his father. Verily, the Promise of Allah is true: let not then this present life deceive you, nor let the chief deceiver deceive you about Allah.

اللهَ مُخْلِصِیْنَ لَهُ الدِّیْنَ ۚ

فَلَمَّا نَجّٰهُمْ اِلَی الْبَرِّ فَمِنْهُمْ

مُّقْتَصِدٌ ؕ وَمَا یَجْحَدُ بِاٰیٰتِنَاۤ اِلَّا

كُلُّ خَتَّارٍ كَفُوْرٍ ۝ یٰۤاَیُّهَا النَّاسُ

اتَّقُوْا رَبَّكُمْ وَاخْشَوْا یَوْمًا لَّا

یَّجْزِیْ وَالِدٌ عَنْ وَّلَدِهٖ ۫ وَلَا

مَوْلُوْدٌ هُوَ جَازٍ عَنْ وَّالِدِهٖ شَیْئًا ؕ

اِنَّ وَعْدَ اللهِ حَقٌّ فَلَا تَغُرَّنَّكُمُ

الْحَیٰوةُ الدُّنْیَا ۫ وَلَا یَغُرَّنَّكُمْ بِاللهِ

appointed; and that Allah is Well-Acquainted with all that you do?

30. That is because Allah is the (only) Reality, and because whatever else they invoke besides Him is Falsehood; and because Allah, - He is the Most High, Most Great.

31. Do you see not that the ships sail through the ocean by the Grace of Allah? - that He may show you of His Signs? Verily in this are Signs for all who constantly persevere and give thanks.

32. When a wave covers them like the canopy (of clouds), they call to

مُسَمًّى وَّ اَنَّ اللّٰهَ بِمَا تَعْمَلُوْنَ

خَبِيْرٌ ۲۸ ذٰلِكَ بِاَنَّ اللّٰهَ هُوَ

الْحَقُّ وَ اَنَّ مَا يَدْعُوْنَ مِنْ

دُوْنِهِ الْبَاطِلُ وَاَنَّ اللّٰهَ هُوَ

الْعَلِیُّ الْكَبِيْرُ ۵ اَلَمْ تَرَ اَنَّ

الْفُلْكَ تَجْرِیْ فِی الْبَحْرِ بِنِعْمَتِ

اللّٰهِ لِيُرِيَكُمْ مِّنْ اٰيٰتِهِ ۚ اِنَّ فِیْ

ذٰلِكَ لَاٰيٰتٍ لِّكُلِّ صَبَّارٍ شَكُوْرٍ

۳ وَاِذَا غَشِيَهُمْ مَّوْجٌ كَالظُّلَلِ دَعَوُا

pens and the ocean (were ink), with seven oceans behind it to add to its (supply), yet would not the Words of Allah be exhausted (in the writing): for Allah is Exalted in Power, full of Wisdom.

28. And your creation or your resurrection is in no wise but as an individual soul: for Allah is He Who hears and sees (all things).

29. Do you see not that Allah merges Night into Day and He merges Day into Night; that He has subjected the sun, and the moon (to his Law), each running its course for a term

اَقْلَامٌ وَّالْبَحْرُ يَمُدُّهٗ مِنْ
بَعْدِهٖ سَبْعَةُ اَبْحُرٍ مَّا نَفِدَتْ
كَلِمٰتُ اللّٰهِ ؕ اِنَّ اللّٰهَ عَزِيْزٌ
حَكِيْمٌ ۝ مَا خَلْقُكُمْ وَلَا بَعْثُكُمْ
اِلَّا كَنَفْسٍ وَّاحِدَةٍ ؕ اِنَّ اللّٰهَ
سَمِيْعٌ بَصِيْرٌ ۝ اَلَمْ تَرَ اَنَّ اللّٰهَ
يُوْلِجُ الَّيْلَ فِی النَّهَارِ وَيُوْلِجُ
النَّهَارَ فِی الَّيْلِ وَسَخَّرَ الشَّمْسَ
وَالْقَمَرَ ۙ كُلٌّ يَّجْرِیْۤ اِلٰۤی اَجَلٍ

for Allah knows well all that is in (men's) hearts.

24. We grant them their pleasure for a little while: in the end shall We drive them to a Chastisement unrelenting.

25. If you ask them, who it is that created the heavens and the earth. They will certainly say, "Allah". Say: "Praise be to Allah!" But most of them understand not.

26. To Allah belong all things in heaven and earth: verily Allah is He (that is) Free of all wants, Worthy of all praise.

27. And if all the trees on earth were

اِنَّ اللّٰهَ عَلِیْمٌۢ بِذَاتِ الصُّدُوْرِ ۞

نُمَتِّعُهُمْ قَلِیْلًا ثُمَّ نَضْطَرُّهُمْ اِلٰی

عَذَابٍ غَلِیْظٍ ۞ وَلَئِنْ سَاَلْتَهُمْ

مَّنْ خَلَقَ السَّمٰوٰتِ وَالْاَرْضَ

لَیَقُوْلُنَّ اللّٰهُ ؕ قُلِ الْحَمْدُ لِلّٰهِ ؕ

بَلْ اَكْثَرُهُمْ لَا یَعْلَمُوْنَ ۞ لِلّٰهِ

مَا فِی السَّمٰوٰتِ وَالْاَرْضِ ؕ اِنَّ

اللّٰهَ هُوَ الْغَنِیُّ الْحَمِیْدُ ۞ وَلَوْ

اَنَّ مَا فِی الْاَرْضِ مِنْ شَجَرَةٍ

(the Revelation) that Allah has sent down, they say: "No, we shall follow the ways that we found our fathers (following)." What! Even if it is Satan beckoning them to the Chastisement of the (Blazing) Fire?

22.　Whoever submits his whole self to Allah, and is a doer of good, has grasped indeed the most trustworthy hand-hold: and to Allah shall all things return.

23.　But if any reject Faith, let not his rejection grieve you: to Us is their return, and We shall tell them the truth of their deeds:

مَآ أَنْزَلَ اللهُ قَالُوا بَلْ نَتَّبِعُ

مَا وَجَدْنَا عَلَيْهِ اٰبَآءَنَا ۚ أَوَلَوْ

كَانَ الشَّيْطٰنُ يَدْعُوهُمْ إِلَى

عَذَابِ السَّعِيرِ ۞ وَمَنْ يُّسْلِمْ

وَجْهَهُ إِلَى اللهِ وَهُوَ مُحْسِنٌ

فَقَدِ اسْتَمْسَكَ بِالْعُرْوَةِ الْوُثْقٰى ۗ

وَإِلَى اللهِ عَاقِبَةُ الْأُمُورِ ۞ وَمَنْ

كَفَرَ فَلَا يَحْزُنْكَ كُفْرُهٗ ۚ إِلَيْنَا

مَرْجِعُهُمْ فَنُنَبِّئُهُمْ بِمَا عَمِلُوا ۚ

19. "And be moderate in your pace, and lower your voice; for the harshest of sounds without doubt is the braying of the ass."

20. Do you not see that Allah has subjected to your (use) all things in the heavens and on earth, and has made His bounties flow to you in exceeding measure, (both) seen and unseen? Yet there are among men those who dispute about Allah, without knowledge and without guidance, and without a Book to enlighten them!

21. When they are told to follow

وَاقْصِدْ فِىْ مَشْيِكَ وَاغْضُضْ

مِنْ صَوْتِكَ ۖ اِنَّ اَنْكَرَ الْاَصْوَاتِ

لَصَوْتُ الْحَمِيْرِ ۝ اَلَمْ تَرَوْا اَنَّ

اللّٰهَ سَخَّرَ لَكُمْ مَّا فِى السَّمٰوٰتِ

وَمَا فِى الْاَرْضِ وَاَسْبَغَ عَلَيْكُمْ

نِعَمَهٗ ظَاهِرَةً وَّبَاطِنَةً ۗ وَمِنَ

النَّاسِ مَنْ يُّجَادِلُ فِى اللّٰهِ

بِغَيْرِ عِلْمٍ وَّلَا هُدًى وَّلَا كِتٰبٍ

مُّنِيْرٍ ۝ وَاِذَا قِيْلَ لَهُمُ اتَّبِعُوْا

or (anywhere) in the heavens or on earth, Allah will bring it forth: for Allah is Subtle and Aware.

17. "O my son! Establish regular Prayer, enjoin what is just, and forbid what is wrong: and bear with patient constancy whatever befall you; for this is firmness (of purpose) in (the conduct of) affairs."

18. "And swell not your cheek (for pride) at men, nor walk in insolence through the earth; for Allah loves not any arrogant boaster."

أَوْ فِى السَّمٰوٰتِ أَوْ فِى الْأَرْضِ

يَأْتِ بِهَا اللَّهُ ؕ إِنَّ اللَّهَ لَطِيفٌ

خَبِيرٌ ۝ يٰبُنَىَّ أَقِمِ الصَّلٰوةَ وَأْمُرْ

بِالْمَعْرُوفِ وَانْهَ عَنِ الْمُنْكَرِ

وَاصْبِرْ عَلٰى مَآ أَصَابَكَ ؕ إِنَّ

ذٰلِكَ مِنْ عَزْمِ الْأُمُورِ ۝ وَلَا

تُصَعِّرْ خَدَّكَ لِلنَّاسِ وَلَا تَمْشِ

فِى الْأَرْضِ مَرَحًا ؕ إِنَّ اللَّهَ لَا

يُحِبُّ كُلَّ مُخْتَالٍ فَخُورٍ ۝

(hear the command), "Show gratitude to Me and to your parents: to Me is (your final) Goal."

15. "But if they strive to make you join in worship with Me things of which you have no knowledge, obey them not; yet bear them company in this life with justice (and consideration), and follow the way of those who turn to Me (in love): in the end the return of you all is to Me, and I will tell you the truth (and meaning) of all that you did."

16. "O my son!" (said Luqman), "If there be (but) the weight of a mustard-seed and it were (hidden) in a rock,

اَنِ اشكُر لِي وَلِوَالِدَيكَ اِلَيَّ

الْمَصِيرُ ۝ وَاِن جَاهَدٰكَ عَلَى

اَن تُشرِكَ بِي مَا لَيسَ لَكَ بِهِ

عِلمٌ فَلَا تُطِعهُمَا وَصَاحِبهُمَا فِي

الدُّنيَا مَعرُوفًا وَّاتَّبِع سَبِيلَ

مَن اَنَابَ اِلَيَّ ثُمَّ اِلَيَّ مَرجِعُكُم

فَاُنَبِّئُكُم بِمَا كُنتُم تَعمَلُونَ ۝

يٰبُنَيَّ اِنَّهَآ اِن تَكُ مِثقَالَ حَبَّةٍ

مِّن خَردَلٍ فَتَكُن فِي صَخرَةٍ

12. We bestowed (in the past) wisdom on Luqman: "Show (you) gratitude to Allah." And who is (so) grateful does so to the profit of his own soul: but if any is ungrateful, verily Allah is Free of all wants, Worthy of all praise.

13. Behold, Luqman said to his son by way of instruction: "O my son! Join not in worship (others) with Allah: for false worship is indeed the highest wrong-doing."

14. And We have enjoined on man (to be good) to his parents: in travail upon travail did his mother bear him, and in years twain was his weaning:

وَلَقَدْ اٰتَيْنَا لُقْمٰنَ الْحِكْمَةَ اَنِ

اشْكُرْ لِلّٰهِ ط وَمَنْ يَّشْكُرْ فَاِنَّمَا

يَشْكُرُ لِنَفْسِهٖ ج وَمَنْ كَفَرَ فَاِنَّ

اللّٰهَ غَنِيٌّ حَمِيْدٌ ۞ وَاِذْ قَالَ

لُقْمٰنُ لِابْنِهٖ وَهُوَ يَعِظُهٗ يٰبُنَیَّ

لَا تُشْرِكْ بِاللّٰهِ ط اِنَّ الشِّرْكَ

لَظُلْمٌ عَظِيْمٌ ۞ وَوَصَّيْنَا الْاِنْسَانَ

بِوَالِدَيْهِ ۚ حَمَلَتْهُ اُمُّهٗ وَهْنًا

عَلٰى وَهْنٍ وَّفِصٰلُهٗ فِیْ عَامَيْنِ

and He is Exalted in Power, Wise.

10. He created the heavens without any pillars that you can see; He set on the earth mountains standing firm, lest it should shake with you; and He scattered through it beasts of all kinds. We send down rain from the sky, and produce on the earth every kind of noble creature, in pairs.

11. Such is the Creation of Allah: now show Me what is there that others besides Him have created: nay, but the Transgressors are in manifest error.

وَهُوَ الْعَزِیْزُ الْحَكِیْمُ ۞ خَلَقَ

السَّمٰوٰتِ بِغَیْرِ عَمَدٍ تَرَوْنَهَا

وَاَلْقٰی فِی الْاَرْضِ رَوَاسِیَ اَنْ

تَمِیْدَ بِكُمْ وَبَثَّ فِیْهَا مِنْ كُلِّ

دَآبَّةٍ ۚ وَاَنْزَلْنَا مِنَ السَّمَآءِ مَآءً

فَاَنْۢبَتْنَا فِیْهَا مِنْ كُلِّ زَوْجٍ

كَرِیْمٍ ۞ هٰذَا خَلْقُ اللّٰهِ فَاَرُوْنِیْ

مَاذَا خَلَقَ الَّذِیْنَ مِنْ دُوْنِهٖ ۚ

بَلِ الظّٰلِمُوْنَ فِیْ ضَلٰلٍ مُّبِیْنٍ ۞

from the Path of Allah and throw ridicule (on the Path): for such there will be a humiliating Chastisement.

7. When Our Signs are rehearsed to such a one, he turns away in arrogance, as if he heard them not, as if there were deafness in both his ears: announce to him a grievous Chastisement.

8. For those who believe and work righteous deeds, there will be Gardens of Bliss, -

9. To dwell therein. The Promise of Allah is true:

عَنْ سَبِيْلِ اللّٰهِ بِغَيْرِ عِلْمٍ

وَّيَتَّخِذَهَا هُزُوًا ۚ أُولٰٓئِكَ لَهُمْ

عَذَابٌ مُّهِيْنٌ ۞ وَإِذَا تُتْلٰى

عَلَيْهِ اٰيٰتُنَا وَلّٰى مُسْتَكْبِرًا كَأَنْ

لَّمْ يَسْمَعْهَا كَأَنَّ فِيْٓ أُذُنَيْهِ

وَقْرًا ۚ فَبَشِّرْهُ بِعَذَابٍ أَلِيْمٍ ۞

إِنَّ الَّذِيْنَ اٰمَنُوْا وَعَمِلُوا

الصّٰلِحٰتِ لَهُمْ جَنّٰتُ النَّعِيْمِ ۞

خٰلِدِيْنَ فِيْهَا ۚ وَعْدَ اللّٰهِ حَقًّا ۚ

Luqman (Lokman)

Bismillahir-Rahmanir-Rahim

1. Alif. Lam. Mim.

2. These are Verses of the Wise Book, -

3. A Guide and a Mercy to the doers of good, -

4. Those who establish regular Prayer, and give regular Charity, and have (in their hearts) the assurance of the Hereafter.

5. These are on (true) guidance from their Lord: and these are the ones who will prosper.

6. But there are, among men, those who purchase idle tales, without knowledge (or meaning), to mislead (men)

بِسْمِ اللهِ الرَّحْمٰنِ الرَّحِیْمِ

الٓمّٓ ۝ تِلْكَ اٰیٰتُ الْكِتٰبِ الْحَكِیْمِ ۝

هُدًی وَّ رَحْمَةً لِّلْمُحْسِنِیْنَ ۝

الَّذِیْنَ یُقِیْمُوْنَ الصَّلٰوةَ وَ یُؤْتُوْنَ

الزَّكٰوةَ وَ هُمْ بِالْاٰخِرَةِ هُمْ

یُوْقِنُوْنَ ۝ اُولٰٓئِكَ عَلٰی هُدًی

مِّنْ رَّبِّهِمْ وَ اُولٰٓئِكَ هُمُ

الْمُفْلِحُوْنَ ۝ وَ مِنَ النَّاسِ مَنْ

یَّشْتَرِیْ لَهْوَ الْحَدِیْثِ لِیُضِلَّ

no excuse of theirs will avail the transgressors, nor will they be allowed to make amends.

58. Verily We have propounded for men, in this Qur'an every kind of parable: but if you bring to them any Sign, the unbelievers are sure to say, "You do nothing but talk vanities."

59. Thus does Allah seal up the hearts of those who understand not.

60. So patiently persevere: for verily the Promise of Allah is true: nor let those shake your firmness, who have (themselves) no certainty of faith.

الَّذِیْنَ ظَلَمُوْا مَعْذِرَتُهُمْ وَلَا هُمْ

یُسْتَعْتَبُوْنَ ۞ وَلَقَدْ ضَرَبْنَا لِلنَّاسِ

فِیْ هٰذَا الْقُرْاٰنِ مِنْ کُلِّ مَثَلٍ ؕ

وَلَئِنْ جِئْتَهُمْ بِاٰیَةٍ لَّیَقُوْلَنَّ

الَّذِیْنَ کَفَرُوْۤا اِنْ اَنْتُمْ اِلَّا

مُبْطِلُوْنَ ۞ کَذٰلِکَ یَطْبَعُ اللّٰهُ

عَلٰی قُلُوْبِ الَّذِیْنَ لَا یَعْلَمُوْنَ

۞ فَاصْبِرْ اِنَّ وَعْدَ اللّٰهِ حَقٌّ وَّلَا

یَسْتَخِفَّنَّکَ الَّذِیْنَ لَا یُوْقِنُوْنَ ۞

He creates as He wills, and it is He Who has all knowledge and power.

55.   On the Day that the Hour (of Reckoning) will be established, the transgressors will swear that they tarried not but an hour: thus were they used to being deluded!

56.   But those endued with knowledge and faith will say: "Indeed you did tarry, within Allah's Decree, to the Day of Resurrection, and this is the Day of Resurrection: but you were not aware!"

57.   So on that Day

يَخْلُقُ مَا يَشَاءُ وَهُوَ الْعَلِيمُ

الْقَدِيرُ ۞ وَيَوْمَ تَقُومُ السَّاعَةُ

يُقْسِمُ الْمُجْرِمُونَ مَا لَبِثُوا غَيْرَ

سَاعَةٍ كَذَٰلِكَ كَانُوا يُؤْفَكُونَ ۞

وَقَالَ الَّذِينَ أُوتُوا الْعِلْمَ

وَالْإِيمَانَ لَقَدْ لَبِثْتُمْ فِي كِتَبِ

اللَّهِ إِلَىٰ يَوْمِ الْبَعْثِ فَهَٰذَا

يَوْمُ الْبَعْثِ وَلَٰكِنَّكُمْ كُنْتُمْ

لَا تَعْلَمُونَ ۞ فَيَوْمَئِذٍ لَا يَنْفَعُ

52. So verily you can not make the dead to hear, nor can you make the deaf to hear the call, when they show their backs and turn away.

53. Nor can you lead back the blind from their straying: only those will you make to hear, who believe in Our Signs and submit (their wills in Islam).

54. It is Allah Who created you in a state of (helpless) weakness, then gave (you) strength after weakness, then, after strength, gave (you) weakness and a hoary head:

فَإِنَّكَ لَا تُسْمِعُ الْمَوْتٰى وَلَا

تُسْمِعُ الصُّمَّ الدُّعَآءَ إِذَا وَلَّوْا

مُدْبِرِيْنَ ۟ وَمَاۤ أَنْتَ بِهٰدِ

الْعُمْيِ عَنْ ضَلٰلَتِهِمْ ۗ إِنْ تُسْمِعُ

إِلَّا مَنْ يُّؤْمِنُ بِاٰيٰتِنَا فَهُمْ

مُّسْلِمُوْنَ ۟ اللّٰهُ الَّذِيْ خَلَقَكُمْ

مِّنْ ضَعْفٍ ثُمَّ جَعَلَ مِنْ

بَعْدِ ضَعْفٍ قُوَّةً ثُمَّ جَعَلَ

مِنْۢ بَعْدِ قُوَّةٍ ضَعْفًا وَّشَيْبَةً ۚ

His servants as He wills behold, they do rejoice! -

49. Even though, before they received (the rain) - just before this - they were dumb with despair!

50. Then contemplate (O man!) the memorials of Allah's Mercy! - how He gives life to the earth after its death: verily the same will give life to the men who are dead: for He has Power over all things.

51. And if We (but) send a wind from which they see (their tilth) turn yellow, - behold, they become, thereafter, ungrateful (unbelievers)!

عِبَادِهٖۤ اِذَا هُمْ یَسْتَبْشِرُوْنَ ۝

وَاِنْ كَانُوْا مِنْ قَبْلِ اَنْ یُّنَزَّلَ

عَلَیْهِمْ مِّنْ قَبْلِهٖ لَمُبْلِسِیْنَ ۝

فَانْظُرْ اِلٰۤی اٰثٰرِ رَحْمَتِ اللّٰهِ

كَیْفَ یُحْیِ الْاَرْضَ بَعْدَ مَوْتِهَا ؕ

اِنَّ ذٰلِكَ لَمُحْیِ الْمَوْتٰی ۚ وَهُوَ

عَلٰی كُلِّ شَیْءٍ قَدِیْرٌ ۝ وَلَىِٕنْ

اَرْسَلْنَا رِیْحًا فَرَاَوْهُ مُصْفَرًّا

لَّظَلُّوْا مِنْ بَعْدِهٖ یَكْفُرُوْنَ ۝

before you, Apostles to their (respective) peoples, and they came to them with clear Signs: then, to those who trans-gressed, We meted out Retribution: and it was due from Us to aid those who believed.

48. It is Allah Who sends the Winds, and they raise the Clouds: then does He spread them in the sky as He wills, and break them into fragments, until you see rain-drops issue from the midst thereof: then when He has made them reach such of

قَبۡلِكَ رُسُلًا اِلٰی قَوۡمِهِمۡ

فَجَآءُوۡهُمۡ بِالۡبَیِّنٰتِ فَانۡتَقَمۡنَا

مِنَ الَّذِیۡنَ اَجۡرَمُوۡا ؕ وَکَانَ حَقًّا

عَلَیۡنَا نَصۡرُ الۡمُؤۡمِنِیۡنَ ۟ اَللّٰهُ

الَّذِیۡ یُرۡسِلُ الرِّیٰحَ فَتُثِیۡرُ

سَحَابًا فَیَبۡسُطُهٗ فِی السَّمَآءِ کَیۡفَ

یَشَآءُ وَیَجۡعَلُهٗ کِسَفًا فَتَرَی

الۡوَدۡقَ یَخۡرُجُ مِنۡ خِلٰلِهٖ ۚ فَاِذَاۤ

اَصَابَ بِهٖ مَنۡ یَّشَآءُ مِنۡ

from that rejection: and those who work righteousness will make provision for themselves (in heaven):

45.   That He may reward those who believe and work righteous deeds, out of His Bounty. For He loves not those who reject Faith.

46.   Among His Signs is this, that He sends the Winds, as heralds of glad tidings, giving you a taste of His (Grace and) Mercy, - that the ships may sail (majestically) by His Command and that you may seek of His Bounty: in order that you may be grateful.

47.   We did indeed send,

كُفْرُهٗ ۚ وَمَنْ عَمِلَ صَالِحًا

فَلِاَنْفُسِهِمْ يَمْهَدُوْنَ ۝ لِيَجْزِیَ

الَّذِيْنَ اٰمَنُوْا وَعَمِلُوا الصّٰلِحٰتِ

مِنْ فَضْلِهٖ ۚ اِنَّهٗ لَا يُحِبُّ

الْكٰفِرِيْنَ ۝ وَمِنْ اٰيٰتِهٖۤ اَنْ يُّرْسِلَ

الرِّيَاحَ مُبَشِّرٰتٍ وَّلِيُذِيْقَكُمْ مِّنْ

رَّحْمَتِهٖ وَلِتَجْرِیَ الْفُلْكُ بِاَمْرِهٖ

وَلِتَبْتَغُوْا مِنْ فَضْلِهٖ وَلَعَلَّكُمْ

تَشْكُرُوْنَ ۝ وَلَقَدْ اَرْسَلْنَا مِنْ

that (Allah) may give them a taste of some of their deeds: in order that they may turn back (from Evil).

42. Say: "Travel through the earth and see what was the end of those before (you): most of them worshipped others besides Allah."

43. But set you your face to the right Religion before there come from Allah the Day which there is no chance of averting: on that Day shall men be divided (in two).

44. Those who reject Faith will suffer

اَيْدِى النَّاسِ لِيُذِيْقَهُمْ بَعْضَ

الَّذِىْ عَمِلُوْا لَعَلَّهُمْ يَرْجِعُوْنَ ۞

قُلْ سِيْرُوْا فِى الْاَرْضِ فَانْظُرُوْا

كَيْفَ كَانَ عَاقِبَةُ الَّذِيْنَ مِنْ

قَبْلُ ۛ كَانَ اَكْثَرُهُمْ مُشْرِكِيْنَ ۞

فَاَقِمْ وَجْهَكَ لِلدِّيْنِ الْقَيِّمِ

مِنْ قَبْلِ اَنْ يَّاْتِىَ يَوْمٌ لَّا

مَرَدَّ لَهٗ مِنَ اللّٰهِ يَوْمَئِذٍ

يَّصَّدَّعُوْنَ ۞ مَنْ كَفَرَ فَعَلَيْهِ

will have no increase with Allah: but that which you lay out for Charity, seeking the Countenance of Allah, (will increase): it is these who will get a recompense multi-plied.

40. It is Allah Who has created you: further, He has provided for your sustenance; then He will cause you to die; and again He will give you life. Are there any of your (false) "partners" who can do any single one of these things? Glory to Him! And High is He above the partners they attribute (to him)!

41. Mischief has appeared on land and sea because of (the meed) that the hands of men have earned,

فَلَا يَرْبُوْا عِنْدَ اللّٰهِ ۚ وَمَاۤ اٰتَيْتُمْ

مِّنْ زَكٰوةٍ تُرِيْدُوْنَ وَجْهَ اللّٰهِ

فَاُولٰٓئِكَ هُمُ الْمُضْعِفُوْنَ ۞ اَللّٰهُ

الَّذِیْ خَلَقَكُمْ ثُمَّ رَزَقَكُمْ ثُمَّ

يُمِيْتُكُمْ ثُمَّ يُحْيِيْكُمْ ؕ هَلْ مِنْ

شُرَكَآئِكُمْ مَّنْ يَّفْعَلُ مِنْ ذٰلِكُمْ

مِّنْ شَیْءٍ ؕ سُبْحٰنَهٗ وَتَعٰلٰى

عَمَّا يُشْرِكُوْنَ ۞ ظَهَرَ الْفَسَادُ

فِی الْبَرِّ وَالْبَحْرِ بِمَا كَسَبَتْ

behold, they are in despair!

37. See they not that Allah enlarges the provision and restricts it, to whomsoever He pleases? Verily in that are Signs for those who believe.

38. So give what is due to kindred, the needy, and the wayfarer. That is best for those who seek the Countenance of Allah, and it is they who will prosper.

39. That which you lay out for increase through the property of (other) people,

اَیْدِیْہِمْ اِذَا ہُمْ یَقْنَطُوْنَ ۝ اَوَ

لَمْ یَرَوْا اَنَّ اللہَ یَبْسُطُ الرِّزْقَ

لِمَنْ یَّشَاۤءُ وَ یَقْدِرُ ؕ اِنَّ فِیْ ذٰلِكَ

لَاٰیٰتٍ لِّقَوْمٍ یُّؤْمِنُوْنَ ۝ فَاٰتِ

ذَا الْقُرْبٰی حَقَّہٗ وَ الْمِسْکِیْنَ وَ ابْنَ

السَّبِیْلِ ؕ ذٰلِكَ خَیْرٌ لِّلَّذِیْنَ

یُرِیْدُوْنَ وَجْہَ اللہِ ؗ وَ اُولٰٓئِكَ ہُمُ

الْمُفْلِحُوْنَ ۝ وَ مَاۤ اٰتَیْتُمْ مِّنْ

رِّبًا لِّیَرْبُوَا۠ فِیْۤ اَمْوَالِ النَّاسِ

turning back to Him in repentance: but when He gives them a taste of Mercy as from Himself, behold, some of them pay part-worship to other god's besides their Lord, -

34. (As if) to show their ingratitude for the (favours) We have bestowed on them! Then enjoy (your brief day); but soon will you know (your folly).

35. Or have We sent down authority to them, which points out to them the things to which they pay part-worship?

36. When We give men a taste of Mercy, they exult thereat: and when some evil afflicts them because of what their (own) hands have sent forth,

مُنِيبِيْنَ اِلَيْهِ ثُمَّ اِذَآ اَذَاقَهُمْ

مِّنْهُ رَحْمَةً اِذَا فَرِيْقٌ مِّنْهُمْ

بِرَبِّهِمْ يُشْرِكُوْنَ ۞ لِيَكْفُرُوْا

بِمَآ اٰتَيْنٰهُمْ ۗ فَتَمَتَّعُوْا ۗ فَسَوْفَ

تَعْلَمُوْنَ ۞ اَمْ اَنْزَلْنَا عَلَيْهِمْ

سُلْطٰنًا فَهُوَ يَتَكَلَّمُ بِمَا كَانُوْا

بِهٖ يُشْرِكُوْنَ ۞ وَاِذَآ اَذَقْنَا

النَّاسَ رَحْمَةً فَرِحُوْا بِهَا ۗ وَاِنْ

تُصِبْهُمْ سَيِّئَةٌ بِمَا قَدَّمَتْ

no change (let there be) in the work (wrought) by Allah: that is the standard Religion: but most among mankind understand not.

31.   Turn you back in repentance to Him, and fear Him: establish regular prayers, and be not you among those who join gods with Allah, -

32.   Those who split up their Religion, and become (mere) sects, - each party rejoicing in that which is with itself!

33.   When trouble touches men, they cry to their Lord,

لَا تَبْدِيلَ لِخَلْقِ اللّٰهِ ذٰلِكَ

الدِّينُ الْقَيِّمُ وَلٰكِنَّ اَكْثَرَ

النَّاسِ لَا يَعْلَمُونَ ۞ مُنِيبِيْنَ

اِلَيْهِ وَاتَّقُوهُ وَاَقِيمُوا الصَّلٰوةَ

وَلَا تَكُونُوا مِنَ الْمُشْرِكِينَ ۞

مِنَ الَّذِينَ فَرَّقُوا دِينَهُمْ

وَكَانُوا شِيَعًا كُلُّ حِزْبٍ بِمَا

لَدَيْهِمْ فَرِحُونَ ۞ وَاِذَا مَسَّ

النَّاسَ ضُرٌّ دَعَوْا رَبَّهُمْ

Do you fear them as you fear each other? Thus do we explain the Signs in detail to a people that understand.

29. No, the wrong-doers (merely) follow their own lusts, being devoid of knowledge. But who will guide those whom Allah leaves astray? To them there will be no helpers.

30. So set you your face steadily and truly to the Faith: (establish) Allah's handiwork according to the pattern on which He has made mankind:

فَأَنتُمْ فِيهِ سَوَآءٌ تَخَافُونَهُمْ

كَخِيفَتِكُمْ أَنفُسَكُمْ ۚ كَذَٰلِكَ

نُفَصِّلُ ٱلْآيَاتِ لِقَوْمٍ يَعْقِلُونَ ۝

بَلِ ٱتَّبَعَ ٱلَّذِينَ ظَلَمُوٓا

أَهْوَآءَهُم بِغَيْرِ عِلْمٍ ۖ فَمَن

يَهْدِى مَنْ أَضَلَّ ٱللَّهُ ۖ وَمَا

لَهُم مِّن نَّاصِرِينَ ۝ فَأَقِمْ

وَجْهَكَ لِلدِّينِ حَنِيفًا ۚ فِطْرَتَ

ٱللَّهِ ٱلَّتِى فَطَرَ ٱلنَّاسَ عَلَيْهَا ۚ

26.　To Him belongs every being that is in the heavens and on earth: all are devoutly obedient to Him.

27.　It is He Who begins (the process of) creation; then repeats it; and for Him it is most easy. To Him belongs the loftiest similitude (one can think of) in the heavens and the earth: for He is Exalted in Might, full of Wisdom.

28.　He does propound to you a similitude from your own (experience): do you have partners among those whom your right hands possess, to share as equals in the wealth We have bestowed on you?

وَلَهٗ مَنْ فِى السَّمٰوٰتِ وَالْاَرْضِ ۖ

كُلٌّ لَّهٗ قٰنِتُوْنَ ۞ وَهُوَ الَّذِىْ

يَبْدَؤُا الْخَلْقَ ثُمَّ يُعِيْدُهٗ

وَهُوَ اَهْوَنُ عَلَيْهِ ۖ وَلَهُ الْمَثَلُ

الْاَعْلٰى فِى السَّمٰوٰتِ وَالْاَرْضِ ۖ

وَهُوَ الْعَزِيْزُ الْحَكِيْمُ ۞ ضَرَبَ

لَكُمْ مَّثَلًا مِّنْ اَنْفُسِكُمْ ۖ هَلْ

لَّكُمْ مِّنْ مَّا مَلَكَتْ اَيْمَانُكُمْ

مِّنْ شُرَكَآءَ فِىْ مَا رَزَقْنٰكُمْ

that are Signs for those who hearken.

24. And among His Signs, He shows you the lightning, by way both of fear and of hope, and He sends down rain from the sky and with it gives life to the earth after it is dead: verily in that are Signs for those who are wise.

25. And among His Signs is this, that heaven and earth stand by His Command: then when He calls you, by a single call, from the earth, behold, you (straight way) come forth.

ذٰلِكَ لَاٰيٰتٍ لِّقَوْمٍ يَّسْمَعُوْنَ ۞

وَمِنْ اٰيٰتِهٖ يُرِيْكُمُ الْبَرْقَ

خَوْفًا وَّطَمَعًا وَّيُنَزِّلُ مِنَ السَّمَآءِ

مَآءً فَيُحْيٖ بِهِ الْاَرْضَ بَعْدَ

مَوْتِهَا ۚ اِنَّ فِيْ ذٰلِكَ لَاٰيٰتٍ لِّقَوْمٍ

يَّعْقِلُوْنَ ۞ وَمِنْ اٰيٰتِهٖۤ اَنْ

تَقُوْمَ السَّمَآءُ وَالْاَرْضُ بِاَمْرِهٖ ۚ

ثُمَّ اِذَا دَعَاكُمْ دَعْوَةً مِّنَ

الْاَرْضِ ۖ اِذَاۤ اَنْتُمْ تَخْرُجُوْنَ ۞

mates from among yourselves, that you may dwell in tranquillity with them, and He has put love and mercy between your (hearts): verily in that are Signs for those who reflect.

22. And among His Signs is the creation of the heavens and the earth, and the variations in your languages and your colours: verily in that are Signs for those who know.

23. And among His Signs is the sleep that you take by night and by day, and the quest that you (make for livelihood) out of His Bounty: verily in

اَنْفُسِكُمْ اَزْوَاجًا لِّتَسْكُنُوْٓا اِلَيْهَا

وَجَعَلَ بَيْنَكُمْ مَّوَدَّةً وَّرَحْمَةً ؕ

اِنَّ فِیْ ذٰلِكَ لَاٰيٰتٍ لِّقَوْمٍ

يَّتَفَكَّرُوْنَ ۞ وَمِنْ اٰيٰتِهٖ خَلْقُ

السَّمٰوٰتِ وَالْاَرْضِ وَاخْتِلَافُ

اَلْسِنَتِكُمْ وَاَلْوَانِكُمْ ؕ اِنَّ فِیْ

ذٰلِكَ لَاٰيٰتٍ لِّلْعٰلِمِيْنَ ۞ وَمِنْ

اٰيٰتِهٖ مَنَامُكُمْ بِالَّيْلِ وَالنَّهَارِ

وَابْتِغَآؤُكُمْ مِّنْ فَضْلِهٖ ؕ اِنَّ فِیْ

you reach eventide and when you rise in the morning;

18. Yes, to Him be praise, in the heavens and on earth; and in the late afternoon and when the day begins to decline.

19. It is He Who brings out the living from the dead, and brings out the dead from the living, and Who gives life to the earth after it is dead: and thus shall you be brought out (from the dead).

20. Among His Signs in this, that He created you from dust; and then, - behold, you are men scattered (far and wide)!

21. And among His Signs is this, that He created for you

تُمْسُونَ وَحِينَ تُصْبِحُونَ ۝ وَلَهُ

الْحَمْدُ فِي السَّمٰوٰتِ وَالْأَرْضِ

وَعَشِيًّا وَّحِينَ تُظْهِرُونَ ۝ يُخْرِجُ

الْحَيَّ مِنَ الْمَيِّتِ وَيُخْرِجُ الْمَيِّتَ

مِنَ الْحَيِّ وَيُحْيِ الْأَرْضَ بَعْدَ

مَوْتِهَا ۚ وَكَذٰلِكَ تُخْرَجُونَ ۝

وَمِنْ اٰيٰتِهٖ أَنْ خَلَقَكُمْ مِّنْ تُرَابٍ

ثُمَّ اِذَآ أَنْتُمْ بَشَرٌ تَنْتَشِرُونَ ۝

وَمِنْ اٰيٰتِهٖ أَنْ خَلَقَ لَكُمْ مِّنْ

13. No intercessor will they have among their "partners" and they will (themselves) reject their "partners".

14. On the Day that the Hour will be established, - that Day shall (all men) be sorted out.

15. Then those who have believed and worked righteous deeds, shall be made happy in a Mead of Delight.

16. And those who have rejected Faith and falsely denied Our Signs and the meeting of the Hereafter, - such shall be brought forth to Punishment.

17. So (give) Glory to Allah, when

الْمُجْرِمُوۡنَ ۞ وَلَمۡ يَكُنۡ لَّهُمۡ مِّنۡ

شُرَكَآئِهِمۡ شُفَعٰٓؤُا وَكَانُوۡا بِشُرَكَآئِهِمۡ

كٰفِرِيۡنَ ۞ وَيَوۡمَ تَقُوۡمُ السَّاعَةُ

يَوۡمَئِذٍ يَّتَفَرَّقُوۡنَ ۞ فَاَمَّا الَّذِيۡنَ

اٰمَنُوۡا وَعَمِلُوا الصّٰلِحٰتِ فَهُمۡ فِيۡ

رَوۡضَةٍ يُّحۡبَرُوۡنَ ۞ وَاَمَّا الَّذِيۡنَ

كَفَرُوۡا وَكَذَّبُوۡا بِاٰيٰتِنَا وَلِقَآئِ

الۡاٰخِرَةِ فَاُولٰٓئِكَ فِی الۡعَذَابِ

مُحۡضَرُوۡنَ ۞ فَسُبۡحٰنَ اللّٰهِ حِيۡنَ

than these have done: then there came to them their Apostles with clear (Signs). (Which they rejected, to their own destruction): it was not Allah Who wronged them, but they wronged their own souls.

10. In the long run evil in the extreme will be the End of those who do evil; for that they rejected the Signs of Allah, and held them up to ridicule.

11. It is Allah Who begins (the process of) creation; then repeats it; then shall you be brought back to Him.

12. On the Day that the Hour will be established, the guilty will be struck dumb with despair.

مِمَّا عَمَرُوۡهَا وَجَآءَتْهُمۡ رُسُلُهُمۡ

بِالْبَيِّنٰتِ ۚ فَمَا كَانَ اللهُ

لِيَظْلِمَهُمۡ وَلٰكِنۡ كَانُوۡۤا اَنۡفُسَهُمۡ

يَظْلِمُوۡنَ ۞ ثُمَّ كَانَ عَاقِبَةَ

الَّذِيۡنَ اَسَآءُوا السُّوۡۤاٰۤى اَنۡ

كَذَّبُوۡا بِاٰيٰتِ اللهِ وَكَانُوۡا بِهَا

يَسْتَهۡزِءُوۡنَ ۞ اللهُ يَبۡدَؤُا الۡخَلۡقَ

ثُمَّ يُعِيۡدُهٗ ثُمَّ اِلَيۡهِ تُرۡجَعُوۡنَ ۞

وَيَوۡمَ تَقُوۡمُ السَّاعَةُ يُبۡلِسُ

8. Do they not reflect in their own minds? Not but for just ends and for a term appointed, did Allah create the heavens and the earth, and all between them: yet are there truly many among men who deny the meeting with their Lord (at the Resurrection)!

9. Do they not travel through the earth, and see what was the end of those before them? They were superior to them in strength: they tilled the soil and populated it in greater numbers

أَوَلَمْ يَتَفَكَّرُوا فِيٓ أَنْفُسِهِمْ ۗ مَا

خَلَقَ اللّٰهُ السَّمٰوٰتِ وَالْأَرْضَ

وَمَا بَيْنَهُمَآ إِلَّا بِالْحَقِّ وَأَجَلٍ

مُّسَمًّى ۗ وَإِنَّ كَثِيرًا مِّنَ النَّاسِ

بِلِقَآئِ رَبِّهِمْ لَكٰفِرُونَ ۞ أَوَلَمْ

يَسِيرُوا فِي الْأَرْضِ فَيَنْظُرُوا

كَيْفَ كَانَ عَاقِبَةُ الَّذِينَ مِنْ

قَبْلِهِمْ ۚ كَانُوٓا أَشَدَّ مِنْهُمْ قُوَّةً

وَّأَثَارُوا الْأَرْضَ وَعَمَرُوهَآ أَكْثَرَ

will soon be victorious -

4. Within a few years. With Allah is the Command, in the past and in the future: on that Day shall the believers rejoice -

5. With the help of Allah. He gives victory to whom He wills, and He is Exalted in Might, Most Merciful.

6. (It is) the promise of Allah. Never does Allah depart from His promise: but most men understand not.

7. They know but the outer (things) in the life of this world: but they are heedless of the Hereafter.

سَيَغْلِبُونَ ۞ فِیْ بِضْعِ سِنِیْنَ ؕ

لِلّٰهِ الْأَمْرُ مِنْ قَبْلُ وَمِنْ بَعْدُ ؕ

وَيَوْمَئِذٍ يَّفْرَحُ الْمُؤْمِنُوْنَ ۞

بِنَصْرِ اللّٰهِ ؕ يَنْصُرُ مَنْ يَّشَآءُ ؕ وَهُوَ

الْعَزِیْزُ الرَّحِیْمُ ۞ وَعْدَ اللّٰهِ ؕ لَا

يُخْلِفُ اللّٰهُ وَعْدَهٗ وَلٰكِنَّ أَكْثَرَ

النَّاسِ لَا يَعْلَمُوْنَ ۞ يَعْلَمُوْنَ

ظَاهِرًا مِّنَ الْحَیٰوةِ الدُّنْیَا ۚ

وَهُمْ عَنِ الْأٰخِرَةِ هُمْ غٰفِلُوْنَ ۞

68. And who does more wrong than he who invents a lie against Allah or rejects the Truth when it reaches him? Is there not a home in Hell for those who reject Faith?

69. And those who strive in Our (cause), - We will certainly guide them to Our Paths: for verily Allah is with those who do right.

Ar-Rum (The Romans)

Bismillahir-Rahmanir-Rahim

1. Alif. Lam. Mim.

2. The Roman Empire has been defeated -

3. In a land close by; but they, (even) after (this) defeat of theirs,

وَمَنْ أَظْلَمُ مِمَّنِ افْتَرَى عَلَى

اللهِ كَذِبًا أَوْ كَذَّبَ بِالْحَقِّ لَمَّا

جَاءَهُ ۚ أَلَيْسَ فِي جَهَنَّمَ مَثْوًى

لِّلْكَٰفِرِينَ ۝ وَالَّذِينَ جَاهَدُوا

فِينَا لَنَهْدِيَنَّهُمْ سُبُلَنَا ۚ وَإِنَّ

اللهَ لَمَعَ الْمُحْسِنِينَ ۝

بِسْمِ اللهِ الرَّحْمَٰنِ الرَّحِيمِ

الٓمٓ ۝ غُلِبَتِ الرُّومُ ۝ فِي أَدْنَى

الْأَرْضِ وَهُم مِّنۢ بَعْدِ غَلَبِهِمْ

is life indeed, if they but knew.

65.   Now, if they embark on a boat, they call on Allah, making their devotion sincerely (and exclusively) to Him; but when He has delivered them safely to (dry) land, behold, they give a share (of their worship to others)! -

66.   Disdaining ungratefully Our gifts, and giving themselves up to (worldly) enjoyment! But soon will they know.

67.   Do they not then see that We have made a Sanctuary secure, and that men are being snatched away from all around them? Then, do they believe in that which is vain, and reject the Grace of Allah?

وقضى أن

الْحَيَوَانُ ۚ لَوْ كَانُوا يَعْلَمُونَ ۝ فَإِذَا

رَكِبُوا فِي الْفُلْكِ دَعَوُا اللّٰهَ

مُخْلِصِينَ لَهُ الدِّينَ ۚ فَلَمَّا نَجّٰهُمْ

إِلَى الْبَرِّ إِذَا هُمْ يُشْرِكُونَ ۝

لِيَكْفُرُوا بِمَا آتَيْنٰهُمْ ۙ وَلِيَتَمَتَّعُوا ۖ

فَسَوْفَ يَعْلَمُونَ ۝ أَوَلَمْ يَرَوْا

أَنَّا جَعَلْنَا حَرَمًا آمِنًا وَّيُتَخَطَّفُ

النَّاسُ مِنْ حَوْلِهِمْ ۚ أَفَبِالْبَاطِلِ

يُؤْمِنُونَ وَبِنِعْمَةِ اللّٰهِ يَكْفُرُونَ ۝

the sustenance (which He gives) to whichever of His servants He pleases; and He (similarly) grants by (strict) measure, (as He pleases): for Allah has full knowledge of all things.

63. And if indeed you ask them: "Who it is that sends down rain from the sky, and gives life therewith to the earth after its death?" they will certainly reply, "Allah". Say, "Praise be to Allah!" But most of them understand not.

64. What is the life of this world but amusement and play? But verily the Home in the Hereafter, - that

الرِّزْقَ لِمَنْ يَشَآءُ مِنْ عِبَادِهِ

وَيَقْدِرُ لَهُ ۚ إِنَّ اللَّهَ بِكُلِّ شَيْءٍ

عَلِيمٌ ۞ وَلَئِنْ سَأَلْتَهُمْ مَّنْ

نَّزَّلَ مِنَ السَّمَآءِ مَآءً فَأَحْيَا

بِهِ الْأَرْضَ مِنْ بَعْدِ مَوْتِهَا

لَيَقُولُنَّ اللَّهُ ۚ قُلِ الْحَمْدُ لِلَّهِ

بَلْ أَكْثَرُهُمْ لَا يَعْقِلُونَ ۞ وَمَا

هَٰذِهِ الْحَيَوٰةُ الدُّنْيَآ إِلَّا لَهْوٌ

وَّلَعِبٌ ۚ وَإِنَّ الدَّارَ الْآخِرَةَ لَهِيَ

rivers, - to dwell therein for ever; - an excellent reward for those who do (good)! -

59. Those who persevere in patience, and put their trust, in their Lord and Cherisher.

60. How many are the creatures that carry not their own sustenance? It is Allah Who feeds (both) them and you: for He hears and knows (all things).

61. If indeed you ask them: "Who has created the heavens and the earth and subjected the sun and the moon (to his Law)?" they will certainly reply, "Allah". How are they then deluded away (from the truth)?

62. Allah enlarges

اِلَّا اَنَّهُمۡ خٰلِدِیۡنَ فِیۡهَا ؕ نِعۡمَ اَجۡرُ

الۡعٰمِلِیۡنَ ۙ الَّذِیۡنَ صَبَرُوۡا وَ عَلٰی

رَبِّهِمۡ یَتَوَكَّلُوۡنَ ۟ وَ كَاَیِّنۡ مِّنۡ

دَآبَّةٍ لَّا تَحۡمِلُ رِزۡقَهَا ۖ ۟ اَللّٰهُ

یَرۡزُقُهَا وَ اِیَّاكُمۡ ۖؗ وَ هُوَ السَّمِیۡعُ

الۡعَلِیۡمُ ۟ وَ لَئِنۡ سَاَلۡتَهُمۡ مَّنۡ

خَلَقَ السَّمٰوٰتِ وَ الۡاَرۡضَ وَ سَخَّرَ

الشَّمۡسَ وَ الۡقَمَرَ لَیَقُوۡلُنَّ اللّٰهُ ۚ

فَاَنّٰی یُؤۡفَكُوۡنَ ۟ اَللّٰهُ یَبۡسُطُ

the rejecters of Faith! -

55. On the Day that the Punishment shall cover them from above them and from below them, and (a Voice) shall say: "Taste you (the fruits) of your deeds!"

56. O My servants who believe! Truly, spacious is My Earth: therefore serve you Me - (and Me alone)!

57. Every soul shall have a taste of death: in the end to Us shall you be brought back.

58. But those who believe and work deeds of righteousness - to them shall We give a Home in Heaven, - lofty mansions beneath which flow

بِالْكَفِرِينَ ۞ يَوْمَ يَغْشَهُمُ الْعَذَابُ

مِنْ فَوْقِهِمْ وَمِنْ تَحْتِ أَرْجُلِهِمْ

وَيَقُولُ ذُوقُوا مَا كُنْتُمْ تَعْمَلُونَ ۞

يَعِبَادِيَ الَّذِينَ آمَنُوا إِنَّ أَرْضِى

وَاسِعَةٌ فَإِيَّايَ فَاعْبُدُونَ ۞

كُلُّ نَفْسٍ ذَآئِقَةُ الْمَوْتِ ثُمَّ

إِلَيْنَا تُرْجَعُونَ ۞ وَالَّذِينَ آمَنُوا

وَعَمِلُوا الصَّالِحَاتِ لَنُبَوِّئَنَّهُمْ مِّنَ

الْجَنَّةِ غُرَفًا تَجْرِى مِنْ تَحْتِهَا

52.   Say: "Enough is Allah for a witness between me and you: He knows what is in the heavens and on earth." And it is those who believe in vanities and reject Allah, that will perish (in the end).

53.   They ask you to hasten on the Punishment (for them): had it not been for a term (of respite) appointed, the Punishment would certainly have come to them: and it will certainly reach them, - of a sudden, while they perceive not!

54.   They ask you to hasten on the Punishment: but, of a surety, Hell will encompass

قُلْ كَفَىٰ بِاللهِ بَيْنِي وَبَيْنَكُمْ

شَهِيدًا ۚ يَعْلَمُ مَا فِي السَّمَاوَاتِ

وَالْأَرْضِ ۗ وَالَّذِينَ آمَنُوا بِالْبَاطِلِ

وَكَفَرُوا بِاللهِ أُولَٰئِكَ هُمُ

الْخَاسِرُونَ ۝ وَيَسْتَعْجِلُونَكَ

بِالْعَذَابِ ۚ وَلَوْلَا أَجَلٌ مُّسَمًّى

لَّجَاءَهُمُ الْعَذَابُ ۚ وَلَيَأْتِيَنَّهُم بَغْتَةً

وَهُمْ لَا يَشْعُرُونَ ۝ يَسْتَعْجِلُونَكَ

بِالْعَذَابِ ۚ وَإِنَّ جَهَنَّمَ لَمُحِيطَةٌ

Signs self-evident in the hearts of those endowed with knowledge: and none but the unjust reject Our Signs.

50. Yet they say: "Why are not Signs sent down to him from his Lord?" Say: "The Signs are indeed with Allah: and I am indeed a clear warner."

51. And is it not enough for them that We have sent down to you the Book which is rehearsed to them? Verily, in it is mercy and a reminder to those who believe.

ايٰتٌ بَيِّنٰتٌ فِىْ صُدُوْرِ الَّذِيْنَ
اُوْتُوا الْعِلْمَ ۚ وَمَا يَجْحَدُ بِاٰيٰتِنَآ
اِلَّا الظّٰلِمُوْنَ ۞ وَقَالُوْا لَوْ لَآ
اُنْزِلَ عَلَيْهِ اٰيٰتٌ مِّنْ رَّبِّهٖ ۚ
قُلْ اِنَّمَا الْاٰيٰتُ عِنْدَ اللّٰهِ ۚ
وَاِنَّمَآ اَنَا نَذِيْرٌ مُّبِيْنٌ ۞ اَوَ
لَمْ يَكْفِهِمْ اَنَّآ اَنْزَلْنَا عَلَيْكَ
الْكِتٰبَ يُتْلٰى عَلَيْهِمْ ۚ اِنَّ فِىْ ذٰلِكَ
لَرَحْمَةً وَّذِكْرٰى لِقَوْمٍ يُّؤْمِنُوْنَ ۞

to you; our Allah and your Allah is One; and it is to Him we bow (in Islam)."

47. And thus (it is) that We have sent down the Book to you. So the People of the Book believe therein, as also do some of these (pagan Arabs): and none but unbelievers reject Our Signs.

48. And you were not (able) to recite a Book before this (Book came), nor are you (able) to transcribe it with your right hand: in that case, indeed, would the talkers of vanities have doubted.

49. No, here are

اِلَيْكُمْ وَالٰهُنَا وَالٰهُكُمْ وَاحِدٌ

وَّنَحْنُ لَهٗ مُسْلِمُوْنَ ۞ وَكَذٰلِكَ

اَنْزَلْنَآ اِلَيْكَ الْكِتٰبَ ۚ فَالَّذِيْنَ

اٰتَيْنٰهُمُ الْكِتٰبَ يُؤْمِنُوْنَ بِهٖ ۚ

وَمِنْ هٰٓؤُلَآءِ مَنْ يُّؤْمِنُ بِهٖ ۗ وَمَا

يَجْحَدُ بِاٰيٰتِنَآ اِلَّا الْكٰفِرُوْنَ ۞

وَمَا كُنْتَ تَتْلُوْا مِنْ قَبْلِهٖ مِنْ

كِتٰبٍ وَّلَا تَخُطُّهٗ بِيَمِيْنِكَ اِذًا

لَّارْتَابَ الْمُبْطِلُوْنَ ۞ بَلْ هُوَ

45. Recite what is sent of the Book by inspiration to you, and establish regular Prayer: for Prayer restrains from shameful and unjust deeds; and remembrance of Allah is the greatest (thing in life) without doubt. And Allah knows the (deeds) that you do.

46. And dispute you not with the People of the Book, except with means better (than mere disputation), unless it be with those of them who inflict wrong (and injury): but say, "We believe in the revelation which has come down to us and in that which came down

اُتْلُ مَآ اُوْحِیَ اِلَیْكَ مِنَ

الْكِتٰبِ وَ اَقِمِ الصَّلٰوۃَ ؕ اِنَّ

الصَّلٰوۃَ تَنْهٰى عَنِ الْفَحْشَآءِ

وَ الْمُنْكَرِ ؕ وَلَذِكْرُ اللّٰهِ اَكْبَرُ ؕ

وَ اللّٰهُ یَعْلَمُ مَا تَصْنَعُوْنَ ۝ وَ لَا

تُجَادِلُوْۤا اَهْلَ الْكِتٰبِ اِلَّا

بِالَّتِیْ هِیَ اَحْسَنُ ۖ اِلَّا الَّذِیْنَ

ظَلَمُوْا مِنْهُمْ وَ قُوْلُوْۤا اٰمَنَّا

بِالَّذِیْۤ اُنْزِلَ اِلَیْنَا وَ اُنْزِلَ

تلك الكتاب الإسلامية

پاره

اُتْلُ مَاۤ اُوْحِیَ

(۲۱)

بِسْمِ اللَّهِ الرَّحْمَنِ الرَّحِيمِ

PART 22
Wamañy-Yaqnut

18. The (people) said: "For us, we augur an evil omen from you: if you desist not, we will certainly stone you. And a grievous punishment indeed will be inflicted on you by us."

19. They said: "Your evil omens are with yourselves: (deem you this an evil omen). If you are admonished? No, but you are a people transgressing all bounds!"

20. Then there came running, from the farthest part of the City, a man, saying, "O my people! Obey the Apostles:

21. "Obey those who ask no reward of you (for themselves), and who have themselves received Guidance.

قَالُوٓا إِنَّا تَطَيَّرْنَا بِكُمْ لَئِن لَّمْ

تَنتَهُوا لَنَرْجُمَنَّكُمْ وَلَيَمَسَّنَّكُم

مِّنَّا عَذَابٌ أَلِيمٌ ۝ قَالُوا

طَٰٓئِرُكُم مَّعَكُمْ أَئِن ذُكِّرْتُم

بَلْ أَنتُمْ قَوْمٌ مُّسْرِفُونَ ۝

وَجَآءَ مِنْ أَقْصَا الْمَدِينَةِ

رَجُلٌ يَسْعَىٰ قَالَ يَٰقَوْمِ اتَّبِعُوا

الْمُرْسَلِينَ ۝ اتَّبِعُوا مَن لَّا

يَسْـَٔلُكُمْ أَجْرًا وَهُم مُّهْتَدُونَ ۝

Behold! There came Apostles to it.

14. When We (first) sent to them two Apostles, they rejected them: but We strengthened them with a third: they said, "Truly, we have been sent on a mission to you."

15. The (people) said: "You are only men like ourselves; and (Allah) Most Gracious sends no sort of revelation: you do nothing but lie."

16. They said: "Our Lord does know that we have been sent on a mission to you:"

17. "And our duty is only to proclaim the clear Message."

اِذْ جَآءَهَا الْمُرْسَلُوْنَ ۞ اِذْ

اَرْسَلْنَاۤ اِلَيْهِمُ اثْنَيْنِ فَكَذَّبُوْهُمَا

فَعَزَّزْنَا بِثَالِثٍ فَقَالُوْۤا اِنَّاۤ

اِلَيْكُمْ مُّرْسَلُوْنَ ۞ قَالُوْا مَاۤ

اَنْتُمْ اِلَّا بَشَرٌ مِّثْلُنَا ۙ وَمَاۤ اَنْزَلَ

الرَّحْمٰنُ مِنْ شَيْءٍ ۙ اِنْ اَنْتُمْ

اِلَّا تَكْذِبُوْنَ ۞ قَالُوْا رَبُّنَا

يَعْلَمُ اِنَّاۤ اِلَيْكُمْ لَمُرْسَلُوْنَ

۞

وَمَا عَلَيْنَاۤ اِلَّا الْبَلٰغُ الْمُبِيْنُ ۞

10. The same is it to them whether you admonish them or you do not admonish them: they will not believe.

11. You can but admonish such a one as follows the Message and fears the (Lord) Most Gracious, unseen: give such a one, there-fore, good tidings, of Forgiveness and a Reward most generous.

12. Verily We shall give life to the dead, and We record that which they send before and that which they leave behind, and of all things have We taken account in a clear Book (of evidence).

13. Set forth to them, by way of a parable, the (story of) the Companions of the City.

وَسَوَآءٌ عَلَيْهِمْ ءَأَنذَرْتَهُمْ أَمْ

لَمْ تُنذِرْهُمْ لَا يُؤْمِنُونَ ۝

إِنَّمَا تُنذِرُ مَنِ اتَّبَعَ الذِّكْرَ

وَخَشِيَ الرَّحْمَٰنَ بِالْغَيْبِ ۖ فَبَشِّرْهُ

بِمَغْفِرَةٍ وَّأَجْرٍ كَرِيمٍ ۝ إِنَّا

نَحْنُ نُحْيِ الْمَوْتَىٰ وَنَكْتُبُ مَا

قَدَّمُوا وَءَاثَارَهُمْ ۚ وَكُلَّ شَيْءٍ

أَحْصَيْنَاهُ فِىٓ إِمَامٍ مُّبِينٍ ۝

وَاضْرِبْ لَهُم مَّثَلًا أَصْحَابَ الْقَرْيَةِ

Most Merciful.

6. In order that you may admonish a people, whose fathers had received no admonition, and who therefore remain heedless (of the Signs of Allah).

7. The Word is proved true against the greater part of them: for they do not believe.

8. We have put yokes round their necks right up to their chins, so that their heads are forced up (and they can not see).

9. And We have put a bar in front of them and a bar behind them, and further, We have covered them up; so that they can not see.

الرَّحِيمِ ۞ لِتُنْذِرَ قَوْمًا مَّا

أُنْذِرَ اٰبَآؤُهُمْ فَهُمْ غٰفِلُوْنَ ۞

لَقَدْ حَقَّ الْقَوْلُ عَلٰى اَكْثَرِهِمْ

فَهُمْ لَا يُؤْمِنُوْنَ ۞ اِنَّا جَعَلْنَا

فِيْٓ اَعْنَاقِهِمْ اَغْلٰلًا فَهِىَ اِلَى

الْاَذْقَانِ فَهُمْ مُّقْمَحُوْنَ ۞

وَجَعَلْنَا مِنْ بَيْنِ اَيْدِيْهِمْ

سَدًّا وَّمِنْ خَلْفِهِمْ سَدًّا

فَاَغْشَيْنٰهُمْ فَهُمْ لَا يُبْصِرُوْنَ ۞

men according to what they deserve. He would not leave on the back of the (earth) a single living creature: but He gives them respite for a stated Term: when their Term expires, verily Allah has in His sight all His servants .

Ya-Sin

Bismillahir-Rahmanir-Rahim

1.   Ya. Sin.

2.   By the Qur'an, full of wisdom,-

3.   You are indeed one of the Apostles,

4.   On a straight way.

5.   It is a Revelation sent down by (Him), the Exalted in Might,

اللهِ النَّاسَ بِمَا كَسَبُوا مَا

تَرَكَ عَلَى ظَهْرِهَا مِنْ دَآبَّةٍ

وَّلَكِنْ يُّؤَخِّرُهُمْ إِلَى أَجَلٍ

مُّسَمًّى فَإِذَا جَآءَ أَجَلُهُمْ فَإِنَّ

اللهَ كَانَ بِعِبَادِهِ بَصِيرًا ﴿﴾

بِسْمِ اللهِ الرَّحْمٰنِ الرَّحِيمِ

يٰسٓ ﴿١﴾ وَالْقُرْآنِ الْحَكِيمِ ﴿٢﴾ إِنَّكَ

لَمِنَ الْمُرْسَلِينَ ﴿٣﴾ عَلَى صِرَاطٍ

مُّسْتَقِيمٍ ﴿٤﴾ تَنْزِيلَ الْعَزِيزِ

But no change will you find in Allah's Way (of dealing): no turning off will you find in Allah's Way (of dealing).

44. Do they not travel through the earth, and see what was the End of those before them, - though they were superior to them in strength? Nor is Allah to be frustrated by anything whatever in the heavens or on earth: for He is All-Knowing, All-Powerful.

45. If Allah were to punish

فَلَنْ تَجِدَ لِسُنَّتِ اللّٰهِ تَبْدِيلًا ۖ

وَلَنْ تَجِدَ لِسُنَّتِ اللّٰهِ تَحْوِيلًا ۞

اَوَلَمْ يَسِيْرُوْا فِى الْاَرْضِ

فَيَنْظُرُوْا كَيْفَ كَانَ عَاقِبَةُ

الَّذِيْنَ مِنْ قَبْلِهِمْ وَكَانُوْٓا

اَشَدَّ مِنْهُمْ قُوَّةً ؕ وَمَا كَانَ

اللّٰهُ لِيُعْجِزَهٗ مِنْ شَىْءٍ فِى

السَّمٰوٰتِ وَلَا فِى الْاَرْضِ ؕ اِنَّهٗ

كَانَ عَلِيْمًا قَدِيْرًا ۞ وَلَوْ يُؤَاخِذُ

thereafter: verily He is Most Forbearing, Oft-Forgiving.

42.   They swore their strongest oaths by Allah that if a warner came to them, they would follow his guidance better than any (other) of the Peoples: but when a warner came to them, it has only increased their flight (from righteousness), -

43.   On account of their arrogance in the land and their plotting of evil, but the plotting of evil will hem in only the authors thereof. Now are they but looking for the way the ancients were dealt with?

أَحَدٍ مِّنْ بَعْدِهٖۤ ۗ اِنَّهٗ كَانَ حَلِيْمًا

غَفُوْرًا ۩ وَاَقْسَمُوْا بِاللّٰهِ جَهْدَ

اَيْمَانِهِمْ لَىِٕنْ جَآءَهُمْ نَذِيْرٌ

لَّيَكُوْنُنَّ اَهْدٰى مِنْ اِحْدَى

الْاُمَمِ ۚ فَلَمَّا جَآءَهُمْ نَذِيْرٌ مَّا

زَادَهُمْ اِلَّا نُفُوْرَا ۩ اسْتِكْبَارًا فِى

الْاَرْضِ وَمَكْرَ السَّيِّئِ ۚ وَلَا يَحِيْقُ

الْمَكْرُ السَّيِّئُ اِلَّا بِاَهْلِهٖ ۚ فَهَلْ

يَنْظُرُوْنَ اِلَّا سُنَّتَ الْاَوَّلِيْنَ ۚ

whom you call upon besides Allah? Show me what it is they have created in the (wide) earth. Or have they a share in the heavens? Or have We given them a Book from which they (can derive) clear (evidence)?- no, the wrong-doers promise each other nothing but delusions.

41. It is Allah Who sustains the heavens and the earth, lest they cease (to function): and if they should fail, there is none - not one - can sustain them

قُلِ الَّذِيْنَ تَدْعُوْنَ مِنْ دُوْنِ
اللهِ أَرُوْنِيْ مَاذَا خَلَقُوْا مِنَ
الْأَرْضِ أَمْ لَهُمْ شِرْكٌ فِي
السَّمٰوٰتِ أَمْ اٰتَيْنٰهُمْ كِتٰبًا فَهُمْ
عَلٰى بَيِّنَتٍ مِّنْهُ بَلْ اِنْ يَّعِدُ
الظّٰلِمُوْنَ بَعْضُهُمْ بَعْضًا اِلَّا
غُرُوْرًا ۞ اِنَّ اللهَ يُمْسِكُ
السَّمٰوٰتِ وَالْأَرْضَ اَنْ تَزُوْلَا ۚ
وَلَئِنْ زَالَتَا اِنْ اَمْسَكَهُمَا مِنْ

for the wrong-doers there is no helper."

38. Verily Allah knows (all) the hidden things of the heavens and the earth: verily He has full knowledge of all that is in (men's) hearts.

39. He it is that has made you inheritors in the earth: if, then, any do reject (Allah), their rejection (works) against themselves: their rejection but adds to the odium for the unbelievers in the sight of their Lord: their rejection but adds to (their own) undoing.

40. Say: "Have you seen (these) 'partners' of yours

فَمَا لِلظَّالِمِينَ مِنْ نَصِيرٍ ۝ اِنَّ

اللّٰهَ عٰلِمُ غَيْبِ السَّمٰوٰتِ وَالْاَرْضِ

اِنَّهٗ عَلِيْمٌۢ بِذَاتِ الصُّدُوْرِ ۝

هُوَ الَّذِىْ جَعَلَكُمْ خَلٰٓئِفَ فِى

الْاَرْضِ ۚ فَمَنْ كَفَرَ فَعَلَيْهِ كُفْرُهٗ ۚ

وَلَا يَزِيْدُ الْكٰفِرِيْنَ كُفْرُهُمْ

عِنْدَ رَبِّهِمْ اِلَّا مَقْتًا ۚ وَلَا

يَزِيْدُ الْكٰفِرِيْنَ كُفْرُهُمْ اِلَّا

خَسَارًا ۝ قُلْ اَرَءَيْتُمْ شُرَكَآءَكُمُ

therein."

36. But those who reject (Allah) - for them will be the Fire of Hell: no term shall be determined for them, so they should die, nor shall its Chastisement be lightened for them. Thus do We reward every ungrateful one!

37. Therein will they cry aloud (for assistance): "Our Lord! Bring us out: we shall work righteousness, not the (deeds) we used to do!" - "Did We not give you long enough life so that he that would should receive admonition? And (moreover) the warner came to you. So taste now (the fruits of your deeds):

فِيهَا لُغُوبٌ ۞ وَالَّذِينَ كَفَرُوا

لَهُمْ نَارُ جَهَنَّمَ ۚ لَا يُقْضَى عَلَيْهِمْ

فَيَمُوتُوا وَلَا يُخَفَّفُ عَنْهُمْ مِّنْ

عَذَابِهَا ۚ كَذَٰلِكَ نَجْزِي كُلَّ

كَفُورٍ ۞ وَهُمْ يَصْطَرِخُونَ فِيهَا

رَبَّنَآ أَخْرِجْنَا نَعْمَلْ صَالِحًا

غَيْرَ الَّذِي كُنَّا نَعْمَلُ ۚ أَوَلَمْ

نُعَمِّرْكُم مَّا يَتَذَكَّرُ فِيهِ مَن

تَذَكَّرَ وَجَآءَكُمُ النَّذِيرُ ۖ فَذُوقُوا

in good deeds; that is the highest Grace.

33. Gardens of Eternity will they enter: therein will they be adorned with bracelets of gold and pearls; and their garments there will be of silk.

34. And they will say: "Praise be to Allah, Who has removed from us (all) sorrow: for our Lord is indeed Oft-Forgiving, Ready to appreciate (service):"

35. "Who has, out of His Bounty, settled us in a Home that will last: no toil nor sense of weariness shall touch us

بِالْخَيْرَتِ بِاِذْنِ اللّٰهِ ذٰلِكَ هُوَ
الْفَضْلُ الْكَبِيْرُ ۞ جَنّٰتُ عَدْنٍ
يَّدْخُلُوْنَهَا يُحَلَّوْنَ فِيْهَا مِنْ
اَسَاوِرَ مِنْ ذَهَبٍ وَّلُؤْلُؤًا وَلِبَاسُهُمْ
فِيْهَا حَرِيْرٌ ۞ وَقَالُوا الْحَمْدُ لِلّٰهِ
الَّذِيْۤ اَذْهَبَ عَنَّا الْحَزَنَ اِنَّ
رَبَّنَا لَغَفُوْرٌ شَكُوْرٌ ۞ الَّذِيْۤ
اَحَلَّنَا دَارَ الْمُقَامَةِ مِنْ فَضْلِهٖ
لَا يَمَسُّنَا فِيْهَا نَصَبٌ وَّلَا يَمَسُّنَا

that will never fail:

30. For He will pay them their meed, no, He will give them (even) more out of His Bounty: for He is Oft-Forgiving, Most Ready to appreciate (service).

31. That which We have revealed to you of the Book is the Truth, - confirming what was (revealed) before it: for Allah is assuredly - with respect to His servants - Well Acquainted and fully Observant.

32. Then We have given the Book for inheritance to such of Our servants as We have chosen: but there are among them some who wrong their own souls; some who follow a middle course; and some who are, by Allah's leave, foremost

كُنْ تَبُورَ ۩ لِيُوَفِّيَهُمْ أُجُورَهُمْ

وَيَزِيدَهُم مِّن فَضْلِهِ ۚ إِنَّهُ

غَفُورٌ شَكُورٌ ۩ وَالَّذِي أَوْحَيْنَا

إِلَيْكَ مِنَ الْكِتَابِ هُوَ الْحَقُّ

مُصَدِّقًا لِّمَا بَيْنَ يَدَيْهِ ۗ إِنَّ

اللَّهَ بِعِبَادِهِ لَخَبِيرٌ بَصِيرٌ ۩ ثُمَّ

أَوْرَثْنَا الْكِتَابَ الَّذِينَ اصْطَفَيْنَا

مِنْ عِبَادِنَا ۖ فَمِنْهُمْ ظَالِمٌ لِّنَفْسِهِ

وَمِنْهُم مُّقْتَصِدٌ وَمِنْهُمْ سَابِقٌ

are tracts white and red, of various shades of colour, and black intense in hue.

28. And so amongst men and crawling creatures and cattle, are they of various colours. Those truly fear Allah, among His servants, who have knowledge: for Allah is Exalted in Might, Oft-Forgiving.

29. Those who rehearse the Book of Allah, establish regular Prayer, and spend (in Charity) out of what We have provided for them, secretly and openly, hope for a commerce

جُدَدٌ بِيضٌ وَّ حُمْرٌ مُّخْتَلِفٌ

اَلْوَانُهَا وَغَرَابِيبُ سُودٌ ۞ وَمِنَ

النَّاسِ وَالدَّوَآبِّ وَالْاَنْعَامِ

مُخْتَلِفٌ اَلْوَانُهٗ كَذٰلِكَ اِنَّمَا

يَخْشَى اللهَ مِنْ عِبَادِهِ الْعُلَمٰٓؤُا

اِنَّ اللهَ عَزِيزٌ غَفُوْرٌ ۞ اِنَّ

الَّذِيْنَ يَتْلُوْنَ كِتٰبَ اللهِ وَاَقَامُوا

الصَّلٰوةَ وَاَنْفَقُوْا مِمَّا رَزَقْنٰهُمْ

سِرًّا وَّعَلَانِيَةً يَّرْجُوْنَ تِجَارَةً

was a people, without a warner having lived among them (in the past).

25. And if they reject you, so did their predecessors, to whom came their Apostles with clear Signs, Books of dark prophecies, and the Book of Enlightenment.

26. In the end did I punish those who rejected Faith: and how (terrible) was My rejection (of them)!

27. Do you not see that Allah sends down rain from the sky? With it We then bring out produce of various colours. And in the mountains

مِّنْ أُمَّةٍ إِلَّا خَلَا فِيهَا نَذِيرٌ ۞

وَإِنْ يُّكَذِّبُوْكَ فَقَدْ كَذَّبَ

الَّذِيْنَ مِنْ قَبْلِهِمْ ۚ جَآءَتْهُمْ

رُسُلُهُمْ بِالْبَيِّنٰتِ وَبِالزُّبُرِ

وَبِالْكِتٰبِ الْمُنِيْرِ ۞ ثُمَّ أَخَذْتُ

الَّذِيْنَ كَفَرُوْا فَكَيْفَ كَانَ نَكِيْرِ ۞

أَلَمْ تَرَ أَنَّ اللّٰهَ أَنْزَلَ مِنَ

السَّمَآءِ مَآءً ۚ فَأَخْرَجْنَا بِهٖ ثَمَرٰتٍ

مُّخْتَلِفًا أَلْوَانُهَا ۚ وَمِنَ الْجِبَالِ

for the benefit of his own soul; and the destination (of all) is to Allah.

19.   The blind and the seeing are not alike;

20.   Nor are the depths of Darkness and the Light;

21.   Nor are the (chilly) shade and the (genial) heat of the sun:

22.   Nor are alike those that are living and those that are dead. Allah can make any that He wills to hear; but you can not make those to hear who are (buried) in graves.

23.   You are no other than a warner.

24.   Verily We have sent you in truth, as a bearer of glad tidings, and as a warner: and there never

لِنَفْسِهٖ ۚ وَاِلَى اللهِ الْمَصِيْرُ ۞

وَمَا يَسْتَوِى الْاَعْمٰى وَالْبَصِيْرُ ۞

وَلَا الظُّلُمٰتُ وَلَا النُّوْرُ ۞ وَلَا

الظِّلُّ وَلَا الْحَرُوْرُ ۞ وَمَا يَسْتَوِى

الْاَحْيَاءُ وَلَا الْاَمْوَاتُ ۚ اِنَّ اللهَ

يُسْمِعُ مَنْ يَّشَاءُ ۚ وَمَا اَنْتَ

بِمُسْمِعٍ مَّنْ فِى الْقُبُوْرِ ۞ اِنْ

اَنْتَ اِلَّا نَذِيْرٌ ۞ اِنَّا اَرْسَلْنٰكَ

بِالْحَقِّ بَشِيْرًا وَّنَذِيْرًا ۚ وَاِنْ

is the One Free of all wants, Worthy of all praise.

16. If He so pleased, He could blot you out and bring in a new Creation.

17. Nor is that (at all) difficult for Allah.

18. Nor can a bearer of burdens bear another's burdens. If one heavily laden should call another to (bear) his load. Not the least portion of it can be carried (by the other). Even though he be nearly related. You can but admonish such as fear their Lord unseen and establish regular Prayer. And whoever purifies himself does so

هُوَ الْغَنِيُّ الْحَمِيدُ ۝ اِنْ يَّشَأْ

يُذْهِبْكُمْ وَيَأْتِ بِخَلْقٍ جَدِيدٍ ۝

وَمَا ذٰلِكَ عَلَى اللهِ بِعَزِيزٍ ۝

وَلَا تَزِرُ وَازِرَةٌ وِّزْرَ أُخْرٰى

وَاِنْ تَدْعُ مُثْقَلَةٌ اِلٰى حِمْلِهَا

لَا يُحْمَلْ مِنْهُ شَيْءٌ وَّلَوْ كَانَ

ذَا قُرْبٰى ﻁ اِنَّمَا تُنْذِرُ الَّذِيْنَ

يَخْشَوْنَ رَبَّهُمْ بِالْغَيْبِ وَاَقَامُوا

الصَّلٰوةَ ﻁ وَمَنْ تَزَكّٰى فَاِنَّمَا يَتَزَكّٰى

each one runs its course for a term appointed. Such is Allah your Lord: to Him belongs all Dominion. And those whom you invoke besides Him have not the least power.

14. If you invoke them, they will not listen to your call, and if they were to listen, they can not answer your (prayer). On the Day of Judgment they will reject your "partnership". And none, (O man!) can tell you (the Truth) like the One Who is Acquainted with all things.

15. O you men! It is you that have need of Allah: but Allah

كُلٌّ يَّجْرِيْ لِاَجَلٍ مُّسَمًّى ۖ ذٰلِكُمُ

اللّٰهُ رَبُّكُمْ لَهُ الْمُلْكُ ۖ وَالَّذِيْنَ

تَدْعُوْنَ مِنْ دُوْنِهٖ مَا يَمْلِكُوْنَ

مِنْ قِطْمِيْرٍ ۩ اِنْ تَدْعُوْهُمْ لَا

يَسْمَعُوْا دُعَآءَكُمْ ۚ وَلَوْ سَمِعُوْا

مَا اسْتَجَابُوْا لَكُمْ ۚ وَيَوْمَ الْقِيٰمَةِ

يَكْفُرُوْنَ بِشِرْكِكُمْ ۚ وَلَا يُنَبِّئُكَ

مِثْلُ خَبِيْرٍ ۩ يٰٓاَيُّهَا النَّاسُ

اَنْتُمُ الْفُقَرَآءُ اِلَى اللّٰهِ ۖ وَاللّٰهُ

12. Nor are the two bodies of flowing water alike, - the one palatable, sweet, and pleasant to drink, and the other, salty and bitter. Yet from each (kind of water) do you eat flesh fresh and tender, and you extract ornaments to wear; and you see the ships therein that plough the waves, that you may seek (thus) of the Bounty of Allah that you may be grateful.

13. He merges night into day, and He merges day into night, and He has subjected the sun and the moon (to His Law):

يَسِيرٌ ۝ وَمَا يَسْتَوِى الْبَحْرَانِ

هٰذَا عَذْبٌ فُرَاتٌ سَآئِغٌ شَرَابُهُ

وَهٰذَا مِلْحٌ أُجَاجٌ ۖ وَمِنْ كُلٍّ

تَأْكُلُونَ لَحْمًا طَرِيًّا وَتَسْتَخْرِجُونَ

حِلْيَةً تَلْبَسُونَهَا ۖ وَتَرَى الْفُلْكَ

فِيهِ مَوَاخِرَ لِتَبْتَغُوا مِنْ فَضْلِهِ

وَلَعَلَّكُمْ تَشْكُرُونَ ۝ يُولِجُ الَّيْلَ

فِى النَّهَارِ وَيُولِجُ النَّهَارَ فِى

الَّيْلِ ۙ وَسَخَّرَ الشَّمْسَ وَالْقَمَرَ ۖ

Those that lay plots of evil, - for them is a Penalty terrible; and the plotting of such will be void (of result).

11. And Allah did create you from dust; then from a sperm-drop; then He made you in pairs. And no female conceives, or lays down (her load), but with His knowledge. Nor is a man long-lived granted length of days, nor is a part cut off from his life, but is in a Book (ordained). All this is easy to Allah.

يَرْفَعُهُ وَالَّذِيْنَ يَمْكُرُوْنَ
السَّيِّئَاتِ لَهُمْ عَذَابٌ شَدِيْدٌ ط
وَمَكْرُ أُولَئِكَ هُوَ يَبُوْرُ ۞ وَاللهُ
خَلَقَكُمْ مِّنْ تُرَابٍ ثُمَّ مِنْ
نُّطْفَةٍ ثُمَّ جَعَلَكُمْ أَزْوَاجًا وَمَا
تَحْمِلُ مِنْ أُنْثَى وَلَا تَضَعُ إِلَّا
بِعِلْمِهِ وَمَا يُعَمَّرُ مِنْ مُّعَمَّرٍ
وَّلَا يُنْقَصُ مِنْ عُمُرِهِ إِلَّا
فِيْ كِتَابٍ ط إِنَّ ذَلِكَ عَلَى اللهِ

So let not your soul go out in (vainly) sighing after them: for Allah knows well all that they do!

9. It is Allah Who sends forth the Winds, so that they raise up the Clouds, and We drive them to a land that is dead, and revive the earth therewith after its death: even so (will be) the Resurrection!

10. If any do seek for glory and power, - to Allah belong all glory and power. To Him mount up (all) Words of Purity: it is He Who exalts each Deed of Righteousness.

فَلَا تَذْهَبْ نَفْسُكَ عَلَيْهِمْ

حَسَرَاتٍ ۖ إِنَّ اللَّهَ عَلِيمٌ بِمَا

يَصْنَعُونَ ۞ وَاللَّهُ الَّذِي أَرْسَلَ

الرِّيَاحَ فَتُثِيرُ سَحَابًا فَسُقْنَاهُ

إِلَىٰ بَلَدٍ مَّيِّتٍ فَأَحْيَيْنَا بِهِ

الْأَرْضَ بَعْدَ مَوْتِهَا ۚ كَذَٰلِكَ

النُّشُورُ ۞ مَن كَانَ يُرِيدُ الْعِزَّةَ

فَلِلَّهِ الْعِزَّةُ جَمِيعًا ۚ إِلَيْهِ يَصْعَدُ

الْكَلِمُ الطَّيِّبُ وَالْعَمَلُ الصَّالِحُ

is an enemy to you: so treat him as an enemy. He only invites his adherents, that they may become Companions of the Blazing Fire.

7.   For those who reject Allah, is a terrible Chastisement: but for those who believe and work righteous deeds, is Forgiveness, and a magnificent Reward.

8.   Is he, then, to whom the evil of his conduct is made alluring, so that he looks upon it as good, (equal to one who is rightly guided)? For Allah leaves to stray whom He wills, and guides whom He wills.

لَكُمْ عَدُوٌّ فَاتَّخِذُوهُ عَدُوًّا

اِنَّمَا يَدْعُوا حِزْبَهُ لِيَكُوْنُوْا

مِنْ اَصْحٰبِ السَّعِيْرِ ۞ اَلَّذِيْنَ

كَفَرُوْا لَهُمْ عَذَابٌ شَدِيْدٌ ۖ

وَالَّذِيْنَ اٰمَنُوْا وَعَمِلُوا الصّٰلِحٰتِ

لَهُمْ مَّغْفِرَةٌ وَّاَجْرٌ كَبِيْرٌ ۞

اَفَمَنْ زُيِّنَ لَهٗ سُوْٓءُ عَمَلِهٖ

فَرَاٰهُ حَسَنًا ۚ فَاِنَّ اللّٰهَ يُضِلُّ

مَنْ يَّشَآءُ وَيَهْدِيْ مَنْ يَّشَآءُ ۖ

is there a creator, other than Allah, to give you sustenance from heaven or earth? There is no god but He: how then are you perverted away from the Truth?

4. And if they reject you, so were Apostles rejected before you: to Allah back for decision all affairs.

5. O men! Certainly the Promise of Allah is true. Let not then this present life deceive you, nor let the chief deceiver deceive you about Allah.

6. Verily Satan

هَلْ مِنْ خَالِقٍ غَيْرُ اللّٰهِ

يَرْزُقُكُمْ مِّنَ السَّمَآءِ وَالْأَرْضِ

لَآ إِلٰهَ إِلَّا هُوَ فَأَنّٰى تُؤْفَكُوْنَ ۞

وَإِنْ يُّكَذِّبُوْكَ فَقَدْ كُذِّبَتْ

رُسُلٌ مِّنْ قَبْلِكَ ۚ وَإِلَى اللّٰهِ

تُرْجَعُ الْأُمُوْرُ ۞ يٰٓأَيُّهَا النَّاسُ

إِنَّ وَعْدَ اللّٰهِ حَقٌّ فَلَا تَغُرَّنَّكُمُ

الْحَيٰوةُ الدُّنْيَا ۖ وَلَا يَغُرَّنَّكُمْ

بِاللّٰهِ الْغَرُوْرُ ۞ إِنَّ الشَّيْطٰنَ

and the earth, Who made the Angels, messengers with wings, - two, or three, or four (pairs): He adds to Creation as He pleases: for Allah has power over all things.

2.   What Allah out of his Mercy does bestow on mankind there is none can withhold: what He does withhold, there is none can grant, apart from Him: and He is the Exalted in Power, full of Wisdom.

3.   O men! Call to mind the Grace of Allah unto you!

وَالْأَرْضِ جَاعِلِ الْمَلَائِكَةِ رُسُلًا

أُولِي أَجْنِحَةٍ مَّثْنَى وَثُلَثَ وَرُبَعَ

يَزِيدُ فِي الْخَلْقِ مَا يَشَاءُ إِنَّ

اللّٰهَ عَلَى كُلِّ شَيْءٍ قَدِيرٌ ۞ مَا

يَفْتَحِ اللّٰهُ لِلنَّاسِ مِن رَّحْمَةٍ

فَلَا مُمْسِكَ لَهَا وَمَا يُمْسِكْ

فَلَا مُرْسِلَ لَهُ مِن بَعْدِهِ وَهُوَ

الْعَزِيزُ الْحَكِيمُ ۞ يَا أَيُّهَا النَّاسُ

اذْكُرُوا نِعْمَتَ اللّٰهِ عَلَيْكُمْ

in the (Truth)"; but how could they receive (Faith) from a position (so far off, -

53. Seeing that they did reject Faith (entirely) before, and that they (continually) cast (slanders) with regard to the unseen from a position far off?

54. And between them and their desires, is placed a barrier, as was done in the past with their partisans: for they were indeed in suspicious (disquieting) doubt.

Fatir (The Originator of Creation)

Bismillahir-Rahmanir-Rahim

1. Praise be to Allah, Who created (out of nothing) the heavens

بِهِ ۚ وَأَنَّىٰ لَهُمُ التَّنَاوُشُ مِن

مَّكَانٍۭ بَعِيدٍ ۝ وَقَدْ كَفَرُوا بِهِ

مِن قَبْلُ ۖ وَيَقْذِفُونَ بِالْغَيْبِ

مِن مَّكَانٍۭ بَعِيدٍ ۝ وَحِيلَ

بَيْنَهُمْ وَبَيْنَ مَا يَشْتَهُونَ كَمَا

فُعِلَ بِأَشْيَاعِهِم مِّن قَبْلُ ۚ

إِنَّهُمْ كَانُوا فِي شَكٍّ مُّرِيبٍ ۝

بِسْمِ اللَّهِ الرَّحْمَٰنِ الرَّحِيمِ

الْحَمْدُ لِلَّهِ فَاطِرِ السَّمَاوَاتِ

Witness to all things."

48. Say: "Verily my Lord does cast the (mantle of) Truth (over His servants), - He that has full knowledge of (all) that is hidden."

49. Say: "The Truth has arrived, and Falsehood neither creates anything new, nor restores anything."

50. Say: "If I am astray, I only stray to the loss of my own soul: but if I receive guidance, it is because of the inspiration of my Lord to me: it is He Who hears all things, and is (ever) near."

51. If you could but see when they will quake with terror; but then there will be no escape (for them), and they will be seized from a position (quite) near.

52. And they will say, "We do believe (now)

شَهِيْدٌ ۝ قُلْ اِنَّ رَبِّيْ يَقْذِفُ

بِالْحَقِّ عَلَّامُ الْغُيُوْبِ ۝ قُلْ

جَآءَ الْحَقُّ وَمَا يُبْدِئُ الْبَاطِلُ

وَمَا يُعِيْدُ ۝ قُلْ اِنْ ضَلَلْتُ

فَاِنَّمَآ اَضِلُّ عَلَى نَفْسِيْ وَاِنِ

اهْتَدَيْتُ فَبِمَا يُوْحِيْ اِلَيَّ رَبِّيْ

اِنَّهٗ سَمِيْعٌ قَرِيْبٌ ۝ وَلَوْ تَرَىٰٓ

اِذْ فَزِعُوْا فَلَا فَوْتَ وَاُخِذُوْا

مِنْ مَّكَانٍ قَرِيْبٍ ۝ وَّقَالُوْٓا اٰمَنَّا

of what We had granted to those: yet when they rejected My Apostles, how (terrible) was My rejection (of them)!

46. Say: "I do admonish you on one point: that you do stand up before Allah, - (it may be) in pairs, or (it may be) singly, - and reflect (within yourselves): your companion is not possessed: he is no less than a warner to you, in face of a terrible Chastisement."

47. Say: "No reward do I ask of you: it is (all) in your interest: my reward is only due from Allah: and He is

مَآ ءَاتَيْنَهُمْ فَكَذَّبُوا رُسُلِى

فَكَيْفَ كَانَ نَكِيرِ ۩ قُلْ إِنَّمَآ

أَعِظُكُمْ بِوَاحِدَةٍ أَن تَقُومُوا لِلَّهِ

مَثْنَى وَفُرَادَى ثُمَّ تَتَفَكَّرُوا

مَا بِصَاحِبِكُم مِّن جِنَّةٍ إِنْ هُوَ

إِلَّا نَذِيرٌ لَّكُم بَيْنَ يَدَىْ عَذَابٍ

شَدِيدٍ ۩ قُلْ مَا سَأَلْتُكُم مِّنْ

أَجْرٍ فَهُوَ لَكُمْ إِنْ أَجْرِىَ إِلَّا

عَلَى اللَّهِ وَهُوَ عَلَى كُلِّ شَىْءٍ

a man who wishes to hinder you from the (worship) which your fathers practised." And they say, "This is only a falsehood invented!" And the unbelievers say of the Truth when it comes to them, "This is nothing but evident magic!"

44. But We had not given them Books which they could study, nor sent Apostles to them before you as warners.

45. And their predecessors rejected (the Truth); these have not received a tenth

رَجُلٌ يُرِيدُ أَنْ يَصُدَّكُمْ عَمَّا

كَانَ يَعْبُدُ اٰبَآؤُكُمْ وَقَالُوا مَا

هٰذَآ إِلَّآ إِفْكٌ مُّفْتَرًى ۚ وَقَالَ

الَّذِينَ كَفَرُوا لِلْحَقِّ لَمَّا جَآءَهُمْ ۙ

إِنْ هٰذَآ إِلَّا سِحْرٌ مُّبِينٌ ۝

وَمَآ

اٰتَيْنٰهُمْ مِّنْ كُتُبٍ يَّدْرُسُونَهَا

وَمَآ أَرْسَلْنَآ إِلَيْهِمْ قَبْلَكَ مِنْ

نَّذِيرٍ ۝ وَكَذَّبَ الَّذِينَ مِنْ

قَبْلِهِمْ ۙ وَمَا بَلَغُوا مِعْشَارَ

worship?"

41. They will say, "Glory to You! Our (tie) is with You - as Protector- not with them. No, but they worshipped the Jinns: most of them believed in them."

42. So on that Day no power shall they have over each other, for profit or harm: and We shall say to the wrong-doers, "Taste you the Chastisement of the Fire, - the which you were wont to deny!"

43. When Our clear Signs are rehearsed to them, they say, "This is only

يَعْبُدُونَ ۞ قَالُوا سُبْحَنَكَ أَنْتَ

وَلِيُّنَا مِنْ دُونِهِمْ بَلْ كَانُوا

يَعْبُدُونَ الْجِنَّ أَكْثَرُهُمْ بِهِمْ

مُؤْمِنُونَ ۞ فَالْيَوْمَ لَا يَمْلِكُ

بَعْضُكُمْ لِبَعْضٍ نَفْعًا وَّلَا ضَرًّا

وَنَقُولُ لِلَّذِينَ ظَلَمُوا ذُوقُوا

عَذَابَ النَّارِ الَّتِي كُنْتُمْ بِهَا

تُكَذِّبُونَ ۞ وَإِذَا تُتْلَى عَلَيْهِمْ

اَيَتُنَا بَيِّنَاتٍ قَالُوا مَا هَذَا إِلَّا

38. Those who strive against Our Signs, to frustrate them, will be given over into Punishment.

39. Say: "Verily my Lord enlarges and restricts the Sustenance to such of his servants as He pleases: and nothing do you spend in the least (in His cause) but He replaces it: for He is the Best of those who grant sustenance.

40. One Day He will gather them all together, and say to the Angels, "Were it you that these men used to

وَالَّذِيْنَ يَسْعَوْنَ فِيْ اٰيٰتِنَا

مُعٰجِزِيْنَ اُولٰٓئِكَ فِي الْعَذَابِ

مُحْضَرُوْنَ ۞ قُلْ اِنَّ رَبِّيْ

يَبْسُطُ الرِّزْقَ لِمَنْ يَّشَآءُ

مِنْ عِبَادِهٖ وَيَقْدِرُ لَهٗ ۚ وَمَآ

اَنْفَقْتُمْ مِّنْ شَيْءٍ فَهُوَ يُخْلِفُهٗ ۚ

وَهُوَ خَيْرُ الرّٰزِقِيْنَ ۞ وَيَوْمَ

يَحْشُرُهُمْ جَمِيْعًا ثُمَّ يَقُوْلُ

لِلْمَلٰٓئِكَةِ اَهٰٓؤُلَآءِ اِيَّاكُمْ كَانُوْا

"We have more in wealth and in sons, and we can not be punished."

36. Say: "Verily my Lord enlarges and restricts the Provision to whom He pleases, but most men understand not."

37. It is not your wealth nor your sons, that will bring you nearer to Us in degree: but only those who believe and work righteousness - these are the ones for whom there is a multiplied reward for their deeds, while secure they (reside) in the dwellings on high!

نَحْنُ اَكْثَرُ اَمْوَالًا وَّ اَوْلَادًا وَّمَا
نَحْنُ بِمُعَذَّبِيْنَ ۞ قُلْ اِنَّ رَبِّيْ
يَبْسُطُ الرِّزْقَ لِمَنْ يَّشَاءُ وَيَقْدِرُ
وَلٰكِنَّ اَكْثَرَ النَّاسِ لَا يَعْلَمُوْنَ ۞
وَمَآ اَمْوَالُكُمْ وَلَا اَوْلَادُكُمْ بِالَّتِيْ
تُقَرِّبُكُمْ عِنْدَنَا زُلْفٰى اِلَّا مَنْ
اٰمَنَ وَعَمِلَ صَالِحًا فَاُولٰٓئِكَ
لَهُمْ جَزَاءُ الضِّعْفِ بِمَا عَمِلُوْا
وَهُمْ فِى الْغُرُفٰتِ اٰمِنُوْنَ ۞

behold! you (constantly) ordered us to be ungrateful to Allah and to attribute equals to Him!" They will declare (their) repentance when they see the Chastisement: We shall put yokes on the necks of the unbelievers: it would only be a requital for their (ill) deeds.

34. Never did We send a warner to a population, but the wealthy ones among them said: "We believe not in the (Message) with which you have been sent."

35. They said:

إِذْ تَأْمُرُونَنَا أَن نَّكْفُرَ بِاللَّهِ

وَنَجْعَلَ لَهُ أَندَادًا ۚ وَأَسَرُّوا

النَّدَامَةَ لَمَّا رَأَوُا الْعَذَابَ ۖ

وَجَعَلْنَا الْأَغْلَالَ فِي أَعْنَاقِ

الَّذِينَ كَفَرُوا ۚ هَلْ يُجْزَوْنَ

إِلَّا مَا كَانُوا يَعْمَلُونَ ۝ وَمَا

أَرْسَلْنَا فِي قَرْيَةٍ مِّن نَّذِيرٍ

إِلَّا قَالَ مُتْرَفُوهَا إِنَّا بِمَا

أُرْسِلْتُم بِهِ كَافِرُونَ ۝ وَقَالُوا

their Lord, throwing back the word (of blame) on one another! Those who were deemed weak will say to the arrogant ones: "Had it not been for you, we should certainly have been believers!"

32. The arrogant ones will say to those who had been deemed weak: "Was it we who kept you back from Guidance after it reached you? No, rather, it was you who transgressed."

33. Those who had been deemed weak will say to the arrogant ones: "No! It was a plot (of yours) by day and by night:

رَبِّهِمْ يَرْجِعُ بَعْضُهُمْ إِلَى بَعْضٍ

الْقَوْلَ يَقُوْلُ الَّذِيْنَ اسْتُضْعِفُوْا

لِلَّذِيْنَ اسْتَكْبَرُوْا لَوْلَا أَنْتُمْ

لَكُنَّا مُؤْمِنِيْنَ ۝ قَالَ الَّذِيْنَ

اسْتَكْبَرُوْا لِلَّذِيْنَ اسْتُضْعِفُوْا

أَنَحْنُ صَدَدْنَاكُمْ عَنِ الْهُدَى بَعْدَ

إِذْ جَآءَكُمْ بَلْ كُنْتُمْ مُّجْرِمِيْنَ ۝

وَقَالَ الَّذِيْنَ اسْتُضْعِفُوْا لِلَّذِيْنَ

اسْتَكْبَرُوْا بَلْ مَكْرُ الَّيْلِ وَالنَّهَارِ

giving them glad tidings, and warning them (against sin), but most men understand not.

29. They say: "When will this promise (come to pass) if you are telling the truth?"

30. Say: "The appointment to you is for a Day, which you can not put back for an hour nor put forward."

31. The unbelievers say: "We shall neither believe in this scripture nor in (any) that (came) before it." Could you but see when the wrong-doers will be made to stand before

بَشِيرًا وَّنَذِيرًا وَّلٰكِنَّ اَكْثَرَ

النَّاسِ لَا يَعْلَمُوْنَ ۞ وَيَقُوْلُوْنَ

مَتٰى هٰذَا الْوَعْدُ اِنْ كُنْتُمْ

صٰدِقِيْنَ ۞ قُلْ لَّكُمْ مِّيْعَادُ يَوْمٍ

لَّا تَسْتَاْخِرُوْنَ عَنْهُ سَاعَةً وَّلَا

تَسْتَقْدِمُوْنَ ۚ وَقَالَ الَّذِيْنَ

كَفَرُوْا لَنْ نُّؤْمِنَ بِهٰذَا الْقُرْاٰنِ

وَلَا بِالَّذِيْ بَيْنَ يَدَيْهِ ۗ وَلَوْ

تَرٰى اِذِ الظّٰلِمُوْنَ مَوْقُوْفُوْنَ عِنْدَ

and certain it is that either we or you are on right guidance or in manifest error!"

25. Say: "You shall not be questioned as to our sins, nor shall we be questioned as to what you do."

26. Say: "Our Lord will gather us together and will in the end decide the matter between us (and you) in truth and justice: and He is the One to decide, the One Who knows all."

27. Say: "Show me those whom you have joined with Him as partners: by no means (can you). No, He is Allah, the Exalted in Power, the Wise."

28. We have not sent you but as a universal (Messenger) to men,

وَإِنَّا أَوْ إِيَّاكُمْ لَعَلَىٰ هُدًى أَوْ

فِى ضَلَالٍ مُّبِينٍ ۝ قُل لَّا

تُسْـَٔلُونَ عَمَّا أَجْرَمْنَا وَلَا نُسْـَٔلُ

عَمَّا تَعْمَلُونَ ۝ قُلْ يَجْمَعُ بَيْنَنَا

رَبُّنَا ثُمَّ يَفْتَحُ بَيْنَنَا بِالْحَقِّ

وَهُوَ الْفَتَّاحُ الْعَلِيمُ ۝ قُلْ أَرُونِىَ

الَّذِينَ أَلْحَقْتُم بِهِۦ شُرَكَآءَ كَلَّا

بَلْ هُوَ اللَّهُ الْعَزِيزُ الْحَكِيمُ ۝

وَمَآ أَرْسَلْنَاكَ إِلَّا كَآفَّةً لِّلنَّاسِ

the heavens or on earth: no (sort of) share have they therein, nor is any of them a helper to Allah."

23.   "No intercession can avail in His Presence, except for those for whom He has granted permission. So far (is this the case) that, when terror is removed from their hearts (at the Day of Judgment, then) will they say, 'What is it that your Lord commanded?' They will say, 'That which is true and just; and He is the Most High Most Great'."

24.   Say: "Who gives you sustenance, from the heavens and the earth?" Say: "It is Allah;

السَّمٰوٰتِ وَلَا فِى الْاَرْضِ وَمَا

لَهُمْ فِيْهِمَا مِنْ شِرْكٍ وَّمَا

لَهٗ مِنْهُمْ مِّنْ ظَهِيْرٍ ۝ وَلَا

تَنْفَعُ الشَّفَاعَةُ عِنْدَهٗٓ اِلَّا لِمَنْ

اَذِنَ لَهٗ ۚ حَتّٰى اِذَا فُزِّعَ عَنْ

قُلُوْبِهِمْ قَالُوْا مَاذَا ۙ قَالَ

رَبُّكُمْ ۗ قَالُوا الْحَقَّ ۚ وَهُوَ الْعَلِىُّ

الْكَبِيْرُ ۝ قُلْ مَنْ يَّرْزُقُكُمْ

مِّنَ السَّمٰوٰتِ وَالْاَرْضِ ۗ قُلِ اللّٰهُ

20. And on them did Satan prove true his idea, and they followed him, all but a party that believed.

21. But he had no authority over them, - except that We might test the man who believes in the Hereafter from him who is in doubt concerning it: and your Lord does watch over all things.

22. Say: "Call upon other (gods) whom you fancy, besides Allah: they have no power, - not the weight of an atom, - in

وَلَقَدْ صَدَّقَ عَلَيْهِمْ إِبْلِيسُ

ظَنَّهُ فَاتَّبَعُوهُ إِلَّا فَرِيقًا مِّنَ

الْمُؤْمِنِينَ ۞ وَمَا كَانَ لَهُ عَلَيْهِم

مِّنْ سُلْطَانٍ إِلَّا لِنَعْلَمَ مَنْ

يُؤْمِنُ بِالْآخِرَةِ مِمَّنْ هُوَ مِنْهَا

فِي شَكٍّ ۚ وَرَبُّكَ عَلَىٰ كُلِّ شَيْءٍ

حَفِيظٌ ۞ قُلِ ادْعُوا الَّذِينَ

زَعَمْتُم مِّن دُونِ اللَّهِ ۖ لَا

يَمْلِكُونَ مِثْقَالَ ذَرَّةٍ فِي

do We give (such) requital except to such as are ungrateful rejecters.

18. Between them and the Cities on which We had poured our blessings, We had placed Cities in prominent positions, and between them We had appointed stages of journey in due proportion: "Travel therein, secure, by night and by day."

19. But they said: "Our Lord! Place longer distances between our journey - stages": but they wronged themselves (therein). At length We made them as a tale (that is told), and We dispersed them all in scattered fragments. Verily in this are Signs for every (soul that is) patiently constant and grateful.

نُجْزِىٓ إِلَّا الْكَفُوْرَ ۝ وَجَعَلْنَا

بَيْنَهُمْ وَبَيْنَ الْقُرَى الَّتِىْ بٰرَكْنَا

فِيْهَا قُرًى ظَاهِرَةً وَّقَدَّرْنَا

فِيْهَا السَّيْرَ ۚ سِيْرُوْا فِيْهَا لَيَالِىَ

وَاَيَّامًا اٰمِنِيْنَ ۝ فَقَالُوْا رَبَّنَا

بٰعِدْ بَيْنَ اَسْفَارِنَا وَظَلَمُوْٓا

اَنْفُسَهُمْ فَجَعَلْنٰهُمْ اَحَادِيْثَ

وَمَزَّقْنٰهُمْ كُلَّ مُمَزَّقٍ ۚ اِنَّ فِىْ

ذٰلِكَ لَاٰيٰتٍ لِّكُلِّ صَبَّارٍ شَكُوْرٍ ۝

15. There was, for Saba, aforetime, a Sign in their home-land - two gardens to the right and to the left. "Eat of the Sustenance (provided) by your Lord, and be grateful to Him: a territory fair and happy, and a Lord Oft-Forgiving!

16. But they turned away (from Allah), and We sent against them the Flood (released) from the dams, and We converted their two garden (rows) into "gardens" producing bitter fruit, and tamarisks, and some few (stunted) Lote-trees.

17. That was the requital We gave them because they ungratefully rejected Faith: and never

لَقَدْ كَانَ لِسَبَإٍ فِيْ مَسْكَنِهِمْ

اٰيَةٌ ۚ جَنَّتٰنِ عَنْ يَّمِيْنٍ وَّشِمَالٍ ؕ

كُلُوْا مِنْ رِّزْقِ رَبِّكُمْ وَاشْكُرُوْا

لَهٗ ؕ بَلْدَةٌ طَيِّبَةٌ وَّرَبٌّ غَفُوْرٌ ۝

فَاَعْرَضُوْا فَاَرْسَلْنَا عَلَيْهِمْ سَيْلَ

الْعَرِمِ وَبَدَّلْنٰهُمْ بِجَنَّتَيْهِمْ

جَنَّتَيْنِ ذَوَاتَيْ اُكُلٍ خَمْطٍ وَّاَثْلٍ

وَّشَيْءٍ مِّنْ سِدْرٍ قَلِيْلٍ ۝

ذٰلِكَ جَزَيْنٰهُمْ بِمَا كَفَرُوْا ؕ وَهَلْ

(making) arches, images, basons as large as reservoirs, and (cooking) cauldrons fixed (in their places): "Work you, sons of David, with thanks! But few of My servants are grateful!"

14. Then, when We decreed (Solomon's) death, nothing showed them his death except a little worm of the earth, which kept (slowly) gnawing away at his staff: so when he fell down, the Jinns saw plainly that if they had known the Unseen, they would not have tarried in the humiliating Chastisement (of their task).

مَّحَارِيبَ وَتَمَاثِيلَ وَجِفَانٍ

كَالْجَوَابِ وَقُدُورٍ رَّاسِيَتٍ ۚ

اِعْمَلُوٓا اٰلَ دَاوٗدَ شُكْرًا ۚ وَقَلِيْلٌ

مِّنْ عِبَادِيَ الشَّكُوْرُ ۝ فَلَمَّا

قَضَيْنَا عَلَيْهِ الْمَوْتَ مَا دَلَّهُمْ

عَلٰى مَوْتِهٖٓ اِلَّا دَآبَّةُ الْاَرْضِ

تَأْكُلُ مِنْسَاَتَهٗ ۚ فَلَمَّا خَرَّ تَبَيَّنَتِ

الْجِنُّ اَنْ لَّوْ كَانُوْا يَعْلَمُوْنَ الْغَيْبَ

مَا لَبِثُوْا فِى الْعَذَابِ الْمُهِيْنِ ۝

"Make you coats of mail, balancing well the rings of chain armour, and work you righteousness; for be sure I see (clearly) all that you do."

12. And to Solomon (We made) the Wind (obedient): its early morning (stride) was a month's (journey), and its evening (stride) was a month's (journey); and We made a font of molten brass to flow for him; and there were Jinns that worked in front of him, by the leave of his Lord, and if any of them turned aside from our command, We made him taste of the Chastisement of the Blazing Fire.

13. They worked for him as he desired,

اعْمَلْ سٰبِغٰتٍ وَّقَدِّرْ فِي السَّرْدِ

وَاعْمَلُوْا صَالِحًا ؕ اِنِّيْ بِمَا تَعْمَلُوْنَ

بَصِيْرٌ ۝ وَلِسُلَيْمٰنَ الرِّيْحَ غُدُوُّهَا

شَهْرٌ وَّرَوَاحُهَا شَهْرٌ ۚ وَاَسَلْنَا لَهٗ

عَيْنَ الْقِطْرِ ؕ وَمِنَ الْجِنِّ مَنْ

يَّعْمَلُ بَيْنَ يَدَيْهِ بِاِذْنِ رَبِّهٖ ؕ

وَمَنْ يَّزِغْ مِنْهُمْ عَنْ اَمْرِنَا

نُذِقْهُ مِنْ عَذَابِ السَّعِيْرِ ۝

يَعْمَلُوْنَ لَهٗ مَا يَشَآءُ مِنْ

that are in (real) Chastisement, and in farthest error.

9. See they not what is before them and behind them, of the sky and the earth? If We wished, We could cause the earth to swallow them up, or cause a piece of the sky to fall upon them. Verily in this is a Sign for every devotee that turns to Allah (in repentance).

10. We bestowed Grace aforetime on David from Ourselves: "O you Mountains! Sing you back the Praises of Allah with him! And you birds (also)! And We made the iron soft for him; -

11. (Commanding),

فِي الْعَذَابِ وَالضَّلَلِ الْبَعِيدِ ۞

أَفَلَمْ يَرَوْا إِلَى مَا بَيْنَ أَيْدِيهِمْ

وَمَا خَلْفَهُم مِّنَ السَّمَاءِ وَالْأَرْضِ

إِن نَّشَأْ نَخْسِفْ بِهِمُ الْأَرْضَ

أَوْ نُسْقِطْ عَلَيْهِمْ كِسَفًا مِّنَ

السَّمَاءِ ۚ إِنَّ فِي ذَٰلِكَ لَآيَةً لِّكُلِّ

عَبْدٍ مُّنِيبٍ ۞ وَلَقَدْ آتَيْنَا دَاوُدَ

مِنَّا فَضْلًا ۖ يَٰجِبَالُ أَوِّبِي مَعَهُ

وَالطَّيْرَ ۖ وَأَلَنَّا لَهُ الْحَدِيدَ ۞ أَنِ

most humiliating.

6. And those to whom knowledge has come see that the (Revelation) sent down to you from your Lord - that is the Truth, and that it guides to the Path of the Exalted (in Might), Worthy of all praise.

7. The unbelievers say (in ridicule): "Shall we point out to you a man that will tell you, when you are all scattered to pieces in disintegration, that you shall (then be raised) in a new Creation?"

8. "Has he invented a falsehood against Allah, or is he afflicted with madness?" - No, it is those who believe not in the Hereafter,

ٱلِيْمٌ ۞ وَيَرَى ٱلَّذِيْنَ أُوتُوا ٱلْعِلْمَ

ٱلَّذِيْ أُنْزِلَ إِلَيْكَ مِنْ رَّبِّكَ

هُوَ ٱلْحَقَّ وَيَهْدِيْ إِلَى صِرَاطِ

ٱلْعَزِيْزِ ٱلْحَمِيْدِ ۞ وَقَالَ ٱلَّذِيْنَ

كَفَرُوا هَلْ نَدُلُّكُمْ عَلَى رَجُلٍ

يُنَبِّئُكُمْ إِذَا مُزِّقْتُمْ كُلَّ مُمَزَّقٍ

إِنَّكُمْ لَفِيْ خَلْقٍ جَدِيْدٍ ۞ أَفْتَرَى

عَلَى ٱللَّهِ كَذِبًا أَمْ بِهِ جِنَّةٌ

بَلِ ٱلَّذِيْنَ لَا يُؤْمِنُوْنَ بِٱلْآخِرَةِ

say, "No! But most surely, by my
Lord, it will come upon you; - by
Him Who knows the Unseen, -
from Whom is not hidden the
least little atom in the heavens or
on earth: nor is there anything
less than that, or greater, but is in
the Record perspicuous."

4.   "That He may reward those
who believe and work deeds of
righteousness: for such is
Forgiveness and a Sustenance
most generous."

5.   But those who strive against
Our Signs, to frustrate them, - for
such will be a Chastisement, - a
Punishment

قُلْ بَلٰى وَرَبِّىْ لَتَأْتِيَنَّكُمْ عٰلِمِ

الْغَيْبِ ۚ لَا يَعْزُبُ عَنْهُ مِثْقَالُ

ذَرَّةٍ فِى السَّمٰوٰتِ وَلَا فِى الْأَرْضِ

وَلَا أَصْغَرُ مِنْ ذٰلِكَ وَلَا أَكْبَرُ

إِلَّا فِىْ كِتٰبٍ مُّبِيْنٍ ۙ لِّيَجْزِىَ

الَّذِيْنَ اٰمَنُوْا وَعَمِلُوا الصّٰلِحٰتِ ۚ

أُولٰٓئِكَ لَهُمْ مَّغْفِرَةٌ وَّرِزْقٌ كَرِيْمٌ ۚ

وَالَّذِيْنَ سَعَوْ فِىْٓ اٰيٰتِنَا مُعٰجِزِيْنَ

أُولٰٓئِكَ لَهُمْ عَذَابٌ مِّنْ رِّجْزٍ

Saba (Sheba)

Bismillahir-Rahmanir-Rahim

1.   Praise be to Allah, to Whom belong all things in the heavens and on earth: to Him be Praise in the Hereafter: and He is full of Wisdom, Acquainted with all things.

2.   He knows all that goes into the earth, and all that comes out thereof; all that comes down from the sky and all that ascends thereto and He is the Most Merciful, the Oft-Forgiving.

3.   The unbelievers say, "Never to us will come the Hour":

بِسْمِ اللهِ الرَّحْمٰنِ الرَّحِيمِ

الْحَمْدُ لِلّٰهِ الَّذِى لَهُ مَا فِى

السَّمٰوٰتِ وَمَا فِى الْأَرْضِ وَلَهُ

الْحَمْدُ فِى الْاٰخِرَةِ ۚ وَهُوَ الْحَكِيمُ

الْخَبِيرُ ۞ يَعْلَمُ مَا يَلِجُ فِى

الْأَرْضِ وَمَا يَخْرُجُ مِنْهَا وَمَا

يَنْزِلُ مِنَ السَّمَآءِ وَمَا يَعْرُجُ

فِيهَا ۗ وَهُوَ الرَّحِيمُ الْغَفُورُ ۞ وَقَالَ

الَّذِينَ كَفَرُوا لَا تَأْتِينَا السَّاعَةُ ۖ

the highest achieve-ment.

72. We did indeed offer the Trust to the heavens and the earth and the mountains; but they refused to undertake it, being afraid thereof: but man undertook it; - he was indeed unjust and foolish; -

73. (With the result) that Allah has to punish the Hypocrites, men and women, and the unbelievers, men and women, and Allah turns in Mercy to the believers, men and women: for Allah is Oft-Forgiving, Most Merciful.

فَوۡزًا عَظِيۡمًا ۞ اِنَّا عَرَضۡنَا الۡاَمَانَةَ

عَلَى السَّمٰوٰتِ وَالۡاَرۡضِ وَالۡجِبَالِ

فَاَبَيۡنَ اَنۡ يَّحۡمِلۡنَهَا وَاَشۡفَقۡنَ

مِنۡهَا وَحَمَلَهَا الۡاِنۡسَانُ ؕ اِنَّهٗ كَانَ

ظَلُوۡمًا جَهُوۡلًا ۞ لِّيُعَذِّبَ اللّٰهُ

الۡمُنٰفِقِيۡنَ وَالۡمُنٰفِقٰتِ وَالۡمُشۡرِكِيۡنَ

وَالۡمُشۡرِكٰتِ وَيَتُوۡبَ اللّٰهُ عَلَى

الۡمُؤۡمِنِيۡنَ وَالۡمُؤۡمِنٰتِ ؕ وَكَانَ اللّٰهُ

غَفُوۡرًا رَّحِيۡمًا ۞

double Chastisement and curse them with a very great Curse!"

69. O you who believe! Be you not like those who vexed and insulted Moses, but Allah cleared him of the (calumnies) they had uttered: and he was honourable in Allah's sight.

70. O you who believe! Fear Allah, and (always) say a word directed to the Right:

71. That He may make your conduct wholesome and forgive you your sins: he that obeys Allah and His Apostle, has already attained

ضِعْفَيْنِ مِنَ الْعَذَابِ وَالْعَنْهُمْ

لَعْنًا كَبِيرًا ۝ يَـٰٓأَيُّهَا الَّذِينَ

ءَامَنُوا لَا تَكُونُوا كَالَّذِينَ ءَاذَوْا

مُوسَىٰ فَبَرَّأَهُ اللَّهُ مِمَّا قَالُوا ۚ

وَكَانَ عِندَ اللَّهِ وَجِيهًا ۝ يَـٰٓأَيُّهَا

الَّذِينَ ءَامَنُوا اتَّقُوا اللَّهَ وَقُولُوا

قَوْلًا سَدِيدًا ۝ يُصْلِحْ لَكُمْ

أَعْمَٰلَكُمْ وَيَغْفِرْ لَكُمْ ذُنُوبَكُمْ ۗ

وَمَن يُطِعِ اللَّهَ وَرَسُولَهُ فَقَدْ فَازَ

the Hour is nigh!

64. Verily Allah has cursed the unbelievers and prepared for them a Blazing Fire, -

65. To dwell therein for ever: no protector will they find, nor helper.

66. The Day that their faces will be turned upside down in the Fire, they will say: "Woe to us! Would that we had obeyed Allah and obeyed the Apostle!"

67. And they would say: "Our Lord! We obeyed our chiefs and our great ones, and they misled us as to the (right) Path."

68. "Our Lord! Give them

السَّاعَةَ تَكُونُ قَرِيبًا ۩ إِنَّ

اللَّهَ لَعَنَ الْكَفِرِينَ وَأَعَدَّ لَهُمْ

سَعِيرًا ۩ خَلِدِينَ فِيهَآ أَبَدًا

لَا يَجِدُونَ وَلِيًّا وَّلَا نَصِيرًا ۩

يَوْمَ تُقَلَّبُ وُجُوهُهُمْ فِي النَّارِ

يَقُولُونَ يَلَيْتَنَآ أَطَعْنَا اللَّهَ

وَأَطَعْنَا الرَّسُولَا ۩ وَقَالُوا رَبَّنَآ

إِنَّآ أَطَعْنَا سَادَتَنَا وَكُبَرَآءَنَا

فَأَضَلُّونَا السَّبِيلَا ۩ رَبَّنَآ أِتِهِمْ

is a disease, and those who stir up
sedition in the City, desist not,
We shall certainly stir you up
against them: then will they not
be able to stay in it as your neighbours for any length of time:

61. They shall have a curse on
them: whenever they are found,
they shall be seized and slain
(without mercy).

62. (Such was) the Practice
(approved) of Allah among those
who lived aforetime: no change
will you find in the Practice
(approved) of Allah.

63. Men ask you concerning the
Hour: say, "The knowledge
thereof is with Allah (alone)":
and what will make you understand? - perchance

مَّرَضٌ وَّالْمُرْجِفُونَ فِي الْمَدِيْنَةِ

لَنُغْرِيَنَّكَ بِهِمْ ثُمَّ لَا يُجَاوِرُوْنَكَ

فِيْهَآ اِلَّا قَلِيْلًا ۚ ﴿٦٠﴾ مَّلْعُوْنِيْنَ ۛ اَيْنَمَا

ثُقِفُوْٓا اُخِذُوْا وَقُتِّلُوْا تَقْتِيْلًا ﴿٦١﴾

سُنَّةَ اللّٰهِ فِي الَّذِيْنَ خَلَوْا

مِنْ قَبْلُ ۚ وَلَنْ تَجِدَ لِسُنَّةِ

اللّٰهِ تَبْدِيْلًا ﴿٦٢﴾ يَسْـَٔلُكَ النَّاسُ

عَنِ السَّاعَةِ ۚ قُلْ اِنَّمَا عِلْمُهَا

عِنْدَ اللّٰهِ ۚ وَمَا يُدْرِيْكَ لَعَلَّ

believing men and women unde-
servedly, bear (on themselves) a
calumny and a glaring sin.

59.   O Prophet! Tell your wives
and daughters, and the believing
women, that they should cast
their outer garments over their
persons (when out of doors): that
is most convenient, that they
should be known (as such) and
not molested. And Allah is Oft-
Forgiving, Most Merciful.

60.   Truly, if the Hypocrites, and
those in whose hearts

الْمُؤْمِنِينَ وَالْمُؤْمِنَاتِ بِغَيْرِ مَا

اكْتَسَبُوا فَقَدِ احْتَمَلُوا بُهْتَانًا

وَّإِثْمًا مُّبِينًا ۝ يَا أَيُّهَا النَّبِيُّ

قُلْ لِّأَزْوَاجِكَ وَبَنَاتِكَ وَنِسَاءِ

الْمُؤْمِنِينَ يُدْنِينَ عَلَيْهِنَّ

مِنْ جَلَابِيبِهِنَّ ذَلِكَ أَدْنَى أَنْ

يُّعْرَفْنَ فَلَا يُؤْذَيْنَ وَكَانَ اللَّهُ

غَفُورًا رَّحِيمًا ۝ لَئِنْ لَّمْ يَنْتَهِ

الْمُنَافِقُونَ وَالَّذِينَ فِي قُلُوبِهِمْ

Whom their right hands possess. And, (ladies), fear Allah; for Allah is Witness to all things.

56.   Allah and His Angels send blessings on the Prophet: O you that believe! send you blessings on him, and salute him with all respect.

57.   Those who annoy Allah and His Apostle - Allah has cursed them in this world and in the Hereafter, and has prepared for them a humiliating Punishment.

58.   And those who annoy

مَلَكَتْ أَيْمَانُهُنَّ وَاتَّقِينَ اللَّهَ

إِنَّ اللَّهَ كَانَ عَلَى كُلِّ شَيْءٍ

شَهِيدًا ۞ إِنَّ اللَّهَ وَمَلَٰئِكَتَهُ

يُصَلُّونَ عَلَى النَّبِيِّ يَٰٓأَيُّهَا

الَّذِينَ ءَامَنُوا صَلُّوا عَلَيْهِ وَسَلِّمُوا

تَسْلِيمًا ۞ إِنَّ الَّذِينَ يُؤْذُونَ

اللَّهَ وَرَسُولَهُ لَعَنَهُمُ اللَّهُ فِى

الدُّنْيَا وَالْءَاخِرَةِ وَأَعَدَّ لَهُمْ

عَذَابًا مُّهِينًا ۞ وَالَّذِينَ يُؤْذُونَ

or that you should marry his widows after him at any time. Truly such a thing is in Allah's sight an enormity.

54. Whether you reveal anything or conceal it, verily Allah has full knowledge of all things.

55. There is no blame (on these ladies if they appear) before their fathers or their sons, their brothers, or their brothers' sons, or their sisters' sons, or their women, or the (slaves)

اللهِ وَلَا أَنْ تَنْكِحُوٓا اَزْوَاجَهٗ

مِنْ بَعْدِهٖۤ اَبَدًا ؕ اِنَّ ذٰلِكُمْ

كَانَ عِنْدَ اللهِ عَظِيْمًا ۞ اِنْ

تُبْدُوْا شَيْئًا اَوْ تُخْفُوْهُ فَاِنَّ

اللهَ كَانَ بِكُلِّ شَىْءٍ عَلِيْمًا ۞

لَا جُنَاحَ عَلَيْهِنَّ فِىْۤ اٰبَآئِهِنَّ

وَلَاۤ اَبْنَآئِهِنَّ وَلَاۤ اِخْوَانِهِنَّ

وَلَاۤ اَبْنَآءِ اِخْوَانِهِنَّ وَلَاۤ اَبْنَآءِ

اَخَوَاتِهِنَّ وَلَا نِسَآئِهِنَّ وَلَا مَا

to wait for its preparation: but when you are invited, enter; and when you have taken your meal, disperse, without seeking familiar talk. Such (behaviour) annoys the Prophet: he is ashamed to dismiss you, but Allah is not ashamed (to tell you) the truth. And when you ask (his ladies) for anything you want, ask them from before a screen: that makes for greater purity for your hearts and for theirs. Nor is it right for you that you should annoy Allah's Apostle,

نَاظِرِينَ اِنَاهُ وَلٰكِنْ اِذَا دُعِيتُمْ

فَادْخُلُوا فَاِذَا طَعِمْتُمْ فَانْتَشِرُوا

وَلَا مُسْتَأْنِسِينَ لِحَدِيثٍ اِنَّ

ذٰلِكُمْ كَانَ يُؤْذِى النَّبِيَّ فَيَسْتَحْىِ

مِنْكُمْ وَاللّٰهُ لَا يَسْتَحْىِ مِنَ

الْحَقِّ وَاِذَا سَاَلْتُمُوهُنَّ مَتَاعًا

فَسْـَٔلُوهُنَّ مِنْ وَّرَآءِ حِجَابٍ

ذٰلِكُمْ اَطْهَرُ لِقُلُوبِكُمْ وَقُلُوبِهِنَّ

وَمَا كَانَ لَكُمْ اَنْ تُؤْذُوا رَسُولَ

that is in your hearts: and Allah is All-Knowing, Most Forbearing.

52.   It is not lawful for you (to marry more) women after this, nor to change them for (other) wives, even though their beauty attract you, except any your right hand should possess (as handmaidens): and Allah does watch over all things.

53.   O you who believe! Enter not the Prophet's houses, - until leave is given you, - for a meal, (and then) not (so early as)

مَا فِى قُلُوبِكُمْ ۚ وَكَانَ اللّٰهُ عَلِيْمًا

حَلِيْمًا ۞ لَا يَحِلُّ لَكَ النِّسَآءُ

مِنْ بَعْدُ وَلَآ أَنْ تَبَدَّلَ

بِهِنَّ مِنْ أَزْوَاجٍ وَّلَوْ أَعْجَبَكَ

حُسْنُهُنَّ إِلَّا مَا مَلَكَتْ يَمِيْنُكَ ۗ

وَكَانَ اللّٰهُ عَلٰى كُلِّ شَىْءٍ

رَّقِيْبًا ۞ يٰٓأَيُّهَا الَّذِيْنَ اٰمَنُوْا لَا

تَدْخُلُوْا بُيُوْتَ النَّبِيِّ إِلَّآ أَنْ

يُّؤْذَنَ لَكُمْ إِلٰى طَعَامٍ غَيْرَ

what We have appointed for them as to their wives and the captives whom their right hands possess; - in order that there should be no difficulty for you. And Allah is Oft-Forgiving, Most Merciful.

51. you may defer (the turn of) any of them that you please, and you may receive any you please: and there is no blame on you if you invite one whose (turn) you had set aside. This were closer to the cooling of their eyes, the prevention of their grief, and their satisfaction - that of all of them - with that which you have to give them: and Allah knows (all)

مَا فَرَضْنَا عَلَيْهِمْ فِىٓ اَزْوَاجِهِمْ

وَمَا مَلَكَتْ اَيْمَانُهُمْ لِكَيْلَا يَكُوْنَ

عَلَيْكَ حَرَجٌ ۖ وَكَانَ اللّٰهُ غَفُوْرًا

رَّحِيْمًا ۝ تُرْجِىْ مَنْ تَشَآءُ مِنْهُنَّ

وَتُـٔوِىٓ اِلَيْكَ مَنْ تَشَآءُ ۖ وَمَنِ

ابْتَغَيْتَ مِمَّنْ عَزَلْتَ فَلَا جُنَاحَ

عَلَيْكَ ۚ ذٰلِكَ اَدْنٰىٓ اَنْ تَقَرَّ

اَعْيُنُهُنَّ وَلَا يَحْزَنَّ وَيَرْضَيْنَ

بِمَآ اٰتَيْتَهُنَّ كُلُّهُنَّ ۚ وَاللّٰهُ يَعْلَمُ

to you your wives to whom you have paid their dowers; and those whom your right hand possesses out of the prisoners of war whom Allah has assigned to you; and daughters of you paternal uncles and aunts, and daughters of your maternal uncles and aunts, who migrated (from Makkah) with you; and any believing woman who dedicates her soul to the Prophet if the Prophet wishes to wed her; - this only for you, and not for the believers (at large); We know

لَكَ اَزْوَاجَكَ الّٰتِىٓ اٰتَيْتَ اُجُوْرَهُنَّ

وَمَا مَلَكَتْ يَمِيْنُكَ مِمَّاۤ اَفَآءَ

اللّٰهُ عَلَيْكَ وَبَنٰتِ عَمِّكَ وَبَنٰتِ

عَمّٰتِكَ وَبَنٰتِ خَالِكَ وَبَنٰتِ

خٰلٰتِكَ الّٰتِىْ هَاجَرْنَ مَعَكَ

وَامْرَاَةً مُّؤْمِنَةً اِنْ وَّهَبَتْ

نَفْسَهَا لِلنَّبِىِّ اِنْ اَرَادَ النَّبِىُّ

اَنْ يَّسْتَنْكِحَهَا خَالِصَةً لَّكَ

مِنْ دُوْنِ الْمُؤْمِنِيْنَ ؕ قَدْ عَلِمْنَا

48. And obey not (the behests) of the unbelievers and the Hypocrites, and heed not their annoyances, but put your trust in Allah. For enough is Allah as a Disposer of affairs.

49. O you who believe! When you marry believing women, and then divorce them before you have touched them, no period of 'Iddat have you to count in respect of them: so give them a present. And set them free in a handsome manner.

50. O Prophet! We have made lawful

كَبِيْرًا ۞ وَلَا تُطِعِ الْكٰفِرِيْنَ

وَالْمُنٰفِقِيْنَ وَدَعْ اَذٰىهُمْ وَتَوَكَّلْ

عَلَى اللّٰهِ ط وَكَفٰى بِاللّٰهِ وَكِيْلًا ۞

يٰاَيُّهَا الَّذِيْنَ اٰمَنُوْا اِذَا نَكَحْتُمُ

الْمُؤْمِنٰتِ ثُمَّ طَلَّقْتُمُوْهُنَّ مِنْ

قَبْلِ اَنْ تَمَسُّوْهُنَّ فَمَا لَكُمْ

عَلَيْهِنَّ مِنْ عِدَّةٍ تَعْتَدُّوْنَهَا ج

فَمَتِّعُوْهُنَّ وَسَرِّحُوْهُنَّ سَرَاحًا

جَمِيْلًا ۞ يٰاَيُّهَا النَّبِيُّ اِنَّا اَحْلَلْنَا

on you, as do His Angels, that He may bring you out from the depths of Darkness into Light: and He is full of Mercy to the believers.

44. Their salutation on the Day they meet Him will be "Peace!"; and He has prepared for them a generous Reward.

45. O Prophet! Truly We have sent you as a witness, a bearer of glad tidings, and warner,-

46. And as one who invites to Allah's (Grace) by His leave, and as a lamp spreading light.

47. Then give the glad tidings to the believers, that they shall have from Allah a very great Bounty.

عَلَيْكُمْ وَمَلَآئِكَتُهُ لِيُخْرِجَكُمْ

مِّنَ الظُّلُمٰتِ إِلَى النُّوْرِ ۚ وَكَانَ

بِالْمُؤْمِنِيْنَ رَحِيْمًا ۞ تَحِيَّتُهُمْ

يَوْمَ يَلْقَوْنَهُ سَلٰمٌ ۚ وَاَعَدَّ لَهُمْ

اَجْرًا كَرِيْمًا ۞ يٰۤاَيُّهَا النَّبِيُّ

اِنَّاۤ اَرْسَلْنٰكَ شَاهِدًا وَّمُبَشِّرًا

وَّنَذِيْرًا ۙ وَّدَاعِيًا اِلَى اللهِ بِاِذْنِهٖ

وَسِرَاجًا مُّنِيْرًا ۞ وَبَشِّرِ الْمُؤْمِنِيْنَ

بِاَنَّ لَهُمْ مِّنَ اللهِ فَضْلًا

and fear Him, and fear none but Allah. And enough is Allah to call (men) to account.

40. Muhammad is not the father of any of your men, but (he is) the Apostle of Allah, and the Seal of the Prophets: and Allah has full knowledge of all things.

41. O you who believe! Celebrate the praises of Allah, and do this often;

42. And glorify Him morning and evening.

43. He it is Who sends blessings

وَيَخْشَوْنَهُ وَلَا يَخْشَوْنَ أَحَدًا

إِلَّا اللّٰهَ ۗ وَكَفَىٰ بِاللّٰهِ حَسِيبًا ۞

مَا كَانَ مُحَمَّدٌ أَبَآ أَحَدٍ مِّنْ

رِّجَالِكُمْ وَلَٰكِنْ رَّسُولَ اللّٰهِ

وَخَاتَمَ النَّبِيِّنَ ۗ وَكَانَ اللّٰهُ

بِكُلِّ شَىْءٍ عَلِيمًا ۞ يَٰٓأَيُّهَا

الَّذِينَ ءَامَنُوا اذْكُرُوا اللّٰهَ

ذِكْرًا كَثِيرًا ۞ وَسَبِّحُوهُ بُكْرَةً

وَّأَصِيلًا ۞ هُوَ الَّذِى يُصَلِّى

in order that (in future) there may be no difficulty to the believers in (the matter of) marriage with the wives of their adopted sons, when the latter have dissolved with the necessary (formality) (their marriage) with them. And Allah's Command must be fulfilled.

38. There can be no difficulty to the Prophet in what Allah has indicated to him as a duty. It was the Practice (approved) of Allah amongst those of old that have passed away. And the Command of Allah is a decree determined.

39. (It is the practice of those) who preach the Messages of Allah,

لِكَىْ لَا يَكُوْنَ عَلَى الْمُؤْمِنِيْنَ

حَرَجٌ فِىْٓ اَزْوَاجِ اَدْعِيَآبِهِمْ

اِذَا قَضَوْا مِنْهُنَّ وَطَرًا ۚ وَكَانَ

اَمْرُ اللّٰهِ مَفْعُوْلًا ۞ مَا كَانَ

عَلَى النَّبِىِّ مِنْ حَرَجٍ فِيْمَا

فَرَضَ اللّٰهُ لَهٗ ۖ سُنَّةَ اللّٰهِ فِى

الَّذِيْنَ خَلَوْا مِنْ قَبْلُ ۚ وَكَانَ

اَمْرُ اللّٰهِ قَدَرًا مَّقْدُوْرَا ۞

الَّذِيْنَ يُبَلِّغُوْنَ رِسٰلٰتِ اللّٰهِ

have any option about their decision: if any one disobeys Allah and His Apostle, he is indeed on a clearly wrong Path.

37. Behold! You did say to one who had received the Grace of Allah and your favour: "Retain you (in wedlock) your wife, and fear Allah." But you did hide in your heart that which Allah was about to make manifest: you did fear the people, but it is more fitting that you should fear Allah. Then when Zaid had dissolved (his marriage) with her, with the necessary (formality), We joined her in marriage to you:

يَكُونَ لَهُمُ الْخِيَرَةُ مِنْ أَمْرِهِمْ ۗ

وَمَنْ يَّعْصِ اللّٰهَ وَرَسُولَهُ فَقَدْ

ضَلَّ ضَلٰلًا مُّبِينًا ۝ وَإِذْ تَقُولُ

لِلَّذِىٓ أَنْعَمَ اللّٰهُ عَلَيْهِ وَأَنْعَمْتَ

عَلَيْهِ أَمْسِكْ عَلَيْكَ زَوْجَكَ

وَاتَّقِ اللّٰهَ وَتُخْفِى فِىْ نَفْسِكَ

مَا اللّٰهُ مُبْدِيهِ وَتَخْشَى النَّاسَ ۖ

وَاللّٰهُ أَحَقُّ أَن تَخْشٰهُ ۗ فَلَمَّا

قَضٰى زَيْدٌ مِّنْهَا وَطَرًا زَوَّجْنٰكَهَا

for true men and women, for men and women who are patient and constant, for men and women who humble themselves, for men and women who give in Charity, for men and women who fast (and deny themselves), for men and women who guard their chastity, and for men and women who engage much in Allah's praise, - for them has Allah prepared Forgiveness and great Reward.

36.   It is not fitting for a believer, man or woman, when a matter has been decided by Allah and His Apostle, to

وَالصّٰدِقِينَ وَالصّٰدِقٰتِ وَالصّٰبِرِينَ

وَالصّٰبِرٰتِ وَالْخٰشِعِينَ وَالْخٰشِعٰتِ

وَالْمُتَصَدِّقِينَ وَالْمُتَصَدِّقٰتِ

وَالصّٰٓئِمِينَ وَالصّٰٓئِمٰتِ وَالْحٰفِظِينَ

فُرُوجَهُمْ وَالْحٰفِظٰتِ وَالذّٰكِرِينَ

اللّٰهَ كَثِيرًا وَّالذّٰكِرٰتِ ۙ اَعَدَّ اللّٰهُ

لَهُمْ مَّغْفِرَةً وَّاَجْرًا عَظِيمًا ۝ وَمَا

كَانَ لِمُؤْمِنٍ وَّلَا مُؤْمِنَةٍ اِذَا

قَضَى اللّٰهُ وَرَسُولُهٗٓ اَمْرًا اَنْ

and establish regular Prayer, and give regular Charity; and obey Allah and His Apostle. And Allah only wishes to remove all abomination from you, you members of the Family, and to make you pure and spotless.

34. And recite what is rehearsed to you in your homes, of the Signs of Allah and His Wisdom: for Allah understands the finest mysteries and is Well-Acquainted (with them).

35. For Muslim men and women, - for believing men and women, for devout men and women,

الْأُولَىٰ وَأَقِمْنَ الصَّلٰوةَ وَاٰتِيْنَ

الزَّكٰوةَ وَأَطِعْنَ اللّٰهَ وَرَسُوْلَهٗ ۚ

اِنَّمَا يُرِيْدُ اللّٰهُ لِيُذْهِبَ عَنْكُمُ

الرِّجْسَ اَهْلَ الْبَيْتِ وَيُطَهِّرَكُمْ

تَطْهِيْرًا ۚ ٣٣ وَاذْكُرْنَ مَا يُتْلٰى فِيْ

بُيُوْتِكُنَّ مِنْ اٰيٰتِ اللّٰهِ وَالْحِكْمَةِ ۚ

اِنَّ اللّٰهَ كَانَ لَطِيْفًا خَبِيْرًا ۚ ٣٤ اِنَّ

الْمُسْلِمِيْنَ وَالْمُسْلِمٰتِ وَالْمُؤْمِنِيْنَ

وَالْمُؤْمِنٰتِ وَالْقٰنِتِيْنَ وَالْقٰنِتٰتِ

31. But any of you that is devout in the service of Allah and His Apostle, and works righteousness, - to her shall We grant her reward twice: and We have prepared for her a generous Sustenance.

32. O consorts of the Prophet! You are not like any of the (other) women: if you do fear (Allah), be not too complaisant of speech, lest one in whose heart is a disease should be moved with desire: but speak you a speech (that is) just.

33. And stay quietly in your houses, and make not a dazzling display, like that of the former times of ignorance;

وَمَنْ يَّقْنُتْ مِنْكُنَّ لِلَّهِ وَرَسُوْلِهٖ

وَتَعْمَلْ صَالِحًا نُّؤْتِهَآ أَجْرَهَا

مَرَّتَيْنِ ۙ وَأَعْتَدْنَا لَهَا رِزْقًا

كَرِيْمًا ۞ يٰنِسَآءَ النَّبِيِّ لَسْتُنَّ

كَأَحَدٍ مِّنَ النِّسَآءِ إِنِ اتَّقَيْتُنَّ

فَلَا تَخْضَعْنَ بِالْقَوْلِ فَيَطْمَعَ

الَّذِيْ فِيْ قَلْبِهٖ مَرَضٌ وَّقُلْنَ

قَوْلًا مَّعْرُوْفًا ۞ وَقَرْنَ فِيْ بُيُوْتِكُنَّ

وَلَا تَبَرَّجْنَ تَبَرُّجَ الْجَاهِلِيَّةِ

پاره

وَمَن يَّقنُت

(۲۲)

بِسْمِ اللّٰهِ الرَّحْمٰنِ الرَّحِيْمِ

PART 23
Wama Liya

every kind of parable, in order that they may receive admonition.

28. (It is) a Qur'an in Arabic, without any crookedness (therein): in order that they may guard against Evil.

29. Allah puts forth a parable - a man belonging to many partners at variance with each other, and a man belonging entirely to one master: are those two equal in comparison? Praise be to Allah! But most of them have no knowledge.

30. Truly you will die (one day), and truly they (too) will die (one day).

31. In the end will you (all), on the Day of Judgment, settle your disputes in the presence of your Lord.

كُلِّ مَثَلٍ لَّعَلَّهُمْ يَتَذَكَّرُونَ ۝

قُرْاٰنًا عَرَبِيًّا غَيْرَ ذِيْ عِوَجٍ

لَّعَلَّهُمْ يَتَّقُونَ ۝ ضَرَبَ اللّٰهُ مَثَلًا

رَّجُلًا فِيْهِ شُرَكَآءُ مُتَشٰكِسُوْنَ

وَرَجُلًا سَلَمًا لِّرَجُلٍ هَلْ

يَسْتَوِيٰنِ مَثَلًا اَلْحَمْدُ لِلّٰهِ بَلْ

اَكْثَرُهُمْ لَا يَعْلَمُوْنَ ۝ اِنَّكَ مَيِّتٌ

وَّاِنَّهُمْ مَّيِّتُوْنَ ۝ ثُمَّ اِنَّكُمْ يَوْمَ

الْقِيٰمَةِ عِنْدَ رَبِّكُمْ تَخْتَصِمُوْنَ ۝

24. Is, then, one who has to fear the brunt of the Chastisement on the Day of Judgment (and receive it) on his face, (like one guarded therefrom)? It will be said to the wrong-doers: "Taste you (the fruits of) what you earned!"

25. Those before them (also) rejected (revelation), and so the punishment came to them from directions they did not perceive.

26. So Allah gave them a taste of humiliation in the present life, but greater is the Punishment of the Hereafter, if they only knew!

27. We have put forth for men, in this Qur'an

اَفَمَنْ يَّتَّقِيْ بِوَجْهِهٖ سُوْٓءَ الْعَذَابِ

يَوْمَ الْقِيٰمَةِ ۖ وَقِيْلَ لِلظّٰلِمِيْنَ

ذُوْقُوْا مَا كُنْتُمْ تَكْسِبُوْنَ ۞ كَذَّبَ

الَّذِيْنَ مِنْ قَبْلِهِمْ فَاَتٰىهُمُ

الْعَذَابُ مِنْ حَيْثُ لَا يَشْعُرُوْنَ ۞

فَاَذَاقَهُمُ اللّٰهُ الْخِزْيَ فِي الْحَيٰوةِ

الدُّنْيَا ۖ وَلَعَذَابُ الْاٰخِرَةِ اَكْبَرُ

لَوْ كَانُوْا يَعْلَمُوْنَ ۞ وَلَقَدْ ضَرَبْنَا

لِلنَّاسِ فِيْ هٰذَا الْقُرْاٰنِ مِنْ

to those whose hearts are hardened against celebrating the praises of Allah! They are manifestly wandering (in error)!

23. Allah has revealed (from time to time) the most beautiful Message in the form of a Book, consistent with itself, (yet) repeating (its teaching in various aspects): the skins of those who fear their Lord tremble thereat; then their skins and their hearts do soften to the celebration of Allah's praises. Such is the Guidance of Allah: He guides therewith whom He pleases, but such as Allah leaves to stray, can have none to guide.

لِلْقَاسِيَةِ قُلُوبُهُم مِّن ذِكْرِ اللّٰهِ

أُوْلَٰٓئِكَ فِى ضَلَٰلٍ مُّبِينٍ ۞ اللّٰهُ

نَزَّلَ أَحْسَنَ الْحَدِيثِ كِتَٰبًا

مُّتَشَٰبِهًا مَّثَانِىَ تَقْشَعِرُّ مِنْهُ

جُلُودُ الَّذِينَ يَخْشَوْنَ رَبَّهُمْ

ثُمَّ تَلِينُ جُلُودُهُمْ وَقُلُوبُهُمْ

إِلَىٰ ذِكْرِ اللّٰهِ ذَٰلِكَ هُدَى اللّٰهِ

يَهْدِى بِهِ مَن يَشَآءُ وَمَن

يُضْلِلِ اللّٰهُ فَمَا لَهُ مِنْ هَادٍ ۞

does Allah fail in (His) promise.

21. Do you see not that Allah sends down rain from the sky, and leads it through springs in the earth? Then He causes to grow, therewith, produce of various colours: then it withers; you will see it grow yellow; then He makes it dry up and crumble away. Truly, in this, is a Message of remembrance to men of understanding.

22. Is one whose heart Allah has opened to Islam, so that he has received Enlightenment from Allah, (no better than one hard-hearted)? Woe

يُخْلِفُ اللهُ الْمِيْعَادَ ۞ اَلَمْ تَرَ

اَنَّ اللهَ اَنْزَلَ مِنَ السَّمَآءِ مَآءً

فَسَلَكَهُ يَنَابِيعَ فِى الْاَرْضِ

ثُمَّ يُخْرِجُ بِهِ زَرْعًا مُّخْتَلِفًا

اَلْوَانُهُ ثُمَّ يَهِيجُ فَتَرٰىهُ مُصْفَرًّا

ثُمَّ يَجْعَلُهُ حُطَامًا ۚ اِنَّ فِى ذٰلِكَ

لَذِكْرٰى لِاُولِى الْاَلْبَابِ ۞ اَفَمَنْ

شَرَحَ اللهُ صَدْرَهُ لِلْاِسْلَامِ

فَهُوَ عَلٰى نُوْرٍ مِّنْ رَّبِّهٖ ۚ فَوَيْلٌ

so announce the good news to My servants, -

18. Those who listen to the Word, and follow the best (meaning) in it: those are the ones whom Allah has guided, and those are the ones endued with understanding.

19. Is, then, one against whom the decree of Punishment is justly due (equal to one who eschews Evil)? Would you, then, deliver one (who is) in the Fire?

20. But it is for those who fear their Lord. That lofty mansions, one above another, have been built: beneath them flow rivers (of delight): (such is) the Promise of Allah: never

فَبَشِّرْ عِبَادِ ۝ الَّذِيْنَ يَسْتَمِعُوْنَ

الْقَوْلَ فَيَتَّبِعُوْنَ اَحْسَنَهٗ ؕ اُولٰٓئِكَ

الَّذِيْنَ هَدٰىهُمُ اللّٰهُ وَاُولٰٓئِكَ هُمْ

اُولُوا الْاَلْبَابِ ۝ اَفَمَنْ حَقَّ عَلَيْهِ

كَلِمَةُ الْعَذَابِ ؕ اَفَاَنْتَ تُنْقِذُ

مَنْ فِى النَّارِ ۝ لٰكِنِ الَّذِيْنَ

اتَّقَوْا رَبَّهُمْ لَهُمْ غُرَفٌ مِّنْ

فَوْقِهَا غُرَفٌ مَّبْنِيَّةٌ ۙ تَجْرِىْ مِنْ

تَحْتِهَا الْاَنْهٰرُ ؕ وَعْدَ اللّٰهِ ؕ لَا

besides Him." Say: "Truly, those in loss are those who lose their own souls and their people on the Day of Judgment: ah! that is indeed the (real and) evident Loss!

16. They shall have Layers of Fire above them, and Layers (of Fire) below them: with this does Allah warn off His servants: "O My servants! Then fear you Me!"

17. Those who eschew Evil, - and fall not into its worship, - and turn to Allah (in repentance), - for them is good news:

مِّن دُونِهِ ۚ قُلْ إِنَّ الْخَاسِرِينَ
الَّذِينَ خَسِرُوا أَنفُسَهُمْ وَأَهْلِيهِمْ
يَوْمَ الْقِيَامَةِ ۗ أَلَا ذَٰلِكَ هُوَ
الْخُسْرَانُ الْمُبِينُ ۞ لَهُم مِّن
فَوْقِهِمْ ظُلَلٌ مِّنَ النَّارِ وَمِن
تَحْتِهِمْ ظُلَلٌ ۚ ذَٰلِكَ يُخَوِّفُ اللَّهُ بِهِ
عِبَادَهُ ۚ يَا عِبَادِ فَاتَّقُونِ ۞ وَالَّذِينَ
اجْتَنَبُوا الطَّاغُوتَ أَن يَعْبُدُوهَا
وَأَنَابُوا إِلَى اللَّهِ لَهُمُ الْبُشْرَىٰ

In this world. Spacious is Allah's earth! Those who patiently persevere will truly receive a reward without measure!"

11. Say: "Verily, I am commanded to serve Allah with sincere devotion;"

12. "And I am commanded to be the first of those who bow to Allah in Islam."

13. Say: "I would, if I disobeyed my Lord, indeed have fear of the Penalty of a Mighty Day."

14. Say: "It is Allah I serve, with my sincere (and exclusive) devotion:"

15. "Serve you what you will

فِى هٰذِهِ الدُّنْيَا حَسَنَةٌ وَأَرْضُ

اللهِ وَاسِعَةٌ اِنَّمَا يُوَفَّى الصّٰبِرُوْنَ

اَجْرَهُمْ بِغَيْرِ حِسَابٍ ۝ قُلْ اِنِّىٓ

اُمِرْتُ اَنْ اَعْبُدَ اللهَ مُخْلِصًا

لَّهُ الدِّيْنَ ۝ وَاُمِرْتُ لِاَنْ اَكُوْنَ

اَوَّلَ الْمُسْلِمِيْنَ ۝ قُلْ اِنِّىٓ اَخَافُ

اِنْ عَصَيْتُ رَبِّى عَذَابَ يَوْمٍ

عَظِيْمٍ ۝ قُلِ اللهَ اَعْبُدُ مُخْلِصًا

لَّهُ دِيْنِىْ ۝ فَاعْبُدُوْا مَا شِئْتُمْ

Allah's Path. Say, "Enjoy your blasphemy for a little while: verily you are (one) of the Companions of the Fire!"

9. Is one who worships devoutly during the hours of the night prostrating himself or standing (in adoration), who takes heed of the Hereafter, and who places his hope in the Mercy of his Lord - (like one who does not)? Say: "Are those equal, those who know and those who do not know? It is those who are endued with understanding that receive admonition."

10. Say: "O you My servants who believe! Fear your Lord, good is (the reward) for those who do good

سَبِيلِهِ ۚ قُلْ تَمَتَّعْ بِكُفْرِكَ

قَلِيلًا ۖ إِنَّكَ مِنْ أَصْحَابِ النَّارِ ۞

أَمَّنْ هُوَ قَانِتٌ آنَاءَ الَّيْلِ

سَاجِدًا وَّ قَآئِمًا يَّحْذَرُ الْاٰخِرَةَ

وَيَرْجُوْا رَحْمَةَ رَبِّهٖ ۗ قُلْ هَلْ

يَسْتَوِى الَّذِيْنَ يَعْلَمُوْنَ وَالَّذِيْنَ

لَا يَعْلَمُوْنَ ۗ إِنَّمَا يَتَذَكَّرُ أُولُوا

الْأَلْبَابِ ۞ قُلْ يٰعِبَادِ الَّذِيْنَ

اٰمَنُوا اتَّقُوْا رَبَّكُمْ ۚ لِلَّذِيْنَ أَحْسَنُوْا

you are grateful, He is pleased with you. No bearer of burdens can bear the burden of another. In the end, to your Lord is your Return, when He will tell you the truth of all that you did (in this life). for He knows well all that is in (men's) hearts.

8.   When some trouble touches man, he cries unto his Lord, turning to Him in repentance: but when He bestows a favour upon him as from Himself, (man) does forget what he cried and prayed for before, and he does set up rivals unto Allah, thus mis-leading others from

تَشْكُرُوا يَرْضَهُ لَكُمْ ۗ وَلَا تَزِرُ

وَازِرَةٌ وِزْرَ أُخْرَىٰ ۗ ثُمَّ إِلَىٰ

رَبِّكُمْ مَّرْجِعُكُمْ فَيُنَبِّئُكُمْ بِمَا

كُنْتُمْ تَعْمَلُونَ ۚ إِنَّهُ عَلِيمٌ بِذَاتِ

الصُّدُورِ ۞ وَإِذَا مَسَّ الْإِنْسَانَ

ضُرٌّ دَعَا رَبَّهُ مُنِيبًا إِلَيْهِ ثُمَّ

إِذَا خَوَّلَهُ نِعْمَةً مِّنْهُ نَسِيَ مَا

كَانَ يَدْعُوا إِلَيْهِ مِنْ قَبْلُ

وَجَعَلَ لِلَّهِ أَنْدَادًا لِّيُضِلَّ عَنْ

6. He created you (all) from a single person: then created, of like nature, his mate; and he sent down for you eight head of cattle in pairs: He makes you, in the wombs of your mothers, in stages, one after another, in three veils of darkness. Such is Allah, your Lord and Cherisher: to Him belongs (all) dominion. There is no Allah but He: then how are you turned away (from your true Centre)?

7. If you reject (Allah), truly Allah has no need of you; but He likes not ingratitude from His servants: if

خَلَقَكُمْ مِّنْ نَّفْسٍ وَّاحِدَةٍ ثُمَّ

جَعَلَ مِنْهَا زَوْجَهَا وَ اَنْزَلَ لَكُمْ

مِّنَ الْاَنْعَامِ ثَمٰنِيَةَ اَزْوَاجٍ ؕ

يَخْلُقُكُمْ فِیْ بُطُوْنِ اُمَّهٰتِكُمْ خَلْقًا

مِّنْۢ بَعْدِ خَلْقٍ فِیْ ظُلُمٰتٍ ثَلٰثٍ ؕ

ذٰلِكُمُ اللّٰهُ رَبُّكُمْ لَهُ الْمُلْكُ ؕ لَاۤ

اِلٰهَ اِلَّا هُوَ ۚ فَاَنّٰی تُصْرَفُوْنَ ۞ اِنْ

تَكْفُرُوْا فَاِنَّ اللّٰهَ غَنِیٌّ عَنْكُمْ ۫

وَلَا یَرْضٰی لِعِبَادِهِ الْكُفْرَ ۚ وَاِنْ

Allah guides not such as are false and ungrateful.

4.　　Had Allah wished to take to Himself a son, He could have chosen whom He pleased out of those whom He does create: but Glory be to Him! (He is above such things.) He is Allah, the One, the Irresistible.

5.　　He created the heavens and the earth in true (proportions): He makes the Night overlap the Day, and the Day overlap the Night: He has subjected the sun and the moon (to His law): each one follows a course for a time appointed. Is not He the Exalted in Power - He Who forgives again and again?

اللَّهَ لَا يَهْدِي مَنْ هُوَ كَاذِبٌ

كَفَّارٌ ۞ لَوْ أَرَادَ اللَّهُ أَنْ يَّتَّخِذَ

وَلَدًا لَّاصْطَفَى مِمَّا يَخْلُقُ مَا

يَشَاءُ ۙ سُبْحٰنَهُ ۚ هُوَ اللَّهُ الْوَاحِدُ

الْقَهَّارُ ۞ خَلَقَ السَّمٰوٰتِ وَالْأَرْضَ

بِالْحَقِّ ۚ يُكَوِّرُ الَّيْلَ عَلَى النَّهَارِ

وَيُكَوِّرُ النَّهَارَ عَلَى الَّيْلِ وَسَخَّرَ

الشَّمْسَ وَالْقَمَرَ ۖ كُلٌّ يَّجْرِى لِأَجَلٍ

مُّسَمًّى ۗ أَلَا هُوَ الْعَزِيزُ الْغَفَّارُ ۞

Az-Zumar (The Groups)
Bismillahir-Rahmanir-Rahim

1.   The revelation of this Book is from Allah, the Exalted in Power, full of Wisdom.

2.   Verily it is We Who have revealed the Book to you in Truth: so serve Allah, offering Him sincere devotion.

3.   Is it not to Allah that sincere devotion is due? But those who take for protectors other than Allah (say): "We only serve them in order that they may bring us nearer to Allah." Truly Allah will judge between them in that wherein they differ. But

سُورَةُ الزُّمَر مَكِّيَّة بِسۡمِ اللهِ الرَّحۡمٰنِ الرَّحِيۡمِ

تَنۡزِيۡلُ الۡكِتٰبِ مِنَ اللهِ الۡعَزِيۡزِ الۡحَكِيۡمِ ۝ اِنَّاۤ اَنۡزَلۡنَاۤ اِلَيۡكَ الۡكِتٰبَ بِالۡحَقِّ فَاعۡبُدِ اللهَ مُخۡلِصًا لَّهُ الدِّيۡنَ ۝ اَلَا لِلّٰهِ الدِّيۡنُ الۡخَالِصُ ۚ وَالَّذِيۡنَ اتَّخَذُوۡا مِنۡ دُوۡنِهٖۤ اَوۡلِيَآءَ ۘ مَا نَعۡبُدُهُمۡ اِلَّا لِيُقَرِّبُوۡنَاۤ اِلَى اللهِ زُلۡفٰى ؕ اِنَّ اللهَ يَحۡكُمُ بَيۡنَهُمۡ فِيۡ مَا هُمۡ فِيۡهِ يَخۡتَلِفُوۡنَ ۬ؕ اِنَّ

of the Time appointed."

82. (Iblis) said: "Then, by Your power, I will put them all in the wrong, -

83. "Except Your servants amongst them, sincere and purified (by Your Grace)."

84. (Allah) said: "Then it is just and fitting - and I say what is just and fitting" -

85. "That I will certainly fill Hell with you and those that follow your, - every one."

86. Say: "No reward do I ask of you for this (Qur'an), nor am I a pretender."

87. "This is no less than a Message to (all) the Worlds."

88. "And you shall certainly know the truth of it (all) after a while."

الْوَقْتِ الْمَعْلُومِ ۞ قَالَ فَبِعِزَّتِكَ

لَأُغْوِيَنَّهُمْ أَجْمَعِينَ ۞ إِلَّا عِبَادَكَ

مِنْهُمُ الْمُخْلَصِينَ ۞ قَالَ فَالْحَقُّ

وَالْحَقَّ أَقُولُ ۞ لَأَمْلَأَنَّ جَهَنَّمَ مِنكَ

وَمِمَّن تَبِعَكَ مِنْهُمْ أَجْمَعِينَ ۞

قُلْ مَا أَسْئَلُكُمْ عَلَيْهِ مِنْ أَجْرٍ

وَمَا أَنَا مِنَ الْمُتَكَلِّفِينَ ۞ إِنْ

هُوَ إِلَّا ذِكْرٌ لِّلْعَالَمِينَ ۞ وَلَتَعْلَمُنَّ

نَبَأَهُ بَعْدَ حِينٍ ۞

"O Iblis! What prevents you from prostrating yourself to one whom I have created with My hands? Are you haughty? Or are you one of the high (and mighty) ones?"

76. (Iblis) said: "I am better than he: You created me from fire, and him You created from clay."

77. (Allah) said: "Then get you out from here: for you are rejected, accursed."

78. "And My curse shall be on you till the Day of Judgment."

79. (Iblis) said: "O my Lord! Give me then respite till the Day the (dead) are raised."

80. (Allah) said: "Respite then is granted you -

81. "Till the Day

يَا إِبْلِيسُ مَا مَنَعَكَ أَنْ تَسْجُدَ لِمَا

خَلَقْتُ بِيَدَيَّ ٱسْتَكْبَرْتَ أَمْ كُنْتَ

مِنَ الْعَالِينَ ۝ قَالَ أَنَا خَيْرٌ

مِّنْهُ خَلَقْتَنِي مِنْ نَّارٍ وَّخَلَقْتَهُ

مِنْ طِينٍ ۝ قَالَ فَاخْرُجْ مِنْهَا

فَإِنَّكَ رَجِيمٌ ۝ وَّإِنَّ عَلَيْكَ لَعْنَتِى

إِلَى يَوْمِ الدِّينِ ۝ قَالَ رَبِّ

فَأَنْظِرْنِى إِلَى يَوْمِ يُبْعَثُونَ ۝ قَالَ

فَإِنَّكَ مِنَ الْمُنْظَرِينَ ۝ إِلَى يَوْمِ

knowledge have I of the Chiefs on high, when they discuss (matters) among themselves."

70.   'Only this has been revealed to me: that I am to give warning plainly and publicly.'"

71.   Behold, your Lord said to the Angels: "I am about to create man from clay:"

72.   "When I have fashioned him (in due proportion) and breathed into him of My spirit, fall you down in prostration before him."

73.   So the Angels prostrated themselves, all of them together:

74.   Not so Iblis: he was haughty, and became one of those who reject Faith.

75.   (Allah) said:

لِّيَ مِنْ عِلْمٍ بِالْمَلَإِ الْأَعْلَىٰ إِذْ

يَخْتَصِمُونَ ۝ إِنْ يُوحَىٰ إِلَيَّ إِلَّا

أَنَّمَا أَنَا نَذِيرٌ مُّبِينٌ ۝ إِذْ قَالَ

رَبُّكَ لِلْمَلَائِكَةِ إِنِّي خَالِقٌ بَشَرًا

مِّن طِينٍ ۝ فَإِذَا سَوَّيْتُهُ وَنَفَخْتُ

فِيهِ مِن رُّوحِي فَقَعُوا لَهُ

سَاجِدِينَ ۝ فَسَجَدَ الْمَلَائِكَةُ كُلُّهُمْ

أَجْمَعُونَ ۝ إِلَّا إِبْلِيسَ اسْتَكْبَرَ

وَكَانَ مِنَ الْكَافِرِينَ ۝ قَالَ

whom we used to number among
the bad ones?"

63. "Did we treat them (as such)
in ridicule, or have (our) eyes
failed to perceive them?"

64. Truly that is just and fitting, -
the mutual recriminations of the
People of the Fire!

65. Say: "Truly am I a warner:
no god is there but the One Allah,
Supreme and Irresistible, -

66. "The Lord of the heavens
and the earth, and all between, -
Exalted in Might, able to enforce
His Will, forgiving again and
again."

67. Say: "That is a teremendous
tiding, -

68. "From which you do turn
away!"   **69.**   "No

كُنَّا نَعُدُّهُم مِّنَ الأَشْرَارِ ۞

أَتَّخَذْنَاهُمْ سِخْرِيًّا أَمْ زَاغَتْ

عَنْهُمُ الأَبْصَارُ ۞ إِنَّ ذَٰلِكَ لَحَقٌّ

تَخَاصُمُ أَهْلِ النَّارِ ۞ قُلْ إِنَّمَآ

أَنَا مُنذِرٌ ۖ وَمَا مِنْ إِلَٰهٍ إِلَّا اللَّهُ

الْوَاحِدُ الْقَهَّارُ ۞ رَبُّ السَّمَاوَاتِ

وَالأَرْضِ وَمَا بَيْنَهُمَا الْعَزِيزُ

الْغَفَّارُ ۞ قُلْ هُوَ نَبَؤٌا عَظِيمٌ ۞

أَنتُمْ عَنْهُ مُعْرِضُونَ ۞ مَا كَانَ

then shall they taste it, - a boiling fluid, and a fluid dark, murky, intensely cold! -

58. And other penalties of a similar kind, to match them!

59. Here is a troop rushing headlong with you! No welcome for them! Truly, they shall burn in the Fire!

60. (The followers shall cry to the misleaders:) "No, you (too)! No welcome for you! It is you who have brought this upon us! Now evil is (this) place to stay in!"

61. They will say: "Our Lord! Whoever brought this upon us, - Add to him a double Chastisement in the Fire!"

62. And they will say: "What has happened to us that we see not men

فَلْيَذُوقُوهُ حَمِيمٌ وَّغَسَّاقٌ ۞ وَّاٰخَرُ

مِنْ شَكْلِهٖٓ اَزْوَاجٌ ۞ هٰذَا فَوْجٌ

مُّقْتَحِمٌ مَّعَكُمْ ۚ لَا مَرْحَبًاۢ بِهِمْ ۚ

اِنَّهُمْ صَالُوا النَّارِ ۞ قَالُوْا

بَلْ اَنْتُمْ ۚ لَا مَرْحَبًاۢ بِكُمْ ۚ اَنْتُمْ

قَدَّمْتُمُوهُ لَنَا ۚ فَبِئْسَ الْقَرَارُ

۞ قَالُوْا رَبَّنَا مَنْ قَدَّمَ لَنَا هٰذَا

فَزِدْهُ عَذَابًا ضِعْفًا فِى النَّارِ ۞

وَقَالُوْا مَا لَنَا لَا نَرٰى رِجَالًا

Place of (final) Return, -

50.   Gardens of Eternity, whose doors will (ever) be open to them;

51.   Therein will they recline (at ease): therein can they call (at pleasure) for fruit in abundance, and (delicious) drink;

52. And beside them will be chaste women restraining their glances, (companions) of equal age.

53.   Such is the Promise made to you for the Day of Account!

54.   Truly such will be Our Bounty (to you); it will never fail; -

55.   Yes, such! But - for the wrong-doers will be an evil place of (final) Return!-

56.   Hell! - they will burn therein, - an evil bed (indeed, to lie on)! -

57.   Yes, such! -

مَاٰبٍ ۟ جَنّٰتِ عَدْنٍ مُّفَتَّحَةً

لَّهُمُ الْاَبْوَابُ ۟ مُتَّكِئِيْنَ فِيْهَا

يَدْعُوْنَ فِيْهَا بِفَاكِهَةٍ كَثِيْرَةٍ

وَّشَرَابٍ ۟ وَعِنْدَهُمْ قٰصِرٰتُ

الطَّرْفِ اَتْرَابٌ ۟ هٰذَا مَا تُوْعَدُوْنَ

لِيَوْمِ الْحِسَابِ ۟ اِنَّ هٰذَا لَرِزْقُنَا

مَا لَهٗ مِنْ نَّفَادٍ ۟ هٰذَا ۟ وَاِنَّ

لِلطّٰغِيْنَ لَشَرَّ مَاٰبٍ ۟ جَهَنَّمَ

يَصْلَوْنَهَا ۚ فَبِئْسَ الْمِهَادُ ۟ هٰذَا

and Break not (your oath)." Truly
We found him full of patience and
constancy. How excellent in Our
service! Ever did he turn (to Us)!

45. And commemorate Our servants Abraham, Isaac, and Jacob,
possessors of Power and Vision.

46. Verily We did choose them for
a special (purpose) - proclaiming
the Message of the Hereafter.

47. They were, in Our sight,
truly, of the company of the Elect
and the Good.

48. And commemorate Isma'il,
Elisha, and Zul-Kifl: each of them
was of the Company of the Good.

49. This is a Message (of admonition): and verily, for the righteous, is a beautiful

وَلَا تَحْنَثْ ۗ إِنَّا وَجَدْنَاهُ صَابِرًا

نِعْمَ الْعَبْدُ ۖ إِنَّهُ أَوَّابٌ ۝ وَاذْكُرْ

عِبَادَنَا إِبْرَاهِيمَ وَإِسْحَاقَ وَيَعْقُوبَ

أُولِي الْأَيْدِي وَالْأَبْصَارِ ۝ إِنَّا

أَخْلَصْنَاهُمْ بِخَالِصَةٍ ذِكْرَى الدَّارِ ۝

وَإِنَّهُمْ عِنْدَنَا لَمِنَ الْمُصْطَفَيْنَ

الْأَخْيَارِ ۝ وَاذْكُرْ إِسْمَاعِيلَ وَالْيَسَعَ

وَذَا الْكِفْلِ ۖ وَكُلٌّ مِّنَ الْأَخْيَارِ ۝

هَٰذَا ذِكْرٌ ۚ وَإِنَّ لِلْمُتَّقِينَ لَحُسْنَ

no account will be asked."

40. And he enjoyed, indeed, a Near Approach to Us, and a beautiful place of (final) Return.

41. Commemorate Our servant Job. Behold he cried to his Lord: "The Satan has afflicted me with distress and suffering!"

42. (The command was given:) "Strike with your foot: here is (water) wherein to wash, cool and refreshing, and (water) to drink."

43. And We gave him (back) his people, and doubled their number, - as a Grace from Ourselves, and a thing for commemoration, for all who have understanding.

44. "And take in your hand a little grass, and strike therewith:

بِغَيْرِ حِسَابٍ ۞ وَإِنَّ لَهُ عِنْدَنَا

لَزُلْفَى وَحُسْنَ مَآبٍ ۞ وَاذْكُرْ

عَبْدَنَا أَيُّوبَ إِذْ نَادَى رَبَّهُ

أَنِّى مَسَّنِيَ الشَّيْطَانُ بِنُصْبٍ

وَعَذَابٍ ۞ ارْكُضْ بِرِجْلِكَ هٰذَا

مُغْتَسَلٌ بَارِدٌ وَشَرَابٌ ۞ وَوَهَبْنَا

لَهُ أَهْلَهُ وَمِثْلَهُمْ مَعَهُمْ رَحْمَةً

مِنَّا وَذِكْرَى لِأُولِى الْأَلْبَابِ ۞

وَخُذْ بِيَدِكَ ضِغْثًا فَاضْرِبْ بِهِ

We did try Solomon: We placed on his throne a body (without life); but he did turn (to Us in true devotion):

35. He said, "O my Lord! Forgive me, and grant me a kingdom which, (it may be), suits not another after me: for You are the Grantor of Bounties (without measure).

36. Then We subjected the wind to his power, to flow gently to his order, whithersoever he willed, -

37. As also the evil ones, (including) every kind of builder and diver, -

38. As also others bound together in fetters.

39. "Such are Our Bounties: whether you bestow them (on others) or withhold them,

فَتَنَّا سُلَيْمٰنَ وَ اَلْقَيْنَا عَلٰى كُرْسِيِّهٖ

جَسَدًا ثُمَّ اَنَابَ ۞ قَالَ رَبِّ

اغْفِرْ لِيْ وَهَبْ لِيْ مُلْكًا لَّا يَنْۢبَغِيْ

لِاَحَدٍ مِّنْۢ بَعْدِيْ اِنَّكَ اَنْتَ

الْوَهَّابُ ۞ فَسَخَّرْنَا لَهُ الرِّيْحَ

تَجْرِيْ بِاَمْرِهٖ رُخَآءً حَيْثُ اَصَابَ

۞ وَ الشَّيٰطِيْنَ كُلَّ بَنَّآءٍ وَّغَوَّاصٍ

۞ وَ اٰخَرِيْنَ مُقَرَّنِيْنَ فِى الْاَصْفَادِ ۞

هٰذَا عَطَآؤُنَا فَامْنُنْ اَوْ اَمْسِكْ

which We have sent down to you, full of blessings, that they may mediate on its Signs, and that men of understanding may receive admonition.

30. To David We gave Solomon (for a son), - how excellent in Our service! ever did he turn (to Us in repentence).

31. Behold, there were brought before him, at eventide coursers of the highest breeding, and swift of foot; **32.** And he said, "Truly do I love the love of good, with a view to the Glory of my Lord," - until (the sun) was hidden in the veil (of night):

33. "Bring them back to me." Then began he to pass his hand over (their) legs and their necks.

34. And

أَنْزَلْنَهُ إِلَيْكَ مُبَرَكٌ لِّيَدَّبَّرُوا

اٰيَتِهِ وَلِيَتَذَكَّرَ أُولُوا الْأَلْبَابِ ۞

وَوَهَبْنَا لِدَاؤُدَ سُلَيْمَنَ نِعْمَ

الْعَبْدُ اِنَّهُ اَوَّابٌ ۞ اِذْ عُرِضَ

عَلَيْهِ بِالْعَشِيِّ الصّٰفِنٰتُ الْجِيَادُ ۞

فَقَالَ اِنِّيْ اَحْبَبْتُ حُبَّ الْخَيْرِ

عَنْ ذِكْرِ رَبِّيْ حَتّٰى تَوَارَتْ

بِالْحِجَابِ ۞ رُدُّوْهَا عَلَيَّ فَطَفِقَ

مَسْحًا بِالسُّوْقِ وَالْأَعْنَاقِ ۞ وَلَقَدْ

wander astray from the Path of Allah, is a Chastisement grievous, for that they forget the Day of Account.

27. Not without purpose did We create heaven and earth and all between! That were the thought of unbelievers! But woe to the unbelievers because of the Fire (of Hell)!

28. Shall We treat those who believe and work deeds of righteousness, the same as those who do mischief on earth? Shall We treat those who guard against evil, the same as those who turn aside from the right?

29. (Here is) a Book

يُضِلُّونَ عَنْ سَبِيلِ اللّٰهِ لَهُمْ
عَذَابٌ شَدِيدٌ بِمَا نَسُوا يَوْمَ
الْحِسَابِ ۞ وَمَا خَلَقْنَا السَّمَآءَ
وَالْاَرْضَ وَمَا بَيْنَهُمَا بَاطِلًا ذٰلِكَ
ظَنُّ الَّذِينَ كَفَرُوا فَوَيْلٌ لِّلَّذِينَ
كَفَرُوا مِنَ النَّارِ ۞ اَمْ نَجْعَلُ
الَّذِينَ اٰمَنُوا وَعَمِلُوا الصّٰلِحٰتِ
كَالْمُفْسِدِينَ فِي الْاَرْضِ اَمْ
نَجْعَلُ الْمُتَّقِينَ كَالْفُجَّارِ ۞ كِتٰبٌ

not so do those who believe and
work deeds of righteousness, and
how few are they?"...and David
gathered that We had tried him:
he asked forgiveness of his Lord,
fell down, bowing (in prostration), and turned (to Allah in
repentance).

25. So We forgave him this
(lapse): he enjoyed, indeed, a
Near Approach to Us, and a
beautiful place of (final) Return.

26. O David! We did indeed
make you a vicegerent on earth:
so judge you between men in
truth (and justice): nor follow you
the lusts (of your heart), for they
will mislead you from the Path of
Allah: for those who

إِلَّا الَّذِينَ أَمَنُوا وَعَمِلُوا الصَّلِحَتِ

وَقَلِيلٌ مَّا هُمْ وَظَنَّ دَاوُدُ أَنَّمَا

فَتَنَّهُ فَاسْتَغْفَرَ رَبَّهُ وَخَرَّ رَاكِعًا

وَأَنَابَ ۩ فَغَفَرْنَا لَهُ ذَلِكَ وَإِنَّ

لَهُ عِندَنَا لَزُلْفَى وَحُسْنَ مَآبٍ ۞

يَدَاوُدُ إِنَّا جَعَلْنَكَ خَلِيفَةً فِى

الْأَرْضِ فَاحْكُم بَيْنَ النَّاسِ

بِالْحَقِّ وَلَا تَتَّبِعِ الْهَوَى فَيُضِلَّكَ

عَن سَبِيلِ اللَّهِ إِنَّ الَّذِينَ

"Fear not: we are two disputants, one of whom has wronged the other: decide now between us with truth, and treat us not with injustice, but guide us to the even Path."

23. "This man is my brother: he has nine and ninety ewes, and I have (but) one: yet he says, 'commit her to my care,' and is (moreover) harsh to me in speech."

24. (David) said: "He has undoubtedly wronged you in demanding you (single) ewe to be added to his (flock of) ewes: truly many are the partners (in business) who wrong each other:

تَخَفْ خَصْمٰنِ بَغٰى بَعْضُنَا عَلٰى

بَعْضٍ فَاحْكُمْ بَيْنَنَا بِالْحَقِّ وَلَا

تُشْطِطْ وَاهْدِنَآ اِلٰى سَوَآءِ الصِّرَاطِ ۲۲

اِنَّ هٰذَآ اَخِیْ لَهٗ تِسْعٌ وَّتِسْعُوْنَ

نَعْجَةً وَّلِیَ نَعْجَةٌ وَّاحِدَةٌ فَقَالَ

اَكْفِلْنِیْهَا وَعَزَّنِیْ فِی الْخِطَابِ ۲۳

قَالَ لَقَدْ ظَلَمَكَ بِسُؤَالِ نَعْجَتِكَ

اِلٰى نِعَاجِهٖ وَاِنَّ كَثِیْرًا مِّنَ

الْخُلَطَآءِ لَیَبْغِیْ بَعْضُهُمْ عَلٰى بَعْضٍ

what they say, and remember Our servant David, the man of strength: for he ever turned (to Allah).

18. It was We that made the hills declare, in unison with him, Our Praises, at eventide and at break of day,

19. And the birds gathered (in assemblies): all with him did turn (to Allah).

20. We strengthened his kingdom, and gave him wisdom and sound judgment in speech and decision.

21. Has the Story of the Disputants reached you? Behold, they climbed over the wall of the private chamber;

22. When they entered the presence of David, and he was terrified of them, they said:

مَا يَقُولُونَ وَاذْكُرْ عَبْدَنَا دَاوُدَ

ذَا الْأَيْدِ إِنَّهُ أَوَّابٌ ۝ إِنَّا سَخَّرْنَا

الْجِبَالَ مَعَهُ يُسَبِّحْنَ بِالْعَشِيِّ

وَالْإِشْرَاقِ ۝ وَالطَّيْرَ مَحْشُورَةً

كُلٌّ لَهُ أَوَّابٌ ۝ وَشَدَدْنَا مُلْكَهُ

وَآتَيْنَاهُ الْحِكْمَةَ وَفَصْلَ الْخِطَابِ ۝

وَهَلْ أَتَاكَ نَبَؤُا الْخَصْمِ إِذْ

تَسَوَّرُوا الْمِحْرَابَ ۝ إِذْ دَخَلُوا عَلَى

دَاوُدَ فَفَزِعَ مِنْهُمْ قَالُوا لَا

12. Before them (were many who) rejected Apostles, - the People of Noah, and 'Ad, and Pharaoh the lord of Stakes,

13. And Thamud, and the People of Lut, and the Companions of the Wood; - such were the Confederates.

14. Not one (of them) but rejected the Apostles, but My Punishment came justly and inevitably (on them).

15. These (today) only wait for a single mighty Blast, which (when it comes) will brook no delay.

16. They say: "Our Lord! Hasten to us our sentence (even) before the Day of Account!"

17. Have patience at

الْاَحْزَابُ ۞ كَذَّبَتْ قَبْلَهُمْ قَوْمُ

نُوحٍ وَّعَادٌ وَّفِرْعَوْنُ ذُو الْاَوْتَادِ ۞

وَثَمُوْدُ وَقَوْمُ لُوْطٍ وَّاَصْحٰبُ لْئَيْكَةِ ۫

اُولٰٓئِكَ الْاَحْزَابُ ۞ اِنْ كُلٌّ اِلَّا

كَذَّبَ الرُّسُلَ فَحَقَّ عِقَابِ ۞

وَمَا يَنْظُرُ هٰٓؤُلَآءِ اِلَّا صَيْحَةً

وَّاحِدَةً مَّا لَهَا مِنْ فَوَاقٍ ۞

وَقَالُوْا رَبَّنَا عَجِّلْ لَّنَا قِطَّنَا

قَبْلَ يَوْمِ الْحِسَابِ ۞ اِصْبِرْ عَلٰى

among the people of these latter days: this is nothing but a made-up tale!"

8. "What! Has the Message been sent to him - (of all persons) among us?"...but they are in doubt concerning My (Own) Message! No, they have not yet tasted My Punishment!

9. Or have they the treasures of the mercy of your Lord, - the Exalted in Power, the Grantor of Bounties without measure?

10. Or have they the dominion of the heavens and the earth and all between? If so, let them mount up with the ropes and means (to reach that end)!

11. They are but a host of confederates and they will be put to flight.

فِى الْمِلَّةِ الْاٰخِرَةِ ۖ اِنْ هٰذَاۤ اِلَّآ

اخْتِلَاقٌ ۚ ءَ اُنْزِلَ عَلَيْهِ الذِّكْرُ

مِنْ بَيْنِنَا ؕ بَلْ هُمْ فِىْ شَكٍّ

مِّنْ ذِكْرِىْ ۚ بَلْ لَّمَّا يَذُوْقُوْا

عَذَابِ ۞ اَمْ عِنْدَهُمْ خَزَآئِنُ

رَحْمَةِ رَبِّكَ الْعَزِيْزِ الْوَهَّابِ ۚ اَمْ

لَهُمْ مُّلْكُ السَّمٰوٰتِ وَالْاَرْضِ وَمَا

بَيْنَهُمَا ۫ فَلْيَرْتَقُوْا فِى الْاَسْبَابِ ۞

جُنْدٌ مَّا هُنَالِكَ مَهْزُوْمٌ مِّنَ

3. How many generations before them did We destroy? In the end they cried (for mercy) - when there was no longer time for being saved!

4. So they wonder that a warner has come to them from among themselves! And the unbelievers say, "This is a sorcerer telling lies!"

5. "Has he made the gods (all) into one Allah? Truly this is a wonderful thing!"

6. And the leader among them go away (impatiently), (saying), "Walk you away, and remain constant to your gods! For this is truly a thing designed (against you)!"

7. "We never heard (the like) of this

كَمْ اَهْلَكْنَا مِنْ قَبْلِهِمْ مِّنْ قَرْنٍ

فَنَادَوْا وَّلَاتَ حِيْنَ مَنَاصٍ ۝

وَعَجِبُوْٓا اَنْ جَآءَهُمْ مُّنْذِرٌ مِّنْهُمْ

وَقَالَ الْكٰفِرُوْنَ هٰذَا سٰحِرٌ

كَذَّابٌ ۚ ۝ اَجَعَلَ الْاٰلِهَةَ اِلٰهًا

وَّاحِدًا ۖ اِنَّ هٰذَا لَشَيْءٌ عُجَابٌ ۝

وَانْطَلَقَ الْمَلَاُ مِنْهُمْ اَنِ امْشُوْا

وَاصْبِرُوْا عَلٰٓى اٰلِهَتِكُمْ ۚ اِنَّ هٰذَا

لَشَيْءٌ يُّرَادُ ۝ مَا سَمِعْنَا بِهٰذَا

it descends into the open space before them, evil will be the morning for those who were warned (and heeded not)!

178. So turn you away from them for a little while,

179. And watch (how they fare) and they soon shall see (how you fare).

180. Glory to your Lord, the Lord of Honour and Power! (He is free) from what they ascribe (to Him)!

181. And Peace on the Apostles!

182. And Praise to Allah, the Lord and Cherisher of the Worlds.

Saad

Bismillahir-Rahmanir-Rahim

1.   Saad: by the Qur'an, Full of Admonition: (this is the Truth).

2.   But the unbelievers (are steeped) in self-glory and opposition.

نَزَلَ بِسَاحَتِهِمْ فَسَآءَ صَبَاحُ

الْمُنْذَرِينَ ۝ وَتَوَلَّ عَنْهُمْ حَتّٰى

حِينٍ ۝ وَأَبْصِرْ فَسَوْفَ يُبْصِرُونَ ۝

سُبْحَانَ رَبِّكَ رَبِّ الْعِزَّةِ عَمَّا

يَصِفُونَ ۝ وَسَلَامٌ عَلَى الْمُرْسَلِينَ ۝

وَالْحَمْدُ لِلّٰهِ رَبِّ الْعَالَمِينَ ۝

سُورَةُ صۤ مَكِّيَّةٌ اٰيَاتُهَا ۸۸ رُكُوعَاتُهَا ۵

بِسْمِ اللّٰهِ الرَّحْمٰنِ الرَّحِيمِ

صۤ وَالْقُرْاٰنِ ذِى الذِّكْرِ ۝ بَلِ

الَّذِينَ كَفَرُوا فِى عِزَّةٍ وَشِقَاقٍ ۝

were those who said,

168. "If only we had had before us a Message from those of old,"

169. "We should certainly have been servants of Allah, sincere (and devoted)!" **170.** But (now that the Qur'an has come), they reject it: but soon will they know!

171. Already has Our Word been passed before (this) to Our servants sent (by Us),

172. That they would certainly be assisted, **173.** And that Our forces, - they surely must conquer.

174. So turn you away from them for a little while, **175.** And watch them (how they fare), and they soon shall see (how you farest)!

176. Do they wish (indeed) to hurry on Our Punishment?

177. But when

كَانُوْا لَيَقُوْلُوْنَ ۟ لَوْ اَنَّ عِنْدَنَا

ذِكْرًا مِّنَ الْاَوَّلِيْنَ ۟ لَكُنَّا عِبَادَ

اللّٰهِ الْمُخْلَصِيْنَ ۟ فَكَفَرُوْا بِهٖ

فَسَوْفَ يَعْلَمُوْنَ ۟ وَلَقَدْ سَبَقَتْ

كَلِمَتُنَا لِعِبَادِنَا الْمُرْسَلِيْنَ ۟ اِنَّهُمْ

لَهُمُ الْمَنْصُوْرُوْنَ ۟ وَاِنَّ جُنْدَنَا

لَهُمُ الْغٰلِبُوْنَ ۟ فَتَوَلَّ عَنْهُمْ حَتّٰى

حِيْنٍ ۟ وَّاَبْصِرْهُمْ فَسَوْفَ يُبْصِرُوْنَ

اَفَبِعَذَابِنَا يَسْتَعْجِلُوْنَ ۟ فَاِذَا

a blood-relationship between Him and the Jinns: but the Jinns know (quite well) that they have indeed to appear (before his Judgment-Seat)! **159.** Glory to Allah! (He is free) from the things they ascribe (to Him)! **160.** Not (so do) the servants of Allah, sincere and devoted. **161.** For, verily, neither you nor those you worship -

162. Can lead (any) into temptation concerning Allah,

163. Except such as are (themselves) going to the blazing Fire!

164. (The Angels say): "Every one of us but has a place appointed;"

165. "And we are verily ranged in ranks (for service);" **166.** "And we are verily those who declare (Allah's) glory!" **167.** And there

بَيْنَهُ وَبَيْنَ الْجِنَّةِ نَسَبًا ۚ وَلَقَدْ

عَلِمَتِ الْجِنَّةُ إِنَّهُمْ لَمُحْضَرُوْنَ ۞

سُبْحٰنَ اللّٰهِ عَمَّا يَصِفُوْنَ ۞ إِلَّا

عِبَادَ اللّٰهِ الْمُخْلَصِيْنَ ۞ فَإِنَّكُمْ

وَمَا تَعْبُدُوْنَ ۞ مَا أَنْتُمْ عَلَيْهِ

بِفٰتِنِيْنَ ۞ إِلَّا مَنْ هُوَ صَالِ

الْجَحِيْمِ ۞ وَمَا مِنَّا إِلَّا لَهُ مَقَامٌ

مَّعْلُوْمٌ ۞ وَّإِنَّا لَنَحْنُ الصَّآفُّوْنَ ۞

وَإِنَّا لَنَحْنُ الْمُسَبِّحُوْنَ ۞ وَإِنْ

149. Now ask them their opinion: is it that your Lord has (only) daughters, and they have sons? -

150. Or that We created the Angels female, and they are witnesses (thereto)?

151. Behold, that they say, from their own invention,

152. "Allah has begotten children"? But they are liars!

153. Did He (then) choose daughters rather than sons?

154. What is the matter with you? How judge you?

155. Will you not then receive admonition?

156. Or have you an authority manifest?

157. Then bring you your Book (of authority) if you be truthful!

158. And they have invented

فَاسْتَفْتِهِمْ اَلِرَبِّكَ الْبَنَاتُ وَلَهُمُ

الْبَنُونَ ۝ اَمْ خَلَقْنَا الْمَلٰئِكَةَ اِنَاثًا

وَهُمْ شٰهِدُونَ ۝ اَلَا اِنَّهُمْ مِّنْ

اِفْكِهِمْ لَيَقُولُونَ ۝ وَلَدَ اللّٰهُ

وَاِنَّهُمْ لَكٰذِبُونَ ۝ اَصْطَفَى الْبَنَاتِ

عَلَى الْبَنِينَ ۝ مَا لَكُمْ كَيْفَ

تَحْكُمُونَ ۝ اَفَلَا تَذَكَّرُونَ ۝ اَمْ لَكُمْ

سُلْطٰنٌ مُّبِينٌ ۝ فَأْتُوا بِكِتٰبِكُمْ

اِنْ كُنْتُمْ صٰدِقِينَ ۝ وَجَعَلُوا

(fully) laden,

141. He (agreed to) cast lots, and he was condemned:

142. Then the big Fish did swallow him, and he had done acts worthy of blame.

143. Had it not been that he (repented and) glorified Allah,

144. He would certainly have remained inside the Fish till the Day of Resurrection.

145. But We cast him forth on the naked shore in a state of sickness,

146. And We caused to grow, over him, a spreading plant of the gourd kind.

147. And We sent him (on a mission) to a hundred thousand (men) or more.

148. And they believed; so We permitted them to enjoy (their life) for a while.

الْمَشْحُونِ ۝ فَسَاهَمَ فَكَانَ مِنَ

الْمُدْحَضِينَ ۝ فَالْتَقَمَهُ الْحُوتُ

وَهُوَ مُلِيمٌ ۝ فَلَوْ لَآ أَنَّهُ كَانَ

مِنَ الْمُسَبِّحِينَ ۝ لَلَبِثَ فِى بَطْنِهِ

إِلَىٰ يَوْمِ يُبْعَثُونَ ۝ فَنَبَذْنٰهُ بِالْعَرَآءِ

وَهُوَ سَقِيمٌ ۝ وَأَنْبَتْنَا عَلَيْهِ

شَجَرَةً مِّنْ يَّقْطِينٍ ۝ وَأَرْسَلْنٰهُ

إِلَىٰ مِائَةِ أَلْفٍ أَوْ يَزِيدُونَ ۝

فَأَمَنُوا فَمَتَّعْنٰهُمْ إِلَىٰ حِينٍ ۝

131. Thus indeed do We reward those who do right.

132. For he was one of our believing servants.

133. So also was Lut among those sent (by Us).

134. Behold, We delivered him and his adherents, all

135. Except an old woman who was among those who lagged behind:

136. Then We destroyed the rest.

137. Verily, you pass by their (sites), by day -

138. And by night: will you not understand?

139. So also was Jonah among those sent (by Us).

140. When he ran away (like a slave from captivity) to the ship

إِنَّا كَذٰلِكَ نَجْزِى الْمُحْسِنِيْنَ ۝

إِنَّهٗ مِنْ عِبَادِنَا الْمُؤْمِنِيْنَ ۝

وَإِنَّ لُوْطًا لَّمِنَ الْمُرْسَلِيْنَ ۝

إِذْ نَجَّيْنٰهُ وَأَهْلَهٗ أَجْمَعِيْنَ ۝

إِلَّا عَجُوْزًا فِى الْغٰبِرِيْنَ ۝ ثُمَّ

دَمَّرْنَا الْاٰخَرِيْنَ ۝ وَإِنَّكُمْ لَتَمُرُّوْنَ

عَلَيْهِمْ مُّصْبِحِيْنَ ۝ وَبِالَّيْلِ ۚ أَفَلَا

تَعْقِلُوْنَ ۝ وَإِنَّ يُوْنُسَ لَمِنَ

الْمُرْسَلِيْنَ ۝ إِذْ أَبَقَ إِلَى الْفُلْكِ

those who do right.

122. For they were two of our believing servants.

123. So also was Elias among those sent (by Us).

124. Behold, he said to his people, "Will you not fear (Allah)?"

125. "Will you call upon Baal and forsake the Best of Creators," -

126. "Allah, your Lord and Cherisher and the Lord and Cherisher of your fathers of old?"

127. But they rejected him, and they will certainly be called up (for punishment), -

128. Except the sincere and devoted servants of Allah (among them).   **129.** And We left (this blessing) for him among generations (to come) in later times:

130. "Peace and salutation to such as Elias!"

الْمُحْسِنِينَ ۞ اِنَّهُمَا مِنْ عِبَادِنَا

الْمُؤْمِنِينَ ۞ وَاِنَّ اِلْيَاسَ لَمِنَ

الْمُرْسَلِينَ ۞ اِذْ قَالَ لِقَوْمِهٖٓ اَلَا

تَتَّقُونَ ۞ اَتَدْعُونَ بَعْلًا وَّتَذَرُونَ

اَحْسَنَ الْخَالِقِينَ ۞ اللّٰهَ رَبَّكُمْ

وَرَبَّ اٰبَآئِكُمُ الْاَوَّلِينَ ۞ فَكَذَّبُوْهُ

فَاِنَّهُمْ لَمُحْضَرُوْنَ ۞ اِلَّا عِبَادَ اللّٰهِ

الْمُخْلَصِينَ ۞ وَتَرَكْنَا عَلَيْهِ فِي

الْاٰخِرِينَ ۞ سَلٰمٌ عَلٰىٓ اِلْ يَاسِينَ ۞

their progeny are (some) that do right, and (some) that obvious-ly do wrong, to their own souls.

114. Again (of old) We bestowed Our favour on Moses and Aaron,

115. And We delivered them and their people from (their) Great Calamity;

116. And We helped them, so they were victorious;

117. And We gave them the Book which helps to make things clear;

118. And We guided them to the Straight Way.

119. And We left (this blessing) for them among generations (to come) in later times:

120. "Peace and salutation to Moses and Aaron!"

121. Thus indeed do We reward

ذُرِّيَّتِهِمَا مُحْسِنٌ وَّظَالِمٌ لِّنَفْسِهٖ

مُبِيْنٌ ۞ وَلَقَدْ مَنَنَّا عَلٰى مُوْسٰى

وَهٰرُوْنَ ۞ وَنَجَّيْنٰهُمَا وَقَوْمَهُمَا

مِنَ الْكَرْبِ الْعَظِيْمِ ۞ وَنَصَرْنٰهُمْ

فَكَانُوْا هُمُ الْغٰلِبِيْنَ ۞ وَاٰتَيْنٰهُمَا

الْكِتٰبَ الْمُسْتَبِيْنَ ۞ وَهَدَيْنٰهُمَا

الصِّرَاطَ الْمُسْتَقِيْمَ ۞ وَتَرَكْنَا عَلَيْهِمَا

فِى الْاٰخِرِيْنَ ۞ سَلٰمٌ عَلٰى مُوْسٰى

وَهٰرُوْنَ ۞ اِنَّا كَذٰلِكَ نَجْزِى

105. "You have already fulfilled the dream!" - thus indeed do We reward those who do right.

106. For this was obviously a trial -

107. And We ransomed him with a momentous sacrifice:

108. And We left (this blessing) for him among generations (to come) in later times:

109. "Peace and salutation to Abraham!"

110. Thus indeed do We reward those who do right.

111. For he was one of our believing servants.

112. And We gave him the good news of Isaac - a Prophet, - one of the Righteous.

113. We blessed him and Isaac: but of

قَدْ صَدَّقْتَ الرُّءْيَا ۚ إِنَّا كَذٰلِكَ

نَجْزِى الْمُحْسِنِيْنَ ۝ إِنَّ هٰذَا

لَهُوَ الْبَلٰٓؤُا الْمُبِيْنُ ۝ وَفَدَيْنٰهُ

بِذِبْحٍ عَظِيْمٍ ۝ وَتَرَكْنَا عَلَيْهِ فِى

الْاٰخِرِيْنَ ۝ سَلٰمٌ عَلٰى اِبْرٰهِيْمَ ۝

كَذٰلِكَ نَجْزِى الْمُحْسِنِيْنَ ۝ اِنَّهُ

مِنْ عِبَادِنَا الْمُؤْمِنِيْنَ ۝ وَبَشَّرْنٰهُ

بِاِسْحٰقَ نَبِيًّا مِّنَ الصّٰلِحِيْنَ ۝

وَبٰرَكْنَا عَلَيْهِ وَعَلٰى اِسْحٰقَ ۚ وَمِنْ

will go to my Lord! He will surely guide me!"

100. "O my Lord! Grant me a righteous (son)!"

101. So We gave him the good news of a boy ready to suffer and forbear.

102. Then, when (the son) reached (the age of) (serious) work with him, he said: "O my son! I see in dream that I offer you in sacrifice: now say what is your view!" (The son) said: "O my father! Do as you are commanded: you will find me, if Allah so wills, one practising patience and constancy!"

103. So when they had both submitted their wills (to Allah), and he had laid him prostrate on his forehead (for sacrifice),

104. We called out to him "O Abraham!"

ذَاهِبٌ اِلٰى رَبِّيْ سَيَهْدِيْنِ ۹۹ رَبِّ

هَبْ لِيْ مِنَ الصّٰلِحِيْنَ ۱۰۰ فَبَشَّرْنٰهُ

بِغُلٰمٍ حَلِيْمٍ ۱۰۱ فَلَمَّا بَلَغَ مَعَهُ

السَّعْىَ قَالَ يٰبُنَيَّ اِنِّيْٓ اَرٰى فِى

الْمَنَامِ اَنِّيْٓ اَذْبَحُكَ فَانْظُرْ مَا ذَا

تَرٰى ۗ قَالَ يٰٓاَبَتِ افْعَلْ مَا تُؤْمَرُ ۗ

سَتَجِدُنِيْٓ اِنْ شَآءَ اللّٰهُ مِنَ

الصّٰبِرِيْنَ ۱۰۲ فَلَمَّآ اَسْلَمَا وَتَلَّهٗ

لِلْجَبِيْنِ ۱۰۳ وَنَادَيْنٰهُ اَنْ يّٰٓاِبْرٰهِيْمُ ۱۰۴

and departed.

91. Then did he turn to their gods and said, "Will you not eat (of the offerings before you)?" ...

92. "What is the matter with you that you speak not (intelligently)?" **93.** Then did he turn upon them, striking (them) with the right hand. **94.** Then came (the worshippers) with hurried steps, and faced (him).

95. He said: "Worship you that which you have (yourselves) carved?" **96.** "But Allah has created you and your handwork!"

97. They said, "Prepare him a furnace, and throw him into the blazing fire!" **98.** (This failing), they then devised a plot against him, but We made them the ones most humiliated! **99.** He said: "I

مُدْبِرِينَ ۝ فَرَاغَ اِلٰۤى اٰلِهَتِهِمْ

فَقَالَ اَلَا تَاْكُلُونَ ۝ مَا لَكُمْ لَا

تَنْطِقُونَ ۝ فَرَاغَ عَلَيْهِمْ ضَرْبًا

بِالْيَمِينِ ۝ فَاَقْبَلُوۤا اِلَيْهِ يَزِفُّونَ ۝

قَالَ اَتَعْبُدُونَ مَا تَنْحِتُونَ ۝

وَاللّٰهُ خَلَقَكُمْ وَمَا تَعْمَلُونَ ۝

قَالُوا ابْنُوا لَهُ بُنْيَانًا فَاَلْقُوهُ

فِى الْجَحِيمِ ۝ فَاَرَادُوا بِهِ كَيْدًا

فَجَعَلْنٰهُمُ الْاَسْفَلِينَ ۝ وَقَالَ اِنِّى

those who do right.

81. For he was one of Our believing servants.

82. Then the rest We overwhelmed in the Flood.

83. Verily among those who followed his way was Abraham.

84. Behold! He approached his Lord with a sound heart.

85. Behold! He said to his father and to his people, "What is that which you worship?"

86. "Is it a falsehood - gods other than Allah - that you desire?"

87. "Then what is your idea about the Lord of the Worlds?"

88. Then did he cast a glance at the stars.

89. And he said, "I am indeed sick (at heart)!"

90. So they turned away from him,

الْمُحْسِنِينَ ۝ إِنَّهُ مِنْ عِبَادِنَا

الْمُؤْمِنِينَ ۝ ثُمَّ أَغْرَقْنَا الْأَخَرِينَ ۝

وَإِنَّ مِنْ شِيعَتِهِ لَإِبْرَٰهِيمَ ۝

إِذْ جَآءَ رَبَّهُ بِقَلْبٍ سَلِيمٍ ۝

إِذْ قَالَ لِأَبِيهِ وَقَوْمِهِ مَاذَا

تَعْبُدُونَ ۝ أَئِفْكًا ءَالِهَةً دُونَ

اللَّهِ تُرِيدُونَ ۝ فَمَا ظَنُّكُم بِرَبِّ

الْعَٰلَمِينَ ۝ فَنَظَرَ نَظْرَةً فِي النُّجُومِ ۝

فَقَالَ إِنِّي سَقِيمٌ ۝ فَتَوَلَّوْا عَنْهُ

We sent aforetime, among them, (Apostles) to admonish them; -

73.   Then see what was the end of those who were admonished (but heeded not), -

74.   Except the sincere (and devoted) servants of Allah.

75.   (In the days of old), Noah cried to Us, and We are the best to hear prayer.

76. And We delivered him and his people from the great Calamity,

77.   And made his progeny to endure (on this earth)

78.   And We left (this blessing) for him among generations to come in later times:

79.   "Peace and salutation to Noah among the nations!"

80.   Thus indeed do We reward

أَرْسَلْنَا فِيهِمْ مُّنْذِرِينَ ۝ فَانْظُرْ

كَيْفَ كَانَ عَاقِبَةُ الْمُنْذَرِينَ ۝

إِلَّا عِبَادَ اللّٰهِ الْمُخْلَصِينَ ۝ وَلَقَدْ

نَادَانَا نُوحٌ فَلَنِعْمَ الْمُجِيبُونَ

۝ وَنَجَّيْنَاهُ وَأَهْلَهُ مِنَ الْكَرْبِ

الْعَظِيمِ ۝ وَجَعَلْنَا ذُرِّيَّتَهُ هُمُ

الْبَاقِينَ ۝ وَتَرَكْنَا عَلَيْهِ فِي

الْآخِرِينَ ۝ سَلَامٌ عَلَىٰ نُوحٍ فِي

الْعَالَمِينَ ۝ إِنَّا كَذٰلِكَ نَجْزِى

that springs out of the bottom of Hell-Fire:

65. The shoots of its fruit-stalks are like the heads of devils:

66. Truly they will eat thereof and fill their bellies therewith.

67. Then on top of that they will be given a mixture made of boiling water.

68. Then shall their return be to the (Blazing) Fire.

69. Truly they found their fathers on the wrong Path;

70. So they (too) were rushed down on their footsteps!

71. And truly before them, many of the ancients went astray;

72. But

تَخْرُجُ فِىْ اَصْلِ الْجَحِيْمِ ۞

طَلْعُهَا كَاَنَّهٗ رُءُوْسُ الشَّيٰطِيْنِ ۞

فَاِنَّهُمْ لَاٰكِلُوْنَ مِنْهَا فَمَالِـٔوْنَ

مِنْهَا الْبُطُوْنَ ۞ ثُمَّ اِنَّ لَهُمْ عَلَيْهَا

لَشَوْبًا مِّنْ حَمِيْمٍ ۞ ثُمَّ اِنَّ

مَرْجِعَهُمْ لَاِلَى الْجَحِيْمِ ۞ اِنَّهُمْ

اَلْفَوْا اٰبَآءَهُمْ ضَآلِّيْنَ ۞ فَهُمْ

عَلٰٓى اٰثَارِهِمْ يُهْرَعُوْنَ ۞ وَلَقَدْ

ضَلَّ قَبْلَهُمْ اَكْثَرُ الْاَوَّلِيْنَ ۞ وَلَقَدْ

56. He said: "By Allah! You were little short of bringing me to perdition!"

57. "Had it not been for the Grace of my Lord, I should certainly have been among those brought (there)!

58. "Is it (the case) that we shall not die,"

59. "Except our first death, and that we shall not be punished?"

60. Verily this is the supreme achievement!"

61. For the like of this let all strive, who wish to strive.

62. Is that the better entertainment or the tree of Zaqqum?

63. For We have truly made it (as) a trial for the wrong-doers.

64. For it is a tree

قَالَ تَاللّٰهِ إِنْ كِدْتَّ لَتُرْدِينِ ۩

وَلَوْلَا نِعْمَةُ رَبِّي لَكُنْتُ مِنَ

الْمُحْضَرِينَ ۩ أَفَمَا نَحْنُ بِمَيِّتِينَ ۩

إِلَّا مَوْتَتَنَا الْأُولَىٰ وَمَا نَحْنُ

بِمُعَذَّبِينَ ۩ إِنَّ هٰذَا لَهُوَ الْفَوْزُ

الْعَظِيمُ ۩ لِمِثْلِ هٰذَا فَلْيَعْمَلِ

الْعَامِلُونَ ۩ أَذٰلِكَ خَيْرٌ نُزُلًا أَمْ

شَجَرَةُ الزَّقُّومِ ۩ إِنَّا جَعَلْنَاهَا

فِتْنَةً لِّلظَّالِمِينَ ۩ إِنَّهَا شَجَرَةٌ

48. And besides them will be chaste women, restraining their glances, with big eyes (of wonder and beauty).

49. As if they were (delicate) eggs closely guarded.

50. Then they will turn to one another and question one another.

51. One of them will start the talk and say: "I had an intimate companion (on the earth),"

52. "Who used to say, 'What! Are you among those who bear witness to the Truth (of the Message)?"

53. "'When we die and become dust and bones, shall we indeed receive rewards and punishments?'"

54. (A voice) said: "Would you like to look down?"

55. He looked down and saw him in the midst of the Fire.

وَعِنْدَهُمْ قٰصِرٰتُ الطَّرْفِ عِيْنٌ ۙ ۝

كَاَنَّهُنَّ بَيْضٌ مَّكْنُوْنٌ ۝ فَاَقْبَلَ

بَعْضُهُمْ عَلٰى بَعْضٍ يَّتَسَآءَلُوْنَ ۝

قَالَ قَآئِلٌ مِّنْهُمْ اِنِّيْ كَانَ لِيْ

قَرِيْنٌ ۙ ۝ يَّقُوْلُ اَءِنَّكَ لَمِنَ

الْمُصَدِّقِيْنَ ۝ ءَاِذَا مِتْنَا وَكُنَّا

تُرَابًا وَّعِظَامًا ءَاِنَّا لَمَدِيْنُوْنَ ۝

قَالَ هَلْ اَنْتُمْ مُّطَّلِعُوْنَ ۝

فَاطَّلَعَ فَرَاٰهُ فِيْ سَوَآءِ الْجَحِيْمِ ۝

and he confirms (the Message of) the Apostles (before him).

38. You shall indeed taste of the grievous Chastisement; -

39. But it will be no more than the retribution of (the Evil) that you have wrought; -

40. But the sincere (and devoted) servants of Allah,-

41. For them is a Sustenance determined,

42. Fruits (Delights); and they (shall enjoy) honour and dignity,

43. In Gardens of Felicity,

44. Facing each other on thrones (of Dignity):

45. Round will be passed to them a cup from a clear-flowing fountain,

46. Crystal-white, of a taste delicious to those who drink (thereof),

47. Free from headiness; nor will they suffer intoxication therefrom.

وَصَدَّقَ الْمُرْسَلِيْنَ ۩ اِنَّكُمْ لَذَآئِقُوا

الْعَذَابِ الْاَلِيْمِ ۩ وَمَا تُجْزَوْنَ اِلَّا

مَا كُنْتُمْ تَعْمَلُوْنَ ۩ اِلَّا عِبَادَ اللّٰهِ

الْمُخْلَصِيْنَ ۩ اُولٰٓئِكَ لَهُمْ رِزْقٌ

مَّعْلُوْمٌ ۩ فَوَاكِهُ ۚ وَهُمْ مُّكْرَمُوْنَ ۩

فِيْ جَنّٰتِ النَّعِيْمِ ۩ عَلٰى سُرُرٍ

مُّتَقٰبِلِيْنَ ۩ يُطَافُ عَلَيْهِمْ بِكَأْسٍ مِّنْ

مَّعِيْنٍ ۩ بَيْضَآءَ لَذَّةٍ لِّلشّٰرِبِيْنَ ۩

لَا فِيْهَا غَوْلٌ وَّلَا هُمْ عَنْهَا يُنْزَفُوْنَ ۩

any authority over you. No, it was you who were a people in obstinate rebellion!"

31. "So now has been proved true, against us, the word of our Lord that we shall indeed (have to) taste (the punishment of our sins)."

32. "We led you astray: for truly we were ourselves astray."

33. Truly, that Day, they will (all) share in the Chastisement.

34. Verily that is how We shall deal with Sinners.

35. For they, when they were told that there is no god except Allah, would puff themselves up with Pride,

36. And say: "What! Shall we give up our gods for the sake of a Poet possessed?"

37. No! He has come with the (very) Truth,

مِّنْ سُلْطَانٍ ۚ بَلْ كُنْتُمْ قَوْمًا

طَاغِينَ ۝ فَحَقَّ عَلَيْنَا قَوْلُ رَبِّنَا ۖ

إِنَّا لَذَائِقُونَ ۝ فَأَغْوَيْنَاكُمْ إِنَّا كُنَّا

غَاوِينَ ۝ فَإِنَّهُمْ يَوْمَئِذٍ فِي الْعَذَابِ

مُشْتَرِكُونَ ۝ إِنَّا كَذَٰلِكَ نَفْعَلُ

بِالْمُجْرِمِينَ ۝ إِنَّهُمْ كَانُوا إِذَا قِيلَ

لَهُمْ لَا إِلَٰهَ إِلَّا اللَّهُ يَسْتَكْبِرُونَ ۝

وَيَقُولُونَ أَئِنَّا لَتَارِكُوا آلِهَتِنَا

لِشَاعِرٍ مَّجْنُونٍ ۝ بَلْ جَاءَ بِالْحَقِّ

and their wives, and the things they worshipped -

23. "Besides Allah, and lead them to the Way to the (fierce) Fire."

24. "But stop them, for they must be asked:"

25. "'What is the matter with you that you help not each other?'"

26. No, but that day they shall submit (to Judgment);

27. And they will turn to one another, and question one another.

28. They will say: "It was you who used to come to us from the right hand (of power and authority)!"

29. They will reply: "No, you yourselves had no Faith!"

30. "Nor had we

وَاَزْوَاجَهُمْ وَمَا كَانُوْا يَعْبُدُوْنَ ۞

مِنْ دُوْنِ اللّٰهِ فَاهْدُوْهُمْ اِلٰى

صِرَاطِ الْجَحِيْمِ ۞ وَقِفُوْهُمْ اِنَّهُمْ

مَّسْئُوْلُوْنَ ۞ مَا لَكُمْ لَا تَنَاصَرُوْنَ

بَلْ هُمُ الْيَوْمَ مُسْتَسْلِمُوْنَ ۞ وَاَقْبَلَ

بَعْضُهُمْ عَلٰى بَعْضٍ يَّتَسَآءَلُوْنَ ۞

قَالُوْا اِنَّكُمْ كُنْتُمْ تَأْتُوْنَنَا عَنِ

الْيَمِيْنِ ۞ قَالُوْا بَلْ لَّمْ تَكُوْنُوْا

مُؤْمِنِيْنَ ۞ وَمَا كَانَ لَنَا عَلَيْكُمْ

a Sign, turn it to mockery,

15. And say, "This is nothing but evident sorcery!"

16. "What! When we die, and become dust and bones, shall we (then) be raised up (again)?"

17. "And also our fathers of old?"

18. Say you: "Yes, and you shall then be humiliated (on account of your evil)."

19. Then it will be a single (compelling) cry; and behold, they will begin to see!

20. They will say, "Ah! Woe to us! This is the Day of Judgment!"

21. (A voice will say,) "This is the Day of Sorting Out, whose truth you (once) denied!"

22. "Bring you up", it shall be said, "The wrong-doers

اٰيَةً يَّسْتَسْخِرُوْنَ ۖ وَقَالُوْۤا اِنْ

هٰذَاۤ اِلَّا سِحْرٌ مُّبِيْنٌ ۖ ءَاِذَا مِتْنَا

وَكُنَّا تُرَابًا وَّعِظَامًا ءَاِنَّا لَمَبْعُوْثُوْنَ ۖ

اَوَ اٰبَآؤُنَا الْاَوَّلُوْنَ ۖ قُلْ نَعَمْ

وَاَنْتُمْ دَاخِرُوْنَ ۖ فَاِنَّمَا هِيَ زَجْرَةٌ

وَّاحِدَةٌ فَاِذَا هُمْ يَنْظُرُوْنَ ۖ وَقَالُوْا

يٰوَيْلَنَا هٰذَا يَوْمُ الدِّيْنِ ۖ هٰذَا

يَوْمُ الْفَصْلِ الَّذِيْ كُنْتُمْ بِهٖ

تُكَذِّبُوْنَ ۖ اُحْشُرُوا الَّذِيْنَ ظَلَمُوْا

all obstinate rebellious Satans.

8. (So) they should not strain their ears in the direction of the Exalted Assembly but be cast away from every side,

9. Repulsed, for they are under a perpetual Chastisement,

10. Except such as snatch away something by stealth, and they are pursued by a flaming fire, of piercing brightness.

11. Just ask their opinion: are they the more difficult to create, or the (other) beings We have created? Them have We created out of a sticky clay!

12. Truly do you marvel, while they ridicule,

13. And, when they are admonished, pay no heed, -

14. And, when they see

مِنْ كُلِّ شَيْطٰنٍ مَّارِدٍ ۚ لَّا يَسَّمَّعُوْنَ

اِلَى الْمَلَاِ الْاَعْلٰى وَ يُقْذَفُوْنَ مِنْ

كُلِّ جَانِبٍ ۚ دُحُوْرًا وَّ لَهُمْ عَذَابٌ

وَّاصِبٌ ۚ اِلَّا مَنْ خَطِفَ الْخَطْفَةَ

فَاَتْبَعَهٗ شِهَابٌ ثَاقِبٌ ۚ فَاسْتَفْتِهِمْ

اَهُمْ اَشَدُّ خَلْقًا اَمْ مَّنْ خَلَقْنَا ۚ

اِنَّا خَلَقْنٰهُمْ مِّنْ طِيْنٍ لَّازِبٍ ۚ

بَلْ عَجِبْتَ وَ يَسْخَرُوْنَ ۚ وَ اِذَا

ذُكِّرُوْا لَا يَذْكُرُوْنَ ۚ وَ اِذَا رَاَوْا

"be", and it is!

83. So Glory to Him in Whose hands is the dominion of all things: and to Him will you be all brought back.

As-Saffat
(Those Ranged in Ranks)
Bismillahir-Rahmanir-Rahim

1. By those who range themselves in ranks, **2.** And so are strong in repelling (evil), **3.** And thus proclaim the Message (of Allah)! **4.** Verily, verily, your Allah is One! - **5.** Lord of the heavens and of the earth and all between them, and Lord of every point at the rising of the sun!

6. We have indeed decked the lower heaven with beauty (in) the stars, - **7.** (For beauty) and for guard against

يَقُولُ لَهُ كُنْ فَيَكُونُ ۝ فَسُبْحَٰنَ

الَّذِى بِيَدِهِ مَلَكُوتُ كُلِّ شَىْءٍ

وَإِلَيْهِ تُرْجَعُونَ ۝

بِسْمِ اللهِ الرَّحْمٰنِ الرَّحِيمِ

وَالصّٰٓفّٰتِ صَفًّا ۝ فَالزّٰجِرٰتِ زَجْرًا ۝

فَالتّٰلِيٰتِ ذِكْرًا ۝ إِنَّ إِلٰهَكُمْ لَوَاحِدٌ ۝

رَّبُّ السّمٰوٰتِ وَالْأَرْضِ وَمَا بَيْنَهُمَا

وَرَبُّ الْمَشَارِقِ ۝ إِنَّا زَيَّنَّا السَّمَآءَ

الدُّنْيَا بِزِينَةٍ الْكَوَاكِبِ ۝ وَحِفْظًا

can give life to (dry) bones and decomposed ones (at that)?"

79. Say, "He will give them life Who created them for the first time! For He is Well-Versed in every kind of creation! -

80. "The same Who produces for you fire out of the green tree, when behold! you kindle therewith (your own fires)!"

81. "Is not He Who created the heavens and the earth able to create the like thereof?" - Yes, indeed! for He is the Creator Supreme, of skill and knowledge (infinite)!

82. Verily, when He intends a thing, His Command is,

يُّحْيِ الْعِظَامَ وَهِىَ رَمِيْمٌ ۞ قُلْ

يُحْيِيْهَا الَّذِىٓ اَنْشَاَهَآ اَوَّلَ مَرَّةٍ ۚ

وَهُوَ بِكُلِّ خَلْقٍ عَلِيْمٌ ۙ۞ الَّذِىْ

جَعَلَ لَكُمْ مِّنَ الشَّجَرِ الْاَخْضَرِ

نَارًا فَاِذَآ اَنْتُمْ مِّنْهُ تُوْقِدُوْنَ ۞

اَوَلَيْسَ الَّذِىْ خَلَقَ السَّمٰوٰتِ

وَالْاَرْضَ بِقٰدِرٍ عَلٰٓى اَنْ يَّخْلُقَ

مِثْلَهُمْ ۚ بَلٰى وَهُوَ الْخَلّٰقُ الْعَلِيْمُ ۞

اِنَّمَآ اَمْرُهٗٓ اِذَآ اَرَادَ شَيْئًا اَنْ

(other) profits (besides), and they get (milk) to drink. Will they not then be grateful?

74. Yet they take (for worship) gods other than Allah, (hoping) that they might be helped!

75. They have not the power to help them: but they will be brought up (before Our Judgment-seat) as a troop (to be condemned).

76. Let not their speech, then, grieve you. Verily We know what they hide as well as what they disclose.

77. Does not man see that it is We Who created him from sperm? Yet behold! He (stands forth) as an open adversary!

78. And he makes comparisons for Us, and forgets his own (origin and) Creation: he says, "Who

مَنَافِعُ وَ مَشَارِبُ ۖ أَفَلَا يَشْكُرُونَ ۝

وَاتَّخَذُوا مِنْ دُونِ اللهِ اٰلِهَةً

لَّعَلَّهُمْ يُنْصَرُونَ ۝ لَا يَسْتَطِيعُونَ

نَصْرَهُمْ وَ هُمْ لَهُمْ جُنْدٌ مُّحْضَرُونَ ۝

فَلَا يَحْزُنْكَ قَوْلُهُمْ ۘ إِنَّا نَعْلَمُ مَا

يُسِرُّونَ وَ مَا يُعْلِنُونَ ۝ أَوَلَمْ يَرَ

الْإِنْسَانُ أَنَّا خَلَقْنٰهُ مِنْ نُّطْفَةٍ

فَإِذَا هُوَ خَصِيمٌ مُّبِينٌ ۝ وَضَرَبَ

لَنَا مَثَلًا وَّ نَسِيَ خَلْقَهُ ۖ قَالَ مَنْ

could they have returned (after error).

68. If We grant long life to any, We cause him to be reversed in nature: will they not then understand?

69. We have not instructed the (Prophet) in Poetry, nor is it meet for him: this is no less than a Message and a Qur'an making things clear:

70. That it may give admonition to any (who are) alive, and that the Word may be proved True against those who reject (Truth).

71. See they not that it is We Who have created for them - among the things which Our hands have fashioned - cattle, which are under their dominion? -

72. And that We have subjected them to their (use)? Of them some do carry them and some they eat:

73. And they have

يَرْجِعُوْنَ ۞ وَمَنْ نُّعَمِّرْهُ نُنَكِّسْهُ فِی

الْخَلْقِ ؕ اَفَلَا يَعْقِلُوْنَ ۞ وَمَا عَلَّمْنٰهُ

الشِّعْرَ وَمَا يَنْۢبَغِیْ لَهٗ ؕ اِنْ هُوَ اِلَّا

ذِكْرٌ وَّقُرْاٰنٌ مُّبِيْنٌ ۙ ۞ لِّيُنْذِرَ مَنْ

كَانَ حَيًّا وَّيَحِقَّ الْقَوْلُ عَلَی

الْكٰفِرِيْنَ ۞ اَوَلَمْ يَرَوْا اَنَّا خَلَقْنَا

لَهُمْ مِّمَّا عَمِلَتْ اَيْدِيْنَاۤ اَنْعَامًا فَهُمْ

لَهَا مٰلِكُوْنَ ۞ وَذَلَّلْنٰهَا لَهُمْ فَمِنْهَا

رَكُوْبُهُمْ وَمِنْهَا يَاْكُلُوْنَ ۞ وَلَهُمْ فِيْهَا

a great multitude of you. Did you not, then, understand?"

63. "This is the Hell of which you were (repeatedly) warned!"

64. "Embrace you the (Fire) this Day, for that you (persistently) rejected (Truth)."

65. That Day shall We set a seal on their mouths. But their hands will speak to us, and their feet bear witness, to all that they did.

66. If it had been our Will, We could surely have blotted out their eyes; then should they have run about groping for the path, but how could they have seen?

67. And if it had been Our Will, We could have transformed them (to remain) in their places; then should they have been unable to move about, nor

جِبِلًّا كَثِيْرًا ۖ اَفَلَمْ تَكُوْنُوْا تَعْقِلُوْنَ ۝

هٰذِهٖ جَهَنَّمُ الَّتِيْ كُنْتُمْ تُوْعَدُوْنَ ۝

اِصْلَوْهَا الْيَوْمَ بِمَا كُنْتُمْ تَكْفُرُوْنَ ۝

اَلْيَوْمَ نَخْتِمُ عَلٰى اَفْوَاهِهِمْ وَتُكَلِّمُنَآ

اَيْدِيْهِمْ وَتَشْهَدُ اَرْجُلُهُمْ بِمَا كَانُوْا

يَكْسِبُوْنَ ۝ وَلَوْ نَشَآءُ لَطَمَسْنَا عَلٰى

اَعْيُنِهِمْ فَاسْتَبَقُوا الصِّرَاطَ فَاَنّٰى

يُبْصِرُوْنَ ۝ وَلَوْ نَشَآءُ لَمَسَخْنٰهُمْ عَلٰى

مَكَانَتِهِمْ فَمَا اسْتَطَاعُوْا مُضِيًّا وَّلَا

56. They and their associates will be in groves of (cool) shade, reclining on thrones (of dignity);

57. (Every) fruit (enjoyment) will be there for them; they shall have whatever they call for;

58. "Peace!" - a word (of salutation) from a Lord, Most Merciful!

59. "And O you in sin! Get you apart this Day!"

60. "Did I not enjoin on you, O you Children of Adam, that you should not worship Satan; for that he was to you an enemy avowed?"-

61. "And that you should worship Me, (for that) this was the straight way?

62. "But he did lead astray

هُمْ وَاَزْوَاجُهُمْ فِىْ ظِلٍّ عَلَى

الْاَرَآئِكِ مُتَّكِـُٔوْنَ ۞ لَهُمْ فِيْهَا

فَاكِهَةٌ وَّلَهُمْ مَّا يَدَّعُوْنَ ۞ سَلٰمٌ

قَوْلًا مِّنْ رَّبٍّ رَّحِيْمٍ ۞ وَامْتَازُوا

الْيَوْمَ اَيُّهَا الْمُجْرِمُوْنَ ۞ اَلَمْ اَعْهَدْ

اِلَيْكُمْ يٰبَنِىْٓ اٰدَمَ اَنْ لَّا تَعْبُدُوا

الشَّيْطٰنَ اِنَّهٗ لَكُمْ عَدُوٌّ مُّبِيْنٌ

۞ وَّاَنِ اعْبُدُوْنِىْ ؕ هٰذَا صِرَاطٌ

مُّسْتَقِيْمٌ ۞ وَلَقَدْ اَضَلَّ مِنْكُمْ

from the sepulchres (men) will rush forth to their Lord!

52. They will say: "Ah! Woe unto us! Who has raised us up from our beds of repose?"... (A voice will say:) "This is what (Allah) Most Gracious had promised. And true was the word of the Apostles!"

53. It will be no more than a single Blast, when lo! they will all be brought up before Us!

54. Then, on that Day, not a soul will be wronged in the least, and you shall but be repaid the meeds of your past Deeds.

55. Verily the Companions of the Garden shall that Day have joy in all that they do;

هُم مِّنَ الْأَجْدَاثِ إِلَى رَبِّهِمْ

يَنسِلُونَ ۝ قَالُوا يَٰوَيْلَنَا مَنۢ

بَعَثَنَا مِن مَّرْقَدِنَا ۗ هَٰذَا مَا وَعَدَ

الرَّحْمَٰنُ وَصَدَقَ الْمُرْسَلُونَ ۝ إِن

كَانَتْ إِلَّا صَيْحَةً وَٰحِدَةً فَإِذَا هُمْ

جَمِيعٌ لَّدَيْنَا مُحْضَرُونَ ۝ فَالْيَوْمَ

لَا تُظْلَمُ نَفْسٌ شَيْئًا وَلَا تُجْزَوْنَ

إِلَّا مَا كُنتُمْ تَعْمَلُونَ ۝ إِنَّ أَصْحَٰبَ

الْجَنَّةِ الْيَوْمَ فِي شُغُلٍ فَٰكِهُونَ ۝

of (the bounties) with which Allah has provided you," the unbelievers say to those who believe: "Shall we then feed those whom, if Allah had so willed, He would have fed, (Himself)? - you are in nothing but manifest error."

48. Further, they say, "When will this promise (come to pass), if what you say is true?"

49. They will not (have to) wait for anything but a single Blast: it will seize them while they are yet disputing among themselves!

50. No (chance) will they then have, by will, to dispose (of their affairs), nor to return to their own people!

51. The trumpet shall be sounded, when behold!

مِمَّا رَزَقَكُمُ اللّٰهُ قَالَ الَّذِينَ

كَفَرُوا لِلَّذِينَ اٰمَنُوا اَنُطُعِمُ مَنُ

لَّوُ يَشَآءُ اللّٰهُ اَطُعَمَهٗ اِنُ اَنُتُمُ اِلَّا

فِي ضَلٰلٍ مُّبِيُنٍ ۞ وَيَقُولُونَ مَتٰى

هٰذَا الُوَعُدُ اِنُ كُنُتُمُ صٰدِقِيُنَ ۞

مَا يَنُظُرُونَ اِلَّا صَيُحَةً وَّاحِدَةً

تَاُخُذُهُمُ وَهُمُ يَخِصِّمُونَ ۞ فَلَا

يَسُتَطِيُعُونَ تَوُصِيَةً وَّلَاۤ اِلٰۤى اَهُلِهِمُ

يَرُجِعُونَ ۞ وَنُفِخَ فِي الصُّورِ فَاِذَا

the loaded Ark;

42. And We have created for them similar (vessels) on which they ride.

43. If it were Our Will, We could drown them: then would there be no helper (to hear their cry), nor could they be delivered,

44. Except by way of Mercy from Us, and by way of (world) convenience (to serve them) for a time.

45. When they are told, "Fear you that which is before you and that which will be after you, in order that you may receive Mercy," (they turn back).

46. Not a Sign comes to them from among the Signs of their Lord, but they turn away therefrom.

47. And when they are told, "Spend you

الْفُلْكِ الْمَشْحُونِ ۝ وَخَلَقْنَا لَهُمْ

مِّنْ مِّثْلِهٖ مَا يَرْكَبُوْنَ ۝ وَاِنْ نَّشَأْ

نُغْرِقْهُمْ فَلَا صَرِيْخَ لَهُمْ وَلَا هُمْ

يُنْقَذُوْنَ ۝ اِلَّا رَحْمَةً مِّنَّا وَمَتَاعًا

اِلٰى حِيْنٍ ۝ وَاِذَا قِيْلَ لَهُمُ اتَّقُوْا

مَا بَيْنَ اَيْدِيْكُمْ وَمَا خَلْفَكُمْ لَعَلَّكُمْ

تُرْحَمُوْنَ ۝ وَمَا تَأْتِيْهِمْ مِّنْ اٰيَةٍ

مِّنْ اٰيٰتِ رَبِّهِمْ اِلَّا كَانُوْا عَنْهَا

مُعْرِضِيْنَ ۝ وَاِذَا قِيْلَ لَهُمْ اَنْفِقُوْا

they have no knowledge.

37. And a Sign for them is the Night: We withdraw therefrom the Day, and behold they are plunged in darkness;

38. And the sun runs his course for a period determined for him: that is the Decree of (Him), the Exalted in Might, the All-Knowing.

39. And the Moon, - We have measured for her mansions (to traverse) till she returns like the old (and withered) lower part of a date-stalk.

40. It is not permitted to the Sun to catch up the Moon, nor can the Night outstrip the Day: each (just) swims along in (its own) orbit (according to Law).

41. And a Sign for them is that We bore their race (through the Flood) in

لَا يَعْلَمُوْنَ ۞ وَاٰيَةٌ لَّهُمُ الَّيْلُ ۚ نَسْلَخُ

مِنْهُ النَّهَارَ فَاِذَا هُمْ مُّظْلِمُوْنَ ۞

وَالشَّمْسُ تَجْرِىْ لِمُسْتَقَرٍّ لَّهَا ۗ ذٰلِكَ

تَقْدِيْرُ الْعَزِيْزِ الْعَلِيْمِ ۞ وَالْقَمَرَ

قَدَّرْنٰهُ مَنَازِلَ حَتّٰى عَادَ كَالْعُرْجُوْنِ

الْقَدِيْمِ ۞ لَا الشَّمْسُ يَنْۢبَغِىْ لَهَآ

اَنْ تُدْرِكَ الْقَمَرَ وَلَا الَّيْلُ سَابِقُ

النَّهَارِ ۗ وَكُلٌّ فِىْ فَلَكٍ يَّسْبَحُوْنَ ۞

وَاٰيَةٌ لَّهُمْ اَنَّا حَمَلْنَا ذُرِّيَّتَهُمْ فِى

of them all - will be brought before Us (for judgment).

33. A Sign for them is the earth that is dead: We do give it life, and produce grain therefrom, of which you do eat.

34. And We produce therein orchard with date-palms and vines, and We cause springs to gush forth therein:

35. That they may enjoy the fruits of this (artistry): it was not their hands that made this: will they not then give thanks?

36. Glory to Allah, Who created in pairs all things that the earth produces, as well as their own (human) kind and (other) things of which

لَّمَّا جَمِيعٌ لَّدَيْنَا مُحْضَرُونَ ۞ وَاٰيَةٌ

لَّهُمُ الْاَرْضُ الْمَيْتَةُ ۚ اَحْيَيْنٰهَا

وَاَخْرَجْنَا مِنْهَا حَبًّا فَمِنْهُ يَاْكُلُونَ ۞

وَجَعَلْنَا فِيْهَا جَنّٰتٍ مِّنْ نَّخِيْلٍ

وَّاَعْنَابٍ وَّفَجَّرْنَا فِيْهَا مِنَ الْعُيُوْنِ ۞

لِيَاْكُلُوْا مِنْ ثَمَرِهٖ ۙ وَمَا عَمِلَتْهُ

اَيْدِيْهِمْ ۗ اَفَلَا يَشْكُرُوْنَ ۞ سُبْحٰنَ

الَّذِيْ خَلَقَ الْاَزْوَاجَ كُلَّهَا مِمَّا

تُنْۢبِتُ الْاَرْضُ وَمِنْ اَنْفُسِهِمْ وَمِمَّا

those held in honour!"

28. And We sent not down against his People, after him, any hosts from heaven, nor was it needful for Us so to do.

29. It was no more than a single mighty Blast, and behold! they were (like ashes) quenched and silent.

30. Ah! Alas for (My) servants! There comes not an Apostle to them but they mock him!

31. See they not how many generations before them we destroyed? Not to them will they return:

32. But each one

الْمُكْرَمِينَ ۞ وَمَآ أَنْزَلْنَا عَلَى قَوْمِهِ

مِنْ بَعْدِهِ مِنْ جُنْدٍ مِّنَ السَّمَاءِ

وَمَا كُنَّا مُنْزِلِينَ ۞ إِنْ كَانَتْ

إِلَّا صَيْحَةً وَّاحِدَةً فَإِذَا هُمْ

خَامِدُونَ ۞ يَحَسْرَةً عَلَى الْعِبَادِ

مَا يَأْتِيهِمْ مِّنْ رَّسُولٍ إِلَّا كَانُوا

بِهِ يَسْتَهْزِءُونَ ۞ أَلَمْ يَرَوْا كَمْ

أَهْلَكْنَا قَبْلَهُمْ مِّنَ الْقُرُونِ أَنَّهُمْ

إِلَيْهِمْ لَا يَرْجِعُونَ ۞ وَإِنْ كُلٌّ

22. "It would not be reasonable in me if I did not serve Him Who created me, and to Whom you shall (all) be brought back."

23. "Shall I take (other) gods besides Him? If (Allah) Most Gracious should intend some adversity for me, of no use whatever will be their intercession for me, nor can they deliver me."

24. "I would indeed, if I were to do so, be in manifest error."

25. "For me, I have faith in the Lord of you (all): listen, then, to me!"

26. It was said: "Enter you the Garden." He said: "Ah me! Would that my People knew (what I know)!" -

27. "For that my Lord has granted me forgiveness and has enrolled me among

وَمَا لِيَ لَا أَعْبُدُ الَّذِي فَطَرَنِي

وَإِلَيْهِ تُرْجَعُونَ ۞ ءَأَتَّخِذُ مِنْ

دُونِهِ ءَالِهَةً إِنْ يُرِدْنِ الرَّحْمَنُ

بِضُرٍّ لَا تُغْنِ عَنِّي شَفَاعَتُهُمْ شَيْئًا

وَّلَا يُنْقِذُونِ ۞ إِنِّي إِذًا لَّفِي

ضَلَالٍ مُبِينٍ ۞ إِنِّي ءَامَنْتُ بِرَبِّكُمْ

فَاسْمَعُونِ ۞ قِيلَ ادْخُلِ الْجَنَّةَ

قَالَ يَالَيْتَ قَوْمِي يَعْلَمُونَ ۞

بِمَا غَفَرَ لِي رَبِّي وَجَعَلَنِي مِنَ

مكتبة الكتب الإسلامية

پاره

وَمَالِيَ

(۲۳)

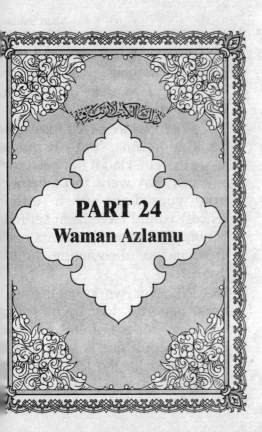

ان راك الكتب الاسلاميه

PART 24
Waman Azlamu

a deafness in their ears, and it is blindness in their (eyes): they are (as it were) being called from a place far distant!"

45. We certainly gave Moses the Book aforetime: but disputes arose therein. Had it not been for a Word that went forth before from your Lord, (their differences) would have been settled between them: but they remained in suspicious disquieting doubt thereon.

46. Whoever works righteousness benefits his own soul; whoever works evil, it is against his own soul: nor is your Lord ever unjust (in the least) to His servants.

وَقْرٌ ۚ وَهُوَ عَلَيْهِمْ عَمًى ۚ أُولٰٓئِكَ

يُنَادَوْنَ مِنْ مَّكَانٍۭ بَعِيدٍ ۞

وَلَقَدْ اٰتَيْنَا مُوسَى الْكِتٰبَ

فَاخْتُلِفَ فِيهِ ۚ وَلَوْلَا كَلِمَةٌ

سَبَقَتْ مِنْ رَّبِّكَ لَقُضِىَ

بَيْنَهُمْ ۚ وَاِنَّهُمْ لَفِىْ شَكٍّ مِّنْهُ

مُرِيْبٍ ۞ مَنْ عَمِلَ صَالِحًا

فَلِنَفْسِهٖ وَمَنْ اَسَآءَ فَعَلَيْهَا ۗ

وَمَا رَبُّكَ بِظَلَّامٍ لِّلْعَبِيْدِ ۞

by One full of Wisdom, Worthy of all praise.

43. Nothing is said to you that was not said to the Apostles before you: that your Lord has at His Command (all) Forgiveness as well as a most grievous Chastisement.

44. Had We sent this as a Qur'an (in the language) other than Arabic, they would have said: "Why are not its verses explained in detail? What! (a Book) not in Arabic and (a Messenger) an Arab?" Say: "It is a Guide and a Healing to those who believe; and for those who believe not, there is

مِنْ حَكِيْمٍ حَمِيْدٍ ۝ مَا يُقَالُ

لَكَ اِلَّا مَا قَدْ قِيْلَ لِلرُّسُلِ

مِنْ قَبْلِكَ ۚ اِنَّ رَبَّكَ لَذُوْ

مَغْفِرَةٍ وَّ ذُوْ عِقَابٍ اَلِيْمٍ ۝

وَ لَوْ جَعَلْنٰهُ قُرْاٰنًا اَعْجَمِيًّا

لَّقَالُوْا لَوْ لَا فُصِّلَتْ اٰيٰتُهٗ ؕ

ءَاَعْجَمِيٌّ وَّ عَرَبِيٌّ ؕ قُلْ هُوَ

لِلَّذِيْنَ اٰمَنُوْا هُدًى وَّ شِفَآءٌ ؕ

وَ الَّذِيْنَ لَا يُؤْمِنُوْنَ فِيْٓ اٰذَانِهِمْ

pervert the Truth in Our Signs are not hidden from Us. Which is better? - he that is cast into the Fire, or he that comes safe through, on the Day of Judgment? Do what you will: verily He sees (clearly) all that you do.

41. Those who reject the Message when it comes to them (are not hidden from Us). And indeed it is a Book of exalted power.

42. No Falsehood can approach it from before or behind it: it is sent down

يُلْحِدُونَ فِيْۤ اٰيٰتِنَا لَا يَخْفَوْنَ

عَلَيْنَا ۗ اَفَمَنْ يُّلْقٰى فِى النَّارِ

خَيْرٌ اَمْ مَّنْ يَّاْتِيْۤ اٰمِنًا يَّوْمَ

الْقِيٰمَةِ ۗ اِعْمَلُوْا مَا شِئْتُمْ ۙ

اِنَّهٗ بِمَا تَعْمَلُوْنَ بَصِيْرٌ ۞ اِنَّ

الَّذِيْنَ كَفَرُوْا بِالذِّكْرِ لَمَّا

جَآءَهُمْ ۖ وَاِنَّهٗ لَكِتٰبٌ عَزِيْزٌ ۞

لَّا يَاْتِيْهِ الْبَاطِلُ مِنْۢ بَيْنِ

يَدَيْهِ وَلَا مِنْ خَلْفِهٖ ۗ تَنْزِيْلٌ

wish to serve.

38. But is the (unbelievers) are arrogant, (no matter): for in the presence of your Lord are those who celebrate His praises by night and by day. And they never flag (nor feel themselves above it).

39. And among His Signs in this: that you see the earth barren and desolate; but when We send down rain to it, it is stirred to life and yields increase. Truly, He Who gives life to the (dead) earth can surely give life to (men) who are dead. For He has power over all things.

40. Those who

تَعْبُدُوْنَ ۩ فَاِنِ اسْتَكْبَرُوْا

فَالَّذِيْنَ عِنْدَ رَبِّكَ يُسَبِّحُوْنَ

لَهٗ بِالَّيْلِ وَالنَّهَارِ وَهُمْ لَا

يَسْـَٔمُوْنَ ۩ وَمِنْ اٰيٰتِهٖۤ اَنَّكَ

تَرَى الْاَرْضَ خَاشِعَةً فَاِذَاۤ

اَنْزَلْنَا عَلَيْهَا الْمَآءَ اهْتَزَّتْ

وَرَبَتْ ۭ اِنَّ الَّذِيْۤ اَحْيَاهَا

لَمُحْيِ الْمَوْتٰى ۭ اِنَّهٗ عَلٰى كُلِّ

شَيْءٍ قَدِيْرٌ ۞ اِنَّ الَّذِيْنَ

except those who exercise patience and self-restraint, - none but persons of the greatest good fortune.

36. And if (at any time) an incitement to discord is made to you by the Evil One, seek refuge in Allah. He is the One Who hears and knows all things.

37. Among His Signs are the Night and the Day, and the Sun and the Moon. Adore not the sun and the moon, but adore Allah, Who created them, if it is Him you

اِلَّا الَّذِيْنَ صَبَرُوْا وَمَا يُلَقّٰهَآ

اِلَّا ذُوْ حَظٍّ عَظِيْمٍ ۩ وَاِمَّا

يَنْزَغَنَّكَ مِنَ الشَّيْطٰنِ نَزْغٌ

فَاسْتَعِذْ بِاللّٰهِ ؕ اِنَّهٗ هُوَ

السَّمِيْعُ الْعَلِيْمُ ۩ وَمِنْ اٰيٰتِهِ

الَّيْلُ وَالنَّهَارُ وَالشَّمْسُ وَالْقَمَرُ ؕ

لَا تَسْجُدُوْا لِلشَّمْسِ وَلَا

لِلْقَمَرِ وَاسْجُدُوْا لِلّٰهِ الَّذِيْ

خَلَقَهُنَّ اِنْ كُنْتُمْ اِيَّاهُ

therein shall you have all that you ask for! -

32. "A hospitable gift from One Oft-Forgiving, Most Merciful!"

33. Who is better in speech than one who calls (men) to Allah, works righteousness, and says, "I am of those who bow in Islam"?

34. Nor can Goodness and Evil be equal. Repel (Evil) with what is better: Then will he between whom and you was hatred become as it were your friend and intimate!

35. And no one will be granted such goodness

وَلَكُمْ فِيهَا مَا تَدَّعُونَ ۞ نُزُلًا

مِنْ غَفُورٍ رَّحِيمٍ ۞ وَمَنْ

أَحْسَنُ قَوْلًا مِّمَّن دَعَا إِلَى

اللَّهِ وَعَمِلَ صَالِحًا وَّقَالَ

إِنَّنِي مِنَ الْمُسْلِمِينَ ۞ وَلَا

تَسْتَوِى الْحَسَنَةُ وَلَا السَّيِّئَةُ

ادْفَعْ بِالَّتِي هِيَ أَحْسَنُ فَإِذَا

الَّذِي بَيْنَكَ وَبَيْنَهُ عَدَاوَةٌ

كَأَنَّهُ وَلِيٌّ حَمِيمٌ ۞ وَمَا يُلَقَّىٰهَا

we shall crush them beneath our feet, so that they become the vilest (before all)."

30.   In the case of those who say, "Our Lord is Allah", and, further, stand straight and steadfast, the Angels descend on them (from time to time): "Fear you not!" (they suggest), "Nor grieve! But receive the glad tidings of the Garden (of Bliss), the which you were promised!

31.   "We are your protectors in this life and in the Hereafter: therein shall you have all that your souls shall desire;

نَجْعَلْهُمَا تَحْتَ أَقْدَامِنَا لِيَكُونَا

مِنَ الْأَسْفَلِينَ ۝ إِنَّ الَّذِينَ

قَالُوا رَبُّنَا اللّٰهُ ثُمَّ اسْتَقَامُوا

تَتَنَزَّلُ عَلَيْهِمُ الْمَلَٰئِكَةُ أَلَّا

تَخَافُوا وَلَا تَحْزَنُوا وَأَبْشِرُوا

بِالْجَنَّةِ الَّتِي كُنْتُمْ تُوعَدُونَ ۝

نَحْنُ أَوْلِيَاؤُكُمْ فِي الْحَيَوٰةِ

الدُّنْيَا وَفِي الْآخِرَةِ وَلَكُمْ

فِيهَا مَا تَشْتَهِي أَنْفُسُكُمْ

that you may gain the upper hand!"

27. But We will certainly give the unbelievers a taste of a severe Chastisement, and We will requite them for the worst of their deeds.

28. Such is the requital of the enemies of Allah, - the Fire: therein will be for them the Eternal Home: a (fit) requital, for that they were wont to reject Our Signs.

29. And the unbelievers will say: "Our Lord! Show us those, among Jinns and men, who misled us:

لَعَلَّكُمْ تَغْلِبُوْنَ ۞ فَلَنُذِيْقَنَّ

الَّذِيْنَ كَفَرُوْا عَذَابًا شَدِيْدًا

وَّلَنَجْزِيَنَّهُمْ اَسْوَاَ الَّذِىْ كَانُوْا

يَعْمَلُوْنَ ۞ ذٰلِكَ جَزَآءُ اَعْدَآءِ

اللّٰهِ النَّارُ ۚ لَهُمْ فِيْهَا دَارُ

الْخُلْدِ ۖ جَزَآءًۢ بِمَا كَانُوْا بِاٰيٰتِنَا

يَجْحَدُوْنَ ۞ وَقَالَ الَّذِيْنَ

كَفَرُوْا رَبَّنَاۤ اَرِنَا الَّذَيْنِ

اَضَلّٰنَا مِنَ الْجِنِّ وَالْاِنْسِ

for them! and if they beg to be received into favour, into favour will they not (then) be received.

25. And We have destined for them intimate companions (of like nature), who made alluring to them what was before them and behind them; and the sentence among the previous generations of Jinns and men, who have passed away, is proved against them; for they are utterly lost.

26. The unbelievers say: "Listen not to this Qur'an, but talk at random in the midst of its (reading),

لَهُمْ وَإِن يَّسْتَعْتِبُوا فَمَا هُم
مِّنَ الْمُعْتَبِينَ ۞ وَقَيَّضْنَا لَهُمْ
قُرَنَآءَ فَزَيَّنُوا لَهُم مَّا بَيْنَ
أَيْدِيهِمْ وَمَا خَلْفَهُمْ وَحَقَّ
عَلَيْهِمُ الْقَوْلُ فِىٓ أُمَمٍ قَدْ
خَلَتْ مِن قَبْلِهِم مِّنَ الْجِنِّ
وَالْإِنسِ إِنَّهُمْ كَانُوا خَاسِرِينَ
۞ وَقَالَ الَّذِينَ كَفَرُوا لَا تَسْمَعُوا
لِهَٰذَا الْقُرْآنِ وَالْغَوْا فِيهِ

He created you for the first time, and unto Him were you to return.

22. "You did not seek to hide yourselves, lest your hearing, your sight, and your skins should bear witness against you! but you did think that Allah knew not many of the things that you used to do!

23. "But this thought of yours which you did entertain concerning your Lord, has brought you to destruction, and (now) have you become of those utterly lost!"

24. If, then, they have patience, the Fire will be a home

وَهُوَ خَلَقَكُمْ اَوَّلَ مَرَّةٍ وَّاِلَيْهِ

تُرْجَعُوْنَ ۞ وَمَا كُنْتُمْ تَسْتَتِرُوْنَ

اَنْ يَّشْهَدَ عَلَيْكُمْ سَمْعُكُمْ وَلَا

اَبْصَارُكُمْ وَلَا جُلُوْدُكُمْ وَلٰكِنْ

ظَنَنْتُمْ اَنَّ اللّٰهَ لَا يَعْلَمُ كَثِيْرًا

مِّمَّا تَعْمَلُوْنَ ۞ وَذٰلِكُمْ ظَنُّكُمُ

الَّذِيْ ظَنَنْتُمْ بِرَبِّكُمْ اَرْدٰىكُمْ

فَاَصْبَحْتُمْ مِّنَ الْخٰسِرِيْنَ ۞

فَاِنْ يَّصْبِرُوْا فَالنَّارُ مَثْوًى

earned.

18.   But We delivered those who believed and practised righteousness.

19.   On the Day that the enemies of Allah will be gathered together to the Fire, they will be marched in ranks.

20.   At length, when they reach the (Fire), their hearing, their sight, and their skins will bear witness against them, as to (all) their deeds.

21.   They will say to their skins: "Why bear you witness against us?" They will say: "Allah has given us speech, - (He) Who gives speech to everything:

يَكْسِبُوْنَ ۝ وَ نَجَّيْنَا الَّذِيْنَ

اٰمَنُوْا وَ كَانُوْا يَتَّقُوْنَ ۝ وَ يَوْمَ

يُحْشَرُ اَعْدَآءُ اللّٰهِ اِلَى النَّارِ

فَهُمْ يُوْزَعُوْنَ ۝ حَتّٰى اِذَا مَا

جَآءُوْهَا شَهِدَ عَلَيْهِمْ سَمْعُهُمْ

وَ اَبْصَارُهُمْ وَ جُلُوْدُهُمْ بِمَا كَانُوْا

يَعْمَلُوْنَ ۝ وَ قَالُوْا لِجُلُوْدِهِمْ لِمَ

شَهِدْتُّمْ عَلَيْنَا قَالُوْا اَنْطَقَنَا

اللّٰهُ الَّذِيْ اَنْطَقَ كُلَّ شَيْءٍ

to reject Our Signs!

16. So We sent against them a furious Wind through days of disaster, that We might give them a taste of a Chastisement of humiliation in this life; but the Chastisement of the Hereafter will be more humiliating still: and they will find no help.

17. As to the Thamud, We gave them Guidance, but they preferred blindness (of heart) to Guidance: so the stunning Punishment of humiliation seized them, because of what they had

بِاٰيٰتِنَا يَجْحَدُوْنَ ۞ فَاَرْسَلْنَا

عَلَيْهِمْ رِيْحًا صَرْصَرًا فِيْ اَيَّامٍ

نَّحِسَاتٍ لِّنُذِيْقَهُمْ عَذَابَ

الْخِزْيِ فِي الْحَيٰوةِ الدُّنْيَا

وَلَعَذَابُ الْاٰخِرَةِ اَخْزٰى وَهُمْ

لَا يُنْصَرُوْنَ ۞ وَاَمَّا ثَمُوْدُ

فَهَدَيْنٰهُمْ فَاسْتَحَبُّوا الْعَمٰى

عَلَى الْهُدٰى فَاَخَذَتْهُمْ صٰعِقَةُ

الْعَذَابِ الْهُوْنِ بِمَا كَانُوْا

before them and behind them, (preaching): "Serve none but Allah." They said, "If our Lord had so pleased, He would certainly have sent down Angels (to preach). Now we reject your mission (altogether)."

15. Now the 'Ad behaved arrogantly through the land, against (all) truth and reason, and said: "Who is superior to us in strength?" What! Did they not see that Allah, Who created them, was superior to them in strength? But they continued

أَيْدِيهِمْ وَمِنْ خَلْفِهِمْ أَلَّا

تَعْبُدُوۤا إِلَّا اللَّهَ ۖ قَالُوا لَوْ

شَآءَ رَبُّنَا لَأَنْزَلَ مَلَٰٓئِكَةً

فَإِنَّا بِمَاۤ أُرْسِلْتُمْ بِهِ كَٰفِرُونَ ۝

فَأَمَّا عَادٌ فَاسْتَكْبَرُوا فِي

الْأَرْضِ بِغَيْرِ الْحَقِّ وَقَالُوا

مَنْ أَشَدُّ مِنَّا قُوَّةً ۖ أَوَلَمْ

يَرَوْا أَنَّ اللَّهَ الَّذِي خَلَقَهُمْ

هُوَ أَشَدُّ مِنْهُمْ قُوَّةً ۖ وَكَانُوا

or unwillingly." They said: "We do come (together), in willing obedience."

12. So He completed them as seven firmaments in two Days, and He assigned to each heaven its duty and command. And We adorned the lower heaven with lights, and (provided it) with guard. Such is the Decree of (Him) the Exalted in Might, full of Knowledge.

13. But if they turn away, say you: "I have warned you of a stunning Punishment (as of thunder and lightning) like that which (overtook) the 'Ad and the Thamud!"

14. Behold, the Apostles came to them, from

اَوْ كَرْهًا ۚ قَالَتَاۤ اَتَيْنَا طَآئِعِيْنَ ۝

فَقَضٰهُنَّ سَبْعَ سَمٰوَاتٍ فِىْ

يَوْمَيْنِ وَ اَوْحٰى فِىْ كُلِّ سَمَآءٍ

اَمْرَهَا ۚ وَ زَيَّنَّا السَّمَآءَ الدُّنْيَا

بِمَصَابِيْحَ ۖ وَ حِفْظًا ۚ ذٰلِكَ تَقْدِيْرُ

الْعَزِيْزِ الْعَلِيْمِ ۝ فَاِنْ اَعْرَضُوْا

فَقُلْ اَنْذَرْتُكُمْ صٰعِقَةً مِّثْلَ

صٰعِقَةِ عَادٍ وَّ ثَمُوْدَ ۝ اِذْ

جَآءَتْهُمُ الرُّسُلُ مِنْ بَيْنِ

fail.

9. Say: Is it that you deny Him Who created the earth in two Days? And do you join equals with Him? He is the Lord of (all) the Worlds.

10. He set on the (earth), mountains standing firm, high above it, and bestowed blessings on the earth, and measure therein its sustenance in four Days, alike for (all) who ask.

11. Moreover He comprehended in His design the sky, and it had been (as) smoke: He said to it and to the earth: "Come you together, willingly

مَمْنُوْنٍ ۞ قُلْ اَئِنَّكُمْ لَتَكْفُرُوْنَ

بِالَّذِيْ خَلَقَ الْاَرْضَ فِيْ يَوْمَيْنِ

وَتَجْعَلُوْنَ لَهٗٓ اَنْدَادًا ذٰلِكَ

رَبُّ الْعٰلَمِيْنَ ۞ وَجَعَلَ فِيْهَا

رَوَاسِيَ مِنْ فَوْقِهَا وَبٰرَكَ فِيْهَا

وَقَدَّرَ فِيْهَآ اَقْوَاتَهَا فِيْٓ اَرْبَعَةِ

اَيَّامٍ ۖ سَوَآءً لِّلسَّآئِلِيْنَ ۞ ثُمَّ

اسْتَوٰٓى اِلَى السَّمَآءِ وَهِيَ دُخَانٌ

فَقَالَ لَهَا وَلِلْاَرْضِ ائْتِيَا طَوْعًا

between us and you is a screen: so do you (what you will); for us, we shall do (what we will!)"

6. Say you: "I am but a man like you: it is revealed to me by Inspiration, that your Allah is one Allah: so stand true to Him, and ask for His Forgiveness." And woe to those who join gods with Allah, -

7. Those who practise not regular Charity, and who even deny the Hereafter.

8. For those who believe and work deeds of righteousness is a reward that will never

بَيْنِنَا وَ بَيْنِكَ حِجَابٌ فَاعْمَلْ

اِنَّنَا عٰمِلُوْنَ ۝ قُلْ اِنَّمَاۤ اَنَا

بَشَرٌ مِّثْلُكُمْ يُوْحٰىۤ اِلَيَّ اَنَّمَاۤ

اِلٰهُكُمْ اِلٰهٌ وَّاحِدٌ فَاسْتَقِيْمُوْۤا

اِلَيْهِ وَ اسْتَغْفِرُوْهُ ؕ وَ وَيْلٌ

لِّلْمُشْرِكِيْنَ ۙ۝ الَّذِيْنَ لَا يُؤْتُوْنَ

الزَّكٰوةَ وَ هُمْ بِالْاٰخِرَةِ هُمْ

كٰفِرُوْنَ ۝ اِنَّ الَّذِيْنَ اٰمَنُوْا

وَ عَمِلُوا الصّٰلِحٰتِ لَهُمْ اَجْرٌ غَيْرُ

And even thus did the rejecters of Allah perish (utterly)!

Ha-Mim Sajda

Bismillahir-Rahmanir-Rahim

1.　Ha-Mim.

2.　A Revelation from (Allah), Most Gracious, Most Merciful; -

3.　A Book, whereof the verses are explained in detail; - a Qur'an in Arabic, for people who understand; -

4.　Giving good news and admonition: yet most of them turn away, and so they hear not.

5.　They say: "Our hearts are under veils, (concealed) from that to which you does invite us, and in our ears in a deafness, and between us

وَخَسِرَ هُنَالِكَ الْكَفِرُوْنَ ۞

بِسْمِ اللهِ الرَّحْمٰنِ الرَّحِيْمِ

حٰمٓ ۞ تَنْزِيْلٌ مِّنَ الرَّحْمٰنِ الرَّحِيْمِ ۞ كِتٰبٌ فُصِّلَتْ اٰيٰتُهٗ قُرْاٰنًا عَرَبِيًّا لِّقَوْمٍ يَّعْلَمُوْنَ ۞ بَشِيْرًا وَّنَذِيْرًا فَاَعْرَضَ اَكْثَرُهُمْ فَهُمْ لَا يَسْمَعُوْنَ ۞ وَقَالُوْا قُلُوْبُنَا فِيْ اَكِنَّةٍ مِّمَّا تَدْعُوْنَآ اِلَيْهِ وَفِيْ اٰذَانِنَا وَقْرٌ وَّمِنْ

83. For when their Apostles came to them with clear Signs, they exulted in such knowledge (and skill) as they had; but that very (wrath) at which they were wont to scoff hemmed them in.

84. But when they saw Our Punishment, they said: "We believe in Allah, - the One Allah - and we reject the partners we used to join with Him."

85. But their professing the Faith when they (actually) saw Our Punishment was not going to profit them. (Such has been) Allah's Way of dealing with His servants (from the most ancient times).

يَكْسِبُونَ ۝ فَلَمَّا جَآءَتْهُمْ رُسُلُهُمْ

بِالْبَيِّنَاتِ فَرِحُوا بِمَا عِنْدَهُمْ

مِنَ الْعِلْمِ وَحَاقَ بِهِمْ مَّا كَانُوا

بِهِ يَسْتَهْزِءُونَ ۝ فَلَمَّا رَأَوْا

بَأْسَنَا قَالُوا آمَنَّا بِاللّٰهِ وَحْدَهُ

وَكَفَرْنَا بِمَا كُنَّا بِهِ مُشْرِكِينَ ۝

فَلَمْ يَكُ يَنْفَعُهُمْ إِيْمَانُهُمْ

لَمَّا رَأَوْا بَأْسَنَا سُنَّتَ اللّٰهِ

الَّتِي قَدْ خَلَتْ فِي عِبَادِهِ

(other) advantages in them for you (besides); that you may through them attain to any need (there may be) in your hearts; and on them and on ships you are carried.

81. And He shows you (always) His Signs: then which of the Signs of Allah will you deny?

82. Do they not travel through the earth and see what was the End of those before them? They were more numerous than these and superior in strength and in the traces (they have left) in the land: yet all that they accomplished was of no profit to them.

فِيهَا مَنَافِعُ وَلِتَبْلُغُوا عَلَيْهَا

حَاجَةً فِي صُدُورِكُمْ وَعَلَيْهَا

وَعَلَى الْفُلْكِ تُحْمَلُونَ ۝ وَيُرِيكُمْ

اٰيٰتِهٖ فَاَيَّ اٰيٰتِ اللّٰهِ تُنْكِرُونَ ۝

اَفَلَمْ يَسِيْرُوْا فِي الْاَرْضِ

فَيَنْظُرُوا كَيْفَ كَانَ عَاقِبَةُ

الَّذِيْنَ مِنْ قَبْلِهِمْ كَانُوْا اَكْثَرَ

مِنْهُمْ وَاَشَدَّ قُوَّةً وَّاٰثَارًا فِي

الْاَرْضِ فَمَآ اَغْنٰى عَنْهُمْ مَّا كَانُوْا

it is to Us that they shall (all) return.

78. We did aforetime send Apostles before you: of them there are some whose story We have related to you, and some whose story We have not related to you. It was not (possible) for any Apostle to bring a Sign except by the leave of Allah: but when the Command of Allah issued, the matter was decided in truth and justice, and there perished, there and then those who stood on falsehoods.

79. It is Allah Who made cattle for you, that you may use some for riding and some for food;

80. And there are

فَاِلَيْنَا يُرْجَعُوْنَ ۞ وَلَقَدْ اَرْسَلْنَا

رُسُلًا مِّنْ قَبْلِكَ مِنْهُمْ مَّنْ

قَصَصْنَا عَلَيْكَ وَمِنْهُمْ مَّنْ لَّمْ

نَقْصُصْ عَلَيْكَ ۗ وَمَا كَانَ لِرَسُوْلٍ

اَنْ يَّاْتِيَ بِاٰيَةٍ اِلَّا بِاِذْنِ اللّٰهِ ۚ

فَاِذَا جَآءَ اَمْرُ اللّٰهِ قُضِيَ بِالْحَقِّ

وَخَسِرَ هُنَالِكَ الْمُبْطِلُوْنَ ۞ اَللّٰهُ

الَّذِيْ جَعَلَ لَكُمُ الْاَنْعَامَ لِتَرْكَبُوْا

مِنْهَا وَمِنْهَا تَاْكُلُوْنَ ۞ وَلَكُمْ

we invoked not, of old, any-thing (that had real existence)." Thus does Allah leave the unbelievers to stray.

75. "That was because you were wont to rejoice on the earth in things other than the Truth, and that you were wont to be insolent."

76. "Enter you the gates of Hell, to dwell therein: and evil is (this) Abode of the arrogant!"

77. So persevere in patience; for the Promise of Allah is true: and whether We show you (in this life) some part of what We promise them, - or We take your soul (to Our Mercy) (before that), - (in any case)

لَمْ نَكُنْ نَّدْعُوا مِنْ قَبْلُ شَيْئًا ۚ

كَذَلِكَ يُضِلُّ اللهُ الْكَافِرِينَ ۞

ذَلِكُمْ بِمَا كُنْتُمْ تَفْرَحُونَ فِي

الْأَرْضِ بِغَيْرِ الْحَقِّ وَبِمَا كُنْتُمْ

تَمْرَحُونَ ۞ اُدْخُلُوا أَبْوَابَ جَهَنَّمَ

خَالِدِينَ فِيهَا ۖ فَبِئْسَ مَثْوَى

الْمُتَكَبِّرِينَ ۞ فَاصْبِرْ إِنَّ وَعْدَ

اللهِ حَقٌّ ۚ فَإِمَّا نُرِيَنَّكَ بَعْضَ

الَّذِي نَعِدُهُمْ أَوْ نَتَوَفَّيَنَّكَ

those that dispute concerning the Signs of Allah? How are they turned away (from Reality)? -

70. Those who reject the Book and the (revelations) with which We sent Our Apostles: but soon shall they know, -

71. When the yokes (shall be) round their necks, and the chains; they shall be dragged along -

72. In the boiling fetid fluid: then in the Fire shall they be burned;

73. Then shall it be said to them: "Where are the (deities) to which you gave part- worship" -

74. "Besides Allah?" They will reply: "They have left us in the lurch: No,

اِلَى الَّذِيْنَ يُجَادِلُوْنَ فِیْۤ اٰيٰتِ

اللّٰهِ ؕ اَنّٰى يُصْرَفُوْنَ ۖ ۙ الَّذِيْنَ

كَذَّبُوْا بِالْكِتٰبِ وَبِمَاۤ اَرْسَلْنَا بِهٖ

رُسُلَنَا ۚ فَسَوْفَ يَعْلَمُوْنَ ۙ اِذِ

الْاَغْلٰلُ فِیْۤ اَعْنَاقِهِمْ وَالسَّلٰسِلُ ؕ

يُسْحَبُوْنَ ۙ فِى الْحَمِيْمِ ۙ ثُمَّ فِى

النَّارِ يُسْجَرُوْنَ ۚ ثُمَّ قِيْلَ لَهُمْ

اَيْنَ مَا كُنْتُمْ تُشْرِكُوْنَ ۙ مِنْ

دُوْنِ اللّٰهِ ؕ قَالُوْا ضَلُّوْا عَنَّا بَلْ

has created you from dust then from a sperm-drop, then from a leech-like clot; then does he get you out (into the light) as a child: then lets you (grow and) reach your age of full strength; then lets you become old, - though of you there are some who die before; - and lets you reach a term appointed; in order that you may learn wisdom.

68. It is He Who gives Life and Death; and when He decides upon an affair, He says to it, "Be", and it is.

69. Do you see not

خَلَقَكُمْ مِنْ تُرَابٍ ثُمَّ مِنْ

نُطْفَةٍ ثُمَّ مِنْ عَلَقَةٍ ثُمَّ

يُخْرِجُكُمْ طِفْلًا ثُمَّ لِتَبْلُغُوا

أَشُدَّكُمْ ثُمَّ لِتَكُونُوا شُيُوخًا

وَمِنْكُمْ مَنْ يُتَوَفَّى مِنْ قَبْلُ

وَلِتَبْلُغُوا أَجَلًا مُسَمًّى وَّلَعَلَّكُمْ

تَعْقِلُونَ ۞ هُوَ الَّذِى يُحْىٖ

وَيُمِيتُ فَإِذَا قَضٰى أَمْرًا فَإِنَّمَا

يَقُولُ لَهُ كُنْ فَيَكُونُ ۞ أَلَمْ تَرَ

Allah your Lord. So Glory to Allah, the Lord of the Worlds!

65. He is the Living (One): there is no god but He: call upon Him, giving Him sincere devotion. Praise be to Allah, Lord of the Worlds!

66. Say: "I have been forbidden to invoke those whom you invoke besides Allah, - seeing that the clear Signs have come to me from my Lord; and I have been commanded to submit (in Islam) to the Lord of the Worlds."

67. It is He Who

اللهُ رَبُّكُمْ فَتَبَارَكَ اللهُ رَبُّ

الْعٰلَمِيْنَ ۞ هُوَ الْحَىُّ لَاۤ اِلٰهَ

اِلَّا هُوَ فَادْعُوْهُ مُخْلِصِيْنَ

لَهُ الدِّيْنَ ۚ اَلْحَمْدُ لِلّٰهِ رَبِّ

الْعٰلَمِيْنَ ۞ قُلْ اِنِّيْ نُهِيْتُ اَنْ

اَعْبُدَ الَّذِيْنَ تَدْعُوْنَ مِنْ

دُوْنِ اللهِ لَمَّا جَآءَنِيَ الْبَيِّنٰتُ

مِنْ رَّبِّيْ وَ اُمِرْتُ اَنْ اُسْلِمَ

لِرَبِّ الْعٰلَمِيْنَ ۞ هُوَ الَّذِيْ

to men: yet most men give no
thanks.

62.   Such is Allah, your Lord, the
Creator of all things, there is no
Allah but He: then how you are
deluded away from the Truth!

63.   Thus are deluded those who
are wont to reject the Signs of
Allah.

64.   It is Allah Who has made for
you the earth as a resting place,
and the sky as a canopy, and has
given you shape - and made your
shapes beautiful, - and has
provided for you Sustenance, of
things pure and good; - such is

عَلَى النَّاسِ وَلَٰكِنَّ اَكْثَرَ النَّاسِ

لَا يَشْكُرُوْنَ ۩ ذٰلِكُمُ اللهُ رَبُّكُمْ

خَالِقُ كُلِّ شَيْءٍ لَّا اِلٰهَ اِلَّا هُوَ

فَاَنّٰى تُؤْفَكُوْنَ ۩ كَذٰلِكَ يُؤْفَكُ

الَّذِيْنَ كَانُوْا بِاٰيٰتِ اللهِ

يَجْحَدُوْنَ ۩ اَللهُ الَّذِيْ جَعَلَ

لَكُمُ الْاَرْضَ قَرَارًا وَّالسَّمَآءَ

بِنَآءً وَّصَوَّرَكُمْ فَاَحْسَنَ صُوَرَكُمْ

وَرَزَقَكُمْ مِّنَ الطَّيِّبٰتِ ذٰلِكُمُ

Little do you learn by admonition!

59. The Hour will certainly come: therein is no doubt: yet most men believe not.

60. And your Lord says: "Call on Me; I will answer your (prayer): but those who are too arrogant to serve Me will surely find themselves in Hell - in humiliation!"

61. It is Allah Who has made the Night for you, that you may rest therein, and the Day, as that which helps (you) to see. Verily Allah is full of Grace and Bounty

قَلِيلًا مَّا تَتَذَكَّرُونَ ۝ إِنَّ

السَّاعَةَ لَآتِيَةٌ لَّا رَيْبَ فِيهَا

وَلَـٰكِنَّ أَكْثَرَ النَّاسِ لَا يُؤْمِنُونَ ۝

وَقَالَ رَبُّكُمُ ادْعُونِي أَسْتَجِبْ

لَكُمْ ۚ إِنَّ الَّذِينَ يَسْتَكْبِرُونَ

عَنْ عِبَادَتِي سَيَدْخُلُونَ جَهَنَّمَ

دَاخِرِينَ ۝ اللَّهُ الَّذِي جَعَلَ لَكُمُ

اللَّيْلَ لِتَسْكُنُوا فِيهِ وَالنَّهَارَ

مُبْصِرًا ۚ إِنَّ اللَّهَ لَذُو فَضْلٍ

Allah without any authority bestowed on them, - there is nothing in their breasts but (the quest of) greatness, which they shall never attain to: seek refuge, then, in Allah: it is He Who hears and sees (all things).

57. Assuredly the creation of the heavens and the earth is a greater (matter) than the creation of men: yet most men understand not.

58. Not equal are the blind and those who (clearly) see: nor are (equal) those who believe and work deeds of righteousness, and those who do evil.

اللّٰهِ بِغَيْرِ سُلْطٰنٍ اَتٰهُمْ اِنْ

فِیْ صُدُوْرِهِمْ اِلَّا كِبْرٌ مَّا هُمْ

بِبَالِغِيْهِ فَاسْتَعِذْ بِاللّٰهِ اِنَّهٗ

هُوَ السَّمِيْعُ الْبَصِيْرُ ۞ لَخَلْقُ

السَّمٰوٰتِ وَالْاَرْضِ اَكْبَرُ مِنْ

خَلْقِ النَّاسِ وَلٰكِنَّ اَكْثَرَ

النَّاسِ لَا يَعْلَمُوْنَ ۞ وَمَا يَسْتَوِی

الْاَعْمٰی وَالْبَصِيْرُ ۙ وَالَّذِيْنَ اٰمَنُوْا

وَعَمِلُوا الصّٰلِحٰتِ وَلَا الْمُسِیْٓءُ

to wrong-doers to present their excuses, but they will (only) have the Curse and the Home of Misery.

53. We did aforetime give Moses the (Book of) Guidance, and We gave the Book in inheritance to the Children of Israel, -

54. A Guide and a Message to men of understanding.

55. Patiently, then, persevere: for the Promise of Allah is true: and ask forgiveness for your fault, and celebrate the Praises of your Lord in the evening and in the morning.

56. Those who dispute about the Signs of

الظّٰلِمِيْنَ مَعْذِرَتُهُمْ وَلَهُمُ

اللَّعْنَةُ وَلَهُمْ سُوْٓءُ الدَّارِ ۞

وَلَقَدْ اٰتَيْنَا مُوْسَى الْهُدٰى

وَاَوْرَثْنَا بَنِيْۤ اِسْرَآءِيْلَ الْكِتٰبَ ۞

هُدًى وَّذِكْرٰى لِاُولِى الْاَلْبَابِ ۞

فَاصْبِرْ اِنَّ وَعْدَ اللّٰهِ حَقٌّ

وَّاسْتَغْفِرْ لِذَنْبِكَ وَسَبِّحْ بِحَمْدِ

رَبِّكَ بِالْعَشِيِّ وَالْاِبْكَارِ ۞ اِنَّ

الَّذِيْنَ يُجَادِلُوْنَ فِيْۤ اٰيٰتِ

to the Keepers of Hell: "Pray to your Lord to lighten us the Penalty for a day (at least)!"

50. They will say: "Did there not come to you your Apostles with clear Signs?" They will say, "Yes". They will reply, "Then pray (as you like)! But the prayer of those without Faith is nothing but (futile wandering) in (mazes of) error!"

51. We will, without doubt, help Our Apostles and those who believe, (both) in this world's life and on the Day when the witnesses will stand forth, -

52. The Day when no profit will it be

النَّارِ لِخَزَنَةِ جَهَنَّمَ ادْعُوا

رَبَّكُمْ يُخَفِّفْ عَنَّا يَوْمًا مِّنَ

الْعَذَابِ ۞ قَالُوا أَوَلَمْ تَكُ

تَأْتِيكُمْ رُسُلُكُم بِالْبَيِّنَاتِ

قَالُوا بَلَى قَالُوا فَادْعُوا وَمَا

دُعَاؤُا الْكَافِرِينَ إِلَّا فِي ضَلَالٍ ۞

إِنَّا لَنَنصُرُ رُسُلَنَا وَالَّذِينَ

آمَنُوا فِي الْحَيَوةِ الدُّنْيَا وَيَوْمَ

يَقُومُ الْأَشْهَادُ ۞ يَوْمَ لَا يَنفَعُ

"Cast you the People of Pharaoh into the severest Chastisement!"

47. Behold, they will dispute with each other in the Fire! The weak ones (who followed) will say to those who had been arrogant, "We but followed you: can you then take (on yourselves) from us some share of the Fire?"

48. Those who had been arrogant will say: "We are all in this (Fire)! Truly, Allah has judged between (his) servants!"

49. Those in the Fire will say

السَّاعَةُ اَدْخِلُوٓا اٰلَ فِرْعَوْنَ

اَشَدَّ الْعَذَابِ ۞ وَاِذْ يَتَحَآجُّوْنَ

فِى النَّارِ فَيَقُوْلُ الضُّعَفٰٓؤُا

لِلَّذِيْنَ اسْتَكْبَرُوٓا اِنَّا كُنَّا

لَكُمْ تَبَعًا فَهَلْ اَنْتُمْ مُّغْنُوْنَ

عَنَّا نَصِيْبًا مِّنَ النَّارِ ۞ قَالَ

الَّذِيْنَ اسْتَكْبَرُوٓا اِنَّا كُلٌّ

فِيْهَآ اِنَّ اللّٰهَ قَدْ حَكَمَ بَيْنَ

الْعِبَادِ ۞ وَقَالَ الَّذِيْنَ فِى

whether in this world, or in the Hereafter; our return will be to Allah; and the transgressors will be Companions of the Fire!

44. "Soon will you remember what I say to you (now). My (own) affair I commit to Allah: for Allah (ever) watches over His servants."

45. Then Allah saved him from (every) ill that they plotted (against him), but the burnt of the penalty encompassed on all sides the People of Pharaoh.

46. In front of the Fire will they be brought, morning and evening: and (the sentence will be) on the Day that Judgment will be established:

فِى الدُّنْيَا وَلَا فِى الْأَخِرَةِ وَاَنَّ

مَرَدَّنَآ اِلَى اللهِ وَاَنَّ الْمُسْرِفِيْنَ

هُمْ اَصْحٰبُ النَّارِ ۞ فَسَتَذْكُرُوْنَ

مَآ اَقُوْلُ لَكُمْ وَاُفَوِّضُ اَمْرِىْ اِلَى

اللهِ ۚ اِنَّ اللهَ بَصِيْرٌۢ بِالْعِبَادِ ۞

فَوَقٰىهُ اللهُ سَيِّاٰتِ مَا مَكَرُوْا

وَحَاقَ بِاٰلِ فِرْعَوْنَ سُوْٓءُ

الْعَذَابِ ۞ اَلنَّارُ يُعْرَضُوْنَ عَلَيْهَا

غُدُوًّا وَّعَشِيًّا ۚ وَيَوْمَ تَقُوْمُ

woman - and is a believer - such will enter the Garden (of Bliss): therein will they have abundance without measure."

41. "And O my People! How (strange) it is for me to call you to salvation while you call me to the Fire!"

42. "You do call upon me to blaspheme against Allah, and to join with Him partners of whom I have no knowledge; and I call you to the Exalted in Power, Who forgives again and again!"

43. "Without doubt you do call me to one who is not fit to be called to,

اُنْثٰى وَهُوَ مُؤْمِنٌ فَاُولٰٓئِكَ

يَدْخُلُوْنَ الْجَنَّةَ يُرْزَقُوْنَ فِيْهَا

بِغَيْرِ حِسَابٍ ۞ وَيٰقَوْمِ مَالِيْٓ

اَدْعُوْكُمْ اِلَى النَّجٰوةِ وَتَدْعُوْنَنِيْٓ

اِلَى النَّارِ ۞ تَدْعُوْنَنِيْ لِاَكْفُرَ

بِاللّٰهِ وَاُشْرِكَ بِهٖ مَا لَيْسَ

لِيْ بِهٖ عِلْمٌ وَّاَنَا اَدْعُوْكُمْ اِلَى

الْعَزِيْزِ الْغَفَّارِ ۞ لَاجَرَمَ اَنَّمَا

تَدْعُوْنَنِيْٓ اِلَيْهِ لَيْسَ لَهٗ دَعْوَةٌ

in Pharaoh's eyes, the evil of his deeds, and he was hindered from the Path; and the plot of Pharaoh led to nothing but perdition (for him).

38. The man who believed said further: "O my People! Follow me: I will lead you to the Path of Right."

39. "O my People! This life of the present is nothing but (temporary) convenience: it is the Hereafter that is the Home that will last."

40. "He that works evil will not be requited but by the like thereof: and he that works a righteous deed - whether man or

لِفِرْعَوْنَ سُوٓءُ عَمَلِهِ وَصُدَّ عَنِ
السَّبِيلِ ۗ وَمَا كَيْدُ فِرْعَوْنَ إِلَّا
فِى تَبَابٍ ۞ وَقَالَ الَّذِىٓ اٰمَنَ
يٰقَوْمِ اتَّبِعُوْنِ أَهْدِكُمْ سَبِيلَ
الرَّشَادِ ۞ يٰقَوْمِ اِنَّمَا هٰذِهِ
الْحَيٰوةُ الدُّنْيَا مَتَاعٌ وَّاِنَّ
الْاٰخِرَةَ هِىَ دَارُ الْقَرَارِ ۞ مَنْ
عَمِلَ سَيِّئَةً فَلَا يُجْزٰىٓ اِلَّا مِثْلَهَا
وَمَنْ عَمِلَ صَالِحًا مِّنْ ذَكَرٍ اَوْ

Allah, without any authority that has reached them, grievous and odious (is such conduct) in the sight of Allah and of the believers. Thus does Allah, seal up every heart - of arrogant and obstinate transgressors."

36. Pharaoh said: "O Haman! Build me a lofty palace, that I may attain the ways and means"-

37. "The ways and means of (reaching) the heavens, and that I may mount up to the Allah of Moses: but as far as I am concerned, I think (Moses) is a liar!" Thus was made alluring,

اللهِ بِغَيْرِ سُلْطَانٍ اٰتَٮهُمْ

كَبُرَ مَقْتًا عِنْدَ اللهِ وَعِنْدَ

الَّذِيْنَ اٰمَنُوْا ۚ كَذٰلِكَ يَطْبَعُ

اللهُ عَلٰى كُلِّ قَلْبِ مُتَكَبِّرٍ

جَبَّارٍ ۞ وَقَالَ فِرْعَوْنُ يٰهَامٰنُ

ابْنِ لِيْ صَرْحًا لَّعَلِّيْ أَبْلُغُ

الْأَسْبَابَ ۞ أَسْبَابَ السَّمٰوٰتِ

فَأَطَّلِعَ اِلٰى اِلٰهِ مُوْسٰى وَاِنِّيْ

لَأَظُنُّهٗ كَاذِبًا ۚ وَكَذٰلِكَ زُيِّنَ

any whom Allah leaves to stray, there is none to guide ..."

34. "And to you there came Joseph in times gone by, with clear Signs, but you ceased not to doubt of the (mission) for which he had come: at length, when he died, you said: 'No Apostle will Allah send after him.' Thus does Allah leave to stray such as transgress and live in doubt," -

35. "(Such) as dispute about the Signs of

مِنْ عَاصِمٍ ۖ وَمَنْ يُّضْلِلِ اللهُ

فَمَا لَهُ مِنْ هَادٍ ۞ وَلَقَدْ

جَآءَكُمْ يُوسُفُ مِنْ قَبْلُ

بِالْبَيِّنٰتِ فَمَا زِلْتُمْ فِىْ شَكٍّ

مِّمَّا جَآءَكُمْ بِهٖ ۖ حَتّٰى إِذَا هَلَكَ

قُلْتُمْ لَنْ يَّبْعَثَ اللهُ مِنْۢ

بَعْدِهٖ رَسُوْلًا ۚ كَذٰلِكَ يُضِلُّ

اللهُ مَنْ هُوَ مُسْرِفٌ مُّرْتَابُ ۞

الَّذِيْنَ يُجَادِلُوْنَ فِىْٓ اٰيٰتِ

to the Path of Right!"

30. Then said the man who believed: "O my people! Truly I do fear for you something like the Day (of disaster) of the Confederates (in sin)! -

31. "Something like the fate of the People of Noah, the 'Ad, and the Thamud, and those who came after them: but Allah never wishes injustice to His servants."

32. "And O my People! I fear for you a Day when there will be mutual calling (and wailing), -

33. "A Day when you shall turn your backs and flee: no defender shall you have from Allah:

سَبِيلَ الرَّشَادِ ۝ وَقَالَ الَّذِىٓ

اٰمَنَ يٰقَوْمِ اِنِّىٓ اَخَافُ عَلَيْكُمْ

مِّثْلَ يَوْمِ الْاَحْزَابِ ۝ مِثْلَ

دَاْبِ قَوْمِ نُوْحٍ وَّعَادٍ وَّثَمُوْدَ

وَالَّذِيْنَ مِنْ بَعْدِهِمْ ۚ وَمَا

اللّٰهُ يُرِيْدُ ظُلْمًا لِّلْعِبَادِ ۝

وَيٰقَوْمِ اِنِّىٓ اَخَافُ عَلَيْكُمْ

يَوْمَ التَّنَادِ ۝ يَوْمَ تُوَلُّوْنَ

مُدْبِرِيْنَ ۚ مَا لَكُمْ مِّنَ اللّٰهِ

on him is (the sin of) his lie: but, if he is telling the Truth, then will fall on you something of the (calamity) of which he warns you: truly Allah guides not one who transgresses and lies!"

29. "O my People! Yours is the dominion this day: you have the upper hand in the land: but who will help us from the Punishment of Allah, should it befall us?" Pharaoh said: "I but point out to you that which I see (myself); nor do I guide you but

فَعَلَيْهِ كَذِبُهُ ۚ وَإِنْ يَّكُ

صَادِقًا يُّصِبْكُمْ بَعْضُ الَّذِى

يَعِدُكُمْ ۚ إِنَّ اللّٰهَ لَا يَهْدِى

مَنْ هُوَ مُسْرِفٌ كَذَّابٌ ۞ يٰقَوْمِ

لَكُمُ الْمُلْكُ الْيَوْمَ ظٰهِرِيْنَ

فِى الْاَرْضِ ۖ فَمَنْ يَّنْصُرُنَا

مِنْ بَأْسِ اللّٰهِ إِنْ جَآءَنَا ۚ

قَالَ فِرْعَوْنُ مَآ أُرِيْكُمْ إِلَّا

مَآ اَرٰى وَمَآ اَهْدِيْكُمْ إِلَّا

your religion, or lest he should cause mischief to appear in the land!"

27. Moses said: "I have indeed called upon my Lord and your Lord (for protection) from every arrogant one who believes not in the Day of Account!"

28. A believer, a man from among the people of Pharaoh, who had concealed his faith, said: "Will you slay a man because he says, 'My Lord is Allah'? - When he has indeed come to you with clear (Signs) from your Lord? And if he be a liar,

دِيْنَكُمْ اَوْ اَنْ يُّظْهِرَ فِى الْاَرْضِ

الْفَسَادَ ۞ وَقَالَ مُوْسٰى اِنِّى

عُذْتُ بِرَبِّى وَرَبِّكُمْ مِّنْ

كُلِّ مُتَكَبِّرٍ لَّا يُؤْمِنُ بِيَوْمِ

الْحِسَابِ ۞ وَقَالَ رَجُلٌ مُّؤْمِنٌ ۙ

مِّنْ اٰلِ فِرْعَوْنَ يَكْتُمُ اِيْمَانَهٗۤ

اَتَقْتُلُوْنَ رَجُلًا اَنْ يَّقُوْلَ رَبِّىَ

اللّٰهُ وَقَدْ جَآءَكُمْ بِالْبَيِّنٰتِ

مِنْ رَّبِّكُمْ ؕ وَاِنْ يَّكُ كَاذِبًا

manifest,

24. To Pharaoh, Haman, and Qarun; but they called (him) "a sorcerer telling lies!"...

25. Now, when he came to them in Truth, from Us, they said, "Slay the sons of those who believe with him, and keep alive their females," but the plots of unbelievers (end) in nothing but errors (and delusions)!...

26. Said Pharaoh: "Leave me to slay Moses; and let him call on his Lord! what I fear is lest he should change

مُّبِيْنٍ ۞ اِلٰى فِرْعَوْنَ وَهَامٰنَ

وَقَارُوْنَ فَقَالُوْا سٰحِرٌ كَذَّابٌ ۞

فَلَمَّا جَآءَهُمْ بِالْحَقِّ مِنْ

عِنْدِنَا قَالُوا اقْتُلُوْٓا اَبْنَآءَ

الَّذِيْنَ اٰمَنُوْا مَعَهٗ وَاسْتَحْيُوْا

نِسَآءَهُمْ ۚ وَمَا كَيْدُ الْكٰفِرِيْنَ

اِلَّا فِيْ ضَلٰلٍ ۞ وَقَالَ فِرْعَوْنُ

ذَرُوْنِيْٓ اَقْتُلْ مُوْسٰى وَلْيَدْعُ

رَبَّهٗ ۚ اِنِّيْٓ اَخَافُ اَنْ يُّبَدِّلَ

before them? They were even superior to them in strength, and in the traces (they have left) in the land: but Allah did call them to account for their sins, and none had they to defend them against Allah.

22. That was because there came to them their Apostles with clear (Signs), but they rejected them: so Allah called them to account: for He is full of Strength, Strict in Punishment.

23. Of old We sent Moses, with Our Signs and an authority

كَانُوْا مِنْ قَبْلِهِمْ ۚ كَانُوْا هُمْ

اَشَدَّ مِنْهُمْ قُوَّةً وَّاٰثَارًا فِي

الْاَرْضِ فَاَخَذَهُمُ اللّٰهُ بِذُنُوْبِهِمْ ۚ

وَمَا كَانَ لَهُمْ مِّنَ اللّٰهِ مِنْ

وَّاقٍ ۞ ذٰلِكَ بِاَنَّهُمْ كَانَتْ

تَّاْتِيْهِمْ رُسُلُهُمْ بِالْبَيِّنٰتِ

فَكَفَرُوْا فَاَخَذَهُمُ اللّٰهُ ۚ اِنَّهٗ

قَوِيٌّ شَدِيْدُ الْعِقَابِ ۞ وَلَقَدْ

اَرْسَلْنَا مُوْسٰى بِاٰيٰتِنَا وَسُلْطٰنٍ

the throats to choke (them); no intimate friend nor intercessor will the wrong-doers have, who could be listened to.

19. (Allah) knows of (the tricks) that deceive with the eyes, and all that the hearts (of men) conceal.

20. And Allah will judge with (justice and) Truth: but those whom (men) invoke besides Him, will not (be in a position) to judge at all. Verily it is Allah (alone) Who hears and sees (all things).

21. Do they not travel through the earth and see what was the End of those

الْحَنَاجِرِ كَظِمِينَ ۖ مَا لِلظَّلِمِينَ

مِنْ حَمِيمٍ وَّلَا شَفِيعٍ يُّطَاعُ ۝

يَعْلَمُ خَائِنَةَ الْأَعْيُنِ وَمَا

تُخْفِي الصُّدُوْرُ ۝ وَاللّٰهُ يَقْضِي

بِالْحَقِّ ۖ وَالَّذِيْنَ يَدْعُوْنَ مِنْ

دُوْنِهٖ لَا يَقْضُوْنَ بِشَيْءٍ ۗ إِنَّ

اللّٰهَ هُوَ السَّمِيْعُ الْبَصِيْرُ ۝ أَوَلَمْ

يَسِيْرُوْا فِي الْأَرْضِ فَيَنْظُرُوْا

كَيْفَ كَانَ عَاقِبَةُ الَّذِيْنَ

to any of His servants He pleases,
that it may warn (men) of the Day
of Mutual Meeting, -

16.   The Day whereon they will
(all) come forth: not a single thing
concerning them is hidden from
Allah. Whose will be the dominion that Day?" That of Allah, the
One, the Irresistible!

17.   That Day will every soul be
requited for what it earned; no
injustice will there be that Day,
for Allah is Swift in taking
account.

18.   Warn them of the Day that is
(ever) drawing near, when the
hearts will (come) right up to

أَمْرِهِ عَلَىٰ مَن يَشَآءُ مِنْ

عِبَادِهِ لِيُنذِرَ يَوْمَ التَّلَاقِ ۝

يَوْمَ هُم بَٰرِزُونَ لَا يَخْفَىٰ عَلَى

اللَّهِ مِنْهُمْ شَيْءٌ لِّمَنِ الْمُلْكُ

الْيَوْمَ لِلَّهِ الْوَاحِدِ الْقَهَّارِ ۝

الْيَوْمَ تُجْزَىٰ كُلُّ نَفْسٍ بِمَا

كَسَبَتْ لَا ظُلْمَ الْيَوْمَ إِنَّ اللَّهَ

سَرِيعُ الْحِسَابِ ۝ وَأَنذِرْهُم

يَوْمَ الْأَزِفَةِ إِذِ الْقُلُوبُ لَدَى

12. (The answer will be:) "This is because, when Allah was invoked as the Only (object of worship), you did reject Faith, but when partners were joined to Him, you believed! the Command is with Allah, Most High, Most Great!"

13. He it is Who shows you his Signs, and sends down sustenance for you from the sky: but only those receive admonition who turn (to Allah).

14. Call you, then, upon Allah with sincere devotion to Him, even though the unbelievers may detest it.

15. Raised high above ranks (or degrees), (He is) the Lord of the Throne (of Authority): by His Command does He send the Spirit (of inspiration)

ذٰلِكُمْ بِاَنَّهُ اِذَا دُعِيَ اللّٰهُ وَحْدَهُ

كَفَرْتُمْ وَاِنْ يُّشْرَكْ بِهِ تُؤْمِنُوْا

فَالْحُكْمُ لِلّٰهِ الْعَلِيِّ الْكَبِيْرِ ۝

هُوَ الَّذِيْ يُرِيْكُمْ اٰيٰتِهِ وَيُنَزِّلُ

لَكُمْ مِّنَ السَّمَآءِ رِزْقًا ۚ وَمَا

يَتَذَكَّرُ اِلَّا مَنْ يُّنِيْبُ ۝ فَادْعُوا

اللّٰهَ مُخْلِصِيْنَ لَهُ الدِّيْنَ وَلَوْ

كَرِهَ الْكٰفِرُوْنَ ۝ رَفِيْعُ الدَّرَجٰتِ

ذُو الْعَرْشِ ۚ يُلْقِى الرُّوْحَ مِنْ

from (all) ills; and any whom You does preserve from (all) ills that Day, - on them will You have bestowed Mercy indeed: and that will be truly (for them) the highest Achievement".

10. The unbelievers will be addressed: "Greater was the aversion of Allah to you than (is) your aversion to yourselves, seeing that you were called to the Faith and you used to refuse."

11. They will say: "Our Lord! Twice have you made us without life, and twice have you given us Life! Now that have we recognised our sins: is there any way out (of this)?"

السَّيِّئَاتِ ۖ وَمَن تَقِ السَّيِّئَاتِ

يَوْمَئِذٍ فَقَدْ رَحِمْتَهُ ۚ وَذَٰلِكَ

هُوَ الْفَوْزُ الْعَظِيمُ ۞ إِنَّ الَّذِينَ

كَفَرُوا يُنَادَوْنَ لَمَقْتُ اللَّهِ أَكْبَرُ

مِن مَّقْتِكُمْ أَنفُسَكُمْ إِذْ تُدْعَوْنَ

إِلَى الْإِيمَانِ فَتَكْفُرُونَ ۞ قَالُوا

رَبَّنَا أَمَتَّنَا اثْنَتَيْنِ وَأَحْيَيْتَنَا

اثْنَتَيْنِ فَاعْتَرَفْنَا بِذُنُوبِنَا

فَهَلْ إِلَىٰ خُرُوجٍ مِّن سَبِيلٍ ۞

their Lord; believe in Him; and implore Forgiveness for those who believe: "Our Lord! Your Reach is over all things, in Mercy and Knowledge. Forgive, then, those who turn in repentance, and follow Your Path; and preserve them from the Chastisement of the Blazing Fire!"

8.   "And grant, our Lord! That they enter the Gardens of Eternity, which You have promised to them, and to the righteous among their fathers, their wives, and their posterity! For You are (He), the Exalted in Might, full of Wisdom."

9.   "And preserve them

رَبِّهِمْ وَيُؤْمِنُوْنَ بِهِ وَيَسْتَغْفِرُوْنَ

لِلَّذِيْنَ اٰمَنُوْا رَبَّنَا وَسِعْتَ كُلَّ

شَيْءٍ رَّحْمَةً وَّعِلْمًا فَاغْفِرْ

لِلَّذِيْنَ تَابُوْا وَاتَّبَعُوْا سَبِيْلَكَ

وَقِهِمْ عَذَابَ الْجَحِيْمِ ۞ رَبَّنَا

وَاَدْخِلْهُمْ جَنّٰتِ عَدْنِ الَّتِيْ

وَعَدْتَّهُمْ وَمَنْ صَلَحَ مِنْ

اٰبَآئِهِمْ وَاَزْوَاجِهِمْ وَذُرِّيّٰتِهِمْ اِنَّكَ

اَنْتَ الْعَزِيْزُ الْحَكِيْمُ ۞ وَقِهِمُ

the People of Noah, and the Confederates (of Evil) after them; and every People plotted against their Prophet, to seize him, and disputed by means of vanities, therewith to condemn the Truth; but it was I that seized them! and how (terrible) was My Requital!

6.   Thus was the Decree of your Lord proved true against the unbelievers; that truly they are Companions of the Fire!

7.   Those who sustain the Throne (of Allah) and those around it sing Glory and Praise to